Anatomy
of
Wonder

Anatomy
of
Wonder 4
A Critical Guide
to Science Fiction

Edited by

Neil Barron

R. R. Bowker
New Providence, New Jersey

Published by R. R. Bowker,
a Reed Reference Publishing Company
Copyright © 1995 by Neil Barron
All rights reserved
Printed and bound in the United States of America
Bowker® is a registered trademark of Reed Reference Publishing, a division of
Reed Elsevier Inc. Anatomy of Wonder™ is a trademark of Reed Elsevier
Properties Inc., used under license.

Library of Congress Cataloging-in-Publication Data
Anatomy of wonder 4: a critical guide to science fiction / edited by
    Neil Barron.
        p.   cm.
        Includes bibliographical references and indexes.
        ISBN 0-8352-3288-3 :
        1. Science fiction–Bibliography.   2. Science fiction–History and
criticism.   I. Barron, Neil, 1934–   . II. Title: Anatomy of
wonder four.
Z5917.S36A52   1995
[PN3433.8]
016.80883'876–dc20   94-42363
                                                                   CIP

ISBN 0 - 8352 - 3288 - 3

9 780835 232883

TO CAROLYN

. . . listen: there's a hell
of a good universe next door; let's go

—e.e. cummings, *1 x 1 [one times one]*, 1944, poem xiv

Contents

Secondary Literature and Research Aids

How to Use This Guide Effectively

Anatomy of Wonder is divided into two parts, fiction and nonfiction. Chapters 1–4 are chronological, from the 16th century through early 1994. A narrative introduction provides a historical and critical overview, followed by an annotated bibliography describing and evaluating the best, better, or historically important books. Chapter 5 is devoted to fiction written for teenagers. Chapters 6–15 provide thorough coverage of the multiple topics shown in the table of contents. Here is a sample annotation, with each of the most common elements explained:

① ② ③ ④ ⑤ ⑥
*4-207. Herbert, Frank. **Dune**. Chilton, 1965. ⑩
⑦ The first volume of this seven-volume bestselling series is the story of a selectively bred messiah who acquires paranormal powers by the use of the spice that is the main product of the desert planet Arrakis, and uses them to prepare for the ecological renewal of the world. Politics and metaphysics are tightly bound into a remarkably detailed and coherent pattern; an imaginative tour de force. The series as a whole is overinflated, the later revisitations of the theme being prompted more by market success than the discovery of new things to do with it. The series demonstrates how a good SF writer's ability to build a coherent and convincing hypothetical world can serve the purpose of making philosophical and sociological questions concrete; the series thus becomes a massive thought experiment in social philosophy, and is more considerable as

such than Asimov's Foundation ⑧ Series [3-12] and Bradley's Darkover ⑧ series [4-63]. HW, 1966; NW, 1965. ⑨
⑪ [For other books by this author see chapter 3.]

1. Asterisk denotes a best book selection; see complete best book listing in chapter 15.

2. Entry Number. The number preceding the hyphen is the chapter number; the number following is the number of the book in that chapter.

3. Author, with less-used portion of name shown in parentheses. All books are entered under the most common name used by the author, even if a pseudonym. A master list of all fiction authors at the end of chapter 9 shows nationality, birth and death years, and in which of ten biocritical reference works more information about the author can be found.

4. Title in boldface.

5. Publisher of the first edition of book. Many books have been reprinted repeatedly. In some cases specific editions are recommended because the text is more reliable or there is an introduction by the author or a critic.

6. Year of the first book publication; earlier magazine publication is usually noted.

7. Annotation providing a succinct plot summary/description and evaluation.

8. Books with similar or contrasting plots or themes are usually suggested, with cross-references to their entry numbers.

9. Awards or nominations received. See preface for abbreviations used and chapter 15 for an explanation and listing of the major awards.

10. Sequels and books in series are usually shown, with complete series information found in chapter 15.

11. Fifty-three authors are split between chapters, usually 3 and 4. This generic cross-reference links all such authors. The author index also lists all books of an author split between two or more chapters.

Preface

Most science fiction, like fiction generally, is undistinguished, which is why this guide exists. *Anatomy of Wonder* is intended to assist·readers, from the devoted fan to the casually curious, as well as to help librarians answer questions and build collections of the best, better, or historically important science fiction works in English. Teachers, from el-hi to college, can also benefit from the guide, especially chapter 13, which is even more strongly oriented to classroom use in this edition. The second (1981) and third (1987) editions were extensively revised, as is this newest edition. There are new contributors of chapters 3, 4, and 8–14. New eyes mean new perceptions, and although many of the standard or outstanding works are critically reevaluated, hundreds of books are new to this edition, many of them published prior to the third edition. And whenever the earlier annotations could be improved or updated, this was done to make the guide as current, balanced, and useful as possible. Coverage is through fall 1993, with last-minute revisions added in November 1994.

To enhance the usefulness of this guide further, many other improvements were made:

1. A comprehensive theme index to novels, theme anthologies, and some works of nonfiction was added, encouraging readers to explore works with similar themes. Up to three themes are assigned to each annotated book.

2. A series index by author and series title lists all annotated series with three or more components. This appears in chapter 15.

3. Because this guide provides only minimal information about fiction authors, a comprehensive tabulation of all fiction authors in chapters 1–5 is keyed to ten authoritative sources of more information about the authors and their books. This tabulation is found at the end of chapter 9.

4. The awards listing in chapter 15 is much more detailed, supplementing the best books listings.

5. Descriptions of the more important organizations associated with science fiction are found in chapter 15, along with a discussion of some of the many conventions at which fans, writers, and others gather.

6. Many SF films have been based on SF novels or short stories. A table in chapter 10 lists such films and their literary sources.

7. The magazines chapter now lists the best or most important magazines *formerly* as well as currently published, both fiction and magazines about SF. Holdings are shown, keyed to the library collections chapter.

8. A discussion of SF poetry concludes chapter 4, and an analysis of SF comic books, comic strips, and graphic novels is included in chapter 11.

9. A list of all translated, annotated books is included in chapter 15, a measure of SF's worldwide influence.

10. To alert users that some authors' listings are divided between chapters, a cross-reference is included at the end of the annotations of all such authors. Most of them are found in chapters 3 and 4.

11. The chapter on classroom aids includes more detailed guidance for junior/senior high school and college instructors.

12. Guidance to audiovisual materials is provided in chapter 13 and more briefly in chapter 10.

13. A quick guide to effective use precedes the preface.

Those familiar with the previous edition of *Anatomy of Wonder* will note the elimination of coverage of SF not translated into English, which occupied 206 pages in the third edition. There were several reasons for the exclusion of untranslated SF. The audience for this guide is almost entirely English-speaking, mostly readers in North America and the United

Kingdom. Non-English SF is rarely found in libraries in these areas, even in the specialized collections described in chapter 14. Acquiring non-English SF, especially if out of print, is very difficult. But the third edition (like the second edition, a Hugo nominee) is found in hundreds of libraries in the United States and abroad, and the determined reader of foreign-language SF can probably locate a copy for guidance. A final reason is essentially economic: to have included updated coverage of untranslated SF would have meant a book well over 1,000 pages in length and at a price few libraries or individuals could afford. Although it is no substitute for the excluded coverage, chapter 15 includes a list of English translations, many of them of the more important works in their respective tongues. See also the revised and enlarged *Encyclopedia of Science Fiction* [7-22], which has entries for 300 foreign-language authors.

Hundreds of new books have been added to this edition. A minimum of 2,100 works of fiction for adults and young adults, from the 16th century through early 1994, are critically evaluated, including many published prior to the third edition of *Anatomy of Wonder*. More than 800 works of nonfiction are also evaluated. Many weaker or merely representative or superseded titles from earlier editions have been dropped. The large number of SF books in recent years (see chapter 6) has required greater selectivity, particularly in chapters 3 and 4. Beyond a few hundred titles about which there would be relatively widespread agreement (see the best book lists in chapter 15), the element of individual judgment is inevitably involved, as it should be. Although outside readers (see below) were used to ensure comprehensive and balanced coverage, the individual contributors had final responsibility for their selections.

Introductions. These provide the historical and analytical perspective on the periods or subjects covered, although they are not intended to replace the more comprehensive accounts annotated in chapter 8. Collectively, however, they provide an excellent overview of the development of science fiction from the earliest times to the late 20th century.

Annotated Bibliographies. These follow the chapter introductions and evaluate the books and other materials judged most significant for literary, extraliterary, or historical reasons. Although some plot summary is usually provided to suggest what fiction books are "about," the emphasis throughout is on critical evaluation.

The annotations include these elements:

Name of author or editor. Any unused or lesser-used portion is shown in parentheses, as in Heinlein, Robert A(nson). Books are listed under the name most commonly used by the author, even if a pseudonym (in which case the real name is shown in parentheses). Cross-references are provided in the author index. Library cataloging practices for anthologies favor the title as main entry, but in this guide anthologies are generally listed by editor.

Entry number. This specifies chapter and sequence, as in [3-147], [8-46], and so on.

Title. Better-known variant titles have been included. Title changes are very common in SF. The two bibliographies by Reginald [7-8] and the newly revised *Encyclopedia of Science Fiction* [7-22] provide extensive guidance in this area.

Publisher and year of first edition. These rely, when possible, on the bibliographies by Reginald, Currey, and Bleiler or the *Locus* annuals (see chapter 7). Collectors and dealers should realize that *no attempt has been made to record the points necessary to distinguish between first and later or variant editions*. The Currey bibliography [7-7] is the most authoritative such guide currently available. Somewhat more detailed bibliographic information is provided for some of the early works in chapter 1 and for nonprint materials. As a rule, any edition is acceptable, but in some cases a specific edition is recommended because of notes, a more reliable text, or other reasons. Books were selected regardless of in/out-of-print status.

Succinct plot summary. Summaries note principal themes, critical strengths and weaknesses, and comparable works. Notable stories in collections or anthologies are usually mentioned. Novels derived from earlier short fiction, often rewritten with connecting text, are referred to as "fix-ups."

Awards or nominations received. Key award winners and nominees are designated by these abbreviations:

HN—Hugo nominee
HW—Hugo winner
IFA—International Fantasy Award
JWC—John W. Campbell Jr. Memorial Award
NN—Nebula nominee
NW—Nebula winner
SFHF—Science Fiction Hall of Fame [see 3-223]

See also chapter 15, which provides a list of winners for the more important awards.

Series. Brief information is given, with chapter 15 providing lists by author and series title for any annotated series with three or more components.

Cross-references. Works with similar or contrasting themes are usually cross-referenced by entry number, as [4-126]. See also the theme index.

First-purchase (best books) titles. An asterisk precedes the entry number of each such book. Starred fiction titles were selected on the basis of one or more of these characteristics: awards or nominations received, influence of the work, outstanding or unique treatment of a theme, critical or popular acceptance, importance to the author's total body of work, or historical importance, especially for early works. *Rarity, scarcity, and collectibility are not criteria for inclusion in this guide.* Nonfiction works were judged by the usual criteria of scope, accuracy, currency, ease of use, balance, insight, clarity, and so on. All best books are listed in chapter 15 along with the judgments of outside readers. Those judged most essential for smaller libraries have two stars.

Nonstarred titles. These are relatively less important but might be found in a more comprehensive collection. This large category includes many of the less distinguished but still respectable efforts and necessarily reflects the substantial personal judgment noted earlier.

Because this is a selective guide to the best and better works, all books can be assumed to be recommended with whatever critical qualifications are included in the annotations. In a few instances, works that have achieved some prominence, but that are judged meretricious here, are annotated as warnings.

Coverage of the secondary literature is more selective in this fourth edition because of the large number of books that have been published in recent years. A recent and valuable guide to an important part of that literature is the *Reference Guide to Science Fiction, Fantasy, and Horror* [7-11]. Because the annotations in the Burgess guide are much fuller than space in *Anatomy of Wonder* will allow, cross-references are provided to works annotated in both, most of them in chapters 7 and 9.

Illustrators of fantastic fiction are the subjects of the recent biographical guide by Weinberg, *A Biographical Dictionary of Science Fiction and Fantasy Artists* [11-18], and all illustrators in chapter 11 about whom works have been written are discussed in this guide.

From the first edition in 1976, *Anatomy of Wonder* has always been a collaborative effort, drawing on the knowledge and enthusiasm of contributors and outside readers. Because this is the last edition I will edit, I wish to acknowledge the help of the many individuals who have made this guide a standard in its field (editions to which they contributed or assisted with are shown in parentheses):

Walter Albert (4th)
Brian W. Aldiss (2nd, 3rd, 4th)
Muriel Rogow Becker (3rd, 4th)
Nachman Ben-Yehuda (3rd)
Jon Bing (3rd)
Everett F. Bleiler (2nd, 3rd, 4th)
Paul A. Carter (2nd, 4th)
Thomas D. Clareson (1st, 2nd, 3rd, 4th)
John Clute (2nd, 3rd, 4th)
William Contento (4th)
Peter M. Coogan (4th)
Lloyd Currey (2nd, 4th)
Niels Dalgaard (3rd)
J. A. Dautzenberg (3rd)
Joe De Bolt (1st, 2nd, 3rd)
Danny De Laet (3rd)
Vincent Di Fate (3rd)
Pascal Ducommun (3rd)
Steve Eng (4th)
Margaret Esmonde (2nd)
James Gunn (2nd, 4th)
Hal W. Hall (1st, 2nd, 3rd, 4th)

David Hartwell (4th)
Ion Hobana (3rd)
Maxim Jakubowski (3rd)
Ken Kessler (2nd)
Michael A. Klossner (3rd, 4th)
Dennis M. Kratz (4th)
Rob Latham (4th)
Russell Letson (4th)
Michael A. Levy (4th)
David Lewis (2nd, 3rd)
Sam J. Lundwall (3rd)
Patrick L. McGuire (2nd, 3rd)
Ed Meskys (3rd)
Susan G. Miles (4th)
Francis J. Molson (1st, 2nd, 3rd, 4th)
Gianni Montanari (2nd, 3rd)
Michael A. Morrison (4th)
Sam Moskowitz (3rd)
Alexander B. Nedelovich (3rd)
Peter Nicholls (2nd, 3rd, 4th)
Frederick Patten (2nd)

John R. Pfeiffer (1st, 2nd, 3rd)
Robert M. Philmus (1st)
Frederik Pohl (3rd)
David Pringle (3rd)
Robert Reginald (2nd)
Ivor A. Rogers (1st)
Franz Rottensteiner (2nd, 3rd)
Joe Sanders (4th)
Randall A. Scott (4th)
Robert Silverberg (2nd)
Mike Smith (2nd)
Philip E. Smith III (2nd)
Brian Stableford (2nd, 3rd, 4th)
Pascal Thomas (3rd)
Donald H. Tuck (2nd)
Frank H. Tucker (2nd)
Marshall B. Tymn (2nd)
Robert Weinberg (3rd)
Mary Weinkauf (2nd)
Jack Williamson (2nd)
David Wingrove (4th)
Gary K. Wolfe (2nd, 3rd, 4th)
Ye Yiong-lie (2nd)

For this latest edition I particularly want to thank the following outside readers, whose suggestions were carefully considered by the contributors:

Lloyd A. Currey, compiler of the standard collector's guide to SF [7-7], bibliographer, and SF's premier antiquarian dealer.

John Clute, co-editor and contributor to both editions of the *Encyclopedia of Science Fiction* [7-22], one of SF's most knowledgeable critics, and winner of the 1994 Pilgrim award.

David Hartwell, co-editor of the *New York Times Review of Science Fiction* [12-27], premier anthologist, and book editor.

Russell Letson, *Locus* reviewer, computer maven, and collector of toy robots.

Michael A. Levy, co-editor of the *Science Fiction & Fantasy Book Review Annual* [7-23] and a professor of English at the University of Wisconsin–Stout.

Thanks are also due the best book selectors, profiled in chapter 15, and to Bill Contento, whose cumulative listings from the *Locus* bibliographies [7-2] proved invaluable.

Contributors

Neil Barron was an active fan in the late 1940s and early 1950s. He edited the three previous editions of *Anatomy of Wonder*, two companon guides to fantasy and horror literature, and in 1982 received the Pilgrim award for his overall contributions to SF and fantasy scholarship.

Walter Albert is retired from the University of Pittsburgh, where he taught French and Italian literature. His interest in the visual arts dates back to an early obsession with horror and fantasy films.

Paul A. Carter was professor of history at the University of Arizona until his retirement. His *The Creation of Tomorrow* [8-34] is a highly regarded history of American SF in magazines.

Thomas D. Clareson was one of the most distinguished scholars of science fiction until his death in July 1993. A number of his works are discussed in this guide.

Peter M. Coogan's specialty is American Studies, and he has long had an interest in comics.

Steve Eng has had hundreds of poems published and won the Rhysling award for SF poetry in 1979. Other interests include country music and western Americana.

James Gunn, now retired from the University of Kansas's English Department, is one of the SF field's outstanding scholars, teachers, and SF authors.

Michael Klossner is a librarian at the Arkansas State Library, Little Rock, and has an extensive knowledge of fantastic cinema, having reviewed many books in this specialty.

Dennis M. Kratz, a specialist in medieval culture, is a professor of Arts and Humanities at the University of Texas, Dallas, where he teaches graduate and undergraduate courses in SF and fantasy and is a specialist in translation.

Rob(ert) Latham co-edited the *Science Fiction & Fantasy Book Review Annual* [7-23] for its first four years. He contributed to chapters 4 and 10. He is working on his doctorate in literature at Stanford.

Michael M. Levy is now co-editor of the *Science Fiction & Fantasy Book Review Annual* [7-23] and is a professor of English at the University of Wisconsin–Stout.

Susan G. Miles is a reference librarian and coordinator of database services at Central Michigan University.

Francis J. Molson is a professor of English at Central Michigan University and the author of *Children's Fantasy* (1989).

Michael A. Morrison is a professor of physics and general education and an adjunct professor of English at the University of Oklahoma. He is the author of *Understanding Quantum Physics*, reviews SF and horror fiction, and is the co-editor of the forthcoming *Understanding Contemporary American Gothic.*

Joe Sanders is a professor of English at Lakeland Community College in Mentor, Ohio. He wrote the Starmont guide to E. E. Smith [9-106] and edited *Science Fiction Fandom* (1994).

Randall W. Scott, a longtime reader of fantastic literature, is a cataloger for the Russel B. Nye Popular Culture Collection of Michigan State University Libraries.

Brian Stableford is the author of considerable fantastic fiction and is one of SF's most knowledgeable critics. In 1987 he received the Distinguished Scholarship Award of the International Association for the Fantastic in the Arts.

Gary K. Wolfe has been a dean and professor at Roosevelt University, Chicago, for some years and is the author of *The Known and the Unknown* [8-145]. He received the Pilgrim award in 1987.

Introduction:
The Strange Journey

James Gunn

The first edition of *Anatomy of Wonder* appeared in 1976, in the midst of a flowering of academic consideration of science fiction. The fourth edition of this classic reference work comes forth when the SF garden is mature, when the most significant contributions may be updatings or filling in the gaps. It wasn't always so.

Science fiction got its identity as a genre in 1926 when Hugo Gernsback published *Amazing Stories* [12-2], the first SF magazine. Up to that time it had been produced as scattered examples of travel stories, satires, utopias, extraordinary voyages, and scientific romances. Gernsback brought it all together—the Poe inspiration, the Verne technological innovation and adventure, the Wells idea—and focused the interests of writers and readers on the stuff itself. In the process he associated this new material—first scientifiction, then, in 1929 when he founded *Science Wonder Stories*, science fiction—with the paraliterary reputation of the pulps. Mainstream critics made no nice distinctions, and still have not observed that science fiction emerged not from the pulp tradition but from the tradition of popular science. Clayton Magazines' *Astounding Stories of Super Science* (1930) [12-3] revealed what SF would have been had it evolved from those origins, but Street & Smith, when it purchased the magazine from the bankrupt Clayton, restored it to its original inspiration, particularly under the editorship of John W. Campbell, Jr., beginning in 1937.

World War II, however, was required to validate SF's vision. Sam Moskowitz began teaching evening classes at the City College of New York in 1953 and 1954; the first class taught as part of a college's standard offerings was by Mark Hillegas at Colgate University in 1962, shortly followed by Jack Williamson's classes at Eastern New Mexico University and Tom Clareson's at Wooster. My own did not begin until 1969.

The first ten years of that period, like that of any youngster, was a time of discovery, both for teachers and students. The second decade, like that of any adolescent, was a time of expansion. It was marked by enthusiasm and experimentation, uncertainty and suspicion. The fact that this period coincided with the great expansion in book publishing of science fiction and fantasy, from 348 books a year in 1972 to 1,288 a year in 1979, may be a coincidence.

The decade from 1972 to 1982 saw a significant increase in the teaching of science fiction not only in colleges but in high schools, although no one knows just how much teaching went on. Jack Williamson did an informal survey in the early 1970s, but no accurate count was ever undertaken. Only the effects can be measured: the slow but steady growth in membership in the Science Fiction Research Association (see chapter 15), founded in 1970, and the interest in teaching conferences and workshops, such as the sessions organized under the auspices of the National Council of Teachers of English, workshops offered by Marshall Tymn at Eastern Michigan University, and a famous conference at Kean College in Union, New Jersey.

It was a period when adventurous teachers wanted to teach science fiction courses, when all but the most conservative colleges and high schools wanted to offer science fiction courses, and when students by the hundreds wanted to enroll in science fiction courses. But it was also a time when few teachers knew what to teach or how to teach it. I was president of the Science Fiction Writers of America 1971–1972, and every week I received a letter from some distraught teacher saying that he or she had been assigned a class in science fiction, and what should be taught? In 1972, we should remember, there were virtually no histories (Donald Wollheim's personal history *The Universe Makers* [8-147], was published in 1971) and few books of criticism. The general anthologies available were *The Science Fiction Hall of Fame* (volume 1 only) [3-223], Robert Silverberg's *Mirror of Infinity* (1970), Dick Allen's *Science Fiction: The Future* (1971, 1983), and a few others intended for the mass market that went rapidly in and out of print. Novels were also ephemeral as far as the classroom was concerned, so even if there had been a consensus about what to teach, teachers would still question whether the books would be out of print.

So much for uncertainty. The suspicion came from both sides: the academic establishment considered science fiction "sub-literary" and the science fiction establishment considered science fiction teachers unqualified and their involvement possibly the kiss of death to the category. The latter reaction was summed up at the founding meeting of the Science Fiction Research Association in the exhortation Dena Brown wrote on the blackboard: "Let's take science fiction out of the classroom and put it back in the gutter where it belongs." A number of writers at the Kean College conference complained about what was being taught and who was teaching it, and Ben Bova published his concerns in an *Analog* editorial.

An outgrowth of that environment of suspicion (and of a guest *Analog* editorial I wrote in response to Ben's) was the Intensive English Institute on the Teaching of Science Fiction, which I organized at the University of Kansas and have offered for twenty years (skipping a couple of years after the first experimental offering). Its intent was to make up for the deficiencies in the academic backgrounds of would-be teachers of science fiction and the fact that they had not discovered science fiction, as they should have, when they were children. We set out to teach the teachers.

Meanwhile, the scholarly consideration of science fiction—which had begun with Philip Babcock Gove's *The Imaginary Voyage in Prose Fiction* (1941), J. O. Bailey's *Pilgrims Through Space and Time* (1947) [8-15], and Majorie Hope Nicolson's *Voyages to the Moon* (1948) [8-97]—got a major boost into respectability from Kingsley Amis's Christian Gauss lectures at Princeton in 1959, which were published the following year as *New Maps of Hell* [8-7]. Oxford University Press, not only the oldest but one of the most prestigious of the academic presses, published several books on science fiction in the mid-1960s, including Bruce Franklin's *Future Perfect* [1-36], I. F. Clarke's *Voices Prophesying War* [8-41], and Mark Hillegas's *The Future As Nightmare* [8-67], and in the 1980s published an ambitious series of single-author studies.

By 1975, when my Science Fiction Institute had its first session, I could prepare for my students a list of fifty-five books of academic interest or usefulness just from those I could see on my shelves. One of them was my own illustrated history, *Alternate Worlds* (1975) [8-62], which had been preceded as the first book-length history of the field by Brian W. Aldiss's *Billion Year Spree* (1973) [8-5]. Two academic journals had been created, *Extrapolation* and *Science-Fiction Studies*, and several more, especially

Foundation and *Fantasy Newsletter* (even more after it became *Fantasy Review*), published much of academic interest [see chapter 12 for details].

The first authoritative magazine indexes began publication in 1952. Cole's *A Checklist of Science-Fiction Anthologies* was superseded by Contento's *Index to Science Fiction Anthologies and Collections* [7-13]. Tuck's *The Encyclopedia of Science Fiction and Fantasy* [7-9] was followed by Nicholls's *The Science Fiction Encyclopedia* [7-22], Reginald's two-volume *Science Fiction and Fantasy Literature* [7-8], and my own *The New Encyclopedia of Science Fiction* [7-26], Bleiler's update of his 1948 *Checklist of Fantastic Literature* [7-1], the Dictionary of Literary Biography's two-volume *Twentieth Century American Science-Fiction Writers*, edited by Cowart and Wymer [7-24], Smith's *Twentieth Century Science-Fiction Writers* [7-30], and many more, including Williamson's *Teaching Science Fiction: Education for Tomorrow* [13-16] and a number of more specialized teaching guides, Tymn's *Science Fiction Reference Book* (1981), and Magill's five-volume *Survey of Science Fiction Literature* [7-27], followed by a five-volume *Survey of Modern Fantasy Literature* [7-36]. And, of course, *Anatomy of Wonder*.

Bibliographies, single-author studies, reprints of classic works in hard covers, even such specialized scholarly materials as bibliographies of first printings, compilations of the year's scholarly production, and book review indexes had appeared by 1982. Annual conferences offering opportunity for academics to share their research and ideas began in 1970 with the Science Fiction Research Association annual meeting now held at various locations, usually in June, and continued with the International Conference on the Fantastic in the Arts now held in March in the Fort Lauderdale area; the Eaton Conference held in April at the University of California at Riverside; the John W. Campbell Conference held in July at the University of Kansas; and a variety of special conferences held overseas as well as in the United States (see chapter 15 for details).

Add to all of these tools of scholarship and teaching various, more popular treatments of the field in text and pictures—covering film, radio, and television, compilations of critical essays, various how-to books, a wider selection of anthologies, including my own four-volume *The Road to Science Fiction* (1977-1982) [13-25], news journals such as *Locus* [12-24] and *Science Fiction Chronicle* [12-29], and novels that stayed longer in print— and the academic paraphernalia of science fiction was complete.

Meanwhile, academic interest in science fiction moved into its third and fourth decades. If the first decade represented experiment and the second decade expansion, the third and fourth decades might be expected to bring maturity. In many ways they did. But with maturity comes a

decline in exuberance, in the spirit of youthful adventure, and even sometimes in enthusiasm. How this will affect the teaching and study of science
fiction is still uncertain, but some indications may already be evident.

Enrollments in science fiction classes that once numbered in the hundreds, when enrollments were allowed to run that high, seem to have
tapered off to more normal numbers. There is only anecdotal evidence to
support this statement, just as was true of the situation in the 1970s. At the
University of Kansas, however, enrollments have dropped from 100 and
150 to 90, 85, 75, and now approximately 30 to 35. In many ways this
makes for better classes (and many colleges and universities never have
permitted really big classes), but it suggests a shift in attitude.

The teaching of science fiction also declined in high schools, with the
"return to basics" movement and the decreased use of half-semester mini-
courses.

The cause of these shifts is even more difficult to pin down. In high
schools, a greater emphasis on more traditional offerings, competency
testing, and merit salaries may have dampened the spirit of adventure. In
colleges, the conservatism of students, particularly in choosing courses
with career preparation and employability in mind, may have reduced
their willingness to take risks. Or, looking at the picture from the opposite
side, the fact that science fiction courses have become commonplace may
mean that teaching such a course, or taking one, no longer seems daring.
The pioneers may have moved on or simply retired.

By 1994, then, SF faced the problem of many once-unacceptable subjects that wedged their way into the curriculum: it had to maintain itself as
a suitable area of study on its own merits.

Academics involved in science fiction have filled their kits with all the
tools they need. Some of these tools, to be sure, must be sharpened periodically or replaced: Contento published a supplement to his index to
anthologies and collections [7-13] and was publishing with Charles Brown
of *Locus* an annual index to all works published, taken from the pages of
Locus [7-2]; and Robert Collins has turned *Fantasy Review* into an annual
[7-23].

Other major reference works must be regularly revised or redone.
Aldiss (with David Wingrove) produced in 1986 a new edition of *Billion
Year Spree* titled *Trillion Year Spree* [8-5]. Everett F. Bleiler published in 1990
a massive survey of *Science-Fiction: The Early Years* [7-21]; Noelle Watson and
Paul E. Schellinger edited in 1991 a third edition of *Twentieth-Century
Science-Fiction Writers* [7-30]; and Alexei and Cory Panshin produced in
1989 their long-in-the-works study *The World Beyond the Hill: Science Fiction
and the Quest for Transcendence* [8-101]. Peter Nicholls and John Clute

updated and expanded their *Science Fiction Encyclopedia* [7-22]; Robert Reginald compiled a massive supplement to his *Science Fiction and Fantasy Literature* [7-8]; and the fourth edition of *Anatomy of Wonder* is in your hands.

Anatomy of Wonder is a guide to the literature by periods and categories, with introductory essays and brief descriptions and evaluations written by knowledgeable authorities. Its value is attested by the four editions through which the book has come and the SFRA Pilgrim award its editor earned in 1982.

Single-author studies and theme-oriented collections of essays may be the most prevalent form of academic publishing today. Oxford allowed its single-author series to end at four volumes, but major programs still are under way at a variety of academic presses.

Definition, the heart of genre studies, has not yet been resolved to the satisfaction of everyone, maybe anyone, in spite of Scholes's "structural fabulation," Suvin's "cognitive estrangement," and Delany's "literal metaphor." I look for continued effort in this area, though perhaps not to produce anything final or revolutionary. Not only the subject matter but the essence of science fiction may be protean.

The teaching of science fiction will have to come to terms with two new elements: science fiction is somewhere between its former status as a minority literature (Damon Knight called it "the mass medium for the few") and a new situation as a significant part of everybody's experience. When the top grossing films of all time are called science fiction, and when as many as 2,000 books considered science fiction, fantasy, or horror are published every year and a few frequently appear on bestseller lists, teachers must cope with popular preconceptions rather than lack of information. The teacher and the scholar must ask, for instance, in what ways *Star Wars* and *E.T.* are science fiction, and in what ways they are something else, and why Isaac Asimov's *Foundation's Edge*, Arthur C. Clarke's *2010*, and Robert A. Heinlein's *Friday* were all on the bestseller list—and at the same time.

The science fiction teacher and student could have worse problems, as many of them remember. Science fiction may indeed be a mature academic discipline, with the principal task remaining to update and fill in the gaps. That may be good news for scholars looking for sources, citations, and dates, not so good for those who want to perform pioneer research. And yet maturity is often the illusion brought on by a lack of perspective. A revolutionary new vision is always possible; Young Turks may be gathering at this moment.

Nothing would delight SF people more.

Primary Literature

CHAPTER 1

The Emergence of Science Fiction: The Beginnings Through 1915

Thomas D. Clareson

The early history of science fiction has been explored much more fully since the publication of the first edition of *Anatomy of Wonder* in 1976. The bibliographies annotated in Chapter 7, notably those by Reginald, Clarke, and Clareson, as well as the important historical studies by Suvin, Clareson, and Stableford, provide abundant information about the evolution of English-language SF. These studies document in detail what my chapters in the previous editions of *Anatomy of Wonder* argued more briefly, "that between the Civil War and the 1920s in America alone as many as a thousand books were published that reflected directly the impact of scientific theory and technology on the literary imagination, and must be considered, at the least, as precursors of modern science fiction" (*Anatomy of Wonder*, 2nd ed., p. 3).

Because of the ready availability of these studies, this chapter is considerably more selective in its coverage, with a number of the titles simply mentioned more briefly in this introduction.[1] These deleted titles retain literary and historical value in themselves, but often that value lay in the individual work's uniqueness or in the close relationship it revealed between SF and the general body of fiction. The retained titles indicate the main thrust of the field as it acquired its modern identity.

The academic and popular attention given to SF has not proved an unmixed blessing, for some of the individuals have concentrated on literary theory and exclusive definitions instead of emphasizing historical perspective. Genre criticism, for example, tends to isolate SF in the present century as much as those who would confine SF to the specialist magazines. Some of the most enthusiastic devotees of the modern (post-1926) period would exclude the "lost-race" motif from the field, although increasingly throughout the 19th century the growing interest in prehistory, archaeology, geology, anthropology, and exploration created a wide audience for that type of fiction. Those areas of science and scientific speculation—concern for the "lost continent" of Atlantis, reaction to the discovery of prehistoric, non-European civilizations, reconciliation of such discoveries with the account given in Genesis—captured the literary and popular imaginations of the period as much as did the technological wonders pouring out of the laboratories of Bell and Edison and Tesla.

Nor is it helpful to insist that critics/literary historians find special criteria by which to evaluate science fiction because somehow, due to its subject matter, it differs from other literature. Again, that is divisive and makes as much sense as the outcries after the lunar landings and space probes that space travel should no longer be written about *as fiction* because of scientific findings. Such a judgment ignores the idea that SF has never been concerned with scientific discovery and the nuts and bolts of technology per se, but has tried instead to examine the effects of those developments on the individual person and on society as a whole. Perhaps the chief problem facing the student/reader of SF remains the recent attempt to distinguish sharply and completely between science fiction and fantasy instead of seeing them as intermingling in a complex literary tradition borrowing from and equal in importance to the tradition of social realism and literary naturalism. The most obvious examples occur in that fiction dealing with horror—from the gothic novel, at least, to the contemporary best-seller; from Mary Shelley and Edgar Allan Poe to the film *Aliens.*

Without calling for a strict definition, one can establish several characteristics to aid in understanding the historical development of the field. First, writers of SF make use of the discoveries, theories, and speculations in the fields of science that appeal to the imagination at the time the story is written. So long as something is thought to be scientific at the time the story is written, it should not be discarded subsequently as mere fantasy. Second, no society can develop a science fiction until it reaches a certain stage of scientific inquiry and technological development; before that time, it will not have the writers or the audience for SF because, individually and collectively, the literary interest lies elsewhere. Granting these premises, one must recall that fiction is a continuum having certain established conventions that writers and readers expect and make use of. Examples abound: the voyage to the moon in the 17th century, the "future history" created in the specialist magazines of the 1940s, the encounter with a supposedly vanished (alien) culture, be it terrestrial (19th century) or extraterrestrial (20th century).

One other ingredient is necessary to the emergence of a science fiction: belief in ongoing change. So long as Western civilization did not basically question the static mythos in which Earth is the center of creation and humanity's life and destiny are framed by the Fall and Final Judgment, there could be little speculation about alternative possibilities in the future. The Renaissance changed all that, although the beginning, ironically, came with the Crusades and found expression in the subsequent "travel books" of men like Sir John Mandeville and Marco Polo, which pictured the wonders lying beyond the European peninsula and provided glimpses of exotic kingdoms like Cathay and that of Prester John. Hard on the discovery of America, Sir Thomas More raised the island of Utopia [1-68], whose communistic society served as a vehicle for an implicit attack on England. One cannot overestimate the importance of More's *Utopia*. It gave its name to those innumerable societies portrayed well into the 20th century that advocated change and foresaw the perfectibility of the political state; moreover, it transformed the travel book into the "imaginary voyage," that narrative framework that has remained one of the essential literary forms of SF, whatever the destination of the voyager.

The imaginary voyage was never the exclusive domain of British writers; as Philip Babcock Gove has pointed out in *The Imaginary Voyage in Prose Fiction* (1941), it became the most popular form of fiction in the 17th century. While Sir Francis Bacon's *The New Atlantis* (1627) emphasized the importance science was beginning to assume, Andrae's *Christianopolis* (1619) portrayed an ideal Christian commonwealth on an island near the South Pole, and Tommaso Campanella's *The City of the Sun* (1623) described a metropolis in Central Asia where such subjects as mathematics, geology, geography, botany, and the mechanical arts were studied. Not until *Gulliver's Travels* [1-89], in which Swift satirized the Royal Societies of London and Dublin, did a major writer of a *terrestrial* imaginary voyage sharply question the increasing stature science was assuming in the intellectual milieu.

Generally speaking, the most notable voyages stemmed from the impact of Copernican astronomy. In 1610 Galileo had published *Sidereus Nuncius*, with its vivid descriptions of the heavens as seen through the telescope. Johannes Kepler's *Somnium* [1-54] postulates an inhabited moon, but in no way does his narrative contradict what might be observed. In that same year, 1634, there appeared the first English translation of Lucian's *True History*, important for its satiric accounts of voyages to the moon. The first English-language journey was Bishop Francis Godwin's *The Man in the Moone* [1-39]. During his visit to the lunar world, its protagonist, Domingo Gonsales, confirms the theories of Kepler and Galileo before turning his interest to the inhabitants who live in "another Paradise" amid their scientific researches. Perhaps no other single work proved so popular; Marjorie Nicolson has pointed out that J. B. D. (Jean Baudoin) translated it as *L'Homme dans la lune* (1648); it was this translation with which both Poe and Verne were familiar.[2]

Another British cleric, Bishop John Wilkins, used *A Discourse Concerning a New World and Another Planet* (1638) to argue that the moon may be "habitable" and went so far as to suggest that one day man would fly and establish a colony on the moon.[3] The third important title of the period was Cyrano de Bergerac's *Histoire comique des états et empires de la lune*, translated into English first by Tho. St. Serf and then by A. Lovell [1-12]. Emphasizing that Cyrano de Bergerac "had his feet on the new ground of science," Nicolson asserts that his narrative must be recognized as "the most brilliant of all the seventeenth century parodies of the cosmic voyage."[4] When Cyrano's first attempt to reach the Moon fails, he falls among the barbarians of New France in Canada, where, having built a new ship, he is propelled to the Moon by rocket power—caused by firecrackers sending his ship aloft. In the lunar kingdoms he finds himself classified with the lowest creatures, as does Lemuel Gulliver in *Gulliver's Travels*. Cyrano takes as his guide Godwin's Domingo Gonsales.

In *Iter Lunare* (1703), David Russen, a teacher at Hythe, in Kent, felt compelled to criticize the scientific inaccuracies of such fictions as those by de Bergerac and Godwin and to entertain the scientific data making spaceflight a probability. In this, of course, he echoed Bishop Wilkins. Other titles might be cited. Daniel Defoe's *The Consolidator* (1705) attacks both Wilkins and Godwin. He turns to the libraries of China, where he finds the record of a lunarian who had long ago been persuaded to be an intellectual leader in the court of the emperor; his own protagonist reaches the Moon in a ship powered by a gaseous *fuel*. Samuel Brunt's *A Voyage to Cacklogallinia* (1727) employs the project of a lunar flight as a means of satirizing the South Sea Bubble.

A century later George Tucker, writing as Joseph Atterley, made the first American contribution to the motif with *A Voyage to the Moon* [1-4], chiefly distinguished for the scientific accuracy of the conditions of the journey. He stressed that the ship "must cross an airless void in bitter cold."[5] In 1835, although not itself a description of a voyage, "Discoveries in the Moon Lately Made at the Cape of Good Hope, by Sir John Herschel"—published in the New York *Sun* by Richard Adams Locke and subsequently known simply as "The Moon Hoax"—created something of a sensation by describing at length the variety of life on the Moon. One cannot be certain of its exact relationship to Poe's "The Unparalleled Adventures of One Hans Pfaall" [1-75]. Although Poe gives an account of Pfaall's ascent by balloon, he concludes by explaining why the manuscript of Pfaall must be a hoax and continues with an attack on both Locke and Godwin. He demands that such narratives exhibit a verisimilitude as well as scientific accuracy. Edward Everett Hale attained so effective a degree of realism in "The Brick Moon" [1-48] that it can be read as the first story to deal with an artificial satellite. The narrative also proves to be the most delightfully comic parody of both the cosmic voyage and the post-Darwinian intellectual controversies written in the 19th century.

When Nicolson reminds her readers that Godwin, Wilkins, and Cyrano de Bergerac "established the conventions of the moon voyage for more than a century,"[6] she might have said that they dominated the extraterrestrial voyage until the 1870s, when Asaph Hall discovered the two moons of Mars and the Italian astronomer Giovanni Schiaparelli announced that he had observed "canali" on Mars. Although the Italian word implies no more than channels, a controversy arose that included such individuals as the American astronomer Percival Lowell, for *canals* on Mars implied intelligence and civilization; the ensuing debate has not been silenced completely even by recent space probes. Overnight Mars replaced the Moon as the most frequent destination of cosmic voyagers. Percy Greg's *Across the Zodiac* [1-40] inaugurated many new conventions, including the use of "apergy"—an electrical force counteracting gravity.

If the imaginary voyages went outward toward the Moon and Mars, they had also gone to subterranean worlds, as might be supposed in a society having the myths of Hades and the underworld. In the first of these, Holberg's *A Journey to the World Under-Ground* [1-50], Nicolas Klimius finds a hollow Earth and lands on the planet Nazar, which becomes a typical vehicle for satire. Holberg achieves much of his effectiveness by inverting the customs of European countries. Robert Paltock's *The Life and Adven-*

tures of Peter Wilkins [1-73], which enjoyed a popularity second only to those of *Robinson Crusoe* and *Gulliver's Travels*, took its narrator-protagonist by a river through extensive caverns to a deep valley near the South Pole, where he found a species of humanoid having the ability to fly. (By inventing mechanical wings, the Vril-ya of Bulwer-Lytton's *The Coming Race* [1-61] share the ability to fly; more importantly, they understand the nature and use of "vril," a kind of electrical force that is the essence of all matter.)

The polar regions have long attracted those who wrote of imaginary voyages. The myth of *terra australis incognita* (the land mass that medieval geographers thought must exist to balance the heavily laden northern hemisphere in order to prevent the Earth from turning over) kept the Antarctic a vital part of the Western imagination. After the discovery of America not only was there the added attraction of the hazardous passage of the Strait of Magellan, but an obsession to find the Northwest Passage around the American continent to Asia lured innumerable explorers into the Arctic. Captain Cook's explorations of the South Seas late in the 18th century fueled the concepts of the noble savage and idyllic lands somewhere beyond the limitations of Europe. As the 19th century ended, the race to the poles themselves made headlines. While these historical matters made the Antarctic and Arctic settings attractive, the decisive literary factor arose from the first American utopia, *Symzonia: A Voyage of Discovery* [1-81] by Captain Adam Seaborn, possibly the pseudonym of John Cleves Symmes of Ohio. He proposed that the Earth is hollow, containing seven inhabitable spheres, and that the innermost, utopian sphere is accessible through openings at both poles. The idea sparked the American and British imaginations. In 1826, with a collaborator, he published *Symmes Theory of Concentric Spheres*; in 1827 he lectured at Union College; in 1834, after his death, J. N. Reynolds—a friend of Poe—appealed to Congress. By the end of that decade officers of American and British ships were under orders to watch for the polar openings, especially in Antarctica. As late as 1873 an article in the *Atlantic Monthly* argued the existence of "Symmes Hole"; in perhaps a more learned fashion, the debate was repeated in an Ohio journal in 1909.[7] Yet one infers that the theory would have become another of those dry, 19th century scholarly exchanges had it not been for the imagination of Edgar Allan Poe, especially as it gained expression in his longest, though fragmentary, work, *The Narrative of Arthur Gordon Pym of Nantucket* [1-74].

One characteristic of these early imaginary voyages must be noted. They occurred "here-and-now," even *Symzonia* and *Arthur Gordon Pym*. Several explanations come to mind. First, the new astronomy and the physical exploration of the world gave the writers settings not needing a time shift. Second, as a literary vehicle with an emphasis on utopia, the voyage provided a means of social criticism having no need of the future. Finally, the implications for change inherent in the industrial and political revolutions had only begun to be realized by the early 19th century.

The earliest fictions to make conscious predictions about the future were, as I. F. Clarke has pointed out [7-5], two 18th-century British projections emphasizing the continuity of European affairs and, quite naturally, the continuing ascendancy of Great Britain. Samuel Madden's *Memoirs of the Twentieth Century* (1733) pictures a continent dominated by the pope and Jesuits (the latter control Russia), although "everywhere" the United Kingdom continued to have power and prestige. *The Reign of George VI, 1900–1925* [1-2] gives a jingoistic Tory description of an ideal monarch who defeats all of Europe after repelling a Russian invasion near Durham. (America, incidentally, remains a loyal colony.)

In that these two narratives ignore the concept of progress—of dramatic change, particularly in terms of differences resulting from the industrial revolution—they fail to take heed of that mood which increasingly dominated the 18th century. As the Renaissance deepened into the Enlightenment, the concept that reason was the highest faculty of the mind drew increasing favor in intellectual circles—and a rational mind *must* exist in a rational universe whose laws could be discerned by further investigation. Such a view envisioned the perfectibility both of humanity and of the sociopolitical state, creating an optimism that remains even in the 1990s at the heart of much SF. (To the extent that this optimism faltered, the dystopian mood of the present century, especially in Europe and especially in the late 1960s, has gained supporters.)

The first vision of a change bringing about the betterment of society came in Louis Sebastien Mercier's *L'An 2440* [1-63], translated into English as *Memoirs of the Year Two Thousand Five Hundred* (1771; America, 1795). The "first influential story of the future in world literature, [it] became one of the most widely read books of the last quarter of the eighteenth century."[8] Its protagonist falls asleep, awakening in a Paris transformed by science and invention. In the United States Mary Griffith's "Three Hundred Years Hence" [1-43] foresees a society in which all advancements have resulted from technological achievements and changes in attitude toward such social issues as women's rights. Between them these novels set the pattern for many of the subsequent portraits of future societies—particularly that legion of utopian states created in the last decades of the 19th century, climaxing, perhaps, with H. G. Wells's *A Modern Utopia* [1-101]. Clarke suggests that beginning with Mercier's

novel, this body of fiction is "an extension of the scheme Bacon had presented in *The New Atlantis.*"[9] It grew out of that faith in inevitable progress,
which became so much a part of the makeup of the 19th-century mind. By
projecting utopia into the future, Mercier and Mrs. Griffith—and their
successors—gave substance to J. O. Bailey's insight that utopia "shifted
from a place to be found to a condition to be achieved."[10]

Yet even as this optimism took shape, the gothic intruded, giving to the
emerging SF a new dimension and an emotional intensity it had not previously known. The dream of the Enlightenment balanced precariously on
the razor's edge of the debate involving epistemology that grew out of
Locke's "Essay concerning Human Understanding" (1690). If one ignores
the paraphernalia of the gothic plots, beginning with Walpole's *The Castle
of Otranto* (1765), then one realizes that its enduring core comes out of
the disquieting conclusions of the 18th-century psychological empiricists.
As a fictional mode it reawakened the demonic and the irrational. Man,
the solitary individual, was marooned in a vast, brooding nature, which
one could not be sure was "reality." In romantic art the situation is typified
by the lone figure dwarfed against vast mountains or the sea. In addition
to this isolation, he also could not be certain that his mind functioned
properly. The issue was simple: could he comprehend reality if; indeed,
he actually perceived it? A negative answer opens up the world of the
absurd.

Poe's *The Narrative of Arthur Gordon Pym of Nantucket* [1-74] dramatizes
this dilemma. During the first portion of the narrative, Pym, telling his
own story, emphasizes his heightened psychological excitement and
uncertainties until the reader questions whether Pym's reports are reliable, if sane. Once aboard the *Lady Guy* headed into the Antarctic wastes,
however, Pym becomes a veritable personification of rationality as he
records the details of an external world different from anything he (or his
reader) has ever known. The story breaks off abruptly when Pym and his
companions, in a canoe, find themselves drawn toward a cataract and a
chasm near the South Pole; the imagery evokes only associations with
Symmes's theory of polar openings. The lasting impact of Poe's story may
be seen by the number of later authors who attempted sequels, ranging
from Charles Romyn Dake's *A Strange Discovery* (1899) to Verne's *An
Antarctic Mystery* (American edition, 1899).

Successful as Poe was, however, Mary Shelley's *Frankenstein; or, The
Modern Prometheus* [1-84] had an even greater effect on SF. In asserting
that SF "was born from the Gothic mode [and] is hardly free from it now,"
Brian Aldiss argues that *Frankenstein* was the first science fiction novel.[11] In
the island kingdom of Utopia, Sir Thomas More gave SF its first myth;

Mary Shelley gave the field its second myth in her tale of a being patched together from cadavers and given life by a scientist who has trespassed beyond those limits set for man. Her monster is Dr. Frankenstein, who conjures up the image of Faust as he plays God and then recoils in horror from the creature he has created. Through the technique of the story-within-a-story, the heart of the novel becomes the unnamed creature's account of his repeated rejection by all those whom he meets, including Victor Frankenstein. Becoming increasingly demented (by error he was given the brain of a criminal), he gives himself to his craze for revenge, pursuing Frankenstein across the vast Arctic ice floe. Despite the appearance and seeming madness of the creature, some persons read the novel as Mary Shelley's plea on behalf of individualism. She brings her indictment against Dr. Frankenstein, who, crazed himself, seeks to kill the being he has created. Guilt-ridden, he recognizes that, like Faust, he has committed the sin of intellectual pride in his zeal to be the first to create another being.

Mary Shelley seized on a second, apocalyptic theme in her final novel, *The Last Man* [1-85], in which a plague sweeps through Europe annihilating humanity. Her protagonist, believing himself the only survivor, struggles toward Rome in search of someone alive. Hers was not the first such catastrophe. As a reaction to Dr. Edward Jenner's published results of his work with vaccine, as well as Thomas Malthus's dire predictions of over-population, Jean-Baptiste Cousin de Grainville wrote *Le Dernier Homme* (1805; English translation, 1806), called by Clarke the "earliest account in fiction of the last days of mankind."[12] Between them they created what may be called the "catastrophe motif," a kind of story permeating Wells's fiction and forming the basis of such individual novels as Doyle's *The Poison Belt* [1-32] and London's *The Scarlet Plague* [1-60]. To read the motif as nothing more than the dark side of the vision of humanity's perfectibility is an oversimplification, for it does not take into account that in the late 19th and early 20th centuries—especially before World War I—the scientist/engineer saved at least a segment of humanity from some natural disaster, as in Garrett P. Serviss's *The Second Deluge* [1-83], or helped survivors to rebuild a devastated world, as in George Allan England's *Darkness and Dawn* trilogy [1-33].

Although de Grainville and Mary Shelley introduced a third lasting motif, their works stand unique in the early part of the century, for the gothic mode more typically concentrated on the aberrations of the individual mind, as best illustrated by the short tales of Poe, like "The Black Cat" and "The Tell-Tale Heart," where first-person narrators reveal the depths to which they have sunk because of their obsessions. Therein lies the heritage of terror coming down from the gothic to contemporary fiction, as in Stephen King's *Pet Sematary* (1983). In the mid-19th century the writer who most nearly equaled Poe was Fitz-James O'Brien, whose "The Diamond Lens" [1-72] introduces a new world to SF. Using a perfect lens, its protagonist, the microscopist Linley, discovers in a drop of water a subatomic world in which the beautiful nymph, Animula, dwells; he falls in love with her but inadvertently allows the water to evaporate so that she dies. He goes mad, ending up in a madhouse. Perhaps the best-known story using the subatomic world remains Ray Cummings's *The Girl in the Golden Atom*, first serialized in *All-Story Weekly* in 1919. Unquestionably the most terrible remains Mark Twain's pessimistic "The Great Dark" [1-25], not published until long after his death. Its first-person protagonist falls through his microscope into the subatomic world of a drop of water, where he and his family must sail forever aboard a ship that has no port as a haven. Against nothing but intense heat and light or intense darkness and cold, great monsters rise occasionally from the water, sometimes threatening the ship itself. (They are, of course, microbes.) No story better captures Twain's hatred and fear of the concept of determinism, which increasingly haunted his imagination. Nor did he offer himself or his reader surcease by relying on the shopworn convention of awakening from a dream. There was no respite.

In the 1890s fear unified the best fiction of Ambrose Bierce. Throughout his stories Bierce refers to racial memory, particularly in terms of the human inheritance of a terrible dread of death and the unknown. He gave a new dimension to horror by drawing on biology in "The Damned Thing" [1-13]; he assigned to the traditional creatures of such stories as O'Brien's "What Was It" (1859) and Maupassant's "Le Horla" (1887) a scientific explanation: just as there are sounds that man cannot hear, so, too, "at each end of the spectrum the chemist can detect what are known as 'actinic rays,' representing colors man cannot see. And, God help me [writes the diarist] The Damned Thing is of such a color."

Although Henry James gave little or no explicit attention in his texts to scientific data, like Bierce he showed an awareness of the new psychology in his ghost stories dealing with obsession and hallucination. "Maud Evelyn" (1900) seems inexplicably neglected by critics, while the incomparable ambiguity of "The Turn of the Screw" (1898) marks one of the high points of turn-of-the-century fiction. Ford Madox Ford's reference to James's technique as the "analysis of an anxious state of mind"[13] applies almost as well to much of the fiction of Bierce. Between them the two did more than any of their contemporaries to transform the traditional ghost story into a psychological case study.

The concern for abnormal states of mind had taken another turn as early as Oliver Wendell Holmes's *Elsie Venner* (1861) with its medical interest in multiple personality. The classic example from the 19th century remains Stevenson's *The Strange Case of Dr. Jekyll and Mr. Hyde* [1-86], in which a London physician hopes to use a drug to rid himself of that streak of evil within him which has marred his personality since his youth; unwittingly he "frees a monster of evil who finally dominates him."[14] As one examines a spectrum of American stories from Thomas Bailey Aldrich's "The Queen of Sheba" (1877) to Albert Bigelow Paine's *The Mystery of Evelin Delorme* (1894) and Vincent Harper's *The Mortgage on the Brain* (1905), one does not know how to interpret the fact that most of the fiction dealing with multiple personality builds around a love story in which the young woman suffers from some mental quirk. Except for amnesia, one cannot describe the condition as any kind of breakdown. Intriguingly, only in such novels as *Some Ladies in Haste* (1908) and *The Green Mouse* (1910) does the fashionable New York writer Robert W. Chambers add an element of comedy to his love stories. The protagonist of *Some Ladies in Haste* uses posthypnotic suggestion to induce the first five young women he sees from the windows of his club to fall in love with some of his friends. One of the young women is, of course, his fiancée. The protagonist of *The Green Mouse* develops a machine capable of intercepting psychic waves, thereby assuring that one falls in love with the person one *should* love and marry. An advertisement for the machine reads in part: "Wedlock by Wireless. Marriage by Machinery. A Wonderful Wooer without Words." In a sense Chambers anticipates the computer-dating fad, although his own central couples follow the impulses of their irrational hearts.

In and of themselves the novels concerned with psychological abnormalities make up a cul-de-sac. To begin with, they dated very quickly. Since their settings and action involved everyday life—thus the popularity of the love story—they were soon lost among substantive concerns and narrative techniques, like the stream of consciousness, which led to modern psychological realism. One strand developed into novels—which some persons label fantasy, others, SF—such as Jack London's *The Star Rover* (1915), whose protagonist, a prisoner in solitary confinement, teaches himself "astral projection"; with his spirit freed from his body, he experiences a number of incarnations. In terms of SF, psychological aberrations were replaced by the motif dealing over the years with mutants, androids, "supermen," and clones. A pair of scientists in Wells's *The Food of the Gods* [1-99] develops a food supplement causing giantism and producing individuals who are superior to Homo sapiens. More typical of the motif is John Davys Beresford's *The Hampdenshire Wonder* [1-11], whose youthful protagonist, a mutant, has a mind far in advance of those of his contemporaries. The motif includes such later titles as Stapledon's *Odd John* [2-120] and van Vogt's *Slan* [3-180]. A noteworthy early American example has never been republished: Edgar Fawcett's *Solarion* [1-34] gives a new twist to the Frankenstein story in that one of its main characters is a dog possessing an artificially enhanced intelligence.

During the last decades of the 19th century the interest in psychology remained peripheral to what seemed at the time more central, vital concerns. The first motif to dominate the emerging SF dramatized the portrayal of future wars. In May 1871, *Blackwood's* published anonymously *The Battle of Dorking: Reminiscences of a Volunteer* [1-21]. Coming fresh upon the surprising result of the Franco-Prussian War, amid a growing hysteria of nationalism and imperialism, as I. F. Clarke has pointed out in *Voices Prophesying War* [8-41], *The Battle of Dorking* caught the British populace in a mood of foreboding and uncertainty regarding the future of the empire. Published throughout the English-speaking world and widely translated, it triggered a reaction throughout Europe, serving as the prototype for innumerable books predicting an imminent holocaust. Its author, Sir George Tomkyns Chesney, who had been recalled from India to establish the Royal Indian Engineering College at Staines, warned his countrymen against a German invasion and British defeat because Britain had refused to accept the cost of building her defenses and so had remained militarily unprepared. Most importantly, he predicted that the use of new weapons would decide the outcome of such a struggle. This attention to the "hardware" of the period proved to be the distinctive innovation of the story.

As one might expect, most of the British authors forecast a war that would be decided in a great sea battle: *The Great Naval War of 1887* (serialized in *St. James Gazette* in 1887) and *Trafalgar Refought* (1905), both by William Laird Clowes and A. H. Burgoyne; *The Captain of the 'Mary Rose'* (1892) by Clowes; *Blake of the 'Rattlesnake'* (1895) by Frederick T. Jane, who gained his fame through his annual books describing the standing navies in *Jane's Ships*. The authors showed their fascination with the new "ironclads," those "dreadnaughts" that became the battleships of the line by the turn of the century, although they also gave much attention to the tiny "torpedo boats," like Jane's *Rattlesnake*, whose speed and mobility made them the despair of the ponderous, seemingly invincible ironclads.

Rear Admiral P. Colomb gave his name to the collaboration of a number of military men and journalists who produced *The Great War of 189-: A*

Forecast [1-26], first published in the illustrated magazine *Black and White*. It was widely translated immediately. By 1894, according to Clarke, its German version, *Der grosse Krieg von 189-*, had reached its fifth edition; in a special introduction General von Below praised it because it concerned itself not only with tomorrow's battles but also with "'the subject of international politics in Europe.'"[15] It portrayed an Anglo-Saxon struggle against a Franco-Russian alliance; its fighting engulfed the Eurasian continent from the approaches to Paris and the Riviera to Vladivostok. These tales have an importance for intellectual history not only for the insights that they give into the military strategy and armaments race at the turn of the century, but for their reflection of the uncertain, shifting alliances of the period.

In the earlier works France continued to be the primary, traditional enemy. As early as Robert Cromie's *For England's Sake* (1889), British forces fought the good fight against Russia in Asia, a result of the tensions involving India; in his *The Next Crusade* (1896), Britain teamed with Austria to defeat Russia and Turkey, thereby making the Mediterranean "a British lake." If one names a single factor that tipped the scales, it must be the naval race between Britain and Germany, which led to the alignments caught up in the debacle of World War I. The persistent fear of invasion of the British Isles, strengthened by the prophecy and immediacy—in terms of realistic detail (the kind of emotional impact Wells achieved by destroying the villages around the city of London in *The War of the Worlds* [1-105])—of *The Battle of Dorking*, may have triggered the decision to side with France against Germany. If so, then the matter-of-fact tone of Erskine Childers's *Riddle of the Sands* [1-24] may have been the literary achievement of the period; its protagonist supposedly discovers a German plot to invade England and reports in detail the method that Germany would use to gain surprise and victory. The plot—or, rather, the public's shift in allegiance—seemed to be confirmed by the publication of August Niemann's *Der Weltkrieg—Deutsche Traume* (1904), translated as *The Coming Conquest of England.*

Niemann's success reminds us that other voices than British clamored for war. In France, for example, as early as 1892–1893, Capitaine Danrit (E. A. Driant) published his first trilogy of books outlining his concepts of the next conflict with Germany: *La Guerre en forteresse, La Guerre en rase campagne,* and *La Guerre en ballon.* In 1888 he had been appointed adjutant to General Boulanger at the Ministry of War and married Boulanger's youngest daughter in the autumn of that year. From 1892 to 1896 he served as an instructor at St. Cyr before being recalled to active duty. He wrote with equal ease of wars against the Germans or the British. The

urge to express an intense nationalism that brought glory to the homeland, whoever the enemy, seemed to provide adequate motivation for
these writers. Driant, incidentally, died at Verdun.

Clarke points out that the future war motif had its greatest impact
when it captured the imagination of the public; this occurred when journalists, like George Griffith and Louis Tracy, made use of mass circulation
journals and papers. He singles out William Le Queux, who first gained
fame with *The Great War in England in 1897* [1-57], but achieved an even
greater success with *The Invasion of 1910* (1906), a cliché-ridden diatribe
against those persons—especially those in government—whom he
accused of ignoring Lord Roberts's warning that Great Britain had not
prepared itself for modern warfare.[16] Clarke explains the success of the
"new mythology of imaginary wars" in terms of "the nationalistic emotions
of the period." Of the writers themselves, he declares, "[They] were trying
to create a Beowulf myth for an industrial civilization of ironclads and
high-speed turbines, a new and violent *chanson de geste* for an age of imperialism, told in the inflammatory language of the mass press."[17] The
European writers won many a land battle, however, with cavalry charges—
just as the cavalry waited impatiently behind the trenches to charge to victory in World War I. The most terrible irony of the future war motif in
Europe, at least, is that no writer foresaw the impasse of trench warfare,
the gas attacks, the aerial warfare. Trapped by past glories (or infamous
defeats, as in the case of France) and the surge of nationalism, they failed
to see the implications of the new weaponry. Irony on irony: one wonders
whether the Battle of Jutland was cut short because those in command
remembered the widespread prediction that the next major war would be
finished by a single, glorious battle at sea. As one might expect, Wells
proved to be the exception; in *The War in the Air* [1-104], he expressed the
fear that social collapse would follow the expected world conflict because
men would not have the ability to solve their social and political problems
or to control such new weapons as the airplane. In contrast—perhaps in
desperation—although his *The World Set Free* (1914) envisions atomic warfare, ultimately a rational settlement of world affairs establishes a utopian
state, for international politics and devastating armaments have made sovereign, fragmented nations and empires untenable.

Because of the persistence of the concept of Manifest Destiny and the
consequent flirtation with imperialism at the turn of the century, the
United States did not escape the wildfire. With the advent of World War I,
writers allowed German hordes to occupy the continental United States.
Cleveland Moffett's *The Conquest of America* [1-67], serialized in *McClure's
Magazine,* typifies the response; he used Thomas A. Edison by name as the

inventor who turned the tide. In that Edison was a member of a special board appointed to overcome the crisis, Moffett reflects the probable influence of Frank Stockton's *The Great War Syndicate* [1-88], in which appointed businessmen lead the United States to victory over Britain.

From the first, American treatments of the motif had a distinctive quality that grew out of its own dreams and nightmares. As early as 1880, in *Last Days of the Republic* [1-30], P. W. Dooner had warned of an "impending catastrophe" resulting from the importation into California of cheap coolie labor. Because the Chinese keep together even when their number increases and because they remain loyal to their homeland, China eventually conquers the United States. The theme of "the yellow peril"[18]—this time Japanese—recurred in such novels as J. U. Giesy's *All for His Country* (1915), in which a Mexican-Japanese invasion is beaten back only after the invention of an "aero destroyer," and in Hector C. Bywater's essaylike tome, *The Great Pacific War: A History of the American-Japanese Campaign of 1931–33* (1925), which is often cataloged by libraries as nonfiction. It persisted in Gawain Edwards's *The Earth Tube* (1929), in which nameless "Mongol" legions stalk across both American continents, and during the 1930s found a haven in such pulp magazines as *Dusty Ayres and His Battle Birds* and *Operator #5*, whose heroes thwarted every effort of Asiatic hordes to ravage the United States. The obsession with the yellow peril had also gained expression as early as a three-part, "factual" prediction in *Cosmopolitan* (1908), "If War Should Come," whose author, Captain Pierson Hobson, identified as "one of the greatest living experts in the sciences of war,"[19] described a sneak attack on Hawaii. One infers that this body of popular literature made conflict with Japan inevitable. Certainly it contributed to the imprisonment of Nisei Americans during World War II; one wonders how a continued portrayal of rampaging Asiatic armies would have influenced the public reaction toward Vietnam.

The second American variation found expression as early as Stanley Waterloo's *Armageddon* (1898). American scientists develop a dirigible-like craft to defeat a European coalition and promise to keep up the good work until they invent a weapon "so terrible" that fear of it will bring all war to an end. American politicians form an Anglo-Saxon alliance with Great Britain and decree that their councils will direct the affairs of the world, perhaps for generations, until the "lesser breeds" are capable of governing themselves. One can catalog the permutations of these themes: Benjamin Rush Davenport's *Anglo-Saxons Onward* (1898), Simon Newcomb's *His Wisdom: The Defender* (1900), Hollis Godfrey's *The Man Who Ended War* (1908), Roy Norton's *The Vanishing Fleets* (1908), and J. Stewart Barney's *L.P.M.: The End of the Great War* [1-6].

In *The Vanishing Fleets*, Norton permits a recalcitrant Kaiser to become part of an Anglo-Saxon triumvirate, but only after he has repented following internment in a lumber camp in the Pacific Northwest, where he glimpses intuitively those higher truths that should govern humanity. At the other end of the limited spectrum, in *L.P.M.: The End of the Great War* [1-6], Barney's protagonist, the American scientist Edestone, first defeats all the warring nations with his advanced weapons and then calls for an authoritarian world government to be ruled by "the Aristocracy of Intelligence," presumably made up of businessmen and scientists. Only in Arthur Cheyney Train and Robert Williams Wood's *The Man Who Rocked the Earth* [1-91], serialized in the *Saturday Evening Post* in the autumn of 1914, does a conference of nations assemble in Washington to abolish war and form a federated, utopian world state. However racist and jingoistic this concept of alliances and conferences may seem more than 80 years later, one wonders what influence, if any, it may have had on Henry Ford's peace mission or the thinking of President Wilson.

While some writers celebrated their nationalism and the new technology in the future war motif, others gave new vitality to the established imaginary voyage and created the second dominant motif of the period. Before one reaches H. Rider Haggard and the lost-race novel, however, one must confront the problem of Jules Verne. In Britain, as early as 1877, he gained a devoted following because he presented "to the public, in a series of fantastic romances and marvelous travels, the results of the wonderful discoveries and theories of modern men of science."[20] The prefatory "In Memoriam" to the posthumous collection of W. H. Rhodes's short stories, *Caxton's Book* [1-78], suggests that had Rhodes been able to devote himself more to his fiction than to the practice of law, even by the late 1860s "the great master of scientific fiction, Jules Verne, would have found the field of his efforts already sown and reaped." For some persons, like the American editor Hugo Gernsback, who emphasize the prophetic nature of SF—especially its accuracy in extrapolating technological achievement—Verne became the founder of a new field of fiction, SF. Even after Gernsback lost control of *Amazing Stories*, a sketch of "Jules Verne's Tombstone at Amiens Portraying His Immortality" graced the masthead of the magazine.

By the early 1860s Verne had written a number of comedies and comic operettas for various theaters in Paris, as well as a few short stories. In 1862 he wanted to complete a factual article dealing with African exploration, incorporating into it the idea that the use of a balloon would make such a venture easier. The publisher, Pierre Hetzel, asked that he change the article into fiction; apparently, too, it was Hetzel who spoke of an

adventure story based on scientific fact. The result was *Cinq semaines en ballon* (1863; published in the United States as *Five Weeks in a Balloon*, 1869),
the first of *Les Voyages extraordinaires*. Its protagonist, Dr. Samuel Ferguson,
an English explorer, becomes the source of vast amounts of information
as he and his companions drift from Zanzibar across the interior of Africa,
sighting Lake Victoria. Ferguson declares the lake to be the source of the
Nile (in the same year John Speke confirmed that observation). The narrative establishes the basic conventions Verne employed throughout his
fiction: a man of reason (a scientist) both invents the necessary gadgetry
and provides an abundance of factual information; a journey to some
exotic destination provides the narrative frame, while a series of largely
disconnected episodes, usually involving the threat of pursuit and capture, makes up the story.

By 1864 Hetzel had launched a new magazine for younger readers—
Magasin d'éducation et de récréation—and in the initial March issue there
appeared the first installment of Verne's second story, *Les Aventures du
Capitaine Hatteras* (*The Adventures of Captain Hatteras* [1-92], published in
book form in 1867), whose explorers find the elusive North Pole at the
cost of Hatteras's sanity. It was not issued in book form until after the success of *Voyage au centre de la terre* (*A Journey to the Center of the Earth*, 1864 [1-
94]) and *De la terre a la lune* (*From the Earth to the Moon*, 1865 [1-93]). In
the former he relied on the theory that volcanoes are joined by subterranean passages permitting them to be fed from some fiery source within
the Earth. His "gadget" was the so-called Ruhmkorff coil, for which the
German physicist Heinrich Ruhmkorff received a cash award in the same
year that Verne wrote the story. One can certainly call it a rudimentary
form of the flashlight, but at that time such an application of electricity
was unknown to the public. (As with so many of his contemporaries, electricity fascinated Verne; he relied on it again and again.) He also displayed the 19th-century fascination with geology, for as his explorers go
deeper into the Earth, they find relics of the prehistoric past, ranging
from the bones of extinct animals and men to the sight of a gigantic man-
like creature acting as a shepherd of a herd of mastodons. In this way
Verne dramatized, to some extent at least, the highly controversial theory
of evolution.

In *From the Earth to the Moon* he spends much of the narrative developing a cannon capable of firing a projectile at a velocity of seven miles per
second—that is, escape velocity. He later defended his practice while condemning Wells's use of a metal negating the power of gravity. In the second part of the novel, *Autour de la lune* (*Round the Moon*, 1870 [1-93]), the
projectile orbits the Moon because it is deflected by a comet; it returns to

Earth and splashes down in the Pacific, where its voyagers, not unlike modern astronauts, are picked up by a U.S. naval vessel. Published in the same year, *Vingt milles lieues sous les mers* (*Twenty Thousand Leagues Under the Sea*, 1870 [1-95]) undoubtedly remains his best-known and most popular *voyage extraordinaire*. It features his most notable protagonist, Captain Nemo, that self-willed outcast of society who loves freedom and hates despotism and at least echoes the earlier gothic heroes. The novel remains a veritable encyclopedia of oceanography, a kind of underwater travelogue ranging from the sunken Atlantis to shipwrecks and Spanish bullion, from descriptions of underwater life to the fierce encounter with the giant squid. He named the *Nautilus* for the submarine Robert Fulton built in France under the sponsorship of Napoleon I.

When one examines Verne's major work closely, a single question looms ever larger: in what way was Verne so original that he earned the reputation of founding a new form of fiction? He himself never claimed that he had done so. One notices that he made use of knowledge available to the scientific community of his period—and to anyone else who bothered to look it up—and that he relied on a narrative frame long available and frequently used. He gave enthusiastic voice to the obvious accomplishments of the new technology, although like most of his contemporaries he does not seem to appreciate the full implications of the science giving rise to that technology. To say these things does not detract from the vividness of his imagination or the impact of his ability as a storyteller. It does ask, however, in what way he differed from his contemporary writers: how was he unique? As Everett Carter reminded his readers in *Howells and the Age of Realism*, the scientist—that is, medical men, engineers, inventors, machinists, archaeologists, and even students of such exotic subjects as the occult and Egyptology—became protagonists of popular fiction in the last decades of the 19th century.[21] Except for his encyclopedic presentation of the "latest" facts—and, perhaps, his impressionable young audience, although research indicates that adults read his books as frequently as did children—one cannot immediately perceive what distinguishes Verne from the many other authors who made use of the imaginary voyage framework.

For example, James De Mille's *A Strange Manuscript Found in a Copper Cylinder* [1-28] echoes Symmes and Poe, for an unknown culture survives in the Antarctic, and a group of educated Englishmen aboard a becalmed yacht rescue from the sea a manuscript giving an account of a marooned sailor's experience among the people. Three times they interrupt the narrative of the sailor—"Thomas More"—to speculate about the feasibility of its contents. By this means De Mille introduces a variety of scientific and

technical data from the period as the Englishmen debate the story's validi-
ty. The resulting fusion of known fact and imagination makes the novel
one of the most effective of its kind; indeed, the technique makes De
Mille's novel unique.

Other voyagers had long found enchanting cities and countries that
provided them with a means of criticizing their own societies. By the end
of the century many writers employing the imaginary voyage framework
championed a neoprimitivism, condemning the new urban-industrial society. In Albert Bigelow Paine's *The Great White Way* (1901), an American
expedition finds a people in Antarctica who live in close harmony with
nature in a valley so beautiful that the narrator calls it "the land of heart's
desire." The people have developed the power of telepathy. The young
technologist chooses to marry the queen of this agrarian society instead of
returning to the outer world. In Henry Drayton's *In Oudemon* (1901), the
narrator stumbles across a group of British colonists in the mountains of
South America; they possess an advanced technology of a sort and have
access to the outer world, but they, too, choose to deny the materialism of
the Western world. As with the future war motif, one could catalog titles.

One writer—Sir H. Rider Haggard—gave the lost-race motif its lasting,
most popular form. After writing *King Solomon's Mines* [1-45], a panorama
of Africa drawing on his personal knowledge of the land, Haggard created
She: A History of Adventure [1-46] and *Allan Quatermain* [1-44]. In *She* his
explorers reach the Valley of Kor in the unknown heart of the continent,
where they find descendants of a lost colony of Egyptians living near the
ruins of a once-great city. They are ruled by Ayesha—"She-Who-Must-Be-
Obeyed." Given immortality by the Flame of Life, she languishes impatiently, awaiting the reincarnation of her beloved Kallikrates, who lives
again in Haggard's protagonist, Leo Vincent. Her accidental death cuts
short their renewed love. *Allan Quatermain* changes that, for the protagonist takes as his wife the lovely queen of the sun-worshipping Zu-Vendris,
Nyleptha, who bears him a son—"a regular curley-haired, blue-eyed young
Englishman in looks . . . destined to inherit the throne of the Zu-Vendris."
In short, Haggard created a form that focused on a love story of a modern
Western man for a primitive beauty, a pagan princess so beautiful that
"language fails me when I try to give some idea of the blaze of loveliness
[possessed by Nyleptha and her sister]." He was immediately parodied
and endlessly imitated. Only Bellamy's *Looking Backward* [1-8] drew a
greater literary response; there was, however, a difference, because after a
few parodies, other novelists followed Haggard's basic plot, as late as
James Hilton's *Lost Horizon* [2-52]. If the future-war motif played out the
fantasies of Western nationalism, then the lost-race motif played on one of

the fantasies emerging in part, at least, during the high tide of imperialism: the fascination of the British or American man for the non-European woman.[22]

Haggard's imitators did not confine themselves to terrestrial voyages. Between Percy Greg's *Across the Zodiac* (1880) and Garrett P. Serviss's *A Columbus of Space* (1911), the interplanetary voyage had become the province of those mystics, like the Theosophists under Madame Blavatsky, who seized on the concept of parallel evolution advanced by John Fiske in *Outline of Cosmic Philosophy* (1874) to resolve the differences between traditional religion and Darwinian theory. For them Mars became heaven, as in Louis P. Gratacap's *The Certainty of a Future Life on Mars* (1903) and Mark Wicks's *To Mars Via the Moon* (1911). Both books express the divided interests of their authors in that the early chapters of each read like an astronomy text, while mysticism dominates after the protagonists encounter Martians who are reincarnations of the voyagers' friends and relatives. For such writers Mars is heaven, one of the chain of worlds leading eventually to a spiritual unity with the godhead. Although in a prefatory note to *Journey to Mars* [1-76], Gustavus W. Pope insisted that no matter what world serves as its home, "Humanity, created in the Image of God, must always and necessarily be the same in Esse," he allows his protagonist, an audacious American naval officer, to marry a Martian princess in *Wonderful Adventures on Venus* (1895). Despite his emphasis of the love story, Pope defended the scientific romance as a distinct type of fiction; he apparently planned to write a series of novels, using a different planet of the solar system as the setting for each one. A decade later, in *Lieut. Gullivar Jones: His Vacation* (1905), Edwin L. Arnold sends his naval officer to Mars on a flying carpet; there, in a pastoral kingdom, Princess Heru wants him to be her husband. He stays with her until her kingdom is threatened by barbarians; just before its destruction he returns by carpet to Earth, where he gains promotion and marries his faithful fiancée. Although a number of details, including the title, suggest that Arnold intended the book as a parody, a few critics, especially Richard Lupoff, believe that Arnold influenced Edgar Rice Burroughs's "Under the Moons of Mars" (1912), published in book form as *A Princess of Mars* [1-17].

What Rider Haggard was to one generation, Burroughs was to the next. Perhaps the most obvious distinction between them lies in Haggard's reliance on his personal experience and his desire for verisimilitude, whereas Burroughs created imaginary worlds, even his unexplored Africa. Erling B. Holtsmark has shown that Burroughs's protagonists—from John Carter, Warlord of Mars, and Tarzan of the Apes [1-18] to the least of them—echo the heroes of classical myth.[23] In so doing, he has not emphasized that throughout Burroughs's fiction an implicit neoprimitivism rejects early 20th-century society because somehow its industrial urbanization and its effete code of manners—particularly those of the European aristocracy, though not exclusively so—have deprived the male of some aspect of a masculinity looking back to those times when he roamed as a warrior-hunter and supposedly through his physical prowess and cunning controlled his destiny. Both men established the erotic code for the popular fiction of their generations. Whereas Haggard always focused on the ambiguous mysteries of such an exotic woman as Ayesha, Burroughs used the desire for a woman to fulfill male fantasies of a heightened masculinity by making his stories an endless series of captures/kidnappings, separations, and rescues. The promise—without explicit fulfillment—lies at the heart of the eroticism in his fiction.

With the notable exception of Jane Porter of Baltimore, Tarzan's mate, Burroughs's principal women reign in some jungle world or on another planet, be it Barsoom (Mars) or Amtor (Venus). In the Tarzan stories, in fact, Jane is replaced by such lovely barbarians as La, priestess of Opar, lost colony of Atlantis, or half-mad Nemone, queen of the City of Gold. They fall in love with the protagonist at first sight. With the exception of the sometimes indifferent Tarzan, Burroughs's protagonists are gallant and devoted lovers (their code of conduct often seems as formal and prissy as anything in the Victorian/American world of the early 20th century); nevertheless, Burroughs's primitive beauties—"this half-naked little savage"; "this beautiful animal"—are reduced to sex objects, although no one—villain or hero—does more than abduct/rescue and desire/adore them.

In Burroughs's first published work, *A Princess of Mars*, to escape death at the hands of Apaches, John Carter literally wishes himself to Mars, where Dejah Thoris awaits his love. In *At the Earth's Core* [1-15], David Innes finds Dian the Beautiful in Pellucidar, that strangely prehistoric world within the Earth, which shares the polar openings of "Symmes Hole." Whether or not from a sense of American Manifest Destiny,[24] he attempts to unite that vast jungle into federated states. Carson Napier journeys to another world by mistake in *Pirates of Venus* [1-16] to reach Duare, princess of Vepaja, though he is most often separated from her. *The Land That Time Forgot* [2-10]—that is, the island of Caspek in the Antarctic—focuses on the love of a young American for a cave girl. *The Moon Maid* [2-11] begins a trilogy in which the first spaceship (*The Barsoom*) finds a Symmesian world within the hollow Moon, where warring peoples plan the eventual devastation of Earth. Burroughs's intolerance of the yellow lunar race negates his sympathy for the American Indian.

While establishing the time period as 1967, he declared that the 1914 war in his imaginary world "terminated in the absolute domination of the Anglo-Saxon race over all the other races of the world." Nonetheless, the story attempts to bring the protagonist and the beloved Nah-ee-lah together. *The Monster Men* (1929) reworks the Frankenstein theme in that its scientists try to create people chemically. Fortunately for the American heroine, her lover—Number 13—is not a monster but an amnesiac.

With good reason many critics have called Burroughs a one-plot author; Holtsmark notices that by the late 1930s, the "narrative formula [had been] worked to exhaustion."[25] From the first his stories served as a kind of proving ground for his protagonists' masculinity—survival in an exotic yet hostile environment, physical victory over sundry opponents, and the devotion of a sensuous and primitive woman (as someone said, Jane goes ape very readily). Granting the formulaic pattern—caused, in part at least, by the demands of the mass market pulps—one must acknowledge that he freed the lost race–imaginary world novel from outdated themes. Perhaps the most significant characteristic of his fiction is the way in which he adapted all of the conventions coming to him from the 19th century to his own ends. By stripping away the dead thematic wood, so to speak, he focused on the actions of a series of heroes, carefully placing them on the epic stages of imagined worlds, where they could escape the limitations of modern civilization.

Others had tried to do the same. During the 19th century the discoveries in archaeology dwarfed the legendary Kingdom of Prester John or the lost cities of Cibola and El Dorado. In terms drawn from the new sciences the period revitalized the myth of a golden age. For popular, "latest" authority the writers turned to *Atlantis: The Antediluvian World* (1882) by Ignatius Donnelly. The concept of a lost, central homeland proved indispensable to the theory of diffusion, the only possible way, so theorized many experts, to explain the similarities between the Mayans and the ancient Egyptians. They had to be *colonies* of a motherland, wherever that might lie. Such theorizing reinforced the lost-race motif, but it also raised the continent of Atlantis—from Cutcliffe Hyne's *The Lost Continent* [1-52] to Arthur Conan Doyle's *The Maracot Deep* [2-33]. A variety of writers peopled pre-Columbian America with vast empires, although many of them tied themselves to a rapidly dating mysticism, as in the instance of Froma Eunice Wait's *Yermah the Dorado* (1897).

Doyle created the classic tale of the survival of a remnant from prehistory in *The Lost World* [1-31]. Still others wrote of the caveman himself, for geology and an emerging paleontology had created a new myth—the "missing link"—which fascinated the popular imagination. Both Stanley

Waterloo's *The Story of Ab* [1-97] and Jack London's *Before Adam* [1-58] dramatize that moment when a single individual, possessing a higher intelligence because of the size of its brain—a theory the sciences of the period insisted on—transformed the beast into the first human. Their protagonists learned the use of fire, clothing, boats, and weapons, and they felt the first emotions of brotherhood and love (not animal lust) as they began the climb toward modern man. Waterloo gave the theme its most original treatment in *A Son of the Ages* [1-96] when by combining the conventions of racial memory and reincarnation, he took his hero through a number of lives. All of these tales have survived into contemporary fiction, as exemplified by William Golding's *The Inheritors* (1962) and the "Atlan" novels of Jane Gaskell, but in SF they have undergone a number of permutations. Perhaps the influence of Robert E. Howard was most important; following the lead of Burroughs toward imaginary worlds, he placed his "Hyperborian world" somewhere/sometime in prehistory after Atlantis, thereby liberating himself and his successors from inherited conventions. The various motifs—from lost race to Atlantis itself—have fused together in what is now the "sword-and-sorcery" portion of SF or fantasy, as the individual critic/reader decides.

Contemporary critics look back at what some of them—unfortunately, perhaps—still call the "prehistory" of SF and insist that the main thrust of the field has always concentrated on scientists and their achievements, whether the event itself or its effects. As previously noted, in all their guises, scientists became heroes of popular fiction in the last decades of the 19th century, more so in the United States than in Britain or France. (One notices in the future war motif, for example, that European writers made use of the new "hardware," but they did not give as much emphasis to the inventor as did Americans.) An explanation of the difference may lie in America's increasing infatuation with the machine. British writers had long shown an ambivalence toward the machine; Richard Jefferies had already destroyed industrial Britain in *After London* [1-53], while the protagonists of W. H. Hudson's *A Crystal Age* [1-51] and William Morris's *News from Nowhere* [1-69] dream of a pastoral England that has rejected industrialization. In *The Napoleon of Notting Hill* [1-23], G. K. Chesterton projected his pastoral scene a century into the future and specifically attacked Wells.

In contrast, advanced technology played a key part in many American visions of utopia, such as Chauncey Tinker's *The Crystal Button* (1891). More importantly, by the 1890s boy inventors proliferated, the most important being Frank Reade, Jr. He was followed by Tom Swift and made individual appearances in such weeklies as *Pluck and Luck* and as late as Richard B. Montgomery's *A Sheet of Blotting Paper; or, The Adventures of a*

Young Inventor (August 2, 1916). An amusing blending of motifs resulted, for the youths produced a dazzling variety of vehicles to transport them to exotic parts of the Earth, many of which had not been explored by the turn of the century. At one end of the spectrum the protagonists of Charles E. Bolton's posthumous *The Harris-Ingram Experiment* (1905) not only developed the finest electrically run steel mill in the world, but they also built a utopian community shared by workers and managers. At the other end, Hugo Gernsback had enshrined the scientist as a hero of the state in *Ralph 124C41+* [1-37]. During the period of World War I probably the most popular scientist in the United States was Craig Kennedy, "the scientific detective" created by Arthur B. Reeve [1-77]; from 1910 until late in 1915 (with the single exception of November 1912) his exploits inside the laboratory and out graced the pages of *Cosmopolitan* and were collected in book form as late as 1926. It seems safe to say that in the United States at that time a scientist could do no wrong—unless, of course, he was a "mad," villainous descendant of Dr. Frankenstein, whose schemes threatened the balance of civilization. (Almost never an American, such a figure had appeared in the weeklies as early as the 1890s to thwart the boy prodigies, but he did not move toward center stage until after World War I.)

Unlike Craig Kennedy, Doyle's Professor George Challenger seems to confront the establishment rather than to ease its way with new inventions. In *The Lost World* [1-31] he leads an expedition into the interior of Venezuela to prove to the members of the Zoological Institute that prehistoric creatures still live on Earth. In *The Poison Belt* [1-32], he reminds readers of the *Times* that the Earth floats "towards some unknown end, some squalid catastrophe which will overwhelm us at the ultimate confines of space" and suggests that the world may be entering a strange belt of ether. He is denounced. But the world does undergo a "death" for 28 hours and then awakens from a cataleptic trance caused by the changed atmosphere. After Doyle's traumatic reaction to his son's death during the war, Challenger becomes more passive in *The Land of Mist* [2-32], a denunciation of materialism and an expression of pathetic hope in life after death.

The voice that endures from the period before World War I is that of H. G. Wells, but he, more than any other writer in SF, questioned the comfortable presumptions of the Victorian and Edwardian periods. Repeatedly he dramatized the precariousness of humanity's very existence amid universal flux and change, of which even science had only partial knowledge. Mark Hillegas quite rightly has identified him as the principal literary source of the dystopian mood that gained prominence after

World War I in Europe and after World War 11 in the United States.[26] On the one hand, his story "The Star" [1-102] permits the Earth to survive a cosmic catastrophe and gives humanity a chance to rebuild, calling attention to the spirit of brotherhood following the ordeal. On the other hand, "The Sea Raiders" (1896) reports the appearance of *Haploteuthis ferox* in the English Channel in order to symbolize "the violence of a changeable nature and the complacency with which man views his immutable world."[27] *The Time Machine* [1-103] climaxes with the vision of a dying world where only dark shapes scuttle across the beach of a tideless ocean. So much attention has been given the Eloi and Morlocks during that passing moment—the year 802,701—that too many critics read the novel solely as a statement of the inevitable fate of Western industrial society—the evolution of humanity into two distinct species. This Marxian projection is but one of the dichotomies of the period that the Eloi and Morlocks may suggest. *The Island of Dr. Moreau* [1-100], in which Moreau transforms various animals into the Beast People, may be read at the level of the Frankenstein myth, but Robert Philmus teases the imagination with his assertion that it is a symbolic reinstatement of God into "the tortuous process of evolution"—that is, "God becomes Moreau, a vivisectionist insensitive beyond all humanity to the pain of his creatures" who are "irrational creature[s] motivated by fear and desire."[28] *The War of the Worlds* [1-105]—written at the height of the popularity of the future war motif—suggests to its narrator that "our views of the human future must be greatly modified by these events. We have learned now that we cannot regard this planet as being fenced in and a secure abiding place."

Repeatedly Wells sounded the same basic warning, but his contemporaries did not heed it, caught up as they were in their fevers of imperialism and outrage, demanding social reforms that did not address the issues Wells raised. Wells may have had too profound an insight; the implications regarding the future may have slipped past his readers who knew Verne and Haggard as well as, if not better than, they knew him. One infers that the events of the 20th century had to take place before the stature of his early romances could be fully appreciated. Although neither Wells nor the narrator of *The Time Machine* shares the metaphysical background and stance of Camus, the narrator concludes: the traveler "saw in the growing pile of civilization only a foolish heaping that must inevitably fall back upon and destroy its makers in the end. If that is so, it remains for us to live as though it were not so." One can read into that assertion the courage to face the absurd.

As the new century brought the old establishment to a fiery end at Passenchendale, Verdun, and the Somme, the parameters of SF had been marked out by Verne, Wells, Haggard, and Burroughs—from the adulation of the inventor and his gadgetry, whether used in peace or war, to a love story in an exotic, primitive setting. During the last decades of the 19th century and the first years of the 20th, science fiction had grown into a widely popular literary form. Perhaps not always immediately apparent, the roots of the dystopian mood were already present. In 1922 Evgenii Zamiatin praised Wells highly in a brief study, *Herbert Wells*; in 1924 the English-language edition of Zamiatin's novel *We* [2-157] was published in the United States by Dutton. Its portrayal of the United States in the 26th century, a glass-enclosed city-state inhabited by those who survived a great war and are kept regimented and separate from the irrational, "ugly" natural world, is obviously an attack not only on Soviet Russia of the day but on all technocratic states. With *We*, utopia died. Aldous Huxley and George Orwell merely added hymns of anger and despair.

Ironically, the English-language edition of *We* appeared two years before American SF was relegated, by and large, to the pulp specialist magazines until after World War Il. To dismiss its writers of that period as bland optimists is to misread them. To some extent they did express the enduring optimism in their own terms, but they also raised their own questions, and in the privacy of the specialist magazines—so to speak—those who cared for the field made even more complex a literary form that may well have become the vehicle most able to inform readers about themselves, their technical societies, and the awesome universe vast about them.

Notes

1. Most of these earlier works are likely to be of less interest to this guide's audience—Ed.
2. Marjorie Hope Nicolson, *Voyages to the Moon* (Macmillan, 1948), p. 265.
3. Ibid., pp. 265–266.
4. Ibid., p. 159.
5. J. O. Bailey, *Pilgrims Through Space and Time* (Argus, 1947), p. 45.
6. Nicolson, *Voyages to the Moon*, p. 94.
7. P. Clarke, "Symmes Theory of the Earth," *Atlantic Monthly* 31 (1873): 471–480; and John Weld Peck, "Symmes Theory," *Ohio Archaeological and Historical Society Publications* 18 (1909): 29–142.
8. I. F. Clarke, *The Pattern of Expectation: 1644–2001* (Basic Books, 1979), p. 16. Everett C. Wilkie, Jr., provides a detailed discussion in *Mercier's "L'An 2440," Its Publishing History During the Author's Lifetime*, Harvard

University Library, 1986, an 87-page study reprinted from the *Harvard Library Bulletin.*

9. Ibid., pp. 23–24.

10. J. O. Bailey, as cited by Thomas D. Clareson, *A Spectrum of Worlds* (Doubleday, 1972), p. 13.

11. Brian W. Aldiss, *Billion Year Spree* (Doubleday, 1973), pp. 18, 19.

12. I. F. Clarke, *The Pattern of Expectation*, p. 43.

13. Ford Madox Ford, *Henry James: A Critical Study* (London: 1913), p. 225.

14. Robert Philmus, *Into the Unknown* (Univ. of California Press, 1970), p. 90.

15. I. F. Clarke, *Voices Prophesying War: 1763–1984* (Oxford, 1966), p. 67.

16. Ibid., p. 148.

17. Ibid., pp. 120–21, 127.

18. Brian Stableford, "The Yellow Danger," in Frank Magill, ed., *Survey of Science Fiction Literature* (Salem Press, 1979), vol. 5, p. 2527.

19. Hobson Pierson, "If War Should Come," *Cosmopolitan* 45 (June 1908): 38.

20. *Men of Mark* (London: 1877). Verne is number 24.

21. Everett Carter, *Howells and the Age of Realism* (Lippincott, 1950), pp. 92–93.

22. This phrasing seems appropriate. With the exception of Pierre Benoit's *L'Atlantide* (1919; English-language edition, 1920), dealing with the French in the Sahara, one cannot recall a title published before World War I written by any but a British or American author. That fact may in itself give insight into the cultures. The pattern within the motif becomes amusingly complex; if the woman's people could in any way have contributed to the bloodstream of northern Europe, the protagonist may stay with her as her husband; if not, she usually commits suicide before the end of the narrative. The only exception to the pattern that comes to mind is Frank Aubrey's *The Devil-Tree of El Dorado* (1896). The term "non-European" should not be read as a euphemism. It applies to Polynesians, Asians, Africans, and Amerinds. As might be imagined, few novels in the motif discussed explicitly the problems of race or women's rights. See Thomas D. Clareson, *Some Kind of Paradise* (Greenwood, 1985), especially chapter 6.

23. Erling B.Holtsmark, *Tarzan and Tradition* (Greenwood,1981) and *Edgar Rice Burroughs* (Twayne, 1986, TUSAS 499).

24. Holtsmark, *Edgar Rice Burroughs*, p. 81.

25. Ibid., pp. 76–77.

26. Mark Hillegas, *The Future as Nightmare* (Oxford, 1967), p. 4.
27. Clareson, *A Spectrum of Worlds*, p. 60.
28. Philmus, *Into the Unknown*, p. 17.

Bibliography

1-1.   Abbott, Edwin A. (as A Square). **Flatland: A Romance of Many Dimensions.** Seeley, 1884.
The narrator, citizen of a two-dimensional world, uses the land for some satire, especially of education and women. He briefly envisions a one-dimensional world (Lineland) where motion is impossible. A three-dimensional man (Sphere) intrudes into the plane of Flatland, thereby giving knowledge of Spaceland. The two speculate about a world of four dimensions. The book becomes a mathematician's delight, an exercise in the limits of perception. Compare the ingenious speculations in A. K. Dewdney's *The Planiverse* (1984).

1-2.   Anonymous. **The Reign of George VI, 1900–1925.** Nicholl, 1763. Ed. by Charles Oman. Rivingtons, 1899.
I. F. Clarke suggests that this first "future history" provided a working model illustrating the political theories of Bolingbroke. Unlike typical SF it neither portrays nor advocates change, but simply projects Britain's 18th-century political problems into the 20th century. The story has value as an expression of wish fulfillment and as an example of the themes that will grow from *The Battle of Dorking* [1-21].

1-3.   Astor, John Jacob. **A Journey in Other Worlds.** Appleton, 1894.
After vivid descriptions of a utopian Earth in A.D. 2000, the narrative shifts to voyages to Jupiter and Saturn. The travelers explore prehistoric Jupiter and hunt its game. Mysticism dominates the stop at Saturn. The novel affirms Fiske's concept of parallel evolution. Astor borrows the antigravity force "apergy" from Greg's *Across the Zodiac* [1-40].

1-4.   Atterley, Joseph (pseud. of George Tucker). **A Voyage to the Moon: With Some Account of the Manners and Customs, Science and Philosophy of the People of Morosophia, and Other Lunarians.** Elam Bliss, 1827.
In this initial American interplanetary journey, Atterley's ship is the first to

use an antigravity coating. He includes the discussion of more scientific data for its own sake than did his British predecessors. After visits to Morosophia (whose inhabitants are trying to perfect an internal combustion engine) and to utopian Okalbia, the voyagers return to Earth. Atterley was dean of the faculty at the University of Virginia when Poe was a student there; a reference in "Hans Pfaall" [1-75] indicates that his writing influenced Poe to some extent.

1-5. Aubrey, Frank (pseud. of Frank Atkins). **A Queen of Atlantis: A Romance of the Caribbean Sea.** Hutchinson, 1899.

Abandoned in the Sargasso Sea, two young boys and a girl find an island that they name Atlantis. Threatened by giant cuttlefish and warring factions of a primitive people, they befriend a faerielike race of "flower dwellers" who are descendants of Atlantis. In *King of the Dead: A Weird Romance* (1903) the remnant of a *white* race that ruled all the Americas when Egypt was at her fullest glory fails in an attempt to resurrect the dead of untold generations in order to regain their lost empire. In *The Devil-Tree of El Dorado* (1896), youthful explorers find a lost city in Venezuela on Mount Raraima, the same site Conan Doyle was to use in *The Lost World* [1-31]. One youth remains behind when his friends return to civilization; he marries the princess Uluma. As Fenton Ash, Atkins wrote *A Trip to Mars* (1909), in which two boys are taken to a Mars where various nations are fighting. In *The Encyclopedia of Science Fiction* [7-22], John Eggeling points out that this "wartorn" Mars precedes Burroughs's use of the idea in *A Princess of Mars* [1-17].

1-6. Barney, J(ohn) Stewart. **L.P.M.: The End of the Great War.** Putnam, 1915.

An American scientist, Edestone, defeats all warring nations and calls for an authoritarian world government to be ruled by "the Aristocracy of Intelligence." He goes beyond the advocacy of Anglo-Saxon supremacy, a favorite theme of the period, to denounce "majority rule, equality of man, and perpetual peace through brotherly love"; he asserts that government should be organized and administered like "the great corporations of America." The novel is unique, at least in American fiction, because of the extreme position Edestone takes. For other fictional portraits of Thomas Edison, see Serviss's *Edison's Conquest of Mars* [1-82]. Compare Wells's *A Modern Utopia* [1-101] for a different view of a special ruling class.

1-7. Bellamy, Edward. **Equality.** Appleton, 1897.

This sequel to *Looking Backward* [1-8] served as a rebuttal to Bellamy's critics. It argues that economic equality is the cornerstone on which the complete life of an industrial democracy rests—political, intellectual, ethical. Although it emphasizes the place of religion in the world of A.D. 2000, society needs no organized church or ordained ministry. Despite the thread of a love story, this is more an essay than a novel. In *The Blindman's World and Other Stories* (1898), "To Whom This May Come" describes a utopian society on a Pacific island whose people have mastered telepathy.

*1-8.   Bellamy, Edward. **Looking Backward: A.D. 2000–1887.** Ticknor, 1888.

Without doubt the most famous of the American utopias, this was the progenitor of several hundred works, both in the United States and Europe, as individuals sided with Bellamy or attacked him. Science is incidental to the text, although technology has made the utopian state possible. The controversial issue centered on socialism. See Roemer's *The Obsolete Necessity* (1976) for the most detailed contemporary discussion of Bellamy and the United States in utopian literature at the end of the century. For very different treatments of socialism, see Morris's *News from Nowhere* [1-69], Donnelly's *Caesar's Column* [1-29], and London's *The Iron Heel* [1-9].

1-9.   Benson, Robert Hugh. **Lord of the World.** Pitman, 1907.

An ardent Catholic, Benson attacked the humanistic utopias of Wells and Bellamy. The narrative dramatizes the apocalyptic encounter between the Antichrist and the Catholic church. Rome is razed by bombing, and the pope and his few remaining followers retreat to Palestine. The novel ends with an ambiguous vision that may be the Second Coming and the end of the world. Benson envisioned an alternative future in a far less well known novel, *The Dawn of All* (1911), portraying a utopian society under papal rule. For a very different treatment of Catholicism in contemporary SF, see Silverberg's "Good News From the Vatican" (1971).

1-10.   Beresford, John Davys. **Goslings.** Heinemann, 1913. U.S. title: *A World of Women*, Macauley, 1913.

A plague sweeps from China through Russia to Western Europe, almost wiping out the male population. The attempt of women to reorganize society obviously changes a number of conventions. Stableford regards *Goslings* as the first effort in British fiction to depict an all-female society seriously and sympathetically. The premise is cut short when the existence of an appreciable number of men is discovered; men and women together, with, it is hoped, better understanding of one another, will rebuild, a favorite British theme. Compare Gilman's *Herland* [1-38] and Lane's *Mizora* [1-56] for earlier treatments of feminist utopias; see Wylie's *The Disappearance* [3-198] for a more recent speculation.

*1-11. Beresford, John Davys. **The Hampdenshire Wonder.** Sidgwick & Jackson, 1911. U.S. title: *The Wonder*, Doran, 1917.
Long celebrated as one of the earliest "superman" novels, the narrative tells of a boy whose mind is thousands of years in advance of his society. Adults regard him as little better than a macrocephalic idiot because of his silence. His chief enemy is the local vicar. His death leaves open the question of murder. Compare Stapledon's *Odd John* [2-120], Wylie's *Gladiator* [2-155], and van Vogt's *Slan* [3-180].

1-12. Bergerac, Cyrano Savinien de. **The Comical History of the States and Empires of the Worlds of the Moon and Sun.** Trans. by A. Lovell, 1687. The original authorized version was titled *Histoire comique des états et empires de la lune*, 1656. The first English trans. was by Tho. St. Serf, 1659. Recommended trans. by Geoffrey Strachan, *Other Worlds*, Oxford, 1965.
Marjorie Hope Nicolson praises this book as the finest of the 17th-century "parodies" of the cosmic voyage, but also insists that it proved highly important to Swift [1-89]. Once on the Moon, the hero becomes the companion of Godwin's Domingo Gonsales [1-39] and witnesses conventional actions such as warfare. One high point comes when the lunarian "philosophers" debate whether he is a human being; another, when he is tried for "heresy" because he asserts the Earth is inhabited. Despite any element of parody, the narrative expresses Cyrano's scientific curiosity.

1-13. Bierce, Ambrose. **In the Midst of Life** (1891); **Can Such Things Be?; Works.** Neale Publishing, 1909–1911, vols. 2 and 3.
Bierce remains one of the most significant writers in the evolution of the ghost story to the psychological case study. His "Moxon's Master" is the closest to Poe's "Maelzel's Chess Player." The automaton in Bierce is a variation on the Frankenstein theme. "The Damned Thing" (1893) draws on biology and is his purest SF, notable for both its use of the Frankenstein theme and its narrative technique. "The Man and the Snake" is his most ironic dramatization of fear. Franklin discusses his importance to early SF in *Future Perfect* [1-36], as does Clareson in *Some Kind of Paradise* [8-37].

1-14. Bradshaw, William Richard. **The Goddess of Atvatabar.** Douthitt, 1892.
Arctic explorers discover a Symmesian world. Extravagant magic and mys-

ticism provide the background to the narrator's wooing of Queen Lyone. As king he opens trade negotiations with the outside world. Julian Hawthorne's introduction denounces Zola and the literary naturalists, predicting that the future of literature lies with such romances as Bradshaw's.

Bulwer-Lytton, Edward. **The Coming Race** [see 1-61].

*1-15.   Burroughs, Edgar Rice. **At the Earth's Core.** McClurg, 1922.
First published in *All-Story* (1914), this novel introduces David Innes to the Symmesian world of Pellucidar, where the first-person narrator searches the jungles for Dian the Beautiful. It is a Darwinian world where assorted beast-men and animals—some dinosaurs—struggle for survival. Innes attempts to unify the various tribes into a loose federation. At the end he returns to the surface without Dian. To gain credibility, Burroughs employs a framing device: an Englishman has found Innes's manuscript. Six novels make up the Pellucidar series.

1-16.   Burroughs, Edgar Rice. **Pirates of Venus.** Burroughs, 1934.
Published in *Argosy* (1931), this novel takes Carson Napier, the weakest of Burroughs's major protagonists, to Venus (Amtor); his beloved is Duare, princess of the treetop kingdom of Vepaja. The central action involves a fight against the criminal Thor, who incited the workers to kill the ruling class (this attack on communism marks one of the few occasions when Burroughs commented explicitly on contemporary affairs). Five novels make up the Venus series. He may have delayed using that planet because of the earlier novels of Otis Adelbert Kline.

*1-17.   Burroughs, Edgar Rice. **A Princess of Mars.** McClurg, 1917.
Published under the pseudonym Norman Bean as "Under the Moons of Mars" in *All-Story* (1912), *A Princess of Mars* introduces Burroughs's most epic adventure and his finest imaginary world, Barsoom, a construct based loosely on Percival Lowell's theories. Against a dying planet torn by strife, John Carter fights his way across the deserts, gaining the friendship of such warriors as Tars Tarkas of Thark and the love of the incomparable Dejah Thoris, princess of Helium. They live happily for nine years until by accident Carter ends up on Earth at the cave where he escapes marauding Apaches by willing himself to Mars. *The Gods of Mars* (1918) and *The Warlord of Mars* (1919), both seeing magazine publication in 1914, complete the personal saga of Carter. Eight other novels follow the adventures of his family and friends. This first novel introduced the conventions

Burroughs used throughout his various series, including some of the tales of Tarzan, but no other series proved so effective. Permutations of Barsoom survive in the worlds of "swords and sorcery" so popular in contemporary SF.

1-18. Burroughs, Edgar Rice. **Tarzan of the Apes.** McClurg, 1914.
Published in *All-Story* (October 1912) and serialized in the New York *Evening World* before book publication, the novel emphasizes the boyhood and youth of Tarzan, Lord Greystoke, Burroughs's most famous (and most macho) hero, the only one to attain mythic proportions and become a part of worldwide popular culture. Burroughs claimed that Tarzan combines the best of environments (unknown Africa) and the best of heredities (British aristocracy). Because D'Arnot is his teacher, taking him to Paris, one cannot fail to compare him to Rousseau's *Émile* (1762), especially in terms of education, to contrast the 18th and 20th centuries, both emphasizing the "natural man." Tarzan saves Jane Porter from an unwanted marriage, but does not wed her in this first novel. Because attention to Jane and Jack (Korak the Killer), the son of Tarzan, aged the apeman, his family was omitted from most of the later novels, while Tarzan roamed the jungles and veldt, always beloved by a conveniently available primitive beauty. One should compare the Africas and the love stories of Burroughs and H. Rider Haggard [1-46] to see the contrasts. For other treatments of Tarzan, one should consult Philip José Farmer's *Lord Tyger* (1970) and *Tarzan Alive* (1972), as well as Gene Wolfe's "Tarzan of the Grapes" (1972). Among the innumerable films are Bo Derek's feminist *Tarzan*—which attempts the story from Jane's point of view—and the neo-behaviorist *Greystoke: The Legend of Tarzan* (1984), with its brilliant cinematography. [For other works of this author see chapter 2.]

*1-19. Butler, Samuel. **Erewhon; or, Over the Range.** Trubner, 1872; **Erewhon Revisited Twenty Years Later**. Richards, 1901. Ed. by Desmond MacCarthy. Dutton, 1965.
In New Zealand, the narrator, Higgs, finds an agrarian, utopian society that has destroyed its machines because of a fear that machines will supersede humanity. Those chapters titled "The Book of the Machine" attack both Darwinian theory and the deist view that the Universe (and, by implication, humanity) is a mechanism set in motion and then abandoned by God. The central fear is that machines will undergo a mechanical evolution until they replace humanity. The Erewhonians abhorred dependence on machines and so destroyed theirs. Higgs escapes in a balloon. In *Erewhon Revisited*, Higgs's return is reported by his son, whose own

visit makes up an epilogue. Higgs's escape triggered a new religion, Sunchildism. This fact leads to a satire of the clerical establishment, Christianity's origins, and the concept of the Second Coming. Compare the attitude toward machines and industrialization in W. H. Hudson [1-51], William Morris [1-69], E. M. Forster [1-35], and more recently Vonnegut's *Player Piano* [3-191].

1-20.   Campanella, Tommaso. **City of the Sun.** Trans. of *Civitas Solis*, 1623. In *Ideal Commonwealths*, Kennikat, 1968.

A sea captain describes a communistic utopian community in central Asia ruled by a philosopher-king (Metaphysicus) aided by three magistrates— Power, Wisdom, and Love. Education focuses on mathematics, geology, geography, botany, and the mechanical arts. Eugenics determines the citizens' mating selections, and the physicians have a secret method of "renovating" life about the seventieth year. Campanella wrote *Civitas Solis* about 1602, when he was a prisoner of the Inquisition.

*1-21.   Chesney, Sir George (Tomkyns). **The Battle of Dorking: Reminiscences of a Volunteer.** Blackwood, 1871.

Published anonymously in *Blackwood's* (May 1871), *The Battle of Dorking* laid the foundation of the future war motif. Clarke's *Voices Prophesying War* [8-41] gives the fullest account of its impact throughout Britain, Europe, and America. The 64-page pamphlet gained much of its effect from Chesney's choice of a participant-observer as narrator; he dramatizes the invasion by German forces in realistic detail. In part its success occurred because Germany had just crushed France in the first conflict fought *in* Western nations since the time of Napoleon I. While Bellamy's *Looking Backward* [1-8] could appeal to the dreams of idealists, Chesney spoke to the fears of a society that believed a catastrophic war was imminent and inevitable.

1-22.   Chester, George Randolph. **The Jingo.** Bobbs-Merrill, 1912.

In a delightful spoof of the lost-race motif, the jingoistic Jimmy Smith, representative of the Eureka Manufacturing Company, brings "improvements" to the kingdom of Isola in the Antarctic. Even his love for the reigning princess is (gently) satirized. Isola becomes a loyal territorial republic waiting to be discovered by the United States. For satire of a more serious tone, see Cowan's earlier *Revi-Lona* [1-27].

1-23. Chesterton, G(ilbert) K(eith). **The Napoleon of Notting Hill.** J. Lane, 1904.

In his first novel Chesterton attacks the notion of progress and the superiority of the sciences, commenting on the inept prophecies of "H. G. Wells and others, who thought that science would take charge of the future." His London a century in the future is "almost exactly as it is now." His central theme insists that to avert disaster, society must return to local patriotism and the universal ideas of the Middle Ages.

*1-24. Childers, Erskine. **The Riddle of the Sands: A Record of Secret Service Recently Achieved.** Smith, Elder, 1903.

In *Voices Prophesying War* [8-41], Clarke names Childers's novel "undoubtedly the best" since *The Battle of Dorking* [1-21]. Instead of another glimpse of clashing armies, Childers presents a work of detection. Realism of detail (plausibility) and characterization also set it apart from its contemporaries, as does the quality of Childers's style. He adopts the ruse of being the editor of a friend's manuscript. This book was republished in 1940 during another threat of invasion.

*1-25. Clemens, Samuel Langhorne (Mark Twain). **A Connecticut Yankee in King Arthur's Court.** Webster, 1889. Recommended ed. by Bernard L. Stein, Univ. of California, 1979.

Hank Morgan suffers a blow on the head and goes backward in time to Arthur's Camelot in the sixth century. Starting as a celebration of modern progress and a denunciation of both British aristocracy and the church-dominated society, Hank's efforts—as "the Boss"—to transform Arthurian Britain into a facsimile of the 19th century end in slaughter and death. The novel voices Twain's confusion and despair. It should be compared with de Camp's classic tale of time travel, *Lest Darkness Fall* [3-58], a return to the Rome of Augustus. Twain's shorter pieces were usefully collected and edited by David Ketterer in *The Science Fiction of Mark Twain* (Archon, 1984). The most important of the 15 stories is "The Great Dark," first published in 1962. It captures the dark side of Twain's imagination and his hatred of the concept of determinism. Edwards's nightmare voyage in a drop of water becomes symbolic of the absurdity of the universe. "The Curious Republic of Gondour" (1874) provides Twain's statement about utopias, while "From the 'London Times' of 1904" (1898) allows him to invent a "gadget," the "telectroscope," and thus is his closest approach to early SF. Ketterer includes excerpts from *A Connecticut Yankee in King Arthur's Court.*

1-26.   Colomb, Rear Admiral P(hilip Howard), and others. **The Great War of 189-: A Forecast.** Heinemann, 1893.

Originally serialized in 1892 in the illustrated magazine *Black and White*, this forecast of imminent war, a collaboration of military men and journalists, attempted to calculate what the next conflict would be like. Many incidents were presented as though they were reports from the scene by news correspondents and officers. The novel closes with the warning that Germany has begun to rearm and that weaknesses in the British army have been glossed over.

1-27.   Cowan, Frank. **Revi-Lona: A Romance of Love in a Marvelous Land.** Tribune Press, 1879; Arno, 1976.

Apparently privately printed, this narrative remains one of the most successful parodies of the lost-race motif, utopian societies, and exploration of the Antarctic. The first-person narrator discovers a society dominated by women and ruled by a council of 25, each of whom becomes his hostess and his mistress. The language and action are sexually explicit for the period. The father of many children by many women, he inadvertently brings about the destruction of the society and its principal city before a ship picks him up and returns him to the outside world. This should not be dismissed as a masculine fantasy but read as a commentary on the literature and society of the 1880s. Compare it with Gilman's *Herland* [1-38], Lane's *Mizora* [1-56], or Beresford's *Goslings* [1-10].

Cyrano de Bergerac, Savinien. **The Comical History of the States and Empires of the Worlds of the Moon and Sun** [see 1-12].

*1-28.   De Mille, James. **A Strange Manuscript Found in a Copper Cylinder.** Harper, 1888.

A shipwrecked sailor, Thomas More, who indicates that he has knowledge of previous "wild works of fiction about lands in the interior of the earth," proceeds to give a portrait of the Kosekin, a society antipodal to the outside world. To escape the stigma of such fictions, De Mille adopts a clever frame: in 1850, passengers aboard the becalmed yacht *Falcon*, property of Lord Featherstone, rescue More's manuscript from the sea. Three times they interrupt its reading to debate scientific data and theory in order to substantiate incidents in the narrative.

*1-29.   Donnelly, Ignatius (as Edmund Boisgilbert). **Caesar's Column.** Schulte, 1890. Ed. by Walter B. Rideout. Harvard, 1960.

Only Bellamy's *Looking Backward* [1-8] had greater popularity or influence than *Caesar's Column*. Donnelly portrayed an actual revolution in 1988; improved technology had separated the elitist capitalist class from the squalor of the working class, but the "heartlessness" of the ruling class caused the revolution. The narrator rescues some machines and compatriots, flying them to Africa, where he hopes to found a Socialist state. Dirigibles and poison gas had been used in the fighting. New York had been a city of wonders. For another account of the class struggle, see London's *The Iron Heel* [1-59].

1-30. Dooner, P(ierton) W. **Last Days of the Republic.** Alta California, 1880.

Written as a protest against importing coolie labor, the narrative suggests that the workers remain agents of the Chinese government. This is the first discussion of "the yellow peril," although Dooner does not use that term. A "fifth column" becomes active, and the United States is destroyed as a nation. The book is presented as a history without individualized characterization or fully developed dramatic scenes.

*1-31. Doyle, Arthur Conan. **The Lost World.** Hodder & Stoughton, 1912.

Professor George Challenger leads a party of explorers who discover a remnant of the prehistoric world atop a plateau, Raraima, Venezuela (see Aubrey [1-5]). Despite such anachronisms as cavemen living with dinosaurs, both Challenger and the credibility of detail strengthen the narrative, making it the classic of its type. Its tone and material differ sharply from those of Haggard. Challenger is featured in two of the 14 stories collected in *The Best Science Fiction of Arthur Conan Doyle*, edited by Charles G. Waugh and Martin H. Greenberg (1981).

*1-32. Doyle, Arthur Conan. **The Poison Belt.** Hodder & Stoughton, 1913.

Professor Challenger's party survives an apparent worldwide catastrophe to explore a vacant world before all life reawakens. The idea of humanity's having a second chance is present. For a later British treatment of the catastrophe motif, see Wyndham's *The Day of the Triffids* [3-199]. Compare it to Serviss's *The Second Deluge* [1-83], especially for its presentation of the scientists. For the role of science in man-made disasters, see Scortia-Robinson's *The Prometheus Crisis* (1975). [For other works of this author see chapter 2.]

1-33. England, George Allan. **Darkness and Dawn.** Small, Maynard, 1914; Hyperion, 1975.

"The Vacant World," "Beyond the Great Oblivion," and "The Afterglow"— originally published in *Cavalier*—chronicle how, after a thousand years of suspended animation, an American engineer and the typist in the office next door awaken and rebuild a "finer, better" civilization. An explosion of subterranean gases had torn a second moon from the Midwest and left a chasm, where dwelt the remaining "Merucaans." Volume 1 explores the eastern United States. With the aid of a surviving biplane (complete with fuel) the protagonist reestablishes the survivors in Volume 2. The last of the three witnesses the fruition of his efforts. Although extremely dated in language and manner, the trilogy remains the classic example of American optimism before World War I.

1-34. Fawcett, Edgar. **Solarion: A Romance.** Lippincott, 1889.

First published in the September 1889 issue of *Lippincott's Magazine*, *Solarion* was the most original treatment of the Frankenstein theme written in the 19th century. Framed by the narrative of an American residing in Switzerland, it gives the story of Kenneth Rodney Stafford, who reminds one of Victor Frankenstein. He uses the knowledge of another to augment the intelligence of the dog Solarion until the animal has human intelligence and converses with him. Their dialogues recall *Frankenstein* [1-84], both in terms of Solarion's loneliness and Stafford's echoing the Faustian theme. He gives the dog to Cecilia Effingham when she marries. Solarion falls in love with Cecilia and maims Stafford when he attempts to kill the dog in a fit of jealousy and repugnance. For a contrasting treatment of the love of an animal for a woman, see Stapledon's *Sirius* [3-168].

*1-35. Forster, E(dward) M(organ). **"The Machine Stops."** 1909.

Long recognized as an attack on Wells, Forster's story pictures a future in which humanity lives underground in hexagonal cells, where they spend almost their entire adult lives. They rely entirely on pushbuttons to activate various functions of the machine. When it breaks down, humanity perishes. Forster intimates that only a few survivors on the surface—perhaps exiled there for sins against the machine—hold any hope for the future that may exist. See also Tarde's *Underground Man* [1-90]. "The Machine Stops" must be judged the first full-fledged dystopian view of the effects of technology.

*1-36. Franklin, H. Bruce. **Future Perfect: American Science Fiction of the Nineteenth Century.** Oxford, 1966; rev. ed., 1978.

Franklin emphasizes the works of such major 19th-century writers as

Hawthorne and Poe (to whom he gives most attention) and Melville, Bierce, Bellamy, and O'Brien. The 15 stories divide themselves among such topics as "Automata," "Marvelous Inventions," and "Time Travel." He chose works published originally in such magazines as *Harper's*, the *Atlantic Monthly*, *Century*, and *Arena*, which reached wide audiences. The importance of the anthology lies not in its comprehensiveness but in the evidence it gives of the diversity of SF during the last century.

1-37. Gernsback, Hugo. **Ralph 124C41+: A Romance of the Year 2660.** Stratford, 1925.
First published as a serial in *Modern Electrics* (1911), this story serves as the classic expression of American infatuation with the machine; it is a virtual catalog of descriptions of advanced machines. Its protagonist is a state hero, who literally resurrects his sweetheart from the dead after an accident. Unique for the period, the "other man" is a Martian. Compare Serviss's *The Second Deluge* [1-83] and *Edison's Conquest of Mars* [1-82] for similar, if not equal, adulation of the scientist. White's *The Mystery* [1-107] and *The Sign at Six* [1-108] differ in tone.

*1-38. Gilman, Charlotte Perkins. **Herland.** Pantheon, 1979.
Originally published in *The Forerunner* (1915), which Gilman edited, this feminist utopia somewhere in Canada expresses the author's conviction that women could collectively be the moving force in reforming society. To explore her ideas as widely as possible, she introduces three men, each representing a different attitude toward women, into a society where parthenogenesis has been practiced for 2,000 years. One man elevates women to an inhuman pedestal; the second has no luck with them; and the third is the complete chauvinist who believes women wish "to be mastered." The narrator—the second man—comes to understand that the so-called feminine charms of the outside world are entirely artificial. The actions of the chauvinist force the three to leave. The novel gives the most complete, nonviolent statement of the period about the need to recognize women as equal beings and reform society accordingly. Ann J. Lane's introduction has value for its biographical information about Gilman. A sequel, "With Her in Ourland" (*The Forerunner*, 1916), is set in the United States.

1-39. Godwin, Francis. **The Man in the Moone; or, A Discourse of a Voyage Thither.** 1638. Grant McColley, ed. Folcroft, 1973.
Although not sophisticated by modern standards, this narrative by an Anglican bishop is the earliest to give the Moon voyage a quality of scientific credibility. Poe's criticism of Godwin in "Hans Pfaall" [1-75] disguises

his indebtedness. Its protagonist, Domingo Gonsales, introduced the conventions of the journey and became Cyrano de Bergerac's companion [1-12].

*1-40.   Greg, Percy. **Across the Zodiac: The Story of a Wrecked Record.** Trubner, 1880. Hyperion, 1974.

Despite the use of antigravity (Greg called the force "apergy"), Greg's chief concerns lay with the nature of Martian society. A monarchical utopia has replaced communism, which failed because of lack of incentive and strife over the allocation of certain jobs. Martian philosophy is so dominated by a dogmatic positivism that opposition to science is a heresy. The plot explores Martian polygamy and allows Greg to air his views regarding female suffrage and moral reform. The narrative is presented as a manuscript recovered from meteoric debris on a Pacific island.

1-41.   Griffith, George (pseud. of George Chetwynd Griffith-Jones). **The Angel of the Revolution: A Tale of the Coming Terror.** Tower, 1893; Hyperion, 1974.

Originally published in *Pearson's Magazine* (1893), this novel played on two of Britain's gravest nightmares: social revolution and war. When a group of anarchists, the "Terrorists," learn that France and Russia plan to attack Britain, Germany, and Austria, they build a fleet of airplanes in their secret valley—called Aeria—in Africa. While they cause the workers in the United States to rise and bring down the government, with poison gas, dirigibles, and submarines, they establish themselves as rulers in Europe. They make certain that peace and socialism triumph by maintaining their air force to ensure the obedience of the world.

1-42.   Griffith, George (pseud. of George Chetwynd Griffith-Jones). **Olga Romanoff; or, The Syren of the Skies.** Tower, 1894; Hyperion, 1974.

First published in *Pearson's Magazine* (1893–1894), the novel gives an account of the effort of Olga Romanoff, descendant of the czars, to seize power from the Aerians (formerly the "Terrorists") after they have ruled the Anglo-Saxon Federation for more than a century. She is foiled only because a comet devastates much of the Earth. Griffith reveals his indebtedness to Bulwer-Lytton [1-61] when the Aerians indicate they have a force like "Vril." For its treatment of catastrophe, compare it to Wylie and Balmer's *When Worlds Collide* [2-156].

1-43.   Griffith, Mary. "Three Hundred Years Hence" in **Camperdown: or, News From Our Neighborhood.** Carey, Lea & Blanchard, 1836.

Although Griffith was indebted to Mercier's *Memoirs of the Year Two*

Thousand Five Hundred [1-63], her utopia is most notable for the influence of women once they have gained equality, especially in "money matters." One result has been the abolition of killing and war (the blacks did not use force and have been emancipated; the Indians did and have "vanished"); another is improved hygiene, both personal and public. All technological advance resulted from the development of an unspecified force by a woman, which replaced steam and heat as sources of energy. More an essay than a novel, it ends when the dreamer awakens.

1-44. Haggard, H(enry) Rider. **Allan Quatermain.** Longmans Green, 1887.

Allan Quatermain is the prototype for the fully developed lost-race motif. Unlike many of his subsequent imitators, Haggard allows his protagonist to marry Nyleptha, queen of the Zu-Vendris, and remain in the primitive kingdom of Africa. Because the topical concerns of the utopian fiction burned out or grew dated, only the future war motif had wider popularity before World War I. The lost-race motif continued its dominance until World War II sent troops to every corner of the world. In addition to the implications of its neoprimitivism, it became perhaps the chief vehicle for the literary eroticism of Western culture during that period. It seems also to have been primarily, if not uniquely, an expression of British and American culture. The most comprehensive discussion of the motif occurs in Clareson's *Some Kind of Paradise* [8-37].

1-45. Haggard, H(enry) Rider. **King Solomon's Mines.** Cassell, 1885.

In this novel Haggard discovered Africa; his own personal background gives the novel an authenticity of detail lacking in Verne and Burroughs. It did for the story of exploration and adventure what Schiaparelli's announcement of the "canali" of Mars did for the interplanetary voyage: it provided a new setting. Cassell reprinted the novel four times within the first year; it has never been out of print.

*1-46. Haggard, H(enry) Rider. **She: A History of Adventure.** Longmans Green, 1887.

Ayesha, She-Who-Must-Be-Obeyed, is Haggard's most famous character, surpassing even stalwart Allan Quatermain. Her dark beauty certainly influenced the portrayal of many women in popular fiction. Among Haggard's contemporaries one thinks of Griffith's *Olga Romanoff* [1-42]; a generation later, of Lo-Tsen in Hilton's *Lost Horizon* [2-52].

1-47.   Haggard, H(enry) Rider. **When the World Shook: Being an Account of the Great Adventure of Bastin, Bickley, and Arbuthnot.** Cassell, 1919.
Although there is much talk and little drama in the narrative, some critics regard this novel as the closest Haggard came to SF, simply because he made use of the myth of Atlantis. Three companions find the priest of Atlantis, Oro, and his daughter, Yva, in suspended animation in a cavern on an island in the Pacific. Oro sank the ancient kingdom because of its evil, and after seeing wartime Europe, threatens to bring on another deluge. He dies, as do Arbuthnot and Yva, whose love, by implication, will survive death.

1-48.   Hale, Edward Everett. "The Brick Moon" in **Masterpieces of Science Fiction.** Ed. by Sam Moskowitz. World, 1966.
"The Brick Moon" first appeared in the *Atlantic Monthly* (October-December 1869); a single-installment sequel, "Life on the Brick Moon," was published in *Atlantic* (February 1870). Although hailed as the first story of a man-made satellite, a close reading, particularly of the tone of the narrator and the messages received from the Moon, suggests that Hale used it as a vehicle to satirize science and technology, as well as Darwinian theory and, perhaps, fiction dealing with imaginary voyages and utopian societies. Hale gives as much attention to its financing as to its construction and (accidental) launching. Prior to Arthur C. Clarke's *Islands in the Sky* [5-31], it is the longest narrative to deal with an artificial satellite.

1-49.   Hartwell, David G., and Lloyd Currey, eds. **The Battle of the Monsters and Other Stories.** Gregg Press, 1976.
These eight stories published between 1878 and 1908 range from William J. Henderson's "Harry Borden's Naval Monster: A Ship of the Air," in which the United States sides with Venezuela during its war in 1927 with Britain (bombs from a balloon sink a British cruiser), to Leonard Kip's "The Secret of Apollonius Septric," a dream-vision anticipating something of the tone of Olaf Stapledon. The title story by Morgan Robertson describes the warfare of germs, white corpuscles, and antibodies of an inoculation in the human bloodstream. It should be compared with similarly historically oriented anthologies, like Clareson's *A Spectrum of Worlds* (1972), Franklin's *Future Perfect* [1-36], and Menville and Reginald's *Ancestral Voices* [1-62].

*1-50.   Holberg, Ludwig. **A Journey to the World Under-Ground: By Nicolas Klimius.** Trans. anonymously, 1742. Trans. of *Nicolai Klimii Iter*

Subterraneum, 1741. Univ. of Nebraska, 1960, as *The Journey of Niels Klim to the World Underground.*

Falling through a cavern to the center of the world, Klim finds a sun and its planets within the Earth. He observes the "true laws of Motion." On the planet Nazar he learns about various societies. Holberg's satire is comparable to that of Swift [1-89]; his general strategy is to invert human conventions. It was long suppressed in Denmark as a dangerously radical book.

1-51.   Hudson, W(illiam) H(enry). **A Crystal Age.** Unwin, 1887.

The narrator, a botanist, suffers a fall and awakens in an unspecified pastoral society having no knowledge of the 19th century. No industrialization is apparent. Although the unit of society is the matriarchal family, there is no marriage nor recognition of sexual love. In a preface to his collected works, Hudson remarked that such "romances of the future" grew out of "a sense of dissatisfaction with the existing order of things." Compare Hudson with Jefferies's *After London* [1-53], in which modern industrial civilization has also disappeared.

1-52.   Hyne, Cutcliffe (pseud. of Charles John Cutcliffe Wright Hyne). **The Lost Continent.** Hutchinson, 1900.

On one of the Canary Islands two Englishmen find a manuscript, the memoir of Deucalion, last king of Atlantis. He becomes involved with "lovely, sinful" Phorenice, self-proclaimed queen and goddess of Atlantis, and Naïs, daughter of the chief priest. Much attention is given to battles and the schemes of Phorenice, but the world is not vividly or dramatically presented. Deucalion places Naïs in a state of suspended animation and they escape as the continent sinks. Hyne established many of the conventions regarding Atlantis that came down to contemporary SF through the fiction of such writers as Robert E. Howard. The characterization of Phorenice owes much to Haggard's *She* [1-46].

1-53.   Jefferies, Richard. **After London; or, Wild England.** Cassell, 1885.

A trained naturalist who hated industrialization, Jefferies pictures an England that has reverted to a vast woodland after some unspecified catastrophe has left the land dominated by a great lake in the Midlands. No cities survive. The story follows the odyssey of Felix Aquila, whose home is Thyma Castle; it ends as he brings his beloved Aurora to live with him among shepherds. One may trace this theme through Hudson's *A Crystal Age* [1-51] to John Collier's *Tom's A-Cold* (1933).

*1-54.   Kepler, Johannes. **Somnium, seu opus posthumum de astronomia lunari.** 1634. The definitive English trans. is that of Edward Rosen, Univ. of Wisconsin Press, 1967.

The dream-vision of Duracotus, an apprentice to Tycho Brahe, describes the physical appearance of the Moon and its life forms. Most observations agree with those of Galileo, although Kepler gives it water and atmosphere. Wells's *First Men in the Moon* [1-98] uses many similar details and makes specific reference to Kepler.

1-55.   Kipling, Rudyard. **With the Night Mail: A Story of 2000 A.D.** Doubleday, 1909.

In the 1905 title story, dirigible balloons, such as Postal Packet 162 from London to Quebec, fly the air currents of the world. Aviation has changed the world so completely that it is governed by the Aerial Board of Control (A.B.C.), whose laws permit anything—including war—that does not obstruct "traffic and all it implies." A sequel, "As Easy as A.B.C." (1912), describes the unsuccessful attempt by the District of Illinois to break away from the board in 2065. *Kipling's Science Fiction* (Tor, 1992) collects nine stories and a bibliography.

1-56.   Lane, Mary E. Bradley. **Mizora: A Prophecy.** Dillingham, 1890.

A Russian noblewoman sentenced to Siberia escapes to a Symmesian world, where she finds a feminist utopia in which parthenogenesis has been practiced for 3,000 years. Genetic engineering assures that all the women will be uniformly blonde and beautiful (with 30-inch waistlines, a sign of Lane's reaction to the fashions of her time). Lane is angrier than Gilman [1-38]; she denounces the cheap prices and cheap labor that make women and children suffer, calling women "beasts of burden." She insists that universal education will bring freedom and equality. *Mizora* was first published in the Cincinnati *Commercial* in 1880–1881. Its date gives it added historical significance.

1-57.   Le Queux, William. **The Great War in England in 1897.** Tower, 1894.

The most sensational and bloodthirsty novelist using the future war motif; Le Queux made his reputation with this account of a French and Russian invasion. Germany, which aided Britain in this book, became the ruthless enemy in Le Queux's *The Invasion of 1910: With a Full Account of the Siege of London* (1904).

*1-58. London, Jack. **Before Adam.** Macmillan, 1906.

Through racial memory the narrator tells of his life as a caveman. Waterloo accused London of plagiarizing his *The Story of Ab* [1-97].

1-59. London, Jack. **The Iron Heel.** Macmillan, 1907.

Scholars of a Socialist utopian state in the 27th century discover the Everhard Manuscript, which tells of the early struggles in the 20th century against a Fascist-type state ruled by the Trusts. His most emotional outburst, the novel may owe something to his experiences of 1902, when he went "down and out in the under-world of London" and bitterly reported his findings in *The People of the Abyss* (1906).

*1-60. London, Jack. **The Science Fiction of Jack London.** Ed. by Richard Sid Powers. Gregg Press, 1975.

Nine short stories range from "A Relic of the Pliocene" (1901), a kind of tall tale in which a hunter pursues a mammoth in the Arctic, to "The Unparalleled Invasion" (1910), an account of the annihilation of China by Western powers. In addition, the volume contains "The Scarlet Plague" (1915) and "The Red One" (1918), very probably the finest SF by an American author of the period. The elderly narrator of "The Scarlet Plague" recalls the catastrophic plague that decimated the modern world, plunging it into a barbarism from which no recovery can be made. Comparison to Doyle's *The Poison Belt* [1-32] or Wyndham's *The Day of the Triffids* [3-199] favors London and shows how casual the British concept of a "second chance" seems. The protagonist of "The Red One" is lured into the jungles of Guadalcanal by the metallic echo of the god of the savages—called "The Red One" or "The Star-Born." It proves to be a spaceship that crashed some time in the past. The story successfully fuses SF and literary naturalism.

*1-61. Lytton, Edward Bulwer. **The Coming Race.** Blackwood, 1871. Ed. by Emerson M. Clymer. Philosophical Publishing, 1973.

In a subterranean world beneath Britain, an American finds the Vril-ya, a race far in advance of the 19th century, both personally and socially. They do not know sorrow, pain, or passion; war, crime, and poverty do not exist. All of this is made possible by the power of Vril, the essential force behind all things. Because Lytton does not share the antipathy toward the machine, his novel differs from those of Butler [1-19], Hudson [1-51], and Morris [1-69]. The women of the Vril-ya are superior to men physically and are equal to the males in all other ways.

1-62.   Melville, Douglas, and R. Reginald, eds. **Ancestral Voices: An Anthology of Early Science Fiction.** Arno, 1975.
Ten stories, British and American, dating from 1887 to 1915, have been taken from the books rather than the magazines of the period. They range from the humor of John Kendrick Bang's "A Glance Ahead: Being a Christmas Tale of A.D. 3568" (1901) and Robert W. Chambers's "The Third Eye" (1915) to the horror of Cutcliffe Hyne's "The Lizard" (1904).

1-63.   Mercier, Louis Sebastien. **Memoirs of the Year Two Thousand Five Hundred.** Trans. by William Hooper from *L'An deux mille quatre cent quarante*, 1771. Dobson, 1795. Gregg Press, 1977.
A Parisian awakens in the year 2500 (2440 in the original) to find a society dominated by science and lacking in all the abuses of the 18th century. Education concerns itself with "useful knowledge," while "first communion" involves looking through a microscope. Paris serves as a model of the perfect city throughout the 19th century.

1-64.   Milne, Robert Duncan. **Into the Sun & Other Stories.** Ed. by Sam Moskowitz. *Science Fiction in Old San Francisco*, vol. 2. Donald Grant, 1980.
Moskowitz discovered several hundred SF and supernatural stories written by a group of West Coast writers, led by Milne, which were published in the San Francisco papers during the last half of the 19th century. Eleven of Milne's 60 stories are collected here, written between 1882 and 1891. They show his interest in topics such as natural catastrophe and electricity. Milne encouraged Bierce to write some of his science fiction tales.

1-65.   Mitchell, Edward Page. **The Crystal Man.** Ed. by Sam Moskowitz. Doubleday, 1973.
Moskowitz calls Mitchell, an editor of the New York *Sun*, the "Lost Giant of American Science Fiction." These 30 stories, written between 1874 and 1886, make use of the motifs and conventions then popular. "The Ablest Man in the World" (1879) must be one of the earliest cyborg stories; a reasoning machine is placed in the head of an idiot. Multiple personality fascinates Mitchell.

1-66.   Mitchell, J(ohn) A(mes). **The Last American.** Stokes, 1889.
The story parallels Poe's "Mellonta Tauta" [1-75]. A Persian expedition of the 30th century visits America, learning that a climatic change long ago brought about the downfall of the United States. It becomes a vehicle for an attack on American materialism. To see dramatically the shifts in SF in terms of theme and handling of detail, compare Gene Wolfe's "Seven American Nights" (1979), which is also concerned with a Persian's visit to

the United States. Wolfe did not know Mitchell's story when he wrote his novelette.

1-67. Moffett, Cleveland. **The Conquest of America.** Doran, 1916.
The novel joins together two stories serialized in *McClure's Magazine* the previous year. Germany occupies the United States, but Thomas Edison invents a radio-controlled torpedo enabling an "insignificant airforce" to annihilate the German navy. Edison sits with other scientists and politicians, all actual persons, who supervise American victory and recall Stockton's *The Great War Syndicate* [1-88].

*1-68.   More, Thomas. **Utopia.** Trans. by Ralphe Robynson, 1551.
Originally *Libellus vere aureus nec minus salutarisquam festivus de optimo reip[ublicae] statu deq[ue] nova insula Vtopia*, 1516. Of the many trans. of *Utopia* those by H. V. S. Ogden (Appleton) or Edward Surtz and J. H. Hexter (Yale), *Collected Works*, vol. 4, or *Selected Works*, vol. 2, are recommended.
More contrasts the state of England, where men are hanged for theft while the state seizes vast areas of land in enclosure, with the communistic society of Utopia, visited by Ralph Hythloday. Utopia is a planned society governed by the principles of justice in keeping with natural law, and the people concern themselves with personal health. Utopia ("no place") serves both as a model of the ideal state and as a vehicle for criticizing existing societies.

1-69.   Morris, William. **News from Nowhere; or, An Epoch of Rest.**
Roberts, 1890. James Redmond, ed. Routledge, 1970.
First published in the *Commonweal* in 1890 as a direct response to Bellamy's *Looking Backward* [1-8], Morris's dream-vision calls up his beloved 14th century. Squalor, poverty, and all signs of urban industrialization have vanished. Neither politics nor family tyranny constrains humankind. All do as they please in their own manner and have as a reward a sense of creation and service. In an earlier dream-vision, *A Dream of John Ball* (1886–1887), Morris returned to the Peasants' Revolt to declare that the Fellowship of Man must prevail and all must share the fruits of the Earth equally.

1-70.   Moskowitz, Sam, ed. **Science Fiction by Gaslight: A History and Anthology of Science Fiction in the Popular Magazines, 1891–1911.** World, 1968.
After giving a useful survey of British and American magazines of the period, Moskowitz selects 26 stories that give a sound indication of the extent,

variety, and popularity of SF reaching the mass audience at the turn of the century. The *Strand*, *Pearson's*, the *Argosy*, and the *Black Cat* provide most of the titles. The selection covers all the motifs then popular.

1-71.   Moskowitz, Sam, ed. **Under the Moons of Mars: A History and Anthology of "The Scientific Romance" in the Munsey Magazines, 1912–1920.** Holt, 1970.

Moskowitz's valuable anthology, which includes a history of the Munsey pulps, shows why the Munsey magazines were the heart of American SF during the period of World War I. From Burroughs and England to Murray Leinster and Charles B. Stilson, two characteristics stand out in the fiction: the protagonist capable of heroic action, and adventure in an exotic setting, whether of an unknown area of the Earth or in another world or dimension. The stories continue to have impact, though the language and some situations are somewhat dated.

*1-72.   O'Brien, Fitz-James. **The Supernatural Tales of Fitz-James O'Brien.** Ed. by Jessica Amanda Salmonson. Doubleday, 1988.

At least four tales introduce concepts seminal to later SF. "The Diamond Lens" (1858) opens up submicroscopic worlds, although its narrator is labeled a madman. In "What Was It?" an invisible creature, by implication from another dimension, is captured by the narrator. It anticipates Bierce's "The Damned Thing" [1-13] in giving a scientific explanation of invisibility. "The Lost Room" (1858) suggests additional dimensions and coexistent worlds. "The Wondersmith" (1859) animates mannequins possessing lives of their own and thereby being capable of independent action. In terms of language and narrative conventions, O'Brien looks back to Poe and the gothic; in terms of basic premises, he prepares the way for his successors. *The Atlantic Monthly* published many of his too few stories.

1-73.   Paltock, Robert. **The Life and Adventures of Peter Wilkins.** Robinson & Dodsley, 1751.

More imitative of *Robinson Crusoe* than of Swift, Paltock's narrative first shipwrecks Wilkins off Africa and then takes him to a subterranean world before he meets a race of winged humans. He marries Youwarkee and has seven children by her, some of whom have her power of flight. Scott, Dickens, and Thackeray mention Peter Wilkins. Paltock seems the literary source for the convention of people (as opposed to angels) who can fly, a convention embracing the genetically engineered "Fliers" of Silverberg's *Nightwings* [4-412].

*1-74. Poe, Edgar Allan. **The Narrative of Arthur Gordon Pym of Nantucket.** 1838. Ed. by Harold Beaver. Penguin, 1976.

The Narrative may be read as a tale of shipwreck, mutiny, cannibalism, and other horrors of seafaring, told in the first person to gain that heightened psychological excitement so typical of Poe and the gothic. But Pym changes character, so to speak, halfway through the story. Through the mutiny and shipwreck, Pym does not trust the working of his own mind and constantly fears that he will go mad. Once aboard the *Jane Guy*, however, he calmly describes a world that grows ever more strange as the ship ventures into the Antarctic. Almost incidentally, Poe indulges his fondness for premature burial and puzzles before he takes Pym and his companions to the brink of the terrible cataract. *The Narrative* breaks off abruptly, and though a number have tried, not even Verne could end the story satisfactorily. Evidence shows that Poe knew Symmes [1-81], and certainly Poe's ending helped make the Antarctic and Symmes's inner world the favorite settings they were well into the 20th century. In addition to the mayhem of its literal level, *The Narrative* may be read as Poe's symbolic dramatization of the dilemma central to the concern of the 18th-century psychological empiricists: namely, that one cannot know the nature of reality because one cannot trust either one's perception of the external world or the workings of one's mind. If read in this fashion, the ending proves to be Poe's finest hoax, for the dilemma cannot be resolved.

*1-75. Poe, Edgar Allan. **The Science Fiction of Edgar Allan Poe.** Ed. by H. Beaver. Penguin, 1976.

Because Beaver carefully excludes those stories, like "The Black Cat," in which madness and horror are Poe's concerns, this collection shows how much Poe followed the lead of his contemporaries and predecessors. "MS Found in a Bottle" (1833) suggests Symmes's theory of the hollow Earth. Poe criticizes both Godwin and Locke in a postscript to "The Unparalleled Adventures of One Hans Pfaall" (1835), in which he combines close observation with the promise that he may later describe the dwarfish lunarians whom he discovered; he ends the tale by implying that it, too, is a hoax. "The Conversation of Eiros and Charmion" (1839) deals with the catastrophe that overtakes the world when a comet collides with it. "William Wilson" (1839) concerns itself with multiple personalities, while "The Facts in the Case of M. Valdemar" (1845) combines mesmerism and suspended animation. "The Balloon Hoax" (1844) carries four men in a dirigible across the Atlantic in 75 hours. "Mellonta Tauta" (1849) brings Pundita to "Amricca" by balloon in the 29th century; New York is a pleasure island for an emperor since "mob rule" has been replaced by a monarchy. A wide variety of inventions, including propeller-driven boats and a transatlantic cable, indicate an advanced technology. In addition to 15 stories, Beaver includes the essay "Eureka" (1848). Perhaps the chief value of the volume is that it shows how much of Poe is lost when one omits the stories of madness and horror—without involved external trappings.

1-76.   Pope, Gustavus W. **Journey to Mars.** Dillingham, 1894. Arno, 1975.
Although much of Pope's initial sequence in the Antarctic echoes Poe and Symmes, he introduces the completely unexpected when his young protagonist saves a visiting Martian prince. By magnetically driven ship they return to Mars, where the naval lieutenant falls in love with and marries the princess Suhlamia. Political unrest (and a rival suitor) keep them apart for much of the book; they flee to the Antarctic when a meteor shower threatens Mars. Although Pope adapts the lost-race motif to an interplanetary romance, he seems to anticipate Burroughs [1-17] more than he reminds one of Haggard [1-46]. In *Journey to Venus* (1895), the lovers find that world to be comparable to prehistoric Earth. That parallel includes the sinking of an "Atlantean" continent.

1-77.   Reeve, Arthur B(enjamin). **The Silent Bullet.** Dodd Mead, 1912.
This was the first book collection of the adventures of America's best known "scientific detective," Craig Kennedy. Often compared to Sherlock Holmes—a medical doctor, Jameson, is his companion and the story-teller—Kennedy differs sharply from Doyle's hero. From "mechanical wonders" to Freudian theory, he exploited current works in all fields of science, and invented his own "gadgets" when necessary; he made use of wiretapping and developed a "love meter [which] registers the grand passion [because] even love can be attributed to electrical forces." He dealt in assassination and adultery, witchcraft and white slavery. The high point of his career came in "The Dream Doctor" (1914), when he explained in detail Freudian theory for the first time in popular magazine fiction. For the way in which another American scientist handles mysteries, see White's *The Sign at Six* [1-108].

*1-78.   Rhodes, W(illiam) H(enry). **Caxton's Book.** Bancroft, 1876.
In an introduction to this posthumous volume, Daniel O'Connell called Rhodes the potential equal of Verne and named "science fiction" a distinct type of fiction. The stories show interests shared by Poe and Verne, although Rhodes was no mere imitator. The longest and best, "The Case of Summerfield," deals with a mad scientist from San Francisco who

threatens to destroy the oceans and thus the world if he is not paid a ransom. It was published separately in 1918; it made its newspaper appearance in 1871. Rhodes should be compared with Milne [1-64] and Bierce [1-13].

1-79. Rosny aîné, J. H. (pseud. of Joseph-Henri Boëx). **The Xipéhuz** and **The Death of the Earth.** Arno, 1978. Trans. by George Edgar Slusser.

Long neglected because his work was not available in English, Rosny was one of France's most important SF writers. In *The Xipéhuz* (1887) nomadic prehistoric men encounter creatures "totally alien to the animal and vegetable kingdoms as we know them" and fight a war of extinction. In the far future water had almost entirely disappeared from the Earth in *The Death of the Earth* (1912); the last men die among sentient beings who have evolved from iron, the "ferromagnetics," which feed on the blood of humans. Harold Talbott translated *La Guerre de feu* (1909), abridged translation as *The Quest for Fire* (1967), in which different species of cavemen struggle to obtain fire. It was filmed in 1981.

1-80. Russell, Alan K., ed. **Science Fiction by the Rivals of H. G. Wells.** Castle, 1979.

Although Russell includes such noteworthy stories as Grant Allen's "The Thames Valley Catastrophe" (1897), he gives most attention to George Griffith, including his "The Raid of Le Vengeur" (1898) and those stories that made up *A Honeymoon in Space* (1901). It yokes together the future war motif and the interplanetary voyage. Lord Redgrave develops "R force," a kind of antigravity power to motivate his "airship" *Astronef.* While he delivers a treaty to Washington that establishes an Anglo-American alliance and prevents war with France and Russia, he literally kidnaps Zaide Rennick from an ocean liner. They honeymoon to Mars, the Moon, and Venus, meeting a standard assortment of wonders.

*1-81. Seaborn, Adam. **Symzonia: A Voyage of Discovery.** Seymour, 1820. Ed. by J. O. Bailey. Scholars' Facsimile, 1967.

Symzonia, thought by some scholars, like Bailey, to be the work of John Cleves Symmes himself, portrays a voyage to an inner world to a utilitarian utopia governed by the Best Man. He is elected by a legislature of Worthies, chosen for their virtues as the Good, the Wise, and the Useful. Poverty is unknown, while property is shared. The first utopia by an American, its greater value lies in its introduction of a setting popular well into the 20th century. Compare with Mercier [1-63] to see the differences in American thinking.

*1-82.   Serviss, Garrett P(utnam). **Edison's Conquest of Mars.** Carcosa House, 1947.

Serialized in the New York *Evening Journal* (1898), this was a sequel to Wells's *The War of the Worlds* [1-105], which had been published in *Cosmopolitan* (1897). Serviss dismisses technical detail and scientific explanation as being beyond the readers' knowledge and interest. The novel eulogizes Edison's inventiveness. Except for giantism, the evolution of Mars parallels that of Earth. Serviss's terrestrial jingoism declares that the issue at stake is that of Martian evolution against that of Earth. Edison and company incidentally find a young woman, descendant of humans brought to Mars after the giants built the pyramids.

*1-83.   Serviss, Garrett P(utnam). **The Second Deluge.** McBride, Nast, 1912; Hyperion, 1975.

When a watery nebula threatens the Earth, Cosmo Versals builds an ark and chooses the people (no lawyers) who will survive. The public, including other scientists, ridicule him. A geological phenomenon raises a portion of the Rockies so that other Americans live through the flood. The story is told by future historians from the science-dominated society that Versals brought into being. During the flood he incidentally visits lost Atlantis in a submarine. For a contemporary American treatment of the scientist as hero, see White and Adams's *The Mystery* [1-107].

*1-84.   Shelley, Mary Wollstonecraft. **Frankenstein; or, The Modern Prometheus.** 1818; rev. ed. 1831. Ed. by James Rieger. Bobbs-Merrill, 1974. Ed. by Leonard Wolf. Clarkson Potter, 1977.

Whatever her literary indebtedness—classical myth, Faustus, or Milton—Mary Shelley gave form to one of the enduring myths of SF: the creation of life by science. Guilty of the sin of intellectual pride, Victor Frankenstein epitomizes a shift in the scientists of the 19th century in that he turns from alchemy to electrical forces, a phenomenon that fascinated writers throughout the century. Mary Shelley acknowledged an indebtedness to the physiologists of Germany and Dr. Erasmus Darwin. Aldiss has argued that *Frankenstein* is the first SF novel, although Wells called it more magic than science. See Aldiss's *Frankenstein Unbound* [4-4] for a late treatment of the theme. The 1831 edition is commonly reprinted. Rieger and Wolf reprint the 1818 edition. Rieger includes variations and notes, Wolf many illustrations along with notes.

1-85.   Shelley, Mary Wollstonecraft. **The Last Man.** Henry Colburn, 1826. Ed. by Brian Aldiss. Hogarth, 1985.

Mary Shelley's apocalyptic vision, indebted to de Grainville's *Le Dernier homme* (1805), has two central concerns. The first involves the abdication of the final British king. Second, Lionel Verney, "the last man," ends his days in Rome after wandering through deserted cities when he left his last refuge in Switzerland. Aldiss suggests that Mary Shelley "added a little imagination" to an actual cholera pandemic spreading from Calcutta around the world. Although she makes no mention of the industrial revolution, she does refer to the use of balloons.

*1-86. Stevenson, Robert Louis. **The Strange Case of Dr. Jekyll and Mr Hyde.** Scribner, 1886.
This classic 19th-century presentation of dual personality dramatizes the good and evil within each human. Aware from his youth of a certain wickedness within his nature, Dr. Jekyll experiments and develops a drug that brings his alter ego into ascendancy, thereby transforming himself physically into Mr. Hyde. One learns of the mystery through the eyes of the lawyer Utterson, but only a final manuscript, the full statement of Henry Jekyll, explains the relationship between him and Hyde.

1-87. Stockton, Frank. **The Great Stone of Sardis.** Harper, 1898.
Against the backdrop of the utopian world of 1947, a scientist develops a kind of X-ray machine permitting him to see the strata of the Earth. He burrows through the outer shell to find its core to be a great diamond, while friends make a successful submarine trip to the North Pole. An incidental love story features the woman who is also his financial partner and co-builder of his extensive laboratories. One infers that Stockton was thinking of Thomas Edison, at least to some extent. See Moffett [1-67] and Serviss [1-83] for other American scientists.

1-88. Stockton, Frank. **The Great War Syndicate.** Collier, 1889.
Twenty-three American businessmen assume responsibility for the war against Britain. They develop an armored vessel and an electrically powered "instantaneous motor," seemingly a cross between a jet-propelled shell and an atomic bomb. After victory, an Anglo-American alliance outlaws all war. Compare Moffett [1-67].

*1-89. Swift, Jonathan. **Travels in Several Remote Nations of the World . . . by Lemuel Gulliver [Gulliver's Travels].** 1726. Ed. by Robert D. Heilman. Modern Library, 1969.
Drawing on the traditions of the imaginary voyage and travel literature, Swift sends his protagonist to visit Lilliput, Brobdingnag, Laputa, and Houyhnhnmland. Lilliput and Brobdingnag satirize humanity's moral and political pettiness and its physical grossness. Book Three directly

attacks the Royal Societies of London and Dublin, ridiculing the new science and its materialistic premises, making use of the *Transactions* of the societies as well as Newton's *Principia* to achieve its effectiveness. Book Four reduces humanity to its most brutal and absurd—the Yahoos—contrasting it with the utopian community of the perfectly rational hippomorphic beings, the Houyhnhnms. Swift makes his satire effective by giving it the objectivity of a scientific report. *Gulliver's Travels* anticipates the bitterly critical tone of much SF from the contemporary period.

1-90. Tarde, Gabriel de. **Underground Man.** Duckworth, 1905. Trans. by Cloudesley Brereton. Hyperion, 1974.

Published in the same year as Wells's *A Modern Utopia* [1-101], this book opens with a description of a utopian society. The extinction of the sun forces humanity deep into the Earth to survive. The new society, powered by wonderful machines, develops aesthetically and spiritually as it never did on the surface. Wells wrote the book's introduction.

1-91. Train, Arthur Cheyney, and Robert Williams Wood. **The Man Who Rocked the Earth.** Doubleday, 1915.

Serialized in the *Saturday Evening Post* in the autumn of 1914, this gives an account of the efforts of a mad scientist to end the stalemated European war. He increases the length of the sidereal day, disintegrates part of the Atlas mountains, and threatens to change the poles of the Earth. His weapons and airship use atomic power. The narrative describes radiation sickness, apparently for the first time in popular fiction. The story involves the efforts of a German expedition and an American scientist to reach his base in Newfoundland. The Germans are destroyed; the scientist flies the ship—"The Flying Ring"—to Washington, where a conference of nations meets and abolishes war. The mad scientist has died in his own experiments. In a brief sequel, *The Moon Maker* (1916–1917), not published in book form until 1958, the novelists take their protagonist and his companion, the woman scientist Rhoda Gibbs, on a journey through the solar system after they deflect a comet threatening the Earth. It calls to mind Griffith's *A Honeymoon in Space* [1-80] since the subsequent marriage of the two is implied, but it does not have the sweep of the earlier novel.

1-92. Verne, Jules. **The Adventures of Captain Hatteras** (*Les Aventures du Capitaine Hatteras*). 1867.

Verne's second novel owes much to Sir John Ross's *Second Voyage in Search of the North-West Passage* (1835). In the narrative the brig *Forward* follows

Ross's route until it is deflected toward the pole. The venture costs Hatteras his sanity.

1-93.   Verne, Jules. **From the Earth to the Moon** (*De la terre a la lune*). 1865. Recommended trans. by Walter James Miller, Crowell, 1978.

The influence of Poe's "Hans Pfaall" [1-75] on this novel by Verne remains uncertain, for most of the narrative is given to building a cannon and locating the site from which the shot is to be made. The actual shot (flight) provides the climactic action of the novel. Not until *Round the Moon* (*Autour de la lune*) (1870) did the readers learn that because of deflection by a second earthly moon (Verne's invention) the ship merely orbited the Moon and splashed down in the Pacific. Since the dark side of the Moon was invisible to them, the voyagers saw nothing of it. That fact raises a question about Verne's imagination: did he have to depend on factual sources for his works? In this case, like Poe and Locke, he may have pulled his own hoax, for there existed a long tradition of lunar descriptions.

*1-94.   Verne, Jules. **A Journey to the Center of the Earth** (*Voyage au centre de la terre*). 1864. Recommended trans. by Robert Baldick, Penguin, 1965.

More than half the book is given to the preliminaries before the actual descent begins, the first two chapters relying on a standard point of departure, the discovery of a manuscript giving the location of the caverns in Iceland. The narrative shows Verne's intense care in presenting the latest scientific thought of his age, while the sighting of the plesiosaurus and the giant humanoid shepherding mammoths indicates how well he incorporated lengthy imaginary episodes to flesh out the factual report.

*1-95.   Verne, Jules. **Twenty Thousand Leagues Under the Sea** (*Vingt milles lieues sous les mers*). 1870. Recommended trans. by Emanuel J. Mickel, Indiana Univ. Press, 1992.

The voyage of the *Nautilus* permitted Verne to describe the wonders of an undersea world almost totally unknown to the general public of the period. Indebted to literary tradition for his Atlantis, he made his major innovation in having the submarine completely powered by electricity, although the interest in electrical forces goes back to Poe and Shelley. So far as the enigmatic ending is concerned, his readers had to wait for the three-part *The Mysterious Island* (*L'Île mysterieuse*) (1874–1875) to learn that Nemo had been the Indian warrior-prince Dakkar, who had been involved in the Sepoy Mutiny of 1857. The island the Americans "domesticated" may be regarded as Verne's Robinsonade.

1-96. Waterloo, Stanley. **A Son of the Ages.** Doubleday, 1914.
By combining the ideas of racial memory and reincarnation, the stories trace the protagonist through his various lives—from that of Scar, "The Link," to the Phoenicians, Germanic tribes, and Vikings—in keeping with his idea of Anglo-Saxon supremacy. One episode dramatizes the sinking of Atlantis.

1-97. Waterloo, Stanley. **The Story of Ab: A Tale of the Time of the Caveman.** Way & Williams, 1897.
This is apparently the first American pseudo-historical novel of prehistory from which previously dominant religious themes are completely absent. It dramatizes the lifetime of an individual whose inventions and intellectual development helped humankind begin its ascent from savagery. It became a prototype for later novels. Waterloo accused London of plagiarism in *Before Adam* [1-58]. The attitudes of the two authors toward the material provide an interesting contrast.

1-98. Wells, H(erbert) G(eorge). **The First Men in the Moon.** Bowen-Merrill, 1901.
At first this seems the most traditional of Wells's romances because of its inclusion of so many conventions, including negative gravity. The Selenites have evolved a highly complex and insectlike social order. The confrontation between Cavor and The Grand Lunar owes much to Swift in that humanity is found wanting in terms of the Lunar's concept of rational norms. Wells criticizes the Selenite specialization. Cavor is destroyed by his inquiring intellect; his companion, Bedford, is saved by his individuality.

1-99. Wells, H(erbert) G(eorge). **The Food of the Gods.** Macmillan, 1904.
At first reading this account of giantism resulting from deliberate experiments to make growth continuous may seem little more than a horror story. But when the little people (humans) attack the giants—Redwood, the Princess, Cossars, and others—it becomes a symbolic statement of public resistance to change.

1-100. Wells, H(erbert) G(eorge). **The Island of Dr. Moreau.** Heinemann, 1896. Variorum ed. by Robert Philmus. Univ. of Georgia, 1993.
Reading *Moreau* as a version of the Frankenstein myth overlooks the fact that, unlike Faustus or Victor Frankenstein, Moreau has no sense of guilt or controlling humanity. He is the most terrible of the three and cannot be called a tragic hero. Both in the narrator Pendrick and the "Beast

People," Wells shows the uneasy tension between "natural" and "civilized" humanity. "The Law" satirizes any attempt to codify religio-moral concepts intended to curb the natural man. Wells emphasizes through his satire after Moreau's death that only a fragile shell of civilization restrains humanity from its natural bestiality. This thrust undercuts the long-time romantic idealization of the natural man. Compare Aldiss's *Moreau's Other Island* (U.K., 1980; U.S. title: *An Island Called Moreau*, 1981).

*1-101. Wells, H(erbert) G(eorge). **A Modern Utopia.** Chapman & Hall, 1905.
In part a parody of the natural man of Morris's *News From Nowhere* [1-69], the novel asserts as its central theme that rejection of technical invention for a willful primitivism achieves nothing. His volunteer nobility, the Samurai, represents his "men of good will"—he makes no mention of women—who must become the governing body of humanity.

*1-102. Wells, H(erbert) G(eorge). **The Short Stories of H. G. Wells.** Benn, 1927.
The best of Wells's short stories vividly exemplify his basic techniques and themes. "The Sea Raiders" (1896) introduces a predatory species of octopus into the channel near Sidmouth, a well-known resort town, to show that humanity exists in a world that it does not fully know, one filled with threats to humanity's continued existence. "The Empire of the Ants" (1905) echoes this theme in that, by implication, the new species will take over the world. "The Star" (1897) gives humanity a second chance after the approach of a comet devastates modern civilization. "A Story of Days to Come" (1897), whose culture anticipates that of *When the Sleeper Wakes* [1-106], emphasizes his ambivalence toward the concept of inevitable progress. Its companion novella, "A Story of the Stone Age" (1897), stresses the theme of survival in a brutal world. His stories range from the terror of "In the Avu Observatory" (1895) and "The Flowering of a Strange Orchid" (1895) to the predictions of "The Argonauts of the Air" (1895) and "The Land Ironclads" (1903). "The Country of the Blind" (1904) becomes a parable attacking ethnocentric dogmatism. His basic theme stresses that humanity must grow wiser if it is to survive.

*1-103. Wells, H(erbert) G(eorge). **The Time Machine.** Heinemann, 1895. *The Definitive Time Machine*, ed. by Harry M. Geduld. Indiana Univ. Press, 1987.
Critics have emphasized the splitting of humanity into the Eloi and Morlocks so much as Wells's vision of the outcome of the Marxist class struggle that its implication, taken from Thomas Huxley, that humanity

cannot control the cosmic evolutionary process, and is, therefore, its victim, has not been adequately emphasized. One should not overlook the fact that the book's climax is the vivid scene of the dying Earth. It must be read as being extremely pessimistic. The final speech of the traveler reveals the inner tensions within Wells that may explain why he turned increasingly to a heavy didacticism.

1-104.   Wells, H(erbert) G(eorge). **The War in the Air.** Bell, 1908.
In the early 1900s, a German dirigible fleet attacks New York City. In turn, it is attacked by an Oriental fleet. Guerrilla warfare spreads throughout the world, the "Purple Death" follows, and within 30 years humanity has been reduced to barbarism, forgetting even how to operate machinery. At one level simply another future war story, this is Wells's dramatization of the widening gap between humanity's social intelligence and its inability to manage new inventions. Contemporary humanity cannot meet the challenges science offers to it.

*1-105.   Wells, H(erbert) G(eorge). **The War of the Worlds.** Heinemann, 1898. *A Critical Edition of The War of the Worlds*, ed. by David Y. Hughes and Harry M. Geduld. Indiana Univ. Press, 1993.
The dramatic effectiveness of the novel lies in the detailed realism with which Wells destroys Richmond, Kingston, and Wimbledon. He brings horror to very familiar doorsteps. Perhaps more than any of his other works, this dramatizes humanity's fragile place in the universe, a theme that obsessed him from the first and that he desperately tried to communicate to his contemporaries. Filmed in 1953, its most memorable dramatization was the 1938 Orson Welles broadcast.

1-106.   Wells, H(erbert) G(eorge). **When the Sleeper Wakes.** Harper, 1899.
One sees in this novel the beginning of the split that leads to the Eloi and the Morlocks. Mechanized progress has made great strides, but there has been no comparable growth in humanity's social and political awareness. An oligarchy of the rich has replaced the timid capitalists and has regimented the workers into the Labour Company. The dreamer, Graham, awakens to find he owns half the world. When his presence brings unrest, he is killed. [For other works by this author see chapter 2.]

*1-107.   White, Stewart Edward, and Samuel Hopkins Adams. **The Mystery.** McClure, Phillips, 1907.
Most of the narrative is presented as a mystery echoing the Marie Celeste

affair. The narrator finally reports the scientist-hero's successful attempt to find the ultimate energy, *celestium*, on a volcanic island in the Pacific. He and his secret die together. Not only does the novel give one of the most idealized portraits of a scientist; technically it succeeds through its realistic detail and narrative technique.

*1-108.   White, Stewart Edward. **The Sign at Six.** Bobbs-Merrill, 1912.
The narrator of *The Mystery* returns as the protagonist who finds the "mad" scientist threatening to cut off light, sound, and heat from New York City. The protagonist destroys the machine and the notes of the madman because they are too dangerous for humanity to have; they represent an area into which humanity should not trespass. In this sense it repeats the same warning that Mary Shelley voiced in *Frankenstein* [1-84].

CHAPTER 2

Science Fiction Between the Wars: 1916–1939

Brian Stableford

World War I had a considerable impact on the history of speculative fiction. It put an end to the myth of a war to end war, and brought to Europe a profound fear of the catastrophic possibilities of a further war fought with airplanes and poison gas. Although America was not without similar anxieties, they were considerably muted; while neither impossible nor uncontemplated, the invasion and saturation bombing of America seemed much less likely to its citizens than such a fate seemed to the citizens of multinational and fearful Europe.

The utopian optimism that had flourished before the war in the works of such writers as Gabriel Tarde and H. G. Wells (chapters 1 and 2) was almost obliterated in Europe; those writers who held to it as best they could—including Wells—mostly accepted that things would probably get worse before they could begin to get better. Optimism remained buoyant only in America, reflecting the fact that the United States had been the only real winner of the war. The war had ripped the European heart out of the world economy, leaving America to take up the slack. The boom lasted until the Wall Street crash of 1929 and the subsequent Great

Depression, but its effects recoiled upon the fragile economies of Europe in such a way as to intensify their disadvantage. It is hardly surprising that American futuristic fiction after 1918 was driven by a confident spirit of adventurism, which was almost entirely absent from European speculative fiction.

The years following the end of the war saw dramatic changes in the market situation of popular fiction—including, of course, science fiction. The middlebrow magazines that had nurtured scientific romance in Britain had lost the experimental fervor that had encouraged them to seek out the unusual and the imaginative even before the war began; afterward, speculative fiction became virtually taboo, except in the Boys' Papers aimed at juvenile readers. The revitalization of commercial advertising was associated with market research that singled out women as the main exercisers of consumer choice, so that magazines aimed at female readers were held to be the best advertising media. In the United States there emerged a sharp division between the advertising-supported "slick magazines" and the sales-supported pulps. The latter underwent a dramatic diversification, experimenting with dozens of new types in the hope of discovering new "ecological niches" within the ragged spectrum of low-brow literary taste. Science fiction was one of the few experiments that succeeded—in the sense of finding, holding, and gradually expanding an audience of specialist readers—because it was a species of fiction appealing mainly to young male readers; however, it remained confined to the pulps.

The demands of the American pulp marketplace encouraged the production of exotic adventure stories, but the development of a specialist audience permitted science fiction to take on distinctive characteristics of its own. Although *Weird Tales*, founded in 1923, mingled science fiction with supernatural fiction and heroic fantasy, its editors were happy to leave stories of the first kind to the new specialist magazines, which began to appear in 1926. The first of these, Hugo Gernsback's *Amazing Stories*, was an anomaly in the pulp marketplace by virtue of its larger size, the character of its advertising, and the editor's insistence that its fiction should have a didactic component dedicated to the popularization of science and a celebration of the utopian potential of scientific progress. Other SF pulps—especially *Astounding Stories of Super-Science*, founded in 1930—diluted Gernsback's manifesto considerably, preferring a kind of futuristic costume drama, which duplicated the standard characteristics of pulp melodrama, but the genre retained a strong and not-unjustified sense of its own uniqueness and ambition.

There emerged with surprising rapidity a loose set of expectations, common to both readers and writers, regarding the appropriate content and method of pulp science fiction stories. This consensus was in some ways constraining, but in others it was liberating, especially in the way that the development of a stock of standardized story frameworks provided imaginative *lebensraum* for a fast range of hypothetical creations. This scope was by no means fully exploited by the early pulp writers, but it was they who put together the first maps of the new literary territory and began the work of training readers in the skills necessary to orient themselves rapidly and comfortably within texts that referred to worlds very different from our own. In Britain, speculative writers had no such established pattern of imaginative conventions to draw on (although many took some warrant from the precedents laid down by Wells) and thus had to be much more careful in the construction of their hypothetical milieux. Their novels, in consequence, tend to stand up much better as individual entities and are much more varied as a result of the idiosyncratic methods and purposes of the writers.

Despite the different evolution of American and European speculative fiction, there was a considerable flow of material in both directions. Gernsback's early magazines used many reprints from the work of Verne and Wells, and frequent translations from the French and German. Most of the speculative fiction that appeared in book form in English was issued on both sides of the Atlantic, and copies of American pulp magazines regularly made their way into Britain, sometimes by curious routes. (England-bound ships sometimes used surplus pulp magazines as ballast, which were then sold at knockdown prices in Woolworth's department stores as "Yank Mags.") There are, inevitably, some shared influences to be seen in the science fiction produced in the two countries. Nevertheless, the two traditions became and remained distinct between the two world wars to a much greater degree than they previously had, or ever would again. Few important science fiction writers actually died in the war, William Hope Hodgson being the most significant casualty, but the output of all the major British writers changed considerably in its content and tone. The difference is very evident in the works of William Le Queux, John Beresford, M. P. Shiel, Sir Arthur Conan Doyle, and—most significant of all—H. G. Wells. In America a sharp discontinuity was caused even before the advent of the specialist magazines by the emergence in the postwar years of a number of new writers who were to make a significant contribution to the evolution of pulp science fiction and fantasy: A. Merritt, Ray Cummings, Will F. Jenkins (Murray Leinster), Francis Stevens, H. P. Lovecraft, and Homer Eon Flint all made their literary debuts between 1917 and 1919.

The change in the character of subsequent British science fiction offers striking testimony to the impact of the Great War on the consciousness of the nation. Prior to the war, the most prolific species of futuristic fiction produced in Britain had been the future war story, whose leading exponents had included George Griffith, William Le Queux, and Louis Tracy. Most of these stories had looked forward with some enthusiasm to the prospect of large-scale conflict made more exciting and spectacular by the advent of airships, submarines, and more destructive weaponry. Even those writers who had imagined slaughter on a vast scale—Griffith in *The Angel of the Revolution* [1-41], Tracy in *The Final War* (1896), and M. P. Shiel in *The Yellow Danger* (1898)—seemed to relish the prospect. Wells, in *The War in the Air* [1-104] and *The World Set Free* (1914), took no pleasure in the contemplation of huge casualty figures, but thought that a war might be a good thing if it could clear away the old social order and make way for the construction of a socialist world state.

Once the reality of modern warfare had been made manifest, however, deep disillusionment followed. The future war stories of the next decade saw war as an unmitigated evil that threatened to destroy civilization utterly. Early examples include Edward Shanks's *The People of the Ruins* [2-107], Cicely Hamilton's *Theodore Savage* [2-48], and Shaw Desmond's *Ragnarok* [2-31]. As the sequence extended into the 1930s with Neil Bell's *The Gas War of 1940* (1931), John Gloag's *To-Morrow's Yesterday* [2-45], and Joseph O'Neill's *Day of Wrath* (1936), the anxiety became increasingly hysterical and the images of mass destruction ever more repulsive, culminating in the horrors of S. Fowler Wright's *Four Days War* [2-153] and Philip George Chadwick's *The Death Guard* [2-18]. The United States, as might be expected, was hardly touched by this tide of apocalyptic anxiety. The war had been fought a long way from American shores, and U.S. involvement had lasted 18 months rather than four years. The future war stories produced in the United States during this period exhibit a combination of alarmism and documentary fascination similar to that which marked several British prewar novels, such as Le Queux's *The Invasion of 1910* [1-57]. Examples include Hector Bywater's *The Great Pacific War* (1925) and Floyd Gibbons's *The Red Napoleon* [2-42].

In Britain, anxiety concerning the destructive power of contemporary technology was not confined to the contemplation of the possibility of war. Suspicion of the fruits of technological progress was much more general, and fears to the effect that even without a war the advance of technology might have a deleterious effect on the quality of life were commonly expressed. The spread of a similar suspicion in the United States was much less marked, and the balance of opinion in fiction produced there remained more optimistic throughout the period, although the seeds of doubt had certainly been sown.

This change in context helps to explain the fact that so many of the important British speculative writers of the prewar period either stopped producing futuristic works or changed the pattern of their thinking dramatically. Wells continued to write speculative fiction after the war, but nothing remotely similar to his early scientific romances. In general, his postwar work is more polemical and is frequently embittered by what Wells saw as a continuing disaster: the failure of humans to realize how desperate their contemporary historical situation really was. This point of view is dramatized in *The Undying Fire* (1919), which is a materialist's version of the story of Job, and in *Mr. Blettsworthy on Rampole Island* (1928), whose hallucinating hero envisions contemporary humans as savage tribespeople unaware of their own brutality. His later utopian novels, *Men Like Gods* [2-139] and *The Shape of Things to Come* [2-140], present ideal societies much further removed from the contemporary world than *A Modern Utopia* [1-101] and imply that contemporary man is too ignoble a creature to aspire to their rewards. Other speculative fictions Wells wrote in this period, including *The Autocracy of Mr Parham* (1930) and *Star-Begotten* [2-141], are uneasy works, which he categorized as "sarcastic fantasies."

The change that overtook Conan Doyle's work was more directly attributable to the ravages of the war itself; he developed an intense interest in spiritualism following the death of his son. The depth of feeling that lies behind *The Land of Mist* [2-32] is obvious, but its hero, Professor Challenger, is tragically demoralized by comparison to his earlier self. Le Queux never recovered the bloodthirsty ebullience that had characterized his prewar work, and he relaxed into the production of lackluster thrillers and mystery novels for the remainder of his career. John Beresford and M. P. Shiel only returned to science fiction as their careers were winding down, Beresford producing hardly anything of SF interest between 1918 and 1940 and Shiel producing a single tour de force in *The Young Men Are Coming!* [2-109] some 20 years after his important early contributions to the genre.

Compared to the decisive break in the pattern of British science fiction, the development of the American scene was a relatively orderly and gradual unfolding. The variety and scope of pulp SF increased by dramatic and seemingly inexorable stages as new writers and new markets appeared. While new British writers—even those interested in SF as a form of fantastic romance—had to take their place in a tradition that had become argumentative, pessimistic, and acutely concerned with social issues, new American writers came into a medium of entertainment full of exciting and colorful narratives. The pulp magazines became increasingly interested in unreservedly exotic romance following the huge success of Edgar Rice Burroughs, who became for a time the biggest money earner on the popular fiction scene. Interplanetary romance in the vein of Burroughs's Martian series [1-17] proliferated and thrived in spectacular fashion between the end of the war and the founding of *Amazing Stories*, and helped to make the notion of a specialist fiction that would rely heavily on interplanetary adventures more acceptable. Other examples of this subspecies include J. U. Giesy's Palos trilogy [2-43], Homer Eon Flint's interplanetary adventures [2-37], Ralph Milne Farley's Radio Man series [2-34], and Otis Adelbert Kline's Venusian series of Burroughs pastiches (1924–1926). Burroughs, however, did not confine himself to interplanetary scenarios, and neither did his imitators. Ray Cummings hollowed out his own niche within the field by developing a new milieu, even less plausible than the hollow interior of the Earth, in *The Girl in the Golden Atom* [2-28]. Another milieu for exotic adventure that became increasingly popular was the "parallel world," extensively featured in the work of the one writer whose fantasies were even gaudier than Burroughs: A. Merritt. Merritt was one of Hugo Gernsback's favorite authors, although the science fictional element in his work is not very pronounced, and he influenced several of the early recruits to Gernsback's cause, most obviously Jack Williamson.

Advocates of the view that science fiction ought to be a hard-headed, rational, and realistic form of imaginative fiction sometimes exaggerate the difference between Burroughsian romance and the SF that Gernsback promoted in *Amazing Stories*, which was ostensibly faithful to known science and authentically prophetic. The overflow of exotic romance into the early science fiction magazines was, however, rather more than a temporary aberration. Pure fantasy, lightly disguised by a science fictional jargon of apology, was a significant element in genre SF from the beginning, and it has remained so in spite of half-hearted attempts to exclude it. The fact that pulp magazines frankly dedicated to fantasy always fell by the wayside had more to do with the fact that the SF pulps were already serving that kind of demand than with the nonviability of fantasy as a genre. (The post-Tolkien boom in genre fantasy readily disproves the latter thesis.) No SF magazine—not even *Astounding* at the very height of its delusions of grandeur—ever featured a science fiction purified of exotic romanticism. Nor was the incidence of escapist fantasy in the science fiction magazines a response to the gloom and despondency of the Great Depression; this kind of pulp romance enjoyed its heyday in the heady years before the Wall Street crash.

Although Burroughs was popular in Britain, he was regarded there (like Jules Verne before him) as a writer of "boys' books" unfit for adult consumption. Such Burroughs imitations as were produced in Britain mostly appeared in the Boys' Papers and few reached book form; Stacey Blake's *Beyond the Blue* (1920) was a rare exception. No British interplanetary stories ever exhibited the same wholehearted exoticism as Burroughs's Martian fantasies, although a few British imitations of his Tarzan stories contrived a certain depth of feeling. Vivid and unashamed fantasy adventures remained a peculiarly American product for many years, and the startling precocity of American writers in bringing the substance of daydreams into various kinds of commercial mass production was to become an effective factor in the spectacular "coca-colonizatlon" of the world's entertainment media achieved by American comic books, American cinema, and—eventually—American TV.

Of the authors who became the main suppliers of original material to the science fiction magazines in the years between 1925 and 1939, very few were untouched by the lure of exotic romance. The main concession made by many of them to Gernsback's manifesto was simply that they began to devote more time and attention to the hardware featured in their stories. Such writers as A. Hyatt Verrill and S. P. Meek remained firmly anchored within the established pulp tradition even though they appeared almost exclusively in the SF pulps. Space travel, although of some moderate interest as a technological possibility, was principally exploited as a literary device for taking characters into a vast array of exotic environments and spectacular conflicts. This trend led to the rapid development of "space opera" by such writers as Edmond Hamilton, Edward E. "Doc" Smith, Jack Williamson, and John W. Campbell, Jr., who quickly came to realize that a solar system was an inconveniently narrow arena when compared to a galaxy. It was not the inspiration of scientific discovery but the thirst for more exotic territories that gave birth to the fabulous faster-than-light spaceships that soon became pulp SF's most prominent motif.

Among writers who conformed to Gernsback's notion of what science fiction writers ought to be doing, David H. Keller stood out, to the extent that he wrote only one interplanetary story and no Burroughsian romance. Keller, a doctor specializing in psychiatric medicine, had the rare advantage of knowing a good deal about science. What he did not have, however, was Gernsback's optimism; his work remained firmly anchored within the "no good will come of it all" school of thought, and he was by no means alone. Other pulp SF writers disposed to be skeptical about the march of progress were Miles J. Breuer and Nathan Schachner. Three early pulp SF writers who had a sound grasp of science combined with a far bolder temperament were the mathematician Eric Temple Bell who wrote under the pseudonym John Taine, John W. Campbell, Jr., and Stanley G. Weinbaum, but all their careers faltered or were brought to a premature conclusion. Taine, who had published several SF books before turning to the pulp marketplace, found scope there to indulge the remarkable extravagance of his imagination, but he wrote relatively little SF after the mid-1930s because of his other commitments. (Taine's fiction, mathematical work as Eric Temple Bell, and life are the subject of Constance Reid's important study, *The Search for E. T. Bell, Also Known as John Taine* [Mathematical Association of America, 1993].) Weinbaum, who had considerable literary ability and imaginative power, as well as a nice sense of humor, died less than 18 months after publishing his first science fiction story. Campbell, who went on to have by far the most profound effect on the genre as editor of *Astounding* from 1938, was unfortunately forbidden by some absurd quirk of his editorial contract to write for his own magazine; he produced some excellent short SF as Don A. Stuart but was forced to abandon even that semiclandestine activity; the fact that he spent the next thirty years feeding his ideas to other writers could not entirely compensate the field for the loss of the work he might have produced. We can only speculate as to the extent to which the fervent editorial propagandizing that became a major force shaping the genre was a product of creative frustration.

One further factor that needs to be mentioned when considering the different ways in which British and American science fiction evolved between the wars is the influence of speculative nonfiction. In Britain, particularly between 1925 and 1935, there was a boom in what is nowadays called futurology. Numerous essays appeared in which authors attempted to anticipate the changes that the near future would bring. A good deal of this material was reprinted in the United States, but Americans produced far less of it. The reason for this, of course, was the fact that in British intellectual circles anxiety about the future was running high. Although there were numerous works whose tone was ebulliently optimistic—the Earl of Birkenhead's *The World in 2030 AD* (1930) and A. M. Low's *Our Wonderful World of Tomorrow* (1934) are notable examples—many of these essays were highly dubious about the certainty of progress.

A particularly influential contribution to speculative thought about the future was made by Kegan Paul, Trench and Trubner's Today & Tomorrow series (reprinted in the United States by Dutton). The series was initiated by the publication in 1924 of the text of a lecture by J. B. S.

Haldane, *Daedalus: or, Science and the Future*, in which the author argued that by the end of the century social life would be altered beyond recognition (entirely for the better) due to the advancement of biological science. The immediate effect of this publication was to prompt a reply from the philosopher Bertrand Russell, *Icarus: or, The Future of Science*, which argued that scientific advancement, by giving greater power to existing power groups, would more likely result in the annihilation, not the betterment, of the human race. The debate was joined by others, and the publishers eventually extended the series to include more than 100 pamphlets. Contributors to the series included many eminent scientists and literary figures, and between them they discussed the future of virtually every human field of endeavor and many social institutions. The essayists included Sylvia Pankhurst, Vernon Lee, Vera Brittain, C. E. M. Joad, and James Jeans; a significant number of the contributors also wrote speculative fiction (usually, though not invariably, after the essays), including Haldane, Russell, André Maurois, Muriel Jaeger, Leslie Mitchell, A. M. Low, Robert Graves, John Gloag, and Gerald Heard.

Haldane's *Daedalus* influenced several notable works of speculative fiction, sometimes in a negative way. Aldous Huxley's *Brave New World* [2-56] and C. S. Lewis's *Out of the Silent Planet* [3-116] are partly reactions against it. Haldane's later collection of essays, *Possible Worlds* (1927), was also influential; its concluding essay, "The Last Judgment," is a virtual blueprint for Olaf Stapledon's *Last and First Men* [2-119], which was also influenced by J. D. Bernal's Today & Tomorrow pamphlet, *The World, the Flesh and the Devil* (1929). In general, this flow of ideas from futurological speculation into speculative fiction helped to maintain the intellectual seriousness of British science fiction. There were many writers in America who were as intellectually and artistically capable as Huxley, Stapledon, and Gloag, but speculation about the future never became fashionable in the intellectual circles in which they moved. The best pulp SF writers were certainly no fools, but the manner in which they could take inspiration from wider public debates was severely constrained by the nature of their marketplace.

The virtues of the best speculative fiction produced in Britain between the wars are easy enough to see: the novels are serious in intent, ambitious in their attempts to analyze genuine human problems, and frequently subtle in the development of their ideas. They were written within—and made a contribution to—an intellectual climate in which concern for the future prospects of society had a certain urgency. American science fiction did not have the benefit of such an intellectual climate; it had to build its own subculture in order to generate such interest on a more limited scale.

An urgent concern for the future, and for the possibilities implicit in the march of science, remained curiously esoteric in the United States during the 1920s. This situation was transformed as time went by, but there is a sense in which American science fiction has never entirely recovered from its one-time esotericism; to a certain extent, the subculture of fans that formed around the SF pulps of the 1920s and 1930s still values that esotericism, and some of its members resent the way in which many of their favorite motifs have now become common cultural property.

Although literary and intellectual sophistication were not among them, American pulp science fiction of the 1930s had several admirable virtues, including a hectic verve and wide-eyed enthusiasm that were part and parcel of its awkward naïveté. British speculative fiction was far-ranging in time, but for the most part it paid relatively little attention to space. Leaving aside such painstaking visionary fantasies as David Lindsay's *A Voyage to Arcturus* [2-72] and Olaf Stapledon's *Star Maker* [2-121], British writers were too interested in our own world to pay much heed to others. Strange societies were frequently situated on the Moon or on Mars, so that their mode of organization could be contrasted with ours, but imagining space travel as an actual project or trying to construct hypothetical life systems that might plausibly exist on other worlds were minority interests. In the pulps, by contrast, such exercises seemed to be the very heart of the whole endeavor. The pulp SF writers turned the universe into a gigantic playground for the imagination, and sent wave after wave of pioneers into imaginative territories that were literally limitless. These pioneers hardly began to exploit this wonderful wealth of opportunity, but in the grand American tradition they blazed the first trails, put up the first signposts, and cut a violent swath through a host of imagined enemies.

The period following World War I was less fertile for the development of speculative fiction in languages other than English. The longest-standing coherent tradition of scientific romance was, of course, in France, where Jules Verne's *voyages imaginaires* had established the genre in the 1860s. Verne died in 1905, and two of his most important contemporaries, Camille Flammarion and Albert Robida, produced no significant work after the turn of the century, although they survived into the 1920s. The most important writers active before the war who continued their careers afterward were Joseph-Henri Boëx, (who signed his scientific romances J. H. Rosny aîné), Maurice Renard, and Jean La Hire; it is a pity that much of Renard's work and all of La Hire's remains untranslated. Charles Bargone, who signed himself Claude Farrère, also wrote some notable speculative fiction in this period but very few specialist writers emerged between the wars; the most notable French scientific romances of the latter part of the period are those of André Maurois. Hugo Gernsback had a few French novels translated for the SF pulps, but they were all minor; the best was *La Mort du fer* (1931) by S. S. Held, translated by Fletcher Pratt as *The Death of Iron* (1931).

The influence of Rosny, who wrote numerous prehistoric fantasies, was presumably responsible for the fact that works of this kind are extensively featured in French fiction of the 1920s, and more prolifically represented in translated work than SF of other kinds. Max Begouen's *Les Bisons d'argile* (1925; trans. as *Bison of Clay*, 1926) and Claude Anet's *La Fin d'un monde* (1925; trans. as *The End of a World*, 1927), are two of the most notable, and Henri Barbusse's panoramic presentation of human history in *Chains* (1925) includes scenes from prehistory.

No nation underwent a more traumatic transformation as a result of the Great War than Germany, and both the leading German speculative writers of the prewar period died in the second decade of the century, Kurd Lasswitz in 1910 and Paul Scheerbart in 1915. The main ingredient of the futuristic fiction that began to appear in some profusion after the war was technocratic utopianism, which bore a strong resemblance to the kind of fiction that Gernsback wanted to publish in his magazines to inspire the American youth with inventive enthusiasm. The most successful writer of this kind was Hans Dominik, but the only translation of his work used by Gernsback was an article "Airports for World Traffic" in *Air Wonder Stories* in 1930. Gernsback featured far more work by a writer less well known in his native land, Otfrid von Hanstein, five of whose novels appeared in *Wonder Stories* and *Wonder Stories Quarterly*, beginning with *Electropolis* [2-131]. The image of a technocratic utopia was so prevalent in German popular literature of the day that it became the target of a particularly scathing attack in Alexandr Moszkowski's satirical demolition of utopian ideals, *The Isles of Wisdom* [2-91]. Some work of this type became so tainted by the political ideals of Nazism that it has since been blotted out of the historical record.

Interplanetary stories also featured in German science fiction between the wars, largely due to the influence of rocket pioneer Hermann Oberth. Otto Willi Gail's *The Shot into Infinity* [2-39] made some attempt to achieve technical realism, and members of the Society for Space Travel founded by Oberth and others popularized their activities via their involvement with Fritz Lang's film *Die Frau im Mond* (1929). The German cinema of the period produced several notable science fiction films, including Lang's magnificent *Metropolis* (1926), novelized by his wife Thea von Harbou [2-132]. The success of the film version of *F. P. 1 Does Not Reply* (1932) was an important factor in guiding Curt Siodmak toward Hollywood, where he enjoyed a long career scripting movies.

An even more dramatic historical break occurred in Eastern Europe, where the effects of World War I were further complicated by the Russian Revolution of 1917. Despite the industrial underdevelopment of Russia, by comparison with the other European powers, there had been several technological utopian novels published in the late 19th century, including one by N. Chernyshevsky, who translated Karl Marx's *Capital* into Russian. The Russian rocket pioneer Konstantin Tsiolkovsky was encouraged by the new regime, and he completed his Vernian romance *Beyond the Planet Earth* [2-129] not long after the revolution. Other writers whose speculative works enjoyed the support of the U.S.S.R. were Alexei Tolstoi and Aleksandr Beliaev. Two Russian writers of the period who undoubtedly were literary figures of major importance were, however, prophets without honor in their own country because they rapidly became disenchanted with the Communist state. Evgenii Zamiatin quickly fell from favor after writing the brilliant *We* [2-157], and although Mikhail Bulgakov was greatly admired as a playwright by Stalin, he too was silenced after the implementation of the new economic policy led him to publish the satirical novella "The Fatal Eggs" [2-9].

Of all the speculative writers of the period who wrote in languages other than English, however, one man stands out: the Czech Karel Čapek, whose major works include *R. U. R.* [2-16], the play that gave the word *robot* to several languages, and the novels *The Absolute at Large* [2-14], *Krakatit* [2-15], and *War with the Newts* [2-17]. Čapek contrasts sharply with the German and American writers, and outdoes the British pessimists, in respect to his dire suspicion of progress and his unique brand of fatalistic black comedy. His ardent championship of democracy and opposition to the threat of Nazism would have ensured him the same fate as his brother Josef, who died in Belsen, had not his death preceded Hitler's invasion.

Of the science fiction published in the rest of Europe during this period, very little has been translated into English. The prehistoric sections of *The Long Journey* [2-60] by Danish Nobel prize winner Johannes V. Jensen have been published in English, but no futuristic fiction from the Scandinavian countries seems to have been translated, although a good deal was produced there. The same is true of Italy.

The interwar period is given relatively sparse coverage in most reference books and histories of SF. American pulp SF of the period is given full and intelligent consideration in Paul Carter's *The Creation of Tomorrow* [8-34], which provides excellent analytical coverage of its main themes. There is also an abundance of highly detailed historical analysis in *The World Beyond the Hill* [8-101] by Alexei and Cory Panshin. British books are listed and briefly annotated in I. F. Clarke's bibliography *Tale of the Future From the Beginning to the Present Day* [7-5], but Clarke's analytical work *The*

Pattern of Expectation [8-40] is less interested in this period than earlier ones. The most detailed commentary on and analysis of the British tradition is to be found in *Scientific Romance in Britain 1890–1950* by Brian Stableford [8-132]. All the major writers of the period are annotated in John Clute and Peter Nicholls's *Encyclopedia of Science Fiction* [7-22], which includes a good idea of material on SF in languages other than English.

Fred Polak's *The Image of the Future* (1961), which is perhaps the best of all historical studies of futuristic fiction, ceases to give detailed consideration to particular texts when it reaches the interbellum period, and argues that futuristic fiction suffered a crucial deterioration because of the "denaturation" of the image of the future possessed by modern Western culture. This denaturation, according to Polak, was partly a disintegration and framentation reflected in the variety and multiplicity of texts, and partly a decline in hopefulness. It *is* true that this period saw the virtual petering out of the tradition of utopian fantasy, and a dramatic loss of confidence in the ability and readiness of Western society to reorganize itself in such a way as to secure the greater happiness of the greatest number, but it is surely a mistake to see this as a final or fatal deterioration in futuristic thought. It certainly reflects the emergence of a more bitter zeitgeist especially in Britain, but it also reflects the emergence of a new skepticism about the possibility of assuring the happiness of all simply by technological sophistication and sociopolitical reorganization.

Before World War I, prophets could declare that utopian reconstruction was not merely feasible but imminent. Such novels as Edward Bellamy's *Looking Backward* [1-8] and Wells's *A Modern Utopia* [1-101]were near-future visions, replete with advertising copy promoting the idea of a world reborn. As the Great War entered its final phase, it was still possible to hope that it might in some small part be justified if it could prepare the way for such a regeneration as is envisaged in Oliver Onions's *The New Moon* (1918). Unfortunately, it was not to be. Optimism ebbed away in the postwar years as men and women counted the cost of the war and hunted in vain for the profit. The march of technology continued, but its champions—Gernsback, Haldane, Dominik, and others—found themselves arrayed against an army of doubters who wondered whether the advancement of technology really could be counted "progress." It was considered that machines *might*, if responsibly used, help to create heaven on Earth, but it was held to be already proven that they could also create hell. The argument invariably turned on some account of human nature, which was (in the wake of Darwin and Freud) almost invariably held to be rapacious and greedy, not to be trusted either with sophisticated means of destruction or with the means of fully gratifying childish and hedonistic desires.

Many of the utopias imagined in this period, therefore, tend to be fugitive ones, like James Hilton's Shangri-La in *Lost Horizon* [2-52], hiding in some all-but-inaccessible corner of dubious plausibility. There are also ironic utopias, like John Gloag's *The New Pleasure* [2-44], and bizarre visions that call the whole notion of utopia into question, such as Herbert Read's *The Green Child* [2-101]. Rex Warner's surreal allegory of the search for a better world conveys its embittered message in its title: *The Wild Goose Chase* (1937). The most rigorous and thorough of all utopian satires, Moszkowski's *Isles of Wisdom* [2-91], is very much in tune with the zeitgeist, and so are the various tales of "utopia betrayed" in which people simply fail to adjust to the opportunities of an age of abundance; examples include Muriel Jaeger's *The Question Mark* [2-59] and Claude Farrère's *Useless Hands* [2-35].

It had been popular before the war to imagine that the miracles of science might be turned against us, by foreign warlords or mad scientists, but in the period between the wars this anxiety grew deeper and broader. There were still mad scientists and foreign warlords, of course, but the suspicion extended to anyone who had power and might try to keep it. Lord Acton's dictum about power corrupting seemed much more important once it was possible to imagine power groups in control of psychotropic drugs and eugenic programs, as in Huxley's *Brave New World* [2-56], or the gift of immortality, as in Gloag's *Winter's Youth* [2-46] or Bell's *The Seventh Bowl* [2-8]. There was even the possibility that the machines themselves might grow sufficiently powerful to turn against us, as in Miles J. Breuer's pulp novel "Paradise and Iron" (1930), and perhaps the possibility that we might turn against our very selves, as in Fowler Wright's *The Adventure of Wyndham Smith* [2-148].

The utopian works of the period are, for the most part, unimpressive. The most wholehearted of them is *Back to Methuselah* [2-108] by George Bernard Shaw, who renounced Darwinism in favor of the simple faith that human nature might be anything we want it to be, and also embraced the rather fatuous notion—later to become commonplace in pulp SF—that mankind might eventually be able to forsake flesh altogether in becoming beings of "pure energy." Despite Gernsback's propagandizing there are relatively few utopian visions to be found in early pulp SF, although this has more to do with the essential features of melodrama than with any consistent pessimism on the part of the writers. The most interesting account of a hard-won utopia is the climax of Laurence Manning's story sequence, *The Man Who Awoke* [2-77].

In earlier eras, dystopian images of the future had been produced almost entirely in order to attack particular political philosophies. This motive remained important in the production of such anti-socialist polemics as Condé B. Pallen's *Crucible Island* (1919), John Kendall's *Unborn Tomorrow* (1933), and Ayn Rand's *Anthem* [2-100], and such anti-Fascist polemics as Sinclair Lewis's *It Can't Happen Here* [2-71]. A notable feature of the period is, however, the profusion of novels that go beyond the surfaces of particular ideologies to reach more fundamental questions about the nature of the good life and the entanglement of political power and technological instrumentality. The classics of this emergent species are Zamiatin's *We* and Huxley's *Brave New World*, but the same kind of analytical thoughtfulness can be seen to a greater or lesser degree in a host of other works, including Michael Arlen's *Man's Mortality* [2-1] and Joseph O'Neill's *Land Under England* [2-96].

George Bernard Shaw was not the only dissenter from the harsher view of human nature that became established in the wake of Darwin and Freud. The Marxist Henri Barbusse offered a different account of human nature in *Chains* (1925), and J. Leslie Mitchell was passionately eloquent in his rejection of the notion of the inherent bestiality of man in his curious evolutionary parable *Three Go Back* [2-89] and its companion piece *Gay Hunter* [2-88]. The majority, however, was on the other side, and the "theriomorphic image of man" became a warrant for scathing misanthropy in the work of several writers. This attitude is at its most extreme in the work of S. Fowler Wright, particularly *The World Below* [2-154] and *Dream* [2-150], but can also be seen in Olaf Stapledon's *Odd John* [2-120] and the hysterical climax of Claude Houghton's *This Was Ivor Trent* [2-53]. Many dystopian fantasies of the period imply that the citizens of dystopia fully deserve their fate by virtue of being descended from apes rather than angels.

Between the extremes of *Back to Methuselah* and *The World Below* there extends a wide spectrum of works in which writers wonder about the real extent of our less fortunate behavioral dispositions and ask what probability exists that we may overcome them. Most writers in the end, come to the conclusion that even though there is much of the ape in us, there is at least an echo of the angel too. This viewpoint is put forward explicitly enough in Wells's *Undying Fire* (1919), Guy Dent's *Emperor of the If* [2-30], and—most eloquently of all—in E. V. Odle's *The Clockwork Man* [2-94]. The force for good is; usually construed in spiritual or emotional terms rather than as the power of reason; indeed, reason is frequently seen to be allied with the dark side of human nature because of its presumed amorality. Fables attacking the amorality of hyperrational and unemotional superhumans are common; examples include Noëlle Roger's *The New Adam* [2-104] and John Russell Fearn's *The Intelligence Gigantic* [2-36].

Parables in which scientists are betrayed into evil deeds by their excessive dedication to rationalism include *The Weigher of Souls* [2-82] by André Maurois and *The Devil's Highway* [2-147] by Harold Bell Wright and John Lebar. This conflict between the image of the human implied by contemporary biology and psychology and the older image of theological supposition is a central issue in many metaphysical fantasies that import a measure of mysticism into speculative fiction, including Lindsay's *A Voyage to Arcturus* and Čapek's *The Absolute at Large*.

This importation of metaphysical themes and ideas assisted a significant trend in British speculative fiction that partly counterbalanced the pessimism of the future war stories and dystopian fantasies. Although few other writers imagined a transcendence of human weakness as extreme as that in *Back to Methuselah*, many did take refuge in the hope that a new kind of being, equipped with a metahuman nature, might emerge to replace *Homo sapiens*. In misanthropic stories, like Fowler Wright's *The World Below* or Gloag's *To-Morrow's Yesterday* [2-45], the replacement species are not our descendants, but in Houghton's *This Was Ivor Trent* [2-53] and John Beresford's *What Dreams May Come* . . . (1941) they are. The author who adapted scientific romance most comprehensively to the purpose of metaphysical speculation, Olaf Stapledon, remained perennially interested in the possibility that future human species might evolve a finer nature; this is given extensive consideration in *Last and First Men* and its sequel *Last Men in London* (1942), and in the later *A Man Divided* (1950).

The positive side of the speculative fiction produced between the wars is not confined to these images of the future transcendence of crude human nature. What Polak saw as evidence of deterioration—the sheer fecundity of futuristic imagination, especially as displayed in American SF—is actually evidence of a new attitude to the future which is dismissive of such ideas as prophecy and destiny, insisting instead that the future does contain a vast spectrum of possible alternatives.

The exuberant naïveté of pulp SF's escapist romps and melodramas is, in part, testimony to the exhilaration of the discovery that the future is yet to be made and that it will be shaped by human endeavor rather than being condemned to follow the repressive and overdemanding blueprints of jealous gods. The science fiction label is often attached to devout works, and the genre has even provided inspiration to certain would-be messiahs, but as a genre science fiction's cardinal virtue is its insistence on the fact that the shape of things to come depends on human choices and human actions. Its images of doom ought not to be regarded as exercises in pessimism, even when they are so intended by their authors, but rather as warnings issued in the hope of averting doom. The most ardent champions of science fiction take up their position because they realize that fiction about the future—or, rather, fiction about an infinite array of possible futures—might become a significant force in shaping the actual future, and in helping to abort the worst of the threats that loom over our rapidly changing world. This is the chief virtue of the science fiction which was published on both sides of the Atlantic in the period between the wars—and, indeed, of all the works that have been assimilated to the label retrospectively and all the works written under the label since, no matter how little they resemble in other ways the contents of Hugo Gernsback's *Amazing Stories.*

Bibliography

2-1.   Arlen, Michael. **Man's Mortality.** Heinemann, 1933.
Controllers of the world's air traffic have forced peace on the world, but young officers disillusioned by their methods join forces with a rebel who has invented a faster aircraft. The enigmatic hero is ultimately revealed as a kind of Antichrist and the political questions raised are left open. Compare Kipling's "As Easy as A.B.C." [1-55] and Wells's *The Shape of Things to Come* [2-140] for other accounts of air dictatorship.

*2-2.   Asimov, Isaac, ed. **Before the Golden Age.** Doubleday, 1974.
Giant anthology of stories from the SF pulps of 1931–1937, with an autobiographical commentary by Asimov explaining what it felt like to be a science fiction fan in the 1930s. The contents include space opera (Murray Leinster's "Proxima Centauri"), microcosmic romance (Henry Hasse's "He Who Shrank" and S. P. Meek's "Submicroscopic" and "Awlo of Ulm"), encounters with alien beings ("Tetrahedra of Space" by P. Schuyler Miller, "The Moon Era" by Jack Williamson, "Old Faithful" by Raymond Z. Gallun, and "Parasite Planet" by Stanley G. Weinbaum), and extravagant "thought-variants" ("Born of the Sun" by Jack Williamson and "The Accursed Galaxy" by Edmond Hamilton). Easily the best introduction to the romance of early pulp SF. Compare with *From Off This World* [2-78] by Margulies and Friend and *Science Fiction of the Thirties* [2-67] by Knight.

2-3.   Beliaev, Aleksandr. **The Amphibian.** Foreign Languages Publishing, 1959. Trans. by L. Kolesnikov of *Chelovek-amphibiia,* 1928.
An account of a biological experiment in which a human child is adapted

for aquatic life. Beliaev was one of the most prolific Soviet writers of the 1920s. Another translated novel, *The Struggle in Space* (1928; trans. 1965), contrasts a communist utopia with a capitalist dystopia. His work has a certain Vernian enthusiasm, but his characters are wooden.

2-4. Beliaev, Aleksandr. **Professor Dowell's Head.** Macmillan, 1980. Trans. by Antonina W. Bouis of *Golova professora Douelia*, 1925.

A melodrama featuring a scientist who can maintain life in extracted human organs, including the severed head of his old mentor. When he splices the head of a singer to a new body, his female assistant—who has befriended the eponymous head—feels that it is time to put a stop to his activities. *Grand guignol* SF; compare Siodmak's *Donovan's Brain* (1943).

2-5. Bell, Neil (pseud. of Stephen Southwold). **The Lord of Life.** Collins, 1933.

A scientist who discovers a new weapon tries to blackmail the world, and then destroys the world. The people aboard an experimental submarine survive, but their chances of making a new beginning are inhibited because there is only one woman among their number. A maliciously ironic black comedy. Compare Sinclair's *The Millennium* [2-110].

2-6. Bell, Neil (pseud. of Stephen Southwold). **Mixed Pickles.** Collins, 1935.

Collection including two short scientific romances, more notably "The Mouse," about an inventive genius who brings wealth and happiness to an ungrateful world and then gives his fellows the power to destroy themselves. "The Evanescence of Adrian Fulk" is a quirky macrocosmic fantasy. "The Facts About Benjamin Crede" is an effective moral fantasy about a man who can fly. A handful of similarly bitter SF parables are scattered about Bell's other collections.

2-7. Bell, Neil (pseud. of Stephen Southwold). **Precious Porcelain.** Gollancz, 1931.

Mysterious events in a small town are ultimately explained as the result of a series of experiments in the evocation of alternate personalities. A curious elaboration of the Jekyll-and-Hyde motif, similar in structure to Bell's later novels *The Disturbing Affair of Noel Blake* (1932), which involves the recovery of race ancestral memories, and *Life Comes to Seathorpe* (1946), which involves the creation of artificial organisms.

*2-8.   Bell, Neil (as "Miles"; pseud. of Stephen Southwold). **The Seventh Bowl.** Partridge, 1930.

The inventor of an immortality serum is murdered by members of the political elite, who use his discovery to secure their rule and to begin the eugenic reshaping of the human community in the wake of a destructive war. Their methods provoke violent opposition, which is ruthlessly suppressed until a new genius puts up such stern resistance that the world is destroyed. A startling example of postwar cynicism. Southwold wrote a second novel as Miles, *The Gas War of 1940* (1931), based on an episode in *The Seventh Bowl,* and both books were reprinted under the Bell name, the 1931 novel as *Valiant Clay.*

2-9.   Bulgakov, Mikhail. "The Fatal Eggs" in **Diaboliad and Other Stories.** Indiana Univ. Press, 1972. Trans. by Carl R. Proffer from a 1925 story.

The last satirical piece Bulgakov published before his work was suppressed—a sarcastic account of the creation of an absurd catastrophe by reckless and inefficient Soviet bureaucrats mishandling a wonderful scientific discovery. *Heart of a Dog* (written 1925; trans. 1968) is more subtle and more effective, attaching allegorical implications to the story of a fantastic transplant operation, and it was deemed too dangerous to be published.

*2-10.   Burroughs, Edgar Rice. **The Land That Time Forgot.** McClurg, 1924.

Three novellas from *Blue Book* (all 1918) combined in one volume. American and British sailors join forces to capture a German U-boat, which winds up on the lost island of Caprona, where Haeckel's Law ("ontogony recapitulates phylogeny") is literally true, life-forms metamorphosing serially through higher evolutionary stages. The usual Burroughs action-adventure fare, in what is probably his most interesting setting.

2-11.   Burroughs, Edgar Rice. **The Moon Maid.** McClurg, 1926.

Three serials from *Argosy/All-Story* (1923–1925), slightly abridged to make a single volume. More action-adventure in various settings; the middle part, which shows Earth under the dominion of alien conquerors, is one of Burroughs's more interesting works, and might be regarded as his most conventional essay in SF. [For other works of this author see chapter 1.]

2-12.   Campbell, John W(ood), Jr. **The Black Star Passes.** Fantasy, 1953.

Three novelettes originally published in *Amazing Stories* and its quarterly companion in 1930, featuring the exploits of the reformed space pirate Wade and his one-time adversaries, Arcot and Morey. They pit their super scientific talents against various alien foes in typically extravagant space operas. The scale of the action expands in the two full-length novels that continued the series: *Islands of Space* (1931; reprinted 1956) and *Invaders From the Infinite* (1932; reprinted 1961). The books are very much in the tradition of Smith's Skylark series [2-114], although Campbell handles scientific jargon a little better.

*2-13. Campbell, John W(ood), Jr. **Who Goes There?** Shasta, 1948.

Collection of seven stories initially published between 1934 and 1938 under the pseudonym Don A. Stuart. The title novella is a classic tale in which scientific acumen allows scientists to detect and defeat an alien mimic, filmed twice as *The Thing*. "Twilight" (1934) is a highly effective vision of a world in which mankind has degenerated because of excessive reliance on machines; "Night" (1935) provides an intriguing sequel. Seven more Stuart stories from 1935–1939 are in *The Cloak of Aesir*, including the Machine trilogy (1935), which tackles the problem outlined in "Twilight" from another angle, and "Forgetfulness" (1937), which—perhaps unfortunately—introduced to pulp SF the idea that mankind might eventually outgrow technology altogether by cultivating mental powers; the notion later became something of an obsession of his. Many of the stories are reprinted in *The Best of John W. Campbell* (1976), which also features the "The Last Evolution" (1932), the story that initiated the long meditation about man's relationship with technology continued in the Stuart stories. These short stories are much better than the author's novel-length space operas, and constitute a fascinating body of work.

*2-14. Čapek, Karel. **The Absolute at Large.** Macmillan, 1927. Trans. of *Tovarna na absolutno*, 1922.

An account of events following the marketing of atomic engines called "karburators," which annihilate matter in order to produce energy. In so doing, however, the machines liberate the "spirit" previously bound up in the matter, and humans fail miserably to cope with the consequent epidemic of religious inspiration. A classic ironic commentary on human fallibility. Compare Williams's *Many Dimensions* (1931), a sober fantasy with similar theme and moral.

*2-15. Čapek, Karel. **Krakatit.** Bles, 1925. Trans. by L. Hyde, 1924.

The inventor of a new explosive tries to keep it out of the hands of others, knowing that they will misuse it, but ultimately fails. Much more sober in tone than Čapek's other early works, it was still sufficiently pertinent to be reprinted 20 years later with the ominous subtitle "An Atomic Phantasy."

*2-16.   Čapek, Karel. **R.U.R.: A Fantastic Melodrama.** Doubleday, 1923. Trans. by P. Selver, 1920. Unabridged trans. by Norma Comrada in *Toward the Radical Center: a Karel Čapek Reader,* Catbird Press, 1990.

The play that popularized the word *robot* (although the artificial people produced by Rossum's Universal Robots are organic rather than mechanical). The story is a simple allegory: the robots are perfected when they acquire souls, and people then become redundant, ripe for extermination.

*2-17.   Čapek, Karel. **War With the Newts.** Allen & Unwin, 1937. Trans. by M. Weatherall and R. Weatherall of *Valkas mloky,* 1936.

This novel is basically an elaboration of the theme of *R.U.R.* [2-16]. The newts are an alien species liberated from their subterranean home by an accident. They begin to learn human ways, and learn them all too well. Eventually, they replace their models, providing in the meantime a particularly sharp caricature of human habits and politics. Slightly long winded, but remains the most effective of Čapek's works.

2-18.   Chadwick, Philip George. **The Death Guard.** Hutchinson, 1939.

The most horrific of all the future war novels published in the run-up to World War II. So that Britain might be defended against the rapidly advancing weapons of rival European nations, a vegetable species of humanoid automatons is developed to serve as soldiers, but when war comes the "Flesh Guard" proves to be something of a two-edged sword. Copies of the original edition are extremely rare, most of the print run having mysteriously vanished when hostilities actually broke out (possibly because the horrific text was considered a threat to morale), but Penguin reprinted the book in 1992 under its Roc imprint. Compare Joseph O'Neill's *Day of Wrath* [2-96] and S. Fowler Wright's *Four Days War* (1936).

2-19.   Clouston, J(oseph) Storer. **Button Brains.** Jenkins, 1933.

A comedy about a robot that is consistently mistaken for its human model, with appropriate farcical consequences. Most of the standard jokes associated with the theme first appeared here. Clouston wrote several other humorous SF stories.

2-20.   Coates, Robert M(yron). **The Eater of Darkness.** Contact Editions, 1926.

Surreal novel parodying the vogue for thrillers featuring scientific supercriminals. The stylistic fireworks are occasionally irritating, but the preposterous plot is amusing, and the chapter where the mad scientist explains

2. Between the Wars 83

his invention is an excellent parody of science fiction exposition. The genuine article can be found in the novels of Sax Rohmer and in the pulp stories that inspired Hugo Gernsback to found the short-lived *Scientific Detective Monthly* (later *Amazing Detective Tales*). The best individual examples are *The Sign at Six* [1-108] by White and *The Devil's Highway* [2-147] by Wright and Lebar.

2-21. Coblentz, Stanton A(rthur). **After 12,000 Years.** Fantasy Publishing, 1950.

Novel first published in *Amazing Stories Quarterly* in 1929. The hero is catapulted into a future in which the three surviving nations of mankind fight wars to determine the control of the climate, using genetically engineered insects as troops and weapons. The most bizarre and one of the most interesting of Coblentz's futuristic fantasies, whose startling subject matter is not entirely suited to the tongue-in-cheek tone.

2-22. Coblentz, Stanton A(rthur). **Hidden World.** Avalon, 1957.

Originally published in *Wonder Stories* (1935) as *In Caverns Below*, this is perhaps the best of Coblentz's rather heavy-handed satires. Two humans become emperors of the warring subterranean empires of Wu and Zu and fail to convert the people to a more rational way of life. A poke at big business, militarism, and the pretensions of the middle class. Coblentz introduced satirical undertones into his more straightforward adventure stories, of which the best is the Atlantean fantasy *The Sunken World* (1928; reprinted 1949).

2-23. Collier, John. **Tom's A-Cold.** Macmillan, 1933. (U.S. title: *Full Circle.*)

Novel of postcatastrophe primitivism in the quasi-lyrical tradition of Richard Jefferies's *After London* [1-53]. Tribal elders struggle against the odds to preserve something of the heritage of civilized wisdom for future generations, but leadership must now become the prerogative of more virile and pragmatically inclined men. Compare the concluding section of Cicely Hamilton's *Theodore Savage* [2-48].

2-24. Connington, J. J. (pseud. of Alfred Walter Stewart). **Nordenholt's Million.** Constable, 1923.

An early ecocatastrophe story in which denitrifying bacteria inimical to plant growth run wild. The plutocrat Nordenholt creates a refuge for the chosen few in Scotland. Similar in spirit to such disaster stories as Wylie and Balmer's *When Worlds Collide* [2-156] and Serviss's *The Second Deluge* [1-83], it anticipates the theme of Christopher's *The Death of Grass* [3-42].

2-25.   Constantine, Murray (pseud. of Katharine Burdekin). **Proud Man.** Boriswood, 1934.
A proto-feminist fantasy, more speculative essay than fiction, in which three exemplary individuals in contemporary London are closely studied and interrogated by a hermaphrodite visitor from the far future. The psychological theorizing now seems old-fashioned but this unique and unashamedly eccentric book was before its time in many ways. The other major female contributor to the tradition of British scientific romance, Muriel Jaeger (see [2-58/59]), also wrote an intense didactic conversation piece in *Retreat from Armageddon* (1936).

2-26.   Constantine, Murray (pseud. of Katharine Burdekin). **Swastika Night.** Gollancz, 1937. Lawrence & Wishart, 1985.
A strange novel of a future Europe dominated by Nazis, whose rule has resulted in a more extreme social and physical differentiation of the sexes. A young German gradually learns to see the world from a different ideological perspective. Recently reprinted under the author's real name.

2-27.   Cox, Erle. **Out of the Silence**. Vidler, 1925.
Novel originally serialized in the *Melbourne Argus* in 1919. A beautiful superwoman, a relic of an ancient race overwhelmed by natural catastrophes, is discovered lying in suspended animation in a huge buried time capsule. She describes the history of her race and the eugenic program that produced her (and her still-sleeping intended consort), but her plans for world domination go awry. The revised and extended text first published in 1947 is considered inferior by some commentators. Explicit racism makes the novel uncongenial to the majority of modern readers, and the plot is obviously derivative of G. Firth Scott's Australia-set fantasy, *The Last Lemurian* (1898), but it remains the first classic of the fragile and fugitive tradition of Australian SF.

*2-28.   Cummings, Ray(mond King). **The Girl in the Golden Atom.** Methuen, 1922.
The book contains two stories first published in *All-Story Weekly* in 1919 and 1920—the first of Cummings's many microcosmic romances. The initial novelette is heavily indebted to *The Time Machine* [1-103] by Wells for its narrative frame and to O'Brien's "The Diamond Lens" [1-72] for its theme, although it is a poor pastiche. The sequel is standardized pulp

melodrama. The notion of atoms as tiny worlds provided a framework for many stories in the SF pulps, including Festus Pragnell's *The Green Man of Graypec* (1936) and Hall's *People of the Comet* [2-37], and persisted long after the advance of science had made it ridiculous. Cummings's own best work in this vein is *The Princess of the Atom* (1929; reprinted 1950), but it lacks something of the naive charm of the original novelette.

2-29. Cummings, Ray(mond King). **The Shadow Girl.** Swan, 1947.

Originally published in *Argosy* in 1929. Cummings's time travel fantasies are, on average, rather better than his space operas, and this story is perhaps the best of them, although some readers prefer *The Man Who Mastered Time* (1924; reprinted 1929). The characters pursue one another back and forth through time, visiting Peter Stuyvesant's New Amsterdam and fighting a desperate war in 25th-century New York. No attention is paid to the question of paradoxes. Compare Williamson's *The Legion of Time* [2-145].

*2-30. Dent, Guy. **Emperor of the If.** Heinemann, 1926.

A scientist discovers a means of bringing into being the world that might have been if climatic changes favorable to the evolution of humans had never occurred, and he decides to subject men and women to a harsh test of their Darwinian fitness. After concluding this experiment (and canceling out its results), he creates the world of the far future that will result if people remain locked into their contemporary course. Although not fully rationalized, this is a powerful and thought-provoking novel, and one of the first to consider history as a developing series of alternatives.

2-31. Desmond, Shaw. **Ragnarok.** Duckworth, 1926.

A graphic future war story in which air fleets devastate the great cities of the world, using chemical and biological weapons as well as high explosives. The rather confused plot seems to owe something to M. P. Shiel's future war stories. Desmond went on to produce *Chaos* (1938) and *Black Dawn* (1944), near-future fantasies that deal speculatively with the social and metaphysical significance of World War II.

2-32. Doyle, Arthur Conan. **The Land of Mist.** Hutchinson, 1926.

Professor Challenger becomes involved with spiritualism following the death of his wife. Skeptical at first, he is ultimately convinced that life continues after death. A sober and earnest novel, which contrasts sharply with the playful exuberance of *The Lost World* [1-31] and *The Poison Belt* [1-32].

2-33.   Doyle, Arthur Conan. **The Maracot Deep and Other Stories.** Murray, 1929.
The title novel features a descent into the depths of the Atlantic ocean and the discovery of Atlantis. The story begins as a Vernian romance, but the author's interest in spiritualism takes its later chapters in a different direction. The best of the three short stories that accompany it is the Challenger novelette, "When the World Screamed," in which Earth turns out to be a living creature. [For other works of this author see chapter 1.]

2-34.   Farley, Ralph Milne (pseud. of Roger Sherman Hoar). **The Omnibus of Time.** F.P.C.I., 1950.
A collection of stories involving time travel and time paradoxes, including "The Time Traveler" (1931) and "The Man Who Met Himself" (1935). Although somewhat rough-hewn, the stories show off the virtues as well as the pretensions of one of the more prolific pulp SF writers. Excerpts from two of his more readable pulp romances, "The Hidden Universe" (1939) and "The Golden City" (1933), are included. Farley's best-known work is the series of Burroughsian interplanetary adventures set on Venus, begun with *The Radio Man* (1924; in book form 1948), but these are among the weaker examples of the species.

*2-35.   Farrère, Claude (pseud. of Charles Bargone). **Useless Hands.** Dutton, 1926. Trans. by Elizabeth Abbott of *Les Condamnés à mort*, 1920.
A bitter melodrama in which the workers who make bread to feed the United States in the 1990s go on strike, only to find their place taken by mechanical hands. Their subsequent revolt is brutally put down in accordance with the logic of "Darwinian law." It is similar in spirit to Donnelly's *Caesar's Column* [1-29], although its central argument is a little more effective.

2-36.   Fearn, John Russell. **The Intelligence Gigantic.** World's Work, 1943.
Originally published in *Amazing Stories* in 1933. A Frankensteinian fantasy in which a scientist employs a Ray Machine to hasten the evolutionary process that turns organic raw materials into living protoplasm, ultimately producing a superman whose plans for world domination are thwarted by Martians. Fearn was the first British writer to become a regular contributor to the U.S. pulps; he delighted in spectacular effect, unconstrained by the most elementary considerations of plausibility. *Liners of Time* (1935; in book form 1947) and its sequel *Zagribud* (1937; abridged for book publication as *Science Metropolis*) introduced the bold sweep of space opera to

tales of time travel. "Mathematica" and "Mathematica Plus" (both 1936; revised as *To the Ultimate*. 1952) took Fearn's naïve imagination to its extreme, and he subsequently contented himself with more modest projects. Compare the similarly expansive pulp SF of Donald Wandrei [2-133].

2-37. Flint, Homer Eon, and Austin Hall. **The Blind Spot.** Prime Press, 1951.

A confused melodrama dealing with intercourse between two parallel worlds, first published in *Argosy* in 1921. Although stylistically uneven and eccentric in structure, it contrives to be effective in its own fashion. A sequel, by Hall alone, is *The Spot of Life* (1932; reprinted 1964). Both authors wrote other scientific romances for the pulps, Flint supplying an interesting interplanetary series to *All-Story Weekly* and *Argosy*, the best of which are *The Devolutionist* and *The Emancipatrix* (both 1921; reprinted in one volume 1965). Hall's most interesting solo work in this vein is the microcosmic romance *People of the Comet* (1948), first published in *Weird Tales* in 1923 as "Hop o' My Thumb."

2-38. Forester, C(ecil) S(cott). **The Peacemaker.** Little, Brown, 1934.

A bitterly ironic story about an ineffectual schoolmaster whose mathematical genius leads him to construct a machine that will demagnetize iron at a distance. He is led by unfortunate circumstances to use the machine in a hopeless attempt to blackmail England into initiating a program of disarmament.

2-39. Gail, Otto Willi. **The Shot Into Infinity.** Garland, 1975. Trans. by Francis Currier of *Der Schuss ins All*, 1925.

A Vernian romance about a rocket ship that gets stranded in orbit with its pilot trapped. Much attention is given to technical detail, but the narrative is unconvincing. It was first translated for Gernsback's *Wonder Stories Quarterly* in 1929, and Gernsback also reprinted its sequel, *The Stone From the Moon* (1930), although its subject matter is entirely pseudoscientific.

2-40. Gallun, Raymond Z(inke). **The Best of Raymond Z. Gallun.** Ballantine, 1978.

Collection including nine stories from 1934–1939, beginning with the touchingly sentimental "Old Faithful" (1934), which constitutes a curious "ideological reply" to the Darwinian logic of H. G. Wells's *War of the Worlds* [1-105] and the pulp "alien menace stories" it inspired. Here, intellectual kinship overrides the reflexive xenophobia that prejudices the first meeting of human and Martian. (Two sequels, "The Son of Old Faithful,"

1935, and "Child of the Stars," 1936, are not included in the collection.) "Davey Jones' Ambassador" (1935) and "Seeds of the Dusk" (1938) are exercises in speculative biology somewhat akin to the best works of Stanley G. Weinbaum [2-135] but more somber in tone; "Derelict" (1935) is an early robot story anticipating Isaac Asimov's tales of innately moral robots; the novella "Godson of Almarlu" (1936) is a painstaking account of mankind's survival of a cosmic disaster. Unusually thoughtful examples of pulp SF by one of the best contributors to that medium. [For other works of this author see chapter 4.]

2-41.   Gardner, Erle Stanley. **The Human Zero: The Science Fiction Stories of Erle Stanley Gardner.** Morrow, 1981. Ed. by Martin H. Greenberg and Charles G. Waugh.
Collection of seven novellas first published in *Argosy* between 1928 and 1932. Two are borderline tales featuring intelligent apes and one is fantasy; "The Sky's the Limit" (1929) is an interplanetary romance; "A Year in a Day" (1930) transplants H. G. Wells's "New Accelerator" into a crime story much as other pulp writers transplanted *The Invisible Man* (1897); "The Human Zero" (1931) is a supercriminal story; "New Worlds" (1932) is a catastrophe story. Stories from a nonspecialist pulp that exemplify the frank carelessness and ineptitude with which stock SF motifs were used, even by writers who were capable of much better work in other genres.

2-42.   Gibbons, Floyd (Philips). **The Red Napoleon.** Cape & Smith, 1929.
A documentary novel by a war correspondent, featuring a hypothetical world war initiated by a Mongol ruler of the U.S.S.R. The author claims to have been motivated by a horror of war, but he takes the usual fascinated interest in planning the campaigns of the would-be conqueror. Hindsight makes it seem rather absurd, but it remains an interesting exercise in future-history-as-propaganda.

2-43.   Giesy, J(ohn) U(lrich). **Palos of the Dog-Star Pack.** Avalon, 1965.
Burroughsian fantasy first published in *All Story* in 1918. Two sequels are *The Mouthpiece of Zitu* (1919; 1965) and *Jason, Son of Jason* (1921; 1965) The hero, transplanted by occult means to a planet orbiting Sirius, has the usual romantic adventures (complicated by a Merrittesque *femme fatale*) but also sets about masterminding an Industrial Revolution based on his American know-how. The series would have been more interesting had the sequels carried this strand of the plot further.

2-44.   Gloag, John (Edward). **The New Pleasure.** Allen & Unwin, 1933.
The invention of a euphoric drug that stimulates the sense of smell allows

people to realize that modern civilization stinks. A gentle satire using an original notion.

*2-45. Gloag, John (Edward). **To-Morrow's Yesterday.** Allen & Unwin, 1932.
A bitter satire in which a new theater opens in London with a film showing the decline of the human race into degenerate savagery as a result of war. Although related to such novels as Shanks's *The People of the Ruins* [2-107] and Desmond's *Ragnarok* [2-31], it is much more scathing in its attack on the complacency of an England that (in Gloag's opinion) was not taking sufficient notice of such prophets as Wells.

*2-46. Gloag, John (Edward). **Winter's Youth.** Allen & Unwin, 1934.
A political satire in which the British government, seeking to regain popularity following the disastrous promotion of a newly discovered gospel subsequently exposed as a fake, promotes a rejuvenating process that precipitates a conflict between young and old. An excellent essay in polished cynicism. Compare Swayne's *The Blue Germ* [2-123] and Bell's *The Seventh Bowl* [2-8]. [For other works of this author see chapter 3.]

2-47. Gregory, Owen. **Meccania: The Super-State.** Methuen, 1918.
An early dystopian satire describing the overorganized "rational" society of Meccania (obviously Germany), seen through the eyes of a Chinese tourist. The mockery of bureaucratic process still seems pertinent. Not as funny as Moszkowski's *Isles of Wisdom* [2-91] or O'Duffy's *Spacious Adventures of the Man in the Street* [2-95], but more closely focused and more subtle.

2-48. Hamilton, Cicely. **Theodore Savage.** Parsons, 1922.
The eponymous hero's comfortable life is disrupted by a new war; aerial bombing of cities drives their population into rural areas where they must fight for survival as scavengers. Civilization is obliterated and communities re-form at a primitive level, dominated by brutality and superstition. A particularly effective and chilling version of the theme that dominates British speculative fiction between the wars; it was revised as *Lest Ye Die* (1928). Compare Stewart's *Earth Abides* [3-169].

2-49. Hamilton, Edmond. **The Best of Edmond Hamilton.** Ballantine, 1977. Ed. by Leigh Brackett.
Collection including thirteen stories from 1926–1938. "The Man Who Evolved" (1931) is a lurid parable of scientific hubris. "A Conquest of Two Worlds" (1932) was one of the first pulp stories to cast human colonists as exploitative alien invaders. "Thundering Worlds" (1934) is a vivid if some-

what implausible space opera. The elegiac mood touchingly displayed in "In the World's Dusk" (1936) remained Hamilton's greatest virtue as a writer. A particularly interesting inclusion here is "What's It Like Out There?" (1952), which was written in the thirties but proved too grimly realistic to sell to the prewar pulps. Hamilton was one of the few early pulp writers to publish a contemporary collection, *The Horror on the Asteroid* (1936), which was issued in the United Kingdom as a collection of "tales of interplanetary horror." His short stories sometimes exhibit a sharpness and sensitivity lacking in his longer, action-packed space operas; his pioneering work in the latter vein (from *Weird Tales* 1929–1930) was the "Interstellar Patrol" series collected in *Crashing Suns* (1965) and *Outside the Universe* (1964).

2-50.   Hamilton, Edmond. **The Horror on the Asteroid.** Allen, 1936.
One of the earliest collections of pulp SF stories, uniform with the publisher's Creeps series of anthologies, which reprinted some material from *Weird Tales.* The six stories are representative of Hamilton's early work, lively but rather rough-hewn. Hamilton began writing space opera for *Weird Tales* in the 1920s, and five other early stories, all featuring the Interstellar Patrol, are collected in *Crashing Suns* (1965). A novel-length story from the same series is *Outside the Universe* (1929; reprinted 1964). [For other works of this author see chapter 3.]

2-51.   Hargrave, John (Gordon). **The Imitation Man.** Gollancz, 1931.
A scientist creates a homunculus, which grows rapidly to physical maturity. The behavior of the artificial man is entirely imitative, but his telepathic powers allow him to repeat out loud the secret thoughts of others, causing him to become an embarrassment to all who know him. He enjoys a spectacular career but meets an ironic fate. The novel is lighthearted and contrasts sharply with the author's bitter Wellsian novel of ideas, *Harbottle* (1923).

2-52.   Hilton, James. **Lost Horizon.** Morrow, 1933.
A classic escapist novel about an Englishman's adventure in the fabulous utopian valley of Shangri-La, marvelously filmed by Frank Capra. The novel testifies to the retreat of the utopian dream into the realm of dream-fantasy. Similar escapist fantasies include A. Merritt's *Dwellers in the Mirage* (1932) and Hannes Bok's *The Blue Flamingo* (1948), but *Lost Horizon* is the most stylish of the species.

2-53.   Houghton, Claude (pseud. of C. H. Oldfield). **This Was Ivor Trent.** Heinemann, 1935.
A psychological melodrama in which a writer's odd behavior is finally

explained as the result of a vision in which he saw a man of the future and realized that a much better world would rise from the ashes of our own sick civilization. A particularly extreme example of the disenchantment that affected many British writers of the period. Compare Gloag's *To-Morrow's Yesterday* [2-45] and J. D. Beresford's *What Dreams May Come . . .* (1941).

2-54. Hunting, (Henry) Gardner. **The Vicarion.** Unity School of Christianity, 1926.

A novel about America's response to the invention of a machine that can see through time, wholly unconvincing but nevertheless fascinating. It contrasts very sharply with T. L. Sherred's famous story based on an identical premise, "E for Effort" (1947).

2-55. Huxley, Aldous (Leonard). **After Many a Summer.** Chatto & Windus, 1939. (U.S. title: *After Many a Summer Dies the Swan.*)

An English poet unwittingly guides an American oil magnate to the secret of longevity he so earnestly desires to find, but when they discover the person who has been reaping its "rewards" since the 18th century they are sadly disillusioned. The scientist, Dr. Obispo, is a vicious caricature, partly based on J. B. S. Haldane. A classic sarcastic fantasy and a cardinal example of the "no good will come of it all" school of thought.

*2-56. Huxley, Aldous (Leonard). **Brave New World.** Doubleday, 1932.

A devastating criticism of the kind of technological utopia outlined in J. B. S. Haldane's essay "Daedalus; or, Science and the Future." Its principal images are well established in the modern mythology of the future, and it remains the definitive critique of the technologically supported "rational" society, exposing the darker side of scientific humanism. It is a brilliant and perceptive polemic, and the opposing side of the argument has found no advocate of comparable eloquence. It stands alongside *We* [2-157] and *Nineteen Eighty-Four* [3-140] as one of the classic dystopian novels. Many of the concerns of the novel were treated in a later nonfiction work, *Brave New World Revisited* (1958). [For other works of this author see chapter 3.]

2-57. Hyne, C(harles) J(ohn) Cutcliffe. **Man's Understanding.** Ward, Lock, 1933.

Collection including several bitterly sarcastic scientific romances, including two world blackmail stories, "Caterpillars" and "Tribute for the Emperor Solomon." "The Air-Service Restaurant Enquiry" laconically tells the story of the invention of a new power source. "The Island That is Seldom There," "The Eel," and the imaginatively adventurous "My Mermaid and the Giants" are tall tales of the sea. Hyne evidently became rather bilious toward the end of his life but these stories are rather more interesting than his earlier and more frequently reprinted SF stories.

2-58.   Jaeger, Muriel. **The Man with Six Senses.** Hogarth, 1927.
A careful and sensitive novel about a youth who is attempting to develop and utilize a new mode of sensory perception. It contrasts sharply with later post-Rhineian stories of ESP, such as Blish's *Jack of Eagles* (1952) and Tucker's *Wild Talent* (1954).

2-59.   Jaeger, Muriel. **The Question Mark.** Hogarth, 1926.
An interesting novel about the quality of life in a Wellsian utopia, observing that freedom must include the freedom to be foolish and even ridiculous. The question mark of the title attends the question of whether we are actually capable of making a better life for ourselves, even if we acquire the means to do so.

2-60.   Jensen, Johannes V(ilhelm). **The Long Journey: Fire and Ice** and **The Cimbrians.** Knopf, 1923. Trans. by A. G. Chater of parts I–IV of *Den lange rejse*, 1908–1922.
A classic prehistoric fantasy. The fifth part of the series was not translated, but the sixth, translated in 1924, is *Christopher Columbus*. The theme of the whole work is the struggle of evolving humankind to cope with major challenges, including the last glaciation of the Northern Hemisphere. The only other prehistoric fantasies that can compare with it are the best works of Rosny aîné, particularly *La Guerre du feu* [2-105], and William Golding's *The Inheritors* (1955).

2-61.   Johnson, Owen (McMahon). **The Coming of the Amazons.** Longmans, 1931.
One of the many novels featuring a female-dominated society, rather more good-humored than most. It is gently insistent that sex roles are determined by socialization rather than by innate dispositions. Contrast Walter Besant's *The Revolt of Man* (1882) and Charles Eric Maine's *Alph* (1972).

*2-62.   Karinthy, Frigyes. **Voyage to Faremido and Capillaria.** Corvina, 1965. Trans. by Paul Tabori of *Utazás Faremidóba*, 1916, and *Capillaria*, 1922.
Accounts of voyages made by Lemuel Gulliver, the first bringing him into contact with a society of machines that communicate with one another via musical notes and have difficulty understanding organic life, the second

describing a submarine civilization whose sexual politics are based in a very different biology from ours. Two marvelously imaginative social satires, quite without parallel.

2-63. Kaul, Fedor. **Contagion to This World.** Bles, 1933. Trans. by Winifred Ray of *Die Welt ohne Gedächtnis*.

A hunchbacked genius, reviled by others, takes revenge by releasing a bacterium that causes universal amnesia. He watches the collapse of civilization and the eventual emergence of a new human species. The novel is remarkable for the sympathy accorded the protagonist. Contrast McClary's *Rebirth* [2-83], which features a similar project.

2-64. Keller, David H(enry). **The Human Termites.** P. D. A. Enterprises, 1978.

Novel originally serialized in *Science Wonder Stories* in 1929. A lurid tale of war and miscegenation between humans and termites based by Keller (at Hugo Gernsback's suggestion) on Maurice Maeterlincks' quasi-scientific rhapsody on *The Life of the White Ant*. Although a few sentences (reproduced here) were censored before publication, the novel pays scant respect to pulp taboos about sex. A graphic example of the use of the "hive-mind" as a model of totalitarian social organization—a theme recapitulated in the SF pulps by Bob Olsen's "The Ant With the Human Soul" (1932). Giant insects also feature luridly in Keller's novella "The Solitary Hunters" (1934). The unreprinted "The Metal Doom" (1932), an early example of a "benign catastrophe" story, is the best of Keller's pulp novels.

2-65. Keller, David H(enry). **Life Everlasting and Other Tales of Science, Fantasy and Horror.** Avalon, 1947.

The title novel is perhaps the best of Keller's early pulp works—a moral fable in which humans abandon immortality in favor of fertility. The short stories in the collection include several of his best works, all arising out of his interest in psychiatry: "The Dead Woman," "The Thing in the Cellar," and "A Piece of Linoleum." A later collection with more varied contents is *Tales From Underwood* (1952), which shows off his talents to slightly better advantage. His science fiction invariably champions simple human values against the threats posed by "rationalization" of human affairs through scientific management and the use of mechanical technology.

2-66. Kelly, Frank K. **Starship Invincible.** Capra, 1979.

Three novelettes from the mid-1930s SF pulps, all featuring heroism and self-sacrifice in distant parts of the solar system. Sentimental space opera, crude and naive, but exhibiting the kind of wide-eyed charm that sustained the appeal of the early SF pulps.

2-67.   Knight, Damon (Francis), ed. **Science Fiction of the Thirties.**
Bobbs-Merrill, 1975.
Representative anthology of stories from the SF pulps of the period, with
contents that do not overlap with Asimov's superior *Before the Golden Age*
[2-2], although many of the same authors are represented. The better stories (Weinbaum's "The Mad Moon," Gallun's "Davy Jones' Ambassador,"
and Bates's "Alas, All Thinking!") are available elsewhere, and the scarcer
ones are of limited interest. Compare also Margulies and Friend's *From
Off This World* [2-78].

*2-68.   Large, E(dward) C. **Sugar in the Air.** Jonathan Cape, 1937.
An excellent story of the conflict between commercial and scientific interests connected with a project to manufacture carbohydrates by artificial
photosynthesis. A devastating attack on the imaginative blindness of the
English bourgeoisie. *Asleep in the Afternoon* (1939) is a less distinguished
satire about a device that promotes peaceful sleep, but Large's handling
of social satire is more assured in his third fantasy novel, *Dawn in
Andromeda* (1956).

2-69.   Leinster, Murray (pseud. of Will F. Jenkins). **The Forgotten
Planet.** Gnome, 1954.
The first two sections of this fixed-up novel are the novelettes "The Mad
Planet" and "The Red Dust," originally published in *Argosy* in 1920 and
1921, featuring the exploits of primitive humans in a world of giant
insects and arachnids. The logic of the situation provided by the new
material does not help to make them more convincing, but they have a
certain panache. The most dramatic scenes recur in many stories of
human miniaturization, from Edwin Pallander's *Adventures of a Micro-Man*
(1902) to Lindsay Gutteridge's *Cold War in a Country Garden* (1971).

2-70.   Leinster, Murray (pseud. of Will F. Jenkins). **Sidewise in Time.**
Shasta, 1950.
Collection including three early stories. The title novella (1934) is a classic tale of disrupted time in which several alternative histories are abruptly
juxtaposed. "Proxima Centauri" (1935) was the first of Leinster's many
space operas. "The Fourth-Dimensional Demonstrator" (1935) is an
example of humorous SF comparable to Stanley Weinbaum's comedies [2-
135]. [For other works of this author see chapter 3.]

2-71.   Lewis, Sinclair. **It Can't Happen Here.** Doubleday, 1935.
A novel about the destruction of democracy in the United States and the establishment of a quasi-Fascist state. The element of parody in the book does not undermine its seriousness, and although it is not quite up to the standard of Lewis's novels of the early 1920s, it remains an effectively powerful exercise in alternate history, a cautionary warning against a possible American future.

*2-72.   Lindsay, David. **A Voyage to Arcturus.** Methuen, 1920.
A classic allegorical romance in which the landscapes and inhabitants of the planet Tormance provide an externalization of the moral and metaphysical questions that preoccupied the author. Its incarnate theological system influenced Lewis's *Out of the Silent Planet* [3-116], and it also bears some similarity to George Macdonald's *Lilith* (1895), although it is very much a work sui generis. Lindsay's other metaphysical fantasies belong to the same species as Charles Williams's theological fantasies, but generally find Christian theology inadequate to their purpose (an exception is the posthumously published novel *The Violet Apple*, 1978). *Devil's Tor* (1932) is a particularly fine novel in this vein.

2-73.   Lovecraft, H(oward) P(hillips). **At the Mountains of Madness and Other Novels.** Arkham, 1964. Corrected text, 1985.
The title novel first appeared in *Astounding Stories* in 1936 and consists of the report of a scientific expedition to a lost world in the Antarctic, whose members learn the terrifying truth about the human place in the universe. Together with *The Dunwich Horror and Others* (1963), this collection presents the most effective of Lovecraft's stories, which see the universe as an implacably hostile place where quests for knowledge and enlightenment usually prove fatal, revealing in the process that men and women are habitually used for horrible purposes by malevolent alien beings of godlike power. Some readers are alienated by the author's idiosyncratic use of language in the attempt to create a mood of dreadful uncertainty.

2-74.   MacIsaac, Fred. **The Hothouse World.** Avalon, 1965.
First published as a serial in *Argosy* in 1931. The hero wakes from suspended animation to find civilization preserved in a tiny glass-enclosed enclave after most of the world's population has been wiped out by gases in a comet's tail. The sterile autocratic state preserved under glass is contrasted with the anarchy of the world outside; to set history back on course a middle way must be found. MacIsaac was one of the more interesting writers of futuristic stories for the nonspecialist pulps; in "World Brigands"

(1928) the domination of world economic affairs by the United States drives a Europe crippled by war debts to the brink of violent reprisals—an interesting scenario, though soon invalidated by the Wall Street crash.

2-75.   Macpherson, Donald. **Go Home, Unicorn.** Faber, 1935.
The lives of a research scientist and two young women are disrupted by material manifestations of various mental images, which turn out to be connected with his experimental use of radiation to induce mutations in guinea pigs. One result of the manifestations is that the scientist changes girlfriends, thus instilling in the loser a passion for revenge that she indulges to the full with her own thought projection machine in an inferior sequel, *Men Are Like Animals* (1937). The depiction of the world of scientific research is unusually realistic in spite of the bizarre intrusions.

2-76.   Madariaga, Salvador de. **The Sacred Giraffe.** Hopkinson, 1925.
The subtitle, "Being the Second Volume of the Posthumous Works of Julio Arceval," serves to distance the true author from his tongue-in-cheek political satire, in which the world of 6922 A.D. is ruled by black women who find it difficult to believe that there ever was a white race, let alone one in which men were its dominant sex. The anthropologists of the day attempt (among many other projects) to analyze the significance of the eponymous creation myth; there is a romantic subplot, more subtle in its execution than many role-reversal love stories. Very clever in patches, but rather disorganized. Compare O'Duffy's *Spacious Adventures of the Man in the Street* [2-95].

2-77.   Manning, Laurence. **The Man Who Awoke.** Ballantine, 1975.
One of the earliest future histories presented by the science fiction pulps, first published in *Wonder Stories* in 1933. The quality of the writing leaves something to be desired, but the account of future social evolution is imaginative and interesting. Although influenced by Stapledon's *Last and First Men* [2-119], the novel takes a rather different view of human destiny. Manning was one of the more thoughtful of Gernsback's writers and one of the first to attempt to impart a degree of realism into stories of interplanetary adventure, in "The Voyage of the *Asteroid*" and "The Wreck of the *Asteroid*" (both 1932).

2-78.   Margulies, Leo, and Oscar J. Friend, eds. **From Off This World.** Merlin, 1949.
An anthology of the original Science Fiction Hall of Fame stories reprinted in *Startling Stories* from Gernsback's *Wonder Stories*. The stories were

chosen by fans and display the more colorful side of pulp SF. They include "The City of the Singing Flame" and its sequel by Clark Ashton Smith, and work by Weinbaum, Hamilton, Williamson, and others. Comparable to Knight's *Science Fiction of the Thirties* [2-67], but inferior to Asimov's *Before the Golden Age* [2-2].

2-79. Marvell, Andrew (pseud. of Howell Davies). **Minimum Man; or, Time to Be Gone.** Gollancz, 1938.
A race of tiny supermen is protected by the hero, and subsequently wins the gratitude of right-thinking men by helping to overthrow a Fascist government in England. Ultimately, though, they will replace Homo sapiens. One of the cleverer extrapolations of the thesis that only another species can hope to establish a saner society. Contrast Beresford's *What Dreams May Come . . .* (1941). Davies wrote two other novels as Marvell, including *Three Men Make a World* (1939), an equally ironic story in which the heroes save civilization from obliteration by war by destroying it more gently with a bacterium that devours petroleum products.

2-80. Matson, Norman. **Doctor Fogg.** Macmillan, 1929.
A bittersweet satire in which the eponymous hero becomes reluctantly famous after building a device to receive radio messages from other worlds. New knowledge promises a technological revolution, and he accidentally brings to Earth a girl exiled from her home world in the distant past. But he and the author harbor doubts as to whether humans are quite ready for membership in an interstellar community.

2-81. Maurois, André. **The Thought-Reading Machine.** Jonathan Cape, 1938. Trans. by J. Whithall of *La Machine à lire les pensées*, 1937.
An American scientist invents a machine that records subvocalized thoughts and plays them back audibly. The argument of the novel is that our internal reveries are of no real significance in terms of our true feelings and policies of action. A thoughtful and well-written book that contrasts with the assumptions usually taken for granted by stories dealing with telepathy.

*2-82. Maurois, André. **The Weigher of Souls.** Cassell, 1931. Trans. by H. Miles of *Le Peseur d'âmes*, 1931.
An excellent novella concerning a hypothetical meeting of experimental science and theological supposition, bringing into sharp focus questions about the morality of scientific inquiry into human nature. Gary's novel *The Gasp* [4-175] develops the same premise in a more ironic vein.

2-83.   McClary, Thomas Calvert. **Rebirth.** Bartholomew House, 1944.
Originally published in *Astounding* in 1934, this is the story of a colossal
experiment in which a scientist wipes out the memories of everyone on
Earth in order to institute a Darwinian struggle for existence. Within a
generation, the favored few recover the use of the artifacts of civilization
and have supposedly established a better social order. Compare the more
pessimistic account by Kaul in *Contagion to This World* [2-63].

2-84.   McIlraith, Frank, and Ray Connolly. **Invasion From the Air.** Grayson & Grayson, 1934.
One of the more realistic accounts of future warfare involving the use of
poison gas, incendiary bombs, and high explosives. It suggests that the disruption caused by heavy bombing would destabilize governments and
pave the way for a wave of coups and revolutions. Compare S. Fowler
Wright's *Prelude in Prague* [2-153] and its sequels.

2-85.   Merritt, A(braham). **The Face in the Abyss.** Liveright, 1931.
Novel abridged from two stories that read much better in the original versions, "The Face in the Abyss" (*Argosy-All-Story*, 1923) and "The Snake
Mother" (*Argosy*, 1930). The hero, betrayed by his companions while treasure hunting in the Andes, is led by the exotically beautiful Suarra into a
hidden land ruled by the last survivor of a serpentine superrace. The second novella expands the ideas laid down in the first into a gaudy but
stereotyped struggle of good versus evil involving miscellaneous relics of
the ancient superscience. The first novella is very striking; it is a pity that
its powerful climax is lost in the fused version, which creates a single continuous narrative. The use of a jargon of "superscience" to underpin the
fantastic intrusions was to be come a staple of the marginal genre of "science fantasy" developed by writers like Jack Williamson, collaborators
Henry Kuttner and C. L. Moore, and Leigh Brackett.

2-86.   Merritt, A(braham). **The Metal Monster.** Avon, 1946.
The most science fictional of Merritt's exotic romances, originally published in *Argosy* in 1920 and revised for Gernsback's *Science and Invention*
in 1927, where it appeared as *The Metal Emperor.* It involves an encounter
with an inorganic alien being with a hivelike organization.

2-87.   Merritt, A(braham). **The Moon Pool.** Putnam, 1919.
A novel compounded out of a classic novelette and its inferior sequel,
originally published in *Argosy* in 1918–1919. It features extravagant adventures in an exotic underworld, recounted in gaudy purple prose. Al-

though it is sheer dream-fantasy, Gernsback reprinted it in *Amazing Stories* in 1927, and it proved to be one of the most popular stories ever to appear there. The introductory novelette is a celebration of the lure of exotic imaginary worlds—a vital element in the tradition of American pulp science fiction.

2-88. Mitchell, J(ames) Leslie. **Gay Hunter.** Heinemann, 1934.
As in *Three Go Back* [2-89], the heroine is projected through time with two companions, this time into a future oddly akin to the world of the Cro-Magnons in the earlier novel. She learns that civilization has been obliterated by nuclear wars fought between Fascist states, and must fight to prevent her Mosleyite companions from setting the noble savages on the same road to destruction.

2-89. Mitchell, J(ames) Leslie. **Three Go Back.** Jarrolds, 1932.
Two men and a woman are thrown back in time to witness the contrasting lifestyles of our Cro-Magnon ancestors and the brutish Neanderthals. The novel conducts a polemical argument against the notion that humans are innately aggressive by virtue of evolutionary heritage. The version issued as a Galaxy novel in 1953 is bowdlerized. Compare William Golding's *The Inheritors* (1955), which reverses the imagined roles of Cro-Magnon and Neanderthal, pointing to a rather different moral.

2-90. Moore, C(atherine) L(ucile). **Scarlet Dream.** Grant, 1981.
A series of stories featuring interplanetary adventurer Northwest Smith, originally published in *Weird Tales* in the 1930s, and formerly reprinted in *Shambleau* (1953) and *Northwest of Earth* (1954). Lush exotic romances in the tradition later carried on by Leigh Brackett. [For other works of this author see chapter 3.]

2-91. Moszkowski, Alexandr. **The Isles of Wisdom.** Routledge, 1924.
Trans. by H. J. Stenning of *Die Inseln der Weisheit*, 1922.
A marvelously eclectic utopian satire that sets out to demonstrate that all political policies, if taken to extremes, have absurd consequences. The parody of technological utopianism is particularly sharp, and the book, frequently very funny, succeeds in making its point.

2-92. Nicolson, Harold. **Public Faces.** Constable, 1932.
Political fantasy set in 1939 describing the diplomatic and political chicanery surrounding the development of an atomic bomb. As in such stories as Gloag's *Winter's Youth* [2-46] and Chadwick's *The Death Guard*

[2-18], the logic of deterrence is turned on its head; the cowardice and hypocrisy of the self-serving statesmen precipitates disaster. The author was himself a diplomat and politician (but was less successful in those capacities than his father) and was thus able to import a biting realism and a depressing sense of conviction into his work.

2-93.   Nowlan, Philip Francis. **Armageddon 2419 A.D.** Avalon, 1962.
A novel compounded out of the two novelettes that provided the seed of the Buck Rogers comic strip. Originally published in *Amazing Stories* in 1928 and 1929, they tell the story of a revolt by white Americans against the Oriental race that dominates them, with spectacular use of superscientific weaponry.

***2-94.**   Odle, E. V. **The Clockwork Man.** Heinemann, 1923.
An excellent fantasy in which a man of the future, fitted with a "clock" that regulates his existence, is thrown into the England of the 1920s by a malfunction, confronting the inhabitants of a small village with a vision of infinite possibility. A highly imaginative story that is probably a response to Beresford's *The Hampdenshire Wonder* [1-11]. Perhaps the outstanding scientific romance of the 1920s.

2-95.   O'Duffy, Eimar. **The Spacious Adventures of the Man in the Street.** Macmillan, 1928.
A remarkably sharp satire in which Aloysius O'Kennedy is transported to the planet Rathe, where he takes the place of his alter ego. The work is uneven, but it includes scathing parodies of sexual morality, religion, and capitalism, as well as episodes of pure comedy and a climactic allegorical vision pleading the cause of humanism and humanitarian values.

2-96.   O'Neill, Joseph. **Land Under England.** Gollancz, 1935.
The protagonist descends into an underworld in search of his father and finds a totalitarian state where thought-control is facilitated by telepathy. A particularly stylish political allegory, with echoes of the myth of Orpheus and Eurydice. O'Neill's *Day of Wrath* (1936) is a documentary novel charting the course of a new world war and its effects on the civilian population, which invites comparison with Merril's *Shadow on the Hearth* [3-124] and Wylie's *Tomorrow!* (1954).

2-97.   Parkinson, H(arold) F(rederick). **They Shall Not Die.** Constable, 1939.
A new patent medicine makes its users immune to all disease (although

only its inventor knows that it is responsible) but also sterilizes them. The division of the world's population into "Immunes" and "Mortalities" affects social and political change over several decades before the Immunes prove vulnerable to a kind of mental illness that makes them into zombies. Intriguingly understated. Contrast Bell's *The Seventh Bowl* [2-8] and Swayne's *The Blue Germ* [2-123].

2-98. Phillpotts, Eden. **Saurus.** Murray, 1938.
A spaceship from another world contains an egg that hatches into an intelligent lizard. This was the first story that attempted to use an alien visitor as an objective observer to comment on the state of contemporary human civilization, and it is rather more sympathetic than most work in this vein. Saurus is more convincing than Grant Allen's future anthropologist in *The British Barbarians* (1895), but his commentary is not as impressive as that of Stapledon's *Sirius* [3-168]. Phillpotts had earlier written a poor science fiction thriller as Harrington Hext, *Number 87* (1922), but his later science fiction novels, written under his own name, are more impressive. One of them—*Address Unknown* (1949)—is similar in theme to Saurus, but is much more dubious about the entitlement of an alien being to criticize human conduct.

2-99. Priestly, J(ohn) B(oynton). **Three Time Plays.** Pan, 1947.
Omnibus edition of *Dangerous Corner* (1932), *Time and the Conways* (1937), and *I Have Been Here Before* (1938). In the first, a trivial remark precipitates a disastrous sequence of revelations, but time is then wound back to allow the secrets to remain safely buried. The second juxtaposes scenes widely separated in time and then allows the future subtly to affect the past. The third develops the thesis of "eternal recurrence" popularized by P. D. Ouspensky. The author's perennial fascination with time and the possibility of undoing mistakes—which echoes C. H. Hinton's "An Unfinished Communication" (1895)—is further displayed in the surreal *Johnson Over Jordan* (1939) and *An Inspector Calls* (1947), establishing precedents in the English theater that prepared the way for many later works, most notably Tom Stoppard's brilliant *Arcadia* (1993).

2-100. Rand, Ayn. **Anthem.** Cassell, 1938.
In the ultimate collectivist dystopia, where the very concept of the individual self has been banished from the language, a creative genius escapes into the wilderness, rediscovers the word *I*, and becomes a new Prometheus. A striking parable by the would-be messiah of "Objectivism," perhaps best regarded as an exotic daydream fantasy in the noble tradi-

tion of Edgar Rice Burroughs's Tarzan stories. Highly influential SF writer Robert A. Heinlein was occasionally wont to fall prey to a similarly neurotic egomania.

2-101. Read, Herbert. **The Green Child.** Heinemann, 1935.
A strange story whose climax is set in a weird underworld where green-skinned humanoids follow a way of life that culminates in a bizarre transcendence of the human condition. An alternative vision of human possibility is presented in an account of a quasi-utopian state in Latin America. A unique and impressive work by a noted critic of art and literature—a reading of his collection of essays, *Reason and Romanticism* (1926), will help to put *The Green Child* in perspective.

2-102. Ridley, Frank A(mbrose). **The Green Machine.** Douglas, 1926.
The eponymous machine is a bicycle capable of interplanetary flight, which carries the protagonist to Mars. There he finds an advanced civilization of giant telepathic ants; in the company of one of them he undertakes a voyage through the solar system. Obviously inspired by Wells, the story is impressive in its imaginative range but distinctly weak in its scientific underpinnings. Its depiction of hive society is by no means sympathetic, but is more evenhanded than most.

2-103. Robertson, E. Arnot. **Three Came Unarmed.** Doubleday, 1929.
A novel about three children raised as "noble savages" in the Far East, who are sent to England when their father dies. Although superior in mind and body, they are crushed and mutilated by civilization, here seen as implacably soul-destroying. A dramatically misanthropic inversion of the Tarzan myth.

2-104. Roger, Noëlle (pseud. of Hélène Pittard). **The New Adam.** Stanley Paul, 1926. Trans. by P. O. Crowhurst of *Le Nouvel Adam*, 1924.
A novel featuring an artificially created superman, emotionless and intellectually powerful, who poses such a threat to "common" people that his creator is forced to bring about his destruction. It has less in common with Weinbaum's novel of the same title [2-136] than with his "The Adaptive Ultimate."

2-105. Rosny aîné, J. H. (pseud. of Joseph-Henri Boëx). **The Giant Cat; or, The Quest of Aoun and Zouhr.** McBride, 1924. Trans. of *Le Félin géant*, 1918. Reprinted as *Quest of the Dawn Man*, 1964.
A fairly typical example of Rosny's prehistoric romances. The only other

example in English, *The Quest for Fire* (1967; trans. of *La Guerre du feu*, 1909), is considerably abridged from the original, and *Ironcastle* (1976; trans. of *L'Étonnant voyage de Hareton Ironcastle*, 1922), a Vernian SF novel, is also considerably rewritten in the English version.

2-106. Scrymsour, Ella. **The Perfect World.** Nash & Grayson, 1922.

A curious novel blending two related novellas. The first describes the discovery of an underground world and the catastrophic destruction of the Earth; the second describes the escape of the leading characters to Jupiter, where alien inhabitants have achieved a utopian existence.

2-107. Shanks, Edward (Richard Buxton). **The People of the Ruins.** Stokes, 1920.

The first of the many British postwar novels that foresee Britain returned to barbarism by the ravages of war. The hero wants to restore progress, but his usefulness to the ruler of the new world is entirely concerned with his knowledge of armaments. The decline, it seems, cannot be reversed. Compare Gloag's *To-Morrow's Yesterday* [2-45] and Desmond's *Ragnarok* [2-31].

*2-108. Shaw, George Bernard. **Back to Methuselah: A Metabiological Pentateuch.** Constable, 1921.

A classic play, infrequently performed because of its length, in which right-thinking people evolve by determined effort into superhumans, eventually being able to look forward to the day when they may cast off the shackles of vulgar matter and become perfect beings of "pure energy." The play is prefaced by a long essay explaining the neo-Lamarckian theory of evolution, which provides its imaginative basis, and offering reasons for the author's rejection of Darwinism.

*2-109. Shiel, M(atthew) P(hipps). **The Young Men Are Coming!** Allen & Unwin, 1937.

A scientist kidnapped aboard a flying saucer returns to Earth with a rejuvenating serum, under whose influence he founds a social movement, the Young Men, which ultimately becomes embroiled in civil war. The hero challenges a religious fundamentalist to a duel of faiths, and his alien allies release at his behest a storm that devastates the world. A stirring championship of Shiel's idiosyncratic view of the ideology of progress. Compare Wells's *The Holy Terror* [2-138] for an interesting contrast of protagonists.

2-110. Sinclair, Upton. **The Millennium: A Comedy of the Year 2000.** Haldeman-Julius, 1924.

An amusing satirical fantasy in which the survivors of a worldwide catastrophe struggle for control of a food-making machine, recapitulating in the process the various economic states described in the Marxist account of history. Originally written as a play in 1909, and might be deemed the first story to feature a neutron bomb.

2-111. Sinclair, Upton. **Our Lady.** Rodale Press, 1938.

Timeslip fantasy in which the mother of Jesus is precipitated into modern California. Harsh criticism of the modern Roman Catholic Church is alleviated by an element of comedy, which emphasizes rather than undermines the moral seriousness of the project. A bold endeavor that anticipates the conscientiously skeptical explorations carried out in much later works, like Michael Moorcock's *Behold the Man* [4-303] and Barry Malzberg's *Cross of Fire* [4-275].

2-112. Sloane, William (Milligan III). **To Walk the Night.** Farrar, 1937.

The story of a doomed love affair between a young college graduate and the widow of his old teacher (who died under very mysterious circumstances). The woman is attractive but alien, trapped by a web of tragic circumstance that destroys those who become involved with her. The novel is a good blend of mystery and science fiction, and it provides a pessimistic account of human inability to come to terms with the unknown. *The Edge of Running Water* (1939) is similar in tone and implications.

2-113. Smith, Clark Ashton. **Zothique.** Ballantine, 1970.

Smith's brief career as a pulp SF and fantasy writer spanned only a few years in the early 1930s. The interplanetary fiction that he wrote for Gernsback's *Wonder Stories* is relatively weak, and though his lurid tales of Zothique have none of the usual science fictional apparatus, they stand at the head of a tradition of far-future exoticism that extends more moderately through the work of writers like Jack Vance. Compare Vance's *The Dying Earth* [3-185].

*2-114. Smith, E(dward) Elmer), and Lee Hawkins Garby. **The Skylark of Space.** Buffalo Book, 1946.

The archetypal pulp space opera, first published in *Amazing Stories* in 1928. X, the unknown metal, sends Richard Seaton's water bath hurtling through the roof of his laboratory, heading for infinity. He follows it in his own good time, and the galaxy becomes his playground, where he fights monstrous aliens and his archenemy, Blackie DuQuesne. The writing is stilted and the plot absurd, but the adventure has a naïve exuberance that remains appealing to younger readers. The two early sequels are *Skylark Three* (1930; reprinted 1947) and *Skylark of Valeron* (1934; reprinted 1949). Much later, Smith added a fourth volume, *Skylark DuQuesne* (1966).

2-115. Smith, Garret. **Between Worlds.** Stellar, 1929.
First serialized in *Argosy* in 1919. Rebellious females are exported from the ordered Patriarchy of Venus to exile on Earth, where they arrive in time to witness and take a small part in World War I, learning much from the contrast between earthly civilization and their own. Smith was perhaps the most interesting of all the writers producing SF for the nonspecialist pulps, and his stories should have been more widely reprinted; the most extravagant is the serial "After a Million Years" (*Argosy*, 1922).

2-116. Smith, Wayland (pseud. of Victor Bayley). **The Machine Stops.** Hale, 1936.
One of several stories emphasizing the vulnerability of modern civilization by following the imagined consequences of a "plague" that destroys all metals. As the new barbarians gather to sack the last enclaves of rural harmony, a young genius tries to save the world by making an alloy that can resist the corrosion. Two very similar stories based on the same premise are *The Death of Iron* (1931) by S. S. Held and *The Metal Doom* (1932) by David H. Keller.

2-117. Snell, Edmund. **Kontrol.** Benn, 1928.
A lurid mad-scientist thriller involving the transplanting of brains for the purpose of manufacturing a superrace. It begins as a conventional horror story, but changes pace when the action shifts to an island where the dehumanized superbeings are building a technological utopia. Snell's other fantasies are much more conventional, but here he appears to have been quite carried away by his idea.

2-118. Squire, J(ohn) C(ollings), ed. **If; or, History Rewritten.** Viking, 1931. British title: *If It Had Happened Otherwise*.
An excellent series of essays in alternate history inspired by G. M. Trevelyan's essay "If Napoleon Had Won the Battle of Waterloo" (1907). The contributors include G. K. Chesterton, André Maurois, and Hilaire Belloc, but the star of the collection is the double-twist account by Winston Churchill, "If Lee Had Not Won the Battle of Gettysburg." The Sidgwick & Jackson edition of 1972 (which retains the British version of

the title) includes Trevelyan's essay and adds new ones by Charles Petrie and A. J. P. Taylor.

*2-119. Stapledon, (William) Olaf. **Last and First Men.** Methuen, 1930.
An "essay in myth creation" documenting the entire future history of the human race and its lineal descendants. The "eighteenth men," living nearly 2 billion years in the future, look forward with equanimity to the end of the story. The book has dated somewhat, not just because its early chapters have been superseded, but also because evolutionary biology has advanced since the 1920s; nevertheless, it remains something of a masterpiece. The immediate sequel, however—*Last Men in London* (1932)—is less impressive, involving an elaborate commentary on the contemporary world from the imaginary viewpoint of one of the eighteenth men. The 1988 J. P. Tarcher reprint of *Last and First Men* includes a foreword by Greg Benford and an afterword by Doris Lessing.

*2-120. Stapledon, (William) Olaf. **Odd John.** Methuen, 1935.
The story of a superchild born into a contemporary human community, apparently modeled on Beresford's *The Hampdenshire Wonder* [1-11]. The novel is well executed, but the child is too obviously a mouthpiece for Stapledon's own prejudices, and his bitter and waspish commentary on human affairs is overdone. The novel lacks the sensitivity of *Sirius* [3-168]; compare Weinbaum's *The New Adam* [2-136].

*2-121. Stapledon, (William) Olaf. **Star Maker.** Methuen, 1937.
A companion piece to *Last and First Men* [2-119], taking the essay in myth creation still further to present an entire history of the cosmos and an account of its myriad life forms. The narrator's vision expands through a series of phases, each giving him a wider perspective until he finally glimpses the Star Maker at his work, experimenting in the cause of producing new and better creations. A magnificent work by any standards; the most important speculative work of the period. Of related interest is *Nebula Maker*, a preliminary and less mature version of *Star Maker*, written in the mid-1930s but not published until 1976. [For other works of this author see chapter 3.]

2-122. Stevens, Francis (pseud. of Gertrude Bennett). **The Heads of Cerberus.** Polaris, 1952.
A curious story, originally published in *The Thrill Book* in 1919, in which the protagonists pass through a strange parallel world into a hypothetical future where Philadelphia, isolated from the rest of America, has become

a totalitarian state. The novel is unconvincing but nevertheless compelling, and is the work of one of the most interesting of the pulp fantasy writers.

2-123. Swayne, Martin. **The Blue Germ.** Hodder & Stoughton, 1918.
A scientist releases a bacillus that confers immunity to aging and disease, and also causes flesh to take on a blue tinge. But the blessing is mixed—by killing desire the bacillus promises to put an end to progress, and when it is fortuitously wiped out this is seen as the world's salvation. Compare Parkinson's *They Shall Not Die* [2-97].

2-124. Taine, John (pseud. of Eric Temple Bell). **The Crystal Horde.** Fantasy, 1952.
Originally published in *Amazing Stories Quarterly* (1930) as *White Lily*, under which title it was once reprinted, this is an extravagant scientific romance involving crystalline life and social strife in the Far East, with the kind of cataclysmic conclusion that Taine loved.

2-125. Taine, John (pseud. of Eric Temple Bell). **The Iron Star.** Dutton, 1930.
One of Taine's mutational romances, in which a radioactive meteorite causes bizarre metamorphoses in a region of central Africa. Its effects include the reversed evolution of humans into protohuman apes.

2-126. Taine, John (pseud. of Eric Temple Bell). **Seeds of Life.** Fantasy Press, 1951.
A story of mutational metamorphosis first published in *Amazing Stories Quarterly* in 1931, somewhat bolder in theme than those Taine managed to publish in book form around the same time, *The Greatest Adventure* (1929) and *The Iron Star* [2-125]. Radiation transforms an ineffectual human being into a superman, but his adventurous plans for the future go sadly awry when he discovers, horribly, that the radiation's effect on his germ plasm has been markedly different from its somatic effects.

*2-127. Taine, John (pseud. of Eric Temple Bell). **The Time Stream.** Buffalo Book, 1946.
This is the best of Taine's novels, originally published in *Wonder Stories* in 1931–1932. More sober in tone than his extravagant stories of monsters and mutations, it is a complex novel of time travel whose climactic catastrophe is by no means simply an imaginative display of spectacular violence. One of the finest pulp SF novels of the period.

2-128. Tolstoi, Aleksei. **Aelita.** Foreign Languages (Moscow), 1957. Trans. by Lucy Flaxman, 1922.

An interplanetary romance in which an idealistic scientist is upstaged by a down-to-earth engineer, who successfully brings the revolution to Mars. It is crudely written, and the propaganda appears to have been grafted onto the story at a late stage. Tolstoi's other translated scientific romance, *The Death Box* (1926; translated 1936; known in a different translation as *The Garin Death Ray*), is an overlong and confusing thriller about a megalomaniac scientist who is finally overthrown by the workers he attempts to exploit.

2-129. Tsiolkovsky, Konstantin. **Beyond the Planet Earth.** Pergamon, 1960. Trans. by K. Syers of *Vne zemli*, 1920.

A juvenile novel about rocket travel into space, written to popularize Tsiolkovsky's ideas about the possibility of spaceflight and the construction of orbital space colonies. The story is awful, but its basic premise has been amply vindicated—Tsiolkovsky must be regarded as the spiritual father of spaceflight and the myth of the conquest of space. The novel is also reprinted, along with various other essays and pieces of science fiction, under the title *Outside the Earth*, in the definitive collection of Tsiolkovsky's works, *The Call of the Cosmos* (1963).

2-130. Vivian, E(velyn) Charles. **Star Dust.** Hutchinson, 1925.

The best of several cautionary tales about scientists who learn how to perform the alchemical trick of making gold, only to find that the discovery brings unexpected difficulties in its wake. Others include Conan Doyle's *The Doings of Raffles Haw* (1891) and John Taine's *Quayle's Invention* (1927). Vivian was one of the better writers of imaginative thrillers, producing lost-world stories under his own name and some fine supernatural stories as Jack Mann, but this was his only science fiction novel.

2-131. von Hanstein, Otfrid. **Electropolis.** *Wonder Stories Quarterly*, Summer 1930. Trans. by Francis Currier of *Elektropolis*, 1927.

A typical German utopian fantasy of the period, in which an industrialist buys a mountain in Australia and uses the radium he mines from it to provide power for a futuristic city, which he builds nearby in the desert. The greedy Australians try to take their land back, but German superscience prevails.

2-132. von Harbou, Thea. **Metropolis.** Reader's Library, 1927. Trans. 1926.

The book of Fritz Lang's classic film, written by his wife. The film thrives on its magnificent visuals, not on its plot, and the novel falls rather flat. It is an unconvincing melodrama about an industrial dispute in a marvelous city of the future. *The Rocket to the Moon* (1930) is the book of the film *Die Frau im Mond*, an interplanetary romance whose special effects were enhanced by the work of the German Rocket Society, but it is similarly depleted in cold print.

2-133. Wandrei, Donald. **Colossus: The Collected Science Fiction of Donald Wandrei.** Fedogan and Bremer, 1989.

Omnibus collection of Wandrei's SF, including 17 stories from 1927–1937, beginning with the vividly nasty far-future fantasy, "The Red Brain" (1927). The title story and its sequel, "Colossus Eternal" (both 1934), are macrocosmic fantasies displaying Wandrei's typical imaginative exuberance; his fondness for extremes is also garishly displayed in "Finality Unlimited" (1936) and "Infinity Zero" (1936). The better stories had earlier appeared mingled with frankly supernatural stories and some marginal items, in the Arkham House collections, *The Eye and the Finger* (1944) and *Strange Harvest* (1965).

2-134. Weinbaum, Stanley G(rauman). **The Black Flame.** Fantasy, 1948.

The book contains the novelette "Dawn of Flame" as well as the title story, although the latter was a new version of the first, rewritten to boost the fantasy content. Neither version sold while Weinbaum was alive; both appeared posthumously in 1939. The stories belong to the species of exotic romance that includes Haggard's *She* [1-46], Benoit's *Atlantida* (1920), and A. Merritt's *Dwellers in the Mirage* (1932)—the translocation of the myth into science fiction does not show it to any greater advantage, but the story is fondly remembered.

*2-135. Weinbaum, Stanley G(rauman). **A Martian Odyssey and Other Science Fiction Tales.** Hyperion, 1974.

An omnibus edition of Weinbaum's pulp science fiction stories, absorbing the two earlier collections, *A Martian Odyssey and Others* (1949) and *The Red Peri* (1952). The stories featuring exotic alien ecosystems are excellent, written with wit and inventiveness. The title work (1934), "The Lotus Eaters" (1935), and "The Mad Moon" (1935) are among the best stories to appear in the early pulps, and they remain readable today. "The Adaptive Ultimate" (1935 as by John Jessel) is an interesting story about a superwoman and "Proteus Island" (1936) an interesting reprise of Wells's *Island of Dr. Moreau* [1-100]. The three stories that feature the eccentric scientist Haskel van Manderpootz (1935–1936) are among the best examples of humorous pulp SF. Weinbaum's premature death robbed the SF pulps of their most promising writer.

*2-136. Weinbaum, Stanley G(rauman). **The New Adam.** Ziff-Davis, 1939.
A classic "superman" novel, written before Weinbaum commenced his brief career as a pulp writer in 1934 but not published during his lifetime. It is an attempt to examine seriously and thoughtfully the possible career of an evolved man born into the contemporary world, and makes much of the analogy of "feral children." Less devoted to social criticism than Stapledon's *Odd John* [2-120], it appears to have been similarly inspired by Beresford's *The Hampdenshire Wonder* [1-11].

2-137. Wells, H(erbert) G(eorge). **The Croquet Player.** Chatto & Windus, 1936.
A neurotic medical man tells the allegorical story of Cainsmarsh, a village whose inhabitants are cursed by their evolutionary heritage (symbolized by the bones of their remote ancestors, which are sometimes exhumed from the marsh). The protagonist, a man of leisure, cannot see the implications of the allegory. A neat parable presenting the view that human nature is fatally flawed.

2-138. Wells, H(erbert) G(eorge). **The Holy Terror.** Joseph, 1939.
A psychological study of the personality of a revolutionary-turned-dictator, who brings about the destruction of the old social order only to become a threat to the establishment of a better one. The protagonist is modeled on Stalin, with Hitler, Mussolini, and Franco also in mind. Perhaps the most interesting exercise in sociopolitical SF among Wells's later works.

2-139. Wells, H(erbert) G(eorge). **Men like Gods.** Cassell, 1923.
The second of Wells's major utopian fantasies, set in the distant future. Our world has long since collapsed, owing to its failure to convert scientific knowledge into practical wisdom. A new superrace, rather different in psychology, has emerged from the ruins, and its members live amicably in a stateless community.

*2-140. Wells, H(erbert) G(eorge). **The Shape of Things to Come.** Hutchinson, 1933.
The last of Wells's major utopian fantasies is a documentary fiction that attempts to reconnect the utopian future with the present by means of an imaginary future history. It reiterates Wells's conviction that the obliteration of contemporary political intrusions is a necessary first step in social reconstruction, but it relies on war and plague rather than revolution to

accomplish the task. The image of the reborn world is really no more convincing than his previous utopian designs.

2-141.   Wells, H(erbert) G(eorge). **Star-Begotten: A Biological Fantasia.** Chatto & Windus, 1937.

A curious novel in which Wells dallies half-heartedly with neo-Lamarckian ideas. Martians bombard Earth with mutagenic radiation to assist the emergence of a new kind of being. The work has more in common with *In the Days of the Comet* (1906) than with *The Food of the Gods* [1-99], and is entirely lacking in conviction. [For other works of this author see chapter 1.]

2-142.   Williamson, Jack. **The Early Williamson.** Doubleday, 1975.

Collection of 11 stories from 1928–1933 with interesting autobiographical commentary. Longer stories, like the fervently Merrittesque and imaginatively fecund "The Alien Intelligence" (1929) and "The Moon Era" (1932) are necessarily excluded from this representative collection, but it displays all the many facets of the author's early work. "The Girl From Mars" (1929; written in collaboration with Miles J. Breuer) is a first contact story in a sober and sentimental vein; "The Cosmic Express" (1930) displays a liveliness of style as well as imagination; "The Meteor Girl" (1931) is an early story about Einstein's theory of relativity; "Through the Purple Cloud" (1931) is an early parallel-worlds story. Williamson was the only pulp SF writer to survive from the twenties into the nineties, maturing all the while and maintaining all the power of his imagination; his work, taken as a whole, displays all the virtues of the evolving genre.

2-143.   Williamson, Jack. **The Green Girl.** Avon, 1950.

One of Williamson's many early magazine serials, from *Amazing* in 1930. An extravagant adventure enlivened by Merrittesque purple prose and a superbly melodramatic first line. The same naive charm is to be found in two similar novels, *The Stone From the Green Star* (1931) and *Xandulu* (1934).

2-144.   Williamson, Jack. **The Legion of Space.** Fantasy, 1947.

A space opera first published in *Astounding* in 1934, in which characters based on Falstaff and the Three Musketeers try to obtain control of a secret superweapon to save Earth from an alien menace. Two other serials featuring the same characters were reprinted in *The Cometeers* (1950), and the whole series—including a fourth novelette—assembled in *Three from the Legion* (1979). *The Queen of the Legion* was added in 1983.

*2-145. Williamson, Jack. **The Legion of Time.** Fantasy, 1952.
A classic of pulp SF in which a small army of soldiers of fortune is co-opted into a war between alternate futures to settle which of them will really exist. The gaudy costume drama is sustained by the power of the central idea, which was new in 1938 when the novel was serialized in *Astounding.* [For other works of this author see chapters 3, 4 and 5.]

2-146. Winsor, G(eorge) MacLeod. **Station X.** Jenkins, 1919.
A competent thriller in which aliens invade Earth by means of a radio installation. Gernsback reprinted it in *Amazing Stories* in 1926. A similar theme is used in Frank Crisp's *The Ape of London* (1959).

2-147. Wright, Harold Bell, and John Lebar. **The Devil's Highway.** Appleton, 1932.
A marvelously lurid mad-scientist story in which the villain uses a machine to suppress the emotions and conscience of his victims so that they can devote their intellectual energies entirely to his nefarious schemes. Contrast Kaul's treatment of a similarly alienated genius in *Contagion to This World* [2-63].

2-148. Wright, S(ydney) Fowler. **The Adventure of Wyndham Smith.** Jenkins, 1938.
In a remote future the inhabitants of a utopia of comforts find their lives utterly pointless and elect to commit mass suicide. One of their number, whose identity is fused with the psyche of a man of our time, saves himself and a woman, but must then face the threat of mechanical killers programmed to hunt them down. Expanded from the short story "Original Sin;" the most scathing of Fowler Wright's denunciations of the leisure society.

*2-149. Wright, S(ydney) Fowler. **Deluge.** Fowler Wright, 1927.
A self-published book that became a best-seller. Geological upheavals result in widespread flooding, but southern England is elevated to make the Cotswolds a tiny archipelago. The inhabitants' struggle for existence is described with a cold realism not previously seen. The narrative of the sequel, *Dawn* (1929), runs parallel for most of its length. Compare and contrast England's *Darkness and Dawn* [1-33], Wyndham's *The Kraken Wakes* (1953), and Ballard's *The Drowned World* [3-16] to appreciate the full spectrum of this species of romantic pessimism.

2-150. Wright, S(ydney) Fowler. **Dream; or, The Simian Maid.** Harrap, 1931.
A depressed socialite seeks distraction in hypnotically sharing the experi-

ences of individuals long dead—in this case an arboreal humanoid primate. Her lover and sister follow her into the past, incarnated as members of another protohuman species; all three become involved in the affairs of an enclosed kingdom threatened by gargantuan rats. A slightly bitter celebration of the noble savagery of nature, to be contrasted with Mitchell's *Three Go Back* [2-89]. *Vengeance of Gwa* (1935, originally published under the name of Anthony Wingrave) was intended as a sequel, though the prefatory material was cut from the published editions. *Spiders' War* (1954), in which the heroine visits an idiosyncratically utopian future, completes the trilogy.

2-151. Wright, S(ydney) Fowler. **The Island of Captain Sparrow.** Gollancz, 1928.

A castaway on a small island finds the cruel descendants of pirates hunting nonsentient satyrs, while the last fugitive survivors of an antediluvian civilization and a forest-dwelling girl also live in fear of them. After a desperate struggle, hero and heroine inherit this fragment of Eden from those of the Fallen who have usurped it. Contrast Wells's *Island of Dr. Moreau* [1-100], whose philosophical and allegorical themes are touched on.

*2-152. Wright, S(ydney) Fowler. **The New Gods Lead.** Jarrolds, 1932.

One of the few SF collections published in the United Kingdom between the wars, featuring a sequence of stories set in nightmarish futures where a scientistic way of thinking has made life frightful. Added to the main sequence are "The Rat," in which the inventor of an immortality serum decides (too late) that it will not improve the quality of life, and "Choice," an allegory in which two lovers decide that life, for all its pain and uncertainty, is preferable to heaven. A striking collection, reprinted with the addition of two stories as *The Throne of Saturn* (1949). Compare Bunch's *Moderan* [4-82].

2-153. Wright, S(ydney) Fowler. **Prelude in Prague.** Newnes, 1935.

A future war novel, written as a newspaper serial after an investigative tour of Europe. World War II begins with a German invasion of Czechoslovakia, and a group of Britons trapped in Prague witness the effects of blitzkrieg. *Four Days War* (1936) takes up the story with Germany sending its air fleets against Britain, with horrific consequences. In *Megiddo's Ridge* (1937) the Americans get involved, and the two contending forces muster for the final battle. The rather contrived main narrative follows the exploits of a remarkable British spy who wins the confidence of the German High Command, but the virtues of the trilogy are in their description of the effects of high technology warfare. Compare O'Neill's *Day of Wrath* [2-96].

*2-154. Wright, S(ydney) Fowler. **The World Below.** Collins, 1929.
Two short novels, the first of which appeared separately as *The Amphibians* in 1925; the second is also known in one paperback version as *The Dwellers*. A time traveler ventures into the remote future in search of two predecessors. His arrival precipitates a crisis in the affairs of the gentle, telepathic Amphibians, who coexist uneasily with the giant humanoid Dwellers. The account of this bizarre posthuman future draws some imagery from Dante's *Inferno*, which Fowler Wright had recently translated, and was unparalleled in its time for its phantasmagoric quality, but the second part peters out into a few synoptic chapters and a hurried ending. Compare Hodgson's *The Night Land* (1912) and Silverberg's *Son of Man* (1971).

*2-155. Wylie, Philip (Gordon). **Gladiator.** Knopf, 1930.
A novel about the growth to adulthood of a boy who is a physical (although not intellectual) "superman." It is the first important sympathetic superman story, but exhibits the customary pessimism regarding the prospect of the hero's eventual integration into the human world—a pessimism set aside by the creators of the comic book *Superman*, who borrowed the novel's central notion.

2-156.   Wylie, Philip (Gordon), and Edwin Balmer. **When Worlds Collide.** Stokes, 1933.
A celebrated novel of impending cosmic catastrophe and the attempt to save a favored few from sharing the fate of the doomed world. It was filmed by George Pal in 1951. The sequel, dealing with the exploits of the survivors on their new world, is *After Worlds Collide* (1934). Similar themes are developed in McIntosh's *One in Three Hundred* (1954) and James Blish's . . . *And All the Stars a Stage* (1971).

*2-157. Zamiatin, Evgenii. **We.** Dutton, 1924. Trans. by Gregory Zilboorg of *My*.
A magnificent vision of a dystopian society in which life has been totally regulated in the cause of order, harmony, and happiness. The seeds of dissatisfaction have been rooted out, with the sole exception of imagination, which is about to be eliminated from the psyche as humans' noblest project comes to fruition: the building of a spaceship that will allow the "United State" to extend itself throughout the universe. A masterpiece of speculative political philosophy by a disillusioned Russian—not published in the U.S.S.R. itself until 1988. It influenced Orwell's *Nineteen Eighty-Four* [3-140] and provided a prototype for modern dystopian fantasy.

CHAPTER 3

From the Golden Age
to the Atomic Age:
1940–1963

Paul A. Carter

The years were grim as the decade of the thirties drew to a close. "The world was numb under the great depression," Frederik Pohl has written, "I remember the cold city streets, gloveless relief workers shovelling snow outside the second-hand magazine store where I browsed through the old copies of *Amazing Stories* before selecting the one in which I would invest my dime."[1] The New Deal, for all its bright promise, had stalled in its tracks; the economy was running typically at no more than 50 percent of plant capacity, with 10 million Americans still unemployed; and in Africa, Asia, and Europe, aggressor powers marched with such seeming irresistibility that some in the still-democratic West saw them pessimistically as "the wave of the future." A young person in the United States could look forward to, at best, an uncertain future with the strong possibility of being conscripted for war. Mainstream writer Edna Ferber, who had been turning out popular novels since the end of a previous world war, summed up in despair: "Who now envies youth?"

Nevertheless, in the then small world of science fiction, certain youths in America experienced and remembered the turn from the 1930s to the 1940s as a Golden Age.

A word of caution here. One familiar adage in the SF community is that "the 'Golden Age' in science fiction was—about thirteen," that is, the age at which one began to read science fiction, whether that happened in 1940, 1960, 1980, or within the last few days. Arthur Clarke typically testified, in the first sentence of his *Astounding Days: A Science Fictional Autobiography* [9-31–35]: "Sometime toward the end of 1930, in my thirteenth year, I acquired my first science fiction magazine—and my life was irrevocably changed." But we cannot relativize too much, for the name has stuck to the times, even though now we are long past them. Just as there were many cultural renaissances in European history but only one that earned the name *the* Renaissance, so too, although there have been many generations of youths discovering SF at 13 (or younger), there remains a period still denotable as *the* Golden Age.

It began just before World War II, and it ended with the war or not long after. To enlarge upon that connection would be to belabor the obvious. An economically limping nation in a prewar mode helps explain its beginning, and Hiroshima helps explain its end. But there were two developments within American SF that must also be taken into account: the sudden proliferation of pulp science fiction magazines after a long drought, and the advent of John W. Campbell as editor of one of them.

Campbell took charge of *Astounding Stories*, as it was then called, in 1937, and promptly softened its pulp-sounding name to *Astounding Science-Fiction*. Thirty-four years later, when he died, still at the magazine's helm, it had become *Analog*. But the taming of pulp sensationalism went far beyond mere renaming of a product. Out went the gassy, semimetaphysical "thought-variant" stories to which his editorial predecessor had been addicted. In came new writers, some crossing over from non-SF pulps (notably L. Ron Hubbard); others found in their teens and developed under Campbell's stimulating if autocratic tutelage; still others mature writers who simply had never before found a suitable niche. Lester del Rey's and L. Sprague de Camp's first stories appeared in the magazine in 1938; Isaac Asimov's (not counting—as he did not—a slightly earlier sale to *Amazing*), Robert Heinlein's, A. E. van Vogt's, and Theodore Sturgeon's in that *annus mirabilis*, 1939. Older writers who had been a staple of magazine SF earlier in the thirties learned to speak Campbell's language or were quietly turned out to pasture.

Some of this makeover was simply learning how to write better English. The pulps have been so carefully sifted for anthologizing purposes that we mercifully forget just how unspeakably bad so much of the residue was. Campbell also had no truck (usually) with Gernsback's sugar-coated-pill approach to SF, in which the story came to a dead stop while the characters poured forth great gobs of scientific explanation (not always accurate) in lecture form. Campbell's instruction to his writers was refreshing: write him a story that could be published as a contemporary item in a magazine published in the 25th century.

He also told them he wanted stories about aliens who could think as well as humans, but not *like* humans. In practice, this latter axiom didn't work out; Campbell made it plain that he wanted *Homo sapiens* to triumph all over the galaxy, and writers like Asimov adjusted what they wrote accordingly. An occasional beloved senior carryover from the thirties like E. E. Smith could be indulged in peopling his future universe with bizarre life-forms, but otherwise the Stanley Weinbaum tradition of wacky, appealing nonhuman intelligences went into abeyance until long after the Golden Age was over. On the whole, though, the gains under the Campbell regime far outweighed the losses. He fed his writers ideas, worked out concepts with them (such as the "three laws of robotics"), and—so testifies Lester del Rey—loved them best when they could stand up to him in argument.

The other herald of the Golden Age was the arrival of a host of new competitors for Campbell's *Astounding*, in a magazine population explosion.

At the end of the Depression, as at the beginning, there were only three science fiction magazines; four if we count *Weird Tales* (and we should, as a nurturer of writers—Henry Kuttner, Fritz Leiber, and especially Ray Bradbury—who became important in SF as well). So deep was Depression conditioning as to the precariousness of any business venture that when *Astounding*'s June 1938 number was late turning up at the Asimov family's Brooklyn candy store, young Isaac made a pilgrimage to the magazine's editorial office on Manhattan to find out if it had folded, which was how he came to meet John Campbell.

The other survivors, although making it financially, had fallen upon hard times in other ways. *Amazing Stories*, the eldest, shorn of its former folio size, had moved to Chicago and become primarily just another men's adventure pulp with an SF veneer. *Wonder*, Gernsback's second venture, had metamorphosed into *Thrilling Wonder Stories*, consciously aiming at a more juvenile audience, and devoting its cover art to the Eternal Triangle of pulp SF: the Jut-Jawed young man, the not-quite-dressed young woman, and the Bug-Eyed Monster (BEM). Sometimes for variety a larger BEM was shown, Godzilla-style, trashing Washington's capitol dome or the Golden Gate bridge.

But if quality suffered, quantitatively SF at the end of the thirties enjoyed a substantial boom—and eventually that helped the quality also. Older magazines spun off companions: *Fantastic Adventures* from *Amazing*, *Startling Stories* from *Thrilling Wonder*, and the splendidly innovative and impudent *Unknown* from *Astounding*. New ones popped up like dandelions: *Astonishing Stories, Super Science, Planet, Comet, Cosmic Stories, Stirring Science Stories, Science Fiction, Future Fiction.*[2] In economic terms SF had become an expanding market, and for would-be writers (it being axiomatic that all who regularly read SF sooner or later try to write it) this was a godsend, at least until wartime paper shortages swept most of these newcomers away.

At the same time this magazine flood reinforced the ghettoizing of SF in the United States; for unless we count the Sunday funnies (Buck Rogers, Flash Gordon) and the emerging "superhero" comic books, for which indeed some SF writers wrote continuity, there wasn't much else to read *but* the magazines. American hardcover publishers rarely touched SF; an occasional sentimental time travel tale like Robert Nathan's *Portrait of Jennie* (1940) or a tepid update on *Looking Backward* [1-8] such as Granville Hicks's *The First to Awaken* (1940) hardly slaked the science fictionists' thirst. Better stuff was being written in Britain, such as John Gloag's *99%* [3-76] and Olaf Stapledon's *Sirius* [3-168], but with an infrequent exception like C. S. Lewis's lovely Venus tale *Perelandra* (1943) [3-116] most imprints from British publishers never got across the U-boat-infested waters of the Atlantic. That a melodrama as bad as Curt Siodmak's *Donovan's Brain* (1943) could become widely popular is a measure of what the seeker after SF was up against, and it is further indicative of the American SF reader's plight that *Donovan* became a grade B movie. Hollywood, apart from Frank Capra's stylishly filmed *Lost Horizon* (1937) [2-52], remained pretty much stuck in its Mad Scientist mode: *Black Friday*, with Boris Karloff; *Son of Frankenstein*, with Karloff and Bela Lugosi; and *Dr. Cyclops*, which the science fiction professional Henry Kuttner "wrote down" into a novelette for *Thrilling Wonder*, with crudely executed halftone stills from the movie.

If young fans couldn't get enough SF to satisfy their appetites, they would have to make some. After they had read and reread their Verne and Wells and Edgar Rice Burroughs they had to go back to the pulps' letter columns as "letterhacks," find and feud with each other in fan clubs, serve an apprenticeship in fanzine fiction (usually awful) and criticism (sometimes quite good), and eventually settle into the serious business of becoming writers. Damon Knight, summing up the history of a most significant fans-into-writers club, *The Futurians* [9-143], argued that the necessary conditions for the flourishing of that group were poverty, political intransigence, and the just-described proliferation of the science fiction magazines.

The scrappy Futurian Society of New York didn't last long; "as soon as the Futurians began to make a little money," Knight concludes, "the group began to dissolve." However, while it lasted it produced, by Knight's count, "10 novelists, a publisher, 2 agents, 4 anthologists, and 5 editors" out of a total membership of only twenty; not to mention seven intragroup marriages and five divorces! The names are a roll call of later-prominent figures in the SF world: Donald Wollheim, Frederik Pohl, Isaac Asimov, Cyril Kornbluth, Knight himself, Judith Merril, James Blish. By the end of 1942 they had collectively produced 129 science fiction stories, mostly as collaborations and almost all under pseudonyms.

Two observations at this point: most of the Futurians didn't write for *Astounding*, the pacesetter, and much of the early action among emerging writers occurred elsewhere. Indeed, of the entire group only Asimov during the Golden Age regularly published in Campbell's magazine, and the rest of them by Knight's account considered themselves rather counter-cultural to Campbell: stylistically more innovative (within the more general limits of pulp publication) and considerably more radical. Three of them, Pohl, Wollheim, and Robert W. Lowndes, edited magazines that, if small in circulation, were nonetheless in direct competition with *Astounding*. The political intransigence Knight referred to in his memoir was real; there was overlap between the science fictionists and sectarian Left politics in New York City, at least until Stalinist rejoicing at the fall of France in 1940 made that relationship embarrassing.

As writers the Futurians derived a strategic advantage from living in New York, where publishing happened. In the homeliest terms, it was cheaper to spend a nickel on the subway each way to hand carry a manuscript to a pulp publisher, and the same to retrieve it, than to put postage stamps on the going and return envelopes at the rate of 3 cents per ounce (about six typewritten pages, or 1,500 words). Besides, a kindhearted editor after rejecting a story in person might buy the kid lunch; so close were Depression-era financial calculations. However, other science fiction writers' centers had emerged from the fan clubs of the earlier thirties. In the Los Angeles Science Fantasy Society, fans, writers, and wannabes happily mingled in the basement of the grandiloquently named Prince Rupert Hotel; Ray Bradbury came out of that milieu and Leigh Brackett was close to it. Further up the coast in the Bay Area, writers in the early forties congregated in the Mañana Literary Society, so named for the great stories its members talked of writing "mañana." A similar authors' club in Milwaukee nurtured young Robert Bloch, and young Lester del Rey rode the train in from Philadelphia to deliver his manuscripts, sometimes crashing for a weekend on Campbell's couch.

What kind of science fiction did the Golden Age writers, in New York and elsewhere, try to write? Campbell's explicit call for contemporary-sounding futures and implicit demand for a humans-only cosmos was paralleled in a how-to article by *Amazing*'s assistant editor, Jerry Westerfield: "Stories starting in some large U.S. city are better than those starting off in space somewhere. A story starting in the present is better than one starting in the past or the future."[3] So much for Burroughs's Mars or Stapledon's Neptune! All editorial rules are of course made to be broken (as Campbell also knew); *Amazing*'s consort, *Fantastic Adventures*, played by looser rules, publishing Robert Bloch's Runyonesque humor and August Derleth's ghost stories. And some writers blithely disregarded all such strictures. "A large U.S. city like New York is concrete and real to the minds of our readers, while a city off on Mars somewhere is vague and indefinite," Westerfield warned; yet Leigh Brackett in that same time period had great fun in *Planet Stories*, starting and ending her stories in cities off on Mars or elsewhere.

Nonetheless, the limits proposed by Campbell and Westerfield did have an impact. A perceptive reader commented on the difference between E. E. Smith's space opera, *Galactic Patrol*, accepted and published in 1937 before the new era had quite begun, and its sequel, *Gray Lensman*, which appeared late in 1939: *Galactic Patrol* had given "the thoughtful reader an impression of the unimaginably huge size of our galaxy," Lew Cunningham wrote in a letter to *Astounding*: but "in 'Gray Lensman' you proceed to shrivel this monstrous aggregation of stars and dirty it up, so to speak, with . . . throwbacks to the ancient twentieth-century system." The wild Western frontier, with which SF had often paralleled, was becoming the frontier under settlement and domestication.[4]

But the closing of that frontier had opened the way to a revival of social criticism, in place of the gadgeteering of Gernsback and the escapism of Burroughs. The option of social commentary had always been latently present; Verne's classic submarine story was not just a future-gadget yarn, but embodied also in Captain Nemo some serious criticism of historical trends Verne didn't like, and of course in Wells the social politics were always integral to the story. Campbell, whose antennae were always sensitive to current concerns until his own idiosyncrasies got the better of him, immediately followed the publication of *Gray Lensman* in *Astounding* with two very un-Smithlike serials: "If This Goes On—," Heinlein's first long story (1940; included in *The Past through Tomorrow* [3-89]), which described a media-manipulating fundamentalist religious dictatorship in a future United States, and *Final Blackout*, by L. Ron Hubbard (also 1940 [3-96]), a somber forecast of one possible outcome of the European war then raging.

Campbell's magazines were especially hospitable to this kind of social-consequences science fiction but other magazines from time to time also took aim at American cultural shortcomings, especially the ones edited by Futurians. It was of course a highly male-focused kind of social consciousness. To be sure, women were given a bit more to do in the stories than they had been in the earlier thirties, when the typical SF heroine, in Leigh Brackett's words, had done "nothing but have tantrums, shriek, and generally gum up the action." Even "Doc" Smith, that highly conventional Michigan Republican, had learned between the writing of the Skylarks and his Lensman series that, in one *Astounding* reader's words, "a female can, in fact, once in a while, get in there and *do* something." Brackett contended that her own women characters, in contrast to the previous norm, were "gutty and intelligent"—but she continued to construct almost all her stories with male viewpoint characters. In this respect science fiction had yet a long, long way to go.[5]

Furthermore, the acute social forecasting that did appear (to the delight of subsequent anthologists) in Golden Age science fiction magazines was surrounded and sometimes submerged by conventional pulp fare. Yet even the straight action-adventure story, which was the staple of most of the magazines most of the time, could quite insensibly take on an element of social consciousness. A sociological study by Walter Hirsch, "The Image of the Scientist in Science-Fiction," based on a random sample of the SF pulps from 1926 to 1950, found that capitalists, by and large, figured in the stories as disreputable characters: "Scientists comprised the major category of both heroes and villains, but businessmen were, proportionately, more villainous than scientists."[6] In Golden Age SF, greedy, rapacious tycoons or stockbrokers seeking to cash in on their hired scientists' labors became almost a cliché. A classic instance is Theodore Sturgeon's "Microcosmic God" (1941; SFHF) with its maverick scientist hero and its banker villain, although Sturgeon pro forma disclaimed any such intention at the outset by writing, "Don't worry, I'm not going political on you."

One subject about which it had become perfectly acceptable to "go political" was the menace of Fascism. In near-future, Earth-focused SF, Hitler and the Japanese warlords regularly got their comeuppance: in transgalactic SF the alien menaces transmuted into hyper-Nazis. But a disquieting note was sounded alongside these justifications of America's

1941–1945 war: its sheer physical and social destructiveness. Forecasts of reversion to barbarism after such a war, deriving from mainstream writer Stephen Vincent Benét's "By the Waters of Babylon" (1937), attracted a number of magazine writers and prompted during 1941 a serious debate in "Brass Tacks," *Astounding*'s letters to the editor department, as to just how far and fast such a collapse could go.

Pretty far, it turned out, if one knew or guessed of the A-bomb, then actually lurking in the wings. The pulps' predictive record on this subject is impressive, *Astounding*'s in particular. In 1941, "Solution Unsatisfactory," by Robert Heinlein, which asked what must happen to politics and foreign policy when a weapon of war is developed against which there can be no defense; in 1942, "Nerves," by Lester del Rey, which debated the ethics of covering up a potential worse-than-Chernobyl disaster in a nuclear power plant; in 1944, "Deadline," by Cleve Cartmill, bad as a story but so precise in detailing how a uranium bomb could be detonated that it prompted Army counterintelligence to investigate whether anyone on the Manhattan Project had been talking; and early in 1945 (before the war in Europe was yet over), "The Piper's Son," by Henry Kuttner and C. L. Moore, which takes place in a post–nuclear war world of independent city-states, each capable of dusting off any one of the others—a smaller scaled version of the "balance of terror," which would become the actual foundation of post-bomb U.S.-Soviet relations.[7]

When the nightmare actually came to pass, it put science fictionists in an emotional double bind. It showed beyond dispute that the crazy Buck Rogers stuff they had dreamed of for years was real after all, but it was not the kind of dream one would have wanted actually to come true. As Theodore Sturgeon summed up in "Memorial," a short story published less than a year after the war ended (included in his *Without Sorcery* [3-173]) science fiction writers who wrote about atomic energy before the end of the war had been "afraid for humanity, but they themselves were not really afraid, except in a delicious drawing room sort of way, because they couldn't conceive of this Buck Rogers event happening to anything but posterity." But the boy cried wolf, and the wolf came.

So although the Golden Age writers (and artists) came back from the wars and resumed their work, and although the Depression impoverishment in which they had started was gone as pent-up demand for civilian goods produced an economic boom instead of the mass unemployment government experts had predicted—a boom in which science fiction, like other consumer activities, flourished—it may fairly be said that the Golden Age that had begun at the end of the thirties was already over. The innocence was gone; as physicist J. Robert Oppenheimer said on behalf of the scientists who had developed the bomb, "We have known sin." People did not yet realize that "civilization, the civilization we have been born into, lived in, and indoctrinated with, died on July 16, 1945, and that the Death Notice was published to the world on August 6, 1945," John Campbell editorialized in *Astounding.* "The atomic bomb must, inevitably, force upon us an era of international good manners and tolerance—or vast and sudden death."[8]

The years immediately following the first use of the atomic bomb were hardly an era of international good manners and tolerance. Science fiction, however, prospered. The atomic bomb and the space program, another activity that the general public had relegated to Buck Rogers and company in the prewar years, broke down the walls of the SF ghetto. Robert Heinlein began selling stories to the *Saturday Evening Post;* Ray Bradbury branched out from *Weird Tales* and *Planet Stories* to *Harper's,* the *New Yorker,* and *Mademoiselle.* Although the pulps enjoyed a kind of Indian Summer, not fading finally from the scene until 1955, and in the meantime helping to launch some new writing careers, notably that of Philip K. Dick, the real action in the 1950s was in new kinds of SF magazines, and in books.

SF book publication began as an exercise in Golden Age nostalgia. One hardcover publisher devoted almost entirely to reprinting work from the pulps, Arkham House, had been in business since 1939, but its output consisted almost entirely of fantasy and horror, quarried chiefly from *Weird Tales* (fantasy and horror had never been quite as ghettoized and tabooed in America as SF; it was after all an anciently respected branch of literature). In 1946 Arkham took the plunge into science fiction by publishing *Slan* [3-180], a former *Astounding* serial by A. E. van Vogt. Arkham was soon joined by half a dozen small-press publishers, started by long-time SF fans who gambled that readers who had spent 15 cents to 20 cents during the war for copies of SF magazines might be willing to spend $3 or so for hardcover books reprinting serials, or collections of a favorite author's stories, from those same magazines.

Venture capital was on the smallest of scales, and press runs by today's trade publisher standards (although not by those of university presses) were modest, Arkham printed 4,000 copies of *Slan* and 3,000 of Ray Bradbury's first collection, *Dark Carnival* (1947). Fantasy Press usually produced three or four thousand copies, reaching its peak with "Doc" Smith's *Galactic Patrol,* 6,600 copies. Prime Press, which grew out of a conversation at a fan club meeting (the Philadelphia Science Fiction Society), printed 2,000 copies of Lester del Rey's first book, *And Some Were Human* (1948), and 3,000 of Theodore Sturgeon's first, *Without Sorcery* [3-173].

For a time these ventures were economically viable, and new small presses entered the field. Shasta Publishers, originating as a Chicago bookseller, published Heinlein, de Camp, and Alfred Bester; Gnome Press offered Asimov, James Blish, Clifford Simak, and C. L. Moore; other specialty publishers joined in, sometimes with only a book or two—"and as soon as they had made a success of it," author-critic Algis Budrys angrily writes, "Doubleday, Simon & Schuster and the others woke up and with one herbivorous snap took it away from them." In 1950 Doubleday started its long-lasting Science Fiction Book Club, and in the following year Gnome Press, to take but one example, had a 90 percent drop in sales.[9]

Actually the publishing giants had had an eye on this potential market since the end of the war. Random House had entered the lists as early as 1946 with *Adventures in Time and Space* [3-214], and before the end of the forties other mainline publishers had produced omnibus volumes edited by Groff Conklin [3-209, 3-210] and August Derleth [3-211, 3-212]. So far these were all reprint collections; even Ray Bradbury's history-making *Martian Chronicles* in 1950 [3-32] was in essence a "fix-up novel" composed of late-forties stories primarily from *Planet* and *Thrilling Wonder*. Nonspecialist hardcover publishers remained resistant to new, not magazine-derived, SF until 1949, when the ubiquitous Doubleday published Max Ehrlich's *The Big Eye* and followed it up with Asimov's *Pebble in the Sky* [3-15], which two magazine editors had previously rejected. The face of science fiction was thereby changed forever.

It was not quite the end for the small presses; Arkham and Donald Grant would continue after Fantasy Press and Shasta and Gnome were gone. But the bulk of SF that appeared after 1950 came either from mainstream hardcover publishers or, once the paperback houses got wind of this bonanza, from publishers like Ace and Dell. This was the price, perhaps, of the tumbling down of those ghetto walls; it meant, for example, that new U.K. science fiction, as before the war, would be reprinted at once in the United States, so that American readers got a reasonably early look at works by people like John Christopher, John Wyndham, and of course Arthur C. Clarke. However, this power shift also subjected SF thereafter to the marketing pressures of large-scale publishing, which eventually, by packaging for specialized submarkets, in effect reestablished the ghetto. Anything science fictional whose publisher scented best-seller potential had best be promoted as something else, indeed as *anything* else; whence the advertising copy or even the book review that lied through its teeth, stating that since this book is good, by definition it can't be science fiction.

Of equal importance with the entrance of general publishers into the science fiction field in the pivotal year 1950 was the founding of two new magazines, both of which sought to live down the pulp image and at the same time challenge John Campbell's leadership. One of them, *The Magazine of Fantasy & Science Fiction* (*F & SF*), under the cultivated and urbane editorship of Anthony Boucher, appeared in digest size with restrained cover art, discreet typography, a single column book-type page layout, no interior artwork, and no letter column. Boucher gave readers science fiction and fantasy with subtle characterization and a high literary polish, in the process quietly and unsensationally breaking old magazine taboos concerning (among other matters) religion, sex, and race. Although he bought stories from Golden Age figures—Heinlein, Sturgeon, Asimov—Boucher also showcased newer writers like Brian Aldiss, Margaret St. Clair, Philip José Farmer, and Richard Matheson.

Respectable folk who had been closet readers for years could now own up to this kind of SF. Back cover subscription ads for *F & SF* during the fifties carried testimonials from opera singer Gladys Swarthout, band leader Guy Lombardo, *New York Times* book review editor Orville Prescott, classical scholar Gilbert Highet—and Eva Gabor. Confessing "I have been a fan of science fiction all my life," the *Saturday Review*'s Basil Davenport went a long step further and edited a series of guest lectures given in 1957 at the University of Chicago by Robert Heinlein, Cyril Kornbluth, Alfred Bester, and Robert Bloch, titled *The Science Fiction Novel: Imagination and Social Criticism* [8-127]. "This book has given me the pleasure, all too rare since my college days, of being a book that I could argue with," said Davenport in his introduction, and from that initial venture grew all the later involvement of SF with the academic world,

The other new periodical, *Galaxy*, physically looked more like a traditional science fiction magazine than did *F & SF*. But its hard-driving editor, Horace Gold, remembered with fondness and fear by writers for having made them sometimes put story manuscripts through four or five drafts, was just as determined as Boucher to abolish what Gold called "retread private eye, western and Congo Sam stories masquerading as science fiction." Sociological and even psychiatric themes were his forte, and much of the social and political satire that was the great glory of 1950s SF, such as *Fahrenheit 451* [3-31] and *The Space Merchants* [3-147], first appeared in *Galaxy*'s pages or in those of its companion, *If*. In a sense it can be said that in *Galaxy* and *If* the irreverent spirit of the Futurians came at last into its own; indeed a former Futurian, Frederik Pohl, in due course succeeded Gold as editor.

The forties in American SF had emphatically been Campbell's decade; the fifties just as definitely were not. To be sure, *Astounding* continued to discover and publish important new writers, for example Frank Herbert and Poul Anderson. But its editor had lately taken to riding hobby horses:

dowsing, Dianetics (a horse from which he soon dismounted), engines that supposedly violated the conservation of energy and still worked, and especially "psi" powers—precognition, telepathy, psychokinesis, and the rest. He could have been forgiven his increasingly cantankerous, elitist, long-winded editorials had not a high proportion of stories in the magazine begun to sound dull. Some writers did figure out how to cater to Campbell's new preferences while still writing good science fiction, notably Mark Clifton [3-51, 52], and "hard" SF writers like Hal Clement continued to thrive and grow, but if the war years had been golden for *Astounding*, the fifties were at best its Silver Age.

The magazines, including some new ones like *Fantastic Universe* and *Worlds of Tomorrow*, continued to supply the burgeoning paperback field with reprintable material, but the demand was beginning to exceed the supply. It would increasingly become necessary for writers to submit stories directly to the paperback houses for first publication (this also, regrettably, tipped the balance over from short stories to novels). Commercially speaking, a paperback seemed at first to have one advantage over a magazine; with no terminal date on its cover it could be left on the sales rack longer. But in the late seventies the chain bookstores would come into the picture, with relentless absentee owners who gave orders that stock be turned over faster than the magazines ever had—as if books left on a shelf, like groceries, would spoil.

Under either regimen, fast or slow, the paperbacks lacked one vital spark that even the sleaziest of magazines had always possessed: reader input. Writers began to complain that now when they sold a story they no longer knew what anyone out there thought of it. Science fiction was suffering like any rapidly growing aggregate of people: from a small town where everybody knew everybody else, with both the reassurances and the stiflings that go with that kind of life, it was turning into a metropolis, increasingly hard to think of as a community at all.

The Hugo Awards, named after SF founding father Hugo Gernsback and comparable to the Oscars and Edgars and Grammys and Emmys in other genres and media, were among other things an effort to restore that vanishing reader input; if you couldn't write a letter about a favorite story, you could at least cast a vote. Perhaps, one could argue, a quantitative method of rewarding writers was fairer than the capriciousness of letter columns, where the criteria for inclusion had always been the editor's. (Campbell pioneered in this direction, as in so much else, by tabulating his readers' choices in a department called the "Analytical Laboratory," for comparative ranking of the stories in a given issue of *Astounding*.) However, there was a catch: to vote for the Hugo nominees you had to be a contributing member of that year's World Science Fiction Convention, which made convention-going a primary electoral qualification—a dubious proposition, some might say. And Worldcon participation has year by year grown more expensive. Already by the fifties the SF scene was a long way from the Denver Worldcon in 1941, which at least one determined fan reached the hard and dangerous way, "riding the rods" under a freight train!

At least, such long-suffering fans could console themselves, their beloved genre was at last being "noticed" outside the erstwhile ghetto. Futurian veteran Damon Knight viewed this as a mixed blessing: science fictionists, flattered by the notice, were neglecting the issue of quality, in "our delight when the slicks began publishing (bad) science fiction stories, the hardcover houses (worse) science fiction books, and Hollywood began to produce (incredibly awful) science fiction movies." Not all the SF films produced prior to *2001* in 1968 were incredibly awful; they included *On the Beach*, for example, which many viewers found an overpowering emotional experience, and *Forbidden Planet*, which retains a kind of gawky charm. But the great bulk of them were either Creature Features—*Them*, *The Blob*, *The Thing* (an incredible distortion of John Campbell's fine "Who Goes There?")—or else disaster epics, like *When Worlds Collide*, with its absurd spacecraft takeoff; or sometimes both at once, like the English-lipsynched, Tokyo-stomping adventures of Godzilla and his pals. They were not much of an advance, if any, upon—to quote Knight again—the SF movies of the 1930s "about the drafty old castle, the eerie flasks and retorts, the crashing sparks, the deformed servant, and above all the shifty-eyed scientist."[10]

And this situation was a great pity, reinforcing as it did the general reader's or viewer's impression that this was all there was to SF. Unnoticed by Hollywood, magazine and paperback science fiction in the fifties racked up a very creditable achievement. It was both literate and socially critical; more, it was courageous: during "that miserable decade we look back on as the era of McCarthyism," Frederik Pohl recalled in 1968, "about the only people speaking up openly to tell it like it was were Edward R. Murrow, one or two Senators, and just about every science fiction writer alive." Of course its lingering pulp aura may have given it protective coloration; it was, after all, only science fiction.[11]

If it had been no more than political preachment, however, the science fiction of the 1950s would not now be remembered and respected to the extent that it is. It had developed a richness and subtlety of characterization all but unknown in the Golden Age, and at its best it was ingenious and imaginative, within the assumptions of its times. On occasion, in stories by Sturgeon or Fritz Leiber or Philip K. Dick, it went far beyond those assumptions; some of Dick's early stories in particular surprise present-day readers encountering them for the first time that they could have been written so long ago.

It must be countered that maturation involves losses as well as gains. Freud said that the pleasure principle has to give place to the reality principle; are pleasure and reality, then, antithetical terms? "When sf writers began taking themselves seriously, they tended to abandon their imaginations," Brian Aldiss cautions; "the result was a descent into greyness, a loss of the original driving force, an espousal of literalism." Partisans of SF carried into the fifties the old defensive insistence that science fiction, far from being crazy, was good for you; Campbell and his writers in particular "liked to justify sf in terms of how accurately its predictions were fulfilled, or how well it served as propaganda for the space race, or how strongly it influenced American kids to become physicists when they grew up." Important though this influence may have been, the genre's school-teacherish urge to uplift and edify must be offset, Aldiss believes, by the irreverent spirit of *homo ludens*, who knows how to play—and to recapture what Golden Age survivors refer to as the "sense of wonder" in SF.[12]

But entropy moves onward; science fiction, however much committed to the future, also reflects sideways upon its own contemporary present; the SF of the 1950s, no matter how critical of that decade, was also a product of it, and therefore reminds the reader that these writings are now history as well as prophecy. Science fiction writer and professional anthropologist Chad Oliver, writing in 1971 some "Afterthoughts" for a collection of his stories [3-137], the first of which had been written when Harry Truman was president and the last when Dwight Eisenhower was still in office, reflected from across the gulf of the sixties that "in a very real sense, these are stories from another world." They therefore demanded from the reader the anthropologist's knack for empathizing with other cultures: "To the extent that they are successful, you will still be able to hear what they are trying to say—but you may have to listen at a different volume, with an unamplified ear."

The pivotal year 1963—the year of the Nuclear Test Ban Treaty, the civil rights march on Washington, the fall of the Diem family in Saigon, the assassination of John Kennedy—began a new moment in history, for science fiction as for everything else. In that smaller world of SF, the premier British science fiction magazine *New Worlds* under editor Edward John Carnell, as it incubated the work of a new generation of U.K. writers outside the imperial American orbit, was paving the way for a revolution in SF writing. In the following decade it would wash across the Atlantic as the New Wave, but that is a subject for another chapter.

Notes

1. Frederik Pohl, "Ragged Claws," in Brian W. Aldiss and Harry Harrison, eds., *Hell's Cartographers* [9-140].

2. The detailed history of all these magazines is found in the authoritative references edited by Tymn and Ashley [12-36, 46]. See also Carter, *The Creation of Tomorrow: Fifty Years of Magazine Science Fiction* [8-34].

3. Jerry K. Westerfield, "The Sky's No Limit," *Writer's Digest*, January 1940. Magazines for writers are a relatively neglected source for SF history; writers such as Henry Kuttner and Ross Rocklynne augmented their pulp income by sharing their trade secrets with would-be fellow writers, and John Campbell in *The Writer* (September 1968) unburdened himself on the subject of "Science Fiction We Can Buy."

4. Lew Cunningham, letter in "Brass Tacks," *Astounding*, June 1940. The theme of Golden Age SF as a closing of the interplanetary frontier after a more wide-open period of exploration is set forth in an article by Alexei and Cory Panshin, "The Domestication of the Future, 1936–1946," *Fantastic*, December 1972.

5. Leigh Brackett, "The Science-Fiction Field," *Writer's Digest*, July 1944; W. B. Hoskins, letter in "Brass Tacks," *Astounding*, April 1942.

6. Walter Hirsch, "The Image of the Scientist in Science-Fiction: A Content Analysis," *American Journal of Sociology*, 23 (March 1958): 506–12.

7. In fairness it must be conceded that science fictionists were not the only people capable of shrewd guesses, or at least close shots, about nuclear weapons development. In April 1945—three months before the Alamagordo weapons test—Ben Hecht and Alfred Hitchcock settled on a uranium-derived bomb as the "MacGuffin" (gimmick) for the forthcoming Hitchcock film *Notorious*; legend has it that movie producer David Selznick doubted the plausibility of such a weapon.

8. John W. Campbell, "The Editor's Page," *Astounding Science-Fiction*, November 1945. The lead time in magazine production then was months long; this editorial was Campbell's earliest voiced reaction to the actual bomb.

9. Algis Budrys, introduction to Lloyd Arthur Eshbach, *Over My Shoulder: Reflections on a Science Fiction Era* (Philadelphia: Oswald Train, 1983), p. 22. An exhaustive history of the dozens of specialty fantastic fiction publishers is provided by Chalker and Owings, *The Science-Fantasy Publishers* [7-3].

10. Damon Knight, *In Search of Wonder* [8-74], p. 277.

11. Frederik Pohl, remarks as a panelist at the 1968 annual meeting of the Modern Language Association—the first formal panel on science fiction sponsored by a mainstream academic professional national society, incidentally; Robert Silverberg and Isaac Asimov, as well as Pohl, participated.

12. Brian Aldiss, ed., *Galactic Empires* [3-201], v. 1, p. 59; v. 2, p. vii. To the perennial charge that SF of this playful kind can be dismissed as escapist, Aldiss quoted a devastating retort by J. R. R. Tolkien: "What class of men would you expect to be most preoccupied with, and most hostile to, the idea of escape?" "Jailers."

Bibliography

This chapter is slightly shorter than the corresponding section in the third edition of *Anatomy of Wonder*. Some of the cuts resulted from shifting the chapter's beginning from 1938 to 1940, others from combining into one annotation titles that had been spread over two or more, but most from a judgment that the earlier bibliography had grown unwieldy, including too many books that were merely representative or peripheral rather than the best, better, or most significant works of this period.

I have tried to produce a list the entire contents of which can, with a bit of application, be held in the reader's mind. I have also written these annotations with the hope that they can be read straight through; so that, even though they fall into conventional alphabetical order, they also con-stitute in effect a second essay on the SF of the period, parallel to that contained in my introductory essay. I am indebted in particular to Nicholas Ruddick of the University of Regina, Saskatchewan, for advice and recommendations concerning science fiction from the United Kingdom [see 8-122] and to other outside commentators who helped spank this list into shape. Errors of commission or omission that remain are strictly my own.

3-1.   Aldiss, Brian W(ilson). **Best Science Fiction Stories of Brian W. Aldiss.** Faber, 1962. U.S. title: *Who Can Replace a Man?*, Harcourt, 1966. Recommended ed.: Faber, 1971; 2nd rev. ed., 1988 (U.K.); 1990 (U.S., as *Man In His Time*).
Assembling these stories 16 stories (14 in the earlier editions, 22 in the lat-est), Aldiss confessed, made him "realise how rapidly change moves," in

SF as in everything else. The stories are arranged in a rough chronological order which, the author comments, "seems to represent also an order of complexity." From the straightforwardly told "Who Can Replace a Man?" (included also in *The Canopy of Time* [3-2]) to the subtlety of "A Kind of Artistry," or from the hero's anguish at his time-trapped predicament in "Not For an Age," 1957, to the startlingly nonchalant outlook of a chap in a somewhat comparable situation in "Man in His Time," 1966, the reader will perceive the evolutionary process to which Aldiss referred; and yet, a reader of a generation still further down the road from this book's publication will find almost all of these stories fresh and contemporary-sounding, regardless of when they were written.

3-2. Aldiss, Brian W(ilson). **The Canopy of Time.** Faber, 1959. U.S. title: *Galaxies Like Grains of Sand*, Signet, 1960 (substantially rewritten).

Eight early stories, published primarily in British SF magazines in 1957 and 1958, with connecting narrative that weaves them into a history of the galaxy's future. These unifying passages set in italic type, have the sweep and cosmic poise of Olaf Stapledon, for whom Aldiss acknowledged admiration in his history of SF, *Trillion-Year Spree* [8-5]. The stories also have touches of early (and later) Arthur C. Clarke, while retaining a distinctive voice of Aldiss's own that foreshadows in mood and philosophic outlook the British New Wave of a later decade; they would certainly have struck U. S. readers in 1959 as very different from what writers carrying over from the previous SF generation (for example, Pohl, Asimov, Heinlein) were doing at that same time.

*3-3. Aldiss, Brian W(ilson). **Hothouse.** Faber, 1962. U.S. title: *The Long Afternoon of Earth*, Signet, 1962. Recommended ed.: Gregg; ed. by Joseph Milicia, 1976.

In the very far future, with the Earth tidelocked toward a hotter sun on the verge of going nova, ferocious, mutually warring vegetative life fills every ecological niche except beyond the "timberline" at the edge of the planet's perpetual nightside. Diminutive human beings, their once-high civilization not even a memory, pick their way through this ultimate Darwinian nightmare—yet the story is an Odyssey, not a victim's lament. Originating as five connected stories in *The Magazine of Fantasy & Science Fiction*, this was recognized at once a a major work, winning a Hugo for best short fiction of the year (1961). Unfortunately the first American edition (Signet, 1962) badly butchered the manuscript to fit available space, leading Aldiss to remark later that copyediting is a form of rape. HW, 1961

3-4.   Aldiss Brian W(ilson). **Non-Stop.** Faber, 1958. U.S. title: *Starship* (Criterion, 1959).

The title of the American edition unfortunately gives away the game. A tribe of primitive nomadic bowhunters ranges through a "jungle" that has corridors and doors; the jungle is actually a wild overgrowth from the hydroponic tanks of a derelict multigenerational spacecraft. The characters' search for the control room and, ultimately, the stars, is a subtle variant from the similar quest in Heinlein's *Orphans of the Sky* [3-88]. Several U.K. science fictionists have testified that this work was a formative influence in their earlier years. Compare Don Wilcox, "The Voyage That Lasted 600 Years," *Amazing Stories*, October 1940; contrast Frank M. Robinson, *The Dark Beyond the Stars* (Tor, 1991) [4-364]. [For other works of this author see chapter 4.]

3-5.   Anderson, Poul. **Brain Wave.** Ballantine, 1954.

This was Anderson's first major novel, after seven years of well-recieved short stories and novelettes. All intelligence on Earth, animal and human, makes a sudden leap forward as the planet moves out of a belt of radiation, which has hitherto held them all back. As retarded persons develop what had formerly been average intellect while formerly average people become supergeniuses, individuals find that relatively they remain mentally, with respect to one another, where they had been before. This gives Anderson the chance for some quiet observation of the relationship and difference between intellect and character. Compare Keyes, *Flowers for Algernon* [3-98]; contrast Clarke, *Childhood's End* [3-44].

*3-6.   Anderson, Poul. **The Enemy Stars.** Lippincott, 1959. Recommended ed.: Berkley, 1979.

Serialized in *Astounding* in 1958 as "We Have Fed Our Sea" (a title derived from a Kipling poem that is quoted effectively at the story's conclusion), this is Anderson at his tragic-heroic best, blending meticulous astrophysics with brooding romanticism. Four astronauts—Japanese, Russian, Australasian, North European (with the fascinating projected futures of their respective cultures deftly sketched in)—are, in the *Star Trek* sense, "beamed aboard" an ion-drive spacecraft in orbit around a dark star, whose unexpectedly powerful magnetic field cripples both the ship and their means of escape from it. Working against a dwindling stock of rations to make repairs, each crew member in the face of death must come to terms with the universe and with personal fate. The 1979 revision updated the science. Compare Budrys, *Rogue Moon* [3-38]. HN, 1959

3-7.   Anderson, Poul. **Flandry of Terra.** Chilton, 1965.

Three novellas, published in magazine form in 1958, 1959, and 1960, detailing adventures of Captain Sir Dominic Flandry of the Terran Space Navy. Anderson in his Flandry and van Rijn stories assumes that interstellar history will recapitulate Earth history: a new Renaissance and Age of Discovery, a subsequent period of capitalist consolidation, followed by an Earth-centered, Roman-modeled galactic empire doomed to plunge at last into the Long Night. The Dominic Flandry stories are set late enough in this future history that their protagonist knows, under his flip sophistication, that his heroic capers are ultimately futile and that the course of history is in essence tragic. The stories are played out on typically well crafted Andersonian planets with convincingly worked out planetary cultures. Compare his *War of the Wing-Men* [3-9]; contrast Asimov, *The Foundation Trilogy* [3-12].

3-8.   Anderson, Poul. **Time Patrol.** Tor, 1991.

If Jack Williamson's *The Legion of Time* [2-145] represents the "liberal" version of alternate-history SF and Fritz Leiber's *Change War* [3-110] a "radical" approach, Anderson's take can be considered "conservative": better the history we know than another that might have been worse. The role of Williamson's timefighters is to change history for the better; of Leiber's to change it, period; of Anderson's, to maintain the status quo ante. Here, together with a new novel "Star of the Sea," are the alternate pasts that originally appeared in *F & SF* during the 1950s: "Delenda Est" (Carthage might have beaten Rome), "Brave to Be a King" (the Persia of Cyrus might have prevailed over the Alexandrian Greeks), "The Only Game in Town" (Kublai Khan's minions might have discovered America) and "Gibraltar Falls," set in Ice Age Cro-Magnon Europe where Time Patrolmen repair for R&R. The author's impressive knowledge of actual history makes his proposed alternate pasts all the more intriguing. Compare Squire, *If, or History Rewritten* [2-118]; Moore, *Bring the Jubilee* [3-131].

3-9.   Anderson, Poul. **War of the Wing-Men.** Ace, 1958. Recommended ed.: Gregg, 1976.

Serialized in *Astounding* in 1958 as "The Man Who Counts," this was the first full-length novel about fat, Falstaffian interstellar merchant-trader Nicholas van Rijn, who appears at an earlier, more youthful and upbeat phase of Anderson's future Technic History than *Flandry of Terra* [3-7]. This shrewd, sly operator, rather than the story's nominal hero-type viewpoint character, is "the man who counts" because by stealth and guile he manipulates others into doing what must be done. The story's Earthborn castaways on one of Anderson's carefully wrought planets must deal with two convincingly described native avian cultures, one land-based, the other seagoing—the "wing-men" of the title. The Gregg edition restores unauthorized changes in the first edition and includes a detailed chronology by Sandra Miesel of the whole future history, from Near Future to Long Night, with individual stories logged in. This chapter in that history is a joyous romp and would make a terrific movie. [For other works of this author see chapters 4 and 5.]

*3-10.   Asimov, Isaac. **The Caves of Steel.** Doubleday, 1954.

The setting is a far-future New York City, which has become one immense building, to which its human inhabitants are fully adapted—but who suffer paralyzing fear at the thought of going outdoors. The plot is a murder mystery: how could one of these deeply inhibited humans have killed a "Spacer," that is, an off-planet visitor, since this would necessitate crossing considerable open ground to get to the Spacers' self-segregated compound? The case is cracked by NYPD detective Lije Baley and his robot partner Daneel Olivaw. Asimov's Three Laws of Robotics, first worked out in the stories comprising *I, Robot* [3-13], figure prominently. A richly characterized, thoughtfully told story; justifiably a favorite among Asimov's readers. A sequel, *The Naked Sun* (Doubleday, 1957), takes Lije and Daneel to a planet where the social neurosis is exactly the reverse of Earth's: people live in robot-served isolation, unable to bear being in one another's physical presence. Further sequels, *The Robots of Dawn* [4-21] and *Robots and Empire* [4-21], tie these stories to Asimov's *Foundation* universe [3-12].

3-11.   Asimov, Isaac. **The Early Asimov; or, Eleven Years of Trying.** Doubleday, 1972.

Writers do not spring full-armored from the brain of Jove; they creep, they toddle and fall, and eventually they succeed in running. Asimov documented this process both with the stories themselves, drawn from Golden Age pulps (most notably *Astounding*), and with narrative commentary between the stories. Valuable descriptions of the New York science fiction scene in which he learned the trade, both from the formidable editor John Campbell of *Astounding* and from his fellow fans-turning-professional, such as Frederik Pohl. The stories have "workshop" utility; Asimov's accounts of how they were devised and composed can be instructive to would-be SF writers even today.

*3-12. Asimov, Isaac. **The Foundation Trilogy.** Doubleday, 1963.
Asimov described the gradual fall of a galactic empire, and the effort of psychohistorian Hari Seldon to shorten the ensuing Dark Ages by setting up a hidden Foundation in a remote corner of the galaxy, in stories published in *Astounding* in the early 1940s and collected as *Foundation* (Gnome, 1951). Other, longer *Astounding* stories, describing an attempt at reconquest of the Foundation by the last competent imperial general Bel Riose (like Belisarius, who similarly attempted to reconquer the Roman West for East Roman Emperor Justinian, and an initially more successful capture of the Foundation by "the Mule," a mutant not subject as an individual to the statistical "laws of psychohistory," were collected as *Foundation and Empire* (Gnome, 1952). Finally, two *Astounding* serials in the late forties described the Mule's search for a Second Foundation, established by Seldon as a backup in case something went wrong for the First; these became *Second Foundation* (Gnome, 1953). Asimov then laid this theme aside for thirty years, until popular demand and his publisher's prodding led him to compose *Foundation's Edge* [4-19], *Foundation and Earth* [4-19], and a "prequel," *Prelude to Foundation* [4-19], describing how Hari Seldon discovered the laws of psychohistory in the first place. At the time of his death in 1992 Asimov had completed four further adventures of Hari Seldon, which were collected as *Forward the Foundation* [4-19]. Special Hugo Award for all time best series, 1966.

*3-13. Asimov, Isaac. **I, Robot.** Gnome, 1950.
Nine stories from early-forties *Astounding*, which illustrate Asimov's (and, perhaps, John W. Campbell's) "three laws of robotics." With the memorable exception of Eando Binder's "I, Robot" (*Amazing*, 1939), this was the first major breakaway from the robots-as-menace cliché; contrast Shelley, *Frankenstein* [1-84]. Čapek, *R.U.R.* [2-16], and Miles J. Breuer, "Paradise and Iron" (1930). Asimov broke with another genre cliché in this series by introducing a high-powered scientific thinker who was not male, Dr. Susan Calvin. Harlan Ellison wrote a film script from these early robot stories of Asimov, structurally modeled on *Citizen Kane*, published serially in *Isaac Asimov's Science Fiction Magazine*, 1985; Ellison's adaptation of the story "Liar!" is especially powerful. Asimov continued to write robot stories throughout his life; many are collected in *The Rest of the Robots* (Doubleday, 1964).

3-14. Asimov, Isaac. **Nightfall, and Other Stories.** Doubleday, 1969.
Twenty stories, all from the 1950s and 1960s except the title story. Piqued at having "Nightfall" referred to a his "best" story a quarter-century after

its initial publication in *Astounding*, said Asimov in his introduction, he decided to publish it with a succession of other stories, from 1950 onward, each with a sprightly Asimov headnote, and let readers decide whether "Nightfall" really *was* his best. A fairer test for the present-day reader might be the author's earlier collection *Nine Tomorrows* (Doubleday, 1959), which did not include "Nightfall" but did contain such outstanding, frequently anthologized pieces as "The Dying Night," "The Last Question," and "The Ugly Little Boy."

3-15.   Asimov, Isaac. **Pebble in the Sky.** Doubleday, 1950.

Asimov's first published novel—which *Astounding* and *Startling Stories* had both rejected! An old man from the present is projected into a far future in which Earth is a pariah planet confronting a galactic empire. He also finds himself in a culture that euthanizes old people who can't do useful work, and what kind of work can someone with a mere 20th-century education perform in the far future? Loosely connected with the Foundation series [3-12], but the true sociohistorical metaphor in the story is that of ancient Judaea facing the might of Rome. A sentimental favorite among Asimov's fans, but significant also as a transitional step between the relatively miserly world of Golden Age pulps and the relatively lucrative world of mainstream book publication; in Asimov's case, for his multifarious nonfiction work as well as his fiction. [For other works of this author see chapters 4 and 5.]

*3-16.   Ballard, J(ames) G(raham). **The Drowned World.** Berkley, 1962.

Climatic change reverts Earth's ecosystem to early Triassic; an expedition from what remains of the British government in northern Greenland explores submerged London. The viewpoint character, haunted by dreams of an earlier Earth, battles the leader of looters who land in London, but eventually heads southward into even hotter and wetter realms, "a second Adam searching for the forgotten paradises of the reborn Sun." The theme of capricious natural catastrophe rather than human-caused ecological disaster links this story with *The Wind From Nowhere* (Berkley, 1962), also set in London, in which a world-girdling hurricane, despite all efforts by the military and by a mad, Ahab-like entrepreneur, literally blows everything away; and then for no accountable reason simply stops blowing. Mood of both stories anticipates New Wave SF, of which Ballard was a primary founder and maker. Compare Bowen, *After the Rain* [3-27]; contrast Serviss, *The Second Deluge* [1-83]. [For other works of this author see chapter 4.]

*3-17.   Bester, Alfred. **The Demolished Man.** Shasta, 1953.

A Freudian-tinged murder mystery given a science fictional spin: how does one premeditate a murder, knowing that police detectives are all telepaths, and expect to get away with it? A convincing portrait of how a society of mutual mind readers might actually function. Tricks of typography on the page, showing for example the interweaving of thought-conversations at a telepaths' cocktail party, further the impact of this first novel by Bester. Written in close consultation with *Galaxy* editor Horace Gold—as much a midwife of ideas, in a different way, as John Campbell—this story richly earned its Hugo for Best Novel, in the first year that prize was awarded. Compare Silverberg, *Dying Inside* [4-409]. HW, 1952

*3-18.   Bester, Alfred. **The Great Short Fiction of Alfred Bester.** Berkley, 1976. 2 vols., titled *The Light Fantastic* and *Star Light, Star Bright.*

Sixteen stories from 1941 to 1974 in this author's distinctive style. The earliest is his somber "Adam and No Eve." Significant headnotes to each story describe the circumstances and emotions surrounding its composition, although as a good Freudian Bester warns against drawing causal inferences; at the time of writing, your rational composing mind doesn't know what your unconscious is doing. Time travel especially engaged Bester, as in "Hobson's Choice," "Of Time and Third Avenue," and "The Men Who Murdered Mohammed." But here also are "Time Is the Traitor" (1953)—*not* time travel, despite the title, but a wildly neurotic love story; "Fondly Fahrenheit" (1954; SFHF); and "They Don't Make Life Like They Used To" (1963), which in tone and temper came close to the verge of SF's modern period. Bester concluded the collection with a wry, lively, informative essay, "My Affair With Science Fiction."

3-19.   Bester, Alfred. **Tiger! Tiger!** Sidgwick, 1956. U.S. title: *The Stars My Destination*, Signet, 1958.

Although the magazine serial version (in *Galaxy*) and the U.S. edition were both titled *The Stars My Destination*, the U.K. title, with its allusion to Blake, is far more apt. The character "burning bright/In the forest of the night" is Gully Foyle, the protagonist of an escape-from-prison story Bester said he modeled on *The Count of Monte Cristo.* But this story veers in a different direction; whereas the Count's dominant motive after his prison break is to wreak vengeance on the men who framed him, Foyle's is to undercut the entire rapacious class system that brutalized him, by bringing to all humankind the power to teleport—"jaunt," in the story's jargon—anywhere in the universe. The author, in the concluding essay to his short story collection [3-18] called this character an "antihero," contrasting with the cleancut "Doc" Smith type; however, Gully Foyle is perhaps more accurately seen as a *proletarian* hero in the tradition of Victor Hugo. Texts of the U.S. and U.K. editions differ.

3-20.   Blish, James. **The Best Science Fiction Stories of James Blish.** Faber, 1966. Recommended ed.: Faber, 1973.

Eight stories, from 1952 to 1970, with a brief but highly provocative introduction by Blish. Leads off with "Surface Tension" (1952, SFHF), which in reworked form became part of *The Seedling Stars* [3-23]. Stories include "Testament of Andros," which can be taken either as stages in the disintegration of a paranoid schizophrenic or as a succession of science fictional disasters (or both!); "A Work of Art," in which the mind of Richard Strauss is implanted upon another person two hundred years after Strauss's death; and "The Oath," about a post-nuclear-holocaust doctor who would rather be a poet. For the 1973 revision, Blish noted, a werewolf story was dropped and two stories from the next period in SF were added; one of them, "How Beautiful With Banners," simply because Blish loved it. Three of the stories had also appeared in an earlier U.S. collection, *Galactic Cluster* (Signet, 1959).

*3-21.   Blish, James. **A Case of Conscience.** Ballantine, 1958.

Except at the simplest level (the overthrow of the fundamentalist dictatorship in Heinlein's "If This Goes On—") religion in Golden Age SF was almost as taboo a subject as sex. (This is one more demonstration of difference between U.S. and U.K. sensibilities; compare the serious theological argument of C. S. Lewis [3-116] and, in an entirely different way, of Olaf Stapledon [2-119–121].) James Blish tackled the subject head-on. Lithia is a newly discovered planet whose intelligent inhabitants have developed a culture that is completely ethical, rational, and without religion. The very *absence* of visible moral evil in them makes them, in the eyes of Jesuit priest/biologist Ramón Ruiz-Sanchez, creations of the devil. He brings one of them in embryo back to Earth; it grows up traumatized (by Earth's own moral evil?), creates social chaos, flees back to Lithia followed by the priest, who exorcises the planet, which is immediately (coincidentally?) destroyed. A rich, ambiguous, deep-cutting probe into the most ultimate of concerns. HW, 1958

*3-22.   Blish, James. **Cities in Flight.** Avon, 1970. U.K. title: *A Clash of Cymbals.*

This is a tetralogy, of which the stories comprising *Earthman, Come Home* (Putnam, 1955) were written first. John Amalfi is mayor of a future New

York, which flies through interstellar space trading work for supplies; it, and other such itinerant cities, are "Okies." Two "prequels," *They Shall Have Stars* (Faber, 1956) and *A Life For The Stars* (Putnam, 1962) describe respectively the development of the cities' means of propulsion (under cover of a boondoggle construction job on a vividly but archaically described Jupiter) and the subsequent flight of the cities from Earth's dreary totalitarian government. Finally in *The Triumph of Time* (Avon, 1958; U.K. title *A Clash of Cymbals*), Amalfi's can-do New Yorkers are faced with the ultimate challenge of the collapse of the universe, and contrive to solve even *that.* An essay at the end of the four volumes by Richard Mullen, originally published in *Riverside Quarterly,* parallels the youth-maturity-senescence cycle Oswald Spengler charted for the comparative history of civilizations in *The Decline of the West* with a similar cycle for Blish's "Earthmanist" civilization. A major, if ponderous, work.

3-23.   Blish, James. **The Seedling Stars.** Gnome, 1957.
Four magazine-derived stories, blended into an account of "pantropy": the genetic alteration of humans in order to colonize radically non-Earthlike planets. This method of planetary settlement is presented as more viable than creating an artificial Earth environment under domes or terraforming the planet to make it resemble Earth. The opening section, in which Earth's military tries to destroy the initial pantropic experiment as Frankensteinian, and the closing chapter, in which, much later, the environmental devastation of Earth by its own inhabitants has rendered the planet uninhabitable *except* by panatropically Adapted Men, make it clear that Blish was writing not only about biological adaptation in the far future but about racism and social adaptation in the here and now. Blish's characteristic care and craft in revising his own work can be traced from the pulp-era "Sunken Universe," first published in *Super Science Stories* in 1942, through the more mature "Surface Tension" from *Galaxy* in 1952 (SFHF), to Book Three of this work; an example of an author committing a kind of pantropy upon his own literary offspring. [For other works of this author see chapter 5.]

3-24.   Boucher, Anthony (pseud. of William Anthony Parker White). **Far and Away: Eleven Fantasy and Science-Fiction Stories.** Ballantine, 1955.
Before Boucher became a distinguished editor he was an accomplished writer. These stories appeared between 1941 and 1954; he took the helm at *The Magazine of Fantasy & Science Fiction* late in 1949. Boucher was also a devotee of the mystery story, and one of these tales, "Elsewhen," combines the SF and detective genres: a time machine whose range is only 45

minute into the future enables a murderer to do his deed and still be "elsewhen" to establish an alibi. Another short-range time travel piece, fantasy rather than SF, is a humorous story from *Unknown*, "Snulbug." Boucher, political liberal and practicing Catholic, showed his humane religious concerns in "The Anomaly of the Empty Man" and, especially, in "Balaam." The last story in the collection, extrapolating from the politics of the 1950s but unhappily still relevant, is the devastating "The Other Inauguration."

3-25.   Boucher, Anthony (pseud. of William Anthony Parker White). **Rocket to the Morgue.** Duell, Sloan, 1942.
Written under the name "H. H. Holmes," which Boucher used for all his whodunits and some of his book reviews—a pseudonym of a pseudonym, as it were—this book is not science fiction but a murder mystery, with leading SF writers as principal suspects. Thus, "Don Stuart" (John W. Campbell) edits *Surprising Stories* (that is, *Astounding*); "D. Vance Wimpole" (L. Ron Hubbard) is one of *Surprising*'s more prominent authors; "Joe Henderson" (a blend of Edmond Hamilton and Jack Williamson) writes lurid space opera for *Captain Comet* (*Captain Future*); and "Austin Carter" (Robert Heinlein), rather than Henry Kuttner, is married to a writer clearly intended as C. L. Moore. The book is also unabashed missionary work for SF: the fictional writers' shop talk in the then actually existent Mañana Literary Society, to which the book was dedicated, converts the detective character, who had appeared in a previous Boucher whodunit, into a science fiction reader. Compare (and contrast!) Malzberg, *Herovit's World* (1973).

3-26.   Boulle, Pierre. **Planet of the Apes.** Vanguard, 1963. Trans. by Xan Fielding of *La Planète des Singes*.
A good example of the way the visual media can dilute a literary work, science fictional or otherwise. Boulle is a vivid writer and a fine ironist and the author of, among other things, *The Bridge Over the River Kwai*, which happily, thanks to director David Lean and a strong cast that included Alec Guinness and Sessue Hayakawa, was *not* diluted in translation from book to film. But the same can hardly be said of this work. Boulle made the Earth astronauts' visit to a far planet where apes are the dominant species and humans a despised underclass a parable of racial and other social failings on Earth, in the grand satiric tradition of *Gulliver's Travels* [1-89]. Little of the satire came through to the screen and less in each successive film sequel. The one superiority of the movie over the book is that last unforgettable image of the Statue of Liberty buried in the sand. Ignore the film's reputation; the book really is worth your while.

3-27. Bowen, John (Griffith). **After the Rain.** Faber, 1958.
The rains come, and a second deluge covers the Earth. An "ark" carries survivors after many days to an island, but the catastrophe has not been a purgation; they have brought all of humanity's aggression, irrationality, and pettiness through the flood intact. (This shouldn't have surprised them; the Biblical original made the same assumption: after Noah's flood is over God says, "The imagination of man's heart is evil from his youth," Gen. 8:21.) Even the narrator, nominally the hero, falls into a jealous rage over a believably innocent relationship between his wife, a ballet dancer, and the young male bodybuilder with whom she works out. Published also as a stage play (Faber, 1967), and the theatrical structure is evident in the scene-building for this powerful story. Compare Serviss, *The Second Deluge* [1-83]; and Ballard, *The Drowned World* [3-16].

3-28. Brackett, Leigh (Douglass). **The Best of Leigh Brackett.** Nelson Doubleday, 1977. Ed. by Edmond Hamilton.
Ten stories from 1944 to 1957 in Brackett's typical, colorful action-adventure style; with maps of Mars by Margaret Howes. Of biographical interest is "The Last Days of Shandakor," which, Hamilton suggested in his introduction, was Brackett's regretful leave-taking from the imagined Mars she had been building since she first read Edgar Rice Burroughs on a California beach at the age of eight, but which science (already, before *Viking*) had denied her the right to believe in. Other stories take place on a similarly defunct Venus; one on a Mercury with a "Twilight Belt" between darkside and sunside, not finally disproved until the planet's rotation period was nailed down in the 1970s; three on Earth, with imported aliens. Readers who find such an Earth milieu more plausible may prefer the story selection in Brackett's *The Halfling, and Other Stories* (Ace, 1973); its raw, tough pulp title story describes an Earthly carnival, all of whose caged animals and most of whose crew are extraterrestrials. Such readers are warned, however, that *The Halfling* also contains "The Lake of the Gone Forever," which splendidly lives up to the extravagance of its title.

3-29. Brackett, Leigh (Douglass). **Eric John Stark: Outlaw of Mars.** Ballantine, 1982.
Two novellas from the wondrously lurid pages of *Planet Stories* (1949 and 1951), set on the Mars Brackett shared with Ray Bradbury and Edgar Rice Burroughs: a dry, western U.S. landscape, an ancient but socially archaic civilization, and a breathable atmosphere. Eric John Stark, interplanetary wanderer and womanizer like C. L. Moore's Northwest Smith, but a tad more complex and with a saving note of tragedy, paradoxically would not

retire from the stage when the Mariner and Viking spacecraft definitively disproved the existence of that kind of Mars; Brackett simply moved him across the galaxy to the planet Skaith, where in the 1970s he would continue to roam. Meanwhile, the outdated Mars of these stories and of other such tales by Brackett, notably *The Sword of Rhiannon* (Ace, 1953), remains a compelling mythic landscape, created by a master storyteller.

*3-30. Brackett, Leigh (Douglass). **The Long Tomorrow.** Doubleday, 1955.
After nuclear war, the U.S. Constitution has been amended to limit the size of cities (making them less tempting targets from the air), and the predominant religiously conservative culture persecutes would-be scientific researchers as witches. Unlike its treatment in most SF, however, the small-town society—basically composed of Amish folk, who might indeed be among the likeliest to survive a nuclear war—is richly and even sympathetically described, so that the viewpoint character's decision to cut off his home ties and exile himself to the citadel where scientists are redeveloping atomic energy is presented as a real personal struggle, with which any young person who has ever had to grow away from a nurturing but confining community can empathize. Very different, in its matter-of-fact realism, from Brackett's Mars and Venus stories! Compare Wyndham, *Re-Birth* [3-200]; contrast Miller, *A Canticle for Leibowitz* [3-125].

3-31. Bradbury, Ray (Douglas). **Fahrenheit 451.** Ballantine, 1953.
Expanded from a novella "The Fireman" (*Galaxy*, February 1951; SFHF). Firemen no longer put out fires; they start them, for the purpose of burning books. The title refers to the temperature at which paper will catch fire. The hero, a fireman but a closet reader, eventually joins an underground of itinerants who have committed the literary classics to memory and recite them orally. The much admired film made from the novel, by making the firemen into brutal, black-uniformed Nazi types, missed a point made by Bradbury early on: that hostility to books and ideas was generated by ordinary people, not simply imposed upon them by government. Frequently reprinted since its original publication and often used in the classroom, although I consider the original novella from the magazine tighter, more vivid, less diffuse—in short a better literary work than the full-length book.

*3-32. Bradbury, Ray (Douglas). **The Martian Chronicles.** Doubleday, 1950. U.K. title: *The Silver Locusts* (Hart-Davis, 1951).
Even after forty years there is Golden Age magic in *The Martian Chronicles*. What Bradbury did in effect was transplant his boyhood "Green Town,

Illinois" to Mars, and there work out the *two* planets' tragic but ultimately redemptive destiny. The stories worked together into this book had been previously published in the 1940s; some in mainstream magazines, most in SF pulps, notably *Planet Stories*. Several of the chapters have been reprinted in *The Stories of Ray Bradbury* [3-33], but not all; one notable omission, ". . . And the Moon Be Still as Bright," originally in *Thrilling Wonder Stories* (June, 1948), contains the key to Bradbury's entire argument. Conversely, expanded versions of *The Martian Chronicles* published in 1963 (Time, Inc.) and 1977 (Doubleday), added other Mars stories that had not been included in this initial edition, and such stories *do* appear in the *Stories*. In 1980 *The Martian Chronicles* was made into an episodic, uneven, but at times highly effective TV miniseries, starring Rock Hudson as the spaceship captain. By any measure this work is a major landmark, both as SF and as literature.

*3-33.   Bradbury, Ray (Douglas). **The Stories of Ray Bradbury.** Knopf, 1980.
Until somebody undertakes a "complete works of," this is likely to remain the definitive Bradbury collection. One hundred stories, drawn from his previous collections: *The Martian Chronicles, The Illustrated Man, The Golden Apples of the Sun, A Medicine for Melancholy, The October Country* (itself derived from Bradbury's earliest collection, *Dark Carnival*, with the horror in some of those first stories considerably softened), and even a chapter from the nongenre *Dandelion Wine*. A 1969 anthology from which some stories were taken, *I Sing the Body Electric*, should be classed in the modern period covered by our Chapter 4; but here, from pre-1963, are most of the Bradbury favorites: "The Veldt," "Frost and Fire," "The Fog Horn," "The Pedestrian," "A Sound of Thunder," "The Million-Year Picnic," and many more. The magazine credits underlying the anthologies remind us of Bradbury's early breakout from the pulp ghetto, *Weird Tales, Planet Stories, Dime Mystery, Thrilling Wonder,* and *Super Science Stories* jostle *Harper's, Mademoiselle,* the *Saturday Evening Post, McCalls's,* and *Playboy*. Bradbury's introduction leads off with a 1953 fan letter from 89-year-old Bernard Berenson—not bad, for a young man who in 1944, he tells us, had sold forty stories for a grand total of $800!

3-34.   Brown, Fredric. **Space on My Hands.** Shasta, 1951.
Nine stories from 1941, drawn from magazines, with an introduction by Brown on the craft of science fiction writing. "The Star Mouse" is the delightful saga of a mouse fired into space aboard a rocket and found by aliens who raise his intelligence; he comes back to Earth speaking English with a heavy German accent, the speech of the professor who built the

rocket. At the opposite pole is the quiet horror of "Come and Go Mad," about an undercover investigator who infiltrates a mental hospital and is entrapped there. Humor, however, is the dominant note, as in "Nothing Sirius" and "Pi in the Sky." Brown was a thoroughly professional writer who could work within the genre and sometimes transcend it. Some readers may prefer the shorter shaggy-dog vignettes in Brown's *Angels and Spaceships* (Dutton, 1954; Bantam, retitled and abridged *Star Shine*, 1956). A later collection is Robert Bloch, ed., *The Best of Fredric Brown* (Nelson Doubleday, 1976).

3-35. Brown, Fredric. **What Mad Universe.** Dutton, 1949.
After a succession of well-crafted murder mysteries this was Brown's first SF novel. The protagonist, a science fiction magazine editor, is thrown into an alternate universe where space travel was accidentally discovered in 1903 and General Eisenhower is now—1949—leading a space war against invading Arcturans. In this universe every cliché in pulp science fiction exists as a reality: bug-eyed monsters, young women in see-through space suits, a superhero who is also a scientific genius—and who turns out to be a particularly vapid and obnoxious science fiction fan in "our" universe who had been writing nasty letters to the editor-hero's magazine. Brown wrote this story before the pulps were quite extinct, so the satire had a recognizable bite. Vis-à-vis science fiction in the visual media it still does. Compare Adams, *The Hitch Hiker's Guide to the Galaxy* [4-1]; contrast Harrison, *Bill, the Galactic Hero* (1965).

3-36. Brunner, John (Kilian Houston). **No Future in It.** Gollancz, 1962.
Eleven stories from 1955 to 1962; half from the United Kingdom's *New Worlds*, most of the remainder from U.S. SF magazines. Leads off with "No Future in It," a jaunty explanation of "demons" as time travelers who bring casual high tech (for example, transmutation of "base" metals into gold) to would-be magicians residing in more primitive eras. Brunner in this first collection ranged from hard SF, such as the murder mystery "Puzzle for Spacemen," to psychologically penetrating stories like "Elected Silence" and "Protect Me from My Friends." "The Windows of Heaven" is a fresh reprise upon Alfred Bester's "Adam and No Eve" [3-18]; "The Iron Jackass" is a lovely retelling of the American legend of John Henry. A promising start for a writer who would be a major force in the modern period. [For other works of this author see chapter 4.]

3-37. Budrys, Algis. **The Falling Torch.** Pyramid, 1959.
Earth, conquered by interstellar invaders, has a government-in-exile on Alpha Centaurus IV, which exists on sufferance of the local regime. The

son of the exiled president, who left Earth as an infant, returns to fight and finds a faction-ridden guerrilla movement, whose leader aspires to become Earth's dictator. He likes the Spartan militarism of the invaders rather better at first, but they have the typical character flaws of occupation troops; he escapes from them (in Philadelphia!) via a delivery van from Mrs. Lemmon's Teashop. Melodramatic, but nonetheless a *bildungsroman* of especially acute anguish, since it combines political conflict with the usual confusions of coming-of-age. The parallel with the "captive nations" situation during and after World War II is clear, and reflects the author's own ethnic and political heritage. The book also foreshadows Budrys's *Michaelmas* [4-77].

*3-38.   Budrys, Algis. **Rogue Moon.** Gold Medal, 1960.
This probes a major metaphysical problem with the widely used SF concept of matter transmission ("beaming aboard," in *Star Trek* parlance): If a person is "scanned," sent in dissociated form to wherever, and then reassembled, does not the scannee (from his/her own point of view) cease to exist? In this instance a Moon-based receiver merely duplicates the traveler, leaving the original on Earth, resulting eventually in a situation in which the transportee must die, so that there will not be two of him. Budrys cuts deeply into some age-old questions about the nature of the self, or soul. But this is no abstract philosophic discourse; the situation is handled with unsparing realism, and the psychic aberrations of the major characters led James Blish to exclaim when the book first came out that they were all certifiably insane. A major work, well meriting its Hugo nomination and (in novella form) Nebula Award. SFHF, 1974

3-39.   Budrys, Algis. **The Unexpected Dimension.** Ballantine, 1960.
For once, such a title is not the meaningless come-on with which paperback story collections in the 1950s typically were merchandised: it exactly describes what Budrys was doing in each of these seven stories: giving what in less skilled hands could have been a conventional plot situation an "unexpected dimension" of insight, irony, or invention. "Go and Behold Them" does this with the age-old theme of love stronger than death; "The End of Summer" with the frequent SF gambit of biological immortality as stagnation; "The Executioner" with the pompous idiocies of legal ritual; "The Burning World" with the ambiguities of political revolution. Except for "First to Serve," a wry satire on the military mind, the tone is uniformly somber. A thoughtful collection well worth reprinting.

3-40.   Budrys, Algis. **Who?** Pyramid, 1958.
They did not call them "cyborgs" when this story was written; Budrys

blended that theme with the competitive dehumanization inherent in the Cold War. A scientist of humble immigrant origins—a status in itself sufficient to make him suspect in some paranoid, subversiveness-haunted minds—is injured in a laboratory accident and falls into Soviet hands. The Russians equip him with a metal face and other mechanical parts. He returns to the United States and is forbidden to continue his research on the ground that nobody can prove who he really is. A strong indictment of the idiocies dignified at that time (and to a great extent still today) as "security," but a parable also of estrangement and alienation more generally. Compare Bernard Wolfe's *Limbo* [3-196]. [For other works of this author see chapter 4.]

*3-41.   Burgess, Anthony (pseud. of John Anthony Burgess Wilson). **A Clockwork Orange.** Heinemann, 1962.
In highly inventive future slang based on Russian loan-words, the story's hero tells how casual recreational gang violence, including murder, got him into prison and then into super-Pavlovian therapy; after treatment, even the thought of violence makes him sick. But so, as side effects, do sex and his former love for classical music; the point apparently being that it is better to do bad things as a free person than not to do them as the result of conditioning. Recognized by "mainstream" critics who probably wouldn't call it SF, and filmed effectively by Stanley Kubrick, this is a world as bleak and vicious as *Nineteen Eighty-Four*—and disturbingly closer, now, than Orwell's to our own. However, Kubrick's version was based on the first U.S. edition of the book, which omitted the crucial last chapter, in which (as Burgess pointed out in a new introduction, 1987) "my young thuggish protagonist grows up . . . and recognises that human energy is better expended on creation than destruction," which radically changes the meaning of *A Clockwork Orange* from the way it had been received in America. Compare Knight, *Hell's Pavement* [3-101]; contrast Skinner, *Walden Two* [3-166].

3-42.   Christopher, John (pseud. of Christopher Samuel Youd). **The Death of Grass.** Michael Joseph, 1956. U.S. title: *No Blade of Grass* (Simon & Schuster, 1957).
A rapidly mutating virus wipes out all of Earth's grasses, including grain crops. As mass starvation sweeps the world, a London architect leads a small family group toward a valley in the north of England where his brother has barricaded the family farm against looters and planted potatoes, which the virus spared. As they journey northward in the growing social chaos, the characters—while preserving a British stiff upper lip!—descend toward murderous savagery themselves. The story is told with

convincingly realistic detail. The explicit Cain and Abel parallel at the conclusion implies that the cycle of history will resume. Under its American title, *No Blade of Grass*, this novel was made into a film. For the exactly opposite situation, of too much rather than too little plant life, compare Ward Moore, *Greener Than You Think* (Sloane, 1947), and, more successfully, Wyndham, *Day of the Triffids* [3-199]. [For other works of this author see chapter 5.]

*3-43. Clarke, Arthur C(harles). **Against the Fall of Night.** Gnome, 1949.

Science fiction partisans are deeply divided between this early work by Clarke, which first appeared in the plebeian pages of *Startling Stories*, and the completely revised and expanded version published as *The City and the Stars* (Harcourt, 1956); raw first novel versus smoother, more complex finished work. Take your pick. Yes, the initial account of how lonely young Alvin finds his way from the self- satisfied stagnation of the far future city Diaspar to the pastoral community of telepaths known as Lys shows the rough carpentry of its pulp origin. But it also exemplifies in its very simplicity the archetypal quest of a youth for hidden treasure for the regeneration of humanity that is the theme of Joseph Campbell's essay in comparative mythologies, *The Hero With a Thousand Faces*. In the revision that theme is lost in the plot's van Vogtian complexity. It may be significant that when Clarke and Gregory Benford decided upon a sequel, *Beyond the Fall of Night* (Ace, 1990), they chose to base it upon this earlier version. Note also the profound influence, on both versions, of John W. Campbell's "Twilight" (1934; SFHF).

*3-44. Clarke, Arthur C(harles). **Childhood's End.** Ballantine, 1953.

Earth, on the verge of nuclear Mutual Assured Destruction, is saved by the intervention of benevolent aliens who have the form of traditional devils. A calm interregnum prepares the way for the last generation of children, who are telepaths. The adults left behind watch helplessly as the children, outgrowing them as no young generation ever has before, rise up and merge with the spiritual powers of the cosmos. The influence of Olaf Stapledon, who was as formative for Clarke's generation of SF writers, at least in the United Kingdom, as H. G. Wells, is patent. The pedestrian, at times downright static, pace of the novel has apparently not interfered with its immense popularity. Perhaps it has been received not as a story but rather as a scripture: Fallible humanity can't make it without transcendent help. If so, that says a lot about the audience for early nuclear age SF, which would have upset that era's for the most part quite hard-headed writers.

3-45.   Clarke, Arthur C(harles). **The Deep Range.** Harcourt, 1957.
The Malthusian food/population crunch has been averted by domesticating and herding whales as immense cattle. If you're grounded as a spaceman, as the hero of this story is, you become a submarine-riding cowboy, or rather whaleboy. After numerous vividly told adventures with a sea serpent, a giant squid, and the like, he rises to become Director of the Bureau of Whales, where he is confronted by a Buddhist leader who objects to whale killing on Eastern reverence-for-life grounds. In his own, more Western, way the Director decides that creatures as uncomfortably close to human intelligence as whales really ought not to end their days herded into slaughtering pens, a nicety that apparently did not occur to Herman Melville even after comparable brooding about whales' deep, dark intellect. This novel was later incorporated into a fragilely bound, omnibus volume, *From the Ocean, From the Stars* (Harcourt, 1961), which incorporated this work, *The City and the Stars* [3-43], and the story collection *The Other Side of the Sky* [3-46].

3-46.   Clarke, Arthur C(harles). **The Other Side of the Sky.** Harcourt, 1958.
These 24 tales, written between 1947 and 1957, include two series of 1,500-word ministories for the London *Evening Standard*, which represent Clarke's response to the challenge of writing good, terse science fiction for a mass readership at that time unfamiliar with the conventions of SF. Also included are "The Wall of Darkness" (1949), a fascinating variant on the boy's quest theme of *Against the Fall of Night* [3-43], with a very different outcome; "Refugee" (1955), which takes on a special poignance in light of the subsequent history of the British royal family; and such Clarke favorites as "The Star" (NW, 1955), "All the Time in the World," and "The Nine Billion Names of God" (SFHF). The final story in the collection, "The Songs of Distant Earth," would later be developed into one of Clarke's best novels. [For other works of this author see chapters 4 and 5.]

3-47.   Clement, Hal (pseud. of Harry Clement Stubbs). **Close to Critical.** Ballantine, 1964.
One of the subtlest of Clement's far-out planetary environments, narrated rather dryly but with flashes of understated humor. The title refers to the temperature at which water hovers between liquid and gaseous phases, at 800 atmospheres on the planet's surface. Every sunset great thirty-foot "raindrops" start to rain down on the natives, who kindle bonfires to turn the stuff back into steam. Fire is a gift from an Earth expedition orbiting the planet. Complications arise when an Earth scientist's 12-year-old

daughter and her 7-year-old alien companion inadvertently launch themselves to the planet's surface. Rescue operations by the Earth-trained natives are set in motion, but in the end it is the Earth child who figures out how to get aloft with her ET friend, meanwhile assuaging a quarrel between her own and the ET's anxious father and negotiating peace between warring native tribes. Such savvy and self-possession in a 12-year-old may stretch credibility, but remember, this is the future. The reader will need a smattering of physical chemistry to understand what is going on; better read Clement's *Iceworld* [3-49] before tackling this one.

3-48. Clement, Hal (pseud. of Harry Clement Stubbs). **Cycle of Fire.** Ballantine, 1957.

Earthman and alien fare across a planet whose conditions are at the absolute tolerable limits for each; upper limit for the one, lower for the other. The Earthman wants to rescue the alien, but the alien wishes to die at the ritually appropriate time with its people. A more daunting journey than the joyous Tweel/Jarvis pilgrimage across Mars in Stanley Weinbaum's "A Martian Odyssey" (1934; SFHF); unlike Weinbaum's characters, who find each other baffling although likable, these highly diverse trailmates feel and think their way with true Clementian logic toward an understanding of each other's radically different cultural and personal points of view. Compare Forword, *Rocheworld* (1990); Benford, *Tides of Light* [4-44].

3-49. Clement, Hal (pseud. of Harry Clement Stubbs). **Iceworld.** Gnome, 1953.

"Iceworld" is the Earth, from the viewpoint of a being that breathes gaseous sulfur and occasionally drinks molten copper chloride. Aliens based on the sunny side of Mercury (for comfort!) drop a guided torpedo containing a speaker and microphone to Earth's surface, where they trade with the "savages" worthless chunks of platinum and gold in exchange for the illegal drug "tofacco"—evidently an even more dangerous substance in transgalactic commerce than it is on its planet of origin. An alien undercover agent solves the problem of landing and surviving on Earth's frigid surface, where he is found by a human family vacationing in the Idaho panhandle; he inadvertently starts a forest fire but rescues the kids. Perhaps with a YA audience in mind Clement's explanatory science is not obtrusive, and this would make an excellent story with which to introduce an inquisitive, science-minded young person to the realm of "hard" SF.

*3-50. Clement, Hal (pseud. of Harry Clement Stubbs). **Mission of Gravity.** Doubleday, 1954.

Serialized in *Astounding* (April, May, June, July 1953), this novel in its initial form was accompanied by an article, "Whirligig World" (June, 1953; reprinted in some later editions), in which Clement described how, in consultation with Isaac Asimov and others, he concocted the planet on which the story takes place. That is an accurate description of the way writers like Clement work: get the science right and it will drive the plot. But this is also a First Contact story of a very high order, between explorers from Earth and a most unhuman sentient native species, to the benefit of both; rejecting the cliché one still sees in movie and TV science fiction that alienness equals evil. Clement stated on more than one occasion that *Mission of Gravity* was his personal philosophical bottom line, and the novel deserves a careful reading not only for its scientific ingenuity but for the working out of that philosophy. A major work. Sequel is *Star Light* (Ballantine, 1971). Compare Forword, *Dragon's Egg* [4-168]; Anderson, *The Enemy Stars* [3-6].

3-51. Clifton, Mark. **The Science Fiction of Mark Clifton.** Southern Illinois Univ. Press, 1980. Ed. by Barry N(orman) Malzberg and Martin H(arry) Greenberg.

Eleven stories, 1952 to 1962, mainly from *Astounding.* In the earliest, "What Have I Done?," alien visitors made over to pass as humans are thereby psychically destroyed; in the last, "Hang Head, Vandal!," Earth astronauts on Mars, after starting a nuclear experiment that will wipe out the indigenous Martians, leave behind on their abandoned Mars landing field a space suit, "the image of man stuffed with straw." Between the bleakness of these two—the author's first and last published stories— Clifton more optimistically functioned as one of John Campbell's psi-writers of the 1950s, apparently from a belief that latent paranormal powers exist and might emerge in a new generation, possibly even in science fiction fans: compare Clifton and Riley, *They'd Rather Be Right* [3-52]. Judith Merril, who corresponded extensively with Clifton, reproduced a very revealing four-page letter from him (June 19, 1952) in an appreciative memoir, and Barry Malzberg in an afterword urged that Clifton, beginning to be forgotten, deserved greater recognition.

3-52. Clifton, Mark, and Frank Riley. **They'd Rather Be Right.** Gnome, 1957.

Serialized in *Astounding* at the height of editor Campbell's emphasis (many would say, overemphasis) on "psi" powers, at a time when the potential of the computer was just beginning to be grasped, this novel combines those two concepts. "Bossy," the first supercomputer does not merely compute; it heals human beings of their imperfections (possibly an echo here of Dianetics). People thus treated not only are improved physically and mentally but develop their latent psi powers. Such talents, perceived as evil by the media, trigger a witch hunt; the only solution is to give "Bossy" to the world, rather than the presumable alternative of exploiting it as a private property of its inventor and its financial backer. A subtext of the necessity of freedom for scientific research, as against the Cold War fetish of "security," a favorite target of 1950s SF. Compare Bester, *The Stars My Destination* [3-19]; contrast Robinson, *The Power* [3-151]. HW

3-53. Clingerman, Mildred (McElroy). **A Cupful of Space.** Ballantine, 1961.
Sixteen stories, mainly from *Fantasy & Science Fiction*, a few from mainstream slick magazines, all laden with charm, a word not usually descriptive of science fiction. Some critics are put off by them, but in the 1950s they constituted one of the bridges away from the boom-boom pulp tradition. Aliens who mingle happily with kids trick-or-treating on Halloween, in "The Word," and other aliens who in "Minister Without Portfolio" decide to spare Earth after interviewing an elderly lady who, color blind, doesn't mind their being green, were a refreshing contrast to the shriek making aliens on former magazine covers. Time travel stories as deft as "Mr. Sakrison's Halt" and "The Day of the Green Velvet Cloak" certainly deserve to be remembered, and in "A Red Heart and Blue Roses" Clingerman showed she could also write quiet, nonsplattering, but quite hair-raising horror.

3-54. Condon, Richard (Thomas). **The Manchurian Candidate.** McGraw-Hill, 1959.
A Korean War Medal of Honor winner is "brainwashed" by his Communist captors into becoming an assassin, with a U.S. presidential election at stake; he is to be activated by post-hypnotic suggestion. The plan backfires as right-wing elements in America contrive that the assassination of a presidential nominee will throw the country into the hands of their own hawkish vice-presidential candidate, whose fiery speech immediately after his running mate's death will, they hope, precipitate World War III. Powerfully and convincingly told. The story became a film, with Angela Lansbury as a particularly chilling mover and shaker in the world of Washington power. After the assassination of President Kennedy in 1963, and the controversy it generated, the movie was for a long while withdrawn from distribution; one could say that this was a dreadful instance of

life imitating science fiction. Compare Knebel and Bailey, *Seven Days in May* [3-99].

3-55. Davidson, Avram. **The Best of Avram Davidson.** Doubleday, 1979. Ed. by Michael Kurland.

Eleven stories and a book chapter, from 1956 to 1971. Editor Kurland's short, sarcastic introduction reminds us that academicians seek to "classify" a magnificently unorganized writer like Davidson at their peril. "Now Let Us Sleep" and, less convincingly, "Help! I am Dr. Morris Goldpepper," are conventional SF; as for the others, if they are as good as "King's Evil" and "The Golem," does it really matter whether they are SF or fantasy? Peter Beagle, a student of Davidson's during that writer's brief (and quite ungovernable) sojourn as a college professor, testifies in a foreword to Davidson's incredible, casual erudition; Davidson himself wrote a modest afterword. Some readers may prefer the story selection in *Or All the Seas With Oysters* (Berkley, 1962), whose Hugo-winning title story this collection unaccountably omitted.

3-56. Davidson, Avram, and Ward Moore. **Joyleg.** Pyramid, 1962.

The recent political exploitation of fraud, real and imagined, in government entitlements is topped by this saga of a war veteran in the Tennessee foothills who has been drawing a government pension for as far back as records exist, and is, in fact, a veteran of the American Revolutionary War. A congressional fact-finding committee, media reporters, "revenuers," even the ubiquitous Soviets turn up in the vicinity of Issachar Joyleg's moonshine still, whose product dispenses rejuvenating powers. A trunkful of undeniably authentic Revolution-era papers gives Joyleg the upper hand. Social satire, allied to the best of the "Li'l Abner" comic strip tradition (before its creator went sour and conservative), aimed at targets that perennially deserve ridicule, and good clean fun.

3-57. de Camp, L(yon) Sprague. **The Continent Makers and Other Tales of the Viagens.** Twayne, 1953.

By the 22nd century Brazil has become the world's greatest power, so that when space exploration gets under way *Viagens Interplanetarias*, the agency that manages space transport among the planets of Sol, Tau Ceti, and Procyon, uses Portuguese as its *lingua franca*. Guided by something like *Star Trek*'s "Prime Directive," Viagens personnel seek to prevent the contamination of not-fully-developed planetary cultures by Earth technology. As several of these breezy action-adventures demonstrate, these efforts are not always successful. The stories are unusual in assuming the existence of trade and diplomacy over interstellar distances at less than light speed because de Camp, writing in the pre-"wormhole" era, did not believe in the possibility of faster-than-light travel. It is a self-restraint unusual in writer of interstellar stories, but for a mind as fertile as de Camp's the time-lag difficulty gave him a couple of interesting plot twists. Written with this author's characteristic rationality, erudition, and humor.

*3-58. de Camp, L(yon) Sprague. **Lest Darkness Fall.** Holt, 1941.
Originally a novel in *Unknown* (December 1939), this was one of the earliest stories from the pulps to be taken up by a mainstream hardcover publisher. (A specialty house, Prime Press, published it again in 1949.) Aware of a problem with the "Connecticut Yankee" theme, namely that not even a supergenius from the modern era could have singlehandedly introduced the full panoply of modern industrial technology into antiquity, de Camp gave his hero, stranded in A.D. 535 in the post-Roman interregnum, the one indispensable survival skill: he can understand spoken Vulgar Latin! Martin Padway then proceeds to introduce what the primitive technology of the period could actually have absorbed. In his headnote to the *Unknown* version, regrettably omitted from the book, de Camp in scholarly fashion listed his sources: Cassiodorus (who figures as a character in the story), Procopius of Caesarea, Gibbon, Bury; the author's meticulous care in this regard breathes life into what is by all odds de Camp's finest book.

3-59. de Camp, L(yon) Sprague. **The Wheels of If; and Other Science-Fiction.** Shasta, 1948.
The title story, originally from *Unknown* (1940), is one of the most engaging of alternate histories, drawn from the work of philosopher of history Arnold Toynbee. The Franks lose to the Saracens, and a Saxon king chooses the Irish rather than the Roman church calendar. Therefore, eventually, North America is settled (earlier than on our time track, so that Indians met Europeans on technologically equal terms) by members of Toynbee's Abortive Scandinavian and Abortive Far Western Christian Civilizations. The result in the 20th century is seen by a hustling New York lawyer who disconcertedly finds himself in the body of a bishop of the Celtic Christian Church. The story is told with de Camp's usual wit and scholarship. Also included are such early de Camp stories from *Astounding* as "The Merman" (1938), "The Gnarly Man" (1939), and "The Contraband Cow" (1942), which speculates on the consequences of a one-person-one-vote merger between the United States and the then British Commonwealth, a polity in which most of the votes would be cast by orthodox Hindus.

*3-60.   del Rey, Lester. **Early del Rey.** Doubleday, 1975.

A generous helping of 24 stories by a major Golden Age writer, with connecting autobiographical narrative that throws light on much in SF of the period, especially in wartime. The collection contains fantasies that first appeared in *Unknown*—for example, "Carillon of Skulls," "Though Poppies Grow"—and SF from *Astounding*, including the first story del Rey sold, "The Faithful," and such classics as "Though Dreamers Die." Publishing constrictions unfortunately prevented the reprinting of several fine stories from del Rey's first (now exceedingly rare) collection, . . . *And Some Were Human* (Prime, 1948), such as "The Day Is Done," "Helen O'Loy" (SFHF), and, on the fantasy side, "The Pipes of Pan." Del Rey's unabashed sentimentalism in this early work has been compared to a rose arbor built of two-by-fours, but it is an authentic and not unattractive element in the SF of the period. Del Rey had also a somewhat different take on editor John Campbell from that of Isaac Asimov; compare *The Early Asimov* [3-11]. The narrative ends with a story sold to *Galaxy*'s Horace Gold, which was a threshold of maturity for del Rey as for so many other writers.

3-61.   del Rey, Lester. **The Eleventh Commandment.** Regency, 1962. Recommended ed.: Ballantine, 1970.

In the chaos following nuclear war an American variant of the Catholic church has taken over society and decreed that people be fruitful and multiply without restraint. The result, as seen by an immigrant from Mars—a low-density, rational/scientific society—is a world of wretched overcrowding, pollution, and economic depression. Unlike other population explosion scenarios, however, this one concludes that unlimited proliferation has become *necessary*, in order to grow out of the radiation-induced mutation that has contaminated Earth's entire gene pool. Featured are a clear grasp (typical, for del Rey) of the Martian's profession, genetic cytology, and convincing characterization of what could easily have been totally unsympathetic clerical figures. Compare Miller, *A Canticle for Leibowitz* [3-125]; contrast Harrison, *Make Room! Make Room!* [4-200], Brunner, *Stand on Zanzibar* [4-74], or George R. R. Martin's Haviland Tuf stories.

3-62.   del Rey, Lester. **Nerves.** Ballantine, 1956.

Developed from a 1942 novella in *Astounding*. Published in the magazine at about the time the first experimental nuclear pile at the University of Chicago (in utmost wartime secrecy) went critical, this story deals with an accident in a nuclear power plant; not only the accident per se—in this case a runaway transuranic radioisotope—but also the resulting panic and coverup. A vivid melodrama in del Rey's characteristic style, and an example of self-educated chutzpah. He tells the story from the point of view of the plant's doctor, who at one point has to do some heart surgery, and makes it convincing although its technological specifics are now dated. *Nerves* is nevertheless prophetic of the real-life situation Frederick Pohl would later describe in his dramatic, but nonfictional, account *Chernobyl*. Compare Heinlein's "Blowups Happen" (1940), which offered a perhaps still valid solution to such problems: boost all nuclear reactors into satellite orbit. [For other works by this author see chapter 5.]

*3-63. Dick, Philip K(indred). **The Collected Stories of Philip K. Dick.** Underwood-Miller, 1987. 5 vols.
With introductions to its individual volumes by Roger Zelazny, Norman Spinrad, John Brunner, James Tiptree, Jr., and Thomas M. Disch, the appearance of this work was a major publishing event in SF. The 118 stories range from Dick's first published one, from the lurid pages of *Planet Stories* in 1952, to a few that appeared in this collection for the first time. Those in Vols. 1 through 4 were composed in SF's "early modern" period, ending in 1963; those in Vol. 5 in the "modern" period that began in 1964, but Philip Dick was so far ahead of most of his contemporaries in the 1950s that it is hardly appropriate thus to periodize him; and Damon Knight's premature judgment after the earliest of these stories had appeared [*In Search of Wonder*, 8-74], that Dick "writes the trivial, short, bland sort of story that . . . is instantly saleable and instantly forgettable" can now be set aside. The existence of this collection corrects the critical record; much as had happened earlier to Scott Fitzgerald, voluminous discussion of the novels had obscured the author's gifts as a craftsman of shorter tales. Endnotes to individual stories, written by Dick for earlier collections published in 1977 and 1980, are informative and, one must say, wise. To single out particular morsels from this rich banquet would be a disservice; however, the author did state in 1976 that the story "Human Is" (written 1953; in Vol. 2) "is my credo. May it be yours." A trade paper edition shifting two stories between volumes and retitling was published by Citadel Twilight, 1990–1992.

3-64. Dick, Philip K(indred). **Eye in the Sky.** Ace, 1957.
In the security-crazed, McCarthyite, cold-warring United States at the time the novel was written, a freak accident projects the psyches of eight people into the private reality of one of them, which becomes not only psychologically but even in a sense physically the entire universe. The worlds

imagined by a racist religious fanatic, a repressed Victorian lady, and an American Communist are compellingly described, and hold up remarkably well for a reader in the post-McCarthy, post–cold war era. The story also foreshadowed the ambiguity of "reality," which would be a major theme in much of Dick's later work. Compare Dick, *Ubik* [4-140]; Le Guin, *The Lathe of Heaven* [4-253]. A reprint of this work with a new introduction by Sandra Miesel and a bibliography was published by Gregg in 1979, alas, without the Ace edition's cover depicting the creepy, cosmic all-seeing Eye.

*3-65. Dick, Philip K(indred). **The Man in the High Castle.** Putnam, 1962.

An alternate history in which Germany and Japan won World War II and partitioned the United States, except for the Rocky Mountain States, which were left in a kind of political limbo. Faction-ridden Nazism oppressively rules the Eastern United States (and is exploring Mars); the West Coast, however, and its Japanese overlords are working out a modus vivendi, exchanging Oriental and American cultural values. In this cosmos an underground novel circulates, in which the Allies won the war; but, characteristic of Dick's layers-within-layers approach to "reality," it is not quite *our* history. Dick stated that at crucial turning points in the plot he, the author, used *I Ching* to decide what his character would do next, and it may be a testament to that kind of divination that at the end everything does come out in the wash, sort of. This is Dick's most important early book. Younger readers may need to have identified for them the various World War II Nazi leaders who on this alternate time track were still around in 1962. Compare Benford and Greenberg, *Hitler Victorious* [4-525]. HW, 1962

3-66. Dick, Philip K(indred). **Martian Time-Slip.** Ballantine, 1964.

A drab but humanly habitable Mars; a powerful president of a Plumber's Union (powerful because of water's scarcity on Mars); a shrewd old real estate speculator from Earth; farm families that grow crops using the rationed runoff from the canals; and Martians with a culture somewhat like that of an Australian aboriginal who wander through the desert; the ingredients could have been found in many a pulp opus of the 1940s. As usual with Phil Dick, however, things are not quite what they seem. The hero of the story, a schizophrenic in remission, develops a rapport with a boy diagnosed as autistic who lives in a different time frame from other humans, and draws the hero into frightening time displacements in which things happen before they happen. Milder than the truly dizzying dislocations that would take place in some of Dick's later work, these interruptions are resolved into what on the surface is a conventional plot conclusion. But this story, with its magazine appearance in *Worlds of Tomorrow* in 1963 as "All We Mars-Men," effectively illustrated by the veteran SF and fantasy artist Virgil Finlay, stood at the very edge of the divide between Golden and Atomic Age SF and the very different science fictions—in plural—which have since ensued.

3-67. Dick, Philip K(indred). **Solar Lottery.** Ace, 1955.
The initial version of this work appeared as an Ace Double paired with *The Big Jump* by Leigh Brackett, a work about as antithetical to Phil Dick's style and approach as it was possible to get. A reissue, sans Brackett, by Gregg in 1976 contained an appreciation by Thomas Disch. A world supposedly run at the top by the random chances of a great lottery is actually a congeries of rival industrial fiefs; would-be Quizmasters seek to rig the odds, and a former Quizmaster by the rules of the game has the right to assassinate his successor if the assassin can get past the incumbent's telepathic guards. The complex plot is driven by games theory, which at the time of writing was just coming into vogue; von Neumann and Morgenstern's *Theory of Games* had recently been published, as well as a popularization titled *Strategy in Poker, Business, and War.* Dick was concerned lest the mathematics of games theory dissolve all political claims of law, tradition, and morality, leaving only the rules of the game: "Minimax," he said in a statement included with the book, "is gaining on us all the time." Dick's first major work. Contrast van Vogt, *The World of Null-A* [3-183]. [For other works of this author see chapter 4.]

3-68. Farmer, Philip José. **The Green Odyssey.** Ballantine, 1957.
A picaresque novel about a shipwrecked spaceman on a barbarian planet. Refreshingly he does not play the traditional imperialist hero role—pukka sahib among the natives. Quite the reverse; he is enslaved. He finds himself part of a family, with a strong-minded wife and her five children— some sexist stereotyping here—until he learns of the capture of two other Earthmen and sets off to rescue them in one of the wind-driven wheeled ships that sail the planet's grassy plains. The "wind roller" lifeways and other aspects of the planet's culture are vividly realized, in a fast-paced adventure story laced with humor à la de Camp. Compare *The Continent Makers* [3-57] and Poul Anderson's *War of the Wing-Men* [3-9].

*3-69. Farmer, Philip José. **The Lovers.** Ballantine, 1961. Recommended ed.: Ballantine, 1979.
Expanded from a 1952 story in *Fantasy & Science Fiction* that provoked controversy at the time for its sexual content. Hero and his wife, on a

wretchedly overpopulated Earth ruled with fiendish ingenuity by an oppressive state church (the "Sturch") that considers all sex evil except for procreation, are—understandably!—unhappily married. Sent to help kill off an intelligent insect-like race on a planet slated for colonization, the man falls in love with a female of another alien species, which can mimic human appearance and behavior up to and including sex, but the consequences are tragic and horrible. Films like *Alien* and its sequels may have taken the edge off the raw shock this story would have given some readers a generation ago. Compare Gardner Dozois, *Strangers* [4-150]; contrast del Rey, *The Eleventh Commandment* [3-61].

3-70.   Farmer, Philip José. **Strange Relations.** Ballantine, 1960.

Farmer has been praised and reviled as the writer who brought sex into science fiction. More precisely, he wrote *alien* sex and, like an orthodox Freudian, defined *sex* to include sibling and parental relationships as well. This comes through most clearly, some would say blatantly, in the story "Mother," about an Earthly "mama's boy" who is trapped within the womb of an alien female monster. Diametrically opposite is the scenario of "Son," in which a similarly infantilized young man breaks away from the "womb"—that of a robot Russian submarine!—and escapes to the sea's surface in an act of male maturation. Other stories, boxing the sexual compass, are "Daughter," "Father," and "My Sister's Brother." A previous précis of this book pronounced its contents "daring stories for the SF of their time," although only two years later Naomi Mitchison, in *Memoirs of a Spacewoman* [3-127], casually trumped Farmer's ace on this subject of interspecies sex. [For other works by this author see chapter 4.]

*3-71.   Fast, Howard. **The Edge of Tomorrow.** Bantam, 1961.

Seven stories, all but one from *Fantasy & Science Fiction*, superbly told. They deal with such themes as the survival of superhuman children in a human, therefore savage, world ("The First Men"): the faking of three ultra-fashionable stores offering "Martian" goods for sale in order to prompt Earth's nations to unite against the alleged menace; in counterpoint, a grim tale of Martian xenophobia toward Earth, "Cato the Martian"; and a pioneering inquiry into the ethics of cryonically freezing terminally ill persons until a cure for their condition can be found, "The Cold, Cold Box." There are echoes of Stapledon's *Odd John* in "'The First Men" and of Bradbury in "Cato the Martian," but in this first SF collection a well-known mainstream writer (*Citizen Tom Paine, My Glorious Brothers, Spartacus*) speaks with a distinctive voice of his own.

3-72. Finney, Jack (pseud. of Walter Braden Finney). **The Body Snatchers.** Dell, 1955. Variant title: *Invasion of the Body Snatchers.*

It pretends to be your best friend, but it's really an invading seed pod from outer space. The entire population of a city is gradually replaced without anybody noticing. That insidious takeover could be a metaphor for either communism or McCarthyism; it has had ardent partisans on both sides. Other critics find it a metaphor for 20th-century human civilization, without benefit of invasion: We are becoming affectless, loveless pods. Finney's human protagonists eventually prevail, but in two film version (1956, 1979) the pods win. The seed for this story was planted (pun intended) by John W. Campbell in "Who Goes There?" (1937; SFHF); for a superb 1950s rendition, compare Philip K. Dick's terrifying, Freudian "The Father-Thing" (1954).

*3-73. Finney, Jack (pseud. of Walter Braden Finney). **The Third Level.** Rinehart, 1957. U.K. title: *The Clock of Time,* Eyre, 1958.

Most of the dozen stories in this collection deal with time travel; not on the cosmic scale of H. G. Wells and William Hope Hodgson, but small, domestic, with a dominant theme of escape. People from a threatening future escape to a safer present, but may be unraveling the whole future by doing so ("I'm Scared"); people from an unsafe, or simply dull and unpleasant, present escape into the past; others, as in "Of Missing Persons" and the title story, glimpse such an escape but do not achieve it. Humor, like "Quit Zoomin' Those Hands Through the Air," alternates with quiet drama, as in "There Is a Tide . . ." Finally, "Second Chance" is so persuasive in its sentimentalism for classic cars that a reader utterly uninterested in such antiques will nonetheless respond. Deceptively well written, with lower middle class urban characters rather like O. Henry's; themes anticipate Finney's outstanding novel in this subgenre, *Time And Again* [4-167]. Recommended. [For other works by this author see chapter 4.]

3-74. Frank, Pat (pseud. of Harry Hart Frank). **Alas, Babylon.** Lippincott, 1959.

This effective novel, by a writer usually classified as mainstream, may be the most widely read of all postholocaust stories. A small band of people survives a nuclear war in Manhattan's subway tunnels and emerges to start rebuilding civilization. The key to survival, depressing to those who imagine primitiveness as innocence, is discipline. Compare Christopher, *No Blade of Grass* [3-42]; and Stewart, *Earth Abides* [3-169]. Frank also wrote *Mr. Adam* (Lippincott, 1946), lighter in tone, about a nuclear accident that sterilizes all Earth males except one, who thereby becomes a national resource; the foibles of congresspeople and the like, faced with the task of deciding who gets him, seemed hilarious at the time of publication but sound sexist and a bit dated today.

*3-75. Galouye, Daniel. **Dark Universe.** Bantam, 1961. Recommended ed.: Gregg, 1976.
A vividly imagined, carefully worked out cultural and material setting: total darkness, in which human beings subsist on plants that are thermo- rather than photosynthetic, and find their way about by using "click-stones" or by heat-sensing. At the simplest level the story is a parable of the fallout shelter obsession of the 1950s, but the author was after bigger game. His characters, as Robert Thurston points out in his introduction to the Gregg reprint, are like the inmates of Plato's cave in *The Republic*, with their backs to the outside world and able to describe it only inferentially. Lacking firsthand knowledge of light, they deify it, giving rise to some pointed religious satire. The central character's eventual emergence into sunshine and open sky is one of the great epiphanies in science fiction. Compare Heinlein, "Universe" [3-88]; Blish, "Surface Tension" [3-20]; Asimov, "Nightfall" [3-14]. HN, 1962

3-76. Gloag, John (Edward). **99%.** Cassell, 1944.
Written (judging from internal evidence) in 1935/1936 at the time of the Italo-Ethiopian War but not published until late in World War II. Ninety-nine percent of our consciousness is ancestral, a Harley Street physician believes, and so as an experiment he hands to each of seven men a pill that will bring up an ancestral memory in dream form. The resulting adventures in earlier, violent centuries shake up the present-day 1 percent of the minds of these well-characterized conventional Londoners so that each makes a major personal life change, with ironic or ambiguous results. The one who regresses the furthest, to Paleolithic cave-painting times, relives in that remote ancestor's experience a Stapledonian vision of cosmic time (the book was dedicated to Stapledon) and renounces the modern world entirely. The message at least borders on the pessimistic; life is just one damn thing after another and with our 1 percent minds we just keep doing them over and over. Compare Jack London, *Before Adam* [1-58]. [For other works of this author see chapter 2.]

3-77. Gold, H(orace) L. **The Old Die Rich and Other Science Fiction Stories: with Working Notes and an Analysis of Each Story.** Crown, 1955.
Twelve stories from 1939 to 1953 by the distinguished editor of *Galaxy* magazine. In the earliest, "Hero," the modest leading character returns from the first expedition to Mars and receives corrosive media and com-

mercial hype; he flees back to Mars. The vivid title story, with characters Gold said he had known from his youth (except the villain!), is a well plotted time travel cum murder mystery. "The Man With English," "Man of Parts," and "No Charge for Alterations" typify the sardonic medical-meddling SF, which was a prominent theme in *Galaxy* under Gold's editorship. "Love in the Dark" looks freshly at the ancient succubus theme, with a conclusion it would be a pity to give away. A choice collection. Gold's working notes are not the usual after-the-fact headnotes; they could be profitably studied by anyone interested in how one writer proceeded with a story before doing the actual writing.

3-78. Golding, William. **The Brass Butterfly.** Faber, 1958.
A stage play, adapted from the novella "Envoy Extraordinary" in the anthology *Sometime, Never* (Ballantine, 1956). A Leonardo-like genius comes to the court of a Roman emperor, presumably Hadrian, with models of inventions (a steam warship, a pressure cooker, explosives) that could, right at that moment in the Age of the Antonines, unleash a full-scale industrial revolution. The emperor backs off, ostensibly on the ground that these are toys, but also with the insight that down the road beyond them lies the horror of modern industrialism and war. An early instance of the antitechnology science fiction that became a major emphasis in the 1960s to the distress of "Old Wave" partisans, by the author of *Lord of the Flies* and other mainstream-accepted work. Contrast de Camp, *Lest Darkness Fall* [3-58].

3-79. Guin, Wyman (Woods). **Living Way Out.** Avon, 1967.
Seven stories, showcasing this writer's ability to create worlds that are logical and consistent in their details but whose totality is bizarre. The earliest, "Trigger Tide," a James Bond-ish tale of intrigue on a far planet whose specs are essential to the story, appeared in *Astounding* in 1950. The rest were published in *Galaxy* under the exacting editorship of H. L. Gold, who is said to have made the author put "Beyond Bedlam" through four drafts before he was satisfied; that story remains politically and psychiatrically harrowing, even though therapists' assumptions about the nature of schizophrenia have changed substantially since 1951. "The Delegate From Guapanga" (1964), with its Mentalist and Matterist parties caucusing telepathically for an upcoming election, is a deliciously skewed parable of politics much closer to home. "'Volpla" (1956) casts what more recently would have been called a "yuppie" in the mad scientist role of Dr. Moreau, with disconcerting results. The jaunty fantasy "My Darling Hecate" (1953) surely owes something to Kipling's Just So story, "The Butterfly That Stamped." A superior collection.

3-80.   Gunn, James E(dwin). **Some Dreams Are Nightmares.** Scribner, 1974.

Strongly believing that "the ideal length for science fiction is the novelette," James Gunn chose to excerpt from works published as novels four magazine stories of that length. "The Cave of Night" (*Galaxy*, 1955) is a first-man-in-space story with a wry twist at the end. "The Hedonist" (*Thrilling Wonder*, 1954, as "Name Your Pleasure") describes a world dedicated to "happiness," not pursued ad lib à la Jefferson but therapeutically prescribed and coerced, resulting in a peculiarly horrible dystopia. "New Blood" (*Astounding*, 1955) describes a mutation that renders people virtually immune to death. "Medic" (*Venture*, 1957) extrapolates from the then already obscene cost of medical care in America and the corporate insensitivity of hospitals to a really savage future, to which we have in the nineties come perilously close. Although the stories were incorporated into well received novels—the first and second in *Station in Space* (Bantam, 1958) and *The Joy Makers* (Bantam, 1961), respectively, and the other two in the *The Immortals* (Bantam, 1962)—the author makes his case that these tales, like other writers' novelette- or novella-length work in the genre, can stand alone; a point library users attuned to "the book," that is, the novel, should ponder carefully. [For other works of this author see chapter 4.]

3-81.   Hamilton, Edmond. **Battle for the Stars.** Torquil, 1964.

This starts with a threatened space fleet ambush in Star Cluster N-356-44, "a hive of smoking suns," but moves in due course to a dark and folksy village on Earth in which the hero (after an obligatory space battle) vows to settle, maybe even do a bit of farming; a treasure-finding, self-discovering odyssey, but in the opposite direction from most such quests; contrast Clarke's *Against the Fall of Night* [3-43]. *Battle for the Stars* is less flamboyant than the space operas Hamilton had been writing for 30 years; he had come a long way as a writer from the full-length novel that he had turned out every three months in the early 1940s for *Captain Future* magazine. This story, originally copyright by Hamilton in 1961, was reissued in 1989 as a Tor Double; its companion, *The Nemesis From Terra*, was by Leigh Brackett, Hamilton's spouse. Their respective styles make an instructive contrast and comparison.

3-82.   Hamilton, Edmond. **What's It Like Out There? and Other Stories.** Ace, 1974.

Twelve stories from 1941 to 1962. Although a later, larger compilation, *The Best of Edmond Hamilton* (Nelson Doubleday, 1977) has a charming introduction by Leigh Brackett and afterword by Hamilton, the story selection in this one is better. Hamilton grew out of his pulp yarn-spinning of the 1930s, and in the period covered here fashioned sensitive, stylistically distinctive, tales. (Some of this may reflect changing magazine standards; the title story, written in 1933, did not see print until 1952.) Here are "Castaway," in which Edgar Allan Poe meets a time-traveling woman who become the inspiration for all his doom-haunted heroines (Ligeia, Eleanora); and such fine pieces as "The Stars My Brothers," "Sunfire!" "Isle of the Sleeper," and, on the fantasy side "Dreamers Worlds" and "The Inn Outside the World," both from *Weird Tales*, where Hamilton had made his debut. [For other works of this author see chapter 2.]

3-83. Harrison, Harry. **Deathworld.** Bantam, 1960.

Deathworld is a planet whose local life reads the hostile thoughts of Earth settlers and transforms itself into ever more deadly forms. Paradoxically, therefore, the harder the humans fight the more formidable becomes their planetary opposition. (Harrison did not overtly draw the obvious moral about human-versus-human conflict in our own time, but it's there.) In the economics of modern publishing the taming of Deathworld does not lead to peace and quiet but to sequels, *Deathworld 2* (Bantam, 1964; Gollancz, retitled *The Ethical Engineer*) and *Deathworld 3* (Dell, 1968). These are less successful. Nevertheless, the whole became *The Deathworld Trilogy* (Nelson Doubleday, 1974) and continues to turn up among the offerings of the Science Fiction Book Club.

3-84. Heinlein, Robert A(nson). **Beyond This Horizon.** Fantasy, 1948.

Originally in *Astounding*, 1942. After society achieves an economy of abundance for all, what do people do with their time? Especially, how fares the omnicompetent Heinlein hero, who no longer has anything to challenge him? Themes that would occupy Heinlein later on, such as the political pitfalls of human genetic engineering, got a preliminary airing in this novel: also the existential implications of mortality versus immortality (his tentative solution, worked out in science fictional rather than occultish terms: reincarnation). An important early work, toward which a later generation of criticism has been unfairly condescending.

3-85. Heinlein, Robert A(nson). **Citizen of the Galaxy.** Scribner, 1957.

Although marketed as a juvenile novel, this work was serialized for adults in *Astounding*. The Horatio Alger hero is in an interstellar setting, except that this lad starts out closer to the edge than Horatio's bootblacks and newsboys: he is a slave on a far planet of a despotic empire. He escapes into space with a nomadic trading company and eventually gets back to Earth, where he assumes (by inheritance!) the headship of a giant financial corporation. This is a *bildungsroman*, except that the young hero never really grows up; but Heinlein's knack for creating sociologically plausible cultures is well displayed. Alex Panshin in *Heinlein in Dimension*, [9-57] argued that *Citizen of the Galaxy*, with a plot revealed at the end to be essentially circular, is normative for all of Heinlein's longer work.

3-86.   Heinlein, Robert A(nson). **Double Star.** Doubleday, 1956.
A ham actor is persuaded to impersonate the kidnapped prime minister of Earth's government. The actual politician is rescued but dies, and his double must carry on. In the process of dealing objectively with the moral judgments entailed in parliamentary politics he grows out of his stagestruck self-centeredness. *Double Star* offers convincing description of the way a planet-spanning constitutional monarchy (with the *Dutch* sovereign as its titular head!) might actually work. Heinlein's lifelong concern for citizen involvement in politics, shorn of his usual meritocratic elitism, is shown to good advantage. Contrast the 1993 film, *Dave*. HW, 1955

3-87.   Heinlein, Robert A(nson). **The Menace from Earth.** Gnome, 1959.
Eight stories that were *not* part of Heinlein's systematic future history as in *The Past Through Tomorrow* [3-89], except for the title story, whose "menace" is a young woman tourist from Earth who is after the boyfriend of the 15-year-old Moon-dwelling female viewpoint character. The stories don't always work: Jove nods, and Heinlein wrote "Project Nightmare"—come on, *dowsing* for A-bombs? But the collection also contains "By His Bootstraps" (SFHF), the ultimate comic travel-through-time-and-meet-yourself story until Heinlein topped it with "All You Zombies" (1959), and such unique and unduplicable stories as "Year of the Jackpot," "Creation Took Eight Days," and "Columbus Was a Dope," with its lovely punchline.

3-88.   Heinlein, Robert A(nson). **Orphans of the Sky.** Gollancz, 1963.
Based on two novellas from *Astounding* in 1941, "Universe" (SFHF) and "Common Sense," *Orphans* is the only major work from Heinlein's formal future history that is not contained in *The Past Through Tomorrow* [3-89], possibly because in terms of that history it is peripheral. Except for "The Voyage that Lasted 600 Years" by Don Wilcox (*Amazing*, December 1940), this was the first serious treatment of the less-than-lightspeed multigenerational starship whose actual origin and destination have become lost in legend. But it is more; it is a story of the quest for truth, both against orga-

nized superstition and against shortsighted, wrong-headed "realism." It also introduced and, regrettably, killed off one of Heinlein's most intriguing characters, the two-headed mutant Joe-Jim Gregory, who can't play cards with himself because he cheats. Compare Aldiss, *Non-Stop* [3-4]; Robinson, *The Dark Beyond the Stars* [4-363].

*3-89. Heinlein, Robert A(nson). **The Past Through Tomorrow.** Putnam, 1967.
Most of this omnibus compilation had been previously published in four separate books: *The Man Who Sold the Moon* (Shasta, 1950); *The Green Hills of Earth* (Shasta, 1951); *Revolt in 2100* (Shasta, 1953); and *Methuselah's Children* (Gnome, 1958). These in turn derived from magazine stories, starting in 1939 and continuing through the 1940s; mainly in *Astounding*, a few in the *Saturday Evening Post*. Collectively they constitute the bulk of Heinlein's future history: a detailed forecast for the next two centuries, from the "Crazy Years" (which, by Heinlein's calendar, have already happened!) to the beginning of the first "mature" civilization 200 years hence. Other science fiction writers (Poul Anderson, Isaac Asimov, James Blish, H. Beam Piper, Cordwainer Smith) have undertaken future-building of this kind, but rarely with Heinlein's degree of verisimilitude. The one major story omission from the future history is "Universe" (in *Orphans of the Sky*, [3-88], and of that story only its brief prologue is really germane. But "Life-line," "Requiem," "Blowups Happen," "Logic of Empire," "If This Goes On—," "Coventry," "The Green Hills of Earth," "The Man Who Sold the Moon," they're all here.

3-90. Heinlein, Robert A(nson). **Starship Troopers.** Putnam, 1959.
Heinlein's Annapolis and Regular Navy background form the context for the training and baptism-of-fire of future space cadets. A well-told story, this novel won the Hugo in 1959, but, later got caught in the crossfire of powerful pro- and anti-Vietnam War feeling, which divided the SF community as it did the "mainstream." The paradox is that Heinlein, with this work, gave aid and comfort to the war supporters, a group to which he belonged in the sixties; while with another novel, *Stranger in a Strange Land* [3-91], he helped to energize the radical student generation that opposed the war. Compare Smith's Lensman series [3-167]; contrast Pangborn, *A Mirror for Observers* [3-141]. HW, 1959

*3-91. Heinlein, Robert A(nson). **Stranger in a Strange Land.** Putnam, 1961.
Of all Heinlein's works this is the best known. It reached large audiences farther away from his science fiction roots than anything else he wrote,

and inspired insurgencies both right and left. An uncut version was issued posthumously by Putnam in 1991. The contradictory libertarian and authoritarian elements in this writer are both present in the saga of Valentine Michael Smith, born human, raised Martian, who returns to Earth a religious, political, and sexual messiah. The first third of the novel, set in one of Heinlein's typically believable sociopolitical milieus (a world government that has grown out of the present United Nations, with the secretary-general as its focus) is well and suspensefully told. Soon thereafter, however, Heinlein ascends into the pulpit where, sadly, this highly creative writer would remain for the next quarter-century, preaching, with unfortunately few lapses into good storytelling (that is, *showing*, not *telling*) such as *The Moon Is a Harsh Mistress* [4-204]. *Stranger*'s cultural impact on an entire generation is, nonetheless, undeniable. HW, 1961

3-92.   Heinlein, Robert A(nson). **Time for the Stars.** Scribner, 1956.
Although written and marketed as a young adult novel, this book is a mature treatment of the relativistic time-dilation effect in interstellar travel. Identical twin brothers are telepathically linked; one goes into space, the other remains on Earth. The object of the experiment is to determine whether continuing telepathic communication is possible over astronomical distances. It is, up to a point; but the astronaut brother returns, still youthful, to Earth, where the stay-at-home brother has become an old man. And there are other complications. For younger readers, a good, graphic introduction to relativity; for older readers, a very readable yarn on its own terms. Compare Anderson, *Tau Zero* [4-12]. [For other works of this author see chapters 4 and 5.]

3-93.   Henderson, Zenna. **Pilgrimage: The Book of the People.** Doubleday, 1961.
Short stories that originally appeared in *Fantasy & Science Fiction*, with connecting narrative. "The People" are humans who came to Earth after their sun became a nova and went into hiding. They have telepathy and telekinesis, which they use solely for benevolent purposes and conceal most of the time lest they rouse hysteria against them as "witches." The host culture they live among is southern Appalachian, which Henderson understood and portrayed accurately and sympathetically; reminiscent in that regard of the fantasy (not the SF) of Manly Wade Wellman. Confrontations with Earth folk that endanger their cover drive most of the story plots, which are saved from sentimentalism by the People's realization that in any revelation of what they are their existence may be at stake; compare Fast, "The First Men" [in 3-71], and Shiras, "In Hiding"

[in 3-160]. A sequel is *The People: No Different Flesh* (Gollancz, 1966). The saga of the People lent itself readily to a TV series format, which aired in the 1970s.

*3-94. Herbert, Frank. **The Dragon in the Sea.** Doubleday, 1956. Variant titles: *21st Century Sub*, Avon, 1956; *Under Pressure*, Ballantine, 1974.
Originating as an *Astounding* serial titled "Under Pressure," this was Herbert's maiden voyage, so to speak. Far transcending its routine plot—a "subtug" seeks to steal oil deposits from the unspecified enemy's continental shelf, with a crew, one of whom must be a spy (shades of *The Hunt for Red October!*)—the story conflates the deep, closed-in submarine environment with the crew members' psychic stress; they are both materially and mentally "under pressure." The seemingly half-mad captain has echoes of Captain Ahab, and there are allusions also to the Book of Job and Freud. The writer who one day would produce *Dune* was well on his way. [For other works of this author see chapter 4.]

3-95. Hoyle, Fred. **The Black Cloud.** Heinemann, 1957.
A cloud of interstellar matter drifts into the solar system, bringing chaos and destruction. The cloud is sentient; contact is established with it; and realizing what it has been doing it withdraws. Its collective mind is not a wholly original idea but derivative, like so much else in U.K. science fiction, from Stapledon's *Last and First Men* [2-119]. What carries it is the Earth astronomers' jargon and banter, which has the ring of absolute authenticity; as well it might, Hoyle himself having been Britain's Astronomer Royal (or in the story's lingo "A.R."). The book has been used in astronomy classes as supplemental reading, an honor not conferred upon much science fiction. Perhaps one ought to say, not yet.

*3-96. Hubbard, L(afayette) Ron(ald). **Final Blackout.** Hadley, 1948.
Serialized in *Astounding* in 1940 just before the Nazi blitzkrieg struck, this grim novel predicted that World War II would drag on for many more years, reducing Europe to peasant villages and bands of soldier-foragers, much as in the middle portion of Wells's *The Shape of Things to Come* [2-140]. Out of this chaos arises a British officer who leads his ragged troops back to England, deposes its government, and at the cost of his own life thwarts an attempt at colonization by the Americans. Very controversial when published in magazine form. Several reprintings have been done, most recently by Bridge in 1989 with an introduction by Algis Budrys and a helpful glossary of now-forgotten military terms. With the possible exception of *Fear* (*Unknown*, July 1940), this is Hubbard's finest work. Its

theme of the lone officer sacrificing his life for the sake of the regime he has established is echoed in another *Astounding* serial, "The End Is Not Yet" (1947), which, though never making it to book publication, is better than any of the heavily subsidized and promoted Hubbard novels of the 1980s, which are self-parody forty years too late. Taking place on an alternate time track, in which Germany gets the Bomb but loses World War II anyway, "The End Is Not Yet" pits a group of concerned scientists against evil international cartel master Jules Fabrecken, who came to power by promoting a U.S.-Russian nuclear war. But the Science Government of the World they establish after the deaths of Fabrecken and the hero must, as two surviving characters realize, in turn become a tyranny. An important and curiously neglected work, which deserves the book publication it has never received; its theme of the ambiguity of all revolutions, even of "good" revolutions (compare Budrys, "The Burning World," in [3-39]), has taken on new meaning since the collapse of the East European Communist system, especially in the Balkans.

3-97.   Huxley, Aldous (Leonard). **Ape and Essence.** Harper, 1948.
What *Brave New World* might look like after a nuclear war, told in the form of a prophetic motion picture screenplay. A Rediscovery Expedition from a relatively sane New Zealand encounters the denizens of what's left of Los Angeles, who dig up the perfectly preserved bodies in Forest Lawn cemetery (an echo of Huxley's satiric *After Many a Summer Dies the Swan* [2-55], and dress in elegant, stolen funeral attire. Humanity's breeding habits have changed to a seasonal rut during which orgy is expected with strict celibacy the rest of the time; a dissident minority who can have sex at any time of year are reviled as the "Hots" and pursued as witches. The worst of Dark Ages clericalism combined with social idiocies that could only have been made in America. Not quite the polished polemic of *Brave New World*, but effective on it own satiric terms. Compare del Rey, *The Eleventh Commandment* [3-61]; contrast Robinson, *The Wild Shore* [4-367]. [For other works of this author see chapter 2.]

*3-98.   Keyes, Daniel. **Flowers for Algernon.** Harcourt, 1966.
Developed from a Hugo-winning short story with the same title (SFHF). A mentally retarded man's intelligence enhanced, to that of a normal adult and then to supergenius. "Progress reports" in his diary, with successive changes in diction and spelling as well as intellectual content, chronicle his triumphant progress; and then, as the treatment fails, the reports record his collapse back into subnormality. A sensitively told, low-key masterpiece that was made into a surprisingly good film, given Hollywood's usual heavy-handed ways with "sci-fi." Compare Anderson's *Brain Wave* [3-

5] and Sturgeon's "Maturity" (in *Without Sorcery*, [3-173]), contrast Fast's "The First Men" (in *The Edge of Tomorrow*, [3-71]) and Shiras's *Children of the Atom* [3-160].

3-99. Knebel, Fletcher, and Charles W. Bailey, II. **Seven Days in May.** Harper, 1962.
This realistically detailed account, by two Washington-wise news professionals, of an attempted coup d'etat by a chairman of the Joint Chiefs impatient with the president's "softness" toward the Russians, still has a disturbing ring, even though the long U.S.-Soviet superpower confrontation that made such scenarios imaginable is over. A few coincidences help save the day, but the one real implausibility in the story is that both the conspiracy and its foiling could have taken place in flap-mouthed Washington without anybody but the immediate participants knowing about it. The novel was made into a successful film, with strong performances by Kirk Douglas, Ava Gardner, and especially Burt Lancaster as the general.

*3-100. Knight, Damon (Francis). **The Best of Damon Knight.** Nelson Doubleday, 1976.
Twenty-two stories, ranging from 1949 to 1972—"most of the best work I did" during that time, Knight attests. They include "To Serve Man," which became a memorable *Twilight Zone* episode; the sardonic "Not With a Bang"; "The Analogues," which became the first chapter of "Hells Pavement" [3-101]; "Babel II," in which a visiting alien that looks like Happy Hooligan scrambles all human speech and writing; "Special Delivery," in which a pregnant woman learns she is carrying a fetal supergenius; several time travel stories "that God sent me," Knight writes, "as a punishment for having said that the time-travel story was dead"; "The Handler," about a socially rejected dwarf who inside a "big man" humanoid shell is the life of the party; and, somewhat atypically for Knight, "Mary," a powerful love story with a quite unexpected happy ending. Barry Malzberg's introduction, "Dark of the Knight," is short and laudatory; Knight's own headnotes are disconcertingly frank about his personal life at the time the stories were written, but that has always been his way.

3-101. Knight, Damon (Francis). **Hell's Pavement.** Lion, 1955. Variant title: *Analogue Men*, Berkley, 1962.
The coming of a bland totalitarianism that does not need to resort to the crude tortures of a *Nineteen Eighty-Four* was a favorite theme in 1950s SF. This novel also exemplifies a political theme we have heard in mainstream

life more recently: the unintended consequences of successful action. Disturbed individuals are provided with "analogues" within their own psyches that prevent them from antisocial or dysfunctional behavior. The motive for such therapy is exemplary: to forestall the alcoholic from drinking, the kleptomaniac from stealing, the pedophile from molesting. Then it goes on to mass treatment against crimes of violence and immunization from corruption for all candidates for public office, and it is a short step from there to conditioning against any attempt to overthrow the government. The inevitable tyranny that results permeates the entire society except for an underground of "immunes" who cannot respond to such therapy. Compare Burgess, *A Clockwork Orange* [3-41]; contrast Skinner, *Walden Two* [3-166]. [For other works of this author see chapters 4, 8 and 9.]

*3-102. Kornbluth, C(yril) M. **The Best of C. M. Kornbluth.** Nelson Doubleday, 1976. Ed. by Frederik Pohl.
Nineteen stories, from 1941 to 1958, attest to the high quality of what Kornbluth wrote in his tragically short career: "The Adventurer," with its devastating punchline, as well as "The Little Black Bag" (SFHF), "The Luckiest Man in Denv," "Gomez" (perhaps the first SF story set in a New York City Hispanic milieu), "The Marching Morons" (SFHF), "With These Hands," and one he had barely completed at the time of his death, "Two Dooms." Most have been repeatedly anthologized. Pohl, Kornbluth's frequent collaborator, selected the stories and wrote the introduction. Only a rubric against annotating pure fantasy stories prevented listing also *Thirteen O'Clock* (Dell, 1970), which reproduced the sprightly tales Kornbluth (under the name "Cecil Corwin") wrote in the early forties as a teenager; no one should be denied the pleasure of reading them.

3-103. Kornbluth, C(yril) M. **Not This August.** Doubleday, 1955. U.K. title: *Christmas Eve*, M. Joseph, 1956. Recommended ed.: Pinnacle, 1981.
Serialized in *Maclean's*, a Canadian mainstream magazine. For U.S. publication the Battle of Yellowknife, at which U.S. and Canadian forces surrendered to the victorious Russians and Chinese, became (less plausibly) the Battle of El Paso. The action takes place in upstate New York under Soviet occupation; not the first or last such awful-warning story, but one of the few that showed some inkling of what rule by Russians under Stalinist principles might actually have been like. Kornbluth's knack for characterization and description saves the story from routine melodrama. As with the Nazi-battling epics of a decade earlier, virtue triumphs: a Resistance develops on the order of the French *maquis* in World War II, and on Christmas Eve the underground strikes. Widely noticed in the mainstream

media, for self-serving purposes as a cold war wake-up call. The 1981 revision included a foreword and afterword by Frederik Pohl.

3-104. Kornbluth, C(yril) M. **The Syndic.** Doubleday, 1953.
A very different reading of the New York underworld from that of *The Godfather*! In a New York of the future, Syndic (that is, the old "Syndicate") has evolved into a free, highly permissive society, with what used to be "protection" functioning as a mild form of taxation. Chicago's regime, the Mob, is quite the opposite, a brutal police state. A U.S. government-in-exile on the Irish coast—a parody of the then recently established Nationalist Chinese regime on Taiwan—launches nuisance raids on Cape Cod and maintains an underground terrorist organization, the Daughters (of the American Revolution). Faced with all these menaces, Syndic is told by the hero that it must prepare for war and, in violation of its permissive principles, institute a military draft; but its genial philosopher-king refuses on the ground that Syndic would then no longer be Syndic. Kornbluth at his wickedly fun-poking best.

3-105. Kornbluth, C(yril) M., and Judith Merril (published under the name Cyril Judd). **Outpost Mars.** Abelard, 1952.
First serialized in *Galaxy* as "Mars Child," this well-characterized novel pits a utopia against a dystopia, both of them on Mars. The utopia is a small cooperative commonwealth; its antithesis is a large mining corporation that brings to Mars the same brutality with which such outfits operated in the American West. One focus of the co-op is the first baby born there, which nearly dies before its parents realize it is over- not under-supplied with oxygen (given the assumption as to the density and composition of the Martian atmosphere the medical symptomology is quite accurately done). Before the story is over native Martians appear, of a nonthreatening kind. Mood and conclusion are upbeat, in an old-fashioned American leftist way; a pleasant tale. Compare Dick, *Martian Time-Slip* [3-66]; contrast Brackett, *Eric John Stark: Outlaw of Mars* [3-29].

*3-106. Kuttner, Henry. **The Best of Henry Kuttner.** Nelson Doubleday, 1975.
Seventeen stories, mostly from 1940s *Astounding*. Science fiction with an acute psychological sensibility, straightforwardly told. Ray Bradbury contributes an appreciative introduction. Here are stories originally penned under Kuttner's mordant Lewis Padgett pseudonym, such as "The Twonky," "The Proud Robot," and the haunting "Mimsy Were the Borogoves" (SFHF)—the most plausible explanation yet of where Lewis Carroll *really* got that nonsense poem. Other stories had first been pub-

lished under Kuttner's own name, including the powerful "Absalom." There are no stories under the "Lawrence O'Donnell" *nom de plume* (that is, co-written with C. L. Moore), although that is always a hard judgment call with that highly symbiotic husband-wife writing team.

3-107. Kuttner, Henry, and C(atherine) L. Moore (published under the name Lewis Padgett). **Mutant.** Gnome, 1953.

These are the "Baldy" stories, published in *Astounding* between 1945 and 1953; the first, which assumed a post-atomic-war "balance of terror" among independent city-states linked by commerce, interestingly appeared in the magazine just *before* the actual atomic bomb. Radiation-induced mutation has begotten a race of telepaths, with a secondary genetic trait of baldness, hence the name. To wear a wig or go proudly naked-headed signifies an ideological division, between living as harmoniously as may be with the nontelepath majority and aggressively asserting superiority on Nazi "superman" lines. The rational working out of this dilemma created a warm, socially and politically thoughtful story. Compare Bester, *The Demolished Man* [3-17]; contrast Henderson, *Pilgrimage* [3-93].

3-108. Kuttner, Henry, and C(atherine) L. Moore. **Tomorrow and Tomorrow; and, The Fairy Chessmen.** Gnome, 1951.

After the socially hopeful tone of "The Piper's Son" (1945; see *Mutant*, [3-107]) it was a surprise when Kuttner and Moore in 1946 and 1947 turned out two short novels as grim as these; conceivably a reflection of the dashed end-of-World-War-II hopes and beginning of the cold war. *Tomorrow*, from *Astounding* in 1947, presents the achievement of world government under a Global Peace Commission at the cost of suppressing "dangerous" scientific research that might promote war or social instability. This society's underground therefore decides that the only way to reopen the path to progress is by starting a nuclear war. Compare Aldiss, *Earthworks* (1965). *Chessmen*, in *Astounding* in 1946, describes a weird, even psychotic future world in which conventional scientists trying to solve a crucial mathematical equation go mad. The only person who can face that challenge with equanimity is someone who enjoys playing "fairy chess," in which the game's conventional rules are livened by differently powered chessmen and differently shaped boards. The ESP so central in 1950s Campbellian SF is broached, not as a bright promise but as a frightening irreality.

*3-109. Leiber, Fritz (Reuter). **The Best of Fritz Leiber.** Nelson Double-day, 1974.

Twenty-two stories from the mid-1940s through the 1960s. Poul Anderson contributes an appreciative introduction; Leiber wraps it up in an afterword. Stories range from fiendish *Astounding* puzzlers ("Sanity," "The Enchanted Forest") through early-fifties dystopias ("Coming Attraction," "Poor Superman") to atmospheric tales from the late fifties such as that ultimate tribute to Marilyn Monroe, "A Deskful of Girls," and the quietly creepy "Little Old Miss Macbeth." Only one story is in Leiber's supernatural horror vein, and there are none of his sword-and-sorcery tales. Readers may argue endlessly, however, as to whether "The Man Who Never Grew Young"—the only story retained from Leiber's first, long-out-of-print collection *Night's Black Agents* (Arkham, 1947)—is SF or fantasy.

*3-110. Leiber, Fritz (Reuter). **The Change War.** Gregg, 1978.

Serialized in *Galaxy* in 1957, "The Big Time," a saga of soldiers from all times who have been recruited as "Spiders" or "Snakes" to battle each other and alter past events to the advantage of their own side, won the Hugo for that year. The primary action takes place in a Spider R&R center outside the cosmos and is staged theatrically, no doubt reflecting Leiber's own experience in his father's repertory Shakespeare company. That novel (*The Big Time*, Ace, 1961) and a collection of shorter stories on the Spiders-versus-Snakes theme, *The Mind Spider* (Ace, 1961), were combined with other related pieces in this collection from Gregg. Jack Williamson had anticipated the theme of time-soldiers battling to change events in *The Legion of Time* [2-145], but Williamson's version assumed a conventional Good-Evil dualism. Leiber's vision was breathtakingly relativist; one principal character in *The Big Time*, from a World War II that turned out differently, is the Nazi *gauleiter* of Chicago! A major and disturbing work. Contrast Anderson, *Time Patrol* [3-8], and Leiber's own *Destiny Times Three* [3-111]. HW

3-111. Leiber, Fritz (Reuter). **Destiny Times Three.** Galaxy, 1956.

Originally a serial in *Astounding*, 1945, this was an important precursor to Leiber's *Change Wars*, but it came to a diametrically opposite conclusion: Don't mess with a world's future. Thirty years before the story opens, Earth has discovered "subtronic power." Mysterious Experimenters use a Probability Engine to split time and actualize three future worlds. In the first, the new energy source is public property; in the second, it is in the hands of a ruling elite; in the third, an attempt to eradicate the discovery has resulted in devastation. Ultimately, all are failures: a stagnant, complacent utopia, a cruel totalitarianism, and a wrecked landscape ravaged by intelligent cats: "three botched worlds." Yet once in existence they must be left free to work out their destinies in their own ways. The story is darkly told, with chapter epigraphs from the Elder Edda, the *Rubaiyat*, and H. P. Lovecraft. An unduly neglected work of which Leiber was personally fond.

3-112.   Leiber, Fritz (Reuter). **Gather, Darkness!.** Pellegrini & Cudahy, 1950.

This was first a serial in *Astounding* in 1943, and built on the religious dictatorship theme pioneered by Robert Heinlein in "If This Goes On—" (*Revolt in 2100*, in *The Past Through Tomorrow* [3-89]). Unlike the fundamentalist Protestant regime envisioned by Heinlein the structure of this one is basically Catholic, although with the magazine taboos of the time Leiber was careful to fuzz the details. His real innovation, which drives the plot, is a revolutionary underground whose goal is the restoration of political and particularly scientific freedom, but which wraps itself in the trappings of Satanism, complete with witches who zap around on jet-propelled broomsticks. A brainwashing of the hero that temporarily recruits him into the power elite he opposes ("memory can link anything") raises darker issues of social control, although at the end of the story the forces of enlightenment do prevail. Compare del Rey, *The Eleventh Commandment* [3-61]. [For other works by this author see chapter 4.]

3-113.   Leinster, Murray (pseud. of Will[iam] F[itzgerald] Jenkins). **The Best of Murray Leinster.** Ballantine, 1978. Ed. by J. J. Pierce.

Thirteen stories from 1934 to 1956 by one of the most consistent lifetime practitioners of SF. His earliest work had appeared in 1920, before there were any science fiction magazines. The stories well reflect transformations in SF's outlook over that time span. "Proxima Centauri" (*Astounding*, 1935) confronts the first Earth visitors to our nearest stellar neighbor with a race of particularly nasty aliens, whereas "First Contact" (SFHF; *Astounding*, 1945) poses and solves the problem of how two mutually suspicious alien species meeting in space for the first time can manage *not* to engage in hostilities; an early, hopeful parable of the cold war. (But see Ivan Yefremov's response to "First Contact," titled "Cor Serpentis," in Magidoff, *Russian Science Fiction* [3-219].) There is also "Sidewise in Time" (*Astounding*, 1934), one of the earliest—and wildest!—of alternate history stories. [For other works by this author see chapter 2.]

3-114.   Lem, Stanislaw. **The Investigation.** Seabury, 1974. Trans. by Adele Milch of '*Sledztwo*, 1959.

In a sense this is a homage to Sherlock Holmes. The scene opens at fog-shrouded Scotland Yard, its investigators baffled by circumstances that would have challenged and delighted Holmes: Corpses are disappearing from mortuaries all over Greater London. An outside consultant, the brilliant but unstable Dr. Sciss, has been called in. But this is not an amateur-outsmarts-professionals tale in the tradition of Holmes or of Poe's M. Dupin. The 19th-century closed universe of cause and effect, which both Holmes and his confreres in the police assumed, no longer works for solving such a case as this. However, rather than accept Dr. Sciss's proposed solution (that the corpses are being collected by visitors from outer space) the Scotland Yard inspectors accept a plausible explanation that they know is probably false but that will "give a semblance of order to this disorder and mark an open case closed." The sciences in this work of SF are the 20th-century investigative tools of information theory and statistics, about which Lem was very knowledgeable. A stimulating work.

*3-115. Lem, Stanislaw. **Solaris.** Walker, 1970. Trans. (from a French translation) by Joanna Kilmartin and Steve Cox.
Written in Polish in 1961, this novel combines profound philosophic speculation with the structure of traditional action-adventure SF, embodied in a clear, vivid writing style that somehow survives two translations. A planet under study by Earth scientists for many decades is swathed in a world-girdling ocean, which, the scientists have realized after initial skepticism, is one immense sentient organism. For purposes of its own (never disclosed), this ocean "reads" the deepest memories of the four men housed at Station Solaris and sends each a double—"Phantom"—of a woman in his past; in the case of the viewpoint character his estranged and since deceased wife, Rheya. But the phantom Rheya thinks she is the real Rheya. And the mysterious world-ocean, constantly flinging up strange shapes that defy the savants' efforts at classification, may be the first, infantile phase of an emerging "imperfect God." A major work by any measure. In the Soviet Union *Solaris* was made into a well-received film. Compare Silverberg, *The Face of the Waters* (1991). [For other works by this author see chapter 4.]

*3-116. Lewis, C(live) S(taples). **Out of the Silent Planet.** Bodley Head, 1938.
This was the initial volume of Lewis's acclaimed Space Trilogy, which constitutes as a whole a highly sophisticated Christian rebuttal to the world-view—today called "secular humanism"—of H. G. Wells. The religious dimension is least evident in this first volume, set on a well-realized, ecologically distinctive Mars. It is more so in the second, *Perelandra* (Bodley Head, 1943; variant title *Voyage to Venus*, Pan, 1953), in which the Garden

of Eden temptation is replayed on a marvelously described ocean-covered Venus (this time humankind does not fall), and centrally so in the third, *That Hideous Strength* (Bodley Head, 1945; abridged as *The Tortured Planet*, Avon, 1958), which angered some American science fictionists when it first appeared because they misread it as an attack on science. Lewis's actual target was scientism. The trilogy has been compared to Tolkien's *Lord of the Rings*, but that would be to throw it into a "heroic fantasy" mold, which really does not fit. It can, however, be contrasted with James Blish's religious fantasies such as *Black Easter* (Doubleday, 1968) and *The Day After Judgment* (Doubleday, 1971).

3-117.   Long, Frank Belknap, Jr. **The Early Long.** Doubleday, 1975.
Seventeen stories by a member of H. P. Lovecraft's circle, heavily overlapping with Long's initial—and now very rare—collection, *The Hounds of Tindalos* (Arkham, 1946). Heavy on *Weird Tales* supernaturalism, some of it very good (for example, "The Peeper"); little SF. From a science fictionist's point of view it is a pity that in addition to such excellent tales as "The Census Taker" and "Dark Vision" this collection did not include more of the interestingly off-trail SF by Long that appeared in the pulps during the 1940s—very different in style and theme from most other Golden Age stories. An example is "To Follow Knowledge" (*Astounding*, 1942), which baffled editor John Campbell pronounced "utterly strange" in its story blurb.

3-118.   MacDonald, John D(ann). **The Girl, the Gold Watch, & Everything.** Gold Medal, 1962.
This novel by a widely read popular writer in the "mainstream" derives, as must all such stories, from H. G. Wells's "The New Accelerator." A "watch" slows time for its possessors, to a rate of about half an hour per second, speeding them up accordingly from the rest of the world's point of view. This confers the power of moving invisibly to anyone else; a power fantasy, in a sense, except that to lose the "watch" would be to cut oneself off from normal contact with the rest of humankind. Practical scientific problems with such acceleration/deceleration—inertia, metabolism, the effect of friction—are touched on rather lightly. Originally a novella in *Super Science Stories*, 1950; shows signs of its pulp origin, but as always with MacDonald, a well told story. Compare Wells, *The Invisible Man* (1897).

*3-119.   Matheson, Richard (Barton). **Born of Man and Woman.** Chamberlain, 1954. Variant title: *Third From the Sun*, Bantam, 1955.
Seventeen stories, the best of this author's early work, including the hor-

rific title story. Of this story, his first, the editors of *Fantasy & Science Fiction* (Summer, 1950) said in their headnote that the protagonist "tells it with a mind such as you have never met, housed in a body you have never imagined." Diction and punctuation help convey an aura of chill alienness. SFHF. Almost equally terrifying is "Lover When You're Near Me." In a more reflective mood are "Third From the Sun" and "The Traveller," a tale comparable to Bradbury's "The Man," which was regrettably among the four stories dropped from the Bantam edition. A fresh and distinctive new voice, in whom it was clear that the 1950s would not be simply a continuation of SF's Golden Age. A massive (900-page) collection of Matheson's short fiction was published by Scream/Press in 1989.

3-120. Matheson, Richard (Barton). **I Am Legend.** Fawcett, 1954.

What Jack Williamson's *Darker Than You Think* [3-193] was to lycanthropy, this novel was to vampirism—an attempt to give what had been considered purely supernatural horror a scientific basis. (Matheson's explanation is today more scientifically persuasive than Williamson's, but then Williamson had the harder job.) Since vampires flee from light, the hero goes forth by day to destroy them. Reversing the Dracula theme, *he* becomes an object of terror to *them*. This should have been a sure-fire movie prospect, but two attempts to translate it for the screen failed, casualties of Hollywood simple-mindedness. Visual horror has become equated with grossness; the metaphysical and psychological implications of the novel are lost.

3-121. Matheson, Richard. **The Shrinking Man.** Gold Medal, 1956.

Radioactive fallout, which in the 1950s covered a multitude of sins, with a little help from a new pesticide, causes the hero gradually to shrink. His psychological dilemma as friends and family, including his wife, start treating him according to his size rather than his personality, as a "little boy," is quite sensitively shown. After a narrow escape from a cuddly kitten, which to one his size is a ferocious predator, he retires to the basement, still shrinking, for a climactic battle with a spider. The comparative sizes of objects in this part of the story are inconsistent and the physics of size change is passed over in silence. The open-ended conclusion prompted some criticism in the SF community for its implicit religious overtone. A movie, *The Incredible Shrinking Man*, was much better than average 1950s SF films. An encounter midway through the shrinking journey with a female midget who is the same size as the hero, but whom he must shrink on past, is rendered with poignancy in a rather Bradburyish way. [For other works by this author see chapter 4.]

3-122.   McKenna, Richard M(ilton). **Casey Agonistes, and Other Science Fiction and Fantasy Stories.** Harper, 1973.

Five fine stories; three from *Fantasy & Science Fiction*, two from *Orbit*. The title story is not SF but a superbly told ghost story. "Hunter, Come Home" and "Mine Own Ways" deal with interplanetary cultural anthropology and, in the former, with the clash of native versus human-introduced ecosystems, anticipating Le Guin's "The Word for the World Is Forest" but from a male viewpoint. Damon Knight's introduction argues that McKenna, eschewing "the trivial puzzles and adventures" of so much SF, "tackled the basic problems of philosophy"; both "Fiddler's Green" and the partly autobiographical "The Secret Place" bear out this judgment. McKenna is a superior literary craftsman, author also of non-SF works such as *The Sand Pebbles.*

*3-123.   Merril, Judith. **The Best of Judith Merril.** Warner, 1976.

Nine stories including "That Only a Mother" (SFHF), the author's first; two poems; and an informative memoir by Virginia Kidd, who at one time roomed with Merril. Readers attuned to modern (or postmodern) feminist sensibilities may find these tales somewhat old-fashioned; readers with awareness of SF's prior history will enjoy their dramatic break with earlier male-sexist genre clichés. Indeed, stories like "Whoever You Are" and "Dead Center" carry dramatic tragic power even today. One fine novella, detailing the conflict between venturesome daughters and protective mothers over going into space, exploring, colonizing, and exploring again, is also the title story of another fine Merril collection, *Daughters of Earth* (Gollancz, 1968; Doubleday, 1969).

3-124.   Merril, Judith. **Shadow on the Hearth.** Doubleday, 1950. Recommended ed.: Roberts & Vintner, 1966.

Rather than write a post–nuclear war story on the collapse of civilization, with bands of survivors stumbling through cities' radioactive rubble, Merril narrowed the focus to that of a housewife in suburbia. The imprisoning circle so typical of that life-style in the 1950s is intensified by the outbreak of war. The radio impersonally announces doom, the voices on the telephone cease, the utilities fail, and the bratty teenager in the family persists in brattiness. With the "shadow" of the novel's title—radiation sickness—hanging over one of her children, the mother copes as best she can. The banal familiarity of the suburban setting made this book accessible for people who normally would not have been attracted to science fiction. Compare Shute, *On the Beach* [3-161]; contrast Frank, *Alas, Babylon* [3-74].

*3-125. Miller, Walter M(ichael), Jr. **A Canticle for Leibowitz.** Lippincott, 1960.

Novelized from three *F & SF* stories in the fifties; happily, the seams do not show. The Earth plunges into a new dark age after nuclear war. Scientists, scapegoats blamed for the war, flee to monasteries, which shelter them; as in the previous downfall, the one coherent surviving social institution is the Catholic church. A new Renaissance, in a context of warfare between city-states, sees the rediscovery of electricity and, as an inescapable consequence, weapons development. Still later, a new high-tech civilization falls once again into nuclear war, although missionaries on a starship that got away will plant a new, autonomous church on a far planet. Bare-bones criticism cannot do justice to this outstanding work; it must be read, or rather experienced. Compare Orson Scott Card, *Folk of the Fringe* (1989), for a different church as the chrysalis of a new civilization. HW, 1960

3-126. Miller, Walter M(ichael), Jr. **The Science Fiction Stories of Walter M. Miller, Jr.** Gregg, 1978.

The Gregg edition comprises the stories included in two previous collections, *Conditionally Human* (Ballantine, 1962) and *View From the Stars* (Ballantine, 1964). Even before *A Canticle for Leibowitz* [3-125] it was apparent from Miller's shorter fiction that in his depth of feeling and characterization this writer had moved decisively away from the space opera tradition, while retaining the ability to write strongly plotted action stories. Typically, "The Darfstellar" (HW, 1954) sensitively explores the psychology of occupational obsolescence, in this case an aging actor displaced from the stage by computer-programmed androids. When Miller did venture into space, to the moon in his powerful story "The Lineman" or to Mars in "Crucifixus Etiam," it was to depict people struggling on the outermost edge—in the Mars story, the heir of a culture in the high Andes whose high altitude life on Earth has prepared him to survive, just barely, on Mars. Introduction by David Samuelson. Highly recommended.

3-127. Mitchison, Naomi. **Memoirs of a Spacewoman.** Gollancz, 1962. U.S. paperback edition, Berkley, 1973.

The viewpoint character's scientific specialty is communication with aliens. Women, in this intergalactic future, are by and large better at that kind of work than men; likelier to perceive the reality of sentience in bizarre lifeforms, and more adroit at devising ways of making contact. Extraterrestrials in this novel include a starfish-like, radially symmetrical species whose mathematics and philosophy differ profoundly from Earth's simple, on-off, yes-no bilateralism, and a caterpillars-and-butterflies race whose adult form abuses and lays guilt trips upon the sentient larval stage from which it metamorphosed. This story also explores, more boldly even than Philip Farmer, the possibilities of interspecies sex (and parenting). Considered a pioneering proto-feminist work; certainly the female protagonist's outlook differs markedly from that of the extroverted aggressive male heroes of most space opera.

*3-128. Moore, C(atherine) L. **The Best of C. L. Moore.** Nelson Doubleday, 1975.
Ten stories from 1933 to 1946 Lester del Rey, a longtime admirer, selected them and wrote a biographical introduction; Moore added a personal afterword. Outstanding are three stories from *Astounding*: "The Bright Illusion" (1934), a human-alien love story that anticipates issues raised by Le Guin's *Left Hand of Darkness* [4-254]; "No Woman Born" (1944), about the triumphant return to the stage of a singer-dancer all but destroyed in a fire, whose brain has been transplanted into a robot body; and "Vintage Season" (1946; SFHF)—originally bylined as Lawrence O'Donnell, the pseudonym employed for collaborations between Moore and her spouse Henry Kuttner, here claimed as Moore's alone—about time traveling tourists and the present-day man who rents his house to them with tragic results. From *Weird Tales* the collection includes Moore's first story, "Shambleau" (1933), which introduced her popular interplanetary roamer, Northwest Smith, and two tales of her medieval female knight Jirel of Joiry. A highly satisfying collection.

3-129.   Moore, C(atherine) L. **Doomsday Morning.** Doubleday, 1957.
Strikingly different from Moore's usual interplanetary or medieval locales: realistic action-adventure on a near-present Earth. May be taken as representative of a science fiction theme common in the 1950s: the authoritarian state based on central control of the national communications network, abetted by subliminal manipulation, against which a ragged but dedicated underground rises. Most such stories, however useful they may then have been as cautionary tales, are eminently forgettable. What makes this one "work," in the show business sense of that verb, is the traveling theater company, which is the story's immediate foreground locale. This was a milieu Moore understood very well, and her description of it will speak to anyone who has ever been even minimally stagestruck. For the theme of an apparently necessary regime (it came to power in the chaos following a brief nuclear war) that became corrupt in the exercise of power, compare Knight, *Hell's Pavement* [3-101]; for the lively theater subculture, compare Fritz Leiber's fine fantasy "Four Ghosts in *Hamlet*"

(*Fantasy & Science Fiction*, January 1965), or the chapter titled "Pageant Wagon" in Card, *Folk of the Fringe* (1989).

3-130. Moore, C(atherine) L. **Judgment Night.** Gnome, 1952.
What Moore did in the title story, in effect, was to translate her medieval warrior-woman Jirel (renaming her Juille) from the *Weird Tales* realm of fantasy to the *Astounding* world of space opera, where this tale ran as a serial in 1943. It works spectacularly; the destruction of a pleasure satellite (a more aesthetic version of Las Vegas/Disneyland) is made a metaphor for the downfall of an entire galactic civilization. The other four stories anthologized here, however, are not vintage Moore, except for "The Code," in which a reversal of biological aging leads not to recapitulation of one's own youth on Earth but to that of someone in a parallel and quite alien universe. Otherwise, for better examples of her shorter work, see *The Best of C. L. Moore* [3-128]. [For other works by this author see chapter 2.]

*3-131. Moore, Ward. **Bring the Jubilee.** Farrar, 1953.
With the possible exception of Sir Winston Churchill's brilliant essay in *If, or History Rewritten* [2-118], this is far and away the best story ever written on the theme of the South having won the Civil War. Moore's fine historical sense led him to describe some perhaps unexpected consequences; in a less affluent North the presidency is won three times by William Jennings Bryan, and in a backlash against the prewar antislavery movement the Grand Army of the Republic, the Union veterans' organization, becomes a terrorist outfit like the Klan. Imaginative rethinking of real history; highly recommended. (This annotator, born and raised in Yankeeland, trembles at the thought of "Johnston's terrible march to Boston"; serves us right, a staunch Southron might reply.)

3-132. Nearing, Homer, Jr. **The Sinister Researches of C. P. Ransom.** Doubleday, 1954.
Eleven stories from *Fantasy & Science Fiction*, humorously describing the self-absorbed rivalry of two all-too-typical academicians—Professor Ransom, a mathematician, and Professor Tate, a philosopher. They try to develop inventions that blend the arts and sciences, for example, a poetry machine (to which, in fact, computer programming has since come perilously close) and hilariously fail. Gentle in tone, but reflective of a deadly serious quarrel within the intelligentsia: the "Two Cultures" conflict sketched by C. P. Snow in his 1956 Reith Lectures, with partisans of the sciences and the humanities each denying the legitimacy of the other. Some of the humor may be too "inside" for nonacademic readers (for

example, the outrageously lit.-crit. combination of names, Cleanth Penn Ransom, applied to the *non*humanities character), but the book's influence could be subtly salutary on university types outside the SF orbit.

3-133. Nesvadba, Josef. **The Lost Face: Best Science Fiction From Czechoslovakia.** Taplinger, 1971. Trans. by Iris Urwin.
Most of these stories were published in a Czech magazine; this translation dates from 1964 and was issued in the United Kingdom as *In the Steps of the Abominable Snowman* (Gollancz, 1970). Science fiction with an East European accent, but drawing upon the Anglo-American SF tradition also. One story, "Dr. Moreau's Other Island," is a variant on one of H. G. Wells's grimmer tales, and another owes much to Tarzan-and-Jane. Two— "Expedition in the Opposite Direction," a time travel story, and "The Lost Face," about some startling consequences of plastic surgery—deal in fresh ways with the perennial question of determinism versus freedom of the will. In that discussion, Marxist considerations are minimal; the only figure in the book who quotes Engels (in the time travel story) is a rather unsympathetic character. The stories are told with verve, humanity, and wit.

3-134. Neville, Kris (Ottman). **Bettyann.** Tower, 1970.
Based on stories published in 1951 and 1954. The estrangement of the lone alien on Earth, common in 1950s SF, here receives a warm and winning twist. Unintentionally abandoned on Earth (like Spielberg's *E.T.* !), an alien child is raised as a crippled human girl. When her people return for her and tell her of her heritage out among the stars, she decides to remain on the adopted world she has learned to love, but where she will nevertheless always be an alien. A story of loneliness and connectedness with a touch of both Bradbury and Sturgeon, and even a bit of Sherwood Anderson, but in a distinctive singing poetry that is the author's own. A sequel is "Bettyann's Children," in Roger Elwood, ed., *Demon Kind*, Avon, 1973. Compare Henderson, *Pilgrimage* [3-93].

*3-135. Neville, Kris (Ottman). **The Science Fiction of Kris Neville.** Southern Illinois Univ. Press, 1984. Ed. by Barry Malzberg and Martin H(arry) Greenberg.
Eleven stories, 1949–1967. In addition to preserving in more permanent form than the evanescent paperback the two novellas comprising *Bettyann* [3-134], this collection showcases the variety of styles and themes in this writer's work, from "Cold War" (*Astounding*, 1949), forecasting an unexpected difficulty in the "balance of terror" nuclear foreign policy, to chill-

ing exposition, in "From the Government Printing Office" (*Dangerous Visions*, 1967), of what three-and-a-half-year-olds *really* think of adults; from the creeping horror of "Underground Movement" (*F & SF*, 1952); to the hilarious and all too true cultural satire of "New Apples in the Garden" (*Analog*, 1963). If, as Malzberg states in his introduction, Neville became totally frustrated at being unable to sell work that went beyond current SF conventions in the market of his day, that does not speak well for the genre. Contains a useful, accurate bibliography of all of Neville's writings.

3-136. Norton, Andre (pseud. of Alice Mary Norton). **The Beast Master.** Harcourt, 1959.
Hosteen Storm is one of the few survivors of an Earth incinerated by interstellar war. He is also of the *Dineh*—a Navajo—and thus doubly alone in the universe. Terrans have, however, spread to other solar systems, and it is to one of those colony-worlds that Storm emigrates, with his team of highly mutated Earth fighting and scouting animals. The planetary scene for the story's action is very like the half-mythical American West, complete with box canyons, horses, and ranching spreads. This story is saved from stereotyping by Norton's vivid descriptive and action writing and her evident empathy for Navajo folkways, like that of Tony Hillerman in a different genre. (However, "Hosteen" is not usually a given name in Navajo; it is a term of address, meaning "respected elder.") Probably the first science fiction novel in which the viewpoint character was a Native American. Norton followed up with another Hosteen Storm story, *Lord of Thunder* (Ace, 1962), and—less successfully—branched out to a different tribe in *The Sioux Spaceman* (Ace, 1960). [For other works by this author see chapter 5.]

3-137. Oliver, Chad. **Another Kind.** Ballantine, 1955.
Oliver's first story collection, which Anthony Boucher termed the best SF book published that year. The seven stories, written early in Oliver's career as an anthropologist, reflect his training and expertise in that field, which in the 1950s was probably the freshest and most creative of the social sciences. In "Rite of Passage," an apparently primitive culture turns out to be a highly advanced society that has deliberately edited itself down to the essentials; in "Artifact," Paleolithic-type flint scrapers turn up in the unlikely sands of Mars. "A Star Above It" is a "time patrol" story à la Poul Anderson, but goes beyond the Patrol's status quo ethics: Do not the people in a newly created alternate past also have a claim on existence? A related anthology is Oliver's *The Edge of Forever: Classic Anthropological Science Fiction* (Sherburne 1971), with an "I knew him when" biographical

introduction by William F. Nolan and a checklist of all Oliver's science fiction published up to that time. Its focus is more on the manipulation of a culture by external agencies unknown to it, as in "Transfusion," a startling revision of conventional wisdom about Earth's own prehistoric past. Both are stimulating collections.

*3-138. Oliver, Chad. **Shadows in the Sun.** Ballantine, 1954.

A field anthropologist learns that the South Texas community he has been studying is a colony of a galactic civilization; its inhabitants convincingly come on as small-town folk of appropriately diverse ages and conditions, but hold nightly meetings in which they commune with the interstellar home country. The story is in sharp contrast, however, to the popular paranoid "aliens are among us" theme, for the hero has an honest inner conflict between leaving to join the galactic culture and remaining on Earth as, in effect, an "Indian." Oliver used to good advantage his training as a anthropologist and his residence in Texas—not the small-town Texas of *The Last Picture Show*, to be sure—in this impressive first novel. Compare Simak, *Way Station* [3-165]; contrast Finney. *The Body Snatchers* [3-72].

3-139.   Oliver, Chad. **The Winds of Time.** Doubleday, 1957.

A burned-out M.D. on a fishing trip up the Gunnison River in Colorado encounters space visitors stranded on Earth when their starship crashed. The human-habitable planets they have visited thus far have either been pretechnological and unable to repair their spacecraft, have been embroiled in war, or have been empty wastelands as the result of war; an early use in SF of "Fermi's paradox" to explain why we have never been visited by ET's. The extraterrestrials left their own world because war seemed imminent, and now are stuck on an Earth that's in the same fix. A cautious venture out to civilization verifies that present-level technology is incapable of putting them back on their journey; it can, however, synthesize the drug the visitors use for suspended animation, and perhaps they will find salvation in Earth's far future (if there has not in the interim been a world-destroying war). The doctor, whose wife has taken up with another man in his absence, decides to go with them. The existential resolution for this viewpoint character is thus the diametric opposite of that in Oliver's *Shadows in the Sun* [3-138]. This story has a mixed mood of estrangement, nostalgic leave-taking, and desperate hope. Contrast Neville, *Bettyann* [3-134]. [For other works by this author see chapter 5.]

*3-140. Orwell, George (pseud. of Eric Arthur Blair). **Nineteen Eighty-Four.** Secker, 1949.

One of the greatest novels of the 20th century, which anti-SF critics still insist is not science fiction. Although British in flavor, this is a universal future projection of the totalitarian state: its nature, purposes, and prospects. Plotted like a suspenseful pulp thriller, but with characters with whom the reader empathizes, it carries one along to it last ironic line. And it should be read that way, freshly, even though a substantial cottage industry of criticism has grown up around it like suburbs at the base of a lofty mountain. The fact that the actual year 1984 came and found not a Big Brother watching in London but an indulgent and inattentive Old Uncle in Washington does not diminish the importance of the warning; eternal vigilance, well before the event, is still the price of liberty. This story was made into an effective motion picture in which Richard Burton played his last screen role as the inquisitor, O'Brien. Compare Huxley, *Brave New World* [2-66], and Knight, *Hell's Pavement* [3-101].

*3-141. Pangborn, Edgar. **A Mirror for Observers.** Doubleday, 1954.

Martians in underground cities for thousands of years have manipulated Earth's historical development. Martian Elmis foresees a great new ethical age for Earth under the leadership of a Gandhi/M. L. King saint-figure; Martian Namir looks toward a "final solution" for the Earth problem in mutually annihilative war. The conflict between Elmis and Namir has been compared with that of God and Satan in the Book of Job; and beyond that, wrote Peter S. Beagle in afterword to a later edition of the novel (Bluejay, 1983, p. 228), it reflects "the endless internal battle that everyone fights who cannot quite abandon hope of one day waking from the nightmare of our species' history." Contrast Vonnegut, *The Sirens of Titan* [3-192].

3-142. Pangborn, Edgar. **West of the Sun.** Doubleday, 1953.

A spacecraft crash-lands on a planet inhabited by two different sentient humanoid species, intelligent but preliterate. One forceful crew member wishes to "bring them civilization," that is, exploit them; the others, although of necessity becoming involved in fierce intertribal war, envision a harmonious community of all three species. Given a chance to return to Earth rather than remain with their aboriginal friends, they refuse. Convincing description of planetary milieu; good characterization. Last chapter gets a tad didactic, but this first novel of Pangborn's still reads well today. Compare Piers Anthony's trilogy, *Omnivore, Orn,* and *Ox* (1968, 1971, 1976). [For other works by this author see chapter 4.]

3-143. Piper, H(enry) Beam (pseud. of John J. McGuire). **Crisis in 2140.** Ace, 1957.

Serialized in *Astounding*, 1953, as "Null-ABC." Idiotic, systematically applied learning theories have resulted in paradox: an advanced high-tech civilization in which the great majority of people are illiterate. Political conflict is between those who support the status quo, in which Literates (like the "scribes" of Biblical antiquity) are a licensed, closed guild, and the radicals, who want Socialized Literacy, that is, that the necessary few who can read and write should become government employees. It does not occur to either side that children at large could simply be taught to read! Good satire on the U.S. teacher-training establishment and on other hidebound, self-serving guilds such as the American Medical Association. Published as an Ace Double, paired with an unrelated novel, *Gunner Cade* by Cyril Judd (Cyril Kornbluth and Judith Merril), itself a neglected gem that undercuts the militaristic ideology of such books as Heinlein's *Starship Troopers* [3-90].

3-144. Piper, H(enry) Beam. **Federation.** Ace, 1981.

Five stories by an unduly neglected writer who broke into print in 1947 with the frequently anthologized "Time and Time Again" (not included here) and whose career tragically ended with his suicide in 1964. Human-alien communication is the theme of three of the tales: "Oomphel in the Sky," "Naudsonce," and most notably "Omnilingual," about the cracking of a long-dead Martian language by a woman scientist who must also battle an ambitious, sexist male colleague. John F. Carr in his introduction describes how he pieced together from Piper's fiction and from recalled conversations between Piper and Jerry Pournelle a centuries-spanning future history, cyclical in nature like Poul Anderson's, with a Terran Federation that eventually thickens into empire. A followup collection edited by Carr, *Empire* (Ace, 1981), leads off in the near-present with "The Edge of the Knife," about a history professor who remembers future events and gets into trouble for absentmindedly referring to them in class! Other, longer works in the Federation saga include *Space Viking* (Ace, 1963) and *Junkyard Planet* (Putnam, 1963; variant title *The Cosmic Computer*).

*3-145. Pohl, Frederik. **The Best of Frederik Pohl.** Nelson Doubleday, 1975.

Sixteen stories from 1954 to 1967, selected by Lester del Rey. An afterword by Pohl describes the genesis of some of them. "The Midas Plague" (SFHF) inverts the values of our present consumer society: wealth is defined as the right to consume *less*; as you rise in social rank you move into a smaller house. "The Census Takers" have the job, in an overcrowded world, of killing off every 300th person; the surplus folk are referred to, in chilling bureaucratese, as Overs. "The Day the Martians Came" makes a pointed comment on racism, from an unusual angle. Pohl's mordant wit, masking an old-fashioned moral concern, is shown to advantage in this choice collection.

3-146. Pohl, Frederik. **Drunkard's Walk.** Ballantine, 1960.
The hero, a math teacher, repeatedly attempts to kill himself, but with no known motivation of his own. He discovers that a closed corporation of immortal telepaths exists, which seeks to prevent the spread of telepathy into the species in general and has been sending suicidal messages to him in particular. A state of drunkenness protects him temporarily against mental control; but the "drunkard's walk" of the title is also a mathematical concept, referring to the irregular motion of small particles under random molecular collision (Brownian movement). Straight-line social progress, which the immortal elite will attempt to carry out if they win, is doomed to peter out, exhausted; for society to continue evolving, uncontrolled randomness—the "drunkard's walk"—is necessary. A thoughtful argument wrapped in an action-adventure plot. A shorter version appeared in *Galaxy* in 1960. Compare Robinson, *The Power* [3-151]. [For other works by this author see chapters 4 and 5.]

*3-147. Pohl, Frederik, and C(yril) M. Kornbluth. **The Space Merchants.** Ballantine, 1953.
Serialized in *Galaxy*, 1952, as "Gravy Planet." Between the 1930s and the 1950s the target of social criticism in America shifted from Wall Street to Madison Avenue. In this novel, reflecting that shift, the world of the future—an overcrowded, resources-starved future—is ruled by two rival advertising agencies. Thematically related to the mainstream novel (and film) *The Hucksters*, but carried out to a satiric *reductio ad absurdem*. Kornbluth later stated that he and Pohl packed into this story everything they hated about advertising, and it came out with Swiftian savagery. One of the first novels by writers with primary roots in the pulps to make an impact in mainstream circles, and, by mainstream measurements a bestseller. A sequel by Pohl (after Kornbluth's death), is *The Merchants' War* (St. Martin's, 1984); both are collected as *Venus, Inc.* (Nelson Doubleday, 1985).

3-148. Pohl, Frederik, and C(yril) M. Kornbluth. **Wolfbane.** Ballantine, 1959. Recommended ed.: Baen, 1986.
This was, regrettably, the last collaboration between Pohl and Kornbluth

before the latter's too-early death. It is one of their strangest. The Earth has been hauled farther out from the sun by pyramidal, solid-state robots, which from time to time kidnap individual humans and plug them into their control system as, in effect, high-grade computers. Meanwhile the rest of humanity develops a culture (driven essentially by malnutrition!) of ritual speech and gesture and Zen-like meditation. A few, however, are not docile Citizens but Wolves, and some of them end up in the robots' comm net and begin to sabotage it. The largely unintelligible activities of the Pyramids, and the stealthy gnawing at their fortress by the human mice in their midst, strikingly resemble the incomprehensible doings of the "mechs" and the effort of humans to survive among them in Greg Benford's memorable *Great Sky River* [4-44]. Pohl addressed himself to the problem of a too-compressed second half in the 1986 revision.

3-149.   Pohl, Frederik, and C(yril) M. Kornbluth. **The Wonder Effect.** Ballantine, 1962.

Nine stories from 1940 to 1961; the later ones were completed by Pohl from manuscripts left unfinished at the time of Kornbluth's death (1958). Of the early ones, "Best Friend" is a touching story of human-canine relationships in an urban, mechanized future, told from the viewpoint of the dog; compare Simak's *City* [3-163]. The authors' acute political consciousness is apparent in stories like "The Engineer," which explains why Mexico *wins* a future war with the United States; and especially "Critical Mass," which explores the stagnancy of a society organized around fallout shelters and "massive retaliation" from the standpoint of Arnold Toynbee's philosophy of history. (But they could be cold warriors too, as in "The Quaker Cannon.") Pohl's introduction also describes how some of their novel-length collaborations were written.

*3-150.   Reynolds, Mack. **The Best of Mack Reynolds.** Pocket, 1976.

Foreword by Barry Malzberg; introduction and headnotes by the author. Versatility and a knack for the O. Henry surprise ending, which on first reading actually does surprise, mark this collection of 22 stories from 1950 to 1974 featuring time travel paradoxes; a Sherlock Holmes pastiche; utopias and dystopias; deals-with-the-devil stories; speculations on the Soviet future, surprisingly fresh despite the demise of the U.S.S.R. ("Freedom," "Revolution," and the wickedly satiric "Subversive"); an ostensibly postnuclear war story, "Survivor," in which the war turns out to have been a false alarm but social disaster happens anyway; a parody tourist guide, for Mars; and "Fad," which tells what happens when the motivational researchers con the American woman once too often.

Starting out in SF in 1950, too late (he believed) to catch up with what Asimov and Clarke already knew about the physical sciences, Reynolds elected to go with the social sciences, and with extensive foreign travel; it shows. A tale like "Pacifist" may start a furious argument among readers but there isn't a dull story in the bunch. [For other works by this author see chapter 4.]

3-151.   Robinson, Frank M. **The Power.** Lippincott, 1956.

An emerging-psi-powers story, well told as a suspense thriller. A Navy Committee for Human Research sees actual telekinesis performed; ergo, the holder of the power must be one of its own members, the likeliest of whom, the son of a dowser and a faith healer, is promptly murdered. The unknown psychic evidently wishes to keep the power for himself. Other deaths follow, and the story becomes a chase, particularly through the gritty environs of Chicago (which Robinson knew well). Surprise twists lead to a disconcerting climax in which the fugitive hero learns *he* has "the power"—and therefore faces the same temptation as his late antagonist. Compare Wells, *The Invisible Man* (1897). After a long absence from SF writing Robinson weighed in again in 1992 with *The Dark Beyond the Stars*, an impressive work [4-363], and indicated in private correspondence later that year that his next project would be a sequel to *The Power*. [For other works by this author see chapter 4.]

3-152.   Russell, Eric Frank. **The Best of Eric Frank Russell.** Ballantine, 1978.

Thirteen stories, almost all from *Astounding*, starting with the touching far-future tale "Mana" (1937), of the last man on Earth bestowing the gift of fire and technology upon humanity's heirs. Good sampling of the Russell range, from humor ("Jay Score," or the hilarious if slightly unbelievable "Homo Saps") to high drama ("Late Night Final," "I Am Nothing," "Fast Falls the Eventide"). Alan Dean Foster contributed an introduction on this writer who deserves to be remembered more for these thoughtfully worked out shorter pieces than for his hokey works such as *Sinister Barrier*, whose great impact when it first appeared in 1939 (in the first issue of *Unknown*) is a mystery, unless a high proportion of readers then were true believers in the revelations of Charles Fort.

3-153.   Russell, Eric Frank. **The Great Explosion.** Dobson, 1962.

An expansion of ". . . And Then There Were None" (*Astounding*, 1951; SFHF). The "explosion" of the title is that of Earth's mavericks and mal-contents—convicts, nudists, what have you—carried by faster-than-light drive to the far corners of the universe. Belatedly, Earth's military and diplomatic forces go after four such disreputable worlds only to find that the colonists' answer to the stock question "Take me to your leader" is "What's *that?*" The political economy of such settlements is what in the United States nowadays would be called Libertarian; their psychological condition is a happy anarchy. A fine, government-deflating, satirical romp. Would it could be true.

3-154. St. Clair, Margaret. **Agent of the Unknown.** Ace, 1956.
On a remote planetoid made up as a rundown tropical resort (palm trees, a lagoon, and all that) beachcomber Don Haig acquires an exquisite doll made by a mysterious artificer named Vulcan at the other end of the galaxy. Mulciber, head of the police, wants the doll, which reputedly heals diseases. In the course of subsequent adventures Don learns he is a pawn between Vulcan, who works for further human progress, and Mulciber, who wants to continue the status quo. A darkly told tale that confutes the whole Golden Age derring-do tradition; Don is the antithesis to Heinlein's or "Doc" Smith's omnicompetent hero, and the story's atmosphere and mood sound much like J. G. Ballard, with a conclusion that is an echo of Philip K. Dick. Appropriately the other half of the Ace Double in which this story was first published was an early Dick novel, *The World Jones Made*, thematically related both to this story and to Dick's *Martian Time-Slip* [3-66].

*3-155. St. Clair, Margaret. **Change the Sky, and Other Stories.** Ace, 1974.
Eighteen stories, 1951 to 1961, mostly from *Fantasy & Science Fiction*, written with irony, sophistication, and at times real bite. "Age of Prophecy" opens in a new Dark Ages with a "prophets' contest." A contestant pretending to levitate by supernatural power is actually a scientist wearing antigravity equipment. Unmasked, he is stoned to death, and the story then follows the career of his young unmasker. On a lighter note, "The Wines of Earth" introduces galactic wine tasters to the pleasures of California's Napa Valley. St. Clair had a knack for fresh twists on older science fiction ideas: "Asking" is a variation on Henry Kuttner's "The Proud Robot"; "Lazarus" is a particularly grisly reworking of the original Frankenstein theme; "Thirsty God" is thematically related to St. Clair's own earlier gem, here uncollected, "Garden of Evil" (*Planet Stories*, Summer 1949). The title story, whose wealthy, restless hero hires an artist to make a succession of "ideal" worlds to inhabit, in none of which can the hero find real happiness, is especially memorable. A superior collection. Contrast Clingerman, *A Cupful of Space* [3-53].

*3-156. Sarban (pseud. of John W. Wall). **The Sound of His Horn.** Davies, 1952. Recommended ed.: Ballantine, 1960.

A British POW "escapes" from a Nazi prison camp into an alternate future world in which the Nazis won World War II. Kingsley Amis aptly pointed out in his introduction to this story that although most U.S. SF dystopias of the 1950s (for example, those of Pohl and Kornbluth) were urban in setting and tone, rural life can know horrors of its own; in this case, a forested estate where feudal barons stage great hunts with human beings as prey (hence the story's title, quoted from the Scottish fox hunting ballad "John Peel"). An understated but quite harrowing tale. Compare the even more chilling "Weihnachtsabend" by Keith Roberts (in Hartwell, *World Treasury of Science Fiction* [4-539]); contrast the Japanese-occupied San Francisco locale in Dick, *The Man in the High Castle* [3-65].

3-157. Sheckley, Robert. **Immortality, Inc.** Bantam, 1959. Variant title: *Immortality Delivered* (Avalon, 1958).

"Immortality" in SF has usually meant biological longevity, as in Vance's *To Live Forever* [3-187], Heinlein's "Methuselah's Children" (in *The Past Through Tomorrow* [3-89]) or Anderson's *The Boat of a Million Years* [4-11]. In Sheckley's variant, science has discovered an actual afterlife complete with real ghosts, and an ever-ingenious capitalism has figured out a way to market it. A 20th-century ad man is snatched into this amoral, hustling, violent future society and finds his own well-honed but archaic survival skills barely able to cope. Dark comedy, of which Sheckley was a master, with serious social commentary underlying the fast-moving surface adventure. Compare Pohl and Kornbluth's *The Space Merchants* [3-147]; contrast Heinlein's *Stranger in a Strange Land* [3-91].

3-158. Sheckley, Robert. **Notions: Unlimited.** Bantam, 196.

Twelve stories from 1952 to 1957, primarily from *Galaxy*. The dangerous folly of quick technological fixes is a common theme, as in "The Leech" and "Watchbird"; the maladaptability of humans to alien planets is another, as in "A Wind is Rising," "Morning After," "Dawn Invader," and especially "The Native Problem," in which a religiously and culturally rigid shipload of colonists cannot bring themselves to believe that the only human being on the planet they are invading is in fact an Earthman who has successfully adapted to its native ways. Some readers may better enjoy the story choices in another Sheckley anthology, *Pilgrimage to Earth* (Bantam, 1957); its title story and the first item in this collection, "Gray Flannel Armor," have the same basic idea, but in "Pilgrimage to Earth" it is given a sharp, savage and, some would say, sexist twist at the end. The selections in the earlier collection have a flavor like that of New York standup comedy routines, but more coherent and blacker in their humor.

*3-159. Sheckley. Robert. **Untouched by Human Hands.** Ballantine, 1954.
Sheckley's first story collection, and a brilliant debut, contains "Seventh Victim," in which an otherwise conventional near-future society sanctions the lethal but apparently stress-reducing game of Hunter and Victim; it was made into an effective movie, *Tenth Victim.* "The Monsters," a straight-faced exercise in cultural relativism, has one of the most startling opening lines in all science fiction (or, indeed, in all fiction). "Specialist" carries Adam Smith's stodgy Division of Labor to its ultimate logical conclusion; "Cost of Living" does the same with the problem, already severe in the 1950s, of mounting consumer debt. The U.K. edition published by M. Joseph, 1955, drops and replaces two stories. Sheckley's voice represented an early break with, and fresh contrast to, the styles and themes of Golden Age SF. Compare Tenn, *Of All Possible Worlds* [3-175]. Sheckley enthusiasts should investigate *The Collected Short Stories of Robert Sheckley*, a five-volume set issued in 1991. [For other works by this author see chapter 4.]

3-160. Shiras, Wilmar H. **Children of the Atom.** Gnome, 1953.
Originally a series in *Astounding* that began with "In Hiding" (SFHF), whose supergenius young hero carefully conceals his higher intelligence from the normals around him; a situation familiar to anyone who was a bright kid roughly handled by parents, other adults, or peers. Most prodigies do work their way through the problem, and so it is with David and a handful of other supernormal children who were produced as mutants by an atomic power plant explosion. They are helped out of their isolation by a sympathetic psychiatrist and emerge into society to make the world better; the world's willingness to take their advice is, alas, less plausible. Compare Kuttner and Moore, *Mutant* [3-107]; contrast Stapledon, *Odd John* [2-120].

*3-161. Shute, Nevil (pseud. of Nevil Shute Norway). **On the Beach.** Heinemann, 1957.
A nuclear war has happened. Australia is spared material damage and continues a semblance of normal life, but the radiation level has risen to such a point that all of humanity is doomed. A U.S. submarine that survived the war sets out to discover whether anyone is alive elsewhere on Earth. It puts in at San Francisco, which is physically intact but dead; follows an irregular radio signal that turns out to be an *ignis fatuus*; and returns to Australia, where the government has prepared euthanasia

tablets for all who want to avoid the last ravages of radiation sickness. An effective warning of an all-too-real possibility; even more effective as a film, with understated images of a civilization shutting down. Conceivably in this instance science fiction may have had an indirect impact on foreign policy.

3-162. Simak, Clifford D(onald). **The Best of Clifford D. Simak.** Sidgwick & Jackson, 1975. Ed. by Angus Wells.

Ten stories from 1939 to 1971. Simak in a modest introduction noted the newspaper experience that influenced his early (not so much his later) work, and accepted with pleasure the "pastoral" label critics have hung on him; one writes about what one loves. Except for "Sunspot Purge" (1940), which builds on a theory taken seriously at one time that economic booms and busts can be correlated with the sunspot cycle, most of these stories deal with alien-human encounters usually benign in a rural Midwest setting, as in "The Sitters," "A Death in the House," and "Shotgun Cure." Simak's Hugo-winning story of this type, "The Big Front Yard," is unaccountably omitted; it may be found in *The Worlds of Clifford Simak* (Simon & Schuster, 1960). Even though the present collection is a "best of" volume, some readers may prefer the story selection in *Strangers in the Universe* (Simon & Schuster, 1956), the thematic emphasis of which was on outgrowing human-centered arrogance; its initial story, "Shadow Show," was in effect a powerful rebuttal to the premise of Blish's *The Seedling Stars* [3-23].

*3-163. Simak, Clifford D(onald). **City.** Gnome, 1952.

Eight quietly told stories from *Astounding*, 1944 to 1951, which describe the decline and disappearance of humanity once it abandons its most characteristic habitat, the city. Some of the more venturesome leave civilization to imprint their psyches on wild, non-tool-using animals native to Jupiter ("Desertion"); others retreat to automated estates, as in "Huddling Place" (SFHF), a locale that recurs in later stories, run by an ageless robot butler named Jenkins and inhabited by sentient, peaceable dogs who are taking over humans' erstwhile role of planetary custodians. (Meanwhile the ants, also evolved into sentience, pursue bizarre and incomprehensible goals of their own.) In book form, the stories are framed as "legends," told around campfires by the dogs, who politely debate whether humans in fact ever existed. A haunting, elegiac tale, diametrically opposed to the "can do" spirit of most Golden Age SF. An additional story, "Epilog," was added for a later edition (Ace, 1981). A major work, which in 1953 won the International Fantasy Award.

3-164. Simak, Clifford D(onald). **Time Is the Simplest Thing.** Doubleday, 1961.

Materially barred from space by the Van Allen belts and other sources of lethal radiation (as many in the non-SF world assumed would be the case in the era before manned spacecraft), humans can travel to the stars only telepathically. Fishhook, the organization that sends its employees out on these mental missions, has acquired great economic and political power through its monopoly of the goodies these agents find in space. Then one of its operatives returns from a far planet with his mind linked to that of a benevolent but very strange alien. The novel becomes an extended chase, with the viewpoint character fleeing not only from Fishhook but also from mobs hostile to all "parries"—paranormals—in part, ironically, because of their own legitimate resentment of Fishhook's power. Parallels are drawn, implicitly, with the Salem witch craze and with the Nazi *Kristallnacht* in 1934. Simak's message, as in so much of his work: trust the unknown; embrace the strange. Compare Henderson, *Pilgrimage* [3-93]; van Vogt, *Slan* [3-180]. Contrast Robinson, *The Power* [3-151].

*3-165. Simak, Clifford D(onald). **Way Station.** Doubleday, 1963.

A Civil War veteran comes home to the family farm, which becomes a station or stop for interstellar travelers. Time passes more slowly inside the disguised farmhouse, so that the stationmaster's longevity in the outside world (which he enters to pick up his mail!) attracts the attention of hostile neighbors and of an implausibly understanding CIA agent. The story gets its effect from casual juxtaposition of bizarre alien visitors and artifacts with realistic southwestern Wisconsin locale. It carries Simak's perennial message that all sentient beings can and must get along, or perish; the various galactic races face the same danger from themselves as do Earth's own warring peoples. A tragic counterpoint is a bittersweet, thwarted love between the hero and a composite "ghost" of two women from his wartime past. A sentimental story, but effective; it won the Hugo Award in 1963 for best novel. HW, 1963 [For other works by this author see chapter 4.]

3-166. Skinner, B(urrhus) F(rederick). **Walden Two.** Macmillan, 1948.

Unlike most post–World War II science fiction, which considered social control by psychological conditioning to be a form of hell on Earth, Skinner presented it grandly as utopian. The structure of the story (which, as a story, doesn't amount to much) is a debate between an advocate of human free choice and a champion of behavioral manipulation, which is offered as the answer to all of society's ills. The choice of title, from that most unconditionable of Americans, Henry David Thoreau, is simply incomprehensible. Unrepentant, Skinner returned to this thesis 23 years later in a nonfiction work, *Beyond Freedom and Dignity* (Knopf, 1971), and again in the third volume of his autobiography, *A Matter of Consequences* (Knopf, 1983). Contrast Huxley, *Brave New World* [2-56]; Burgess, *A Clockwork Orange* [3-41]; Knight, *Hell's Pavement* [3-101]; Orwell, *Nineteen Eighty-Four* [3-140]. At the opposite ideological extreme from Skinner, contrast Ayn Rand, *Atlas Shrugged* (Random, 1957), which is even more didactic and talky but at least has a story line.

*3-167. Smith, E(dward) E(lmer). **The Lensman Series.** Fantasy Press, 1948–1954.
The space opera to end all space operas, with humans and aliens arrayed (some on each side) in a cosmic war of Good and Evil, which even George Lucas would be hard put to top. For all its implausibilities, this series represents a vast improvement in "Doc" Smith's novelistic skills of storytelling and character portrayal over his archetypal, but crude, *Skylark of Space* [2-114]. Readers' response to the "Civilization" vs. "Boskonia" theme as an allegory of the "West" vs. "Fascism" during World War II was an important factor in the stories' initial reception. The novels are best read in the order in which they appeared in *Astounding: Galactic Patrol* (1937–1938), *Gray Lensman* (1939–1940), *Second-Stage Lensmen* (1942), and *Children of the Lens* (1947–1948). *Triplanetary* is a fix-up novel, which converts an earlier, previously unrelated serial in *Amazing* into a "prequel" to the series; it and *First Lensman*, written after the initial tetralogy but preceding its chronology, give away Smith's conceptual scheme, which his Lensman-hero had to puzzle out the hard way through four long novels. *Vortex Blaster* (1960) is peripheral to the main series, although occurring in the same future universe; it grew out of short stories in the more obscure pulps (*Comet, Super Science*) in 1941.

*3-168. Stapledon, W(illiam) Olaf. **Sirius: A Fantasy of Love and Discord.** Secker, 1944.
Related to Stapledon's *Odd John* [2-120] in its portrayal of the estrangement of a superbeing among limited, unimaginative normals. In this case the superbeing is a surgically enhanced dog, thus even more isolated from humanity than the evolved-from-people superhuman in *Odd John*. The dog Sirius also becomes, in effect, an outside observer commenting on the shortcomings of civilization. His ultimately tragic love relationship with a human young woman, which in our own more explicit era might have been simply gross, is tastefully handled. Lacking the cosmic sweep of

Stapledon's *Star Maker* [2-121] and *Last and First Men* [2-119], it is far more satisfying—more so even than *Odd John*—in the qualities that make for a good novel. Compare Neville, *Bettyann* [3-134]; contrast Shiras, *Children of the Atom* [3-160]. [For other works by this author see chapter 2.]

*3-169. Stewart, George R(ippey). **Earth Abides.** Random, 1949.

In a near future, a plague devastates humankind, leaving isolated pockets of survivors. The story follows the fortunes of one group in the San Francisco Bay area, who subsist for quite some time on the bounties of civilization that have remained intact. But the subtler social fabric, formerly held together by the cooperation of large numbers of people, is too much for this handful to sustain. With a mournful backward look at the millions of now-doomed volumes in the University of California library, the protagonist teaches the new children how to make bows and arrows. He lives long enough to see society forming itself anew at the tribal level. He himself is fated to be misremembered as a legendary culture-hero. The quotation from which the title derives (Ecclesiastes 1:4) is apt. Compare Jack London, "The Scarlet Plague" (in *The Science Fiction of Jack London* [1-60]; Stephen King's *The Stand* [4-233]; Shelley, *The Last Man* [1-85]. First winner of the International Fantasy Award, 1951; a major work. IFA, 1951

3-170.   Sturgeon, Theodore. **The Dreaming Jewels.** Greenberg, 1950. Variant title: *The Synthetic Man*, Pyramid, 1957. Recommended ed.: Gregg, 1978.

Sturgeon's first novel, published initially in *Fantastic Adventures* (February 1950). It was expanded by about 17 percent and rewritten for book publication in August of that same year. In the interim L. Ron Hubbard in *Astounding* (May 1950) launched Dianetics, which may have made some contribution to the story. Paul Williams' introduction to the Gregg edition discusses the revision from magazine to book version in detail, useful to anyone interested in a writer's working methods, and points also to the autobiographical elements in the story. Horty, the young hero, runs away from "home" (and an evil stepfather) and grows up in a carnival (over which presides an even more evil stepfather). The story nevertheless exemplifies Sturgeon's conviction, which would be expressed often in later work, that "a touch of kindness is not cancelled out by all the villainy in the world."

*3-171. Sturgeon, Theodore. **E Pluribus Unicorn.** Abelard, 1953.

Thirteen fine, emotionally intense stories, ranging from "The World Well Lost," probably the first serious and sympathetic treatment in magazine

SF of homosexuality, to "The Professor's Teddy Bear," in the most horrific *Weird Tales* tradition; from the touching love story "A Saucer of Loneliness" to a celebration of jazz musicianship (by one who understood what he was writing about), "Die, Maestro, Die!" Sturgeon's forte was telling stories about people at the edge, and treating them with compassion and nonjudgmentally even when they acted as shockingly as at the climax of "A Way of Thinking." A showcase for a very talented writer, which can be interestingly compared with the earlier collection of Sturgeon's Golden Age work, *Without Sorcery* [3-173].

*3-172. Sturgeon, Theodore. **More Than Human.** Farrar, 1953.
Winner of the International Fantasy Award in 1954, and deservedly so. Growing out of the acclaimed novella, "Baby Is Three" (SFHF), this excellent work describes the rise, against all the meanness and bigotries of the surrounding world, of *Homo Gestalt*, an individual composed of the blended intelligences of numerous people, each of whom retains personal identity while contributing a particular special strength or talent to the whole. An emergence-of-the-superhuman story; made more of a struggle than it was for the superchildren in Clarke's *Childhood's End* [3-44], but shorn also of the inevitable tragedy forecast for the superhumans in Stapledon's *Odd John* [2-120]. Arguably Sturgeon's best book, and frequently on lists for school courses in SF. IFA, 1954

*3-173. Sturgeon, Theodore. **Without Sorcery.** Prime, 1948.
Thirteen of Sturgeon's earliest stories, from 1939 to 1948, including "Microcosmic God" (SFHF); "Poker Face," one of the earliest stories to portray future time travelers going native in the present; "It," a truly oppressive horror story based on the theory of spontaneous generation—scientifically outmoded, of course (or is it?)—and "The Ultimate Egoist," an exercise in philosophical solipsism with an incredible shaggy dog last line. Introduction by Ray Bradbury. Three fine stories from this collection, "Shottle Bop," "Memorial," and "Maturity," reappear in *The Worlds of Theodore Sturgeon* (Ace, 1972), along with specimens of his later, more developed style, such as "The Perfect Host" and "The Other Man," both of which explore the psychiatric frontiers on which Sturgeon was one of SF's boldest pioneers. [For other works by this author see chapter 4.]

3-174. Temple, William F(rederick). **Four-Sided Triangle.** John Long, 1949.
Derives from a novelette in *Amazing*, (1939), and written at a time when the concept of cloning did not yet exist in the non-SF world. Only in science fiction, in 1939, could such a plot have been devised: boy, A, loves

girl, B; boy, C, also loves B, but she loves only A; C therefore duplicates B in the laboratory; but alas, since girl, D, is an exact duplicate of B, therefore D also loves only A. (The situation recalls the Gilbert & Sullivan song from *The Mikado*: "See how the fates their gifts allot/For A is happy, B is not.") However, this story, realistically told and richly characterized, far transcends its pulp origin and remains readable today. It can also be read as an interesting variant on del Rey's classic "Helen O'Loy" (SFHF).

*3-175. Tenn, William (pseud. of Philip Klass). **Of All Possible Worlds.** Ballantine, 1955.

Seven stories and an essay, "On the Fiction in Science Fiction," in this first collection by a writer with an even more savage wit than Robert Sheckley, if that be possible. Memorable items include "Down Among the Dead Men," in which recycled soldiers' corpses are fitted out to fight again because the world is running out of cannon fodder; "The Custodian," a last-person-on-earth story, sort of a jazz variant on Mary Shelley's *The Last Man* [1-85]; and "The Liberation of Earth," a sarcastic parable on the hapless fate of small nations invaded and counterinvaded by ideologically well-intentioned superpowers. A U.K. edition (M. Joseph, 1956) drops two stories and adds three, including "Project Hush," a satire on the fetish of military security, and "Party of the Two Parts," which makes fun of prurience from an unusual angle. Those two stories may also be found in another U.S. collection of Tenn's work, *The Human Angle* (Ballantine, 1956).

3-176. Tenn, William (pseud. of Philip Klass). **Time in Advance.** Bantam, 1958.

Four strong novelettes. Highly advanced aliens, in "Firewater" (*Astounding*, 1952), visit Earth and demoralize humans just by being there. "Precriminals," in "Time in Advance" (*Galaxy*, 1956), are permitted to do prison time *prior* to committing the crime, which they may then do without interference from the law. In "The Sickness" (*Infinity*, 1955) a precariously coexistent Russian-American expedition to Mars finds a dead city and is infected with a Martian disease, with unexpected results. Finally, "Winthrop Was Stubborn" (*Galaxy*, 1957) depicts the plight of five ordinary 20th-century people allowed to time travel by exchanging places with the same number (and mass) of 25th-century folk, all of whom for symmetry's sake must return to their time of origin together—but one won't go home. The successive efforts of each of the other four to persuade the ornery holdout make for some of Tenn's funniest writing. A highly satisfactory collection. [For other works by this author see chapter 4.]

3-177. Tucker, (Arthur) Wilson. **The Long Loud Silence.** Rinehart, 1952.
The United States east of the Mississippi has been devastated by nuclear
and biological weapons. A few surviving immunes are quarantined and
refused reentry to civilization because they are carriers of disease, as
becomes disastrously apparent when the narrator sneaks across the river
and discovers he is leaving a trail of plague behind him. Returning to the
wasteland he becomes reconciled to a life of savagery. Cannibalism implicit in his situation, deleted from the initial edition, reappears in a revision
(Lancer, 1970). Even without that denouement this is a grim unsparing
postholocaust scenario. Compare Christopher, *The Death of Grass* [3-42];
contrast Frank, *Alas, Babylon* [3-74].

3-178. Tucker, (Arthur) Wilson. **The Time Masters.** Rinehart, 1953.
Derives from a well-told short story, "The Job Is Ended." An effective presentation of a taken-for-granted sexual chauvinism, which it is to be hoped
the genre has by now outgrown. A troubled man confesses to a psychiatrist that his wife is his mental superior, which women are not "naturally"
supposed to be. The psychiatrist, also male, a 10,000-year-old survivor of a
spaceship crash, spots the wife as his own spouse (and enemy!) from that
ages-old marooning; of course she's the intellectual superior of her short-
lived husband, she's had longer to work at it. But *he*, the psychiatrist, who
ages ago was the legendary folk hero Gilgamesh, can be presumed to have
the edge over her as they battle for control of Earth's destiny. Historically
significant as a document of the prejudice SF shared with other literature
and with the "real world" in the early 1950s. Followed by a sequel, *Time
Bomb* (1955). The 1971 Nelson Doubleday (SF Book Club) edition
restored missing text. Contrast Mitchison, *Memoirs of a Spacewoman* [3-
127], Le Guin, *The Dispossessed* [4-252], and anything by Joanna Russ,
Vonda McIntyre, Pamela Sargent, or indeed by most male SF writers since
about 1970.

3-179. van Vogt, A(lfred) E(lton). **Away and Beyond.** Pellegrini, 1952.
Nine stories, 1940 to 1948, primarily from *Astounding*. Includes van Vogt's
first-written (but not first-published) SF story, "Vault of the Beast," an
alien-monster-from-the-monster's-viewpoint story; "Asylum," in which a
newspaper reporter (who is not quite what he seems) must deal with high-
IQ, energy-stealing interstellar vampires; and "Secret Unattainable," told
in the form of interoffice memos among the Nazi bureaucracy in World
War II, which offers a novel explanation for Hitler's suicidal invasion of
Russia. Some readers may prefer the story selection in *Destination Universe*
(Pellegrini, 1952), from a wider array of sources—*Startling Stories, Other*

Worlds, Avon Fantasy Reader, Arkham Sampler—as well as some from *Astounding*, such as "The Search," with its memorable image of the down staircase that ends in a void. Van Vogt is not to everybody's taste, but these story collections are worth looking into.

3-180.   van Vogt, A(lfred) E(lton). **Slan.** Arkham, 1946.
The author's first novel-length work, serialized in *Astounding* in 1940, was also one of the first SF stories from the magazines to make it into hardcover publication. According to editor John Campbell, van Vogt used a "trick" to solve the problem of how a merely human writer convincingly describes a superhuman being who by definition is beyond human comprehension: compare Weinbaum, *The New Adam* [2-136]; Stapledon, *Odd John* [2-120]. The trick was to cast the superbeing as a 9-year-old boy on the lam from the human dictator's cops, and tell the story as a don't-pause-for-breath chase sequence. Another explanation, offered van Vogt himself at the 1946 Worldcon, was that he took the interstellar alien monster viewpoint character he had used in several previous stories, made it sympathetic, and installed it in a human body. Whatever the explanation, it worked, in 1940, 1946, and 1951; the reader will have to decide whether it still works today. Simon & Schuster published a revised edition, in 1951, but the first edition is preferred. (Note: *Slan, The Voyage of the Space Beagle*, and *The World of Null-A* were assembled as *Triad: Three Complete Science Fiction Novels*, Simon & Schuster, 1959.)

3-181.   van Vogt, A(lfred) E(lton). **The Voyage of the Space Beagle.** Simon & Schuster, 1950.
This *Beagle* is of course named after HMS *Beagle*, aboard which on a five-year cruise (1831-1836) Charles Darwin gathered much of the data that went into *The Origin of Species*. The fearsome interstellar beasts encountered by the crew of the future *Beagle*, which might have made Darwin give it all up as a bad job, made their first bow in magazine stories, most notably "Black Destroyer" (*Astounding*, July 1939). The stories stood up better as separate entities; van Vogt himself, in *Reflections of A. E. van Vogt* (Fictioneer Books, 1975) called this a "fix-up" novel. The fixer-up—the viewpoint character who knits the various episodes together, at first kibitzing from the sidelines and eventually taking charge—is one of van Vogt's rather obnoxious know-it-all superheroes, who lacks the appeal of young Jommy Cross in *Slan* [3-180]. The book, by example, raises the question of the tendency of critics, teachers and bibliographers to focus on writers' novel-length work, to the neglect of shorter pieces that often may have been better crafted. See James Gunn on this same point, in his introduction to *Some Dreams Are Nightmares* [3-80].

3-182. van Vogt, A(lfred) E(lton). **The Weapon Shops of Isher.** Greenberg, 1951.

The bibliographic history of this work is complex. Two short stories, "The Seesaw" and "'The Weapon Shop" (SFHF) appeared in *Astounding* in 1941 and 1942. These were incorporated with a magazine version of "The Weapon Shops of Isher" (*Thrilling Wonder*, 1949), plus new material, to make up a book of the same title. However, a magazine version of "The Weapon Makers," originally a sequel to the two short stories, appeared in *Astounding* in 1943; then that story, even though published *before* "The Weapon Shops of Isher," was rewritten to make it a *sequel* to *Shops*; a publishing history that matches the intricacy of van Vogt's plots. Greenberg published *The Weapon Makers* as a sequel in 1952. The National Rifle Association should love this series about the Weapon Shops with their slogan "The right to buy weapons is the right to be free." A van Vogtian superhero named Hedrock defends the Shops against the machinations of the wily Empress Innelda . . . but it turns out that *he*, Hedrock, centuries ago founded the Empire in the first place, as well as the Shops. So schizoid a balance between libertarianism and authoritarianism may unconsciously say more about our own culture than about that of van Vogt's far future.

*3-183. van Vogt, A(lfred) E(lton). **The World of Null-A.** Simon & Schuster, 1948. Recommended ed.: Berkley, 1970.

"Null-A"—non-Aristotelianism—was supposed to be the new way of thinking that would permeate humankind with the acceptance of General Semantics, for which a considerable vogue existed among science fictionists in the 1940s. This story, serialized in *Astounding* in 1945, capitalized on that vogue. However, it is not the logical rigor of Alfred Korzybski's *Science and Sanity* that comes through to the present-day reader. The entire novel exemplifies what psychologists today call "magical thinking"—not scientific, and not, except superficially, semanticist. For a supposed superbeing, master of his fate through the power of non-Aristotelian positive thinking, Gilbert Gosseyn acts for most of the story like a pawn in the hands of vast unknown forces, recurrently crying "I do not know who I am!" His superman qualities emerge more clearly in sequels, *The Pawns of Null-A* (Ace, 1948; as *The Players of Null-A*, Berkley, 1966) and *Null-A Three* (DAW, 1985); the latter after prior publication in France, a nation whose SF community, I admit, takes van Vogt far more seriously than I am taking him here. van Vogt, in his introduction to the revised Berkley edition of *World of Null-A*, pointed out in the novel's defense that this was, after all, the first magazine-derived SF novel to be offered in hardcover by a major mainstream publisher after World War II; that choice also speaks volumes about publishers' assessment of the potential U.S. SF audience.

3-184. Vance, Jack (pseud. of John Holbrook Vance). **The Dragon Masters.** Ace, 1963. Recommended ed.: Gregg, 1976.
Hugo for best novella, 1962. At the edge of the galaxy, what is possibly the last human-controlled world is periodically invaded by the lizardlike "Basics"; in the interm, the humans fight each other. The Basics use as their troops genetically engineered humans; the planet's human defenders deploy dragons, of several sizes and degrees of ferocity, which have been developed from "Basics" eggs. However, no summary can do justice to the richness of Vance's atmospherics. Critics have pigeonholed his style as "baroque"; anyhow, it is uniquely his. This book is a landmark in the transformation of SF away from both Golden Age and 1950s themes, yet in a different direction from the emerging "New Wave." The advent of the dragon as a popular theme, foreshadowing Anne McCaffrey's "Weyr Search" (HW, 1968) and its many sequels. The Gregg edition features an introduction by Norman Spinrad.

3-185. Vance, Jack (pseud. of John Holbrook Vance). **The Dying Earth.** Hillman, 1950.
A hauntingly beautiful story of a far future Earth "steeped," as Norman Spinrad has put it, "in magic born of rotting history." Scientific experiment has given place to charms and enchantments that really work. Six loosely connected episodes derive not from technophile Golden Age SF but from a quite antithetical tradition: the world-ends-in-magic milieu explored in the 1930s by Clark Ashton Smith, and picaresque sword-and-sorcery such as Fritz Leiber's early-forties Fafhrd and Gray Mouser tales, with a dash (Chapter 5) of Lord Dunsany. A slender thread of scientific hope is held out in the concluding episode, whose hero, given since childhood to how and why questions and driven by doubts about an approach to reality in which magic spells are learned by rote, makes his way through strange landscapes and degenerate towns to the Museum of Man. But that hope of a scientific renaissance was not to be realized in this novel's several sequels, good as some of them were as stories. Little noticed at initial publication, this work launched a whole subgenre of fictional futures in which magic replaces science, a development not altogether healthy for science fiction or implicitly for the place of science in modern civilization. Interestingly, a countertrend has appeared in the fantasy field, of *formerly* effective magic that became displaced by the emergent scientific world view of the 17th century, as in Tim Powers's *On Stranger Tides* (Ace, 1988).

3-186. Vance, Jack (pseud. of John Holbrook Vance). **The Languages of Pao.** Avalon, 1958.

Having grown to a population of 15 billion, which presses against the edge of subsistence, the planet Pao has developed a stagnant, passive culture under hereditary rule through an omnipresent civil service—rather resembling that of premodern Mandarin China, although Vance doesn't press the point—with a language having no formal comparatives and no verbs. By developing entire new languages, with grammars and vocabularies appropriate to particular vocations (soldiers, scholars, technicians), the way is paved for breaking the cultural mold. Relying on studies such as Benjamin Whorf's pioneering work on the grammar of Hopi and more recent scholarship by Edward Sapir, Vance applies the insight cryptically anticipated also by Nietzsche, that the structure of language shapes a culture's *weltanschauung* far more than the other way around. The first full-scale use in SF of linguistics as a "hard" science. Compare Delany's *Babel-17* [4-126]; contrast Piper's "Omnilingual," in *Federation* [3-144].

*3-187. Vance, Jack (pseud. of John Holbrook Vance). **To Live Forever.** Ballantine, 1956.

In a far future following what is remembered as the "Malthusian Chaos," biological immortality is possible, but if generally allowed it would precipitate a new population explosion. Therefore it has to be earned. One rises in rank, with a set number of years added to life, by civic participation, productive employment, or some spectacular public achievement, through a possible five grades culminating in "Amaranth," indefinite longevity. People who fail to make the grade are visited by their assassins at the end of their allotted time. Of course one may choose to be a "glark"—a nonparticipant in the scheme—and live out one's natural, probably short, life unmolested. Vance works this all out and much more, in terms of a stratified society driven by a covertly vicious form of social climbing. A logical, imaginative work; very possibly Vance's best book. Compare Heinlein, "Methuselah's Children" (in *The Past Through Tomorrow* [3-89]); Anderson, *The Boat of a Million Years* [4-11]. [For other works by this author see chapters 4 and 5.]

3-188. Vercors (pseud. of Jean Bruller). **You Shall Know Them.** Little, Brown, 1953. Trans. by Rita Barisse of *Les animaux dénaturés*, 1952. Variant titles: *Borderline*, Macmillan, 1954; *The Murder of the Missing Link*, Pocket, 1958.

A tribe of "missing links" between ape and human is discovered in a remote corner of New Guinea. Transported to London, one of them is artificially inseminated with human sperm and gives birth. Is *he* a baby boy, or is *it* a little ape? Can it be christened according to the rites of the Church of England? When it is killed, was that act a murder? To the growing dismay of the characters, all dwellers at one or another level of the British Establishment, no generally accepted legal, scientific, or philosophical definition of "man" exists. A court of law, Parliament, and the United Kingdom's famous penny-dreadful press all grapple with the problem. Perhaps only a French writer could so keenly have dissected the ways of his cross-Channel cousins, in a manner both witty and wise. Scientific knowledge of prehuman hominids has grown considerably since 1952, but this book still raises some fundamental questions as to who and what we are.

3-189.   Vidal, Gore. **Messiah.** Dutton, 1954.

A mainstream writer's most impressive venture into science fiction. A new religion proclaims the worship of death, with suicide as the ultimate sacrament. Starting in (stereotypically?) California, the faith spreads across America—is especially strong in Texas—and eventually most of the world. The story is told by the founder's PR man, who does not believe in the religion but goes along for the ride, like the hapless Jack Burden tagging along after Willie Stark in *All the King's Men.* Eventually he flees to Egypt, where a stern, archaic Muslim fundamentalism bars the entrance of any and all infidel notions. A chilling, plausible novel; it anatomizes in particular the amoral, for-hire potential of the mass media at the service of an unscrupulous fanatic. Recommended. Revised in a 1965 edition. Compare Heinlein, *Revolt in 2100* [in *The Past Through Tomorrow,* 3-89]; Leiber, *Gather Darkness!* [3-112]. [For other works by this author see chapter 4.]

3-190.   Vonnegut, Kurt. **Cat's Cradle.** Holt, 1963.

The absurdist vision, going beyond mere satire, that had been subtly implicit even in straightforwardly extrapolative SF by Vonnegut like *Player Piano* [3-191], is unabashed in this novel, published at the dividing line on the calendar between "early modern" and "modern" SF. Not that Vonnegut's earlier satiric targets escape unscathed here, including both organized religion and the organized corporate idiocies of "Ilium" (that is, Troy), New York. But in this novel Vonnegut has more in common with Ballard and Dick than with, say, Pohl and Kornbluth. The irresponsible invention of Ice-9, whose melting point above 100 degrees Fahrenheit spells doom for all life except in the most sizzling tropics, drives what there is of a conventional plot. Like other Vonnegut works, the story also has traceable roots in traditional American folk humor, especially the Southwestern "tall tale."

*3-191. Vonnegut, Kurt. **Player Piano.** Scribner, 1952. Variant title: *Utopia 14*, Bantam, 1954.

It used to be called "technological unemployment"; then "automation"; now, euphemistically, "job displacement." Vonnegut in this first novel realistically traced the personal and political consequences of such transformation, with most working people forced into a future WPA while the upper class languishes in the vapid corporate culture of William C. Whyte's *The Organization Man*. In his opposition to replacing people with machines, the rebellious hero identifies with the Luddites of the Industrial Revolution and with the native Americans' last Ghost Dance uprising: quixotic, but necessary "for the record." The story has touches of the absurdism that would become manifest in Vonnegut's later work, but on the whole it can be read simply as science fictional extrapolation into a quite possible future. Compare Pohl and Kornbluth, *The Space Merchants* [3-147].

3-192. Vonnegut, Kurt. **The Sirens of Titan.** Dell, 1959.

In this second novel Vonnegut took some of the standard gambits of SF (time travel, interplanetary exploration, an invasion from Mars) and put a reverse-English spin on them. This is not so much a work of science fiction as a takeoff from, or jazz variation on, the genre; this novel's closest kin in the modern period may be the works of Douglas Adams. But Vonnegut is after bigger game than is Adams: "I was a victim of a series of accidents," the story's stumbling hero proclaims. "As are we all." Monuments on Earth and on Saturn's satellite Titan exist only to convey a message from one galactic civilization to another; and the message is utterly banal. The high "Tralfamadorian" culture that spans all time simultaneously will reappear as the matrix for the adventures of Billy Pilgrim in Vonnegut's most bitterly autobiographical novel, *Slaughterhouse-Five* [4-479]. The journeyings in this earlier work, from Earth to Mars to Mercury to Titan, are not the jaunty adventures they would have been in the pulp; they are darkly disturbing, which may be a reason conventional science fictionists were slow to respond to this work. The Dell paperback *preceded* hardcover publication by Houghton Mifflin (1961). [For other works by this author see chapter 4.]

3-193. Williamson, Jack. **Darker Than You Think.** Fantasy, 1948.

Originally published in *Unknown* in 1940, this may be Williamson's finest work—a pioneering effort to give "supernatural" phenomena, in this case lycanthropy, a scientific rationale. The science is a bit shaky from today's perspective, but the felt response of the viewpoint character as a werewolf and in his other shape-changes, is vivid and convincing. The experience also converts his purpose from a stock pulp-heroic defense of humanity against the encroaching lycanthropes to a Nietzschean "beyond good and evil" embrace of his antihuman role, reminiscent of the change in the way the young giants are perceived in the course of Wells's *The Food of the Gods* [1-99]. In a sense this is a variation on the Superman theme, except that it does not depict the superbeings as benevolent toward humanity; their coming regime truly will be "darker than you think." A Dell edition in 1979 reproduced the original magazine illustrations by Edd Cartier. Compare Matheson, *I Am Legend* [3-120]; contrast Stapledon, *Odd John* [2-120].

*3-194. Williamson, Jack. **The Humanoids.** Simon & Schuster, 1949. Recommended ed.: Avon, 1980.
"To serve and obey, and guard men from harm." This slogan of Williamson's highly efficient Humanoids sounds at first like Asimov's Three Laws of Robotics; the catch is that these robots interpret "guarding" as preventing humans from doing anything that could possibly get them into trouble; in short, anything at all. John Campbell was so upset by the downbeat ending of the first humanoids story, "With Folded Hands" (*Astounding*, 1947, SFHF), that he insisted Williamson write a happy-ending sequel, ". . . And Searching Mind," out of which this novel grew. The author, however, balked at the editor's mandated upbeat conclusion (humans regain their freedom by developing psi powers, which was the robots benevolent purpose all along), and in later stories on the humanoid theme persisted in regarding the robots as inimical. The story can also be taken as a parable about the effect of ever-increasing mechanization on our own present-day civilization. The 1980 edition includes "With Folded Hands" and a new introduction by the author. Compare Čapek, *R.U.R.* [2-16]; Vonnegut, *Player Piano* [3-191].

3-195. Williamson, Jack (as Will Stewart). **Seetee Ship.** Gnome, 1951.
The earliest SF to deal systematically with the concept of antimatter, then called *contraterrene* matter—C.T.—hence, "seetee." One of the early-forties *Astounding* stories that were combined into this work was titled "Opposites—React!"; oppositions not only of matter-antimatter but of human beings and governments. (Williamson's future geopolitics envisioned a monopoly capitalist Earth, a Martian Reich, an Oriental empire on Venus, and a Union of Soviet Satellites of Jupiter, with the liberty-loving asteroid frontiersmen chafing under a High Space Mandate of the four great powers.) *Seetee Ship* features stereotyped man-woman relationships and national traits, but an absorbing story; the pulp tradition at its best. The sequel, *Seetee Shock*, which by the vagaries of publishing appeared in

print *before* the work it followed (Simon & Schuster, 1950), combined a typical melodramatic Williamson story line, in which all is lost until the last page, with a serious philosophical debate, couched in terms of the suppression or release of seetee-based energy; between stability under elite stewardship and the promise and risks of social freedom. [For other works by this author see chapters 2, 4 and 5.]

*3-196. Wolfe, Bernard. **Limbo.** Random, 1952. U.K. title: *Limbo 90,* Secker, 1953. Recommended ed.: Carroll & Graf, 1987.
Hailed as America's answer to the two greatest British dystopias, *Nineteen Eighty-Four* and *Brave New World,* this remarkable novel blends satire, Freudian psychoanalysis, outrageous puns, literary allusions, and straight-line scientific and technical extrapolation. After World War III, allegedly pacifist regimes come to power in what is left of the United States and the U.S.S.R., based on voluntary quadruple amputation. The assumption is that people cannot march against each other if they have no legs; to dis-arm it is necessary, literally, to dis-arm. Of course, as a doctor learns who returns to this mad culture after 18 years on a remote island, the actual state of affairs is not one of peace and joy. All that was dysfunctional in the world of 1950 as Wolfe saw it is carried forward forty years into an appalling future, including a truly dismal forecast of the future of sex. Although lapsing at times into didacticism, especially toward the conclusion, the narrative is hard-driving and dramatic. The "author's notes" in the 1987 reprint describing the intellectual influences upon him when he wrote the story include both Norbert Wiener and A. E. van Vogt! By any measure, including that of "mainstream" literature, this is a major achievement.

3-197. Wright, Austin Tappan. **Islandia.** Farrar, 1942.
This is a worthy conclusion to the "lost continent" literary tradition, which was excluded from SF by geographic exploration and satellite mapping in the 20th century. The Islandians, after a long history in isolation (like Tokugawa Japan), are debating the extent to which they should allow relations with the (real) nations of the modern world as the novel opens; viewpoint character is an American who aspires to become the first U.S. consul to Islandia. The story unfolds in leisurely fashion, convincing the reader of its social "reality" by its accumulation of careful brushstrokes. Islandia's people, literature, politics, place names, and much else, were a lifelong project of the author, and the published novel is a posthumous abridgement of a 400,000-word original. It thus compares in scope and texture with Tolkien's Middle Earth and Herbert's Arrakis, but is more conventionally realistic than either. A unique work; not to everyone's

taste, but one that will always find readers. *Islandia* has earned the compliment of semi-sequels, all by Mark Saxton: *The Islar* (1969), *The Two Kingdoms* (1979), and *Havoc in Islandia* (1982), all from Houghton Mifflin.

3-198. Wylie, Philip (Gordon). **The Disappearance.** Rinehart, 1951.
For no scientifically (or otherwise!) explained reason, all of Earth's men and women suddenly disappear from each other's worlds. With his own critical agenda, the author traces the evolution of these two single-sex societies; the deterioration of the men, the necessary empowerment of the women, and the creative consequences of their eventual, equally unexplained reunion. There are a few miscalls from today's perspective; Wylie was basically an antifeminist who criticized Simone de Beauvoir, for example, as admittedly brilliant but totally wrongheaded! But on the whole this was, *for the time,* a compassionate commentary on what used to be called the "battle of the sexes" and on the prurient, hung-up society that made the rules by which that battle had traditionally been fought. Compare Le Guin's *Left Hand of Darkness* [4-254] and Michaela Roessner's *Vanishing Point* (1993); contrast Russ's *The Female Man* [4-375].

3-199. Wyndham, John (pseud. of John Beynon Harris). **The Day of the Triffids.** Doubleday, 1951. Variant title: *Revolt of the Triffids*, Popular Library, 1952.
No SF bibliography would be complete without at least one tale of monsters from a botched experiment marching over the world; let this one, expanded from a serial in *Collier's*, be representative of the breed. The Things in the story are sentient plants that walk about, sting, and feast on carrion. To even the odds, a shower from space, probably from one of the erstwhile dominant species' own secret military satellites, has rendered most of humanity blind. What raises this novel head and shoulders over almost all others in the subgenre is the quality of the writing and characterization. Details unfold with leisurely novelistic richness and the characters' actions make logical and psychological sense. At the end the narrator, his spouse, their children, and a few others have retreated to the Isle of Wight, leaving England to the triffids and a few enclaves of militarized human survivalists. In today's publishing climate there could—probably would—be a sequel, but some stories really are better left open-ended. Compare Christopher, *The Death of Grass* [3-42].

3-200. Wyndham, John (pseud. of John Benyon Harris). **Re-Birth.** Ballantine, 1955. U.K. title (with altered text): *The Chrysalids*, M. Joseph, 1955.
Nuclear warfare has not only reverted civilization to a Dark Age village

culture but unleashed a flood of mutations. In a resurgence of religious bigotry, mutants are cursed as the fruit of sin. They must not be allowed to contaminate the gene pool by reproducing their kind; the imagery is that of the "clean"-"unclean" dichotomy in the Mosaic code. The mutants, however, are not sub- but superhuman, since they carry telepathic ability. At their point of greatest danger two mutant children make contact by telepathy with a distant community, high-tech as well as telepathic; this triggers a climactic rescue scene, strongly reminiscent of *Things to Come*, the SF motion picture for which H. G. Wells wrote the screenplay, very loosely adapting it from his own *The Shape of Things to Come* [2-140]. And the message is the same as with Wells: old ways, no matter how comfortably familiar, must give way to the rational new. Compare Brackett, *The Long Tomorrow* [3-30]; Clarke, *Childhood's End* [3-44]. Contrast Miller, *A Canticle for Leibowitz* [3-125], in which mutation has an entirely different social function and theological meaning.

Anthologies

As with the novels and single-writer collections, this list has been substantially curtailed from that which appeared in the third edition. One important category, that of collections of stories from particular magazines, has been regrouped into the chapter in which the magazines themselves are discussed. Another, the single-theme anthology (all of its stories are about space travel, or time travel, or matriarchs, or robots, or war, or whatever) has been dropped, with few exceptions, in agreement with Brian Aldiss's observation that anthologists by and large seem to have confined their reading to other anthologists. With the excellent bibliographic tools now available for SF, individual stories are more readily traced through other categories. Moreover, each generation in SF finds different areas for emphasis in the work of its predecessors, and the canon is never closed.

3-201. Aldiss, Brian W(ilson), ed. **Space Opera: An Anthology of Way-Back-When Futures.** Weidenfeld, 1974.
Long-term science fictionists do not forget their roots. Aldiss, in this and the volumes that succeeded it, remembered the excesses of youth with affection rather than disdain. Although including conventionally space-opera items like an excerpt from Edmond Hamilton's *Star of Life*, he also sought out good stories not already overanthologized such as Jack Vance's brief, beautiful, heartbreaking "The Mitr." *Space Odysseys*, which followed

in 1975, included both Arthur Clarke's "The Sentinel," containing the germ of the important SF film *2001*, and Leigh Brackett's unashamedly romantic-nostalgic "The Lake of the Gone Forever." *Evil Earths* (Weidenfeld, 1975) turned to the Dark Side of the Force, as exemplified in Campbell's "Night" and Tenn's matter-of-factly horrifying "Down Among the Dead Men." *Galactic Empires* (Weidenfeld, 1976), introduced by Aldiss with the provocative comment, "Galactic empires represent the ultimate absurdity in science fiction," ranged in its two volumes from the technocratic optimism of Asimov's "Foundation"—and, in an entirely different way, of James Blish's cogently argued "Beep"—to the quiet sadness of Algis Budrys's "To Civilize" and Arthur Clarke's "The Possessed." An outstanding and distinctive series, boldly arguing that SF was at its best when least respectable.

3-202.   Aldiss, Brian W(ilson), and Harry Harrison, eds. **Decade: The 1940s.** Macmillan, 1975.
Eight stories, all from *Astounding*—which in the forties, the editors argue, was all we had—by Asimov, Fredric Brown, van Vogt, Clement, Simak, Philip Latham (pseudonym of the astronomer R. S. Richardson), Russell, and the present annotator. In contrast, the same editors' *Decade: The 1950s* (Macmillan, 1976) contained *no* stories from *Astounding*; a characteristic choice instead is Cordwainer Smith's "Scanners Live in Vain" (SFHF). *Decade: The 1960s* (Macmillan, 1977) carried their selections on into the New Wave, although the editors did not use that term. An excellent series, foreshadowing other retrospective "decade" collections such as Pohl, Greenberg, and Olander's *Science Fiction of the Forties* (Avon, 1978), which in contrast to Aldiss and Harrison chose less than half its 21 stories from *Astounding*; Barry Malzberg and Bill Pronzini's *The End of Summer: Science Fiction of the Fifties* (Ace, 1979); and Terry Carr's *Classic Science Fiction: The First Golden Age* (Harper, 1978). The judicious, but idiosyncratic, choices of all these editors bring to life the *zeitgeist* of the periods they anthologize; and their own diversity of temperaments and tastes assure that those periods are presented with appropriate variety.

3-203.   Amis, Kingsley (William), and Robert Conquest, eds. **Spectrum.** Gollancz, 1961, and annually to 1966.
Designed to introduce U.K. readers to science fiction, primarily from U.S. magazines and authors, as an acceptable literary medium. Contrary to notions of fundamental Anglo-American cultural divergences, this British-selected fiction meshed with the U.S. genre consensus: items like Pohl's "The Midas Plague," Kuttner and Moore's "Vintage Season," Anderson's

"Call Me Joe," Bester's "Fondly Fahrenheit," and Kornbluth's "The Marching Morons" all made it also into the United States' SF writers' own self-balloted Science Fiction Hall of Fame [3-223]; and stories that did not, such as Sheckley's "Pilgrimage to Earth," Wyman Guin's "Beyond Bedlam," and Theodore Sturgeon's "Killdozer" were very much in the American grain. By the third of the volumes, however, harbingers of the coming British New Wave, such as Ballard's "Voices of Time," were beginning to appear. A special departure in *Spectrum 4* was "Unreal Estates," a debate on SF among Amis, Brian Aldiss, and C. S. Lewis, who here was in effect renewing his old feud with H. G. Wells.

*3-204. Asimov, Isaac, ed. **The Hugo Winners.** Doubleday, 1962 (Vol. I); 1971 (Vol. II).

Short stories and novelettes that won the Hugo, SF's equivalent of Hollywood's Oscars, awarded by ballot of delegates to the annual World Science Fiction Convention (Worldcon), and vulnerable to critical objections similar to those raised from time to time against the Academy Awards [see Lupoff, 3-218]. Nevertheless, this is a guide to what was well-received in the SF community in particular years, most of it of enduring value. Asimov, echewing comment on the stories—which he contended spoke for themselves—supplied introductions, usually fun-poking, to the stories' authors. Volume I, covering 1955 through 1961, omitted 1957, when the Worldcon was in London. Winning stories included Walter Miller's "The Darfstellar," Clarke's "The Star," Davidson's "Or All the Seas With Oysters," Simak's "The Big Front Yard," and Keyes's "Flowers For Algernon." Volume II covered 1963 through 1970, when the field was undergoing rapid change; the very titles of some winners—"Repent, Harlequin! Said the Ticktockman," "The Sharing of Flesh," "The Beast That Shouted Love at the Heart of the World," "Time Considered as a Helix of Semi-precious Stones"—would have been unimaginable in the magazines of the forties. The series would continue, still presided over by Asimov [4-522].

*3-205. Asimov, Isaac, and Martin H(arry) Greenberg, eds. **Isaac Asimov Presents the Great Science Fiction Stories: Volume 1, 1939.** DAW, 1979.

Differs from all previous "best of the year" anthologies, which typically had reprinted stories first published in the immediately prior year. In contrast, Asimov and Greenberg began their series *forty* years after the stories' initial appearance, giving plenty of time for reflection and recall. Each story is supplied with helpful critical and biographical notes. The initial volume, covering the pivotal year 1939, is noteworthy for several debut stories in *Astounding* by van Vogt, Asimov, Heinlein, Sturgeon, and Lee Gregor (Milton A. Rothman) and early work by de Camp and del Rey, as well as three strong stories from *Amazing* by Robert Bloch, William F. Temple, and Nelson S. Bond. The succeeding volumes have chronicled the Golden Age SF of the forties, the shift to social criticism and satire in the fifties, and by the 1963 volume at the edge of the modern period (DAW, 1990) were including the U.S. and U.K. writers who were about to launch SF's perceptual revolution. A must purchase for any library's reading room.

3-206.   Bleiler, Everett F., and T(haddeus) E(ugene) Dikty, eds. **The Best Science-Fiction Stories: 1949.** Fell, 1949.
The pioneering "year's best" series. Mainly from U.S. genre sources but within that limitation well-selected; the first two years, for example, collected Asimov, Bradbury, Leinster, Fredric Brown, John D. MacDonald, Poul Anderson, and Wilmar Shiras. Conventional choices are interspersed with a few offbeat items like Martin Gardner's "Thang," in Vol. 1, and Robert W. Krepp's "Five Years in the Marmalade," in Vol. 2. Outstanding stories included J. J. Coupling's "Period Piece" and a virtuoso performance by Henry Kuttner, "Happy Ending," in Vol. 1, and Theodore Sturgeon's jolly "The Hurkle Is a Happy Beast" as well as Clifford Simak's darkly ironic "Eternity Lost" in Vol. 2. These two volumes were combined as *Science Fiction Omnibus* (Doubleday, 1952), but the series continued into 1956 (Bleiler dropping out as editor after 1954), with a final volume appearing (from Advent) in 1958, thus overlapping with Judith Merril's *SF: The Year's Greatest* [3-220]. Dikty's solo editions included yearly review essays, a practice taken up by Merril and, in more recent series, by Terry Carr and Donald Wollheim.

3-207.   Bleiler, Everett F., and T(haddeus) E(ugene) Dikty, eds. **Imagination Unlimited: Science-fiction and Science.** Farrar, 1952.
Thirteen stories, grouped under particular scientific disciplines: mathematics and philosophy; physical sciences; biological sciences; social sciences. This approach could result in a series of arid puzzle-stories, and of course the scientific premises of any SF story can become outdated. (That happened to Ross Rocklynne's "Pressure.") On the whole, however, these seasoned anthologists simply chose good, strong, well-told tales, with the paradoxical result that the science in most of them is surprisingly undated. Under mathematics, we get Theodore Sturgeon's "What Dead Men Tell"; under psychology, Peter Phillips's "Dreams Are Sacred"; under anthropology Frank Robinson's quietly melancholy, "The Fire and the Sword"; under philosophy, Ray Bradbury's "Referent"; under physics,

Philip Latham's "Xi Effect"; and under biochemistry, Julian May's quite marvelous (and too little known) "Dune Roller." A good book to place in the hands of a humanities-oriented reader who is skittish about the science in science fiction.

3-208. Boucher, Anthony (pseud. of William Anthony Parker White), ed. **A Treasury of Great Science Fiction.** Doubleday, 1959. 2 vols.

This generous collection by the longtime editor of *Fantasy & Science Fiction* reprints four book-length works (Wyndham's *Re-Birth* [3-200], van Vogt's *Weapon Shops of Isher* [3-182], Anderson's *Brain Wave* [3-5], and Bester's *Tiger! Tiger!* under its American title, *The Stars My Destination* [3-19], along with 21 shorter works, some of which had been largely or entirely overlooked by previous anthologists. They included Nelson Bond's "Magic City," Heinlein's "Waldo," Poul Anderson's "The Martian Crown Jewels," Philip K. Dick's psychiatrically terrifying "The Father-Thing," Kornbluth's Hispanic-focused "Gomez," E. B. White's coolly sarcastic "The Morning of the Day They Did It," and Theodore Sturgeon's engagingly titled "The (Widget), the (Wadget), and Boff." Offered repeatedly as a free bonus for book club enrollment, this anthology has over the years given many readers their first in-depth introduction to SF.

3-209. Conklin, Groff, ed. **The Best of Science Fiction.** Crown, 1946.

Intended to introduce previous nonreaders of SF to the genre (and to lure secret readers out of the closet), this generous (40 stories) reprint anthology opened with an essay, "Concerning Science Fiction," by *Astounding* editor John W. Campbell, and included notable mainstream writers such as Wells, Poe, Conan Doyle, Julian Huxley, and Frank R. Stockton, as well as pulp stalwarts like Leinster ("First Contact"), Sturgeon ("Killdozer"), Heinlein ("Solution Unsatisfactory"), and Kuttner/Moore ("The Piper's Son"). Conklin divided the stories into categories: "The Atom—and After"; "Wonders of Earth"; "Dangerous Inventions"; "Adventures in Dimension," etc., a format he would repeat in *A Treasury of Science Fiction* [3-210]. *The Big Book of Science Fiction* (Crown, 1950), and *The Omnibus of Science Fiction* (Crown, 1952), comprising with this volume 2,400 pages, well covering the short story field prior to the 1950s. These large books, together with some 30 smaller collections (often in the form of "theme" anthologies), made Conklin the leading reprint anthologist in the field prior to the advent of the indefatigable Martin H. Greenberg.

*3-210. Conklin, Groff, ed. **A Treasury of Science Fiction.** Crown, 1948.

The editor inadvertently gave the impression in his introduction that this was a collection of "leftovers" from his earlier compilation, *The Best of*

Science Fiction [3-209]. Far from it; this is by far the better anthology. With only one concession to "mainstream" writing, H. F. Heard's thoughtful and haunting "The Great Fog," Conklin launched boldly into the pulps, notably *Astounding*, for his 30 stories, and came up with Chan Davis's "The Nightmare"; Poul Anderson's debut story, with F. N. Waldrop, "Tomorrow's Children"; Williamson's "With Folded Hands"; C. L. Moore's "No Woman Born," and Moore/Kuttner's "Mimsy Were the Borogoves"; William Tenn's black-comic "Child's Play"; H. Beam Piper's memorable first story, "Time and Time Again"; Heinlein's "It's Great to Be Back"; and Clifford Simak's somber "Tools." Reprintings of this collection as late as the 1980s indicate how well these stories have stood the test of time.

3-211.   Derleth, August (William), ed. **The Other Side of the Moon.** Pellegrini & Cudahy, 1949.

Twenty stories selected by the founder and director of Arkham House. This anthology has been perceived by another critic as a reflection of that editor's preference for science fiction on the horror side: Bradbury's "Pillar of Fire," in which the last vampire resists an antiseptic future society's effort to cleanse the world of all fantasy, for example, or in another fashion van Vogt's "Vault of the Beast." However, there is also straightforward extrapolative SF, like H. G. Wells's "The Star," keen satire, as in S. Fowler Wright's "Original Sin"; and post–A-bomb social criticism, in Sturgeon's "Memorial" and in nongenre writer Gerald Kersh's "The Monster," a pointed commentary on, in Kersh's words, "that disgusting weapon." Clark Ashton Smith's poetic "City of the Singing Flame," F. B. Long's wondrously deranged robot story, "The World of Wulkins," and Nelson S. Bond's "Conqueror's Isle," with its great exit line, help to round out a balanced collection, which picked up a few stories anthologists Bleiler/Dikty, Conklin, and Healy/McComas had missed.

3-212.   Derleth, August (William), ed. **Strange Ports of Call.** Pellegrini & Cudahy, 1948.

Derleth was already recognized in the mainstream as a major anthologist of ghost and horror stories (for example, *Sleep No More*, Rinehart, 1944; *Who Knocks?*, Rinehart, 1946; *The Night Side*, Rinehart, 1947) when he turned his attention to science fiction in this still eminently readable collection. Twenty stories, of which the centerpiece is H. P. Lovecraft's longest tale, "At the Mountains of Madness," making an editorial point that HPL was entitled to be counted also as a science fiction writer. The anthology also included Bradbury's "The Million Year Picnic," Heinlein's "The Green Hills of Earth," Kuttner/Moore's disturbing "Call Him Demon," and Theodore Sturgeon's powerful plea against the nations' mutual nuclear suicide,"Thunder and Roses." Derleth also showed a knack for picking up worthy stories other collectors had (and have) overlooked, such as "Forgotten," P. Schuyler Miller's tale of a grizzled uranium prospector on Mars, and "The Lost Street," by Clifford Simak and Carl Jacobi (originally in the short-lived pulp *Comet* under the title "The Street That Wasn't There"), an effective dramatization of one of the classic problems of philosophy.

3-213. Harrison, Harry, ed. **The Light Fantastic: Science Fiction Classics from the Mainstream.** Scribner, 1971.

Thirteen stories, mostly from the fifties and early sixties, by authors not commonly thought of as genre SF writers. Avoiding frequently anthologized works (except Forster's "The Machine Stops" and John Cheever's "The Enormous Radio"), Harrison chose items like "The Muse" by Anthony Burgess; "The End of the Party" by Graham Greene; "Something Strange" by Kingsley Amis; "The Shout" by Robert Graves; and the quietly unsettling "The Shoddy Lands" by C. S. Lewis. Gerald Kersh's pseudoscientific hokum about "Fluorine 80+" in his otherwise excellent tale "The Unsafe Deposit Box" raises a question of whether mainstream writers are permitted more sloppiness in their science than are genre writers, and one could argue that "The Circular Ruins," by Jorge Luis Borges, is fantasy rather than SF. A fine collection, nonetheless, with keen social satire in the selections by Forster, E. B. White, and Leo Szilard. Rudyard Kipling's "The Finest Story in the World" will strike a responsive chord in any author who has ever been accosted by a would-be writer purporting to have some great story ideas; you write 'em down and we'll split fifty-fifty. James Blish's introduction offered persuasive explanation of the ghettoizing of American SF; Harrison's afterword argued optimistically that that situation was about to change.

*3-214. Healy, Raymond J., and J. Francis McComas, eds. **Adventures in Time and Space.** Random, 1946. Retitled *Famous Science-Fiction Stories,* 1957.

Published in the respected Modern Library Giant format, this hefty 33-story anthology, quarried entirely from genre magazines, represents one of the earliest breakouts from SF's erstwhile pulp ghetto. To general readers, and to libraries that might not in 1946 have purchased any other SF, it introduced Asimov's "Nightfall," Bester's "Adam and No Eve," Heinlein's "Requiem" and "By His Bootstraps," van Vogt's "Black Destroyer," P. Schuyler Miller's "As Never Was," del Rey's "Nerves," Campbell's "Who

Goes There?," Raymond Z. Gallun's dark Darwinist parable, "Seeds of the Dusk," and many more, together with two nonfiction pieces. Overwhelmingly the selections were from Campbell's *Astounding*, further reinforcing the reputation of that editor and magazine as founders and shapers of SF's Golden Age. Fredric Brown's humorous story "The Star-Mouse," from *Planet Stories*, is exceptional in this collection in *not* having been reprinted from Campbell's magazines. A Golden Age collection drawn entirely from *Astounding*'s rivals—*Planet, Startling Stories, Amazing, Super Science, Future*, and the rest—would have read very differently from this one and not always to the other magazines' and stories' discredit.

3-215.   Healy, Raymond J., ed. **New Tales of Space and Time.** Holt, 1951.
The first venture by a major hardcover publisher into anthologizing *original* SF stories, in contrast to the purely reprint collections, which by 1951 had become fairly common. Kris Neville's lovely, bittersweet "Bettyann" might never have seen publication otherwise [see also 3-134 and 3-135]. In contrast, R. Bretnor's "Little Anton" introduced the great-nephew of that other great comic creation by Bretnor, Papa Schimmelhorn. P. Schuyler Miller, *Astounding*'s veteran book reviewer, made his first fiction appearance in five years with "Status Quondam," about a 20th-century visitor to ancient Greece who discovers that the Age of Pericles experienced raw is rather less glorious than its modern reputation. Anthony Boucher's "The Quest of Saint Aquin" (SFHF), reprinted several times since its initial appearance here, rounds out an excellent collection. Introduction by Anthony Boucher. Compare Pohl, *Star Science Fiction Stories* [3-222].

3-216.   Knight, Damon (Francis), ed. **A Century of Science Fiction.** Simon & Schuster, 1962.
Only three items in this collection by Ambrose Bierce, H. G. Wells, and Fitz-James O'Brien, are actually a century old; nearly half fall within the 1950s. Arranging the 26 stories and excerpts in a manner similar to Groff Conklin's anthologies (robots, time travel, space, etc.), the editor grouped the stories within each category chronologically and added incisive and informative commentary. Even though most of the stories, by Aldiss, Asimov, Bester, Clarke, Hamilton, and others, appear in other collections, this way of looking at them provides fresh insight. A companion volume, *One Hundred Years of Science Fiction* (Simon & Schuster, 1968), is organized the same way but without editorial commentary; the stories have to speak for themselves. Again only three go back a hundred years, or nearly so; one is Kipling's "With the Night Mail" happily published here with the ads from the magazine of the year 2000 in which it purportedly appeared. Other tales, less familiar than those chosen for *A Century . . .*, include

Sturgeon's creepy "The Other Celia," Anderson's powerful and tragic "The Man Who Came Early," Leinster's sentimental but effective "The Other Now," Kornbluth's chilling "The Mindworm," Budrys's melancholy "Nobody Bothers Gus," and Ralph Williams's economic thought-provoker, "Business as Usual, During Alterations."

3-217. Knight, Damon (Francis), ed. and trans. **Thirteen French Science Fiction Stories.** Bantam, 1965.
Since Jules Verne's time France has had an independent science fiction tradition that is largely unknown to the English-speaking world. In 1959 Knight found stories like these "more or less by accident" in the French magazine *Fiction: la revue littéraire de l'étrange,* the Paris affiliate of the American *Fantasy & Science Fiction.* The oldest, however, Pierre Mille's "After Three Hundred Years," a believable portrait of a far-future French society that has regressed to barbarism, dates from 1922, long before the time of *Fiction* or *F & SF.* Three stories are by (Nathalie) Charles-Henneberg, including the subtle time travel tale, "Moon-Fishers." Gérard Klein, a Bradbury-influenced prodigy in the 1950s and a major mover and shaper of French SF today, contributed the suspenseful "The Monster"; Alain Dorémieux, a frequent contributor to *Fiction* (and translator into French of stories in that magazine by Richard Matheson, Zenna Henderson, and others) is represented by the deeply erotic, ultimately tragic tale "The Vana"; Boris Vian, notable as the translator of van Vogt's work into French, by the absurdist "The Dead Fish." And Claude Cheinisse, in "Juliette," shows that America's young males are not the only ones who fall in love with their cars.

3-218. Lupoff, Richard A(llen), ed. **What If?: Stories That Should Have Won the Hugo.** Pocket, 1980.
The editor's introduction, "Earned Glory" describes the history of the movement toward annual awards in SF culminating in the Hugo, which is conferred by vote of the members of each year's World Science Fiction Convention. Although Lupoff believes the Hugo Award is rightly "here to stay," he cautions that the selection process by the fans is not flawless; it is subject to fads, sentimentalism, electioneering, and slow response to avant-garde writing. That stories as good as Sturgeon's "Golden Helix," Anderson's "The Man Who Came Early," and Kornbluth's "Two Dooms" were overlooked gives credibility to Lupoff's thesis. Volume I tracked the years 1952–1958; Volume II (Pocket, 1981) covered 1959 through 1965, and made the further point that the United Kingdom and other non-U. S. sources were slighted by the conventions' mostly American attendees; witness the fine stories "Where Is the Bird of Fire," by Thomas Burnett Swan,

from *Science Fantasy*, and "All the King's Men," by Barrington J. Bayley, from *New Worlds*. This condition has been somewhat alleviated in more recent years by sometimes holding the Worldcons in cities overseas, with awards going to writers like the Strugatskii brothers from the former U.S.S.R.

3-219. Magidoff, Robert, ed. **Russian Science Fiction.** Allen & Unwin, 1963. Trans. by Doris Johnson (except three stories).

Eleven stories, ranging from an archaic piece by Konstantin Tsiolkovsky, the father of astronautics in the U.S.S.R. and, indirectly in the West, to Vladimir Dudintsev's allegory, fable, or whatever, "A New Year's Fairy Tale," which when it first appeared in 1960 baffled both Soviet literary censors and U.S. literary critics. Includes strong work by Mikhail Vasilyev, Anatoly Dnieprov, and Valentina Zhuravleva. American SF gets an ideological lecture from Ivan Yefremov in "Cor Serpentis" (Heart of the Serpent), specifically Murray Leinster's "First Contact" (1945; SFHF), which had raised the question whether starships from different civilizations meeting in deep space would be motivated to destroy each other to safeguard the home world from invasion. No society sufficiently advanced to develop interstellar travel (under planet-wide communism), Yefremov's future cosmonauts agree, would need even to consider such an action. Soviet SF was, however, in even more rapid flux in the 1960s than that in the West as Judith Merril discovered only three years later when editing *Path Into the Unknown: The Best of Soviet Science Fiction* (MacGibbon & Kee, 1966; Dell, 1968). In stories like G. Gor's "The Boy," Merril argued, "you may prepare to have your magazine-article notions of daily life in the U.S.S.R. severely shaken up."

*3-220. Merril, Judith, ed. **SF: The Year's Greatest.** Dell, 1956, and annually to 1968, skipping 1967.

Merril's care for balance between genre and nongenre sources (among the latter: Shirley Jackson, Steve Allen, Bertrand Russell, Conrad Aiken, John Dos Passos, John Ciardi, Roald Dahl; among the former: Davidson's "The Golem," Knight's "The Country of the Kind," Sturgeon's "The Man Who Lost the Sea," Cordwainer Smith's "A Planet Named Shayol") and between U.S. and U.K. writers helped make this the most outstanding of all "best of last year" collections. Merril also included "honorable mention" listings, modeled on the O'Brien and O. Henry mainstream short story annuals, and wrote provocative, well-founded essays on the state of the art (and of the world). Orson Welles gave the series an introductory sendoff; Anthony Boucher in numbers 6, 7, 8, and 9 (1961–1964) surveyed the year's best SF books. Title changed in 1960 to *The (5th) Annual of the Year's Best SF*. Series continued through number 11, 1966; a final volume, *SF 12*, appeared from Delacorte in 1968. Although this series then ended, worthy successors Terry Carr and Donald A. Wollheim, among others, took up the annual anthology format in the modern period.

3-221. Pohl, Frederik, ed. **The Expert Dreamers.** Doubleday, 1962.
Sixteen science fiction stories by scientists, some of them regular practitioners in the genre: Asimov, Clarke, R. S. Richardson (Philip Latham), Hoyle, and George O. Smith; others who have published SF only occasionally, such as George Gamow, Leo Szilard, and most poignantly Norbert Wiener, who in his autobiography expressed categoric *disapproval* of all SF as "vicious daydreaming" that leads youths astray who might otherwise learn to think like good scientists! (Wiener, *I Am a Mathematician*, Doubleday, 1956, p. 270). A cognate anthology is Groff Conklin's *Great Science Fiction by Scientists* (Collier, 1962), with stories by some of the same authors as in the Pohl collection, as well as Eric Temple Bell (John Taine), J. B. S. Haldane, Sir Julian Huxley, John R. Pierce (J. J. Coupling), and—stretching "science" to include anthropology—Chad Oliver. Conklin's introduction briefly but persuasively speculates as to why more scientists do not write science fiction; happily, his reasons are not the same as Wiener's. Both collections contain helpful biographical and story notes.

*3-222. Pohl, Frederik, ed. **Star Science Fiction Stories.** Ballantine, 1953.
The first of six original-story anthologies by Pohl, an expert editor in addition to his prolific writing career (*Super Science Stories*, early 1940s; *Galaxy*, later 1960s), which well epitomized the state of 1950s science fiction. Stories that appeared here for the first time included Clarke's "The Nine Billion Names of God" (SFHF) and Kuttner/Moore's "A Wild Surmise" in number 1; Bixby's "It's a *Good* Life" (SFHF) and Richard Wilson's "Friend of the Family" (with its narrative hook, "They had passed a law making babies illegal"), in number 2: Arthur Clarke's "The Deep Range," core of the later novel having the same name [3-45] and Philip K. Dick's truly depressing "Foster, You're Dead," in number 3; and Howard Koch's subtle "Invasion From Inner Space" in number 6, which in 1960 concluded the series. Concerned for the viability in the SF marketplace of works that fell between short story and book length, Pohl also launched *Star Short Novels* (Ballantine, 1954), which showcased three new novellas: a sprightly thought experiment "Little Men," by Jessmyn West; "To Here and the Easel," by Theodore Sturgeon; and a powerful and memorable statement on religion, "For I Am a Jealous People!" by Lester del Rey.

*3-223. Science Fiction Hall of Fame. Vol. I, Doubleday, 1971; Vols. IIA and IIB, Doubleday, 1974.

Volume 1 edited by Robert Silverberg consisted of 26 short stories and novelettes chosen by ballot of the Science Fiction Writers of America as the best shorter works in the field to have been published before 1965. The oldest story in the collection is Stanley Weinbaum's "A Martian Odyssey" (1934); the newest is Roger Zelazny's "A Rose for Ecclesiastes" (1963). An editorial decision to limit the collection to one story from each author may have slightly skewed the selection. Is "The Roads Must Roll" *the* story by which we wish to remember Robert Heinlein? On the whole, however, this anthology may be taken as definitive, and it works effectively in the classroom, except among the worldly-wise who "have read all those stories before." For Volume 2, Ben Bova edited 22 novellas chosen the same way, 11 in each sub-volume. They range from Wells's indispensable *The Time Machine* (1895), through Golden Age classics like Heinlein's "Universe" and Campbell's "Who Goes There?" to strong works from the early 1960s such as Jack Vance's "'The Moon Moth." In both Bova's and Silverberg' anthologies there is surprisingly little overlap with the Hugo winners [3-204]; in fact, but one short story, "Flowers for Algernon," and one novella "The Big Front Yard," which may say something about the differences between fans' and writers' literary tastes. Stories mentioned elsewhere in this chapter and chapter 4 that are collected here are designated SFHF.

3-224. Stong, Phil(ip Duffield), ed. **The Other Worlds.** Wilfred Funk, 1941. Variant title: *25 Modern Stories of Mystery and Imagination,* Garden City, 1942.

This was a pioneering attempt by a mainstream publishing house to draw upon the pulps for hardcover publication; marred, from SF's point of view, by one fatal flaw: Stong's avowed conviction that "the first requirement of a good fantastic story . . . is that it should not be even remotely possible." The result is a collection weighted toward fantasy and ghost stories, some of them excellent, by such writers as Sturgeon, del Rey, Manly Wade Wellman, Henry Kuttner, and H. P. Lovecraft; but the science fiction selection is, to say the least, capricious. Stong did reprint Harry Bates's awkwardly told but still powerful "Alas, All Thinking," and such neglected items as Donald Bern's "The Man Who Knew All the Answers" and Weinbaum's "The Adaptive Ultimate" (under the pseudonym John Jessel), but a truly representative *science fiction* anthology was yet to come. Contrast Wollheim, *The Pocket Book of Science Fiction* [3-225]; Wollheim, significantly, roasted the Stong collection as "cynical," in a book review for *Astonishing Stories*, September 1941.

3-225. Wollheim, Donald A(llen), ed. **The Pocket Book of Science Fiction.** Pocket, 1943.

The first modern, pulp-derived *science fiction* anthology, not fantasy or horror. Hedging his bet with work by mainstreamers Stephen Vincent Benét, Ambrose Bierce, John Collier, and H. G. Wells, Wollheim included three stories from the SF pulps of the day now listed in the Science Fiction Hall of Fame: Weinbaum's "A Martian Odyssey," Campbell's "Twilight," and Sturgeon's "Microcosmic God," as well as Heinlein's lighthearted "—And He Built a Crooked House." Of the ten stories, the only real dud is a long-winded opus from mid-1930s *Amazing*, T. S. Stribling's "The Green Splotches." Two years later Wollheim edited *The Portable Novels of Science* (Viking, 1945), which reprinted four longer works: Stapledon's *Odd John* [2-120], Wells's *First Men in the Moon* [1–98], Taine's *Before the Dawn*, and *The Shadow Out of Time*, one of two Lovecraft novellas to have first appeared in *Astounding*. In 1949 Wollheim also edited one of the earliest (and sadly ignored) anthologies of *original* SF stories, *The Girl With Hungry Eyes and Other Stories* (Avon). It included William Tenn's "Venus and the Seven Sexes": bizarre, hilarious, and at that time quite unconventional. All of this was seasoning for the regular and industrious best-of-the-year anthologizing Wollheim would be doing in the modern period, beginning in 1965 and continuing more than two and a half decades.

CHAPTER 4

The New Wave, Cyberpunk, and Beyond: 1963–1994

Michael M. Levy

For those of us born between the end of World War II and the early 1950s, the "sixties," that strange period that ran from approximately 1963 to 1972, *was* science fiction. New technologies like nuclear power, television, computers, and spaceflight were changing our lives at an incredible rate. In 1964, after reading Philip Wylie's *Triumph* (1963), I got into a violent argument with my parents over their unwillingness to build an elaborate fallout shelter in our backyard. A few years later, in my high school math class, a teacher flapped a stack of punch cards in our faces, proclaimed that computers were the wave of the future, and ceremonially (and perhaps a bit prematurely) tossed his expensive slide rule in the trash can. In my college freshman English class, a university professor made reference to the psychedelic ending of the new Stanley Kubrick film, *2001: A Space Odyssey*, and hinted that he'd been to that bizarre, unearthly place himself under the auspices of a new drug named LSD. An article in the newspaper that year (1968) mentioned that Pan Am was taking reservations for trips to the moon. On a more serious note, Vietnam was heating up and, although we had as yet no real notion of that war's true horror, we did recognize its strangeness. With no front lines and dazzling new military technology, it seemed to my rather naïve mind to have more in common with Heinlein's *Starship Troopers* [3-90] than it did with World War II or Korea. And then, in 1969, I stayed up all night watching as a human being walked on the moon. Responsible scientists, flushed with optimism, were even promising us Mars in the not-too-distant future.

It can be argued, of course, that the world is always undergoing change and that every generation sees its own time period as standing in some special relationship to the universe. For every generation, the millennium, or its secular equivalent, seems to be just around the corner. How else, after all, do we account for the periodic visits to the bestseller list of the prophecies of Nostradamus? Still, the 1960s seemed different, at least to those of us who came of age during that period. Perhaps it was the influence of Marshall McLuhan, whose *Understanding Media* (1964) argued that the electronic media generally and television specifically were causing an actual and permanent change in the way that humanity comprehended the world. Perhaps it was the somewhat later influence of Alvin Toffler, whose *Future Shock* (1970) emphasized that the rate of change was picking up dramatically. Perhaps it was the high-tech nature of the change: computers, moon landings, and such. Perhaps it was the violence: the war in Vietnam, the student riots, the assassinations of the Kennedys, Martin Luther King, and Malcolm X. Or maybe it was the music; to a teenager growing up on the South Side of Chicago in the mid-1960s, the Beatles and the Rolling Stones seemed nearly as strange and wonderful as any being from Arcturus or Deneb.

Other equally important changes were occurring in the 1960s. In the United States the rise of the civil rights movement and then of the women's movement altered forever the way our laws are written and the way decent people think about human interactions. President Lyndon Johnson's Great Society programs, along with similar efforts in Britain and elsewhere, were sparking the enormous growth of public welfare with all its attendant advantages and disadvantages. The Soviet Union, after a brief thaw under Khrushchev, was falling back into that dark, repressive stagnation that would both prolong the Cold War and lead inevitably to the eventual collapse of the Soviet state.

In the mid-1960s a phenomenon variously called the Youth Culture and the Counter-Culture forced its way onto the public stage, gaining moral force from anti-Vietnam protests, vague theological underpinnings from a watered-down version of Buddhism, visibility from media hype, and economic clout from the sheer size of the baby boom generation. Many of the different components of the youth culture were themselves, at least in part, direct outgrowths of technological change. The sexual revolution would have been highly unlikely if not for conveniently timed breakthroughs in birth control technology. Drug use, always common in some parts of American society, did not become a topic of general concern until it entered the middle class, especially when technology once again took a hand, creating new kinds of highs. The explosive growth of the rock'n'roll industry, fueled by the increased buying power of young people, was also made possible, in part, by new developments in sound reproduction technology. Even the antiwar movement was technology-related. World War II and Korea were distant affairs that the voters back home read about in the newspapers or saw on carefully edited newsreels. Vietnam occurred on television, in our homes, its horrors less well disguised by distance and government control.

The social, political, economic, and technological changes of the 1960s were diverse, but they all had an effect on science fiction. The genre always had its political differences, of course. John W. Campbell, Jr., the editor of *Astounding SF*, which became *Analog* in 1960, was a technophile and a political conservative; with a few notable exceptions the stories he published tended to follow his bent. In the 1950s *Galaxy*, edited by H. L. Gold and later by Frederik Pohl and others, published stories by writers like Pohl, Damon Knight, Robert Sheckley, and Fritz Leiber that were less highly enamored of technology and that satirized some of the more conservative and established elements in our society, including government, the military, and big business. Although many of the genre's biggest names published in both *Analog* and *Galaxy* throughout the 1950s and 1960s, the ideological rivalry was quite real. It came to a head with the outbreak of the Vietnam War and the eventual growth of the antiwar movement. Much of the political rhetoric of American SF soon centered on the need to either oppose or support U.S. government policy in Southeast Asia. In June 1968 two groups of science fiction writers with opposing views on U.S. involvement in Vietnam published angry advertisements in *Galaxy*. Among the signers of the antiwar advertisement were Ursula K. Le Guin, Philip K. Dick, Joanna Russ, Ray Bradbury, and Harlan Ellison. Among those signing the ad supporting U.S. government policy were John W. Campbell, Jr., Robert Heinlein, Poul Anderson, Larry Niven, and Jerry Pournelle. This debate was to achieve the ultimate in public irony nearly a decade later at the 1976 World Science Fiction Convention in Kansas City, where Vietnam veteran Joe Haldeman's bitter antiwar story *The Forever War* [4-193] received the Hugo Award for best novel of the year the same weekend the convention's guest of honor, Robert A. Heinlein, was booed for, in essence, arguing that nuclear war was inevitable and may in fact improve the species.

The youth culture, with its attendant drug use and alternative life-styles, had an enormous effect on the genre as well. One of the most influential writers of the period, Philip K. Dick, had demonstrated an interest in altered states of consciousness from his earliest published fiction—see, for example *Eye in the Sky* [3-64]—and this interest only intensified as Dick explored more fully the use of mind-altering substances. The result, of course, was an entire body of literary work in which reality is at best a fragile consensus and drugs can be the key to transcendental knowledge. Among the most notable of Dick's drug-related novels are *The Three Stigmata of Palmer Eldritch* (1965), *Now Wait for Last Year* (1966), and the powerful *Flow My Tears, the Policeman Said* [4-137]. Following Dick's lead and, perhaps, their own contemporary experiences, many SF writers made the drug culture a standard component of their novels to an extent that today comes across as rather naïve. Indeed, when David Gerrold rewrote his successful 1972 novel, *When HARLIE Was One* [4-179] in 1988, he went so far as to remove virtually all mention of casual drug use by his scientist protagonist. With or without drug use, characters who lived decidedly alternate life-styles also became common in science fiction, especially in the work of Samuel R. Delany. See, for example, *Nova* [4-130] or the somewhat later *Dhalgren* [4-127].

In Britain, a nation that had never fully recovered from World War II and that was still coming to terms with the gradual, but painful, loss of its colonial empire, a new generation of science fiction writers was creating what came to be called the "New Wave." Reacting in direct opposition to what they saw as the SF establishment—authors like Arthur C. Clarke, James White, and John Wyndham perhaps—these "new wave" writers had relatively little interest in science and technology per se and were frequently technophobic. They tended toward leftist political values and they prized stylistic experimentation above all else. Infected, perhaps, by the general depression left by the loss of empire, their work also tended toward a depiction of disasters and decay, entropy in all its forms. On the brighter side, they were also interested in sex, drugs, and rock'n'roll.

Although some of the writers who later gained fame as part of the New Wave had been publishing since the mid-1950s, most notably Brian Aldiss and J. G. Ballard, the movement found its focus in 1964 when Michael Moorcock became editor of the British SF magazine *New Worlds* [12-13]. Moorcock didn't simply publish avant-garde work, however; he also publicized it widely and produced a series of manifestos in support of what the New Wave writers were doing. Moorcock's own vision of science fiction was both experimental and politically radical. He saw apocalyptic possibilities in contemporary British life and explored them in a series of bitingly satirical stories, most notably the first of the Jerry Cornelius tales (1965) [4-304] and the award-winning "Behold the Man" (1966) [4-302]. Although Ballard and Aldiss are the most estimable authors connected with the British New Wave, Moorcock helped develop a large roster of talented younger writers, including Langdon Jones, Barrington J. Bayley, M. John Harrison, and David I. Masson. He also published work by a number of Americans, most notably Thomas M. Disch and John Sladek. Despite its literary excellence, it should be noted, *New Worlds* was always pretty much a failure from a financial point of view. Still, the magazine's value as a pioneer was enormous. It provided a venue for writers eager to try new and important approaches to the genre and helped found several major careers.

In America a number of writers were similarly involved in a radical revisioning of science fiction, though they lacked the focal point provided by Moorcock's *New Worlds*. Among these authors were Disch, Samuel R. Delany, and Harlan Ellison, all of whom published some of their best early work in *New Worlds*. Two other American writers associated with the New Wave were Roger Zelazny and Robert Silverberg. Disch, Zelazny, and Delany demonstrated high artistic ambitions virtually from their first published stories. Ellison and Silverberg served apprenticeships writing more standard fare before spreading their wings. Among them, however, these five writers produced some of the best American science fiction of the 1960s. Although the New Wave writers were at first roundly criticized by both long-time genre readers and other science fiction authors, the gradual acceptance of their work can be seen in the sheer number of awards they received between 1965 and 1969. Zelazny, for example, picked up two Hugos and two Nebulas, as did Harlan Ellison; Aldiss and Moorcock each received a Nebula, while Silverberg was awarded both the Hugo and the Nebula. Samuel R. Delany earned an amazing four Nebulas as well as a Hugo. Lacking a magazine comparable to *New Worlds*, American New Wave writers published much of their best fiction in the original anthologies, Damon Knight's *Orbit* series [4-540], for example, and, particularly, Harlan Ellison's groundbreaking *Dangerous Visions* [4-535], which appeared in 1967 and included superb experimental fiction by Philip José Farmer, Silverberg, Delany, Norman Spinrad, Ballard, and R. A. Lafferty, as well as somewhat more traditional work by a number of other major talents.

Although radical changes occurred in the science fiction of the mid- to late-1960s, more traditional writers continued to produce excellent stories throughout the period, as they do to this day. Among the longtime veterans working at the top of their form were Clifford D. Simak, Fritz Leiber, Philip José Farmer, and Robert A. Heinlein, all of whom took home Hugo Awards for what may well be their best novels. Simak received the Hugo in 1964 for *Way Station* [3-165], a quiet tale of alien-human interaction; Leiber's large-scale disaster novel, *The Wanderer* [4-259], took the award in 1965; Farmer's tale of life after death, *To Your Scattered Bodies Go* [4-165], saw magazine publication in 1965–1966, but picked up a Hugo after its book publication in 1971; and Heinlein's much imitated tale of revolution on Luna, *The Moon Is a Harsh Mistress* [4-204], was the 1967 Hugo winner. Another veteran, Frank Herbert, produced one of the most important SF novels of the modern period in *Dune* [4-207], which won the Nebula in 1965. Other veterans publishing excellent more-or-less-traditional science fiction in the 1960s included Jack Vance, Poul Anderson, Cordwainer Smith, Arthur C. Clarke, James White, and Gordon R. Dickson.

Nor did all of the newer writers make a complete break with traditional methods and themes. Among the most important SF authors to begin publishing in the mid-1960s was Larry Niven, who was largely responsible for redefining the concept of hard science fiction for the modern period. Niven's first story appeared in 1964, and he went on to win a handful of major awards, most notably both the Hugo and Nebula for his influential 1970 novel, *Ringworld* [4-316]. SF writers have always had a penchant for the gigantic, the tendency to toss planets and stars around as if they were peanuts, but in *Ringworld* Niven went a step further, creating what may well have been at that time the largest inhabitable artifact in the history of the genre, a ring many miles wide that quite literally circles a star at approximately the same distance that Earth circles our sun. Niven's influence continues to this day and can be traced in the careers of such hard SF writers as his frequent collaborator Jerry Pournelle, Charles Sheffield, Robert L. Forward, David Brin, and Greg Bear.

The 1960s saw changes not merely in the kind of science fiction that was written, but also in how the genre was marketed, both in the United States and in Britain. Since Hugo Gernsback founded *Amazing Stories* in 1926, the majority of American science fiction stories had been published in magazines. Although relatively few of them are remembered today, dozens of SF magazines flourished from 1930 to 1960. When paperback fiction began to appear in the late 1930s and 1940s, collections of SF short stories reprinted from magazines soon became popular and, indeed, one of the first paperback volumes issued was a collection of previously published SF stories, *The Pocket Book of Science Fiction* [3-225], edited by Donald A. Wollheim in 1943. Throughout the 1950s and early 1960s magazine reprints continued to be the dominant form of science fiction in book format. Even the relatively few novels that were printed as often as not saw their first publication in magazines; both Pohl and Kornbluth's *The Space Merchants* [3-147] and Heinlein's *Double Star* [3-86], for example, had previously appeared as serials in *Galaxy* and *Astounding*, respectively. This, changed gradually, in part as a result of the gutting of the American News Company in the late 1950s and the increased distribution difficulties that resulted. By the early 1960s most of the magazines were gone and more and more original and reprint novels were appearing, in part because publishers began to recognize the drawing power of big-name writers with a number of books constantly kept in print. Publishing houses such as Ace and Ballantine led the way, the former being especially remembered for its back-to-back "Ace Double" format: two original short SF novels for just a quarter! Ballantine and Ace both had considerable success in promoting reprint editions of the work of Edgar Rice Burroughs, and Ace also turned a profit on its original paperback novels by Andre Norton. Heinlein, E. E. Smith, Asimov, Ray Bradbury, and a few other writers began receiving promotion and fairly large print runs. Then, in 1965, Ace and Ballantine went to war over the publication of an immensely long, heroic fantasy novel by a heretofore virtually unknown writer. J. R. R. Tolkien's monumental, three-volume *The Lord of the Rings*, had been published in hardcover in Britain in the mid-1950s to a lukewarm reception and modest sales. In 1965, however, Ace brought out a paperback edition in the United States and did so without paying royalties because of a loophole in the copyright law. Within months Ballantine issued a revised edition of the trilogy with a note from the author castigating Ace Books and asking readers to buy only the new version of his novel. Between them the Ace and Ballantine paperback editions of *The Lord of the Rings* sold more than a quarter of a million copies in their first year in print, an unheard-of figure for a work of genre fiction. The major publishers, of course, took notice, and the publication of quality original science fiction and fantasy became a growth industry. By the mid- to late-1970s the number of original titles published annually had tripled and works of science fiction and fantasy by such authors as Tolkien, Frank Herbert, Stephen R. Donaldson, and Terry Brooks were achieving bestseller status. By the early 1980s, Asimov, Heinlein, Clarke, and Piers Anthony had also become fixtures on the bestseller lists.

Among the outgrowths of this mid-1960s boom period were the establishment of the highly successful Ballantine Adult Fantasy series and, of more relevance here, the creation by editor Terry Carr of the Ace Science Fiction Specials series. Carr published original SF novels of considerable literary merit and, perhaps just as importantly, put covers on the books by top-rated illustrators Leo and Diane Dillon, which appealed to an adult audience. Between 1968 and 1971, he edited some of the finest novels ever to appear in the genre, among them Ursula K. Le Guin's *The Left Hand of Darkness* [4-254], R. A. Lafferty's *Past Master* [4-244], Keith Robert's *Pavane* [4-362], Joanna Russ's *And Chaos Died* [4-373], and Alexei Panshin's *Rite of Passage* [4-325]. Other publishers in both the United States and Britain soon developed similar quality SF lines with varying results. Another outgrowth of the mid-1960s SF boom was the original anthologies. Dozens of them appeared in the 1960s and early 1970s. Among the best were the already mentioned *Orbit* (beginning in 1966), edited by Damon Knight, and *Dangerous Visions* (1967), edited by Harlan Ellison. Terry Carr's *Universe* series [4-530] and Robert Silverberg's *New Dimensions* [4-550] (both beginning in 1971) also published large quantities of superb short fiction. Unfortunately, copycat publishers quickly flooded the market, producing numerous mediocre original anthologies, half of them edited by the notorious Roger Elwood. By the early 1980s very few such volumes were being published.

The decades following 1963 saw any number of new themes gaining importance within the genre, but two stand out in particular, one largely sociological in nature, the other largely technological. I am referring, of course, to science fiction's increasing interest in feminism and gender issues and the evolving technology of computers, microprocessors, and cybernetics.

It has often been written about science fiction that prior to the 1960s it was essentially a boys' club, both in terms of its readership and its writers. There is some truth to that assertion, although even a brief examination of the magazines of the 1950s will turn up a surprisingly long list of female authors, among them C. L. Moore, Leigh Brackett, Judith Merril, Andre Norton, Katherine MacLean, Mildred Clingerman, Zenna Henderson, Marion Zimmer Bradley, and Margaret St. Clair. Some of these writers, Moore, Brackett, Norton, and Bradley, for example, hid behind initials or gender-obscure first names and wrote what was essentially traditional science fiction and fantasy, utilizing generally male protagonists and catering to an essentially male audience. Others, Clingerman and Henderson in particular, were seen in their day, at least in part, as women's writers and published primarily in *The Magazine of Fantasy and Science Fiction*, which, since its founding in 1949, had adhered to a more urbane, polished, and mainstream literary style than other magazines in the field, a style somewhat more calculated perhaps to win a female readership.

What changed in the mid-1960s and early 1970s, then, was not just the number of women writers in the field but also the kinds of things they wrote about. The women's movement transformed science fiction, affecting even those writers who were hostile to it or simply uninterested. The careers of Ursula K. Le Guin and Joanna Russ typify the change that occurred. Le Guin entered the field with a number of well-done but fairly traditional science fiction and fantasy stories and novels written somewhat in the manner of Andre Norton, for example *Rocannon's World* in 1966. But in 1969, as part of Terry Carr's Ace SF Specials series, she published what may well be the most influential science fiction novel of the the latter half of the 20th century, *The Left Hand of Darkness* [4-254], a brilliant examination of, among many other things, gender stereotypes. Similarly, Joanna Russ, although she had begun publishing short fiction as early as 1959, first came to general notice with stories in *Orbit* in the mid- to late-1960s and with two Ace Specials, 1968's *Picnic on Paradise* [4-372] and 1970's *And Chaos Died* [4-373]. These later stories generally revolved around strong female protagonists heretofore rare in science fiction. Russ's controversial third novel, *The Female Man* [4-375], a much more radical and bitter feminist critique of contemporary gender roles, appeared in 1975. It had been written some years earlier but had considerable trouble finding a publisher.

Other women writers began to establish increasingly high profiles throughout the late-1960s and 1970S. Kate Wilhelm, who had been publishing with relatively little notice since the mid-1950s, blossomed into one of the genre's finest stylists, first in the pages of *Orbit* and eventually in such novels as the *Where the Sweet Birds Sang* [4-497] and *The Clewiston Test* [4-492]. Wilhelm's work has rarely addressed gender issues as directly as the works of Le Guin or Russ, but it has always been clear that she writes from a feminist perspective. Alice Sheldon, writing first under the pseudonym James Tiptree, Jr., and later as Raccoona Sheldon, beginning in the late 1960s produced a series of cutting feminist-oriented short stories, including "The Girl Who Was Plugged In," "The Women Men Don't See," and "Houston, Houston, Do You Read?" In 1974 Suzy McKee Charnas published *Walk to the End of the World* [4-99], which featured what might well be the most hideous patriarchal dystopia ever conceived by an SF writer. In 1976, Marge Piercy, a well-known mainstream novelist and poet, published *Woman on the Edge of Time* [4-330], which, like Russ's *The Female Man*, displayed glimpses of a variety of better and worse universes for women. Other female, feminist-oriented writers who entered, and helped to change, the field in the 1960s and 1970s included Pamela Sargent, Lisa Tuttle, and Elizabeth Lynn. The process continues to this day with newer authors like Octavia Butler, Sheri Tepper, Joan Slonczewski, Eleanor Arnason, and Judith Moffett producing increasingly sophisticated fiction that deals meaningfully with, among other things, the relationship between gender and such topics as violence, race, ecology, pacifism, religion, and child abuse. Also of note has been the increasing number of male authors who write from a feminist perspective, for example, John Varley, Samuel R. Delany, and Kim Stanley Robinson, as well as writers who introduce gay or lesbian characters into their fiction, including Delany, Thomas M. Disch, Lynn, Arnason, and, somewhat unexpectedly, Marion Zimmer Bradley, whose work underwent a major transformation in the early to mid-1970s, changing gradually from fairly standard science fantasy in the tradition of Leigh Brackett and Andre Norton to a more serious exploration of women's and gay issues. It should be noted, perhaps, that as was the case with the New Wave, the emergence of so many strong female and feminist writers in the genre has led to a fair amount of anger. This criticism has come primarily, though not entirely, from male writers who either disagree with the entire feminist message or see women writers as responsible for publishing fantasy disguised as SF and thus somehow damaging the genre's legitimacy.

In his *Skylark of Space* series [2-114] E. E. Smith could describe gigantic spaceships powered by hundreds of towering vacuum tubes. Even as late as 1966, Robert A. Heinlein in *The Moon Is a Harsh Mistress* [4-204] and D. F. Jones in *Colossus* could write of computers that took up entire buildings. But with the invention of the microprocessor in 1969, and the marketing of the first microcomputers in 1971, sheer size was no longer synonymous with computing power and further enormous breakthroughs in computer technology seemed to be right around the corner. In the 1960s and early 1970s computers were primarily of interest to science fiction writers in terms of the quest for artificial intelligence (AI). The Heinlein and Jones novels are examples of this interest, which was often coupled with a fear that if an AI were created, it might, for better or worse, take control of the human race, a fear that is, of course, traceable as far back as Jack Williamson's *The Humanoids* [3-194], Karel Čapek's *R.U.R.* [2-16], and perhaps even *Frankenstein* [1-84]. Other 1970s examples of the interest in artificial intelligence include David Gerrold's *When HARLIE Was One* [4-179] and, of course, Isaac Asimov's "The Bicentennial Man" (1976). In the 1960s scientists were fairly sanguine concerning their ability to create true AIs in the near future, but little real progress was made over the next two decades and genre interest in artificial intelligence gradually declined. AIs, whether housed in stationary computers or configured as robots, became, for the most part, an assumed background element in stories largely about other things. The major exception to this trend would be in film and television, where artificial intelligences continued to be popular, most often in the form of highly attractive young "women," brawny "men," or cute robots, and who were most frequently cast as police officers, faithful sidekicks, or villains.

Even in the 1970s programmers routinely expected to spend hours punching cards and poring over yards of printout before they could run all but the simplest programs. Gradually, however, as programming became easier and turned into a matter of keyboards and screens, direct, tactile connection between user and machine made it increasingly possible to sink into an almost trance-like creative state. The hardware came to be seen as secondary, a mere interface between the user and both the software (the programs themselves) and the networked electronic space in which those programs were increasingly being run (which came to be called cyberspace). Perhaps the first SF author to make use of this concept in its modern form was Vernor Vinge in his fine 1981 novella "True Names" [4-476]. The idea of cyberspace didn't really catch fire, however, until 1984, when science fiction was turned upside down by its first highly organized, high-profile literary movement since the New Wave.

The term *cyberpunk* was created by Bruce Bethke in a story of that name, which appeared in *Amazing* in 1983, but it was almost immediately appropriated by the editor Gardner Dozois to label the early fiction of the new literary movement, much of which he was publishing in *Isaac Asimov's SF Magazine*. The cyberpunks fused a strong interest in technology, and particularly in cybernetics and biotechnology, a generally left-wing or libertarian (antigovernment, anti-big business) political stance, and down-and-dirty punk attitudes with a literary aesthetic borrowed, at least in part, from Raymond Chandler, Dashiell Hammett, and *film noir*. They also claimed as progenitors writers as diverse as Alfred Bester, Harlan Ellison, William Burroughs, Anthony Burgess, and J. G. Ballard, not to mention Ridley Scott's 1982 film, *Bladerunner*. Their main theorist and author of manifestos was Bruce Sterling, their finest writer William Gibson. Other writers closely associated with the cyberpunks were John Shirley, though his career dated back to 1973, Lewis Shiner, Rudy Rucker, Pat Cadigan, Marc Laidlaw, and Richard Kadrey. A number of other SF writers have claimed or been claimed to have occasional connections with the cyberpunks, including Samuel R. Delany, Walter Jon Williams, Michael Swanwick, George Alec Effinger, and Greg Bear.

The work that most epitomized cyberpunk was William Gibson's 1984 novel, *Neuromancer* [4-184] which, fittingly enough, initiated the second group of Terry Carr-edited Ace SF specials. The book, a stylish and complex tale of computer cowboys hacking their way through cyberspace to commit a variety of computer crimes, won the Hugo, Nebula, and Philip K. Dick awards and is clearly the most influential (and most imitated) SF novel since Le Guin's *The Left Hand of Darkness*. Many of the major cyberpunk stories appeared in *Isaac Asimov's SF Magazine*, edited by Gardner Dozois. The core cyberpunk anthology, however, was Bruce Sterling's *Mirrorshades* [4-551]. Although, or perhaps because, the more talented proponents of the movement quickly branched off in a variety of different literary directions, cyberpunk soon became a rather standardized set of tropes to be readily imitated by less ambitious writers and, by 1990, it was fashionable in academic and book review circles to proclaim the subgenre dead. Not surprisingly, however, one or two excellent new cyberpunk novels continue to appear each year, most recently Neal Stephenson's *Snow Crash* [4-437]. The concept of cyberspace as a place where an artificial or virtual reality can be constructed and where human and machine intelligences can interact and, in effect, live their lives is not limited in its use merely to the cyberpunk writers. In becoming the common coin of SF, cyberpunk has also lent itself to spectacular use by writers as diverse as Dan Simmons in *The Fall of Hyperion* [4-419], Charles Platt in *The Silicon Man* [4-332], Norman Spinrad in *Deus X* (1993), and Marge Piercy in *He, She, and It* [4-329].

From its earliest days, most obviously in *Frankenstein* [1-84], science fiction has concerned itself with such Faustian ambitions as the creation of new life forms and the transformation of already existing life into something either superior to or more specialized than what has gone before. Early writers, like Shelley and H. G. Wells in *The Island of Doctor Moreau* [1-100], more often than not saw such actions within the context of surgical science, and contemporary authors have continued to use this concept with some frequency, especially whenever new advances in transplant techniques or the use of prosthetics attracted their attention. Notable examples of the use of surgery to keep alive, augment, or simply change the human body include, in the 1970s, Heinlein's *I Will Fear No Evil* (1970), Clarke's "A Meeting with Medusa" (1972) and Pohl's *Man Plus* [4-335]. In the 1980s, improvements in microtechnology brought renewed popularity to this concept, especially in the work of the cyberpunks, who often assumed the widespread adoption of implants to create a direct computer/brain interface; see, for example, Walter Jon Williams's *Hardwired* [4-499], George Alec Effinger's *When Gravity Fails* [4-154], and Pat Cadigan's *Synners* [4-89]. The potential for surgically altering the human form to build a superior warrior has also been an ongoing interest of SF and was well-handled most recently in Benford's *Great Sky River* [4-44].

The concept of creating some form of *Homo superior* through surgery has, throughout the history of science fiction, been paralleled by the desire to make genetic alterations—alterations that will breed true. The early-modern period is full of superman tales; in some cases the new form of humanity is seen as a spontaneous mutation, but in others, for example, A. E. van Vogt's *Slan* [3-180], the changes are the result of what appears to be (van Vogt's language is rather imprecise) an experiment in genetic manipulation. In the 1950s and 1960s, spurred perhaps by breakthroughs in DNA research, a number of writers produced excellent stories centered on an improved understanding of genetic engineering, most notably James Blish's *The Seedling Stars* [3-23] and, on a more modest level, Frank Herbert's *Dune* [4-207] and the Instrumentality of Man stories of Cordwainer Smith [4-427]. Lacking specifics on how such engineering should be done, however, these stories tended to concentrate on the spectacular, and at times rather unlikely, end products of the process. In the late 1960s and 1970s the aspect of genetic engineering that was most widely used in science fiction was cloning; see, for example, Le Guin's "Nine Lives" (1969), Pamela Sargent's *Cloned Lives* (1976), Ira Levin's *The Boys From Brazil* [4-265], and Kate Wilhelm's *Where Late the Sweet Birds Sang* [4-497]. In more recent years, stories involving genetic engineering have generally broken into two groups, those concerned with relatively limited and entirely possible near-future attempts to create *Homo superior*, for example Robert Reed's *Black Milk* [4-353], Lois McMaster Bujold's *Falling Free* [4-79], George Turner's *Brain Child* (1991), and Nancy Kress's *Beggars in Spain* [4-238], and more spectacular tales of wholesale genetic transformation, including, for example, Charles Sheffield's *Sight of Proteus* [4-399], Bruce Sterling's *Schismatrix* and his Shaper and Mechanist stories [4-440], and Geoff Ryman's *The Child Garden* [4-377]. Although set in the far future, C. J. Cherryh's *Cyteen* [4-102] may be the most realistic portrayal we have of the psychological and sociological ramifications of cloning.

In what is undoubtedly his weakest novel, *Fantastic Voyage* (1966), written as a film tie-in, Isaac Asimov told the basically silly story of the miniaturization of a surgical team, which was then sent into the body of a dying man to save his life. In the 1970s, however, a number of scientists, most notably K. Eric Drexler, began writing about the concept of nanotechnology, the creation of machines on a molecular level, and primitive forms of this technology quickly came into existence in our world (see Drexler's *Engines of Creation*, 1987). Interest in nanotechnology within the science fiction community was immediate and, when combined with research in both genetic engineering and microprocessors, resulted in a number of fine new stories like Greg Bear's *Blood Music* [4-38], which involves a scientist who uses genetic engineering techniques to transform a virus into an intelligent nanocomputer. Replicating rapidly, the virus takes over the scientist's body, transforming it to its own specifications. Within a very few years nanotechnology has become, like faster-than-light space travel and artificial intelligence, one of the standard tropes of science fiction and a major background element in such works as Paul Preuss's *Human Error* [4-343], Bear's *Queen of Angels* [4-41], Walter Jon Williams's *Aristoi* [4-498], and Michael Swanwick's *Stations of the Tide* [4-450].

In the thirty years since 1963 new scientific breakthroughs have transformed science fiction, as have the great sociological and political changes of the period. One of the pleasures of the genre, however, involves discovering the ways in which authors can take some of the older ideas, dust them off, do a little genetic manipulation, perhaps, and present them to us in new and exciting forms. The earliest popular tales of Mars, for example, those of Edgar Rice Burroughs and, somewhat later, Leigh Brackett, were gorgeous, generally lightweight romantic romps. Then, in the decade after World War II, we saw a number of more or less realistic portrayals of the exploration and colonization of Mars, for example, Heinlein's *Red Planet* (1949) and Clarke's *The Sands of Mars* (1951). In the years that followed, however, other kinds of stories became popular. Ray Bradbury, taking his cue in part from Brackett, but with a more serious purpose, published the highly romantic *The Martian Chronicles* [3-32] in 1950. He in turn was emulated by any number of other writers, most notably Roger Zelazny in his classic, "A Rose for Ecclesiastes" (1963). Neither Bradbury nor Zelazny, it should be noted, made any attempt at depicting a scientifically accurate Mars; such accuracy was simply irrelevant to their purposes. Still other authors used a not-very-realistically portrayed Mars as a backdrop for stories in which the location was of secondary importance, for example Philip K. Dick's *Martian Time-Slip* [3-66] and *The Three Stigmata of Palmer Eldritch* [4-137]. The romanticized Mars of Brackett and Bradbury continues to fascinate SF writers, as was most recently demonstrated by Ian McDonald in his novel *Desolation Road* [4-292]. Periodically, however, writers armed with new data about the red planet have returned to attempt to describe its exploration and colonization in realistic terms, as, for example, in Pohl's 1976 *Man Plus* [4-335], Lewis Shiner's 1984 *Frontera*, and, most recently, in Kim Stanley Robinson's *Red Mars* [4-366], *Green Mars* (1993), and the forthcoming *Blue Mars*. The updating that goes on when an author returns to one of science fiction's perennial themes, however, is often much more than merely technological. Shiner, for example, uses *Frontera* not merely to describe the colonization of Mars, but also to make some of the standard cyberpunk criticisms concerning the inherent corruption of big business and big government. Similarly, Robinson, while presenting perhaps the most detailed and believable description of planetary colonization ever to appear in a work of fiction, is also pursuing a well-thought out ecological agenda.

Other venerable genre topics also received periodic updating between 1963 and 1993, among them nuclear war and militarism. The post-nuclear holocaust theme handled so well by Walter M. Miller, Jr., in *A Canticle for Leibowitz* [3-125] and by Edgar Pangborn in *Davy* [4-324] in the 1950s and 1960s, reappeared in the 1980s in powerful new tales such as Russell Hoban's *Riddley Walker* [4-210] and Neal Barrett, Jr.'s *Through Darkest America* [4-31]. Given impetus by the Vietnam War and responding to Heinlein's earlier novel *Starship Troopers* [3-90], Joe Haldeman explored with great insight the dangers of militarism in his 1975 novel, *The Forever War* [4-193]. Then, ten years later, Orson Scott Card published what was, at least in part, another installment in the same argument, his award-winning *Ender's Game* [4-92]. Science fiction's debate over militarism continues to this day. In his Mercenary series [4-338] and his *There Will Be War* anthologies, for example, Jerry Pournelle continues to conduct a campaign against what he sees as the liberal betrayal of the United States in Vietnam and elsewhere. Although it rarely receives award nominations or serious reviews, military fiction by Pournelle, David Drake, and similar writers comprises a significant percentage of the SF published each year.

A final theme that has become increasingly important in science fiction during the modern period is ecology. Genre warnings of potential ecological disaster go back at least as far as Ward Moore's *Greener Than You Think* (1947) and John Christopher's 1956 *The Death of Grass* [3-42]. It wasn't until the 1960s, however, that our society's ability to cause overwhelming ecological damage began to gain a more general public attention. Nonfiction works such as Rachel Carson's *The Silent Spring* (1962) and, somewhat later, Paul Ehrlich's *The Population Bomb* (1968) gained enormous readership. Among the earlier works of science fiction that helped promulgate this new environmental awareness were J. G. Ballard's *The Drowned World* [3-16], *The Drought* [4-27], and *The Crystal World* [4-26], each of which depicted horrifying ecological disasters; Frank Herbert's *Dune* [4-207], with its serious discussion of the possibilities for transforming a planetary ecology; John Brunner's two disaster novels, *Stand on Zanzibar* [4-74], which concentrates on the population explosion, and *The Sheep Look Up* [4-72], which portrays an America collapsing beneath the weight of its own pollution; and Ursula K. Le Guin's 1972 novella, *The Word for World Is Forest* [4-256], which depicts the accidental destruction of an alien ecology by colonists from Earth. In the late 1980s and 1990s the topic of ecology has been virtually ubiquitous in near-future SF, appearing as a major element in such important novels as Le Guin's *Always Coming*

Home [4-251], George Turner's *Drowning Towers* [4-462], Joan Slon-czewski's *A Door into Ocean* [4-425], Judith Moffett's *Pennterra* [4-300], David Brin's *Earth* [4-64], and Kim Stanley Robinson's *Pacific Edge* [4-367].

The preceding pages are at best a partial introduction to the new developments that have occurred in science fiction since 1963. When I first began exploring the genre in the late 1950s, it was still possible to read almost everything of importance in the field, but the quantity of new science fiction books being published each year has grown considerably since the days of my youth. Since 1985 the number of original SF titles appearing annually, according to the trade magazine *Locus*, has varied between 239 and 317 volumes, and that's excluding all anthologies, collections, and novelizations, not to mention works of fantasy and horror. Though I write two of the most comprehensive "SF Year in Review" articles in the field for annual reference books, I don't pretend to have read more than a minority of the new books that appear. It is my hope and belief, however, that I have managed to read all, or at least most, of the major new novels, short story collections, and anthologies worthy of inclusion in this edition of *Anatomy of Wonder*.

To do justice to the tremendous flowering of new and important science fiction during the past decade, it has been necessary to cut many of the entries from the 1987 third edition. In pursuit of this goal, I have attempted to retain entries for all of the genre's true classics, nonetheless I was forced to remove or to combine entries for many excellent books. The practicalities of publishing simply forced us to make some very difficult cuts.

In writing this essay and the entries that appear here for the first time, my model first and foremost was the work of Brian Stableford, who handled the modern period in the third edition of *Anatomy of Wonder*. As I read Brian's work in preparation for beginning my own, it became apparent to me that our tastes differ in a number of areas—he appears to have a higher tolerance than I do for military science fiction and a greater love of hard SF. I apparently feel more comfortable than he does with the cyberpunks and with feminist SF. I came away from reading Brian's work, however, believing that he did a superb job, and it seemed a waste both of my time and his effort to simply rewrite all of his entries from scratch. Therefore I've left many of Brian's entries largely unchanged. In a few cases I've retained the bulk of an entry, but changed parts of it to reflect further publications by the author under consideration or my own occasional disagreements with what Brian wrote. I would also like to thank Rob Latham for providing a number of fine entries for books I simply didn't have time to cover. In preparing my entries and article, I have made use of a variety of publications for background data, especially *Twentieth-Century Science-Fiction Writers,* second edition, edited by Curtis C. Smith [7-30], and the marvelous new *Encyclopedia of Science Fiction,* edited by John Clute and Peter Nicholls [7-22]. I have also received help from reviews published in the *SFRA Review, Locus* (particularly the fine work of Russ Letson and Faren Miller), the late, lamented *Fantasy Review, The New York Review of SF, SF Eye,* and *Science Fiction & Fantasy Book Review Annual,* edited by Robert A. Collins and Robert Latham. I would also like to thank my wife, Sandra Lindow, for her editorial help; she always makes me put in semicolons when the sentences get too long.

Bibliography

This is approximately 80 percent of the length of the corresponding bibliography in the third edition of *Anatomy of Wonder,* a reduction reflecting the greater selectivity in this edition, for the reasons suggested earlier in this introduction and for the same reasons chapter 3 is more selective.

Approximately 330 of Brian Stableford's annotations from the third edition were selected by Michael Levy for retention, often with minor revisions; these entries show the initials BS at the end of the annotation. Approximately 45 entries were more extensively revised by Levy and are designated by dual initials. Michael Levy selected approximately 180 books from the 1987–1993 period, assisted by Rob Latham, and their initials follow these annotations.

4-1.   Adams, Douglas. **The Hitchhiker's Guide to the Galaxy.** Pan, 1979.

Adaptation of a much-loved and very funny British radio series. Earth is demolished to make way for a new hyperspatial bypass, but the hero stows away on a starship with a reporter for the eponymous reference book. Their outrageous extraterrestrial adventures are part satire, part slapstick. *The Restaurant at the End of the Universe* (1980) completed the adaptation of the original radio scripts, but Adams then added *Life, the Universe and Everything* (1982), *So Long, and Thanks for All the Fish* (1984), and *Mostly Harmless* (1992). Although all five books sold well, the later volumes seem less inspired and tend increasingly toward dark humor and irony. Readers who can't get enough of this series should investigate Neil Gaiman's *Don't Panic: The Official Hitchhiker's Guide to the Galaxy Companion* (1988). Compare Sheckley's *Options* (1975). (BS/ML)

4-2. Aldiss, Brian W(ilson). **Barefoot in the Head: A European Fantasia.** Faber, 1969.
The Acid Head War, fought with psychotropic weapons, has left all Europe crazy. The hero journeys back and forth across the continent, becoming a guru in the Gurdjieff tradition and acquiring quasi-messianic status. A Joycean celebration of the vivid eccentricities of the 1960s counterculture, brilliantly phantasmagoric. Based on materials published in *New Worlds*; a fine testament to the stimulus provided by the magazine. (BS)

4-3. Aldiss, Brian W(ilson). **Best SF Stories of Brian Aldiss.** Gollancz, 1988. U.S. title: *Man in His Time: Best SF Stories of Brian W. Aldiss*, Atheneum, 1989.
Aldiss has written many fine stories, far too many to be contained in one collection, but this volume includes some of the best: among them "Who Can Replace a Man," "Poor Little Warrior," and the Nebula Award-winning "The Saliva Tree." Many of the earlier stories, dating from the late 1960s, are superior examples of the New Wave. The later stories, dating from the mid-1980s, "My Country 'Tis Not Only of Thee" or "The Gods in Flight," for example, are often intensely political and rather idiosyncratic. Other excellent collections of Aldiss's work include *A Romance of the Equator: Best Fantasy Stories of Brian W. Aldiss* (1989), *Seasons in Flight* (1984), *Last Orders, and Other Stories* (1977), and *The Moment of Eclipse* (1970). Compare Jones's *The Eye of the Lens* [4-220]. (ML)

4-4. Aldiss, Brian W(ilson). **Frankenstein Unbound.** Cape, 1973.
The protagonist timeslips from the 21st century into a past where Mary Shelley coexists with the monster of her imagination. An interesting extrapolation of Aldiss's fascination with Mary Shelley and her book; more successful than his later attempt to reconsider the philosophical import of a Wells novel, *Moreau's Other Island* (1980; U.S. title: *An Island Called Moreau*). (BS)

*4-5. Aldiss, Brian W(ilson). **Graybeard.** Faber, 1964.
Unwise experimentation with nuclear devices has led to the sterilization of mankind, and there seems to be no hope for the future. The central characters, waiting for the end, consider the ironies and frustrations of their situation. A key work in the tradition of British disaster stories. Compare F. Wright Moxley's *Red Snow* (1930) for an earlier variation of the theme. (BS)

*4-6. Aldiss, Brian W(ilson). **Helliconia Spring.** Cape, 1982.
The first volume in a trilogy continued in *Helliconia Summer* (1983) and

Helliconia Winter (1985; NN, 1985). Helliconia is a planet whose sun eccentrically orbits a much brighter start and thus has a "great year" extending over hundreds of generations. Its societies undergo vast changes, interrupted by periodic plagues, and the relationship between humans and the cold-loving phagors also alters dramatically. Observers from Earth watch with interest from an orbital station and relay the story of one great year back to an avid audience on Earth. The dedication states that the trilogy takes up themes from Aldiss's non-SF novel *Life in the West* (1980) in attempting to analyze the "malaise" from which our time is suffering. Superb world-building SF. Compare Paul Park's *Starbridge Chronicles* [4-327] and Michael Swanwick's *Stations of the Tide* [4-450]. (BS/ML) JWC, 1983; NN, 1982

4-7.   Aldiss, Brian W(ilson). **Report on Probability A.** Faber, 1968.
An attempt to write a novel based on Heisenberg's uncertainty principle. A series of observers sustain alternative realities with their unwavering inquisitiveness. An enigmatic work that has affinities with the French anti-novel. Compare Robert Anton Wilson's modeling of modern physical theory in narrative, *Shrödinger's Cat* [4-504]. (BS) [For other works by this author see chapter 3.]

4-8.   Amis, Kingsley. **The Alteration.** Cape, 1976.
Alternate world story of Catholic-dominated Europe; the central character is a young singer who faces the possibility of being castrated to preserve his voice. A nice balance is struck between the hard-edged plot and the ironic background. Compare Phyllis Eisenstein's *Shadow of Earth* (1979). (BS) John W. Campbell Award, 1977

4-9.   Anderson, Chester. **The Butterfly Kid.** Pyramid, 1967.
Psychedelic adventures in Greenwich Village, with aliens intervening to materialize the phantoms of hallucination. An engaging expression of countercultural exuberance. The author and two friends are the main characters; the friends added their own contributions to an unusual trilogy in *The Unicorn Girl* (1969) by Michael Kurland and *The Probability Pad* (1970) by T. A. Waters. (BS) HN, 1968

4-10.   Anderson, Poul. **The Avatar.** Berkley, 1978.
Progress on Earth is being stifled by a paternalistic regime, and the hero must embark on a transgalactic odyssey to find an alien species sufficiently sophisticated to bring him home adequately enriched with knowledge. Compare Charles Sheffield's *Between the Strokes of Night* (1985). (BS)

4-11. Anderson, Poul. **The Boat of a Million Years.** Tor, 1989.
Through the ages random genetic mutation has bestowed immortality on a small number of human beings. Beginning in 310 B.C., Anderson chronicles the lives of a number of such immortals, some who partake in society, some who remain aloof from it. Eventually, tiring of an Earth that has grown too tame, the immortals build a starship and go off to explore the universe. Although the novel is a bit rambling, Anderson's historical detail is endlessly fascinating. Compare Zelazny's *This Immortal* [4-518]. (ML) HN, 1989; NN 1990

*4-12. Anderson, Poul. **Tau Zero.** Doubleday, 1970.
A malfunctioning starship continues to accelerate as it nears light speed, and its crew observes relativistic effects, ultimately being carried beyond the time frame of the universe, while the cruel circumstances force psychological and interpersonal adaptations. An archetypal example of hard SF with a visionary element. Compare Bear's *Eon* [4-39]. (BS) HN, 1971 [For other works by this author see chapters 3 and 5.]

4-13. Anthony, Patricia. **Cold Allies.** Harcourt, 1993.
Fine first novel. The world is in sorry shape because of the climatic changes of the greenhouse effect. Famine is widespread, and just about every nation is at war with another, struggling over the planet's dwindling resources. Then enigmatic aliens appear; they are seen only as cold blue lights, floating over the battlefields, occasionally kidnapping people. Anthony is a fine prose stylist with a knack for creating believable characters in a small space, evident also in her second novel *Brother Termite* (Harcourt, 1993). Compare Kessel's *Good News from Outer Space* [4-227] and Slonczewski's *The Wall Around Eden* [4-426]. (ML)

4-14. Anthony, Piers (pseud. of Piers Anthony Jacob). **Chthon.** Ballantine, 1967.
The plot and counterplot, running in close parallel, tell of the protagonist's escape from a hellish prison and the transgalactic odyssey that ultimately confronts him with the chemical nature of his own being. A stylized futuristic fable. The sequel, *Phthor* (1975), is much less successful. (BS) HN, 1968; NN, 1967

4-15. Anthony, Piers (pseud. of Piers Anthony Jacob). **Macroscope.** Avon, 1969.
The macroscope is an instrument allowing human observers access to the wonders of the universe. When Homo sapiens is relocated in this cosmic

perspective, the narrative shifts to a quasi-allegorical mode in which the symbolic significance of astrological lore is reworked. A more extended exercise in the same vein is the trilogy *God of Tarot* (1979), *Vision of Tarot* (1980), and *Faith of Tarot* (1980), which similarly attempts to display a modern philosophy of life by reinterpreting the apparatus of an occult system. A future series of this type, using even more baroque apparatus and taking its pretensions even more seriously, is The Incarnations of Immortality, a seven-volume saga begun with *On a Pale Horse* (1983). (BS) [For other works by this author see chapter 5.]

4-16.   Arnason, Eleanor. **Ring of Swords.** Tor, 1993.
Humanity and the alien *hwarhath* are on the verge of war and diplomats are working desperately to avoid bloodshed. The key to negotiations may be Nicholas, a human prisoner of war whom the *hwarhath* leader has taken as his lover. Fine anthropological SF. Arnason is one of the most original writers in the field working on gender issues. A sequel is expected to appear in 1995. Compare Jones's *White Queen* [4-219]. Contrast Niven and Pournelle's *The Mote in God's Eye* [4-320]. (ML)

4-17.   Arnason, Eleanor. **A Woman of the Iron People.** Morrow, 1991.
Co-winner of the first annual James Tiptree Award for science fiction, which examines problems of gender. An anthropological team from Earth discovers an alien society where women create all culture and technology, while men live in primitive style on the fringes of civilization. Compare Tepper's *The Gate to Women's Country* [4-453] and Sargent's *Venus of Dreams* [4-382] for other variations on this idea. (ML)

*4-18.   Asimov, Isaac. **The Complete Stories.** Doubleday, 1990–1992.
Volume one assembles 46 stories from three Asimov collections, *Earth Is Room Enough* (1957), *Nine Tomorrows* (1957), and *Nightfall and Other Stories* (1959). Although not everything here is memorable, there are a number of excellent pieces, including two of the author's own favorite short stories, "The Last Question" and "The Ugly Little Boy," plus the classic "Nightfall" and "Dreaming Is a Private Thing." Volume two collects an additional 40 stories. (ML)

4-19.   Asimov, Isaac. **Foundation's Edge.** Doubleday, 1982.
Fourth volume of the Foundation series [3-12], uncomfortably extending its themes and beginning the work of binding it into a common future history with Asimov's robot stories. In the 1940s the series seemed sophisticated in introducing political themes into space opera, but SF has evolved so far in the meantime that the new book seems rather quaint

despite its popularity. It is a feast of nostalgia for longtime readers. The story continues in *Foundation and Earth* (1986), with the hero pursuing his quest to track down the origins of mankind and gradually learning the truth about Earth. *Prelude to Foundation* (1988) and *Forward the Foundation* (1993), which Asimov left unfinished at his death, predate the other novels in the series in terms of internal chronology, describing the early life of Hari Seldon. (BS/ML) HW, 1983; NN, 1982

*4-20.   Asimov, Isaac. **The Gods Themselves.** Doubleday, 1972.

A novel reflecting Asimov's fascination with the sociology of science, reminiscent in parts of J. D. Watson's *The Double Helix* (1968). The energy crisis is "solved" by pumping energy from a parallel universe, whose alien inhabitants must try to communicate with humans in order to tell them that both races are in deadly peril. Written with a verve and economy that are missing from Asimov's later novels. Compare Bob Shaw's *A Wreath of Stars* (1976). (BS) HW, 1973; NW, 1972

4-21.   Asimov, Isaac. **The Robots of Dawn.** Phantasia, 1983.

The heroes of Asimov's earlier robot detective stories, *The Caves of Steel* [3-10] and *The Naked Sun* [3-10], undertake a new investigation on the utopian world of Aurora, where men live in harmony with their machines. The murder mystery becomes a peg on which to hang part of the argument connecting the robot series with the Foundation series. The argument is further extended in *Robots and Empire* (1985), in which robots renegotiate the famous laws of robotics and set humankind on the road to galactic empire. Prolix, but better connected with their antecedents than the new Foundation novels [4-19]. (BS) HN, 1984 [For other works by this author see chapters 3 and 5 (French).]

4-22.   Attanasio, A. A. **Radix.** Morrow, 1981.

Earth is much altered by the loss of its magnetic "shield" against cosmic radiation, and the changes are accelerated by a burst of energy from a "collapsar," which brings about a wholesale metamorphosis of Earth's life system. Many beings transcend the limitations of frail flesh in different ways, and the plot follows one such transcendent maturation. Attanasio has published three further novels that he defines as thematic sequels to *Radix*—*In Other Worlds* (1984), *Arc of Dreams* (1986), and *The Last Legends of Earth* (1989)—none of which has received comparable acclaim. Compare Silverberg's *Son of Man* (1971) and Delany's *The Einstein Intersection* [4-129]. (BS/ML) NN, 1981

*4-23.　Atwood, Margaret. **The Handmaid's Tale.** McClelland & Stewart, 1985.

Dystopian novel of a world ruled by militaristic fundamentalism in which sexual pleasure is forbidden. Conception and childbirth have become difficult and the handmaid of the title belongs to a specialist breeding stock. The story is annotated by a historian in a further future, whose shape is not revealed. The 1990 film was somewhat sterile. Compare Wyndham's "Consider Her Ways" (1956) and Charnas's *Walk to the End of the World* [4-99]. (BS) NN, 1986

4-24.　Ballard, J(ames) G(raham). **The Atrocity Exhibition.** Cape, 1970. U.S. title: *Love and Napalm: Export U.S.A.*, 1972.

A series of "condensed novels"—collages of images presenting a kaleidoscopic pattern of 20th century myths and motifs, particularly those that dominated the 1960s. Political assassinations, customized cars, the space program, the arms race, the media as brokers of celebrity—all are juxtaposed here in a nightmarish panorama of a culture out of control, subject to a cancerous malaise. Compare Burroughs's *Nova Express* [4-83]. (BS)

*4-25.　Ballard, J(ames) G(raham). **Chronopolis and Other Stories.** Putnam, 1971.

Ballard's short fiction is distributed over more than a dozen collections, in various combinations, but this selection—which overlaps considerably with *The Best Short Stories of J. G. Ballard* (1978)—preserves the best of his early work. Alienated protagonists bear witness to the world's descent into a perverse decadence; if they attempt to resist (many do not), they are likely to be maddened by the consciousness of their hopeless entrapment. "The Terminal Beach" (1964) marked a turning point in the concerns of British SF, and signaled the start of the era of avant-garde methods. (BS)

*4-26.　Ballard, J(ames) G(raham). **The Crystal World.** Cape, 1966.

Completes a quartet of apocalyptic novels begun with *The Wind From Nowhere* (1962) and continued with *The Drowned World* [3-16] and *The Drought* [4-27]. Time begins to "crystallize out," causing vast tracts of African rain forest to undergo a metamorphosis that echoes and contrasts with the metamorphosis of human flesh that is leprosy. The hero's symbolic odyssey, like that of the protagonist in Conrad's *Heart of Darkness*, brings him to a more fundamental existential level. Superb imagery. (BS) NN, 1966

*4-27.　Ballard, J(ames) G(raham). **The Drought.** Cape, 1965. U.S. title (of a considerably shorter version): *The Burning World*, Berkley, 1964.

Evaporation from the world's oceans is inhibited by pollutants, and inland areas are devastated by drought. Humans adapt psychologically in various ways, and the protagonist's personal life becomes spiritually desiccated in tune with his surroundings. The narrative is suitably dry and laconic. (BS)

4-28. Ballard, J(ames) G(raham). **Vermilion Sands.** Berkley, 1971.
A collection of stories showing the more colorful and romantic side of Ballard's imagination. In a decadent resort town, avant-garde artists and the jetsam of faded star-cults play out their casual tragedies. Elegantly ironic and overripe; *Sunset Boulevard* transposed into the SF idiom. Compare Lee Killough's *Aventine* (1982). (BS) [For other works by this author see chapter 3.]

*4-29. Banks, Iain M. **Consider Phlebas.** Macmillan, 1987.
After publishing a series of highly experimental literary novels, Banks changed gears and produced a series of sophisticated space operas. Horza, an alien shape changer and one of the most feared spies and assassins in the galaxy, is hired by another alien race, the Idirans, to further their religious crusade against the Culture, a technologically advanced, liberal-minded human civilization. Banks combines wit, political acumen, and nonstop action with complete success. Equally good are the later books in the series: *The Player of Games* (1988), *Use of Weapons* (1990), *The State of the Art* (1991), and *Against a Dark Background* (1993). Compare Vinge's *A Fire Upon the Deep* [4-474]. (ML)

4-30. Barnes, John. **A Million Open Doors.** Tor, 1992.
The Thousand Cultures, once separated by interstellar distances, are now being connected by instantaneous matter transmission, and each formerly isolated planet is going through intense culture shock. Giraut, who comes from a high-tech, pseudomedieval culture of duels, troubadours, and chivalry, finds himself employed on Caledony, a grim, no-frills world run according to the utilitarian dictates of Rational Christianity. The clash of cultures is fascinating, though too much of the novel's action occurs offstage. Compare Heinlein's *Beyond This Horizon* [3-84]. (ML) NN, 1992

*4-31. Barrett, Jr., Neal. **Through Darkest America.** Congdon and Weed, 1986.
When his isolated farm is destroyed and his family is murdered, young Howie Ryder sets off to seek revenge. As he travels across a continent still recovering from a nuclear war in the past, Howie discovers a horrifying world of government-sanctioned cannibalism, slavery, and child abuse. This is one of the bleakest and most powerful post-holocaust novels ever written. *Dawn's Uncertain Light* (1989) is a competent, but somewhat less

harrowing sequel. Compare Miller's *A Canticle for Leibowitz* [3-125] and Pangborn's *Davy* [4-324]. (ML)

4-32.   Barth, John. **Giles Goat-Boy: or, The Revised New Syllabus.** Doubleday, 1966.
A fabulation in which the world is a university and the hero an experimental embodiment of the theriomorphic image of human nature. A clever satire, very much the product of its time. One of the works that began drawing science fiction ideas into the American literary mainstream. See also Pynchon's *Gravity's Rainbow* [4-348]. (BS)

4-33.   Batchelor, John Calvin. **The Birth of the People's Republic of Antarctica.** Dial, 1983.
As civilization collapses, an odd assortment of characters sets sail for Sweden in search of a better world. Their journey ultimately takes them into the icy wastes of Antarctica, but even there they find no escape from the troubles that afflict humankind. Compare Vidal's *Kalki* [4-471]. (BS)

4-34.   Batchelor, John Calvin. **The Further Adventures of Halley's Comet.** Congdon & Lattes, 1980.
Members of a wealthy bourgeois family plot to extend their empire into space. Their Machiavellian schemes require the kidnapping and incarceration of assorted idealists. Meanwhile, an extraordinary trio of mages associated with Halley's Comet look on. A baroque tale. Compare Pynchon's *Gravity's Rainbow* [4-348].

4-35.   Baxter, Stephen. **Raft.** Grafton, 1991.
Generations ago an interstellar spacecraft from Earth accidentally broke through into another universe, one only five thousand miles across, where gravity is much more intense than it is in our universe. At its center is the Core, a planetoid some 50 miles in diameter, with a black hole at its center. Surrounding the Core is a nebula of breathable air. With no inhabitable planets available, the survivors live on rock fragments and bits of wreckage from their ship that have been tied together into a ring of sorts about the kernel of a dead star. The nebula, however, is dying, its limited air supply going bad. The bizarre native life forms are preparing to shift to another universe and, if the humans trapped with them are to survive, they will have to move as well. Despite a few typical first-novel problems, *Raft* features some of the most startling hard SF content in recent years and was a nominee for the 1991 Arthur C. Clarke Award. Compare Niven's *The Integral Trees* [4-312] and its sequel. (ML)

4-36. Bayley, Barrington J(ohn). **The Fall of Chronopolis.** DAW, 1974.
An autocratic empire extends across time, its armies deployed in time traveling citadels, but its attempts to control change are subverted. A colorful adventure story with metaphysical themes woven into the plot. Compare Harness's *Ring of Ritornel* [4-197]. (BS)

4-37. Bayley, Barrington J(ohn). **The Knights of the Limits.** Allison & Busby, 1978.
Stories, mostly from the *New Worlds* anthologies, showing the versatility of Bayley's fertile imagination. "The Exploration of Space" is a strange dimensional fantasy; "Me and My Antronoscope" is a bizarre exercise in speculative cosmology; "The Cabinet of Oliver Naylor" is a baroque space opera exhibiting the author's fascination with philosophical problems. A 1979 collection, *The Seed of Evil*, is slightly less dazzling, but has the gruesome "Sporting with the Child" and the fine *conte philosophique* "Man in Transit." (BS)

*4-38. Bear, Greg. **Blood Music.** Arbor House, 1985.
A genetic engineer conducts unauthorized experiments that result in the creation of intelligent microorganisms. Having infected himself, he become a "universe" of sentient cells, and when his "disease" becomes epidemic the whole living world undergoes an astonishing transformation. A brilliant novel, expanded from a novelette (HW, 1984) that extends the SF imagination to new horizons. Compare Clarke's *Childhood's End* [3-44] and Attanasio's *Radix* [4-22]. (BS) HN, 1986; NN, 1985

4-39. Bear, Greg. **Eon.** Bluejay, 1985.
World War III looms as an asteroid starship mysteriously orbiting Earth is taken over by Americans, who discover that it is an artifact from the future that offers a gateway to infinite opportunity. Hard SF unfolding into vast realms of possibilities. In the sequel, *Eternity* (1988), humans explore the seemingly endless corridor of the Way and the alternate universes and time periods that lead off it. Compare Reed's *Down the Bright Way* [4-354]. (BS/ML)

*4-40. Bear, Greg. **The Forge of God.** Tor, 1987.
Bear has occasionally been compared to the pulp writer Edmond Hamilton because of his propensity for destroying entire worlds during the course of his novels. This book is the ultimate example of the tendency. In the near future, a series of strange events occurs: one of the moons of Jupiter disappears; an exact duplicate of the Ayers rock appears in the

Australian desert; strange robots and aliens show up at various sites. One of the aliens explains that a gigantic machine is approaching through space, its sole purpose to destroy all planets that harbor life and thus make the universe safe for those who built it. The machine appears and, as the novel ends, Earth is destroyed. Although lacking the focus provided by strong central characters, this is a powerful novel, with magnificently described scenes of destruction. The sequel, *Anvil of Stars* (1992), details the quest by a small number of human children who were saved from Earth's destruction to uncover those responsible for their planet's death and gain revenge. Compare Clarke's *Childhood's End* [3-44]. (ML) HN, 1988

*4-41.   Bear, Greg. **Queen of Angels.** Warner, 1990.
Because of the virtually universal use of therapy to promote mental health and the prosperity brought on by the perfection of nanotechnology, crime is virtually unknown in the 21st century. Then the famous poet Emanuel Goldsmith commits mass murder and flees the country; police investigator Mary Choy is sent to track him down. Psychologist Martin Burke is preparing to enter Goldsmith's mind to uncover the cause of his actions. Meanwhile, out in space, headed for distant worlds, the AXIS probe broods over the nature of its own intelligence. An engrossing story as well as a complex meditation on the nature of intelligence, free will, and sin. Probably Bear's best novel to date. Compare Zelazny's *The Dream Master* [4-515]. (ML) HN, 1991

4-42.   Bear, Greg. **Tangents.** Warner, 1989.
The centerpiece of this fine collection of ten mostly hard SF stories is the Hugo and Nebula Award-winning short story, "Tangents," a beautifully understated piece about the relationship between a fugitive scientist and a young refugee from a future war. Other strong fiction includes "Sleepside Story," "Schrodinger's Plague," and "Sisters." An equally strong earlier collection is *The Wind From a Burning Woman* (1983), which includes Bear's superb Hugo and Nebula Award-winning novella, "Hardfought," as well as the title story, "Scattershot," and three other pieces. Yet another fine hard SF novella, *Heads,* received separate book publication in 1990. (ML)

4-43.   Benford, Gregory. **Against Infinity.** Timescape, 1983.
The first part of this Ganymede-set novel draws its inspiration from Faulkner's novella, "The Bear," with an adolescent and an aging hunter tracking down a strange alien creature. Inevitably, the story moves to new ground when it gives more attention to the nature of the alien and the kind of world into which the hero's rite de passage will take him. An inter-

esting attempt to infuse SF with narrative realism. Compare Clarke's *Rendezvous with Rama* [4-109]. (BS) NN, 1967

*4-44. Benford, Gregory. **Great Sky River.** Bantam, 1987.

Across the galaxy humanity is on the run from the encroaching Mech civilization. On the planet Snowglade, family Bishop and other bionically enhanced human survivors are treated as vermin by the Mechs, either ignored or "harvested." Killeen, leader of the Bishops, must find some way of defeating, communicating with, or escaping from the Mantis, an advanced artificial intelligence, which seems set upon tracking them down. In the sequel, *Tides of Light* (1989), Killeen and family Bishop flee to a new planet where they discover more Mechs who are at war with a race of alien cyborgs. In these fine novels Benford presents a sophisticated and endlessly fascinating portrayal of the multiple forms that intelligence might take. *Furious Gulf* (1994) concluded the series. (ML) HN, 1988

4-45. Benford, Gregory. **In the Ocean of Night.** Dial, 1977.

A fix-up novel in which the hero looks for evidence of the existence of aliens, and ultimately meets one; contact may invigorate a world becoming gradually decadent. In a sequel, *Across the Sea of Suns* (1984), the difficulty of coming to terms with alien beings, and the necessity of so doing, lie at the heart of a complex plot involving the confrontation of alternative human philosophies of life. Thoughtful hard SF, its visionary element less wide-eyed than in Anderson's *The Avatar* [4-10] and other like-minded works. (BS) NN, 1977

*4-46. Benford, Gregory. **Timescape.** Simon & Schuster, 1980.

As the world lurches toward disaster, scientists in 1998 try to transmit a warning message to 1962 by means of tachyons. Their story is told in parallel with that of the scientists trying to decode the transmission, and the two plots converge on the possibility of paradox. Unusual for the realism of its depiction of scientists at work; admirably serious in handling the implications of its theme. Compare Carter Scholz and Glen A. Harcourt's *Palimpsests* (1985). (BS) JWC, 1981; NW, 1980 [For other works by this author see chapter 5.]

4-47. Benford, Gregory, and David Brin. **Heart of the Comet.** Bantam, 1986.

Scientists exploring Halley's Comet in 2061 are marooned when plague breaks out and monsters attack but they survive and thrive in extraordinary fashion. Colorful space adventure that diversifies into speculative metaphysics. Compare Williamson's *Lifeburst* [4-500]. (BS)

4-48.   Bishop, Michael. **Ancient of Days.** Arbor House, 1985.
Expanded from the novella, "Her Habiline Husband" (NN, 1983), this book continues themes first tackled in *No Enemy But Time* [4-51] in a more lighthearted vein. A modern woman falls in love with a relic of the prehistoric past, outraging the neighbors. Funny and sentimental. Compare Farmer's "The Alley Man" (1959). (BS)

4-49.   Bishop, Michael. **Blooded on Arachne.** Arkham, 1982.
The first of two collections of short stories, followed by *One Winter in Eden* (1984). Bishop claims to be stressing the "palpability" of alien landscapes and transfigured futures in these atmospheric stories, which do indeed seem infatuated with strangeness. The title story draws on anthropological material after the fashion of *Transfigurations* [4-53], while the novella "The White Otters of Childhood" (HN, 1974; NN, 1973) has a leading character named after the protagonist of *The Island of Dr. Moreau* [1-100]. A later collection is *Close Encounters With the Deity* (1986). (BS)

4-50.   Bishop, Michael. **Catacomb Years.** Berkley, 1979.
Fix-up novel extrapolating themes from *A Little Knowledge* (1977) and introducing new insights into an elaborate study of the culture of 21st-century Atlanta. The diffuse and richly detailed text presents an unusually convincing picture of future life in a period of crisis. Compare Pohl's *Years of the City* [4-337]. (BS)

*4-51.   Bishop, Michael. **No Enemy But Time.** Timescape, 1982.
A strange, alienated child has lurid dreams of the Pleistocene era, and discovers the truth of them when he becomes a time traveler in adulthood. He joins forces with a band of habiline protohumans and fathers a child, which he brings back to the present. Brilliant and memorable, written with great conviction. Compare Vercors's *You Shall Know Them* [3-188]. (BS) NW, 1982

4-52.   Bishop, Michael. **The Secret Ascension; or Philip K. Dick Is Dead, Alas.** Tor, 1987.
In the late 1980s Richard Nixon is in the fourth term of his "imperial Presidency," and an obscure, but talented mainstream novelist named Philip K. Dick has recently died in California. Soon after his death, however, Dick, apparently suffering from amnesia, makes an appearance in a

psychiatrist's office in Georgia. Bishop covers most of Dick's major themes in this well-done pastiche and also does a fine job of copying Dick's somewhat idiosyncratic style. Compare Dick's *Ubik* [4-140] and other novels. (ML)

4-53. Bishop, Michael. **Transfigurations.** Berkley, 1979.
Expanded from the novella, "Death and Designation Among the Asadi" (NN, 1973; HN, 1974). One of the more impressive SF novels using perspectives and themes drawn from anthropology to aid depiction of an enigmatic alien culture. Compare Le Guin's *The Word for World Is Forest* [4-256]. (BS)

4-54. Bisson, Terry. **Fire on the Mountain.** Arbor, 1988.
The Civil War as we know it never occurred in this alternate universe because John Brown, with Harriet Tubman acting as his lieutenant, sparked a successful slave rebellion. The outcome was a divided United States with an African-American-dominated South emerging as a socialist utopia. This somehow led to a Europe that avoided world war and to an Africa that developed free from the worst results of colonial rule. The viewpoint alternates between Yasmin, a successful anthropologist and citizen of the utopian South; her great grandfather Abraham, who, born a slave, took part in the rebellion; and Dr. Hunter, a white abolitionist who served as Abraham's mentor. The novel's basic premise seems a bit far-fetched, but Bisson's alternate 20th century is endlessly fascinating and well worth a visit. Compare Harry Turtledove's *The Guns of the South* (1992). (ML)

4-55. Bisson, Terry. **Voyage to the Red Planet.** Morrow, 1990.
A Mars ship was built, but the mission was mothballed at the onslaught of the worldwide Grand Depression, and all the astronauts were laid off. Years later, an on-the-cheap mission has been commissioned by sleazy Pellucidar Pictures, which plans to use the trip to film a pulp adventure flick about, you guessed it, the first trip to Mars. Bisson manages the difficult job of writing a hilariously funny spoof that still takes the grandeur of Mars seriously. For a more deadpan description of the first exploration of the Red Planet, compare Ben Bova's *Mars* [4-60]. (ML)

4-56. Blaylock, James P. **The Digging Leviathan.** Ace, 1984.
A complicated adventure story that plays affectionately with supposedly antiquated pulp ideas, including the hollow Earth. Evil conspirators try to use the imaginative power of a young genius for their own nefarious ends.

Breezy homage to the delights and eccentricities of pulp SF, witty and well-written. Compare Mark Helprin's *Winter's Tale* (1983). (BS)

4-57.   Blaylock, James P. **Homunculus.** Ace, 1986.
Intricately plotted action-adventure story set in Victorian England where the natural philosophers of the Trismegistus Club battle a sinister reanimator of corpses and a greedy entrepreneur while a tiny alien imprisoned in one of four identical boxes is passed unwittingly from hand to hand, causing havoc wherever he goes. A witty and very stylish combination of SF and Victorian melodrama. In the sequel, *Lord Kelvin's Machine* (1992), the Earth is nearly destroyed by a passing comet. Compare Power's *The Anubis Gates* [4-339] and K. W. Jeter's *Infernal Devices* (1987). (BS/ML) Philip K. Dick Award, 1987

4-58.   Blumlein, Michael. **The Brains of Rats.** Scream/Press, 1990.
Twelve stories, three previously unpublished, from the 1984–1990 period. Title story and "Tissue Ablation and Variant Regeneration: A Case Report," both published first in *Interzone*, are corrosively brilliant studies of biotechnology, extrapolating the impact of medical research on sexual and national politics. Though other tales are solid but unexciting, these two clearly mark Blumlein as a major talent. His knowledge and experience as a practicing physician are also evident in *The Movement of Mountains* (1987), an ambitious if uneven novel about genetic engineering and future class warfare. Compare the stories of Tiptree and Ballard. (RL)

4-59.   Bova, Ben. **Colony.** Pocket Books, 1978.
Carries forward themes from *Millennium* (1976) and *Kinsman* (1979); with Earth in trouble the future of humankind seems tied up with the fortunes of orbital space habitats—stepping stones to the colonization of the solar system, and focal points of desperate power struggles. The wide-ranging story takes in many convincing near-future scenarios; an attempt to incorporate the format of mainstream bestsellers into SF. Compare Dickson's *The Far Call* [4-143]. (BS)

4-60.   Bova, Ben. **Mars.** Bantam, 1992.
An international mission to Mars is undertaken in this highly realistic novel by one of the leading exponents of the manned exploration of outer space. Bova's characters are not very well developed, but they're secondary to his detailed and at times breathtaking descriptions of the Red Planet. Compare Kim Stanley Robinson's *Red Mars* [4-366] for a more lit-

erary, but equally hard-science description of the colonization of Mars. Contrast Terry Bisson's *Voyage to the Red Planet* [4-55] for a somewhat more satirical approach. (ML) [For other works by this author see chapter 5.]

4-61.   Boyd, John (pseud. of Boyd Upchurch). **The Last Starship From Earth.** Weybright & Talley, 1968.
An alternate Earth is ruled by a dictatorship that employs religion and the insights of social science to secure its hegemony, exporting dissidents to the planet Hell. The hero plans to save the world by striking at the very heart of the despised order, preventing Christ's conquest of Rome. Clever development of an interesting premise. Compare Brian Earnshaw's *Planet in the Eye of Time* (1968). (BS)

4-62.   Boyd, John (pseud. of Boyd Upchurch). **The Pollinators of Eden.** Weybright & Talley, 1969.
A repressed female scientist is liberated and fulfilled, thanks to alien orchids. Sexual mores and the working of the scientific community are gently satirized. Compare Ronald Fraser's classic fantasy, *Flower Phantoms* (1926). (BS)

4-63.   Bradley, Marion Zimmer. **The Heirs of Hammerfell.** DAW, 1989.
The disappointing latest novel in the Darkover series, which began with the Ace Double, *The Planet Savers/The Sword of Aldones* (1962). Associated materials include a number of Darkover anthologies, edited by Bradley, with stories by various friends and associates. *The Planet Savers* first appeared in 1958, and the series thus extends across more than 35 years. It has evolved as the changing market situation of SF has altered. The early novels are generally action-adventure stories confronting ordinary humans with the psi-powered descendants of colonists whose world has been long out of touch with galactic civilization, although *Darkover Landfall* (1972) is notable for its early inclusion of homosexuality as a theme. Bradley gradually elaborated the history of Darkover and began to write longer, denser novels that focus more and more on the relationships between characters, diversifying into an elaborate discussion of sexual politics and exploring the ramifications of the intimacy permitted by telepathic communication. In the later novels, therefore, psychological melodrama replaces action-adventure and female protagonists replace male ones. The history cobbled together from the earlier novels eventually proved unsatisfactory and *The Heritage of Hastur* (1975; NN)—generally considered the best book in the series—became the first novel assuming the fully worked out and coherent history. *Sharra's Exile* (1981) was subse-

quently rewritten to replace *The Sword of Aldones* in the "official canon." The series is fascinating as an exercise in world building, and as a testament to changing fashions in SF during the modern period. Compare McCaffrey's *Dragonflight* [4-289] and sequels. (BS/ML)

*4-64.   Brin, David. **Earth.** Bantam, 1990.

This is a big, engrossing novel with half a dozen fully developed plot lines. Fifty years in the future the ozone layer is gone, sea levels are rising, and the ecology is on the verge of collapse. An engineer struggles to save the world through large-scale technology. A biologist sets up gigantic indoor refuges to preserve at least a few of the many species that face extinction. Neo-Luddites stage raids on scientific laboratories, making no attempt to differentiate between technologies that will help or will damage the environment. Worst of all, scientist Alex Lustig has created a black hole and then lost it—inside the Earth. The end of the world may be at hand. *Earth* has a few structural weaknesses and tends towards the didactic, but it's enormously readable. Compare Brunner's *Stand on Zanzibar* [4-74]. (ML) HN, 1991

4-65.   Brin, David. **Glory Season.** Bantam, 1993.

The planet Stratos was founded centuries ago by feminist separatists who set up a matriarchal civilization based on families of female clones. A limited number of noncloned females, called vars, provide genetic variety and a small number of men are used both to impregnate clonal women with vars and to "spark" clonal reproduction itself. Although neither vars nor men have complete equality, the society of Stratos is generally benign and nonviolent. Tensions are growing, however, due to the rise of the Perkinites, who would eliminate all men, and due to the appearance of a male emissary from human space. Against this background, two young var twins come of age and attempt to make a life for themselves. Compare Tepper's *The Gate to Women's Country* [4-453], Sargent's *The Shore of Women* [4-381], and Orson Scott Card's *The Memory of Earth* (1992). (ML)

4-66.   Brin, David. **The Postman.** Bantam, 1985.

Expanded from a novella (HN, 1983). In postholocaust America a scavenger picks up the uniform of a dead postman, triggering the myth that the Post Office still survives and that order might soon be restored to the shattered world. By degrees he is forced reluctantly to accept the responsibility of his peculiar charismatic authority. An antidote to postholocaust romanticism, but not without a romanticism of it own. Compare and con-

trast the trilogy beginning with Robinson's *The Wild Shore* [4-367]. (BS)
HN, 1986; JWC, 1986; *Locus* Award, 1986

*4-67. Brin, David. **Startide Rising.** Bantam, 1983.
The intelligent species of Earth (men, apes, and dolphins) seem to be
highly exceptional in having advanced to technological sophistication
without the alien Patrons that generally supervise the "uplift" of sentient
species throughout the galactic culture. Now a dolphin-commanded starship has made a significant discovery in deep space, but must take refuge
in an alien ocean from its rivals. While the dolphins struggle desperately
to survive, the starships of a number of alien races do battle overhead for
the prize. Superior space opera of a very high order. Brin's "Uplift" universe was first introduced in *Sundiver* (1980). Compare Niven's Known
Space series [4-314]. (BS/ML) HW, 1984; NW, 1983; *Locus* Award, 1984

*4-68. Brin, David. **The Uplift War.** Phantasia Press, 1987.
Whoever owns the secret discovered by the dolphins of *Startide Rising* [4-
67] can gain control of the entire galactic civilization. The planet Garth
lies on the other side of the galaxy from the site of that discovery, but the
alien Gubru, in a bold move to force humanity to give up the secret, have
taken that planet and its population of human beings and neo-chimps
hostage. Only a small band of humans and chimps stands between the
Gubru and success. The setting here is less exotic than those of the previous two books in the Uplift series, but Brin's character development is
particularly good and the neo-chimps especially are a wonderful creation.
(ML) HW, 1988; NN, 1987; *Locus* Award, 1988

4-69. Broderick, Damien. **The Dreaming Dragons: A Time Opera.**
Pocket Books, 1980.
An aborigine anthropologist and his nephew discover an alien artifact
that gives them access to a vault beneath Ayers Rock. The boy is changed
by the experience and becomes the key to scientific study of the vault and
its builders. An intriguing combination of SF motifs and mythological references. Compare Zelazny's *Eye of Cat* (1982). (BS)

4-70. Broderick, Damien. **The Judas Mandala.** Pocket Books, 1982. Rev.
ed., Mandarin, 1990.
Carries forward themes from *The Dreaming Dragons* [4-69]; in a far future
benevolently ruled by powerful computers some humans find a way to
escape their governance by dimensional side-stepping. They gradually
extend their ability to travel in time until they begin trying to alter and

control history. A convoluted and effective SF mystery. Compare van Vogt's *Masters of Time* (1950). (BS)

4-71.   Brunner, John. The Jagged Orbit. Ace, 1969.
A dystopian black comedy of a culturally fragmented near-future United States whose citizens are armed to the teeth and have made fortresses of their homes. As the personal arms race threatens to escalate yet again, an investigative journalist and a psychologist combine forces to strike a blow for sanity. The bitter alarmism, very much a product of the 1960s, makes the novel a striking period piece. Compare Stephen Barnes's *Streetlethal* (1983) and Bunch's *Moderan* [4-82]. (BS)

*4-72.   Brunner, John. The Sheep Look Up. Harper, 1972.
The most elaborate alarmist novel about industrial pollution. Uses techniques similar to *Stand on Zanzibar* [4-74] to present a kaleidoscopic image of future America drowning in its own wastes. Relentlessly angry and anguished. Compare Philip Wylie's *The End of the Dream* (1972). (BS) NN, 1972

4-73.   Brunner, John. The Shockwave Rider. Harper, 1975.
The third of Brunner's massive alarmist fantasies, partly inspired by Alvin Toffler's *Future Shock*, warning against the loss of individual freedom that might result from widespread use of information technology and against the psychological effects of rapid technological change. Brunner complained bitterly about Harper's insensitive editing; the 1976 Ballantine reprint restored the author's text. (BS)

*4-74.   Brunner, John. Stand on Zanzibar. Doubleday, 1968.
A complex novel borrowing techniques from John Dos Passos and ideas from Marshall McLuhan and other 1960s commentators to provide a multifaceted image of an overpopulated near future. Clever, highly detailed, and frequently very witty, the book is a successful experiment and one of the key works of the period. Compare *A Torrent of Faces* (also 1968) by James Blish and Norman L. Knight. (BS) Prix Apollo, 1973; HW, 1969; NN, 1968

4-75.   Brunner, John. The Whole Man. Ballantine, 1964. British title: *Telepathist*, 1965.
Developed from two novellas. A crippled and deformed social outcast is nearly destroyed by his telepathic powers, but learns to use them to create therapeutic dreams for others and eventually to create a new art form.

Good characterization and sensitive narration. Compare Silverberg's *Dying Inside* [4-409] and Zelazny's *The Dream Master* [4-515]. (BS) HN, 1965 [For other works by this author see chapter 3.]

4-76. Bryant, Edward. **Cinnabar.** Macmillan, 1976.

A "mosaic novel" about a decadent far-future city where aesthetic motives are paramount and ennui reigns supreme. Equally well done is the short fiction found in Bryant's several collections, most importantly *Particle Theory* (1980). Compare Harrison's Viriconium series [4-202] and Carr's *Cirque* [4-95]. (BS/ML)

4-77. Budrys, Algis. **Michaelmas.** Berkley, 1977.

The hero and his machine-intelligence sidekick secretly rule the world, but their subtle dictatorship is threatened by insidious alien intruders. A slick power fantasy. Compare van Vogt's *The Anarchistic Colossus* (1977). (BS) [For other works by this author see chapter 3.]

*4-78. Bujold, Lois McMaster. **Barrayar.** Baen, 1991.

Cordelia Naismith and Aral Vorkosigan were once enemies in an interstellar war. Now a fragile peace has been established and they're a married couple expecting their first child. Cordelia, a liberated woman, is ill at ease among the more conservative, less civilized people of Barrayar and, when her husband is named regent, she realizes that she, Aral, and their unborn baby are in great danger. Traditional space opera at its very best. Bujold's highly competent first novel, *Shards of Honor* (1986), details Cordelia and Aral's first meeting in the midst of war. Compare C. J. Cherryh's *Rimrunners* [4-107] and other novels. (ML) HW, 1992; NN, 1992; *Locus* Award, 1992

*4-79. Bujold, Lois McMaster. **Falling Free.** Baen, 1988.

Leo Graf, a welding engineer hired to train workers on a space station, is astonished to discover that his new pupils are "quaddies," genetically engineered living tools with extra arms where normal people have legs. Designed by the GalacTech corporation to be perfect zero-gravity employees, the quaddies unfortunately have failed to turn a profit for their owner/employers. Soon after Graf's arrival, the corporation decides to cut its losses and return the quaddies to Earth, where they will presumably be dumped in nursing homes on a small pension. The quaddies, however, have other ideas, and convince Graf to join them in revolt. Originally published as a serial in *Analog* in 1987–1988, this is an example of old-fashioned, Campbell-style hard SF at its best, but with a fascinating feminist twist. Compare Steele's *Orbital Decay* [4-436]. (ML) HN, 1989; NW, 1988

4-80.   Bujold, Lois McMaster. **The Vor Game.** Baen, 1990.
The culture of the planet Barrayar values men only to the extent that they prove themselves in the military, and Miles Vorkosigan, the disabled son of Lord Aral and Lady Cordelia Vorkosigan, has determined to succeed in such a career despite his disability. Miles proves his worth, first at an isolated weather station and then in space, where he rescues his runaway cousin, the Emperor Gregor, from possible death. This is superior space opera with a touch of humor. Earlier books in the series include *The Warrior's Apprentice* (1986), *Brothers in Arms* (1989), and *Borders of Infinity* (1989), one previously published section of which, "The Mountains of Mourning," won both the Hugo and Nebula Awards for best novella in 1990. All the Miles Vorkosigan books make for fine reading. *Mirror Dance* was published in 1994, and more volumes are promised. Compare C. S. Forester's Hornblower novels. (ML) HW, 1991

4-81.   Bull, Emma. **Bone Dance: A Fantasy for Technophiles.** Ace, 1991.
Sparrow, a sexless, artificial person who makes a living tracking down and selling videos and other aging technological artifacts in punked-out, postnuclear war Minneapolis, accidentally becomes involved with the Horsemen, U.S. government-developed secret agents capable of entering the minds of others. In the past the Horsemen were secretly used to destabilize foreign governments until their actions triggered the nuclear war; now they serve other masters, and Sparrow, simply having discovered their existence, is at risk. To complicate matters, there is evidence that at least some of what's going on is supernatural, rather than merely weird science. Bull's world is gritty, well realized, and a lot of fun. For a variant on the possession motif, see Cadigan's *Fools* [4-89]. (ML) HN, 1992; NN, 1991

*4-82.   Bunch, David. **Moderan.** Avon, 1971.
Collection of linked stories of a future world completely altered by the progressive cyborgization of its inhabitants and artificialization of its environments. Humanity is lost with the discarded "flesh-strips" and the nightmare progresses to its inevitable conclusion. A magnificent work full of striking imagery and fine prose. Compare Wright's *The New Gods Lead* [2-152]. (BS)

4-83.   Burroughs, William S(eward). **Nova Express.** Grove, 1964.
A novel of future violence and corruption, in which the anarchic Nova Mob descend like the Furies on hapless humankind, while the Nova

Police try to match them. Carries forward themes from the famous avant-garde trilogy, *The Naked Lunch* (1959), *The Soft Machine* (1961), and *The Ticket That Exploded* (1962). Burroughs influenced the work of J. G. Ballard, especially *The Atrocity Exhibition* [4-24]. (BS)

4-84. Busby, F(rancis) M(arion). **Star Rebel.** Bantam, 1984.
Fast-paced adventure in which the tough hero must go to extraordinary lengths to survive and hit back against his enemies, repeating the theme of the author's earlier *The Demu Trilogy* (Pocket Books, 1980). Three sequels follow *Star Rebel*, with the last, *Rebel's Seed*, connecting this series to another, whose heroine, Rissa Kerguelen, generally features in more ironic accounts of extreme individual assertiveness in a space opera setting. Compare Mike Resnick's *Santiago* (1986). (BS)

*4-85. Butler, Octavia. **Dawn.** Warner, 1987.
Lilith Iyapo, a contemporary African American and survivor of the recent nuclear war that has destroyed virtually all life on Earth, awakes to find herself one of a small number of human beings "rescued" by aliens. The Oankali, however, are not entirely altruistic. It is part of their genetic imperative that they must mate with other species, thus sharing genetic material. This fine, if at times harrowing, novel, like much of Butler's work, can be read as an allegory of sorts for the African-American experience in the United States. The two outstanding sequels are *Adulthood Rites* (1988) and *Imago* (1989). Butler explores somewhat similar ideas in *Clay's Ark* (1984). (ML)

4-86. Butler, Octavia. **Kindred.** Doubleday, 1979.
Dana, a well-educated contemporary African-American woman, suddenly finds herself pulled into the past to save the life of a distant ancestor, an early-19th-century southern white boy named Rufus Weylin. Although she returns to the present moments later, she soon finds herself saving Rufus again and again. Although only a short time passes for her between each bout of time travel, years pass for Rufus, who gradually grows into adulthood and becomes a slave owner. This sometimes painful novel features superb character development. By forcing Dana to confront her own white ancestry, Butler points out the necessity of coming to terms with the past without oversimplifying it. Compare Lisa Tuttle's *Lost Futures* (1992) and Jane Yolen's *The Devil's Arithmetic* (1988). (ML)

4-87. Butler, Octavia. **Wild Seed.** Doubleday, 1980.
The first story in Butler's Patternist series in terms of internal chronology, though not in terms of publication. In ancient Africa, Doro, an immortal

telepath, begins the work of genetic manipulation that will help him create an empire. Doro's work comes to apparent fruition with the creation of his telepathic daughter, Mary, in *Mind of My Mind* (1977). In *Patternmaster* (1976) we see an entire telepathic society. *Survivor* (1978) is another book in this well-done series. Although *Clay's Ark* (1984) is not a Patternist novel, it explores similar themes. Compare Sturgeon's *More Than Human* [3-172]. (ML)

*4-88.   Cadigan, Pat. **Patterns.** Ursus Imprints, 1989.

Fourteen stories from the 1980s. Some are horror, but most—including "Angel," "Rock On," and "Pretty Boy Crossover," all award nominees—are hard-edged, ferociously inventive cyberpunk ranking with the best of Gibson and Sterling. Cadigan's milieu is a gritty urban zone where the funky street life and slick corporate power interact unpredictably. Her most recent collection is *Dirty Work* (Ziesing, 1993). Compare Gibson's *Burning Chrome* [4-181]. (RL)

4-89.   Cadigan, Pat. **Synners.** Bantam, 1991.

In near-future United States, an obsessed video artist pioneers brain-socket implants that allow electronic "uploading" of consciousness, but the artist suffers a stroke while psychically online, releasing a destructive virus into the worldwide computer network. A loose fraternity of teen hackers, aging rock-and-rollers, and corporate moguls struggles to eradicate the virus and restore the "crashed" system. Tense and complex, brilliantly wedding cyberpunk with the disaster story; along with *Mindplayers* (1987) and *Fools* (1992), this establishes Cadigan as a visionary explorer of high technology, pop culture, and cyborg consciousness. Compare Spinrad's *Little Heroes* [4-430] and Laidlaw's *Kalifornia* [4-247]. (RL) A. C. Clarke Award, 1992

4-90.   Callenbach, Ernest. **Ecotopia.** Banyan Tree, 1975.

A utopian novel of ecologically sensitive political reorganization. The West Coast states have seceded from the Union and have established a life-style based on small-scale technology and environmental conservation. A visitor from the East is gradually converted to these ideals. The 1981 sequel, *Ecotopia Emerging*, fills in (and revises) the historical background. This is perhaps the most important modern addition to the tradition of Bellamy's *Looking Backward* [1-8] and an interesting development of the ideologies that have since been adopted by various European "green" parties. Compare Robinson's *Pacific Edge* [4-367]. (BS)

4-91. Calvino, Italo. **Cosmicomics.** Harcourt, 1968. Trans. by William Weaver of *Le Cosmicomiche*, 1965.
The childlike Qfwfq has the entire cosmos and all eternity as his playground, and naïvely confronts the great mysteries of time and space in 12 bizarre tales. *t zero* (1969) offers more of the same. Zestful modern fabliaux with a unique charm. Weaver won the National Book Award for translation for *Cosmicomics*. (BS)

4-92. Card, Orson Scott. **Ender's Game.** Tor, 1985.
The child hero is subjected to horrific manipulation by the military in order to make him the perfect commander able to annihilate the insectile aliens who have twice attacked the solar system. Based on a novelette (HN, 1978), the expanded version includes much discussion of moral propriety and undergoes a dramatic ideological shift at the end, but remains in many ways a sophisticated power fantasy. Grimly fascinating. The sequel, *Speaker for the Dead* (1986; HW, 1987; NW, 1986), takes off from the climactic shift in perspective to construct a very different story in which Ender becomes a more Christ-like savior. The third book in the series, *Xenocide* (1991; HN, 1992), is most notable for a new subplot, the story of a world whose future leaders are genetically engineered for brilliance, but also for a crippling Obsessive-Compulsive Disorder designed to limit their power. The ending of the novel is weak, shifting into wish fulfillment fantasy. Compare Heinlein's *Starship Troopers* [3-90], Haldeman's *Forever War* [4-193], and Dave Wolverton's *On My Way to Paradise* (1989). (ML/BS) HW, 1986; NW, 1985

4-93. Card, Orson Scott. **Maps in a Mirror: The Short Fiction of Orson Scott Card.** Tor, 1990.
This enormous volume, some 46 stories, represents most of Card's short fiction. Included are such well-known pieces as the award-winning "Lost Boys" and "An Eye for an Eye," "Dogwalker," "Unaccompanied Sonata," "Ender's Game," "The Originist," and "Kingsmeat." Some of the early fiction and particularly the non-science fiction is minor but, generally speaking, this is an excellent collection from a controversial and important writer, who provides commentary on the stories. (ML) *Locus* Award, 1991

4-94. Carr, Jayge. **Leviathan's Deep.** Doubleday, 1979.
An alien female whose society is matriarchal embarks on a doomed love affair with a human male, whose species is busily employed in the conquest of the galaxy. An intelligent novel, spiced with wit, that brings a measure of conviction to a difficult theme. More even-handed in its treat-

ment of sexual politics than most exemplary adventures in interstellar miscegenation. Contrast Farmer's *The Lovers* [3-69] and Lee's *The Silver Metal Lover* [4-257]. (BS)

4-95.   Carr, Terry. Cirque. Bobbs-Merrill, 1977.
A decadent far-future city faces a crisis that demands heroic action from some of its strange citizens. Clever and colorful, with a rich underlay of moral and metaphysical questions. Compare Bryant's *Cinnabar* [4-76] for another version of the far-future *civitas solis* and Dick's *Galactic Pot-Healer* [4-138] for some similar play with metaphysical anxiety. (BS)

4-96.   Carter, Angela. Heroes and Villains. Heinemann, 1969.
After the holocaust, the flame of culture and learning is kept alight by Professors guarded by Soldiers, while barbarians and mutants threaten to extinguish it. The heroine, a Professor's daughter, runs off with a barbarian and enjoys her just desserts. A strange combination of the lyrical, the ironic, and the author's usual flirtation with horrors. (BS)

*4-97.   Carter, Angela. The Infernal Desire Machines of Doctor Hoffman. Hart-Davis, 1972. U.S. title: *The War of Dreams*, Harcourt, 1974.
The hero, Desiderio, sets out to find and defeat Dr. Hoffman, whose machines are the fountainhead of troublesome illusions. His journey is an odyssey into the unconscious, where he is alternatively (sometimes simultaneously) seduced and threatened in a phantasmagoric variety of ways. A gothic black comedy, elaborating and decoding much of the erotic symbolism of fantastic fiction; a disturbing tour de force. (BS)

4-98.   Carter, Angela. The Passion of New Eve. Gollancz, 1977.
The English hero loses himself in a decadent near-future New York, undergoes a forced sex change at the hands of sex war guerrillas, is captured by a brutal masculinist nihilist, and meets the transvestite film star who incarnated in celluloid the perfect image of feminine frailty, before floating away from the California coast as the holocaust destroys America. Wonderfully phantasmagoric. Compare Ballard's *Vermilion Sands* [4-28] and *Hello America* (1981). (BS)

4-99.   Charnas, Suzy McKee. Walk to the End of the World. Ballantine, 1974.
In a grim, postholocaust world, the Holdfast is a nightmarish, intensely patriarchal society where women are treated as no more than subhuman breeders of the next generation of men. The symbolically named Alldera escapes from captivity to the wilderness and a new life. In *Motherlines*

(1978) she discovers a number of all-female societies, none of them utopian. Although both novels have occasional weaknesses in style and plot, they serve as powerful indictment of patriarchal attitudes. *The Furies* (1994), set much later, chronicles Alldera's return to the Holdfast at the head of a conquering army. Compare Sally Miller Gearhart's *The Wanderground* (1978) and Tepper's *The Gate to Women's Country* [4-453]. (ML)

4-100. Chayefsky, Paddy. **Altered States.** Hutchinson, 1978.
First novel by a well-known film scriptwriter, subsequently filmed. Experiments in hallucination induced by sensory deprivation ultimately lead the hero into a psychic and physical regression to the protohuman. An interesting development of theme from the work of John Lilly. Compare James Kennaway's *The Mind Benders* (1963) and Ian Watson's *The Martian Inca* (1977). (BS)

4-101. Cherryh, C. J. (pseud. of Carolyn Janice Cherry). **Cuckoo's Egg.** Phantasia, 1985.
A member of a cat-like race rears an unlovable alien child, training him for membership in an elite corps of judges. The child resents his status as a stranger, but ultimately learns the whys and wherefores of his situation, and that he must accept it. The cool, mannered narrative suits the theme. (BS) HN, 1986

*4-102. Cherryh, C. J. (pseud. of Carolyn Janice Cherry). **Cyteen.** Warner, 1988.
The rulers of the planet Cyteen have a monopoly on the creation of Azi, the artificial human beings who have featured so prominently in such earlier Cherryh novels as *Downbelow Station* [4-103] and the underrated *Forty Thousand in Gehena* (1983), and they also have the rarely used ability to clone human beings. When the aging Ariane Emory, ruthless director of the planet's genetic labs and a major political figure, decides to have herself cloned, the resulting child becomes a pawn in a complex series of political manipulations. This powerful psychological study is Cherryh's longest novel and her most difficult, but there's plenty of meat here to reward the diligent reader. For a very different novel that nonetheless asks similar questions about genetic determinism, compare Levin's *The Boys From Brazil* [4-265]. (ML) HW, 1989; *Locus* Award, 1989

*4-103. Cherryh, C. J. (pseud. of Carolyn Janice Cherry). **Downbelow Station.** DAW, 1981.
Political space opera set on the star station Pell, caught in the middle of

the conflict for control of humankind's fragile interstellar "empire." Complex and multifaceted: the many-sided conflict provides action and intrigue while the central characters try to construct viable personal relationships and work out careers in a fluid situation. The novel is a key work in an elaborate future history used as a background for several other novels, including *Merchanter's Luck* [4-105] and *Voyager in Night* (1984). (BS) HW, 1982

4-104.   Cherryh, C. J. (pseud. of Carolyn Janice Cherry). **The Faded Sun: Kesrith.** DAW, 1978.
The first volume in a three-part novel, completed in *The Faded Sun: Shon 'Jir* (1979) and *The Faded Sun: Kutath* (1980). An alien society organized somewhat in the fashion of an anthill hires out its warriors as mercenaries. But when its clients get into a war with humankind, the warriors and their kin are virtually wiped out. The client species sues for peace, but the survivors go their own way. One human involves himself with their cause and their quest to save their race. Compare Carr's *Leviathan's Deep* [4-94]. (BS)

4-105.   Cherryh, C. J. (pseud. of Carolyn Janice Cherry). **Merchanter's Luck.** DAW, 1982.
The alienated hero of this sophisticated space opera is moved to extraordinary action by erotic fascination, and is tested to the full by the adventures that follow. A study of ambition and self-esteem, set in a richly detailed, exotic background. Compare Bear's *Beyond Heaven's River* (1980). (BS)

4-106.   Cherryh, C. J. (pseud. of Carolyn Janice Cherry). **The Pride of Chanur.** DAW, 1982.
The Chanur books are relatively lightweight when compared to Cherryh's major work, but they are still superior space opera. The series follows the adventures of a female starship commander in a politically corrupt, multi-species interstellar civilization. A fascinating exercise in speculative cultural anthropology, with Cherryh's usual deft and intense plotting. Sequels are *Chanur's Venture* (1984), *The Kif Strike Back* (1985), *Chanur's Homecoming* (1986), and *Chanur's Legacy* (1992). Compare Crowley's *Beasts* [4-121] and Walter Jon Williams's *Angel Station* (1989). (ML/BS)

4-107.   Cherryh, C. J. (pseud. of Carolyn Janice Cherry). **Rimrunners.** Warner, 1989.
One of the strongest additions to Cherryh's fine Union-Alliance series, *Rimrunners* is the tale of tough-as-nails Bet Yeager, a soldier separated from

her ship and stranded on a dying space station. Out of work, desperate, and close to starvation, Bet takes a berth on the *Loki*, nominally an enemy ship, where she must hide her past. Things turn even more difficult for her, however, when she takes as her lover the ship's scapegoat, an unstable loser with a lot of enemies on board. This is gritty, small-scale hard SF at its best. Cherryh's characters are memorable and her portrayal of life on a warship seems very real. Compare Heinlein's *Starship Troopers* [3-90] and Robinson's *The Dark Beyond the Stars* [4-363]. (ML)

*4-108. Clarke, Arthur C(harles). **The Fountains of Paradise.** Gollancz, 1979.
An engineer succeeds in building a space elevator connecting a tropical island (modeled on Sri Lanka, where Clarke lives, but moved for geographical convenience) to a space station in geosynchronous orbit. Imposing propaganda for high technology as the means of human progress and salvation. Charles Sheffield's *The Web Between the Worlds* (1979) develops the same premise in a more conventional fashion. (BS) HW, 1980; NW, 1979

*4-109. Clarke, Arthur C(harles). **Rendezvous with Rama.** Gollancz, 1973.
A vast alien spaceship passes through the solar system, using the Sun's gravity to boost its velocity. Human explorers witness the brief blossoming of its artificial life system, but do not meet its makers. Ten years later, in *Rama II* (1989) by Clarke and Gentry Lee, a second spaceship repeats the maneuver and a second group of human explorers is dispatched. When the Raman ship departs the solar system, however, three of the explorers go along for the ride. In Clarke and Lee's *The Garden of Rama* (1991), by far the most successful of the two writers' collaborations, the three humans aboard the Raman vessel spend 13 years on their journey. Not expecting to see Earth again, they settle in, have babies, and explore in much greater depth. They also meet other alien residents of the vessel, though not the Ramans themselves. Eventually reaching a gigantic space station, they learn much more about the Ramans, though enough mysteries remain for a promised fourth volume. Compare Niven's *Ringworld* [4-316] and Shaw's *Orbitsville* [4-389] for similarly charismatic artifacts. (ML/BS) HW, 1974; NW 1973; JWC 1974

4-110. Clarke, Arthur C(harles). **2001: A Space Odyssey.** New American Library, 1968.
Novelization of the Stanley Kubrick film partly based on the short story "The Sentinel." Alien monoliths mysteriously influence human evolution

and entice a space mission into the outer solar system, where the computer HAL breaks down and the lone survivor undergoes a psychedelic encounter with strangeness: a symbolic transcendence of the human condition. In the sequel, *2010: Odyssey Two* (1982), a joint Russian/American expedition to Jupiter resurrects HAL and discovers life on Europa; then the intelligence controlling the monoliths of *2001* begins to move in its characteristically mysterious way, sending a messiah to Earth to save humankind and issuing a new commandment forbidding access to Europa. The combination of technological realism and awed mysticism works as well in these novels as anywhere else in Clarke's work, and the religious imagery is even more pronounced than in *Childhood's End* [3-44]. Somewhat less successful is *2061: Odyssey Three* (1988), which describes events after a human spacecraft accidentally crashes on Europa. Compare Gregory Benford and Gordon Eklund's *If the Stars Are Gods* (1977) and Wilson's *The Harvest* [4-506]. (BS/ML) [For other works by this author see chapters 3 and 5.]

*4-111. Compton, D(avid) G(uy). **The Continuous Katherine Mortenhoe.** Gollancz, 1974. U.S. title: *The Unsleeping Eye*, DAW, 1974.

In a world from which pain and disease have been banished, the heroine contracts a terminal illness and has to cope with the intense media interest her condition provokes. Her attempts to hide come to nothing when a reporter with cameras implanted in his eyes wins her confidence, but he becomes bitterly disillusioned with his mission. Brilliantly filmed in France as *Death Watch*, under which title it was once reprinted. One of the finest examples of the SF novel. A 1979 sequel, *Windows*, further develops the reporter's crisis of conscience; he has his camera-eyes put out, but ironically makes himself the object of the same kind of curiosity to which he once pandered. Contrast Silverberg's more stylized and hyperbolic *Thorns* [4-413]. (BS)

4-112.   Compton, D(avid) G(uy). **The Electric Crocodile.** Hodder & Stoughton, 1970. U.S. title: *The Steel Crocodile*, Ace, 1970.

Two workers at a secret research institute act as agents for a dissident group, but ultimately cannot oppose the claustrophobic conservatism that has sterilized both scientific and moral progress. Subtle and very convincing. Compare Kate Wilhelm's "April Fool's Day Forever" (1970). (BS)

4-113.   Compton, D(avid) G(uy). **Synthajoy.** Hodder & Stoughton, 1968.

A machine is developed that can record emotional experiences for later transmission into the minds of others. Abused by its inventor, it is subsequently used in the psychiatric treatment of his wife and murderer. Intricately constructed, with fine characterization and compelling cynicism. Compare Malzberg's *Cross of Fire* [4-274]. (BS)

4-114. Coney, Michael G(reatrex). **The Celestial Steam Locomotive.** Houghton Mifflin, 1983.

The first part of a tetralogy. A far-future Earth is inhabited by several humanoid species; "true" humans have retreated into seclusion, dreaming their lives away with the aid of the great computer, Rainbow, while the godlike alien, Starquin, despite imprisonment, interferes extensively with Earth's affairs. The central characters embark on a quest to bring out the network of alternative possibilities (the "Ifalong") and a new destiny for all humankind. A curious combination of mythical fantasy and SF. *Cat Karina* (1982) is an independent novel with the same background. Compare Smith's *Norstrilia* [4-427] and Crowley's *Engine Summer* [4-122]. (BS)

4-115. Constantine, Storm. **The Enchantments of Flesh and Spirit: The First Book of Wraeththu.** Macdonald, 1987.

Civilization is on the skids and technology is in decline. A spontaneous mutation occurs all over the world producing the Wraeththu, hermaphrodites with psionic powers and an affinity for down-and-dirty, punk lifestyles. Humanity's natural enemy, the Wraeththu soon overcome our species, but then engage in violent confrontations with each other in an attempt to achieve dominance. There are many logical problems with the Wraeththu books of a sort calculated to annoy the traditional SF reader, but the series succeeds on the strength of Constantine's somewhat decadent prose style, her powerful depiction of character, and her frequent and unusually graphic portrayal of some very strange sex. Other books in the series include *The Bewitchments of Love and Hate* (1988) and *The Fulfillments of Fate and Desire* (1989). Compare Hand's *Winterlong* [4-196] and its sequels. Contrast Doris Lessing's *The Fifth Child* (1988). (ML)

4-116. Cover, Arthur Byron. **The Platypus of Doom and Other Nihilists.** Warner, 1976.

A bizarre collection of four novellas, including a parody of Barry Malzberg (the title story) and an ironic homage to the angst-ridden private eye novel ("The Aardvark of Despair"). "The Clam of Catastrophe" introduces some of Cover's literary heroes into a chaotic and absurd adventure story. Other exercises in the same vein are *Autumn Angels*

(1975; NN, 1975) and the more pretentious *An East Wind Coming* (1979). Compare Philip José Farmer's *Venus on the Half-Shell* (1975). (BS)

4-117. Cowper, Richard (pseud. of John Middleton Murry, Jr.). **The Custodians, and Other Stories.** Gollancz, 1976.
The first of Cowper's collections, followed in Britain by *The Web of the Magi and Other Stories* (1980) and *The Tithonian Factor and Other Stories* (1984); the U.S. collection, *Out There Where the Big Ships Go* (1980), combines materials from the first two. Cowper displays a poetic style and an unusual delicacy of touch in featuring encounters between his characters and the speculative situations in which they are placed. He frequently builds tragic images of people dehumanized by technophilia and the lust for power; "The Custodians" (HN, 1976; NN, 1975) is one such lament for lost sanity. (BS)

4-118. Cowper, Richard (pseud. of John Middleton Murry, Jr.). **The Road to Corlay.** Gollancz, 1978.
The first (NN, 1979) of three novel-length sequels to the fine novella, "Piper at the Gates of Dawn" (HN, 1977; NN, 1976), which deals with the revival of a heretical cult in a postholocaust Britain dominated by oppressive religious orthodoxy. The cult, organized around the symbol of the White Bird of Kinship, enjoys the advantage that its most talented members can invoke and use a paranormal empathy, often associated with music. In *A Dream of Kinship* (1981) the cult has been transformed by the passing of centuries into an alternative orthodoxy, but in *A Tapestry of Time* (1982) it undergoes a further renewal. The books are lyrical fantasies affirming the author's conviction that it is spiritual rather than technological development that truly constitutes human progress. U.S. editions include "Piper at the Gates of Dawn" as a prelude. Compare Le Guin's *Also Coming Home* [4-251]. (BS)

4-119. Crichton, Michael. **The Andromeda Strain.** Knopf, 1969.
A satellite returns to Earth harboring a deadly plague, and worldwide catastrophe is narrowly averted. Realistic and suspenseful, this was made into an effective film. *The Terminal Man* (1972) is similar in its convincing handling of technical matters. (BS)

4-120. Crichton, Michael. **Jurassic Park.** Knopf, 1990.
A wealthy industrialist bankrolls an attempt to recreate dinosaurs using Cray computers, the latest in gene sequencing technology, and DNA recovered from prehistoric insects trapped in amber. Succeeding, he

builds a glorified theme park to house them but, just as the park is about to open, things begin to go wrong and the dinosaurs break loose. Although somewhat predictable, the novel is tremendous fun. It's also much more intelligent than viewers of the Spielberg film might be led to believe. Compare Larry Niven's *Dream Park* (1981). (ML)

4-121. Crowley, John. **Beasts.** Doubleday, 1976.
In a balkanized near-future America various outsiders, including hybrid beast-men left over from an experiment in genetic engineering, resist the recentralization of authority. Displays the same romantic nostalgia as Crowley's other work, but in a less expansive fashion. (BS)

*4-122. Crowley, John. **Engine Summer.** Doubleday, 1979.
In a far-future America returned to agrarian primitivism by disaster, the hero has recorded for future generations the story of his youthful quest for enlightenment. Beautifully written and eloquently argued; it can be appreciated even by those who lack sympathy with the ideology behind its Arcadian romanticism. Compare Le Guin's *Always Coming Home* [4-251]. (BS)

4-123. Crowley, John. **Novelty.** Doubleday, 1989.
This collection contains four stories, the novella "Great Work of Time," and three shorter pieces, "In Blue," "Novelty," and "The Nightingales Sing at Night." "Great Work of Time," winner of the 1990 World Fantasy Award and the centerpiece of the book, is an alternate history story in which Cecil Rhodes, founder of Rhodesia, also set up the Otherhood, a secret society of time travelers whose purpose is to preserve the British Empire. Due to their meddling, England wins World War I without help and dominates the world to this day. Eventually, however, the Otherhood discovers that its present course will lead to disaster and that, to save the Earth, the Empire must fall. Crowley is one of science fiction's finest stylists and these stories are a delight. Compare Michael Flynn's *In the Country of the Blind* (1990) and Poul Anderson's *Time Patrol* (1991). (ML)

4-124. Dann, Jack. **The Man Who Melted.** Bluejay, 1984.
A man searches for his lost wife in a world where social order has been torn apart by outbreaks of hysterical collective consciousness, which have spawned a new religiosity and an epidemic of schizophrenia. An ironic reconstruction of the voyage of the *Titanic* is featured in the plot. Aggressively decadent, with a hint of Jacobean tragedy. Compare Zelazny's *Dream Master* [4-515]. (BS) NN, 1984

4-125.   Deighton, Len. **SS-GB: Nazi-Occupied Britain 1941.** Cape, 1978.
Bestselling alternate history describing Britain occupied by Nazis in 1941.
Compare Martin Hawkin's *When Adolf Came* (1943), Frederick Mullally's
Hitler Has Won (1975), and Benford and Greenberg's *Hitler Victorious* [4-
525]. (BS)

*4-126.   Delany, Samuel R(ay). **Babel-17.** Ace, 1966.
An unorthodox heroine must come to terms with an artificial language
whose constraints on thought and behavior make it an effective weapon of
war. Clever, colorful, and highly original; it updates and sophisticates the
theme of Vance's *The Language of Pao* [3-186]. Compare also Watson's *The
Embedding* [4-483]. (BS)

*4-127.   Delany, Samuel R(ay). **Dhalgren.** Bantam, 1975.
To the depopulated city of Bellona, which is subjected to occasional distortions of time and space, comes a youthful hero hungry for experience
and keen to develop his powers as a creative artist. A dense and multilayered novel that alienated some readers who had previously applauded
Delany's colorful fantastic romances, but that reached a much wider audience. Convoluted and fascinating, it remains one of the key works of
avant-garde SF, by an author determined to extend the limits of the genre.
(BS) NN, 1975

4-128.   Delany, Samuel R(ay). **Driftglass.** Doubleday, 1971.
A collection of shorter works, including the brilliant "Time Considered as
a Helix of Semi-Precious Stones" (HN, 1970; NW, 1969) and "The Star
Pit" (HN, 1968). A later, slightly overlapping collection is *Distant Stars*
(1981), which includes the short novel, *Empire Star* (1966), a highly sophisticated space opera. (BS)

*4-129.   Delany, Samuel R(ay). **The Einstein Intersection.** Ace, 1967.
In the far future the nonhuman inhabitants of Earth mine the mythologies of the ancient past in search of meanings appropriate to their own
existence; the hero must undertake an Orphean quest into the underworld of the collective unconscious, confronting its archetypes. A fabulous
tour de force of the imagination. Compare Zelazny's *This Immortal* [4-518]
and Carter's *Infernal Desire Machines of Dr. Hoffman* [4-97]. (BS) HN, 1968;
NW, 1967

*4-130.   Delany, Samuel R(ay). **Nova.** Doubleday, 1968.
A grail epic as space opera, whose hero must trawl the core of an exploding star for the fabulous element that is the power source of the galactic

civilization. The most romantic and action-packed of Delany's novels, but no less sophisticated for that. Beautifully written. (BS) HN, 1969

4-131. Delany, Samuel R(ay). **Stars in My Pocket Like Grains of Sand.** Bantam, 1984.
The first part of a novel that accepts the impossible task of describing, analyzing, and bringing to life the culture of a galactic civilization, meanwhile telling a story of love and conflict at the individual level. An awesome project, with all the density and richness accompanying Delany's determination to stretch the limits of the genre. Presumably to be completed in *The Splendor and Misery of Bodies, of Cities.* (BS)

4-132. Delany, Samuel R(ay). **Triton: An Ambiguous Heterotopia.** Bantam, 1976.
This complex novel considers the problems that might arise for an individual trying with difficulty to orient himself in a culture where people have almost unlimited choice of identity and social role. The uncertainty of the protagonist's life is reflected in the unstable politics of the solar system, which ultimately becomes embroiled in a brief but catastrophic war. A rich, dense dramatization of issues in existential philosophy and sexual politics. (BS)

*4-133. Denton, Bradley. **Buddy Holly Is Alive and Well on Ganymede.** Morrow, 1991.
Oliver Vale, in his late twenties and not terribly successful, has spent his entire life acutely aware that his mother conceived him at the very moment in 1959 when rock star Buddy Holly's plane crashed in Iowa. Now, in 1989, the deceased Holly has inexplicably begun to appear "live" on every TV set in the world. Apparently broadcasting from one of Jupiter's moons, he informs the Earth that Oliver is responsible for Holly's usurpation of the airwaves. Needless to say, Vale soon ends up on the run, pursued by the police, angry neighbors, secret agents, his therapist, a cyborg doberman named Ringo, and some very strange aliens. This is gonzo, absurdist fiction at its best. For similar delights compare John Kessel's *Good News From Outer Space* [4-227]. (ML) JWC, 1991

4-134. Dick, Philip K(indred). **The Divine Invasion.** Timescape, 1981.
The chief characters return to Earth from a space colony, setting in train a remarkable second coming, which heralds a strange millennium. The religious philosophy interwoven with the plot is idiosyncratic, but Dick's usual fervor of sympathy and anxiety is here strengthened by a powerful injection of faith and hope as well as charity. The religious themes were

carried forward into Dick's last (non-SF) novel, *The Transmigration of Timothy Archer* (1982; NN, 1982). (BS)

*4-135.   Dick, Philip K(indred). Do Androids Dream of Electric Sheep? Doubleday, 1968.

In a future where technological sophistication has made the ersatz virtually indistinguishable from the real, the hero is a bounty hunter who must track down and eliminate androids passing for human. But android animals are routinely passed off as real by people trying to purge human guilt for having exterminated so many living species, and the new messiah is an artificial construct; so what is the difference between the human and the android? A key novel in Dick's canon. The film, *Blade Runner*, is a very pale echo. *We Can Build You* (1972) further explores the ambiguity of such distinctions as human/android and sane/schizophrenic in a haunting story of people who create machines more human than themselves. (BS) NN, 1968

4-136.   Dick, Philip K(indred). Dr. Bloodmoney; or How We Got Along After the Bomb. Ace, 1965.

A striking postholocaust novel in which the United States, despite awful devastation, sticks perversely to the same old social ruts. The characters struggle manfully to get by in appalling circumstances, wondering where the blame for it all truly lies. Compare Swanwick's *In the Drift* (1985). (BS) NN, 1965

4-137.   Dick, Philip K(indred). Flow My Tears, the Policeman Said. Doubleday, 1974.

The protagonist is drawn into the reconstructed reality of a woman's drug-induced dream where he has been stripped of his identity and made vulnerable to persecution by her policeman brother. Written with the author's customary fervor, more emotionally charged than the earlier drug story, *Now Wait for Last Year* (1966), but less nightmarish than *The Three Stigmata of Palmer Eldritch* (1965; NN, 1965). (BS) NN, 1974; HN, 1975; JWC, 1975

4-138.   Dick, Philip K(indred). Galactic Pot-Healer. Berkley, 1969.

A very curious novel in which the hero, a dissatisfied mender of pots, joins a group of misfits assembled by a godlike alien to raise a sunken cathedral, while other aliens read the runes that may indicate the destiny of the universe. A prefiguration of the metaphysical themes of Dick's last novels, developed in a mock-naïve fashion slightly reminiscent of Vonnegut's *The*

Sirens of Titan [3-192]. *A Maze of Death* (1970) picked up the theological issues for more earnest development. *Our Friends From Frolix 8* (1970) reassigned them to a throwaway role as an alien god is discovered dead in the void and his human messiah plays an essentially ambiguous role. (BS)

4-139. Dick, Philip K(indred). **A Scanner Darkly.** Doubleday, 1977.
The protagonist is, as usual in Dick's novels, gradually enmeshed by a web of circumstance in which he ceases to be able to distinguish between reality and hallucination. The fascination with which the author had previously contemplated such situations is here replaced by horrified revulsion. An affecting, powerful novel. (BS)

*4-140. Dick, Philip K(indred). **Ubik.** Doubleday, 1969.
The dead can be reactivated into a kind of half-life where they must construct their own shared realities, competing with one another to impose their own patterns. In this Schopenhaueresque world of will and idea, it is not easy for the characters to formulate a policy of psychological adaptation. Takes up themes from *Eye in the Sky* (1957) and is closely related to his hallucinatory novels but is more tightly plotted than many Dick novels. (BS)

4-141. Dick, Philip K(indred). **VALIS.** Bantam, 1981.
A convoluted novel in which the author figures as character, though his role is subservient to that of his alter ego, Horselover Fat, who achieves miraculous enlightenment courtesy of the godlike Vast Active Living Intelligence System, but has difficulty communicating his insights to others. *Radio Free Albemuth* (1985) uses similar materials, apparently being a different draft for the same purpose. (BS) [For other works by this author see chapter 3.]

4-142. Dickson, Gordon R(upert). **Dorsai!** DAW, 1976.
Revised version of *The Genetic General* (1960), the first volume in one of the more popular science fiction series. Some of the later books in the series are, in whole or in part, revised versions of earlier books. The Dorsai are the greatest soldiers in the galaxy, having developed a mercenary culture in order to gain the capital necessary to survive on a resource-poor planet. In Dickson's universe humanity has fragmented into three basic genetically determined types—men of faith, of war, and of philosophy—with the Dorsai exemplifying men of war. The three types, however, are destined to come together again to form a new, higher type of human being called the Ethical-Responsible Man. Donal Graeme,

Dorsai, military genius, and psychic superman, is the first of this new kind of human being. Dickson has outlined an ambitious plan to write a dozen novels describing the evolution of the Ethical-Responsible Man from our past, through the present, and into the future, called the Childe Cycle. So far none of the novels set in the past or present have appeared, and it seems unlikely that they will. The early Dorsai novels were primarily action-adventure of a superior sort. The later novels have become increasingly philosophical and perhaps a bit long-winded. Compare David Drake's *Hammer's Slammers* (1979) and its sequels and Jerry Pournelle's *The Mercenary* [4-338] and sequels. (ML)

4-143. Dickson, Gordon R(upert). **The Far Call.** Dial, 1978.
Political fantasy about a mission to Mars that is doomed to fail by the chicanery of its promoters. The book version is much expanded from a 1973 *Analog* serial, the private lives of the characters being mapped out extensively, presumably with the intention of appealing to a wider audience. Interesting for its study of the clash between the ideals of scientific progress and the follies of political pragmatism. Compare Bova's *Colony* [4-59]. (BS) [For other works by this author see chapter 5.]

*4-144. Disch, Thomas M(ichael). **Camp Concentration.** Hart-Davis, 1968.
A political prisoner is a guinea pig in an experiment that uses a syphilis-related spirochete to boost IQ to unparalleled levels. The author boldly presents the story as first-person narrative and carries it off brilliantly. A key work of avant-garde SF, written with its serialization in *New Worlds* in mind. Compare Keyes's *Flowers for Algernon* [3-98]. (BS)

4-145. Disch, Thomas M(ichael). **The Man Who Had No Idea.** Bantam, 1982.
The most recent collection of Disch's shorter fiction follows *One Hundred and Two H Bombs* (1966; enlarged as *White Fang Goes Dingo and Other Funny SF Stories*, 1971); *Under Compulsion* (1968; U.S. title: *Fun With Your New Head*), *Getting Into Death* (1973; U.K. and U.S. editions differ), and *Fundamental Disch* (1980). Disch is a master of black comedy, but can also write with nightmarish intensity or with a cool weltschmertz. This collection has nothing to match the classic "The Asian Shore" (NN, 1970; in *Getting Into Death* and *Fundamental Disch*) but it has the ironic and satirical title story and another novelette, "Concepts," in which people separated by a vast gulf of space fall in love via a hyperspatial link, and the bleakly horrific "The Apartment Next to the War." Disch is one of the best contemporary American short story writers. Compare Ellison's *Deathbird Stories* [4-159]. (BS)

*4-146. Disch, Thomas M(ichael). **On Wings of Song.** St. Martin's, 1979.

The hero, growing up in the ideologically repressive Midwest, yearns to learn the art of "flying," by which talented individuals can sing their souls out of their bodies. He loses his freedom, his wife, and his dignity to this quest, but in a cruelly ambiguous climax might have achieved an absurd triumph. Clever and compelling; a disturbing satire subverting SF myths of transcendence. Contrast *Stardance* [4-368] by the Robinsons and Clarke's *Childhood's End* [3-44]. (BS) HN, 1980; JWC,1980; NN, 1979

*4-147. Disch, Thomas M(ichael). **334.** MacGibbon & Kee, 1972.

A dystopian vision of future New York, focusing on various residents of a huge apartment house and other parties interested in it. A brilliant work, utterly convincing in its portraits of people trying to get by in a world they are powerless to influence or control. The most eloquent display of the pessimism that became newly acceptable in New Wave SF. Compare Brunner's *Stand on Zanzibar* [4-74]. (BS)

4-148. Dorsey, Candas Jane. **Machine Sex and Other Stories.** Porcépic, 1988.

A first collection of short fiction by a highly promising new Canadian writer. Dorsey experiments widely and wildly, ranging from cyberpunk to surrealism. Among the better stories in the book are "The Prairie Wanderers," "Machine Sex," "Time Is the School in Which We Learn," "Time Is the Fire in Which We Burn," and "Black Dog." Compare Cadigan's *Patterns* [4-88]. (ML)

4-149. Dowling, Terry. **Rynosseros.** Aphelion, 1990.

Collection of linked stories set in future Australia, which has reverted to Ab'O rule, and featuring Tom Tyson, captain of the immense "sandship" *Rynosseros*, which plies desert wastes separating balkanized tribes. Political background is shadowy and volatile, involving artificial intelligences, which meddle in conflicts between clashing principates. Exquisitely detailed, lushly baroque, elliptical to the point of unintelligibility. Compare Herbert's *Dune* [4-207] and Wolfe's *Fifth Head of Cerberus* [4-508]. *Blue Tyson* (1992) is a sequel. (RL)

4-150. Dozois, Gardner. **Strangers.** Berkley, 1978.

Expansion of a novella (HN, 1975; NN, 1974) tracking the love affair between a man and an alien woman whose reproductive biology is exotic. A virtual reprise of Farmer's *The Lovers* [3-69], with added depth of characterization. (BS)

4-151.   Dunn, Katherine. **Geek Love.** Knopf, 1989.

Although widely reviewed as a work of horror, this fine novel clearly qualifies as science fiction. It concerns the Binewski Fabulon freak show, a family-run business where the father intentionally creates mutants by exposing his frequently pregnant wife to toxic materials. The resulting children include an albino hunchback dwarf (the novel's fascinating protagonist), a flipper boy, and others. At least one child has paranormal powers. *Geek Love* was nominated for the National Book Award and the Bram Stoker Award. Compare Tod Browning's classic film *Freaks* (1932). Contrast Tom Reamy's *Blind Voices* [4-351]. (ML)

4-152.   Durrell, Lawrence. **The Revolt of Aphrodite.** Faber, 1974.

Omnibus edition of *Tunc* (1968) and *Nunquam* (1970). The inventor of a supercomputer is hired by a multinational corporation that wants him to predict the future, but he is corrupted by greed. He reemerges from the madhouse in the second volume in order to make a duplicate of the corporation head's lost love. Mannered and convoluted. Compare Barth's *Giles Goat-Boy* [4-32]. (BS)

4-153.   Effinger, George Alec. **What Entropy Means to Me.** Doubleday, 1972.

A complex set of interwoven stories in which the central character invents the tale of his brother's search for his father, while beset by problems of his own. Highly unusual, reminiscent in some ways of Flann O'Brien's *At-Swim-Two-Birds* (1939). Effinger's penchant for surrealism and the intricate interweaving of story lines is further demonstrated in *Relatives* (1973) and *The Wolves of Memory* (1981), which exhibit the same sharp imagery and the same conscientious failure to achieve coherency. (BS) NN, 1972

*4-154.   Effinger, George Alec. **When Gravity Fails.** Arbor, 1987.

Marid, a small-time hood, is a citizen of the Budayeen, the redlight district of an unnamed 21st-century Arabic city. He is also something of an anomaly; virtually all of his friends and acquaintances have had their brains wired to accept "moddies," behavior modules that can be chipped in to give the wearer an entirely different set of skills or personality. One day, someone Marid is conducting business with is murdered and he finds himself caught up in a complex web of intrigue and death. This is a fine, gritty, violent novel borrowing equally from the cyberpunks and Raymond Chandler. *A Fire in the Sun* (1989), also a Hugo Award nominee, is an excellent sequel. Somewhat weaker, but still worth reading is the third book in the series, *The Exile Kiss* (1991). Compare Gibson's *Neuromancer* [4-184]. (ML) HN, 1988; NN, 1987

4-155. Elgin, Suzette Haden. **Communipath Worlds.** Pocket Books, 1980.

Omnibus containing *The Communipaths* (1970), *Furthest* (1971), and *At the Seventh Level* (1972). The telepathic hero is a reluctant agent for a galactic federal government, but his particular missions remain subservient to the author's interest in general issues of communication and the way in which communication systems and languages are implicated in social stratification. Coyote Jones, the hero of *Communipath Worlds*, also features in *Star Anchored, Star Angered* (1979), which deals with questions of theology, and in *Yonder Comes the Other End of Time* (1986), which links the series to her Ozark trilogy of fantasies. Elgin's plots are rough-hewn, but the ideas in them are intriguing and sometimes challenging. Compare the works of C. J. Cherryh. (BS)

4-156. Elgin, Suzette Haden. **Native Tongue.** DAW, 1984.

This angry and moving feminist dystopian novel assumes a powerful backlash against women's rights in the 1980s and 1990s, culminating in the loss of the vote and the complete domination of American women by men. Centuries later, living in virtual slavery, women have developed a secret language that allows them to continue the struggle for freedom. When humanity is contacted by aliens, the linguistic facility of women makes them the logical choice to conduct negotiations, under the watchful eyes of their male oppressors. The sequel, *The Judas Rose* (1987), shows the women making some progress toward attaining their freedom. A third volume, *Earthsong*, was published in 1994. Compare Atwood's *The Handmaid's Tale* [4-23], and Hellen Collins's *Mutagenesis* (1993). (ML)

4-157. Ellison, Harlan. **Alone Against Tomorrow.** Macmillan, 1971.

Short stories dramatizing situations of acute alienation, including many of Ellison's best. "I Have No Mouth and I Must Scream" (HW, 1968) and "'Repent, Harlequin!' Said the Ticktockman" (HW, 1966; NW, 1965) are among them. Intense, filled with Sartrian nausea but by no means lacking in caritas. Compare James Sallis's *A Few Last Words* (1969). (BS)

4-158. Ellison, Harlan. **Angry Candy.** Houghton, 1988.

Most of these stories are vintage Ellison, all centering on the theme of death. Among the best are the Hugo Award-winning "Paladin of the Lost Hour," the Edgar Award-winning "Soft Monkey," "With Virgil Oddum at the East Pole," "Broken Glass," and the very funny "Prince Myshkin, and Hold the Relish." (ML) World Fantasy Award, 1989; *Locus* Award 1989

*4-159. Ellison, Harlan. **Deathbird Stories: A Pantheon of Modern Gods.** Harper, 1975.

A collection of stories said to display "a pantheon of modern gods"; angry reactions against aspects of the contemporary world. Outstanding are "The Deathbird" (HW, 1974; NN, 1973), "Pretty Maggy Moneyeyes" (HN, 1968; NN, 1967), "Shattered Like a Glass Goblin" (NN, 1969), and "Paingod." Demonstrates Ellison's brilliance as a short story writer, able to generate great affective power. Compare Spinrad's *No Direction Home* (1975). (BS)

*4-160. Ellison, Harlan. **The Essential Ellison: a 35-Year Retrospective.** Nemo Press, 1987. Ed. by Terry Dowling, Richard Delap, and Gil Lamont.

More than one thousand pages of Ellison's work as a science fiction and fantasy writer, essayist, screenwriter, television and film critic, and all-purpose social commentator. Most of the classics and award winners are here, including "Pretty Maggie Moneyeyes," "I Have No Mouth and I Must Scream," "'Repent Harlequin!' Said the Ticktockman," "A Boy and His Dog," and "Deathbird." Less well known are some of Ellison's earlier stories and his nonfiction. (ML)

4-161. Ellison, Harlan. **Shatterday.** Houghton Mifflin, 1980.

Collection continuing a trend in Ellison's work toward surrealism and psychological study, including the ironic non-SF novella, "All the Lies That Are My Life" (HN, 1981), and the bitter fable, "Count the Clock That Tells the Time." Compare Disch's *The Man Who Had No Idea* [4-145]. (BS)

4-162. Emshwiller, Carol. **The Start of the End of It All.** Women's Press, 1990.

The most recent (and best) of the author's story collections, following *Joy in Our Cause* (1974) and *Verging on the Pertinent* (1989); gathers 18 stories from sixties, seventies, and eighties. Some are straight mimetic fiction, but most construct absurdist SF scenarios enabling brilliantly pointed observations of sexual politics, such as the cat-hating aliens of the title story, whose attitudes converge with those of human men toward women. The text of the 1990 U.K. and 1991 U.S. editions differs. Compare the stories of Russ [4-374]. (RL) World Fantasy Award, 1991

4-163. Engh, M. J. **Arslan.** Warner, 1976. U.K. title: *A Wind From Bukhara*, 1979.
Having already defeated the Soviet Union and the United States in battle, Arslan, a charismatic young Asian conqueror, personally oversees mopping-up operations in the American Midwest. Deciding to make a small town in Illinois his temporary headquarters, Arslan at first rapes and terrorizes the citizens, but then seduces them by the force of his personality. This frightening and disconcerting novel features superb character development and fascinating political insights. Compare Sinclair Lewis's *It Can't Happen Here* [2-71]. Engh's recent novel, *Rainbow Man* (1993), deals with the theme of personal responsibility in a radically different but equally fascinating manner. (ML)

4-164. Farmer, Philip José. **A Feast Unknown: Volume IX of the Memoirs of Lord Grandith.** Essex House, 1969.
Superheroic rivals Lord Grandith (that is, Tarzan) and Doc Caliban (that is, Doc Savage) tensely join forces to battle a shadowy cult. Brilliant satire of superhero fantasies, first (despite its subtitle) in a loosely related series including *Lord of the Trees* (1970), *The Mad Goblin* (1970), *Tarzan Alive: A Definitive Biography of Lord Greystoke* (1972), *Doc Savage: His Apocalyptic Life* (1973), and (less certainly) many other texts, elaborating a potent celebration-cum-critique of SF's fascination with supermen. Compare Spinrad's *The Iron Dream* [4-429]. (RL)

*4-165. Farmer, Philip José. **To Your Scattered Bodies Go.** Putnam, 1971.
The entire human race is reincarnated along the banks of a huge river. Sir Richard Francis Burton sets off to find out who accomplished this remarkable feat, and why (HW, 1972). In *The Fabulous Riverboat* (1971), Sam Clemens undertakes a similar quest. Both characters, and others who become involved in further books of the series, *The Dark Design* (1977) and *The Magic Labyrinth* (1980), are continually sidetracked by violent conflicts in which characters from various phases of Earth's history are idiosyncratically matched against one another, causing the main issue to be constantly confused, sometimes to the detriment of the story. Associated stories outside the main sequence are "Riverworld" in *Riverworld and Other Stories* (1979) and *Gods of Riverworld* (1983). An early version of the story, written in the early 1950s for an ill-fated competition, was rediscovered and issued as *River of Eternity* (1983). Like a number of authors of successful, long-running series, Farmer has recently franchised out the River World, editing a shared-universe anthology, *Tales of the Riverworld* (1992), which features a new novella by Farmer, "Crossing the

Dark River," plus solid fiction by Phillip C. Jennings, Harry Turtledove, Allen Steele, and others. (BS/ML) HW, 1972

4-166.   Farmer, Philip José. **The Unreasoning Mask.** Putnam, 1981.
A swashbuckling space opera with heavy metaphysical overtones; the ambiguous hero undertakes a fabulous quest despite the suspicions of his crew that he is committing awful crimes and exposing them to great danger. Much more tightly organized than most of Farmer's later works, with a suitably apocalyptic climax. Compare Ian Watson's *The Gardens of Delight* [4-485]. (BS) [For other works by this author see chapter 3.]

4-167.   Finney, Jack. **Time and Again.** Simon & Schuster, 1970.
Timeslip romance whose plausibility is enhanced by making the time travel part of an experimental project and by unusually scrupulous research. Excellent historical detail and a compelling plot make this the outstanding work of the subgenre. *From Time to Time*, a sequel, was announced for 1995. Compare Matheson's *Bid Time Return* [4-285]. (BS) [For other works by this author see chapter 3.]

4-168.   Forward, Robert L(ull). **Dragon's Egg.** Ballantine, 1980.
A race that evolves on the surface of a neutron star lives on a vastly compressed time scale, but nevertheless manages to make contact with human observers. A fascinating and ingenious example of hard SF. Its representation of scientists at work compares with Benford's *Timescape* [4-46]. In the sequel, *Starquake* (1985), the aliens achieve technological sophistication, are returned to primitivism by a "starquake," and rebuild their civilization—a process that takes several of their generations but only 24 hours of our time. Compare Brunner's *The Crucible of Time* (1984). (BS)

4-169.   Foster, Alan Dean. **The Tar-Aiym Krang.** Ballantine, 1972.
First part of a trilogy continued in *Orphan Star* (1977) and *The End of the Matter* (1977), following the adventures of a young psi-powered hero who takes on mighty adversaries and wins by ingenuity and audacity. Entertaining picaresque space opera in a modern vein. Foster has used the same background and sometimes the same characters in other novels, including *Bloodhype* (1973), *Nor Crystal Tears* (1982), and *For Love of Mother-Not* (1983). The more recent works move away from pure space opera toward more thoughtful consideration of the relationships between different species in the interstellar commonwealth. (BS)

4-170.   Foster, M(ichael) A(nthony). **The Morphodite.** DAW, 1981.
On a planet where change is suppressed by a determined totalitarian gov-

ernment, revolution is precipitated by an assassin whose calculation of social stresses tells him where to strike and whose shape-shifting power keeps him one step ahead of his pursuers. In the sequels, *Transformer* (1983) and *Preserver* (1985), the morphodite's mission is carried further, into the wider reaches of interstellar civilization. Action-adventure fiction enlived by the protagonist's dramatic changes of identity and the problems that ensue. (BS)

4-171. Foster, M(ichael) A(nthony). **Waves.** DAW, 1980.
An enigmatic intelligent ocean interferes with Slavic colonists on an alien world. Apparently inspired by Lem's *Solaris* [3-115]. The author draws on his background as a Russian linguist with the U.S. Air Force in setting up the situation. An interesting novel of ideas. (BS)

4-172. Fowler, Karen Joy. **Artificial Things.** Bantam, 1986.
It's rare for a new SF author's first published book to be a short story collection, but Fowler's polished tales have had a powerful and immediate impact within the genre. Included are the hysterically funny "The Faithful Companion at Forty," which gives us the truth about the Lone Ranger's relationship with Tonto, as well as such fine pieces as "The Gate of Ghosts," "The View From Venus," "Praxis," and "The Lake Is Full of Artificial Things." Compare Wilhelm's *The Infinity Box* [4-494] and other collections. (ML)

*4-173. Fowler, Karen Joy. **Sarah Canary.** Holt, 1991.
In 1873 an apparent madwoman stumbles into a Chinese labor camp in Washington state and is led to a nearby insane asylum. The woman, named Sarah Canary at the asylum, escapes and wanders the Pacific coast, accompanied by a host of fascinating characters. But who is Sarah, a broken victim of male oppression, the simple madwoman she first appeared to be, or something more sinister, a vampire perhaps, or something not of this planet? We never find out for sure, which has frustrated critics bent on sticking the book into a generic pigeonhole. What is certain, however, is that *Sarah Canary* is a brilliantly conceived, beautifully written book. Compare Robert Charles Wilson's *A Hidden Place* (1986). (ML) NN, 1992

4-174. Gallun, Raymond Z(inke). **The Eden Cycle.** Ballantine, 1974.
A novel that investigates the common assertion that evolution into superhumanity would take the spice out of life; the central characters struggle to find meaning and purpose in a situation in which they can effectively have anything they want. Contrast Moorcock's Dancers at the End of Time series [4-305]. (BS) [For other works by this author see chapter 2.]

4-175.   Gary, Romain (pseud. of Romain Kassevgari). **The Gasp.** Putnam, 1973.

A scientist succeeds in isolating the *élan vital* that is the human soul, and it is exploited as an energy source. Satirical black comedy with a fast-paced plot, apparently following up the central idea of Maurois's *The Weigher of Souls* [2-82]. (BS)

4-176.   Gawron, Jean Mark. **Dream of Glass.** Harcourt, 1993.

An amnesiac young woman finds herself a major player in a convoluted conflict among extraterrestrials, renegade artificial intelligences, and a future police state, battle-joined in quasi-mystical computer cyberspace. Meditative and striking; weds the metaphysical space opera of the author's earlier *Algorithm* (1978) with cyberpunk. Contrast Gibson's *Neuromancer* [4-184]. (RL)

4-177.   Gentle, Mary. **Golden Witchbreed.** Gollancz, 1983.

Lynne Christie, envoy of Earth Dominion, has been sent to Orthe to determine whether its humanoid inhabitants are ready for diplomatic and economic relations. She discovers a complex world with factions both friendly to and hostile to her goal. Gentle's Orthe is a superb example of world building, comparable in many ways to Herbert's *Dune* [4-207] or Le Guin's *The Left Hand of Darkness* [4-254]. Compare also Cherryh's *The Faded Sun* [4-104]. The excellent sequel is *Ancient Light* (1987). (ML)

4-178.   Gerrold, David (pseud. of Jerrold David Friedman). **The Man Who Folded Himself.** Random, 1973.

A time traveler shuttles back and forth, replicating himself many times over and creating practical and existential problems for himselfs. A playfully narcissistic treatment of the time paradox theme, developing ideas from Heinlein's "By His Bootstraps" (1941) and "All You Zombies . . ." (1959). (BS)

4-179.   Gerrold, David (pseud. of Jerrold David Friedman). **When HARLIE Was One.** Doubleday, 1972.

The hero supervises the making and education of a sentient computer, which eventually designs an artificial intelligence even more powerful in order to demonstrate its usefulness. *When HARLIE Was One (Release 2.0)* (1988) is a rewrite of the earlier novel, which updates the book's computer technology and jettisons its early 1970s drug culture milieu. Opinions are mixed as to which version is superior. Compare Thomas J. Ryan's

Adolescence of P-1 (1977) and Maddox's *Halo* [4-272]. (ML/BS) HN, 1973; NN, 1972

4-180. Geston, Mark S(ymington). **Lords of the Starship.** Ace, 1967.
In the far future a nation whose ancestors once built starships attempts to duplicate their achievement, though it no longer has the appropriate technology and must expend many generations in the project. *Out of the Mouth of the Dragon* (1969) is set in the same desolate far future and deals with the last of the many wars that have laid it waste. Grim and somber stories, with some fine imagery and a uniquely bitter ennui. (BS)

*4-181. Gibson, William. **Burning Chrome.** Arbor, 1986.
Ten short stories by the most innovative new voice to enter the science fiction field in decades. Included here are such superb short fictions as "Burning Chrome," "The Winter Market," "Dogfight" (co-authored with Michael Swanwick), and "Hinterlands," as well as collaborations with Bruce Sterling and John Shirley. Several are award nominees. Many of these stories are set in the sleazy, cyberpunk future made famous in Gibson's novels. Compare Sterling's *Crystal Express* [4-438] and *Global Head* (1992). (ML)

*4-182. Gibson, William. **Count Zero.** Arbor House, 1985.
A complex adventure story set in the same future as *Neuromancer* [4-184]. The eponymous hero gets into trouble as a result of a weird experience in cyberspace, while two other protagonists follow their own projects to the entangled climax; clever and slick. The same settings also feature in many of Gibson's short stories, collected in *Burning Chrome* [4-181]. (BS)

*4-183. Gibson, William. **Mona Lisa Overdrive.** Gollancz, 1988.
Gibson's third cyberpunk novel, following *Neuromancer* [4-184] and *Count Zero* [4-182], features a complex plotline and four separate protagonists: a teenage runaway, an artist who creates kinetic sculpture from scrap, the daughter of a wealthy Japanese industrialist, and a Sense/Net star. A number of characters from the earlier stories also reappear. Although not generally regarded as highly as is *Neuromancer, Mona* is engrossing. A novel of dark settings and pointed details, it features Gibson's usual superb style. (ML) HN, 1989; NN, 1988

*4-184. Gibson, William. **Neuromancer.** Ace, 1984.
In a highly urbanized future dominated by cybernetics and bioengineering, anti-hero Case is rescued from wretchedness and given back the abili-

ty to send his persona into the cyberspace of the world's computer networks, where he must carry out a hazardous mission for an enigmatic employer. An adventure story much enlivened by elaborate technical jargon and sleazy, streetwise characters—the pioneering "cyberpunk" novel. Compare Vinge's *True Names* [4-476], Sterling's *Islands in the Net* [4-439], and the film *Blade Runner*. (BS/ML) HW, 1985; NW, 1984; JWC, 1985

4-185. Gibson, William. **Virtual Light.** Viking, 1993.
In post-quake San Francisco the badly damaged Golden Gate Bridge has become home for hundreds of dropouts and counterculture types. One such, Chevette, while working as a bicycle messenger, steals a pair of virtual reality glasses that contain a secret that a number of people are willing to kill for. This is relatively minor Gibson, but his early-21st-century California is wonderfully well realized, and the action plot is nicely handled. Compare Richard Paul Russo's *Destroying Angel* (1992). Contrast Pat Murphy's *The City, Not Long After* [4-308]. (ML)

4-186. Gibson, William, and Bruce Sterling. **The Difference Engine.** Gollancz, 1990.
The Victorian scientist Charles Babbage designed a primitive but workable mechanical computer. He never built it, of course, but what if he had? The novel postulates an enormously accelerated Industrial Revolution fueled by construction of gigantic Babbage machines and, as a result, a social revolution as well. Lord Byron, leader of the Industrial Radical party, has become Prime Minister, and the country is largely run by a science-based meritocracy. Against this wonderfully complex backdrop, the authors work a fairly straightforward mystery plotline. It seems that a valuable deck of programming cards has been stolen and a variety of powerful people are willing to do virtually anything to recover them. One of the joys of this rather erudite novel lies in spotting the many historical personages and figuring out exactly how their lives have changed. Compare Michael Flynn's use of the Babbage machine in *In the Country of the Blind* (1990). (ML) NN, 1991

4-187. Goldstein, Lisa. **A Mask for the General.** Bantam, 1987.
Twenty-first-century America, plunged into a permanent depression by the collapse of computer technology, struggles under the repressive rule of the General, while in Berkeley, California, a group of artists and latter-day hippies do their best to promote revolution. Foremost among them is Layla, a mask maker whose creations appear to have almost mystical powers. This is a subtle, but moving novel, lacking much in the way of action,

but making up for it with fine writing. Compare two very similar books, Murphy's *The City, Not Long After* [4-308] and Russo's *Subterranean Gallery* [4-376]. (ML)

4-188. Goulart, Ron. **After Things Fell Apart.** Ace, 1970.

A detective pursues a gang of feminist assassins through the eccentric sub-cultures of a balkanized future United States. The best of the author's many humorous SF novels, with a genuine satirical element to add to the usual slapstick. Compare Robert Sheckley's *Journey Beyond Tomorrow* (1962). (BS)

4-189. Grant, Richard. **Rumors of Spring.** Bantam, 1987.

A strange blend of satire, fable, science fiction, and fantasy set on a far-future Earth where technology is in a state of collapse, entropy seems to be gaining, and a badly damaged ecology is actively fighting back. The First Biotic Crusade, a group of eccentrics worthy of a Mervyn Peake novel, sets out in a huge Rube Goldberg-like vehicle to uncover the truth behind the strange goings-on in the world's last woodland, the Carbon Bank Forest. At once a cutting attack on government bureaucracy, a sprightly and somewhat silly adventure story, and an ecological fable, *Rumors of Spring* is beautifully written and constantly surprising. Compare John Crowley's *Little, Big* (1981). (ML)

4-190. Greenland, Colin. **Take Back Plenty.** Unwin, 1990.

This sophisticated and enormously funny postmodernist space opera owes a debt not only to the pulp tradition, but also to Lewis Carroll. Tabitha Jute, a free-lance space trucker with a penchant for partying and choosing unsuitable lovers, is hired to transport a rather shady troupe of entertainers from the decaying space habitat Plenty to the surface of Titan. The entertainers, however, are not what they claim to be, and Tabitha soon finds herself up to her neck in intrigue. Compare Iain M. Banks's *The Player of Games* [4-29]. (ML) A. C. Clarke, 1990; British SF Association, 1990

4-191. Gunn, James E(dwin). **The Dreamers.** Simon & Schuster, 1980.

Once the mechanism of memory is known, the business of learning is technologically transformed, but the acquisition of information by ingestion and injection mechanizes the personality. Thoughtful development of fascinating premises; similar in structure and import to the author's *The Joy Makers* (1961). (BS)

4-192.   Gunn, James E(dwin). **The Listeners.** Scribner, 1972.
A fix-up novel about the radio astronomers who pick up and decode a message from an alien civilization, and about the public reaction to the event. The work is heavy with religious symbolism and literary allusion. Compare Clarke's *2010* (1982) and Michael Kube-McDowell's *Emprise* (1985). (BS) [For other works by this author see chapter 3.]

*4-193.   Haldeman, Joe. **The Forever War.** St. Martin's, 1975.
Fix-up novel of interstellar war against hive-organized aliens. Realistic descriptions of military training and action, with interesting use of relativistic time distortions. A reprise of and ideological counterweight to Heinlein's *Starship Troopers* [3-90]. Compare also Card's *Ender's Game* [4-92]. (BS) HW, 1976; NN, 1975; *Locus* Award, 1976

4-194.   Haldeman, Joe. **The Hemingway Hoax.** Morrow, 1990.
John Baird, a Hemingway specialist at Boston University with severe financial problems, falls in with some shady characters who persuade him to fake and then claim to have rediscovered a series of stories that Hemingway is known to have lost on a train trip. Unbeknown to Baird or his confederates, however, some very strange people—people not from our world—have a stake in Baird's *not* writing the stories. Haldeman's intimate knowledge and love of Hemingway and his work is highly apparent in this very short, very intense novel based on a Hugo and Nebula Award-winning novella of the same name. Compare MacDonald Harris's non-SF novel, *Hemingway's Suitcase* (1990). (ML)

4-195.   Haldeman, Joe. **Worlds.** Viking, 1981.
The first volume of a trilogy, followed by *Worlds Apart* (1983). Earth lurches toward World War III, after which devastation the future of humankind will become dependent on the society of the "Worlds"—orbital space colonies. Near-future realism combined with loosely knit action-adventure. The long-delayed and very well done concluding volume, *Worlds Enough and Time* (1992), describes the difficult journey of one of those colonies to another star system. Compare Bova's *Colony* [4-59]. (BS/ML)

4-196.   Hand, Elizabeth. **Winterlong.** Bantam, 1990.
Hand's first novel features gorgeous prose reminiscent of Gene Wolfe and an exotic and decadent setting, the City of the Trees in the Northeastern Federated Republic of America, in essence a far-future Washington, D.C., half destroyed by global warming, biological warfare, and time. Among the characters are Wendy Wanders, half-mad victim of a government-spon-

sored parapsychology program, and Margalis Tast'annin, the Mad Aviator, hero of the Archipelago Conflict. Tast'annin has been sent to close down the parapsychology program and execute all those involved in it. When Wendy escapes, he must pursue her through the nightmarish City. Two loose sequels to *Winterlong* are *Aestival Tide* (1992) and *Icarus Descending* (1993). Compare Ryman's *The Child Garden* [4-377] and Constantine's *The Enchantments of Flesh and Spirit* [4-115]. ML

4-197. Harness, Charles L(eonard). **The Ring of Ritornel.** Gollancz, 1968.
A fine space opera in which a corrupt galactic empire faces apocalyptic destruction as the contending forces of chance and destiny (personalized in rival deities) resolve their conflict. Will the cosmos be reborn and renewed when the cycle ends? The themes echoed here from the earlier *Flight Into Yesterday* (1953) recur in *Firebird* (1981), and these three works are among the most stylish modern space operas. Compare Ian Wallace's Croyd series [4-481] and Barrington J. Bayley's *The Pillars of Eternity* (1982). (BS)

4-198. Harrison, Harry. **Captive Universe.** Putnam, 1969.
A well-done variation on the concept of the generation ship that spends years, possibly centuries, reaching another star system at sub-light speeds. Many such novels suggest that the society of such a ship will break down over the years, leading to barbarism. Harrison postulates a ship with an artificially constructed, conservative social order patterned on the Aztecs. Most citizens aren't even aware they're on a starship. Only the priests who lead the culture know the true nature of their environment. Compare Heinlein's *Orphans of the Sky* [3-88] and Aldiss's *Non-Stop* [3-4]. (ML)

4-199. Harrison, Harry. **The Daleth Effect.** Putnam, 1970. U.K. title: *In Our Hands, the Stars*, 1970.
An Israeli scientist invents antigravity and flees to Denmark to develop his invention for peaceful purposes rather than allowing it to become a hot pawn in the cold war. Action-adventure with a political slant. Compare Bob Shaw's *Ground Zero Man* (1971). (BS)

4-200. Harrison, Harry. **Make Room! Make Room!** Doubleday, 1966.
A classic novel of overpopulation and pollution, reprinted in connection with the film version (which certainly fails to do the book justice) as *Soylent Green*. An archetypal example of 1960s alarmism. Compare Brunner's *Stand on Zanzibar* [4-74]. (BS) NN, 1966

4-201. Harrison, Harry. **West of Eden.** Bantam, 1984.

Alternate history story in which the dinosaurs were not killed off and ultimately produced sentient, humanoid descendants devoted to biotechnology. Their civilized race is ultimately forced into contact and conflict with savage human beings, adding culture shock to crisis. Inventive, fast-paced narrative. Followed by two sequels. (BS)

4-202. Harrison, M(ichael) John. **A Storm of Wings.** Sphere, 1980.

A sequel to the downbeat sword and sorcery novel *The Pastel City* (1971). It begins the transformation of the city Viriconium into a milieu for more sophisticated literary exercise, extended in *In Viriconium* (1982; U.S. title: *The Floating Gods*) and *Viriconium Nights* (1984). Images of decadence and exhaustion abound in this series, which contrasts with other images of far-future cities in Bryant's *Cinnabar* [4-76] and Carr's *Cirque* [4-95] and has strong affinities with certain aspects of Michael Moorcock's work. SF motifs are relatively sparse in what is essentially a fantasy series, but the use of entropic decay as a prevalent metaphor sustains the bridge between genres. (BS)

4-203. Heinlein, Robert A(nson). **Friday.** Holt, 1982.

An artificially created superwoman, courier for a secret organization, has to fend for herself when the decline of the West reaches its climax; she ultimately find a new raison d'être on the extraterrestrial frontier. Welcomed by Heinlein fans as action-adventure respite from his more introspective works, but actually related very closely to some sections of *Time Enough for Love* [4-205] and refers to much earlier material ("Gulf," 1949). (BS) HN, 1983; NN, 1982

*4-204. Heinlein, Robert A(nson). **The Moon Is a Harsh Mistress.** Putnam, 1966.

Colonists of the Moon declare independence from Earth and contrive to win the ensuing battle with the aid of a sentient computer. Action-adventure with some exploration of new possibilities in social organization and fierce assertion of the motto "There Ain't No Such Thing as a Free Lunch." Though not a true sequel, *The Cat Who Walks Through Walls* (1985) is a much weaker novel set in the same universe and with some of the same characters. Compare John Varley's *Steel Beach* [4-469] and Greg Bear's *Moving Mars* (1993). (BS/ML) HW, 1967; NN, 1966

4-205. Heinlein, Robert A(nson). **Time Enough for Love.** Putnam, 1973.

Partial biography of Lazarus Long, the long-lived hero of *Methuselah's*

Children [3-89], involving the promiscuous multiplication of his genes and a journey into the past that affords him the opportunity to seduce his mother and die a hero's death (not final, of course) in World War I. An extravagant exercise in the production of an idealized fantasy self, drawing on the repertoire of SF ideas to support and sanction extraordinary forms of imaginary self-indulgence. Powerful because of the wish fulfillment aspect of the composition. Compare "Baron Corvo's" *Hadrian VII* (1904). (BS) HN, 1974; NN, 1973. [For other works by this author see chapters 3 and 5.]

4-206. Herbert, Frank. **Destination: Void.** Berkley, 1966.
The computers guiding a starship en route to a new world fail, and the crew must construct an artificial intelligence to repair the damage, but the intelligence defines itself as God and demands worship as the price of looking after its human cargo. In three sequels written with Bill Ransom, *The Jesus Incident* (1979), *The Lazarus Effect* (1983), and *The Ascension Factor* (1988), this artificial God and its human subjects draw on biblical lore in order to explore the possibilities of worship, trying to figure out how it should be appropriately done. Compare Chris Boyce's *Catchworld* (1975) and Gerrold's *When HARLIE Was One* [4-179]. (BS/ML)

*4-207. Herbert, Frank. **Dune.** Chilton, 1965.
The first of a seven-volume bestselling series is the story of a selectively bred messiah who acquires paranormal powers by use of the spice that is the main product of the desert planet Arrakis, and uses these powers to prepare for the ecological renewal of the world. Politics and metaphysics are tightly bound into a remarkably detailed and coherent pattern; an imaginative tour de force. The series as a whole is overinflated, the later revisitations of the theme being prompted more by market success than the discovery of new things to do with it. The series demonstrates how a good SF writer's ability to build a coherent and convincing hypothetical world can serve the purpose of making philosophical and sociological questions concrete; the series thus becomes a massive thought experiment in social philosophy, and is more considerable as such than Asimov's Foundation series [3-12] and [4-19] or Bradley's Darkover series [4-63]. (BS) HW, 1966; NW, 1965

4-208. Herbert, Frank. **Whipping Star.** Putnam, 1970.
The awesome basic premise of Herbert's novel is that some stars are merely one part of an intelligent, extra-dimensional life-form. When a star dies, one of these super-aliens dies. The aliens also manifest themselves physi-

cally in our universe as Calebans and, in this form, have introduced humanity to teleportation via jumpdoors. Now, however, the last Caleban is dying and humanity finds out too late that, when it does die, everyone who has ever used a jumpdoor will die with it. The novel's protagonist must find a way to save the Caleban's life, thus saving his own and those of untold millions of other intelligent beings. A lesser, but still worthwhile sequel is *The Dosadi Experiment* (1977). (ML)

4-209.   Herbert, Frank. **The White Plague.** Putnam, 1982.
A molecular biologist driven mad by cruel circumstances unleashes a plague that will universalize his personal tragedy and destroy the women of the world. The terrorism that initially provoked him is reproduced on a grand scale: an appalling visitation of a kind of "justice." Compare Christopher Priest's *Fugue for a Darkening Island* (1972). (BS) [For other works by this author see chapter 3.]

4-210.   Hoban, Russell. **Riddley Walker.** Cape, 1980.
A postholocaust story in which gunpowder is rediscovered but set aside by the naïvely wise hero, who believes that mankind must find a new path of progress this time. The first-person narrative is presented in the decayed and transfigured dialect of the day and represents a fascinating linguistic experiment. Compare Aldiss's *Barefoot in the Head* [4-2]. (BS) JWC, 1982

4-211.   Hogan, James P(atrick). **The Minervan Experiment.** Nelson Doubleday, 1981.
Omnibus SFBC edition of a trilogy: *Inherit the Stars* (1977), *The Gentle Giants of Ganymede* (1978), and *Giants' Star* (1981). A humanoid corpse discovered on the moon presents a puzzle that unravels into the story of an ancient civilization whose colonies in the solar system were destroyed by war. The trilogy starts well but deteriorates gradually into unexceptional space opera; in the third volume humans and alien allies resist absorption into a nasty galactic empire. The strength of the first volume is its portrayal of scientists battling with a mystery, producing and testing hypotheses until the solution is found. Compare Benford's *Timescape* [4-46]. (BS)

4-212.   Holdstock, Robert. **Where Time Winds Blow.** Faber, 1981.
Time winds carry objects back and forth in time on an alien planet; the detritus they leave is eagerly investigated during periods of calm. Investigators, though, live in constant peril of being caught up by the

winds. The story is heavy on dialogue and philosophical discussion. Compare Priest's *An Infinite Summer* [4-346]. (BS)

4-213.   Jablokov, Alexander. **Carve the Sky.** Morrow, 1991.
It is the 24th century, and Earth has colonized both the inner planets and the larger moons of the gas giants. In the distant past our solar system was visited by starfaring aliens, but humanity has not yet developed interstellar travel. The ability to do so lies in the possession of a fabulously rare metal found in artifacts left by the aliens. Now, some of that metal has turned up in a new sculpture by a supposedly long-dead artist. Several powerful organizations are searching for the artist's source of materials and are willing to stop at nothing to find it. Jablokov has created a complex and fascinating culture here, and his knowledge of the art world is considerable. The mannered style and use of anachronistic technology recall the work of Jack Vance. Compare Simmons' *Hyperion* [4-419]. (ML)

4-214.   Jennings, Phillip C. **The Bug Life Chronicles.** Baen, 1989.
Fifteen interconnected stories set in a future where nanotechnology, very large-scale engineering feats, personality downloading, and computer-generated virtual reality environments are the norm. Character development is not necessarily his strong point, but Jennings sets a hectic and fascinating pace in these stories, demanding of his readership considerable scientific literacy and the ability to appreciate a very odd sense of humor. The average Jennings story contains enough ideas to flesh out two or three longer works by other writers. Among the highlights: convicted felons, their minds downloaded into miniature spacecraft, sent out to explore the solar system; and "fictoids," artificial characters, originally developed for computer games, which have now gained legal status and "human" rights. Equally compelling is Jennings's novel set in the same future history, *Tower to the Sky* (1988). Compare Bear's *Queen of Angels* [4-41]. (ML)

4-215.   Jeschke, Wolfgang. **The Last Day of Creation.** Century, 1982.
Trans. of *Der letzte Tag der Schöpfung*, 1981, by Gertrud Mander.
Time travel story in which Americans try to hijack the Middle East's oil from the past; when paradoxes accumulate, the travelers are cut off from futures that no longer exist. A fast-paced adventure story with a touch of weltschmertz. Compare Silverberg's *Up the Line* [4-415]. (BS)

4-216.   Jeter, K. W. **Dr. Adder.** Bluejay, 1984.
Quasi-pornographic novel of a decadent future Los Angeles and the attempt made by a video evangelist to clean it up, with the protagonist

caught in the exotic crossfire. Compare Steven Barnes's *Streetlethal* (1983). (BS)

4-217.   Jeter, K. W. Madlands. St. Martin's, 1991.
For reasons unknown—though a government conspiracy is rumored—part of southern California has been warped into the Madlands, a place where dreams, particularly nightmares, come true and where a variety of gruesome diseases run rampant. Identrope, a corrupt televangelist, controls the city from a copy of the Hindenburg, which burns perpetually in the sky above. Then Trayne, a private eye with a bizarre secret, runs afoul of the televangelist and a series of odd and violent events is set in motion. This compelling example of postmodernist SF reads very much like a bad acid trip and owes an obvious debt to both the cyberpunks and Raymond Chandler. A more subtle connection may be with the work of Barry Malzberg, who is Jeter's only equal when it comes to bleakness of the spirit. Compare, also, Newman's *The Night Mayor* [4-311]. (ML)

4-218.   Jones, Gwyneth. Divine Endurance. Allen & Unwin, 1984.
On a far-future Earth, in an isolated citadel in central Asia, live the immortal cat Divine Endurance and the last of the manufactured humans, Chosen Among the Beautiful. When the machines that imprison them finally cease functioning, they venture forth into the wasteland to see the world. In Southeast Asia they find what might well be the last human civilization on Earth. Cho was created with the need to fulfill human desires, but the people she meets find her presence to be at best a mixed blessing. A densely written and difficult novel, with a touch of Jack Vance, though lacking his wittiness and of radically different political sensibility. Compare Slonczewski's *A Door into Ocean* [4-425]. ML

4-219.   Jones, Gwyneth. White Queen. Gollancz, 1991.
This gender-bending story concerns a reporter who, blackballed from his profession and living a hand-to-mouth existence in a second-rate African city, is contacted by an apparently female alien who offers him an interview and later seduces/rapes him. Although the aliens look human, their thought patterns are radically different from ours, and Jones does a particularly good job of portraying them. Compare Dozois's *Strangers* [4-150]. (ML) James Tiptree Award, 1992; Arthur C. Clarke nominee, 1992

4-220.   Jones, Langdon. The Eye of the Lens. Macmillan, 1972.
A collection of New Wave stories by a *New Worlds* writer, including the controversial "I Remember, Anita" and such fine surreal stories as "The Great Clock" and "The Time Machine." (BS)

4-221. Joseph, M(ichael) K(ennedy). **The Hole in the Zero.** Gollancz, 1967.
Surreal SF novel, set largely outside time and space, in which the characters can and do create their own subjective realities, searching therein for some kind of existential anchorage. Compare Dick's *Ubik* [4-140] and Stableford's *Man in a Cage* (1976). (BS)

4-222. Kadrey, Richard. **Metrophage: A Romance of the Future.** Ace, 1988.
A streetwise drug dealer in grittily decadent 21st-century Los Angeles becomes enmeshed in a wobbly, convoluted plot involving aliens and a mysterious wasting disease. Self-conscious cyberpunk marked by zestful surrealism and witty allusiveness. Compare Gibson's *Neuromancer* [4-184] and Jeter's *Dr. Adder* [4-216]. (RL)

4-223. Kagan, Janet. **Mirabile.** Tor, 1991.
The designers behind Mirabile colony thought they had developed a foolproof way to guarantee the colonists a wide range of Earth life-forms to choose from on their new world. Each Earth species was engineered to carry the genes of other species piggybacked within its own. Thus, under controlled conditions, one species would beget another, daffodils giving birth to bugs, for example. Unfortunately, due to an accident that destroyed many of their records, the colonists never know what they're going to get and often end up with bizarre mutations and unwanted pests. Take for example the Loch Moose Monster, Kangaroo Rex, or the ever-dangerous Frankenswine. These enormously popular stories, all originally published in *Asimov's SF*, engagingly combine broad humor and fascinating genetics. Compare Varley's *Titan* [4-470]. (ML)

4-224. Kandel, Michael. **Strange Invasion.** Bantam, 1989.
Shapeshifting alien invaders turn Earth into a tourist site, bizarrely unsettling the global political balance. Wildly funny satire with a sting in its tail from the renowned English translator of Lem. Contrast Fredric Brown's *Martians, Go Home!* (1955). (RL)

4-225. Kavan, Anna (pseud. of Helen Woods Edmonds). **Ice.** Owen, 1967.
A dreamlike story whose narrator pursues a fragile girl through increasingly icebound war zones while harboring nostalgic feelings about the warm and gentle world of the indri of Madagascar. A classic surreal novel of existential catastrophe. Contrast Ballard's *The Drowned World* [3-16]. (BS)

4-226.   Kelly, James Patrick. **Look Into the Sun.** Tor, 1989.

A talented young American architect suffers a crisis of confidence because he fears he will never be able to equal his masterpiece, a floating sculpture called the Glass Cloud. When the alien Messengers, powerful but not entirely competent evangelists, offer him a job creating a shrine for a dying goddess on another planet, Wing jumps at the chance to escape Earth. Kelly's characters are well developed and his alien religion is extremely interesting, though the book is at times a bit talky. An earlier, relatively minor novel set in the same universe is *Planet of Whispers* (1984). (ML)

*4-227.   Kessel, John. **Good News From Outer Space.** Tor, 1989.

The millennium is at hand and America is in bad economic and spiritual shape. To make matters worse, the aliens have apparently landed, though they refuse to show themselves and their purposes remain highly ambiguous. At once chilling and very funny, this novel is notable for its portrayal of aliens whose motives are beyond our comprehension. For other portraits of millennial fervor, compare James Morrow's *Only Begotten Daughter* (1990) and Mark Geston's *Mirror to the Sky* (1992). (ML) NN, 1989

4-228.   Kessel, John. **Meeting in Infinity.** Arkham, 1992.

At once erudite and witty, Kessel has a particular genius for literary pastiche. Among the best of the 14 short stories are the Nebula Award-winning "Another Orphan," in which a commodities broker finds himself in the world of *Moby Dick*; the Sturgeon Award-winning (and Hugo- and Nebula-nominated) "Buffalo," in which the author envisions a meeting between his father and H. G. Wells; and the hilarious "Faustfeathers," which successfully combines the Marx brothers and Christopher Marlowe with truly amazing results. Compare Swanwick's *Gravity's Angels* [4-449]. (ML)

4-229.   Kilworth, Garry. **The Songbirds of Pain: Stories from the Inscape.** Gollancz, 1984.

A collection of short stories including the time travel story, "Let's Go to Golgotha," which won a *Sunday Times* SF story competition in 1975. The title story and some others show the author in a lyrical vein that contrasts with the taut adventure fiction of his novels. Compare the short fiction of Richard Cowper [4-117]. (BS)

4-230.   Kilworth, Garry. **A Theatre of Timesmiths.** Gollancz, 1984.

A closed-world story; the inhabitants of a city completely surrounded by vast walls of ice face crisis as their central computer becomes unreliable and they must rediscover their history in search of a solution. (BS)

4-231. King, Stephen. **Carrie.** Doubleday, 1974.
The story of an alienated teenage girl whose latent psychokinetic power bursts forth in an orgy of destruction when she is humiliated at a high school prom. A graphic and satisfying revenge fantasy. Contrast van Vogt's *Slan* [3-180]. (BS)

4-232. King, Stephen. **The Dead Zone.** Viking, 1979.
The juvenile hero acquires the gift of precognition, although his talent is almost entirely limited to disastrous events; but can the holocaust he foresees in connection with the campaign of a presidential candidate be averted? Compare Cherryh's "Cassandra" in *Visible Light* (1986). (BS)

4-233. King, Stephen. **The Stand.** Doubleday, 1978. Recommended ed.: Doubleday, 1990.
This new edition not only restores cut material, but updates the book as well, setting it in the 1990s and improving the science content. The basic plot remains unchanged: a killer flu escapes from a bio-weapons facility and 99 percent of the human race dies. In the United States, most of the good people who are left gather in Boulder while most of the evil people end up in Las Vegas. Armageddon follows. The novel's greatest strength lies in King's ability to portray characters who are either highly believable or chillingly twisted. Contrast Brin's *The Postman* [4-66]. (ML)

4-234. Kingsbury, Donald. **Courtship Rite.** Timescape, 1982. U.K. title: *Geta*, 1984.
A colony on an arid world is in cultural extremis because of its lack of resources, and the central characters become involved with a challenge to its established order. An unusually detailed and complex novel, interesting because of its carefully worked political and anthropological themes. Compare Herbert's *Dune* [4-207]. (BS) HN, 1983

4-235. Klein, Gérard. **The Day Before Tomorrow.** DAW, 1972. Trans. of *Le Temps n'a pas d'odeur*, 1967, by P. J. Sokolowski.
Interplanetary peace is secured by transtemporal agents who alter the history of worlds likely to prove troublesome, but a team on one such mission finds unexpected problems with paradoxes and a peculiar alien culture. Compare Michael Jeury's *Chronolysis* (1973; trans. 1980). (BS)

4-236.   Knight, Damon. CV. Tor, 1985.
At first *CV* reads much like a Michael Crichton thriller. A gigantic, high-tech ocean habitat, on its maiden voyage, hauls an artifact up from the ocean floor, which contains something not of this world, a disease of some sort, or perhaps something worse. Soon many passengers and crew are falling into a coma and the habitat's physician, Dr. McNulty, notices a strange pattern of infection emerging. In the sequels, *The Observers* (1988) and *A Reasonable World* (1991), it becomes clear that those who have survived McNulty's Disease are changed by it forever, made more rational, less violent. When the infection begins to make its way through the general population, doing so in a way which implies conscious intent, radical change occurs throughout the world. Compare Crichton's *Sphere* (1987) and Heinlein's *The Puppet Masters* (1951). (ML) [For other works by this author see chapter 3.]

4-237.   Kress, Nancy. An Alien Light. Arbor, 1987.
Humanity is at war with the alien Ged and apparently winning. Unable to understand the human propensity for violence, the Ged conduct an experiment on two isolated and primitive human societies that are hereditary enemies, hoping to uncover the key to defeating a more advanced human foe. They build a gigantic maze-like structure, lure humans from both cultures into it, and then study their interactions. Kress's characters are well developed and sympathetically portrayed. Her ideas on the nature of human violence are thoughtful, though she differs from many of the recent feminist SF writers who have examined the issue. Contrast Tepper's *The Gate to Women's Country* [4-453] and her *Raising the Stones* [4-454]. (ML)

4-238.   Kress, Nancy. Beggars in Spain. Morrow, 1993.
Based on a Hugo Award-winning novella, *Beggars in Spain* concerns the creation of a brilliant new race of genetically enhanced supermen who have no need to sleep. The Sleepless gradually take over the government of the United States, but must deal with increasing hostility from normal human beings. Kress breathes new life into one of the most tired SF plots. The excellent sequel is *Beggars and Choosers* (1984). Compare van Vogt's *Slan* [3-180] and Reed's *Black Milk* [4-353]. (ML)

4-239.   Kube-McDowell, Michael P. The Quiet Pools. Ace, 1990.
The purpose of the Diaspora Project is to send humanity to the stars. One starship has already left and a second, the *Memphis*, is nearly completed. Many people are opposed to the project, however, in part because of the

enormous cost and in part because of the ecological damage humanity might do to another planet. Anti-Project terrorism has become common. Chris McCutcheon, an archivist working on the *Memphis's* library, but not himself scheduled to take the journey, must make up his own mind as to the rightness of the Diaspora Project. He must also unravel the frightening biological secret that makes the project a necessity. Compare Vonda McIntyre's *Starfarers* (1989). (ML) HN, 1991

4-240. Lafferty, R(aphael) A(loysius). **Annals of Klepsis.** Ace, 1983.
A minor historian comes to Klepsis but is told that it has no history for him to write, because its existence is merely a prelude to the beginning of time, and the universe to which he belongs is only a figment of the imagination of its founder. Typical wild adventure with apocalyptic undertones. Compare Dick's *Galactic Pot-Healer* [4-138]. (BS)

4-241. Lafferty, R(aphael) A(loysius). **Apocalypses.** Pinnacle, 1977.
Two novels: *Where Have You Been, Sandaliotis?* and *The Three Armageddons of Enniscorthy Sweeny.* The first is a Fortean romance about a Mediterranean nation that is only occasionally accessible; the second a fine surrealist account of the apocalyptic reshaping of human destiny by an inspired artist. Marvelous fabulations by a writer sui generis. (BS)

***4-242.** Lafferty, R(aphael) A(loysius). **Fourth Mansions.** Ace, 1969.
An innocent tries to understand the enigmatic events and secret organizations that are symbolic incarnations of the forces embodied in the (highly problematic) moral progress and spiritual evolution of humankind. A bizarre tour de force; one of the finest examples of American avant-garde SF. Compare Zelazny's *This Immortal* [4-518] and Delany's *The Einstein Intersection* [4-129]. (BS)

***4-243.** Lafferty, R(aphael) A(loysius). **Nine Hundred Grandmothers.** Ace, 1970.
The first and best of Lafferty's collections, followed by *Strange Doings* (1971), *Does Anyone Else Have Something Further to Add?* (1974), *Ringing Changes* (1984), and various collections issued by small presses. Lafferty's shorter works tend to be highly distinctive and idiosyncratic, often mixing materials from Celtic or Amerindian folklore with SF motifs in order to produce tall stories with a philosophical bite. At his most stylized he is comparable to Calvino's *Cosmicomics* [4-91], but he is rarely so abstracted and his stories have a characteristic warmth as well as a breezy imaginative recklessness and a good deal of wit. (BS)

4-244.   Lafferty, R(aphael) A(loysius). **Past Master.** Ace, 1968.
St. Thomas More is snatched out of the past in order to save a decidedly ambiguous utopia—if its enemies can't prevent his doing so. A heartfelt but lighthearted exercise in the theater of the absurd: bewildering, funny, and thought-provoking. (BS) NN, 1968; HN, 1969

4-245.   Lafferty, R(aphael) A(loysius). **Space Chantey.** Ace, 1968.
The *Odyssey* transposed into bizarre space opera, omnivorously devouring bits and pieces from other mythologies, to construct a futuristic mythos open to all possibilities, where the outrageous can only be commonplace and characters who are innocent and worldly wise at the same time can stroll through the tallest tales ever told. (BS)

4-246.   Laidlaw, Marc. **Dad's Nuke.** Donald Fine, 1985.
Mock soap opera set in a near future where the domestic scene has been transformed by all manner of new technologies and every man's home is a fortress. Clever black comedy, taking themes from such novels as Brunner's *The Jagged Orbit* [4-71] to absurd extremes. (BS)

4-247.   Laidlaw, Marc. **Kalifornia.** St. Martin's, 1993.
In 21st-century United States, where nerve implants allow mass audiences to share the sense perceptions of media stars, a cyborgized baby (who may be an incarnation of the goddess Kali) threatens to become the omnipotent puppet-master of the "livewired" populace. Hilarious satire of media landscape, with a dark undercurrent; carries forward themes from *Neon Lotus* (1988). Compare the "Sense/Net" media of Gibson's *Mona Lisa Overdrive* [4-183]. (RL)

4-248.   Lake, David J(ohn). **The Right Hand of Dextra.** DAW, 1977.
A New Jerusalem is built in a green and pleasant alien land, where the emigrant pilgrims from Earth face the prospect of mingling and merging with the unfallen telepathic natives. In the sequel, *The Wildings of Westron* (1977), their hopes seem to have come to nothing because the legacy of their earthly existence has not been entirely set aside. Action-adventure SF with considerable metaphorical weight. Compare and contrast Lewis's *Out of the Silent Planet* and *Perelandra* [3-116]. (BS)

4-249.   Lanier, Stephen. **Hiero's Journey.** Chilton, 1973.
The world, wasted by nuclear war, is dominated by horrid mutants; the protagonist goes questing for the legendary computers that might save humankind. *The Unforsaken Hiero* (1983) presents his further adventures.

Boisterous picaresque adventure fiction, comparable to Pier Anthony's Xanth fantasy novels as well as SF postholocaust romances like Zelazny's *Damnation Alley* (1969). (BS)

4-250. Laumer, Keith. **Reward for Retief.** Baen, 1989.
Although he's written a wide variety of SF novels over a career spanning 30 years, Laumer will always be remembered primarily for his stories about the diplomat Jaime Retief. A somewhat smug variation on Heinlein's competent man, Retief invariably finds himself surrounded by stupid fellow diplomats, eccentric aliens, and near-psychotic military men. In this volume Retief is posted to a planet inhabited by xenophobic caterpillars on which is located a "trans-temporal flux," a strange phenomenon that allows reality to be changed by a thought. Other volumes in the series include *Envoy to New Worlds* (1963), *Retief's Ransom* (1971), *Retief: Diplomat at Arms* (1982), *Retief to the Rescue* (1983), and *The Return of Retief* (1985). For equally inspired silliness, compare Ron Goulart's *The Chameleon Corps* (1972) and *Starpirate's Brain* (1987). (ML)

*4-251. Le Guin, Ursula K(roeber). **Always Coming Home.** Harper, 1985.
An elaborate account of the culture of the Kesh—people living in "the Valley" in northern California in a postindustrial future. The main narrative sequence concerns the experience of a girl fathered on a woman of the Valley by an outsider, but there is a great wealth of supplementary detail to set this story in context; the environment, mythology, and arts of the imaginary society are scrupulously described. A fabulously rich work, the most elaborate exercise in imaginary anthropology ever undertaken, even including a cassette recording. Compare Wright's *Islandia* [3-197] and Brunner's *Stand on Zanzibar* [4-74]. (BS)

*4-252. Le Guin, Ursula K(roeber). **The Dispossessed: An Ambiguous Utopia.** Harper, 1974.
This story contrasts the poverty-stricken world of Anarres, whose political order is anarchist and egalitarian, with its rich neighbor Urras, from whose capitalist and competitive system the settlers of Anarres initially fled. A physicist who must travel from one world to the other serves as a self-conscious and anxious viewpoint character. A dense and very careful work, arguably the best example of how SF can be used for serious discussion of moral and political issues. The quality of the writing is also outstanding. Compare Lessing's Canopus in Archives series [4-264] and Hermann Hesse's *Magister Ludi* (1943). (BS) HW, 1973; JWC, 1974; NW, 1974

4-253. Le Guin, Ursula K(roeber). **The Lathe of Heaven.** Scribner, 1971.

A psychiatrist sets out to use a patient whose dreams can alter reality to create utopia, but in usurping this power he is gradually delivered into madness. Compare Dick's *Flow My Tears, the Policeman Said* [4-137] and *Ubik* [4-140]. (BS)

*4-254. Le Guin, Ursula K(roeber). **The Left Hand of Darkness.** Ace, 1969. Recommended ed.: Walker, 1994.

Humans on the world of Winter are hermaphrodite, able to develop male or female sexual characteristics during periodic phases of fertility. An envoy from the galactic community becomes embroiled in local politics and is forced by his experiences to reconsider his attitudes toward human relationships. Serious, meticulous, and well written, the book has been much discussed and praised because of its timely analytic interest in sexual politics. The 1994 Walker reprint includes a new afterword and approximately 60 pages in four appendixes. Compare Sturgeon's *Venus Plus X* (1960). (BS) HW, 1970; NW, 1969

*4-255. Le Guin, Ursula K(roeber). **The Wind's Twelve Quarters.** Harper, 1975.

The first of Le Guin's short fiction collections. The stories are various in theme but uniformly well written, ranging from the philosophical "Vaster Than Empires and More Slow" (HN, 1972) and the moving story of clone siblings, "Nine Lives" (NN, 1969), to a brief prelude to *The Dispossessed* [4-252], "The Day Before the Revolution" (NW, 1974; HN, 1975), and the dark fable, "The Ones Who Walk Away From Omelas" (HW, 1974). Within the SF field their elegance is matched by some of the work of Thomas Disch [4-145], but their earnest seriousness is without parallel. Le Guin's more recent collection, *Buffalo Gals and Other Animal Presences* (1987), includes a number of stories available in her earlier collections but is notable for her Hugo award-winning fantasy tale, "Buffalo Girls, Won't You Come Out Tonight?" (BS) *Locus* Award, 1976

4-256. Le Guin, Ursula K(roeber). **The Word for World Is Forest.** Berkley, 1976.

Short novel originally published in *Again, Dangerous Visions* [4-535]. Human colonists on an alien world cause untold damage to the innocent natives and their environment. A harsh comment on the ethics and politics of colonialism, making good use of anthropological perspectives. Compare Bishop's *Transfigurations* [4-53]. NN, 1972; HW, 1973

4-257. Lee, Tanith. **The Silver Metal Lover.** Nelson Doubleday, 1981.
A teenage girl finds the perfect soul mate—but how is she going to explain to her mother that he is a robot? An ironic inversion of del Rey's "Helen O'Loy" [3-60] told in earnest fashion, ultimately facing (as del Rey's story does not) the issues involved in its premise. (BS)

*4-258. Leiber, Fritz. **The Leiber Chronicles: Fifty Years of Fritz Leiber.** Dark Harvest, 1990. Ed. by Martin H. Greenberg.
This definitive collection of Fritz Leiber's science fiction and fantasy contains 44 stories that span the author's career, among them such acknowledged classics as "The Girl With the Hungry Eyes," "Coming Attraction," "A Bad Day for Sales," "The Man Who Made Friends with Electricity," "Gonna Roll Them Bones," "Ship of Shadows," and "Ill Met in Lankhmar." The book gives evidence, if such were needed, that Leiber is one of our very finest short story writers. Another excellent, if somewhat smaller, collection of the author's work is *The Ghost Light* (1964). Compare Ellison's *The Essential Ellison* [4-160]. (ML)

4-259. Leiber, Fritz. **The Wanderer.** Ballantine, 1964.
Worldwide disaster occurs when a mysterious, planet-sized spaceship appears out of nowhere, goes into Earth orbit, and begins to take the Moon apart, apparently for fuel. Leiber's characters and dialogue haven't held up all that well over the years, but his description of a large-scale catastrophe still impresses. Compare Wylie and Balmer's *When Worlds Collide* [2-156] and Greg Bear's *The Forge of God* [4-40]. (ML) HW, 1965 [For other works by this author see chapter 3.]

4-260. Lem, Stanislaw. **The Cyberiad: Fables for the Cybernetic Age.** Seabury, 1974. Trans. of *Cyberiada*, 1967, by Michael Kandel.
A series of fables about two robot "constructors" who build marvelous machines that usually fulfill their appointed tasks, but with unforeseen side effects. Futuristic folklore akin to Lafferty's *Space Chantey* [4-245] but with a satirical element more akin to the work of John Sladek. *Mortal Engines* (trans. 1977) is a similar collection of 14 tales. (BS)

4-261. Lem, Stanislaw. **The Futurological Congress: (From the Memoirs of Ijon Tichy).** Seabury, 1974. Trans. of *Ze wspomnien Ljona Tichego, Kongres Futrologiczny*, 1971, by Michael Kandel.
A story of Ijon Tichy, whose adventures can also be found in *The Star Diaries* (trans. 1976; also published as *Memoirs of a Space Traveller*). A convention of futurologists is disrupted by terrorism, and the release of psy-

chotropic chemicals hurls the protagonist into a dream of a violent and decadent dystopian future. Satire of the "no-good-will-come-of-it-all" school pioneered by Karel Čapek. (BS)

4-262.   Lem, Stanislaw. **His Master's Voice.** Secker, 1983. Trans. of *Glos pana*, 1968, by Michael Kandel.
A stream of "signals" from outer space is the subject of various attempted decodings and an excuse for all kinds of wild hypotheses about who might have sent the message and why, in which are reflected various human hopes and fears. Good satire; contrast Sagan's *Contact* [4-379]. (BS) [For other works by this author see chapter 3.]

4-263.   Lessing, Doris. **The Memoirs of a Survivor.** Octagon, 1974.
The heroine watches the slow disintegration of civilization while a teenage girl left in her care slowly matures, the two processes of decay and growth being carefully contrasted. Compare and contrast Disch's *334* [4-147]. (BS)

4-264.   Lessing, Doris. **Shikasta.** Cape, 1979.
First of the Canopus in Argos: Archives five-volume series. Shikasta is Earth, whose history—extending over millions of years—is here put into the cosmic perspective, observed by Canopeans who seem to be in charge of galactic history although responsible to some higher, impersonal authority. The sequels follow the exploits of various human cultures whose affairs are subtly influenced by the Canopeans; all share the remotely detached perspective that transforms the way in which individual endeavors are seen. Thoughtful and painstaking. Compare Stapledon's *Last and First Men* [2-119] and *Last Men in London* [2-119] and Pangborn's *A Mirror for Observers* [3-141]. (BS)

4-265.   Levin, Ira. **The Boys From Brazil.** Random, 1976.
An aging Nazi hunter discovers Dr. Mengele's plot to produce a whole series of Hitler clones when the boys' adoptive fathers have to be killed to reproduce the key event in Hitler's upbringing. A thriller that cleverly questions genetic determinism. (BS)

4-266.   Longyear, Barry B(rookes). **Manifest Destiny.** Berkley, 1980.
Collection including "Enemy Mine" (NW, 1979; HW, 1980), in which an alien and a human stranded on a hostile world must cooperate although their species are at war. "The Jaren" expresses a similar conviction that if different races cannot achieve a proper sympathy for one another the

results must be tragic. *The Tomorrow Testament* (1983) is a novel set against the same background as "Enemy Mine" and similarly deals with the cultivation of understanding; "Enemy Mine" itself was expanded to novel length by David Gerrold, the resultant 1983 book being issued as a collaboration, in connection with the film version. (BS)

4-267.   Longyear, Barry B(rookes). **Sea of Glass.** St. Martin's, 1987.
Longyear's most powerful novel and one of the grimmest stories of overpopulation ever written. When seven-year-old Thomas Windom's parents are discovered to have committed the crime of having an illegal child in the grossly overpopulated 21st century, they are put to death gruesomely on public television, and Thomas is sent to spend his life in a brutal labor camp. Compare Harrison's *Make Room! Make Room!* [4-200] and Brunner's *Stand on Zanzibar* [4-74]. (ML)

4-268.   Lundwall, Sam J(errie). **2018 A.D.: or, The King Kong Blues.** DAW, 1975.
In a polluted future world dominated by crass commercialism, the hero struggles to make a living in the corrupt advertising profession, while a bored oil sheik plays games with the world economy. Satirical black comedy with considerable bite. Compare Pohl and Kornbluth's *The Space Merchants* [3-147] and Snoo Wilson's *Spaceache* (1984). (BS)

4-269.   Lupoff, Richard A(llen). **Space War Blues.** Dell, 1978.
A fix-up novel in which human colonies fight a race war in space, disrupting the lives of the peaceful tribesmen who have adapted to life as spacefaring nomads. A deliberate mingling of the avant-garde and romantic aspects of 1970s SF, based on a short novel that appeared in Ellison's *Again, Dangerous Visions* [4-535]. (BS)

4-270.   Lynn, Elizabeth. **The Sardonyx Net.** Putnam, 1981.
On the one planet in the galactic community where slavery still survives, political adversaries fight over the drug that sustains the system. The chief protagonist is caught in a conflict of loyalties, finding his principles and emotions continually at odds as he moves through the convoluted plot. Colorful action-adventure with pretensions to moral seriousness. Compare Jayge Carr's *Navigator's Syndrome* (1983). (BS)

4-271.   MacLean, Katherine. **The Missing Man.** Berkley, 1975.
Expanded from a novella (NW, 1971). The psychic hero, although a social outcast, uses his powers for the public good but has still to achieve full

development of his superhuman nature. Compare Brunner's *The Whole Man* [4-75] and Sellings's *Telepath* (1962). (BS)

4-272.   Maddox, Tom. **Halo.** Tor, 1991.
Mikhail Gonzales, an auditor, is dispatched to the Halo space station to keep an eye on a daring but costly experiment, the attempt to download the personality of a dying man into the station's artificial intelligence, Aleph. The experiment is fraught with difficulties, but things get worse when the corporation that owns both the station and Aleph decides to pull the plug. *Halo* features a number of engaging characters, several of whom are artificial intelligences, and an engrossing examination of the nature of consciousness. Compare Lisa Mason's *Arachne* (1990), Gerrold's *When HARLIE Was One* [4-179], and Bear's *Queen of Angels* [4-41]. (ML)

*4-273.   Malzberg, Barry N(orman). **Beyond Apollo.** Random, 1972.
Winner of the first John W. Campbell Memorial Award (1973), causing controversy because it is a wickedly funny undermining of the SF myth of the conquest of space, of which Campbell was one of the principal promoters. The sole survivor of a Venus mission cannot explain what became of his companions. *The Falling Astronauts* (1971) and *Revelations* (1972) also challenge with mockery the values implicit in the space program. (BS)

4-274.   Malzberg, Barry N(orman). **The Cross of Fire.** Ace, 1982.
Expanded from the novella "Le Croix." A dissident in a future totalitarian state undergoes a kind of psychotherapy involving induced illusions, which allow him to play Christ, in which role he ardently but hopelessly seeks meaning through self-sacrifice. Mordant wit and graphic imagery combine in a powerful and disturbing story. Compare Moorcock's *Behold the Man* [4-302]. (BS)

4-275.   Malzberg, Barry N(orman). **Galaxies.** Pyramid, 1975.
Expanded from the novelette "A Galaxy Called Rome." The plot, deliberately designed as a hard SF story, involves a spaceship endangered by a black hole, on whose fate much depends; this is blended with an elaborate commentary on the psychology and sociology of SF writing, using the story as paradigm. It thus becomes a brilliantly self-conscious work of art, more telling in many ways than Malzberg's *Herovit's World* (1973). (BS)

4-276.   Malzberg, Barry N(orman). **The Man Who Loved the Midnight Lady.** Doubleday, 1980.
Perhaps the best of Malzberg's several collections; also outstanding is the

earlier *Down Here in the Dream Quarter* (1976). Most of Malzberg's stories contrive to be anguished and witty at the same time—classic examples of ironic weltschmertz. Compare the short fiction of John Sladek [4-421] and the work of nongenre writers like Bernard Malamud. (BS)

4-277. Malzberg, Barry N(orman). **The Remaking of Sigmund Freud.** Ballantine, 1985.

A fix-up novel featuring an alternate world where Freud psychoanalyzes Emily Dickinson from afar and is assassinated by a disappointed patient, and a future where he is reincarnated aboard a spaceship to save its crew members from the kind of extraterrestrial angst that was suffered by the protagonist of *Beyond Apollo* [4-273]. Lacks the fluency of Malzberg's early novels but gains in complexity by way of compensation. Compare Jeremy Leven's *Satan* (1982). (BS) NN, 1985

4-278. Mann, Phillip. **The Eye of the Queen.** Gollancz, 1982.

A painstaking account of contact between humans and a very strange alien culture. The text consists of a diary written by a scientist who tries to understand the aliens, interrupted by a commentary by his assistant. Slow-moving but intriguing and commendably ambitious. Compare Bishop's *Transfigurations* [4-53] and Cherryh's *Voyager in Night* (1984). (BS)

4-279. Mann, Phillip. **Wulfsyarn: A Mosaic.** Gollancz, 1990.

In this strangely metaphysical and heavily symbolic tale, Captain Jon Wilberfoss, commanding the starship *Nightingale*, is sent on a mission of mercy to return home hundreds of refugees who were scattered across the galaxy by the recently ended War of Ignorance. En route, the *Nightingale* inexplicably vanishes, only to reappear a year later, ruined and devoid of life with the exception of its captain, who has gone mad. Wulf, an artificial intelligence that has devoted itself to Wilberfoss, must try to heal him and discover what really happened. Compare Wallace's *Croyd* [4-481] and Farmer's *The Unreasoning Mask* [4-166]. (ML)

4-280. Martin, George R(aymond) R(ichard). **Dying of the Light.** Simon & Schuster, 1977.

On a wandering world, briefly brought to light by its temporary association with a sun, several races have built cities for a great festival. The self-pitying protagonist pursues his lost love here and becomes involved with the alien tribe into which she has married as the long night closes in again. Compare Elizabeth Lynn's *A Different Light* (1978). (BS) HN, 1978

4-281.   Martin, George R(aymond) R(ichard). **A Song for Lya and Other Stories.** Avon, 1976.

The title story of this collection (HW, 1975) is one of several notable studies of an alien species whose biology is such that their religious faith in life after death has material foundation. One of the protagonists goes native to take advantage of this opportunity, but her lover cannot. Martin is generally at his best in medium-length stories. *Nightflyers* (HN, 1981; reprinted as a book, 1985) is another story of contact with mysterious aliens, while the title story of the collection *Sandkings* (1981; HW, 1980) is a memorable account of insectile "pets" learning to see their "owners" in a new light. His other collections are *Songs of Stars and Shadows* (1977), *Songs the Dead Men Sing* (1983), and, most recently, *Portraits of His Children* (1987), whose Nebula-winning title story concerns an author whose stories quite literally come alive. (BS/ML)

4-282.   Martin, George R(aymond) R(ichard), and Lisa Tuttle. **Windhaven.** Timescape, 1981.

A fix-up novel including "One-Wing" (HN, 1981). On a stormy world humans struggle to survive on the islands of an archipelago, their communications depending on the flyers who use artificial wings. The heroine has a turbulent time on the ground as well as in the air. Compare McCaffrey's Pern series [4-289]. (BS)

4-283.   Martin, Valerie. **Mary Reilly.** Doubleday, 1990.

All the actual science fiction content in this brilliant revisioning of Robert Louis Stevenson's classic novella exists off stage and in the mind of the reader. The title character is Dr. Jekyll's maid, a kind, competent, but sadly damaged young woman who is herself the victim of a monster, her father's alcoholism. Despite their differences in class and education, Mary's background makes her an ideal companion for Dr. Jekyll as he journeys into the heart of evil. Compare Stevenson's *The Strange Case of Dr. Jekyll and Mr. Hyde* [1-86]. (ML)

4-284.   Masson, David. **The Caltraps of Time.** Faber, 1968.

Notable short stories by a writer associated with Moorcock's *New Worlds*, including the fine "Traveller's Rest," about a war fought on a world where time passes at different rates in different places. Polished and original. Compare Bayley's *The Knights of the Limits* [4-37] and James Sallis's *A Few Last Words* (1964). (BS)

4-285.   Matheson, Richard. **Bid Time Return.** Viking, 1975.

Timeslip romance in which a young author is allowed to meet (briefly) the actress from the past with whose photographic image he's fallen in love. Compare Finney's *Time and Again* [4-167]. (BS) World Fantasy Award, 1976 [For other works by this author see chapter 3.]

4-286. May, Julian. **The Many-Colored Land.** Houghton, 1981.
Misfits flee by time warp from the 22nd century, ending up in the Pliocene, where they and other time travelers are caught up in a conflict between two alien species, members of an interstellar civilization called the Galactic Milieu. Although May's language is occasionally overly elaborate, the rich background is well worked out and her characters are engaging. The Pliocene novels were followed by *Intervention* (1987), a transitional novel exploring events on Earth in the 20th and 21st centuries and leading to the Galactic Milieu Trilogy, the first volume of which, *Jack the Bodiless* (1992), deals with contacts between Earth and the Milieu in the near future. (ML/BS) HN, 1982; NN, 1981

4-287. McAllister, Bruce. **Dream Baby.** Tor, 1989.
Based on an award-nominated short story, *Dream Baby* is the disturbing tale of Mary Damico, a trauma nurse in Vietnam who, discovered to have psychic powers that appear under extreme stress, finds herself co-opted into a top-secret, CIA-led experiment in parapsychology. Eventually she becomes one of a team of psychics sent on a grueling and desperate terrorist mission into North Vietnam. At least some of McAllister's material is apparently based on the real experiences of men and women who served in Vietnam. Compare Elizabeth Ann Scarborough's *The Healer's War* (1988) and Lucius Shepard's *Life During Wartime* [4-402]. (ML)

4-288. McAuley, Paul J. **Four Hundred Billion Stars.** Ballantine, 1988.
Explorers from Earth discover a planet that doesn't seem old enough geologically to have developed its complex native ecology. Adding to the mystery, abandoned, hive-like cities are discovered, even though the dominate life-form, the nomadic herders, seem to be only semi-sentient. Humanity is currently engaged in an interplanetary war elsewhere in the galaxy, and the naval officers in charge of the expedition fear there may be some connection between the primitive herders and humanity's enemy. This seems unlikely until someone notices that the abandoned hive-cities are coming to life and the herders are beginning to change their age-old behavior patterns. McAuley's exploration of the complex herder species is fascinating and his protagonist, the astronomer Dorthy Yoshida, an unwilling psychic, is well developed. *Eternal Light* (1991) is a direct sequel to *Four Hundred Billion Stars* and is every bit as good. *Of the Fall* (1989), titled *Secret Harmonies* (1991) in its British edition, is a solid, but relatively minor tale

set in the same universe as the other two novels. All three books, along with McAuley's first short story collection, *The King of the Hill* (1991), demonstrate the author's genius for creating fascinating aliens. Compare Gregory Benford's *Great Sky River* [4-44] and its sequels. (ML) Philip K. Dick Award, 1989

4-289.   McCaffrey, Anne. **Dragonflight.** Ballantine, 1968.
First of the Pern series, combining the novellas "Weyr Search" (NN, 1967; HW, 1968) and "Dragonrider" (NW, 1968; HN, 1969). Immediate sequels are *Dragonquest* (1971, HN, 1972) and the best-selling *The White Dragon* (1978; HN, 1979); these novels appear in an omnibus as *The Dragonriders of Pern* (1978). An associated trilogy aimed at younger readers is *Dragonsong* (1976), *Dragonsinger* (1977), and *Dragondrums* (1979) [5-109]. Later novels set on Pern include *Moreta, Dragonlady of Pern* (1983; HN, 1984), *Nerika's Story* (1986), *Dragonsdawn* (1988), *The Renegades of Pern* (1989), and *All the Weyrs of Pern* (1991; HN, 1992). Pern is a lost colony where dragons telepathically bonded to male riders breathe fire to burn up the spores of deadly vegetable invaders that appear at long intervals. The dragons can also travel through time whenever the plots require a deus ex machina. Despite the commercial success of later volumes, the quality and originality of the books decline somewhat as the series proceeds, although the most recent addition, *All the Weyrs of Pern*, represents something of an improvement. The author appears to have achieved in these novels a mode and intensity of feeling that broke new ground in fitting SF to the imaginative needs of alienated teenage girls, thus helping to break the masculine mold of most previous SF. Compare Jacqueline Lichtenberg's Sime/Gen series, beginning with *House of Zeor* (1974) and C. J. Cherryh's Morgaine series, beginning with *Gates of Ivrel* (1976), both of which show McCaffrey's influence. (BS/ML)

4-290.   McCaffrey, Anne. **The Ship Who Sang.** Walker, 1969.
A fix-up novel in which the severely disabled heroine is the cyborg guidance system of a spaceship, in which role she can construct more fulfilling relationships with male pilots than she ever could have hoped to find in her fleshly incarnation. The initial story is genuinely poignant, but the later sections are more strained. McCaffrey has recently published a number of sequels, books largely written by a junior collaborator based on her outlines. These include *PartnerShip* (1992) with Margaret Ball, *The Ship Who Searched* (1992) with Mercedes Lackey, and *The City Who Fought* (1993) with S. M. Stirling. Compare McIntyre's *Superluminal* [4-296] and Jennings's *The Bug Life Chronicles* [4-214]. (BS/ML) [For other works by this author see chapter 5.]

4-291. McDonald, Ian. **The Broken Land.** Bantam, 1992. U.K. title: *Hearts, Hands and Voices,* 1992 (first edition).

The Broken Land is an oppressed colonial nation, ripped apart by strife between its two major religious groups, the Proclaimers and the Confessors. It's a land of amazing biotechnology, where new homes can be grown and where the heads of the newly dead can be planted in pots and continue to offer their wisdom to their families. It's a land of terrible suffering, revolution, mass deportations, and the murder of innocents. *The Broken Land* is also an allegory of sorts for McDonald's homeland, Northern Ireland. This is a beautifully written but at times very painful novel. Compare Geoff Ryman's *The Unconquered Country* (1987) and Paul Park's *Starbridge Chronicles* [4-327]. (ML)

4-292. McDonald, Ian. **Desolation Road.** Bantam, 1988.

Lost in the desert of a terraformed Mars after having met an alien, Dr. Alimantando decides to found a settlement. To Desolation Road are attracted many of the red planet's eccentrics, refugees, and dreamers. As the town grows, conflicts arise between those with differing visions of its future. This beautifully written, somewhat mystical, and at times very witty tale, has occasionally been criticized as a pastiche of Bradbury, García Márquez, and early Roger Zelazny. Compare Bradbury's *The Martian Chronicles* [3-32]. Contrast Robinson's more realistic *Red Mars* [4-366]. (ML) *Locus* Award, 1989

4-293. McDonald, Ian. **Empire Dreams.** Bantam, 1988.

A first collection by one of the most brilliant new stylists to enter the field in years. Included here are "King of Morning, Queen of Day," the basis for McDonald's Philip K. Dick Award-winning fantasy novel of the same name, as well as the Nebula Award-nominated "Unfinished Portrait of the King of Pain by Van Gogh," "The Catherine Wheel," "The Island of the Dead," and six others. McDonald's second collection, *Speaking in Tongues* (1992), is equally impressive. For sheer poetic exuberance compare the short fiction of Harlan Ellison. (ML)

4-294. McHugh, Maureen F. **China Mountain Zhang.** Tor, 1992.

The title character of McHugh's first novel is a Chinese American living in a United States that has fallen to third-world status just as China has risen, through apparently peaceful means, to dominate the world. In this hierarchical culture, Zhang's ancestry automatically places him above most Caucasians in status (though below native-born Chinese). Zhang, however, has a couple of dirty secrets. First, he's only half-Chinese, though his parents had him genetically adjusted to hide his Hispanic ancestry.

Second, he's gay, and both China and Chinese-dominated America are puritanical societies. As the story progresses, we follow Zhang's rise from construction worker to successful architect. The novel's two greatest strengths lie in its depiction of a believable and sympathetic gay character and in its equally believable portrayal of a Chinese-dominated 21st century. Besides receiving nominations for the Hugo and Nebula, *China Mountain Zhang* won both the Tiptree Award and the *Locus* Award for best first novel. Compare Wingrove's *Chung Kuo* [4-508]. (ML) HN, 1993; NN, 1992

4-295.   McIntyre, Vonda N(eel). **Dreamsnake.** Houghton Mifflin, 1978.
Novel based on the short story "Of Mist and Grass and Sand" (NW, 1973; HN, 1974). A healer whose instruments are metabolically engineered snakes must journey to a city that has contacts with the star worlds in the hope of replacing the dreamsnake that eases the pain of her clients. A convincing mixture of stoicism and sentimentality, rather highly strung. Compare Tiptree's *Up the Walls of the World* [4-458]. (BS) NW, 1978; HW, 1979, *Locus* Award, 1979

4-296.   McIntyre, Vonda N(eel). **Superluminal.** Houghton Mifflin, 1984.
Novel based on the novella "Aztecs" (NN, 1977; HN, 1978). The heroine surrenders her real heart for an artificial one in order to become a starship pilot. Her subsequent struggles against the effects of this voluntary alienation ally her with other social outsiders, but in the end she wins a spectacular victory over the natural and technological handicaps afflicting humankind. Intense to the point of feverishness. Compare Cordwainer Smith's "Scanners Live in Vain" [4-427]. (BS)

4-297.   McKillip, Patricia A(nne). **Fool's Run.** Warner, 1987.
Cyberpunk SF by a writer better known for her high fantasy. Several years ago Terra Viridian murdered some 1,500 innocent people in response to an overwhelming but unexplained vision. Now, apparently psychotic, she bides her time in the Underground, a grim orbital penal colony. When a high-tech band is brought up to the Underground to give a performance, the stage is set for some very strange goings-on. Although the plot of *Fool's Run* is occasionally a bit confusing, this is a beautifully written novel with lots of lush visual imagery. Compare Pat Cadigan's *Synners* [4-89] and Norman Spinrad's *Little Heroes* [4-430]. (ML) [For other works by this author see chapter 5.]

4-298.   McQuay, Mike. **Memories.** Bantam, 1987.
David Wolf, a psychiatrist with a troubled personal history, is approached

by Silv, a woman from the far future, who asks his help. An experiment in pharmacotherapy has gone wrong in her own age, and an aggressive, unstable soldier, Hersh, has escaped into the distant past where, as Napoleon, he is using his knowledge of military tactics to change history. Silv wants Wolf to follow Hersh into the past and convince the soldier to enter therapy with him. Although a bit unwieldy in its construction, this Philip K. Dick Award runner-up is both wise and emotionally satisfying. Compare Willis's *Doomsday Book* [4-501] and Moorcock's *Behold the Man* [4-302]. (ML)

4-299. Merle, Robert. **Malevil.** Simon & Schuster, 1974. Trans. of *Malevil*, 1972, by Derek Coltman.

Survivors of a nuclear holocaust are drawn to the medieval castle of Malevil, where a charismatic leader supervises the progress of their community. Dense and thoughtful. Compare Stewart's *Earth Abides* [3-169]. (BS) JWC, 1974

4-300. Moffett, Judith. **Pennterra.** Congdon & Weed, 1987.

The planet Pennterra was originally settled by Quakers who were entirely willing to accept the native *hrossa*'s strict rules for the maintenance of their environment. Trouble breaks out, however, when a shipload of non-Quaker colonists arrive and begin tearing up the landscape. Moffett's desire to give a powerful environmental message occasionally overwhelms her artistic sense in this first novel, but her strong character development and poetic style never falter. Compare Slonczewski's *Still Forms on Foxfield* (1980) and *The Wall Around Eden* [4-427]. (ML)

4-301. Moffett, Judith. **The Ragged World: A Novel of the Hefn on Earth.** St. Martin's, 1991.

A starship commanded by the alien Gafr, but crewed by a different race, the Hefn, returns to Earth to retrieve Hefn mutineers left behind centuries ago and to stop humanity's destruction of the ecosystem. The aliens decree that no more human babies will be born until we cease polluting. Originally a series of short stories, including two award nominees, this fix-up novel is a powerful indictment of humanity's ability to foul its own nest. In the more unified sequel, *Time, Like an Ever-Rolling Stream* (1992), two young people grow up in the more primitive world that has resulted from the Hefn's stay on Earth. Moffett continues her ecological theme, but also deals movingly with the topic of sexual abuse. Compare Slonczewski's *The Wall Around Eden* [4-427]. (ML)

*4-302. Moorcock, Michael. **Behold the Man.** Allison & Busby, 1969.
Expanded from a novella (NW, 1967). The alienated hero travels back to
the time of Christ in the hope of enlightenment, but he finds Jesus
grotesquely ill-fitted to the role of messiah and must take his place. Darkly
ironic; a fascinating exercise in the psychology of martyrdom. Compare
Malzberg's *The Cross of Fire* [4-274]. (BS)

4-303. Moorcock, Michael. **The Black Corridor.** Mayflower, 1969.
Novel actually written in collaboration with Hillary Bailey, whose contribution is acknowledged in some later (revised) editions. A crewman aboard
a starship carrying frozen survivors away from a ruined Earth is beset by
guilt-stricken dreams and delusions. An innovative work of avant-garde SF.
Compare Cherryh's *Voyager in Night* (1984) and Stableford's *Man in a Cage*
(1976). (BS)

4-304. Moorcock, Michael. **The Cornelius Chronicles.** Avon, 1977.
Omnibus containing *The Final Programme* (1969), *A Cure for Cancer* (1971),
The English Assassin (1972), and *The Condition of Muzak* (1977), the first
three in slightly revised form. Jerry Cornelius, the contemporary and
near-future avatar of the multifaceted Moorcockian hero, features in the
tetralogy in various roles: secret agent, messiah, corpse, dreary teenager,
and even a negative image of himself. The first novel begins as a parody of
heroic fiction, its events running parallel to two of Moorcock's early Elric
stories, but moves on to parody other themes in popular fiction. The middle volumes present a kaleidoscopic display of 20th-century motifs, and
the fourth moves on again to subvert the fantasy elements in the first
three and add its own theme of tragedy, symbolized with the aid of images
drawn from harlequinade. The series is a sprawling masterpiece: a dream
story loaded with all the threads of contemporary consciousness and modern mythology, bearing an appropriate burden of nightmare and irony.
The ubiquitous Jerry can also be found in associated materials (see series
listing in chapter 15). (BS)

4-305. Moorcock, Michael. **The Dancers at the Edge of Time.** Granada,
1981.
Omnibus containing *An Alien Heat* (1972), *The Hollow Lands* (1974), and
The End of All Songs (1976). At the end of time all-powerful immortals
have no problems except how to amuse themselves, which they do in exotically contrived fashion, mining the past for its quaint inspirations.
Colorful, witty, and boisterously decadent, with a certain distinctive
weltschmerz. See series listing for related works. (BS)

4-306. Morrow, James. **This Is the Way the World Ends.** Holt, 1986.
Satirical apocalyptic fantasy in which the few survivors of the holocaust are put on trial by those who would have lived if only their ancestors had ordered their affairs more reasonably. Clever and elegant. Compare Vonnegut's *Cat's Cradle* [3-190]. (BS)

4-307. Murakami, Haruki. **Hard-Boiled Wonderland and the End of the World.** Kodansha, 1991. Trans. of *Sekai No Owari to Hado-Boirudo Wandarando* by Alfred Birnbaum.
An unnamed, but decidedly hard-boiled detective takes on a strange case involving a brilliant, but naïve elderly scientist, his beautiful, apparently mute granddaughter, some very strange technology, and what appear to be kappas, traditional Japanese monsters. In alternating chapters a different unnamed narrator visits a town at the end of the world, where things aren't what they seem and unicorns are common. This strange and surrealistic novel is heavily influenced by the cyberpunks. Compare Neal Stephenson's *Snow Crash* [4-437] and Michael Swanwick's *Stations of the Tide* [4-450]. (ML)

4-308. Murphy, Pat. **The City, Not Long After.** Doubleday, 1989.
San Francisco has been decimated by plague and virtually abandoned. Those who remain are mostly artists and counterculture types. Word arrives, however, that a power-mad military officer has determined to retake the city, and a mixed coalition of oddballs, mystics, and artists forms to defeat him. Murphy manages to carry the spirit of the late 1960s into the late 1980s with considerable success. Compare two similar works, Goldstein's *A Mask for the General* [4-187], and Russo's *Subterranean Gallery* [4-376]. (ML)

4-309. Murphy, Pat. **Points of Departure.** Bantam, 1990.
Nineteen short stories by a writer whose work ranges widely over the genres of science fiction, fantasy, and horror. Among the best are the Nebula and *Locus* Award-winning novelette, "Rachel in Love," the heartbreaking story of a young girl trapped in a chimpanzee's body; the Nebula-nominated "Dead Men on TV"; "Bones"; and "His Vegetable Wife." Compare Swanwick's *Gravity's Angels* [4-449] and Fowler's *Artificial Things* [4-172]. (ML) Philip K. Dick Award, 1991

4-310. Nelson, Ray Faraday. **Timequest.** Tor, 1986.
A revised and extended version of *Blake's Progress* (1975). The heroine is the wife of William Blake, who becomes his guide and mentor in the

dreamlike excursions into time and space that provide the basis for his visionary poems. An unusual and idiosyncratic philosophical adventure story, crafted with care. Nelson's concern with utopianism is displayed more crudely in *Then Beggars Could Ride* (1976) and negatively in a novel of rebellion against dystopian organization, *The Prometheus Man* (1982). (BS)

4-311.   Newman, Kim. **The Night Mayor.** Simon & Schuster, 1989.
The brilliant but psychopathic criminal Truro Daine, incarcerated for life on 8,921 counts of first-degree murder, has used advanced dream technology to escape into virtual reality, and the government sends two agents in after him. They discover a run-down city like something out of Cornell Woolrich or American *film noir*, populated exclusively by characters from classic gangster films, where it is always 2:30 in the morning, where it's always raining, and where Daine is the all-powerful title character. Newman is an expert on horror movies and *film noir* and it shows in this brilliant tour de force of a first novel. Compare Zelazny's *The Dream Master* [4-515] and David Thompson's *Suspects* (1985). (ML)

4-312.   Niven, Larry. **The Integral Trees.** Ballantine, 1984.
The descendants of humans shipwrecked in an alien solar system eke out a difficult living in a bizarre worldless ecosystem. One group, forced into exile, undergoes a series of adventures culminating in their meeting with a strange spacefarer. The plot is mainly a vehicle to display the intricately worked out environment; the book is thus an imaginative exercise comparable to *Ringworld* [4-316]. The 1987 sequel, *The Smoke Ring*, continues the story and further explores the unusual environment. Compare Baxter's *Raft* [4-35]. (BS) HN, 1985; NN, 1984; *Locus* Award, 1985

4-313.   Niven, Larry. **The Long ARM of Gil Hamilton.** Ballantine, 1976.
Collection of novellas featuring a hero whose amputated and replaced arm is more versatile in spirit than it was in the flesh. Although the series is integrated into the Known Space future history they are earthbound mysteries set against the background of the development of organ-bank technology, and they are among the finest examples of the SF detective story. The series continues in *The Patchwork Girl* (1980), an excellent story of futuristic detective work set on the moon. The criminal activities usually involve "organlegging," which also features in other short stories and in the Known Space novel *A Gift From Earth* (1969). (BS)

4-314.   Niven, Larry. **Neutron Star.** Ballantine, 1968.
The first collection of Niven's hard SF stories, early works developing the

Known Space future history. The title story (HW, 1967) is one of several in which Beowulf Shaeffer is blackmailed into taking on a dangerous mission in an exotic environment. The bibliography of Niven's collections is complex, stories being recombined into some later selections, but *The Shape of Space* (1969), *All the Myriad Ways* (1971), and *A Hole in Space* (1974) preserve most of the important early fiction. *Tales of Known Space* (1975) is useful for the notes about the future-historical background. The title story of *Inconstant Moon* (1973) (HW, 1972; also in *All the Myriad Ways*) is a marvelously vivid story in which people on the night side of the world realize that the sun has gone nova when the Moon becomes much brighter. A more recent, but relatively minor collection is *Limits* (1985), which includes a number of collaborative stories. *N-Space* (1990) and *Playgrounds of the Mind* (1991) are retrospective collections covering Niven's entire career. These volumes include essays, novel excerpts, appreciations by other writers, and bibliographies, but leave out some of Niven's better early stories. (BS/ML)

4-315. Niven, Larry. **Protector.** Ballantine, 1973.
Part of the Known Space series. Here the Pak Protectors, remote ancestors of humankind and builders of *Ringworld* [4-316], are introduced; the discovery of a Pak ship leads to the creation of a human/alien "hybrid" whose subsequent career threatens to alter the course of human destiny. (BS) HN, 1974

*4-316. Niven, Larry. **Ringworld.** Ballantine, 1970.
An exploration team consisting of an exotic mix of humans and aliens investigates a huge artifact occupying a planetary orbit around a sun. A novel of imaginary tourism; its real hero is the artifact, whose nature is further explored and explained in *Ringworld Engineers* (1980; HN, 1981). Compare Clarke's *Rendezvous With Rama* [4-109]. (BS) HW, 1971; NW, 1970

4-317. Niven, Larry, and Steven Barnes. **The Descent of Anansi.** Tor, 1982.
Near-future melodrama in which a space shuttle delivering a monomolecular cable from the Moon to Earth becomes a pawn in a political power play. Taut and suspenseful (in more ways than one). Compare Bova's *Colony* [4-59]. (BS)

4-318. Niven, Larry, and Jerry Pournelle. **Footfall.** Ballantine, 1985.
The aliens displaced from the outline of *Lucifer's Hammer* [4-319] come into their own here, in an invasion story that aspires to be the definitive

modern version of the theme, just as *The Mote in God's Eye* [4-320] attempted to provide a definitive first-contact story. Spectacular in scale and
detail. Compare Wells's *The War of the Worlds* [1-105] and Heinlein's *The
Puppet Masters* (1951) to put the story in historical perspective. (BS) HN,
1986

4-319.   Niven, Larry, and Jerry Pournelle. **Lucifer's Hammer.** Playboy,
1977.
The world is badly damaged by a meteor strike, but the survivors manage
to get things going again. An SF book that cashed in on the Hollywood
boom in (more localized) disaster stories and became a bestseller, though
the aliens who were in the original outline had to be left out. A tough-
minded exercise in imaginary social Darwinism. Compare and contrast R.
C. Sherriff's *The Hopkins Manuscript* (1939). (BS)

4-320.   Niven, Larry, and Jerry Pournelle. **The Mote in God's Eye.** Simon
& Schuster, 1974.
Superior space opera in which Earth's interstellar navy contacts and does
battle with an enormously hostile alien race. The scenes of space warfare
are well handled, and the alien Moties are fascinating. The sequel, *The
Gripping Hand* (1993), is more mundane. Compare C. J. Cherryh's
Downbelow Station [4-103] or Vernor Vinge's *A Fire Upon the Deep* [4-474].
(ML)

4-321.   Nolan, William F(rancis), and George Clayton Johnson. **Logan's
Run.** Dial, 1967.
In a world where population control requires euthanasia at 21, a police-
man puts to good use his expertise in hunting down those who won't sub-
mit when he becomes a "runner" himself. A slickly written and lively
entertainment, horribly mangled in the long-delayed film version.
Inferior sequels by Nolan alone are *Logan's World* (1977) and *Logan's
Search* (1980). (BS)

4-322.   Ore, Rebecca. **Becoming Alien.** Tor, 1987.
Tom Red Clay, a smart young hillbilly kid with unsavory relatives, is kid-
napped/rescued by aliens, emissaries from a galactic federation sent to
Earth undercover to judge whether humanity is ready for contact. Tom
starts out as a test case and eventually becomes a recruit in the federation's alien contact agency. Ore is a fine stylist and her characters, both
human and alien, are well developed and quirky. Two more volumes in
the series are *Being Alien* (1989), and the less well-known but equally good

Human to Human (1990). Compare Brin's *The Uplift War* [4-68] and James White's *Hospital Station* (1992) and sequels. (ML)

4-323. Palmer, David R. **Emergence.** Bantam, 1984.
A juvenile genius is enabled by her superhumanity to survive a nuclear holocaust and sets off across the blasted United States to search for others of her kind. Compare George O. Smith's *The Fourth "R"* (1959). (BS) HN, 1986

***4-324.** Pangborn, Edgar. **Davy.** St. Martin's, 1964.
Nuclear war is now 300 years in the past, but the world is still a primitive place. The title character begins life as a bondsman and grows to become a great leader. Though his intent is serious, Pangborn's tone is satirical and a bit bawdy throughout. Numerous critics have noticed similarities between *Davy* and Fielding's *Tom Jones.* Set in the same postholocaust world are *The Judgment of Eve* (1966), *The Company of Glory* (1975), and stories found in the collection *Still I Persist in Wondering* (1978). Compare Miller's *A Canticle for Leibowitz* [3-125] and Crowley's *Engine Summer* [4-122]. (ML) [For other works by this author see chapter 3.]

***4-325.** Panshin, Alexei. **Rite of Passage.** Ace, 1968.
The heroine belongs to a starfaring culture, and her rite de passage into adulthood involves her descent into a colony world whose culture is very different. A homage to Heinlein's juveniles but more carefully and painstakingly constructed than most of his models; compare especially his *Tunnel in the Sky* [5-65]. (BS) HN, 1969; NW, 1968

4-326. Park, Paul. **Coelestis.** HarperCollins, 1993.
On a distant world human colonists have converted the natives to Christianity, molded them into a servant class, and used surgery and drug therapy to transform them into close approximations of human beings. Simon, an aide to the British consul, and Katherine, a talented and beautiful native who can pass for human, are captured by terrorists. Under the press of circumstances they fall in love. Then Katherine, deprived of her regular drug therapy, begins to change and, worse yet, to see things the Earthman can't. Comparisons between Park's aliens and the native peoples of Africa and Australia are obvious, but his superb style and his strong characters make this novel much more than a mere polemic. Compare Bradbury's *Martian Chronicles* [3-32] and Resnick's *Paradise* [4-356]. (ML)

4-327. Park, Paul. **Soldiers of Paradise.** Arbor, 1987.
On a planet called Earth by its inhabitants, though it and its solar system

differ dramatically from our own, the seasons last for lifetimes and, as in Aldiss's Helliconia series [4-6], they change with such violence that entire civilizations are in danger of dying or being transformed. Two misfit members of the Starbridge family, the planet's ruling class, wander through the confusion and growing revolution of the oncoming springtime, pondering the ills of their society. *Soldiers of Paradise* is nearly plotless, but its beautifully wrought prose, carefully etched characters, and strong moral sense make it an unforgettable experience. Two fine sequels are *Sugar Rain* (1989) and *The Cult of Loving Kindness* (1991). Compare Aldiss's Helliconia series, Swanwick's *Stations of the Tide* [4-450], and Wolfe's *Book of the New Sun* [4-510]. (ML)

4-328. Percy, Walker. **Love in the Ruins: The Adventures of a Bad Catholic at a Time Near the End of the World.** Farrar, 1971.
Dr. Thomas More invents a device that might cure the world of its chemically induced collective insanity, but things are too far gone. In the sequel, *The Thanatos Syndrome* (1987), More deals with a series of strange phenomena, including female patients who exhibit unusual sexual behavior and a conspiracy to improve humanity by placing drugs in the water supply. Allegorical social comment. Compare Jeremy Leven's *Satan* (1982). (BS/ML)

4-329. Piercy, Marge. **He, She, and It.** Knopf, 1991. U.K. title: *Body of Glass*, 1992.
Scarred by a painful divorce and custody fight, Shira Shipman leaves her 21st-century urban, male-dominated corporation and returns to the egalitarian Jewish enclave of Tikva, where she takes part in the programming of a revolutionary and illegal new cyborg named Yod. As part of Yod's education, Shira's grandmother narrates the story of the 17th-century Prague golem; the lives of the two artificial beings have obvious connections. Piercy uses many techniques borrowed from the cyberpunks and, although her usage is occasionally clumsy, it's fun to watch her put them into the service of ideas radically different from those generally touched on by Gibson and company. Compare Gibson's *Neuromancer* [4-184] and Asimov's "The Bicentennial Man" [4-18]. (ML) Arthur C. Clarke Award, 1992

*4-330. Piercy, Marge. **Woman on the Edge of Time.** Knopf, 1976.
A Hispanic-American mother undergoes experimental psychosurgery. She makes psychic contact with the 22nd-century world that has resulted from a feminist revolution whose success may depend on the subversion of the

experiments in which she is involved. Outstanding for the elaborate description of the future utopia and the graphic representation of the inhumanity inherent in the way that contemporary people can and do treat one another. Compare Russ's *The Female Man* [4-375]. (BS)

4-331. Piserchia, Doris. **Mister Justice.** Ace, 1973.
A time traveling vigilante superman tires of delivering criminals to institutionalized justice and takes on the role of judge and executioner. An intense and striking work. Compare Bester's *Tiger! Tiger!* [3-19]. (BS)

4-332. Platt, Charles. **The Silicon Man.** Bantam, 1991.
An FBI agent finds himself captured by unscrupulous scientists who download his mind into a computer and murder his body. The scientist who heads the illicit project has set up his own little virtual reality kingdom and the agent at first finds himself a helpless prisoner, but determines to fight back. Platt's depiction of a computer-generated environment comes across as much more believable than William Gibson's cyberspace. Compare Gibson's *Neuromancer* [4-184] and Philip K. Dick's *Eye in the Sky* [3-64]. (ML)

*4-333. Pohl, Frederik. **Gateway.** St. Martin's, 1977.
Mankind "inherits" the stars by finding and exploiting (with considerable difficulty) the starships and gadgets left behind by the alien Heechee. The flippant, guilt-ridden hero has greatness thrust upon him by degrees as he picks up his winnings in the game of Russian roulette that men must play in gaining control of the Heechee artifacts. His luck continues to hold in *Beyond the Blue Event Horizon* (1980; HN, 1981; NN, 1980), which ends with his finding out why the Heechee ran away. This is fine contemporary space opera, with some neatly ironic characterization. Less successful are the later volumes in the series, *Heechee Rendezvous* (1984), in which the aliens finally arrive on stage, *Annals of the Heechee* (1987), and *The Gateway Trip: Tales and Vignettes of the Heechee* (1990). (BS/ML) HW, 1978; NW, 1977; JWC, 1978; *Locus* Award, 1978

4-334. Pohl, Frederik. **JEM: The Making of Utopia.** St. Martin's, 1979.
A new planet is ripe for exploitation by Earth's three power blocs: food-exporting nations, oil-exporting nations, and people's republics. Three species of intelligent natives enter into appropriate associations with the three colonizing groups, and are thus drawn into the web of conflicts and compromises that reproduces all the evils of earthly politics. A cynical ide-

ological counterweight to stories of human/alien cooperation along the lines of Poul Anderson's *People of the Wind* (1973). (BS)

*4-335.   Pohl, Frederik. **Man Plus.** Random, 1976.
The protagonist is technologically adapted for life on Mars. The process by which he is made into an alien is revealed, ironically, to be part of a plan to save humanity from the coming self-destruction of a nuclear war. A convincing and critical reexamination of the theme of Bradbury's *The Martian Chronicles* [3-32]. A less successful sequel, *Mars Plus* (1994), was outlined by Pohl and written by Thomas J. Thomas. (BS) NW, 1977

4-336.   Pohl, Frederik. **Pohlstars.** Ballantine, 1984.
Twelve short stories most dating from the late 1970s and early 1980s. Among the best tales here are "Spending a Day at the Lottery Fair," "We Purchase People," and "The Sweet, Sad Queen of the Grazing Isles." Among Pohl's other collections in the modern period are *Digits and Dastards* (1966), *Day Million* (1970), *The Gold at the Starbow's End* (1972), *The Best of Frederik Pohl* (1975), and *In the Problem Pit* (1976). In recent years Pohl has concentrated on novels, but has also produced two fine, individually published novellas, *Stopping at Slowyear* (1991) and *Outnumbering the Dead* (1992), both of which deal in a very thoughtful manner with the problems of old age and impending death. (ML)

4-337.   Pohl, Frederik. **The Years of the City.** Simon & Schuster, 1984.
Five novellas tracking the future of New York City as its leading citizens grapple with the problems of armies, urban decay, and pollution using the electronic media to create a new style of democracy. A fascinating set of extrapolations, determinedly constructive. Compare Niven and Pournelle's *Oath of Fealty* (1981). (BS) JWC, 1985 [For other works by this author see chapter 3.]

4-338.   Pournelle, Jerry. **The Mercenary.** Pocket, 1977.
Fix-up novel about space mercenaries led by a charismatic military genius. Other novels in the series include *West of Honor* (1976; rev. 1980), *Prince of Mercenaries* (1989), *Falkenberg's Legion* (collects *The Mercenary* and *West of Honor,* 1976) (1990), and *Go Tell the Spartans* (1991; written in collaboration with S. M. Stirling). One of the most fascinating things about this series is the way it has merged with the universe of Pournelle and Larry Niven's *The Mote in God's Eye* [4-320]. Similar works include *Janissaries* (1979), in which involuntary mercenaries serve alien masters, and that novel's two sequels, written in collaboration with Roland Green, *Clan and Crown* (1982) and *Storms of Victory* (1987). The stories present a polemical

glorification of militarism and libertarian tough-mindedness. Compare Heinlein's *Starship Troopers* [3-90], David Drake's *Hammer's Slammers* (1979) and sequels, and the work of imitators too numerous to mention. (ML/BS)

*4-339. Powers, Tim. **The Anubis Gates.** Ace, 1983.
An academic interested in a minor Victorian poet named William Ashbless is recruited as a kind of tour guide to a time traveling expedition whose members expect to hear Coleridge lecture. When he is marooned in 1810 he has to fight a multitude of enemies, including the man who marooned him. His struggle for survival, which necessitates his becoming Ashbless, makes a fabulous adventure story with some excellent gothic elements. More fantasy than SF, but the ingeniously constructed paradox-avoiding time-tripping draws heavily on the SF tradition. Compare Blaylock's *Homunculus* [4-57]. (BS) Philip K. Dick Award, 1984

4-340. Powers, Tim. **Dinner at Deviant's Palace.** Ace, 1985.
A hardboiled version of the story of Orpheus and Eurydice set in postholocaust California, with a bizarre alien presiding over an exotic hell. A fast-moving adventure with the author's usual gothic touches; a key example of the new postholocaust romanticism. Compare Zelazny's *Damnation Alley* (1969). (BS) Philip K. Dick Award, 1986; NN, 1985

4-341. Pratchett, Terry. **Strata.** Colin Smythe, 1981.
The heroine, a "worldbuilder," deserts her work in order to investigate the mysterious works of others (presumably aliens) in the same vein—in particular, a flat Earth enclosed within a crystal sphere, complete with monsters and demons. She sets out with two alien companions to explore it, attempting to find out who built it and why. An absurdist *Ringworld* [4-316], subverting SF clichés. (BS)

4-342. Preuss, Paul. **Broken Symmetries.** Timescape, 1983.
A brilliant theoretical physicist becomes involved in controversy—and ultimately conflict—generated by the discovery of a new subatomic particle. Technically detailed; its fascinating scientific and technological speculations are virtues making up for the rather makeshift plot. Compare Benford's *Timescape* [4-46]. (BS)

4-343. Preuss, Paul. **Human Error.** Tor, 1985.
A biologist and a computer scientist combine their artistry to produce a powerful biochip microcomputer. Inevitably, though, the potential of the new creation extends far beyond the purpose for which it was intended.

Not as apocalyptic as Bear's *Blood Music* [4-38] but very effective in its fashion. (BS)

4-344.   Priest, Christopher. **The Affirmation.** Faber, 1981.
The protagonist exists simultaneously in London and the exotic Dream Archipelago. As the state of his affairs in the former deteriorates he finds new opportunities in the latter, but he does not know whether this represents a viable solution to his predicament. Compare Saxton's *Queen of the States* [4-383]. (BS)

4-345.   Priest, Christopher. **The Glamour.** Cape, 1984.
Outcasts of society, who pass unnoticed in "the hierarchy of visual interest," can make themselves invisible, a talent that is, ironically, the "glamour" of the title. The amnesiac hero gradually relearns the use of this talent and rediscovers his love for the heroine. A delicately ambivalent tale of welcome alienation. The U.S. edition (Doubleday, 1985) is substantially revised. Compare Fritz Leiber's *The Sinful Ones* (1953; revised 1980). (BS)

4-346.   Priest, Christopher. **An Infinite Summer.** Faber, 1979.
Priest's second collection, superior to *Real-Time World* (1974). The mundane lives of the characters are usually interrupted by fantastic distortions of time and space, whose consequences are seductive but possibly subversive of sanity. Includes "Palely Loitering" (HN, 1980) and "The Watched" (HN, 1979). (BS)

4-347.   Priest, Christopher. **Inverted World.** Faber, 1974.
A city is subject to space-time distortions that force its inhabitants to move it en masse, pursuing a point of stability across a hyperbolic surface, although observers from outside see it progressing across Europe. A fascinating juxtaposition of incompatible worldviews, with some fine imagery in the description of the hero's mission away from the city. Compare Dick's *Martian Time-Slip* [3-66]. (BS)

4-348.   Pynchon, Thomas. **Gravity's Rainbow.** Viking, 1973.
A sprawling novel about a World War II psychological warfare unit full of weird characters, one of whom seems to be determining the pattern of V-2 rocket attacks by his sexual activities but refuses to submit to study and possible control. Extraordinarily elaborate black comedy. Compare the research establishment in Carter Scholz and Glen A. Harcourt's *Palimpsests* (1985). (BS)

4-349. Randall, Marta. **Islands.** Pocket Books, 1980.
Revised edition of a novel first published in 1976. A mortal woman, a freak in a world of immortals, immerses herself in archaeological studies and makes a discovery that might give her access to a better kind of immortality, in which a kind of transcendence will utterly defeat existential angst. Compare Richard Cowper's *The Tithonian Factor and Other Stories* (1984). (BS)

4-350. Rankin, Robert. **Armageddon: The Musical.** Bloomsbury, 1990.
Truly bizarre aliens have been secretly televising life on Earth for centuries, and intentionally manipulating human development whenever the ratings have begun to slip. The alien production staff eventually decides to bolster their ratings by sending someone to Earth with a Time Sprout. Elvis is involved in the attempt to avoid world catastrophe. One of the silliest works of science fiction ever published. Several sequels have been reported. Compare Adams's *The Hitch Hiker's Guide to the Galaxy* [4-1] and Denton's *Buddy Holly Is Alive and Well on Ganymede* [4-133]. (ML)

4-351. Reamy, Tom. **Blind Voices.** Berkley, 1978.
A small Kansas town is visited during the depression by a circus whose freaks have been produced by psionic genetic engineering. A moving study of exotic evil vanquished by exotic saintliness, very much in the tradition of Sturgeon's *The Dreaming Jewels* [3-170]. Contrast Dunn's *Geek Love* [4-151]. (BS)

4-352. Reed, Kit. **Armed Camps.** Faber, 1969.
Warfare is institutionalized as a means of social control and a product of technological imperatives. The two protagonists move from opposite political poles toward a climactic meeting. Reed's forte is the production of SF fabulations in which characters struggle to retain and assert their humanity in a mechanized and devalued world, but she can also be very witty—both aspects of her writing are displayed in her collections: *The Killer Mice* (1976), *Other Stories, and the Attack of the Giant Baby* (1981), and *The Revenge of the Senior Citizens, **Plus* (1986). (BS)

4-353. Reed, Robert. **Black Milk.** Donald Fine, 1989.
Ryder, Cody, Marshall, and their friends live a happy, pastoral life, hardly aware of the fact that they're different, superior, the result of Dr. Aaron Florida's experiments in genetic engineering. As the children learn more about some of their surrogate father's other experiments, however, they begin to see that not everything is sweetness and light. When Dr. Florida's

Sparkhounds escape confinement, all humankind is at risk. Well-developed, complex characters and fascinating scientific concepts are the hallmark of this satisfying novel. Compare Lois McMaster Bujold's *Falling Free* [4-79] and Nancy Kress's *Beggars in Spain* [4-238]. (ML)

4-354.   Reed, Robert. Down the Bright Way. Bantam, 1991.
In the unimaginably distant past a departed race of superbeings created the Way, a road of sorts that cuts across a seemingly endless number of parallel worlds. The Founders, distant relatives of ours from one of those worlds, discovered the Way and began a quasi-religious quest to find its creators. These Wanderers have traveled through an enormous number of parallel worlds, recruiting pilgrims as they go. Kyle, who comes from a world that may well be ours, is not sure whether he wants to be a Wanderer, but then finds himself kidnapped by a secret organization out to use the Way for its own dark purposes. This is large-scale sense-of-wonder SF of a rather old-fashioned sort. It is also a meditation on the nature of violence. Compare Greg Bear's *Eon* [4-39] and *Eternity* [4-39]. (ML)

4-355.   Reed, Robert. The Remarkables. Bantam, 1992.
When the damaged starship *Pitcairn* makes an emergency landing on a new world its crew discovers the Remarkables, the only other intelligent species in known space. Unable to digest native foods on their own, the survivors enter into a permanent symbiotic relationship with the Remarkables and create a successful joint civilization. Rediscovered by Earth years later, the Pitcairners have no interest in rejoining the human race, though they periodically invite humans to their planet to contribute genetic material by taking part in a momentous ritual called a passion. Reed has created a fascinating alien species, and one of the most intriguing examples of alien-human symbiosis in recent science fiction. Compare Butler's *Dawn* [4-85] and its sequels. (ML)

4-356.   Resnick, Mike. Ivory: A Legend of Past and Future. Tor, 1988.
The sacred ivory of the Kilimanjaro Elephant, the largest tusks ever recorded, were in the keeping of the Masai for thousands of years until one such keeper, proving himself unworthy, lost them in a card game. Now, 7,000 years after the elephant died, Bukoba Mandaka, the last Masai, wants them back, and he hires Duncan Rojas, a computer expert who specializes in authenticating interstellar hunting trophies, to get them back. This is an intelligent tale that treats African culture with considerable respect. Resnick has also written two novels, *Paradise* (1989) and *Purgatory* (1993), that take the history of individual African nations and reinterpret

them in SF terms, as well as a series of award-winning short stories set on an artificially created world, Kirinyaga, intended to duplicate precolonial East Africa. Compare the stories in the anthology *Future Earths: Under African Skies* (1993), which Resnick co-edited with Gardner Dozois. (ML) NN, 1989

4-357. Reynolds, Mack. **Lagrange Five.** Bantam, 1979.
An O'Neill space colony develops an effective social system, but its key role in the power politics of the solar system makes it the target of subversive conspiracy. The theme is further developed in *The Lagrangists* (1983), *Chaos in Lagrangia* (1984), and *Trojan Orbit* (1985), all edited by Dean Ing from posthumously discovered manuscripts. Compare Haldeman's Worlds series [4-195]. (BS) [For other works by this author see chapter 3.]

4-358. Roberts, Keith. **The Chalk Giants.** Hutchinson, 1974.
Fix-up postholocaust novel in which Britain is rent apart and barbarism reigns. The final sequence, like the final sequence of *Pavane* [4-362], is set at Corfe Gate. A brilliant and disturbing book that develops the grimly realistic aspect of British catastrophic fiction. To be sharply contrasted with Cowper's Kinship trilogy [4-118]. (BS)

4-359. Roberts, Keith. **Kiteworld.** Gollancz, 1985.
Fix-up novel set in a pseudomedieval world dominated by a religious elite, in which men are carried aloft by giant kites to look out for invading demons. Has affinities with *Pavane* [4-362] and *The Chalk Giants* [4-358], although it sets aside the idea of historical cyclicity that underlies these novels. (BS)

4-360. Roberts, Keith. **The Lordly Ones.** Gollancz, 1986.
A recent collection, following *Machines and Men* (1973), *The Grain Kings* (1976), and *Ladies From Hell* (1979) (in addition to various fix-up novels). The title story and "The Comfort Station" both deal with the collapse of civilized order—one of Roberts's favorite themes—and do so with much feeling. "Diva" and "Sphairistike" are more playful, as is the author's wont when dealing with the leisurely aspects of life. Compare Richard Cowper's short fiction [4-117]. (BS)

4-361. Roberts, Keith. **Molly Zero.** Gollancz, 1980.
The adolescent heroine escapes from intense and enigmatic education in "the Blocks," living as a working girl, a gypsy, and ultimately as an urban outlaw, but her apparent escape turns out to be simply one more phase in

her rite de passage. A grimly earnest version of a common SF theme, exhibiting Roberts's fondness for young female protagonists threatened by the forces of corruption. (S)

*4-362. Roberts, Keith. **Pavane.** Hart-Davis, 1968.
Fix-up novel describing what appears to be an alternate world where the Catholic church retained its hegemony in Europe because of the victory of the Spanish Armada. But this technologically retarded world also harbors fairies who know the real truth, and when progress rears its ugly head again, its value is brought sharply into question. A rich, many-faceted narrative, written with great care and delicacy; one of the finest SF novels of the period. U.S. editions add an extra episode. Compare Miller's *A Canticle for Leibowitz* [3-125] and Amis's *The Alteration* [4-8]. (BS)

4-363. Robinson, Frank M. **The Dark Beyond the Stars.** Tor, 1991.
Robinson's first SF novel in decades concerns the starship *Astron*, which has searched the galaxy for alien life for 2,000 years. The ship is now falling apart and its crew, all born during the voyage, are ripe for mutiny. Unfortunately the *Astron*'s immortal captain has been conditioned to refuse to turn back until he finds evidence of life, evidence that apparently does not exist. Sparrow, a 17 year-old crewman who suffers from amnesia, is caught up in the mounting discontent and soon discovers that his lost past may hold a clue to what has gone wrong with the mission. This gritty, moving variation on the generation starship concept features an unusually adept handling of the same-sex relationships as well as a well-constructed mystery plotline. Compare Heinlein's *Orphans of the Sky* [3-88]. (ML) [For other works by this author see chapter 3.]

4-364. Robinson, Kim Stanley. **The Memory of Whiteness.** Tor, 1985.
An inspired musician tours the solar system with a one-man orchestra designed by a brilliant physicist, whose theory of the universe is strongly linked to the fundamentals of musical aesthetics. The protagonist's friends must try to protect him from threats that appear to come from a strange religious cult, though he seems not unwilling to accept a messianic role in their unfolding psychodrama. A highly original and delicately fashioned novel whose exotic settings are remarkably convincing. (BS)

4-365. Robinson, Kim Stanley. **The Planet on the Table.** Tor, 1986.
Collection of early fiction by one of the genre's finest literary writers, including Robinson's World Fantasy Award-winning story about the Spanish Armada, "Black Air," and the fine alternate history tale, "The

Lucky Strike," which is set in a world where the bomb was not dropped on Hiroshima. Robinson's other major collections are *Escape From Kathmandu* (1989), which includes the Hugo- and Nebula Award-nominated title novella, and *Remaking History* (1991), which includes the Nebula-nominated "Before I Wake," as well as "Vinland the Dream," "Glacier," and 12 other fine stories. Compare Kessel's *Meeting in Infinity* [4-228]. (ML)

*4-366. Robinson, Kim Stanley. **Red Mars.** HarperCollins, 1992.
This novel, the first of a projected trilogy, is, without a doubt, the most detailed and impressive portrayal of the exploration and colonization of another planet ever published. Robinson is in complete control of his materials, whether he is describing the engineering difficulties involved in the building of a large-scale underground habitat or the political wheeling and dealing involved in placating a wide range of political, religious, ethnic, and commercial interests, all of which want a slice of the Martian pie. The novel features a large cast of well-developed characters, breathtaking descriptions of the Martian landscape, and a sophisticated understanding of the complex interplay between technology and politics. *Red Mars* may well be the finest hard-science fiction novel of the last decade. Sequels are *Green Mars* (1994) and *Blue Mars* (*Locus* Award). For a competent, smaller-scale approach to the exploration of the Red Planet, compare Ben Bova's *Mars* [4-60]. (ML) HN, 1993

*4-367. Robinson, Kim Stanley. **The Wild Shore.** Ace, 1984.
After the nuclear holocaust the United States is quarantined by the United Nations, and the survivors must remake their civilization in isolation. The protagonist, his role analogous to that of Huckleberry Finn, explores this new frontier world. The most sophisticated example of contemporary American romantic catastrophism. Compare Powers's *Dinner at Deviant's Palace* [4-340] and Brin's *The Postman* [4-66]. Robinson followed *The Wild Shore* with two more novels set in the same location in Southern California, thematic sequels considering alternate historical possibilities. *The Gold Coast* (1988) describes a near-future Orange County of superhighways and designer drugs that is only marginally different from our own. *Pacific Edge* (1990), which won the JWC Award, is set in a postdisaster, small-scale community where everything is done with an eye toward its effect on the ecology. (ML/BS) NN, 1984

4-368. Robinson, Spider, and Jeanne Robinson. **Stardance.** Dial, 1979.
Based on a novella (HW, 1978; NW, 1977). A story of exotic redemption in which a crippled dancer becomes involved in humanity's first contact

with aliens, and helps set the stage for a mystical communion between the species. The sequel, *Starseed* (1991), is much less successful. Compare Orson Scott Card's *Songmaster* (1980). (BS/ML)

4-369.   Rucker, Rudy. **The Hollow Earth.** Morrow, 1990.
Edgar Allan Poe and others head out on a mad, sometimes hilarious expedition to seek the polar hole that will allow them to enter the hollow Earth. Succeeding, they find a bizarre interior world, a number of unusual civilizations, some mindbending physical phenomena, flying saucers, and special effects of a sort usually associated with a trip on LSD. Compare Burroughs' *At the Earth's Core* [1-15], Poe's *The Narrative of Arthur Gordon Pym* [1-74], and Seaborn's *Symzonia: A Voyage of Discovery* [1-81]. (ML)

4-370.   Rucker, Rudy. **Software.** Ace, 1982.
Artificial intelligence has developed to the point where computers can begin the inevitable power struggle with mankind. Should we be prepared to put aside our frail flesh in favor of inorganic forms that will preserve our personalities in their software? The extravagant plot is well spiced with wit. The equally well done sequel is *Wetware* (1988), and a third volume is expected. Both *Software* and *Wetware* won the Philip K. Dick Award. Compare Piercy's *He, She, and It* [4-329]. (BS/ML)

4-371.   Rucker, Rudy. **White Light.** Ace, 1980.
A strange fantasy of life after death that has abundant SF interest by virtue of the author's use of "higher dimensions" as a milieu for displaying ideas drawn from number theory and other areas of higher mathematics. The author suggests that this exercise in "transrealism" can be regarded as the first element in a trilogy completed by *The Sex Sphere* (1983), in which a hypersphere trapped into an intersection with our 3-D space obligingly responds to the sexual fantasies of the male characters, and *The Secret of Life* (1985). Rucker's work invites comparison with some very early SF writers, including Camille Flammarion and C. H. Hinton, as well as avantgarde figures like John Shirley and Bruce Sterling. (BS)

4-372.   Russ, Joanna. **Alyx.** Gregg Press, 1976. Variant title: *The Adventures of Alyx.*
Incorporates the novel *Picnic on Paradise* (1968; HN, 1969) with four short stories featuring the same heroine. Alyx's native land is the cradle of civilization, where she is an outlaw because her ideas are so far ahead of her time, but in the novel she is snatched out of context to become a time

traveling agent charged with rescuing a group of tourists trapped on a resort planet where local politics have turned sour. Clever and lively. Another similar novel is *The Two of Them* (1978), in which a female agent is dispatched to a quasi-Islamic world where she rescues a girl from a harem. (BS)

4-373. Russ, Joanna. **And Chaos Died.** Ace, 1970.
A castaway on a colony world, whose inhabitants have been taught telepathy by mysterious aliens, picks up the gift himself, but then finds himself alienated from ordinary humans, able to remain sane only among members of what is now his own kind. A determined attempt to examine psi power from a new angle. Compare Arthur Sellings's *The Uncensored Man* (1964). (BS) NN, 1970

4-374. Russ, Joanna. **Extra(ordinary) People.** St. Martin's, 1984.
A collection of linked stories, deliberately didactic in form, in which liberated women in different societies challenge the forces of oppression. Includes "Souls" (HW, 1983). As with *The Female Man* [4-375], the result is multifaceted and the call for a revolution in sexual politics is eloquent even though the stories retain a full appreciation of the difficulty of compiling a manifesto for a nonsexist society. Other, more varied, collections are *The Zanzibar Cat* (1984), which features the Nebula Award-winning "When It Changed," the seed story for *The Female Man*, and *The Hidden Side of the Moon* (1988), which includes such stories as "The Dirty Little Girl" and "Reasonable People." (BS/ML)

*4-375. Russ, Joanna. **The Female Man.** Bantam, 1975.
A contemporary woman encounters three "alternative selves," including a version from the feminist utopia Whileaway, a version from a world where patriarchy is more powerful and more brutally imposed, and a version from a world where the sex war has exploded into armed conflict. The juxtaposition of these alternatives, phantasmagoric and very witty, provides an extraordinarily rich and thought-provoking commentary on sexual politics. A key novel of feminist SF. Compare Piercy's *Woman on the Edge of Time* [4-330] and Saxton's *Queen of the States* [4-383]. (BS)

4-376. Russo, Richard Paul. **Subterranean Gallery.** Tor, 1989.
Rheinhardt, a San Francisco-based sculptor living in a repressive, near-future America, has tried to keep out of politics, but a series of events makes this increasingly difficult. A close friend is drafted to fight in a gruesome South American war. Much of the best work by local artists is

systematically destroyed or suppressed. Police helicopters circle overhead nightly. Then a mysterious Vietnam veteran named Justinian persuades Rheinhardt to fight back. This novel is very dark and packs a powerful emotional wallop. Compare two similar books, Murphy's *The City, Not Long After* [4-308] and Goldstein's *A Mask for the General* [4-187]. (ML) Philip K. Dick Award, 1989

*4-377. Ryman, Geoff. **The Child Garden: A Low Comedy.** Unwin, 1989.

This brilliant postmodernist extravaganza takes place in a tropical future London where genetic engineering has abolished cancer, mastered the art of passing on knowledge through viruses, allowed human beings to photosynthesize and, tragically, caused an irreversible change in human genetics, which leads most human beings to die in their mid-thirties. The complex plot centers on a pair of artist-lovers—Milena, a mediocre actress with a talent for directing, and Rolfa, a huge, genetically engineered Polar Woman who sings opera. For comparably audacious speculation about bioengineering, see Bear's *Blood Music* [4-38]. For a comparable picture of a city transformed by the greenhouse effect, see Hand's *Winterlong* [4-196]. Winner of the 1990 Arthur C. Clarke Award and the JWC Award and a nominee for the British SF Association Award. (ML)

4-378. Saberhagen, Fred. **Berserker.** Ballantine, 1967.

A collection, the first book in an extensive series of novels and collections (see series listing). Berserkers are automated war machines programmed to destroy life, whose perennial and inescapable threat unites the life forms of the galaxy and stimulates their collective technological progress. The power of the premise, and its fecundity in generating plots, is aptly demonstrated by the expansion of the series to take in work by other writers. The series has become an archetypal example of the SF myth that opposes man and machine, and also develops the common assumption of SF writers that without some kind of challenge men might use their technology to become lotus eaters, stagnating in evolutionary decadence. The early stories tend to be a little clumsy, but Saberhagen's writing skills have developed; the series testifies, like Bradley's Darkover series [4-63], to the sophistication and changing concerns of the SF field during the modern period. Compare Benford's *Great Sky River* and sequels [4-44]. (BS/ML)

4-379. Sagan, Carl. **Contact.** Simon & Schuster, 1985.

Much-touted first novel by the noted popularizer of science, concerning the deciphering of a message from the stars and the voyage to a fateful rendezvous. The fervor of the story exceeds that of Gunn's *The Listeners*

[4-192] and Kube-McDowell's *Emprise* (1985). It can also be compared to Clarke's *2010: Odyssey Two* [4-110]. (BS) *Locus* Award, 1986

4-380. Sargent, Pamela. **The Golden Space.** Timescape, 1982.
In a world of near-immortal humans, biologists experiment with the design of a "more rational" human species, but the fate of the experiment becomes problematic while society adapts to man's new relationship with death. Thoughtful and neatly understated. Compare Wilhelm's *Welcome Chaos* [4-496]. (BS)

4-381. Sargent, Pamela. **The Shore of Women.** Crown, 1986.
In a postholocaust world women live in high-tech cities, while men dwell among ruins and wilderness, worshiping women as gods. Birana is cast out from the city into the wilderness. There she meets Arvil and, eventually, falls in love. *The Shore of Women* differs from most of the separatist novels that have appeared in the past decade in that it sees the separation of men and women as less than desirable and takes strong exception to the concept of the all-female state as utopia. Compare Tepper's *The Gate to Women's Country* [4-453] and Brin's *Glory Season* [4-65]. (ML)

4-382. Sargent, Pamela. **Venus of Dreams.** Bantam, 1986.
A long novel about the relationship between two people involved in a project to terraform Venus. The book is carefully constructed and delicately handled, with some striking imagery to set off the love story. The political background is complex. In the sequel, *Venus of Shadows* (1988), humans have descended to the partially terraformed surface, living in domed cities. Although the settlers are able to control the planet, they are unable to control themselves, and political and religious rivalries begin to tear the colony apart. Compare Robinson's *Red Mars* [4-366]. (ML/BS) [For other works by this author see chapter 5.]

4-383. Saxton, Josephine. **Queen of the States.** Women's Press, 1986.
Magdalen is confined in a mental hospital because people think she suffers from delusions; she coexists in several realities, in one of which she is politely studied by aliens interested in the mysteries of human sexuality. Lively and witty, with a profusion of deft ironies. Compare Vonnegut's *Slaughterhouse-Five* [4-479] and Piercy's *Woman on the Edge of Time* [4-330]. (BS)

4-384. Saxton, Josephine. **The Travails of Jane Saint and Other Stories.** Women's Press, 1986.
In the title short novel (first published separately in 1980) the heroine,

imprisoned in a sensory deprivation tank awaiting brainwashing, embarks on a dream-quest in search of her lost children, hoping perhaps also to save the world. The sequel novella is *Jane Saint and the Backlash* (1989), published jointly with the novella "The Consciousness Machine." It concerns Jane's second trip into the Unconscious, which she takes in a quest to counteract renewed hostility toward women. Saxton has stated that both the Jane Saint stories and "The Consciousness Machine" are attempts to explore the Collective Unconscious as if it were an actual physical place. Compare and contrast Russ's *Extra(ordinary) People* [4-374]. (ML/BS)

4-385. Schenck, Hilbert. **At the Eye of the Ocean.** Pocket Books/Timescape, 1980.
A novel about individuals whose extraordinary sensitivity to the sea enables them to locate the places and times at which a mystical moment of enlightenment is available to those who ardently desire it. Finely realized background (Cape Cod at widely spaced intervals of history) and effective writing; mystical SF at its best. (BS)

4-386. Schenck, Hilbert. **A Rose for Armageddon.** Pocket Books/Timescape, 1982.
As a new dark age looms, a handful of aging intellectuals race to finish a project in the computer simulation of social relationships in the history of a small island. A mystery emerges whose solution may offer an opportunity for redemption not only to the unhappy characters but also to their unhappy era. Poignant and beautifully written; highly original in its recompilation of the timeslip romance. Compare and contrast Finney's *Time and Again* [4-167]. (BS)

4-387. Scott, Jody. **Passing for Human.** DAW, 1977.
A rhapsodic essay in misanthropy, engagingly indiscriminate in finding human beings despicable (especially the males) and then forgiving them for it. Ribald and zestful. The sequel, *I, Vampire* (1984), whose narrator rejoices in the name Sterling O'Blivion, is equally sharp and has the same ebullient charm. Compare Saxton's *The Travails of Jane Saint and Other Stories* [4-384]. (BS)

4-388. Sellings, Arthur (pseud. of Robert Arthur Ley). **Junk Day.** Dobson, 1970.
Postholocaust story in which survivors in London are exploited by the junkman, whose gangsterism restores a kind of social order before his evil role is usurped by scientists, who take over by means of behavioral engi-

neering techniques. An exercise in polished cynicism. Compare Van Greenway's *graffiti* (1983). (BS)

4-389. Shaw, Bob. **Orbitsville.** Gollancz, 1975.
The protagonist is forced to flee from Earth when he incurs the wrath of his imperious employer, and discovers a vast artificial sphere surrounding a sun, which offers apparently unlimited opportunities for human colonists. A sequel, *Orbitsville Departure* (1983), is a taut thriller in whose climax the purpose of Orbitsville is revealed. The trilogy concludes with *Orbitsville Judgment* (1990). Inevitably invites comparison with Niven's *Ringworld* [4-316], although the books are very different in tone and technique, and a more apt comparison is to Simak's *Ring Around the Sun* (1953). (BS)

4-390. Shaw, Bob. **Other Days, Other Eyes.** Gollancz, 1972.
A fix-up novel featuring one of the most ingenious SF inventions: "slow glass," which is quite transparent but lets light through so slowly that the image may take years to emerge. The book presents a marvelous study of the possible applications of the substance and its impact on society, incorporating some fine vignettes (including the brilliant "Light of Other Days," NN, 1966). A thoughtful and painstaking exercise in extrapolation, demonstrating how an apparently trivial and by no means implausible innovation would have dramatic and far-reaching effects; a key thought-experiment in the sociology of technology. (BS)

4-391. Shaw, Bob. **The Palace of Eternity.** Ace, 1969.
Thriller in which it transpires that humans have alien commensals that secure a kind of life after death—but the aliens are under threat of destruction as a side effect of a new technology. Thematically fascinating; compare Simak's *Time and Again* (1951) and Martin's *A Song for Lya* [4-281]. (BS)

4-392. Shaw, Bob. **The Ragged Astronauts.** Gollancz, 1986.
In a planetary system where two worlds share a common atmosphere the inhabitants of one are forced by circumstance to migrate to the other in hot air balloons. An unusual adventure story in which good characterization helps to make extraordinary events plausible. The somewhat less successful sequels are *The Wooden Spaceships* (1988) and *The Fugitive Worlds* (1989). (BS/ML) HN, 1987

4-393. Shaw, Bob. **The Two-Timers.** Ace, 1968.
The protagonist, traumatized by the death of his wife, transports himself

into an alternate world where he saves her, but then faces a problematic confrontation with his other self when the unforeseen side effects of his displacement disrupt the space-time continuum. A tense and dramatic thriller, convincingly handled. (BS)

4-394.   Shaw, Bob. **Who Goes Here?** Gollancz, 1977.
Warren Peace has joined the Space Legion to forget, but can't help wondering what it was that was so awful he had to forget it. Finding out involves him with monsters, mad scientists, and time paradoxes. Pure fun, very readable, and highly enjoyable. *Warren Peace*, a new novel, was published in 1993. Compare Harry Harrison's *Bill, the Galactic Hero* (1965). (BS)

4-395.   Shea, Robert, and Robert Anton Wilson. **The Illuminatus! Trilogy.** Dell, 1984.
An omnibus edition of a three-decker novel whose separate parts—*The Eye in the Pyramid, The Golden Apple,* and *Leviathan*—first appeared in 1975. A wild extravaganza that hypothesizes that all the secret societies claiming access to a special enlightenment were and are part of a huge conspiracy that will take over Earth unless the heroes of the counterculture can stop them. A crazy compendium of contemporary concerns. Compare Pynchon's *Gravity's Rainbow* [4-348]. (BS)

4-396.   Sheckley, Robert. **Dimensions of Miracles.** Dell, 1968.
The winner of a galactic sweepstake finds problems returning home with his prize, passing through various absurd alternate Earths, perennially threatened by imminent death. Less chaotic than the later bizarre odyssey, *Options* (1977), and more imaginative than the convoluted *Dramocles* (1983), but not up to the standard of the earlier *Journey Beyond Tomorrow* (1962). Sadly demonstrates the difficulty that Sheckley has in developing his brilliant comic writing at novel length. (BS)

4-397.   Sheckley, Robert. **Is *That* What People Do?** Holt, 1984.
This collection recombines stories from earlier collections, as did *The Wonderful World of Robert Sheckley* (1979). A five-volume set collected 132 stories, *The Collected Short Stories of Robert Sheckley* (Pulphouse, 1991). His stories are very funny, but the humor is generally underlaid with a dark and serious suspicion of the follies of human vanity. His robot stories are exceptionally fine and should be compared and contrasted with the Asimov stories, whose themes they often subvert and mock. Compare also the short fiction of John Sladek [4-421]. (BS) [For other works by this author see chapter 3.]

4-398. Sheffield, Charles. **Brother to Dragons.** Baen, 1992.
In a future America where the Royal Hundred run everything from their luxurious Mall compound, most Americans live in polluted, disintegrating slums. Job Salk, the deformed child of one such slum dweller, is saved by a nurse in a charity ward and ends up in an orphanage. Father Bonifant, Chief Steward of Cloak House, teaches him the value of hard work and sends the boy, now six years of age, out into the streets to borrow, earn, or otherwise acquire the necessities of life for the orphanage. Sheffield has a reputation as a hard SF writer, but this touching novel owes more to Charles Dickens than it does to John W. Campbell. (ML) JWC, 1993

4-399. Sheffield, Charles. **Sight of Proteus.** Ace, 1978.
Tracks the 23rd-century development and eventual application of a technology of transmutation allowing human bodies to be reshaped and augmented. Although treated with great suspicion, the techniques ultimately prove themselves of immense value. In the sequel, *Proteus Unbound* (1989), 30 years have passed and a revolutionary has discovered a way to interfere with the delicate computers that govern human transformation. Behrooz Wolf, the protagonist of the earlier novel, is called out of retirement to stop him. Sheffield isn't strong on character development, but his novels invariably feature superb scientific speculation. (ML/BS)

4-400. Shepard, Lucius. **Green Eyes.** Ace, 1984.
Scientific researchers reanimate corpses biotechnologically, introducing new personalities. One of these "zombies" escapes in the company of a female doctor and gradually acquires superhuman powers that enable him to find out the truth behind voodoo mythology and the true purpose of the project that created him. Upmarket melodrama. Compare Matheson's *I Am Legend* [3-120]. (BS)

*4-401. Shepard, Lucius. **The Jaguar Hunter.** Arkham, 1987.
One of the finest collections of fantasy and science fiction published in the 1980s. Probably the best story included is the Nebula- and *Locus* Award-winning "R&R," the tale of an American soldier on leave from a future war in Central America, which was later incorporated into Shepard's second novel, *Life During Wartime* [4-402]. Other outstanding stories, many of them award nominees, include "The End of Life as We Know It," "A Traveler's Tale," "The Man Who Painted the Dragon Griaule," and "A Spanish Lesson." *The Jaguar Hunter* won the 1988 World Fantasy Award for best collection. Shepard's second volume of short stories, *The Ends of the Earth* (1991), also a World Fantasy Award nominee, includes such fine pieces as "Delta Sly Honey," the award-nominated

"Shades," "The Ends of the Earth," and "Surrender." Compare Tiptree's *Tales of the Quintana Roo* (1986). (ML) World Fantasy Award, 1988; *Locus Award*, 1988

*4-402. Shepard, Lucius. **Life During Wartime.** Bantam, 1987.
Based in part on Shepard's Nebula Award-winning novella, "R&R," and several other short stories, this is the tale of David Mingolla, a psychic drafted to fight in a near-future, Vietnam-style conflict in Central America. Like many fix-up novels, *Life During Wartime* suffers from occasional discontinuities, but the language is brilliant, and Shepard's searing portrayal of the soul-destroying immorality of contemporary warfare rivals that to be found in films like *Apocalypse Now* and *Platoon*. Compare also McAllister's *Dream Baby* [4-287]. (ML)

4-403. Shiner, Lewis. **Frontera.** Baen, 1984.
Fairly traditional SF novel written by a member of the cyberpunk movement. Frontera, NASA's Mars colony, has been abandoned for ten years, but the giant corporation Pulsystems has now mounted a dangerous mission hoping to bring back a mysterious treasure from the Red Planet, possibly some form of new technology. Kane, a corporate mercenary hired for the trip, finds himself programmed to do Pulsystems' bidding no matter how strange things get. A well-done, gritty adventure story. Compare Allen Steele's *Labyrinth of Night* (1992) and Terry Bisson's *Voyage to the Red Planet* [4-55]. (ML) NN, 1984

4-404. Shirley, John. **Eclipse.** Bluejay, 1985.
In Shirley's A Song Called Youth series, set in the early 21st century, the United States is bogged down in a nonnuclear war with the Soviet Union while Europe has been taken over by the intensely racist, neo-Fascist Second Alliance. Led by a motley crew of rock musicians, anarchists, and counterculture types, the Resistance struggles valiantly to stem the tide of right-wing domination. The second and third volumes, *Eclipse Penumbra* (1988) and *Eclipse Corona* (1990), play down the cyberpunkish special effects of volume one as Shirley concentrates on a more straightforward presentation of guerrilla warfare. Compare Sinclair Lewis's *It Can't Happen Here* [2-71] and Williams's *Hardwired* [4-499]. (ML)

4-405. Shirley, John. **Heatseeker.** Scream/Press, 1989.
A mixed collection of reprint and original science fiction, horror, and surrealism, by one of the genre's more radical innovators and a cofounder of the cyberpunk movement. Particularly powerful are the very dark new story "Equilibrium" and the stunning cyberpunk tale, "Wolves of the

Plateau." Few writers are capable of getting away with so much over-the-top craziness. Compare Ellison's *Alone Against Tomorrow* [4-157] and *Shatterday* [4-161]. (ML)

4-406. Silverberg, Robert. **The Book of Skulls.** Scribner, 1972.

A student finds an ancient manuscript in the rare books room at the university library, which seems to promise immortality if he and three friends can track down the Brotherhood of the Skull. They travel to Arizona on their quest, only to find that what awaits is not immortality but terror and death. Very much a product of the late-1960s and early-1970s fascination with the occult and hallucinogenic transcendent experience, this novel still packs a considerable emotional punch. Compare Attanasio's *Radix* [4-22]. (ML)

*4-407. Silverberg, Robert. **The Collected Stories of Robert Silverberg** Volume One: **Secret Sharers.** Bantam, 1992. In U.K. published as two volumes—*The Collected Stories of Robert Silverberg*, Volume One: *Pluto in the Morning Light* (Grafton, 1992) and Volume Two: *Secret Sharers* (Grafton, 1993).

There are 24 stories collected here, all published between 1981 and 1988. Approximately half made one or more of the "best of the year" anthologies, and a number were award winners or nominees. Among the most memorable stories included are: "Chip Runner," "The Secret Sharer," "Sailing to Byzantium," "A Sleep and a Forgetting," "Enter a Soldier. Later: Enter Another," "The Pardoner's Tale," and "Homefaring." Silverberg is one of the finest writers of short fiction. A second volume is planned. Numerous earlier collections of Silverberg's work are also available, among the best of them *Moonferns and Starsongs* (1971), *The Reality Trip and Other Implausibilities* (1972), *Born With the Dead* (1974), *The Conglomeroid Cocktail Party* (1984), and *Beyond the Safe Zone: Collected Short Fiction of Robert Silverberg* (1986). (ML)

*4-408. Silverberg, Robert. **Downward to the Earth.** Doubleday, 1970.

The guilt-stricken protagonist returns to the alien world where he was once a colonial officer and where he committed crimes for which he now seeks forgiveness and redemption. To become truly human, he must become alien, sharing the religious rituals of the natives and the related processes of physical metamorphosis. A superb novel; one of the best examples of the use of hypothetical biology and alien culture to symbolize problematic aspects of human existence. Compare Le Guin's *The Word for World Is Forest* [4-256] and Shaw's *The Palace of Eternity* [4-391]. (BS)

*4-409. Silverberg, Robert. **Dying Inside.** Scribner, 1972.
The story of a telepath whose powers are fading—a loss that may allow him to overcome his alienation from the human world. Told with great intensity and merciless realism; one of the finest works of the period and one of the best examples of the SF novel. Compare Russ's *And Chaos Died* [4-373]. *The Stochastic Man* (1975; HN, 1976; NN, 1975) is a similar but less impressive story of ESP-related alienation, this time embodied in a story of the acquisition of precognitive abilities. (BS) NN, 1972; HN, 1973

4-410. Silverberg, Robert. **Hawksbill Station.** Doubleday, 1968. U.K. title: *The Anvil of Time,* 1969.
A future government sends dissidents back in time to a Cambrian prison camp; moves for their repatriation are made—but can they really be rescued from their spiritual wasteland? A grim story of exile, told with compassion. (BS)

4-411. Silverberg, Robert. **The Masks of Time.** Ballantine, 1968. U.K. title: *Vornan-19,* 1970.
As the millennial year 2000 approaches, an enigmatic visitor from the future comes to study the 20th-century man and is trapped in a quasi-messianic role. Compare Russell Griffins's *Century's End* (1981). Another enigmatic messiah figure is the industrialist in *Tower of Glass* (1970; NN, 1970; HN, 1972), who builds a new Tower of Babel and is deified by oppressed androids. (BS)

4-412. Silverberg, Robert. **Nightwings.** Avon, 1969.
A fix-up novel (first novella, HW, 1969) in which a decadent Earth is taken over by aliens who have old scores to settle, but who might offer humankind a path to salvation too. Lushly romantic and elegiac far-future fantasy. (BS)

4-413. Silverberg, Robert. **Thorns.** Ballantine, 1967.
Two lonely people alienated by awful experiences are brought together by a psychic vampire in order that their anguish might feed his extraordinary lust, but they achieve a remarkable transcendence of their predicament. A highly stylized SF fable, comparable to Charles Harness's *The Rose* (1966). (BS)

4-414. Silverberg, Robert. **A Time of Changes.** Doubleday, 1971.
A colony world preserves a strange culture based on self-hatred, but the protagonist learns individualism from a visiting Earthman and becomes a

revolutionary advocate of a new kind of community. Unlike Ayn Rand's *Anthem* [2-100], with which it inevitably invites comparison, it is not a political allegory but an exploration of the value of human relationships. (BS) HN, 1972; NW, 1971

4-415. Silverberg, Robert. **Up the Line.** Ballantine, 1969.
A satirical and sexy extrapolation of the "time patrol" theme, in which the protagonist turns outlaw, trying to alter history instead of protecting it, and is appropriately punished. Compare Poul Anderson's *Guardians of Time* (1961). (BS) HN, 1970; NN, 1969

*4-416. Silverberg, Robert. **The World Inside.** Doubleday, 1971.
In a crowded future, populations have to be gathered together in massive Urbmons: compact high-rise cities whose culture has set aside ideas of privacy. For some this is a kind of hell, but there can be no escape from it, even to the world outside. Compare T. J. Bass's *Half Past Human* (1971). (BS) HN (withdrawn), 1972 [For other works by this author see chapter 5.]

4-417. Simak, Clifford D(onald). **A Choice of Gods.** Putnam, 1971.
In a depopulated post-technological world, robots have taken over man's religious quest. An interesting example of SF mysticism, carrying forward themes from *City* [3-163]; rather more ambitious, despite its relative orthodoxy, than Schenck's *At the Eye of the Ocean* [4-385]. (BS)

4-418. Simak, Clifford D(onald). **The Visitors.** Ballantine, 1980.
Alien "black boxes" descend on Earth in droves, peacefully reproducing themselves and minding their own business. They pay for what they consume, but their payments threaten to precipitate economic chaos. An ironic story to be compared and contrasted with the Strugatskiis's *Roadside Picnic* [4-443]. (BS) [For other works by this author see chapter 3.]

*4-419. Simmons, Dan. **Hyperion.** Doubleday, 1989.
Hyperion is the first half of one of the most complex space operas ever written. With a structure based on the *Canterbury Tales*, it tells the story of a pilgrimage of sorts to the planet Hyperion, where the Time Tombs, alien artifacts that run backward through time, are about to open. As in Chaucer, each pilgrim has his or her own story to tell; stories that are individually riveting and contribute thematically to the novel as a whole. The book ends just as the travelers reach their destination. *The Fall of Hyperion* (1990) takes its inspiration from Keats's poem of the same name. It con-

tinues the narration of events at the tombs, but also opens up into a portrait of a sophisticated interstellar culture where teleportation is so basic that people routinely build homes with rooms on more than one planet. Powerful players are interested in the events on Hyperion, and the individual crises faced by the pilgrims may have galaxy-spanning outcomes. The *Hyperion* books suffer from occasional problems of continuity, but they are beautifully written and have few equals for sheer, large-scale sense of wonder. A third volume is promised. On a somewhat smaller scale, compare Alexander Jablokov's *Carve the Sky* [4-213]. (ML) *Hyperion*: HW, 1990; *Locus* Award, 1990. *Fall of Hyperion*: HN, 1991; NN, 1990; *Locus* Award, 1991

4-420.   Skal, David J. **Antibodies.** Congdon & Weed, 1988.
The San Francisco art underground becomes the vanguard of a Cybernetic Temple cult, which prophesies wholesale conversion of fallible humans into immortal machines. A savage if overblown critique of cyborg fantasies, continuing the exploitation of SF tropes for horror purposes begun in *Scavengers* (1980) and *When We Were Good* (1981). Contrast Cadigan's *Synners* [4-89]. (RL)

4-421.   Sladek, John T(homas). **The Lunatics of Terra.** Gollancz, 1984.
Sladek's most recent collection, following *The Steam-Driven Boy and Other Strangers* (1973), *Keep the Giraffe Burning* (1977), and *Alien Accounts* (1982). His main theme is the invasion of the human environment and usurpation of human prerogatives by machines, but he also has a strong interest in peculiar logics and creative illogicalities, which often supply him with ideas for short stories. He is a surreal humorist; no one in SF has a finer feeling for the aesthetics of the incongruous. Compare the short fiction of Robert Sheckley [3-158 and 4-397] and Kit Reed [4-352]. (BS)

4-422.   Sladek, John T(homas). **The Müller-Fokker Effect.** Hutchinson, 1970.
Computer tapes on which a man's personality is stored are bootlegged about, causing havoc wherever they go, until the millionaire who caused all the trouble reintegrates the personality in a new body. Wild and intricate satire. Compare Russell Griffin's *Century's End* (1981). (BS)

4-423.   Sladek, John T(homas). **The Reproductive System.** Gollancz, 1968. U.S. title: *Mechasm*, 1969.
Metal-eating, self-replicating robots threaten to destroy the fabric of civilization if they cannot be controlled and contained, although if used responsibly they might pave the way to paradise. A satirical parable of

man/machine relationships. Compare and contrast Rucker's *Software* [4-370]. (BS)

4-424. Sladek, John T(homas). **Roderick.** Granada, 1980. Original U.S. edition (1982) was abridged, but 1987 reprint was complete.
First part of a two-decker novel completed in *Roderick at Random* (1983). A satirical bildungsroman in which the title character, a robot, slowly develops through eccentric infancy to detached maturity while various enemies attempt to locate and destroy him. Very funny, picking up themes from *The Reproductive System* [4-423] in presenting its satirical account of man/machine relationships but extrapolating them to new extremes. If Roderick is the epitome of the good robot, his opposite is found in Sladek's *Tik-Tok* (1983). Tik-Tok is a robot whose "asimov circuits" malfunction, allowing him to become as morally defective as the humans who made him and thus enabling him to build a spectacular career for himself. A fine black comedy. Compare Gerrold's *When HARLIE Was One* [4-179]. (BS/ML)

*4-425. Slonczewski, Joan. **A Door Into Ocean.** Arbor, 1986.
The planet Valedon is ruled by a highly militaristic patriarchy. The water world of Shora is all-female, pacifist, lacking any military. When Valedon invades Shora, the women's world seems helpless to stop its advance, but appearances can be deceiving. Slonczewski is one of the best of the second generation of feminist SF writers who are examining such important issues as pacifism, environmentalism, and the relationship between language and violence. Although somewhat slow moving, this is a very wise novel with interesting characters and plenty of food for thought. The sequel is *Daughters of Elysium* (1993). Compare Moffett's *Pennterra* [4-300] and Tepper's *The Gate to Women's Country* [4-453]. (ML) JWC, 1987

*4-426. Slonczewski, Joan. **The Wall Around Eden.** Morrow, 1989.
Twenty years ago full-scale war broke out and the world was plunged into nuclear winter. Simultaneously, aliens appeared and preserved a few scattered towns and cities from destruction by means of force fields. Some think that the aliens, who have made virtually no attempt to communicate with humanity, triggered the war intentionally. In tiny Gwynwood, Pennsylvania, the people go on with their lives, practicing a pacifist, ecologically sound lifestyle heavily influenced by the Quaker faith. But one young woman isn't satisfied with things as they are, and vows to discover the aliens' secrets. One of Slonczewski's purposes here, as in *A Door Into Ocean* [4-425], is to suggest practical alternatives to violence. Her novel can be seen as a welcome rejoinder to the current glut of military SF nov-

els. Compare Moffett's *Pennterra* [4-300]. Contrast Drake's *Hammer's Slammers* (1979). (ML)

*4-427. Smith, Cordwainer (pseud. of Paul Myron Anthony Linebarger). **The Rediscovery of Man: The Complete Short Science Fiction of Cordwainer Smith.** Ed. by J. J. Pierce. NESFA Press, 1993.
Gathers 33 stories, including two previously unpublished, thus replacing *The Best of Cordwainer Smith* (1975; U.K. title: *The Rediscovery of Man*) and *The Instrumentality of Mankind* (1979). Most tales belong to an elliptical, vaguely allegorical future history, relating colonization of space and achievement of virtual immortality, both purchased at the price of growing class division between Instrumentality and Underpeople, genetically engineered slaves. Most tales can stand alone, and many are classics: "Scanners Live in Vain," "The Dead Lady of Clown Town," "The Ballad of Lost C'Mell," and others. *Norstrilia* (1975), a novel relating the accession of Underpeople to full civil rights, continues the overarching story. The future history is evocative, baroquely brilliant (though at times politically dubious), moving between the early scientific romances of Wells and sixties New Wave. (RL)

4-428. Spinrad, Norman. **Bug Jack Barron.** Walker, 1969.
A TV personality makes a powerful enemy when he attacks a plutocrat who is trying to develop an immortality treatment. Taboo-breaking in its day because of its sexual frankness and extravagant cynicism; remains significant as an early examination of the growing media and their manipulators. Compare Sterling's *The Artificial Kid* (1980). (BS) HN, 1970; NN, 1969

4-429. Spinrad, Norman. **The Iron Dream.** Avon, 1972.
A futuristic fantasy supposedly written by Adolf Hitler, who is here said to have become a pulp SF writer after emigrating to the United States in the 1920s. Here the ideas that inspired the Third Reich are rendered harmlessly into a pulp adventure fiction—but how harmless, then, is such fiction? Hitler's *Lord of the Swastika* is similar enough to much real pulp SF to make us look again at the ideologies embedded in the genre. Compare Malzberg's *Herovit's World* (1973). (BS) NN, 1972

4-430. Spinrad, Norman. **Little Heroes.** Bantam, 1987.
In a grim near-future United States, soulless corporations that manage culture conspire to replace unruly rock stars with computer-generated "Artificial Personalities," but encounter resistance from the "Reality Liberation Front"—not to mention from the ungovernable spirit of rock

and roll itself. Energetic and hard-edged; weds *Bug Jack Barron*'s [4-428] scathing critique of cynical media establishment with cyberpunk. Compare Shirley's *Eclipse* [4-404] and Cadigan's *Synners* [4-89]. (RL)

4-431. Spinrad, Norman. **Other Americas.** Bantam, 1988.
Collection of four novellas, including "The Lost Continent of America" (1970), "Street Meat" (1983), "World War Last" (1985), and the fine original story "La Vie Continue," which concerns a writer named Spinrad exiled to Paris in the near future as a result of his left-wing political writings and his attempts to gain readmittance into the United States. Spinrad's stories are frequently satiric and often touched by bitterness. Two excellent early collections are *No Direction Home* (1975) and *The Last Hurrah of the Golden Horde* (1970). *The Star-Spangled Future* (1979) combines stories from Spinrad's first two collections. (ML)

4-432. Spinrad, Norman. **Russian Spring.** Bantam, 1991.
In a 21st century where an intact, liberalized Soviet Union prospers and a United States weighted down by Reagan-era paranoia is on the verge of collapse, a U.S. space scientist tries desperately to maintain a place for himself in an international space program, where Americans are increasingly persona non grata. Although he may have gotten the actual historical events wrong, Spinrad's novel comes across as intensely realistic. He's particularly good on the behind-the-scenes politics. Compare Robinson's *Red Mars* [4-366] for another realistic portrayal of the near future of the space program.

*4-433. Spinrad, Norman. **The Void Captain's Tale.** Pocket Books/ Timescape, 1983.
Like *The Iron Dream* [4-429], this novel delves beneath the surface of SF mythology looking for the psychological drives within—and presents a phallic starship that really does have a psychological drive! A fabulous erotic fantasy deployed in SF dream-symbolism; very clever and written with much verve. Set in the same universe as *The Void Captain's Tale* and a thematic sequel to that novel, *Child of Fortune* (1985) is an exotic bildungsroman whose heroine falls in for a time with the ageless storyteller and philosopher Pater Pan, and undertakes a journey across the psychedelic Bloomenveldt, before attaining her particular enlightenment. A fabulously ornamented and compelling story, carrying forward the erotic themes of its predecessor and developing them in a broader context. Compare Carter's *The Infernal Desire Machines of Doctor Hoffman* [4-97] and Delany's *Stars in my Pocket Like Grains of Sand* [4-131]. (BS/ML) NN, 1983

4-434. Stableford, Brian. **The Empire of Fear.** Simon & Schuster, 1988.

A big, sprawling alternate-history novel in which vampirism has a scientific basis and vampires, among them Vlad Dracul and Richard the Lionhearted, have ruled much of the world since the Middle Ages. A 17th-century scholar searches for the cause of vampirism, and his quest takes him to the heart of darkest Africa. Stableford has done a fine job of working out his alternate history, continuing it up to the present day. The African chapters of the novel read like H. Rider Haggard at his best. Compare Haggard's *Allan Quatermain* [1-44]. For other scientific vampires, compare Matheson's *I Am Legend* [3-120] and Charnas's *The Vampire Tapestry* (1980). (ML)

4-435. Stableford, Brian. **Sexual Chemistry: Sardonic Tales of the Genetic Revolution.** Simon & Schuster U.K., 1991.

Stableford is by training a biologist and sociologist, and the ten tales (six reprinted from *Interzone*) and one essay collected here effectively blend his specialties. Black comedy is the tone, whether he is telling us about a researcher with the unlikely name of Casanova in "A Career in Sexual Chemistry" or about assorted disasters by well-meaning scientists. Stableford has argued that biotechnology will affect our world far more than, say, space travel, and these somewhat bloodless intellectual exercises make his points well. An American edition would be welcome. (ML)

4-436. Steele, Allen. **Orbital Decay.** Ace, 1989.

The first novel by a writer who has quickly established himself as a leading exponent of realistic, near-future hard SF of a sort that harks back to science fiction's golden age. In the year 2016 a group of competent but not very well-mannered construction workers are engaged in the building of a new orbital solar-powered satellite. To succeed they often have to work against both the interference of their superiors and the machinations of the various government agents who want to use the satellite as a weapons platform. Steele has followed *Orbital Decay* with a number of similar tales, including *Clarke County, Space* (1990), and *Lunar Descent* (1991). Compare Clarke's *A Fall of Moondust* (1961). (ML) *Locus* Award, 1990

*4-437. Stephenson, Neal. **Snow Crash.** Bantam, 1992.

An outrageous combination of cyberpunk tropes, sophisticated linguistics theory, and postmodernist satire, *Snow Crash* is set in a near-future America where government has broken down and just about everything is done by franchise. The main character, Hiro Protagonist, a.k.a. the Deliverator, is a genius hacker and samurai warrior, but he makes his living delivering pizza for the Mafia. When a deadly disease, the snow crash virus, begins to take out hackers and threatens virtual reality itself, Hiro is the man to tame it. The novel is a complex stew of cyberspace high jinks, religion, off-the-wall humor, and action-adventure sequences. It's crammed with delightful throwaway ideas, such as Mafia-enforced, potentially deadly, 30-minute pizza delivery deadlines and semi-intelligent, nuclear-powered watchdogs. Although not calculated to bring pleasure to fans of old-fashioned, meat and potatoes hard SF, *Snow Crash* is a genuinely dazzling novel. Compare Gibson's *Neuromancer* [4-184] and Cadigan's *Synners* [4-89]. (ML)

*4-438. Sterling, Bruce. Crystal Express. Arkham, 1989.
Early short fiction by one of the confounders of the cyberpunk movement. Included is Sterling's entire Shaper/Mechanist series, most importantly "Swarm," as well as such excellent stories as "The Flowers of Edo," "Dinner in Audoghast," "Green Days in Brunei," and "Twenty Evocations." A number of these are award nominees and all are worth reading. A more recent, equally good collection of Sterling's short fiction is *Globalhead* (1992). Compare Gibson's *Burning Chrome* [4-181] and Cadigan's *Patterns* [4-88]. (ML)

*4-439. Sterling, Bruce. Islands in the Net. Arbor, 1988.
There's a perfectly fine plot here, involving data piracy, and some nicely developed characters, including Laura, who goes out and has adventures while her husband takes care of the baby. What stands out in Sterling's novel, however, is the extraordinarily detailed and highly believable world he has created. The almost universal presence of the data Net, the widespread use of creative ecological engineering, the economic and cultural interpenetration of formerly separate societies, the fads and styles, all come together in one of the most fascinating sociological and political SF novels in recent years. Compare Stephenson's *Snow Crash* [4-437]. (ML) HN, 1990; JWC, 1989

*4-440. Sterling, Bruce. Schismatrix. Arbor House, 1985.
The hero, in the course of a long and eventful life, witnesses the political and technological evolution of the solar system after Earth has been devastated. The long struggle between the biotechnologically inclined Shapers and the electronically expert Mechanists is complicated by the arrival of aliens and the eruption of new ideological movements. A marvelous compendium of ideas; an imaginative tour de force. Compare Williamson's *Lifeburst* [4-500]. (BS)

4-441. Stith, John. **Redshift Rendezvous.** Ace, 1990.

When the starship *Redshift* moves into hyperspace, it enters a universe where the speed of light is measured in meters per second and various relativistic effects, from time dilation to doppler shifting images, become part of the crew's everyday surroundings. When the ship's first officer must investigate an onboard murder, an understanding of those relativistic effects is the key to finding a solution. Stith is not a particularly good prose stylist, and his characters aren't that well developed, but he tells a compelling tale and has created an intriguing science fiction mystery. Compare Larry Niven's short hard SF mysteries, for example "Neutron Star" [4-314], and Robert J. Sawyer's *Golden Fleece* (1991). (ML) NN, 1991

4-442. Strugatskii, Arkadii Natanovich, and Boris Natanovich Strugatskii. **Definitely Maybe.** Macmillan, 1978. Trans. of *Za milliard let do kontsa sveta*, 1976–1977, by Antonina W. Bouis.

The work of the world's leading scientists is radically disrupted by inexplicable events. Can they mount an investigation of what is happening, or must any such project be disrupted in its turn? As in other Strugatskii works, characters must bring rationality to bear on the irrational, and must accept the probability that it will prove inadequate. (BS)

*4-443. Strugatskii, Arkadii Natanovich, and Boris Natanovich Strugatskii. **Roadside Picnic & The Tale of the Troika.** Macmillan, 1977. Trans. of *Piknik na obochine*, 1972, and *Skazka o troike*, 1968, by Antonina W. Bouis.

Two short novels. In the first, human scavengers try to make capital out of the rubbish left behind by alien tourists, which poses awful dangers as well as promising fabulous rewards. Human vanity is satirized but credit is given where it is due. Filmed as *Stalker*, 1979. The second, which is linked to the novel *Monday Begins on Saturday* (trans. 1977), mixes motifs from SF and folklore in order to satirize the bureaucratic process in scientific research and society. As usual, the scientific method proves no match for the arbitrarily miraculous. (BS)

4-444. Strugatskii, Arkadii Natanovich, and Boris Natanovich Strugatskii. **The Snail on the Slope.** Bantam, 1980. Trans. of *Ulitka na sklone*, 1966–1968, by Alan Meyers.

Two interlocked stories offer different views of a strange alien forest, the perspectives embodying contrasting ideologies of intellectual method and social organization. A dense and complex work, comparable in many ways to Lem's *Solaris* [3-115]. (BS)

4-445. Strugatskii, Arkadii Natanovich, and Boris Natanovich Strugatskii. **The Ugly Swans.** Macmillan, 1979. Trans. of *Gadkie lebedi*, 1972, by Alexander Nakhimovsky and Alice Stone Nakhimovsky.
In a decadent future strange weather conditions bring fantastic changes to a region where children appear to be evolving into superhumanity. Contrast Clarke's *Childhood's End* [3-44]. (BS)

*4-446. Sturgeon, Theodore. **Sturgeon Is Alive and Well . . .** Putnam, 1971.
Among the finest short story writers in America, Sturgeon was never very prolific and is now in danger of being forgotten. This collection, one of his best, includes his Hugo- and Nebula Award-winner "Slow Sculpture," the earlier classic "To Here and the Easel," and a variety of other fine stories. Two other late collections are *Case and the Dreamer* (1974), which includes the title novella, plus "If All Men Were Brothers, Would You Let One Marry Your Sister?" and "When You Care, When You Love," and *The Stars Are the Styx* (1979), which features the title story, "Occam's Scalpel," "Tandy's Story," "Granny Won't Knit," and others. Compare Ellison's *Alone Against Tomorrow* [4-157] and *Deathbird Stories* [4-159]. (ML) [For other works by this author see chapter 3.]

4-447. Sucharitkul, Somtow. **Light on the Sound.** Pocket Books, 1982.
First of a series. A galactic civilization is dominated by the all-powerful Inquestors, who cruelly exploit the sentient Windbringers to sustain their hegemony. The Windbringers' only defense is the beauty of light and sound, so the Inquestors use deaf and dumb humans as their agents. The heroes and heroines of the books are rebels against this monstrous tyranny, but their resistance is a complicated business. An understanding of their enemies slowly emerges. Baroque, highly ornamented SF, original in style and outlook. Compare Smith's *Norstrilia* [4-427] and Delany's *Stars in My Pocket Like Grains of Sand* [4-131]. (BS)

4-448. Sucharitkul, Somtow. **Starship & Haiku.** Pocket Books, 1984.
An extraordinary work in which Earth has suffered ecocatastrophe, men rediscover their kinship with whales, and a dubious messiah urges the entire Japanese nation to expiate their historical sins in seppuku. Compare Watson's *The Jonah Kit* [4-486] and Bear's *Beyond Heaven's River* (1980). (BS) *Locus* Award, 1985

*4-449. Swanwick, Michael. **Gravity's Angels.** Arkham, 1991.
This collection of Swanwick's major short fiction includes such fine stories as "The Feast of St. Janis," "The Transmigration of Philip K," "Mummer's

Kiss," "The Edge of the World," and "Trojan Horse." A number of these stories are award nominees and all are beautifully written. One of the best collections in recent memory. Compare Sterling's *Crystal Express* [4-438] and Gibson's *Burning Chrome* [4-181]. (ML)

*4-450. Swanwick, Michael. **Stations of the Tide.** Morrow, 1991.
The jubilee tides are coming, and the heavily populated lowlands of the planet Miranda are about to be drowned. Entire cities must relocate to the highlands. Against this chaotic background a government agent known only as the bureaucrat searches for the outlaw Gregorian who, although locally rumored to be a magician, is actually the possessor of stolen and very dangerous nanotechnology. Swanwick presents a marvelously complex world in a very small space, filling it with finely drawn characters, superb stylistic flourishes, tantric sex, literary allusions galore, and fascinating bits of cybernetic technology, including an almost magical artificial intelligence briefcase and a government office complex located exclusively in virtual reality. For similar literary excellence, albeit on a much larger scale, compare Simmons's *Hyperion* [4-419]. (ML) HN, 1992; NW, 1991

4-451. Swanwick, Michael. **Vacuum Flowers.** Arbor, 1987.
Rebel Elizabeth Mudlark is a persona bum; she's addicted to the use of persona wafers, computer chips that, when clipped into the brain, can radically reprogram an individual's personality. Rebel is responsible for the destruction of the master copy of an important new persona wafer, and the megacorporation, Deutsche Nakasone, which owns rights to the wafer, is after her. Swanwick's venture into cyberpunk is well-written and exciting, though the plot is somewhat on the picaresque side. Compare Effinger's *When Gravity Fails* [4-154] and Cadigan's *Fools* [4-89]. (ML)

4-452. Tenn, William (pseud. of Philip Klass). **Of Men and Monsters.** Ballantine, 1968.
After Earth is invaded and colonized by gigantic aliens, humanity is driven to live a ratlike existence within the walls of the invaders' dwellings. Years later, a few courageous human beings steal an alien spaceship and head for the stars. A fine novel by a talented writer who largely dropped out of the field in the late 1960s and whose work is little remembered today. Compare Disch's *The Genocides* (1965) and Benford's *Great Sky River* [4-44]. (ML) [For other works by this author see chapter 3.]

4-453. Tepper, Sheri S. **The Gate to Women's Country.** Doubleday, 1988.
After the nuclear war women rebuilt society with themselves in control of

all government, commerce, agriculture, and art. The men live in garrisons outside the city walls devoting themselves to games, parades, military training, and occasional, strictly controlled, small-scale wars. When they come of age, boys are given the choice of leaving the city to join the men or remaining as servants. One young woman takes exception to this system and runs away with her male lover. Although Tepper has occasionally been criticized for the stridency of her message, *The Gate to Women's Country* is in reality a subtle and sophisticated novel. Compare Slonczewski's *A Door Into Ocean* [4-425] and Arnason's *A Woman of the Iron People* [4-17]. Contrast David Brin's *Glory Season* (1993) and Orson Scott Card's *The Memory of Earth* (1992). (ML)

*4-454. Tepper, Sheri S. **Grass.** Doubleday, 1989.

Diplomats are dispatched to the planet Grass in search of the cure for a deadly disease that is spreading throughout inhabited space. The human settlers, xenophobic and conservative landed gentry, lead an existence tightly structured around the Hunt, a complex and violent ritual involving the use of alien mounts that seem nearly demonic in their malevolence. The presence of a number of not particularly sympathetic religious groups adds complexity to the situation. This is a beautifully written novel with well-developed characters and a number of very interesting aliens. It's also a serious study of the relationship between gender and violence. Two other fine novels set in the same universe and examining similar themes are *Raising the Stones* (1990) and *Sideshow* (1992). Compare Butler's *Dawn* and its sequels [4-85] and Robert Reed's *The Remarkables* [4-355]. (ML) HN, 1990

4-455. Tepper, Sheri S. **A Plague of Angels.** Bantam, 1993.

The novel opens in what appears to be a village from a typical fantasy novel, but eventually is revealed to be something much stranger. A farm boy named Abasio sets out on an adventure to the wicked big city where a supposed witch is assembling an army of androids equipped with high-tech weapons from a long-abandoned space station. Tepper has mixed fantasy and science fiction tropes before, and she does it particularly well here. Compare Wolfe's *The Book of the New Sun* [4-510]. (ML)

4-456. Tevis, Walter S(tone). **Mockingbird.** Doubleday, 1980.

In a decadent future whose inhabitants have abandoned literacy, the alienated hero becomes a rebel, while one of the robots that keep things going acquires human sensibilities (to his cost). A further study of alienation using SF motifs is *The Steps of the Sun* (1983). (BS) NN, 1980

4-457.   Tiptree, James, Jr. (pseud. of Alice Sheldon). **Brightness Falls From the Air.** Tor, 1985.

A thriller in which a lonely outpost of galactic civilization is taken over by gangsters while the debris of a nova comes ever closer. The violent oppression recalls old sins committed and old hurts sustained by the human and alien characters. Seemingly modeled on the 1948 film *Key Largo.* Compare Cherryh's *Downbelow Station* [4-103]. *The Starry Rift* (1986), although billed as a sequel, is actually a collection of three novellas with the same background, including "The Only Neat Thing to Do" (HN, 1986). (BS)

*4-458.   Tiptree, James, Jr. (pseud. of Alice Sheldon). **Her Smoke Rose Up Forever: The Great Years of James Tiptree, Jr.** Arkham, 1990.

More than 500 pages of the best fiction of one of the best short story writers in the genre, including such award winners as "The Women Men Don't See," "Love Is the Plan, the Plan Is Death," "The Screwfly Solution," and "Houston, Houston, Do You Read?" Among Tiptree's other fine collections are *Ten Thousand Light Years From Home* (1973), *Warm Worlds and Otherwise* (1975), *Star Songs of an Old Primate* (1978), *Out of the Everywhere and Other Extraordinary Visions* (1981), the World Fantasy Award-winning *Tales of the Quintana Roo* (1986), *The Starry Rift* (1986), and *Crown of Stars* (1988). Her most effective stories seem motivated by outrage, using SF motifs to set up situations in which the injustices and tragedies of our world are magnified. Scientism, cruelty, and sexism are all attacked. Among those writers currently publishing, the closest in spirit to Tiptree may well be Sheri Tepper. Compare her *Grass* [4-454] and its sequels. Compare also Russ's *Extra(ordinary) People* [4-374]. (ML/BS)

4-459.   Tiptree, James, Jr. (pseud. of Alice Sheldon). **Up the Walls of the World.** Berkley, 1978.

Airborne aliens who enjoy a utopian existence are threatened with extinction when a sun-destroying entity nears their home. Telepathic explorers set up a psychic pipeline to Earth, which might allow some of them to escape by appropriating human bodies. Meanwhile, the human contactees have problems of their own. A rather shrill and high-strung story. Compare Jeffrey Carver's *The Infinity Link* (1984). (BS) HN, 1979

4-460.   Tucker, Wilson. **The Year of the Quiet Sun.** Ace, 1970.

Time travelers trying to figure out a way to subvert the future armageddon that their researches may actually be initiating. Their researches also stir up, ironically, controversy regarding the authenticity of the biblical Book of Revelations. A grimly realistic and cleverly constructed story, unusual in its subtlety. Compare Silverberg's *The Masks of Time* [4-411]. (BS) JWC (retrospective), 1976; HN, 1971; NN, 1970

4-461. Turner, George. **Beloved Son.** Faber, 1978.
The first part of a trilogy also including *Vaneglory* (1981) and *Yesterday's Men* (1983). Social reconstruction has followed ecocastrophe, international relations being conducted on the basis of a strict ethic of noninterference, but order and control are threatened by the results of experiments in biotechnology and research into the possibility of immortality (already possessed by the mutants who are the main characters of *Vaneglory*). Cynical and downbeat, convinced of the imperfectability of humankind and inclined to be maudlin about it. Compare Compton's *The Electric Crocodile* [4-112]. (BS)

4-462. Turner, George. **The Sea and the Summer.** Faber, 1987. U.S. title: *Drowning Towers*, Arbor House, 1988.
A boy grows up in a future Australia where global warming has raised the level of the sea, drowning most of the coastline, and where out-of-control population growth has led to mass starvation. Despite the hellishness of the situation, we're told that Australia is better off than most places. This is a powerful, depressing, and intensely didactic novel. Compare Harrison's *Make Room! Make Room!* [4-200] and Brunner's *Stand on Zanzibar* [4-74]. (ML) Arthur C. Clarke Award, 1988

4-463. Vance, Jack. **Araminta Station.** Tor, 1987.
Araminta Station on the planet Cadwal was founded as a nature preserve with a strictly limited population of conservationists and research scientists. Over the centuries, however, using a series of legal subterfuges, its now hereditary administrators have allowed enormous population growth, and society has taken on an almost Byzantine complexity. As social unrest begins to spread across the planet, one young police officer attempts to solve a murder. Vance is one of science fiction's premier stylists, though his often wayward plotting and cynical characters aren't to everyone's taste. Sequels include *Ecce and Old Earth* (1991) and *Throy* (1992). (ML)

4-464. Vance, Jack. **Emphyrio.** Doubleday, 1969.
The protagonist must travel to Earth to recover the knowledge necessary to free his world from the cultural rigidity imposed on it by alien rulers. Picks up themes from earlier Vance novels, including *The Languages of Pao* [3-186], to further illustrate the author's fascination with colorful, exotic cultures and messianic rebels against their stagnation. (BS)

4-465. Vance, Jack. **The Last Castle.** Ace, 1967.
A novella in which far-future Earth is recolonized by humans who establish themselves as an aristocracy supported by alien underclasses, but become vulnerable to revolution. Elegant exoticism with an underlying political message. Compare Smith's *Norstrilia* [4-427]. (BS) HW, 1967; NW, 1966 [For other works by this author see chapters 3 and 5.]

*4-466. Varley, John. **Millennium.** Berkley, 1983.
Slick time travel story based on "Air Raid" (NN, 1977; HN, 1978) in which the damaged citizens of a ruined future Earth try to save humankind by kidnapping people from the past whose disappearance cannot create paradoxes. While they are snatching passengers from a doomed jumbo jet, an object is left behind sparking off changes that may destroy the universe if the time stream is not healed. Clever and tightly constructed, acknowledging its debt to the long tradition of time paradox stories by using famous titles as chapter headings. (BS) HN, 1984

4-467. Varley, John. **The Ophiuchi Hotline.** Dial, 1977.
Contact with aliens at first brings new opportunities, but then come the Invaders, determined to take over the solar system and expel humankind. What future can there be for displaced persons in the galactic civilization? Compare Brin's *Startide Rising* [4-67]. (BS)

*4-468. Varley, John. **The Persistence of Vision.** Dial, 1978. U.K. title: *In the Hall of the Martian Kings*, 1978.
The first of Varley's short story collections, followed by *The Barbie Murders and Other Stories* (1980) and *Blue Champagne* (1986). The title story (NW, 1978; HW, 1979) is a parable in which men are so alienated that the path of true enlightenment is reserved for the handicapped. "In the Hall of the Martian Kings" (HN, 1978) has castaways on Mars saved by the advent of miraculous life-forms. Varley almost always deals in extremes, and the fervent inventiveness of his early stories made them very striking. Compare the short fiction of James Tiptree, Jr. [4-458]. (BS/ML)

4-469. Varley, John. **Steel Beach.** Ace/Putnam, 1992.
Innovations in nanotechnology and medicine have turned the moon into a near-utopia, but our protagonist, the flippant, angst-ridden Hildy Johnson, 100-year-old ace reporter for *The News Nipple*, is onto a hot story. Suicide rates are way up (Hildy himself has committed suicide several times recently) and Luna's Central Computer is afraid that it too may be on the verge of killing itself, permanently. Hildy, who undergoes sex

change surgery during the story, must, in effect, track down the Meaning of It All in order to save his/her own life, the life of the Central Computer, and, perhaps, the entire Lunar civilization. What stands out in *Steel Beach*, however, is not the plot or the somewhat arch characters, but rather the amazingly complex society of the moon. The plot is in effect Varley's excuse to give the reader a guided tour of a marvel-filled new world. Compare Heinlein's *The Moon Is a Harsh Mistress* [4-204] and *Time Enough for Love* [4-205]. Contrast Bear's *Queen of Angels* [4-41]. (ML) HN, 1993

4-470. Varley, John. **Titan.** Putnam, 1979.
First of a trilogy (NN, 1979; HN, 1980) completed in *Wizard* (1980; HN, 1981) and *Demon* (1984). The heroine finds an artificial world among the satellites of Saturn and becomes an agent of its resident intelligence, the godlike Gaea, before being forced to turn against "her." Conscientiously nonsexist action-adventure SF. Compare Doris Piserchia's *Earthchild* (1977). (BS) *Locus* Award, 1980

4-471. Vidal, Gore. **Kalki.** Random, 1978.
A would-be avatar of the eponymous deity annihilates humankind save for a chosen few, but the New Order quickly founders in betrayal and cruel circumstance. Bleakly ironic. Compare Neil Bell's *The Lord of Life* [2-5]. (BS) [For other works by this author see chapter 3.]

4-472. Vinge, Joan D(ennison). **Eyes of Amber and Other Stories.** Signet, 1979.
A collection whose title novella (HW, 1978) is the story of communication between a human linguist and a strange female alien. "To Bell the Cat" also revolves around problems of human/alien communication, while "Tin Soldier" is a curious tale of alienation in which the hero falls out of touch with those around him by aging more slowly. Vinge's short fiction is also found in *Fireship* (1978) and *Phoenix in the Ashes* (1985). (BS)

*4-473. Vinge, Joan D(ennison). **The Snow Queen.** Dial, 1980.
A colorful amalgam of SF and heroic fantasy borrowing the structure of Hans Christian Andersen's famous story, set on a barbarian world exploited by technologically superior outworlders, against the background of a fallen galactic empire. The convoluted plot makes heavy use of ideas drawn from Robert Graves's classic *The White Goddess*. *World's End* (1984), a more modest sequel, relates the adventures of an important secondary character from the first book. *The Summer Queen* (1991; HN, 1992) ties

together plot threads from both of the previous novels. Lacking the fairy-tale-like qualities of *The Snow Queen*, it is a well-done but somewhat more conventional story of planetary intrigue and interstellar politics. Compare Herbert's *Dune* [4-207] and Mary Gentle's *Golden Witchbreed* [4-177]. (ML/BS) HW, 1981; NN, 1980 [For other works by this author see chapter 5.]

*4-474. Vinge, Vernor. **A Fire Upon the Deep.** Tor, 1992.
The Milky Way is divided into four concentric zones, the Unthinking Depths, the Slow Zone, the Beyond, and the Transcend. Inherent in the basic physics of these zones are limitations to intelligence; intellect increases as one moves outward. Humanity, originally from the Slow Zone, is merely one of uncounted races on the Known Net. It is a mark of our success, however, that we have planted thriving colonies well into the Beyond. A human research team exploring the edge of the Transcend accidentally releases a Power, a malevolent superbeing that begins laying waste to the galaxy, wiping out entire intelligent species in a matter of days. Two human children, survivors of the accidental release of the Power, hold the key to its defeat, but they have been shipwrecked on a distant planet on the edge of the Slow Zone and their rescue will be difficult. Vinge's plot is big and bold, almost in the manner of E. E. Smith, but his scientific content is quite sophisticated and his character development is solid. His doglike aliens, with their limited group minds, are endlessly fascinating. Compare Brin's *Startide Rising* [4-67]. (ML) HW, 1993; NN, 1992

4-475. Vinge, Vernor. **The Peace War.** Bluejay, 1984.
The superhuman protagonist can augment his talents even further by interfacing with computers, and must exploit such advantages to the full in order to survive in a future transformed (and wrecked) by the exploitation of elaborate information technology, new biotechnologies, and "bobbles"—stasis fields. Bobbles offer a means of suspended animation, and thus become the starting point of a sequel, *Marooned in Realtime* (1986), which features an Earth abandoned save for those committed, voluntarily or involuntarily, to such imprisonment. The books combine interesting extrapolations with lively plotting. (BS) HN, 1985

4-476. Vinge, Vernor. **True Names.** Bluejay, 1984.
Novella first published in 1981 (HN, 1982). Clever computer hackers have established their own fantasy world within the data matrix of the world's computers, where they can work mischief and enjoy themselves—until someone (or maybe something) tries to take over the world and the hero,

blackmailed into cooperating with the FBI, has to stop the rot. A lively and fascinating extrapolation of the idea that advanced technology opens up the opportunities traditionally associated with wizardry. A precursor of Gibson's *Neuromancer* [4-184]. (BS)

4-477. Vonarburg, Elisabeth. **The Silent City.** Press Porcépic, 1988. Trans. of *Le Silence de la Cité*, 1981, by Jane Brierley.

In this award-winning novel, life on Earth has nearly been destroyed by a massive ecological collapse. Elisa has grown up in a high-tech underground city under her father's tight control. Utilizing the city's technology to change herself into a man and to create children who can change sex at will, Elisa attempts to end patriarchal control of the remaining human enclaves on the planet's surface. Vonarburg's Tiptree Award-nominated *In the Mother's Land* (1992) is set in the same world, but many years later, after the establishment of a matriarchal society. Both novels are rather slow moving, but their examination of gender issues is both earnest and intelligent. Compare Wilhelm's *Where Late the Sweet Bird Sang* [4-497], Charnas's *Walk to the End of the World* [4-99], and Louise Lawrence's *Children of Dust* [5-92]. (ML)

4-478. Vonnegut, Kurt. **Galápagos.** Delacorte, 1985.

A group of tourists on a cruise survive the end of the world, settling on a small Galapagos island and beginning a new evolutionary sequence. The ghostly narrator looks back on things from a perspective one million years later. Compare Bernard Malamud's *God's Grace* (1982). (BS)

*4-479. Vonnegut, Kurt. **Slaughterhouse-Five; or, The Children's Crusade.** Delacorte, 1969.

Billy Pilgrim survives the Dresden firestorm as a POW but subsequently becomes unstuck in time after being kidnapped by Tralfamadorians and caged with a blue movie starlet. Thus he learns that everything is fixed and unalterable, and that one simply has to make the best of the few good times one has. A masterpiece, in which Vonnegut penetrated to the heart of the issues developed in his earlier absurdist fabulations. A key work of modern SF. (BS) NN, 1969; HN, 1970 [For other works by this author see chapter 3.]

*4-480. Waldrop, Howard. **Night of the Cooters: More Neat Stories.** Ursus, 1990.

Most recent collection, following *Howard Who?* (1986) and *All About Strange Monsters of the Recent Past* (1987; U.S. paperback, *Strange Monsters of the Recent Past* (1991) adds novella "A Dozen Tough Jobs"), gathering ten stories from the eighties. All are outrageously imagined and narrated with scathingly deadpan humor. The title story retells Wells's *War of the Worlds* in a Texas setting; "Thirty Minutes Over Broadway" recreates the atmosphere of early comic books; "French Scenes" hilariously applies sampling/mixing technologies to film. The three collections are filled with deceptively lightweight but ingeniously crafted gems, marking Waldrop as one of best new short story writers of the eighties. Compare stories of Lafferty [4-243]. (RL)

4-481.   Wallace, Ian (pseud. of John W. Pritchard). **Croyd.** Putnam, 1967. First of a series of sophisticated van Vogtian superman stories, in which the eponymous hero must continually save the galaxy. *Dr. Orpheus* (1968) is a particularly fine blend of SF and quasi-mythological themes, strongly recalling Charles Harness's casually embellished van Vogtian adventure stories. (BS)

4-482.   Watson, Ian. **The Book of the River.** Gollancz, 1984. First part of a trilogy completed in *The Book of the Stars* (1985) and *The Book of Being* (1985). Societies on the two banks of a vast river are kept apart by the living "black current," which also intervenes to make females dominant in the economic life of one shore. The heroine manages to cross to the other side, where she finds a cruelly oppressive male-dominated society, and then must play a crucial role in the events following the withdrawal of the alien divider. In the later volumes she gradually learns the truth behind the enigmatic mythology of her world and must join in a cosmic conflict between the Worm and the Godmind, suffering death and rebirth in her quest to save humankind from the fate planned for it by the latter. Echoes themes from Watson's earlier work, but the tone is much lighter and the plotting more easily paced; the central character is appealing. Compare Varley's Titan trilogy [4-470]. (BS)

*4-483.   Watson, Ian. **The Embedding.** Gollancz, 1973. An intricately constructed novel about the power of language to contain and delimit "reality." It features an experiment in which children are taught an artificial language to alter their perception of the world; an Amerindian tribe whose use of psychotropic drugs is associated with transformations of their native tongue; and alien visitors who seek to understand humans via their communicative artifacts. Original and mind stretching, something of an imaginative tour de force. Compare Delany's *Babel-17* [4-126]. (BS) NN, 1975

4-484. Watson, Ian. **The Flies of Memory.** Gollancz, 1990.
Aliens who look very much like human-sized flies visit the Earth and spend most of their time viewing our great works of art and architecture, as well as our natural wonders. They say their purpose is simply to record what they're seeing, but then some of the objects begin to disappear, including a significant part of the city of Munich. Compare Mark S. Geston's *Mirror to the Sky* (1992). (ML)

*4-485. Watson, Ian. **The Gardens of Delight.** Gollancz, 1980.
A colony world visited after many years by a starship from Earth is found to have been remade in the image of the Bosch triptych, whose centerpiece is the famous "Garden of Earthly Delights"; here the characters (human, nonhuman, and mechanical) undergo continual metamorphic reincarnations, apparently striving to ascend an evolutionary ladder to transcendental enlightenment. Despite the fabulous trappings and the use of alchemical metaphors, the story is provided with a sound SF explanation and has the sense of discipline that is (or ought to be) characteristic of SF. Marvelous imaginative and intellectual showmanship, unparalleled in its exoticism. Compare and contrast Silverberg's *Son of Man* (1971). (BS)

4-486. Watson, Ian. **The Jonah Kit.** Gollancz, 1975.
Men open communication with whales by imprinting a human thought pattern on the brain of a sperm whale, but when the whales learn what we have to tell them—including an astronomer's recent discovery that ours is only an echo of the "true" universe—their worldview is devastated. A highly original novel with some effective description of nonhuman consciousness. Compare Sucharitkul's *Starship & Haiku* [4-448]. (BS)

4-487. Watson, Ian. **Miracle Visitors.** Gollancz, 1978.
A novel developing the hypothesis that UFO experiences are altered states of consciousness that tantalize rationality and beckon humankind to further mental evolution. Some fine imagery displayed in a careful and orderly narrative. Picks up themes from the earlier novels, *The Martian Inca* (1977) and *Alien Embassy* (1977), which feature more melodramatic images of emerging metahumanity. (BS)

4-488. Watson, Ian. **Queenmagic, Kingmagic.** Gollancz, 1986.
In a universe ordered according to the rules of chess, rival pawns discover how to preserve themselves from the apocalyptic checkmate, and experience universes embodying the logic of several other games before discov-

ering the fundamental truths of their mode of existence. The more play-ful element in Watson's work, introduced in *Deathhunter* (1981) and con-tinued in the Black Current trilogy [4-482], is here taken to a lighthearted extreme. (BS)

4-489. Watson, Ian. **The Very Slow Time Machine.** Gollancz, 1979.
Watson's first collection, followed by *Sunstroke and Other Stories* (1982) and *Slow Birds and Other Stories* (1985). The stories display his delight in novel and startling ideas, filling a spectrum from the flippant "My Soul Swims in a Goldfish Bowl" to the extravagant title story about a most unusual jour-ney through time. The versatility of Watson's imagination is well suited to short fictions of the "idea as hero" variety. Compare Bayley's *The Knights of the Limits* [4-37]. (BS)

4-490. White, James. **The Dream Millennium.** Michael Joseph, 1974.
Colonists in suspended animation aboard a generation starship experi-ence dreams that unlock a way into the collective unconscious and allow them to obtain new insights into their past lives and their human nature. Painstaking and neatly understated. Contrast Michael Moorcock's *The Black Corridor* [4-303]. (BS)

4-491. White, James. **The Watch Below.** Ballantine, 1966.
Descendants of people trapped in the hold of a sunken cargo ship have developed a worldview that make them suitable contactees of aquatic aliens in search of a new home. Intriguing development of an unusual premise, showing White's preoccupation with the idea of establishing har-monious relationships between species with very different biologies. Other extrapolations of the theme can be found in *All Judgement Fled* (1968) and his stories about the multi-environmental galactic hospital Sector General, featured in *Ambulance Ship* (1979) and *Star Healer* (1985). (BS)

***4-492.** Wilhelm, Kate. **The Clewiston Test.** Farrar, 1976.
The protagonist, recovering from a serious accident, throws herself into her scientific work but becomes increasingly frustrated by the personal and professional problems that develop as her experiments with behavior-controlling drugs produce ambiguous result. A first-rate novel presenting an excellent picture of scientists at work, developing a compelling argu-ment about the conflict that can arise between the objectivity of the scien-tific outlook and the need for warmth and concern within human relationships. Compare Leven's *Satan* (1982). (BS)

4-493. Wilhelm, Kate. **Death Qualified: A Mystery of Chaos.** St. Martin's, 1991.

Barbara Holloway, a former lawyer who quit in disgust with the legal system, is persuaded to take her first case in five years. A woman is accused of murdering her husband, whom she had not seen for seven years prior to the day of his death. There's no real motive, however, and Holloway quickly discovers that someone doesn't want her on the case. Further, there is evidence that the deceased husband may have been involved in some very peculiar scientific experiments in perception. For another novel that puts chaos theory to good use, compare Clarke's *The Ghost From the Grand Banks* (1990). (ML)

*4-494. Wilhelm, Kate. **The Infinity Box.** Harper, 1975.

Perhaps Wilhelm's best early short story collection, including the fine title novella (NN, 1971) and "April Fool's Day Forever" (NN, 1970), the latter presenting a characteristic Wilhelm theme: a new and promising discovery with tragic side effects. The earlier collections, *The Downstairs Room* (1968) and *Abyss* (1971), also have some strong material; the former includes "The Planners" (NW, 1968), one of many convincing stories of scientists at work in the forefront of genetic and behavioral research. Other collections are *Somerset Dreams and Other Fictions* (1978); *Listen, Listen* (1981); *Children of the Wind* (1989), which includes the Nebula Award-winning "The Girl Who Fell Into the Sky" and the Nebula-nominated "The Gorgon Field;" and *And the Angels Sing* (1992), which features the Nebula-winning "Forever Yours, Anna." Wilhelm has no peer as a writer of realistic near-future SF stories examining the human implications of possible biological discoveries. Compare Fowler's *Artificial Things* [4-172]. (BS/ML)

4-495. Wilhelm, Kate. **Juniper Time.** Harper, 1979.

The heroine is a linguist sought by the authorities because they need her to help translate an alien "message," but she has fled decaying civilization for the simpler life of the Indians, who have again come into their own in the returning wilderness. Compare Crowley's *Engine Summer* [4-122] for a similar celebration of the pastoral. (BS) NN, 1979

4-496. Wilhelm, Kate. **Welcome Chaos.** Houghton Mifflin, 1983.

A serum that immunizes against all disease and stops aging is kept secret by a group of scientists because many people cannot survive the initial administration. Their hopes of increasing its success rate and overcoming the sterility that is its main side effect are dashed when the world comes to the brink of nuclear war because the Soviet government apparently has the secret, and they must decide whether to make public what they know. A gripping account of individuals wrestling with a novel moral dilemma; excellent characterization. Parkinson's *They Shall Not Die* [2-97] provides an interesting contrast of perspectives. (BS)

4-497.   Wilhelm, Kate. **Where Late the Sweet Birds Sang.** Harper, 1976.
Ecocatastrophe destroys the United States, but a family of survivalists comes through the crisis, using cloning techniques to combat a plague of sterility. But are their descendants really victors in the struggle for existence, or has their artificial selection simply delivered them into a different kind of existential sterility? Compare Herbert's *Hellstrom's Hive* (1973) and Pamela Sargent's *Cloned Lives* (1976). (BS) NN, 1976; HW, 1977

4-498.   Williams, Walter Jon. **Aristoi.** Tor, 1992.
In the far future, a galaxy-spanning human empire is ruled by the Aristoi, supercompetent geniuses with vast psychic powers and sophisticated technological support. Although the rule of the Aristoi is far from democratic, humanity has achieved unprecedented comfort and harmony under them. When the Aristo Gabriel uncovers a plot to overthrow the system from within, he takes it upon himself to defeat the traitors. This is a beautifully written, morally complex novel, that explores the nature of personal power and its ability to corrupt. Compare Moorcock's *The Dancers at the End of Times* [4-305]. (ML)

4-499.   Williams, Walter Jon. **Hardwired.** Tor, 1986.
Earth's surface has been devastated in a war against orbiting space stations; the survivors live in a violent world of petty tyrants and black marketeers. The tough hero, who can enter into cyborg symbiosis with his high-tech transport, and the equally tough heroine are outlaws caught up in renewed world conflict. The novella *Solip:System* (1989) is a direct sequel, recounting the last part of *Hardwired*'s plot from another character's perspective. *Voice of the Whirlwind* (1987) is an indirect sequel. All three volumes are excellent examples of the fusion of military SF with cyberpunk. Compare John Shirley's *Eclipse* [4-404] and sequels. (BS/ML)

4-500.   Williamson, Jack. **Lifeburst.** Ballantine, 1984.
Intelligent space opera in which the human conquest of the solar system is inhibited by violent political disputes and interrupted by the arrival of a gravid alien queen of a powerful and rapacious species, while gentler aliens stand on the sidelines. An illustration of the way in which Williamson's work has become gradually more sophisticated with the evolution of

the genre; compare *The Legion of Space* [2-144] and *The Reefs of Space* (1964). (BS) [For other works by this author see chapters 2, 3, and 5.]

*4-501. Willis, Connie. **Doomsday Book.** Bantam, 1992.
Kivrin, a time traveling history student from 21st-century Oxford, is sent back to the 14th century for her Practicum. It's supposed to be a routine trip, but everything seems to go wrong at once. Kivrin is accidently set down in the heart of the Black Plague and soon falls ill. Worse still, 21st-century Oxford is also hit by some sort of plague, making her immediate retrieval impossible. This is a grim, but beautifully written novel, full of carefully drawn characters and fascinating historical detail. It's one of the best time travel stories ever written. The title piece from Willis's collection *Fire Watch* [4-502] is set in the same universe as *Doomsday Book*. Compare McQuay's *Memories* [4-298] and Bishop's *No Enemy but Time* [4-51]. (ML) HW 1993; NW, 1992; *Locus* Award, 1993

4-502. Willis, Connie. **Fire Watch.** Bluejay, 1985.
The title story (HW, 1983; NW, 1982) of this collection has time traveling students discovering the real texture of history and shows off the author's main strength: her ability to import warmth and intimacy into classic SF themes. Compare C. J. Cherryh's *Visible Light* (1986). (BS)

4-503. Wilson, Colin. **The Mind Parasites.** Arkham, 1967.
A scientist discovers that antilife entities have been preventing humans from achieving their true potential and have perverted human nature. The heroes begin to set things right. A similar parable, more extensively dressed up with pseudoscientific materials, is *The Philosopher's Stone* (1969). Wilson found in the works of A. E. van Vogt and H. P. Lovecraft themes echoing his own beliefs, and his SF is essentially a series of pastiches; *The Space Vampires* (1976) is virtually a sequel to van Vogt's "Asylum" and is less weighed down by hints that it all might be true. (BS)

4-504. Wilson, Robert Anton. **Schrödinger's Cat: The Universe Next Door.** Pocket Books, 1979.
First part of a three-decker novel continued in *The Trick Top Hat* (1981) and *The Homing Pigeons* (1981). The three stories run more or less in parallel, and the workings of their convoluted plots model alternative interpretations of the strange world of subatomic physics. Funny and clever carrying forward some of the countercultural fascination of *The Illuminatus! Trilogy* [4-395]. Compare Aldiss's *Report on Probability A* [4-7] and Wilhelm's *Huysman's Pets* (1986). (BS)

4-505. Wilson, Robert Charles. **The Divide.** Doubleday, 1990.

Benjamin appears to be a normal man, trying to lead a normal life, but appearances are deceiving. He's also John Shaw, a gene-engineered super-man created by an unscrupulous scientist. The division between the two personalities is extensive; each is only vaguely aware of the other's exis-tence, and each has a life of his own. When the scientist who created Shaw and then abandoned him when funding ran out sends Susan, a graduate student, to reestablish contact, both personalities are in crisis. Wilson's trademark strong and sympathetic character development is very much in evidence in this well-done tale of a crippled superman. Compare *The Strange Case of Dr. Jekyll and Mr. Hyde* [1-86] and Keyes's *Flowers for Algernon* [3-98]. (ML)

4-506. Wilson, Robert Charles. **The Harvest.** Bantam, 1993.

The Alien Travelers have arrived in a planet-sized spaceship and they bring with them god-like possibilities. Humanity is invited to join them on their journey through the universe; all that is required is that we give up our material bodies, merge with the group mind, and achieve immortality. Within a short time most people accept the Travelers' offer. Wilson con-centrates, however, on the one in ten thousand who turn it down and who must watch their world gradually fall to pieces. This is a somber, almost elegiac tale, filled with interesting characters. Comparisons with Clarke's *Childhood's End* [3-44] are almost inevitable, and it is to Wilson's credit that he holds his own when that comparison is made. (ML)

4-507. Wingrove, David. **The Middle Kingdom.** New English Library, 1989.

The Middle Kingdom is merely the first installment in the Chung Kuo series, which, when complete, will total nine volumes. It is the 22nd century and China rules the Earth. In many ways the great mass of humanity has never had it better; poverty and civil strife are virtually eliminated, though at the cost of limited personal freedom and progress. A mixed group of younger Chinese and Europeans want change and are willing to start the War of Two Directions to get it. The book's greatest strength lies in its detailed depiction of a complex and fascinating culture, though some readers will find the plot a bit slow. Compare McHugh's *China Mountain Zhang* [4-294]. (ML)

*4-508. Wolfe, Gene. **The Fifth Head of Cerberus.** Scribner, 1972.

Three linked novellas (title novella HN, 1973; NN, 1972) forming a coher-ent whole (whose coherence has not been obvious to all readers). The key issue is the identity of the main characters. One is a boy who is the latest in a series of clones whose failure to achieve success in life has become the focal point of obsessive "self"-examination; the other is apparently an anthropologist who offers a strange "reconstruction" of the life of the alien aborigines that were supposedly wiped out by human colonists but actually used their shape-shifting powers to mimic and displace the humans (including the anthropologist). A supremely delicate exercise in narrative construction; not easy to follow, but one of the true classics of SF. (BS)

4-509. Wolfe, Gene. **The Island of Doctor Death and Other Stories and Other Stories.** Pocket Books, 1980.
Collection, including the title story (NN, 1970) and a novella that inverts its themes, "The Death of Doctor Island" (NW, 1973; HN, 1974). They deal with the subtle interaction of "private" fictional worlds and "public" real ones. Wolfe is playing, as in *The Fifth Head of Cerberus* [4-508], with relationships between appearance and reality more subtle and mystifying than those to be found in such Philip Dick novels as *Martian Time-Slip* [3-66] and *Do Androids Dream of Electric Sheep?* [4-135]. This preoccupation recurs in many of his other stories. Later Wolfe collections, all of them excellent, include *Gene Wolfe's Book of Days* (1981), *Storeys From the Old Hotel* (1988), *Endangered Species* (1989), and *Castle of Days* (1992). (BS/ML)

*4-510. Wolfe, Gene. **The Shadow of the Torturer.** Simon & Schuster, 1980.
The first volume of The Book of the New Sun, a superb four-volume novel completed in *The Claw of the Conciliator* (1981; HN, 1982; NW, 1981), *The Sword of the Lictor* (1982; HN, 1983; NN, 1982), and *The Citadel of the Autarch* (1983; NN, 1983; JWC, 1984). SF and fantasy motifs are combined here in a far-future scenario akin to Vance's *The Dying Earth* [3-185], but much more ambitious; planetary resources are exhausted and civilization is in the final stages of decline. The hero, Severian, is a disgraced torturer who embarks on a long journey, becoming involved with a religious order that preserves a relic of a long-gone redeemer, and eventually with a plan to renew the Sun. A rich, many-layered story; the detail and integrity of the imagined world invite comparison with Herbert's *Dune* [4-207] and Tolkien's "Middle Earth," but it is a unique literary work that transcends issues of categorization. *The Urth of the New Sun* (1987), a separate novel detailing Severian's later, off-Urth quest for transcendence, is a lesser, but still worthwhile story. *Nightside the Long Sun* (1993), first volume of The Book of the Long Sun, is set on an extremely baroque generation starship and supposedly has connections to the earlier series, though they aren't yet apparent. (BS/ML) NN, 1980; BSFA, 1981

4-511. Womack, Jack. **Ambient.** Weidenfeld, 1987.

In a future milieu as gritty and dark as that of the cyberpunks, but minus their ubiquitous computer technology, the Dryco Corporation dominates the world through its control of the recreational drug market. The various members of the Dryden family, owners of Dryco, seem to be involved in endless, borderline-psychotic plots to increase their power over the world around them. Later books in the series, not all of which are tightly connected to *Ambient,* include *Terraplane* (1988), *Heathern* (1990), and *Elvissey* (1993). Womack's books are difficult because he writes in a futuristic slang, much as Anthony Burgess did in *A Clockwork Orange* [3-41]. (ML)

4-512. Yarbro, Chelsea Quinn. **False Dawn.** Doubleday, 1978.

A grim tale of social misfits winning a brief moment of joy from dire circumstances in a future California ruined by ecocatastrophe. Compare Michael Swanwick's *In the Drift* (1985). (BS)

4-513. Zebrowski, George. **Macrolife.** Harper, 1979.

Humans are forced by cosmic catastrophe to quit Earth, dispersing into the galaxy in space habitats hollowed out of asteroids. As much essay as story, providing a sociology of these quasi-utopian "macroworlds" as they continue the human story across vast reaches of future time. Comparable in scope to Stapledon's *Last and First Men* [2-119] and very impressive in the breadth of its vision despite being a bit of a stylistic patchwork. (BS)

*4-514. Zelazny, Roger. **The Doors of His Face, The Lamps of His Mouth and Other Stories.** Doubleday, 1971.

A fine collection; the title story (HN, 1966; NW, 1965) concerns a man facing up to his fears in the shape of a Venerian sea monster, and "A Rose for Ecclesiastes" (HN, 1964) is a poignant story about a man who unwittingly brings faith to a Martian race on the brink of extinction. The earlier collection, *Four for Tomorrow* (1967), is equally good, but two subsequent short story volumes, *My Name Is Legion* (1976) and *The Last Defender of Camelot* (1980), are weaker, although the former does feature "Home Is the Hangman" (HW, 1976; NN, 1975)—a suspenseful story about an enigmatic robot executioner. Zelazny's most recent collections are *Unicorn Variations* (1983), which features "Unicorn Variation" (HW; 1981), and *Frost and Fire* (1989), which contains "Permafrost" (HW, 1986) and "24 Views of Mt. Fuji by Hokusai" (HW, 1985). (BS/ML)

*4-515. Zelazny, Roger. **The Dream Master.** Ace, 1966.

Expanded from the novella "He Who Shapes" (NW, 1965). A psychiatrist links minds with disturbed patients to construct therapeutic dream experiences. He tries to train a blind woman in the relevant techniques, despite opposition from her intellectually augmented guide dog, and finds his own balance of mind threatened. Compare Le Guin's *The Lathe of Heaven* [4-253] and Bear's *Queen of Angels* [4-41]. (BS)

4-516. Zelazny, Roger. **Isle of the Dead.** Ace, 1969.

The human hero has learned the alien power of "worldscaping," embracing a new religion along with his godlike powers, but a resentful alien sets out to destroy him. The hero's psychological hang-ups are incarnated in one of his creations, and his inner and outer conflicts are fused. (BS) NN, 1969

*4-517. Zelazny, Roger. **Lord of Light.** Doubleday, 1967.

A colony world has used its powerful technology to recreate Hindu culture, its elite assuming the roles of the god. The hero first rebels against these "gods" on their own terms, but then opposes them more successfully with a new faith. Pyrotechnically dramatic and imaginatively fascinating. The similar *Creatures of Light and Darkness* (1969), which draws heavily on Egyptian mythology, is less successful. (BS) HW, 1968; NN, 1967

*4-518. Zelazny, Roger. **This Immortal.** Ace, 1966.

Expanded from a shorter version titled ". . . And Call Me Conrad" (HW, 1966). The superhuman hero must defend an extraterrestrial visitor against the many dangers of a wrecked Earth where mutation has reformulated many mythical entities. A fascinating interweaving of motifs from SF and mythology—perhaps the most successful of Zelazny's several exercises in that vein. Compare Delany's *The Einstein Intersection* [4-129]. (BS) NN, 1966

4-519. Zoline, Pamela. **Busy About the Tree of Life.** Women's Press, 1988. U.S. title: *The Heat Death of the Universe and Other Stories*, 1988.

Zoline doesn't write very much, but what she does produce is superb. Her first story, "The Heat Death of the Universe," was hailed as a masterpiece when it appeared in *New Worlds* in 1967. In the following decades, however, she published only three more stories. This first collection includes five stories, all of Zoline's previously published fiction plus the new title story, a cutting satire on evolution. Compare Langdon Jones's *The Eye of the Lens* [4-220] and Pat Cadigan's *Patterns* [4-88]. (ML)

Anthologies

In the early years of the modern period the primary purpose of the science fiction anthology was to preserve in a more permanent form the best stories that had previously appeared in the SF magazines. Thus we had anthologies that collected the finest stories published in a given year by a specific magazine, see (chapter 12); best-of-the-year anthologies that collected fiction from many different sources, for example Donald Wollheim's *World's Best SF* series [4-553]; anthologies of award-winning stories, for example *The Hugo Winners* [4-522], edited by Isaac Asimov; theme anthologies, such as Leon Stover and Harry Harrison's *Apeman, Spaceman* (1968), which featured short stories centering on the topic of anthropology; and, finally, general reprint anthologies, which might be structured historically or which might contain stories having nothing more in common than the fact that the editor liked them, for example Norman Spinrad's *Modern Science Fiction* (1974).

Anthologies of original short fiction were uncommon in the early modern period. Frederik Pohl had edited six volumes of *Star Science Fiction Stories* [3-222] between 1953 and 1960 with considerable critical success but only passable sales, and there had been few imitators. By the mid-1960s, however, the number of science fiction magazines was at a low point and original anthologies began to appear in greater numbers, among them John Carnell's *New Writings in SF* series [4-528], Damon Knight's *Orbit* series [4-540], Harlan Ellison's *Dangerous Visions* [4-535], and a host of others. The original anthologies were perceived as having several advantages over the magazines. First, since the anthologist wasn't trapped within the framework of a monthly publication schedule, it was assumed that he could simply do a better job of finding quality fiction. Second, it was believed that books containing original fiction would both have a longer shelf life than magazines and be more appealing to libraries. Finally, it was hoped that original anthologies would attract a different, perhaps more mature readership, a readership willing to pay somewhat more and interested in a more varied selection of stories than the traditional magazines were willing to publish. Thus Damon Knight was able to include a variety of experimental, sometimes New Wave stories in *Orbit*, which would have seemed entirely out of place in *Analog* or *The Magazine of Fantasy and Science Fiction*. This was even more true of Ellison's *Dangerous Visions*, which included a number of stories that were explicitly sexual in nature, stories no SF magazine would have considered publishing at that time. In 1971 three more important original anthology series began publication, Terry Carr's *Universe* [4-530], Robert Silverberg's *New Dimensions* [4-550], and Michael Moorcock's *New Worlds* [12-13], recently defunct as a magazine but now newly reconstituted as a quarterly paperback series.

Increasingly popular as well were one-shot theme anthologies composed either of entirely original stories or a mixture of classic reprints and original fiction. Among the most successful such in the late 1960s and 1970s were Joseph Elder's *The Farthest Reaches* (1968), which featured stories set far away in space and time; Harry Harrison's *The Year 2000* (1970); Thomas M. Disch's *The Ruins of Earth* [4-533], which concerned itself with ecological disasters; Roger Elwood's *Future City* (1973); and Jack Dann's *Wandering Stars* (1974), which contained stories on Jewish themes. Elwood was by far the most prolific editor of original SF anthologies in the 1970s, publishing an estimated 70 to 80 volumes within a very brief time span. At one point he supposedly controlled some 25 percent of the market for original short science fiction. A number of the volumes he produced were excellent, or at least contained some excellent fiction. *Epoch* [4-536], co-edited with Robert Silverberg, and the *Continuum* series (1974–1975) were particularly notable. Unfortunately Elwood's theme anthologies were frequently crowded with mediocre fiction and this shortcoming, combined with the sheer number of books he was producing, more than one a month over a two-year period, quickly led to a glut on the market. Elwood left science fiction editing in the late 1970s, made the jump to Christian publishing, and soon found a long-term niche as the author and editor of inspirational books. Unfortunately he left behind him a near-moribund market for original science fiction anthologies, and he remains to this day one of the least popular figures in the history of science fiction.

When the third edition of *Anatomy of Wonder* appeared in 1987, Brian Stableford's comments on the contemporary anthology market were basically negative. "When the recession put a brake on the expansion of SF publication and forced a certain pruning, anthologies were cut back much more severely than novels," he states. "Anthology production has received very little investment in terms of cash or publicity. Reprint anthologies now flourish only in association with the selling power of Isaac Asimov's name." This last comment is still true despite Asimov's death in 1992. In actual fact the work of prolific editor Martin H. Greenberg and a variety of collaborators, dozens upon dozens of reprint anthologies now bear Asimov's name, many of them theme anthologies covering topics in which Asimov had never showed any previous interest. In fact, one of the growth industries of the mid-1980s and 1990s has been the mass marketing of the names of major authors. Dozens of shared-world anthologies have appeared in recent years featuring stories set in the universe of Asimov's Foundation series [3-12], or Marion Zimmer Bradley's Darkover series [4-63], or Fred Saberhagen's Berserker series [4-378] or, in some cases, a universe created by a famous writer purely for the purpose of publishing a shared-world anthology. A few of these volumes have produced excellent stories, Harlan Ellison's *Medea* (1985) being one such, but most have been decidedly mediocre.

The mid-1980s and 1990s did see a partial revival of the market for quality original SF anthologies, however, and several of these deserve to be singled out. The four volumes of *Full Spectrum* [4-521], edited by Lou Aronica and others, have produced any number of award-nominated stories and clearly constitute the top current original SF series. Gregory Benford and Martin H. Greenberg's What Might Have Been series [4-424] of alternate history stories has also included a considerable quantity of good fiction. Robert Silverberg and Karen Haber's attempts to revive the Universe series (1990) have not yet met with the same success that Terry Carr achieved in the 1970s, but they've showcased the work of a number of promising new writers. Among the one-shot original anthologies, the books that most stand out for me are Jeanne Van Buren Dann and Jack Dann's superb *In the Field of Fire* [4-531], a collection of Vietnam-related stories, Jen Green and Sarah LeFanu's feminist-oriented *Despatches From the Frontiers of the Female Mind* [4-538], and Ellen Datlow's sometimes horrific *Alien Sex* [4-532].

The majority of the anthologies chosen for annotation in this section are recent, though I've included the most important original and reprint volumes from the 1960s and 1970s. My suggestion for readers with relatively little experience in the field is that they look first to the anthologies that collect award winners, the Hugo Winners series [4-522] edited by Asimov and the Nebula Award volumes [4-544], which have various editors. Readers particularly interested in the current state of the art are directed to Gardner Dozois's enormous annual volumes, *The Year's Best Science Fiction* [4-534]. As the editor of *Isaac Asimov's SF Magazine*, Dozois has published more award-winning fiction than any other editor in recent memory, and his superb taste is equally evident in the stories he chooses for his yearly anthologies.

4-520. Aldiss, Brian W., and Sam J. Lundwall, eds. **The Penguin World Omnibus of Science Fiction.** Penguin, 1986.
Anthology of stories from many nations, assembled in connection with the World SF organization founded in 1976 (see chapter 15). Most of the material is recent, though some dates back to the 1950s. Notable for fea-

turing material from South America and Southeast Asia as well as more familiar points of origin, and fascinating in its diversity. (BS)

*4-521. Aronica, Lou, and Shawna McCarthy, eds. **Full Spectrum.** Bantam, 1988–.
A fine continuing series of original science fiction and fantasy stories. James Morrow's "Bible Stories for Adults, No. 17: The Deluge," won the 1988 Nebula Award, while Norman Spinrad's "Journals of the Plague Years," Pat Murphy's "Dead Men on TV," Jack McDevitt's "The Fort Moxie Branch," and Thomas M. Disch's "Voices of the Kill," were also award nominees. *Full Spectrum* itself won the 1989 *Locus* Award for best SF anthology. Four volumes had appeared by 1993, each containing a number of excellent stories. (ML)

*4-522. Asimov, Isaac, and Martin H. Greenberg, eds. **The New Hugo Winners.** Wynwood (vol. 1), Baen (vol. 2), 1989, 1991.
Most recent in the series of anthologies collecting Hugo award winners in the novella, novelette, and short story categories, assembling stories published 1983–1985 and 1986–1988, the last including Silverberg's "Gilgamesh in the Outback," Zelazny's "Permafrost," Bear's "Tangents," and others. Preceded by the series edited by Asimov alone, *The Hugo Winners*, all Doubleday, vol. 1, 1962, 1955–1961; vol. 2, 1971, 1962–1970 [3-204]; vol. 3, 1977, 1971–1975; vol. 4, 1985, 1976–1979; and vol. 5, 1986, 1980–1982. Together with the annual *Nebula Awards* anthologies [4-544], these two series provide a valuable record of the best short SF to appear in the United States. Note that both Hugo and Nebula awards have a history of ignoring stories published outside the United States. See awards listing in chapter 15 for winners. (ML)

4-523. Asimov, Isaac, Patricia Warrick, and Martin H. Greenberg, eds. **Machines That Think: The Best Science Fiction Stories About Robots and Computers.** Holt, 1984.
Perhaps the best of the retrospective theme anthologies using Asimov's name as a selling point. The contents span the entire history of SF and although many of the stories have also appeared in earlier theme anthologies, this large volume (29 stories, 627 pages) currently offers the best historical overview. (BS)

4-524. Benford, Gregory, and Martin H. Greenberg, eds. **Alternate Empires.** Bantam, 1989.
Each volume of the What Might Have Been? original short fiction series

focuses on a different aspect of alternate history. The stories in volume one are designed to explore the changed world that would have occurred as the result of some "grand event that did not come about." Two stories from the book received Hugo Award nominations, George Alec Effinger's "Everything but Honor" and Larry Niven's "The Return of William Proxmire." The impressive list of contributors also includes Poul Anderson, Kim Stanley Robinson, Harry Turtledove, Gregory Benford, Robert Silverberg, Karen Joy Fowler, and Frederik Pohl. Later volumes in the series are *Alternate Heroes* (1990), *Alternate Wars* (1991), and *Alternate Americas* (1992). (ML)

4-525.   Benford, Gregory, and Martin H. Greenberg, eds. **Hitler Victorious: Eleven Stories of the German Victory in World War II.** Garland, 1986.
Theme anthology mixing reprints and originals dealing with the most popular of all alternate history premises. (BS)

4-526.   Bishop, Michael, ed. **Light Years and Dark: Science Fiction and Fantasy of and for Our Time.** Berkley, 1984.
A large anthology mixing reprints and originals and providing a good cross section of the concerns and modes of modern imaginative fiction. Authors featured include Spinrad, Niven, Tiptree, Wolfe, Ballard, and Dozois. (BS) *Locus* Award, 1985

4-527.   Broderick, Damien, ed. **Strange Attractors: Original Australian Speculative Fiction.** Hale & Iremonger, 1985.
One of several collections of SF stories by Australian writers. Such collections provide a significant market for writers whose domestic opportunities for publication are limited. Broderick's material is rather more avant-garde than that featured in the trio edited by Paul Collins, *Envisaged Worlds* (1978), *Distant Worlds* (1981), and *Frontier Worlds* (1983). This work can be placed in historical context with the aid of Van Ikin's interesting retrospective survey of Australian SF writing from 1945 to 1979, *Australian Science Fiction* (Univ. of Queensland Press, 1982). (BS)

4-528.   Bulmer, Kenneth, ed. **New Writings in SF.** Dobson & Corgi; Sidgwick & Jackson, 1964–1977.
Begun under the editorship of E. J. Carnell (nos. 1–21, 1964–1972) and continued by Bulmer (nos. 22–30, 1973–1977). The series was an important market for lesser British SF writers, especially those whose careers were launched after the demise of *New Worlds* [12-13] and those who were more traditionally inclined. (BS)

*4-529. Carr, Terry, ed. **The Best Science Fiction of the Year.** Ballantine, Holt, Pocket Books, Timescape, Baen, Tor, 1965–1987.
Carr first began editing this peripatetic series with Donald Wollheim. He struck a good balance between big names and not-yet-established writers and was always sensitive to originality of approach. When published by Ballantine a supplemental volume was issued, *Best Science Fiction Novellas of the Year*, 1979–80. (BS)

*4-530. Carr, Terry, ed. **Universe.** Doubleday, 1971–1987.
Terry Carr's Universe series of original SF anthologies began publication in 1971 and, along with Damon Knight's somewhat more experimental Orbit series [4-540], helped redefine the science fiction short story. The last volume in the series features a number of excellent tales, including Marta Randall's "Lapidary Nights," James Tiptree, Jr.'s "Second Going," and Jack McDevitt's "In the Tower." Carr tended to shy away from both highly experimental fiction and hard SF, preferring stories that featured traditional storytelling techniques and fine style. Writers identified with the later volumes in the series include Howard Waldrop, Lucius Shepard, and Kim Stanley Robinson. Carr died in 1987, but the series was revived in 1990 with a renumbered *Universe 1* (Doubleday), edited by Robert Silverberg and Karen Haber. New volumes followed from Bantam in 1992 and 1993. Silverberg has stated that his goal is to publish stories similar to those that appeared when Carr was editor, but the new *Universe* has yet to achieve comparable critical acclaim. (ML)

4-531. Dann, Jeanne Van Buren, and Jack Dann, eds. **In the Field of Fire.** Tor, 1987.
This well-done collection of short science fiction stories about the war in Vietnam includes the Hugo and Nebula Award-nominated novelette "Dream Baby" by Bruce McAllister, which was later expanded into a successful novel [4-287] and the World Fantasy Award-nominated "Shades" by Lucius Shepard, as well as stories by Kim Stanley Robinson, Lucius Shepard, Karen Joy Fowler, Kate Wilhelm, Harlan Ellison, Joe Haldeman, Brian Aldiss, and others. Compare Joe Haldeman's *The Forever War* [4-193] and Lucius Shepard's *Life During Wartime* [4-402]. (ML)

4-532. Datlow, Ellen, ed. **Alien Sex.** Dutton, 1990.
Nineteen science fiction and horror stories about sex with the alien. The most memorable story in the book is undoubtedly Pat Murphy's Nebula Award-nominated "Love and Sex Among the Invertebrates." Other fine pieces include Leigh Kennedy's "Her Furry Face," Harlan Ellison's "How's the Night Life on Cissalda?" Larry Niven's bizarre "Man of Steel, Woman

of Kleenex," Edward Bryant's "Dancing Chickens," and Connie Willis's extremely controversial "All My Darling Daughters." Compare *Strange Bedfellows: Sex and Science Fiction*, ed. by Thomas N. Scortia (1972). (ML)

4-533. Disch, Thomas M., ed. **The Ruins of Earth.** Putnam, 1971.
First of a series of theme anthologies edited by Disch in the 1970s. The others are *Bad Moon Rising* (1975), *The New Improved Sun* (1975), *New Constellations* (1976), and *Strangeness* (1977), the last two in collaboration with Charles Naylor. The books mix original and reprinted material, focusing on themes of contemporary concern and fashion. They are interesting because they operate on the boundary between SF and the literary mainstream, juxtaposing SF with more conventional avant-garde items. The material is high in quality, heavy on irony, and (despite the title of the third volume) bleak in outlook. (BS)

*4-534. Dozois, Gardner, ed. **The Year's Best Science Fiction.** St. Martin's, 1984–.
Dozois's enormous best-of-the-year collections have dominated the field virtually since their inception. The editor's taste is impeccable, reflected in his Hugo awards, and he simply has more room than anyone else around to include a wide range of outstanding fiction. The 1993 volume features the editor's usual summation of the year in science fiction, Connie Willis's Nebula- and Hugo Award-winning "Even the Queen," plus stories by (among many others) Michael Swanwick, Nancy Kress, Joe Haldeman, Maureen F. McHugh, Ian Watson, Robert Silverberg, Robert Reed, Bradley Denton, Ian McDonald, and Pat Cadigan. (ML)

*4-535. Ellison, Harlan, ed. **Dangerous Visions.** Doubleday, 1967.
The first big hardcover anthology of original SF stories—a classic that launched a publishing vogue as well as providing a manifesto for the American New Wave. Ellison's combative introductions set off the stories superbly, though some of the efforts at "taboo-breaking" now seem a little sophomoric. A very influential book, followed by the even bigger and equally fine *Again, Dangerous Visions* (1972). An endlessly promised volume, *The Last Dangerous Visions*, was the subject of a scathing pamphlet by Christopher Priest, *The Last Deadloss Visions* (1987), reprinted with revisions as *The Book on the Edge of Forever* (Fantagraphics Books, 1994). (BS)

4-536. Elwood, Roger, and Robert Silverberg, eds. **Epoch.** Berkley, 1975.
Elwood was one of the most prolific SF anthologists of all time, but few of the books he produced were memorable. *Epoch*, by far the best of his anthologies, included excellent original stories by Niven, Pohl, Wilhelm,

Martin, Russ, Attanasio, Bishop, Malzberg, Benford, Aldiss, Vance, Le Guin, and others. (ML) *Locus* Award, 1976

4-537. Evans, Christopher, and Robert Holdstock, eds. **Other Edens.** Unwin, 1987.
Excellent British all-original anthology. Among the best stories included are Tanith Lee's "Crying in the Rain," Brian Aldiss's "The Price of Cabbages," Michael Moorcock's "The Frozen Cardinal," and Lisa Tuttle's "The Wound." *Other Edens II* (1988) was equally strong, though *Other Edens III* (1989) tailed off somewhat in quality. (ML)

4-538. Green, Jen, and Sarah Lefanu, eds. **Despatches From the Frontiers of the Female Mind.** Women's Press, 1985.
Original anthology of feminist SF including American as well as British writers. The stories range from the heavily didactic to the sensitively sentimental. Russ, Tiptree, and Tanith Lee are among those featured. This feminist anthology was preceded by those of Sargent [4-549], *Aurora: Beyond Equality* (ed. by Vonda N. McIntyre and Susan Janice Anderson, 1976) and *Cassandra Rising* (ed. by Alice Laurance, 1978). (BS)

*4-539. Hartwell, David, ed. **The World Treasury of Science Fiction.** Little Brown, 1989.
A large and masterful selection of 52 stories by one of the genre's finest editors. Most of the best-known American writers are represented by classic stories that are nonetheless available elsewhere. What makes this anthology important is Hartwell's inclusion of so much work from outside the English-language tradition. Among the authors present in translation who have reached an American audience previously are Borges, Calvino, the Strugatskii brothers, Gérard Klein, and Kiril Bulychev, but a number of less well known and highly talented authors are also included. Equally important is Hartwell's anthology of hard SF, *The Ascent of Wonder* (Tor, 1994), co-edited with Kathryn Cramer. Compare Aldiss and Lundwall's *The Penguin World Omnibus of SF* [4-520]. A Book of the Month Club selection. (ML)

*4-540. Knight, Damon F., ed. **Orbit.** Putnam (nos. 1–12), Berkley (no. 13), Harper (nos. 14–21), 1966–1980.
The last of the pioneering original anthology series. Knight's relationship with the Clarion workshops ensured that he was often in a position to find talented new writers as their careers were just getting under way, and the series played a major role in establishing the careers of several major writers, including Kate Wilhelm and Gene Wolfe. R. A. Lafferty was also

extensively featured. An early preference for material with particularly polished literary style gradually gave way to an interest in esoteric material, sometimes without much discernible speculative content, but the series was a worthy experiment whose early volumes feature some very fine material. (BS)

*4-541. Le Guin, Ursula K., and Brian Attebery, eds. **The Norton Book of Science Fiction.** Norton, 1993.

Unlike the usual Norton anthology, this enormous, 67-story, 864-page volume makes no pretense of establishing a canon of standard classics. The selection, although excellent, is somewhat idiosyncratic, excluding such expected names as Bradbury, Asimov, Heinlein, and Clarke (only North American authors are included), with coverage limited to the 1960–1990 period. Many of the genre's acknowledged masters are here, however, among them Sturgeon, Blish, Dick, Benford, Butler, Gibson, and Le Guin herself, but also included are stories by less well known writers such as Eleanor Arnason, Molly Gloss, Andrew Weiner, and Diane Glancy. The book places an unusually strong emphasis on women, minority and, oddly, Canadian writers. The 129-page paperback teacher's guide, by Attebery alone, provides one-page commentaries on each story and short chapters on teaching SF, SF history and marketing, critical approaches to SF, primary and secondary bibliographies, and a list of resources. Compare Hartwell's *The World Treasury of Science Fiction* (52 stories, 1,083 pages [4-539]); contrast the 1946 golden age Healy/McComas classic, *Adventures in Time and Space* (33 stories, 997 pages [3-214]). (ML)

4-542. Martin, George R. R., ed. **New Voices in Science Fiction: Stories by Campbell Award Nominees.** Macmillan (no. 1), Jove/Berkley (nos. 2–4), Bluejay (no. 5), 1977–1984.

Each volume featured long stories by the authors nominated for the John W. Campbell Award for the best new writer in the years 1973–1976. The final volume in the series was titled *The John W. Campbell Award Volume 5.* The award is still given. (BS)

4-543. Merril, Judith, ed. **Tesseracts.** Press Porcépic, 1985.

Representative anthology of stories by Canadian writers, mixing originals and reprints. More famous names include William Gibson, Spider Robinson, and Phyllis Gotlieb, but the main interest is in the juxtaposition of unusual genre material with speculative work by mainstream writers—a mix similar to that which distinguished Merril's famous best-of-the-year anthologies of the 1950s and early 1960s [3-220], which were renowned for their eclecticism and favoring of avant-garde material. Some stories here have been translated from French. *Tesseracts 2* (1987) and *Tesseracts 3* (1991) continue the series by different editors. Compare Broderick's *Strange Attractors* [4-527]. (BS)

*4-544. Morrow, James, ed. **Nebula Awards.** Harcourt, 1993.
The annual Nebula Awards volumes collect each year's winning short stories and a selection of the other nominees. Various volumes in the series have also included excerpts from the winning novel, the winners of the Rhysling Award for outstanding SF poetry, essays on a variety of SF-related subjects, including film, and bibliographies of past winners and runners up. The most recent volume, number 28, covers the year 1992. Previous volumes, with editors and years of publication, include: 1 (Knight, 1966); 2 (Aldiss and Harrison, 1967); 3 (Zelazny, 1968); 4 (Anderson, 1969); 5 (Blish, 1970); 6 (Simak, 1971); 7 (Biggle, 1972); 8 (Asimov, 1973); 9 (Wilhelm, 1974); 10 (Gunn, 1975); 11 (Le Guin, 1976); 12 (Dickson, 1978); 13 (Delany, 1980); 14 (Pohl, 1980); 15 (Herbert, 1981); 16 (Pournelle, 1982); 17 (Haldeman, 1983); 18 (Silverberg, 1983); 19 (Randall, 1984); 20 (Zebrowski, 1985); 21 (Zebrowski, 1986); 22 (Zebrowski, 1988); 23 (Bishop, 1989); 24 (Bishop, 1990); 25 (Bishop, 1991); 26–28 (Morrow, 1992–1994). There is also a *Best of the Nebulas* (Bova, 1989). (ML)

4-545. Nolane, Richard D., ed. **Terra SF: The Year's Best European SF.** DAW, 1981, 1983.
DAW's head, Donald A. Wollheim, read French, and his was the only mass market imprint to occasionally publish translations. Most of these stories are from France and Germany, although the net is cast wide enough to include Finland and Italy. Although not all published in a single year, the stories are all recent. The *Terra SF* anthologies follow Wollheim's earlier *The Best From the Rest of the World* (1976). Franz Rottensteiner, a Viennese attorney active in European SF (he's Lem's agent), edited *View From Another Shore* (1973), which includes some East European SF. Compare also Aldiss and Lundwall's *Penguin World Omnibus* [4-520]. (BS)

4-546. Pournelle, Jerry, and John F. Carr, eds. **There Will Be War.** Tor, 1983–.
Theme anthologies, each with a distinctive subtitle, mixing original and reprinted stories with poems and essays, which had reached volume 9 by 1990. Reflects a strong commitment to militarism and its associated codes of behavior; features propaganda for the Strategic Defense Initiative and similar political/military programs. Comparable to British future war fiction of the bombastic kind produced in the wake of Chesney's *The Battle*

of Dorking [1-21] until the outbreak of World War I. Compare Reginald Bretnor's less didactic three-volume series, *The Future of War* (1979–1980). Contrast Harry Harrison and Bruce McAllister's *There Won't Be War* (1991), 19 mostly antiwar stories, and Lewis Shiner's *When the Music's Over* (1991), 18 original antiwar stories, proceeds from which were to be donated to Greenpeace. (BS/ML)

4-547. Ryan, Alan, ed. **Perpetual Light.** Warner, 1982.
Theme anthology offering 23 original stories dealing with aspects of "religious experience." Modern SF writers have been curiously fascinated by the phenomena of religious observance and questions of theology and metaphysics. This anthology revisits the themes of some of the better anthologies of the 1970s, including Mayo Mohs' *Other Worlds, Other Gods* (1971; reprints) and Terry Carr's *An Exaltation of Stars* (1973; original novellas). Ryan includes particularly fine stories by Silverberg, Benford, and Schenck. (BS)

4-548. Sargent, Pamela, ed. **Women of Wonder: Science Fiction Stories by Women About Women.** Vintage, 1974.
Twelve reprinted short stories by women writers, all devoted to the examination of sex roles. Included are a number of classics, among them Judith Merril's "That Only a Mother," Anne McCaffrey's "The Ship Who Sang," Sonya Dorman's "When I Was Miss Dow," Kate Wilhelm's "Baby, You Were Great," Carol Emshwiller's "Sex and/or Mr. Morrison," Ursula K. Le Guin's "Vaster Than Empires and More Slow," and Vonda N. McIntyre's "Of Mist, and Grass, and Sand." Sargent's long introductory essay is particularly valuable. A second reprint volume, *More Women of Wonder* (1976), featured another introduction by Sargent and seven novelettes, including C. L. Moore's "Jirel Meets Magic," Joanna Russ's "The Second Inquisition," and Le Guin's "The Day Before the Revolution." A collection of original fiction, *The New Women of Wonder* (1978), included Dorman's "Building Block," Eleanor Arnason's "Warlord of Saturn's Moons," and others. Two new *Women of Wonder* anthologies were nearing completion in late 1993 and will be published in 1995. Compare *Cassandra Rising* (1978) edited by Alice Laurance, *Millennial Women* (1978), edited by Virginia Kidd, and *Aurora: Beyond Equality* (1976), edited by Vonda N. McIntyre and Susan J. Anderson. (ML)

4-549. Sargent, Pamela, and Ian Watson, eds. **Afterlives.** Vintage, 1986.
Theme anthology mixing a few reprints with mostly original stories of life after death. SF and fantasy approaches mingle in many of the tales, demonstrating again the fascination many SF writers have with questions

of metaphysics and with the possibility that technology might one day provide opportunities that humans have long yearned for in the context of the theological imagination. (BS)

4-550. Silverberg, Robert, and Marta Randall, eds. **New Dimensions.** Doubleday, Signet, Harper, Pocket Books, 1971–1981.
The early volumes of this series helped establish the careers of Barry Malzberg, James Tiptree, Jr., and Gardner Dozois, and the series continued to promote new writers to the end, much as did Terry Carr in his *Universe* series [4-530]. Randall co-edited the last two of the dozen volumes. (BS)

4-551. Sterling, Bruce, ed. **Mirrorshades: The Cyberpunk Anthology.** Arbor, 1986.
Reprint anthology of the latest New Wave movement in American SF, edited by one of the major proponents and theorists for "cyberpunk," which features a streetwise and cynical assessment of future possibilities generated by new information and biotechnology. Other leading figures in the movement—William Gibson, Pat Cadigan, and John Shirley prominent among them—are of course represented. (BS/ML)

4-552. Sturgeon, Theodore, ed. **New Soviet Science Fiction.** Macmillan, 1979.
A representative anthology of modern Soviet SF, featuring most of the major writers from the U.S.S.R. with the exception of the Strugatskiis, whose work was independently featured in the collection, *Noon: 22nd Century* (1978). Early anthologies along the same lines include *The Ultimate Threshold* (1970), ed. by Mirra Ginsburg. Darko Suvin's anthology *Other Worlds, Other Seas* (1970) also features considerable Soviet SF alongside stories from eastern Europe. These anthologies provide an interesting contrast of perspectives with American SF. (BS)

4-553. Wollheim, Donald A., Terry Carr, and Arthur W. Saha, eds. **World's Best Science Fiction.** Ace, DAW, 1970–1990.
A long-running best-of-the-year anthology, with Saha replacing Carr with the 1972 annual, and DAW taking over with 1973. The title has varied slightly over the years. Despite Wollheim's reputation for favoring traditional material he was reasonably eclectic in selecting stories for these anthologies, and although he was slightly inclined to favor DAW authors, he was a reliable spotter of stories that subsequently won awards. Compare the best-of anthologies edited by Dozois. (BS)

The Speculative Muse: An Introduction to Science Fiction Poetry

Steve Eng

On first consideration, can *anything* seem more unsuited to poetry than themes of science or scientific speculation? Certainly the stereotype of the dreamy, impractical poet contrasts sharply with that of the austere, precise, orderly scientist.

Yet past a point, such a dichotomy is false. Often, the tangible, cold technology of science derives from some nigh-impossible vision born in someone's fevered imagination. The poets themselves have, many times, been among the first to intuit and ponder the mysteries of the universe. Various Romantic poets dabbled in science, some of whom believed that the meter of their muse was throbbing with the rhythm of the spheres.

Finally, as mathematician Tord Hall observed, "the mechanical 19th-century model of the universe has vanished. . . . The physicist of today does not think according to a given model, but instead employs abstract mathematical concepts such as tensors, matrices, and potentials." Hall offered these opinions in his introduction to the English translation of *Aniara* [4-565], a book-length science fiction poem by Harry (Edmund) Martinson.[1]

Stodgy, rigid, scientific thinking had already been toppled by Einstein, who asserted that matter was really energy, that time equaled space. If there is a Valhalla for visionaries, Einstein and the poet William Blake should be enjoying instinctive rapport. For it was Blake who wrote in "Auguries of Innocence" (ca. 1801–1803) that it was possible to "see a World in a Grain of Sand," as well as "Eternity in an hour."

As far back as the first century B.C., Lucretius guessed correctly about the atomic theory of the universe, in his poem *De Rerum Natura* (On the nature of things).[2]

Astrology was an early preoccupation of poets, such as Anglo-Norman bard Phillipe de Thaon (ca. 1121) and Chaucer (the Wife of Bath blames her amorousness on her horoscope!). A new star (supernova) appeared in 1572, and again in 1604, and these plus the earthquake of 1580 quite unsettled conventional European thinking about the cosmos. Astrologers shrieked bleak warnings, according to Dennis R. Dean, but astronomers Tycho Brahe, Johannes Kepler, and Galileo courageously offered new perspectives of the heavens.[3] Galileo's first telescope was constructed in 1609, and poets began reflecting the new science, such as John Donne in his "The First Anniversary" ("And in these constellations there arise / New stars, and old do vanish from our eyes"). Milton's *Paradise Lost* is rich in scientific allusion, and critic Marjorie Nicolson suggests that his third Hell may invoke Kepler's grim vision of the moon. She calls the journey of Milton's Satan through Chaos a "cosmic" voyage.[4] Samuel Butler's poem, "The Elephant in the Moon," lampoons both Kepler's *Somnium* [1-54] and the Royal Society, by having a mouse invade a telescope, where it is mistaken for a lunar elephant—and the scientists won't admit it!

In the 18th century, the poets increasingly acknowledged the awesome omnipresence of astronomy. John Reynolds, in *Death's Vision* (1709; enlarged 1725), has the poet looking down upon himself from the heavens. In "To the Memory of Sir Isaac Newton" James Thomson alludes to "whirling vortices and circling spheres," expressing the debt many poets were feeling toward Newton's *Opticks* (1704). Thomson celebrates the vast chain-of-being revealed by the microscope in *The Seasons* (1726–1730), while speculating on the existence of atoms too small to see. Edward Young, in "Night IX" of his *Night Thoughts* (1742–1746), attempts to reconcile science with religion ("an undevout astronomer is mad") while addressing the "starr'd and planeted inhabitants" of the other worlds.[5]

But the most striking Enlightenment poet of science was Erasmus Darwin, grandfather of Charles Darwin. His *The Botanic Garden* (1789–1791) has been criticized for its monotonous meter (Popean heroic couplets), but it contains many splendid flashes of cosmic description.

Erasmus Darwin influenced Shelley, Southey, Coleridge, and Byron, among others.[6]

William Blake was an engraver, a graphic artist, and a poet. He illustrated Young's *Night Thoughts*, as well as part of Darwin's *Botanic Garden*. His poem "Mock on, Mock on, Voltaire, Rousseau" challenges the smugness of the Enlightenment:

> The Atoms of Democritus
> And Newton's Particles of light
> Are sands upon the Red sea shore Where Israel's tents do shine so bright.

While Blake may attack science as being anti-imaginative, at least one critic sees him as fashioning his own rationalized scheme of the universe.[7]

A minor poet from this same period, Henry Kirke White, who died at 21 in 1806, left behind his philosophic "Time," which shows trivial humankind dwarfed by "boundless space," and speculates that telescopes may reveal each planet to be "stock'd / With living beings."

William Wordsworth ushered in Romanticism with his preface to *Lyrical Ballads*, whose second edition (1800) affirms that "Poetry is the breath and finer spirit of all knowledge; it is the impassioned expression which is in the countenance of all Science," adding that chemistry, botany, and mineralogy would be suitable topics for the poet.

More than any other Romantic poet, Percy Bysshe Shelley pursued science so fanatically that it became, for him, something almost supernatural. At Eton his eccentric instructor Adam Walker had enchanted his students with the "marvels of science." He invited them to peer through his telescope at the planet Saturn, which he believed was inhabited. Walker thought fire, light, and heat were the same—a unity that would later inform Shelley's *Prometheus Unbound*. Shelley became an impassioned scientific amateur—tinkering with an electrical machine, flying fire balloons, toying with gunpowder, and poisoning himself with chemicals, with which he was frequently stained and corroded. His microscope was rigged with a magic lantern device, throwing objects on the wall in a darkened room.

Shelley also constructed a steam engine, which blew up. In 1820 he helped an inventor finish building a steamboat engine, capturing this in his poem, "Letter to Marcia Gisborne." In his preface to "The Wandering Jew," Shelley voices his belief in alchemy. His novel *St. Irvyne; or, The Rosicrucian* (1811) affirms his conviction (borrowed from Benjamin Franklin) that one day the human mind will defeat the aging process. In the first Canto of *Queen Mab* (1813) Mab and Ianthe drive off to the "black concave" of interplanetary space. *Prometheus Unbound* (1819) is alive with scientific imagery. Shelley's friend, Thomas Jefferson Hogg, recalled the madcap-scientist atmosphere of Shelley's cluttered room . . . chemicals, papers, and instruments everywhere. Shelley himself was one of the obvious prototypes for Doctor Victor Frankenstein in his wife's famous novel, *Frankenstein* [1-84], which he greatly influenced. (Shelley's teacher Adam Walker was perhaps Frankenstein's remote, real-life ancestor—in the same way that Arthur Conan Doyle's teacher, Dr. Joseph Bell, inspired Sherlock Holmes.)[8]

Lord Byron was much less interested in science than Shelley was—but Shelley had discussed with him the "Last Man" theme, which was then in vogue. This may have inspired Byron's "Darkness" (1816), with its gloomy, apocalyptic view of a planet cataclysmically destroyed by earthquakes, volcanoes, and other upheavals ("The bright sun was extinguished, and the stars / Did wander darkling in the eternal space"). Michael Tritt suggests that Isaac Asimov's short story "Nightfall" (1941) may have really been inspired by Byron's "Darkness," instead of the Emerson quotation used as an epigraph to open the tale.[9]

A similar poem in tone and subject was Thomas Campbell's "The Last Man," one of many works with this title, such as Mary Shelley's novel [1-84]. Campbell himself claimed to have inspired Byron's "Darkness" in an earlier conversation. Also in this vein is Thomas Lovell Beddoes's "Doomsday" ("Ye lakes and oceans, and ye lava floods / That have o'erwhelmed great cities, now roll back!").

That most popular of Victorian poets, Alfred, Lord Tennyson, loved telescopes and microscopes—and his poetry often emphasized evolutionary change. Verses from his juvenilia convey the prophetic, doomsday mood of some of his Romantic predecessors, such as "Armageddon," which sees "The Moon's white cities" and hears "The hum of men / Or other things talking in unknown tongues, / And notes of busy Life in distant worlds." His "The Coach of Death" (written in 1824) erupts with volcanic and other upheavals, and "Chorus" (1830) has a SF atmosphere of riotous planets, with the cosmos itself reeling in "wildest anarchy." In a posthumously published poem Tennyson foresees the destruction of London.

His masterpiece, *In Memoriam* (1850), deals heavily with evolution. *Locksley Hall* (1842) predicts the League of Nations-United Nations concept ("the Parliament of Man, the Federation of the World"). The poem's famous passage, "a ghastly dew / From the nations' airy navies grappling in the central blue," was presumed by earlier writers to anticipate gas or germ warfare—more recently, Isaac Asimov has suggested it predicts nuclear war. Tennyson's disturbing sequel, *Locksley Hall Sixty Years After* (1886), waxes iconoclastic with "Reversion ever dragging Evolution in the mud," forecasting that "Far away beyond her myriad coming changes earth will be / Something other than the wildest modern guess of you and me."

Some other Victorian poems that treat science imaginatively include Robert Browning's "Prince Hohenstiel-Schwangan" (1871), with evolutionary speculations ("new teeming growth, surprises of strange life"), and George Meredith's "The Olive Branch" ("Let Science, swiftly as she can, / Fly seaward on from shore to shore").

Of 19th-century American writers, Edgar Allan Poe was of course the most fantastic in both prose and verse. Yet his prose poem "Eureka" anticipates modern science (non-Euclidian geometry, relativity, and quantum theory). And his "Sonnet—To Science" calls science a vulture that preys upon the poet's heart.

Some actual SF poetry was written by two late 19th-century American poets. Kentuckian Madison Cawein's "Hieroglyphics" (1893) has "superior planets" whose inhabitants converse by telepathy. And Richard Burton (not the *Arabian Nights* translator) may have written the first modern, full-scale SF poem in "A Legend of the Moon" (1899). By using his imagination, the narrator learns that primal gods once peopled the moon with a dominant "elder race" of beings—all but one of whom was destroyed by a rain of fire.

Modern SF poetry has its beginnings in what we might call the "stellar" school of poetry. Its founder was California romantic George Sterling, whose "The Testimony of the Suns" (1903) may be the most ambitious SF poem ever written. Sterling is late Victorian, pre-Raphaelite in his manner, but his love of sky and surf reflects a Pacific Coast spaciousness. His 162-stanza poem follows Tennyson's *In Memoriam* form. It depicts the planets themselves at war, colliding, exploding . . . but new suns will evolve, and perhaps new civilizations with them. Sterling's mentor was short story master Ambrose Bierce, who wrote him on March 15, 1902: "The tremendous phenomena of Astronomy have never had adequate poetic treatment. . . . You shall be the poet of the skies, the prophet of the suns." Sterling discovered and promoted the more modern Robinson Jeffers, whose "Nova" shows Sterling's astronomical influence.

Sterling was the mentor and poetic model for another Californian, Clark Ashton Smith. He carried the "stellar imperative" even further in his voluminous poetry and poetic SF short stories (which influenced Jack Vance). Smith's career began with "The Star-Treader" (1912), where planetary space is traversed in a dream. His "The Last Night" foresees the end of the universe. And his masterpiece, "The Hashish-Eater" (1922), expands in cosmic, astronomic energy. Smith wrote for *Weird Tales*, as did his close friend H. P. Lovecraft, whose famous "Fungi From Yuggoth" (1929–1930) sonnet-cycle concludes with "Continuity" (XXXVI). For once, the pessimistic Lovecraft perceives a discernible pattern in the universe, obeying the laws of time and space.

Smith's hero Sterling had lived in San Francisco. Stanton A. Coblentz was born there, and as a young man witnessed the tumbling walls and gutting fires of the great 1906 earthquake. Coblentz would relive these childhood traumas in numerous poems that warn humankind against Armageddon. Coblentz was an admirer of Sterling and an ally of Smith, and furthered the "stellar" tradition in countless volumes of his own verse, and in his magazine *Wings* (1933–1961). This poetic impulse probably motivated his pioneer science fiction novels—Frederik Pohl credits Coblentz and others with "opening a new vantage point from which to observe the human race."[10] Coblentz told *Who's Who*, "The longer I have lived and drunk of the fountains of man's knowledge, the more I have felt like a space traveler adrift amid the mazes of innumerable galaxies."

Coblentz's close colleague was Lilith Lorraine (Mary M. Wright), who for decades wrote poems defiantly "stellar" in content, and arch-traditional in form. She edited magazines such as *Challenge, Flame,* and *Different,* as well as anthologies.[11] Her "Avalon" poetry campaigns based in Texas and Arkansas resembled somewhat those of Larry Farsace (Litterio B. Farsaci), whose *Golden Atom* was a persistent SF poetry journal in the 1940s. Two latter-day "stellar" poets in the sonnet form are Raymond McCarty, poetry leader in Memphis, and Lee Becker, whose sonnets appeared in *Fantasy Commentator* [12-21] in the 1980s.

The "stellar" bards are more concerned with cosmic wonder than with technology, and at their worst can be stilted, vague, and in the cases of Coblentz and Lorraine, sentimental and fluffy. But they kept the Miltonic-Shelleyan ideal alive, and took it farther into outer space than any of their contemporaries.

At first glance it would seem that modern poetry lacks the expansiveness necessary for soaring, cosmic themes. Certainly the modern vision is often directed inward, but a systematic review of 20th-century poets reveals that many of them have written at least one SF poem.

The SF magazines themselves have carried poetry, as far back as *Unknown Worlds* (1939–1943), and especially *The Magazine of Fantasy and Science Fiction* [12-6], anthologies from which carried poetry (as did the Judith Merril anthologies in the 1950s–1960s).

A milestone publishing event was the appearance in 1963 of *Aniara* [4-565] by Harry Martinson. This book-length poem about space travel was a translation from the Swedish of a bestseller first published in 1956.

Then in 1969 appeared the first two major SF poetry anthologies. John Fairfax's *The Frontier of Going* was a paperback published in England, but Edward Lucie-Smith's *Holding Your Eight Hands* [4-464] was a mainstream U.S. hardcover book, reprinted in England. The following year Robert Van Dias's anthology, *Inside Outer Space: New Poems of the Space Age*, appeared.

Poet and editor Robert Frazier has traced the genre's modern development, recognizing its interaction with fiction—whether inspiring stories like Kuttner's "All Mimsy Were the Borogoves," or augmenting novels like Marilyn Hacker's epigraphs in Samuel K. Delany's *Babel-17* [4-126], or encouraging novelists to add their own verses to their prose, as with Le Guin's *Left Hand of Darkness* [4-424], or Herbert's *Dune Messiah* [4-207]. Brian Aldiss's *Barefoot in the Head* [4-2] includes considerable poetry and Joyce-influenced prose.[12]

The 1970s witnessed a small press explosion throughout the fantasy field—from horror, heroic fantasy, and sword-and-sorcery, to SF. As a complement to fiction and graphic art, poetry was published profusely. Like nowhere else in contemporary literature, it was being written and published for readers, and not for critics. The magazines survived (when they did) by subscriptions and not by institutional support. Virginia Kidd's *Kinesis* used poetry, and so did *Eternity* (1973–1975). Frazier identifies Mark Rich's *Treaders of Starlight* (1974–1976) as being the first "speculative" poetry magazine, as SF poetry was now frequently being called. Peter Dillingham's *Cthulhu Calls* featured a SF verse contest in this period. And Frazier's own *The Anthology of Speculative Poetry* (1977–1980; originally *Speculative Poetry Review*) broke new ground. Also, isolated critical articles began to give momentum to the genre, notably the seminal "What Rough Beast: SF-Oriented Poetry" by Dick Allen in *Extrapolation* (December 1975).

The year 1978 was a "rite of passage" or "watermark" year according to Frazier. Suzette Haden Elgin had already transmuted her linguistic interests into fiction with her *Communipath* novels [4-155], and in 1978 she founded the Science Fiction Poetry Association (see Chapter 15). Simultaneously she established its journal, *Star*Line* [4-569], and inaugurated its "Rhysling" awards. That same year Steve Rasnic Tem's speculative poetry magazine, *Umbral* (1978–1981), was launched, and later anthologized [4-571]. Also in 1978, at the World Science Fiction Convention, Frederick J. Mayer instigated a poetry panel, and also created the

International Clark Ashton Smith Poetry Awards (1979–1985). And in 1978 anthologists like Jerry Pournelle and Reginald Bretnor began taking poems.

In 1979 Ace Books began buying poetry for its anthologies, and *Isaac Asimov's Science Fiction Magazine* [12-4] began accepting poems. (Asimov's penchant for limericks, his own and others', is a reminder that "serious" poetry need not be solemn.) *Amazing* started taking poems in the 1980s, and poets like Peter Payack, Roger Dutcher, Steve Rasnic Tem, and Bruce Boston (one of the most prolific of genre poets) achieved recognition. A large-format SF poetry issue of *Portland Review* [4-567] appeared in 1981, mixing poetry and criticism. Book reviews and witty debates became a staple with *Star*Line*, especially under Robert Frazier's editorship. Suzette Haden Elgin supplied the Science Fiction Poetry Association with the *Science Fiction Poetry Handbook* [4-560] in 1986. The following year *Extrapolation* published an article by Patrick D. Murphy, which asked rhetorically, "The Monsters Are There, Where Are the Critics?" Murphy dared to answer his own question in 1989, with an edited collection of essays, *The Poetic Fantastic* [4-566]. Also in 1989 Scott E. Green supplied the first SF reference work, *Contemporary Science Fiction, Fantasy, and Horror Poetry* [4-562]. And by the 1990s poet Lee Ballantine (*Dream Protocols*) had emerged as the major publisher of SF poetry books. His Ocean View Books, founded in 1981, dignified the genre with the same sort of permanence and taste that August Derleth's Arkham House bestowed upon horror and fantasy poetry. Another evidence of genre recognition are the Nebula anthologies [4-544], which for several years have been reprinting Rhysling Award winners.

But has SF or "speculative" verse really established its beachhead in the outer space of mainstream poetry? "Poetry is in some ways the most difficult, the most dangerous territory for SF to colonize," warned Andrew Joron in 1981 in *Portland Review*. "It is very difficult to join the two forms and not have one of them cancel the other out." But enough bards have already seized the challenge to mount a movement that has lasted over two decades—such as Bruce Boston, probably the most successful SF poet alive. His poems dramatize mankind's terrifying confrontation with science and with the future, and yet retain a fresh, e. e. cummings quality of lyricism. Other poets, in the tradition of Martinson's *Aniara*, have attempted to transcend the ghetto of genre and speak importantly to our age with mainstream books, such as Ackerman's *Planets* [4-554] and Turner's *The New World* [4-572].

Since SF itself is regarded with suspicion by the academy, the poetry of SF is rarely included in any literature course. But Dick Allen, professor of

English at the University of Bridgeport (and a prize-winning mainstream poet), featured SF poems in his landmark teaching anthology, *Science Fiction: The Future*. He and Bruce McAllister, a novelist and fellow poet (both of whom are represented in the *Umbral Anthology of Science Fiction Poetry* [4-571]), assembled a massive SF poetry anthology manuscript, drawing from both the SF field and from mainstream poetry. Their unrealized hope was to create a standard text, along the lines of the prestigious Norton anthologies.

But any poetry movement depends ultimately on the committed creativity of its members. The SF or speculative poetry community has struggled and sustained itself since the 1970s. While speculating upon humankind's scientific future it has made its bold poetic claim upon posterity.

Notes

Special thanks to Mark Rich for publishing an earlier version of this essay in the spring 1992 issue of *The Magazine of Speculative Poetry*, and for research assistance to Diane Ackerman, Lee Ballantine, Bruce Boston, Bety Fisher (Nashville Public Library), Robert Frazier, Theresa Hambrick (Tennessee State Library and Archives), Andrew Joron, Marge B. Simon, Steve Sneyd, and Steve Rasnic Tem.

1. Harry Martinson, *Aniara: A Review of Man in Time and Space* (Knopf, 1963), p. x.
2. Richard Minedo, *The Lyre of Science: Form and Meaning in Lucretius'* De Rerum Natura (Wayne State Univ. Press, 1969).
3. Dennis R. Dean, "Science and Poetry," in *Critical Survey of Poetry*, ed. Frank N. Magill (Salem Press, 1982), vol. 8, pp. 3489–98.
4. Marjorie Nicolson, *Voyages to the Moon* (Macmillan, 1948), p. 54; see also Kester Svendsen, *Milton and Science* (Harvard Univ. Press, 1956).
5. Marjorie Nicolson, *Newton Demands the Muse: Newton's "Opticks" and Eighteenth Century Poets* (Princeton Univ. Press, 1946); Nicolson, *Science and Imagination* (Great Seal Books, 1956); Douglas Bush, *Science and English Poetry: A Historical Sketch, 1590–1950* (Oxford Univ. Press, 1950).
6. Donald M. Hassler, *Erasmus Darwin* (Twayne, 1973).
7. Donald M. Ault, *Visionary Physics: Blake's Response to Newton* (Univ. of Chicago Press, 1974).
8. Thomas Medwin, *The Life of Percy Bysshe Shelley* (Oxford Univ. Press, 1913); Carl Grabo, *A Newton Among Poets: Shelley's Use of Science in Prometheus Unbound* (Univ. of North Carolina Press, 1930); Desmond King-Hele, *Shelley: His Thought and Work*, 3rd ed. (Fairleigh Dickinson

4. Science Fiction Poetry 387

Univ. Press, 1984).

9. Michael Tritt, "Byron's 'Darkness' and Asimov's 'Nightfall'," *Science-Fiction Studies* 8 (March 1981): 26–28.

10. Donald M. Hassler, *Comic Tones in Science Fiction: The Art of Compromise With Nature* (Greenwood Press, 1982), p. 3.

11. Steve Sneyd, "Empress of the Stars: A Reassessment of Lilith Lorraine, Pioneering Fantasy Poetess," *Fantasy Commentator* 7 (Spring 1992): 206–29.

12. Robert Frazier and Terry Hansen, "A Silent Evolution: Speculative Verse," *PSFQ,* no. 5 (Spring 1981), 10–13; see also Steve Eng, "Fantasy Genre Poetry," in *Survey of Modern Fantasy,* ed. by Frank N. Magill (Salem Press, 1983), vol 5, pp. 2415–21; Gary William Crawford and Steve Eng, "Small Press Magazines," in *The Penguin Encyclopedia of Horror and the Supernatural,* ed. by Jack Sullivan (Viking, 1986), pp. 391–92; Scott E. Green, "Poetry," *The New Encyclopedia of Science Fiction,* ed. by James Gunn (Viking, 1988), pp. 359–60; and Robert Frazier, "Poetry," *Encyclopedia of Science Fiction,* ed. by John Clute and Peter Nicholls (St. Martin's, 1993), pp. 941–42.

Bibliography

*4-554. Ackerman, Diane. **The Planets: A Cosmic Pastoral.** Morrow, 1976. Major poetry cycle celebrating the planets, as well as asteroids, and Cape Canaveral. Ackerman drew considerable inspiration from the space sciences faculty at Cornell University, especially Carl Sagan, who praised *The Planets'* blend of art and science in *The New Republic. Contemporary Poets* (1985) said *The Planets* was the most successful poetic work of its type since the 18th century, when poets were influenced by Newton's *Opticks* to write verses about astronomy. Since 1980 Ackerman has served on the advisory board of the Planetary Society, and in 1986 was a Regional Semi-Finalist in the Journalist-in-Space Project. Her verse is at once scientifically precise, yet lucid and lyrical, written with Millayesque directness and warmth. Compare Martinson [4-565], Turner [4-572].

*4-555. Ballentine, Lee, ed. **POLY: New Speculative Writing.** Ocean View Books (Box 102650, Denver, CO 80250), 1989. Historically important anthology of 69 poems by 25 poets, plus 19 collaborations or translations. The title *POLY* signifies the many voices expressed within the compilation, according to the provocative and philosophical introduction. *POLY* contains valuable introductory notes on each of the contributors, who range from Ray Bradbury, Tom Disch, and Diane Ackerman to Andrew Darlington, Peter Dillingham, Jonathan Post, and John Oliver Simon. Includes some prose poetry as well as interviews, including one with William Stafford (Poetry Consultant to the Library of Congress, 1970). Impressively designed and astutely edited. Compare Frazier [4-562], Lucie-Smith [4-564], Simon [4-569], Tem [4-571].

4-556.   Boston, Bruce. **All the Clocks Are Melting.** Velocities Chapbook Series, 1984.

Representative collection by probably the most fecund and critically acclaimed SF or speculative poet. Boston has long been identified with the Berkeley Poets Workshop and Press, and is a Rhysling Award winner (1985, 1988, 1989) and "Best Writer: Poetry" (1988, 1989), Small Press Writers and Artists Organization (SPWAO). This 40-page chapbook of 23 poems was included, along with *Alchemical Texts* (1988), in *The Bruce Boston Omnibus* (1988). (Neither chapbook is contained in its successor, *The New Bruce Boston Omnibus* [4-557], however.) Compare Sneyd [4-570].

4-557.   Boston, Bruce. **The New Bruce Boston Omnibus.** Ocean View Books (Box 102650, Denver, CO 80250), 1991.

Slip-cased, boxed set of five items from other publishers, two of them SF poetry. *Nuclear Futures* (Velocities Chapbook Series, 1987), is a stapled, 18-page booklet of eight poems in the mood of nuclear protest. *Time* (*Titan Press Magazine*, no. 5, 1988, 20 pp.) collects 15 poems dealing with time.

4-558.   Coblentz, Stanton A. **Strange Universes: New Selected Poems.** Redwood Press, 1977.

Valuable for its excerpt from *The Pageant of Man* (1936), Coblentz's major SF poem, which exemplifies soaring, "stellar" poetry at its best. Some of the other selections, however, display the histrionic sentimentality that too often alienates modern critics from traditional rhymed and metered verse.

4-559.   Dutcher, Roger, and Mark Rich, eds. **The Magazine of Speculative Poetry** (Box 564, Beloit, WI 53512), 1984–.

Quarterly journal whose typical 26-page issue contains a dozen poems, four book reviews, and a critical or scholarly essay of seminal importance. Compare *Star*Line* [4-569], *Velocities* [4-563].

4-560. Elgin, Suzette Haden. **Science Fiction Poetry Handbook.** Science Fiction Poetry Association, 1986.

The founder of SFPA offers a capsule history of the group, a theoretical discussion of the genre, as well as highly opinionated commentary on versification and poetic aesthetics. Bibliography. Compare Murphy [4-566], Green [4-562].

4-561. Frazier, Robert, ed. **Burning With a Vision: Poetry of Science and the Fantastic.** Owlswick, 1984.

Wide-ranging anthology of 130 poems by 56 poets, including such genre bards as Michael Bishop, Janet Fox, Le Guin, Elissa Hamilton Malcohn, Lois Wickstrom, Jane Yolen, as well as mainstream poets John Ciardi, Adam Cornford, and Loren Eisley. Frazier has edited *Star*Line* [4-569], and is a Rhysling winner (1980, 1989). *Co-orbital Moons* is a collection of 12 of his rather eerie poems, several of them dealing with paleontology (Ocean View Press, 1987). Compare Ballentine [4-555], Lucie-Smith [4-564], Simon [4-569], Tem [4-571].

*4-562. Green, Scott E. **Contemporary Science Fiction, Fantasy and Horror Poetry: A Resource Guide and Biographical Directory.** Greenwood, 1989.

First genre reference work, concentrating primarily upon the 1970s–1980s. Poets who have been published in leading commercial SF magazines, such as *Amazing* and *Isaac Asimov's Science Fiction Magazine,* are listed with dates of their appearances. Similar listings are given for such small press journals as *The Magazine of Speculative Poetry* and *Star*Line.* Numerous SF anthologies with poetry inclusions are listed, as well as several SF poetry anthologies, including Rhysling nomination anthologies. Winners of Rhysling and SPWAO (Small Press Writers and Artists Organization) awards are given. Poets' directory records 155 then-active poets, with mailing addresses (circa 1988) but lacking in other biographical details. Includes pithy, if sometimes subjective, critical assessments of their work, as well as awards, key magazine and anthology appearances, and titles of major collections. Overall, this directory is biased toward poets publishing in commercial markets, resulting in stronger coverage of SF or speculative poetry than of horror or other fantasy verse. Compare Elgin [4-560], Murphy [4-566].

4-563. Joron, Andrew, ed. **Velocities: Boxed Set.** Ocean View Books (Box 102650, Denver, CO 80250), 1991.

Complete run (nos. 1-5, 1982-1988) of *Velocities: A Magazine of Speculative*

Poetry, edited by poet Andrew Joron (Rhysling winner, 1978, 1986). Includes verse by Michael Collings, Tom Disch, Joe Haldeman; issue no. 4 is devoted to science poetry (guest editor: Robert Frazier), and no. 5 to prose poetry. Joron's anthology, *Terminal Velocities: An Anthology of Speculative Poetry* (Pantograph Press [Box 9643, Berkeley, CA 94709], 1993) contains 19 poems by 12 poets, plus an index to *Velocities*, nos. 1–5. Joron's own first collection (21 poems) is *Force Fields* (Starmont House, 1987); his *Science Fiction* (38 poems) includes the lengthy "Antenna," and several translations (Pantograph Press, 1992).

*4-564. Lucie-Smith, Edward, ed. **Holding Your Eight Hands: An Anthology of Science Fiction Verse.** Doubleday [1970 U.K. paperback ed. available from Ocean View Books, Box 102650, Denver, CO 80250], 1969.
Major anthology of catalytic impact. Included are 58 poems by 36 poets, including Brian W. Aldiss, John Brunner, Thomas M. Disch, C. S. Lewis, Brian Patten, and D. M. Thomas (whose "The Head-Rape" published here gained considerable renown). Good biographical notes, and perceptive introduction, which points out that many mainstream poets grew up reading SF. Compare Ballentine [4-555], Frazier [4-561], Simon [4-568], Tem [4-571].

*4-565. Martinson, Harry (Edmund). **Aniara: A Review of Man in Time and Space.** Knopf, 1963. Trans. by Hugh MacDiarmid and Elspeth Hurley Schubert.
Space travel epic of 103 cantos in free verse. Martinson's space travelers, headed for Mars, end up instead on an endless voyage into space. This affords them plenty of time for philosophical discussion, and they keep in touch with Earth through Mima, a magically powerful woman with a computer brain. *Aniara* sold 36,000 copies in its 1956 Swedish edition—which inspired an opera by Karl-Birger Blomdahl (1959) and won Martinson a Nobel prize for literature (1974). Compare Ackerman [4-554], Turner [4-572].

*4-566. Murphy, Patrick D., and Vernon Hyles, eds. **The Poetic Fantastic: Studies in an Evolving Genre.** Greenwood, 1989.
First major collection of critical essays dealing with fantastic verse. Reprints Murphy's seminal article from *Extrapolation*, which demands that more critics address the field. Contains several non-SF essays, but Murphy on Le Guin and Carl Schaffer on Abba Kovner's holocaust poetry are of interest. Professor and poet Michael Collings offers three approaches to writing SF poetry, in a chapter buttressed with a bibliography of 20 prima-

ry and 26 secondary sources. General bibliography of 253 sources. Compare Elgin [4-560], Green [4-562].

4-567. Portland Review. 1981 (vol. 27, no. 2, Science Fiction Poetry Issue). (Portland State Univ., Box 751, Portland, OR 97207)
Poet and editor Gene Van Troyer, a frequent poetry panelist at SF conventions, assembled a special SF poetry section, with Robert Frazier. Included are articles by Andrew Joron ("Is This Poetry, or Is This Science Fiction?"), Douglas Barbour, as well as numerous poems, including excerpts from William S. Doxey's "Star Poem" epic.

4-568. Simon, Marge, and Steve Eng, eds. **Poets of the Fantastic: An Anthology of Horror, Fantasy, and Science Fiction [Speculative] Verse.** Small Press Writers and Artists Organization (SPWAO; Wayne Edwards, Box 158, Lynn, IN 47355), 1992.
Chapbook (stapled) containing 57 poems, including SF or speculative poems by Robert Frazier, Steve Sneyd, James S. K. Dorr, Walter M. Sharrock, and others. Appendix features SF bibliographical entries by Frazier, and Lilith Lorraine tribute by Sneyd. Compare Ballentine [4-555], Frazier [4-561], Tem [4-571].

*4-569. Simon, Marge B., ed. **Star*Line.** Science Fiction Poetry Association (c/o Marge B. Simon, 1412 NE 35th St., Ocala, FL 34479), 1978–.
Official organ of the SFPA, whose typical 20-page issue publishes 16 poems, 4 book reviews, market and other genre news, and member letters. *Star*Line* has exerted leadership for a decade and a half, from publishing the annual *Rhysling Anthology*, to airing responsible debates (that is, over the potentials of computer-created verse, and over the competition of free verse with rhymed and metered verse). Fiction writers Brian W. Aldiss, Michael Bishop, Marion Zimmer Bradley, Ursula K. Le Guin, Gene Wolfe (former SFPA president), Jane Yolen, and Roger Zelazny have been among *Star*Line*'s contributors. Compare *The Magazine of Speculative Poetry* [4-559], *Velocities: Boxed Set* [4-563].

4-570. Sneyd, Steve. **Bad News From the Stars.** Ocean View Books (Box 102650, Denver, CO 80205), 1991.
Seventeen-poem collection by the Yorkshire poet, who appears frequently in American markets. Critic Scott E. Green [4-562] notes that Sneyd's "rather dry English humor" has its dark side, as he shows humankind struggling with an impersonal universe. Sneyd is also Lilith Lorraine's biographer. Compare Boston [4-557].

*4-571. Tem, Steve Rasnic, ed. **The Umbral Anthology of Science Fiction Poetry.** Umbral Press (Ocean View Books, Box 102650, Denver, CO 80250), 1982.

Milestone anthology of 141 poems by 61 poets including Sonya Dorman, Tom Disch, Dick Allen, Duane Ackerson, Robert Frazier, Ray Bradbury—and mainstream poets David Wagoner, Mark Jarman, William Stafford, and Archibald Macleish. With introduction and afterword. Compare Ballentine [4-555], Frazier [4-561], Simon [4-568].

4-572. Turner, Frederick. **The New World: An Epic Poem.** Princeton Univ. Press, 1985.

Narrative poem that begins in A.D. 2376, in a fragmented America riven by war and choked by energy shortages. New York City lies in rubble—but an intellectual aristocracy of Free Counties tenders future hope. Written in unrhymed, five-stressed lines, by an English professor, Shakespeare scholar, and science fiction novelist (*A Double Shadow*, 1978). Turner's several poetry collections contain occasional SF entries; and his *Genesis: An Epic Poem* (1988) is another futuristic chronicle, featuring a trip to Mars, which one day may become habitable to humans. Compare Martinson [4-365], Ackerman [4-554].

CHAPTER 5

Young Adult Science Fiction

Francis J. Molson and Susan G. Miles

Rocket Ship Galileo [5-62] by Robert Heinlein, published in 1947, is generally considered the first American juvenile science fiction work to merit serious critical attention. For the first time—at least, as far as specialists knew—an author expertly blended characters, subject matter, and plot in a way that was novel, relevant, and appealing to young readers. Ross, Art, and Morrie, the protagonists in the story, were believable teenagers. The subject matter—a trip to the Moon in an atomic engine–powered rocket—was plausible extrapolation from current scientific knowledge; for who in 1947 had not heard of atomic power and the V-1 and V-2 rockets, technological breakthroughs that rendered possible a variety of schemes and proposals previously judged illusory or harebrained? The plot of the novel was both exciting and timely: not only a trip to the Moon and the discovery there of an extinct civilization, but the destruction of a lunar base from which a band of Nazis plotted World War III.

There was another reason why the specialists were willing to praise *Rocket Ship Galileo*. The novel fit nicely into a recently developed genre, the junior novel, designed to appeal to teenagers by acknowledging their existence and speaking to their special needs. For Ross, Art, and Morrie, like many other American teenagers, fretted over vocational goals. They even debated whether they should obey their parents, who at first would not allow the boys to accompany Dr. Cargraves, eminent scientist and Morrie's uncle, on his flight to the Moon; however, Cargraves convinced the boys' parents that going to the Moon would be not only adventurous but educational and character building. Seen as a junior novel, then, *Rocket Ship Galileo* easily met the important didactic requirements demanded of literature aimed at young readers. Thus, science fiction, once it was demonstrated that it could be written competently and contain didactic elements, was allowed to enter the mainstream of children's literature.

The publication of *Rocket Ship Galileo* may have marked mainstream children's literature recognition of SF and its potential for engaging youth, but the book did not initiate children's and young adult (YA) SF. Prior to 1947 young readers had ready access to popular SF literature specifically written for them or easily comprehensible. As early as the late 1870s, for instance, the Frank Reade and Frank Reade, Jr., stories, perhaps the most important SF series in 19th-century America, began to appear. Begun by Harry Eaton and continued by Luis Senarens, who contributed most of the 187 Reade stories (reprinted in ten volumes by Garland Publishing; see Bleiler [7-21] for a detailed discussion), these adventures not only chronicled the exploits of a boy genius responsible for many remarkable inventions, but in Jules Verne-like fashion strewed the exploits over a wide geographic area. Other science adventure stories, modeled on or similar to the successful Reade pattern, could be found in the Tom Edison, Jr., Happy Days, Pluck and Luck, and the British The Boys' Own Paper series.

Not long after the heyday of the Reade stories, the Edward Stratemeyer syndicate, alert to new trends in youths' reading tastes, decided that science adventure might still attract young readers. Accordingly, in 1906 Stratemeyer published in hard cover the first volume in what came to be called the Great Marvel series, *Through the Air to the North Pole* [5-132], written by Roy Rockwood, a syndicate house name and, most likely, actually Howard Garis, Stratemeyer's most effective author. Perhaps the most interesting of early SF for boys, the Great Marvel books, with their distinctive Jules Verne flavor, eventually numbered nine. Stratemeyer, apparently convinced that the juvenile market for science adventure was real and might sustain a regular series, released in 1910 five titles of a proposed series focused on another boy inventor and his "marvelous" achievements—Tom Swift [5-6]. Written by Victor Appleton, another house name and, again, really Howard Garis, the Tom Swift books proved most successful, totaling 38 titles before their demise in 1941 and becoming one of the two or three most popular series of the 20th century.

There were other series competing with Tom Swift and the Great Marvel adventures for the attention of young boys enthusiastic for SF. (Girls, as was typical of the time, were deemed a priori "uninterested or unsuited for science or strenuous adventure.") Prominent among these were: Hancock's The Conquest of the United States [5-58]; Bonner's The Boy Inventors; two called The Radio Boys (one by Gerald Breckinridge, the other by Allen Chapman); Howard Garis's Rocket Riders; and Snell's Radiophone Boys. Perhaps the most imaginative of these rivals to Tom Swift were the four volumes of Claudy's Adventures in the Unknown [5-33], actually expansions and revisions of stories first published in *American Boy*. Finally, youngsters' dreams of interplanetary adventure were realized during the 1930s in tales of Buck Rogers and Flash Gordon in the comics and then in Big Little Books.

Youngsters, however, did not have to limit their reading to series books. What would be called today adult SF, often in pulp form, was available to the young. It was not until the last decades of the 19th century that distinctions between children's books and adult ones began to be drawn with any kind of precision. Thus, young and old readers might be reading Verne, Wells, or Burroughs. Further, some youngsters, even when popular children's SF was available, probably skipped it and read adult SF. Isaac Asimov, for example, when speaking of his youth, does not mention reading children's SF, but he does vividly recall reading copies of *Science Wonder Stories*, *Amazing Stories*, and *Air Wonder Stories*, which were for sale on his father's newsstand.

Within the mainstream itself, certain books, usually fantasies, indirectly contributed to the development of space fantasy or SF. For instance, Robinson Crusoe's narrative of survival on a strange island and Gulliver's adventures among the astonishing miniature and gigantic peoples were read also by children and soon became staples of their reading fare, presumably whetting an appetite for similar adventure tales. Charles Delorme (pseudonym of Charles Rumball) in *The Marvelous and Incredible Adventures of Charles Thunderbolt in the Moon* (1851) implied the possibility of space adventure and to that extent predated Verne. Elbert Perce's *Gulliver Loi, His Three Voyages: Being an Account of His Marvelous Adventures in Kailo, Hydrogenia, and Ejano* (1852) contains one of the very first references to space travel by rocket. Charles Kingsley's *The Water Babies* (1863) moralized excessively, but it did utilize the fantasy mode to inform its readers of both the science of underwater life and the theory of evolution; thus, the latter appeared for the first time as a topic in children's literature. The stories of Alice's journeys not only introduced children to wonderlands where ordinary reason is eschewed, but, by entertaining their young readers, sought to undermine the dictum that children's books had to teach earnestly and ought not waste or "murder" time. In *Up the Moonstair* (1890) Albert E. Hooper placed lunar inhabitants on the hidden side of the Moon to escape the prying eyes of Earth's astronomers; in Howard Pyle's *The Garden Behind the Moon*, moonlight functions as a bridge from Earth to the Moon; and in Frances Montgomery's *The Electrical Elephant* (1903) and its sequel, *On a Lark to the Planets* (1904), the young protagonists, because of the electrically powered mechanical elephant, traveled worldwide and in space. L. Frank Baum, attempting in many of his books an indigenous American fantasy, saw in electricity peculiarly appropriate American material for imaginative treatment and wrote *The Master Key: An Electrical Fairy Tale* (1901). Baum should also be given credit for creating one of the first fully realized robots in children's literature, Tik-Tok, who was introduced in *Ozma of Oz* (1902) and seven years later had its own book, *Tik-Tok of Oz*. And, as a final instance, Hugh Lofting, in *Doctor Dolittle in the Moon* (1929), recounted the lunar adventures and observations of his inestimable and much-traveled hero.

After the popular and critical success of *Rocket Ship Galileo*, mainstream publishers did not take long to realize that juvenile science fiction might prove profitable. By 1958, at least 90 additional science fiction titles, excluding series books, were published in the United States alone. Although this amount hardly seems impressive, the total was indeed large in comparison to preceding years, when virtually nothing appeared, and it indicated that science fiction was well on its way to becoming an important subgenre of both American and British children's and YA literature. The relatively sudden popularity and acceptance of young people's science fiction in the 1950s can be attributed to many causes: the pioneering work of Heinlein, who went on writing other good juveniles; the emergence of a handful of genuinely talented writers, such as Andre Norton and Alan Nourse, who wanted to write for young audiences; the continuing development of preteens and teenagers as separate groups requiring their own reading material (most of the new titles being addressed to these groups); the growing popularity of science fiction not only in novels and short stories but in film and comics, the two media that drew teenagers and preteens as avid fans. For example, 1950 saw in the British *The Eagle* the initial appearance of the hugely successful Dan Dare comic; and the Sputnik phenomenon and resulting interest in space and its exploration rendered less suspect and flamboyant the speculation of science fiction.

It would be pleasant to claim that most of the science fiction for young people in the 1950s was well done, but the truth is the opposite.

Children's literature, historically, has been burdened with hackwork, and juvenile science fiction is no exception. Too many publishers, eager to take advantage of the interest in science fiction, were willing to accept any manuscript dealing with a first trip to the Moon, life on Venus, or a visitor from Mars or some other planet, provided the story had for its protagonist youngsters (sometimes even animals), virtually eschewed all references to sex, and ostensibly had some educational or moral value. For instance, in Leslie Greener's *Moon Ahead* (1951), Noel, Frank, and their fathers are invited to go along on a rocket flight to the Moon. A plethora of scientific and procedural information clogs the narrative, and the adventures on the Moon are tepid and predictable. In Carl Biemiller's *The Magic Ball from Mars* (1953), J meets a mysterious visitor from Mars, who gives him a magic ball because the young boy believed in the stranger. The U.S. military appeals to J's patriotism in order to obtain the ball, which will grant any wish, but the Martians, fearing the possibility of planetwide war, take back the ball without even allowing the youth to decide whether he might voluntarily return it. Martians and a first trip to the Moon are combined subject matter in Mary Patchett's *Send for Johnny Danger* (1956). The first humans on the Moon, Johnny Danger and his crew readily escape from their Martian captors, who, although able to colonize the Moon because of their very advanced technology, are inexplicably unable to cope with human beings. Or, in Ruthven Todd's *Space Cat* (1952), Flyball, a cat, accidentally becomes a crew member on a rocket to the Moon, finds sentient life there, saves his captain, and returns to Earth a hero. This work, incidentally, illustrates the problems confronting anyone who wants to write science fiction for the younger child. Generally speaking, trying to organize a picture book around a scientific principle or technological procedure is difficult because of the intended audience's lack of scientific knowledge. Consequently, the author opts for little or no science at all, and the result is best labeled space fancy—for example, a picture book about talking cats or monkeys acting as space pilots or metal-eating monsters from space.

Three features of children's and YA science fiction from the 1950s deserve particular attention. The first is the contribution that the John C. Winston Company made to the emerging subgenre. Under the editorial direction of Cecile Matschat and Carl Carmer, Winston published 26 novels in the 1950s, almost one-third of the juvenile SF released during the decade. (Gregg Press reprinted several of them.) As a group, the novels still make for interesting and mildly entertaining reading; some of the novels—for example, Raymond Jones's *Planet of Light* (1953), Oliver's *Mists of Dawn* [5-125], Anderson's *Vault of the Ages* [5-4], and North's *The*

Ant Men [5-112]—compare quite favorably, in imaginative conception, style, and narrative pace, with the typical YA SF novel written today. The format of the Winston novels clearly reveals the editors' perspicacity. Usually each of the stories was preceded by an introduction in which the author summarized briefly then-current information about a particular planet (such as Venus or Saturn), or natural phenomena (such as ESP or the possibility of timeslips), or a particular scientific discipline (such as archaeology or oceanography), and then, even more briefly, speculated about future changes or applications. The narrative which followed supposedly embodied or illustrated the speculation; thus, whatever entertainment or escape the narrative provided would be justified by the speculation. In this way, the didacticism expected of juvenile books was incorporated into the Winston novels, and science fiction—"cheapened" in the eyes of librarians, teachers, and concerned parents by its association with pulps, series books, and comics—would be elevated and made respectable. Fortunately for the reader, the narratives are, generally speaking, relatively unencumbered by ill-digested blocks of information and speculation; and they succeed, or fail, primarily as storytelling and not as instruction.

The second noteworthy feature of young people's SF in the 1950s was the rekindling of interest in SF series fiction. The same year *Rocket Ship Galileo* was released, Grosset & Dunlap published John Blaine's *The Rocket Shadow* [5-14] and three other titles as part of a prospective series devoted to Rick Brant's Electronic Adventures, which ultimately included 23 volumes. Other series were begun: Carey Rockwell's Tom Corbett, Space Cadet books, Jay Williams and Raymond Abrashkin's still popular Danny Dunn adventures, and, perhaps most appropriately, a new Tom Swift series. Interestingly, for the new series the "sons" of both the author and the hero were involved: Victor Appleton II wrote 33 stories about Tom Swift, Jr. At the end of the decade, two additional series were inaugurated: Dig Allen by Joseph Greene and Mike Mars by Donald Wollheim. Clearly, the renewal of interest in series SF and its acceptance by youngsters suggest that mainstream children's and YA SF in its short history already has assisted in the spinning off of popular culture manifestations of science fiction.

The third feature that should be noted concerning SF for young readers in the 1950s is the high proportion of titles—about one-third (including many of the Winston novels)—produced by already established authors of science fiction. The names of those who have written for both children and adults include some of the most prominent authors of science fiction: Isaac Asimov, Robert Silverberg, Donald Wollheim, Poul

Anderson, James Blish, Ben Bova, Arthur Clarke, Lester del Rey, Gordon Dickson, Murray Leinster, Andre Norton, Jack Vance, and Harry Harrison. Of more than passing interest is the possibility that some of these "name" authors might have been forced, were it not for their juvenile SF output, to cease writing science fiction. Unfortunately, the evidence also suggests that several were not above placing hackwork in the supposedly lucrative juvenile market. On the other hand, the competent work of Heinlein, Norton, Bova, del Rey, and Dickson provided direction to and some prestige for children's and YA science fiction until new talent, seriously committed to writing for youth and unwilling to compromise, entered the field in the next four decades.

Since the 1950s YA and children's science fiction has definitely come of age. An overreliance on first trips to the Moon or meeting Martians has been abandoned, and new and wider-ranging topics have been essayed. The political abuses of behavior modification and mind control, for instance, are a central concern in John Christopher's novels, Sleator's *House of Stairs* [5-144] and Ames's *Anna to the Infinite Power* [5-2]. ESP has become a favorite topic; especially fine examples are Virginia Hamilton's *Justice and Her Brothers* and its two sequels [5-57], and Joan Vinge's *Psion* [5-162]. Theological speculation can be found in the novels of Madeleine L'Engle, in particular her time trilogy [5-95] and *The Young Unicorns* (1968), and those of Alexander Key [5-86, 87]. The sexism historically so endemic in children's books (as well as in SF in general) is also under attack, especially in the novels of Sylvia Engdahl, H. M. Hoover, and Monica Hughes, whose central protagonists are girls or young women who are assigned tasks usually given males, and in Robert O'Brien's *Z for Zachariah* [5-123], which depicts the tragic shortcomings of conventional male-female relationships even in the aftermath of catastrophe. The evils of racism are explored candidly in Piers Anthony's *Race Against Time* [5-5], Monica Hughes's *The Keeper of the Isis Light* and its two sequels [5-76], A. M. Lightner's *The Day of the Drones* [5-96], Craig Strete's *The Bleeding Man and Other Science Fiction Stories* [5-151], and Laurence Yep's *Sweetwater* [5-179]. The ecological movement, as expected, has become a common topic. For example, James R. Berry's *Dar Tellum: Stranger From a Distant Planet* (1973), one of the few SF picture books that work, argues for conservation; Adrien Stoutenburg's *Out There* [5-150] is a study of human destruction of other species and its effect on a future where expeditions are organized to find any traces of animal life; Caroline Macdonald's *The Lake at the End of the World* [5-101] intertwines the story of a world ravaged by chemical pollution with that of the machinations of a "mad scientist"; and Jean Ure's *Plague* [5-159] graphically depicts an England devastated by a plague brought about by human error. Not surprisingly, electronic games too have become plot material; witness Gillian Rubenstein's *Space Demons* [5-134] and its sequel, *Skyway*, in which four teens enter into experimental computer games, testing their courage and learning tolerance. Finally, as might be anticipated in fiction designed for youth, the conflict between the demands of society and individual freedom continues to be portrayed but in more contemporary terms: Dale and Danny Carlsons' *The Shining Pool* [5-22], Hoover's *The Lost Star* [5-70], John Rowe Townsend's *The Creatures* [5-156], Robert Westall's *Futuretrack 5* [5-168], and Gregory Maguire's *I Feel Like the Morning Sun* [5-104].

Perhaps the best evidence that YA and children's science fiction has become a permanent, important segment of YA and children's literature is twofold. One aspect is that science fiction for youth, at ease with itself and confident of its value, can make fun of itself as in the Matthew Looney books of Jerome Beatty, which, describing Moon inhabitants debating whether Earth can support any life, gently parody stock situations and attitudes. The other aspect is that the mainstream has granted science fiction its highest awards. For example, William Pene du Bois' *The Twenty-One Balloons* [5-44], a humorous, Jules Verne-like, richly imaginative science fantasy, won the 1948 Newbery Medal as the best children's book of the year. L'Engle's *A Wrinkle in Time* [5-95], with its talk of time warps and its depiction of a world ruled by a computer that exemplifies the worst features of behavior modification and mind control, won the same award in 1963. Robert C. O'Brien's *Mrs. Frisby and the Rats of NIMH* [5-122], the story of rats who have become superintelligent through psychological and biological experimentation and who build themselves a utopian society, was awarded the 1972 Newbery Medal.

It is easy to understand why YA fiction, successor to the junior or teen novel of the 1940s and 1950s, some of whose major conventions Heinlein incorporated into his pioneering juveniles, continues to feature SF. In their *Literature for Today's Young Adults*, fourth edition (1993), Kenneth L. Donelson and Alleen Pace Nilsen claim that SF enjoys tremendous popularity among teens and cite as evidence the popularity of not just the fiction itself but also SF film, TV tie-ins, and SF conventions. Donelson and Nilsen believe that the reasons for the popularity of SF among young adults are that SF is exciting reading, refuses to patronize its audience, permits young adults to read imaginative fiction without feeling it is "kid stuff," presents attractive, real heroes at a time when the world is too often perceived as devoid of anyone worth admiring, and encourages its readers to be intellectually curious. Among the authors judged most appealing to young adults are Heinlein, L'Engle, and H. M. Hoover.

The list of annotated titles that follows is very selective. We have personally handled and read all the books in the annotated bibliography. As the chapter title indicates, we limited our selection to books written for junior/senior high school age readers, a minimum age of about 11 or 12 years. This change eliminated 16 books in the third edition that fell below this age range. We considered approximately 100 books published since the third edition and selected 18 for this new edition, a few of them mentioned in parent annotations.

We have also limited our selections to books that are clearly science fiction, even if the science is not as "hard" as in some books written for adult readers, and even if in some cases there is an admixture of fantasy. We therefore excluded distinguished works like Le Guin's Earthsea series, which subjects magic to the sort of strict laws typical of science. Peter Nicholls, in his entry on children's SF in his new encyclopedia [7-22], argues for the inclusion of such works. We discussed them in "Modern Fantasy for Young Adults, 1950–1988," a chapter in Barron's *Fantasy Literature: A Reader's Guide* [7-33].

In making these selections, we have been guided more by the needs of the general reader, the classroom teacher, and the librarian, and less by those of the specialist or "fan" of SF. There are several consequences of this approach. First, we have consulted extensively the reviews and commentary in *Horn Book Magazine, School Library Journal, Booklist, Bulletin of the Center for Children's Books, Language Arts, The Alan Review,* and *Children's Literature.* At the same time, we have consulted the various bibliographic and critical resources of adult science fiction; particularly helpful have been *Locus* [12-24], *Luna Monthly, Delap's SF and F Review, Science Fiction and Fantasy Book Review, Fantasy Review,* and *The Year's Scholarship in Science Fiction and Fantasy* [7-19]. Second, the books selected, in addition to being within the conventional age levels—for example, 12 and above—are those that are well written; illustrate aptly a particular theme, approach, and direction in science fiction; or represent the multivolume work of an author such as Norton, Heinlein, or Walters. Third, most of the books annotated have been published since 1947, for reasons that should be clear from what has been said above.

Readers seeking further information about children's and YA science fiction have several sources. First is the book-length study, four of which have appeared in very recent years. In 1981 Lillian Biermann Wehmeyer's *Images in a Crystal Ball: World Futures in Novels for Young People* (Libraries Unlimited) was published. Containing over 150 annotations and extensive commentary, Biermann's book is didactic and classroom-oriented as she lays out a rather elaborate program built around children's and YA science fiction for developing or supplementing instructional units in futuristics. Obviously the value of Biermann's program depends on teachers' conviction that not only does futuristics belong in the classroom but the didactic potential of SF should be tapped even at the risk of neglecting or distorting its potential to entertain. More critical than Biermann's study is Janice Antczak's *Science Fiction: The Mythos of a New Romance* (1985). Focusing on novels for children 8 to 14, Antczak argues that SF can be read as the story of a modern quest and, hence, is organized around the structure and pattern of the quest. This new manifestation of an ancient pattern, along with the romantic nature of SF, presumably attracts young readers and provides them a way to cope with the possible futures confronting them. Unfortunately, Antczak's emphasis on SF as traditional quest in modern form, regardless of her stated intent, tends to present SF as essentially conservative rather than estranging or critical. In *Nuclear Age Literature: The Quest for a Life-Affirming Ethic* (American Library Association, 1990), Millicent Lenz advocates the importance of finding for youth an ethic "adequate to forestall global catastrophe" likely to occur from ecosystem pollution and thermonuclear disaster. C. W. Sullivan III compiled a very useful collection of original essays, *Science Fiction for Young Readers* (Greenwood, 1993), dealing with the history of SF for youth, individual authors, and recurring themes.

A second source of information is the individual essay. Most helpful are:

Adams, John, "Linkages: Science Fiction and Science Fantasy," *School Library Journal* 26 (May 1980): 23.

The Alan Review, Spring 1992 issue devoted to SF, which includes Monica Hughes, "Science Fiction as Myth and Metaphor"; Laurence Yep, "A Garden of Dragons"; William Sleator, "From Interstellar Pigs to Spirit Houses"; Pamela F. Service, "On Writing Sci Fi and Fantasy for Kids"; and Suzy McKee Charnas, "A Case for Fantasy."

Brians, Paul, "Nuclear War Fiction for Young Readers: A Commentary and Annotated Bibliography," in *Science Fiction, Social Conflict and War*, ed. by Philip John Davies, (Manchester Univ. Press, 1990) [8-44].

Children's Literature Association Quarterly, Winter 1981 issue devoted to SF, which includes Eleanor Cameron, "Fantasy, SF and the Mushroom Planet Books"; Francis Molson, "Writing for the 'Electric Boy': Notes on the Origins of Children's SF"; David Greene, "L. Frank Baum: SF and Fantasy"; and Carol Stevens, "SF in the Classroom."

Children's Literature Association Quarterly, Summer 1985 issue devoted to SF, which includes Francis Molson, "Three Generations of Tom

Swift"; C. W. Sullivan, III, "Heinlein's Juveniles: Still Contemporary After All These Years"; Virginia Wolf, "Andre Norton: Feminist Pied Piper"; and Janice Antczak, "The Visions of H. M. Hoover."

Engdahl, Sylvia L., "The Changing Role of Science Fiction in Children's Literature," *Horn Book Magazine* 47 (October 1971): 450.

Erisman, Fred, "Robert Heinlein, the Scribner Juveniles, and Cultural Literacy," *Extrapolation* 32 (Spring 1991): 45.

Esmonde, Margaret, "From Little Buddy to Big Brother: The Icon of the Robot in Children's Science Fiction," in *The Mechanical God: Machines in Science Fiction*, ed. by Thomas P. Dunn and Richard D. Erlich (Greenwood, 1982) [8-51].

Greenlaw, M. Jean, "Science Fiction: Impossible! Improbable! or Prophetic," *Elementary English* 48 (April 1971): 201.

McCaulet, Virginia, "Out of This World: A Bibliography of Space Literature for Boys and Girls," *Elementary English* 36 (February 1959): 98.

Molson, Francis J., "Great Marvel: The First American Hardcover Science Fiction Series," *Extrapolation* 34 (Summer 1993): 101–22.

————"The Winston Science Fiction Series and the Development of Children's Science Fiction," *Extrapolation* 25 (Spring 1984): 34.

Moskowitz, Sam, "Teen-Agers: Tom Swift and the Syndicate," in *Strange Horizons: The Spectrum of Science Fiction*, ed. by Sam Moskowitz (Scribner, 1976) [8-92].

Nodelman, Perry, "Out There in Children's Science Fiction: Forward into the Past," *Science-Fiction Studies* 12 (November 1985): 255.

Roberts, Thomas, "Science Fiction and the Adolescent," *Children's Literature* 2 (1973): 86.

Svilpis, Janis, "Authority, Autonomy, and Adventure in Juvenile Science Fiction," *Children's Literature Association Quarterly* 8 (Fall 1983): 22.

A third source of information is the work of adult SF criticism or commentary. The varied essays assembled by Sullivan were mentioned earlier. The most detailed information about young adult SF in a book not limited to YA literature is found in the newly revised and enlarged *Encyclopedia of Science Fiction*, which has entries for most of the authors in this chapter. But see our earlier comments on our selection criteria, which differ from those used in the *Encyclopedia*. Also useful, if dated, is Tuck's pioneering encyclopedia [7-9].

Bibliography

(The age level is indicated after the bibliographic information for each entry.)

5-1.   Allum, Tom. **Boy Beyond the Moon.** Bobbs-Merrill, 1960. Illus. by Jack Russell. British title: *Emperor of Space,* 1959 (11–14).
Guy Abbot meets Professor Harvey, a famous expert in interplanetary travel whose innovative spaceship is rejected as unworkable by the government. Unexpectedly the professor dragoons four escaped prisoners and Guy as a crew, and they take off for Emperor, the mysterious planet. The journey out, the sudden death of Harvey, encountering prehistoric fish and tremendous purplish fires, a mutiny by the prisoners, a rescue party, and a novel return to Earth make up the adventures. Accurate scientific information; an above-average space adventure with a refreshingly different set of characters. Contrast Claudy's *The Mystery Men of Mars* [5-33].

5-2.   Ames, Mildred. **Anna to the Infinite Power.** Scribner, 1981 (12 up).
Perfect student, superintelligent, amoral Anna suddenly begins to question her identity when she spots an exact look-alike, and sets out, with the help of her brother, to solve the mystery. Credible characterization and poignant conclusion enhance a gripping story of cloning experimentation. Compare Bova's *Exiled From Earth* [5-18]; contrast Hoover's *Children of Morrow* [5-69].

5-3.   Ames, Mildred. **Is There Life on a Plastic Planet?** Dutton, 1975 (13 up).
Overweight and friendless, Holly meets the proprietor of a strange doll shop and accepts from her a lifelike doll identical to Holly to substitute for the girl in school and then at home. Becoming afraid when the doll insists it is Holly, the girl must struggle to escape the shop, which, she realizes, contains dolls of some of her classmates. Ominous in tone, suspenseful and sensitive in its characterization of troubled children, the novel effectively combines science fiction and the gothic. Contrast Sleator's *The Duplicate* [5-143].

5-4.   Anderson, Poul. **Vault of the Ages.** Winston, 1952 (12 up).
Five hundred years after the "Doom," the Lann army from the north invades the peaceful Dale country and threatens the vestiges of civiliza-

tion. Escaping from marauding Lanns, Carl stumbles among the ruins of a city on a time vault, which summarizes in books and containers past scientific and human knowledge for the use of survivors of the nuclear holocaust. Carl determines that this store of knowledge should be open to the people. However, both the Lann army and the people's ignorance must be overcome before the time vault can open its riches. Brisk adventure, well written, effective in dramatizing human ambivalence before the potential of knowledge. Contrast Norton's *Star Man's Son* [5-116]. [For other works by this author see chapters 3 and 4.]

*5-5. Anthony, Piers. **Race Against Time.** Hawthorn, 1973 (14 up).
Six teens, representing "true Caucasians, Negroids, and Mongoloids," suspect that they are being brought up in a zoo-like setting. Breaking out and painfully learning the true reason for their segregation, the youths decide to return to the "banks" where they resolve to master their distinctive cultures and prepare to become an elite. An exceptionally well paced opening highlights a provocative look at a possible future grounded in racial purity and cultural equality. Compare Lightner's *The Day of the Drones* [5-96]. [For other works by this author see chapter 4.]

5-6. Appleton, Victor (pseud. of Edward Stratemeyer Syndicate). **Tom Swift and His Electric Rifle.** Grosset & Dunlap, 1911 (9–12).
Having perfected his new electric rifle, Tom decides to try it out on an elephant hunt in Africa. With friends Ned Newton, Mr. Damon, and Durvan, who is an elephant hunter, Tom takes off for Africa in the Black Hawk, his newest airship. There he becomes embroiled in native attacks, rescuing various whites, and tracking down lions and elephants. One of a group of five books published concurrently and written by the Edward Stratemeyer Syndicate, the story features a young, inventive genius, Tom Swift, who is easily superior to his contemporaries and able to overcome all dangers. So popular were the books that they eventually totaled 38 volumes and were continued in subsequent series. Like series fiction then and now, the Tom Swift books emphasize rapidity of incident and stereotypical characterization. Oddly, none of the books deals with space travel or extraterrestrial life, the two most common topics of science fiction. There have been three successor series: Tom Swift, Jr. (33 titles, 1954–1971); Tom Swift (11 titles, 1981–1984) Tom Swift (11 titles to date, 1991–).

5-7. Baird, Thomas. **Smart Rats.** Harper, 1990 (12 up).
Embittered 17-year-old Laddie, living with his parents and younger sister, learns several of his friends are being terrorized as the Big Brother–like

government goes about removing one child from all two-progeny house-holds for "conservation" purposes. Laddie plots to save himself and his parents by pretending to collaborate with the government. Gripping and suspenseful, the story is one in which readers will identify with the complaining, sarcastic, yet idealistic hero. Contrast Westall's *Futuretrack 5* [5-168].

5-8.   Ballou, Arthur W. **Bound for Mars.** Little, Brown, 1970 (12–14).
The Pegasus, under command of Colonel Sanborn, is scheduled to place the first permanent station on Mars. For this historically important mission, the crew has been most carefully screened, physically and psychologically. However, George Foran, the youngest crew member, cracks under the strain and threatens the ship's safety. Carefully the commander entraps Foran, and the mission continues. Actual incidents are not, per se, much above routine; what is impressive is the authentic detailing of on-board procedures, especially the in-space repair of one sled that malfunctions. Highly recommended for hard science fiction devotees. Compare Pešek's *The Earth Is Near* [5-128]. This is a sequel to *Marooned in Orbit* (1968).

5-9.   Bell, Clare. **Ratha's Creature.** Atheneum, 1983 (12 up).
Long ago in an alternate world, a band of intelligent wild cats, the Named, survive because Ratha dares to use fire as a weapon against predatory cat raiders, the UnNamed. Believable characterization, vivid, accurate details, and plausible incidents make for a fascinating story. Sequels are *Clan Ground* (1984), in which Ratha faces challenges to her leadership and use of fire, and *Ratha and the Thistle-Chaser* (1990). Contrast O'Brien's *Mrs. Frisby and the Rats of NIHM* [5-122]. 1984 International Reading Association Children's Book Award.

5-10.   Bell, William Dixon. **The Moon Colony.** Goldsmith, 1938 (12–14).
Julian and Joan Epsworth, captured by the great, evil scientist Toplinsky, are forced to accompany him to the Moon, where a colony is being formed and eventual invasion of Earth organized. Before the brother and sister can return to Earth, they survive attacks by Toplinsky's colonists and crickets, controlled by a beauteous and evil Amazon-like queen, Carza, and lead lunar pygmies and their queen, Moawha, against Carza. Nonmainstream children's space adventure; constantly shifts from fact and informed extrapolation (such as rocket technology) to brutal violence and romance with even a hint of sex. Compare Burroughs's "Under the Moons of Mars" [1-17] and Craigie's *The Voyage of the Luna I* [5-35].

*5-11. Benford, Greg(ory). **Jupiter Project.** Nelson, 1975 (14 up).
What prevents the shutting down of the Astronautical-Biological Laboratory orbiting Jupiter, which has had no luck in finding life and justifying its high cost, is young Matt Bowles's accidental discovery of Jovian bacteria. Expertly and plausibly, the novel weaves together details of the operations of a scientific expedition in space, the problems of a closed-in society, and the challenges and difficulties of growing up. Through additional material—in particular, scenes of explicit sexual activity—the second edition (Berkley, 1980) amplifies the sociological and rite-of-passage dimensions. Compare Williamson's *Trapped in Space* [5-175] and Marsten's *Rocket to Luna* [5-106]; contrast Stone's *The Mudhead* [5-148]. [For other works by this author see chapter 4.]

*5-12. Bethancourt, T. Ernesto. **The Mortal Instruments.** Holiday, 1977 (13 up).
Humanity in the far future, evolving into bodiless energy, sends those few who cannot evolve into the past where they become geniuses or great leaders, both good and evil. Eddie Rodriguez is revealed as an evil genius who seeks to take over the computers of I.G.O. in order to dominate the world. Suspenseful, quick moving, well plotted, and superbly written, this is one of the best science fiction novels for young people. The sequel is *Instruments of Darkness* (1979), which manifests the same high level of craftsmanship and interest. Contrast Suddaby's *Village Fanfare* [5-152].

5-13. Biemiller, Carl L. **The Hydronauts.** Doubleday, 1970 (12 up).
A postcatastrophe story. Because of great changes brought about by radiation, the seas have become the major source of food. Kim, Toby, Genright, and Tuktu are trainees in the Warden Service, which oversees the harvesting of the oceans. Patrolling the kelp forests, guarding the shark pens, and tracking down a mysterious hostile power provide the four ample adventure and experience. Provocative look at future marine life, harvesting the sea, and water-survival techniques; taut writing; credible characterization. Compare Clarke's *Dolphin Island* [5-30]. Subsequent adventures of the quartet are found in *Follow the Whales: The Hydronauts Meet the Otter People* (1973) and *Escape from the Crater: More Adventures of the Hydronauts* (1974).

5-14. Blaine, John (pseud. of Harold L. Goodwin). **The Rocket's Shadow.** Grosset, 1947 (8–12).
Rick Brant, a young inventor of electronic devices, is caught up in intrigue aimed at preventing, if not destroying, his father's experimental

Moon rocket. Although atypical in that the hero's inventive skills are modest, the narrative is typical series fiction in its emphasis on incident, routine characterization, and bland style. The first of 23 volumes, most having nothing to do with SF, and the first of the second wave of series science fiction for boys that began after World War II. Contrast Appleton's Tom Swift series [5-6].

5-15.   Blish, James. **Mission to the Heart Stars.** Putnam, 1965 (14 up).
The flight of the starship *Argo* across the galaxy is the occasion for an investigation into the various forms taken by societies that Earth might face in the future. Stability versus change, self-satisfaction versus curiosity, and coercion versus tolerance are the poles around which these societies are organized; another topic of investigation is the way society is affected by technological advancement and sheer lasting power. Although lacking in exciting adventures, the novel contains ample, provocative speculation and discussion. Compare Heinlein's *Citizen of the Galaxy* [5-60]. [For other works by this author see chapter 3.]

*5-16.   Bond, Nancy. **The Voyage Begun.** Atheneum, 1981 (13 up).
In a future where pollution, energy shortages, and changes in the climate severely affect the economy, Paul takes part in an apparently harebrained scheme to help old Walter Jepson build a boat. Impressive narrative; distinctive characters, most of whom are rendered to a degree rarely found in science fiction; especially sensitive nature description; convincing study of impact of changing environment on human life. Compare Corlett's *Return to the Gate* [5-34]; contrast Christopher's *Empty World* [5-25]. 1982 Boston Globe Horn Book Award/fiction honor.

5-17.   Bonham, Frank. **The Forever Formula.** Dutton, 1979 (12 up).
Awakening in a strange hospital and an even stranger world, dominated by the "super-old," Evan Clark realizes that he had been secretly frozen, misplaced, found, and then thawed so that his mind could be probed to reveal his father's formula to ensure hyperlongevity. The boy becomes a pawn in a struggle between those demanding "immortality" and those preferring mortality. Fast-paced, suspenseful, and fascinating portrait of a world where life for those 200 or more years old is privileged and for the "younger" is degrading and squalid. Contrast Heinlein's *Tunnel in the Sky* [5-65].

*5-18.   Bova, Ben(jamin William). **Exiled from Earth.** Dutton, 1971 (13 up).
A world suffering from overpopulation fears genetic engineering, so the best geneticists and support scientists are banished to an orbiting satellite.

Some scientists are mysteriously reprieved but, Lou Christopher discovers, only to aid unwittingly a revolt that fails. Again banished, Lou convinces his associates that the only hope for the race's preservation is to aim for the stars, and they depart Earth. Tight, suspenseful writing, especially the description of Lou's escape attempt; thoughtful examination of science's need to be free. Compare Norton's *The Stars Are Ours* [5-117]. Story of the long flight to the stars and a new home is continued in two subsequent novels—*Flight of Exiles* (1972) and *End of Exile* (1975)—that conclude the Exiles trilogy.

5-19.   Bova, Ben(jamin William). **The Winds of Altair.** Dutton, 1972 (12 up).

A plan to alter the hostile environment of Altair to one suitable for colonization by the teeming millions of Earth is thwarted by Jeff Holman. Having had his mind electronically channeled into that of a giant wolfcat, Jeff realizes how benign and supportive Altair's environment actually is to its native life. Quick-moving narrative, with low-keyed technological passages, reflects engagingly contemporary concern for conserving Earth's resources, in particular, animals. Compare Stoutenburg's *Out There* [5-150] and Lightner's *The Space Ark* [5-98]. [For other works by this author see chapter 4.]

5-20.   Capon, Paul. **Flight of Time.** Heinemann, 1960 (12–14).

A Wellsian time travel book. Four children, accidentally blundering into a UFO, travel to 2260 England. Then follows a glance both at futuristic cities, travel, and communication, and at alterations to the country's geography. More interesting is the adventure in the past, 1960 B.C. While observing a bloody battle between two Stone Age peoples over the talisman spaceship, the children are under attack and, just managing to activate the controls, return to the present. Above average in style. Compare Severn's *The Future Took Us* [5-138].

5-21.   Capon, Paul. **Lost: A Moon.** Bobbs-Merrill, 1956. British title: *Phobos the Robot Planet* (13 up).

Three vacationers are picked up by a small spaceship and brought to Phobos, the Martian satellite, which they discover is a highly complex automated machine that speaks English, learned from another person previously kidnapped. Outwitting the machine, the four escape to Earth while bringing about the satellite's destruction. Well written stylistically, the novel features interesting, somewhat humorous characterization that instills some freshness into familiar Martian subject matter. Compare Wollheim's *The Secret of the Martian Moons* [5-178].

5-22.   Carlson, Dale, and Danny Carlson. **The Shining Pool.** Atheneum, 1979 (14 up).

A light suddenly appearing in a nearby pool begins to dominate every youth in town except Ben, a teenager given to stubborn independence and reflection. Encouraged by a teacher versed in spirituality, Ben manages to fend off the light, actually an alien force seeking to expand itself at the expense of human individuality, and convinces it to leave Earth. Although a bit static, the novel is still unusual science fiction for youth in that it eschews routine approaches and uses instead philosophic speculation to articulate themes of individuality and freedom. Compare Bethancourt's *The Mortal Instruments* [5-12].

5-23.   Chetwin, Grace. **Collidescope.** Bradbury, 1990 (12 up).

The lives of a young girl and Sky-Fire-Trail (a Native American from precolonial America) intertwine because of an accident to Hahn, a cyborg from the future sent to "check out" Earth's viability and, if necessary, preserve it from greedy planet developers. Interesting, almost too trendy characterization and dialogue, but clever in its handling of time shifts. Contrast Huddy's *The Humboldt Effect* [5-75].

5-24.   Chilton, Charles. **Journey Into Space.** Jenkins, 1954 (10–14).

With a crew of four, the *Luna* takes off on the first lunar flight. Arriving on the Moon, the crew encounters another spacecraft, attempts to escape, but is forced by the aliens to land on a planet that turns out to be Earth—but centuries ago. Competently written; suspenseful handling of on-board procedures; plausible details of time and space travel. Based on a very popular British radio series. Contrast Bell's *The Moon Colony* [5-10] or Heinlein's *Rocket Ship Galileo* [5-62].

5-25.   Christopher, John (pseud. of Christopher Samuel Youd). **Empty World.** Hamish Hamilton, 1977 (14 up).

In spite of personal problems, Neil gradually realizes that virtually the entire world may soon die from plague. One of the few survivors, the teenager forces himself to master survival techniques. Even though the future of the race is literally at stake, Neil also learns that getting along with people, especially girls, is still not easy for him. Tersely written, somber in mood, and always believable, the novel vividly recreates a postholocaust world; the final note of hope is convincing. Compare O'Brien's *Z for Zachariah* [5-123]; contrast Parker's *The Hendon Fungus* [5-126] or Ure's *Plague* [5-159].

5-26.   Christopher, John (pseud. of Christopher Samuel Youd). **Fireball.**
Gollancz, 1981 (12 up).

Drawn into a parallel world, similar to Roman Britain, Brad and Simon
participate in the Bishop of London's successful revolt. When the ensuing
regime promises to be repressive, the boys and two friends escape to the
New World. Vintage Christopher: terse, plausible story continues author's
investigation of various political systems and their treatment of individual
rights. Sequels are *New Found Land* (1983) and *Dragon Dance* (1986), in
which the friends journey to California, then China, and finally an alternate world. Compare Silverberg's *The Gate of Worlds* [5-140]; contrast
Oliver's *Mists of Dawn* [5-125]. *New Found Land*: 1983 Parents' Choice
Award.

*5-27.   Christopher, John (pseud. of Christopher Samuel Youd). **The
Guardians.** Hamish Hamilton, 1970 (12–14).

England of 2052 is divided into two parts: the Conurb, a megalopolis
teeming with unrest and pacified by bread and games, and the County,
where the gentry pursue a rural life-style. Conurban Rob flees, after the
mysterious death of his father, to the County, where he is befriended by
the Giffords and passed off as gentry. In the course of an uprising, Rob
learns the terrifying facts of the guardians' systematic repression of all dissident elements and, giving up an opportunity to become a guardian,
leaves for the Conurb to join the revolutionary movement. Tautly written;
thoughtful study of the potentially evil implications of behavioral modification and mind control. Contrast Severn's *The Future Took Us* [5-138].
1971 Guardian Children's Fiction Award; 1971 Christopher Award; 1976
Deutscher Jugendliteraturpreis (German Youth Literature Prize).

5-28.   Christopher, John (pseud. of Christopher Samuel Youd). **The
Prince in Waiting.** Hamish Hamilton, 1970 (12–14).

After a series of earthquakes destroys much of civilization, England
rebuilds following the pattern of medieval walled cities ruled over by the
Spirits as they are interpreted by the seers. Thirteen-year-old Luke suddenly finds himself recognized when his father is selected Prince of
Winchester. After his father's sudden death, Luke is forced to flee to the
Sanctuary, where science and technology are preserved and augmented
and the seers practice trickery to keep the people malleable. Luke also
discovers that he is to be groomed to become prince of princes and
reunite the cities. The first of a trilogy; the others, *Beyond the Burning
Lands* (1971) and *The Sword of the Spirits* (1972), continue Luke's career as
he fails at reunification through force and becomes content to wait and

use peaceful means. As is typical of this author, featured are dramatic interplay and ample incidents, investigation of both proper use of science and technology and individual rights versus society's needs. Compare Dickinson's *The Weathermonger* [5-42].

*5-29.   Christopher, John (pseud. of Christopher Samuel Youd). **The White Mountains.** Hamish Hamilton, 1967 (12–14).
The first volume in the Tripod trilogy about a successful invasion of Earth by aliens and the eventual triumph by humans over the invaders. The tripods consolidate their control by inserting metal communicators into the heads of all adults; thus, behavior modification is quick and brutal if need be. Will, Henry, and Jean Paul all fear the ceremony of capping that marks rites of passage and set out to join a small band of humans at the White Mountains who resist the tripods. The picture of future life in England after an alien invasion is convincing and troubling; the journey of boys is exciting and suspenseful; tripods are suggestive of Wells. In *The City of Gold and Lead* (1967), Will and Fritz enter the city of the masters to discover the nature of tripods and ascertain whether there is any way they can be overthrown. *The Pool of Fire* (1968) describes the overthrow of tripods and their masters. However, an ominous note enters at the end when the various nations squabble among themselves. Prequel is *When the Tripods Came* (1988). 1977 George G. Stone Center for Children's Books Recognition of Merit. [For other works by this author see chapter 3.]

5-30.   Clarke, Arthur C(harles). **Dolphin Island.** Holt, 1963 (12–14).
A story of experiments on Dolphin Island to open up more effective communication with the dolphins. Johnny Clinton, unloved runaway, discovers a special affinity with dolphins when they rescue him from a sinking hovercraft. Later, after a great storm, he uses the dolphins to surf across to the mainland to bring medical aid. Characterization of humans and the incidents are routine; what is above average is the depiction of various experiments, current and future, with dolphins, all of which assume that one day dolphins and humans will communicate freely. Compare Robert Merle's *The Day of the Dolphin* (1967).

5-31.   Clarke, Arthur C(harles). **Islands in the Sky.** Winston, 1952 (12–15).
As his prize for winning a television quiz show in the second half of the 21st century, Roy Malcolm goes to an orbiting space station. There he has several adventures involving space pirates, the making of a space film, and a runaway rocket ship. The strength of the book, despite its publication date, is in the details, all plausibly explained, of the procedures of space travel and life on an orbiting station. The same thoroughness later seen in

2001: A Space Odyssey [4-110] is clearly evident. As an adventure story, routine; as an investigation into the required technology necessary for space travel, exceptional. [For other works by this author see chapters 3 and 4.]

5-32. Clarke, Joan B. **The Happy Planet.** Cape, 1963 (12–15).
A postcatastrophe story. Three future societies are contrasted: the Tuanians, descendants of the Getaways who left before the great destruction, are a technologically advanced, highly regimented people; the hombods, descending from holocaust survivors, have established a semipastoral life that may make Earth a "happy planet"; and the Dredfooters, descended from cyborgs, attempt to prey on the Hombods. A Tuanian attempt to investigate Earth's utility is thwarted, and the planet is spared the joyless, rationalistic life of Tuan. Although a relatively thoughtful study of possible societies, its excessive length may hamper enjoyment. Contrast Lawrence's *The Warriors of Taan* [5-94].

5-33. Claudy, Carl H(arry). **The Mystery Men of Mars.** Grosset, 1933 (11–13).
Ted and Adam are recruited by Professor Lutyens to accompany him on a rocket trip to Mars, where they are imprisoned by buglike, superintelligent Martians, whose plan to join human brains to the gigantic brain ruling the planet is foiled by the professor, who gives his life to save the boys. Expanded from a story in *American Boy* and one of the Adventures in the Unknown, the novel aptly represents one of the two authors writing before Heinlein (the other is Roy Rockwood) whose imagination and storytelling ability still stand out. There are three sequels.

*5-34. Corlett, William. **Return to the Gate.** Bradbury, 1977 (14 up).
This conclusion to a trilogy dramatizing growth in self-knowledge and the necessity of risking friendship—the highly praised *The Gate of Eden* (1975) and *The Land Beyond* (1976) being the other segments—takes place in a not-too-distant future of violent social disintegration and painful rebuilding. Focus is on old age and its natural, although often unrealized, alliance with youth. The visionary is subordinate, but the portrait of love's insistence on no conditions is memorable for its lyrical terseness and allusiveness. Compare L'Engle's *A Wrinkle in Time* [5-95], where unconditional love is also demanded and the young and old are allies.

5-35. Craigie, David (pseud. of Dorothy M. Craigie). **The Voyage of the Luna 1.** Eyre & Spottiswoode, 1948 (12–14).
Martin and Jane Ridley, members of a British family famous for exploring, stow away on board a test rocket that precedes the first manned flight to the Moon. Once there the children encounter lunar ants, ash forests,

snakes, and bats. While they explore the Moon, the second rocket is readied for their rescue, and the children return world-famous. A Jules Verne-like adventure with a premium on fanciful incidents and not science; firm and very British characterization; slowly developing story because of time devoted to background and minor characters. Compare Heinlein's *Rocket Ship Galileo* [5-62].

*5-36.   Cross, John Keir. **The Angry Planet.** Peter Lunn, 1945 (13–15).
Three children stow away on an experimental rocket ship bound for Mars. There they encounter the Beautiful People, who are mobile plant life, and the Terrible Ones, ugly mushroom-like plants. In spite of their best efforts, the humans and the Beautiful People are overcome in battle, the rocket crew barely managing to escape. Finally, a volcanic explosion seemingly terminates all Martian life. A British book influenced by Wells and one of the very first science fiction mainstream novels, it precedes even *Rocket Ship Galileo* [5-62]. Use of journal device for a multiple perspective provides effective change of mood and narrative pace. Careful, speculative discussion of possible life on Mars. Compare Claudy's *The Mystery Men of Mars* [5-33]. Sequel: *The Red Journey Back* (1954).

5-37.   del Rey, Lester. **The Infinite Worlds of Maybe.** Holt, 1966. Ghost-written by Paul W. Fairman (12 up).
Bill Franklin's father has disappeared into one of the infinite possible worlds, leaving a cryptic note for his son. Assisted by Professor Adams, Bill studies his father's notes until the pair figure out how they, too, can enter the possible worlds. Following his father's track, Bill travels into the future, a second war between the states, a simian-dominated land, a society with a technology that satisfies all wants (where Adams remains), an ice age, and finally a society devoted to individual perfection, where his father awaits him. Investigation both of a variety of alternative societies that humans might select if comfort, ease, and pleasure are goals, and of the nature of time. Compare Capon's *Flight of Time* [5-20].

5-38.   del Rey, Lester. **Step to the Stars.** Winston, 1954 (12 up).
Eschewing space opera gadgetry and employing then-current knowledge and techniques, the book plausibly and convincingly lays out the various stages and dangers of constructing the first space station. The narrative involves Jim Stanly's growth from a lonely, skilled mechanic, too poor to pursue his goal of becoming a space pilot, to a confident, poised man who earns his space pilot wings. A subplot of espionage and sabotage by a pacifist group opposed to military uses of space is too conventional to add

much to the book's impact. Compare Heinlein's *Starman Jones* [5-64] or Norton's *Star Man's Son: 2250 A.D.* [5-116]. [For other works by this author see chapter 3 and Van Lhin in this chapter.]

5-39. del Rey, Lester, Cecile Matschatt, and Carl Carmer, eds. **The Year after Tomorrow: An Anthology of Science Fiction Stories.** Winston, 1954 (11–13).

Pioneering collection of short science fiction for youth. Important because most stories were actually written for young readers, unlike the vast majority of subsequent anthologies for the juvenile market whose contents were written for adults and then deemed, on perfunctory editing, "suitable" for youth. Special features are four stories reprinted from the *American Boy*: three by Carl Claudy, "The Master Minds of Mars" (later expanded into *The Mystery Men of Mars* [5-33]), "The Land of No Shadow," (later expanded into *The Land of No Shadow*) and "Tongues of Beast"; and one by P. van Dresser, "By Virtue of Circumference."

5-40. Dereske, Jo. **The Lone Sentinel.** Atheneum, 1989 (9–14).

Unexpectedly left the keeper of Lone Sentinel by which terran colonists on Azure protect a valuable plant, Erik fends off an attack by enemies of Earth's allies. Somewhat bland and predictable characterization is easily offset by effective depiction of a lonely, routine-filled way of life in the future. Contrast Hughes's *The Keeper of the Isis Light* [5-76].

*5-41. Dickinson, Peter. **Eva.** Gollancz, 1988 (12 up).

After a terrible car accident, 13-year-old Eva's neuron memory is transferred into a chimp. The girl successfully adjusts to her new body, so successfully that she learns to live with chimps, mates with them, and becomes their leader. Brilliant in concept and execution, the novel is both emotionally shocking and intellectually provocative: exemplary SF for young readers. Compare Bell's *Ratha's Creature* [5-9]; contrast Hughes's *The Keeper of the Isis Light* [5-76]. 1989 Boston Globe Horn Book Award/fiction.

*5-42. Dickinson, Peter. **The Weathermonger.** Gollancz, 1968 (12–14).

The first volume in the Changes trilogy. Geoffrey and Sally, brother and sister, having been abandoned to die as witches, escape to France. There they are urged to return to England and discover the cause of the changes that have thrown the British Isles back into the Middle Ages, where ignorance and superstition again rule, all things mechanical are feared, and even the weather is controlled by incantation. The children find out that

Merlin's sleep has been disturbed, and, unhappy with what he sees, Merlin has sent England back to a time he knows. Geoffrey and Sally convince him to wait for a more suitable time to return and he relents, freeing England from its curse. A brilliantly imaginative combination of myth and science fiction. *Heartsease* (1969) recounts the successful rescue of a witch by a group of children. In *The Devil's Children* (1970), Nicky and a band of Sikhs, free of the madness caused by the changes, become allies, settle on a farm, and beat off various threats to their safety. Compare Mayne's *Earthfasts* [5-108] or Christopher's *The Prince in Waiting* [5-28].

5-43.   Dickson, Gordon R. **Space Winners.** Holt, 1965 (12–14).
Jim, Curt, and Ellen are selected by the Alien Federation for a secret training mission of great moment. They are joined by Atakit, a small, squirrel-like, but strong alien. Crash landing on Quebahr, a planet closed to technological knowledge, the four, after various adventures, assist in establishing cooperation among the several hostile peoples. They discover also that their mission actually was to Quebahr, and the three teenagers become part of an advance cadre for bringing Earth into the federation. Well-paced narrative, competently written, many surprises. Contrast Heinlein's *Tunnel in the Sky* [5-65] for a less sanguine adult view of teenagers. [For other works by this author see chapter 4.]

*5-44.   du Bois, William Pene. **The Twenty-One Balloons.** Viking, 1947 (10 up).
Krakatoa in the late 19th century is the site of an amazing civilization that combines outlandish but workable household devices to save labor and a utopian social organization built around eating tastes and financed by a diamond hoard. Professor Sherman, a retired teacher on a balloon tour over the Pacific, is forced down near Krakatoa and invited to join the group. The eruption of the volcano ends the utopian experiment and the professor escapes to inform a curious country why he was found in the ocean amid twenty-one balloons. A humorous, Jules Verne-like, richly imaginative book that can be enjoyed by all. 1947 Spring Book Festival Award; 1948 Newbery Award.

*5-45.   Engdahl, Sylvia Louise. **Enchantress From the Stars.** Atheneum, 1970 (13-15).
A long, detailed novel built around the notion that a traditional fairy tale may actually refer to incidents involving a wise, superior race visiting a younger race and world to spare it contamination. To Georyn, a youngest son, Elana is an enchantress who would help him destroy a ravaging dragon, actually a rock-destroying machine of the Imperial Exploration Corps.

Elana and her father instruct Georyn in utilizing his latent psychological power, which frightens the materialistic Imperial colony, who are a Youngling people, into leaving the planet—Earth? Strong features are the working out of correspondences between fairy tale and the mission, anti-colonizing theme, and the preeminence of Elana; thus, a rare nonsexist novel. Compare L'Engle's *A Wrinkle in Time* [5-95]; contrast Heinlein's *Tunnel in the Sky* [5-65] and Huddy's *Time Piper* [5-75]. 1971 Newbery Award Honor Book; 1990 Phoenix Award.

5-46. Engdahl, Sylvia Louise. **The Far Side of Evil.** Atheneum, 1971 (13-15).
Another long, detailed story devoted to Elana and the Anthropological Service. Now graduated from the academy, Elana is sent on a mission to Toris, a Youngling planet, split between liberal and reactionary factions and on the brink of war. As usual, she is to observe and not interfere. However, a second agent, Randil, becoming too involved, falls in love, and interferes. Before matters can be set right and Toris can turn its attention to space travel and not war, Elana is imprisoned and tortured and Randil killed. Good but drawn-out depiction of Elana's interrogation through brainwashing; the length may offset this admirable attempt to fuse science fiction and conventional romance formulas. Contrast Chetwin's *Collidescope* [5-23].

5-47. Fairman, Paul W. **The Runway Robot.** Westminster, 1964. Ghost-written for Lester del Rey (12–14).
Sixteen-year-old Paul Simon must return to Earth from Ganymede and leave behind his robot, Rex. Paul jumps ship and is reunited with Rex, who also has been pining for Paul. After several adventures in which the pair is forced to separate, the two are again happily reunited on Earth. A feature that sets the book off from the commonplace is that it is told from Rex's perspective. Humor also abounds because of the robot's habit of assuming, even against the evidence of his "eyes," that his human masters are superior in all respects to robots, since masters by definition never make errors and know all. Contrast Van Lhin's *Battle on Mercury* [5-160].

5-48. Faville, Barry. **The Return.** Oxford Univ. Press, 1987 (12 up).
Teenage Jonathan, befriending the strange boy, Karl, discovers that they share paranormal powers. Gradually Jonathan realizes that Karl and Myra, his "mother," are really aliens come to determine if there are any earthly descendants of those upon whom their predecessors performed brain tissue transplants. A suspenseful, carefully plotted story; deft characterization; surprise ending. Contrast Freeman's *Alien Thunder* [5-54].

5-49. Fisk, Nicholas. **A Rag, a Bone and a Hank of Hair.** Kestrel, 1982 (12 up).
Superintelligent Brin, required to take part in experiments manipulating Reborns, artificially created humans of the 23rd century, is increasingly resentful of their inhumane treatment. Although the impact of this insightful critique of social engineering is muted by point-of-view problems and an inconclusive ending, the story is worthwhile, at times very moving. Compare Ames's *Anna to the Infinite Power* [5-2]; contrast Sargent's *Alien Child* [5-135].

5-50. Fisk, Nicholas. **Space Hostages.** Hamish Hamilton, 1967 (11–13).
A group of nine children, kidnapped by a "flying saucer," discover that their kidnapper is a crazed pilot of a secret British craft. Arrogant Tony and intelligent Brylo contend for leadership but are forced to cooperate to save the craft. An eerie opening, insightful study of differing personalities clashing, and plausible description of life aboard spacecraft make for superior science fiction for preteens. Contrast Capon's *Lost: A Moon* [5-21].

5-51. Fisk, Nicholas. **Time Trap.** Gollancz, 1976 (14 up).
In 2079, English life is possible only within Ecoshield, where regimentation stifles liberty, and moral permissiveness and cowardice encourage teenage rioting and mugging. Dano Gazzard, who becomes privy to the secret of time travel through drugs, is driven to choose between "idyllic" past (1942) and an uncertain future. Tautly written and somewhat horrifying portrait of a possible future blends Anthony Burgess's moral vision and John Christopher's terse readability.

*5-52. Fisk, Nicholas. **Trillions.** Hamish Hamilton, 1971 (12–14).
Countless numbers of strange geometric objects, called trillions by the children, fall from the skies on Earth. Thirteen-year-old Scott Houghton, who has extraordinary ability to observe and think, discovers that the trillions have intelligence, are from a destroyed planet, and have come to Earth seeking work and a new home. General Hartman is the leader of those who see the trillions as invaders seeking to destroy, and he proposes to exterminate them. Scott, however, who communicates with the trillions, has them leave to continue their search. Suspenseful, well-written narrative, political overtones, and ecological orientation. Contrast Finney's *The Body Snatchers* [3-72] or Wyndham's *The Day of the Triffids* [3-199].

5-53. Forman, James D. **Call Back Yesterday.** Scribner, 1981 (12 up).
The only survivor of a hostile seizing of an American embassy in the Mideast in the near future, Cindy is forced finally to accept that her ill-

advised flirtation with a young Arab may have precipitated nuclear conflagration. Suspenseful, plausible, and ultimately believable account of what could have been an absurd young adult romance. Compare the Johnsons' *Prisoner of Psi* [5-80]. The sequel is *Doomsday Plus Twelve* (1984).

5-54.　Freeman, Gaail. **Alien Thunder.** Bradbury, 1982 (12–14).
In a future in which Earth is dying, Walker learns that his mother has actually become an alien sent to gather as many children as possible for transportation to another world where humanity may have a chance to survive. The first-person narration gives mystery, suspense, poignancy to an otherwise ordinary plot. Contrast the Carlsons' *The Shining Pool* [5-22].

5-55.　French, Paul (pseud. of Isaac Asimov). **David Starr: Space Ranger.** Doubleday, 1952 (12 up).
To an Earth suffering from overpopulation, its Martian colony is a necessary breadbasket. When poisoned food begins to turn up, David Starr, agent of the Council of Science, is sent to investigate and uncovers an alien conspiracy. Routine adventure story, among the first space operas for children; significant also because of the special status of its author. There are five other David Starr adventures: *Lucky Starr and the Pirates of the Asteroids* (1953), *Lucky Starr and the Oceans of Venus* (1954), *Lucky Starr and the Big Sun of Mercury* (1956), *Lucky Starr and the Moons of Jupiter* (1957), and *Lucky Starr and the Rings of Saturn* (1958). [For other works by this author (Asimov) see chapters 3 and 4.]

5-56.　Halacy, D(aniel) S(tephen), Jr. **Return from Luna.** Grosset, 1969 (13 up).
Rob Stevens arrives at the Moon colony to find it discouraged by cutbacks in funds that have severely curtailed the colony's aim to become independent. Nuclear war breaks out on Earth, and the colony, along with its Russian counterpart, is forced to go it alone. Dissension festers and some men crack and mutiny; only cooperation with the Russians enables the colony to survive until all are rescued. A survival story translated into a lunar and technological setting. Writing and characterization adequate; quite good re-creation of lunar life and terrain; technological passages mesh smoothly into the narrative. Contrast Craigie's *The Voyage of the Luna 1* [5-35].

*5-57.　Hamilton, Virginia. **Justice and Her Brothers.** Greenwillow, 1978 (14 up).
Justice and her older brothers, who are identical twins, along with a fourth child, slowly realize that they are gifted with ESP. Conflict ensues as one brother cruelly manipulates his weaker twin, and Justice senses that

she, not the older boys, is to become leader of the linked group and possible progenitor of a new life form. In this exceptionally good book, strong writing and characterization and brooding, convincing atmosphere and setting accompany themes familiar in adult science fiction, for example, Clarke's *Childhood's End* [3-44] or Sturgeon's *More Than Human* [3-172], but still novel in SF for young readers. Sequels: *Dustland* (1980) and *The Gathering* (1981).

5-58.   Hancock, Harrie Irving. **The Invasion of the United States; or, Uncle Sam's Boys at the Capture of Boston.** Altemus, 1916 (12–14).
Invading an unprepared United States, the Germans enjoy smashing victories near Boston. Regardless of American courage, particularly as exhibited by Bert Howard and the boys from Gridley High, the seemingly invincible German Army advances on New York. First of four volumes in The Conquest of the United States series, which, combining prowar propaganda, school story, and the visionary, depicts a German invasion. The series abruptly ended when actual war (World War I) broke out. Proto-science fiction, which atypically eschews space adventure and technological marvels and instead focuses on futuristic politics and sociology.

*5-59.   Harding, Lee. **Misplaced Persons.** Harper, 1979. Australian title: *Displaced Person* (13 up).
Aware that he cannot make contact with people and that the world is turning gray, Graeme soon finds himself alone, except for an alcoholic ex-teacher and a frightened girl, in a terrifying world where food must be scavenged and darkness is becoming total. Suddenly returned to the normal world, the boy retains a few shreds of evidence that the bizarre events did actually happen. Convincing psychological study of timeslip; well plotted and written; fresh characterization. Contrast Engdahl's *The Far Side of Evil* [5-46]. 1978 Alan Marshall Award for narrative fiction.

5-60.   Heinlein, Robert A(nson). **Citizen of the Galaxy.** Scribner, 1957 (13 up).
Before Thorby Baslim can enter into his rightful inheritance as head of Rudbek, a Terran financial corporation, he is first a slave boy on Jubbul in the Nine Worlds, a quasi-Roman empire, then an adopted son of the People, an intergalactic trading company organized around matriarchy, and finally a guardsman in a futuristic foreign service. Emphasis is not on characterization or incident, but on explaining alternate ways of organizing society and dramatizing distinctions between owning and controlling, having power and using it. Early instance of using children's science fiction for explaining and pushing ideas rather than merely relating exciting incidents.

5-61. Heinlein, Robert A(nson). **Farmer in the Sky.** Scribner, 1950 (13–15).

Emigration to Ganymede and the opportunity to homestead are the choices of Bill and his family. The flight out is long, and disappointment awaits Bill when the colonists discover that land and equipment are not ready. Bill is lucky to be assigned an early plot and begins the process of making soil. In spite of the setback of a massive quake, Bill decides to continue farming rather than return to Earth for further schooling. Subplots concerning Bill's relationship with father and stepmother and setting up scouting on Ganymede make the book, supposedly, more attractive to young readers. Chief interest is description of futuristic agricultural techniques.

*5-62. Heinlein, Robert A(nson). **Rocket Ship Galileo.** Scribner, 1947 (13 up).

Ross, Art, and Morrie, all amateur rocketeers, become involved with Morrie's uncle, Doctor Cargraves, and his plan to fly to the Moon. Having worked together in building an experimental, atomic-powered rocket, the three boys and Cargraves set off for the Moon. There they are attacked by a few Nazis plotting World War III from a secret lunar base. The boys overcome the Nazis and, having also discovered the ruins of a dead lunar civilization, return to Earth famous. A pioneering novel that began American mainstream science fiction for children and combined young protagonists, gadgetry, current science, and adventure in such a way that even today the book retains interest. Contrast Bell's *The Moon Colony* [5-10].

5-63. Heinlein, Robert A(nson). **The Rolling Stones.** Scribner, 1952 (13 up).

The Stone family, at the instigation of the twins, Castor and Pollux, reconditions a spaceship as a family yacht, *The Rolling Stone*, and embarks on various adventures, including selling used bikes on Mars and flat cats (which proliferate hugely) in the asteroids. Its humor and wit still fresh, its portrait of family life still winning although sexist, and its hard science plausible and detailed, the novel aptly illustrates the author's eminence as writer of science fiction for young readers.

*5-64. Heinlein, Robert A(nson). **Starman Jones.** Scribner, 1953 (13-15).

Story of Max Jones's rise from hillbilly runaway to acting captain of a starship. What makes Max's rise possible is a phenomenal memory that retains all the astrogator's tables, needed for astronavigation, and the cunning of Sam, an older man who befriends the runaway and gets him aboard the *Asgard* with fake credentials. Striking are the detailed, convincing picture of spaceship operational procedures and the suspense whenever the ship must pass through an anomaly. A subplot involving colonization of Charity, an unexplored planet, provides a change of pace and conventional adventure. Compare Marsten's *Rocket to Luna* [5-106].

*5-65.   Heinlein, Robert A(nson). **Tunnel in the Sky.** Scribner, 1955 (12–14).

Rod Walker and his classmates, having been sent into an unknown world as part of a survival test, find themselves stranded. Banding together, as many as 50 teenagers are forced to make their own laws and rules. Just as the new society is viable and children are born, the young people are rescued and returned to Earth where many, including Rod, are forced back into teen roles. A provocative book, especially in its portrait of adults who fail to discern the maturity of young people. One unfortunate flaw is the stereotyped and sexist characterization. Contrast Engdahl's *Enchantress From the Stars* [5-45] or Anthony's *Race Against Time* [5-5]. [For other works by this author see chapters 3 and 4.]

5-66.   Hill, Douglas. **Galactic Warlord.** Gollancz, 1979 (12 up).

Shocked to learn that he is the only legionary to survive the destruction of Moros, Keill Randor, assisted by the alien Glr, smashes Thr'un, one of the evil Deathwing, and begins his search for the dreaded Warlord. Perhaps the best of current space opera for young readers; quick moving, suspenseful, action-filled. Followed by *Day of the Starwind* (1980), in which Randor contends with bogus legionaries, *Deathwing over Veynaa* (1980), *Planet of the Warlord* (1981), in which Randor and Glr finally destroy The One, responsible for destroying Moros, and *Young Legionary* (1983). Compare Vance's *Vandals of the Void* [5-160].

5-67.   Hill, Douglas. **The Huntsman.** Heinemann, 1982 (12 up).

Relying on his uncanny ability to survive in the open, Finn Ferral sets out to rescue his foster father, Josh, and sister, Jena, stolen by brutal, ugly aliens who have enslaved Earth. Fast-paced adventure with enough originality and diversity of character to make for very entertaining reading. Sequels are *Warriors of the Wasteland* (1983), in which Finn finds his sister, and *Alien Citadel* (1984), in which guerrilla warfare, directed by Finn, forces the Slavers to leave Earth for more profitable ventures elsewhere. Compare Christopher's Tripod trilogy [5-29], contrast Norton's *Storm Over Warlock* [5-118].

*5-68.   Hoover, H. M. **Another Heaven, Another Earth.** Viking, 1981 (12–14).

Discovering that Xilan, presumably ignored by explorers 400 years earlier, has a human colony, a scientific team learns that the planet is genuinely inhospitable to human life. In spite of the fact that they are doomed, the original colonists will not leave. Intriguing concepts, plausible scenario, and rich and sustained characterization add up to an exceptionally interesting and moving novel. Contrast Sargent's *Earthseed* [5-136]. 1982 Ohioana Book Award.

5-69.   Hoover, H. M. **Children of Morrow.** Four Winds, 1973 (12–14).

Set in a future after widespread nuclear devastation has wiped out civilization, the story contrasts two forms of government and economy that the survivors have adopted. One is afraid, cautious, reactionary, distrustful of what technology survives, and hence, increasingly brutal and stagnant. The other is open, bold, and willing to build on extant science and to utilize genetic mutations to construct a new society, which seems to have successfully combined progress, discipline, justice, and love. The descriptions of the countryside after the Great Destruction are plausible and convincing. In all, a stimulating novel. Compare Clarke's *The Happy Planet* [5-32]. Sequel: *Treasures of Morrow* (1976).

5-70.   Hoover, H. M. **The Lost Star.** Viking, 1979 (13 up).

As part of an archaeological team surveying Blathor, Lian Webster realizes that the indigenous Lumpens, apparently fat and stupid animals, are really intelligent. Soon she uncovers their secret—they are an alien race, the Toapa, protected by a powerful computer brain within a mysterious dome—and must decide whether to share her knowledge with other team members. Multilayered story: mystery, coming of age, and study of racism and xenophobia. Compare Engdahl's *Enchantress from the Stars* [5-45] and Silverberg's *Across a Billion Years* [5-139]; contrast Anthony's *Race Against Time* [5-5].

*5-71.   Hoover, H. M. **The Rains of Eridan.** Viking, 1977 (12 up).

The three experimental stations on Eridan are inexplicably infected by unnatural fear. The cause of and antidote to the fear are discovered by Theo Leslie, a biologist, who also learns the challenge and joy of parenting when she befriends an orphan child. Superior science fiction: plausible alien world, well-paced plotting, sensitive and tactful characterization, in particular, the growth of love between an older woman and a young girl who share a deep commitment to science. Compare Lightner's *The Space Plague* [5-99].

5-72.   Hoover, H. M. **Return to Earth.** Viking, 1980 (14 up).

In 3307, a retiring senior diplomat, Galen Innes, returns to his native Earth seeking peace, but unexpectedly becomes embroiled in conflict between the Dolmen, a dishonest leader of a powerful cult, and Samara, teenage heiress to the gigantic Lloyd Corporation. Befriending the young girl, Galen assists her in outwitting, then destroying the Dolmen. The vision of possible economic and social organizations is disquieting, and the novel presents an appealing portrayal of friendship between youth and old age: evidence of author's continuing success in wedding young adult concerns and science fiction. Contrast Heinlein's *Citizen of the Galaxy* [5-60]; compare L'Engle's *A Wrinkle in Time* [5-95] or Corlett's *Return to the Gate* [5-34].

5-73.   Hoover, H. M. **The Shepherd Moon.** Viking, 1984 (12–14).

Lonely 13-year-old Merry unexpectedly makes friends with her powerful grandfather, and together they stave off an attempt to conquer Earth by a colonist from a forgotten artificial moon. Especially good are sympathetic insight into youth and old age relationship and study of corrosive effects of stagnant social classes. Compare Bond's *The Voyage Begun* [5-16] or Corlett's *Return to the Gate* [5-34].

5-74.   Huddy, Delia. **The Humboldt Effect.** MacRae, 1982 (12–14).

Because the Humboldt Time Machine, working in unexpected ways, sucks his friend Arthur into the past while drawing into the present a fourth-century B.C. man, the project leader, Luke, must travel into the past to set matters straight. Attractive novel: intriguing parallels to the Jonah and the whale story, suspense, and believable characterization. Compare Engdahl's *Enchantress From the Stars* [5-45].

*5-75.   Huddy, Delia. **Time Piper.** Hamish Hamilton, 1976 (13 up).

When Luke goes to work for Humbolt, the brilliant scientist experimenting with a time machine, he again meets Hare, the strange young girl disliked by most of her peers. As the machine is tested, he realizes that Hare and her just-as-strange friends have been transported from the past, actually Hamlin, Germany. Fascinating blend of legend and science fiction, mystery and suspense, the well-plotted novel also examines teenagers at odds with their surroundings and reaching out for sympathy. Compare Mayne's *Earthfasts* [5-108]; contrast Capon's *Flight of Time* [5-20] and Engdahl's *Enchantress from the Stars* [5-45].

5-76. Hughes, Monica. **The Keeper of the Isis Light.** Hamish Hamilton, 1980 (12 up).

Olwen, keeper of the intergalactic lighthouse Isis Light, who has been isolated from humanity except for Guardian, welcomes settlers from Earth only to discover the poignant truth about her capacity to survive on harsh Isis. Likable protagonist, plausible setting, and provocative scenario offset conventional story of lovers' misunderstanding. Sequels are *The Guardian of Isis* (1981) and *The Isis Pedlar* (1982), which continue the story of Olwen's unhappy romance and the fate of Isis's human colony. Contrast Engdahl's *The Far Side of Evil* [5-46]. 1982 IBBY Honour List; the sequel, *The Guardian of Isis*, won the 1981 Canadian Council Children's Literature Prize.

5-77. Hughes, Monica. **The Tomorrow City.** Hamish Hamilton, 1978 (12–14).

C-Three, a computer built to coordinate all power uses in a city, takes literally its charge to do what is best for children, in particular, Caro, daughter of its designer. A reign of terror, instigated by C-Three, is terminated only when the computer, "grief-stricken" at having blinded Caro, blows up. New subject matter for children's science fiction is effectively handled through a convincing, plausible scenario and believable characterization. Compare Bethancourt's *The Mortal Instruments* [5-12].

5-78. Hunter, Evan. **Find the Feathered Serpent.** Winston, 1952 (12–14).

Neil, substituting for his father, the inventor of a time machine, journeys back in time, hoping to find the origin of Quetzalcoatl, the great white god. He meets Eric, who becomes instrumental in assisting the Mayans to resist barbarian invaders and in introducing corn and other agricultural innovations. Returning to the present, Neil realizes that he has participated in the making of legend and myth. A time travel tale involving a Wellsian time machine; patterned also after books describing long-lost peoples. By far, more interesting as an archaeological and anthropological reconstruction than as hard science fiction. Compare Oliver's *Mists of Dawn* [5-125]; contrast Chetwin's *Collidescope* [5-23].

*5-79. Jacobs, Paul Samuel. **Born Into Light.** Scholastic, 1988 (11 up).

When a number of "feral" children suddenly appear in a New England town seventy-five years ago, a young boy, his mother, and the local doctor discover the children are aliens come to Earth to find ways to renew their species "back home." Story's strength is not so much concept but narrative point of view, poignant tone, and believable characterization. Contrast Freeman's *Alien Thunder* [5-54].

5-80.   Johnson, Annabel, and Edgar Johnson. **Prisoner of Psi.** Atheneum, 1985 (12 up).

When the famous psychic Emory Morgan is kidnapped, his previously estranged son, Tristan, assembles a team and, using psi, frees Morgan. Oddball characters, unexpected plotting, and a suggestive portrait of a future America suffering from climatic changes result in fresh, contemporary story. Compare Forman's *Call Back Yesterday* [5-53].

5-81.   Jones, McClure. **Cast Down the Stars.** Holt, 1978 (12–14).

To save her own, the spirit people, Glory, Second Starcaster and someday First Starcaster and First Reader of Solstice Tower, must cast the stones correctly so the Serpent Line that keeps out barbarians and the cold can be repaired. Intertwined are stories of Glory's relation with her grandfather, Sun in Winter, who has rejected her parents, and of her budding love for Honor, Third Geomancer. Fascinating picture of a future world and culture dominated by astrology and geomancy, whose ultimate credibility depends on reader's degree of acceptance of the latter as a science. Contrast Heinlein's *Citizen of the Galaxy* [5-60].

5-82.   Jones, Raymond F. **The Year When Stardust Fell.** Winston, 1958 (12–14).

Cosmic dust from an approaching comet disturbs the surface tension of all metals, causing them to blend together. The resulting destruction of virtually all machinery throughout the world breeds violence and chaos. Ken Maddox, his chemist father, and a few other scientists find a remedy. Except for the prominence of young Ken, the picture of social disintegration and scientific antidote is plausible and convincing, but lacks the emotional impact the British postcatastrophe novel began to have for children in the 1960s. Best of author's three novels in the Winston 1950s series. Contrast Fisk's *Trillions* [5-52].

5-83.   Karl, Jean E. **But We Are Not of Earth.** Dutton, 1981 (12 up).

In training to be Discoverers like their parents, four very bright teens, the Terrible Four, apparently discover Ariel, an Earthlike planet, but soon suspect they have been manipulated for other, devious purposes. Likable characters, quick action, suspenseful plot, and plausible setting and subject matter add up to a winning story. Compare Dickson's *Space Winners* [5-43]; contrast Heinlein's *Tunnel in the Sky* [5-65].

*5-84. Karl, Jean E. **The Turning Place: Stories of a Future Past.** Dutton, 1976 (14 up).

A series of loosely related stories concerning a future Earth, defeated by aliens and forced to rebuild, which decides to forgo materialism and imperial expansion and utilize human intelligence and curiosity to form a new society. Aimed explicitly at youth in terms of themes and interest and thoroughly nonsexist in characterization, the stories are genuinely speculative as they imagine a future extrapolated from humanity's "best" traits; hence, hopeful and even inspiring. Compare Bradbury's *The Martian Chronicles* [3-32]; contrast Simak's *City* [3-163].

5-85. Kestaven, G. R. (pseud. of G. R. Crosher). **The Pale Invaders.** Chatto, 1974 (12 up).

After the Upheavals, the inhabitants of a peaceful valley who are satisfied with a quiet pastoral life are disturbed by strangers asking for permission to dig "coal." The elders must decide whether the past—what young Gerald has accepted as "make-believe"—can be learned from or must be avoided at all costs. Air of mystery, sensitive depiction of coming of age, and probing of morality of technology result in superior children's science fiction. Compare Hoover's *Children of Morrow* [5-69].

5-86. Key, Alexander. **Escape to Witch Mountain.** Westminster, 1968 (11–13).

Tony and Tia, orphan brother and sister, are placed in a home with no possessions except a star box that suggests a mysterious origin and an equally mysterious destination. When a stranger seeks to adopt them, the children run away. Before they reach the safety of Witch Mountain, they realize that they possess parapsychological powers and remember that they are "Castaways" from a destroyed planet. It is also hinted that the children are sought by forces of satanic evil; hence, the book is another of the more recent stories dramatizing a universal struggle between good and evil in which youthful protagonists play active roles. Contrast Jacob's *Born Into Light* [5-79]. A Walt Disney film of the same name was released in 1975. Sequel: *Return From Witch Mountain* (1978).

5-87. Key, Alexander. **The Forgotten Door.** Westminster, 1965 (11–13).

Little Jon falls through a forgotten door into an alien world—Earth. Temporarily forgetting his past, Jon is befriended by the Bean family, who gradually suspect he is from another, peaceful world. Others, not that perceptive, are frightened by, or want for their own uses, Jon's telepathic power. As a mob closes in on him, Jon tries to find the door back; when he does, he takes the Bean family with him. Taut, suspenseful story; firm characterization, depiction of Jon's returning memory especially good; ethical commentary never allowed to take over narrative. Compare Winterfield's *Star Girl* [5-176]; contrast Jacob's *Born Into Light* [5-79]. 1965 American Association of University Women Award in Juvenile Literature; 1972 Lewis Carroll Shelf Award.

5-88.   Knott, William C. **Journey Across the Third Planet.** Chilton, 1969 (12–14).
Laark is forced to abandon ship on Earth, a strange planet. His appearance makes him alien, and his journey to meet a rescuing starship seems impossible except for the help of Peter, a runaway who joins Laark. In addition to the exciting adventure, the depiction of the slowly growing friendship between the two is distinctive, in particular, Laark's realization that Earth, technologically very inferior to his home, can give Krall, an old and tired planet, insights gained from the courage and resourcefulness of a young planet. Contrast Key's *The Forgotten Door* [5-87].

5-89.   Kurland, Michael. **The Princes of Earth.** Nelson, 1978 (14 up).
In the far future, Adam Warrington, from the backwater planet Jasper, wins a scholarship to the University of Sol on Mars. On his way there the teenager becomes entangled in intrigue, aids a prince of Earth, is kidnapped, escapes, and eventually enrolls in school. Always interesting and sometimes witty commentary on future politics and schooling, interlaced with futuristic technology; plausibly based on present events and knowledge. Contrast Anthony's *Race Against Time* [5-5] or Sleator's *House of Stairs* [5-144].

5-90.   Latham, Philip (pseud. of Robert Shirley Richardson). **Missing Men of Saturn.** Winston, 1953 (12–14).
The spaceship *Albatross* is ordered to follow the *Anomaly*, a ghost ship, out to Saturn. Subsequently, the crew is exposed to a series of terrifying incidents, and members disappear. Gradually, it becomes apparent that Saturn is inhabited, and both the Saturnians, an old civilized race, and the descendants of Captain Dearborn, first explorer of Saturn who disappeared mysteriously, do not want any interlopers. The crew, however, is set free as the Saturnians decide rapprochement is inevitable. Suspenseful, well-written mystery for two-thirds of the book; then speculation about the possibility of life on Saturn intrudes.

*5-91.   Lawrence, Louise (pseud. of Elizabeth Rhoda Wintle). **Andra.** Collins, 1971 (12 up).
When far into the future, a brain graft enables Andra to live as well as to

experience the feelings of a boy who had died in 1987 and had been frozen, she incites rebellious change among the young. A conventional story of youthful rebellion and challenge to established order is enhanced by engaging characterization, celebration of the worth of the individual, and, most unusually, a tragic ending. Contrast Dickinson's *Eva* [5-41].

5-92. Lawrence, Louise (pseud. of Elizabeth Rhoda Wintle). **Children of the Dust.** Bodley Head, 1985 (13 up).

The several Harnden daughters and their children, who survive the terrible first years after a nuclear war, represent contrasting approaches to rebuilding society, and then embody the mutations able to thrive in the reconstructed civilization. Compassionate yet honest tone, coupled with effective use of point of view, enriches plausible, detailed plot. Compare Hoover's *Children of Morrow* [5-69]; contrast Clarke's *The Happy Planet* [5-32].

5-93. Lawrence, Louise (pseud. of Elizabeth Rhoda Wintle). **The Power of Stars.** Collins, 1972 (12 up).

The power of the stars, becoming manifest one night, accidentally possesses Jane and seeks to establish itself on Earth. Jimmy and Alan, one suspicious and the other blinded by love, compete to understand and help the girl. Suspense, a surprise ending, and convincing atmosphere and characterization are features of an impressive combination of science fiction and the young adult novel. Contrast Carlson's *The Shining Pool* [5-22].

5-94. Lawrence, Louise (pseud. of Elizabeth Rhoda Wintle). **The Warriors of Taan.** Bodley Head, 1986 (12 up).

Struggling to save their planet for their Goddess and restore peace, the Sisterhood on Taan plot by any means necessary to reconcile natives, Outworlders, and Stonewraiths. Plotting and an alien setting vaguely resembling Earth mark a story extolling the advantages of a matriarchy. Contrast Heinlein's *Citizen of the Galaxy* [5-60].

*5-95. L'Engle, Madeleine. **A Wrinkle in Time.** Farrar, 1962 (13-15).

Meg and Charles Wallace Murray, along with Calvin, Meg's classmate, become involved in an attempt to find Dr. Murray, a brilliant scientist who has mysteriously disappeared. Under the direction of Mrs. Who, Mrs. Whatsit, and Mrs. Which, three "angels," they "tesseract" to Camazotz, a distant star, where the children must save Dr. Murray, held captive by "It" in Central Intelligence. Eventually, it is the self-effacing love of Meg, and not the brilliant intelligence of Charles, that saves their father. One of the contemporary fantasy-science fiction novels that enmesh young people in planetwide struggles between good and evil. Well written, firm characterization, provocative themes. Contrast Heinlein's *The Rolling Stones* [5-63]. Companion novels are *A Wind in the Door* (1973), in which Charles Wallace's bloodstream becomes an arena for a clash between good and evil; *A Swiftly Tilting Planet* (1978), in which an older Charles Wallace, aided by Meg and the unicorn Gaudior, goes back in time to resolve several moral crises and avert nuclear catastrophe; and *An Acceptable Time* (1989). 1963 Newbery Award; 1965 Lewis Carroll Shelf Award; 1965 Sequoyah Children's Book Award; 1980 American Book Award for *A Swiftly Tilting Planet.*

5-96.   Lightner, A(lice) M. **The Day of the Drones.** Norton, 1969 (10–14).

A postcatastrophe story. Afria (once Africa) seems the only land uncontaminated by radioactivity. An expedition sets out to explore the potentially dangerous nearby lands and discovers in an ancient northern country (once England) the Bee-people, a mutant, dwarfed race descended from the predisaster white population, organized around matriarchal principles, and controlled by gigantic mutant bees. A harrowing look at a possible future society adversely affected by radiation, virtually bookless, and unsure of the uses of power and knowledge; a perceptive study of the nature and effects of racial prejudice. Contrast O'Brien's *Z for Zachariah* [5-123].

5-97.   Lightner, A(lice) M. **Doctor to the Galaxy.** Norton, 1965 (11–13).
Young Dr. Garrison Bart becomes, through a mix-up, a veterinarian instead of a physician on a faraway planet. He discovers that lustra, a local moneymaking grain, inhibits growth. To the Assembly of Scientists he announces the discovery, but his findings are rejected; he is also charged with illegally practicing medicine. Bart makes another discovery: lustra inhibits cancerous growth. This time he is honored for his discovery and is able to become a physician. Interesting story that aptly represents the author's ability to find subject matter appealing to preteens. Contrast Heinlein's *Farmer in the Sky* [5-61].

5-98.   Lightner, A(lice) M. **The Space Ark.** Putnam, 1968 (12–14).
Dinkie, Uncle Rol, Cherry, the Rock, and Dr. Binns attempt to establish on another planet several of the unique species of Shikai, whose sun is going nova. Although too episodic and predictable to be an exciting adventure, the narrative profits from fluent style, likable characters, and author's manifest enjoyment of nature and animals. Contrast Heinlein's

The Rolling Stones [5-63]. Sequel and superior to *The Rock of Three Planets* (1963) and *The Planet Poachers* (1965).

5-99.   Lightner, A(lice) M. **The Space Plague.** Norton, 1966 (13 up).
Reflecting the author's knowledge of lepidopterology and entomology, the novel depicts a group of young people caught up in a search for the cause of a space plague on the planet Arcona. Barney, a beetle specialist, and Jenny, a lepidopterist, eventually untangle the causes of the disease, all of which involve the brilliant flutterfly. Deft, entertaining mixture of science and exotic locale, with a touch of romance; convincing and satisfying narrative. Compare Nourse's *Star Surgeon* [5-121].

5-100.   MacArthur, David. **The Thunderbolt Men.** Claridge, Lewis & Jordan, 1947 (12–14).
Kidnapped and brought to a remote island, David and Rosemary find a secret base ruled over by the fanatic Dr. Gruber, who plans to destroy the civilized world through his Thunderbolt cadre, powerful magnetic fields, and an atom destroyer. Along with Logan, a British agent, and Dr. Nicolai, the inventor of the new weaponry, the children manage to foil Gruber's plot. Very early British science fiction for youth echoes Verne and Wells, reflects the recently won war in its proud British patriotism, and expresses concern for possible nuclear war. Contrast White's *The Master* [5-170].

5-101.   Macdonald, Caroline. **The Lake at the End of the World.** Dial, 1988 (12 up).
In a future Earth ravaged by chemical pollution, Hector and Diana discover each other's existence and join forces to save Hector's cave-dwelling people, Diana's family, and the lake itself from the nightmarish plan of a mad scientist. Rescuing the plot from stereotyping are the dual narrative point of view and convincing portrait of teens' growing trust as well as adjustment to reality. Contrast Martel's *The City Under Ground* [5-107] or Stoutenburg's *Out There* [5-102].

5-102.   Mace, Elisabeth. **Out There.** Greenwillow, 1978. British title: *Ransome Revisited*, 1975 (13 up).
Eleven confronts a bleak life after his schooling is finished and he is sent to the quarries. Along with his subnormal older brother and two acquaintances, Susan and Will, Eleven escapes and sets out for a community where, rumor has it, freedom exists. Postholocaust survival story is marked by tough-minded honesty in its depiction of the ways supposedly deprived youth manage to survive with self-respect and dignity fundamentally intact

and continue to hope for a better life. Contrast Clarke's *The Happy Planet* [5-32].

5-103.   MacVicar, Angus. **The Lost Planet.** Burke, 1953 (10–14).

Recently orphaned Jeremy Grant goes to live with his uncle, Dr. Lachlan McKinnon. The teenager becomes part of the crew that, utilizing McKinnon's experimental atom-powered rocket, explores "the lost planet," finding there a flower whose scent promotes gentleness and peace, and iridonium, which can change lead into gold. The briskly moving narrative, engaging characterization, and theme exhorting unity and cooperation aptly represent the work of an early popular British author of children's science fiction. Followed by seven sequels. Contrast Heinlein's *Rocket Ship Galileo* [5-62].

*5-104.   Maguire, Gregory. **I Feel Like the Morning Star.** Harper, 1989 (12 up).

Three teens in The Pioneer Colony, a postholocaust subterranean station that has ironically become virtually a prison, break out, along with the children, to the surface and freedom. Very literate style, rich characterization, and plausibly rendered setting elevate conventional plot to superior status. Contrast Hoover's *Children of Morrow* [5-69].

5-105.   Mark, Jan. **The Ennead.** Crowell, 1978 (14 up).

Three socially deviant characters, Isaac, Eleanor, and Moshe, are destroyed by the rigidly stratified society of Erato, a harsh, stark planet still struggling through to the freedom of spirit its inhabitants have sought. Unusually somber in mood and marked by sharp characterization and distinctive setting, the novel is a ringing statement of the need for individual freedom and the power of human spirit. Contrast Mace's *Out There* [5-102].

5-106.   Marsten, Richard (pseud. of Evan Hunter). **Rocket to Luna.** Winston, 1953 (12–14).

Ted Baker, Space Academy cadet, unexpectedly becomes backup on the first rocket to the Moon. Rejected at first by the crew, Ted is accepted eventually as it is he who pilots the rocket onto the Moon's surface and saves the life of one of the crew. Although time has made obsolete some of the presentation of the technology required for a lunar flight, the technical descriptions are detailed and accurate. Moreover, the story still retains much of the tension and excitement of a journey to the Moon. Compare Heinlein's *Rocket Ship Galileo* [5-62].

5-107. Martel, Suzanne. **The City Under Ground.** Viking, 1964 (11–13).

A postcatastrophe story. Where old Montreal used to be, Surreal, an underground city, survives because of a highly technological and rigidly organized society. Two sets of brothers, Luke and Paul and Eric and Bernard, showing curiosity and initiative, help the city fight a mysterious, hitherto-unknown underground enemy and stumble on a way to the surface where they discover a cleansed Earth and other survivors, the Lauranians, a free, less repressed, and technologically inferior people. Surreal decides to go above ground and ally itself with the Lauranians. Adequately written and mildly engaging incidents. Compare Silverberg's *Time of the Great Freeze* [5-141].

*5-108. Mayne, William. **Earthfasts.** Hamish Hamilton, 1966 (12–14).

David and Keith meet an 18th-century drummer boy emerging from a newly formed grassy mound and carrying a steady, cold, white-flamed candle. Before Keith can return the candle to the past, inexplicable phenomena—"boggarts," heaving ground, moving stones, wild boars, giants, shadowing horsemen, awakening Arthurian knights, and even David's "death"—plague the area. A remarkable combination of fantasy and science fiction; strong characterization; fine depiction of the boys' determination to treat the constantly burning candle scientifically before succumbing to its power; exceptional use of atmosphere; brilliant style. Contrast Huddy's *Time Piper* [5-75]. 1968 Lewis Carroll Shelf Award.

*5-109. McCaffrey, Anne. **Dragonsong.** Atheneum, 1976 (12 up).

Frustrated in her desire to express her musical talent and forced to live as girls are wont to in Half Circle, Menolly injures her hand. Recuperating, she witnesses the birth of fire lizards, survives Thread-fall out in the open, and eventually comes to the attention of the Masterharper, who wants Menolly to utilize her talent. As part of the Pern sequence, the novel provides detailed description of the birth of fire lizards, the small relatives of dragons, and is a slow but sensitive, somewhat unconventional revelation of a girl's coming of age. Compare Engdahl's *Enchantress From the Stars* [5-45]. Two subsequent novels continue portrait of coming of age. *Dragonsinger* (1977) follows Menolly's life in Harper Hall and underscores necessity of discipline in mastering any art or craft. *Dragondrums* (1979) focuses on Piemur, a boy soprano, and details his adventures on the way to becoming a journeyman drummer. 1977 Children's Book Showcase; 1979 Balrog Award for *Dragondrums*. [For other works by this author see chapter 4.]

*5-110. McKillip, Patricia. **Moon-Flash.** Atheneum, 1984 (12 up).
Impelled by questions concerning Riverworld and her own dreams,
Kyreol, accompanied by Terje, a young man, travels beyond the end of the
world and learns the truth: River is a small "primitive" region carefully
observed and guarded by the Dome, a technologically developed civiliza-
tion. A superior story: fascinating application of anthropology; rich,
detailed nature description; sustained mystery. Sequel is *The Moon and the
Face* (1985), in which Kyreol and Terje bring about the commingling of
River and the Dome. Compare Stone's *The Mudhead* [5-148]; contrast
Hunter's *Find the Feathered Serpent* [5-78]. 1984 Parents' Choice Award.
[For other works by this author see chapter 4.]

5-111.   Miklowitz, Gloria. **After the Bomb.** Scholastic, 1985 (12–14).
When a Russian nuclear bomb accidentally explodes over Los Angeles,
young Philip Singer is forced into the unlikely role of leader for his family.
Well-researched and harrowing depiction of immediate aftermath of a
nuclear disaster is joined to attractive characterization. Followed by a
sequel, *After the Bomb: Week One*, 1987. Contrast Swindells's *Brother in the
Land* [5-155].

*5-112. North, Eric (pseud. of B. C. Cronin). **The Ant Men.** Winston, 1955
(12–14).
A scientific expedition is caught in a central Australian desert storm and
whirled into a lost world inhabited by gigantic mantises and antlike creatures struggling up the evolutionary ladder to human intelligence. Vivid
nature description and strong characterization—in particular, the expedition's gradual realization that they are indeed in a lost world—outweigh
routine plotting and scenes of battle. One of the best written of the 1950
Winston series and still enjoyable today. Compare Oliver's *Mists of Dawn*
[5-125].

5-113.   Norton, Andre (pseud. of Alice Mary Norton). **Catseye.** Harcourt,
1961 (13 up).
Temporary work in a strange interplanetary pet shop involves Troy Horan,
a displaced person, in adventure, intrigue, and mystery, hallmarks of typical Norton work. Surprised to learn that he can communicate with animals, Troy stumbles onto the fact that several pets in the shop are being
used as secret weapons in a plot against the rulers of Korwar. Troy is
forced to flee into the wild and a dead, booby-trapped underground city;
only the closest cooperation between Troy and several exotic animals
enables him to survive and become a member of the Rangers, who patrol

the wild. Skillful narrating of science fiction adventure and sympathetic depiction of animal-human relationship. Followed by two sequels.

*5-114. Norton, Andre (pseud. of Alice Mary Norton). **Operation Time Search.** Harcourt, 1967 (13 up).

Ray Osborne is accidentally sent back into a time when the Atlantean Empire sought to overthrow the Murians, and he becomes the instrument whereby the latter, worshipers of the Flame, are able to annihilate Atlantis, where devotees of the false Poseidon traffic in demonic powers. Osborne wonders why Atlantis lingers in legend while the Murian Empire disappeared, but fails to observe that the religion and kings of Mura provide the basis for the Greek pantheon and mythology. Osborne remains in the past, determined to organize in the Barren Lands a colony, ruins of which are the mounds dotting the central United States. An Atlantis legend story, entertaining, especially stimulating in its speculation concerning origin of myth. Compare Hunter's *Find the Feathered Serpent* [5-78].

5-115.   Norton, Andre (pseud. of Alice Mary Norton). **Quest Crosstime.** Viking, 1965. British title: *Crosstime Agent* (13–15).

In a future when moving "crosstime" to parallel universes is possible, one group on Vroom favors crosstiming so that society can rebuild itself after nuclear devastation by using the resources of other universes. The Rogan sisters and Blake Walker, all with various parapsychological abilities, are swept into a revolt organized by those opposed to crosstiming. Before the revolt is put down, the adventure spills over to E625, a crosstime world embroiled in a tense stalemate modeled on the conflict between the American Plains Indians and the pioneers. Exciting and fast-moving story. Blake Walker first appeared in *The Crossroads of Time*, half of a 1956 Ace Double.

*5-116. Norton, Andre (pseud. of Alice Mary Norton). **Star Man's Son: 2250 A.D.** Harcourt, 1952. Variant title: *Daybreak 2250 A.D.* (12 up).

Rejected by his father's clan, young Fors, a mutant, runs away to prove himself a Star Man, or explorer. Along with Arskane, a black youth who befriends him, Fors is successful in uniting the several clans against their common enemy, the Beast Things, and in instilling in the former the dream of starting over without repeating the mistakes of the Old Ones. The author's first SF novel, one of her best, both a fine study of coming of age and a convincing portrait of postholocaust world. Compare Heinlein's *Farmer in the Sky* [5-61] or *Red Planet* (1949).

5-117.   Norton, Andre (pseud. of Alice Mary Norton). **The Stars Are Ours!** World, 1954 (13 up).

Even in a time when Earth has embarked on interplanetary flight, old animosities continue and eventually lead to a devastating war. Scientists are proscribed by the Company of Pax, and a handful of Free Scientists escape to the stars. After exploring a new planet, the humans enter into an alliance with a race of mermen to take up anew the history of humanity. Well plotted, filled with incident, and skillfully written. Sequel: *Star Born* (1957).

5-118.   Norton, Andre (pseud. of Alice Mary Norton). **Storm Over Warlock.** World, 1960 (13 up).

Terrans and the evil, cruel Throgs clash over establishing sovereignty in Warlock, a newly discovered planet. Thorvald and Shann Lantee, the only survivors of a terran survey, along with two wolverines, are forced to flee a band of Throgs. Falling into the hands of Wyvern or witches, the pair is tested but eventually accepted by them. The new allies of Terra assist in pushing the Throgs back to their own planet. Early space adventure featuring one major characteristic of the author: witches and witchcraft, illusion versus dream. Of secondary interest is human-animal coequal relationship. Followed by four sequels. [For other works by this author see chapter 3.]

5-119.   Nourse, Alan E(dward). **The Bladerunner.** McKay, 1974 (13 up).

By the early 21st century, overpopulation has forced sterilization on anyone seeking medical care. A medical black market springs up for those opposed to this kind of medical practice. When a mysterious flu virus threatens a nationwide epidemic, Billy Gimp and other bladerunners—that is, persons who provide black-market physicians with supplies and assistance—are called on to warn the populace. The epidemic is curtailed and humane changes in health care ensue. Suspenseful incidents; fascinating look at future medical care and procedures; responsible handling of overpopulation control problem. Compare Lightner's *Doctor to the Galaxy* [5-97].

5-120.   Nourse, Alan E(dward). **The Mercy Men.** McKay, 1968 (12–14).

In this novel of narrative twists and surprises, Jeff Mayer feels a compulsion to seek out and kill a man he believes has killed his father. Suspecting that the man has entered a research medical center, Jeff decides to enter also as a mercy man, that is, one who allows medical self-experimentation for money. Before Jeff can leave the center, he is shocked to learn that he, like his father, is triggered to go insane and that this insanity affects the laws of probability. Jeff is a carrier of a disorder that must be eradicated or treated. As in other novels by the author, speculation about future medical practice is stimulating; style and characterization are above average. Expanded from a 1955 Ace Double titled *A Man Obsessed.* Compare the Suttons' *The Programmed Man* [5-153].

*5-121. Nourse, Alan E(dward). **Star Surgeon.** McKay, 1960 (12 up).
Expert blending of futuristic medicine, its procedures and organization, and the story of Earth's attempt to enter the Galactic Confederation. Earth, hospital center for the entire galaxy, prides itself on its medical skill and begrudgingly allows Dal, a Garvian and first off-Earth medical student, to intern. After several adventures Dal wins his silver star as a star surgeon, and Earth has passed its probation. Suspenseful in depicting possible future medical technology, especially provocative speculation about possible applications of symbiosis. Compare Lightner's *Doctor to the Galaxy* [5-97].

*5-122. O'Brien, Robert C. **Mrs. Frisby and the Rats of NIMH.** Atheneum, 1971 (10–14).
Mrs. Frisby, head of a family of field mice, is told to consult neighboring rats concerning the illness of her son. Justin, a leader of the rats, agrees to help because Mr. Frisby had been of assistance to the rats. On hearing the whole story of the rats as the object of psychological and biological experimentation by the NIMH laboratories and the rats becoming, as a result, superintelligent, Mrs. Frisby also volunteers to aid the rats. The rats escape from an attempt by the NIMH laboratories to exterminate them and establish a utopian society away from humans. Outstanding combination of fantasy and science fiction; a winning portrait of rats and mice that has little cuteness. *The Secret of NIMH,* a feature film based on the story, was released in 1982, when Scholastic reprinted the book under the film title. 1971 Boston Globe Horn Book Award; 1971 William Allen White Children's Book Award; 1972 Newbery Award; 1972 John and Patricia Beatty Award; 1972 Lewis Carroll Shelf Award; 1973 Mark Twain Award; 1974 Pacific Northwest Young Reader's Choice Award; 1978 Massachusetts Children's Book Award.

*5-123. O'Brien, Robert C. **Z for Zachariah.** Atheneum, 1975 (14–16).
A postcatastrophe story. Believing she may be the only survivor of a devastating war, Ann Burden is pleased to see a man enter the Burden valley and decides to befriend him. Shocked when, after all she has done for

him, he tries to rape her, Ann is forced to leave the valley, hoping to come across other survivors. Sensitive transformation of trite subject into a tragic story of human behavior in the face of destruction and possible extinction. Use of journal to record struggle for understanding, carefully paced narrative, and characterization of protagonist are distinctive. Compare Engdahl's *The Far Side of Evil* [5-46]. 1976 Edgar Allen Poe Award.

5-124.   Offutt, Andrew J. **The Galactic Rejects.** Lothrop, 1973 (13–15).
Rinegan, Berneson, and Cory, all gifted with parapsychological power, but social misfits, find themselves on Bors, a hitherto-unknown agrarian world where crime and the proverbial rat race seem nonexistent and life is utopian. Impressed by the marked contrast to Earth, the three change and become circus performers. The extent of change is tested when they decide not only to preserve Bors's society from the invading Azuli, archenemy of Earth, but to bring peace by offering to immunize the Azulians from a disease fatal to them, but not to terrans. Different and refreshing because of the engaging circus scenes. Compare Lightner's *The Space Plague* [5-99] or Nourse's *Star Surgeon* [5-121].

5-125.   Oliver, Chad (pseud. of Chadwick Symmes Oliver). **Mists of Dawn.** Winston, 1952 (12–14).
A time travel machine accidently transports young Mark Nye 50,000 years into the past. Attacked by brutish Neanderthals and befriended by the relatively civilized Cro-Magnons, Mark learns how to survive by cooperating with nature and with other human beings. The plot is less adventure and more a dramatized and still engrossing presentation of then-current anthropological speculation about primitive peoples. Compare Hunter's *Find the Feathered Serpent* [5-78]. [For other works by this author see chapter 3.]

5-126.   Parker, Richard. **The Hendon Fungus.** Gollancz, 1967 (13 up).
Fungus sent to England by Dr. Hendon accidentally escapes and spreads throughout the countryside with devastating results. Since it feeds on calcium, all concrete and stone buildings in southern England crumble before a bulldozed strip, island-wide, and grubbing pigs finally stop the fungus. Quick-moving, plausible plot, likable characters, and insights into the bureaucratic mind and profiteers make up a deliberately low-keyed, effective story. Compare Christopher's *No Blade of Grass* [3-42] or Jones's *The Year When Stardust Fell* [5-82].

5-127.   Patchett, Mary E. **Adam Troy: Astroman.** Lutterworth, 1954 (12–14).
Early British science fiction for youth is set in a future with Earth about to

be devastated by an asteroid, Object A, and struggling to find some way to survive out in space. Adam is sent to determine whether colonies on artificial satellite E.E.I., the Moon, and Mars can be adapted for tremendously expanded growth. Parallel story deals with survivors on Earth after A's devastation. Above-average writing and characterization, along with variety of incident and detailed setting, provide entertaining reading.

5-128. Pešek, Luděk. **The Earth Is Near.** Bradbury, 1974. Trans. of *Die Erde Ist Nah*, 1970, by Anthea Bell (13 up).

An engrossing adventure, convincing investigation of what happens to an international crew of 20 during a journey to Mars and its exploration. The dramatization of the shifting psychological states of mind on the long trip and during the terrifying dust storms; the explicit and hidden animosities and rivalries that emerge; the loneliness and futility experienced because the crew has depended too much on specialized machines, which fail or prove useless; the frustration resulting from the suspicion that the expedition might have done better if it had attempted to harmonize with Martian ecology; and human courage and endurance all give the novel its distinction. Compare Halacy's *Return From Luna* [5-56]. 1971 Deutscher Jugendliteraturpreis (German Youth Literature Prize).

5-129. Pešek, Luděk. **Trap for Perseus.** Bradbury, 1980. Trans. of *Falle für Perseus*, 1976, by Anthea Bell (13 up).

When the spaceship *Perseus III*, investigating the fate of two previous *Perseus* ships, is trapped by the presumably lost Argo, Commander Blair undergoes brainwashing, eventually accepting both the totalitarian society of Argo and a role in entrapping *Perseus IV*. Impressive narrative, fascinating psychological study, richly detailed setting, Kafkaesque atmosphere. Compare Malzberg's *Beyond Apollo* [4-273]; contrast Sleator's *House of Stairs* [5-144].

*5-130. Randall, Florence Engel. **The Watcher in the Woods.** Atheneum, 1976 (12 up).

From the day the Carstairs family inhabits an old house, individual members sense a mysterious, powerful, and potentially dangerous force in the woods watching them. Increasingly bizarre electronic and other disturbances culminate in the discovery of a time-trapped visitor from space in the woods. Stylistic excellence, plausible use of science fiction and ghost story elements, and fresh characterization, especially of warm family life, make for superior storytelling. Compare L'Engle's *A Wrinkle in Time* [5-95]; contrast Jacob's *Born Into Light* [5-79].

5-131. Reynolds, Alfred. **Kiteman of Karanga.** Knopf, 1985 (12–14).
Failing his ordeal and charged with cowardice after choosing banishment
instead of death, Karl finds a new opportunity to prove himself by helping
the people of Eftah wrest their freedom from the lizard-riding Hrithdon.
Attractive and sympathetic characters, distinctive setting, and adventure
mark the fast-moving narrative. Compare Norton's *Star Man's Son: 2250
A.D.* [5-116].

5-132. Rockwood, Roy (pseud. of Edward Stratemeyer Syndicate).
Through the Air to the North Pole; or, The Wonderful Cruise of the Electric Monarch. Cupples & Leon, 1906 (9–11).
Orphans Mark Sampson and Jack Darrow, befriended by Professor Amos
Henderson, accompany him and African-American assistant Washington
(in a secret airship) to the North Pole. The voyagers encounter assorted
adventures, from attack by eagles to capture by "Esquimaux," before
attaining success. First of the nine Great Marvel books, these Verne-like
adventures, from the Edward Stratemeyer Syndicate, both predated the
Tom Swift series and often surpassed it in literary quality and imaginative
scope, although they never equaled it in popularity.

*5-133. Rubinstein, Gillian. **Beyond the Labyrinth.** Hyland House, 1988
(12 up).
An extraterrestrial anthropologist, Cal, precipitates and then resolves tension within 14-year-old Breton's family, as the former, shifting her studies
from aboriginal to contemporary life and falling ill, invites the youth to
come to her home. Intriguing use of alternate points of view and conclusions; provocative investigation of social and cultural issues affecting individuals and families alike. Contrast Engdahl's *The Far Side of Evil* [5-46].
1989 Children's Book of the Year Award of Australia; 1990 National
Children's Literature Award of Australia.

*5-134. Rubinstein, Gillian. **Space Demons.** Omnibus, 1986 (12 up).
Literally caught up in Space Demons, an experimental computer game,
four temperamentally and socially ill-suited teens need every skill and
resource they possess to win the game and save each other's lives. Brilliant
concept; engaging style sensitive to actual teen talk; rounded, honest
characterization. Contrast Key's *The Forgotten Door* [5-87]. A sequel, *Skyway*
(1989), which uses the challenges of a second computer game to continue
exploring the changes within the four teenagers, is just as well written and
exciting as its predecessor. 1988 National Children's Literature Award of
Australia.

5-135. Sargent, Pamela. **Alien Child.** Harper, 1988 (12 up).
Having been revived by their alien-guardians from a frozen embryonic status, Nita and Sven, discovering they are the only living human beings on Earth, decide after some misgivings to revive the other frozen human embryos and restore human life to Earth. Provocative concept and plausible depiction of adolescent sexuality, both human and alien. Contrast Hamilton's *Justice and Her Brothers* [5-57].

*5-136. Sargent, Pamela. **Earthseed.** Harper, 1983 (13 up).
Zoheret and her young companions, artificially born and raised aboard ship, struggle to colonize Hollow, contending against their own inner doubts and the hostility of other human colonizers. Attractive characters, unexpected plotting, and perceptive insight into social and political organizations make the narrative superior storytelling. Compare Karl's *But We Are Not of Earth* [5-83]; contrast Ames's *Anna to the Infinite Power* [5-2]. [For other works by this author see chapter 4.]

*5-137. Schlee, Ann. **The Vandal.** Macmillan, 1979 (12 up).
Placed under psychological care because of his act of vandalism, Paul slowly realizes that the daily Drink, which all must take, no longer is making him immune to the "contamination" of memory, the past, and history. Impressive story: taut narrative pace, Kafkaesque atmosphere, and insightful study of once-benevolent government gone bad. Compare Westall's *Futuretrack 5* [5-168]; contrast Fisk's *Time Trap* [5-51].

5-138. Severn, David (pseud. of David Unwin). **The Future Took Us.** Bodley Head, 1957 (12 up).
A timeslip narrative. Two boys, Peter and Dick, are carried forward into the Great Britain of A.D. 3000 via a machine devised by the Calculators, who venerate mathematics and reason and dominate the masses growing increasingly restive and seeking liberty under the leadership of a handful of aristocrats. A provocative look at a future England controlled by an elite and devastated by social unrest, which predates similar portraits by both Peter Dickinson (the Changes trilogy) [5-42] and John Christopher (the Luke trilogy) [5-28].

5-139. Silverberg, Robert. **Across a Billion Years.** Dial, 1969 (14 up).
Story of a dig in 2375 on Higby V for further evidence of the High Ones is narrated by Tom Rice, apprentice archaeologist. Although Tom is often an amusing narrator and wry observer of the team made up half of humans and half of aliens—evidence of attempt to engage young read-

ers—the book is replete with information about archaeology, present and future. Speculation about origin of life, ESP, and a superrace is also interesting. Compare Hunter's *Find the Feathered Serpent* [5-78]; contrast Oliver's *Mists of Dawn* [5-125].

5-140.   Silverberg, Robert. **The Gate of Worlds.** Holt, 1967 (13–15).
Europe and the rest of the world in an alternative history where the Black Death of 1348 killed three-fourths instead of one-quarter of Europe's population. Dan Beauchamp of New Istanbul (London) leaves to make his fortune in Mexico. Accepting the patronage of a rascally nephew of King Moctezuma, Dan never quite makes his fortune. Of more interest than Dan's adventures is the portrait of the New World, non-Christian, less dependent on machinery, and non-Westernized; anthropological and archaeological information and speculation are sound and challenging. Compare Dick's *The Man in the High Castle* [3-65].

5-141.   Silverberg, Robert. **Time of the Great Freeze.** Holt, 1964 (12–14).
By A.D. 2230, because of the fifth ice age, cities were forced underground. Centuries later the inhabitants of these cities, afraid and suspicious, were content with their living conditions and the lack of communication with each other. Jim Barnes, his father, and five other men, having made radio contact with London, were as a consequence expelled from New York and determined to make London over the ice. Their many adventures and dangers make up a fast-moving story that also entertains through suggesting what elements in today's civilization might survive after an ice age. Contrast Anderson's *Vault of the Ages* [5-4]. [For other works by this author see chapter 4.]

5-142.   Sleator, William. **The Boy Who Reversed Himself.** Dutton, 1986 (10–17).
Confronting Omar, the strange boy next door, with her suspicions, Laura sets in motion the process by which she too is able to enter the fourth dimension, with near tragic consequences for herself and everyone else. The clever, plausible, and somewhat bizarre tale also has a surprise ending. Contrast Harding's *Misplaced Persons* [5-59].

5-143.   Sleator, William. **The Duplicate.** Dutton, 1988 (10–17).
Coming across an odd-looking machine that he discovers can duplicate living organisms, 16-year-old David decides to duplicate himself, only to find his life at peril when Duplicate A, replicating itself, plots with Duplicate B to eliminate David. Suspenseful, quick-moving, and (after the

initial strain on credibility) plausible twist on the Frankenstein story. Contrast Ames's *Is There Life on a Plastic Planet?* [5-3].

*5-144. Sleator, William. **House of Stairs.** Dutton, 1974 (14 up).

Five 16-year-old orphans find themselves in a house of stairs with a red machine as the only furniture. When the machine light blinks and sounds are emitted, the teenagers realize they must perform in a certain way or the machine will not spit out food pellets. Three of the young people do what the machine wants, use each other, and become brutal and mechanistic. The other two open to and sustain each other as humans. The young people discover that they have been subjects in a psychological conditioning experiment. The language and attitudes of teenagers are captured; the breaking down of all external, protective devices is plausibly rendered. However, the truth of the situation may be too obvious to some readers; hence, the sharpness of the attack on behavioral modification procedures is blunted. Compare O'Brien's *Mrs. Frisby and the Rats of NIMH* [5-122].

5-145. Sleator, William. **Singularity.** Dutton, 1985 (12 up).

Dislocations in time and space, caused by a singularity or passageway to another universe located on their property, alter Barry and Harry, twins trapped in a competitive relationship. Entertaining amalgam of young adult focus on difficult sibling relationship, sympathetically handled, and current speculation concerning black holes. Contrast Randall's *A Watcher in the Woods* [5-130].

5-146. Sleator, William. **Strange Attractors.** Dutton, 1990 (12 up).

Clever twists on time travel and contemporary chaos theory force Max to choose between identical pairs of Eve and her brilliant scientist father, Sylvan—one set, good and relatively dull, from Max's time; the other, fascinating and amoral from an alternate world. Intriguing story, which forthrightly includes sex among "attractions" should prove attractive to teens. Contrast Bethancourt's *The Mortal Instruments* [5-12] and O'Brien's *Z for Zachariah* [5-123].

*5-147. Snyder, Zilpha Keatley. **Below the Root.** Atheneum, 1975 (13 up).

In the first part of the Green Sky trilogy, the Kindar are introduced. They live pleasantly in the large branches and trunks of the great trees of Green Sky; the banished Erdlings live below, barely above subsistence level, and called monsters by the Ol-zhaan, leaders of Green Sky. Young Raamo, destined to be a leader and very curious, descends to the ground and, finding out the truth, sets in motion the rejoining of the two peoples. A low-keyed, leisurely moving narrative pace does not seriously detract from the impact of the very detailed and ultimately convincing portrait of this unique arboreal society. Compare Williams's *The People of the Ax* [5-173] and Hoover's *Children of Morrow* [5-69]. *And All Between* (1976) focuses on two children, Teera and Pomma (Erdling and Kindar, respectively), who utilize their telekinetic powers to smooth over the forces working to keep apart the two groups. *Until the Celebration* (1977) details the growing pains of the peoples' rejoining, finally accomplished when Raamo gives his life to cement the union.

*5-148. Stone, Josephine Rector (pseud. of Jeanne Dixon). **The Mudhead.** Atheneum, 1980 (13 up).
The "purple people-eaters" of Sigma capture Corly when, bored and resentful, the young boy leaves the station established by the terran scientific team. Physically tormented, he is saved by the tribe's shaman, a Mudhead, despised but required by the people, only to realize that he is himself destined to become a Mudhead. Further pain and deprivation must be suffered before Corly and his brother, also captured, can escape. Impressive mingling of anthropology and space exploration; especially effective setting; convincing and moving portrait of a boy's maturation through physical and psychological suffering. Compare Engdahl's *The Far Side of Evil* [5-46].

5-149.   Stone, Josephine Rector (pseud. of Jeanne Dixon). **Praise All the Moons of Morning.** Atheneum, 1979 (10–14).
Via time travel two young women from different pasts join forces on the planet Ix-thlan and, aided by Kiffen, an Aslan-like protector, escape the evil, demonic Tez and his worshipers, the Goldmen, and find a utopian future. Themes of youth's testing, drug addiction, and potentially creative tension between the old and the new are special features. Contrast Strete's *The Bleeding Man and Other Science Fiction Stories* [5-151].

*5-150.   Stoutenburg, Adrien. **Out There.** Viking, 1971 (13–15).
Sometime in the 21st century cities lie sterile under steel and plastic domes. Outside is a land so ravaged by waste and pollution that virtually all wildlife is gone. Into this land Zeb and a handful of youngsters travel on an outing to find animal life. The group does locate ample signs of wildlife, but also meets a hunter. An even more ominous note is sounded at the end: the possibility that the restored land may become recreational land, and the cycle of ecological nightmare begin anew. Well-written and

believable situation; polemic against human selfishness and exploitation balanced. Contrast Norton's *Star Man's Son: 2250 A.D.* [5-116] or Clarke's *The Happy Planet* [5-32].

5-151. Strete, Craig. **The Bleeding Man and Other Science Fiction Stories.** Greenwillow, 1977 (12 up).

One of the relatively rare collections of original science fiction short stories for youth, the book is also superior science fiction. Exceptional among the well-crafted and provocative stories are "The Bleeding Man," about a young Indian male who becomes psychochemically a superman, and "Into Every Rain, A Little Life Must Fall," a portrait of a future city controlled by "wombeops." Added strength is an Amerind dimension that challenges Western logic and reason. Contrast Norton's *The Beast Master* (1959).

*5-152. Suddaby, (William) Donald. **Village Fanfare.** Oxford, 1954 (13 up).

In 1908 the village of Much Swayford becomes the center of activity for Burton, the man from the future. Come to Edwardian England to learn from the past, Burton, through his giant computator and his ability to project images of himself anywhere in the world, relearns and takes back the human attributes—laughter, courage, and love for music—that he believes will enable his time, the age of great brains, to go on. Clearly indebted to Wells not only for its depiction of scientific apparatus and time travel, but for its sympathetic, gently humorous portrayal of British village life. A book that deserves wider reading.

5-153. Sutton, Jean, and Jeff(erson) Sutton. **The Programmed Man.** Putnam, 1968 (13–15).

The conventions of space opera and the novel of espionage are interwoven in this neatly plotted story of suspense and adventure. Various agents feint and counterfeint to discover the secret of the N-Bomb, a weapon that has kept peace in the galaxy. Compounding the intrigue is the existence of the "programmed man," a mysterious agent whose identity and purpose, rumor has it, have been programmed to become known at the moment of great crisis. A double surprise ending caps the fast-paced novel. Contrast del Rey's *Step to the Stars* [5-38].

5-154. Sutton, Jeff(erson). **Beyond Apollo.** Putnam, 1966 (13 up).

Delivery of the first lunar permanent station is on schedule when Logan sickens from weightlessness and *Apollo II* has to return to Earth. Clay, command pilot, decides to go ahead putting Big Lander on the Moon. The landing is successful, but an off-target landing spot and another injury appear to force abandonment of the project until Clay stays behind alone to man the station. A taut, suspenseful story; vivid, believable rendering of landing procedure; good description of Moon scenery, atmosphere, and travel; theme of human endurance and determination easily comes across. Compare Marsten's *Rocket to Luna* [5-106].

*5-155. Swindells, Robert. **Brother in the Land.** Oxford, 1984 (13 up).
In the aftermath of nuclear war in Britain, Danny, his younger brother, Ben, and their friend, Kim, can hope to survive only by adopting "Neanderthal" tactics. Ruthlessly honest extrapolation, realistic characterization, and starkly effective style constitute a powerful story. Compare Mace's *Out There* [5-102]; contrast Lawrence's *Children of the Dust* [5-92]. 1984 Children's Book Award.

5-156. Townsend, John Rowe. **The Creatures.** Lippincott, 1980. British title: *King Creature, Come* (13 up).
Two young Persons, Victor and Harmony, decide to leave Colony, established on Earth by its conquerors from Home Planet, and find out for themselves if life can be less restrictive and more exciting out among the Creatures, those native to Earth and despised by the supercerebral Persons. Becoming entangled in intrigue and open revolt, the young couple side with the Creatures in their fight for freedom. Plausible story of adventure and insight into the nature of real liberty and responsibility.

5-157. Townsend, John Rowe. **Noah's Castle.** Oxford Univ. Press., 1975 (12 up).
The Mortimer family, led by its stubborn father, battens down through hoarding to live out a catastrophe of inflation and scarcity befalling England in the near future. Strains within the family and without force several members to break with the father's plan, and the "castle" is invaded and destroyed. Relentlessly honest in its picture of strong personalities clashing and vivid in depicting society's disintegration, the novel is superior postcatastrophe fiction. Compare Christopher's *The Guardians* [5-27]; contrast Corlett's *Return to the Gate* [5-34].

5-158. Townsend, John Rowe. **The Visitors.** Lippincott, 1977. British title: *The Xanadu Manuscript* (14 up).
While jotting down his rapidly fading memories of the Wyatts and their daughter, ostensibly foreign and very mysterious visitors to Cambridge,

young John Dunham is forced to admit that the latter are actually visitors from the future and can bring only grief to those whose lives they touch. The time travel motif is handled freshly and poignantly; characterization is deft and insightful. Compare Suddaby's *Village Fanfare* [5-152].

*5-159. Ure, Jean. **Plague.** Harcourt, 1991. British title: *Plague 99*, 1989 (10 up).

Three teenagers, Harriet, Fran, and Shahid, struggle to survive when a plague devastates the cities of England. Plausible study of both the pathology of disease and the unpredictability of human response to tragedy is further enhanced by skillful use of multiple points of view. Compare Christopher's *Empty World* [5-25]; contrast Parker's *The Hendon Fungus* [5-126]. 1990 Children's Book of the Year in Great Britain for *Plague 99*.

5-160. Van Lhin, Eric (pseud. of Lester del Rey). **Battle on Mercury.** Winston, 1953 (12–14).

When the rescue ship crashes and a terrible electric storm is imminent, one of the mining domes on Mercury faces extinction. Dick Rogers; his "pet" Johnny Quicksilver, a Wispie, which is an indigenous life form; Pete the Robot; and Hotshot Charlie, a prospector, combine to bring aid successfully after battling the inhospitable terrain, electricity-eating demons, and Silicone Beasts. Still "fun reading," the novel stands out among the Winston series because of its deft style, fast pace, and imaginative characterization. Compare Vance's *Vandals of the Void* [5-160]. [For other works by this author (del Rey) see chapters 3 and 5.]

5-161. Vance, Jack (John Holbrook). **Vandals of the Void.** Winston, 1953 (12–14).

Futuristic piracy and old-fashioned megalomania play prominent roles in this novel of space rockets being attacked, taken, and reconverted into a fleet designed to conquer Earth and its colonies. Young Dick Murdock uncovers the lair of the Basilisk and is able to alert Earth to former's identity and plans. The story, in spite of the vintage space opera elements, is still interesting because of the rich detailing and swift narrative pace. Stylistically one of the best-written Winston 1950s novels. [For other works by this author see chapters 3 and 4.]

*5-162. Vinge, Joan D. **Psion.** Delacorte, 1982 (13 up).

Centuries in the future, Cat, an illiterate slum child, reluctantly undergoes training to utilize his telepathic powers and becomes involved in the struggle both to outwit Robiy, an evil telepath, and to aid the wise telepaths, the Hydrans. Fine characterization, detailed setting, provocative study of psi, and suspenseful plotting; engrossing narrative. The sequel is *Catspaw*, 1988. Compare the Johnsons' *Prisoner of Psi* [5-80]; contrast Norton's *Quest Crosstime* [5-115]. [For other works by this author see chapter 4.]

5-163.   Walters, Hugh (pseud. of Walter Llewellyn Hughes). **Destination Mars.** Faber, 1963 (12–14).
All goes well as Chris Godfrey and his companions find, during investigation into the possibility of Martian life, exciting evidence of life and civilization. However, disembodied Martian life makes its presence known and demands to be taken to Earth. When the crew resists, the new hostile life takes over the minds of all except Chris and begins the flight to Earth. Mysterious space voices, transmitted by the ship's radio, frighten away the Martians and the crew escapes. Effective space adventure, adequately written, ample incident and suspense, representative of the author's quality work in science fiction for young readers. Compare Heinlein's *Rocket Ship Galileo* [5-62] or Capon's *Lost: A Moon* [5-21].

5-164.   Walters, Hugh (pseud. of Walter Llewellyn Hughes). **The Mohole Mystery.** Faber, 1968 (12–14).
Four astronauts, becoming "subterranauts," volunteer to descend 40 miles into Earth's mantle. First Serge, then Chris, via rocket plummeting down a two-feet-in-diameter tube into a forbidding cavern, ascertain the source of a mysterious, deadly bacteria. Perhaps the best written of the author's many books. The narrative moves fast and features interesting technology and training techniques. The only flaw is implausible balloonlike creatures residing in the cavern. One of 24 books in the Chris Godfrey series.

5-165.   Walton, Bryce. **Sons of the Ocean Deeps.** Winston, 1952 (12–14).
Chagrined at having been washed out of the rocket program, Jon West hopes to hide away in the underseas service. Gradually learning underwater survival techniques, suffering patiently the taunts of Sprague, who resents his family, and acquiring self-knowledge, Jon proves himself a man. One of the better 1950s Winston novels. Depiction of aquatic life, real and imagined, and of possible living quarters is extensive and interesting; style is competent; and hero's maturation is plausible and convincing. Compare Norton's *Star Man's Son: 2250 A.D.* [5-116].

5-166.   Watson, Simon. **No Man's Land.** Gollancz, 1975 (12 up).
Set in a future England where progress rules and the countryside is "rationalized" through technology, the story concerns Alan's fight, aided by

another youth, Jay, and the 65-year-old general, to prevent the demolition of an ancient keep by a gigantic robot. Although the fight is successful, the victory over rationalizing is just local. A bit slow moving, the novel impresses because of its plausible scenario and its sympathetic portrait of old age and love of the countryside. Compare Corlett's *Return to the Gate* [5-34]; contrast Christopher's *The Prince in Waiting* [5-28].

5-167. Webb, Sharon. **Earthchild.** Atheneum, 1982 (13 up).
Young people who can become immortal because of the Mouat-Gari process must be protected from their envious elders. Since immortality is no guarantee of creativity, a select few, chosen by Kurt Kraus, one of the immortal leaders, are asked to decide between immortality and creative mortality. Engrossing reading, provocative speculation, and poignant and believable situations. Sequels are *Earth Song* (1983), which focuses on David Defour, a gifted young composer who chooses music over immortality, and *Ram Song* (1984), in which Kurt again intervenes to preserve balance between demands for immortality and society's need for creativity. Compare Bonham's *The Forever Formula* [5-17]; contrast Bethancourt's *The Mortal Instruments* [5-12].

*5-168. Westall, Robert. **Futuretrack 5.** Kestrel, 1983 (13 up).
A young computer genius, Kitson goes "razzle," running away from tending Laura, the master computer, and joining up with Keri, a master cyclist. The couple set out to discover the secret of Scott-Astbury, responsible for much that explains tightly controlled 21st-century England. Powerful novel: nightmarish depiction of future life, especially in the cities; intriguing plot; distinctive, richly allusive, yet colloquial style. Compare Burgess's *A Clockwork Orange* [3-41].

*5-169. Westall, Robert. **Urn Burial.** Viking, 1987 (12 up).
Ralph's accidental discovery of an ancient burial site involves him in a conflict between two alien peoples—an evil one seeking to establish a new home on Earth, and a good one wishing to prevent it. In spite of common plot situation, tale is marked by suspense, deft characterization, wit, and a richly allusive style. Contrast L'Engle's *A Wrinkle in Time* [5-95].

5-170. White, T(erence) H(ansbury). **The Master.** Cape, 1957 (14 up).
Exploring the supposedly barren island Rockall, Nicky and Judy accidentally fall into the water and into the secret headquarters of the Master, a 157-year-old ESP adept who is plotting to conquer the world via powerful vibrators he has invented. Another accident, when the Master slips into the ocean after being bitten by the children's dog, finally saves the world.

Off-beat characterization and psychological probing are revealed through the extensive dialogue; hence, a bit talky for many young readers. Still, the acerbic wit and charm characteristic of the author are present. Compare MacArthur's *The Thunderbolt Men* [5-100].

5-171.   Wibberly, Leonard (pseud. of Patrick O'Connor). **Encounter Near Venus.** Farrar, 1967 (11–13).

Four members of a family must spend their summer vacation with their uncle. Becoming involved with Venusian life forms, children and uncle journey to Nede, a satellite of Venus, where they are caught up in a struggle to keep Ka, the evil Smiler, from corrupting Nede, an innocent world. A struggle-between-forms-of-good-and-evil book, suggestive of the Narnia books by C. S. Lewis. Information about science and ethics is, generally speaking, skillfully meshed into the narrative. Sequel is *Journey to Untor*, 1970. Compare L'Engle's *A Wrinkle in Time* [5-95].

5-172.   Wilder, Cherry (pseud. of Cherry Barbara Grimm). **The Luck of Brin's Five.** Atheneum, 1977 (13 up).

Scott Gale, navigator of a terran bio-survey team on Torin, crash-lands and is found and befriended by Dorn, member of the family called Brin's Five. According to custom, the family considers Scott a Diver and their new "luck." Through the ensuing adventures—in particular, those involving flying machines and air races—and the dangerous intrigue of those opposed to change, Scott proves he is indeed a "luck" and precipitates a new openness to change among the people. Although the narrative pace flags occasionally, the novel creates an original world and culture vaguely Oriental. Sequels are *The Nearest Fire* (1980), which just as engagingly continues to detail Torin, and *The Tapestry Warriors* (1983). Compare Yep's *Sweetwater* [5-179]. 1977 Ditmar Award.

5-173.   Williams, Jay. **The People of the Ax.** Walck, 1974 (12–14).

A postcatastrophe story. Two societies have survived: human beings, or the ax people, who have souls and no longer kill except for food, and the "crom," a human-like people hated by the humans. Arne realizes he possesses "tendo," the ability to sense the spirit of harmony in all, and hence is destined to become a leader of the humans. Arne's first, and revolutionary, intuition is a suspicion that crom may also be human, and he successfully awakens soul in one of their leaders. Competently written, plausible look at possible future societies, except that the author becomes too tendentious when contemporary civilization is blamed for all human failures. Compare Norton's *Star Man's Son: 2250 A.D.* [5-116].

5-174. Williams, Jay. **The Time of the Kraken.** Four Winds, 1977 (12 up).
Spurned by his people as he warns them of the coming of the terrible Kraken, Thorgeir Redhair seeks the gods' help. With three companions, the young hero makes the arduous journey to the Temple of Arveid and learns the surprising truth: his people are descendants of humans escaping from a hopelessly polluted Earth via rockets to new worlds. A brisk retelling, cast in heroic terms, of Icelandic saga that presupposes a scientific explanation for the latter; hence, an adroit blending of fantasy and science fiction. Compare Huddy's *Time Piper* [5-75].

5-175. Williamson, Jack (John Stewart). **Trapped in Space.** Doubleday, 1968 (10–14).
Although resenting Ben, his older and more talented brother, Jeff Stone still volunteers to search for him, missing while exploring Topaz. Accompanied by Lupe Flor, a fellow starman, and a fuzzy alien, Buzzy Dozen-Dozen, Jeff locates his brother among the hostile rock hoppers of Topaz. Before a rescue can be effected, the humans must convince the hoppers to trust Earth and join the galaxywide family. Written economically without sacrificing detail or variety, the story effectively combines adventure, space technology, and the theme of growing up. Compare Marsten's *Rocket to Luna* [5-106]. [For other works by this author see chapters 2, 3 and 4.]

5-176. Winterfeld, Henry. **Star Girl.** Harcourt, 1957. Trans. of *Kommt ein Mädchen Geflogen,* 1956, by Kyrill Schabert (11–13).
Mo, an 87-year-old "girl" from Asra or Venus, accidentally falls out of her father's spaceship. She is found by several German children under a forest tree and they, believing her story, agree to help Mo meet her father that night. The village adults refuse to believe or help Mo, but the children and Mo eventually succeed. Exceptional are the realistic portrayal of adult disbelief and their quick willingness to consider Mo insane, and the sharply distinguished characterization of Mo and the children. Less convincing is the speculation about possible Venusian civilization.

5-177. Wollheim, Donald A. **The Secret of Saturn's Rings.** Winston, 1954 (10–12).
Young Bruce Rhodes accompanies his famous scientist father on a United Nations mission to prove that Saturn's rings were artificially caused. The expedition, although harassed by Terraluna, a corporation seeking to blast into the Moon's core to find precious ores, is successful, and evidence of life on Saturn is uncovered. The scenes describing father and

son marooned in the rings and devising ways to travel are still imaginative; one of the better 1950s Winston books. Compare Latham's *Missing Men of Saturn* [5-90].

5-178.   Wollheim, Donald A. **The Secret of the Martian Moons.** Winston, 1955 (12–14).
Early children's mainstream space opera. A handful of humans, secretly left behind in a final attempt to discover the origin and fate of the Martian cities, become embroiled in a rivalry between the two factions of the cowardly Vegans, who centuries before had placed two artificial spheres, Phobos and Deimos, in orbit near Mars. Before peace can be established, the Star people, the original inhabitants of Mars, return and enter into an alliance with Earth. Minimal characterization and science hardware, but ample incident and a quick-moving story. Contrast Claudy's *The Mystery Men of Mars* [5-33].

*5-179.   Yep, Laurence. **Sweetwater.** Harper, 1973 (12 up).
Young Tyree is torn between pursuing an interest in music encouraged by Amadeus, an Argan (the oldest race on the planet Harmony), and obeying his father, elected captain of the Silkies, descendants of the starship crews from Earth, who are fighting for a life in harmony with the dominant sea. A distinctive narrative that unexpectedly and winningly combines a richly imagined world and its ecology, a boy's rite of passage, and wide-ranging allusions to music and the Old Testament. Compare Norton's *Star Man's Son: 2250 A.D.* [5-116].

*5-180.   Zebrowski, George. **Sunspacer.** Harper, 1984 (14 up).
Unsure whether he wants a career in theoretical physics but aware that he needs adventure and the challenge of hardship and danger, Joe Sorby, a high school student of the future, forgoes college on Bernal to become a maintenance apprentice. Very detailed scenario of possible solar system exploration; convincing portrait of youth unsure of himself and his options. Followed by *The Stars Will Speak*, 1985. Compare Kurland's *The Princes of Earth* [5-89] or Heinlein's *Starman Jones* [5-64].

Secondary
Literature and
Research Aids

CHAPTER 6

Science Fiction
Publishing and Libraries

Neil Barron

SF Publishing

Science fiction has solidly established itself as a staple in publishing and
libraries since the first edition of *Anatomy of Wonder* was published in 1976.
SF routinely appears on hardcover and mass market paperback bestseller
lists. The influence of film and television is reflected in the sales of the
novels based on the *Star Trek* and *Star Trek: The Next Generation* series. The
first book series began in 1979, the second in 1987, and more than 38 million hardcover and paperback copies of more than 100 novels had been
published by summer 1992, with many of them on the bestseller lists. The
Star Trek books have been translated into 15 languages, suggesting the
series' very widespread appeal. The appeal of SF is still heavily to males, if
the annual reader surveys by *Locus* represent the field at large. In 1971 the
split was about 80/20; it's about 70/30 today.

Science fiction's popularity has been tracked in detail by *Locus* [12-24],
for more than 25 years a major source of information about SF and fantastic fiction generally. Over the past decade for example, the number of
original (that is, not reprinted or reissued) SF novels increased from 186

in 1983 to 317 in 1988, hovering around 300 in the years since. SF anthologies, collections, and film novelizations would increase these figures by about 35 percent. The Science Fiction Book Club, founded in 1950, makes available hardcover reprints of original paperbacks as well as printing various omnibus editions, all under the Nelson Doubleday imprint. Libraries might consider joining because of the low prices and the hardcover editions of mass market paperbacks. Quite different from the cheap SFBC editions is the leatherbound, gilt-edged Masterpieces of Science Fiction series issued on a subscription basis by Easton Press.

The increasing popularity of SF has been paralleled by major changes in publishing in the United States and abroad. Publishing is increasingly international in nature, and a wave of mergers and acquisitions has resulted in huge transnational conglomerates, of which publishers are only a part. The age of the gentleman as publisher is a fading memory, and publishers have increasingly been subject to the same short-term, often ruthless bottom-line mentality other businesses have long lived with.

Most authors have rarely had much say in how their books were edited, promoted, or sold, and they are at an increasing disadvantage when dealing with the large corporations that have replaced the more traditional publishers, which were sometimes willing to take a chance on an unknown, a book that didn't fit into a standardized marketing category, or one that departed from the conventional formulas of category fiction. The effects on authors, readers, and libraries of today's SF publishing marketplace were explored in trenchant detail by Cristina Sedgewick in "The Fork in the Road: Can Science Fiction Survive in Postmodern, Megacorporate America," *Science-Fiction Studies* 18 (March 1991): 11–52. The publisher as simply one of many, often disparate subsidiaries in a large, impersonal corporation, combined with the increasing domination of retail book sales by a few large chains that can rapidly track sales by author, category, publisher, or any combination thereof, has led to an increasingly standardized product in trade and mass market publishing (other segments of publishing have been less subject to these influences).

Libraries have a potentially important role in resisting the increasing homogenization of publishing by their collective selection decisions, which have a significant effect on fiction sales other than bestsellers, and of course an overwhelming effect on the sale of children's and young adult books, which are sold mostly to libraries. And guides like *Anatomy of Wonder* attempt to identify the more distinguished works worthy of library dollars and a reader's time, although the replies I received from academic and public libraries indicated that this guide is only infrequently used to build a quality, core collection of science fiction.

Although many publishers issue science fiction, even if not so labeled, most of the originals and reprints are issued by a relatively few companies, which are listed in table 6-1 in approximate rank by number of original books, based on tabulations in the February 1993 *Locus* and my knowledge of publishers of secondary literature.

Table 6-1   Principal U.S. Publishers of Science Fiction

Trade Hardcovers	*Mass Market Paperbacks*	*Nonfiction*
Putnam	Berkley	Greenwood Press
Bantam Spectra	Ace	McFarland & Co.
Doubleday Foundation	Bantam Spectra	Univ. of Georgia Press
Ballantine Del Rey	Dell	Routledge
Tor	Tor	Indiana Univ. Press
St. Martin's	Ballantine Del Rey	Bowling Green Univ.
Random House	Roc/Signet	Popular Press
Penguin/Dutton	Pulphouse	Borgo Press
HarperPrism	Zebra/Pinnacle	Twayne Publishers
Macmillan	Baen	Underwood Books
Harcourt	Leisure	Charles F. Miller
Simon & Schuster	Avon	
Morrow/AvoNova	Pocket Books	
SF Book Club*	DAW	
	Warner/Aspect	

* whose Nelson Doubleday imprint denotes an original hardcover

Specialty publishers of science fiction have existed since the mid-1940s, when fans founded firms to put into hardcovers fiction they'd read in the moldering pulps. Most of these early firms died in the 1950s, when the larger publishers, recognizing a profitable market niche, moved in. Only Arkham House, founded in 1939 to preserve the work of H. P. Lovecraft, survives from this earliest period. The story of the specialty publishers is chronicled in great detail in Chalker & Owings, *The Science-Fantasy Publishers* [7-3], and in the more specialized accounts by Eshbach [8-54] and Harbottle and Holland [8-65]. Books from these publishers often appear today in two editions, a limited, signed, numbered, often slip-cased edition for collectors and an unnumbered trade edition. The principal specialty publishers of SF in 1994 are shown below. Excluded are those that publish only fantasy and/or horror.

Advent Publishers, Box A3228, Chicago, IL 60690. History and criticism, especially the Tuck set [7-9].

Arkham House, Box 546, Sauk City, WI 53583. Originally supernatural fiction; more SF recently.

Borgo Press, Box 2845, San Bernardino, CA 92406. Criticism and bibliographies; absorbed Starmont House winter 1992/93.

Cheap Street, Rt. 2, Box 293, New Castle, VA 24127. Original fiction handset in very fine quality editions; special collections departments should investigate.

Dragon Press, Box 78, Pleasantville, NY 10570.

Chris Drumm, Box 445, Polk City, IA 50226. Pamphlet-length author bibliographies and some short stories, especially by R. A. Lafferty.

Galactic Central Publications, George Benson, Jr., Box 40494, Albuquerque, NM 87196. Pamphlet-length author bibliographies jointly produced with Phil Stephensen-Payne in England.

Donald M. Grant, Box 187, Hampton Falls, NH 03844. Reprints from the pulps, especially Robert E. Howard; emphasis on fantasy/horror rather than SF.

Locus Press, Box 13305, Oakland, CA 94661; annual bibliographies [7-2].

Charles F. Miller, 708 Westover Drive, Lancaster, PA 17601. Nonfiction and illustration.

Mirage Press, Box 1689, Westminster, MD 21158-1689. Mostly nonfiction, most notably the Chalker & Owings bibliography [7-3].

Owlswick Press, Box 8243, Philadelphia, PA 19101.

Pulphouse Publishing, Box 1227, Eugene, OR 97440. A recent (1988) entrant; pamphlet-length works and occasional longer works; mostly fiction, plus the irregular serial, *Monad* [12-25].

Underwood Books, Box 1607, Grass Valley, CA 95945. Nonfiction and illustration.

Reviewing, Selecting, and Collecting SF

In the United States alone more than 3,000 original works of fiction are published each year, from the standard commercial novels of Michener, Steele, and Sheldon to the "serious" fiction of Updike to many types of category fiction, much of the latter issued as original paperbacks. Partly because of its pulp magazine heritage (see chapter 12 and the introductions to chapters 2, 3, and 4), and because about 35–40 percent of SF is still published as original mass market paperbacks, the successors to yesterday's pulp magazines, SF is not taken very seriously as "literature," however much it may sell or contribute to a publisher's profits. Writing in 1974 Norman Spinrad asked, "How *can* a serious, conscientious literary critic sort through the year's mountain-high pile of tacky-looking science fiction paperbacks to find a few real jewels buried in this heap of literary mediocrity?" (from his *Modern Science Fiction* (1974)).

The sheer number of books published each year—more than 30,000 titles in the United States, plus several thousand reprints and reissues (the figures are higher in the United Kingdom)—means that no magazine or newspaper can review more than a very small selection, many of them simply the most heavily hyped. This fact alone, quite apart from the tackiness Spinrad notes, means that little SF will be reviewed in general review media. Library and book trade journals review more, and a few specialty magazines more still, as table 6-2 shows, based on estimates by Michael Levy and by H. W. Hall, who indexes these book reviews (see [7-15]).

Table 6-2   Science Fiction Book Reviewing

Magazine	Frequency	No. SF Books Reviewed/Year
General		
NY Times Book Review	Weekly	40–50
Booklist	Biweekly	200
Choice	Monthly	60
Kirkus	Semi-monthly	120
Kliatt Young Adult Paperback Guide	8 issues/year	120
Library Journal	Biweekly	140
Publishers Weekly	Weekly	250
Voice of Youth Advocates (VOYA)	Quarterly	200
Washington Post Book World	Weekly	50
Specialty (see chapter 12)		
Analog	13 issues/year	130
Asimov's SF Magazine	13 issues/year	50
Extrapolation	Quarterly	15
Foundation	3 issues/year	60
Interzone	Monthly	150
Locus	Monthly	240
Magazine of Fantasy & SF	Monthly	30
The New York Review of SF	Monthly	75
Science Fiction & Fantasy Book Review Annual	Annual	350
Science Fiction Chronicle	Monthly	175
Science-Fiction Studies	3 issues/year	45
SFRA Review	6 issues/year	250

The estimates include SF and books about SF. The academic journals generally review only nonfiction. Library and book trade journals and *Locus* usually provide pre- or on-publication reviews. This is important because of the large number of mass market paperbacks, which rarely remain on the newsstands for more than a few weeks except in the specialty stores found in selected metropolitan areas. Mail order specialty dealers can usually supply paperbacks for many months following publication and naturally have much more depth in their stock. The classified ads in *Locus* include many of the most important dealers. And the comprehensive Books Received listings (U.S. and U.K.) can be used by the knowledgeable person to select originals and reprints.

Anatomy of Wonder has always been a critical guide to the best or better works. Scarcity, rarity, or collectibility were not and are not among the selection criteria, as I stated in the preface. SF has been collected for decades, and over the years various price guides have been issued. As any knowledgeable collector knows, such guides are misleading at best and would never be written by a professional book dealer, who recognizes their inherently suspect nature, particularly in a field that changes as rapidly as SF. Most guides omit the points necessary to identify the collectible editions and fail to note the crucial effect condition has on price. Collectors should acquire a copy of *Science Fiction and Fantasy Authors* [7-7], available from the compiler, L. W. Currey, Elizabethtown, New York 12933, for $68.50 delivered. This provides the essential points for thousands of editions issued through mid-1977. Collectors, dealers, and order librarians know *AB Bookman's Weekly*, long the bible of the used/antiquarian book trade. Since 1983 *AB* has published a special SF and fantasy issue each October, when the World Fantasy Convention is held. These issues contain many articles and advertisements of interest to collectors. See Currey's valuable current survey of the market, "Buying and Selling Fantastic Fiction in the Real World; or SF Versus Sci-Fi," *AB Bookman's Weekly*, 18 October 1993.

Cataloging

Academic libraries usually catalog both hardcovers and paperbacks, but paperbacks in public libraries are apparently judged as something close to expendable supplies, based on the replies I received. SF paperbacks are typically placed on spinner racks or shelves and tagged with a spine label but are infrequently cataloged. Since a user has no way of determining the library's holdings of such paperbacks, simple chance is likely to determine what is found. These volumes cannot be used effectively for interbranch or interlibrary lending.

Although the Library of Congress receives most American SF books in the form of copyright copies, only in 1992 did it begin to catalog SF mass market collections and anthologies, with novels—by far the largest segment—still going to a warehouse unsorted and uncataloged. But at the same time Joseph Mayhew of the Library of Congress wrote me with this information, LC's catalog department bulletin specifically said to exclude from all mass market originals or reprints the cataloging in publication (CIP) information typically found on the copyright page of most hardcovers and trade paperbacks. However, some of the libraries with the largest collections (see chapter 14) contribute cataloging information to the OCLC database for anyone to use, making LC's practices largely irrelevant.

Libraries using the Library of Congress classification scheme that acquire more than an occasional work of SF should consider purchase of *A Guide to Science Fiction and Fantasy in the Library of Congress Classification Scheme*, 2nd ed., Borgo Press, 1988, which is much more detailed than the 1984 first edition. The author is a cataloger and bibliographer (under the name R. Reginald). Classification schedules, subject headings, and author and literature class numbers are provided.

CHAPTER 7

General Reference Works

Neil Barron

The emphasis in this chapter is on books that are referred to but not read continuously and that do not fall within the more specialized chapters: film and TV (chapter 10), magazines (12), the Weinberg directory (11), or the author bibliographies in chapter 9. SF and its major writers have achieved sufficient acceptance in recent years to be the subjects of entries in dozens of general reference works, such as encyclopedias, literary guides, and histories. See, for example, *The Facts on File Bibliography of American Literature*, an ambitious 12-volume set that began publication in 1991 with two volumes covering fiction published from 1919 through 1988, some of it by genre fiction writers such as Heinlein and Dick, some by writers peripheral to SF, such as John Barth or William Burroughs. The coverage here is restricted to works limited to SF, fantastic fiction generally, or utopian studies. Most books annotated in this chapter are evaluated in Burgess's *Reference Guide to Science Fiction, Fantasy, and Horror* [7-11]; the Burgess entry number concludes each annotation.

Bibliographies and Indexes

As science fiction began to be recognized as a distinct type of fiction in the late 1920s, when the specialty pulps began, it wasn't long before fans started listing books and authors, indexing magazines, and engaging in similar hobbyist efforts. Some of these appeared in the fanzines (fan magazines) of the time, others as relatively crude hectographed or mimeographed booklets, for which the term "fugitive" would be extremely optimistic and which have long been superseded. But it was the efforts of these fans that laid the foundations for the more authoritative works of recent years, themselves often created by fans, some turned academics, but no less professional for that. This section is roughly divided into general and specialized bibliographies and indexes.

General

7-1.   Bleiler, Everett F. The Checklist of Science-Fiction and Supernatural Fiction. Firebell Books, 1978.
The Checklist of Fantastic Literature (1948), or Bleiler as it soon became known to collectors and enthusiasts, was for many years the standard bibliography of English-language fantastic fiction. This revised edition deletes 600 presumably marginal or improper titles and adds 1,150 to the original and extends the coverage through 1948. The 5,600 titles are listed by author with a title index. Although Bleiler attempted to list only the first edition, his citations sometimes differ from those of Reginald [7-8], who Bleiler thinks improperly omits approximately a thousand titles in his pioneering compilation. New to this revised edition are approximately 90 codes used to denote the dominant theme or motif of the book. See also Bleiler's masterful annotated bibliography of early SF [7-21]. Burgess 178.

*7-2.   Brown, Charles N., and William G. Contento. Science Fiction, Fantasy, & Horror: A Comprehensive Bibliography of Books and Short Fiction Published in the English Language. Locus Press, 1984–1991.
This annual began as *Science Fiction in Print—1985*, with 1984 added later in order to provide continuity with Contento's second index [7-13]. Each volume assembles, revises, and supplements the material in the preceding year of *Locus* [12-24]. Books and shorter fiction are indexed by author and title, with the contents of all anthologies, collections, and professional magazines shown and indexed. Beginning with the 1988 annual, H. W. Hall's "reference index" to books and articles about fantastic literature and film was included. Appendixes provide valuable surveys of book and magazine publishing, of fantastic cinema, and surveys of the best books by regular *Locus* reviewers, along with the results of reader polls. Harlan McGhan provides a comprehensive listing of awards, supplementing the Mallett & Reginald compilation [7-7]. Weak sales resulting from anemic library budgets forced the editors to seek another publisher, which had

not been found by the end of 1994. *Locus* has provided the most authoritative and comprehensive history of SF and fantastic fiction generally, and these annuals will be essential for any historian and many critics. Burgess 24. Eaton award, 1991

7-3.   Chalker, Jack L., and Mark Owings. **The Science-Fantasy Publishers: A Critical and Bibliographic History.** Mirage Press, 1991. 3rd ed., rev. & enl.

This new edition is almost ten times the length of its two 1966 predecessors, reflecting the rapid growth in specialty publishing since the founding of Arkham House in 1939. The main sequence profiles 148 publishers in almost 500 pages, with books listed alphabetically by publisher, then chronologically. A 135-page appendix lists the work of 48 smaller publishers. There are author-artist and title indexes. Various appendixes provide additional information. Although this compilation provides far more detail about specialty publications than any other source, the text mixes purely factual information—some of it based on the imperfect memories of individuals associated with the publishers—with considerable unsupported opinion, sometimes masquerading as dispassionate fact. The book is very poorly proofread, a major failing in a bibliography. The method of production, by which text is corrected but pagination unaltered, makes it impossible to determine which of the very short-run printings one has and what corrections have been made. A 130-page supplement with corrections and additions, July 1991–June 1992, was released in late 1992 (not seen), followed in fall 1993 by an enlarged supplement, 164 pages, designated July 1991–June 1993. A useful if specialized work to be used with extreme caution. Burgess 237 (for the earlier editions). See Eshbach [8-53] and Harbottle and Holland [8-65] for more specialized publishing histories.

7-4.   Clareson, Thomas D. **Science Fiction in America, 1870s–1930s: An Annotated Bibliography of Primary Sources.** Greenwood, 1984.

Provides descriptive, occasionally evaluative annotations of 838 books, mostly by American writers, although British and some European writers are represented (for example, Haggard, Wells, Verne). Intended as a companion to Clareson's narrative history, *Some Kind of Paradise* [8-37]. The bibliography in chapter 1 of this guide is a selection from this authoritative compilation. Compare Bleiler [7-21]. Contrast Suvin [8-138] and Stableford [8-132], whose focus is British writers. Burgess 199.

7-5. Clarke, I(gnatius) F(rederick). **Tale of the Future From the Beginning to the Present Day: An Annotated Bibliography.** Library Association, 1978. 3rd ed.

A chronological and briefly annotated listing by year from 1644 to 1976 of about 3,900 utopian, political, and scientific romance tales of the future published in Britain, excluding juveniles and serial publications. Clarke's definition excludes alternate histories or parallel world tales unless set in the future. Since books had to be published in the United Kingdom, hundreds and perhaps thousands of American works were excluded. The annotations are often too brief to be of much value. Clarke's narrative survey of the subject, *The Pattern of Expectation: 1644–2001* [8-40], usefully complements this bibliography. Author and title indexes and a brief bibliography. Burgess 212.

7-6. Cottrill, Tim, Martin H. Greenberg, and Charles G. Waugh. **Science Fiction and Fantasy Series and Sequels: A Bibliography.** Volume 1: **Books.** Garland, 1986.

Series and sequels have become increasingly common in SF and fantasy in recent years, reflecting publishers' preferences for guaranteed sales and readers' preferences for more of the same. This compilation builds on the work of Reginald [7-8], Tuck [7-9], and other bibliographies annotated in this chapter and lists approximately 1,160 series and more than 6,900 books, many paperback originals, mostly published in this century. Author, title, year, publisher, and sequence in series are shown through 1985 works. Series and book title indexes enhance the book's usefulness. Because many libraries view popular fiction series with disdain, they will not own—or will not catalog if owned in paperback—most of these books. Useful as a reader's advisory tool and for specialty booksellers. The series listing in *Anatomy of Wonder* updates this guide, which was supposed to (but won't) be followed by a second volume indexing short fiction series and sequels rather than novels. The two Reginald bibliographies provide series indexes [7-8]. A series index is one of several indexes in the Gale Research annual, *What Do I Read Next?* [7-18]. The guide by Vicki Anderson, *Fiction Sequels for Readers 10 to 16: An Annotated Bibliography of Books in Succession* (McFarland, 1990), lists about 1,500 titles by 350 authors, most published since 1960, some of them fantastic fiction. Literary merit was not a basis for selection. Literary merit was one criterion (balanced against popularity) in the more comprehensive guide, *Sequels: An Annotated Guide to Novels in Series* (American Library Association, 2nd ed., 1990), compiled by Janet Husband and Jonathan F.

Husband. Thirty of the approximately 500 authors wrote fantastic novels in series. Burgess 225.

7-7.   Currey, L. W. **Science Fiction and Fantasy Authors: A Bibliography of First Printings of Their Fiction and Selected Nonfiction.** G. K. Hall, 1979.

A comprehensive listing of more than 6,200 printings and editions through June 1977 of books by 215 authors, from Wells to authors prominent by the mid-1970s. Multiple copies of a title were carefully compared to determine first and variant editions, and all essential points are included for collectors, for whom this is an indispensable guide (see chapter 6 for ordering information). Non-SF books by the authors, and significant reference material (notably bibliographies) about them published through June 1979 are also listed, some of it fugitive fan press items rarely recorded elsewhere. Sometimes differs with Reginald [7-8] as to first editions. Single author listings supplementing the book have appeared in *The New York Review of Science Fiction* [12-27]. More specialized is Christopher P. Stephens, *The Science Fiction and Fantasy Paperback First Edition: A Complete List of Them All (1939–1973)* (Ultramarine, 1991; Burgess 222). He includes the usual bibliographic information as well as publisher stock numbers, names of cover illustrators, and cloth reprints published 1969–1973. As authoritative as Currey but much more personal is *A Spectrum of Fantasy: The Bibliography and Biography of a Collection of Fantastic Literature* (Ferret Fantasy, 1980; Burgess 181) by the British dealer/collector, George Locke, who describes, often in fascinating detail, his personal collection of more than 3,100 books. Locke has published other, more specialized guides, such as *Voyages in Space: A Bibliography of Interplanetary Fiction 1801–1914* (Ferret Fantasy, 1975; Burgess 227). Currey and these other books are valuable to collectors and would be useful to any special collections librarian whose holdings include substantial fantastic fiction. Burgess 210.

*7-8.   Reginald, R(obert). **Science Fiction and Fantasy Literature: A Checklist, 1700–1974, with Contemporary Science Fiction Authors II.** Gale Research, 1979. 2 vols.

Volume 1 lists the first editions of 15,884 books published in English from 1700 through 1974. The listed books were examined and, if necessary, read to determine if they fell within the work's broad scope, with more than 4,000 titles rejected as unsuitable, some of them listed in earlier bibliographies, which were effectively superseded with the appearance of this authoritative set. Arrangement is by author, with thorough cross-references among pseudonyms, many newly identified, followed by a title index. Supplemental indexes include those to series, awards, and Ace and Belmont Doubles paperbacks. Volume 2 replaces the compiler's *Stella Nova* (1970), reprinted as *Contemporary Science Fiction Authors* (1974), and is a biographical directory of 1,443 modern SF and fantasy writers, including editors and critics, compiled from questionnaires completed by the authors or their estates. The traditional information—family, education, career, memberships—is supplemented by personal comments, whose length is unrelated to the relative importance of the author. The increasing popularity of fantastic literature led to the compiler's supplement, *Science Fiction and Fantasy Literature 1975–1991: A Bibliography of Science Fiction, Fantasy, and Horror Fiction Books and Nonfiction Monographs* (Gale Research, 1992), a massive volume that lists more than 22,000 English-language works, fiction and related nonfiction, a small percentage omitted from the original bibliography. Note that half again as many books are listed in the supplement, which covers only 17 years. Title, series, doubles indexes, major awards (compare [7-17]). Easily the most authoritative and comprehensive general bibliography of English-language fantastic literature and essential for larger libraries. Heavily used in the preparation of *Anatomy of Wonder.* Collectors will need Currey [7-7] for the points essential for identifying true first or variant editions. See also the pioneering work by Bleiler [7-1]. Burgess 182.

7-9.   Tuck, Donald H(enry). **The Encyclopedia of Science Fiction and Fantasy Through 1968.** Advent, 1974, 1978, 1983. 3 vols.

One of the most important earlier bibliographies, complementing Bleiler's checklist [7-1], this has grown increasingly dated although it is very useful for historians of the field. The first two volumes include a who's who and works, with a 52-page book title index. Volume 3 provides magazine checklists, extensive paperback information, pseudonyms, series, sequels, and other information. Brief biographical information, some of it more recent than the 1968 cutoff, is included for almost all authors, some of them only peripherally linked to fantastic literature. Contents of anthologies and collections are shown, as are series and original magazine sources for many works. Primarily descriptive with some evaluative comment. Much of the bibliographical information has largely been superseded by the authoritative works by Reginald [7-8], and the contents of collections and anthologies are more systematically and thoroughly indexed by Contento [7-13] and Brown and Contento [7-2]. Burgess 10. Hugo award, 1984

Specialized

7-10.   Brians, Paul. **Nuclear Holocausts: Atomic War in Fiction, 1895–1984.** Kent State Univ. Press, 1987.

Reflecting an age of anxiety, Brians provides the most comprehensive overview of this sobering literature. The initial fourth of the 400-page guide provides a history of nuclear warfare in five chapters, followed by a 250-page annotated bibliography of novels and shorter fiction, with entries ranging from a sentence to very full descriptions, with 100 words about average. A chronological checklist, lists of closely related works of fiction (near-war narratives, doubtful cases, reactor disasters, and so on), plus title and subject indexes complete this authoritative survey. Brians is much more comprehensive than John Newman and Michael Unsworth, *Future War Novels: An Annotated Bibliography of Works in English Published Since 1946* (Oryx Press, 1985), which chronologically lists with annotations 191 novels, 1946–1983, with author and title indexes. The selection criteria are different from those used by Brians, and the book therefore includes some books excluded from Brians. The book is based on the Imaginary Wars Collection at the Colorado State University Library [14-10]. Brians continued his work in *Nuclear Texts & Contexts*, an irregular newsletter of the International Society for the Study of Nuclear Texts & Contexts, now ed. by Daniel Zins, 2918 Harts Mill Lane NE, Atlanta, GA 30319-1854. Compare Clarke's *Voices Prophesying War* [8-41] and Dowling's *Fictions of Nuclear Disaster* [8-50]. Burgess 220. Also annotated as [8-30].

*7-11.   Burgess, Michael. **Reference Guide to Science Fiction, Fantasy, and Horror.** Libraries Unlimited, 1992.

Writing under his real name, cataloger/bibliographer R. Reginald has compiled an authoritative guide to hundreds of encyclopedias, dictionaries, bibliographies/indexes (subject, national, magazine, publisher, author) and similar "reference" works. The 551 numbered entries provide very full annotations—far longer than space permits in this guide—of all the standard works as well as the many fan productions unavailable for years or decades. The detailed annotations include full pagination and comparative cross references and evaluations of the relative value of each work. These evaluations are reflected in his core collection choices for large and smaller academic and public libraries as well as personal libraries. Books from his own Borgo Press tend to be overpraised, and bibliographies of authors favor genre authors, omitting important figures like Poe and Shelley. Author, title, and subject indexes, plus an attractive layout, make the book extremely easy to consult. Most books annotated in this chapter are evaluated in Burgess, and the Burgess entry number therefore concludes each annotation for anyone needing more information.

7-12.   Clareson, Thomas D. **Science Fiction Criticism: An Annotated Checklist.** Kent State Univ. Press, 1972.
This was the first book devoted to the secondary literature about SF, listing more than 800 items from both popular and academic sources, excluding fanzines and most European sources. The entries are grouped in nine chapters, such as General Studies, Literary Studies, Visual Arts, Classroom, and Library. The book reviews are from general magazines not indexed by Hall [7-15]. The annotations are primarily descriptive. Continued by Tymn and Schlobin [7-19] and partly superseded by Hall [7-16]. Burgess 87.

*7-13.   Contento, William G. **Index to Science Fiction Anthologies and Collections.** G. K. Hall, 1978.
The first of the Contento volumes indexes approximately 12,000 English-language stories by 2,500 authors in more than 1,900 anthologies and single-author collections published through June 1977. Access is by author, editor, story, and book title. Original magazine sources are shown when known. The supplement (G. K. Hall, 1984) continues the indexing through 1983, providing access to 8,550 works of short fiction, plus poems and plays, by about 2,600 authors. Supersedes Walter Cole's *A Checklist of Science-Fiction Anthologies* (1964), Fred Siemon's *Science Fiction Story Index* (1971), and the unforgivably shoddy index by Marilyn P. Fletcher, *Science Fiction Story Index 1950–1979* (1981). Continued by Brown & Contento [7-2]. Valuable to libraries desiring to locate a source or an elusive short story, and vastly more comprehensive than the *Short Story Index* found in many libraries. Burgess 117. Mike Ashley and Contento have prepared a companion index to more than 2,200 anthologies of supernatural/weird short fiction to be published by Greenwood, probably in 1995.

7-14.   Garber, Eric, and Lyn Paleo. **Uranian Worlds: A Reader's Guide to Alternative Sexuality in Science Fiction and Fantasy.** G. K. Hall, 1990. 2nd ed.
Sexuality was taboo in the pages of most SF pulps, although sometimes present in books, a heritage partly derived from social and literary conventions of the 1920–1960 period, and partly because of the heavily male adolescent readership of pulp magazines. If sexuality was taboo, homosexuality was almost unthinkable until recent years. The second edition

includes 935 numbered entries, the increase over the 1983 first edition's 568 novels and shorter stories containing "images of and attitudes toward homosexuality" suggesting the greater social acceptance of such fiction. (The stance of the compilers is dismissive of those who find homosexual themes in fiction distasteful.) The second edition also adds films and a list of fan organizations. Arranged by author with title and chronological indexes, the annotations are both descriptive and evaluative, not only of the fiction but of the authors. See also the 33-page annotated bibliography in Palumbo's *Erotic Universe* [8-99], which includes both fiction and nonfiction and is not limited to homosexuality. Burgess 226.

7-15.   Hall, H. W. **Science Fiction and Fantasy Book Review Index 1923–1973.** Gale Research, 1975.

Supplementing his reference index is this comprehensive index to book reviews of fantastic fiction. The initial volume indexes almost 14,000 book reviews of about 6,900 books appearing in SF magazines since 1923 and in general reviewing sources since 1970. A 1974–1979 cumulation (Gale, 1981) indexes 15,600 reviews of 6,220 books, followed by a 1980–1984 cumulation (Gale, 1985), with another 13,800 reviews from more than 70 journals. The third cumulation included Hall's initial reference index, later expanded as a separate index [7-16]. Hall, a librarian at Texas A&M, originally issued these indexes as annuals and has continued the annuals through vol. 20, 1989 (year of reviews) as of 1993; future annuals are uncertain. Although traditional library tools such as the *Book Review Digest* and *Book Review Index* have provided some access to reviews of fantastic fiction, their coverage is limited to more generally available magazines. Hall provides access to the dozens of pulps and fanzines featuring reviews over almost a 60-year period. Clareson indexed some reviews in sources not covered by Hall [7-12], and Gale Research's annual, *What Do I Read Next?* [7-18] also provides review citations more current than Hall. Burgess 92.

*7-16.   Hall, H. W. **Science Fiction and Fantasy Reference Index, 1878–1985: An International Author and Subject Index to History and Criticism.** Gale Research, 1987. 2 vols.

By far the most comprehensive index to the secondary literature about fantastic literature, this indexes by author (vol. 1) and subject (vol. 2) 19,000 books, articles, interviews, and other material. Particularly valuable is his indexing of the principal fan news magazines (fanzines) from the 1940s on. Fanzines have for decades served as an informal, unrefereed but invaluable forum. The four-page list of sources shows which magazines and books were indexed, and a 12-page list in vol. 2 shows the indexing terms used. Although Hall's intent is the same as that of his predecessors, Clareson [7-12] and Tymn [7-19], he did not "raid" their indexes, and there are therefore some unique entries in Clareson and Tymn not otherwise identified by Hall, but the number is relatively few. Hall continued his index in the form of separate self-published annuals, later including the index as part of the 1988–1991 Brown-Contento annuals [7-2]. Borgo Press began annual publication in 1994 with vol. 10, covering 1992. The contents of these annuals, and additional citations uncovered later, were cumulated as *Science Fiction and Fantasy Reference Index: 1985-1991* (Libraries Unlimited, 1993), which adds 16,000 more citations. A major achievement, Hall's indexes provide scholars comprehensive access to the secondary literature, and all large libraries should own them. Burgess 93.

7-17. Mallett, Daryl F., and Robert Reginald. **Reginald's Science Fiction and Fantasy Awards: A Comprehensive Guide to the Awards and Their Winners.** Borgo, 1993. 3rd ed.

Because fantastic fiction is not generally recognized by standard literary awards, fans have felt the need to recognize their own, beginning with the International Fantasy Awards in 1951. This latest edition supersedes the first edition in 1981 and the second in 1991. Genre awards total 126, non-genre 89. Indexes to award names, to winners, plus appendixes listing SFRA and SFWA officers and locations and dates of World Fantasy and Hugo conventions, plus some statistical tabulations. Most of these awards are obscure beyond belief. See the list of winners of the major awards in chapter 15. Reginald lists the major award winners in his latest bibliography [7-8]. Burgess 38.

7-18. Rosenberg, Betty, and Diana Tixier Herald. **Genreflecting: A Guide to Reading Interests in Genre Fiction.** Libraries Unlimited, 1991. 3rd ed.

Chapter 1 provides an overview of genre fiction and the role of libraries in providing such books or advising readers. The remaining six chapters survey westerns, thrillers, romances, SF, fantasy, and horror, with about a third of the text devoted to fantastic fiction. Each chapter lists books under themes and types, then by topic—anthologies, bibliographies, encyclopedias, history and criticism, background, awards, and so on. Many of the nonfiction books are descriptively annotated, sometimes evaluated, but often too briefly to judge their relative worth. Although revised twice and enlarged since the first edition in 1982, the revisions have failed to adequately update the text, and too much obsolete or incorrect information remains. Compare the British work compiled by Mandy Hicken and

Ray Prytherch, *Now Read On: A Guide to Contemporary Popular Fiction* (Gower, 1990; distributed by Ashgate), whose focus is on writers active today or who died in the 1980s. One of the 19 overlapping theme categories is SF. A necessarily selective guide, which achieves its modest aims well and which would be useful in American libraries, since most of the authors are popular in the United States as well. More inclusive is the annual published by Gale Research since 1990, *What Do I Read Next? A Reader's Guide to Current Genre Fiction*. Westerns, romances, mysteries, fantasy, SF, and horror are the categories covered, with 200–250 books in each category being descriptively profiled and multiply indexed, supplemented by annual surveys providing a limited critical dimension, plus lists of awards in each category.

7-19.   Tymn, Marshall B., and Roger C. Schlobin. **The Year's Scholarship in Science Fiction and Fantasy: 1972–1975.** Kent State Univ. Press, 1979.

This first supplement to Clareson [7-12] cumulates listings that appeared in *Extrapolation* [12-20]. The descriptive annotations are grouped into four sections. Coverage is limited to American and British journals and selected fanzines as well as books and doctoral and selected master's theses. Supplements cover 1976–1979 (1983), 1980, 1981, 1982 (1983–1985). All volumes have author and title indexes. Publication continued in the pages of *Extrapolation*, 1983–1988, but without annotations, and ended in a 1989 issue of the *Journal of the Fantastic in the Arts*. Largely superseded by Hall [7-16]. Burgess 105.

Theme Indexing

Most of the bibliographies and indexes discussed above provide access by author and title only, with some providing access by series or chronologically. A few have provided access by theme or motif, and here I summarize the more important works that provide theme indexing. (For many subject bibliographies not annotated in this chapter, see Burgess [7-11].)

The first significant book to provide theme access was the revised edition of Bleiler's checklist [7-1]. The 90 subject codes were assigned to about 95 percent of the 5,600 books listed, although there is no index by theme, only by title. In Bleiler's magisterial *Science-Fiction: The Early Years* [7-21], however, a very detailed motif and theme index provides access to the more than 3,000 books and magazine stories annotated. (A similar index was provided in Bleiler's *Guide to Supernatural Fiction* [7-34].) The first edition of *The Encyclopedia of Science Fiction* [7-22] provided 175 theme entries, although some are not fictional themes, such as "Anonymous SF Authors" and "Bibliographies and Indexes." The much revised and enlarged second edition provides 212 theme entries (plus 65 shorter terminology entries), each providing a running historical and analytical summary of its topic. The Gunn encyclopedia [7-26] provides access by 96 fictional themes. The Rosenberg, Hicken, and *What Do I Read Next?* guides [all 7-18] provide varying degrees of thematic access, as do my own reader guides, *Fantasy Literature* [7-33] and *Horror Literature* [7-33].

Biocritical Works

The link between SF fans and SF writers is strong, as a work like Hartwell's *Age of Wonders* [8-66] makes very clear. Articles about SF writers appeared with the advent of the pulps. Many of these were little more than puffery profiles, but some provided both biographical and varying amounts of critical evaluation, as in the relatively early magazine profiles by Moskowitz, collected in his *Explorers of the Infinite* (1963) and *Seekers of Tomorrow* (1966). As SF's popularity increased, genre writers were the subject of book-length studies derived from fanzine articles, such as Panshin's 1968 study, *Heinlein in Dimension* [9-57]. Along with the growing number of single author studies, the best of which are evaluated in chapter 9, biocritical works began to appear in which biographical, bibliographic, and critical information was included for multiple authors. The most comprehensive earlier work of this type was Tuck [7-9], although it is primarily bibliographic in nature and is therefore annotated in the first section of this chapter. The books in this section include varying amounts of evaluation along with biographical and bibliographic information. Arrangement is by author/editor.

*7-20. Bleiler, Everett F., ed. **Science Fiction Writers: Critical Studies of the Major Authors From the Early Nineteenth Century to the Present Day.** Scribner, 1982.
Each of these 75 well-written and carefully edited essays by 26 contributors provide biographical information, a critical analysis of the fiction and the author's historical importance in the development of SF, and a basic primary and secondary bibliography. Both SF writers and writers of occasional SF (Huxley, Orwell, C. S. Lewis) are discussed, with Verne, Lem, and Čapek the only non-Anglo-American writers. The youngest author discussed is Samuel Delany. The essays are grouped in seven chronological sections, and the table of contents or the detailed index has to be consulted for the location of a given essay. More critically acute and better edited than the similar work by Cowart and Wymer [7-24]. The quality evident

here is also seen in the companion work devoted to supernatural fiction writers [7-35]. Burgess 56.

*7-21.   Bleiler, Everett F., and Richard J. Bleiler. **Science-Fiction, the Early Years: A Full Description of More Than 3,000 Science-Fiction Stories From Earliest Times to the Appearance of the Genre Magazines in 1930, With Author, Title, and Motif Indexes.** Kent State Univ. Press, 1990.
Although fans such as Moskowitz had explored the early development of SF in various histories and anthologies, the most comprehensive and detailed work by far is this massive reference work by Bleiler, a crowning achievement of his long association with the field. The subtitle provides a succinct description of the book's scope, but only a detailed examination of the contents will reveal the riches therein. What is perhaps most remarkable is that Bleiler read or reread all the stories, many annotated in great detail and many previously undiscovered in numerous rare sources. The arrangement is by author, with novels and short fiction in collections or magazines sequenced by title, with abundant cross-references. The annotations are descriptive and provide a historical context as well as full bibliographic details. But almost every annotation ends with a one-line evaluation, often acerbic. Supplementing the author, title, and motif indexes, keyed to the numbered entries, are a chronological index from Plato to Thomas More to about 1930, with later reprints shown as well, and an index by magazine, most entries predating the founding of *Amazing Stories* [12-2] in 1926 and which shows how widely SF was published in the popular magazines of yesteryear. The only weakness of this work, offset from a clear two-column typescript, is the lack of running heads, slowing quick access to desired entries. An essential work for the scholar and for larger libraries. Burgess 55. *Locus* award for best nonfiction. Also annotated as [8-26].

*7-22.   Clute, John, Peter Nicholls, and Brian Stableford, eds. **The Encyclopedia of Science Fiction.** St. Martin's, 1993. 2nd ed., rev. & enl.
The 1979 edition of this work (titled *The Science Fiction Encyclopedia* in the American edition), a Hugo and *Locus* winner, was the first true English-language encyclopedia, in spite of other books having used *encyclopedia* in their titles. What made it particularly valuable was its reliance on original research and primary sources, thus eliminating much spurious information contained in less carefully compiled works. This new edition retains the virtues of the old and adds many new ones, most notably currency (through 1992) and scope (approximately 1.4 million words versus 730,000 in the first edition versus 475,000 in Gunn [7-26]). In terms of

total text it's the lengthiest single work ever devoted to SF. Approximately 85 percent of the text was written by the three editors, assisted by about 80 other contributors in specialized areas, such as non-English SF (300 author entries, close to 40,000 words). The more than 4,000 entries are linked by 2,100 cross-references in the main text plus thousands of "see also" references. The entries are primarily descriptive, but judicious evaluation is also included.

There are more theme entries (see the earlier discussion of theme indexing), plus 65 shorter terminology entries, plus more than 2,900 entries for authors, editors, critics, and other individuals. In short, there is much more of everything, including much broader coverage of borderline areas such as game worlds, film and TV spinoffs, graphic novels, YA fiction, and science fantasy. All this has led to a 1,400-page, six-pound volume, very well-designed and made, but its $75 cost may limit it to larger libraries. But that figure equals about the cost of four hardcover novels, which will be discarded long before this authoritative reference work becomes seriously dated. The most essential work for any library. A CD-ROM version was in preparation by Grolier Electronic Publishing in 1994, the first SF reference work in this format. Burgess 7 (1979 edition). Hugo winner, *Locus* award

7-23. Collins, Robert A., Robert Latham (1988–1992), and Michael M. Levy (1993–), eds. **Science Fiction & Fantasy Book Review Annual.** Meckler, 1988–.

The impetus for this annual was the demise of the *Fantasy Review* (1981–1987). The first two annuals were issued by Meckler, with rights to the unsold copies and to future annuals bought by Greenwood Press, which issued the third annual in 1991, covering 1989 books. Editorial problems delayed future annuals, with the 1991 annual (1990 books) not published until late 1993. Continued publication is conjectural. The bulk of each book is composed of the reviews, grouped into (adult) fiction, young adult fiction, and nonfiction. Narrative surveys of the year discussing adult and young adult SF, fantasy and horror fiction, and the secondary literature and films, each with a recommended reading list, are supplemented by author profiles and other commissioned articles whose topics vary from year to year. Many of the reviews are reprinted from the *SFRA Review* [12-32], with most written by academics and fans, with a predictably variable quality, given that more than 500 books are reviewed, most of them inevitably undistinguished. Collins has argued that, poor as many of these books are, the annual will provide a permanent historical record of the development of authors whose later works may attain distinction. The Gale Research annual *What Do I Read Next?* [7-18] provides much broader and prompter coverage of category fiction, but does not pretend to be a critical work aside from the brief year-in-review essays. Large libraries should consider this annual, whose quality control should be improved and which should appear by middle of the year following the year of the books reviewed. Burgess 25.

7-24.   Cowart, David, and Thomas L. Wymer, eds. **Twentieth-Century American Science-Fiction Writers.** Gale, 1981. 2 vols. *Dictionary of Literary Biography,* vol. 8.

The 90 alphabetically arranged biocritical essays by 41 contributors discuss writers, 11 of them women, who began writing after 1900 and before 1970, although four writers fall after the 1970 cutoff. Varying in length from two to three pages to 16 pages for prolific or more important authors, each essay includes biographical information, critical evaluation of major works, and a bibliography of books and other writings, including a brief secondary bibliography. Photos of the authors and pages of manuscript are reproduced. Some choices are questionable, such as George R. Stewart, solely for *Earth Abides* [3-169]. Appendixes discuss the New Wave, the fusion of SF and fantasy into science fantasy, SF illustration, paperback SF, SF films, fandom, fanzines, the Science Fiction Writers of America, Hugo and Nebula winners through 1980, a chronology of SF books 1818–1979, details on American and British SF magazines, and a secondary bibliography. The author essays are the core of the book and, while generally sound, lack the critical rigor and acumen of those in Bleiler [7-20], whose scope isn't limited to American writers. The appendixes have grown dated and add little to the set today. Large libraries may want both, but most libraries should prefer Bleiler. A companion set devoted to British writers was in preparation in 1994. Burgess 44.

7-25.   Fletcher, Marilyn P., and James L. Thorson, eds. **Reader's Guide to Twentieth-Century Science Fiction.** American Library Association, 1989.

Fletcher is one of 20 librarians among the 38 contributors who wrote the essays about 131 writers, who should have been listed in a table of contents. The stated selection criteria were ignored when writers like Bloch, Derleth, Robert E. Howard, and H. P. Lovecraft have entries. L'Engle is the sole writer of YA SF. Many minor writers are included, and some more important writers are omitted—Bishop, Butler, Compton, Lupoff, Sterling, and Vernor Vinge, for example. The entries discuss life and works, themes and style, include a secondary bibliography, with most of the entry devoted to potted plot summaries of up to six books, which collectively take up almost three-fourths of this 700-page book. The summaries are slackly edited and lack any critical rigor, unlike the far better essays in the Salem set edited by Magill [7-27]. Students will plagiarize them for "book reports." Fletcher compiled an atrocious SF short fiction index that ALA published in 1981. She did not improve her standing with this botched effort. Prefer the far superior essays in Bleiler [7-20] or the shorter entries in the far more comprehensive Watson and Schellinger [7-30]. Burgess 61.

7-26. Gunn, James, ed. **The New Encyclopedia of Science Fiction.** Viking, 1988.

The title was probably chosen to emphasize its currency over the 1979 Clute/Nicholls work, whose British title was *The Encyclopedia of Science Fiction* and which was retained for the greatly revised and enlarged edition [7-22]. Any careful comparison between the two encyclopedias reveals that, apart from the currency Gunn enjoyed over the first edition of its competitor, this newer encyclopedia is inferior in almost every respect. Gunn is about 60 percent the length of Nicholls, with about a third as many entries. (Both include far too many entries on wretched films.) Nicholls has 1,817 entries for authors, editors, and critics, Gunn 516. Encyclopedia entries should direct users to sources of additional information; Nicholls does, Gunn doesn't. The 175 theme entries in Nicholls are generally much better than their 96 counterparts in Gunn, a few of which deal with modern topics like cyberpunk. Gunn included entries devoted to 53 writers who achieved prominence in the decade following Nicholls, such as Bear, Brin, Gibson, Shirley, and Sterling. The coated stock in Gunn results in better if fewer illustrations, and the book is well designed. Its currency was its major merit, however, and it lost this when the new Clute/Nicholls edition appeared. Larger libraries may want to retain Gunn for its differing viewpoints, but if only one true encyclopedia is to be acquired, the revised Clute/Nicholls is unquestionably the only choice. Burgess 4.

*7-27. Magill, Frank N., ed. **Survey of Science Fiction Literature.** Salem, 1979. 5 vols.

A major reference and critical source, containing 513 essays averaging 2,000 words each. Novels and short fiction by 280 authors, a fourth of them foreign, are analyzed by about 130 contributors, whose work was coordinated by the actual editor, Keith Neilson. Each essay is preceded by basic information: year of first book publication, type of work (novel, and so on), time, locale, one-line summary, and principal characters. Essays are arranged by title with an author index. The references following the essays are mostly to book reviews, an oversight corrected with a 1982 bibliographical supplement compiled by Marshall B. Tymn and now included with the set. A 1981 paperback, *Science Fiction: Alien Encounter*, reprinted the essays dealing with its subject for classroom use. An essential tool, although its price will limit it to larger libraries. A companion set is devoted to fantasy [7-36]. Burgess 69.

7-28.   Pringle, David. **The Ultimate Guide to Science Fiction.** Pharos Books, 1990.

Pringle provides brief evaluations (zero to four stars) of approximately 3,000 novels, collections, and anthologies, most of them published or reprinted since 1970. He largely excluded YA SF, translations, novelizations, and "mainstream" SF. For no apparent reason the sequence is by title with an author index rather than the reverse. Although Pringle's evaluations generally square with the perceived wisdom, it's self-evident that most—I'd estimate at least three-fourths—of the books are undistinguished at best and do not deserve to be annotated. Pringle knows quality when he sees it, and readers would profit far more from his *Science Fiction: The 100 Best Novels* [8-109]. Compare the similar work by Wingrove [7-31]. Burgess 74.

7-29.   Sargent, Lyman Tower. **British and American Utopian Literature 1516-1986: An Annotated Chronological Bibliography.** Garland, 1988.

SF and utopian literature have a parallel and overlapping history, and many of the cited books are SF. Sargent's bibliography was originally published in 1979 by G. K. Hall and included a 124-page secondary multilingual unannotated bibliography of about 600 books and dissertations and 1,600 articles that was unfortunately dropped for the enlarged edition, which chronologically lists close to 2,600 entries, an increase of about 900. Very brief descriptive annotations are provided, along with a code denoting a holding library, or Sargent's or another private collection. Author and title indexes. Both Sargent volumes retain value, the first for its secondary bibliography, and are useful for the utopian scholar. Among the many histories of utopian thought are *Utopian Thought in the Western World* (Harvard, 1979) by Frank E. Manuel and Fritzie P. Manuel, one of the most comprehensive surveys in English; Kenneth M. Roemer's *The Obsolete Necessity: America in Utopian Writings 1888–1900* (Kent State Univ. Press, 1966), whose annotated bibliography is excellent; Krishan Kumar's *Utopia and Anti-Utopia in Modern Times* [8-76]; and Peter Ruppert's *Reader in a*

Strange Land: The Activity of Reading Literary Utopias (Univ. of Georgia Press, 1986). Burgess 232.

7-30. Watson, Noelle, and Paul E. Schellinger, eds. **Twentieth-Century Science-Fiction Writers.** St. James, 1991. 3rd ed.
This new edition has gone to a standard 8 1/2 x 11 inch size, has new editors, and has added about 100,000 words to the 1986 second edition. Seventy-eight English- and foreign-language writers were added, 43 and 4 dropped, for a total of 640 writers, of which 38 are foreign language. The format is unchanged: nationality, birth/death dates, education, pseudonyms, skeletal biographical information. SF publications are listed chronologically, novels and collections separately, followed by "other" publications: non-SF novels, plays, verse, edited works. Published bibliographies are cited, along with locations of MSS and correspondence, and a selective secondary bibliography. Some authors provided a "comment" preceding the descriptive/evaluative section by one of the 187 contributors. Entries range from about two to eight columns, with little relationship between importance of the writer and length, because of the apparent rule that all books of an author must be listed, even if most are unrelated to SF (Heinlein, for example, has two and a half columns, William Dean Howells, who wrote two sort-of-SF novels, has five). A handful of fantasy writers, such as Dunsany and Tolkien, are mysteriously included. A number of writers as "important" as many included are excluded, and few writers of YA SF are profiled. A detailed title index of novels and collections designated SF could be useful. The editorial rules governing what should be listed often give strange results. In spite of its many bibliographic deficiencies, a comprehensive, current, and generally accurate work that less demanding readers should find useful. More demanding readers will prefer the fewer, detailed evaluations of 75 major writers in Bleiler [7-20], the comprehensive coverage of *The Encyclopedia of Science Fiction* [7-22], and the Reginald bibliographies [7-8]. Burgess 47. David Pringle is editing for St. James companion guides to fantasy and horror/Gothic writers.

7-31. Wingrove, David. **The Science Fiction Source Book.** Longmans, 1984.
About 40 percent of this book includes a short history, an essay on SF themes, working habits of authors, magazines, the economics of SF publishing, and the secondary literature. The balance is a consumer's guide to the principal works of 880 authors of SF (and some fantasy) whose works have been available in English since about 1960. The unsigned

entries by 12 British contributors range from 50 to 500 words, with some works mentioned or briefly evaluated in an introductory paragraph, with others shown on a grid assessing by zero to five stars readability, characterization, idea content, and literary merit. A hodgepodge with no clear focus. The consumer's guide is more capably done in Pringle [7-28], but the revised Clute/Nicholls encyclopedia is far preferable to both. Burgess 82.

7-32.   Wolfe, Gary K. **Critical Terms for Science Fiction and Fantasy: A Glossary and Guide to Scholarship.** Greenwood, 1986.
A valuable introduction traces the historical development of fantasy and SF critical discourse. Approximately three-fourths of this book is composed of a glossary of almost 500 terms and concepts, ranging from brief definitions to short essays, keyed to a secondary bibliography and to authors of cited fiction. Clear, concise, and most welcome, it is current enough to include trendy terms like cyberpunk and postmodern. A useful companion to more general works like *A Glossary of Literary Terms* by M. H. Abrams (6th ed., Harcourt, 1992), which defines nearly a thousand terms.

Fantasy and Horror Fiction

The readership for SF, fantasy, and (to a lesser extent) horror fiction heavily overlaps, and many authors write SF and fantasy and occasionally horror as well. Science fantasy is a popular hybrid. Annotated below are a few key works likely to be of value to this guide's users. Since they are outside SF, they haven't been included in the best books listing, but they are recommended for medium and larger libraries. Some of the books annotated in chapters 8–13 are of interest to readers of fantasy and horror fiction.

7-33.   Barron, Neil, ed. **Fantasy Literature: A Reader's Guide.** Garland, 1990.
This and Barron's *Horror Literature: A Reader's Guide* (Garland, 1990) were designed as companions to *Anatomy of Wonder* and have parallel structures: four chronological chapters surveying adult horror and fantasy fiction, a chapter on modern fantasy for young adults, and chapters corresponding to chapters 6–12, 14, and 15 in this guide. Chapters 5, 10, 11, and 12, which compose about 15 percent of each book, are identical, since separation of fantasy and horror was impracticable in these chapters. Coverage is limited to materials available in English. Burgess 52.

7-34.   Bleiler, Everett F. **The Guide to Supernatural Fiction: A Full Description of 1,775 Books From 1750 to 1960, Including Ghost Stories,**

Weird Fiction, Stories of Supernatural Horror, Fantasy, Gothic Novels, Occult Fiction, and Similar Literature With Author, Title, and Motif Indexes. Kent State Univ. Press, 1983.

As authoritative as Bleiler's later guide to early SF [7-21], the subtitle indicates its wide scope. About 7,000 stories are individually described, several thousand from collections and anthologies. The motif index alone has more than 40,000 entries. A remarkable feat of scholarship. Burgess 57.

7-35. Bleiler, Everett F., ed. **Supernatural Fiction Writers: Fantasy and Horror.** Scribner, 1985. 2 vols.

A companion to his guide to SF writers [7-20] in which more than 145 writers—from Apuleius to contemporary writers, American, British, French, and German—are treated, many for the first time in such detail. The carefully edited essays use a variety of approaches, although each includes biography, description, and evaluation of the major works, an assessment of each author's historical position, and a secondary bibliography. Bleiler's supernatural guide (above) treats most of these writers and many others. Burgess 57.

7-36. Magill, Frank N., ed. **Survey of Modern Fantasy Literature.** Salem, 1983. 5 vols.

A companion to Magill's SF set [7-27], this contains about 500 essays devoted to 341 authors of fantasy and horror literature. Lesser titles receive about 1,000 words, most titles about 2,000, with series, trilogies, and major works receiving 3,000 to 10,000 words. Volume 5 contains 19 topical essays, a chronological listing from 1764 through 1981, an annotated bibliography of secondary literature, a list of major anthologies, and a detailed index. Burgess 68.

7-37. Sullivan, Jack, ed. **The Penguin Encyclopedia of Horror and the Supernatural.** Viking, 1986.

An attractively designed work for the layperson, with approximately 600 entries. The biographical profiles emphasize the works, not the lives, of authors, artists, directors, actors, composers, and so on. Approximately 150 films have entries, along with 54 essays on topics such as B movies, ghosts, graveyard poetry, opera, sex, writers of today (a lengthy and difficult-to-use hodgepodge), and zombies. Approximately 300 monochrome illustrations accompany the text, which is thoroughly cross-referenced. Compare Wolf's much more personal work [7-38]. Burgess 9.

7-38.   Wolf, Leonard. **Horror: A Connoisseur's Guide to Literature and Film.** Facts on File, 1989.

Unlike Sullivan's multiply authored reference work, Wolf provides "a partial record of my own listening" chosen for "historical spread, thematic variety, and fun." A bit less than 400 entries are arranged by title and include novels, short fiction, some poetry, and films. Ranging from 100 to 1,000 words, the knowledgeable and gracefully written entries reveal an intelligently enthusiastic guide. A useful companion to Sullivan. Burgess 84.

CHAPTER 8

History and Criticism

Gary K. Wolfe

The reader or scholar approaching the now-considerable body of SF criticism and history may at first be daunted by the plethora of conflicting voices and traditions. The works discussed in this chapter range from the relatively uncritical zeal of obsessive fans to the most abstruse postmodern theorizing and it is evidence of the genre's vitality and broad appeal that nearly all of them have something useful to add to the ongoing discourse. Like SF itself the scholarship and criticism of the field has had its own ghettos, its own warring camps, its own struggle for respectability, and its own ambivalence about whether it really *wants* to be "respectable." Complicating matters further is the fact that critical writing about SF has evolved out of three distinct traditions, and that only in the last couple of decades have these traditions begun to talk to each other at all.

The earliest of these traditions to become clearly identifiable began in the letter columns of the pulp magazines and the hectographed "fanzines" of the 1920s and 1930s. The founder of *Amazing Stories*, Hugo Gernsback, encouraged such feedback and did much to help create the sense of extended community among SF readers that came to be known as fandom. While much of this early commentary was simply a listing of story preferences, it also often touched upon questions of what SF ought to be. Although most of these early fan writings are now inaccessible to all but the most devoted scholars, they helped to establish a tradition of resolutely informal populist criticism that may well have helped shape the genre, and that still informs much that is written about it. Some of the most enthusiastic of these fan scholars, such as Sam Moskowitz, later organized their commentary into books, and scholars approaching SF in the sixties found almost the only source of information about authors in titles like Moskowitz's *Explorers of the Infinite* (1963) and *Seekers of Tomorrow* (1966). Moskowitz has continued to be one of the most assiduous researchers of early SF history, and in 1981 he became fandom's first (and so far only) recipient of the Science Fiction Research Association's Pilgrim Award. (It should be noted, however, that some well-known academic critics of SF, such as Thomas D. Clareson, also began in fandom.)

A second tradition of SF criticism, related to but not quite congruent with the fan tradition, evolved during the 1940s as professional writers began publishing commentaries on each other, on the nature of SF, and on various matters of technique and professional strategy. By now, with the rise of anthologies and specialty presses (and the attendant promise of hardbound immortality), it was becoming apparent to many of these authors that SF was more than one pulp market among many, that it was a genre or mode that had developed its own techniques and themes and an increasingly sophisticated audience. Often appearing side-by-side with fan letters in the same publications, this kind of commentary often took the form of tips to aspiring writers; what may have been the first book about modern SF, Lloyd Arthur Eshbach's *Of Worlds Beyond* [8-54], consisted mostly of a variety of authors doing just that. But the tradition of writer criticism took on a new dimension of sophistication in the early 1950s when James Blish and Damon Knight began seeking to establish critical standards in their various periodical pieces. (Both Blish and Knight later collected these essays in the books listed in this chapter.) This tradition of writer-critics—later carried on by Algis Budrys, Norman Spinrad, and others—added to the fannish discourse a concern with craft and technique, as well as a realistic awareness of the market forces and editorial practices that are crucial to any meaningful discussion of popular fiction. These latter concerns are nowhere more evident than in the various letters and essays that went to make up Theodore Cogswell's "professional fanzine" *Proceedings of the Institute for Twenty-First Century Studies* [8-43] from 1959–1962. This is still the most extensive source of details on what a wide variety of authors thought about the field during that period.

Still a third tradition of discourse came into play as academically trained scholars—and the occasional commentator from the "mainstream"—began to pay increasing attention to popular fantastic literature, to the frequent chagrin and irritation of the writers and fans. Older writers and fans may have remembered—and resented—such early mainstream attacks on the genre as a 1939 *Harper's* essay by Bernard De Voto titled "Doom Beyond Jupiter," but many of them came to admit that the first academic study of SF history, J. O. Bailey's *Pilgrims Through Space and Time* [8-15] helped to give the genre its own archaeology and at least something of a pedigree. (Ever since Bailey, advocates of SF have cheerfully claimed Plato, Lucian, and Kepler as ancestors.) This pedigree was solidified further by the publication, a year after Bailey's book, of Everett Bleiler's massive historical bibliography, *The Checklist of Fantastic Literature* [7-1].

But both the Bailey and Bleiler books were still published by specialty presses, available pretty much only to those who sought them out. Commercial presses published a couple of general studies of SF during the 1950s, including Reginald Bretnor's *Modern Science Fiction: Its Meaning and Future* [8-28] and Basil Davenport's brief *Inquiry Into Science Fiction* (1955), but it wasn't until Kingsley Amis's *New Maps of Hell* [8-7] appeared in 1960 that the SF field began to suspect it was having a substantial impact beyond its own borders. Even though the book was based on lectures given at Princeton, Amis was hardly an academic, but he was at the height of his reputation as one of England's "Angry Young Men," and the attention he paid to SF almost certainly helped to open what would eventually seem the floodgates of academe. (In part because of SF's hunger for respectability, the impact of Amis's book far exceeded its actual contributions to SF scholarship or criticism, and this pattern would be repeated each time a writer or scholar with a substantial mainstream reputation— Leslie Fiedler, Robert Scholes, Harold Bloom—wrote sympathetically of the field.)

SF had never been entirely alien to the academic establishment; Bailey's study was based on his own 1934 dissertation and James Gunn—in a move that seems emblematic of the whole history of SF scholarship— published substantial parts of his master's thesis in the pulp magazine *Dynamic Science Fiction* in 1953 and 1954. In 1958, the Modern Language Association convention featured the first of what would become annual sessions on SF, and the seminars gave rise to the first academic journal on SF (*Extrapolation*, founded 1959 [12-20]) and eventually to the formation of the Science Fiction Research Association in 1970. Soon after, other journals began to appear, most notably the British *Foundation* [12-22] in 1972 and the Canadian-American *Science-Fiction Studies* [12-33] in 1973. Nineteen-seventy also saw what was probably the first history of SF to appear with the imprimatur of a university press, Robert M. Philmus's *Into the Unknown* [8-104] (although Oxford had published H. Bruce Franklin's critical anthology *Future Perfect* [1-36] in 1966). By 1972, enough books and articles about SF had appeared to fill a book-length bibliography by Thomas D. Clareson, *Science Fiction Criticism: An Annotated Checklist* [7-12]. Similar bibliographies have appeared with some regularity since then.

The 1970s saw the flowering of SF scholarship with a vengeance. Major histories of the field appeared from Aldiss [8-5] (the first edition, titled *Billion Year Spree*, appeared in 1973) and Gunn [8-62], and more personal histories from Wollheim [8-147] and del Rey [8-46]. More theoretical works appeared from Suvin [8-136], Ketterer [8-71], Wolfe [8-145], and Rose [8-118]. Essay collections, beginning with Clareson's *SF: The Other Side of Realism* [8-36], vied with and at times outpaced the journals as sources of critical essays, and a string of reference books featuring critical assessments often outpaced the essay collections. (One of the most ambitious of these books, the Salem Press *Survey of Science Fiction Literature* [7-27], is actually not a reference work at all, but a collection of no fewer than 500 essays on key works in the genre.) Several university presses instituted series of studies on SF and fantasy, most notably Oxford, Indiana, Southern Illinois, Kent State, and Bowling Green. (Later the University of Georgia joined this list.) By 1984, UMI Research Press, in a series called "Studies in Speculative Fiction," was even mining unpublished doctoral dissertations, with mixed results. Other presses with series devoted to the genre included Taplinger, Ungar, Borgo, Starmont House, and most notably Greenwood Press, whose series Contributions to the Study of Science Fiction and Fantasy, begun under the editorship of Marshall Tymn in 1982, included 55 titles by early 1993.

It has often been suggested that this boom in SF scholarship was essentially opportunistic, a result of college English departments cynically trying to attract students by finally permitting a once-despised genre to enter the curriculum. The argument makes sense up to a point: certainly the earlier exclusion from the curriculum was accompanied by exclusion from standard reference works and library collections of criticism, and the sudden interest in SF among students and teachers revealed an enormous gap in resources—a gap that was quickly filled to overflowing. Fandom had never provided a substantial market for serious critical commentary (and still does not), so there is little doubt that the academic "discovery" of SF permitted a great many works to be published that otherwise might never have seen the light of day. But other forces besides academia were at work as well. The more traditional universities of England, for example, participated very little in this "academic awakening," and yet England also saw a significant rise in SF studies and even gave birth in 1971 to the Science Fiction Foundation, for which there is still no comparable organization in the United States. (The closest candidate, the Science Fiction Research Association, lacks a central location and research collection.) Elsewhere in Europe—in France and Germany especially—SF studies also took off without benefit of serving as a recruitment strategy for undergraduate students.

Some of the growth in SF studies, then, must be attributed to the growth in stature and the maturation of the genre itself. The mainstream reputation of a Vonnegut; the literary sophistication of a Le Guin (who may still be the most written-about of all modern SF authors); the forays into SF by revered writers such as Doris Lessing; the national bestseller status accorded works by Heinlein, Clarke, Asimov, and Farmer; and the substantial share of the overall fiction market garnered by SF and its related genres of fantasy and horror—estimated by some as being as high as 20 to 25 percent—all helped make SF impossible to ignore in the literary community. In the academic community, the influence of structuralism, feminism, deconstructionism, and a seemingly endless fascination with postmodernism have helped topple the traditional 19th-century-based realistic novel from its privileged status in the canon and opened up critical discourse to a far wider range of texts than might have been discussed a decade or two earlier.

While SF criticism and history remain wildly eclectic, it has become possible to identify a number of emerging schools of thought, although few of them have self-consciously identified themselves as such. For example, the "consensus" view of SF history represented in works listed in this chapter by Gunn, Asimov, Wollheim, and del Rey is essentially a consensus of American writers and fans of a certain age group who tend to agree that "real" SF began with the publication of *Amazing Stories* in 1926, despite a lineage going back to Plato. A radically different view can be found in Aldiss and Wingrove's *Trillion Year Spree* [8-5], which views the genre as descended from the Gothic novel, or the histories of British SF by Stableford [8-132] and Ruddick [8-122], which trace a clear path of evolution independent from the American magazines. Other works, by Lundwall [8-81], Rottensteiner [8-121], and Wuckel and Cassiday [8-148] see a much more international pattern of development; while still others, such as Kumar [8-76], Berger [8-25], and Walsh [8-141] trace the genre to origins in utopian fiction.

Critical theory, too, has developed in a number of different directions. The journal *Science-Fiction Studies* introduced structuralist, narratological, and Marxist approaches to SF, championing authors—Le Guin, Lem,

Dick—whose works yielded most readily to such analyses. This trend in SF criticism paved the way for major theoretical studies by Suvin [8-136/137], Malmgren [8-82], and others. A somewhat less formalistic but equally theory-oriented attempt to grapple with major themes and problems posed by the genre grew up around California's J. Lloyd Eaton conferences, and is reflected in the several volumes of papers drawn from those conferences listed here, edited by George E. Slusser and others. Feminist criticism of SF has grown into a virtual subspecialty of its own, and its variety of approaches is represented by Lefanu [8-79], Barr [8-18, 8-19, 8-20], Bartkowski [8-21], Armitt [8-9], Shinn [8-128], and Weedman [8-176]. Finally, the cyberpunk movement has drawn SF to the attention of a considerable number of scholars who view aspects of the genre as a symptomatic expression of postmodernism; see, for example, Bukatman [8-33], McCaffrey [8-86], and Slusser and Shippey [8-175].

Other works listed in this section may treat SF in terms of myth, popular culture, religion, politics, and philosophy. The body of critical and historical writing on the genre is now substantial enough to sustain internal debates; gone are the days when an author such as Amis could attempt a brief overview of the genre with reference to virtually no prior scholarship—and gone also is the "consensus" that once enabled SF writers and fans to claim virtual ownership of the genre. Much of what passes for academic scholarship is still surprisingly shoddy and piecemeal, but the best of it reflects a deep understanding of the field and many of its most important texts. This chapter lists most of the book-length studies of the genre that have appeared in English, eliminating some of those listed in earlier editions that have become dated, but retaining those whose very age has lent them historical significance for the scholar. The listing is alphabetical by author or editor, with proceedings of specific conferences grouped at the end of the chapter.

Bibliography

8-1.   Albinski, Nan Bowman. **Women's Utopias in British and American Fiction.** Routledge, 1988.
A historical and thematic survey of some 250 works, arranged by period (before 1920, 1920–1960, 1960–1987) and focusing on such major themes as sexuality, marriage, suffrage, and religion. Albinski's approach seems to derive more from the tradition of utopian studies than from feminist the-

ory, and her chronological organization forces her to reintroduce themes throughout the book, but the comprehensiveness of her survey makes this book an indispensable background source for studies such as Bammer's [8-17] and Bartkowski's [8-21].

8-2. Aldiss, Brian W. **. . . And the Lurid Glare of the Comet.** Serconia, 1986.

Essays on Wells, Sturgeon, and Aldiss's own work, including his phantasmagorical *Barefoot in the Head.* Especially interesting is "The Glass Forest," an autobiographical piece expanded from his contribution to *Hell's Cartographers,* which is of particular interest to readers of Aldiss's excellent non-SF novel, *Forgotten Life.*

8-3. Aldiss, Brian W. **The Pale Shadow of Science.** Serconia, 1985.

A collection of 13 essays covering Orwell, Shelley, Stapledon, and other topics, some of them autobiographical. Of particular interest is an essay on Aldiss's acclaimed Helliconia series [4-6]. HN, 1986

8-4. Aldiss, Brian W. **This World and Nearer Ones: Essays Exploring the Familiar.** Weidenfield & Nicolson, 1979.

A collection of 30 essays revised from various sources and including a number of SF writers and topics, including Blish, Dick, Sheckley, Nesvadba, Verne, Vonnegut, British SF, SF art, and SF film. Aldiss, who received the Pilgrim Award in 1978, and the James Blish Award for SF criticism in 1978, is among the most literate and broadly educated of writer-critics in the field, and his essays explore at a more leisurely pace many of the topics covered in his more famous *Trillion Year Spree* [8-5].

*8-5. Aldiss, Brian W., and David Wingrove. **Trillion Year Spree: The History of Science Fiction.** Atheneum, 1986.

A thorough revision and expansion of Aldiss's *Billion Year Spree: The True History of Science Fiction* (1973), which was the first attempt at a coherent critical literary history of the field. Unlike works by Gunn [8-62], del Rey [8-46], and Wollheim [8-147], which tend to view SF history as a prologue to the development of the commercial American genre market, *Trillion Year Spree* sets out to be a comprehensive survey of the evolution of a literary form, with a distinctly personal viewpoint. Some of Aldiss's arguments, such as the contention that SF is a "post-Gothic" genre descended largely from Mary Shelley's *Frankenstein* [1-84], have gained wide currency, while others, such as his comparative treatment of the British and American "New Wave" movements, reveal a slight bias toward the "literariness" of the British SF tradition. Generally, however, the account is remarkably balanced and even-handed. Perhaps in response to complaints that his earlier history slighted more recent SF, Aldiss worked with David Wingrove to assure wider coverage and increased currency; fully two-fifths of the book is devoted to SF after 1960 and includes discussions of films, feminist SF, cyberpunk, mainstream writers such as Doris Lessing, and the growth of SF scholarship as well as an impressive number of younger writers. Some of the more recent writers are treated in a kind of headlong rush, and some inaccuracies result, but most of the judgments have held up well, and the book remains the definitive single-volume history of the field. Sixteen pages of photos, detailed reference and explanatory endnotes, a critical bibliography, and a thorough index add to the book's value as a scholarly reference as well as the most graceful and witty account of the genre to date. HW, 1987; L, 1987; Eaton, 1988

8-6.   Alkon, Paul K. **Origins of Futuristic Fiction.** Univ. of Georgia Press, 1987.

A literate and scholarly analysis of the early history of prose works set in the future, beginning with Jacques Guttin's *Epigone* (1659) and including useful discussions of works little known even to SF historians, by such authors as David Russen, Thomas Burnet, Samuel Madden, Louis Geoffroy, Louis Sébastien Mercier, Jean-Baptiste Cousin de Grainville, Restif de la Bretonne, and Jane Webb, whose 1827 *The Mummy!* represents the latter end of the chronological period covered. Especially interesting is Alkon's discussions of early theorists of future fiction, most notably Félix Bodin, whose 1834 *Le Roman de l'avenir* anticipates many later defenses of SF. Alkon consistently relates his material to current SF scholarship and literary theory, giving his study a degree of relevance unusual among such protohistorical studies, which often focus on social theory more than literary form. This specialized study is drawn on for his excellent short history, *Science Fiction Before 1900* (1994). Compare I. F. Clarke's *The Pattern of Expectation: 1644–2001* [8-40]. Eaton Award, 1989

8-7.   Amis, Kingsley. **New Maps of Hell: A Survey of Science Fiction.** Harcourt, 1960.

Amis's early study, based on his Christian Gauss lectures at Princeton in 1959, is now of more historical than critical interest. It was the first serious treatment of SF by a reputable mainstream novelist and, thanks to a Ballantine mass-market paperback published in 1960, the first critical work on SF to reach a wide audience. Amis sees SF largely as a vehicle for satire, and thus his discussion of contemporaneous writers leans heavily on the work of Pohl and Kornbluth. Though there are clear gaps in his knowledge of the field, Amis does not look down on genre writers, his style remains sharp and acerbic, and his book is justifiably cited as one of the landmarks in gaining broad recognition for the genre. Amis's later *The Alteration* [4-8] is an alternate world SF novel, and he has edited a number of anthologies, both alone and with Robert Conquest.

8-8.   Anisfield, Nancy, ed. **The Nightmare Considered: Critical Essays on Nuclear War Literature.** Bowling Green, 1991.
A collection of 19 essays, eight of them previously published, divided into "Issues and Overviews" and "Specific Texts." The collection is unusual in that it offers perspectives from poets, feminists, environmental activists, historians, and specialists in young adult or Native American literatures—including Louise Erdrich and Michael Dorris—and discussions of mainstream fiction, drama, film, poetry, and even alternative journalism. Although few of the essays take advantage of previous research in the field, many offer unique perspectives on works by Vonnegut, Hoban, Denis Johnson, Arthur Kopit, and Tim O'Brien, and two excellent contributions come from leading scholars in the field, Paul Brians and H. Bruce Franklin. Useful for its broad perspective, but beginning researchers should first consult Brians's *Nuclear Holocausts* [8-30] and Bartter's *The Way to Ground Zero* [8-22].

8-9.   Armitt, Lucie, ed. **Where No Man Has Gone Before: Women and Science Fiction.** Routledge, 1991.
Thirteen original essays by British women writers and academics offer a variety of perspectives on various writers, women characters, and problems of genre writing. The first section, on individual authors, includes a rare discussion of works by Charlotte Haldane and Katherine Burdekin (by Elizabeth Russell), plus essays on C. L. Moore, Ursula Le Guin, and Doris Lessing. The second section offers perspectives on the Frankenstein tradition, Lisa Tuttle on the metamorphosis theme in recent SF, the role of language in SF, and film. The final section considers relations between SF and young adult fiction, horror fiction, and Arthurian romance, and concludes with a lively autobiographical piece by Josephine Saxton. An important collection, which should be consulted together with Lefanu [8-79], Weedman [8-176], and Barr [8-20].

8-10.   Armytage, W(alter) H(arry) G(reen). **Yesterday's Tomorrows: A Historical Survey of Future Societies.** Univ. of Toronto Press, 1968.
Armytage attempts to trace the history of what he calls "conflict models" of prediction and anticipation, as opposed to mere futuristic fantasies. His ambitious agenda, ranging from ancient Greece to J. G. Ballard, leads to

some glib summaries and distorted judgments (Ray Bradbury's teenage fanzine is cited as evidence of the rise of technocracy), but his impressively broad research uncovers useful insights from sources as varied as D. H. Lawrence and William Burroughs. I. F. Clarke's *The Pattern of Expectation* [8-40] and Fred Polak's *The Image of the Future* (1961) are more straightforward but less wide-ranging accounts of past futures.

8-11.   Asimov, Isaac. **Asimov on Science Fiction.** Avon, 1981.
A collection of 55 short pieces, 22 of them editorials from *Isaac Asimov's Science Fiction Magazine* and others from sources as varied as *TV Guide* and liner notes from recordings, that offer provocative glimpses into Asimov's attitudes toward the field, writers, fans, and the process of writing. Written with Asimov's familiar chatty wit, the pieces are mostly directed toward wide, popular audiences, and thus offer little in the way of extended critical arguments or information unfamiliar to SF readers. Taken together, however, they provide a useful overview of the opinions of one of the most prolific and popular authors of this century.

8-12.   Asimov, Isaac. **Asimov's Galaxy: Reflections on Science Fiction.** Doubleday, 1989.
A collection of 66 short editorials originally published in *Isaac Asimov's Science Fiction Magazine* between 1980 and 1985, though not overlapping those in *Asimov on Science Fiction* [8-11]. Like the earlier collection, the tone here is chatty and sometimes a bit windy, and the book as a whole is of more interest to students of Asimov than to students of SF in general.

8-13.   Atheling, William, Jr. (pseud. of James Blish). **The Issue at Hand: Studies in Contemporary Magazine Science Fiction.** Advent, 1964.
From 1952 through 1963, Blish published an ongoing critical commentary on SF magazine fiction, with occasional comments on major novels of the period. His essays, which originally appeared in a variety of fanzines, are here collected together with two convention speeches, and make clear why Blish, along with Damon Knight, is counted as a pioneer in establishing critical standards for the field. While his discussions of stories that have since become famous are of obvious interest, his demolition of less successful stories is often more informative from a technical standpoint. Useful not only for those interested in the history of SF during the 1950s, but for anyone interested in the technique and construction of SF stories.

8-14.   Atheling, William, Jr. (pseud. of James Blish). **More Issues at Hand.** Advent, 1970.
Blish's second collection of "watchdog" reviews emphasizes novels more

than magazine fiction, covering works by Heinlein, Sturgeon, and Budrys as well as earlier authors such as A. Merritt. Of particular interest are his early discussions of SF criticism, SF in translation, and his contribution to the "New Wave" debate. Similar collections by writers as critics include Knight's *In Search of Wonder* [8-74], Budrys's *Benchmarks* [8-31], and Spinrad's *Science Fiction in the Real World* [8-130].

*8-15. Bailey, J(ames) O(sler). **Pilgrims Through Space and Time: Trends and Patterns in Scientific and Utopian Fiction.** Argus, 1947.

Although largely superseded by more recent scholarship, Bailey's adaptation of his own 1934 doctoral dissertation was the first scholarly study of the roots of the genre, and thus exerted a profound influence on later historians and anthologists—as evidenced by the name of the Pilgrim Award, given annually by the Science Fiction Research Association to distinguished scholars in the field. This influence includes not only establishing a pedigree for modern SF, but helping to develop, through its taxonomic organization, a kind of consensus motif-list used by many later scholars. Despite its almost exclusive focus on pre-World War I works, Bailey's study remains readable and useful.

8-16. Bainbridge, William Sims. **Dimensions of Science Fiction.** Harvard, 1986.

Like many attempts at sociological descriptions of the genre, Bainbridge's study—based on surveys of some 600 registrants at the 1978 world SF convention in Phoenix plus followup surveys—tends to offer few new insights, but provides statistical data to support what is already common knowledge among, at least, editors and publishers. The main "dimensions" that Bainbridge isolates, for example, are hard SF, New Wave, and fantasy—a similar survey taken a few years earlier or later might have yielded quite different results. Written with jargon-free clarity, Bainbridge's study offers little in the way of literary theory but provides a useful statistical snapshot of the genre at one point in its history. Compare with Brian Stableford's *The Sociology of Science Fiction* [8-133].

8-17. Bammer, Angelika. **Partial Visions: Feminism and Utopianism in the 1970s.** Routledge, 1992.

One of a number of recent studies of feminist utopias (see also Bartkowski [8-21] and Moylan [8-93]), this book is valuable for its historical perspective and its treatment of little-discussed European writers such as Christa Wolf, Irmtraud Morgner, Helene Cixous, and Monica Wittig. Although Bammer's definition of utopian writing is broader than most, her discussions of works by these writers—as well as Sally Gearhart, Joanna Russ, Marge Piercy, and Rita Mae Brown—are often insightful.

8-18. Barr, Marleen S. **Alien to Femininity: Speculative Fiction and Feminist Theory.** Greenwood, 1987.
Barr's first extended attempt to link feminist theory with SF suffers from a tendency to quote rather than elucidate her theoretical sources, and then to rather mechanically apply these quotations to selected texts—although the texts she has chosen to discuss are often quite interesting. The book is divided into three sections, "Community," "Heroism," and "Sexuality and Reproduction," and authors covered include Tiptree, Wilhelm, and Charnas. Both Barr's own *Feminist Fabulation* [8-9] and Lefanu [8-79] are more consistent.

8-19. Barr, Marleen S. **Feminist Fabulation: Space/Postmodern Fiction.** Univ. of Iowa Press, 1992.
An impassioned and energetic study of speculative feminist works that "unmask patriarchal master narratives," but that are excluded from the postmodern canon because of their genre origins. The first section, "Reclaiming Canonical Space," defines "feminist fabulation" and relates it to earlier traditions of women's literature. The second, "Redefining Gendered Space," includes chapters on flying as portrayed in literature, houses and "domestic spaces," and imaginary societies. The third, "Reconceiving Narrative Space," examines female characters and feminist revisions of traditional "male-centered" stories. A broad range of authors is covered, including Lynn Abbey, Marion Zimmer Bradley, Octavia Butler, Isak Dineson, Gail Godwin, Carol Hill, Doris Lessing, Marge Piercy, Pamela Sargent, and Christa Wolf. Barr's deliberately contentious style and broad overgeneralizations may irritate some readers, but she succeeds in raising a number of provocative issues. Compare Lefanu [8-79].

8-20. Barr, Marleen S., ed. **Future Females: A Critical Anthology.** Bowling Green, 1981.
Like many topics of SF scholarship, the role of women authors and characters began first to be explored in individual essays and then in collections like this one before giving rise to more extended studies, such as Barr's own *Feminist Fabulation* [8-19]. The contributors of her 15 essays—13 of them original—include Joanna Russ, Robert Scholes, and Eric Rabkin, and the bibliography by Roger Schlobin was later expanded and published separately as *Urania's Daughters* (1983). In its way a groundbreaking anthology, designed clearly to redress past omissions, the book

still offers useful insights. Compare with Armitt [8-9] and Weedman [8-176].

8-21. Bartkowski, Frances. **Feminist Utopias.** Univ. of Nebraska Press, 1989.
Bartkowski discusses ten American, Canadian, and French novels by pairing them off in five chapters, sometimes almost arbitrarily. The works discussed are Gilman's *Herland* [1-38] and Monique Wittig's *Les Guérellères*, Russ's *The Female Man* [4-375], and Piercy's *Woman on the Edge of Time* [4-330], Charnas's *Walk to the End of the World* [4-99] and *Motherlines* [4-99], Christian Rochefort's *Archaos, ou le jardin étincelant* and E. M. Broner's *Weave of Women*, and Louky Bersianik's *The Eugélionne* and Atwood's *The Handmaid's Tale* [4-23]. Although Bartkowski's familiarity with other scholarship in the field seems limited, her readings of specific texts are valuable. Compare Bammer [8-17] and Moylan [8-93].

8-22. Bartter, Martha A. **The Way to Ground Zero: The Atomic Bomb in American Science Fiction.** Greenwood, 1988.
In one of the most thoroughly researched and extensive studies of a single theme in American science fiction, Bartter traces the image of the bomb (and related themes of the image of the scientist, future wars, and the return to barbarism) in works ranging from pre–World War I "super-weapon" stories through some works of the 1980s, although her coverage is strongest in the 1940s and 1950s. Although her agenda sometimes seems too ambitious to permit extended treatment of significant works (very short shrift is given to *A Canticle for Leibowitz* [3-125], for example), a chapter comparing 20 stories by Heinlein with 27 by Sturgeon is especially revealing. Although comparisons with Brians [8-30] are inevitable, Bartter's study is more than twice as long as the essay portion of Brians, and more narrowly focused. Franklin's *War Stars* [8-58] is a useful complementary text.

8-23. Becker, Allienne R. **The Lost Worlds Romance: From Dawn Till Dusk.** Greenwood, 1992.
Becker attempts to trace the history of one of SF's most popular early subgenres from its development late in the 19th century to modern echoes in the work of Andrew M. Greeley (who also provides an appreciative introduction). While Becker makes use of almost none of the existing scholarship in this field, and sometimes seems unclear whether she wants to write a literary history or an indictment of sexist and racist themes (her index includes such odd items as "bare-breasted women"), her lively discussions

of the plots of works by Verne, Haggard, Burroughs, and others make this a convenient if incomplete reference. A clearer definition of the form and what it implies can be found in Thomas Clareson's "Lost Lands, Lost Races: A Pagan Princess of Their Very Own" in *Many Futures, Many Worlds* [8-35].

8-24.   Ben-Yehuda Nachman. **Deviance and Moral Boundaries: Witch-craft, the Occult, Science Fiction, Deviant Sciences and Scientists.** Univ. of Chicago Press, 1985.

In an unusual attempt to place SF in the context of a theory of social deviance, an Israeli sociologist argues that an understanding of deviance is central to an understanding of social change. To demonstrate this, he offers case studies of the European witchcraft hysteria, the occult and SF, nontraditional sciences (including UFOs and the search for extraterrestrial intelligence), and fraudulent science. Unfortunately, his discussion of SF is among the weakest aspects of the book, focusing on fandom and a few related cults such as Scientology, mentioning few specific texts, and failing to distinguish between pseudoscience and speculative or imaginary science. Stableford's *The Sociology of Science Fiction* [8-133], though not specifically concerned with deviance, is far more generally informed about the genre.

8-25.   Berger, Harold. **Science Fiction and the New Dark Age.** Bowling Green, 1976.

A relatively early study of some 300 works showing the growing dystopian trend in SF. Berger groups the works into 12 categories (such as Man vs. Machine, the Totalitarian State of the Future, the Revolt of Youth, Race War in America, Nuclear War, the Population Explosion), but offers little detailed analysis of specific works and not much more in the way of theoretical or historical context. Useful as a source of some lesser-known texts. Compare Walsh's more thoughtful *From Utopia to Nightmare* [8-141].

*8-26.   Bleiler, Everett M. **Science-Fiction: The Early Years.** Kent State Univ. Press, 1991.

Bleiler's massive compilation describes more than 3,000 stories and novels (as well as influential works of nonfiction such as Henry George's *Progress and Poverty* and Madame Blavatsky's *The Secret Doctrine*), which define the prehistory of science fiction from ancient Greece through the 1930s. Amazingly, Bleiler does not rely on secondary sources, as have so many historians of early SF, but has actually read the titles he describes and is able to relate them to each other and to later trends in SF, while identifying a number of themes that have long since died out. Covering a wide variety of texts from utopias to dime novels, Bleiler's study is one of the most impressive achievements of SF scholarship to date, and is both definitive and indispensable. Also annotated as [7-21]. HN, 1992; L, 1992

8-27. Blish, James. **The Tale That Wags the God.** Advent, 1987. Ed. by Cy Chauvin.

A posthumous collection of essays on a wide variety of topics, together with an extensive bibliography of Blish's work prepared by his widow, Judith L. Blish. Generally more thoughtful and theoretical than the commentary collected in his *Issue at Hand* volumes (see under Atheling), the topics include the definition of SF, science and the arts in SF, modern music, Poul Anderson, James Branch Cabell, and James Joyce. Of particular interest is a long autobiographical piece and a conversation between Blish and Brian W. Aldiss.

8-28. Bretnor, Reginald, ed. **Modern Science Fiction: Its Meaning and Its Future.** Coward-McCann, 1953. Recommended ed.: Advent, 1979 (2nd ed.).

Primarily of historical interest (this was the first critical overview of SF to come from a mainstream publisher), Bretnor's collection includes pieces on the state of science fiction (by John W. Campbell, Jr., Anthony Boucher, and Don Fabun), literary merit (by Fletcher Pratt, Rosalie Moore, and L. Sprague de Camp), and various philosophical issues (by Isaac Asimov, Arthur C. Clarke, Philip Wylie, Gerald Heard, and Bretnor himself). Of particular interest are Asimov's essay defining "social science fiction" and Boucher's account of SF's "ghettoization," a term that has remained common since.

8-29. Bretnor, Reginald, ed. **Science Fiction, Today and Tomorrow.** Harper, 1974.

Fifteen essays covering much of the same territory as Bretnor's 1953 collection, and with essentially the same subdivisions as that earlier collection ("Science Fiction Today," "Science Fiction, Science, and Modern Man," "The Art and Science of Science Fiction"). Poul Anderson, Hal Clement, Anne McCaffrey, and Gordon R. Dickson offer useful technical discussions of aspects of SF writing; Ben Bova, Frederik Pohl, and George Zebrowski discuss the state of SF in 1974; and Frank Herbert, Theodore Sturgeon, Alan E. Nourse, Thomas N. Scortia, and Bretnor offer more philosophical discussions. Despite the progress apparent in SF and the mainstream (discussed by James Gunn) and SF teaching (discussed by Jack Williamson), the book is in many ways as dated as its predecessor.

*8-30.   Brians, Paul. Nuclear Holocausts: Atomic War in Fiction, 1895–1984. Kent State Univ. Press, 1987.

Brians's definitive study includes a long essay on the theme of nuclear war in fiction (including mainstream works as well as SF), followed by an extensive annotated bibliography of more than 800 stories and novels, together with a chronology, checklists, and detailed title and subject indexes. Brians's critical essay identifies and traces all the major themes associated with nuclear war fiction, but is necessarily rather synoptic in its treatment of individual works and is essentially a work of literary history rather than theory. His bibliography, which includes ephemeral works of survivalist fiction as well as SF and mainstream works, includes admirably succinct and balanced annotations. For more detailed treatment of the theme in American SF, see Martha Bartter, *The Way to Ground Zero: The Atomic Bomb in American Science Fiction* [8-22]. Also annotated as [7-10].

8-31.   Budrys, Algis. Benchmarks: Galaxy Bookshelf. Southern Illinois Univ. Press, 1985.

As reviewer for *Galaxy* magazine from 1965–1971, Budrys established himself as one of the field's most perceptive and influential "in-house critics," as he described himself. His reviews, covering some 161 books, not only provide an overview of a volatile period in SF history, but contribute an important chapter to an informal documentary history of the field which also includes review collections by Knight [8-74], Blish [8-13/14], and Spinrad [8-130]. Though some of the reviews or judgments seem dated— which Budrys acknowledges in occasional notes added to this edition— the comments on the techniques and ideas of the genre are still valid. An introduction by Catherine McClenehan provides a perceptive overview of Budrys's criticism, and Frederik Pohl, Budrys's former editor, adds a brief memoir. An index has also been added. HN, 1986; L, 1986

8-32.   Budrys, Algis. Nonliterary Influences on Science Fiction. Drumm, 1983.

This 12,000-word pamphlet represents Budrys's preferred text of an essay that appeared at less than half that length in *Science-Fiction Dialogues* [8-146]. By "nonliterary influences," Budrys refers not so much to the composition of SF texts as to their frequent corruption, often for purely mechanical reasons, by the chain magazines (both pulp and digest) that originally published them. Although relatively little scholarship has been done on establishing authors' texts for popular magazine fiction, Budrys's examples make clear that any scholar or critic ought to take such matters into account when discussing such stories.

8-33. Bukatman, Scott. **Terminal Identity: The Virtual Subject in Post-modern Science Fiction.** Duke Univ. Press, 1993.
An ambitious, broadly interdisciplinary, and sometimes densely theoretical attempt to trace the disappearance of the traditional narrative "subject" in the face of new technologies. "Terminal identity" (a term borrowed from William S. Burroughs) is defined as "a transitional state produced at the intersection of technology and narration," and is discussed in terms of works by Gibson, Sterling, Ballard, Dick, Tiptree, Zelazny, Bernard Wolfe, Greg Bear, Vernor Vinge, Neal Stephenson, and others. Bukatman draws heavily on theorists from McLuhan to (especially) Baudrillard, and devotes somewhat less attention to fiction than to a variety of postmodern expressions in media: film, TV music, comics, video art, computer games and simulations, virtual reality, alternative journalism. A professor of film, he seems most comfortable in that arena. Although he provides few extended readings of specific SF works, the complex cultural context in which he locates them is provocatively presented and well-documented. Compare McCaffrey's *Storming the Reality Studio* [8-86].

*8-34. Carter, Paul A. **The Creation of Tomorrow: Fifty Years of Magazine Science Fiction.** Columbia Univ. Press, 1977.
A historian as well as an occasional SF author, Carter provides a knowledgeable and witty overview of the major themes and preoccupations of magazine SF from 1919 through the 1950s, including such topics as moon rockets, interplanetary romances, time machines, Hitler and fascism, evolution, dystopia and utopia, postholocaust tales, and the role of women in SF. By focusing on magazine fiction—which defined the genre much more than novels did during most of this period—and by treating the historical background with informed sophistication, Carter has produced a highly readable and essential counterpoint to the more novel-based histories of the field. His treatment of the World War II period is especially informative. Compare with the detailed introductory essays to Michael Ashley's *History of the Science Fiction Magazine*, vols. 1–4 [12-36]. Eaton, 1979

8-35. Clareson, Thomas D. **Many Futures, Many Worlds: Theme and Form in Science Fiction.** Kent State Univ. Press, 1977.
One of the first books of SF criticism to be reviewed in *The New York Times*, this collection of fourteen essays (twelve by academic critics and one each by Stanley Schmidt and Samuel R. Delany) helped define some of the

major issues that accompanied academic criticism's "discovery" of the genre. Delany's essay also appears in his *The Jewel-Hinged Jaw* [8-48], and three of the academic essays discuss topics that were later expanded into books by their authors: S. C. Fredericks [8-59], Gary K. Wolfe [8-145], and Patricia Warrick [8-143]. Other essays still of interest are those by Thomas L. Wymer, Thomas D. Clareson, Robert H. Canary, and Beverly Friend.

8-36.   Clareson, Thomas D., ed. **SF: The Other Side of Realism: Essays on Modern Fantasy and Science Fiction.** Bowling Green, 1972.
Produced in recognition of the first ten years of the MLA Seminar on Science Fiction and the founding of the Science Fiction Research Association, this collection of 26 essays still retains much of its interest. Problems of definition are addressed by Judith Merril, Julius Kagarlitski, Samuel Delany, and Lionel Stevenson; individual works or authors are discussed by Brian Aldiss, Norman Spinrad, Willis McNelly, Bruce Franklin, Richard D. Mullen, and Franz Rottensteiner; themes are explored by Stanislaw Lem and I. F. Clarke; film is covered by Richard Hodgens, Robert Plank, and Alex Eisenstein. Further evidence of the collection's substance is that no fewer than seven of the contributors went on to receive Pilgrim Awards.

*8-37.   Clareson, Thomas D. **Some Kind of Paradise: The Emergence of American Science Fiction.** Greenwood, 1985.
The most comprehensive narrative history of American science fiction of the period 1870–1930, this well-documented study is a companion piece to Clareson's bibliography *Science Fiction in America, 1870s–1930s* [7-4]. Beginning with an overview of the Gothic influence in American SF, Clareson devotes chapters to the future war motif, the growing celebration of science and scientists, utopianism and catastrophism, the imaginary voyage, and the interplanetary romance. Throughout, he remains sensitive to issues of interest to contemporary readers, such as portrayals of women and Native Americans, and often cites the relationships of texts under discussion with relevant European fiction and modern descendants. Though occasionally simplistic in its treatment of historical contexts, the book fills in a useful chapter of American literary history. Eaton Award, 1987

8-38.   Clareson, Thomas D. **Understanding Contemporary American Science Fiction: The Formative Period (1926–1970).** Univ. of South Carolina Press, 1990.
A general, popular survey prepared as part of Matthew Bruccoli's "Understanding Contemporary American Literature" series of mono-

graphs. Except for a cursory overview of the period 1926–1950 in the first chapter, the book is entirely a history of American SF of the 1950s and 1960s. The authors covered in greatest detail are Simak, Bradbury, Vonnegut, Pohl, Bester, Sturgeon, Clement, Anderson, Blish, Asimov, Leiber, Dick, Herbert, Pangborn, Disch, Spinrad, Vance, Cordwainer Smith, Delany, Zelazny, and Silverberg; women's SF is treated almost peremptorily, and some publishing history is offered by way of context. A competent account, with notes and bibliography, of the more-or-less standard view of the period; an interesting contrast is Malzberg's more opinionated *The Engines of the Night* [8-83].

8-39. Clareson, Thomas D., and Thomas L. Wymer (Vol. 3 only), eds. **Voices for the Future: Essays on Major Science Fiction Writers.** Bowling Green, Vol. 1, 1976; Vol. 2, 1979; Vol. 3, 1983.
Intended as a more detailed followup to *SF: The Other Side of Realism* [8-36], this series consists of original essays covering major writers whose work is frequently covered in the classroom. In the first volume, all the authors covered except Kurt Vonnegut began their careers before World War II: Williamson, Stapledon, Simak, Asimov, Heinlein, Sturgeon, Bradbury, Kuttner and Moore, Clarke. The second volume covers eight authors who began in the 1950s and 1960s: Reynolds, Farmer, Ballard, Silverberg, Walter Miller, Le Guin, Brunner, and Zelazny. The third volume broadens its scope to include fantasy and covers Knight, Cordwainer Smith, Gene Wolfe, Mervyn Peake, Frederik Pohl, C. S. Lewis, Delany, and Disch. Though some material is superseded by more extensive studies of the authors covered, much remains valuable.

8-40. Clarke, I. F. **The Pattern of Expectation: 1644–2001.** Basic Books, 1979.
An informed and well-illustrated scholarly study of future speculation from the 18th century to modern SF. Like Berger [8-25] and Walsh [8-141], Clarke traces the shift from technological and scientific optimism to dystopian visions, but his real strength is in portraying earlier historical visions of tomorrow. A comparable study, less focused on fictional texts, is Fred Polak's *The Image of the Future* (1961); more similar is Armytage [8-10]. Clarke's *Tale of the Future* [7-5] is a companion bibliography.

*8-41. Clarke, I. F. **Voices Prophesying War: Future Wars, 1763–3749.** Oxford Univ. Press, 1992.
A revision and updating of Clarke's classic 1966 *Voices Prophesying War: 1763–1984*, this work remains the standard history of future war literature, although Clarke's coverage of more recent material is spotty compared to

the authoritative treatment of pre–World War I works. Beginning with a survey of the period 1763–1871, Clarke then devotes a chapter to *The Battle of Dorking* [1-21], which he convincingly establishes as a benchmark text for this subgenre, and treats science and politics from 1880–1914 in the next two chapters. A heavily revised fifth chapter and a new sixth chapter attempt to bring coverage to the present, and a chronological checklist and index round out the volume (though both prove to be somewhat unreliable with more recent texts). While Clarke's treatment of nuclear war adds little to that of Brians [8-30] or Bartter [8-22], his work as a whole remains one of the core texts of SF historical scholarship.

8-42.   Clute, John. **Strokes: Essays and Reviews, 1966–1986.** Serconia Press, 1988. Introduction by Thomas M. Disch.

The subtitle is somewhat misleading, since all but two of the 19 pieces collected here originally appeared as reviews. (The exceptions are an essay on Robert Aickman written for a reference book and a short piece on the film *Them.*) But Clute is among the most acerbic and widely read of SF critics, and his strong opinions and energetic prose make this a stimulating update to a somewhat similar collection from an earlier era, Knight's *In Search of Wonder* [8-74]. The pieces collected here, with introductions and occasional interpolations added for this edition, cover some 60 authors, with somewhat more extended treatment given to Blish, Aldiss, and Gene Wolfe. A useful and highly readable overview of the period covered.

8-43.   Cogswell, Theodore R., ed. **PITFCS: Proceedings of the Institute for Twenty-First Century Studies.** Advent, 1992. Introduction by Algis Budrys.

From April 1959 through December 1962, SF writer Cogswell used this mock-pretentious title (there was no Institute, and these are not "proceedings") for his "fanzine for professionals," designed initially to encourage debate about forming an SF writers' organization. This large, well-indexed volume assembles the entire run of the magazine (except for one apparently scurrilous issue), and features often lengthy contributions from most of the major SF figures of the day—including Kurt Vonnegut, Kingsley Amis, and Hugo Gernsback—on topics ranging from problems with editors to controversial books such as Heinlein's *Starship Troopers* [3-90]. As a clearinghouse for professional writers, *PITFCS* offers a wealth of critical comment, as well as a detailed history of the issues that eventually led to the founding of the Science Fiction Writers of America. A final 1979 issue—17 years late, long after the SFWA had been formed—lends poignancy to the lost era portrayed here. An invaluable resource in SF history, and a useful companion piece to Blish's *The Issue at Hand* [8-13] and Knight's *In Search of Wonder* [8-74].

8-44. Davies, Philip John, ed. **Science Fiction, Social Conflict and War.** Manchester Univ. Press, 1990.
A collection of intelligent and informed essays exploring the ways in which SF has examined—and might examine—major contemporary issues of social conflict and international relations. Contributors include Jacqueline Pearson on sexual politics, Edward James (with two essays) on racism and violent revolution as portrayed in American SF, Alasdair Spark on SF and the Vietnam War, H. Bruce Franklin on the ideology of the American superweapon (explored more fully in his *War Stars* [8-58]), and Martha Bartter and Paul Brians on aspects of nuclear war fiction. Many of the essays focus on fictional strategies and methods, and all demonstrate a firm grasp not only of relevant fiction, but of the broader social issues as well.

8-45. De Vos, Luk, ed. **Just the Other Day: Essays on the Suture of the Future.** Restant (Antwerp), 1985.
One of the first truly international symposia on SF criticism, this huge collection of 37 essays and three interviews includes contributors from England, the United States, Holland, Germany, France, Israel, Australia, Belgium, Denmark, Sweden, and Canada. Essays appear in French, Dutch, and German, but about half are in English, making the book valuable for the English-only reader. De Vos divides the book into six parts, the first of which is his own rationale for the collection, leading into a group of other theoretical pieces by Helmut Pesch, Darko Suvin, and others. A third section focuses on literary history, a fourth on religious and metaphysical themes, a fifth on individual writers, and a final miscellany. Useful for its treatments of many European writers little discussed in Anglo-American criticism and for its European perspective.

8-46. del Rey, Lester. **The World of Science Fiction, 1926–1976: The History of a Subculture.** Ballantine and Garland, 1979.
Despite its title, this history of American commercial SF does not focus in any significant way on the "subculture" of fans and writers during SF's formative years, but instead is an opinionated and very informal survey, divided into 12-year periods, of what the author regards as key works from the periods in question. Offering little in the way of context, broader critical perspective, or discussion of international science fiction, the book is of

504 *Gary K. Wolfe*

primary interest when viewed as an example of a significant insider's view of the field's development. As a more or less "official" representation of the perspective of that generation of writers who helped shape American popular SF, it is generally less balanced and comprehensive than James Gunn's *Alternate Worlds* [8-62], which covers much of the same territory, and is far less complete as a general history than Aldiss and Wingrove's *Trillion Year Spree* [8-5].

8-47. Delany, Samuel R. **The American Shore: Meditations on a Tale of Science Fiction by Thomas M. Disch—Angouleme.** Dragon Press, 1978.
By devoting more than 200 pages of close analysis to a 20-page story (which appears as part of Disch's novel *334* [4-147]), Delany has produced the most detailed deconstruction of a single SF text to date. Written at the height of Delany's preoccupation with European structuralism and semiotics, the analysis attempts to identify the varying "discourses" of the story by dividing it into some 287 lexical units; some, but not all, of these discourses reflect Delany's notion that SF can be characterized by its unique use of language. Of primary interest to scholars of critical theory, the book represents an extreme application of techniques apparent in some of Delany's other criticism and in Christine Brooke-Rose's *A Rhetoric of the Unreal* (1981).

*8-48. Delany, Samuel R. **The Jewel-Hinged Jaw: Notes on the Language of Science Fiction.** Dragon Press, 1977.
Thirteen essays, revised from their appearances in various anthologies and journals between 1966 and 1976, plus one original essay on reading Le Guin's *The Dispossessed* [4-252]. After an opening "Letter to a Critic," Delany describes his language-based approach to SF in three general essays (one more in the form of an extended meditation), then deals with technical concerns of plot, character, and storytelling, and focuses in individual pieces on works by Disch, Zelazny, Russ, and Le Guin. An "autobiographical postscript" provides a context for his experience with SF, anticipating the more extended autobiographical material in *The Motion of Light on Water* (1988; rev. ed. 1990).

8-49. Delany, Samuel R. **Starboard Wine: More Notes on the Language of Science Fiction.** Dragon Press, 1984.
Ten essays, plus an introduction and three letters to *Science-Fiction Studies*, on major writers and theoretical questions. Two of the author essays, "Heinlein" and "Sturgeon," originally appeared as introductions to Gregg Press reprints of novels by these authors; the others concern Russ and

Disch. Of the more theoretical essays, the most important are *"Dichtung and Science Fiction,"* which proposes an ideal SF class; "Science Fiction and 'Literature,'" which continues Delany's exploration of the unique use of language in the genre; and "Reflections on Historical Models," which concerns problems in writing SF history. An influential and provocative book, far more accessible than *The American Shore* [8-47].

8-50. Dowling, David. **Fictions of Nuclear Disaster.** Univ. of Iowa Press, 1987.

A well-researched and informative study, broader in scope than Bartter [8-22] in that it covers international fiction, fiction not specifically concerned with the bomb, and such nongenre oddities as Raymond Briggs's *When the Wind Blows* or Yorick Blumenfeld's *Jenny: My Diary*; Dowling even finds anticipations of nuclear war in the work of Zola. Following six chapters in which he considers the bomb in fiction, the role of the scientist, depictions of nuclear war, postcatastrophe societies, and eschatological issues, Dowling sets up *A Canticle for Leibowitz* [3-125] and *Riddley Walker* [4-210] as "exemplary fictions" notable for their focus on language and signs. Well-researched and annotated, although the bibliography lists only primary works and the index omits titles.

8-51. Dunn, Thomas P., and Richard D. Erlich, eds. **The Mechanical God: Machines in Science Fiction.** Greenwood, 1982.

The inaugural volume in Greenwood's "Contributions to the Study of Science Fiction and Fantasy" series contains 18 essays grouped rather confusingly according to "Authors" (seven essays), "Children's Science Fiction" (one essay), "Attributes" (seven essays), and "Cyborgs" (three essays). Some of the individual essays are quite good, but the breadth of the topic and the spottiness of coverage limit the book's usefulness as an overview. *Clockwork Worlds* [8-52] is a companion volume, with similar strengths and weaknesses.

8-52. Erlich, Richard D., and Thomas P. Dunn, eds. **Clockwork Worlds: Mechanized Environments in Science Fiction.** Greenwood, 1983.

The companion volume to *The Mechanical God* [8-51] featuring essays that focus on technological or machine-dominated environments more than on individual robots or computers. Erlich and Dunn compiled *Clockworks: A Multimedia Bibliography of Works Useful for the Study of the Human/Machine Interface in SF* (Greenwood, 1993; not seen).

8-53.   Eshbach, Lloyd Arthur, ed. **Of Worlds Beyond: The Science of Science Fiction Writing.** Advent, 1964.

Originally published in 1947, this symposium on SF technique by the leading writers of that era is badly dated as a guidebook for aspiring writers, but invaluable as a historic document of how the field viewed itself in the immediate postwar period, and of the compositional methods of some of its major writers. Heinlein offers the earliest argument for the term "speculative fiction"; Jack Williamson argues for the necessity of internal logic in fantasy; van Vogt gives advice on plot complications; de Camp discusses the use of humor; Edward E. Smith discusses the genesis of his space operas; and John Taine and John W. Campbell discuss science in SF. Researchers on any of these writers should not overlook this absorbing—and oddly innocent—volume of "advice."

8-54.   Eshbach, Lloyd Arthur. **Over My Shoulder: Reflections on a Science Fiction Era.** Oswald Train, 1983.

The founder of the important early specialty publisher Fantasy Press and editor of *Of Worlds Beyond* [8-54] recounts a personal history of SF book publishing from the 1930s to the 1950s, and includes a bibliography of books issued by the fan presses that dominated the field until the 1950s. A useful resource for the collector and the historian of SF publishing, but with little commentary on the literature. An interesting contrast is the situation in England recounted in Harbottle and Holland [8-65].

8-55.   Fischer, William B. **The Empire Strikes Out: Kurd Lasswitz, Hans Dominik, and the Development of German Science Fiction.** Bowling Green, 1984.

A revised doctoral dissertation that provided one of the first accounts in English of the early history of German SF. Lasswitz's major novel, *Two Planets*, appeared in 1897; Dominik gained popularity following World War I and remained popular through the Nazi era. Dominik is probably rightly regarded by Fischer as the lesser SF writer, but his glorification of technology and Germany give his works an ominous edge. A more complete view of pre-Nazi German SF can be found in Fisher [8-56]. Compare also Wuckel and Cassiday [8-148].

8-56.   Fisher, Peter S. **Fantasy and Politics: Visions of the Future in the Weimar Republic.** Univ. of Wisconsin Press, 1991.

An informed and well-documented examination of 30 writers of Weimar Germany, grouped according to "radical nationalists," "technological visionaries," and "socialist and pacifist visions." The first section reveals the growing nationalism of the pre-Nazi era, with swastikas appearing on book covers as early as 1921, while the second deals with fiction that most resembles conventional SF (including an extensive discussion of Thea Von Harbou, author of *Metropolis* [1-132]). The third section concerns leftist writers who never achieved the popularity of the nationalists. Though few of the writers discussed are familiar to English-language readers, Fisher's is an important study of the potential misuses of SF. Compare Fischer [8-55] and Wuckel [8-148].

8-57. Foote, Bud. **The Connecticut Yankee in the Twentieth Century: Travel to the Past in Science Fiction.** Greenwood, 1990.
Foote argues that Twain's *Connecticut Yankee in King Arthur's Court* [1-25], by focusing on a traveler to the past who is determined to change it through technology, established a paradigm for a whole subgenre of SF. Foote does an excellent job of showing the importance of history to SF in general, and discusses a wide variety of works in chapters that are more substantial than their coy titles would indicate (for example, "Dear Old Dad and His Girl," "These Curious Strangers," "Innocents Abroad"). Although Foote does not claim to be definitive either in his text or his bibliography (there are some surprising omissions), he offers insightful treatments of familiar works by Bradbury and Jack Finney, as well as lesser-known texts by Haiblum and Kirk Mitchell. A clearly written and engrossing thematic study.

8-58. Franklin, H. Bruce. **War Stars: The Superweapon and the American Imagination.** Oxford Univ. Press, 1988.
Franklin is one of the few scholars to succeed in raising SF themes to the level of political and social commentary, and in demonstrating that SF modes of thought have formed as well as reflected American social attitudes. *War Stars* is a general cultural history of superweapon ideology, beginning with Robert Fulton and Thomas Edison and ending with Reagan's "Star Wars" campaign. He describes the rise of paranoid future war stories between 1880 and 1917, the developing tradition of nuclear war fiction and film, the contribution of SF writers such as Bova and Pournelle to Reagan's "Star Wars" ideology, and even such works as Joseph Heller's *Catch-22* and Vonnegut's *Slaughterhouse-5* [4-479]. Although Bartter [8-22], Brians [8-30], and Dowling [8-50] provide more extensive discussions of fiction, Franklin's book is crucial to understanding the historical impact of SF-type visions.

*8-59. Fredericks, Casey. **The Future of Eternity: Mythologies of Science Fiction and Fantasy.** Indiana Univ. Press, 1982.
Familiar with both classical scholarship and SF, Fredericks offers the most disciplined and coherent account of the frequently claimed relationships between SF, fantasy, and mythology. Following a discussion of the role of

myths in major historical works—*Frankenstein, Dr. Jekyll and Mr. Hyde, The Time Machine, Last and First Men*—he explores creation myths, echoes of Norse mythology, the superman theme, and the "return to the primitive." The three major myths of SF are identified as man-machine, man-superman, and human-alien encounters. Fredericks offers unusual insights into authors as varied as Poul Anderson, de Camp, Delany, Dick, Ellison, Farmer, Leiber, van Vogt, Weinbaum, and Zelazny.

8-60.   Garnett, Rhys, and R. J. Ellis, eds. **Science Fiction Roots and Branches: Contemporary Critical Approaches.** St. Martin's, 1990.
Eleven essays intended to show a variety of current critical approaches to SF. A historical section includes Darko Suvin on Morris's *News From Nowhere* [1-69], Stanislaw Lem on Wells's *The Time Machine* [1-103], and Garnett on *Dracula*. A second section includes Patrick Parrinder on scientists in SF, Jerzy Jarzebski on Lem, Tom and Alice Clareson on Wyndham, R. J. Ellis on Herbert's *Dune* [4-207], and Robert Philmus on Le Guin's *The Dispossessed* [4-252]. The final section, on feminist criticism, includes Marleen Barr on Marge Piercy and Thomas Berger, Jenny Woolmark on Vonda McIntyre, and Anne Cranny-Francis on Suzy McKee Charnas. Individual essays are quite useful, but the book as a whole lacks structure or focus.

*8-61.   Greenland, Colin. **The Entropy Exhibition: Michael Moorcock and the British "New Wave" in Science Fiction.** Routledge, 1983.
A history of SF's most famous avant-garde movement, based on the author's 1980 Oxford doctoral dissertation. Moorcock is the central figure because it was his editorship of the British magazine *New Worlds* from 1964 to 1970 that defined the "New Wave," but Greenland also includes substantial discussions of two other key writers, Brian Aldiss and J. G. Ballard (all three authors are the subjects of more thorough book-length studies; see Chapter 9). In addition to a history of the magazine and these author studies, Greenland includes chapters on sex in SF, "anti-space" and "inner space" fiction, and stylistic theory and practice. He relates the topics knowledgeably to literary, psychological, and anthropological history, and provides what is close to the standard history of the topic. Eaton Award, 1985

*8-62.   Gunn, James E. **Alternate Worlds: The Illustrated History of Science Fiction.** Prentice-Hall, 1975.
A readable and concise popular history, lavishly illustrated with magazine covers (many in color) and photographs of authors and including lists of

Hugo and Nebula awards through 1974, a short list of major themes and representative works, and a chronology. Like del Rey's *The World of Science Fiction* [8-46], the book reflects a kind of consensus view of the field held by many writers of the postwar period, but Gunn is far more politic and balanced than del Rey. Nearly half the text recounts SF history prior to 1926, with individual chapters on Verne and Wells; later chapters focus on the pulps (with a predictable emphasis on Campbell's *Astounding*) and the 1950s SF boom. Coverage of post-1965 SF is slight. Since Gunn's avowed purpose is not a critical history such as that of Aldiss and Wingrove [8-5], relatively few texts are discussed in depth, and judgments tend to be bland and noncontroversial. Nevertheless, this is the closest thing the SF community of Gunn's generation has to an "official" history. Special Hugo Award, 1976

8-63. Gunn, James E. **Inside Science Fiction: Essays on Fantastic Literature.** Borgo, 1992.
The only person to serve as president of both the Science Fiction Writers of America and the Science Fiction Research Association, Gunn consistently brings his dual perspective to these eighteen essays, which originally appeared between 1971 and 1989. The first five essays deal with historical and autobiographical matters, the next four with academic questions and the teaching of SF, the next four with SF film and television (including an account of the TV movie and series adaptation of Gunn's *The Immortals*), and the final five with social and economic issues related to SF. Gunn's style is informal and reasonable, and his perspective is much the same as that of *Alternate Worlds*. Malzberg [8-83] offers a different perspective on many of the same issues. Also annotated as [13-9].

8-64. Guthke, Karl S. **The Last Frontier: Imagining Other Worlds From the Copernican Revolution to Modern Science Fiction.** Cornell Univ. Press, 1990. Trans. of *Der Mythos der Neuzeit* (Bern, 1983) by Helen Atkins.
An ambitious and scholarly attempt to trace the "plurality of worlds" theme—the idea that there may be other inhabited planets—from its origins in the Renaissance through late 19th-century SF. (The final chapter is on Lasswitz and Wells.) Despite the title, most of the "modern" SF Guthke discusses is treated somewhat cursorily in his introduction. Nevertheless, he views SF as the principal literary and popular expression of a pattern of mythical belief, which has at various times taken the form of theological, scientific, and philosophical debate. Thus he deals with a number of figures not directly connected with the history of SF narrative, as well as with familiar ancestors such as Campanella, Wilkins, Godwin, Cyrano de

Bergerac, and Voltaire. Guthke's European perspective provides a broader context for Nicolson [8-97] and the relevant chapters of Bailey [8-15] and Philmus [8-104]. Eaton Award, 1992

8-65.   Harbottle, Philip, and Stephen Holland. **Vultures of the Void: A History of British Science Fiction Publishing, 1946–1956.** Borgo, 1993.
A fascinating account of an appalling and relatively unexplored chapter in SF history: the postwar British pulp industry, which took advantage of the shortage of popular fiction brought on by paper rationing by issuing large amounts of subliterary genre paperbacks and magazines, usually based on American models and commissioned from poorly paid hack writers working under ridiculous deadlines. A few writers, such as John Russell Fearn, produced considerable bodies of work under these conditions, while more familiar names such as Clarke and Wyndham wrote for the American magazines of the time. Interpolated memoirs from Ted Carnell, Gordon Landsborough, E. C. Tubb, Kenneth Bulmer, and others lend authenticity to this strange history, which focuses more on the industry than on individual works. A valuable complement to more standard histories of the genre.

8-66.   Hartwell, David. **Age of Wonders: Exploring the World of Science Fiction.** Walker, 1984. Recommended ed.: McGraw-Hill, 1985.
Hartwell is arguably the most influential SF book editor of the 1970s and 1980s, and his chatty general introduction to the field mixes a sophisticated insider's understanding with astute critical and academic judgments. Although occasionally self-indulgent, Hartwell's is one of the few guidebooks that does not get weighed down in a mechanical recitation of SF history. Following three chapters on aspects of SF's appeal and readership, he explores common myths about the genre (escapism, predictions of the future) and devotes individual chapters to fandom, the New Wave, and academic criticism. A brief bibliography of critical works is included, and the 1985 paperback adds reading lists and suggestions for developing a course in SF. A more academic treatment of many of the same themes is Stableford's *Sociology of Science Fiction* [8-133].

*8-67.   Hillegas, Mark R(obert). **The Future as Nightmare: H. G. Wells and the Anti-Utopians.** Oxford Univ. Press, 1967.
Despite the considerable body of more recent scholarship on the topics covered here, Hillegas's pioneering text remains significant for having cogently defined the anti-utopian tradition and its connections to SF. In addition to Wells, Forster, Čapek, Zamiatin, Huxley, Orwell, and Lewis,

Hillegas discusses Bradbury, Pohl and Kornbluth, Clarke, and Vonnegut. Compare Walsh [8-141].

8-68. Holdstock, Robert. **Encyclopedia of Science Fiction.** Octopus, 1978.

Neither a reference work nor a true history of the genre, Holdstock's heavily illustrated collection of essays by various British contributors is more comparable to Gunn's *Alternate Worlds* [8-63] or Ash's *Visual Encyclopedia of Science Fiction* [11-2] than to Clute and Nicholls' comprehensive *Encyclopedia of Science Fiction* [7-22]. The essays are generally informed and lively, however, with some useful insights.

8-69. Hume, Kathryn. **Fantasy and Mimesis: Responses to Reality in Western Literature.** Methuen, 1984.

A broad-ranging and highly intelligent argument for the proposition that the fantastic—including SF—represents a historically significant "counter-tradition" to mimesis in literature from the Icelandic sagas to the present. Rejecting the notion that fantasy constitutes a simple genre, Hume makes such a compelling case that the book should be consulted by anyone interested in SF theory and history, or the relation of SF to other modes of the fantastic. The authors discussed range from John Barth, Jorge Luis Borges, Thomas Pynchon, and Franz Kafka to Vonnegut, Calvino, Le Guin, Herbert, Heinlein, and Wells. Eaton Award, 1986

8-70. Huntington, John. **Rationalizing Genius: Ideological Strategies in the Classic American Science Fiction Short Story.** Rutgers Univ. Press, 1989.

Huntington's ambitious attempt to outline the fundamental ideologies of three decades of American SF by analyzing the stories in a single anthology—Volume I of *The Science Fiction Hall of Fame* [3-223]—is valuable chiefly for his intelligent and perceptive readings of such relatively unexamined "classics" as Tom Godwin's "The Cold Equations" or Kornbluth's "The Marching Morons." The implicit argument that an anthology tabulated by a single vote of SFWA members in 1968 can serve as a kind of Rosetta Stone for the genre raises a number of problems, however, since the final selection was further skewed by choices made by the editor, Robert Silverberg, and since it necessarily ignores historical, editorial, and literary contexts. Huntington is aware of this, and relates the stories to other relevant texts. His chapter on "Reading Popular Genres" is especially valuable. Informed readers will find Huntington's analyses often illuminating, although novices may occasionally be misled.

8-71.   Ketterer, David. **Canadian Science Fiction and Fantasy.** Indiana Univ. Press, 1992.

In what is almost inevitably the definitive treatment of its subject, Ketterer offers a broad overview of English and French Canadian authors who have written SF or fantasy, although many of them (such as A. E. van Vogt and Gordon Dickson) spent much of their careers elsewhere, and Ketterer finally acknowledges that "Canadian-ness" is marginal to most of the major authors he discusses, which include Margaret Atwood, Phyllis Gotlieb, and Charles de Lint. The avowedly narrow focus of the study disguises some broadly useful insights—such as a distinction between "hermetic" and "consequential" imaginary worlds—and the treatment of French Canadian SF uncovers a surprisingly rich and little-known tradition. A very informative study, which is one of the first national histories of SF. (Another is Robert Mathews' *Japanese Science Fiction* [8-85].)

*8-72.   Ketterer, David. **New Worlds for Old: The Apocalyptic Imagination, Science Fiction, and American Literature.** Indiana Univ. Press, 1974.

In one of the first rigorous attempts to establish a theoretical context for science fiction, Ketterer argues that "apocalyptic" literature differs from both mimetic and fantastic literature by creating credible imaginary worlds that lead to the "metaphorical destruction" of the reader's real world. He sees this as a broad tradition in American literature (Poe, Melville, Charles Brockden Brown, Mark Twain), whose most significant modern manifestation is SF. Individual chapters treat Le Guin, Lem, Vonnegut, and several SF themes, with substantial discussion of works by Aldiss, Balmer and Wylie, John Boyd, Bradbury, Dick, Heinlein, Sturgeon, Jack London, Edward Bellamy, Walter M. Miller, Jr., and others. An influential work whose theory bears comparison with that of Kathryn Hume [8-69].

8-73.   Klaić, Dragan. **The Plot of the Future: Utopia and Dystopia in Modern Drama.** Univ. of Michigan Press, 1992.

In what is virtually the only extended study of SF and utopian drama, Klaić identifies nearly 50 plays from several countries that focus on portrayals of future societies. Of the playwrights discussed, only George Bernard Shaw and Vladimir Mayakovsky meet the author's criteria as utopian writers, and some of the plays covered, such as John Bowen's *After the Rain*, are as significant for their SF content as for dystopian ideas. Klaić's introductory history of speculation about the future offers little that is new, but his discussion of individual plays under various thematic groupings (for example, "The Menace of Science," "Decay, Catastrophe, and Survival") is quite original. Klaić omits most absurdist and surrealist drama and never quite develops an overall theory of futuristic drama, but his book is invaluable as a source of relatively little-known plays relevant to speculative literature.

8-74. Knight, Damon. **In Search of Wonder: Essays on Modern Science Fiction.** Advent, 1967. 2nd ed., rev. and enl.

A collection of 27 essays, almost all book reviews that appeared in fanzines and *The Magazine of Fantasy and Science Fiction* between 1951–1960. Along with James Blish [8-13, 8-14, 8-27], Knight was among the most influential of writer-critics who sought to impose rigorous and coherent critical standards on the field during one of its most formative decades, often using a review as a platform for broader issues. His piece on van Vogt, for example, led to a serious reassessment of that author's entire reputation. While many of the works he discusses are now nearly forgotten, his insights often remain striking, and these essays helped establish a tradition that has since been continued by Budrys [8-31] and Spinrad [8-130].

8-75. Knight, Damon, ed. **Turning Points: Essays on the Art of Science Fiction.** Harper, 1977.

Until the 1970s, SF theory and criticism was pretty much confined to occasional essays and lectures by practicing authors. Knight's worthwhile intention here was to preserve the most significant of these critical pieces in a historical anthology of SF criticism. He has assembled 21 essays originally published between 1947 and 1973 and added two of his own, on SF definitions and the writing and selling of SF. Other contributors are a mix of familiar SF names (Heinlein, Asimov, Aldiss, Campbell, Poul Anderson, Keith Laumer, Bester, Sturgeon, Clarke, McKenna, Russ), mainstream writers on SF (Huxley, Amis, C. S. Lewis) and critics (H. Bruce Franklin, Pierre Versins). Primarily of historical interest; Nicholls's *Science Fiction at Large* [8-95] and Bretnor's *Science Fiction, Today and Tomorrow* [8-29] are similar collections.

8-76. Kumar, Krishan. **Utopia and Anti-Utopia in Modern Times.** Basil Blackwell, 1987.

This lengthy work by a respected scholar is the most thorough social and cultural analysis of modern utopian literature to date. Following in the tradition of Frank and Fritzie Manuel's monumental *Utopian Thought in the Western World* (1979), Kumar focuses more on social and political philosophy than on literary form and value, often citing such thinkers as Herbert Marcuse and David Riesman to provide a context for discussions of individual texts. The first section of the book offers a historical overview of the development of utopian and anti-utopian traditions through the 19th century; the second section examines Bellamy's *Looking Backward* [1-8], Wells's *A Modern Utopia* [1-101], Huxley's *Brave New World* [2-256], Orwell's *Nineteen Eighty-Four* [3-140], and Skinner's *Walden Two* [3-166]; the concluding section includes discussions of Huxley's *Island* (1962), Vonnegut's *Player Piano* [3-191], and Le Guin's *The Dispossessed* [4-252]. A much more comprehensive study than either Berger [8-25] or Walsh [8-141]. A briefer summary of Kumar's ideas on utopianism, with less reference to SF, is his *Utopianism* (1991).

8-77.   Le Guin, Ursula K. **Dancing at the Edge of the World: Thoughts on Words, Women, Places.** Grove Press, 1989.

In a more broad-ranging collection than *The Language of the Night* [8-78], Le Guin assembles 32 essays and speeches and 17 book reviews on topics such as literature, travel, feminism, and social responsibility. While relatively few essays are obviously about SF, Le Guin offers insights into utopianism ("A Non-Euclidean View of California as a Cold Place to Be"), narrative theory ("The Carrier Bag Theory of Fiction," "Some Thoughts on Narrative"), her role as an SF writer ("The Space Crone"), and the TV-movie version of her novel *The Lathe of Heaven* (1971). Among the authors treated in her reviews are Calvino, C. S. Lewis, Doris Lessing, and Mervyn Peake. Le Guin is as graceful an essayist as novelist, and this collection offers a great deal of wisdom and insight. HN, 1990

*8-78.   Le Guin, Ursula K. **The Language of the Night: Essays on Fantasy and Science Fiction.** Harper, 1992. Rev. ed.

Originally published in 1979 and reissued with corrections and notes in England in 1989 (the 1992 edition adds a useful Le Guin bibliography by L. W. Currey), this collection of essays, speeches, and introductions contains some of the most widely discussed commentary by a modern SF writer, such as "Dreams Must Explain Themselves," "From Elfland to Poughkeepsie," "Science Fiction and Mrs. Brown," and "Is Gender Necessary?" (to which Le Guin adds an extensive gloss for this edition). Le Guin is as elegant in her essays as in her fiction, and the volume is useful to all SF scholars, and indispensable to students of Le Guin. HN, 1980

*8-79.   Lefanu, Sarah. **In the Chinks of the World Machine: Feminism and Science Fiction.** The Women's Press, 1988. U.S. title: *Feminism and Science Fiction.*

Informed by both current feminist theory and a broad familiarity with both U.S. and European SF by women, this is perhaps the most coherent exposition of feminist themes in SF. The first section explores such themes as amazon heroines, feminist utopias and dystopias, romantic love, and treatments of authority in women's SF; while the second consists of more extended discussions of the work of Tiptree, Le Guin, Charnas, and Russ. Although her theoretical observations are persuasive, Lefanu's greatest strength is in her readings of individual texts, including rarely discussed works by Marion Zimmer Bradley, Jayge Carr, Angela Carter, Sally Miller Gearhart, Gwyneth Jones, Vonda McIntyre, Marge Piercy, Josephine Saxton, and Pamela Zoline. Compare Barr's *Feminist Fabulation* [8-19].

*8-80. Lem, Stanislaw. **Microworlds: Writings on Science Fiction and Fantasy.** Harcourt, 1985. Ed. by Franz Rottensteiner.
Ten essays by Poland's leading SF writer include an autobiographical piece (which also discusses Lem's writing methods), individual discussions of Dick, Borges, the Strugatski brothers, and Todorov's theory of the fantastic, and SF themes and structures. As a critic, Lem is best known for his often stringent treatments of SF tropes; his most important pieces here cover time travel, cosmology, structuralism and SF, and the possibilities of the genre (which Lem sees as often betrayed or unrealized). Lem makes a passionate case for the social and philosophical responsibilities of literature, and his perspective is a valuable one. In his introduction, Rottensteiner relates these essays to Lem's other writings in literary theory.

8-81. Lundwall, Sam. **Science Fiction: An Illustrated History.** Grosset, 1978.
One of Europe's most knowledgeable critics and historians of SF offers a popular international survey which, because of its coverage of untranslated European SF, serves as a useful supplement to Gunn's *Alternate Worlds* [8-62] and Aldiss and Wingrove [8-5]. Sometimes Lundwall's claims for early European SF are a bit exaggerated, however, and a chapter of this book reprinted in *Foundation* 34 (Autumn 1985) brought a stinging rebuttal from Sam Moskowitz in *Foundation* 36 (Summer 1986). Some of the material here is included in Lundwall's earlier brief survey, *Science Fiction: What It's All About* (1971).

*8-82. Malmgren, Carl. **Worlds Apart: Narratology of Science Fiction.** Indiana Univ. Press, 1991.
An important if sometimes densely written study that argues that SF is better defined by the worlds it creates than by its narrative conventions. Malmgren first divides SF into "speculative" or "extrapolative" modes, then shows how representative texts of each mode treat four major types of SF narrative: the alien encounter, the alternate society (utopian or

dystopian works in which society, but not the world, is changed), the gadget story, and the alternate world. A separate chapter discusses science fantasy, which doesn't really fit into the scheme. Like all typologies, Malmgren's is debatable, but he offers insightful readings of works by Wells, Lem, Silverberg, Ian Watson, Wilhelm, Russ, Clarke, Ballard, the Strugatskys, Leiber, Benford and Brin, and Gene Wolfe.

*8-83.   Malzberg, Barry. **The Engines of the Night: Science Fiction in the Eighties.** Doubleday, 1982.
Malzberg's reputation as SF's most articulate depressive is borne out by many of the 36 essays collected here, many revised from earlier appearances and none having to do with SF in the 1980s. Although he covers a varied list of topics (sex in SF, SF of the fifties, academia and SF, SF stories about SF) and includes tributes to John W. Campbell, Jr., Cornell Woolrich, and Mark Clifton, his recurrent theme is the plight of the writer and the often destructive effects of the SF industry. Malzberg's iconoclastic wit has often gotten him in trouble, but in retrospect his portrait of the profession of SF, and how it often managed to produce masterworks under the most unlikely conditions, is invaluable and often brilliant. An interesting contrast is Gunn's *Inside Science Fiction* [8-63]. HN, 1983; *Locus* award, 1983

*8-84.   Manlove, Colin. **Science Fiction: Ten Explorations.** Kent State Univ. Press, 1986.
Manlove is a Scottish scholar best known for a series of penetrating studies of fantasy (*Modern Fantasy: Five Studies*, 1975; *The Impulse of Fantasy Literature*, 1983; *Christian Fantasy*, 1992). He sees in SF a unique kind of energy, which he describes as a desire for "more life," and explores this through intelligent and graceful readings of ten representative texts. Some are recognized classics—Asimov's *Foundation* series [3-12], Herbert's *Dune* [4-207], Farmer's first Riverworld novel [4-165], Clarke's *Rendezvous With Rama* [4-109]—but the selections from Pohl, Aldiss, Silverberg, and Simak are not among the authors' best-known works. The most recent works discussed are Attanasio's *Radix* [4-22] and Wolfe's *Book of the New Sun* [4-510]. Manlove sees questions of identity and self in all these books; while this gives his readings some thematic coherence, he does not offer an overall theory of the genre, claiming that in the face of such inventiveness, all criticism can do is describe.

8-85.   Matthew, Robert. **Japanese Science Fiction.** Routledge, 1989.
The first book-length study in English of an extensive, and largely independent, tradition of Japanese SF dating back to the 19th century. Matthew, an Australian professor and translator, shows little familiarity

with other SF scholarship and depends heavily on plot summaries, but such summaries are valuable since many of the works discussed are not available in English. After a historical survey of both fiction and critical attitudes, six chapters deal with characteristic themes of Japanese SF. The themes themselves demonstrate some key ways in which Japanese SF is different: boredom and satiety, advertising and media, economics and trade, "human concerns and values," relations between generations, and sex. Additional chapters discuss religious and ethical concerns and such current anxieties as regimentation, alienation, and the aftermath of the bomb. An extremely useful national-literature study.

8-86. McCaffery, Larry, ed. **Storming the Reality Studio: A Casebook of Cyberpunk and Postmodern Science Fiction.** Duke Univ. Press, 1992.
An odd amalgam of 29 stories or novel excerpts and 20 critical or theoretical essays, some of which appeared in a special cyberpunk issue of *Mississippi Review* in 1988. The collection's main value is as a work of criticism, since many of the brief fictional selections illustrate particular points in the essays. The overall goal is to provide an ambitious theoretical, cultural, and historical context for the cyberpunk movement, ranging from Mary Shelley to MTV. The nonfiction includes excerpts from Jacques Derrida, Fredric Jameson, and Jean François Lyotard; essays by Joan Gordon, Veronica Hollinger, Brooks Landon, Bruce Sterling, and Tom Maddox; an interview with William Gibson; and a very strange piece by Timothy Leary. Compare with Slusser and Shippey's somewhat more focused *Fiction 2000* [8-175].

8-87. McGuire, Patrick. **Red Stars: Political Aspects of Soviet Science Fiction.** UMI Research Press, 1985.
This brief study, revised from a 1977 dissertation, focuses on the political and social context of Soviet science fiction published between 1923 and 1976, complete with extensive bibliographies and six tables showing such things as the number of works published over the years and SF preferences among various population groups. Although McGuire does not focus on literary theory or offer much evaluative commentary on individual works (the only authors treated in much detail are the Strugatskys and Ivan Efremov), he makes useful connections with relevant American SF in his extensive notes. His study is generally more informative and current than John Glad's *Extrapolations From Dystopia: A Critical Study of Soviet Science Fiction* (Kingston, 1982), a dated revision of a 1970 dissertation.

*8-88. Meyers, Walter E. **Aliens and Linguists: Language Study and Science Fiction.** Univ. of Georgia Press, 1980.
A witty and informed study of languages and linguistic evolution as por-

trayed in SF, with substantial treatment of fantasy languages such as Tolkien's elvish as well. Meyers is widely familiar with popular Anglo-American SF as well as with linguistics, and his study demonstrates the crucial importance of communication to many SF narratives. Some of the more enjoyable chapters excoriate famous dumb ideas like implanted knowledge and automatic translators, while others deal with SF's notions of linguistic change. The entry on language in the Nicholls and Clute *Encyclopedia* [7-22] offers updated material on some of the same themes.

8-89.   Mogen, David. **Wilderness Visions: Science Fiction Westerns, Vol. 1.** Borgo, 1982.
A brief but important discussion of the frontier theme in SF—not of westerns with SF elements—based on the author's 1977 dissertation. Following two chapters that summarize the history and prophetic aspects of the frontier myth, Mogen examines works by Heinlein, Asimov, Pohl, and Kornbluth. Though Mogen's is the only extended study of what would seem a major SF theme, the book ends rather abruptly; an expanded second edition was published in 1994 and added three chapters. Its more accurate subtitle is *The Western Theme in Science Fiction Literature.*

8-90.   Moskowitz, Sam. **The Immortal Storm: A History of Science Fiction Fandom.** Atlanta Science Fiction Organization Press, 1954. Recommended ed.: Hyperion, 1974.
Famous for its hyperbolic title, Moskowitz's largely personal and autobiographical account (originally serialized in *Fantasy Commentator* beginning in 1945) is in fact largely confined to the meetings and squabbles of a handful of 1930s East Coast fans whose efforts eventually led to the first World Science Fiction Convention of 1939. Obsessively detailed and deadly serious, Moskowitz's book reveals almost nothing about SF literature, but is an important source for the study of that passionate and more-or-less organized body of SF readership that calls itself "fandom." An equally anecdotal but far more complete account is Warner's *All Our Yesterdays* [8-142]. Special Hugo plaque, 1955

8-91.   Moskowitz, Sam. **Science Fiction in Old San Francisco, Vol. 1: History of the Movement from 1854 to 1890.** Donald M. Grant, 1980.
Moskowitz, a devoted fan historian whose early collections of author profiles and theme essays (*Explorers of the Infinite*, 1963; *Seekers of Tomorrow*, 1966) for a time served as almost the only widely available references on SF history, has also pioneered in resurrecting little-known aspects of early SF history in anthologies such as *Under the Moons of Mars* [1-71], *Science*

Fiction by Gaslight [1-70], and the collection of stories by Robert Duncan Milne [1-64], which is the companion volume to this history. Milne was the chief figure in a group of writers who contributed hundreds of fantastic tales, many of them SF, to San Francisco newspapers in the late 19th century, influencing Ambrose Bierce among others. While Moskowitz's enthusiasm occasionally gets out of hand, his original research here uncovers a genuinely forgotten chapter in SF history.

8-92. Moskowitz, Sam. **Strange Horizons: The Spectrum of Science Fiction.** Scribner, 1976.

Eleven essays, ten revised from earlier magazine appearances, tracing a variety of themes and movements in SF. Although Moskowitz characteristically disdains theory, his broad knowledge of lesser-known works of early SF gives considerable reference value to his treatment of such topics as anti-Semitism, civil rights, religion, matriarchal societies, crime, psychiatry, war, and birth control; other essays discuss Charles Fort, Virgil Finlay, and juvenile SF. Some of these themes are also treated in Carter [8-34].

8-93. Moylan, Tom. **Demand the Impossible: Science Fiction and the Utopian Imagination.** Methuen, 1986.

A thoughtful and intelligent analysis of what Moylan calls the "critical utopia," which he sees as having emerged in the 1970s to lend new life to a tradition earlier characterized by "totalizing blueprints" and dystopias. Critical utopias, represented by extended discussions of Russ's *The Female Man* [4-375], Le Guin's *The Dispossessed* [4-252], Piercy's *Woman on the Edge of Time* [4-330], and Delany's *Triton* [4-132], question both the utopian tradition and their own assumptions. Though some might be put off by Moylan's occasionally rigid Marxist-feminist approach, his readings of these works and his general conclusions constitute a provocative attempt to link modern SF to the utopian tradition. Compare Bartkowski [8-21].

8-94. Myers, Robert E., ed. **The Intersection of Science Fiction and Philosophy: Critical Studies.** Greenwood, 1983.

A collection of 17 essays, arranged in eight thematic sections (for example, "Space-Time and Time Travel"), in which philosophers and scholars of other disciplines seek to explore various philosophical issues as treated in SF. Each piece is followed by a list of recommended readings, and in all some 50 SF authors are touched upon. Most of the essays provide little meaningful criticism, although those by William Schuyler, Adam Frisch, Joann Cob, and Bart Thurber are especially insightful. A similar collection, Nicholas D. Smith's *Philosophers Look at Science Fiction* (Nelson-Hall, 1982), is more heavily oriented toward academic philosophy.

*8-95.   Nicholls, Peter, ed. **Science Fiction at Large.** Gollancz, 1976. U.K. title: *Explorations of the Marvelous* (1978). Recommended ed.: Harper, 1977.

Eleven essays derived from a series of lectures delivered at London's Institute of Contemporary Arts in 1975. Some, such as Le Guin's "Science Fiction and Mrs. Brown," have become classics while others, notably Dick's "Man, Android, and Machine," are indispensable for students of the author involved. Other contributors include SF and fantasy authors Brunner, Harrison, Disch, Alan Garner, and Robert Sheckley, and scholars of SF or related fields Edward de Bono, John Taylor, Alvin Toffler, and Nicholls himself. An excellent overview of major concerns in SF for the general reader, which makes for an interesting comparison with the similar (but much earlier) collection of public lectures *The Science Fiction Novel: Imagination and Social Criticism* [8-127].

8-96.   Nicholls, Peter, David Langford, and Brian Stableford. **The Science in Science Fiction.** Knopf, 1983.

A thorough popular account of scientific principles and concepts underlying SF, replete with enough color illustrations and diagrams to give it value as a popular science book. Twelve chapters cover such topics as space travel, energy sources, aliens, imaginary science, time travel, future wars and nuclear holocausts, computers and robots, biological adaptations, dystopian societies, mental powers, cult science (such as UFOs), and common SF errors. Much of the text is an extension and popularization of similar topics covered in Clute and Nicholls's *Encyclopedia* [7-22]. A bibliography lists relevant fiction and nonfiction for each chapter. While some of the cutting-edge science described in the book is inevitably dated, the authors generally show a sophisticated knowledge of SF and effectively relate their discussions to a variety of fictional texts. Much preferable to Amit and Maggie Goswami, *The Cosmic Dancers: Exploring the Physics of Science Fiction* (Harper, 1983), which is more a popular account of modern physics than an exploration of SF.

8-97.   Nicolson, Marjorie Hope. **Voyages to the Moon.** Macmillan, 1948.

An influential early study of SF prehistory, roughly contemporary with Bailey [8-15] but more oriented toward traditional literary history and far more narrowly focused. Nicolson focuses principally on English-language works of the 17th and 18th centuries and adds a final chapter touching on Poe, Verne, Wells, and Lewis. Illustrated, with primary and secondary bibliographies (the latter now badly dated). A comparable, but more popular work, is Roger Lancelyn Green's *Into Other Worlds: Space Flight in Fiction From Lucian to Lewis* (1958).

8-98. Palumbo, Donald, ed. **Eros in the Mind's Eye: Sexuality and the Fantastic in Art and Film.** Greenwood, 1986.
Eighteen original essays on erotic themes in fantastic art and film, intended as a companion piece to *Erotic Universe* [8-99]. The contributions tend to emphasize films (more than 70 are discussed), but include discussions of more than 50 fantasy illustrators, mainstream artists from the medieval period to the present, and even SF fanzines. A secondary bibliography, compiled by contributors, is included, as well as reference lists of films and artworks.

8-99. Palumbo, Donald, ed. **Erotic Universe: Sexuality and Fantastic Literature.** Greenwood, 1986.
Fifteen essays, most originally delivered at various conferences, organized according to theory, themes, feminist views, and fanzines (which consists of only one essay, on *Star Trek* fanzines). Most of the topics covered are relatively unexplored; James Riemer's essay on homosexuality and Judith Bogert's on sexual comedy are especially unusual. Among the authors treated at some length are Angela Carter, Russ, Le Guin, McCaffrey, Farmer, and Sturgeon. A seven-part bibliography and filmography includes a useful annotated section of primary texts. An unusual and readable collection.

8-100. Panshin, Alexei. **SF in Dimension: A Book of Explorations.** Advent, 1980. Rev. and enl. edition.
A collection of 22 essays from 1969–1980, ranging from broadly theoretical pieces on the nature of SF to somewhat dated book reviews. Authors or editors discussed in some detail include Heinlein, Anderson, Aldiss, Asimov, Clarke, Campbell, Gernsback, Leiber, Cordwainer Smith, van Vogt, Weinbaum, and Zelazny. Mostly of historical interest, since Panshin's major ideas are developed at much greater length in *The World Beyond the Hill* [8-101].

*8-101. Panshin, Alexei, and Cory Panshin. **The World Beyond the Hill: Science Fiction and the Quest for Transcendence.** Jeremy P. Tarcher, 1989.
The authors set out to trace a history of SF as a modern myth of transcendence, from the end of witchcraft trials in England in 1685 through the publication of Asimov's "The Mule" in 1945. They provide little scholar-

ship on myth or intellectual history, citing only Joseph Campbell and two books on Sufism in a tiny bibliography; no secondary sources are indexed. But if their scholarly thesis is finally weak and unconvincing, their contribution to the history of "golden age" SF is invaluable. Fully two-thirds of this huge book is virtually a story-by-story analysis of the development of modern magazine SF, mostly through Campbell's editorship of *Astounding*. The Panshins discuss the stories intelligently, showing in almost obsessive detail Campbell's role in working with such authors as Heinlein, Asimov, van Vogt, and Williamson. As a general history, this is far less complete than Aldiss and Wingrove [8-5], and is often eccentric in its judgments. As a microhistorical portrait of a key period in SF's development, it is unparalleled. HW, 1990

8-102.   Parrinder, Patrick. **Science Fiction: A Critical Guide.** Longmans, 1979.

Twelve academic essays, with notes and bibliographies, focusing mostly on British and European science fiction and covering such topics as early SF history, Verne, Wells, the utopian tradition, SF editors, the scientific worldview, the cold war, religion, characterization, and post-1960 American SF. The essays are generally of high quality and some—such as the Raymond Williams essay on utopian themes—reflect a broad understanding of social and political theory as well as SF. Compare Clareson's *Many Futures, Many Worlds* [8-35] and Garnett and Ellis [8-60].

8-103.   Parrinder, Patrick. **Science Fiction: Its Criticism and Teaching.** Methuen, 1980.

A brief and cogent introduction to SF for the student and teacher. An introductory chapter discusses various definitions and types of SF, from the scientific romance to the New Wave, and subsequent chapters discuss the sociology of SF; SF as romance, fable, or epic; the language of SF, and a possible SF course, with valuable insights on the issue of canon-formation. Particular attention is given to Clarke, Delany, Dick, Heinlein, Lem, Vonnegut, and Wells. Neither oversimplified nor arcane, this is an excellent text, with notes and annotated bibliography, for the beginning student or teacher of the genre. Also annotated as [13-12].

8-104.   Philmus, Robert. **Into the Unknown: The Evolution of Science Fiction From Francis Godwin to H. G. Wells.** Univ. of California Press, 1970.

A more scholarly and current survey of the English prehistory of SF treated more synoptically in Bailey [8-15], and the first general study of SF history to come from a university press. Following a long introductory chapter discussing SF as myth and as rhetorical strategy, Philmus covers important works by Godwin, Swift, Aphra Behn, Samuel Butler, Defoe, Bulwer-Lytton, Robert Louis Stevenson, Verne, and Wells. A partially annotated bibliography is now superseded by Bleiler [8-26], and an introduction added to the 1983 paperback notes the growth of scholarship since 1970. Compare the broader European perspective in Alkon [8-6].

8-105. Pierce, Hazel Beasley. **A Literary Symbiosis: Science Fiction/ Fantasy Mystery.** Greenwood, 1983.
A somewhat confused and already dated account of the relations of SF with mystery and detective fiction, valuable primarily for the texts identified and plot summaries. Pierce takes advantage of relatively little scholarship on either detective fiction or SF, but isolates an important area for research in cross-genre studies.

8-106. Pierce, John J(eremy). **Foundations of Science Fiction: A Study in Imagination and Evolution.** Greenwood, 1987.
Pierce, a critic and professional editor, originally intended his massive study of SF to be published in one volume titled *Imagination and Evolution*. The four volumes that eventually emerged constitute an ambitious attempt to write a popular but well-documented history of the genre organized along thematic rather than strictly chronological lines. The overall thesis seems to be an answer to Aldiss and Wingrove's gothic-based history of the genre [8-5]; Pierce sees SF instead as an evolving fictional portrayal of the scientific worldview. The first volume covers the familiar territory of Plato, Lucian, early utopianists, Verne, Robida, Victorian future war tales and interplanetary voyages, Rosny, Wells, and Lasswitz; and offers useful discussions of imaginary worlds from Burroughs to Herbert, space opera from Hamilton to *Star Wars*, and anti-utopian and dystopian traditions. Although he relies heavily on secondary sources, his study is a far more complete version of "official" SF history than, for example, that of Gunn [8-62].

8-107. Pierce, John J(eremy). **Great Themes of Science Fiction: A Study in Imagination and Evolution.** Greenwood, 1987.
The second volume of Pierce's study identifies eight key themes in SF—aliens and alien worlds, supermen and mutations, eternal or extended life, men like gods (and vice versa), artificial intelligence and robots, future cities, future wars, and disasters. A final chapter concerns works at the margins of SF, in Pierce's view, such as parallel universe tales or tales

with satirical or allegorical intent. A wide variety of texts and films is invoked, with particularly good discussions of works by Anderson, Asimov, Aleksandr Beliaev, Clement, Farmer, Heinlein, Leinster, Niven, and Wells.

8-108.   Pierce, John J(eremy). When World Views Collide: A Study in Imagination and Evolution. Greenwood, 1989.

Pierce's third volume sets out to explore "science fiction as a way of defining and delimiting humanity and human values." It begins with a discussion of the Wellsian tradition in Clarke and Asimov, then treats such "anti-Wellsians" as C. S. Lewis, Walter M. Miller, and Brian Aldiss. Subsequent chapters cover Simak and Sturgeon, social Darwinism in Heinlein and Budrys, the literary experiments of the New Wave and Delany, the protest fiction of Ellison and some feminist writers, Soviet writers, the ideological fiction of Brunner and Ayn Rand, and the "synthetists" Cordwainer Smith and Le Guin. Pierce's odd juxtapositions are often enlightening, but this volume reveals more clearly than the others the consistent "Wellsian" rationalist bias of his overall study, and his impatience with literary matters, or works that he sees as betraying the essential mission of SF. A brief afterword touches upon cyberpunk. As in all his volumes, the notes, bibliographies, and filmographies are extensive. A concluding volume, *Odd Genre*, was published in 1994 (not seen).

*8-109.   Pringle, David. Science Fiction: The 100 Best Novels—An English-Language Selection, 1949–1984. Xanadu, 1985.

A series of two-page essays on works the author considers to be seminal to modern SF, from Orwell's *Nineteen Eighty-Four* to Gibson's *Neuromancer*. Pringle often mentions other works—including short stories and collections—in annotating his selections, and the selections themselves are intelligent and provocative. The guide is especially useful for libraries and those new to the genre, but is likely to be more fully enjoyed by knowledgeable readers who might quibble with some of Pringle's more unexpected selections, such as novels by Harness, Pat Frank, Bob Shaw, Mack Reynolds, Damien Broderick, and John Calvin Batchelor. A companion volume is *Modern Fantasy: The Hundred Best Novels, an English-Language Selection, 1946-1987* (1988).

8-110.   Puschmann-Nalenz, Barbara. Science Fiction and Postmodern Fiction: A Genre Study. Peter Lang, 1992. Trans. of *Science Fiction und ihre Grenzbereiche* (1986).

Although dated both in its selection of primary texts and its discussions of previous scholarship in SF—almost nothing later than the early 1970s is discussed—this theoretical study nevertheless contains some interesting insights on the parallels and contrast between genre SF and more "literary" postmodernist works. Authors covered include Pynchon, Brunner, Aldiss, Ballard, Borges, Lem, and Vonnegut. A more coherent approach, not specifically concerned with SF, is Lance Olsen's *Ellipse of Uncertainty: An Introduction to Postmodern Fantasy* (1987).

8-111. Rabkin, Eric S. **The Fantastic in Literature.** Princeton Univ. Press, 1976.
A lucid theory of the fantastic that arranges relevant genres, including SF, along a continuum according to the extent to which basic "ground rules" are reversed in the fictional world. Rabkin's study is useful for the manner in which it provides a theoretical and historical context for fantastic works, and even though it does not exclusively concern SF and focuses more on theory than analysis of individual texts, it includes insightful discussions of works by Clarke, Asimov, Moorcock, Sturgeon, Wells, and others.

8-112. Rabkin, Eric S., Martin H. Greenberg, and Joseph D. Olander, eds. **The End of the World.** Southern Illinois Univ. Press, 1983.
A collection of six original essays, with notes and a brief overall bibliography, on the various ways SF writers have handled this subject. Contributors are Gary K. Wolfe, Robert Plank, Robert Galbreath, Brian Stableford, and W. Warren Wagar, whose two contributions appear in somewhat shorter form in his *Terminal Visions* [8-140], which in general is a more sustained and coherent approach to the same topic. Nevertheless, these essays offer many useful insights and discussions of works by Clarke, Blish, Wylie, Wyndham, Shiel, Coppel, George R. Stewart, Edmund Cooper, and others.

8-113. Rabkin, Eric S., Martin H. Greenberg and Joseph D. Olander, eds. **No Place Else: Explorations in Utopian and Dystopian Fiction.** Southern Illinois Univ. Press, 1983.
Southern Illinois Univ. Press's ambitious Alternatives series included collections of fiction, reprints of famous magazine issues, papers from various Eaton Conferences (see "Conference Proceedings") and occasional volumes of original essays, including this one and *The End of the World* [8-112]. Most of the essays here consider individual works: *The Coming Race* [1-61], *Erewhon* [1-19], *We* [2-157], *Last and First Men* [2-119], *Brave New World* [2-56], *Nineteen Eighty-Four* [3-140], *The Shape of Things to Come* [2-140], *Player Piano* [3-191], *Lord of the Flies* (1954). Notable are Merritt

Abrash on Silverberg's *The World Inside* [4-416], James Bittner on *The Dispossessed* [4-252]. Little overall theory or context is provided, and the essays are of uneven quality. More coherent studies of the topic include those by Kumar [8-76] and Berger [8-25].

8-114.   Reilly, Robert, ed. **The Transcendent Adventure: Studies of Religion in Science Fiction/Fantasy.** Greenwood, 1984.
An uneven but useful collection of 15 essays, together with primary and secondary bibliographies, on the ways in which SF and fantasy writers use religious themes. Four essays attempt to draw general conclusions about religious and ethical themes in SF; the rest focus on such individual authors as Blish, Lewis, Dick, Farmer, Herbert, Miller, Lessing, Tolkien, Zelazny, and Walter Tevis. Although the essays offer little continuity in terms of a developing argument, they cover a far broader range of texts than either of the more focused studies by Sammons [8-123] or by Frederick A. Kreuziger's *The Religion of Science Fiction* (1986).

8-115.   Riley, Dick, ed. **Critical Encounters: Writers and Themes in Science Fiction.** Ungar, 1978.
The first volume in Ungar's Recognitions series, like many relatively early essay collections, tries to appeal both to fans and academics with nine fairly general essays on familiar topics and authors. The most useful contributions are David Samuelson on *Stranger in a Strange Land* [3-91], Timothy O'Reilly on *Dune* [4-207], and George A. Von Glahn on *The Einstein Intersection* [4-129]. Others cover Asimov, Bradbury, Clarke, Sturgeon, Le Guin, and women SF writers. Most of the material is superseded by later critical treatments, but the insights in the best essays still stand up. Compare Clareson's various collections, especially the Voices for the Future series [8-39].

8-116.   Roberts, Robin. **A New Species: Gender and Science in Science Fiction.** Univ. of Illinois Press, 1993.
While acknowledging the work of Rosinski [8-120], Barr [8-19], Albinski [8-1], and Lefanu [8-79], Roberts promises to add a significant new dimension to feminist studies of SF by covering both 19th-century SF and the pulp era; in fact her coverage of these periods is slight, including only two novels by Mary Shelley and one each by Bulwer-Lytton, Walter Besant, and H. G. Wells for the 19th century and only Philip José Farmer's "The Lovers" and four very minor stories from the early 1950s (apparently chosen on the basis of their cover illustrations) for the "pulp era," which Roberts misidentifies as the post-World War II period. Subsequent chap-

ters discuss feminist utopias, feminist SF, Doris Lessing, and postmodernism (which focuses on Slonczewski, Finch, Atwood, and Le Guin). Roberts offers some useful insights, despite her tendency to make generalizations based on an inadequate sampling of texts. Eleven illustrations complement the text, which is hampered by a very incomplete and unreliable index, not prepared by the author.

8-117. Roberts, Thomas J. **An Aesthetics of Junk Fiction.** Univ. of Georgia Press, 1990.

In one of the first general theories of popular fiction to appear since John Cawelti's *Adventure, Mystery, and Romance* (1976), Roberts divides literature into canonical, serious, "plain," and "junk," with observations about the readership and authorship of each. "Junk" readers, for example—who include SF readers—engage in "thick reading," in which each new text is measured against a wide familiarity with the genre, and in fact redefines the genre. Although his selection of terminology is unfortunate, his discussion of market and editorial forces weak, and his knowledge of SF critical theory deficient (his theory would benefit from some discussion of Delany's critical work), Roberts shows a greater sympathetic awareness of the genre than most general-purpose theorists of fiction and writes in a generally engaging and clear manner. Recommended for those interested in exploring SF in the broader context of commercial literature.

*8-118. Rose, Mark. **Alien Encounters: Anatomy of Science Fiction.** Harvard Univ. Press, 1981.

A brief but cogent theory of SF, which argues that the human-nonhuman encounter is the central paradigm of the genre. Following two introductory chapters that delimit the genre and identify this paradigm, he explores how it is developed in various ways in chapters titled "Space," "Time," "Machine," and "Monster." Few texts are analyzed in detail, although particular attention is paid to works by Asimov, Clarke, Dick, Heinlein, Lem, Stapledon, Verne, and Wells. Rose's theory is more provocative than definitive, but is elegantly developed, and bears comparison with Wolfe's *The Known and the Unknown* [8-145] and Malmgren's *Worlds Apart* [8-82]. Eaton Award, 1983

8-119. Rose, Mark, ed. **Science Fiction: A Collection of Critical Essays.** Prentice-Hall, 1976.

A pioneering but now somewhat dated collection of 11 essays, originally published in various sources between 1960 and 1975 and intended to provide an overview of academic SF criticism in much the same way that

Knight's *Turning Points* [8-75] provides an overview of criticism by SF writers. The pieces by Amis, Scholes, Suvin, Lem, Rabkin, and Ketterer are all included in books by these authors separately annotated in this chapter. Two other influential essays, by Susan Sontag and C. S. Lewis, are also available in books by those authors. Only the pieces by Robert Conquest, Michael Holquist, and John Huntington are not widely available elsewhere, so that the book's chief value is now as a convenient source of important critical writing for smaller libraries lacking an SF collection.

8-120.   Rosinski, Natalie. **Feminist Futures: Contemporary Women's Speculative Fiction.** UMI Research Press, 1984.

This 1982 dissertation inaugurated UMI's project of publishing selected graduate theses on SF topics, and like many of the series it suffers from ponderous use of theoretical machinery. The texts explored—mostly familiar works from the 1960s and 1970s by Le Guin, Russ, Piercy, and others—have been treated more extensively and more recently by Lefanu [8-79], Moylan [8-93], and Barr [8-18, 8-19].

8-121.   Rottensteiner, Franz. **The Science Fiction Book: An Illustrated History.** Seabury, 1975.

A popular illustrated history by Austria's leading scholar of SF. Organized almost randomly into 52 very short chapters, followed by a chronology, bibliography, and awards list (but no index), the book retains some value for its international perspective and Rottensteiner's generally sound judgments, although even many of the illustrations lose their value through an overdesigned layout. Generally more useful than the comparable Wuckel and Cassiday [8-148], but less so than Gunn's American-based illustrated history [8-62].

*8-122.   Ruddick, Nicholas. **Ultimate Island: On the Nature of British Science Fiction.** Greenwood, 1993.

Ruddick sets out to contest the notion that British SF is either an offspring of the American tradition or purely a development of the "scientific romance" as described by Stableford [8-132]. Following introductory chapters in which he tries to outline the unique characteristics of British SF, he argues that Wells's works represented a synthesis of various literary traditions and that later authors self-consciously built upon Wells's work, particularly upon the motif of the island. Subsequent chapters focus on disaster fiction before and after World War II, modern British SF, and apparent future trends. Ruddick offers persuasive and sometimes brilliant readings of works by 13 key authors: Wells, S. Fowler Wright, Golding,

Jacquetta Hawkes, Shiel, Doyle, Edward Shanks, J. J. Connington, John Collier, Alun Llewellyn, R. C. Sherriff, Wyndham, Christopher, and Ballard. This valuable study is a companion to Ruddick's *British Science Fiction: A Chronology, 1478–1990* (Greenwood, 1992), a reference work most useful in conjunction with this study.

8-123. Sammons, Martha C. **A Better Country: The Worlds of Religious Fantasy and Science Fiction.** Greenwood, 1988.
Far more narrowly focused than its subtitle suggests, this brief study focuses heavily on Christian fantasy writers with avowedly didactic intent. References to SF include brief discussions of films such as *Star Wars* and authors such as Cordwainer Smith, Stephen Lawhead, and lesser-known figures published by religious presses, such as David Lawrence, Mark Durstewitz, and Wallace Henley. Blish is mentioned in passing, and Walter Miller, Zelazny, and Gene Wolfe not at all. Sammons has done a thorough job of surveying some major works by Tolkien, C. S. Lewis, and Madeleine L'Engle, but her treatment of SF is less useful than the broader perspective offered by Reilly, and her historical context is far less thorough than that of C. N. Manlove's *Christian Fantasy* (1992).

8-124. Samuelson, David. **Visions of Tomorrow: Six Journeys From Outer to Inner Space.** Arno, 1974.
A detailed analysis, based on the author's 1969 dissertation, of six modern novels representing different theoretical aspects of SF: Clarke's *Childhood's End* [3-44], Asimov's *The Caves of Steel* [3-10] Sturgeon's *More Than Human* [3-172], Miller's *A Canticle for Leibowitz* [3-125], Budrys' *Rogue Moon* [3-38], and Ballard's *The Crystal World* [4-26]. Although a relatively early work, this retains much of its value because of Samuelson's sensitive readings; his discussion of Budrys in particular remains the most cogent extended critical treatment of that novel. A similar "representative novel" approach is taken by Manlove [8-84] and Scholes and Rabkin [8-125].

*8-125. Scholes, Robert. **Structural Fabulation: An Essay on Fiction of the Future.** Univ. of Notre Dame Press, 1975.
Scholes, an influential literary theorist, finds in SF fertile ground for exploring ideas he earlier developed in *The Fabulators* (1967) and *Structuralism in Literature* (1974). This brief study, revised from four lectures delivered in 1974, first outlines a general defense for the study of SF in a postmodern context, followed by two chapters outlining a general definition with examples drawn from Sturgeon, Keyes, Stapledon, and Herbert; the final chapter is a more extended discussion of Le Guin's

Earthsea series (1968–1990) and *The Left Hand of Darkness* [4-254]. Despite his limited familiarity with the field, Scholes's theory has been influential, especially among participants at the annual Eaton conference (see "Conference Proceedings"). A much more detailed and knowledgeable approach, using some of the same methods, is Suvin's *Metamorphoses of Science Fiction* [8-136].

*8-126. Scholes, Robert, and Eric S. Rabkin. **Science Fiction: History/ Science/Vision.** Oxford Univ. Press, 1977.
Intended as an introductory text for the general reader, this clearly written and organized study begins with a general history of SF, followed by a rather weak chapter on SF in nonliterary media. The "science" section offers fairly basic explanations of the scientific method and commonly used concepts from physics, astronomy, computer science, thermodynamics, biology, and psychology, with a brief discussion of pseudosciences. The "vision" section includes discussions of major SF themes and brief analyses of ten representative novels by Shelley, Verne, Wells, Zamiatin, Lindsay, Stapledon, Clarke, Miller, Le Guin, and Brunner. Annotated nonfiction bibliographies and a list of award-winning novels follows. Although it offers little new for the serious student of SF, this is a valuable and lucid brief overview.

8-127.   The Science Fiction Novel: Imagination and Social Criticism. Advent, 1959.
A series of four lectures—by Heinlein, Kornbluth, Bloch, and Bester—originally delivered at the University of Chicago in 1957, and introduced by Basil Davenport. While the book in general is dated, Heinlein's essay remains of particular interest by developing at length his definition of science fiction; and Kornbluth's is a still-vivid attack on the failure of SF of the day to grapple meaningfully with social issues.

8-128. Shinn, Thelma J. **Worlds Within Women: Myth and Mythmaking in Fantastic Literature by Women.** Greenwood, 1986.
Shinn sets out to demonstrate how modern men writers, mostly of SF, have redefined and reinvented traditional "patriarchal" myths, as well as creating original myth systems and transforming female archetypes. The first chapter explores works based on familiar myths (such as Bradley's reworking of Arthurian material), and discusses Jean Auel, Doris Lessing, and Octavia Butler. The second chapter shows how Norton, Van Scyoc, Susan Coon, Vinge, Charnas, Elgin, and others reinvent these myths in SF settings. Mythmaking in Lessing, Le Guin, Van Scyoc, Sargent, Butler, Piercy, and others is covered in Chapter 3, and Chapter 4 concerns new or transformed female archetypes in Tanith Lee, Russ, Butler, Wilhelm, and

others. Shinn's work is persuasive without being polemical, and is of particular value because of the detailed attention she devotes to too-often-ignored writers such as Butler or Vinge. Compare Barr's *Feminist Fabulation* [8-19].

8-129.   Shippey, Tom, ed. **Fictional Space: Essays on Contemporary Science Fiction.** Humanities Press International, 1991.

Eight essays on significant topics and texts in modern SF. Shippey's introductory piece on SF language and neologisms bears comparison with Delany's approach in *The Jewel-Hinged Jaw* [8-48], while Walter E. Meyers' discussion of SF language expands points made in his *Aliens and Linguists* [8-88]. John R. Christie and John Huntington each explore postmodern aspects of SF, emphasizing Gibson's *Neuromancer* [4-184]; Robert Crossley examines SF museum artifacts; Alasdair Spark compares Heinlein's *Starship Troopers* [3-90] with Haldeman's *Forever War* [4-193]; Alan C. Elms explores the biographical sources of Cordwainer Smith's SF; and Shippey's second essay examines the iconography of America in decline. An excellent general collection.

*8-130.   Spinrad, Norman. **Science Fiction in the Real World.** Southern Illinois Univ. Press, 1990.

Assembled mostly from columns written for *Isaac Asimov's Science Fiction Magazine* from 1985 to 1988, these fourteen essays by a major SF novelist show far more coherence than most such collections, since Spinrad used his column to explore ideas rather than merely review books. The three essays in his first section explores SF's relation to the mainstream and to its own easy formulas, which Spinrad terms *sci-fi*. The second covers SF in graphic novels and films, and the third various "modes" such as cyberpunk, hard SF, and space colonies (the only specific theme treated as such). A fourth section discusses power fantasies in SF, including an account of Spinrad's experiences with his *The Iron Dream* [4-429]. The highly personal final group of essays treat individual writers—Sturgeon, Vonnegut, Ballard, and Dick. The Sturgeon and Dick pieces are passionate and moving, and Spinrad's treatment of cyberpunk is among the best available. Despite his contentious reputation, his arguments are reasonable, balanced, and sound. Compare Budrys' *Benchmarks* [8-31], which offers similar coverage of an earlier period. HN, 1991

8-131.   Stableford, Brian M. **Masters of Science Fiction: Essays on Six Science Fiction Authors.** Borgo, 1981.

An informed and well-written series of essays on authors who have made unique contributions to SF, even though not all are widely recognized by scholars; in fact, Vonnegut may be the only "canonical" author discussed. Other essays cover Edmond Hamilton, Leigh Brackett, Mack Reynolds, Silverberg, and Malzberg.

*8-132. Stableford, Brian M. **Scientific Romance in Britain 1890–1950.** Fourth Estate/St. Martin's, 1985.

One of the major works on SF history, and one of the first to establish a British tradition of fantastic literature clearly independent of American pulp history and, in fact, different from SF itself (although Stableford sees the traditions merging by the 1950s). Following two chapters of definition and background, he proceeds chronologically, first discussing the major preoccupations and writers of the pre-World War I period (George Griffith, Wells, Shiel, Doyle, Hodgson, and J. D. Beresford). Economic and cultural changes after the war altered the nature of works published; interwar writers discussed include S. Fowler Wright, E. V. Odle, Stapledon, Neil Bell, and John Gloag. The final chapters trace the decline of scientific romance following World War II, discussing C. S. Lewis, Gerald Heard, and the heritage of the tradition in Clarke, Aldiss, and Ballard. As a sociologist as well as novelist, Stableford not only discusses a great many works with insight, but outlines the changing publishing and market conditions as well. Compare Suvin's *Victorian Science Fiction in the UK* [8-138] and Ruddick [8-122]. Eaton Award, 1987

8-133. Stableford, Brian M. **The Sociology of Science Fiction.** Borgo, 1987.

Stableford's doctoral thesis in sociology, originally completed in 1978 and reprinted here with a new introduction and index. Following two general chapters on the sociology of literature and communication, he briefly traces the development of the SF market, then devotes the heart of his discussion to chapters on what SF readers expect—which Stableford sees as more emotional than cognitive—and on significant themes (machines, aliens, societies, supermen) and trends. His conclusion is that SF doesn't work well as didactic literature, but serves important "directive," "maintenance," and "restorative" functions for its readership. Though not without its academic jargon, this is far more clearly written than most dissertations and offers solid insights into how SF is "used" by its readers.

8-134. Staicar, Tom, ed. **Critical Encounters II: Writers and Themes in Science Fiction.** Ungar, 1982.

A companion volume to Riley [8-115], also directed toward a general audience, offers an essay by Eric Rabkin on the rhetoric of SF plus pieces on Clement, Zelazny, Silverberg, Ian Watson, Doris Piserchia, Vonda McIntyre, Richard Matheson, and the Strugatski's. Similar in approach to

Clareson's *Voices for the Future* volumes [8-39], this is chiefly valuable for treatments of authors (Watson, Matheson, Piserchia) not widely treated elsewhere.

8-135. Staicar, Tom, ed. **The Feminine Eye: Science Fiction and the Women Who Write It.** Ungar, 1982.
An early collection of nine essays on women writers, including Cherryh, Charnas, Elgin, Brackett, Norton, Bradley, Vinge, Tiptree, and Moore. Not overtly feminist in its emphasis, the book is less thorough than Armitt [8-9], Weedman [8-176], or Barr's *Future Females* [8-20].

*8-136. Suvin, Darko. **Metamorphoses of Science Fiction: On the Poetics and History of a Literary Genre.** Yale Univ. Press, 1979.
Revised and expanded from the author's *Pour une poétique de la science-fiction* (Montreal, 1977), this has proved to be one of the most influential theoretical studies of SF to date, although many find the style dense and abstract. Suvin begins by proposing his widely cited notions of "cognitive estrangement" and the "novum," and the differences between SF and utopian literature. The second two-thirds of the book, focusing on SF history, discusses More's *Utopia* [1-68], Shelley's *Frankenstein* [1-84], Morris's *News From Nowhere* [1-69] Wells's *The Time Machine* [1-103], and works by Bellamy, Twain, Poe, Čapek, and Russian SF writers. Suvin's strong opinions are always supported by relentless logic and solid scholarship, and even though some view his approach to SF as narrow and prescriptive, this remains one of the most serious, scholarly, and important attempts to place the genre in a coherent context of intellectual and cultural history.

8-137. Suvin, Darko. **Positions and Presuppositions in Science Fiction.** Kent State Univ. Press, 1988.
A collection of 13 essays originally published between 1973 and 1984. Two essays provide an overview of Suvin's general ideas on social theories of literature, five deal with SF theory in particular, one with teaching SF, and five with various writers (Asimov, Yefremov, Lem, Dick, Le Guin, the Strugatskys, Johanna and Günter Braun). As always, Suvin's criticism is rigorous and theoretically sophisticated, and some readers may find this book a more accessible introduction to his work than his *Metamorphoses of Science Fiction* [8-136].

*8-138. Suvin, Darko. **Victorian Science Fiction in the UK: The Discourses of Knowledge and of Power.** G. K. Hall, 1983.
In what is perhaps the most detailed and rigorous study of a particular period in SF history, Suvin attempts to expand upon ideas developed in *Metamorphoses of Science Fiction* by investigating in great detail the period

1848–1900 in England. He begins with an annotated bibliography of 360 books, then discusses which should and should not be counted as SF; an essay by John Sutherland on the Victorian book trade supplements this. He then offers biographical information on 270 writers and discusses them in terms of social origin, profession, social position, and even longevity. Having thus laid out his data, Suvin devotes the second part of his study to a long essay on the audiences (or "social addressees" of the works discussed) and the major themes of knowledge, ideology, and power. An invaluable source for students of Victorian literature, SF history, and the sociology of SF. Stableford's *The Sociology of Science Fiction* [8-133] and Bainbridge [8-16] touch upon some similar issues for the modern period, although in considerably less detail.

8-139.   Tolley, Michael J., and Kirpal Singh, eds. **The Stellar Gauge: Essays on Science Fiction Authors.** Norstrilia Press, 1980.

An international group of contributors (Australia, England, the United States, and Singapore) cover a variety of SF authors and works in an unusually readable and literate collection, which features a number of novelists on other novelists: George Turner on Pohl, John Sladek on Disch, Brian Aldiss on Blish, and Christopher Priest on Ballard. Other writers covered include Verne, Orwell, Bester, Clarke, Aldiss, Dick, and Silverberg. Only two of the essays (Aldiss and Priest) were previously published. Compare with Clareson's Voices for the Future series [8-39].

*8-140.   Wagar, W. Warren. **Terminal Visions: The Literature of Last Things.** Indiana Univ. Press, 1982.

Wagar, a historian who has also published SF stories, traces the history of secular eschatological fiction through some 300 works, from Mary Shelley's *The Last Man* through the work of Ballard. Wagar is adept at showing how such works reflect the spirit of the times, and makes some unusual but important discoveries: that most doomsday fiction is actually rather upbeat, and that World War I marked a dramatic turning point between fictions predominantly of natural disaster and those predominantly of man-made disasters. He is also unusually knowledgeable among cultural historians about SF. Although there are few extended analyses of individual works, this is the most comprehensive analysis of this major SF theme. Compare with Rabkin, Greenberg, and Olander's *The End of the World* [8-112] (with which there is some overlap in Wagar's two contributions to that volume).

8-141.   Walsh, Chad. **From Utopia to Nightmare.** Harper, 1982.

From an essentially Christian perspective, Walsh discusses the shift from utopian to dystopian literature (his work was the first to popularize the term *dystopia*) in the 19th and 20th centuries. Among the authors he covers are Bellamy, Huxley, Orwell, Vonnegut, Zamiatin, Wells, Bernard Wolfe, E. M. Forster, and Vladimir Nabokov. Although much of the material is covered in more depth in Kumar [8-76], this is still a wide-ranging and elegantly written study.

8-142.   Warner, Harry. **All Our Yesterdays: An Informal History of Science Fiction in the Forties.** Advent, 1969. Introduction by Wilson Tucker.

A somewhat rambling and anecdotal history of fandom, focusing principally on the 1930s and 1940s, and liberally supplemented with photographs, a glossary, profiles of major fans and important conventions, and summaries of regional and international fan activities. Far more thorough than Moskowitz's *The Immortal Storm* [8-90], and probably the most complete compilation of information anywhere about SF's organized readership during this period. (Warner even uncovers information on possible 19th-century fans.) Of limited interest in terms of literary history, but an important ancillary resource for those interested in the culture of SF. Warner continues his history into the 1950s in the generally inaccessible fan-published *A Wealth of Fable: The History of Science Fiction Fandom in the 1950s* (Fanhistorica Press, 1976–1977), which was belatedly awarded the Hugo in 1993.

8-143.   Warrick, Patricia S. **The Cybernetic Imagination in Science Fiction.** MIT Press, 1980.

Warrick surveyed some 225 stories and novels published between 1930 and 1977, all dealing with some aspect of intelligent machines. She discovers two models of the human/machine relationship. The "closed-system" model tends to focus on the indelible opposition between humans and machines, and sees the latter as dehumanizing and threatening. The "open-system" model, more to her liking, sees a potentially creative symbiosis of humans and machines. Warrick focuses more consistently on questions of scientific verisimilitude than of literary merit, and her general theoretical approach is rather vague, permitting her to cite as the two "giants" of this kind of fiction authors as dissimilar as Asimov and Dick. She also sometimes fails to account for the social and psychological significance of certain ideas, or of the conditions under which many of these works were produced. Her broad sampling and often cogent discussions of individual works, however, makes this a significant study of its topic. Compare Dunn and Erlich's two volumes [8-51, 8-52].

8-144.   Wendland, Albert. **Science, Myth, and the Fictional Creation of Alien Worlds.** UMI Research Press, 1984.

A revision of the author's 1980 dissertation divides SF into "conventional" and "experimental" modes, which sound suspiciously like the familiar distinction between escapist and socially engaged SF. Although this approach contributes little to SF theory, discussions of individual works by Clement, Anderson, Wolfe, Anthony, Lem, Clarke, Aldiss, Russ, Bradbury, Ballard, and others are sometimes insightful.

*8-145. Wolfe, Gary K. **The Known and the Unknown: The Iconography of Science Fiction.** Kent State Univ. Press, 1979.

In this fascinating and exceptionally perceptive study, Wolfe explores the recurrent iconic images that SF writers have used with varying degrees of subtlety, complexity, and power. He suggests that the "sense of wonder" so often talked of is generated by the juxtaposition of the known and the unknown, separated by a barrier. Among the iconic images explored in a wide-ranging selection of American and British stories are those of the spaceship, the city, the wasteland, the robot, and the monster. Wolfe transcends a purely formulaic analysis of SF to show how many works blend traditional images and sophisticated development that engage the reader on many levels. The novice will not have sufficient knowledge of SF to appreciate the breadth and subtlety of Wolfe's analysis, but fans and scholars cannot fail to have their insights enriched. A major study worthy of the widest readership. (NB) Eaton Award, 1981

8-146.   Wolfe, Gary K., ed. **Science Fiction Dialogues.** Academy Chicago, 1982.

This is the second volume to collect papers presented at the annual Science Fiction Research Association conferences or written by members (see also Remington [8-164]). Aldiss's original essay on *Frankenstein* [1-84], later collected in his *The Pale Shadow of Science* [8-3], is followed by letters between Stapledon and Wells, the edited version of Budrys's valuable essay [8-32], and pieces on *Galaxy*'s first editor H. L. Gold, Hal Clement, Niven's *Ringworld* [4-316], Piercy's *Woman on the Edge of Time* [4-330], Gardner's *Grendel*, and feminist SF. Sam Moskowitz's 1981 Pilgrim acceptance speech on the development of Bailey's *Pilgrims Through Space and Time* [8-15] is followed by several bibliographical pieces. (NB)

8-147. Wollheim, Donald A. **The Universe Makers: Science Fiction Today.** Harper, 1971.

A personal and anecdotal brief survey by an influential editor and author, notable for its outline of a "consensus cosmogony" of future history drawn from the works of "Golden Age" writers and later picked up by James Gunn and others. Wollheim's approach is both conservative and commercial, and the book is of greater value as a record of his ideas than as a general survey. A similar personal history is del Rey [8-46].

8-148. Wuckel, Dieter, and Bruce Cassiday. **The Illustrated History of Science Fiction.** Ungar, 1989. Trans. and adaptation of *Science Fiction: Eine Illustrierte Literaturgeschichte* (1986) by Jenny Vowles.

This rather odd contribution to Ungar's Recognitions series is a translation of a 1986 East German work with some additional material and "adaptation" by Bruce Cassiday. Its lack of an index and unreliable bibliography severely limit its usefulness as a history, and the plentiful illustrations are nearly useless (many are simply random covers of paperbacks or magazines unrelated to the text). Wuckel's doctrinaire biases also distort his judgments of many texts, and his coverage of Anglo-American SF is often truncated and error-ridden. What gives the book its value is its extensive coverage of European and Soviet writers and its account of developing SF traditions in socialist countries; treatment of SF in the European democracies, however, tends to dismiss it as a pawn of the American SF industry.

8-149. Yoke, Carl B., and Donald M. Hassler, eds. **Death and the Serpent: Immortality in Science Fiction and Fantasy.** Greenwood, 1985.

Intended to cover the theme of immortality in much the same way that Erlich and Dunn's books in the same series [8-51, 8-52] covered machines, this collection of 19 essays focuses on fantasy, myth, and horror as well as SF. Of interest are Marleen Barr on feminist communities, Nick O'Donohue on Shelley and Leiber, Curtis Smith on Stapledon, C. W. Sullivan III on Heinlein, Joseph Sanders on Zelazny, Mark Siegel on Tiptree, and essays on Herbert, Niven, Gunn, and Vance. A useful bibliography covers fiction, nonfiction, and anthologies.

8-150. Yoke, Carl B., and Donald M. Hassler, eds. **Phoenix From the Ashes: The Literature of the Remade World.** Greenwood, 1987.

Like most such symposia, this collection of 19 essays on the theme of renewal following catastrophe suffers both from gaps in coverage and overlap among the contributors. Five essays deal with general topics, and fourteen on particular writers, texts, or films. Most are quite short. Among the more provocative are Yoke's own introduction, Paul Brians on the rediscovery of learning as a theme, and Wyn Wachhorst on films. Others cover such authors as Walter M. Miller, Jr., Ballard, Pat Frank, Nevil Shute, Piers Anthony, Wells, Weinbaum, Poul Anderson, Russell Hoban, and Bernard Malamud. A comparable, but somewhat more theoretically oriented volume, is Rabkin, Greenberg, and Olander's *The End of the World* [8-112]. See also Wagar [8-140].

8-151.   Zaki, Hoda M. **Phoenix Renewed: The Survival and Mutation of Utopian Thought in North American Science Fiction 1965–1982.** Starmont House, 1988. Borgo Press, 1993. Rev. ed.
Zaki, a political scientist whose intended audience seems to be other political scientists, argues that the utopian impulse in fiction is alive in American SF, and sets out to demonstrate this through discussions of 16 Nebula-winning novels from 1965 to 1982, with a separate chapter on Le Guin. Her introductory groundlaying chapter and perfunctory account of SF history reveal the book's sources as a dissertation, and her only principle of selecting texts (the Nebula) severely limits her coverage, but her political science perspective permits her some valuable insights. Compare Moylan [8-93].

Conference Proceedings

Two major academic conferences have regularly published collections of papers derived from their annual meetings. The International Association for the Fantastic in the Arts (IAFA) has met annually since 1980 (in Fort Lauderdale, Florida, since 1988) and is the largest such academic conference, with registered attendance in the 250–300 range; selections of papers (usually about 10 percent of those delivered at any given conference) have been published by Greenwood Press since 1985, and additional conference papers sometimes appear in the association's *Journal of the Fantastic in the Arts*, begun in 1988. The Eaton Conference on Science Fiction and Fantasy Literature, held annually at the University of California–Riverside since 1979, began publishing essays from its conferences with Southern Illinois University Press in 1980, moving to the University of Georgia Press in 1993. In addition, several other conferences have regularly produced papers that eventually saw print in journals, essay collections, or irregular volumes of proceedings; the University of Nice's biennial Colloque International de Science Fiction de Nice, for example, has published the proceedings of its meetings as special issues of the journal *Metaphores* [8-156]. The Science Fiction Research Association (SFRA) holds an annual summer conference at various locations, attracting 75–125 registrants, and it published a volume of *Selected Proceedings* in 1979 [8-164]. The Popular Culture Association has met annually at various location since 1971, and usually features a substantial selection of papers dealing with SF literature and film. The largest of the fan conventions, the World Science Fiction Convention, has been held annually since 1939, and has on occasion published proceedings of individual meetings; since 1982 it has featured a track of academic programming, which has also produced two volumes of essays [8-157, 8-158]. Numerous other "oneshot" conferences on SF topics have also produced volumes of essays. Most of the collections annotated here and earlier in this chapter are indexed by Tymn and Schlobin [7-19] and Hall [7-16].

8-152. Collings, Michael R., ed. **Reflections on the Fantastic: Selected Essays From the Fourth International Conference on the Fantastic in the Arts.** Greenwood, 1986.
The slimmest of the ICFA volumes also reflects the highest proportion of essays on SF. Twelve papers from the 1983 conference include a provocative short piece by Brian Attebery on fantasy and anti-utopia, two on Brian Aldiss, one on Delany, one on Le Guin and Pohl, and one on Zelazny and Saberhagen's *Coils*.

8-153. Collins, Robert A., and Howard D. Pearce, eds. **The Scope of the Fantastic—Culture, Biography, Themes, Children's Literature: Selected Essays From the First International Conference on the Fantastic in Literature and Film.** Greenwood, 1985.
A second selection of 27 essays from the first ICFA includes an interesting essay by Charles Elkins on the social functions of SF and fantasy, Olena Saciuk on the little-known Ukrainian SF writer Oleś Berdnyk, Joseph Sanders on filmmaker Willis O'Brien, and pieces on Zelazny and Le Guin.

8-154. Collins, Robert A., and Howard D. Pearce, eds. **The Scope of the Fantastic—Theory, Technique, Major Authors: Selected Essays From the First International Conference on the Fantastic in Literature and Film.** Greenwood, 1985.
The first of two volumes of papers from the inaugural ICFA, held in 1980, establishes the characteristic pattern of the series. The relative brevity of

many of the essays, the broadly diffuse focus on almost anything that could be called "fantastic," and the frequency with which the proceedings have appeared (11 volumes in seven years) all suggest a hardbound periodical rather than a series of independently conceived volumes. In this volume, a useful introduction by Eric S. Rabkin is followed by 30 essays divided into theory, techniques, and author studies. The few essays that deal with SF touch upon works by Golding, Verne, Zelazny, and Piers Anthony.

8-155.   Coyle, William, ed. **Aspects of Fantasy: Selected Essays From the Second International Conference on the Fantastic in Literature and Film.** Greenwood, 1986.

Coyle organizes 25 papers from the 1981 conference into five broad categories: creators of fantasy, fantastic creatures, fantasy and the media, fantasy and literary tradition, and fantasy and contemporary concerns. Of particular interest are Rosemary Jackson's psychoanalytic reading of *Frankenstein* [1-84], Robert Collins on Thomas Burnett Swann, and Roger C. Schlobin on the figure of the fool in modern fantasy. Only four essays deal significantly with SF, including Herbert, Clarke, Shelley, and language.

8-156.   Emelina, Jean, and Denise Terrel, eds. **Actes du Premier Colloque International de Science-Fiction de Nice: Images de l'ailleurs-espace interieur.** Centre d'etude de la metaphore, 1984.

Eighteen essays and a roundtable discussion from the University of Nice's first biennial conference on SF in 1983; nine of the essays are in English, the rest in French. The English-language essays include significant theoretical and thematic pieces by major scholars and writers such as Robert Scholes, Darko Suvin, John Dean, Brian Stableford, Peter Fitting, Patrick Parrinder, Moria Monteith, David Ketterer, and John Shirley. The proceedings of the fourth Nice conference, with all papers in both French and English versions, were published in a massive two-volume collection, *Science et science-fiction: Actes du 4ème colloque international de science-fiction de Nice*, in 1992.

8-157.   Hassler, Donald M., ed. **Patterns of the Fantastic: Academic Programming at Chicon IV.** Starmont, 1983.

A selection of 12 short papers from the first formally organized track of Worldcon academic programming, at the 1982 Chicon (the complete track is listed in an appendix). Five of the essays deal with women writers or characters; others cover Delany, Ellison, King, Robin Cook, and *2001*. Those most relevant to the convention itself discuss the Moebius Theatre

Company and the sociology of conventions (based on some 700 questionnaires distributed at various midwestern conferences).

8-158. Hassler, Donald M., ed. **Patterns of the Fantastic II: Academic Proceedings at Constellation.** Starmont, 1984.
Hassler's second selection of papers, drawn from the 1983 Baltimore Worldcon, includes ten essays, the best of which is Jan Bogstad's analysis of cross-genre fiction. Two essays compare the film *Blade Runner* with its source, and others cover Wells, mathematics in SF, computers, and Le Guin.

8-159. Hokenson, Jan, and Howard Pearce, eds. **Forms of the Fantastic: Selected Essays From the Third International Conference on the Fantastic in Literature and Film.** Greenwood, 1986.
A selection of 26 essays from the 1982 ICFA, reflecting the usual variety of approaches and topics. SF topics are covered in essays on Lewis, Delany, Le Guin, and Hesse.

8-160. Langford, Michele, ed. **Contours of the Fantastic: Selected Essays From the Eighth International Conference on the Fantastic in the Arts.** Greenwood, 1990.
An unusually strong volume in this series contains 22 essays, including speeches by conference guests Brian Aldiss, Brian Stableford, Nancy Willard, and Vivian Sobchack. Other strong essays are by David Miller, Michael Clifton, and especially Peter Malekin, who lucidly applies post-structuralist theory to works by Lem and Delany. (Malekin does not publish widely elsewhere in the field, and may be regarded as one of the hidden treasures of these ICFA volumes.)

8-161. Morse, Donald E., ed. **The Fantastic in World Literature and the Arts: Selected Essays From the Fifth International Conference on the Fantastic in the Arts.** Greenwood, 1987.
Morse tries to give a more coherent comparative cultural focus to this collection of 16 papers from the 1984 ICFA, and it is one of the few volumes to contain illustrations (particularly valuable for Steven Earl Forry's analysis of 20th-century versions of *Frankenstein*). Other relevant pieces include Donald Palumbo on SF film, Peter Malekin on Wolfe's *Book of the New Sun* [4-510], and Gregory Shreve on Joan Vinge.

8-162. Morse, Donald E., Csilla Bertha, and Marshall B. Tymn, eds. **The Celebration of the Fantastic: Selected Papers From the Tenth Anniversary International Conference on the Fantastic in the Arts.** Greenwood, 1992.
This volume follows the selected papers of the eighth ICFA (the selection

from the ninth conference, in 1988, did not appear), and includes 26 essays. Of particular SF interest are Joan Gordon on Haldeman, Len Hatfield on Greg Bear, H. Bruce Franklin on superweapon fantasies, Robert Latham on SF and modernism, Barbara Mabee on German fantastic literature, and Judith Kerman on "virtual space" in SF film and television.

8-163.   Palumbo, Donald, ed. **Spectrum of the Fantastic: Selected Essays from the Sixth International Conference on the Fantastic in the Arts.** Greenwood, 1988.

Palumbo's selection of 24 papers from the 1985 conference includes a specific section on SF, with papers exploring Platonism in Heinlein and Le Guin, the Foundation [3-12] and Dune [4-207] series, Aldiss, and Tiptree; other essays touch upon Vonnegut, King, Lem, and *Star Trek*.

8-164.   Remington, Thomas J., ed. **Selected Proceedings of the 1978 Science Fiction Research Association National Conference.** Univ. of Northern Iowa, 1979.

The only published proceedings volume of the SFRA includes 17 essays plus Brian Aldiss's Pilgrim acceptance speech; a dialogue between Gordon Dickson and Joe Haldeman; a roundtable discussion with Le Guin, Robert Scholes, Eric Rabkin, Gene Wolfe, and Darko Suvin, and even transcripts of Le Guin's interaction with the audience. Essayists include Marshall Tymn, Andrew Gordon, Patricia Warrick, Jane Weedman, William Hardesty, Natalie Rosinski, Richard Erlich, Darko Suvin, and Gary K. Wolfe. Though much of the material was later published in various books, this remains valuable as a rare record of one of SFRA's most important conferences.

8-165.   Ruddick, Nicholas, ed. **State of the Fantastic—Studies in the Theory and Practice of Fantastic Literature and Film: Selected Essays From the Eleventh International Conference on the Fantastic in the Arts, 1990.** Greenwood, 1992.

Ruddick's selection from the 1990 conference is among the most carefully edited and thematically unified volumes in this series, and may be of greatest value to SF scholars. In addition to contributions from writers Jane Yolen and Elisabeth Vonarburg, substantial theoretical approaches are offered by Peter Malekin, Brian Attebery, and Veronica Hollinger. Other topics covered include gnostic SF, SF film, and works by Dick Zelazny, Russ, Farmer, Ballard, Greg Bear, and Kathy Acker.

8-166. Saciuk, Olena, ed. **The Shape of Fantasy: Selected Essays From the Seventh International Conference on the Fantastic in the Arts.** Greenwood, 1990.

Papers from the 1986 conference are highlighted by Brian Aldiss's cogent "What Should a SF Novel Be About?" and C. N. Manlove's "The Elusiveness of Fantasy." Of the 23 other essays, those of particular interest include Leo Daugherty on SF's still-weak academic reputation, Brooks Landon on SF film, and Carl Shaffer on Brunner's *Stand on Zanzibar* [4-74].

8-167. Slusser, George E., Colin Greenland, and Eric S. Rabkin, eds. **Storm Warnings: Science Fiction Confronts the Future.** Southern Illinois Univ. Press, 1987.

Papers from the 1984 Eaton Conference, which was held in two parts in California and London. Predictably, the major topic of discussion that year was Orwell's most famous novel and its influence. Frederik Pohl's "Coming Up on 1984" debunks the novel as among Orwell's worst, while other contributors, including John Huntington, Elizabeth Maslen, T. A. Shippey, Colin Greenland, and Frank McConnell discuss the work and its successors more favorably.

8-168. Slusser, George E., George R. Guffey, and Mark Rose, eds. **Bridges to Science Fiction.** Southern Illinois Univ. Press, 1980.

The inaugural volume in the Eaton series features papers from the first conference, held in 1979. Of particular interest are Gregory Benford's essay on aliens and Patrick Parrinder's on SF as "truncated epic." Eric S. Rabkin compares SF to fairy tales, Harry Levin (in the keynote address) discusses various literary responses to science, and other contributors discuss Dick, SF's treatment of historical time, SF and Gothic, medieval SF, visionary SF, and philosophical empiricism and SF. The second Eaton Conference volume, *Bridges to Fantasy*, concerns itself almost exclusively with definitions and parameters of fantasy fiction rather than SF, although some of the essays are useful for their theoretical genre distinctions.

8-169. Slusser, George E., and Eric S. Rabkin, eds. **Aliens: The Anthropology of Science Fiction.** Southern Illinois Univ. Press, 1987.

The papers from the 1986 Eaton Conference focus not so much on anthropology, but upon a common SF theme that sometimes involves anthropological speculation. Larry Niven and Gregory Benford reveal their different approaches to the topic (and to SF) as Niven considers why aliens haven't visited Earth and Benford considers stylistic problems of dealing with aliens. Other essays touch upon friendly aliens, "illegal" aliens, robots, telepaths, and even Barbie dolls. One of the livelier volumes in this series.

8-170.   Slusser, George E., and Eric S. Rabkin, eds. **Flights of Fancy: Armed Conflict in Science Fiction and Fantasy.** Univ. of Georgia Press, 1993.
Fifteen essays chosen from those presented at the 1988 Eaton Conference, many of which define the theme "armed conflict" pretty loosely. Eric S. Rabkin's essay tracing the internalization of warfare in SF is the only piece to offer a substantial overview of the topic. Reginald Bretnor and Gary Westfahl focus on problems of semantics and language; four essays deal with earlier imaginary wars; other topics include film, comics, nuclear war, and Third World issues. Of particular interest are Joe Haldeman's account of his own fiction dealing with Vietnam, Louis Pedrotti's discussion of an 1833 Russian SF novel by Osip Senkovsky, and Martha Bartter's treatment of M. J. Engh's *Arslan* [4-163].

8-171.   Slusser, George E., and Eric S. Rabkin, eds. **Hard Science Fiction.** Southern Illinois Univ. Press, 1986.
One of the most focused of the Eaton collections, this selection of 16 essays all address issues of hard SF, which is seldom discussed separately as a form. Four SF writers among the contributors—Brin, Benford, Gunn, and Forward—make a persuasive case for hard SF as a particular kind of craft. Two of the essays, by Alkon [8-6] and Huntington [8-70] are versions of what would become chapters in their books. Slusser's own essay is among the most provocative.

8-172.   Slusser, George E., and Eric S. Rabkin, eds. **Intersections: Fantasy and Science Fiction.** Southern Illinois Univ. Press, 1987.
The 1985 Eaton Conference volume collects 17 essays focusing generally on genre theory as it applies to SF and fantasy. The first group of essays, which try to make distinctions between SF and fantasy, includes Robert Scholes on science fantasy, Michael Collings on horror, Joseph Miller on parallel universes, and a short essay by Zelazny. The second group looks at origins of the forms, and is highlighted by essays by Kathleen Spencer and Frank McConnell. The final section contains essays that seek to make a synthesis, and includes contributions from Slusser, Brian Attebery, and Kathryn Hume.

8-173.   Slusser, George E., and Eric S. Rabkin, eds. **Styles of Creation: Aesthetic Technique and the Creation of Fictional Worlds.** Univ. of Georgia Press, 1993.
Aesthetic and stylistic discussions are surprisingly rare in SF studies, and

this volume from the eleventh Eaton Conference, in 1989, attempts to redress the balance. Benford, a regular at the conference, discusses his own experiments with style, and Paul Carter offers a rare discussion of pulp writer Nat Schachner; other authors covered include Heinlein, Dick, King, and Malzberg. Other provocative essays include Joseph D. Miller on the role of ambiguity in portraying alien mental states, Gary Westfahl on SF neologisms, Patrick Parrinder on landscapes in British SF, Brooks Landon on invisibility, and Robert Crossley on museums in SF narratives. One of the best of the Eaton volumes.

8-174. Slusser, George E., Eric S. Rabkin, and Robert Scholes, eds. **Coordinates: Placing Science Fiction and Fantasy.** Southern Illinois Univ. Press, 1983.

The third Eaton Conference, in 1981, addressed the question of appropriate standards or norms by which to judge SF and fantasy, and this group of 13 essays begins with a lively argument by Leslie Fiedler against the usefulness of traditional elitist vs. popular standards. Rabkin then offers a philosophical, almost biological theory of the origins of fantasy, and later essays cover specific texts by Verne, Delany, Heinlein, Simak, Ayn Rand, Bradbury, Haggard, and Charlotte Perkins Gilman. H. Bruce Franklin's "America as Science Fiction: 1939" is an especially valuable contribution to SF as cultural history.

8-175. Slusser, George E., and Tom Shippey, eds. **Fiction 2000: Cyberpunk and the Future of Narrative.** Univ. of Georgia Press, 1992.

A collection of 17 essays and one roundtable discussion drawn from the proceedings of the 1989 Fiction 2000 conference held in Leeds, England. Gibson's *Neuromancer* trilogy [4-184, 4-182, 4-183] is a central text for more than half the contributions, which are divided into five sections. The first, on the cyberpunk movement, includes pieces by Lewis Shiner, Istvan Csicsery-Ronay, and George Slusser. The second, on SF traditions related to cyberpunk, features Paul Alkon, Gary Westfahl, and Carol McGuirk. The third section looks outside of SF with essays by Lance Olsen, John Huntington, and Brooks Landon. Individual writers, including Shiner, Sterling, and Gibson, are treated in section four along with film and TV. The final section considers the future of narrative and includes a refreshingly debunking piece by Gregory Benford as well as more theoretical essays by David Porush and Eric S. Rabkin. As a whole, the volume is somewhat more focused and less polemical than the comparable *Storming the Reality Studio* [8-86].

8-176. Weedman, Jane, ed. **Women Worldwalkers: New Dimensions of Science Fiction and Fantasy.** Texas Tech Press, 1985.

Sixteen papers originally delivered at a comparative literature symposium at Texas Tech in 1983 and revised for publication, including two by guest writers Marion Zimmer Bradley (on the responsibilities of women SF writers) and Samuel R. Delany (on Joanna Russ). Others cover a wide variety of topics from film and SF illustration to Dick, Aldiss, Lessing, Herbert, Christa Reinig, Elgin, and Bradley. The collection has little overall focus and lacks an index, although the abstracts of each paper are helpful. Both Barr's *Future Females* [8-20] and Armitt [8-9] are more current and less diffuse.

CHAPTER 9

Author Studies

Michael A. Morrison and Neil Barron

This chapter surveys books devoted to individual authors, followed by a discussion of collective biographies and interviews. Coverage is limited to SF writers and to some others who wrote at least one work important in the history of SF, such as Orwell or C. S. Lewis. In the latter case we have annotated primarily those books that focus on the writer's works relevant to SF.

SF writers, as distinct from writers of occasional SF, are now routinely included in literary and other reference works. Some works by SF writers are included among the texts studied in courses devoted to general literary history and criticism, though it would probably be overstating the case to say that such inclusions are routine. Because only a relatively small number of SF writers have been the subject of individual books, this chapter concludes with a tabulation of the 595 authors whose fiction was annotated in chapters 1–5 and for whom more bibliographic, biographical, and critical information is available in ten sources likely to be available in larger libraries. Many authors are discussed in the works of history and criticism annotated in chapter 8 and in the general reference works evaluated in chapter 7. Comprehensive access to material about authors in magazines and books is provided in the authoritative indexes by Hall [7-16].

For this edition we largely excluded purely bibliographic works and instead referred readers to the exhaustive bibliography by Burgess [7-11], which discusses bibliographies of 131 authors, many of them SF authors.

Many single author studies appeared as part of ceased series from publishers such as Oxford, Ungar, and Taplinger. The relatively short (64–150 pages) reader guide series from Starmont House was the longest running. Most of Starmont's backlist was bought in winter 1992/93 by Borgo Press, whose owner hopes to revise and republish some of the earlier studies, along with new author monographs, all under the Borgo imprint.

Many of the studies annotated share a potential weakness: they were often published while their subjects were still active, sometimes relatively early in their careers, and will therefore date fairly rapidly. That should be understood as an implicit comment in many of the evaluations.

Individual Authors

Brian W. Aldiss

9-1. Aldiss, Brian. **Bury My Heart at W. H. Smith's: A Writing Life.** Hodder & Stoughton, 1990. Enlarged edition, Avernus, 1990

*9-2. Aldiss, Margaret. **The Work of Brian W. Aldiss: An Annotated Bibliography and Guide.** Borgo, 1992.

9-3. Collings, Michael R. **Brian W. Aldiss.** Starmont, 1986.

9-4. Griffin, Brian, and David Wingrove. **Apertures: A Study of the Writings of Brian W. Aldiss.** Greenwood, 1984.

With over 100 published books, 300 short stories, and miscellaneous works including plays, poems, travelogues, criticism, and scripts for TV and radio, Brian W. Aldiss challenges biographer, bibliographer, and critic alike. Absent a full biography, Aldiss's charming but unanalytical autobiography *Bury My Heart at W. H. Smith's* usefully updates and complements information in *The Shape of Further Things* (1971) and various scattered essays, of which the most useful appears in *Hell's Cartographers* [9-140] and the most current appears in Margaret Aldiss's exemplary bibliography. This well-organized, complete volume, which includes annotations by Brian Aldiss, a detailed chronology, indexes of titles, and an exhaustive (indexed) list of secondary sources along with selected excerpts from reviews and critical commentaries, will be an essential tool for future students of Aldiss's fiction.

In his introduction, David Wingrove characterizes this bibliography as "a map" to "the territory of Brian Aldiss' psyche"—a view that echoes the critical perspective Michael Collings adopts in his Starmont guide. As the most recent book on Aldiss, Collings supersedes Richard Mathews's *Aldiss Unbound* (1977), although as Collings notes, Mathews's 64-page booklet remains "the best and most accessible introduction to Aldiss." Collings offers a coherent, lucid chronological overview of Aldiss through the Helliconia trilogy (1985) [4-6] informed by the unifying critical perspective of Aldiss as "mapmaker." Collings shows that Aldiss's multiplex fictional excursions serve as maps of the future requiring interpretation by his characters and readers, who in so doing elaborate "the possibilities of space, time, and humanity." Collings identifies the dominant image patterns and major themes of Aldiss's fiction (time, entropy, the role of the artist, transfiguration), is singularly insightful on his use of language, and fails only to clarify his influence on SF during and after the New Wave—a topic best explored in Colin Greenland's *The Entropy Exhibition* [8-61]. Selectively annotated primary and secondary bibliographies, chronology, and index.

Aldiss's place in SF also receives inadequate treatment at the hands of Griffin and Wingrove, who instead try to counter the perception that "as a whole, [Aldiss's canon] seems a contradictory mess that can't be taken seriously" by determinedly contextualizing it in the broad frame of literary Modernism. This sensible approach, however, is energized by what appears to be an excess of adulation that leads the authors to overemphasize the influence of mainstream novelists and poets. *Apertures* benefits from a certain amount of internal conflict with its own (chronological) structure and the tension between the quite different critical methods and perspectives of its authors, but as a whole is ultimately undermined by zeal and incoherence. Chapter notes, bibliography, index. Burgess 265–267. (MAM)

Poul Anderson

9-5. Miesel, Sandra. **Against Time's Arrow: The High Crusade of Poul Anderson.** Borgo, 1978.

Since 1947, when his first story was published, Anderson has been one of the more prolific writers of SF and fantasy and has won or been nominated for many of the field's most prestigious awards. His undergraduate degree was in physics, and a key concept in that field is entropy, which Miesel, following James Blish, argues is the organizing principle of much if not all of Anderson's fiction. Entropy is defined here as the inexorable tendency of systems to become increasingly disordered, leading to the death of individuals and the "heat death" of the universe. But individuals can create, bring order to life, can thus oppose time's arrow, even if only temporarily, and Miesel selects stories published through 1977 that illustrate Anderson's credo that, as Faulkner put it in his 1950 Nobel Prize speech, "I believe that man will not merely endure: he will prevail." A useful, brief (64 pages) if too admiring study of one of the field's more important authors. Burgess 269–70. (NB)

Isaac Asimov

9-6.   Asimov, Isaac. **In Joy Still Felt: The Autobiography of Isaac Asimov 1954–1978.** Doubleday, 1980. Hugo nominee.

9-7.   Asimov, Isaac. **In Memory Yet Green: The Autobiography of Isaac Asimov, 1920–1954.** Doubleday, 1979. Hugo nominee.

9-8.   Gunn, James. **Isaac Asimov: The Foundations of Science Fiction.** Oxford, 1982. Hugo winner.

9-9.   Hassler, Donald M. **Isaac Asimov.** Starmont, 1991. Eaton, 1993

9-10.   Touponce, William F. **Isaac Asimov.** Twayne, 1991.

When Asimov died in 1992 his authored and edited books were approaching 500. His SF, under his own name and that of Paul French (see chapter 5), accounted for approximately 13 percent of the total, among them many of the most popular works in the field (see chapters 3 and 4). His autobiography, totaling more than 1,500 pages, is likely to intimidate most readers, but it is valuable for the historian of SF because of Asimov's central role in the development of modern SF. Published in 1994 was *I. Asimov, A Memoir* (Doubleday), in whose 562 pages Asimov chronicles his entire life, but more impressionistically, and concludes with a useful classified bibliography of his many books.

Gunn is a contemporary of Asimov, a friend of 30 years, and many of his stories were published about the same time. Gunn also likes the type of SF Asimov wrote, and he is good at analyzing its appeal. He discusses the series and nonseries novels, the short fiction, as well as providing biographical information and details about Asimov's dealings with the marketplace. The best of the earlier studies of its subject though now somewhat dated.

Both the Hassler and Touponce are intended to be introductory works, but they are quite different in structure. Hassler discusses Asimov's works by category, such as short fiction, series novels, and juveniles, and examines how they are derived from Enlightenment sources and rationalist philosophy and how they are antiliterary in style. Touponce's emphasis is on the influence on Asimov's fiction of his scientific training. He argues that the paradigms of science (he relies heavily on Thomas Kuhn's work) are present throughout Asimov's many writings, especially evident in the robot and psychohistory stories. The detailed plot summaries in Touponce will help the novice even if they sometimes reveal too much. Touponce is a bit more current than Hassler, whose coverage effectively ends about 1989, and is slightly preferable. Burgess 273–74. (NB)

J. G. Ballard

9-11. Brigg, Peter. **J. G. Ballard.** Starmont, 1985.

9-12. Goddard, James, and David Pringle. **J. G. Ballard: The First Twenty Years.** Bran's Head, 1976.

*****9-13.** Pringle, David. **Earth Is the Alien Planet: J. G. Ballard's Four-Dimensional Nightmare.** Borgo, 1979.

*****9-14.** Pringle, David. **J. G. Ballard: A Primary and Secondary Bibliography.** G. K. Hall, 1984.

9-15. Stephenson, Gregory. **Out of the Night and Into the Dream: A Thematic Study of the Fiction of J. G. Ballard.** Greenwood, 1991.

In many respects the most useful analyses to date of Ballard's challenging, important speculative fiction appear in two works by David Pringle. *Earth Is the Alien Planet* is too brief and quite dated, covering only works through 1978. Still, its elucidation of Ballard's major themes, four-fold symbolism, and use of archetypal characters remains essential to understanding his work old and new—as is Brian W. Aldiss's seminal 1965 essay "The Wounded Land: J. G. Ballard." More up-to-date is the extensive biographical and critical introduction (supplemented by a long interview) Pringle prepared for his invaluable bibliography. This book's primary (fiction, nonfiction, and critical writings) and secondary bibliographic coverage (augmented by excerpts from reviews) is accurate and thorough within the format of this series. Appendixes of foreign editions, index.

None of the more recent studies are entirely satisfactory. Brigg also suffers from brevity (and, unlike Pringle's monograph, from poor writing). More seriously, Brigg fails to satisfactorily explicate Ballard's relationship to contemporary SF and mainstream fiction. On the plus side, he usefully clarifies the influence of surrealist painters on Ballard's creation of landscapes where "inner and outer realities fuse uncompromisingly." And he is insightful on Ballard's post-modern urban horror stories of the eighties, especially those in *The Atrocity Exhibition* [4-24]. Chronological primary and annotated secondary bibliographies, index.

Like Pringle, Stephenson sets out to counter the perception that Ballard is a nihilist. Unlike Pringle, he attempts to render Ballard as the

Aldous Huxley of the late 20th century, a mystic whose principal theme is "the problem of exceeding or escaping the limitations of the material world, the space-time continuum, the body, the senses and ordinary ego consciousness." Elucidating a wider range of influences than do Pringle or Brigg, Stephenson argues that in his fundamentally anti-rationalist works Ballard seeks, in effect, to thrust readers into the ontological Eden of inner space where they, like Ballard's characters, can seek liberation from time and thus find transcendence. Although relevant and energetically argued, this thesis, which neglects the dark satiric wit and urgent moral warnings present in such disparate works as *Crash* (1973) and *Running Wild* (1988), is ultimately a bit too reductive and a good deal too pat. Notes, index, selected bibliography.

All of these works offer important insights and perspectives on Ballard's fiction. Readers seeking a balanced perspective should also seek out Brian McHale's *Postmodernist Fiction* (1987), which succinctly situates Ballard among the postmoderns; Chapter 7 of *The Entropy Exhibition* [8-61], which contextualizes him within the New Wave movement; and Nicholas Ruddick's superb *Ultimate Island* [8-122], which offers an up-to-date account (within the framework of British SF) that counterbalances somewhat the weaknesses of Stephenson's book. Burgess 275. (MAM)

Alfred Bester

9-16.   Wendell, Carolyn. **Alfred Bester.** Starmont, 1982.

Although his first story was published in a 1939 pulp, Bester wrote relatively little SF until his death in 1987. But two of the novels he did write are highly regarded, *The Demolished Man* [3-17] and *The Stars My Destination* [3-19]. Wendell devotes a chapter to each of these novels, one to his weak 1975 novel, *The Computer Connection,* and another to his short stories [3-18]. Annotated bibliography of primary and secondary materials. Wendell favors plot summary over extended analysis, making her short study primarily of use to someone relatively unfamiliar with Bester's fiction. Bester's 30-page autobiographical essay in *Hell's Cartographers* [9-140] provides more insight into the author's work. (NB)

James Blish

*9-17.   Ketterer, David. **Imprisoned in a Tesseract: The Life and Work of James Blish.** Kent State Univ. Press, 1987.

*9-18.   Stableford, Brian M. **A Clash of Symbols: The Triumph of James Blish.** Borgo, 1979.

Both Ketterer and Stableford skillfully position Blish in the pre- and postwar American SF scenes and show his evolution from a disciple of John W.

Campbell to a meticulous craftsman determined through his fiction and criticism (collected in *The Issue at Hand* [8-13] and *More Issues at Hand* [8-14] to drag his chosen literary mode out of the gutter of pulp conventions. Although highly selective, Stableford's fine, brief introduction to the major themes of Blish's work suggests that his central contribution was an emphasis on moral and philosophical (rather than technological) concerns. Ketterer, whose book is almost seven times as long, draws upon exhaustive research in archival materials and extensive interviews with Blish's acquaintances to paint the most detailed portrait yet of a 20th-century SF author. Ketterer gives due attention to Blish's life and views, but the greatest strength of this remarkable book is its detailed analyses of key texts, ranging from (selected) early short stories Blish published in the pulps through his future history *Cities in Flight* [3-22] to the books that comprise his greatest work, *A Case of Conscience* [3-21]. Adumbrating Blish's major themes, motifs, and image patterns, Ketterer reveals the Spenglerian historical consciousness and fundamentally religious sensibility (one at odds with Blish's scientifically informed skepticism) behind this somewhat paradoxical but unarguably important figure in American science fiction. Extensive notes; primary bibliography of fiction, dramatic work, edited books, criticism, and nonfiction; selected secondary bibliography; index and chronology. Burgess 283. (MAM)

Ray Bradbury

9-19. Greenberg, Martin H., and Joseph D. Olander, eds. **Ray Bradbury.** Taplinger, 1980.

9-20. Johnson, Wayne L. **Ray Bradbury.** Ungar, 1980.

*9-21. Mogen, David. **Ray Bradbury.** Twayne, 1986.

9-22. Slusser, George Edgar. **The Bradbury Chronicles.** Borgo, 1977.

9-23. Touponce, William F. **Ray Bradbury and the Poetics of Reverie: Fantasy, Science Fiction, and the Reader.** UMI Research Press, 1984.

9-24. Touponce, William F. **Ray Bradbury.** Starmont, 1989.

As David Mogen shows in his excellent Twayne overview, Bradbury's position vis-à-vis SF is ambiguous. Despite the antitechnological stance of his best-known early works and his recent retreat from the genre, Bradbury is still considered by mainstream critics and readers as the premier exponent of science fiction. Mogen draws on lengthy interviews (conducted for this book) to present Bradbury as a man, as a stylist, and as a member of the SF and mainstream literary communities. With uncommon skill, Mogen combines biographical, philosophical, and critical insights in discussions organized around the diverse genres in which Bradbury has published: the weird tale, science fiction, and so on. Chronology, index, primary and annotated secondary bibliography.

Like Mogen, Slusser and Johnson argue that Bradbury attained the pinnacle of his artistry in the sixties—which makes less important the fact that their studies are dated. Slusser, in two extended essays devoted to Bradbury's short fiction and "fix-up" novels, persuasively positions him as a "tenaciously regional" American writer, primarily of short stories. Noting that throughout his career Bradbury has written "essentially the same kind of story," Slusser dates his artistic decline from his abandonment of the "toughminded optimism" of his early and mid-career prose works. Johnson, too, remarks on the lack of development in Bradbury's fiction. While he considers Bradbury primarily a fantasist, Johnson, like Slusser, broadly contextualizes his subject within the tradition of rural American fiction. Although usefully organized around Bradbury's main themes, Johnson's book is marred by an excess of plot summary, an overemphasis on autobiographical elements in Bradbury's stories, and lack of a coherent critical perspective. Index, selected annotated bibliography

Touponce, by contrast, brings very sharply defined perspectives to bear on Bradbury. In the 1984 revision of his 1981 dissertation—a solid, sophisticated (sometimes to excess) application of the reader-response theories of Wolfgang Iser and Gaston Bachelard to three short stories and *Fahrenheit 451* [3-31]—Touponce shows how reverie, "both core and method in the fantasy of Ray Bradbury," provides a link between author and reader whereby the former draws the latter into the worlds of his fictions. Extensive bibliography, index. Touponce's Starmont study is mislabeled. In no way introductory, it amounts to an extended essay on the influence of Friedrich Nietzsche's aesthetics of tragedy on Bradbury's thought and art. Touponce develops this thesis, somewhat repetitively, in his "biocritical introduction" and in chapters on Bradbury's major works. Although Touponce establishes his point, viewing Bradbury's rich oeuvre exclusively through so narrow a lens tends to distort it. Chronology, bibliography, index. Finally, Greenberg and Olander's collection of essays on Bradbury is one of the best in Taplinger's series, offering particularly useful examinations of structural aspects of Bradbury's fiction and of the themes of religion, science and technology, and the frontier myth. Burgess 290–92. (MAM)

John Brunner

9-25.   De Bolt, Joe, ed. **The Happening Worlds of John Brunner: Critical Explorations in Science Fiction.** Kennikat, 1975.

John Brunner's novels are a good deal more interesting and important than the paucity of critical attention given them would suggest—a neglect not excused by the sharp decline in his productivity since the mid seventies. The best introductions to his work and its place in modern SF are John R. Pfeiffer's essay in Bleiler's *Science Fiction Writers* [7-20] and De Bolt's biocritical introduction to this uneven collection. Its strengths include James Blish's brief introduction, a survey of Brunner's now inaccessible poetry, a long concluding essay by Brunner that combines autobiographical remarks with reflections on science fiction, and a thorough bibliography. Its weaknesses, regrettably, are its critical apparatus: too many of these essays are undercut by pretentious or downright awkward writing, often in the service of pointless or obvious observations. Nevertheless, this book will be of value to readers focusing on Brunner's most significant and controversial work, the dystopian novels *Stand on Zanzibar* [4-74], *The Sheep Look Up* [4-72], and *Shockwave Rider* [4-73]. Index of works and persons. Burgess 297. (MAM)

Edgar Rice Burroughs

9-26.   Holtsmark, Erling B. **Edgar Rice Burroughs.** Twayne, 1986.

9-27.   Lupoff, Richard A. **Edgar Rice Burroughs: Master of Adventure.** Ace, 1968. Rev. ed.

9-28.   Porges, Irwin. **Edgar Rice Burroughs: The Man Who Created Tarzan.** Brigham Young, 1975.

In *Trillion Year Spree* [8-5] Brian Aldiss comments: "Wells is teaching us to think. Burroughs and his lesser imitators are teaching us not to think. Of course, Burroughs is teaching us to wonder. The sense of wonder is in essence a religious state, blanketing out criticism." Burroughs wrote 70 novels, which have sold well over 100 million copies. Yet, as Aldiss also says, "All Burroughs's novels are vaguely similar, wherever they are set, heroes and incidents often transposable, as clips of crocodile fights were transposed from one Tarzan movie to the next."

Published on the one hundredth anniversary of Burroughs's birth, Porges is the authorized and definitive biography, over 100 pages, including more than 250 photos and illustrations. The sources of Burroughs's popularity and the entire scope of his works and life are discussed in detail by Porges, who has relied on many primary sources not previously available.

Readers will find Holtsmark, in the Twayne author series, the most readily available and convenient survey. He includes a short biography and a discussion of the Mars, Tarzan, Pellucidar, and Venus series; discusses literary background and themes; and offers a balanced final assessment. Lupoff treats the entire range of the writings, from Tarzan in 1914 to posthumous works issued in the 1960s. Chapter 19, "A Basic Burroughs

Library," will be helpful to libraries, which usually reject most of the works of this author. Tarzan fans may wish to search out Philip José Farmer's mock serious account, *Tarzan Alive: A Definitive Biography of Lord Greystoke* (Doubleday, 1972). Burgess 300–305. (NB)

John W. Campbell, Jr.

*9-29.   Berger, Albert I. **The Magic That Works: John W. Campbell and the American Response to Technology.** Borgo, 1993.

John W. Campbell, Jr., was by wide agreement the most influential single editor SF has seen in his more than 30 years at *Astounding*, now *Analog*. His importance is discussed in *Trillion Year Spree* [8-5], *The Creation of Tomorrow* [8-34] (see also chapter 3), and Panshin's *The World Beyond the Hill* [8-101], among other sources. A selection of his letters was published as *The John W. Campbell Letters*, vol. 1, ineptly edited by Perry A. Chapdelaine, Sr., and others (AC Projects, 1985), on which Berger draws. (A second volume, letters to/from Asimov and van Vogt, was published in mid-1993.) Berger, a history professor, has provided the first detailed assessment of Campbell, the historical context in which he worked, the commercial pressures to which he was subject, and the influence he and his magazine had on SF. Although published as part of Borgo's Popular Writers to Today series, the work is a case study in American intellectual history derived from a then-despised branch of popular literature. Berger has drawn on his master's and doctoral theses, his published articles, and Campbell's letters to create this detailed and balanced analysis.

He explores how the writers, editor, and readers of *Astounding* interacted with one another and how they were shaped by the shift from the 19th-century tradition of the inventor/tinkerer (recall Tom Swift and similar boy heroes) to the corporate and university laboratories of today, where large budgets and teams dominate. Berger is especially good at dissecting Campbell's attitudes toward science and technology, especially the role of the "amateur" scientist, and even more specifically, the problems Campbell had in distinguishing between "unorthodox" science and outright quackery. (There is considerable discussion of Hubbard's Dianetics and Scientology and other Campbell enthusiasms such as the Dean Drive and parapsychology generally.) An admirable study, transcending the narrowly literary, well-written, exceptionally well-documented, and well-indexed, and easily the best in this Borgo series. (NB)

Orson Scott Card

*9-30.   Collings, Michael R. **In the Image of God: Theme, Characterization, and Landscape in the Fiction of Orson Scott Card.** Greenwood, 1990.

A phenomenally diverse and prolific writer, Card has produced a host of novels, collections, stories, poetry, plays, video and tape presentations, nonfiction books, and articles. Collings's accessible, intelligent advocacy of Card's work rests upon a parallel with C. S. Lewis—another author who fervently affirms the primacy of story, is concerned with theological issues, and whose works manifest an (apparent) deep-seated sense of estrangement. Clearly deeply affected by Card's work, Collings portrays him as "a consummate storyteller whose stories happen to be . . . [about] a world composed of the spiritual as well as the material." He explicates that world via a singularly perceptive account of Card's analogical use of interior and exterior landscapes and an explication of the structural role played by the monomyth in his construction of heroes. Collings further identifies "the need to identify and define community" as Card's dominant theme and deals with such dicey and important issues as his use of the Bible, Mormonism, and violence. For anyone with more than a passing interest in this author, Collings's book is essential, although it is marred by the exclusionary implication that only those sympathetic to the Mormon worldview can meaningfully interpret Card's fiction. Scholars will also need Collings's exhaustive (through 1991) bibliography *The Work of Orson Scott Card: An Annotated Bibliography and Guide* (Borgo, 1992). Extensive primary and secondary bibliography; index. Burgess 311, 312. (MAM)

Arthur C. Clarke

9-31. Hollow, John. **Against the Night, the Stars: The Science Fiction of Arthur C. Clarke.** Ohio Univ. Press, 1987.

9-32. McAleer, Neil. **Arthur C. Clarke: The Authorized Biography.** Contemporary, 1992.

9-33. Olander, Joseph D., and Martin H. Greenberg, eds. **Arthur C. Clarke.** Taplinger lL., 1977.

9-34. Rabkin, Eric S. **Arthur C. Clarke.** Starmont, 1980. 2nd ed., rev.

*9-35. Slusser, George Edgar. **The Space Odysseys of Arthur C. Clarke.** Borgo, 1978.

Infused with optimism about the future of humanity, enthusiasm for technology, and a sense of wonder at the universe, Clarke's fiction is a touchstone of 20th century SF. Rabkin's brief guide, in chapters devoted to Clarke's short fiction and four major novels, usefully situates him in the British SF tradition that followed Wells and Stapledon. Rabkin leans too heavily on plot summary and deals inadequately with the role of science in Clarke's works, but enhances his book by including, in addition to the usual chronology and index, a well-annotated bibliography of Clarke's pre-1980 fiction. Unlike Rabkin, Slusser strives to unify Clarke's fictions of this era by identifying in each "the Odyssey pattern," a modern updating of the archetypal narrative pattern that dates from *The Odyssey*. Slusser's use of Lucien Goldmann's structural sociology not only illuminates Clarke's works and their interconnections but also introduces useful evaluative criteria, a combination that makes this 64-page essay the best extended criticism on Clarke to date.

John Hollow identifies as a unifying theme Clarke's optimistic view of the potential of the human race for understanding the cosmos. But he overemphasizes this rather obvious point to the exclusion of other important aspects of Clarke's fiction and fails to define a context for Clarke as a major modern SF writer. Hollow took the opportunity of the 1987 reprinting of his book (first published in 1983) to add a chapter on Peter Hyams's 1982 film of *2010: Odyssey Two* [4-110] and the various incarnations of *Songs of Distant Earth* (1986) (short story, movie outline, novel) but, unfortunately, did not remedy the defects in its scholarly apparatus, which offers only a list of Clarke's fiction and a bibliography of selected criticism. Readers seeking additional criticism should consult David N. Samuelson's insightful essay in Bleiler's *Science Fiction Writers* [8-20] and Olander and Greenberg's collection, especially the essays by Thomas Clareson on Clarke's vision, by Betsy Harfst on the mythical content of his major novels, and by Samuelson and John Huntington on *Childhood's End* [3-44]. Selected bibliography, index.

Readers seeking biographical information face a problem. Clarke's engaging, somewhat eccentric autobiography *Astounding Days* (Bantam, 1989) adopts the clever strategy of using the issues of *Astounding Science Fiction* that Clarke read from March 1930 through 1945 as triggers for reflections on his life and stories. The result, although fragmented, is fascinatingly chatty and usefully complements the equally fragmentary information in *The View from Serendip* (1977). Most disappointingly, Neil McAleer's well-intended but numbing "authorized biography" offers endless details about Clarke's travels, book contracts, and projects but little insight into his intellectual life or his fiction. List of sources, index. Burgess 315. (MAM)

Hal Clement

9-36.   Hassler, Donald M. **Hal Clement.** Starmont, 1982.

Clement attended technical high school, earned an undergraduate degree in astronomy from Harvard, and has taught science in a private school since 1949, the year before his first novel, *Needle*, was published. His fiction predictably reflects his interest in and extensive knowledge of "hard" science, from his most famous work, *Mission of Gravity* [3-50] to his most recent, *Still River* (1987). Hassler surveys Clement's fiction through *The Nitrogen Fix* in 1980, emphasizing his skill in depicting alien intelligences. Such outsiders sometimes provide an ironic perspective on humanity, a centuries-old literary device. A competent account that should have been more rigorously edited to improve the often awkward prose. Burgess 316–1717. (NB)

Samuel R. Delany

*9-37.   Barbour, Douglas. **Worlds Out of Words: The SF Novels of Samuel R. Delany.** Bran's Head Books, 1979.

9-38.   McEvoy, Seth. **Samuel R. Delany.** Ungar, 1983.

9-39.   Slusser, George Edgar. **The Delany Intersection: Samuel R. Delany Considered as a Writer of Semi-Precious Words.** Borgo, 1977.

9-40.   Weedman, Jane Branhan. **Samuel R. Delany.** Starmont, 1977.

Samuel Delany's paramount contributions to the evolving poetics of SF through his critical essays and multiplex experimental fictions demand critical attention at greater length than is offered in any of these books. None deal adequately with his publications since *Triton* (1976) [4-132], and only Barbour offers insights into that primary novel. Although dated and hard to find, Barbour's remains the best overall introduction to Delany's early works; in particular his insights into *Dhalgren* (1975) [4-127] are sure to benefit perplexed readers. Barbour leads up to this novel with four chapters that approach Delany's novels of the sixties from diverse perspectives: his use of the quest pattern as spatial metaphor, his creation of a self-contained system of allusions, his construction of alien cultures, and his style and structure. Barbour is least satisfactory in dealing with this last topic, but Slusser's essay fills the gap. Most usefully, Slusser clearly explains the essential structuralist features of Delany's art, highlighting the overriding concern for language and structure evident in his self-conscious post-mimetic speculative fictions.

Weedman takes a completely different tack, presenting Delany as primarily as an author of "anthropological SF" whose "double consciousness" (as a black writer working in a dominant white culture) influences both thematic and formal dimensions of his fiction. In hindsight, Weedman's emphasis on race does usefully clarify the sense in which Delany's novels of the late sixties anticipated much heralded developments in American SF of the late eighties. But her overemphasis on this theme creates a perception of Delany that is too distorted for an introductory guide. Chronology, annotated primary and secondary bibliography, index.

Last and least, Seth McEvoy provides a wealth of biographical detail, only some of which he usefully relates to Delany's early novels. But McEvoy's awkward prose, carelessness with facts and details, apparent obliviousness to secondary literature, and frequent lapses into banal generalities undercut and obscure such insights as he has to offer. Inadequate bibliography, index. The most sophisticated critical work to date on Delany and the only extended treatment of his novels since the mid-seventies is Robert Fox's penetrating contextualization of him as a black American postmodernist in *Conscientious Sorcerers: The Black Postmodernist Fiction of LeRoi Jones/Amiri Bakara, Ishmael Reed, and Samuel R. Delany* (Greenwood, 1987). Finally, readers interested in Delany's fiction should definitely read his critical works (see chapter 8). Burgess 322–23. (MAM)

Philip K. Dick

9-41.   Dick, Philip K. **The Selected Letters of Philip K. Dick, 1974.** Underwood-Miller, 1991. Ed. by Paul Williams.

9-42.   Greenberg, Martin H., and Joseph D. Olander, eds. **Philip K. Dick.** Taplinger, 1983.

*9-43.   Mackey, Douglas A. **Philip K. Dick.** Twayne, 1988.

*9-44.   Mullen, R. D., Istvan Csicserny-Ronay, Jr., and Arthur B. Evans, eds. **On Philip K. Dick: 40 Articles From Science-Fiction Studies.** SF-TH, Inc., 1992.

9-45.   Pierce, Hazel. **Philip K. Dick.** Starmont, 1982.

9-46.   Robinson, Kim Stanley. **The Novels of Philip K. Dick.** UMI Research Press, 1984.

*9-47.   Sutin, Lawrence. **Divine Invasions: A Life of Philip K. Dick.** Harmony, 1989.

9-48.   Warrick, Patricia S. **Mind in Motion: The Fiction of Philip K. Dick.** Southern Illinois Univ. Press, 1987.

The explosion of interest in Dick's fiction since his death in 1982 is manifest in the posthumous publication of his mainstream novels, the enshrinement of his major SF novels in Vintage paperback editions, and the accelerating proliferation of biographical and critical works that culminates with Mullen et al.'s collection of articles from *Science-Fiction Studies.* Prefaced by a perceptive introduction on Dick's posthumous reception by critics and its consequences for SF's interpenetration into the mainstream, lists of the manuscript collection at California State University and of Dick's books in chronological order, and a secondary bibliography, this essential volume maps the development of a critical consensus that is still in flux. Index.

The best introduction to Dick's huge oeuvre is Douglas Mackey's Twayne volume. In chapters organized chronologically by decade, Mackey presents accurate summaries of Dick's SF and mainstream novels and of many of his short stories, accompanied by brief but sensible critical insights that often parallel (or quote) the work of previous studies. He falters only when confronted with the complexity of the novels of the seventies. By careful organization and identification of thematic interconnections between various works (primarily Dick's concern for the nature of reality), Mackey brings uncommon coherence to this necessarily brief overview. Chronology, primary and annotated secondary bibliography, index.

Also valuable to newcomers to Dick's fiction are the largely empirical essays collected by Greenberg and Olander. Of special interest are the stimulating essays by three contemporaries of Dick: Brian Aldiss, Michael Bishop, and Thomas Disch. Although this collection suffers from exclusion of novels published after 1974, its 10 accessible, thematically oriented, largely theoretical essays comprise a valuable if fragmented survey of Dick's fiction. Biography, index. Last among introductions comes Pierce's guide, a respectable if sometimes careless effort crippled by the ridiculous length constraints of this series, which here requires dealing with the totality of Dick's novels, short stories, and published critical comments in under 60 pages. Chronology, primary and secondary bibliography, notes.

Like Mackey and other critics who followed her, Warrick contextualizes Dick's works by his turbulent, troubled life and the mid-century American culture in which he lived and wrote. Drawing heavily on personal interviews and correspondence with Dick, Warrick considers his works chronologically in chapters, each of which addresses a primary theme of the period. Her lucid attempt to resolve the considerable ambiguities of Dick's works through the notion of a "dynamic four-chambered metaphor" and to present his "strange, mutant science fiction" as "quantum-reality fiction" generates myriad insights, especially into the eight major novels on which she focuses. But her study is marred by apparent lack of use of and lack of reference to secondary literature and, more seriously, by absence of any discussion of Dick's relationship to and views on American SF, its publishers, and readership. Chronology, primary bibliography, index. Robinson's brief study of Dick's SF and mainstream novels, based on his 1982 doctoral thesis, complements Warrick's book. Robinson is particularly strong on Dick's challenge to the conventions of traditional American SF and on the self-referential and broadly metaphorical character of his later works. In spite of a few minor errors, lack of depth in treatment of some novels, and uneven reference to the secondary literature, Robinson should be read in conjunction with Warrick or after Mackey. Notes, bibliography, index.

The troubled, turbulent nature of Dick's life and its clear importance to his later fiction has provoked several biographical studies, including Greg Rickman's book-length interviews, *Philip K. Dick: In His Own Words* (Fragments West, 1984) and *Philip K. Dick: The Last Testament* (Fragments West, 1985) and his three-part personal biography the first volume of which is *To The High Castle. Philip K. Dick: A Life 1928-1962* (Fragments West/Valentine Press, 1989). The latter, although useful for illuminating Dick's interaction with his SF contemporaries, is flawed by lack of discrimination, repetitiveness, awkward prose, and Rickman's propensity for speculative psychological interpretations. By contrast, Sutin interweaves a compelling, compassionate account of Dick and those who knew him with a narrative of his intellectual life and evolving fictional concerns. He concludes with a very useful "Chronological Survey and Guide," which annotates and rates (on a scale from 1 to 10) every book Dick wrote. Index. Looming large in Sutin's account is the supernatural/religious vision/hallucination Dick experienced in 1974. Dick detailed his efforts to assimilate this extraordinary phenomenon in his journal, the "exegesis," excerpts from which have been edited by Sutin and published as *In Pursuit of Valis: Selections From the Exegesis* (Underwood-Miller, 1991). Although extremely valuable to Dick scholars, this eccentric volume provides a less acute sense of this experience than the three novels that resulted from it, the "Valis trilogy," and the first of Underwood-Miller's proposed series of Dick's letters. Covering a wide range of topics, the latter volume (which omits a few important letters and, more seriously, lacks a topic index) provides a troubling snapshot of an atypical year in the life of a most atypical man. Burgess 326–28. (MAM)

Harlan Ellison

*9-49.   Slusser, George Edgar. **Harlan Ellison: Unrepentant Harlequin.** Borgo, 1977.

Has Harlan Ellison cowed the critics? Or is the reason for the paucity of critical work on American SF's *enfant terrible* due to his chosen fictional form, the short story of scientific fantasy? In this brief but excellent examination of Ellison's work through *Deathbird Stories* (1975) [4-159], George

Slusser details, in sections devoted to Ellison's journalism, fantasy stories, and mythic parables and quests, his evolution of "an intricate, highly personal language of mythical expression." While busily elaborating Ellison's underlying Emersonian dynamic, Slusser slights somewhat the intense topicality of Ellison's work, with its focus on social injustice energized by barely controlled outrage and considerable stylistic gifts. Slusser's essay on Ellison in Bleiler's *Science Fiction Writers* [8-20] brings his analysis only up to 1980. Ellison was uncommonly unprolific during the eighties; still, his more recent stories—primarily those in *Angry Candy* [4-158], which deepen the "mood of reconciliation" and tendency toward "optimistic pessimism" Slusser identifies in works of the mid-1970s—make one wish for an expansion and updating of this singularly insightful booklet. See also essays in *The Book of Ellison*, ed. by Andrew Porter (Algol Press, 1978). Burgess 335. (MAM)

Philip José Farmer

9-50. Brizzi, Mary T. **Philip José Farmer.** Starmont, 1980.

9-51. Chapman, Edgar L. **The Magic Labyrinth of Philip José Farmer.** 1985.

Farmer is fond of the picaresque and the playful and has over the years linked his fictions to those of others, such as Burroughs, Arthur Conan Doyle, and L. Frank Baum. These elements are explored in both books. Brizzi examines his technique and images in works published through mid-1978. Chapman is more current, though now a bit dated, and is more detailed as well, although he omits the Brizzi study from his bibliography. He is strongest in his exploration of Farmer's use of parody and satire. Burgess 336–37. (NB)

William Gibson

*9-52. Olsen, Lance. **William Gibson.** Starmont, 1992.

Although William Gibson is younger and has been less prolific than most in the Starmont series, the impact of his short stories and novels on SF in general and cyberpunk in particular warrant this detailed critical explication. Like Brian McHale in *Constructing Postmodernism* (Routledge, 1993) and several critics who contributed essays to Larry McCaffery's *Storming the Reality Studio* [8-86], Olsen situates Gibson in two overlapping literary schools: SF and postmodernism. Drawing in part on perspectives elaborated in his *Eclipse of Uncertainty* (1987), Olsen explores Gibson's intertextuality, globalism, and eclectic use of genre materials and motifs, particularizing his insights with discussions of style and structure, the dominant aspects of Gibson's art. Best of all, Olsen is balanced; he demonstrates the strengths of several short stories and *Neuromancer* [4-184] but also notes the progressive weakening of Gibson's later novels, excluding *The Difference Engine* [4-186], which he mentions only in passing. Readers seeking a broader view of the cyberpunk phenomenon should supplement this essential guide with aforementioned books by McHale and McCaffery. Chronology, primary and secondary bibliography, index. (MAM)

Joe Haldeman

9-53.   Gordon, Joan. **Joe Haldeman.** Starmont, 1980.

In February 1968, age 24, Haldeman was sent to Vietnam and was seriously wounded in September. This experience shaped all his writings, especially the semiautobiographical novel, *War Year* (1972) and particularly his *The Forever War* [4-193], which won both the Hugo and the Nebula. This early survey discusses his work and life through the 1978 collection, *Infinite Dreams.* His subsequent work, with the possible exception of *The Hemingway Hoax* [4-194], has been less highly regarded. (NB)

Harry Harrison

9-54.   Stover, Leon. **Harry Harrison.** Twayne, 1991.

Harrison is the least well-known SF author yet included in Twayne's United States Authors Series, but his friend and collaborator Leon Stover forcefully argues that he is not merely a fine and prolific SF writer but "a significant American writer"—part of the tradition of classic American adventure fiction that include such heavy hitters as Cooper, Melville, Twain, and Mailer. While acknowledging Harrison's reliance on the traditional Gernsbackian mode of technophilic adventure narratives imbued with scientific rationalism and shaped by pulp forms and conventions, Stover successfully situates Harrison's major works such as *Make Room! Make Room!* [4-200] and *Captive Universe* [4-198] in the stream of social science fiction whose modern incarnations derive from the works of H. G. Wells. Less successful is his argument that Harrison's fiction is sufficiently rich, mature, and sophisticated to warrant the critical attention whose neglect he decries. In part this failure is less the fault of Harrison's works than of Stover's overreliance on advocacy and asides rather than analysis: for example, his skimpy discussion of Harrison's epic alternate history, the West of Eden trilogy [4-201], arguably the best evidence for his claims for Harrison's stature. Stover drew extensively on interviews with Harrison, and his book contains an excellent biographical sketch and provocative asides on Harrison's philosophy. Chronology, notes, primary and (briefly annotated) secondary bibliography, index. Burgess 343–45. (MAM)

Robert A. Heinlein

*9-55. Franklin, H(oward) Bruce. **Robert A. Heinlein: America as Science Fiction.** Oxford Univ. Press, 1980. Eaton, 1982

9-56. Olander, Joseph D., and Martin H. Greenberg, eds. **Robert A. Heinlein.** Taplinger, 1978.

9-57. Panshin, Alexei. **Heinlein in Dimension.** Advent, 1968.

9-58. Slusser, George Edgar. **The Classic Years of Robert A. Heinlein.** Borgo, 1977.

9-59. Slusser, George Edgar. **Robert A. Heinlein: Stranger In His Own Land.** Borgo, 1977. 2nd ed.

9-60. Stover, Leon. **Robert A. Heinlein.** Twayne, 1987.

Heinlein began to publish SF in 1939 and for the next 20 years unquestionably dominated the field, as he moved from the genre magazines to the "slicks" and to book publication of his YA novels by Scribner's and to bestsellerdom in the years preceding his death in 1988. He may have been the first genre author to have had a book devoted to him, Panshin's study, revised from its piecemeal appearance in *Riverside Quarterly.* Although Panshin is limited to Heinlein's earlier works, his assessment of the plots, subjects, literary quality, and influence anticipates the later works and themes.

Slusser examines Heinlein's first two decades in his first study, while the second focuses on later work through the mid-1970s. Both studies explore the central dynamics underlying the surface themes, conventions and doctrines and how they generate the formal structure of the stories. Especially valuable for their close readings and their heterodox interpretations.

The Taplinger collection assembles nine original essays treating the YA novels, his future history series, *Stranger in a Strange Land* [3-91] and *Time Enough for Love* [4-205], human sexuality, and social Darwinism in his fictions. Primary and secondary bibliography and index. A useful synoptic survey and starting point.

Franklin approaches Heinlein from a Marxist standpoint and divides the tales into five periods, relating them to contemporary American history. He is effective in showing how the contradictions in a capitalist American society are reflected and refracted in the stories, examining in detail the familiar Heinlein dualisms of authoritarianism/anarchism, futuristic realism/nostalgia and hardheaded rationalism/mysticism. Like most Marxists, he's a trifle dogmatic, and his study almost wholly neglects the SF genre in which most of his work—and certainly his most important (though not most popular) work—appeared. Nevertheless, an important study of a seminal and influential writer.

Leon Stover is an anthropologist and a decided partisan of Heinlein. He claims his study "is the first to treat him as a significant American author and not merely as a genre writer," an unsupportable assertion. What is most characteristic of Stover's study, in an author series that is supposed to provide balanced assessments of their subjects, is the defensive and tendentious tone throughout. Franklin's study, for example, "turns out to be of more interest to America-hating Marxists than to students of American science fiction." He finds the critical literature on Heinlein "uniformly hostile," another unsupportable claim. Although some of Stover's interpretations are worth the time of Heinlein critics, the uncritical boosterism and dismissal of anyone who disagrees with him makes this an irresponsible work. Burgess 346. (NB)

Frank Herbert

9-61.   Miller, David M. **Frank Herbert.** Starmont, 1980.

9-62.   O'Reilly, Timothy. **Frank Herbert.** Ungar, 1981.

A journalist for many years, Herbert incorporated many of his interests in *Dune* [4-207] and its sequels, the subject of *The Dune Encyclopedia* (Berkley, 1984), edited by Willis E. McNelly, which embroiders an already complex set of novels. Miller's study departs from the usual Starmont format. Biographical details are few, with the focus on critical analysis—often harsh. Miller argues that the concept of dynamic homeostasis is central to an understanding of Herbert's novels, each of which is discussed in two to four pages. In a study three times the length of Miller, O'Reilly explores the philosophical ideas underlying and linking Herbert's fiction, not only the Dune series. The later Dune books would require some revision of both Miller and O'Reilly. Burgess 347–48. (NB)

Ursula K. Le Guin

*9-63.   Cummins, Elizabeth. **Understanding Ursula K. Le Guin.** Univ. of South Carolina, 1990.

9-64.   De Bolt, Joe, ed. **Ursula K. Le Guin: Voyager to Inner Lands and to Outer Space.** Kennikat, 1979.

9-65. Spivack, Charlotte. **Ursula K. Le Guin.** Twayne, 1984.

Of all modern SF writers, Le Guin has been the subject of more articles and books than any other, although Philip K. Dick is—without counting—a close second. Her popularity extends well beyond the confines of genre SF, one reason for the extensive secondary literature. The books began with George Slusser's long 1976 essay, *The Farthest Shores of Ursula K. Le Guin* (Borgo), which provides a careful analysis of her earlier works. A useful overview of her achievement is provided in the De Bolt collection of essays. Spivack's introductory survey provides the usual Twayne features: chronology, life and intellectual background, influences, and some discussion of her key works—fiction, essay, and poetry—through about 1981. The best introduction to Le Guin, other than the author herself (see chapter 8), is Cummins's volume in the Understanding Contemporary American Literature series. Le Guin's ideas have evolved and changed considerably in recent years, and the recency of the Cummins study gives it a decided advantage. She is especially good in her analyses of more recent works, such as *Always Coming Home*, and how they are related to her earlier fiction. (The 1993 trade paperback reprint from USC Press adds a chapter and updates the the bibliography.) Burgess 364. (NB)

Fritz Leiber

*9-66. Byfield, Bruce. **Witches of the Mind: A Critical Study of Fritz Leiber.** Necronomicon, 1991.

Although Fritz Leiber won six Hugos, four Nebulas, and myriad other awards and was one of the pioneers of American sociological science fiction, this importance has been underemphasized by most chroniclers of the field. As Bruce Byfield shows in his splendid critical study, "[Leiber] has paced developments in science fiction as no other writer has done," and "his development is a microcosm of the field's." Byfield's book is a bracing corrective to the vacuity of the first two books on Leiber: an over-reliance on plot summary, paucity of analysis, and an excess of errors mar both Jeff Frane's Starmont House guide (1980) and Tom Staircar's entry in the Ungar Recognitions series (1983). Byfield, however, is excellent. He explicates Leiber's oeuvre (which also includes supernatural horror, fantasy, and sword-and-sorcery yarns) through their symbols and the influence of three major figures—H. P. Lovecraft, Robert Graves (the novels, not the poetry), and Carl Jung—and several secondary ones (for example, Thomas De Quincy, Henrik Ibsen, and Joseph Campbell). This schema fits Leiber's career almost perfectly, since each stage in his development was informed by encounters with the works of these three men. Byfield further illuminates the absolutely central place of personal experience in Leiber's later works. Rich with insights into Leiber's life and works, this is an exemplary critical biography. Primary and secondary bibliography, index. Burgess 365, 366. (MAM)

Stanislaw Lem

9-67.   Davis, J. Madison. **Stanislaw Lem.** Starmont, 1990.

9-68.   Ziegfeld, Richard E. **Stanislaw Lem.** Ungar, 1985.

Critics tackling the writings of Stanislaw Lem face major obstacles. For one thing, the play of commentary in Lem's fiction undermines most critical approaches as effectively as the better known tactics of Thomas Pynchon and Umberto Eco. For another, some of Lem's most important works—notably the futurological treatise *Summa Technologiae* (1964) and his critical analysis *Science Fiction and Futurology* (1971)—remain largely untranslated into English, and existing translations of important novels (notably *The Invincible* (1973)) are seriously flawed. To date, the best critical work on Lem, by critics such as Jerzy Jarzebski and Andrzej Stoff, is available only in monographs and essay collections published in West Germany and in his native Poland.

The best one can say about the first English-language book on Lem is that its author, Richard Ziegfeld, is infectiously keen on Lem's fiction. Unfortunately, he ignores nearly all the subtleties and complexities of Lem's work, and his commentaries generate more confusion than clarity. So determined is Ziegfeld to present Lem's fiction as essentially philosophical that he overemphasizes its themes, a singularly reductive approach to Lem's multifaceted novels, and undervalues other vital features, such as Lem's use of irony. Madison Davis shares Ziegfeld's enthusiasm but brings to his overview a more acute critical sensitivity and less ham-handed prose. Alas, hamstrung by the brevity of the Starmont format, Davis can offer only a cursory biographical sketch followed by 10 brief chapters devoted to individual texts from three phases of Lem's career: early SF, examinations of cognition and self-reference, and recent experimental metafictions. Here Davis emphasizes Lem's use of mystery/detective narratives at the expense of other aspects of his fiction: satire, philosophy, metacommentary, theology, parody, and so on. Davis does about as well as anyone could in 89 pages, but somehow characterizing Lem's writing as "unpredictable, wise, silly, philosophical, but always entertaining" seems inadequate. Chronology, usefully annotated primary and secondary bibliographies, index. See also Lem's collection of critical essays on SF, *Microworlds* [8-80], the special Lem issue of *Science-Fiction Studies* (vol. 13, no. 3, November 1986), and the thorough review by Peter Swirski of several untranslated critical works in *SFS* (vol. 19, no. 3, November 1992). As Swirski wryly notes, "we are still waiting for an English volume of interpretation and criticism that will set a standard for all subsequent Lem scholars." (MAM)

Doris Lessing

9-69. Fishburn, Katherine. **The Unexpected Universe of Doris Lessing: A Study in Narrative Technique.** Greenwood, 1985.

9-70. Pickering, Jean. **Understanding Doris Lessing.** Univ. of South Carolina, 1990.

9-71. Sprague, Claire, and Virginia Tiger, eds. **Critical Essays on Doris Lessing.** G. K. Hall, 1986.

9-72. Whitaker, Ruth. **Doris Lessing.** St. Martin's, 1988.

Someone familiar only with Lessing's earlier works, such as *The Golden Notebook* (1962) or the five-volume Children of Violence sequence (1952–1969), may well wonder what she is doing in this chapter. She is admittedly a peripheral figure for SF. Her 1974 novel, *The Memoirs of a Survivor* [4-263], chronicles a growing social anarchy observed by a woman from her apartment but ends as the characters leave one world to enter another. But it is the five-volume Canopus in Argos series [4-264] that makes her of interest to some SF readers. The books chosen for annotation therefore had to be recent enough to discuss this series.

Whitaker's volume in the Modern Novelists series provides a balanced analysis of all of Lessing's fiction, from the relatively straightforward realism of her earlier works to the metaphysical concerns of *Memoirs* to the conscious use of a galactic empire structure for her Canopus series. Whitaker devotes nine pages to *Memoirs* and 20 pages (a chapter) to the Canopus series, which she regards as "an extraordinary achievement . . . more than an esoteric work of fiction; read aright it may be, quite literally, a handbook for survival."

Pickering's audience is claimed to be "students as well as good nonacademic readers," but I found it too abstract for them and plodding, with no sense that Lessing's fictions might be at least intellectually exciting.

Fishburn devotes one chapter each to Lessing's "fantastic" fiction, beginning with the 1971 novel, *Briefing for a Descent Into Hell*. She writes clearly, and her study isn't clogged with the theoretical posturings that disfigure so much of literary criticism. Since she provides fairly detailed plot summaries, her account will be of more use to someone who's read little of Lessing. She is particularly good at clarifying Lessing's ideas of individuality versus collectivity and how these are embodied in the fiction.

The Sprague/Tiger collection of essays provides an eclectic overview of Lessing's career, with several essays dealing with the Canopus series and *Memoirs* from various perspectives, many of them from nonacademic sources and therefore more readable. Lessing is decidedly an acquired taste, and few of her critics show much knowledge of SF (often referring to her "space" fiction), while SF readers have generally ignored her. (NB)

C. S. Lewis

9-73.   Christopher, Joe R. **C. S. Lewis.** Twayne, 1987.

*9-74.   Dowling, David C. **Planets in Peril: A Critical Study of C. S. Lewis' Ransom Trilogy.** Univ. of Massachusetts Press, 1992.

9-75.   Edwards, Bruce L., ed. **The Taste of the Pineapple: Essays on C. S. Lewis as Reader, Critic, and Imaginative Writer.** Bowling Green State Univ. Press, 1988.

9-76.   Glover, Donald E. **C. S. Lewis: The Art of Enchantment.** Ohio Univ. Press, 1981.

*9-77.   Manlove, C. N,. **C. S. Lewis: His Literary Achievement.** Macmillan, 1987.

*9-78.   Murphy, Brian C. **C. S. Lewis.** Starmont, 1983.

9-79.   Walsh, Chad. **The Literary Legacy of C. S. Lewis.** Harcourt Brace, 1979.

Medievalist Christian apologist, and fantasist and mythmaker second only to fellow Inkling J. R. R. Tolkien, C. S. Lewis remains a problematical if cherished figure in the history of SF. In the mountain of biographical and critical writings on Lewis are a handful that contain either direct explications of or essential background to his fantasies. Christopher's Twayne study, although intelligently organized around the diverse roles Lewis assumed during his career and offering useful readings of Lewis's nonfiction, is really too superficial to serve as an introduction to this complex, multifaceted writer; moreover Christopher deemphasizes Lewis's significance as a fantasist and SF writer. His book does, however, contain annotated bibliography that will well serve newcomers to Lewis studies.

Walsh's study is a fine introduction to Lewis's life and thought. Focusing as much on Lewis the man as Lewis the writer, Walsh (a longtime friend of Lewis and his family) seeks to unify his diverse writings;

readers interested in his fantasies will find, for example, important connections between the Narnia and Ransom novels and his religious polemics. Walsh's particular orientation sometimes leads him to oversimplify the mythic influences on the content of Lewis's fictions, which he almost always sees as Christian allegories—a narrowness of critical view that more severely limits Colin Duriez's otherwise valuable guide *The C. S. Lewis Handbook: A Comprehensive Guide to His Life, Thought, and Writings* (Baker Book House, 1990). Primary and secondary bibliography, index.

Glover frames his study of the didactic elements and technical machinery of Lewis's fiction with a presentation of Lewis's perspectives on art and literature as gleaned from a careful reading of his letters and critical essays. Refusing to see Lewis as mere religious polemicist, Glover emphasizes how he constructed the novels in which he expressed his theological convictions. As such, Glover's book is an important complement to Walsh's. Notes, index. An even broader context for consideration of Lewis's SF can be found in Edwards's collection of essays on how Lewis's premises as a scholar inform his fiction. This collection features examinations of Lewis's critical practice, the rhetorical strategies he used in writing criticism, and the intellectual context in which he wrote, and a fascinating section on how Lewis's critical principles relate to his own fiction, including his interplanetary fantasies. Index.

Readers interested only in Lewis's SF works will find a more focused context in Manlove's lucid explication of the themes in eleven of Lewis's fictional works. Emphasizing the literary rather than theological/moral dimensions of Lewis's novels, Manlove unveils the "image of the universe" that emerges from them. Read consecutively, the seven chapters that constitute the body of this book also reveal Lewis's growth as an artist of fiction "of often considerable literary merit and subtlety" in which myth and image interfuse with religious didacticism. Notes, bibliography, index. In his brief but tightly written Starmont House guide, Murphy manages to cram an amazing amount of information, insights, and thoughtful assessments without ever becoming opaque or confusing. After a competent sketch of Lewis's life and principal philosophical beliefs, Murphy converges on the Ransom trilogy and Lewis's last works concluding with a useful primary and annotated secondary bibliography. Dowling focuses even more narrowly on Lewis's space trilogy, showing how religion and fantasy interpenetrate in these three novels. Dowling's fine, thoughtful study is valuable both for its careful background on Lewis's life and scholarship as it informs the trilogy and for its careful explication of the influences and content of each novel and their critical reception. An appendix on "The Dark Tower," a fragment Lewis apparently began as a dystopian sequel to

Out of the Silent Planet [3-116] then abandoned, rounds out this essential guide to reading or study of Lewis's greatest contribution to SF. Notes, bibliography, index. On Lewis's place in the history of British SF, see Brian Stableford's *Scientific Romance in Britain 1890–1950* [8-132]. (MAM)

David Lindsay

9-80.   Wolfe, Gary K. **David Lindsay.** Starmont, 1982.

Lindsay is best known for one book, *A Voyage to Arcturus* [2-72], which C. S. Lewis said in a letter was the "real father of my planet books" (his space trilogy [3-116]). A complex, demanding novel that has gained greater recognition in recent years, it and Lindsay's handful of other works are clearly explicated by Wolfe in his 64-page study and more briefly in his chapter in Bleiler's *Supernatural Fiction Writers* [7-20]. A decidedly marginal figure to SF, his life and thought is the subject of Bernard Sellin's *The Life and Works of David Lindsay* (Cambridge, 1981), a translation of his doctoral thesis. (NB)

Jack London

*9-81.   Beauchamp, Gorman. **Jack London.** Starmont, 1986.

*9-82.   Labor, Earle. **Jack London.** Twayne, 1974.

Like Mark Twain, Jack London produced a huge corpus of writing only a fraction of which is SF. But the considerable influence of London's social and political extrapolations continues to the present; thus *Before Adam* (1908) [1-58] anticipates the series of anthropological SF novels by Jean M. Auel (1980–1990), and the novella "The Scarlet Plague" (1915) anticipates (among myriad other disaster tales) Stephen King's *The Stand* (1978, rev. 1990) [4-233]. Regrettably, the finest critical book to date on London, Charles N. Watson's *The Novels of Jack London: A Reappraisal* (Wisconsin, 1983), excludes all of London's fantasies except the dystopia *The Iron Heel* (1908) [1-59]. Happily, both Beauchamp's guide and Labor's Twayne study are excellent. Beauchamp focuses exclusively on London's SF works and combines plot summary and accessible critical commentary to elaborate their historical, political, and social themes. Of particular value are his contextual connections, such as parallels to Wells's scientific romances and links to the revolutionary theories of the Russian Anarchist Petr Kropotkin and, more generally to the dominant Social Darwinist intellectual atmosphere of London's *fin de siècle* times. Chronology, annotated primary and secondary bibliography; index. Labor's balanced overview of

London's intensely creative output successfully seeks to recuperate him as "a major figure in American literature." Following a sketch of London's irresistibly American life and an excellent synopsis of the state of American popular fiction at the turn of the century, Labor examines all of London's major works, treating his fantasies as "a symbolic path into the deeper, inchoate reality of the unconscious mind." Even for readers interested only in London's SF, Labor defines an essential context for Beauchamp's more narrowly focused book. Chronology, notes and references, selected primary and annotated secondary bibliography, index. (MAM)

Anne McCaffrey

9-83. Brizzi, Mary T. **Anne McCaffrey.** Starmont, 1986.

9-84. Hargreaves, Mathew D. **Anne Inez McCaffrey: Forty Years of Publishing, An International Bibliography.** Author, Box 66099, Seattle, WA 98166-0099, 1992.

McCaffrey is best known for a series of linked novels set on a lost Earth colony called Pern, whose humans are linked symbiotically with tame, telepathic dragons. It sounds like fantasy, but the dragons are given a bio-engineering rationale, and most of her work, while relatively undemanding adventure with wide appeal to younger and older women, is still SF, although she has won awards for both SF and fantasy.

Brizzi finds the most persuasive metaphor in McCaffrey the "horse-and-rider motif," which takes many forms: ship and brain in *The Ship Who Sang* [4-290], dragon and rider in *Dragonflight* [4-289], and so on. She provides summaries and some analysis of McCaffrey's varied works as of about 1984; McCaffrey has published much since then. Brizzi recognizes the romantic and sentimental elements that are an essential part of McCaffrey's writings and finds these one of her major strengths and the source of her wide appeal. A moderately good introduction.

Hargreaves provides a somewhat detailed short biography and an exhaustive listing of published and unpublished works, secondary literature, and reproductions of 350 book jackets or covers, published anywhere in the world. Marred by too many typos but essential for McCaffrey buffs. A 42-page supplement was issued in 1994. Burgess 381. (NB)

A. Merritt

*9-85. Foust, Ronald. **A. Merritt.** Starmont, 1989.

A Munsey writer of the first rank and, according to Ronald Foust, "the last great writer of scientific romances," A. Merritt was one of the most popular writers of the pulp era (1930–1950), and his novels have intermittently reappeared ever since. Foust's well-written guide supplements but does not quite displace Sam Moskowitz's exasperating *A. Merritt: Reflections in the Moon Pool* (Oswald Train, 1985) as an introduction and overview. Except for its long, awkwardly presented biographical introduction, Moskowitz's mosaic of primary materials concerning Merritt's rise to reader acclaim remains essential to scholars. Foust draws upon Freudian and Jungian psychoanalytic concepts in his examination of the protagonists and rhetorical strategies of each of Merritt's major novels and several incidental pieces. This approach, within the context of Foust's mythic and archetypal critical stance, is certainly appropriate to Merritt's supersaturated lost race fantasies and produces interesting readings, especially of *Dwellers in the Mirage* (1932). Ultimately, however, it fails to earn for Merritt a place in the pantheon of significant SF writers; like Moskowitz's book, Foust's will likely be of more value to scholars of the pulp era than of SF. For a counterbalancing perspective on Merritt, see E. F. Bleiler's essay in *Science Fiction Writers* [7-20]. Chronology, annotated primary and secondary bibliographies, index. Burgess 383. (MAM)

Michael Moorcock

9-86.   Davey, John. **Michael Moorcock: A Reader's Guide.** Author (U.K.), 1992.

9-87.   Greenland, Colin. **Michael Moorcock: Death Is No Obstacle.** Savoy, 1992.

Michael Moorcock is nothing if not prolific. His huge, intricately coupled canon includes SF, fantasy, sword-and-sorcery, suspense and adventure stories, pastiches and satires, and unclassifiable "mainstream" novels. Faced with this literary cornucopia, readers urgently need bibliographical and critical help. What's available is sparse. Davey considers only British and American editions and excludes all but one of Moorcock's edited anthologies and all of his short fiction and nonfiction. Still, with its engaging descriptions of the intricate publication histories of Moorcock's self-contained interconnecting series of novels (including variant titles and often bewildering omnibus collections) and its phenomenal list (containing 85 entries!) recommending an eminently sensible sequence for reading Moorcock's entire output, Davey's guide is an essential map through Moorcock's multiverse. Colin Greenland's book is, unexpectedly, a 143-page interview with Moorcock about the craft of fiction. Greenland is the ideal interviewer—his book *The Entropy Exhibition* [8-61] contains the most extended discussion to date of Moorcock's seminal leadership of the New Wave movement—and Moorcock as interviewee is open and engaging. Reading their dialogue sometimes feels like eavesdropping on a conversation that has been under way for some time. But Moorcock's fiction nevertheless encompasses so many forms—various chapters consider heroic fantasy, comedy and SF, comic strips and commedia dell'arte, didactic fiction, and non-linear fiction, pastiches, and more—that this book amounts to a short course on writing techniques compounded with an overview of Moorcock's career. It contains sufficient nuggets of insight to fascinate readers familiar with Moorcock's works. Others should begin with *The Entropy Exhibition* [8-61] and the somewhat narrower perspectives offered by Brian W. Aldiss in *Trillion Year Spree* [8-5], Warren Wagar in *Terminal Visions* [8-140], John J. Pierce in *When World Views Collide* [8-108], and Peter Nicholls in his perceptive but dated essay in Bleiler's *Science Fiction Writers* [7-20]. As treatments of Moorcock's oeuvre, however, all of these suffer from brevity and narrowness of focus. Burgess 384-86. (MAM)

George Orwell

9-88.   Crick, Bernard. **George Orwell: A Life.** Little, Brown, 1980.

*9-89.   Orwell, George. **Nineteen Eighty-Four.** Clarendon/Oxford, 1984. Ed. by Bernard Crick.

9-90.   Gardner, Averil. **George Orwell.** Twayne, 1987.

*9-91.   Howe, Irving, ed. **Orwell's Nineteen Eighty-Four: Text, Sources, Criticism.** Harcourt, 1963. 2nd ed.

*9-92.   Reilly, Patrick. **Nineteen Eighty-Four: Past, Present, and Future.** Twayne, 1989.

*9-93.   Sheldon, Michael. **Orwell: The Authorized Biography.** Harper, 1991.

9-94.   Stansky, Peter, ed. **On Nineteen Eighty-Four.** W. H. Freeman, 1983.

The literature about Orwell is enormous, and new books and essays appear regularly. Orwell's importance to SF is his contribution to the tradition of dystopia, which has been a prominent feature of this century. *Nineteen Eighty-Four* is a warning, not a prophecy, and has explicitly and by influence energized much discussion of its literary and especially political meanings. I've selected for annotation a handful of the many studies of Orwell that focus on and illuminate his most discussed novel or that provide the context in which it can be most fully understood.

The first authorized biography was by Bernard Crick of the University of London, who was given permission by Orwell's second wife to consult Orwell's papers and quote freely. According to Michael Sheldon (later authorized by Orwell's literary executor), Sonia Orwell "was disappointed. She condemned it as too political, too dry, and too unsympathetic and tried to stop it from being published" but died of cancer when it was published in late 1980. (It was slightly revised for the 1982 Penguin edition.) Sheldon agrees that Crick's biography is a large collection of facts and faults it for not attempting to deal with Orwell's personal character, since he argues that the facts don't speak for themselves. However, Crick is still well worth the time of anyone seriously interested in Orwell, but the additional information available to Sheldon in the 11 years since Crick was published resulted in a better, much more readable biography, the best currently available.

Crick also provided annotations and a critical introduction to the definitive text. The novel itself occupies 272 of the 460 pages and has 103 annotations, which provide the reader with notes on the historical milieu in which the novel took shape and takes place and "how deeply rooted was part of Orwell's satire." Crick devotes 136 pages to his close critical reading, citing also his biography in the revised Penguin edition. Eight brief appendixes include a 1942 outline of the novel, 1948 notes revising the outline, the report of publisher Fredric Warburg, jacket copy of the U.K. and U.S. editions, and other material. His comments are invaluable to all serious students of the novel, and this edition is strongly recommended to academic and larger public libraries. Larger libraries will also want to consider Peter Davison's *Nineteen Eighty-Four: The Facsimile of the Extant Manuscript* (Harcourt, 1984). Davison also edited the standard edition of Orwell's works, 20 volumes published by Penguin, 1984–1993.

Gardner's study in Twayne's long-running author series provides a sound consensus overview of Orwell's life and works. She provides enough biographical detail to show the links between his life and his writings. It draws heavily on the author's research at the Orwell Archive, University College, London, as well as the many books and essays about Orwell listed and partly annotated in a four-page secondary bibliography. A useful starting point for a high school or college student.

Reilly's study in Twayne's Masterwork series vigorously argues that the novel be judged by literary not political criteria, even while recognizing that Orwell was an inherently didactic writer. Reilly says Bernard Crick argues that Orwell's dystopia stands to the 20th century as Hobbes's *Leviathan* does to the 17th. Reilly (Univ. of Glasgow) provides a useful summary of the widely varied critical reception showing how many critics, then as now, used the novel for political purposes, to defend what Orwell dismissed as "smelly little orthodoxies." Reilly devotes approximately 100 pages to a very close and intelligent reading of the novel, sometimes challenging other readings, such as that of Isaac Deutscher, whose essay Howe reprints. He is especially good in his analysis of the novel as "a love story, conducted against the background of a rebellion against God," which appalls rather than inspires. The novel is contrasted with *Paradise Lost* and Christian doctrine generally, with Ingsoc a perversion and repudiation of such doctrine. Reilly also illuminates the novel by showing the parallels with *Gulliver's Travels*. Swift is an obvious influence on Orwell, who discussed Swift in his essays, but it is the bleak pessimism of Swift that permeates the novel, which Reilly aptly calls "the death certificate of Renaissance man." He concludes that *Nineteen Eighty-Four* "is a conditional prophecy, a summons to preventive action, a tocsin to rouse his sleeping fellows." The crystal spirit, argued Orwell, can and must be preserved. Excellent annotated bibliography.

The late Irving Howe assembled for his Harbrace Sourcebook the text of the novel, seven pieces on sources, 13 essays on the novel proper, and two essays on the politics of totalitarianism; most essays are reprinted. The contributors include such influential figures as Lionel Trilling, Isaac Deutscher, Hannah Arendt, and Michael Harrington. Suggestions for papers and for further reading conclude the paperback. Howe recognizes that the novel "has become a major document of contemporary politics," and the emphasis of the essays is on the political rather than the purely literary dimensions of the novel. An especially well chosen collection of important and insightful essays, fortunately still in print.

Stansky, a professor of history and a biographer of Orwell, assembled 22 original essays for his book, published originally as part of a series issued by the alumni association of Stanford. All contributors were then associated with Stanford. The range of concern among the essays is wide, and anyone would gain a deepened and broadened understanding of the novel. The text is enriched with reproductions of apt paintings and cartoons. (NB)

Frederik Pohl

9-95. Clareson, Thomas D. **Frederik Pohl.** Starmont, 1987.

9-96. Pohl, Frederik. **The Way the Future Was: A Memoir.** Ballantine, 1978.

Pohl has been involved with SF since his teens as an editor, writer, and agent. His earlier years, including his life outside SF proper, is discussed in detail in his memoir, and more briefly in his chapter in *Hell's Cartographers* [9-140] and in his 16-page sketch in *Contemporary Authors Autobiographical Series*, vol. 1, 1984. He has written a lot and won every important award, including the Grand Master Nebula awarded by his fellow writers in 1993.

Clareson's 183-page study is one of the best and most detailed of the Starmont guides. He discusses Pohl's works chronologically from the 1940s through 1987, exploring their principal ideas and themes and relating them to the larger world of SF. His influential work as an editor and agent is not neglected. Clareson's friendship for and admiration of Pohl, however, sometimes undercuts the critical distance readers expect him to maintain, with the result that some works are praised excessively. Still, a valuable portrait of a prolific writer who has continued to develop throughout his life. Burgess 399. (NB)

Christopher Priest

*9-97.   Ruddick, Nicholas. **Christopher Priest.** Starmont, 1990.

After his public break in 1980 with science fiction as a genre and an institution and his continuing critical attack on the stories and writers of traditional Campbellian mass-market SF, American readers deserted Christopher Priest in droves. Although Priest is a writer of integrity, courage, and gifts both visionary and stylistic, his novels—philosophical in intent and (mildly) experimental in execution—are critical and popular successes only in Europe (especially in France). Ruddick's exceptional guide should begin to recoup Priest for U.S. readers. In a brief biocritical introduction and separate chapters for Priest's short fiction and each of his seven novels (completed in 1985, this book does not cover *The Quiet Woman* [1990]). Ruddick offers a balanced perspective on Priest's program, begun in his early New Wave fiction and continued in later metafictional novels, of critiquing "the history and politics of literary genre in general and science fiction in particular." Ruddick's insightful, detailed readings clarify how Priest elaborates (in massively recomplicated, organic plots) a universe constructed out of the private interior worlds of his characters, worlds that remain isolated by their creators' incomprehension and misperceptions. Ruddick and Colin Greenland have further situated Priest within broader contexts of British SF and the New Wave in *Ultimate Island* [8-122], and *The Entropy Exhibition* [8-61], respectively; those books and this guide, with its thoroughly annotated bibliography, will serve as essential starting points for readers and scholars interested in this unjustly obscure writer. Index. (MAM)

Mary Shelley

*9-98. Baldick, Chris. **In Frankenstein's Shadow: Myth, Monstrosity, and Nineteenth-Century Writing.** Oxford Univ. Press, 1987.

9-99. Forrey, Steven Earl. **Hideous Progenies: Dramatizations of Frankenstein from Mary Shelley to the Present.** Univ. of Pennsylvania, 1990.

*9-100. Mellor, Ann K. **Mary Shelley: Her Life, Her Fiction, Her Monsters.** Routledge, 1987.

*9-101. Sunstein, Emily W. **Mary Shelley: Romance and Reality.** Little, Brown, 1989.

*9-102. Tropp, Martin. **Mary Shelley's Monster: The Story of Frankenstein.** Houghton Mifflin, 1976.

9-103. Vasbinder, S. H. **Scientific Attitudes in Mary Shelley's Frankenstein.** UMI Research Press, 1984.

The explosion of critical and biographical interest in Mary Shelley during the 1980s presents formidable problems to readers seeking a focus on her contributions to science fiction. The place to start is with Brian W. Aldiss's spirited (widely but not universally accepted) defense in *Trillion Year Spree* [8-5] and in essays in *The Pale Shadow of Science* [8-3] of the progenitive role of *Frankenstein* [1-84]. Mellor, too, credits Mary Shelley with "[initiating] a new literary genre, what we now call science fiction." Mellor's skillful blend of biography and criticism, most of which focuses on *Frankenstein*, is an especially rewarding approach to her subject, for, as became apparent in earlier studies such as Elizabeth Nitchie's critical biography, *Mary Shelley: Author of Frankenstein* (Rutgers Univ. Press, 1953), Mary Shelley's life informed her fiction in complex, essential ways. To prove the revisionist thesis that her fiction is an extended attempt to conjure the (idealized) loving bourgeois family she never knew in life, Mellor recounts in detail her troubled life prior to the composition of *Frankenstein*, then brings a variety of critical approaches to bear on the novel. Of especial importance to scholars is her detailed study of Percy Bysshe Shelley's editorial changes to the original manuscript. Chronology, eight pages of plates, notes, primary and secondary bibliography, index.

Sunstein emphasizes biography over criticism, although her fascinating final chapter shows how Mary Shelley's posthumous reputation was "bent out of shape by admirers and, more lastingly, by traducers." Most important, Sunstein successfully individuates Mary Shelley, removing her once and for all from the shadow of her famous parents and husband and letting her emerge as "a major literary figure of the first half of the nineteenth century." Engaging, well-written, and drawing heavily on her subject's letters, journals, and other writings, Sunstein's "revisionary" biography is the standard for readers more interested in Mary Shelley's life than her fiction. Extensive primary bibliography, notes, index. More directly focused on *Frankenstein* is Vasbinder's brief monograph. Unfortunately, in his analysis of the novel's structure, setting, and science content, Vasbinder exaggerates his thesis concerning the role of the latter, distorting his representation both of the novel and its place in 19th-century fiction. See also Robert M. Philmus' *Into the Unknown* (Univ. of California, 1983) [8-104] and Christopher Small's *Ariel Like a Harpy: Shelley, Mary, and Frankenstein* (Gollancz, 1972).

The enormous and continuing influence of *Frankenstein* is the topic of Martin Tropp's study of the novel's mutation and evolution in the rich media of modern culture. After a discussion of the novel's background (considerably more cursory than Mellor's), Tropp first explicates its dream imagery, technological significance, and use of the *doppelgänger* motif, then turns to its stage and film adaptations. Notes, chronology of Frankenstein films, index, and bibliography. Scholars interested in early adaptations will find Forry's exhaustively researched *Hideous Progenies* to be indispensable; readers will find it great fun. In addition Forry's detailed and superbly illustrated history of adaptations prior to James Whale's 1931 film—a survey drawn in part from Donald F. Glut's vast compendium of minutiae *The Frankenstein Catalogue* (McFarland, 1984)—and a too-cursory survey of "post-Karloffian dramatizations," this book reprints the texts of seven early stage versions and, of all things, an appendix concerning the music for Richard Butler and H. Chance Newton's burlesque melodrama *Frankenstein; or, The Vampire's Victim* (1887). Bibliography, index. Chris Baldick's equally fine book about "adaptations, allusions, accretions, analogues, parodies, and plain misreadings" in works from 1789 to 1917 also contains a fascinating application of the myth theories of Claude Lévi-Strauss to Mary Shelley's novel. Notes, index. (MAM)

Robert Silverberg

9-104. Clareson, Thomas D. **Robert Silverberg.** Starmont, 1983.

9-105. Elkins, Charles L., and Martin H. Greenberg, eds. **Robert Silverberg's Many Trapdoors: Critical Essays on His Science Fiction.** Greenwood, 1992.

Clareson has written on Silverberg in several essays, reworked for his short Starmont guide. The approach is mostly chronological, from his fiction factory years in the 1950s and 1960s to his more "serious" work in the

1970s and later, with 11 novels discussed (about three pages each), along with the shorter fiction (1969–1974) and the Majipoor series of the 1980s. Clareson provides a balanced assessment of one of the field's major figures, who continues to write and edit regularly and has received two Nebulas and one Hugo since Clareson's book. Clareson also compiled a very detailed bibliography issued by G. K. Hall in 1983.

The 1992 book collects seven original essays introduced by Clareson, all dealing with Silverberg's more significant fiction from the 1970s. Russell Letson's overview essay is especially valuable; the other essays focus on individual novels, with one investigating short fiction from all phases of Silverberg's career. The 96-page Starmont guide is especially recommended to those relatively new to Silverberg, the collection to those who have read many of his works, Burgess 413. (NB)

E. E. Smith

9-106.   Sanders, Joe. **E. E. "Doc" Smith.** Starmont, 1986.

Smith was a food chemist, and Gernsback's addition of Ph.D. to his name generated his nickname. Smith's space operas were popular from the 1930s through the 1950s, and even today spinoffs appear that hitchhike on his reputation. Sanders's guide, the first critical study, "is intended to explain Smith's popularity while countering some of the unthinking aversion Smith's work has received" such as the Stableford assessment that he quotes: "aesthetically and intellectually vacuous." Such vacuity has never precluded popularity, and Sanders makes a good case for his subject. Fans of the Lensman and Skylark series may want to investigate *The Universes of E. E. Smith* by Ron Ellik and Bill Evans (Advent, 1966), a concordance and bibliography. (NB)

Olaf Stapledon

9-107.   Fiedler, Leslie. **Olaf Stapledon: A Man Divided.** Oxford, 1983.

*9-108.   Kinnaird, John. **Olaf Stapledon.** Starmont, 1986.

*9-109.   McCarthy, Patrick A. **Olaf Stapledon.** Twayne, 1982.

*9-110.   McCarthy, Patrick A., Martin H. Greenberg, and Charles Elkins, eds. **The Legacy of Olaf Stapledon: Critical Essays and an Unpublished Manuscript.** Greenwood, 1989.

Among the many paradoxes of Olaf Stapledon is the fact that even today this author of philosophical SF on the most expansive scale of space and time yet attempted, whom Brian W. Aldiss called "the ultimate SF writer," should remain, as Patrick McCarthy notes in his introduction to *The Legacy of Olaf Stapledon*, "a marginal figure in his own field." This excellent and important collection of six well-researched, well-written contextual essays covers Stapledon's nonfiction as well as the religious, mythic, historical, political, and, of course, philosophical dimensions of his SF novels. Perhaps most important, it includes a hitherto unpublished philosophical work *by* Stapledon: a series of letters written to his great-grandson concerning "the spiritual crisis he saw in his own civilization."

McCarthy's Twayne volume is the best overall introduction to Stapledon's work, although Kinnaird's guide runs it a close second. McCarthy's overview emphasizes the rich matrix of themes and techniques to be found in Stapledon's novels, and, in a somewhat less satisfactory concluding chapter, explores their influence on subsequent American and British writers. McCarthy's thorough biocritical introduction and chronological chapters devoted to thematic, philosophical, ethical, and literary issues admirably fulfills his goals of "[introducing] general readers to the beauty and subtlety of Stapledon's art" and "[laying] a foundation for more specialized studies." Chronology, notes and references, limited bibliography, index.

John Kinnaird's book clarifies Stapledon's development as a writer and thinker and convincingly renders him as "a mythopoetic writer—one who not only created myth but *thought* in terms of myth." Kinnaird elaborates this view with respect to various aspects of Stapledon's fiction, including his central themes and his symbolism of "abstract configurations." While somewhat uneven, Kinnaird's book offers much both to newcomers and to those familiar with Stapledon's novels—including a singularly fine reading of *Last and First Men* [2-119]. Chronology, annotated primary and secondary bibliography, index.

The subtitle of Leslie Fiedler's book might equally well apply to Fiedler himself. As the book progresses he repeatedly destabilizes his assessment of Stapledon, creating a deeply bifurcated portrait. Although avowedly not a biography, neither is Fiedler's book simply criticism; in fact, the tension between sometimes inaccurate biography and too often imprecise criticism almost rips it asunder. Fiedler sees Stapledon as an acutely "anomalous" writer and, determinedly extrapolating from his subject's texts to his mind and motives, raises specters of sadomasochism, schizophrenia, paranoia, and more. While Fiedler is singularly adept at situating Stapledon within the literary culture of the 1930s and at distinguishing Stapledon's scientific romances from "art novels," his book, among the most troubling and controversial ever written on an SF writer, contains so many generalizations and serious factual errors that it should be read (if at all) only in conjunction with either McCarthy or Kinnaird or, better yet, both. Chronology, selected primary and secondary bibliography, index. A thoroughly researched, well-written biography by Robert Crossley was published in 1994, *Olaf Stapledon: Speaking for the Future*. Readers should also consult Crossley's fascinating collection of Stapledon's letters to his fiancée, *Talking Across the World: The Love Letters of Olaf Stapledon and Agnes Miller, 1913–1919* (Univ. Press of New England, 1987). Finally, none of these books clarifies Stapledon's importance to British SF as well as Brian Stableford's essential *Scientific Romance in Britain 1890–1950* [8-132]; see also Scholes and Rabkin *Science Fiction: History-Science-Vision* [8-126]. Burgess 422. (MAM)

Arkadii and Boris Strugatskii

9-111. Potts, Stephen W. **The Second Marxian Invasion: The Fiction of Strugatsky Brothers.** Borgo, 1991.

In this first book-length study of the best-known and most significant Soviet SF writers, Stephen Potts seeks to shift attention away from the ideological controversies that have swarmed about the works of Arkadii and Boris Strugatskii toward a middle ground that "plac[es] political and artistic matters in perspective relative to one another." In this he is largely successful. The Strugatskiis, whose polemical, often witty novels range from idealistic hard SF to strange absurdist satires that straddle SF and fantasy, exemplify the so-called "warm school" of Soviet writers, a group of less conservative writers who are more concerned with moral issues and literary quality than with technological prediction and who became prominent during the post-Stalinist thaw in the mid-1950s. Potts lucidly introduces and limns the themes of the Strugatskiis' major works and fairly discusses the "esthetic malaise" and "creative exhaustion" of their most recent efforts; but his view of the political, ideological, and global literary contexts of their works is somewhat narrow. Readers should also see *Red Stars: Political Aspects of Society Science Fiction* [8-87] and, more briefly, the fine introduction to the chapter on Russian SF in *Anatomy of Wonder*, 3rd ed.—both by Patrick McGuire—and the article by Gina Macdonald and Darko Suvin in *Twentieth-Century Science Fiction Writers*, 3rd ed.[7-30]. Bibliographical notes, index. (MAM) Eaton, 1993.

Theodore Sturgeon

9-112. Diskin, Lahna. **Theodore Sturgeon.** Starmont, 1981.

9-113. Menger, Lucy. **Theodore Sturgeon.** Ungar, 1981.

For approximately two decades prior to his death in 1985 Sturgeon produced little. The late 1940s and 1950s saw his major work appear(see chapter 3). Diskin's brief study is barely adequate. Menger's account, approximately twice the length (144 pages), provides a short biography, then examines the fiction chronologically, emphasizing four novels and about 25 short stories (the rationale for selection isn't explained). Menger is much preferable, but Sturgeon was a writer important enough to justify a better assessment than either of these. Burgess 424–25. (NB)

James Tiptree, Jr.

9-114.   Siegel, Mark. **James Tiptree, Jr.** Starmont, 1985.

Alice Sheldon came late to SF, her first SF story having been published at age 53 under her well-known pseudonym. She will be remembered for her shorter fiction, which won or was nominated for many awards. The first relatively detailed study of Tiptree was the introduction to the 1976 Gregg Press edition of *10,000 Light-Years From Home* [4-458] by Gardner Dozois, reprinted as a 36-page booklet, *The Fiction of James Tiptree, Jr.*, in 1977. Dozois approaches the stories chronologically and stylistically, whereas Siegel, then a college instructor, "examines Tiptree's works thematically in the order in which they appeared in book-length publications, partly as a matter of convenience." Siegel interviewed Tiptree in mid-1982, and his introduction, presumably written later, says of her marriage, "they continue together happily to this day." Siegel's study, while useful, does not emphasize sufficiently Tiptree's preoccupation with death. Her husband was already suffering from Alzheimer's disease and her own health was poor when he interviewed her. Five years after the interview, she shot her husband and killed herself. Burgess 429. (NB)

Mark Twain

*9-115.   Cummings, Sherwood. **Mark Twain and Science.** Louisiana State Univ. Press, 1989.

Among Mark Twain's contributions to American literature are a small number of science fiction short stories, ranging from satires and humorous hoaxes to more serious and pessimistic utopian and dystopian technological extrapolations—and, of course, *A Connecticut Yankee in King Arthur's Court* (1889) [1-25]. The significance of this seminal work, if not the first time-travel story certainly a progenitive prototype, has been addressed at length in Bud Foote's important, ingratiating study of Twain's novel and subsequence time-travel narratives, *The Connecticut Yankee in the Twentieth Century: Travel to the Past in Science Fiction* [8-57]. Cummings, by contrast, disavows interest in Twain's SF, remarking that it "is a worthy subject . . . but it is not the subject of this book." Yet his examination of Twain's intellectual involvement with science in general and Darwinian evolutionary concepts in particular, part of an ambitious project to track Twain's philosophical development (especially his struggle between Deism and determinism), both illuminates Twain's fiction (SF and otherwise) and demonstrates the wide-ranging influence of science in late 19th-century America. As such it contains valuable background for the study of pre-Gernsback SF. Index. (MAM)

Jack Vance

9-116. Rawlins, Jack. **Demon Prince: The Dissonant Worlds of Jack Vance.** Borgo, 1986.

9-117. Underwood, Tim, and Chuck Miller, eds. **Jack Vance.** Taplinger, 1980.

Vance is one of the more popular writers of SF and fantasy, his fiction expertly blending elements from each. Rawlins quotes Vance as thinking of himself as "writer of adventure stories," which is accurate but incomplete. Rawlins suggests that Vance's career can be divided into three periods: from 1945 to the mid-1950s with a hard science emphasis; a later period emphasizing alien worlds and their cultures; and the post-1973 period. Within about 100 pages Rawlins squeezes in a brief sketch, three chapters dealing with Vance's worlds, words, and plots, a two-page update of the 1981 version of this study, a 1985 interview, a selective secondary bibliography, and an index. Competent, but Vance deserves better. The eight reprinted essays in the Taplinger collection treat various aspects of Vance's SF and fantasy, including an updated version of Richard Tiedman's *Jack Vance: Science Fiction Stylist*, published separately in 1965, whose 44 pages provide a detailed look at Vance's somewhat mannered diction. The latter is the subject of a dictionary of Vance-coined words, *The Jack Vance Lexicon: From Ahulph to Zipangote* by Dan Temianka (Underwood-Miller, 1992). Burgess 434–35. (NB)

Jules Verne

9-118. Butcher, William. **Verne's Journey to the Centre of the Self: Space and Time in the Voyages Extraordinaires.** St. Martin's, 1990.

9-119. Costello, Peter. **Jules Verne: Inventor of Science Fiction.** Scribner, 1978.

*9-120. Evans, Arthur B. **Jules Verne Rediscovered: Didacticism and the Scientific Novel.** Greenwood, 1988. Eaton, 1990.

9-121. Lynch, Lawrence W. **Jules Verne.** Twayne, 1992.

9-122.   Martin, Andrew. The Mask of the Prophet: The Extraordinary Fictions of Jules Verne. Oxford, 1990.

The best critical work in English on Verne is Arthur Evans's study of scientific and moral didacticism in the *Voyages Extraordinaires*. In separate sections devoted to the pedagogical intent, ideological and intellectual content, and narrative and textual mechanics of Verne's works, Evans applies multiple critical strategies to reveal the *Voyages* as "a unique narrative (and social) configuration in the history of nineteenth-century literary prose." Bristling with first-rate scholarship—including notes, an exhaustive bibliography (though less complete than *Jules Verne: A Primary and Secondary Bibliography* by Edward J. Gallagher, Judith A. Misticelli, and John A. Van Eerde [G. K. Hall, 1980]), and a very detailed index—Evans's book is so well-organized that much of it will be accessible even to nonspecialists. Readers as well as scholars will be especially interested in Evans's commentary on the dreadfully distorted English translations—which, he argues, are largely responsible for the lack of attention given Verne by English-language critics and for his comparatively low standing among adult readers—and his clarification of the primary role played by Verne's major publisher, Pierre-Jules Hetzel, in shaping the vast pedagogical project of the *Voyages*.

Like Evans's exemplary study, the monographs by Butcher and Martin show the degree of critical imagination and sophistication Verne's works can call forth. Both are densely argued, highly specialized analyses that draw on recent (untranslated) work by French critics. Butcher uses structuralist and phenomenological criticism to explore "the key question of dimensionality" in Verne's *Voyages* in space and time. Using often abstruse arguments supplemented by graphs, he illuminates narrative patterns, details of grammar and style, and relevant thematic issues, always carefully contextualizing his discussions within the naturalistic genre in which Verne wrote. Martin's witty deconstructive book seems at first capricious in its plan to "read Verne as if it had been written by Napoleon Bonaparte or [Jorge Luis] Borges," and, "by way of compensating for the historical errors thus committed, [to] read Napoleon and Borges as though they had been written by Verne." The unexpected nexus Martin establishes between these three disparate writers is a shared, archetypal ideological narrative: the story of a Masked Prophet who rebels against an Empire "to reveal what is concealed." Surprisingly, this strange strategy leads Martin to fascinating insights into the sub-text of imperialism in Verne's works. Like Butcher's study, Martin's can be recommended to specialized collections and to readers well-versed in contemporary literary theory. Bibliography, index.

Readers seeking a less theoretically formidable introduction to Verne as man and writer will find comparatively slim pickings. Costello's is the best extant biography, but it suffers from an excess of trivial details about Verne's rather sober life and inadequate attention to his novels—particularly unfortunate in light of Costello's intent to present Verne as "the inventor of science fiction." Like Evans, Costello tracks Verne's increasing pessimism and waning faith in science and technology; unlike Evans he fails to follow through when his thesis takes him close to Verne's writings. Although agreeable and readable, Costello's biography leaves one with the inaccurate impression that Verne was a severely limited writer of escapist adventure stories for children. Eight pages of plates, chronological list of Verne's novels, index. Lynch's enthusiastic nonspecialized introduction presents a more accurate impression of Verne's importance than the earlier Twayne study it replaces. After an appropriately brief biographical chapter, Lynch hones in on the context of the composition of the *Voyages*, then turns to a chronological consideration of the plots, themes, and characters of Verne's works and a somewhat superficial discussion of Verne's use of science and technology. But, saddled with an inadequate secondary bibliography and somewhat misleading statements on Verne's stature, this book only intimates at the richness that awaits readers willing to tackle more challenging criticism. The one to read before you read Evans. Chronology, notes, appendix on film adaptations, index. Burgess 436–38. (MAM)

Kurt Vonnegut

*9-123. Klinkowitz, Jerome. **Kurt Vonnegut.** Routledge, 1982.

9-124. Klinkowitz, Jerome, and John Somer, eds. **The Vonnegut Statement.** Delacorte, 1972.

*9-125. Merrill, Robert, ed. **Critical Essays on Kurt Vonnegut.** G. K. Hall, 1990.

9-126. Pieratt, Asa B., Julie Huffman-Klinkowitz, and Jerome Klinkowitz, eds. **Kurt Vonnegut: A Comprehensive Bibliography.** Archon, 1987.

Although Kurt Vonnegut (the Jr. was dropped some years ago) prefers not to be considered a writer of SF, and some critics have followed his lead, any sensible study of his career reveals that he has often written SF or used its techniques and tropes for his dark fables. (Robert Scholes has persuasively argued that black humorists like Vonnegut are fabulators who lack "the rhetoric of moral certainty" claimed by satirists.)

Vonnegut was largely ignored for the first two decades of his literary career, tainted perhaps by his association with SF, but by the 1970s he was the subject of extensive criticism. *The Vonnegut Statement* assembles 13 pieces, some revised from earlier publication, mostly by academics. Valuable for its perspective at a relatively early point in Vonnegut's career. By 1990, when the Merrill collection appeared, Vonnegut, though still popular, was not being ground as actively by the scholarly mills. (So it goes.) Merrill contains a balanced collection of reviews, essays on individual works and general essays, four of them commissioned for this collection. Merrill's own introduction provides a valuable and well-documented 27-page survey of Vonnegut criticism, which is exhaustively recorded in the bibliography, a revision and expansion of its 1974 predecessor.

Klinkowitz has shown a consistent interest in Vonnegut, having edited several collections as well as having written what is the most knowledgeable and balanced study, incorporating new biographical material with reliable judgments, all this in only 96 pages. More current and somewhat better than the similar 1977 studies by James Lundquist, *Kurt Vonnegut* (Ungar), and Richard Giannone, *Vonnegut: A Preface to His Novels* (Kennikat). (NB)

H. G. Wells

9-127. Bergonzi, Bernard, ed. **H. G. Wells: A Collection of Critical Essays.** Prentice-Hall, 1976.

9-128. Costa, Richard Hauer. **H. G. Wells.** Twayne, 1985.

***9-129.** Crossley, Robert. **H. G. Wells.** Starmont, 1986.

9-130. Hammond, J(ohn) R. **H. G. Wells and the Short Story.** St. Martin's, 1992.

***9-131.** Huntington, John. **The Logic of Fantasy: H. G. Wells and Science Fiction.** Columbia, 1982. Eaton, 1984.

9-132. McConnell, Frank. **The Science Fiction of H. G. Wells.** Oxford Univ. Press, 1981.

9-133. Scheick, William J., and J. Randolph Cox. **H. G. Wells: A Reference Guide.** G. K. Hall, 1988.

***9-134.** Smith, David. **H. G. Wells: Desperately Mortal.** Yale Univ. Press, 1986.

***9-135.** Suvin, Darko, and Robert M. Philmus, eds. **H. G. Wells and Modern Science Fiction.** Bucknell Univ. Press, 1977.

9-136. Wells, H. G. **H. G. Wells: Early Writings in Science and Science Fiction.** Univ. of California Press, 1975. Ed. by David Y. Hughes and Robert M. Philmus.

Wells, who as "the Shakespeare of science fiction," left behind a vast oeuvre of fiction and nonfiction including several novels written around the turn of the century—the scientific romances—that proved generative to the subsequent evolution of SF. Biographies of Wells abound, from Geoffrey West's early *H. G. Wells: A Sketch for a Portrait* (Norton, 1930) to Anthony West's controversial biased account *H. G. Wells: Aspects of a Life* (Random House, 1984). The best to date, supplanting even Norman and Jeanne MacKenzie's excellent *H. G. Wells: A Biography* (Simon & Schuster, 1973) (published in the United Kingdom as *Time Traveller: The Life of H. G. Wells* [Weidenfeld & Nicolson, 1973]) is that of historian David Smith. With Wellsian pacing and energy, Smith draws upon the vast paper trail Wells left behind to chronicle his subject's endlessly active life and involvement in a bewildering variety of progressive causes. Smith deals with a number of literary matters, including the argument between Wells and Henry James over the purpose of art, the role of class and social development in his writings, the potential for human betterment he saw inherent in the future, and (briefly) his use of science in the scientific romances—a topic far more thoroughly developed in Roslynn D. Haynes's *H. G. Wells: Discoverer of the Future: The Influence of Science on His Thought* (New York Univ. Press, 1980). But Smith's exhaustively researched and documented thematic biography is less concerned with explicating Wells's fiction (and not at all with its posthumous critical reception) than with tracking his intellectual development and personal, sexual, and professional involvements in wide-ranging social contexts. Appendix, notes, index.

Readers more interested in Wells's fiction can choose from several introductions. Costa's revision of his 1967 Twayne study surveys some of the recent critical work he says motivated it but doesn't coherently incorporate insights from that criticism. Less a revision than an expansion, Costa's book includes fix-ups inserted into earlier material and new sections on Wells's critical reception, his influence as a fabulist, his relationship to feminism, and his science fiction, which Costa considers "in the larger context of science." Unfortunately, this approach to revision somewhat exacerbates the awkward structure and repetitiveness of his first edition, flaws compounded by several careless errors and Costa's curiously ambivalent view of Wells as "a literary figure of almost the first order." Notes, list of primary sources and annotated secondary bibliography, index.

Best among recent introductory books that emphasize Wells's SF is Crossley's historically acute Starmont guide. Crossley focuses on the motifs, characters, and style of five major early SF novels (and a few short stories). Crossley compensates for the narrowness of focus inevitable in a book of this brevity with a particularly fine introductory sketch of Wells's early years and of works written after the five novels he discusses in the chapters that follow. Chronology, annotated primary and secondary bibliography, index. McConnell introduces Wells's life and deftly situates him within well-defined historical and social contexts from the turn of the century through the First World War. He then turns to issues raised by seven key SF works organized into clusters as evolutionary fables, realistic fantasies, and onieric extrapolations. If McConnell fails to illuminate the scope of Wells's scientific views, he nonetheless offers perceptive readings of the scientific romances and illuminates Wells's influence, especially on Olaf Stapledon. Chronology, checklist of publications from 1895–1945, selected bibliography, index.

Studies since the 1960s that emphasize Wells's SF build on earlier scholarship by Bernard Bergonzi, whose *The Early H. G. Wells: A Study of the Scientific Romances* (Manchester Univ. Press, 1961) contextualizes Wells's early SF within the intellectual instability of the late 19th century; Mark Hillegas, whose seminal *The Future as Nightmare: H. G. Wells and the Anti-utopians* (Oxford, 1967) [8-67] examines Wells's impact on 20th-century dystopian thought; Patrick Parrinder, whose *H. G. Wells* (Oliver & Boyd, 1970) offers a succinct overview of the thematic and intellectual concerns of Wells's fiction, including the scientific romances; and Robert Philmus, whose *Into the Unknown: The Evolution of Science Fiction From Francis Godwin to H. G. Wells* [8-104] tracks the origins of the major themes of Wells's SF in British fiction of the 18th and 19th centuries. Notable among recent critical work on Wells's early SF is Huntington's monograph, which essentially supplants the aforementioned 1961 book by Bergonzi as the best formal study of the scientific romances. Central to Huntington's argument is his emphasis on the tension in Wells between opposition and ethics established by the "two world structure" of these works. Huntington appropriately identifies *The Time Machine* [1-103] as the exemplar of "Wells's use of balanced opposition and symbolic mediation as a way of thinking," then develops analyses of the structures and rhetorical devices in scientific romances, and concludes with a chapter on Wells's anti-utopias in conjunction with works by such writers as Zamiatin, Bradbury, and Orwell. Extensive notes, index.

J. R. Hammond—who in *H. G. Wells and the Modern Novel* (St. Martin's, 1988) mounted a spirited case for Wells the novelist as a precursor of the literary modernism of Kafka, Conrad, and the like—has in the successor to that book provided the first book-length study of Wells's capacious short fiction. While Hammond's first book emphasized Wells's realistic novels (of the scientific romances, Hammond considered only *The Time Machine* [1-103]), his second considers many of Wells's important SF stories. In both books Hammond argues that Wells's literary contributions have been under-appreciated, and the thematic links between Wells's short stories and novels that Hammond adumbrates in his second book strongly support this argument. In addition to an overview of the nature of Wells's art in shorter forms (usefully supplemented by Wells's introduction to his collection *The Country of the Blind* [1911], which Hammond reprints as an appendix), Hammond provides a checklist of all of Wells's stories annotated with brief plot summaries and publication data, followed by in-depth analyses of 27 selected tales. If Hammond's judgments lack critical rigor, his books nevertheless offer myriad nuggets of historical and biographical insights into Wells's vast output. Notes, bibliography, index.

Of the enormous number of essays that have been written about Wells, many of the best appear in Bergonzi's 1976 collection, which, usefully for students of SF, emphasizes the period from 1895 to 1910. Somewhat more extensive is the carefully chosen collection of reviews (from 1895–1946) and the accompanying list of criticism in Parrinder's *H. G. Wells: The Critical Heritage* (Routledge, 1972). More recent work can be found in the proceedings of the first world conference on Wells, which was held in 1971 in Montreal; in their volume Suvin and Philmus present essays ranging from inquiries into individual texts to broader perspectives. Particularly valuable are Suvin's introduction, David Y. Hughes and J. Vernier's study of Wells's use of biology (the persistence of which subject in Wells is elaborated by Peter Kemp in *H. G. Wells and the Culminating Ape* [St. Martin's, 1982]), and Komatsu's survey of the impact of Wells's fiction on Japanese SF. This volume is especially noteworthy for two excellent bibliographic essays, one by Hughes and Philmus on Wells's science journalism, the other by R. D. Mullen on his books and pamphlets. Parrinder and Christopher Rolfe have edited proceedings of the second such conference, *H. G. Wells Under Revision: Proceedings of the International Wells Symposium, London, July 1986* (Susquehanna Univ. Press, 1990)—a book that, although a useful snapshot of the currently bifurcating field of Wells studies, offers only a single article on Wells's SF: a close reading by John R. Reed of *The Island of Doctor Moreau*. Finally, Philmus and Hughes's collection of Wells's science journalism from 1887–1901 provides a close track of development in Wells's thought that directly informed his SF. The editors' stimulating introductions carefully frame these reprinted essays and stories (which include early versions of *The Time Machine*), making this an important resource for Wellsians and scholars concerned with attitudes toward science at the turn of the century. Annotated selective bibliography of science writings, indexes of titles and of names.

Further guidance to the critical literature on Wells can be found in Scheick and Cox. Impaired only by the lack of an inadequate index, a somewhat misleading introduction, and a few omissions and deficient

592 *Michael A. Morrison, Neil Barron*

annotations, this volume follows a list of Wells's fiction and nonfiction books with a 3,019-item annotated secondary bibliography, which includes nearly all salient English-language reviews, essays, and books published through 1986 as well as a selection of foreign pieces. (MAM)

Jack Williamson

*9-137. Williamson, Jack. **Wonder's Child: My Life in Science Fiction.** Bluejay, 1984.

This aptly titled, very personal autobiography reveals a life begun in poverty in the Southwest that led to a doctorate in English in 1974 and his election as a Grand Master by fellow SF writers in 1976. Williamson triumphed over poverty, inadequate education, and emotional problems and has continued to publish, often in collaboration with Frederik Pohl. A remarkable and moving odyssey more self-reflective than Pohl's *The Way the Future Was* [9-96] and much less detailed than Asimov's massive autobiography [9-6/7]. Burgess 448–49. (NB) Hugo winner, 1985

Roger Zelazny

9-138. Krulik, Theodore. **Roger Zelazny.** Ungar, 1986.

9-139. Yoke, Carl B. **Roger Zelazny.** Starmont, 1979.

Zelazny is probably best known for his long–running and popular Amber series, although his best works are not part of series. Krulik draws on Zelazny's letters at Syracuse University (see chapter 14) and a 1982 interview. He effectively links Zelazny's life to his fiction, but his book is heavy with plot summaries, often ineptly written (or edited), and stops with 1983. Yoke, a longtime friend, surveys the writings through 1977, discussing with greater insight than Krulik the major novels and important shorter fiction then available. Although the later works do not equal the best of those published prior to 1980, Zelazny remains a figure important enough to justify a current study, such as a revision of Yoke. Burgess 455–57. (NB)

Collective Biography

9-140. Aldiss, Brian W., and Harry Harrison, eds. **Hell's Cartographers: Some Personal Histories of Science Fiction Writers.** Harpers, 1976.

9-141. Greenberg, Martin H., ed. **Fantastic Lives: Autobiographical Essays by Notable Science Fiction Writers.** Southern Illinois Univ. Press, 1981.

*9-142. Jakubowski, Maxim, and Edward James, eds. **The Profession of Science Fiction: SF Writers on their Craft and Ideas.** St. Martin's, 1993.

*9-143. Knight, Damon F(rancis). **The Futurians: The Story of the Science Fiction "Family" of the 30s That Produced Today's Top SF Writers and Editors.** John Day, 1977.

Taking its title from Kingsley Amis's seminal study of SF, Aldiss and Harrison's collection gives free reign to six contemporaneous SF writers, all of whose works, according to Aldiss, share the "unspoken topic" that "the individual's role in society is eroded as society itself becomes wealthier and more powerful." Writing about themselves and their participation in the world of SF, Aldiss, Harrison, Robert Silverberg, Alfred Bester, Damon Knight, and Frederik Pohl produce largely thoughtful pieces supplemented by brief accounts of their working habits and now-dated lists of their writings. See also Aldiss's *The Shape of Further Things* (Doubleday, 1970), "The Glass Forest" in . . . *And the Lurid Glare of the Comet* [8-2], and "A Walk in the Glass Forest" in *The Work of Brian W. Aldiss* [9-2]; Pohl's *The Way the Future Was: A Memoir* [9-96]. Knight, whose *In Search of Wonder: Essays on Modern Science Fiction* [8-74] contains some of the most acute early SF criticism, has also published in *The Futurians* an uncomfortably personal account of his involvement in the Futurian Society of New York, which included such important writers of American pulp SF as Isaac Asimov, James Blish, and Cyril Kornbluth.

Greenberg's sequel to *Hell's Cartographers* gives even more latitude to a wider range of writers. Although a few circle tediously around the perennial question (What is SF?), some like Philip José Farmer offer straightforward autobiography while others articulate their attitudes toward SF as a genre, a field of commercial writing, a compact with a highly interactive readership, and a locus of critical attention. Of particular note are Barry Malzberg's characteristically bitter reflections on the viability of SF— thoughts he has further embellished in *The Engines of the Night: Science Fiction in the Eighties* [8-83]—R. A. Lafferty's caustic assault on John W. Campbell and most of the writers of his ostensible "Golden Age," Harlan Ellison's fervid attack on academic critics, and Norman Spinrad's inadvertently complementary defense of their worth. Like several of the essays in *Hell's Cartographers*, many in Greenberg's collection suggest a disjunction between SF and the mainstream that was more pertinent to the 1980s than to the 1990s, lending the whole enterprise a somewhat dated tone. Moreover the works of several writers in Greenberg's roster (Katherine Maclean, Mack Reynolds, A. E. van Vogt, Margaret St. Clair) have declined in importance today; nevertheless their subjective ruminations remain of interest to scholars. Appended to each essay is a brief biography of primary works.

By far the most interesting and useful of these volumes is the collection Jakubowski and James edited of 16 essays and reminiscences selected from more than 40 published from 1972 to 1990 in *Foundation* [12-22], the premier British journal *about* science fiction, under the rubric "The Profession of Science Fiction." The open-ended invitation offered to contributors to this series allows them to focus on whatever aspect of SF seems most important; the result is a (necessarily somewhat dated) collection that because of its breadth offers a unique snapshot of late 20th-century English-language SF. Its contents embrace autobiographical concerns, the origin of key SF works, the experience of being an SF writer, and, most interestingly, the trials and tribulations of SF during the latter half of this century. Index, notes. (MAM)

Interviews

*9-144. McCaffery, Larry. **Across the Wounded Galaxies: Interviews with Contemporary American Science Fiction Writers.** Univ. of Illinois Press, 1990.

*9-145. Platt, Charles. **Dream Makers: Science Fiction and Fantasy Writers at Work.** Ungar, 1987.

Larry McCaffery is an interviewer with an agenda. As clarified in his controversial pronouncements in the *Columbia Literary History of the United States* (1988), he considers SF the preeminent literature of our age. More specifically, he considers SF the essence of postmodernism. Unfortunately, McCaffery carries this thesis, which parallels the thinking of Brian McHale and other contemporary critics, into each of these nine interviews (conducted between 1983–1988), where it proceeds to throw several askew. Perhaps in consequence the most fruitful interactions occur between McCaffery and William Gibson, Bruce Sterling, and Samuel Delany, all of whom seem in sympathy with McCaffery's argument. Still, except for an uncharacteristically dull encounter with Gene Wolfe and an incoherent one with William Burroughs, the other interviews in this book offer a wealth of insights for readers and scholars as, unleashed from McCaffery's thesis, Ursula Le Guin, Octavia Butler, Thomas Disch, and Gregory Benford discourse on their perspectives on SF and allied matters. As in his earlier books of interviews with American writers *Anything Can Happen* (Univ. of Illinois Press, 1983) and *Alive and Writing* (Univ. of Illinois Press, 1987), the latter of which included early versions of the interviews with Le Guin and Delany printed here, McCaffery's questions evince in-depth preparation, a quick intelligence, and a willingness to give his interviewees space. These qualities raise his conversations to a level of sophistication rarely approached in earlier fannish interview series such as Science Fiction Voices series conducted by Jeffrey M. Elliot and Darrell Schweitzer (Borgo). Index.

If McCaffery's book constitutes a glimpse of the state of SF in the late 1980s, Charles Platt's offers snapshots from previous decades. Ungar's hardcover omnibus reprints (with modest revision) 25 of the 56 profiles previously published in *Dream Makers* (Berkley, 1980) and *Dream Makers II* (Berkley, 1983). Instead of using the conventional question-and-answer format, Platt constructs essays out of material gathered during long taped interviews with his subjects, which includes such luminaries as Isaac Asimov, Arthur C. Clarke, Frank Herbert, Stephen King, and A. E. van Vogt. Platt's deep knowledge of SF, his sense of balance and fairness, and his sensitivity to his subjects' concerns inform each of these witty, penetrating profiles, making this volume indispensable for readers, libraries, and scholars. (MAM)

Sources of Information on Fiction Authors and Editors

Anatomy of Wonder is primarily a guide to books and related materials, not to their authors. For readers desiring more bibliographic, biographical, or critical information about the almost 600 authors whose books were annotated in chapters 1–5, ten sources of such information were checked to create the following tabulation. Most sources will be found in the reference sections of larger libraries. Nine are annotated in chapter 7. *Contemporary Authors*, which is not, has been published for some years by Gale Research and is found in most libraries. Gale regularly issues cumulative indexes to *CA* and its sister publications, such as *Contemporary Literary Criticism*, and the latest such index was consulted for this tabulation. Contemporary means authors (not limited to fiction) writing today as well as writers from earlier periods who are still read today, that is, who are our intellectual if not chronological contemporaries. The coverage of *CA* is largely limited to authors in chapters 3–5.

Sources

1. *Contemporary Authors* (Gale Research)
2. *Encyclopedia of Science Fiction & Fantasy* (Tuck)
3. *The Encyclopedia of Science Fiction* (Clute & Nicholls)
4. *The New Encyclopedia of Science Fiction* (Gunn)

5. *Reader's Guide to Twentieth-Century Science Fiction* (Fletcher)
6. *Science-Fiction: The Early Years* (Bleiler)
7. *Science Fiction Writers* (Bleiler)
8. *Survey of Science Fiction Literature* (Magill)
9. *Twentieth-Century American Science-Fiction Writers* (Cowart & Wymer)
10. *Twentieth-Century Science-Fiction Writers*, 3rd ed. (Watson & Schellinger)

Author, Nationality (if not U.S.)**, Years**

Author, Nationality (if not U.S.), Years	Sources									
	1	2	3	4	5	6	7	8	9	10
Abbott, Edwin A(bbott), UK, 1839–1926		x	x	x		x		x		
Adams, Douglas (Noel), UK, 1952–	x		x	x	x					x
Aldiss, Brian W(ilson), UK, 1925–	x	x	x	x	x		x	x		x
Allum, Tom, UK, ?		x								
Ames, Mildred, 1919–	x									
Amis, Kingsley (William), UK, 1922–	x	x	x	x				x		x
Anderson, Chester, 1932–1991	x	x	x							
Anderson, Poul (William), 1926–	x	x	x	x	x		x	x	x	x
Anthony, Patricia, ?										
Anthony, Piers, 1934–	x		x	x	x			x	x	x
Appleton, Victor [house pseudonym]	x	x	x			x		x		
Arlen, Michael, UK/Armenia, 1895–1956	x	x	x							
Arnason, Eleanor (Atwood), 1942–			x							
Aronica, Lou, 1958–			x							
Asimov, Isaac, 1920–1992	x	x	x	x	x	x	x	x	x	x
Astor, John Jacob, 1864–1912			x	x		x		x		
Attanasio, A(lfred) A(ngelo), 1951–	x		x							x
Atterly, Joseph, 1775–1861			x	x		x				
Atwood, Margaret (Eleanor), Canada, 1939–	x		x							
Aubrey, Frank, UK, 1840–1927			x			x				
Bailey, Charles W(aldo), 1929–		x	x							
Baird, Thomas P., 1923–1990	x									
Ballard, J(ames) G(raham), UK, 1930–	x	x	x	x	x		x	x		x
Ballou, Arthur W., 1915–1981	x	x								
Banks, Iain M(enzies), Scotland, 1954–	x		x							x
Barnes, John, 1957–	x		x							
Barney, John Stewart, 1868–1925			x			x				
Barrett, Neal, Jr., 1929–			x	x						x
Barth, John (Simmons), 1930–	x	x	x					x		
Batchelor, John Calvin, 1948–	x		x							x

Author, Nationality (if not U.S.), Years	1	2	3	4	5	6	7	8	9	10
Baxter, Stephen (M.), UK, 1957–			x							
Bayley, Barrington J(ohn), UK, 1937–	x		x	x						x
Bear, Greg(ory Dale), 1951–	x		x	x						x
Bell, Clare (Louise), UK/US, 1957–			x							
Bell, Neil, UK, 1887–1964		x	x							
Bell, William Dixon, 1865–1951										
Bellamy, Edward, 1850–1898	x	x		x		x		x		x
Beliaev, Alexander, Russia, 1884–?1942		x	x							x
Benford, Gregory, 1941–	x		x	x	x			x		x
Benson, Robert Hugh, UK, 1871–1914		x	x			x				
Beresford, J(ohn) D(avys), UK, 1873–1947	x	x	x	x		x		x		x
Bergerac, Savinien Cyrano de, France, 1619–1655		x	x	x		x				
Bester, Alfred, 1913–1987	x	x	x	x	x		x	x	x	x
Bethancourt, T(omás) Ernesto, 1932–	x									
Biemiller, Carl L(udwig Jr.), 1912–1979	x	x	x							
Bierce, Ambrose, 1842–c.1914	x	x	x	x		x		x		
Bishop, Michael, 1945–	x		x	x						x
Bisson, Terry (Ballantine), 1942–	x		x							
Blaine, John, 1914–1990	x	x	x							
Blaylock, James P., 1950–	x		x							x
Blish, James, 1921–1975	x	x	x	x	x		x	x	x	x
Blumlein, Michael, 1948–			x							
Bond, Nancy (Barbara), 1945–	x									
Bonham, Frank, 1914–1988			x							
Boucher, Anthony, 1911–1968	x	x	x	x	x				x	x
Boulle, Pierre, France, 1912–	x	x	x	x				x		x
Bova, Ben(jamin William), 1932–	x	x	x	x	x					x
Bowen, John (Griffith), UK, 1924–	x	x	x							
Boyd, John, 1919–	x	x	x	x				x	x	x
Brackett, Leigh (Douglass), 1915–1978	x	x	x	x	x			x	x	x
Bradbury, Ray (Douglas), 1920–	x	x	x	x	x		x	x	x	x
Bradley, Marion Zimmer, 1930–	x	x	x	x	x			x	x	x
Bradshaw, William R. 1851–1927			x							
Brin, (Glen) David, 1950–	x		x	x	x					x
Broderick, Damien (Francis), Australia, 1944	x	x	x	x						x
Brown, Fredric (William), 1906–1972	x	x	x	x				x	x	x
Brunner, John (Kilian Houston), UK, 1934	x	x	x	x	x		x	x		x
Bryant, Edward (Winslow Jr.), 1945–	x		x	x						x
Budrys, Algis, 1931–	x	x	x	x	x		x	x	x	x

Author, Nationality (if not U.S.), Years — Sources

Author, Nationality (if not U.S.), Years	1	2	3	4	5	6	7	8	9	10
Bujold, Lois McMaster, 1949–			x							x
Bulgakov, Mikhail, Russia, 1891–1940	x	x						x		x
Bull, Emma, 1954–	x		x							
Bunch, David R(oosevelt), 1925(?)–	x	x	x	x						x
Burdekin, Katharine P(enelope), UK, 1896–1963			x							x
Burgess, Anthony, UK, 1917–1993	x	x	x		x			x		x
Burroughs, Edgar Rice, 1875–1950	x	x	x	x	x	x	x	x	x	x
Burroughs, William S(eward), 1914–	x	x	x					x	x	x
Busby, F(rancis) M(arion), 1921–	x		x	x						x
Butler, Octavia E(stelle), 1947–	x		x	x						x
Butler, Samuel, UK, 1835–1902	x	x	x					x		x
Cadigan, Pat(ricia K.), 1953–			x	x						
Callenbach, Ernest, 1929–	x		x							x
Calvino, Italo, Italy, 1923–1985	x	x	x	x				x		x
Campanella, Tommaso, Italy, 1568–1639			x			x				
Campbell, John W(ood), Jr., 1910–1971	x	x	x	x	x		x	x	x	x
Čapek, Karel, Czechoslovakia, 1890–1938	x	x	x	x	x	x	x	x		x
Capon, (Harry) Paul, UK, 1911–1969	x	x	x							x
Card, Orson Scott, 1951–	x		x	x	x					x
Carlson, Dale, 1935–	x									
Carlson, Danny, 1960–	x									
Carr, Jayge, 1940–			x	x						x
Carr, Terry (Gene), 1937–1987	x	x	x	x						
Carter, Angela, UK, 1940–1992	x	x	x							
Chadwick, P(hilip) G(eorge), UK, 1893–1955			x							
Charnas, Suzy McKee, 1939–	x		x	x						x
Chayevsky, Paddy, 1923–1981	x		x							
Cherryh, C(arolyn) J(anice), 1942–	x		x	x	x					x
Chesney, Sir George T(omkyns), UK, 1830–1895			x	x		x		x		
Chester, George Randolph, 1869–1924	x		x							
Chesterton, G(ilbert) K(eith), UK, 1874–1936	x	x	x			x				
Chetwin, Grace, UK, ?	x									
Childers, (Robert) Erskine, Ireland 1870–1922	x		x							
Chilton, Charles (Frederick William), UK, 1927–		x	x							
Christopher, John, UK, 1922–	x	x	x	x				x		x
Clarke, Arthur C(harles), UK, 1917–	x	x	x	x	x		x	x		x
Clarke, Joan B., UK, 1921–	x	x								
Claudy, Carl H(arry), 1879–1957		x	x							

Author, Nationality (if not U.S.), Years	1	2	3	4	5	6	7	8	9	10
Clement, Hal, 1922–	x	x	x	x	x		x	x	x	x
Clifton, Mark, 1906–1963	x	x	x	x				x		x
Clingerman, Mildred (McElroy), 1918–		x	x							
Clouston, J(oseph) Storer, Scotland, 1870–1944		x	x			x				
Coates, Robert M(yron), 1897–1973	x	x	x			x				
Coblentz, Stanton A(rthur), 1896–1982	x	x	x	x						x
Collier, John (Henry Noyes), 1923–1981	x	x	x	x						
Colomb, P(hilip Howard), UK, 1831–1899		x				x				
Compton, D(avid) G(uy), UK, 1930–	x	x	x	x				x		x
Condon, Richard (Thomas), 1915–	x	x	x							
Coney, Michael G(reatrex), UK, 1932–	x		x					x		x
Connington, J. J., UK, 1880–1947		x	x			x				
Constantine, Storm, UK 1956–			x							x
Corlett, William, UK, 1938–	x		x							
Cover, Arthur Byron, 1950–	x		x	x						x
Cowan, Frank, 1844–1905			x			x				
Cowper, Richard, UK, 1926–	x	x	x	x						x
Cox, Erle, Australia, 1873–1950	x	x	x			x				x
Craigie, David, UK, 1908–		x	x							
Crichton, Michael, 1942–	x		x	x				x		x
Cross, John Kier, UK, 1914–1967	x	x	x							x
Crowley, John, 1942–	x		x	x				x		x
Cummings, Ray, 1887–1957	x	x	x	x		x		x	x	x
Dann, Jack (Mayo), 1945–	x		x	x	x					x
Datlow, Ellen (Sue), 1949–			x							
Davidson, Avram, 1923–1993	x	x	x	x	x			x	x	x
de Camp, L(yon) Sprague, 1907–	x	x	x	x	x		x	x	x	x
De Mille, James, Canada, 1833–1880	x		x			x				
Deighton, Len, UK, 1929–	x		x							
del Rey, Lester, 1915–1993	x	x	x	x	x			x	x	x
Delany, Samuel R(ay), 1942–	x	x	x	x	x		x	x	x	x
Dent, Guy, UK, ?			x			x		x		
Denton, Bradley (Clayton), 1958–			x	x						
Dereske, Jo, US, ?										
Desmond, Shaw, Ireland, 1877–1960	x	x	x							
Dick, Philip K(indred), 1928–1982	x	x	x	x	x		x	x	x	x
Dickinson, Peter, UK, 1927–	x	x	x	x						x
Dickson, Gordon R(upert), Canada/US, 1913–	x	x	x	x	x		x	x	x	x

Author, Nationality (if not U.S.), Years	1	2	3	4	5	6	7	8	9	10
Disch, Thomas M(ichael), 1940–	x	x	x	x	x		x	x	x	x
Donnelly, Ignatius, 1831–1901	x	x	x				x			
Dooner, Pierton W., 1844–1907(?)			x		x					
Dorsey, Candas Jane, Canada, 1952–			x							x
Dowling, Terry, Australia, 1947–			x							x
Doyle, Arthur Conan, UK, 1859–1930	x	x	x			x	x	x		x
Dozois, Gardner, 1947–	x		x							x
du Bois, William Pène, 1916–1993	x		x							
Dunn, Katherine (Karen), 1945–			x							
Durrell, Lawrence, UK, 1912–1990	x		x							x
Effinger, George Alex, 1947–	x		x	x					x	x
Elgin, Suzette Haden, 1936–	x		x	x						x
Ellison, Harlan (Jay), 1934–	x	x	x	x	x		x	x	x	x
Emshwiller, Carol (Fries), 1921–			x	x						
Engdahl, Sylvia Louise, 1933–	x		x							
Engh, M(ary) J(ane), 1933–	x		x							x
England, George Allan, 1877–1936	x	x	x	x		x		x		x
Fairman, Paul W., 1916–1977	x	x	x							x
Farley, Ralph Milne, 1887–1963		x	x	x		x				x
Farmer, Philip José, 1918–	x	x	x	x	x		x	x	x	x
Farrère, Claude, France, 1876–1957		x	x		x					
Fast, Howard, 1914–	x	x	x	x						x
Faville, Barry, New Zealand ?										
Fawcett, Edgar, 1847–1904			x			x		x		
Fearn, John Russell 1908–1960		x	x	x						x
Ferman, Edward L(ewis), 1937–		x	x							
Finney, Jack, 1911	x	x	x	x	x			x	x	x
Fisk, Nicholas, UK, 1923–	x	x	x							
Flint, Homer Eon, 1892–1924	x	x	x			x				x
Forester, C(ecil) S(cott), 1899–1966	x	x	x							
Forman, James D(ouglas), 1932–	x		x							
Forster, E(dward) M(organ), UK, 1879–1970	x	x	x	x				x		
Forward, Robert L(ull), 1932–	x		x	x						x
Foster, Alan Dean, 1946–	x		x	x						
Foster, M(ichael) A(nthony), 1939–	x		x							x
Fowler, Karen Joy, 1950–			x							x
Frank, Pat, 1907–1964	x	x	x	x	x			x		x
Franklin, H(oward) Bruce, 1934–	x	x	x							

Author, Nationality (if not U.S.), Years	1	2	3	4	5	6	7	8	9	10
Freeman, Gaail, US, ?										
Gail, Otto Willi, Germany, 1896–1956		x	x			x		x		x
Gallun, Raymond Z(inke), 1911–1994	x	x	x	x	x					x
Galouye, David, 1920–1976	x	x	x	x				x		x
Gardner, Erle Stanley, 1889–1970	x	x	x			x				
Gary, Romain, France, 1914–1980	x	x	x							
Gawron, Jean Mark, 1953–		x								
Gentle, Mary, UK, 1956–	x	x								x
Gernsback, Hugo, Luxembourg, 1884–1967	x	x	x	x	x	x		x	x	x
Gerrold, David, 1944–	x		x	x					x	x
Geston, Mark S(ymington), 1946–	x	x	x	x				x	x	x
Gibbons, Floyd, 1886–1939		x				x				
Gibson, William (Ford), US/Canada, 1948	x		x	x	x					x
Giesy, J(ohn) U(lrich), 1877–1948		x	x			x				x
Gilman, Charlotte Perkins, 1860–1935	x		x			x				x
Gloag, John (Edwards), UK, 1896–1981	x		x	x						x
Godwin, Francis, UK, 1562–1633		x	x			x				
Gold, H(orace) L(eonard), 1914–		x	x	x						x
Golding, William (Gerald), UK, 1911–	x	x	x	x				x		x
Goldstein, Lisa, 1953–	x		x							x
Goulart, Ron(ald Joseph), 1933–	x	x	x	x						x
Grant, Richard 1952–		x								
Greenland, Colin, UK, 1954–	x		x							x
Greg, Percy, UK, 1836–1889			x	x		x		x		
Gregory, Owen, UK, ?			x			x				
Griffith, George, UK, 1857–1906	x		x	x		x		x		x
Griffith, Mary, 1800(?)–1877		x	x			x				
Guin, Wyman (Woods), 1915–	x	x	x	x						x
Gunn, James E(dwin), 1923–	x	x	x	x				x	x	x
Haggard, H(enry) Rider, UK, 1856–1925	x	x	x	x		x	x	x		x
Halacy, D(aniel) S(tephen) Jr., 1919–	x	x								
Haldeman, Joe, 1943–	x		x	x				x	x	x
Hale, Edward Everett, 1822–1909	x		x	x		x				
Hamilton, Cicely, UK, 1872–1952			x			x				
Hamilton, Edmond, 1904–1977	x	x	x	x	x	x		x	x	x
Hamilton, Virginia (Esther), 1936–	x		x							
Hancock, H(arrie) Irving, 1868–1922			x			x				
Hand, Elizabeth, 1957–	x		x							x
Harding, Lee (John), Australia, 1937–	x	x	x							x

Author, Nationality (if not U.S.), Years	1	2	3	4	5	6	7	8	9	10
Hargrave, John (Gordon), UK, 1894–1982	x		x							
Harness, Charles (Leonard), 1915–	x	x	x	x				x	x	x
Harrison, Harry, 1925–	x	x	x	x	x			x	x	x
Harrison, M(ichael) John, UK, 1945–	x		x					x		x
Heinlein, Robert A(nson), 1907–1988	x	x	x	x	x		x	x	x	x
Henderson, Zenna, 1917–1983	x	x	x	x	x			x	x	x
Herbert, Frank, 1920–1986	x	x	x	x	x		x	x	x	x
Hill, Douglas (Arthur), Canada, 1935–	x	x	x							
Hilton, James, UK, 1900–1954	x	x	x	x				x		
Hoban, Russell (Conwell), 1925–	x		x							x
Hogan, James P(atrick), UK, 1941–	x		x	x	x					x
Holberg, Ludvig, Denmark, 1684–1754		x	x	x		x				
Holdstock, Robert P(aul), UK, 1948–	x		x	x						x
Hoover, H(elen) M(ary), 1935–	x		x							x
Houghton, Claude, UK, 1889–1961			x							
Hoyle, Fred, UK, 1915–	x	x	x	x	x		x	x		x
Hubbard, L(afayette) Ron(ald), 1911–1986	x	x	x	x	x			x		x
Huddy, Delia, UK, 1934–	x									
Hudson, W(illiam) H(enry), UK, 1841–1922	x	x	x			x		x		
Hughes, Monica, UK/Canada, 1925–	x		x							x
Hunter, Evan, 1926–	x	x	x							
Hunting, (Henry) Gardner, 1872–1958	x	x	x			x				x
Huxley, Aldous (Leonard), UK, 1894–1963	x	x	x	x	x		x	x		x
Hyne, C(harles) J(ohn) Cutcliffe, UK, 1866–1944	x	x	x			x				x
Jablokov, Alexander, 1956–			x							
Jacobs, Paul Samuel, ?										
Jaeger, Muriel, UK, ca. 1893–			x							
Jefferies, (John) Richard, UK, 1848–1887	x		x			x				
Jennings, Philip C., 1946–	x		x							
Jensen, Johannes V(ilhelm), Denmark, 1873–1950	x		x							
Jeschke, Wolfgang, Germany, 1936–			x							x
Jeter, K. W., 1950–			x	x						x
Johnson, Annabel, 1921–										
Johnson, Edgar, 1912–										
Johnson, George Clayton, 1929–		x	x	x						
Johnson, Owen M(cMahon), 1878–1952	x		x							
Jones, Gwyneth (Ann), UK, 1952–	x		x							
Jones, Langdon, UK, 1942–			x							

Author, Nationality (if not U.S.), Years	1	2	3	4	5	6	7	8	9	10
Jones, McClure, US, ?	x									
Jones, Raymond F., 1915–1994		x	x	x						x
Joseph, M(ichael) K(ennedy), UK/New Zealand, 1914–1981	x	x	x							x
Kadrey, Richard, 1957–			x							
Kagan, Janet, 1946–			x							
Kandel, Michael, 1941–			x							
Karinthy, Frigyes, Hungary, 1887–1938		x	x			x				
Karl, Jean E(dna), 1927–	x									
Kaul, Fedor, Germany, ?			x							
Kavan, Anna, UK, 1901–1968	x	x	x					x		x
Keller, David H(enry), 1880–1966		x	x	x		x	x			x
Kelly, Frank K(ing), 1914–	x	x	x							
Kelly, James Patrick, 1951–	x									x
Kepler, Johannes, Germany, 1571–1630			x			x				
Kessel, John (Joseph Vincent), 1950–	x		x	x						x
Kesteven, G. R., UK, 1911–	x		x							
Key, Alexander (Hill), 1904–1979	x	x	x							x
Keyes, Daniel, 1927–	x	x	x	x	x			x		x
Kilworth, Gary (Douglas), UK, 1941–	x		x							x
King, Stephen, 1947–	x		x	x						
Kingsbury, Donald (MacDonald), 1929–	x		x							x
Kipling, (Joseph) Rudyard, UK, 1865–1936	x	x	x	x		x		x		
Klein, Gérard, France, 1937–	x		x							
Knebel, Fletcher, 1911–1993	x	x	x							
Knight, Damon (Francis), 1922–	x	x	x	x	x		x	x	x	x
Knott, William C(ecil), 1927–	x									
Kornbluth, C(yril) M., 1923–1958	x	x	x	x	x		x	x	x	x
Kress, Nancy, 1948–	x		x							
Kube-McDowell, Michael P., 1954–			x							x
Kurland, Michael (Joseph), 1938–	x	x	x	x						x
Kuttner, Henry, 1914–1958	x	x	x	x	x		x	x	x	x
Lafferty, R(aphael) A(loysius), 1914–	x	x	x	x	x			x	x	x
Laidlaw, Marc, 1960–	x		x							
Lake, David J(ohn), Australia, 1929–	x		x	x	x					x
Lane, Mary E. Bradley, US, ?			x							
Lanier, Sterling E(dmund), 1927–	x		x	x						x
Large, E(rnest) C(harles), UK, (?)–1976		x	x							x

Author, Nationality (if not U.S.), Years	1	2	3	4	5	6	7	8	9	10
Latham, Philip, 1902–1981	x	x	x							x
Laumer, (John) Keith, 1925–1993	x	x	x	x	x			x	x	x
Lawrence, Louise, UK, 1943–	x		x							
Le Guin, Ursula K(roeber), 1929–	x		x	x	x		x	x	x	x
Le Queux, William (Tufnell), France/UK, 1864–1927	x	x	x			x				
Lee, Tanith, UK, 1947–	x		x	x						x
Leiber, Fritz (Reuter Jr.), 1910–1992	x	x	x	x	x		x	x	x	x
Leinster, Murray, 1896–1975	x	x	x	x	x	x	x	x	x	x
Lem, Stanislaw, Poland, 1921–	x	x	x	x	x		x	x		x
L'Engle, Madeleine, 1918–	x	x	x	x	x					x
Lessing, Doris, Iran/UK, 1919–	x		x	x				x		x
Levin, Ira, 1929–	x	x	x		x					x
Lewis, C(live) S(taples), UK, 1898–1963	x	x	x	x			x	x		x
Lewis, Sinclair, 1885–1951	x	x	x	x				x		
Lightner, A(lice) M(artha), 1904–1988	x	x	x							x
Lindsay, David, UK, 1878–1945	x	x	x	x		x		x		x
London, Jack, 1876–1916	x	x	x	x		x		x	x	x
Long, Frank Belknap, 1903–1994	x	x	x	x		x				x
Longyear, Barry B(rookes), 1942–	x		x	x	x					x
Lovecraft, H(oward) P(hilips), 1890–1937	x	x	x	x	x	x	x	x		x
Lundwall, Sam J(errie), Sweden, 1941–	x	x	x	x				x		x
Lupoff, Richard A(llen), 1935–	x	x	x	x						x
Lynn, Elizabeth A., 1946–	x		x	x						x
Lytton, Edward Bulyer, UK, 1803–1873	x	x	x	x		x		x		
MacArthur, David, UK, 1903–	x									
Macdonald, Caroline, UK, ?										
MacDonald, John D(ann), 1916–1986	x	x	x	x				x	x	x
Mace, Elizabeth, UK, 1933–	x									
MacIsaac, Fred(erick John), 1886–1940		x	x			x				
MacLean, Katherine (Anne), 1925–	x	x	x	x	x				x	x
MacPherson, Donald, Canada, ?			x							
MacVicar, Angus, UK, 1908–	x	x	x							
Madariaga (y Rojo), Salvador de, Spain, 1886–1978	x		x							
Maddox, Tom, US, ?			x							
Maguire, Gregory, 1954–	x									
Malzberg, Barry N(orman), 1939–		x	x	x	x			x	x	x
Mann, (Anthony) Philip, UK, 1942–			x							x

Author, Nationality (if not U.S.), Years	1	2	3	4	5	6	7	8	9	10
Manning, Laurence (Edward), Canada/US, 1899–1972		x	x	x						x
Margulies, Leo, 1900–1975	x	x	x							
Mark, Jan, UK, 1943–	x									
Martel, Suzanne, Canada, 1924–		x								
Martin, George R(aymond) R(ichard), 1948–	x		x	x	x					x
Martin, Valerie, 1948–	x		x							
Marvell, Andrew, UK, 1896–1985			x							
Masson, David, 1924–1974			x							x
Matheson, Richard (Burton), 1926–	x	x	x	x			x	x	x	x
Matson, Norman (Haghejm), 1893–1965		x	x			x				
Maurois, André, France, 1885–1967	x	x	x			x		x		x
May, Julian, 1931–	x	x	x	x	x					x
Mayne, William (James Carter), UK, 1928–	x	x	x							
McAllister, Bruce (Hugh), 1946–	x		x							x
McAuley, Paul J., UK, 1955–			x							x
McCaffrey, Anne (Inez), 1926–	x	x	x	x	x			x	x	x
McClary, Thomas Calvert, 1909(?)–1972		x	x							
McDonald, Ian, UK, 1960–			x							x
McHugh, Maureen F.	x									
McIlraith, Frank, UK, ?										
McIntyre, Vonda N(eel), 1948–	x		x	x	x			x		x
McKenna, Richard M(ilton), 1913–1964	x	x	x	x				x		x
McKillip, Patricia A(nne), 1948–	x		x							x
McQuay, Mike, 1949–			x	x						x
Mercier, Louis Sébastian, France, 1740–1814			x			x				
Merle, Robert, France, 1908–	x		x	x			x			
Merril, Judith, 1923–	x	x	x	x	x		x	x		x
Merritt, A(braham), 1884–1943	x	x	x	x			x	x	x	x
Miklowitz, Gloria D(ubov), 1927–	x									
Miller, Walter M(ichael), 1922–	x	x	x	x	x		x	x	x	x
Milne, Robert Duncan, Scotland/US, 1844–1899			x			x				
Mitchell, Edward Page, 1852–1927			x	x		x				
Mitchell, J(ames) Leslie, Scotland, 1901–1935	x	x	x							
Mitchell, John A(mes), 1845–1918	x	x	x	x		x				
Mitchison, Naomi (Margaret), UK, 1897–	x	x	x							x
Moffett, Cleveland Langston, 1863–1926			x			x				
Moffett, Judith, 1942–	x		x							x
Moorcock, Michael (John), UK, 1939–	x	x	x	x	x		x	x		x

Author, Nationality (if not U.S.), Years — Sources

Author, Nationality (if not U.S.), Years	1	2	3	4	5	6	7	8	9	10
Moore, C(atherine) L(ucille), 1911–1987	x	x	x	x	x		x	x	x	x
Moore, (Joseph) Ward, 1903–1978	x	x	x	x				x	x	x
More, Sir Thomas, UK, 1478–1535			x	x		x				
Morris, William, UK, 1834–1896	x		x			x		x		x
Morrow, James (Kenneth), 1947–	x		x	x						x
Moskowitz, Sam, 1920–	x	x	x	x		x				
Moszowski, Alexander, Germany, 1851–1934		x				x				
Murakami, Haruki, Japan, 1949–		x								
Murphy, Pat, 1955–		x								x
Nearing, Homer, Jr., 1915–		x	x							
Nelson, Ray Faraday, 1931–	x		x	x						x
Nesvadba, Josef, Czechoslovakia, 1926–	x	x	x							x
Neville, Kris (Ottman), 1925–1980	x	x	x	x						x
Newman, Kim (James), UK, 1959–	x		x							
Nicolson, Harold (George), UK, 1886–1968		x								
Niven, Larry, 1938–	x	x	x	x	x		x	x	x	x
Nolan, William F(rances), 1928–	x	x	x							x
North, Eric, Australia, 1884–1968		x	x			x				
Norton, Andre, 1912–	x	x	x	x	x			x	x	x
Nourse, Alan E(dward), 1928–1992	x	x	x	x					x	x
Nowlan, Philip Francis, 1888–1940	x	x	x	x				x		x
O'Brien, Fitz-James, 1828–1862	x	x	x	x		x		x		
O'Brien, Robert C(arroll), 1922–1973	x		x							
Odle, E(dwin) V(incent), UK, 1890–1942		x				x		x		
O'Duffy, Eimar, Ireland, 1893–1935		x								
Offutt, Andrew J(efferson V.), 1937–	x		x	x						x
Oliver, Chad(wick), 1928–1993	x	x	x	x	x		x	x	x	x
O'Neill, Joseph, Ireland, 1886–1953		x								x
Ore, Rebecca, 1948–		x								x
Orwell, George, UK, 1903–1950	x	x	x	x	x		x	x		x
Palmer, David (Reay), 1941–			x	x						
Paltock, Robert, UK, 1697–1767	x		x			x				
Pangborn, Edgar, 1909–1976	x	x	x	x	x			x	x	x
Panshin, Alexei, 1940–	x	x	x	x				x	x	x
Park, Paul (Claiborne), 1954–	x		x							x
Parker, Richard, UK, 1915–	x	x	x							
Parkinson, H(arold) F(rederick), UK, (?)		x								
Patchett, M(ary Osborne) E(lwyn), Australia, 1897–	x	x	x							

Author, Nationality (if not U.S.), Years	Sources									
	1	2	3	4	5	6	7	8	9	10
Percy, (F.) Walker, 1916–1990	x	x						x		
Pešek, Luděk, Czechoslovakia, 1919–	x	x								
Phillpotts, Eden, UK, 1862–1960	x	x		x		x		x		
Piercy, Marge, 1936–	x		x	x				x		x
Piper, H(orace) Beam, 1904–1964		x	x	x	x			x	x	x
Piserchia, Doris (Elaine), 1928–	x		x	x	x					x
Platt, Charles (Michael), 1945–	x	x	x	x						x
Poe, Edgar Allan, 1809–1849	x	x	x	x		x	x	x		
Pohl, Frederik, 1919–	x	x	x	x	x		x	x	x	x
Pope, Gustavus W., ?			x			x				
Pournelle, Jerry E(ugene), 1933–	x		x	x	x					x
Powers, Tim(othy), 1952–	x		x	x						x
Pratchett, Terry, UK, 1948–			x							x
Preuss, Paul, 1942–	x		x	x						x
Priest, Christopher (McKenzie), UK, 1943–	x		x	x	x			x		x
Priestley, J(ohn) B(oynton), UK, 1894–1984	x	x	x	x						x
Pynchon, Thomas, 1937–	x		x	x				x		x
Rand, Ayn, 1905–1982	x	x	x	x						x
Randall, Florence Engel, 1917–	x									
Randall, Marta, 1948–	x		x	x	x					x
Rankin, Robert (Fleming), UK, 1949–			x							
Read, Herbert (Edward), UK, 1893–1968	x	x	x							
Reamy, Tom, 1935–1977	x		x							x
Reed, Kit, 1932–	x	x	x	x						x
Reed, Robert, 1956–	x		x							x
Reeve, Arthur B(enjamin), 1880–1936		x	x			x				
Resnick, Michael D(iamond), 1942–	x	x	x							x
Reynolds, Alfred, ?										
Reynolds, Mack, 1917–1983	x	x	x						x	x
Rhodes, W(illiam) H(enry), 1822–1876			x			x				
Ridley, Frank A(mbrose), UK, 1897–1994			x			x				
Roberts, Keith (John Kingston), UK, 1935–	x	x	x	x				x		x
Robertson, E(ileen) Arnot, UK, 1903–1961			x							
Robinson, Frank M(alcolm), 1926–	x	x	x	x	x					x
Robinson, Kim Stanley, 1952–	x		x	x						x
Robinson, Spider, US/Canada, 1948–	x		x	x						x
Rockwood, Roy [house pseudonym]	x		x			x				
Roger, Noëlle, Switzerland, 1874–1953			x			x				

Author, Nationality (if not U.S.), Years	1	2	3	4	5	6	7	8	9	10
Rosny aîné, J. H., Belgium, 1856–1940		x	x			x		x		
Rubinstein, Gillian, Australia, 1942–	x		x							
Rucker, Rudy, 1946–	x		x	x						x
Russ, Joanna, 1937–	x	x	x	x	x		x	x	x	x
Russell, Eric Frank, UK, 1905–1978	x	x	x	x	x		x	x		x
Russo, Richard Paul, 1954–	x		x							
Ryman, Geoff(rey Charles), Canada/UK, 1951–	x		x							x
Saberhagen, Fred(erick Thomas), 1930–	x	x	x	x	x				x	x
Sagan, Carl, 1934–	x	x	x	x						
St. Clair, Margaret, 1911–	x	x	x	x	x		x			x
Sarban, UK, 1910–1989		x	x							x
Sargent, Pamela, 1948–	x		x	x				x	x	x
Saxton, Josephine (Mary Howard), UK, 1935–	x		x							x
Schenck, Hilbert, 1926–			x							x
Schlee, Ann, UK, 1934–	x									
Scott, Jody (Huegelet Wood), UK/US, 1923–	x		x							
Scrymsour, Ella M., UK, 1888–(?)			x		x					
Seaborn, Adam, ?			x		x		x			
Sellings, Arthur, UK, 1921–1968	x	x	x							x
Serviss, Garrett Putnam, 1851–1929	x	x	x	x		x	x	x		x
Severn, David, UK, 1918–	x	x								
Shanks, Edward (Richard Buxton), UK, 1892–1953		x	x			x				
Shaw, Bob, Northern Ireland, 1931–	x	x	x	x				x		x
Shaw, George Bernard, Ireland, 1856–1950	x		x			x		x		
Shea, Robert (Joseph), 1933–1994	x		x							
Sheckley, Robert (Joseph), 1933–	x	x	x	x	x		x	x	x	x
Sheffield, Charles, UK/US, 1935–			x	x						x
Shelley, Mary Wolstonecraft, UK, 1797–1851	x	x	x	x		x	x	x		x
Shepard, Lucius, 1947–	x		x	x						x
Shiel, M(atthew) P(hipps), UK, 1865–1947	x	x	x	x		x	x	x		x
Shiner, Lewis, 1950–			x							
Shiras, Wilmar H(ouse), 1908–1990		x	x					x		x
Shirley, John (Patrick), 1953–	x		x	x						x
Shute, Neville, UK, 1899–1960	x	x	x	x				x		x
Silverberg, Robert, 1935–	x	x	x	x	x		x	x	x	x
Simak, Clifford D(onald), 1904–1988	x	x	x	x	x		x	x	x	x
Simmons, Dan, 1948–	x		x							
Sinclair, Upton (Beall), 1878–1968	x	x	x			x				x

Author, Nationality (if not U.S.), Years	1	2	3	4	5	6	7	8	9	10
Skal, David, US, ?			x							
Skinner, B(urrhus) F(rederic), 1904–1990	x	x	x					x		
Sladek, John T(homas), 1937–		x	x	x						x
Sleator, William (Warner III), 1945–	x		x							
Sloane, William M(illigan), 1906–1974	x	x	x					x		x
Slonczewski, Joan (Lyn), 1956–		x	x							x
Smith, Clark Ashton, 1893–1961	x	x	x	x		x	x			x
Smith, Cordwainer, 1913–1966	x	x	x	x						x
Smith, E(dward) E(lmer), 1890–1965	x	x	x	x	x		x	x	x	x
Smith, Garret, 1876(?)–1954		x	x			x				
Smith, Wayland, UK, 1880–1972		x	x							
Snell, Edmund, UK, 1889(?)–		x	x			x				
Snyder, Zilpha Keatley, 1927–	x									
Spinrad, Norman (Richard), 1940–	x	x	x	x	x			x	x	x
Squire, J(ohn) C(ollings), UK, 1884–1958		x	x							
Stableford, Brian M(ichael), UK, 1948–	x		x	x				x		x
Stapledon, (William) Olaf, UK, 1886–1950	x	x	x	x	x	x	x	x		x
Steele, Allen (M.), 1958–	x		x							
Stephenson, Neal, 1959–	x		x							
Sterling, Bruce, 1954–	x		x	x						x
Stevens, Francis, 1884–1939(?)		x	x	x		x				
Stevenson, Robert Louis, Scotland, 1850–1894	x	x	x	x		x		x		
Stewart, George R(ippey), 1895–1980	x	x	x	x				x	x	x
Stith, John E(dward), 1947–	x		x							
Stockton, Frank R(ichard), 1834–1902		x	x	x		x				x
Stone, Josephine Rector, 1936–	x									
Stoutenberg, Adrien, 1916–1982	x									
Strete, Craig (Kee), 1950–	x		x	x						x
Strugatskii, Arkadii & Boris, Russia, 1925/1931–	x		x	x	x			x		x
Sturgeon, Theodore, 1918–1985	x	x	x	x	x		x	x	x	x
Sucharitkul, Somtow, Thailand, 1952–	x		x	x						x
Suddaby, (William) Donald, UK, 1900–1964		x	x							
Sutton, Jean, 1917–			x							x
Sutton, Jeff(erson Howard), 1913–1979	x	x	x							x
Swanwick, Michael (Jurgen), 1950–	x		x	x						x
Swayne, Martin, UK, 1884–1953			x			x				
Swift, Jonathan, Ireland, 1667–1745	x	x	x	x		x				
Swindells, Robert E(dward), UK, 1939–	x									

Author, Nationality (if not U.S.), Years	1	2	3	4	5	6	7	8	9	10
Taine, John, 1883–1960		x	x	x		x	x	x		x
Tarde, Gabriel, France, 1843–1904		x				x				
Temple, William F(rederick), 1914–1989		x	x	x						x
Tenn, William, 1920–		x	x	x	x		x	x	x	x
Tepper, Sheri S., 1929–	x	x								
Tevis, Walter (Stone), 1928–1984	x		x	x	x		x	x	x	x
Tiptree, James Jr., 1915–1987	x		x	x	x		x	x	x	x
Tolstoy, Alexei, Russia, 1883–1945	x	x	x			x		x		x
Townsend, John Rowe, UK, 1922–	x	x	x							
Train, Arthur (Cheney), 1875–1945	x	x	x			x				
Tsiolkovsky, Konstantin, Russia, 1857–1935	x	x	x			x				x
Tucker, (Arthur) Wilson, 1914–	x	x	x	x	x			x		x
Turner, George (Reginald), Australia, 1916–	x		x	x						x
Twain, Mark, 1835–1910	x	x	x	x		x		x		x
Ure, Jean (Neville), UK, 1924–	x									
Vance, Jack, 1916–	x	x	x	x	x			x	x	x
van Vogt, A(lfred) E(lton), 1912–	x	x	x	x	x		x	x	x	x
Varley, John (Herbert), 1947–	x		x	x	x			x		x
Vercors, France, 1902–1992	x	x	x	x				x		x
Verne, Jules, France, 1828–1905	x	x	x	x		x	x	x		x
Vidal, Gore, 1925–	x	x	x	x						
Vinge, Joan (Carol) D(ennison), 1948–	x		x	x	x					x
Vinge, Vernor (Steffen), 1944–	x		x	x						x
Vivian, E(velyn) Charles, UK, 1882–1947		x	x			x				
Vonarburg, Elisabeth, Canada, 1947–		x								
von Hanstein, Otfried, Germany, ?		x	x			x		x		
von Harbou, Thea, Germany, 1888–1954		x	x	x		x		x		
Vonnegut, Kurt, 1923–	x	x	x	x	x			x	x	x
Waldrop, Howard, 1946–	x		x	x						x
Wallace, Ian, 1912–	x	x	x							x
Walters, Hugh, UK, 1910–	x	x	x							x
Walton, Bryce, 1918–1988	x	x	x							
Wandrei, Donald, 1908–1957		x	x			x				
Waterloo, Stanley, 1846–1913			x	x		x				
Watson, Ian, UK, 1943–	x		x	x				x		x
Watson, Simon, UK, ?										
Webb, Sharon (Lynn), 1936–	x		x							x
Weinbaum, Stanley G(rauman), 1902–1935	x	x	x	x			x	x	x	x

Author, Nationality (if not U.S.), Years	1	2	3	4	5	6	7	8	9	10
Wells, H(erbert) G(eorge), UK, 1866–1946	x	x	x	x	x	x	x	x		x
Westall, Robert (Atkinson), 1929–1993	x		x							
White, James, UK, 1928–	x	x	x					x		x
White, Stewart Edward, 1873–1946			x			x				
White, T(erence) H(anbury), 1906–1964	x	x	x							
Wibberly, Leonard, UK, 1915–1983	x	x	x							
Wilder, Cherry, New Zealand, 1930–	x		x							x
Wilhelm, Kate, 1928–	x	x	x	x	x			x	x	x
Williams, Jay, 1914–1978	x	x								
Williams, Walter Jon, 1953–			x	x						
Williamson, Jack, 1908–	x	x	x	x	x		x	x	x	x
Willis, Connie, 1945–	x		x	x						x
Wilson, Colin, UK, 1931–	x	x	x	x						x
Wilson, Robert Anton, 1932–	x		x	x						x
Wilson, Robert Charles, 1953–			x							x
Wingrove, David, UK, 1954–	x		x							x
Winsor, G(eorge) McLeod, UK, ?		x	x			x				
Winterfeld, Henry, 1901–1990	x	x								
Wolfe, Bernard, 1915–1985	x	x	x	x				x		x
Wolfe, Gene (Rodman), 1931–	x		x	x	x			x	x	x
Wollheim, Donald A(llen), 1914–1990	x	x	x	x		x				x
Womack, Jack, 1956–			x							
Wright, Austin Tappan, 1883–1931		x	x					x		x
Wright, Harold Bell, 1872–1944			x							
Wright, S(ydney) Fowler, UK, 1874–1965		x	x	x		x	x	x		x
Wylie, Philip (Gordon), 1902–1971	x	x	x	x		x		x		x
Wyndham, John, UK, 1903–1969	x	x	x	x			x	x		x
Yarbro, Chelsea Quinn, 1942–	x		x	x						x
Yep, Laurence (Michael), 1948–	x		x	x						x
Zamiatin, Yevgeny, Russia, 1884–1937	x	x	x	x	x	x		x		x
Zebrowski, George, 1945–	x		x	x					x	x
Zelazny, Roger (Joseph), 1937–	x	x	x	x	x			x	x	x
Zoline, Pamela, 1941–			x							x

CHAPTER 10

Science Fiction in Film, Television, and Radio

Michael Klossner

The science fiction film was one of the last film genres to reach maturity. The film industry was over fifty years old and other genres were long established when regular production of SF films began in 1950. After over forty years of intensive production, it is still not clear whether film is a suitable medium for SF. Peter Nicholls [10-13, p. 34] writes, "Fantastic cinema has always been better able to cope with horror, to which imagery and atmosphere are central, than with science fiction, which in its literary form relies on quite complex intellectual structures." *2001: A Space Odyssey* (1968) was voted the tenth-best film ever made by *Sight & Sound* magazine's 1992 International Critics Poll, but *2001* and other prestigious SF films such as *Metropolis* (1926), *Things to Come* (1936), and *Blade Runner* (1982) have been subjected to the same criticism that is leveled at merely enjoyable entertainment such as *Star Wars* (1977) and disappointing films like *Tron* (1982)—the visual elements are more interesting than the scripts. The SF films with the most secure reputations may turn out to be the best middle-budget productions of the 1950s and 1960s, such as *Invasion of the Body Snatchers* (1956), *The Incredible Shrinking Man* (1957), and the British *Quatermass* trilogy (1955, 1957, 1967), all of which provide suspense rather than spectacle.

Table 10-1 lists 117 significant SF films and television and radio programs, which were chosen by experts or which won awards. Table 10-2 presents statistics drawn from Phil Hardy's *Science Fiction* [10-1] and from Table 10-1, divided into five periods—1895–1949; the first, low-budget boom in Hollywood SF production, 1950–1957; what could be called the interboom period, 1958–1975; the second, big-budget boom, 1976–1984; and the post-boom years, 1985 to 1990. These tables make several trends clear. They show that the years 1950–1957 really were a boom, with great increases over earlier periods in the production of both ordinary and important films. The period after the first boom, 1958–1975, saw an increase in total SF film production but somewhat less quality, at least in America. Hollywood produced only fourteen exceptional films during the eighteen years between the booms, against twelve during the eight years of the first boom and twenty during the nine years of the second boom. On the other hand, television programs and non-U.S. films improved during the period between the booms, contributing twenty-eight of the forty-two important titles. The quality of U.S. films rose during the second boom, while TV and foreign films withered. U.S. quality fell off after the second boom.

Table 10-3, SF film rentals, reminds us that several of the most popular films ever made have been SF. However, a list in the February 22, 1993, issue of *Variety*, which breaks down film rentals by decade, shows that SF was far less popular than other genres during the supposed golden age of SF films in the 1950s. Of 253 films which made $3 million or more in rentals during the 1950s, only two (both based on Jules Verne romances) were SF—Disney's *20,000 Leagues Under the Sea* (1954, in 20th place for the decade with $11,267,000) and *Journey to the Center of the Earth* (1959, in 98th place with $4,777,000). *20,000 Leagues* and *Forbidden Planet* (1956) were the major big-budget SF films of the decade. The failure of *Forbidden Planet* to achieve satisfactory box-office results helped to kill the first SF boom. In the 1960s, of 146 films that made $6 million or more in rentals, the only SF films (aside from several James Bond movies) were *2001* (12th place, $25,522,000), *Planet of the Apes* (1968, 39th place, $15,000,000), and two Disney comedies, *The Love Bug* (1969, 14th place, $23,150,000) and *The Absent-Minded Professor* (1961, 56th place, $11,426,000). SF was commercially important only after 1975.

During the second boom several expensive films failed to meet box-office expectations—*The Black Hole* (1979), *Saturn 3* (1980), *Outland* (1981), *Blade Runner* and *Tron* (both 1982 and both visually innovative), and *Krull* (1983). In 1984 the extremely expensive *Dune*, based on one of the most popular SF novels [4-207], and *2010*, the sequel to the most respected SF film, both did inadequate business. Subsequent box-office disappointments included *Enemy Mine* and *Explorers* (both 1985), *Howard the Duck* (1986), *Innerspace* (1987), *Alien Nation* (1988), *Millennium* and *The Abyss* (both 1989). These failed films were especially alarming to studios because production costs for SF films escalated sharply after 1977. As audiences demanded more elaborate and convincing special effects it became nearly impossible to make SF films without huge budgets and the risk of heavy losses. George Lucas stopped making *Star Wars* films after the budgets rose from $9 million for the first film in 1977 to $32 million for the third film, *Return of the Jedi*, in 1983. He has indicated he will wait until advances in computer-generated special effects greatly reduce costs before resuming the series. In 1991 *Terminator 2: Judgment Day* became the most expensive film to date (estimated $90 million). The crunch between rapidly rising budgets and uncertain returns poses a major problem for makers of SF films.

It is unsurprising that the most expensive film was a sequel. The films of the 1950s could be innovative because they had low budgets and represented small financial risks. Indeed they had to be creative because previous SF films were no longer of interest to the public. Filmmakers of the 1950s jettisoned both the mad scientists of the horror-SF films of the early 1930s and the juvenile heroics of serial films such as *Flash Gordon* (1936). By contrast films made during and after the second boom were often highly derivative. Movies of the Lucas-Spielberg era have drawn not only on earlier SF films but also on a wide variety of old films admired in the California film schools, where many of the new directors studied—"classic Hollywood," foreign art films, and many kinds of B movies. In their annotation of *Star Wars* in the first and second editions of *The Encyclopedia of Science Fiction* [7-22], Peter Nicholls and John Brosnan note that the film contains references to "comic strips, old serials, Westerns, James Bond stories, *The Wizard of Oz*, *Snow White*, Errol Flynn swashbucklers, and movies about WWII," to which they could have added Laurel and Hardy and Japanese samurai films. *E.T.* (1982) and *Close Encounters of the Third Kind* (1977) are both redolent of the most saccharine Disney sentiment. Recent direct remakes of old films have included *Invasion of the Body Snatchers* (1978), *The Thing* (1982), *Invaders From Mars* (1986), *The Blob* (1988), *The Fly* (1986), and *Not of This Earth* (1988). *Alien* (1979) was reminiscent of *The Thing* (1951). *Flash Gordon* (1980) and the *Superman* and *Star Trek* films were of course based on older material. Even *The Terminator* (1984) owed much to *Westworld* (1973). In Brosnan's *The Primal Screen* [10-11, p. 382] John Baxter says of the new directors: "These people don't know anything about science fiction, and have no interest in SF, but they are encyclopedic in their knowledge of SF movies. . . . You can't win in a conversation with Joe Dante on the subject of fifties SF movies because he's seen them all, but I'd be astonished to learn that he's read more than four or five of the basic science fiction novels." The 1950s films, including B movies, have achieved canonical status, for filmmakers if not for critics.

To capture large audiences the Lucas generation had to make a vital alteration in the material they borrowed so freely. The 1950s films appealed to fear; the 1970s films were cheerful and exhilarating. The threat in 1950s films was usually aggressive aliens but occasionally advanced technology. *Forbidden Planet* featured a likable robot but also an alien civilization that was destroyed by its own advanced machines. The decisive change occurred in the late 1960s, when *Star Trek* (1966–1969) and *2001* both featured benevolent aliens (Spock and the monolith makers) and desirable technologically advanced futures. *Star Trek* in particular promised a future of miraculous technology and medicine, no social problems and luxury and adventure for all—a utopia with BEMs. Hollywood was slow to recognize the appeal of these visions and continued to believe that SF was meant to scare people. From the late 1960s through the mid-1970s the threat was usually not aliens but technology and dystopian futures, as shown by *Planet of the Apes* and its sequels (1968–1973), *Colossus, No Blade of Grass* (both 1970), *Andromeda Strain, THX 1138, Silent Running* (all three 1971), *Soylent Green, Westworld* (both 1973), *Zardoz* (1974), *Rollerball, The Stepford Wives* (both 1975), and *Logan's Run* (1976), the disappointing first film of the second boom.

Two fabulously popular 1977 films, *Star Wars* and *Close Encounters of the* *Third Kind*, killed off the dystopian wave and set the new boom on a firm footing of bright futures, friendly aliens, and happy endings. The *Star Wars* trilogy (which is supposedly set in the past but which audiences accept as a vision of a possible future) and the *Star Trek* series (seven films so far, beginning in 1979) provided attractive futures in which the heroes always win, while *Close Encounters, E.T.* (the most popular film ever made), and the *Superman* films (four films, 1978–1987) featured benevolent aliens with miraculous powers. Such feel-good films did not always succeed. *Starman* (1984) and *The Abyss* both offered friendly aliens and both failed. Audiences responded to four grim films, *Invasion of the Body Snatchers, Alien, Mad Max 2: The Road Warrior* (1981), and *The Terminator*, but the most ambitious dystopian film of the period, *Blade Runner*, was a notable box-office fiasco.

The community of serious SF writers and scholars has found only a few films to approve since 1977. *Alien, Blade Runner, The Terminator, Brazil* (1985), and to a lesser degree *Videodrome* (1983) have received the lion's share of critical attention. Table 10-1 suggests some other recent titles that should be considered. Some recent films show encouraging creativity. Tim Burton's two *Batman* movies (1989, 1992) and Paul Verhoeven's *Robocop* (1987) are set in striking dystopian futures that found much more audience approval than *Blade Runner*. Robert Zemeckis's first two *Back to the Future* films (1985, 1989) presented time travel paradoxes of surprising complexity only a few years after *The Final Countdown* (1980) timidly avoided such paradoxes; *Future II* has one of the most complicated plots of any popular film. Verhoeven's *Total Recall* (1990) also has a conceptually sophisticated SF plot. *Terminator 2* features an audaciously complex time paradox and *Groundhog Day* (1993) introduced audiences to the concept of a time loop. Of these, only the first *Back to the Future* and *Terminator 2* are in Table 10-1, but the willingness of studios to risk large budgets on relatively sophisticated concepts and the fact that audiences endorsed all these films suggest the possibility of a new boom in SF films, especially if further miracles in special effects technology reduce budgets to reasonable levels.

SF films have won many Academy Awards for special effects and other technical work but only three major Oscars. Frederic March won Best Actor for *Dr. Jekyll and Mr. Hyde* (1932), Cliff Robertson Best Actor for *Charly* (1968), and Don Ameche Best Supporting Actor for *Cocoon* (1985). Major nominations went to *Jekyll/Hyde* (1932) for Best Screenplay; *The Man in the White Suit* (1952), Screenplay; *Dr. Strangelove* (1964), Best Picture, Director, Screenplay, and Actor; *2001*, Director and Screenplay; *Clockwork Orange* (1971), Picture and Director; *Young Frankenstein* (1974), Screenplay; *Star Wars*, Picture, Director, Screenplay, and Supporting Actor; *Close Encounters*, Director and Supporting Actress; *The Boys from Brazil* (1978), Actor; *The China Syndrome* (1979), Actor, Actress, and Screenplay; *E.T.*, Picture, Director, and Screenplay; *Testament* (1983), Actress; *War Games* (1983), Screenplay; *Starman*, Actor; *Brazil*, Screenplay; *Back to the Future* Screenplay; *Aliens* (1986), Actress; and *Big* (1988), Actor and Screenplay.

SF has always been a commercially weak genre on network television, which requires enormous audiences for success. The number of people who can make a film a big hit is inadequate to keep a TV show alive. With the exception of *Doctor Who* (1963–1989), most SF TV series have been short-lived. Even *Star Trek*, the biggest cult show, lasted only three years on NBC, and its reincarnation, *Star Trek: The Next Generation* (1987–), has flourished not on network TV but in the less demanding syndication market. The best period for SF on TV was the 1960s. Only three new British shows and two U.S. shows made after 1969 appear on Table 10-1. The mostly short-lived cult shows of the 1980s included *V* (1983–1985) and *Quantum Leap* (1989–1993) in America and *Blake's 7* (1978–1981), *Hitch Hiker's Guide to the Galaxy* (1981), and *Red Dwarf* (1988–) in Britain. Since 1992 cable TV's Sci-Fi channel has offered films and reruns of old TV series. Some of the channel's films, such as Japanese animated movies, are hard to find elsewhere.

In 1992 Americans paid $17.2 billion to rent and buy video recordings and only $4.9 billion for film tickets. Videocassettes and the insatiable need for programming on cable TV have given young fans the opportunity to become familiar with most U.S., genre films made as far back as 1950. Fans can become almost as expert as the new breed of directors. Many old movies dating back to the silents, foreign films, serial films, and representative episodes of several old TV series can be bought on video by schools and libraries. Movies Unlimited (6736 Castor Ave., Philadelphia, PA 19149, 800-523-0823) is the largest mail order video dealer. Science Fiction Continuum (P.O. Box 154, Colonia, NJ 07067, 800-232-6002) is a specialized source for videos of Japanese animated SF films.

Radio played a major role in introducing audiences to the basic concepts of SF from the 1930s to the 1950s. Recordings of the 1938 Orson Welles broadcast of *War of the Worlds* and of episodes from the vintage radio series *Superman, Dimension X,* and *X Minus One* are available from Radio Yesteryear (Box C, Sandy Hook, CT 06482, 800-243-0987). In 1989 SF radio drama was revived by a 26-part National Public Radio series, Sci-Fi Radio, featuring stories by Dick, Bradbury, Le Guin, Anderson, and others.

Science fiction is a popular category on "audiobooks," spoken recordings on audiocassttes. Bookstore customers and library patrons can choose between abridged tapes (many read by well-known actors) and unabridged recordings, usually spoken by professional readers who are not necessarily less competent than the famous stars. Some tapes are read by authors, who may have a better understanding of their works but who may be unskilled dramatic speakers. Audio books are reviewed in *Library Journal* and *Booklist.* Bowker's annual *Words on Cassette* lists all current spoken tapes and includes a genre index. The 1993 edition has information on more than 50,000 tapes, both fiction and nonfiction.

Although most films of any importance are available on videocassette, published screenplays are still a convenience. This chapter annotates books containing screenplays of *Things to Come* [10-37], *Invasion of the Body Snatchers* [10-29], *Star Wars* [10-41], *Friendship's Death* [10-34], and *Brazil* [10-32] and the script of the 1938 *War of the Worlds* radio broadcast [10-45]. Philip J. Riley has edited a series of books about Universal's Franken-

Title, Year*, Source, Awards

Planet of the Apes (1968) (TM)
2001: A Space Odyssey (1968) (AC, RC, NF, DG, AJ, MK, TM, PN, DP, BW) (H)
Gladiatorerna (Sweden, 1969) (BA)
Der Grosse Verhau (Germany, 1970) (PH)
A Clockwork Orange (UK, 1971) (BA, AJ, SJ, SJo, TM) (H)
Silent Running (1971) (PH)
Solaris (USSR, 1971) (BA, PN)
Slaughterhouse Five (1972) (H)
Fantastic Planet (France, animated, 1973) (MK)
Sleeper (1973) (H)
Westworld (1973) (BA, DP)
Dark Star (1974) (RC, PH, TMi, PT)
The Parasite Murders (Canada, 1974) (PH, PN, PT)
Young Frankenstein (1974) (H)
A Boy and His Dog (1975) (H)
The Man Who Fell to Earth (UK, 1976) (NF, PH, TMi, KN, PN, BW)
Capricorn One (1977) (BA)
Close Encounters of the Third Kind (1977) (AC, RC, DG, TM, PN, DP, BW)
Demon Seed (1977) (AJ)
Star Wars (1977) (DG, AJ, SJo, MK, BW) (H)
Eraserhead (1978) (MK)
Invasion of the Body Snatchers (1978) (BW)
Superman: The Movie (1978) (DG, DP) (H)
Alien (1979) (BA, AC, AJ, MK, TM, DP) (H)
The Brood (Canada, 1979) (PN)
The Hitch Hiker's Guide to the Galaxy (UK, TV series, 1979) (JJ) (BSFA)
Quintet (1979) (TMi)
Stalker (USSR, 1979) (RC)
The Empire Strikes Back (1980) (BW) (H)
Mad Max 2: The Road Warrior (Australia, 1981) (AJ, SJ, MK, PT)
Time Bandits (UK, 1981) (MK) (BSFA)
Android (1982) (PT) (BSFA)
Blade Runner (1982) (AC, NF, AJ, SJ, SJo, PN, BW) (H, BSFA)
E.T. (1982) (MK)
The Thing (1982) (SJ, SJo, PN)
Videodrome (Canada, 1982) (AJ, SJ, PN)
Return of the Jedi (1983) (BW) (H)
Strange Invaders (1983) (PN)
Dune (1984) (SJo)
The Terminator (1984) (MK, KN)
Trancers (1984) (KN)
2010 (1984) (H)
Back to the Future (1985) (SJo) (H)
Brazil (1985) (NF) (BSFA)
Aliens (1986) (NF, SJo) (H,BSFA)
The Fly (1986) (RC)
Robocop (1987) (AJ)

Title, Year*, Source, Awards

Star Cops (UK, TV miniseries, 1987) (BSFA)
Akira (Japan, animated, 1988) (MK)
The Navigator (New Zealand, 1988) (MK)
Red Dwarf (UK, TV series, 1989) (BSFA)
Edward Scissorhands (1990) (H)
Terminator 2: Judgment Day (1991) (H, BSFA)
The Inner Light (Star Trek episode, 1992) (H)
Jurassic Park (1993) (H)
The X Files (TV series, 1993–) (MK)

* In chronological order.
All are U.S. feature films unless another nationality or form is stated. BA, Brian Aldiss. AC, Arthur C. Clarke. RC, Ramsey Campbell. NF, Nigel Floyd. DG, Denis Gifford. PH, Phil Hardy. AJ, Alan Jones. JJ, top 5 TV series picked by large jury in Javna [10-50], p. 7. SJ, Stefan Jaworzyn. SJo, Stephen Jones. MK, Michael Klossner. TM, Tony Masters. TMi, Tom Milne. KN, Kim Newman. PN, Peter Nicholls. DP, David Pirie. PT, Phil Taylor. BW, Bill Warren. All but JJ and MK are from Best Films lists in Hardy [10-1], p. 461.
H, Hugo Award. BSFA, British Science Fiction Association Award. These awards are not shown for every year since their inception because no awards were made in some years, some awards went to non-SF titles, and some TV series received the same award more than one year.

Table 10-2.   SF Film Production, 1895–1990

	1895-1949	1950-1957	1958-1975	1976-1984	1985-1990	Total
Years	55	8	18	9	6	96
Hardy films[a]	365	150	536	262	171	1,484
Hardy Films/Year	6.64	18.75	29.77	29.11	28.50	—
10-1 US films[b]	8	12	14	20	7	61
10-1 UK films[b]	1	5	9	2	—	17
10-1 other films[b]	3	—	13	4	2	22
	1895-1949	1950-1957	1958-1975	1976-1984	1985-1990	Total
10-1 all films[b]	12	17	36	26	9	100
10-1 TV[b]	—	3	6	1	2	12
10-1 radio[b]	1	1	—	—	—	2
10-1 all titles[b]	13	21	42	27	11	114
10-1 4+ titles[c]	2	5	5	6	1	19

[a] All films listed in Hardy [10-1].
[b] From Table 10-1.
[c] Titles from Table 10-1 with four or more votes or awards.

Table 10-3.   Top Science Fiction Rental Films.

Title, Year	Rental Revenue $ (thousands)
E.T. the Extra-Terrestrial, 1982	228,619
Jurassic Park, 1993	205,000
Star Wars, 1977	193,777
Return of the Jedi, 1983	169,193
Batman, 1989	150,500
The Empire Strikes Back, 1980	141,672
Terminator 2: Judgment Day, 1991	112,500
Back to the Future, 1985	105,496
Batman Returns, 1992	100,100
Superman—the Movie, 1978	82,800
Close Encounters of the Third Kind, 1977	82,750
Back to the Future, Part II, 1989	72,319
Honey, I Shrunk the Kids, 1989	72,007
Teenage Mutant Ninja Turtles, 1990	67,650
Superman II, 1981	65,100
Total Recall, 1990	63,511
The Hunt for Red October, 1990	58,500
Star Trek IV: The Voyage Home, 1986	56,820
Star Trek, the Motion Picture, 1979	56,000
Back to the Future, Part III, 1990	49,072
Aliens, 1986	43,753
Teenage Mutant Ninja Turtles II, 1991	41,900
Alien, 1979	40,300
Star Trek II, The Wrath of Khan, 1982	40,000
Cocoon, 1985	40,000
Star Trek III: The Search for Spock, 1984	39,000
Young Frankenstein, 1975	38,823
WarGames, 1983	38,520
The Rocky Horror Picture Show, 1975	38,096
Superman III, 1983	37,200
Star Trek VI: The Undiscovered Country, 1991	36,000
Octopussy, 1983	34,031
Moonraker, 1979	33,924
Groundhog Day, 1993	32,500
Alien 3, 1992	31,762
Predator, 1987	31,000
Flatliners, 1990	28,800
Abyss, 1989	28,700
Thunderball, 1965	28,621
Never Say Never Again, 1983	28,200
Edward Scissorhands, 1990	27,500
Honey, I Blew Up the Kid, 1992	27,417
Star Trek V: The Final Frontier, 1989	27,100
2001: A Space Odyssey, 1968	25,522
Demolition Man, 1993	25,500
The Black Hole, 1979	25,437
Firefox, 1982	25,000
The Spy Who Loved Me, 1977	24,364

Title, Year	Rental Revenue $ (thousands)
Robocop, 1987	24,037
The Rocketeer, 1991	23,179
The Love Bug, 1969	23,150
Goldfinger, 1964	22,998
Robocop 2, 1990	22,505
Blue Thunder, 1983	21,890
Time Bandits, 1981	20,533
2010, 1984	20,186
Teenage Mutant Ninja Turtles, 1993	19,868
Diamonds Are Forever, 1971	19,727
You Only Live Twice, 1967	19,388
Little Shop of Horrors, 1986	19,300
Spaceballs, 1987	19,027
Medicine Man, 1992	19,000
Red Dawn, 1984	17,938
Mad Max Beyond Thunderdome, 1985	17,900
Short Circuit, 1986	17,878
The Fly, 1986	17,500
Harry and the Hendersons, 1987	17,430
A Clockwork Orange, 1971	17,000
Herbie Rides Again, 1974	17,000
The Terminator, 1984	16,822
Bill & Ted's Excellent Adventure, 1989	16,801
Tron, 1982	16,704
Blade Runner, 1982	16,650
Dune, 1984	16,560
The Running Man, 1987	16,335
Darkman, 1990	16,158
Universal Soldier, 1992	16,000
Batteries Not Included, 1987	15,416
Planet of the Apes, 1968	15,000

Source: *Variety*, Feb. 22, 1993 and Feb. 21, 1994. The figures are rentals paid to the studios, not box-office receipts, for the United States and Canada only, not adjusted for inflation.

Table 10-4.   Science Fiction Films and Their Literary Sources

Film Title, Year(s)	Author, Title (if different)
The Absent-Minded Professor, 1961	Taylor, Samuel W. "A Situation of Gravity"
Aelita, 1924	Tolstoy, Alexei
Alien, 1979	(see note A below)
Alraune, 1928, 1930, 1952	Ewers, Hans Heinz
Altered States, 1980	Chayefsky, Paddy
The Amphibious Man, 1961	Belyayev, Alexander
The Andromeda Nebula, 1968	Efremov, Ivan

Film Title, Year(s)	Author, Title (if different)
The Andromeda Strain, 1970	Crichton, Michael
Animal Farm, 1955	Orwell, George
At the Earth's Core, 1976	Burroughs, Edgar Rice. *Pellucidar*
L'Atlantide, 1932, 1961	Benoit, Pierre
Atlantis, the Lost Continent, 1960	Hargreaves, Gerald. *Atalanta* (play)
The Awful Dr. Orloff, 1962	Kuhne, David
The Beast From 20,000 Fathoms, 1953	Bradbury, Ray. "The Foghorn"
The Bed Sitting Room, 1969	Antrobus, John, and Spike Milligan (play)
Biggles, 1986	Johns, W. E. (several *Biggles* novels)
Billion Dollar Brain, 1967	Deighton, Len
The Birds, 1963	DuMaurier, Daphne
The Black Oxen, 1924	Atherton, Gertrude
The Black Sun, 1979	Čapek, Karel. *Krakatit*
Blade Runner, 1982	Dick, Philip K. *Do Androids Dream of Electric Sheep?*
A Blind Bargain, 1922	Pain, Barry. *Octave of Claudius*
Body Snatchers, 1993	Finney, Jack
A Boy and His Dog, 1975	Ellison, Harlan
The Boys From Brazil, 1978	Levin, Ira
The Brain, 1962	Siodmak, Curt. *Donovan's Brain*
The Brain Eaters,1958	Heinlein, Robert *The Puppet Masters*
Bug, 1975	Page, Thomas. *The Hephaestus Plague*
Carnosaur, 1993	Knight, Harry Adam (pseud. of John Brosnan)
The Chairman, 1969	Kennedy, Jay Richard
Charly, 1968	Keyes, Daniel. *Flowers for Algernon*
Children of the Damned, 1963	Wyndham, John. *The Midwich Cuckoos*
A Clockwork Orange, 1971	Burgess, Anthony
Colossus—the Forbin Project, 1971	Jones, D. F. *Colossus*
Coma, 1978	Cook, Robin
Communion, 1989	Strieber, Whitley (nonfiction)
Condorman, 1981	Sheckley, Robert. *The Game of X*
A Connecticut Yankee, 1931	Twain, Mark
A Connecticut Yankee in King Arthur's Court, 1949	Twain, Mark
The Conquest of Space, 1955	Ley, Willy, and Chesley Bonestell (nonfiction)
Countdown, 1968	Searls, Hank. *The Pilgrim Project*
The Curse of Frankenstein, 1957	Shelley, Mary. *Frankenstein*
Damnation Alley, 1977	Zelazny, Roger
The Damned, 1961	Lawrence, H. L. *The Children of Light*
Day of the Dolphin, 1973	Merle, Robert
Day of the Triffids, 1963	Wyndham, John
The Day the Earth Stood Still, 1951	Bates, Harry. "Farewell to the Master"
Dead-End Drive-In, 1986	Carey, Peter. "Crabs"
The Dead Mountaineer Hotel, 1979	Strugatskii, Boris and Arkadii
The Dead Zone, 1983	King, Stephen
Death Race 2000, 1975	Melchior, Ib. "The Racer"
Deluge, 1933	Wright, S. Fowler
Demon Seed, 1977	Koontz, Dean R.

Film Title, Year(s)	Author, Title (if different)
Destination Moon, 1950	Heinlein, Robert. *Rocket Ship Galileo*
The Devil Commands, 1941	Sloane, William. *The Edge of Running Water*
Devil Girl from Mars, 1954	Maher, John C., and James Eastwood (play)
Diamonds Are Forever, 1971	Fleming, Ian
Die, Monster, Die, 1965	Lovecraft, H. P. "The Colour Out of Space"
Doc Savage, the Man of Bronze, 1975	Robeson, Kenneth
Dr. Jekyll and Mr. Hyde, 1920, 1932, 1941	Stevenson, R. L.
Dr. Jekyll and Sister Hyde, 1972	Stevenson, R. L. *Dr. Jekyll and Mr. Hyde*
Dr. Mabuse, the Gambler, 1922	Jacques, Norbert
Dr. No, 1962	Fleming, Ian
Dr. Strangelove, 1964	George, Peter. *Red Alert*
Donovan's Brain, 1953	Siodmak, Curt
Don't Play with the Martians, 1967	Labty, Michel. *Les Sextuplets de Locqmaria*
Dune, 1984	Herbert, Frank
Earth vs. the Flying Saucers, 1956	Keyhoe, Donald. *Flying Saucers From Outer Space* (nonfiction)
The Electronic Monster, 1957	Maine, Charles Eric. *Escapement*
Empire of the Ants, 1977	Wells, H. G.
The End of the World, 1930	Flammarion, Camille
Enemy Mine, 1985	Longyear, Barry
Engineer Garin's Death Ray, 1965	Tolstoy, Alexei. *The Garin Death Ray*
Escape to Witch Mountain, 1975	Key, Alexander
The Eye Creatures, 1965	Fairman, Paul W. "The Cosmic Frame"
The Fabulous World of Jules Verne, 1958	Verne, Jules. *Facing the Flag*
The Face of Fu Manchu, 1965	Rohmer, Sax
Fahrenheit 451, 1966	Bradbury, Ray
Fail Safe, 1964	Burdick, Eugene, and Harvey Wheeler
Fantastic Planet, 1973	Wul, Stefan. *Oms en Serie*
Fiend Without a Face, 1958	Long, Amelia Reynolds. "The Thought Monster"
The Final Programme, 1973	Moorcock, Michael
Firefox, 1982	Thomas, Craig
Firestarter, 1984	King, Stephen
The First Men in the Moon, 1964	Wells, H. G.
First Spaceship on Venus, 1960	Lem, Stanislaw. *The Astronauts*
The Fly, 1958, 1986	Langelaan, George
Food of the Gods, 1976	Wells, H. G.
Forbidden Planet, 1956	Shakespeare, William. *The Tempest* (play)
Four-Sided Triangle, 1953	Temple, William F.
F.P.1. Doesn't Answer, 1932	Siodmak, Curt
Frankenstein, 1931	Shelley, Mary
Frankenstein Unbound, 1990	Aldiss, Brian
Freejack, 1992	Sheckley, Robert. *Immortality, Inc.*
Friendship's Death, 1987	Wollen, Peter
From the Earth to the Moon, 1958	Verne, Jules
Give Us the Moon, 1944	Brahms, Caryl, and S. J. Simon. *The Elephant Is White*
The Gladiator, 1938	Wylie, Philip
Goldfinger, 1964	Fleming, Ian
The Handmaid's Tale, 1990	Atwood, Margaret

Film Title, Year(s)	Author, Title (if different)
The Hands of Orlac, 1925	Renard, Maurice
Hard to Be a God, 1989	Strugatskii, Boris and Arkadii
High Treason, 1929	Pemberton-Billing, Noel (play)
Homunculus, 1916	Reinert, Robert
I, Monster, 1971	Stevenson, R. L. *Dr. Jekyll and Mr. Hyde*
The Illustrated Man, 1969	Bradbury, Ray
The Incredible Shrinking Man, 1957	Matheson, Richard. *The Shrinking Man*
The Incredible Shrinking Woman, 1981	Matheson, Richard *The Shrinking Man*
Invasion of the Body Snatchers, 1956, 1978	Finney, Jack. *The Body Snatchers*
Invasion of the Saucermen, 1957	Fairman, Paul W. "The Cosmic Frame"
The Invisible Boy, 1957	Cooper, Edmund
The Invisible Man, 1933	Wells, H. G.
The Island at the Top of the World, 1974	Cameron, Ian. *The Lost Ones*
The Island of Dr. Moreau, 1977	Wells, H. G.
The Island of Lost Souls, 1932	Wells, H. G. *The Island of Dr. Moreau*
Island of the Burning Damned, 1967	Lymington, John. *Night of the Big Heat*
It's Alive, 1968	Matheson, Richard. *Being*
It's Great to Be Alive, 1933	Swain, John D.
Journey to the Center of the Earth, 1959	Verne, Jules
Jurassic Park, 1993	Crichton, Michael
Kiss Me Deadly, 1955	Spillane, Mickey
Krakatit, 1948	Čapek, Karel
The Lady and the Monster, 1944	Siodmak, Curt. *Donovan's Brain*
The Last Man on Earth, 1923	Swain, John D.
The Last Man on Earth, 1964	Matheson, Richard. *I Am Legend*
The Lawnmower Man, 1992	King, Stephen
Lifeforce, 1985	Wilson, Colin. *The Space Vampires*
Light Years, 1988	Andrevan, Jean-Pierre. *Robots Against Gandahar*
Logan's Run, 1976	Nolan, William F. and George Clayton Johnson
Lord of the Flies, 1963, 1990	Golding, William
The Lost Continent, 1968	Wheatley, Dennis. *Uncharted Seas*
The Lost World, 1925, 1960	Doyle, Arthur Conan
Mad Love, 1935	Renard, Maurice. *The Hands of Orlac*
Malevil, 1981	Merle, Robert
The Man and the Beast, 1951	Stevenson, R. L. *Dr. Jekyll and Mr. Hyde*
The Man in the White Suit, 1951	MacDougall, Roger (play)
The Man Who Could Work Miracles, 1936	Wells, H. G. "The Man Who Had to Sing"
The Man Who Fell to Earth, 1976	Tevis, Walter
The Man Who Thought Life, 1969	Holst, Valdemar
The Man With the Golden Gun, 1974	Fleming, Ian
The Manchurian Candidate, 1962	Condon, Richard
Marooned, 1969	Caidin, Martin
Mary Shelley's Frankenstein, 1994	Shelley, Mary. *Frankenstein*
The Mask of Fu Manchu, 1932	Rohmer, Sax
Master of the World, 1961	Verne, Jules. *Master of the World* and *Robur the Conqueror*
The Masters of Time, 1982	Wul, Stefan. *L'Orphelin de Perdide*

Film Title, Year(s)	*Author, Title (if different)*
Maximum Overdrive, 1986	King, Stephen. "Trucks"
The Maze, 1953	Sandoz, Maurice
Memoirs of a Survivor, 1981	Lessing, Doris
Memoirs of an Invisible Man, 1992	Saint, H.F.
A Message from Mars, 1913, 1921	Ganthony, Richard (play)
Metropolis, 1926	Von Harbou, Thea
Millennium, 1989	Varley, John. "Air Raid"
The Mind of Mr. Soames, 1970	Maine, Charles Eric
Mission Stardust, 1968	Ernsting, Walter. *Perry Rhodan* series
The Monitors, 1968	Laumer, Keith
Moonraker, 1979	Fleming, Ian
The Most Dangerous Man Alive, 1958	Rock, Philip, and Michael Pate. "The Steel Monster"
The Mysterians, 1957	Okami, Jojiro
Mysterious Island, 1929, 1961	Verne, Jules
Naked Lunch, 1991	Burroughs, William S.
The Navy Vs. the Night Monsters, 1965	Leinster, Murray. *The Monster From Earth's End*
Never Say Never Again, 1983	Fleming, Ian
Nightfall, 1988	Asimov, Isaac
Nightflyers, 1987	Martin, George R. R.
1984, 1956, 1984	Orwell, George
No Blade of Grass, 1970	Christopher, John. *The Death of Grass*
The Nutty Professor, 1963	Stevenson, R. L. *Dr. Jekyll and Mr. Hyde*
The Omega Man, 1971	Matheson, Richard. *I Am Legend*
On Her Majesty's Secret Service, 1969	Fleming, Ian
On the Beach, 1959	Shute, Nevil
On the Comet, 1970	Verne, Jules. *Hector Servadac*
The Perfect Woman, 1949	Geoffrey, Wallace, and Basil Mitchell (play)
Perry Rhodan—SOS, 1967	Ernsting, Walter
The Philadelphia Experiment, 1984	Moore, William I., and Charles Berlitz (nonfiction)
Planet of the Apes, 1968	Boulle, Pierre
The Power, 1967	Robinson, Frank M.
Project X, 1967	Davies, Leslie P. *The Artificial Man* and *Psychogeist*
The Puppet Masters, 1994	Heinlein, Robert
The Quest for Fire, 1981	Rosny, J. H.
Quest for Love, 1971	Wyndham, John. "Random Quest"
The Quiet Earth, 1985	Harrison, Craig
The Ravagers, 1979	Alter, Robert E. *Path to Savagery*
Red Planet Mars, 1952	Balderson, John L., and John Hoare. *Red Planet* (play)
The Return of Dr. X, 1939	Makin, William J. "The Doctor's Secret"
Robinson Crusoe on Mars, 1964	Defoe, Daniel. *Robinson Crusoe*
Rollerball, 1975	Harrison, William. "Rollerball Murders"
The Running Man, 1987	King, Stephen
The Satan Bug, 1965	MacLean, Alistair
Saturn 3, 1980	Barry, John
Scream and Scream Again, 1969	Saxon, Peter. *The Disoriented Man*

Film Title, Year(s)	*Author, Title (if different)*
Seconds, 1966	Ely, David
The Secret of NIMH, 1982	O'Brien, Robert C. *Mrs. Frisby and the Rats of NIMH*
She Devil, 1957	Weinbaum, Stanley G. "The Adaptive Ultimate"
Sinners in Silk, 1924	Glazer, Benjamin
Siren of Atlantis, 1949	Benoit, Pierre. *L'Atlantide*
Six Hours to Live, 1932	Morris, Gordon, and Morton Barteaux. "Auf Wiedersehen"
Skeleton on Horseback, 1937	Čapek, Karel. *The White Disease* (play)
Slapstick of Another Kind, 1984	Vonnegut, Kurt. *Slapstick*
Slaughterhouse Five, 1972	Vonnegut, Kurt
Solaris, 1971	Lem, Stanislaw
Soylent Green, 1973	Harrison, Harry. *Make Room! Make Room!*
The Spy Who Loved Me, 1977	Fleming, Ian
Stalker, 1979	Strugatskii, Boris and Arkadii. *Roadside Picnic*
The Stepford Wives, 1974	Levin, Ira
The Submersion of Japan, 1973	Komatsu, Sakyo. *Japan Sinks*
The Swarm, 1978	Herzog, Arthur
Target Earth! 1954	Fairman, Paul W. "Deadly City"
The Tenth Victim, 1965	Sheckley, Robert. "The Seventh Victim"
The Terminal Man, 1974	Crichton, Michael
The Terminator, 1984	(see note b below)
The Terrornauts, 1967	Leinster, Murray. *The Wailing Asteroid*
Test Pilot Pirx, 1978	Lem, Stanislaw. "Inquiry"
Testament, 1983	Amen, Carol. "The Last Testament"
Them! 1954	Yates, George W.
They Came From Beyond Space, 1967	Millard, Joseph. *The Gods Hate Kansas*
They Live, 1988	Nelson, Ray. "Eight O'Clock in the Morning"
The Thing, 1951, 1982	Campbell, John W. "Who Goes There?"
Things to Come, 1936	Wells, H. G. *The Shape of Things to Come*
This Island Earth, 1955	Jones, Raymond F.
Thunderball, 1965	Fleming, Ian
The Time Machine, 1960	Wells, H. G.
Timeslip, 1956	Maine, Charles Eric. *The Isotope Man*
Total Recall, 1990	Dick, Philip K. "We Can Remember It for You Wholesale"
Transatlantic Tunnel, 1935	Kellermann, Bernhard. *Der Tunnel*
The 27th Day, 1957	Mantley, John
20,000 Leagues Under the Sea, 1916	Verne, Jules. *20,000 Leagues* and *Mysterious Island*
20,000 Leagues Under the Sea, 1954	Verne, Jules
The Two Faces of Dr. Jekyll, 1961	Stevenson, R. L. *Dr. Jekyll and Mr. Hyde*
2001: A Space Odyssey, 1968	Clarke, Arthur C. "The Sentinel"
2010, 1984	Clarke, Arthur C. *2010: Odyssey Two*
The Twonky, 1953	Kuttner, Henry

Film Title, Year(s)	Author, Title (if different)
Unidentified Flying Oddball, 1979	Twain, Mark. *A Connecticut Yankee in King Arthur's Court*
Village of the Damned, 1960	Wyndham, John. *The Midwich Cuckoos*
Village of the Giants, 1965	Wells, H. G. *Food of the Gods*
Virus, 1980	Komatsu, Sakyo
War of the Worlds, 1953	Wells, H. G.
Watchers, 1988	Koontz, Dean R.
When the Wind Blows, 1986	Briggs, Raymond
When Worlds Collide, 1951	Wylie, Philip, and Edwin Balmer
Who? 1974	Budrys, Algis
Wild in the Streets, 1968	Thom, Robert. "The Day It All Happened, Baby"
Woman in the Moon, 1929	Von Harbou, Thea. *By Rocket to the Moon*
The World, the Flesh and the Devil, 1959	Shiel, Matthew P. *The Purple Cloud*
The World Will Shake, 1939	Dumas, C. R., and R. F. Didelot. *La Machine a Predire la Mort*
You Only Live Twice, 1967	Fleming, Ian
The Young Diana, 1922	Corelli, Maria

Anthology films, made-for-TV films and miniseries, films based on comic books, and most sequels are excluded from this list. Most sources are "official." A few were established only by legal action after a film's release. Titles of novels are in italics, titles of shorter fiction in quotes. Consult author index for entry numbers of annotated fiction.

[a] The producers of *Alien* made an out-of-court settlement with A. E. van Vogt for his story "The Black Destroyer," incorporated in his *The Voyage of the Space Beagle* [3-181].

[b] The makers of *The Terminator* were forced to "acknowledge the work of Harlan Ellison," including the story "I Have No Mouth and I Must Scream."

Bibliography

This section is divided into five groups: Reference Works, General Studies, Specialized Studies, TV and Radio, and Periodicals.

Reference Works

*10-1.   Hardy, Phil, ed. **Science Fiction.** Aurum, 1991. 2nd ed. U.S. ed.: *The Overlook Film Encyclopedia: Science Fiction.* Overlook, 1994.
Almost 1,500 entries arranged chronologically from 1895 to 1990 cover almost all English-language SF feature films and hundreds of silents (including short films) and foreign films. Some 1980s films (U.S. B movies and Japanese, Australian, and New Zealand films) are omitted. Annotations are unsigned; besides Hardy, contributors and their areas of

expertise are Denis Gifford on silents; Anthony Masters, the 1950s; Paul Taylor, the 1970s and early 1980s; Paul Willemen, foreign films; and Kim Newman, 1985–1990. Entries include variant titles, running time, color or black-and-white, principal credits, and from 100 to 1,000 words of terse, highly erudite criticism. The title index, in tiny print, includes variant titles. More than 500 well-chosen black-and-white and a few dozen color illustrations supplement the text. Appendixes include box-office champions, best film lists by seventeen experts (used in tables 10-1 and 10-2), Oscar nominees and winners, and a selective bibliography (which is unchanged from the first, 1984 ed.). The most sophisticated critical reference work on the subject, *Science Fiction* is the second volume in the Aurum Film Encyclopedia series. Hardy also edited *Horror* (1985, reprinted as *The Encyclopedia of Horror Movies*), third in the Aurum series, which includes several marginal SF films. Many titles are discussed in both volumes.

10-2.   Lee, Walt. Reference Guide to Fantastic Films: Science Fiction, Fantasy and Horror. Chelsea-Lee Books, 1972–1974. 3 vols.
Many years of fan scholarship lie behind this compilation, the most complete filmography of fantastic films made before the 1970s, which includes many obscure, marginal, silent, short, foreign, animated, and juvenile titles not in other sources. About 15,000 films are arranged by title in three sturdy, 8½ x 11 inch paperbacks. Many entries are incomplete; complete entries include date, country, length, credits (including casts but not names of characters), a brief, nonevaluative note describing the film's fantastic elements (not a complete synopsis), and references to information (not necessarily reviews) found in hundreds of sources listed in the bibliography. About 5,000 more films are listed briefly as "exclusions" (films which appear to have fantastic elements but do not) and "problems" (for which sufficient information could not be found). The approximately 150 illustrations are mainly unfamiliar and interesting. Special Hugo plaque, 1975

10-3.   Lentz, Harris M. Science Fiction, Horror and Fantasy Film and Television Credits. McFarland, 1983. 2 vols.
Lentz lists credits in genre films and TV programs for more than 10,000 actors, directors, producers, writers, cinematographers, special effects and makeup artists, and composers of film scores. Entries for actors include the names of characters portrayed. Vol. 2 is arranged by titles of films and TV series. For films, only the director and actors are listed; it is necessary to consult other works to find who performed other functions on a film. Lentz and Fulton [10-46] are the most complete sources of information

on fantastic TV series. Lentz provides title, actors, character names, and broadcast dates for each episode of each series. This very complete work has been updated by a 1989 supplement, current through 1987, and a second supplement, current through 1993.

10-4. Senn, Bryan, and John Johnson. **Fantastic Cinema Subject Guide: A Topical Index to 2,500 Horror, Science Fiction and Fantasy Films.** McFarland, 1992.

This much-needed guide arranges 2,500 films under eighty-one subject areas, such as Alien Invaders, Frankenstein, the Future, Mars, and Robots. Titles are listed alphabetically under each subject; chronological order would have been preferable. Entries include the film's principal credits and cast, a description emphasizing subject rather than plot, often ludicrous quotes from dialogue and film ads, and "interesting information" (that is, trivia) about the film's production and participants. The authors' often harsh critical opinions are relegated to a numerical rating system in the title index. Includes serial films, TV films and miniseries, and foreign films that have been dubbed or subtitled in English. The *Subject Guide* is less complete than other reference books in the field; Senn and Johnson list hundreds of obscure films but several B films and a few notable films are missing.

10-5. Strickland, A. W., and Forrest J. Ackerman. **A Reference Guide to American Science Fiction Films.** TIS Publications, 1981. Vol. 1, 1897–1929.

The most detailed guide to very early SF films presents a unique picture of a time when audiences and filmmakers were almost totally ignorant of SF (although several films were based on *Frankenstein, Jekyll/Hyde,* and Verne romances) but were clearly disturbed by rapid technological change. Of the 222 films listed (many of them short films or serial films), about one-third are comedies and most of the rest thrillers; most deal with the ludicrous or dangerous effects of futuristic inventions. Strickland is listed in Hardy's [10-1] bibliography, but of Strickland's 222 films, 130 are not in Hardy, indicating how many of these titles are quite marginal SF. The *Reference Guide* has more complete filmographic information than Hardy, including character names; much longer, largely uncritical synopses; references to and often quotes from contemporary reviews; and dozens of illustrations, many full-page. Only the first volume of Strickland's planned set was published.

10-6. **Videohound's Golden Movie Retriever.** Visible Ink, 1991–. Annual.

Many obscure genre films are now available on videocassette. This annual is the most complete of many reasonably priced video guides. The 1993 issue lists 22,000 titles. Indexes provide access by genre and names of directors and leading actors. Each entry includes date, length, director, cast, a terse description, and a numerical critical rating. *The Phantom's Ultimate Video Guide* (1989) by the Phantom of the Movies (B-movie and video critic for the *New York Daily News*) includes 100 pages on SF and fantasy videos. The Phantom's annotations are longer and more critical than the *Retriever's*, but his list is less complete.

10-7. Weldon, Michael. **The Psychotronic Encyclopedia of Film.** Ballantine, 1983.

Weldon includes expensive productions and ranges from the 1930s to the 1980s, but B movies of the 1950s and 1960s are his first love. Many of the over 3,000 films listed are nonfantastic exploitation movies, such as juvenile delinquent and prison films. Except for the very good and the very bad, Weldon describes but does not evaluate most films, recognizing that B-movie fans are attracted by plot elements and stars, not by conventional dramatic and cinematic values. He has something interesting to say about almost every film.

10-8. Willis, Donald. **Horror and Science Fiction Films.** Scarecrow, 1972–1984. 3 vols.

Entries include year, country, running time, credits, cast, variant titles, and citations to reviews and sources of more complete information. Vol. I has about 4,400 films, Vol. II about 2,350, and Vol. III 760, but many entries in Vols. II and III are critical commentaries for films listed briefly in a previous volume. As the number of films in each volume decreased, the length of Willis's commentaries increased. His Vol. I is comparable to but less complete than Lee's Reference Guide [10-2]. Willis's critical annotations are respectable, but less authoritative than those in Hardy's *Science Fiction* [10-1] and *Horror*. Like Willis, John Stanley's *Creature Features Movie Guide Strikes Again* (1994) describes most SF, fantasy, and horror films. Stanley is more fannish than Willis and provides less information (fewer credits, no running times or citations), but his guide is much cheaper and ten years more current.

10-9. Willis, Donald, ed. **Variety's Complete Science Fiction Reviews.** Garland, 1985.

In the 1950s many genre films, even major ones such as *Invasion of the Body Snatchers*, received few reviews in the mainstream press, but almost all were reviewed in *Variety*, the weekly trade paper of the entertainment industry. The approximately 1,000 reviews reprinted here cover films from 1907 to 1984. Most are shrewd, terse, punchy, and extremely knowledgeable about the film industry of their time. *Variety* reviewers were primarily interested in a film's commercial prospects, but they also carefully discussed writing, direction, acting, and what they called "technical credits." Some reviews, such as an unfavorable appraisal of *2001*, are dated, but many have stood the test of time and all are of historical interest. Reviews include more detailed credits than most other sources and give character names as well as the names of actors. Many little-known foreign films are covered. Reviews published since 1984 are collected in biennial volumes of *Variety's Film Reviews*, published by Bowker. Another large set, *The Motion Picture Guide* (CineBooks, 1987, updated by annuals) has even more films than the *Variety* set but also a higher error rate and more lenient film buff criticism. There is no genre index to the biennial collections of *Variety* reviews. A companion volume to the Nash set, *Cinebooks Movie List*, indexes the set by genre through 1988; each subsequent annual volume has its own genre index.

General Studies

10-10. Baxter, John. **Science Fiction in the Cinema.** A. S. Barnes, 1970.
Baxter and Johnson [10-12] were two of the earliest authors to write seriously on the SF film, which in 1970 was just becoming a respectable topic. Baxter's careful examinations of most of the major films to that date, including several foreign films, support his conclusion that "the two fields of sf and cinema do not mesh; sf films usually succeed as cinema in proportion to the degree in which they fail as sf." His belief that written SF is optimistic and pro-science while SF films are pessimistic and anti-science was justified at the time. A British critic, Baxter greatly admires the American SF directors of the 1950s, especially Jack Arnold. Includes a chapter on SF on television.

*10-11. Brosnan, John. **The Primal Screen: A History of Science Fiction Film.** Orbit, 1991.
Primal Screen is greatly expanded from Brosnan's previous history of SF films, *Future Tense* (1978), and, according to the author, is "much more personal" and "should in no way be regarded as a serious reference book." Nonetheless his wit, irreverence, and common sense, leavened with Australian colloquialisms, make this the best current general history of the genre, despite the omission of a few notable films. An ideal critic of popular entertainment, Brosnan holds films to a high standard that few of them meet, but he is fair to the many mediocre films in the genre and understands their appeal. He overthrows some icons, unearths some obscure gems, and concludes that SF films are "equally delighting and

irritating." With many well-chosen illustrations and quotes from filmmakers.

10-12. Johnson, William, ed. **Focus on the Science Fiction Film.** Prentice-Hall, 1972.
The mostly short pieces collected by Johnson include contemporary reviews (some of them quaint); screenplay excerpts; articles on the production of five films; thoughtful comments by directors François Truffaut, Don Siegel, and Stanley Kubrick and authors Brian Aldiss and Kingsley Amis; academic film criticism (some by Europeans); a report on one of the first SF film festivals (Trieste, 1963); and a remarkably old-fashioned 1959 *Film Quarterly* article denouncing almost all 1950s SF films as absurd and "perverse." Some contributors disagree interestingly; for instance, Siegel and a European critic see *Invasion of the Body Snatchers* very differently. A useful overview of informed opinion on the genre two decades after production accelerated in 1950. Johnson's bibliography includes articles and foreign books.

*10-13. Nicholls, Peter. **The World of Fantastic Films: An Illustrated Survey.** Dodd, Mead, 1984. U.K. title: *Fantastic Cinema*, Ebury, 1984.
Nicholls's survey of SF, horror, and fantasy films has an exceptional critical text, carefully selected illustrations representing many periods and types of films, and reference information. The latter is found in a filmography of 700 titles; each entry includes country, date, length, color or black-and-white, production company, principal credits and cast, and a rating based on the average of four critics' opinions. Four hundred films are briefly annotated in the filmography; the other 300 are discussed at greater length in the well-organized text. Nicholls includes almost all significant titles and no trivia. He can be faulted for rushing through several decades; 44 pages cover films from the 1890s to 1967 while 120 pages describe movies from 1968 to 1983. Coverage of foreign films is strong. Nicholls concludes that film is better suited to fantasy and horror than SF. *The World of Fantastic Films* is the best one-volume critical work covering all kinds of fantastic cinema. In his heavily illustrated *Films of Science Fiction and Fantasy* (1988) Baird Searles is rarely as insightful as Nicholls.

10-14. Pohl, Frederik, and Frederik Pohl IV. **Science Fiction Studies in Film.** Ace, 1981.
The Pohls mention bad films only briefly and rush over some good ones; they devote only two pages to *Invasion of the Body Snatchers* and one to *The Incredible Shrinking Man*, against a 25-page chapter on Stanley Kubrick's three SF films. Their mostly conventional, sometimes illuminating comments are supplemented by extensive, well-chosen quotes from filmmak-

ers, contemporary reviews, and current critics. This satisfactory introduction for novices focuses on the differences between written and filmed SF and concludes "science fiction films are usually fun, sometimes very good, once in a while superb." Pohl IV contributes a 31-page appendix on special effects techniques.

10-15.   Strick, Philip. **Science Fiction Movies.** Octopus, 1976.
Arranged thematically, not chronologically, Strick's survey is the only one of many heavily illustrated books on SF films to provide a substantive text as well as attractive illustrations. Chatty, erudite, sometimes facetious, Strick includes many obscure, borderline, silent, and foreign films. He finds most SF films highly pessimistic—a fact of which he approves.

Specialized Studies

10-16.   Adler, Alan. **Science Fiction and Horror Movie Posters in Full Color.** Dover, 1977.
10-17.   Borst, Ronald V., Keith Burns, and Leith Adams, eds. **Graven Images: The Best of Horror, Fantasy and Science Fiction Film Art from the Collection of Ronald V. Borst.** Grove, 1992.

The work of a film poster artist is restricted only by the film's premise and the artist's imagination, not by budgets or physical impossibilities. Not surprisingly, many posters for SF films were more striking than anything in the films they advertised, especially in the early days of limited budgets and primitive special effects. Borst beautifully reproduces about 500 posters from the silents through the 1960s; many of the best are foreign. Adler offers only 46 posters, most of which promoted schlock films of the 1950s, but his collection is much cheaper than Borst's, his reproductions are larger (most a generous 13 by 9 inches), and his brief annotations more informative. Unfortunately neither book identifies the artists responsible for individual posters. Chapter introductions in Borst by celebrities such as Bradbury and Ellison are merely fannish nostalgia, except for Robert Bloch's comments on silent films. *Yesterday's Tomorrows: The Golden Age of Science Fiction Movie Posters, 1950–1964* by Bruce L. Wright (1993) reproduces 75 posters, many 11 by 8 inches. Wright's annotations are longer than Adler's and Borst's but fannish and superficial. He identifies some of the poster artists.

10-18.   Agel, Jerome, ed. **The Making of Kubrick's 2001.** Signet, 1970.
One of the longest books (367 pages) about a single film, Agel's *Making* is misleadingly titled. Articles on the film's production (reprinted from the *New Yorker*) are not very detailed, especially about *2001*'s innovative special effects. The collection also includes Arthur C. Clarke's story, "The

Sentinel," on which *2001* was based; speculation by scientists on the prospects for finding extraterrestrial intelligence; 100 pages of heavily captioned, small, black-and-white stills; 22 pages of "audience response" (fan mail, some of it sophisticated); 78 pages of reviews, presenting a wide variety of reactions to the controversial film; and Stanley Kubrick's celebrated 1968 *Playboy* interview. A necessary resource for the study of the most prestigious SF film.

10-19. Benson, Michael. **Vintage Science Fiction Films, 1896–1949.** McFarland, 1985.

This examination of the decades before SF became a real film genre strays deep into fantasy, horror, and other marginal material. Benson's commentary is anecdotal and only occasionally critical, but quite informative about hundreds of little-known silent and sound films and serials. Includes a good selection of illustrations, detailed credits and cast lists, a very complete index, synopses (including many for serials that Kinnaird [10-25] does not synopsize), and information on many foreign films not in Strickland [10-5]. Benson's full text is available on CD-ROM as part of *The ScanRom Motion Picture Guide to Horror and Science Fiction Films* (1992). John Frazer's *Artificially Arranged Scenes: The Films of George Méliès* (1979) recounts the career of the earliest maker of notable SF films and describes his surviving films in detail.

10-20. Broderick, Mick. **Nuclear Movies: A Critical Analysis and Filmography of International Feature Length Films Dealing With Experimentation, Aliens, Terrorism, Holocaust and Other Disaster Scenarios, 1914–1989.** McFarland, 1991.

After an excellent 45-page critical history of films about nuclear energy, weapons, and warfare, Broderick lists about 850 films from 30 countries (63 percent of them American). His terse descriptions are not complete synopses but focus on the (often slight) nuclear content of each film. The pre-1945 films are mostly about radium, which was seen as an almost magical substance. Includes TV films and miniseries. Large, annotated bibliography. This very complete survey chronicles the amazing diversity of films on this subject. Contrast the equally comprehensive bibliography of nuclear war fictions by Brians [7-10]. In his *Japanese Science Fiction, Fantasy and Horror Films* (1994), Stuart Galbraith IV agrees with Broderick that many Japanese genre films, including some of their disreputable giant monster movies, have been preoccupied with nuclear issues. Galbraith is very knowledgeable about the Japanese film industry and provides detailed synopses, credits, and critiques of 103 films released in the United States 1950–1992. Two less detailed books cover the giant monster films—Donald Glut's *Classic Movie Monsters* (1978) and Stephen Jones's *The Illustrated Dinosaur Movie Guide* (1993), which actually surveys films about all sorts of giant creatures. Galbraith omits Japanese animated films, which are numerous and heavily SF; Helen McCarthy's *Anime! A Beginner's Guide to Japanese Animation* (1993) is short (64 pp.) and was not seen in time for annotation.

10-21. Brosnan, John. **Movie Magic: The Story of Special Effects in the Cinema.** St. Martin's, 1974.
10-22. Harryhausen, Ray. **Film Fantasy Scrapbook.** A. S. Barnes, 1981. 3rd ed.

No other film genre has been more influenced by developments in film-making technology than SF films. Without special effects, SF movies would be far less popular, numerous, and important—and much less expensive. Brosnan's *Movie Magic* is the most detailed history of effects but is of course now outdated. Christopher Finch's *Special Effects: Creating Movie Magic* (1984) and Thomas C. Smith's *Industrial Light & Magic: The Art of Special Effects* (1986) both update Brosnan and provide information on new computer-generated-imagery techniques. Both are much more heavily illustrated and expensive than Brosnan. Finch covers the whole history of effects to 1984; Smith focuses on effects in films produced by George Lucas from 1977 to 1986. All three books thoroughly convince the reader of the truth of an effects artist's boast: "We can do anything. It's just a question of how much it's going to cost." Before his work in fantasy films made him the most famous effects artist, Harryhausen worked in three representative but somewhat superior 1950s SF monster movies—*It Came From Beneath the Sea* (1955), *Earth Vs. the Flying Saucers* (1956), and *20 Million Miles to Earth* (1957); he later did the Vernian *Mysterious Island* (1961) and the Wellsian *First Men in the Moon* (1964). Harryhausen is notable for his time-consuming, relatively cheap "stop-motion" craftsman-ship in a field now dominated by expensive technology. His *Scrapbook* is disappointingly defensive and superficial, with poorly reproduced stills. A videocassette produced by Richard Jones, *Aliens, Monsters & Me: The Fantasy Film World of Ray Harryhausen* (1990), surveys his most important work. Pohl and Pohl [10-14] have an appendix on effects. *Cinefex* [10-58] is a valuable magazine covering current effects work. *Cinefex* editors Don Shay and Jody Duncan cowrote *The Making of Terminator 2: Judgment Day* (1991) and *The Making of Jurassic Park* (1993), detailing the state-of-the-art techniques developed for those very ambitious and expensive films. R. M. Hayes's *3-D Movies: A History and Filmography of Stereoscopic Cinema* (1989) provides detailed technical information and a very complete filmography on films made in a format that (during its two brief periods of popularity) was often associated with SF. *Hollywood and History: Costume Design in Films*, ed. by Edward Maeder (1987), a heavily illustrated survey of costume in historical films, includes a 16-page chapter by Elois Jenssen, "Visions of the Future: Costume in Science Fiction Films."

10-23.   Hickman, Gail Morgan. **The Films of George Pal.** A. S. Barnes, 1977.

George Pal produced *Destination Moon* (1950), *When Worlds Collide* (1951), and *War of the Worlds* (1953) and directed *The Time Machine* (1960). The 14 features and the many innovative short films he produced or directed also included several fantasy titles. Hickman's discussion is fannish and only mildly critical. She tends to exonerate Pal and blame screenwriters and studio executives for whatever faults she finds in his films. Her book is useful mainly for its biographical information on Pal and for the many illustrations. *The Fantasy Film Worlds of George Pal* (1983), a documentary film directed by Arnold Leibovit and available on videocassette, is similarly informative but uncritical and includes the most spectacular scenes from Pal's movies.

10-24.   Kerman, Judith B., ed. **Retrofitting Blade Runner: Issues in Ridley Scott's Blade Runner and Philip K. Dick's Do Androids Dream of Electric Sheep?** Bowling Green State Univ. Popular Press, 1991.

Based on Philip K. Dick's *Do Androids Dream of Electric Sheep?* [4-135], Ridley Scott's *Blade Runner* (1982) was a box-office flop but is regarded by many in the SF community as one of the few serious genre films of the post–*Star Wars* age. For many viewers, the art design of the garish, frightening future city overwhelmed the story. The nineteen essays (all by academics) in *Retrofitting Blade Runner* vary in importance; some are jargon-filled, theoretical, tangential, and repetitious and reach questionable conclusions. Others, especially two long pieces by William Kolb, are enlightening guides to this richly detailed film. An interview with Dick (who died four months before the film's release) by Gregg Rickman records the author's reactions to successive versions of the screenplay. Kolb contributes a very complete annotated bibliography of over 100 critical reviews of *Blade Runner*.

10-25.   Kinnard, Roy. **Fifty Years of Serial Thrills.** Scarecrow, 1983.

Of the 500 serial films made in the United States from 1912 to 1956, dozens had SF plot devices. Only a few serials, such as *Flash Gordon* (1936), were primarily SF, but those few included many of the most famous serials and almost all the few serials made with large budgets. The SF serials were virtually the only American SF films (other than *Frankenstein* and other films regarded as horror by audiences) to achieve popularity before 1950. Kinnard provides filmographic data including date, number of episodes, director, and major players for all 500 serials and intelligently discusses fourteen major serials (eight of them SF or superhero films). Benson [10-19] has more information than Kinnard on several pre-1950 serials. Alan Barbour's *Days of Thrills and Adventure* (1968) and *Cliffhanger* (1977) are heavily illustrated. Raymond Stedman's *The Serials* (1971) has the wittiest criticism of the films. Wayne Schutz's *The Motion Picture Serial: An Annotated Bibliography* (1992) is a guide to the vast body of useful fan scholarship on these once-despised but surprisingly influential films (compare *Star Wars, Indiana Jones*).

10-26. Kuhn, Annette, ed. **Alien Zone: Cultural Theory and Contemporary Science Fiction Cinema.** Verso/Routledge, 1990.

Eighteen essays devoted to sociopolitical analyses, ideological critiques, psychoanalytic diagnoses, reader-response investigations, and intertextual explorations. Six discuss *Alien*, a touchstone for feminist issues, and *Blade Runner*, which displays themes and techniques associated with postmodernist culture. Excellent essays on *The Thing* (1982) and *Videodrome* and by H. Bruce Franklin on SF films of the 1970s and Vivian Sobchack on the sexual politics of the genre, the last two reprinted from Slusser [10-39], which provides a broader perspective. For large film collections. (RL)

10-27. Landon, Brooks. **The Aesthetics of Ambivalence: Rethinking Science Fiction Film in the Age of Electronic (Re)Production.** Greenwood, 1992.

Collects earlier pieces to create a suggestive if diffuse study. The focus is on the relationship of SF film to SF literature and effectively defends the former against detractors who view it as a second-rate echo of the latter. One part considers adaptations, using *The Thing* and *Blade Runner* as examples. Another treats special effects, arguing for their centrality in historically defining SF as a film genre; a third discusses the influence of electronic technology in transforming SF film's parameters and possibilities. Clearly written and well-informed about film, literary, and technical details, but the pieces are not fully integrated into a coherent whole. (RL)

10-28. Larson, Randall D. **Musique Fantastique: A Survey of Film Music in the Fantastic Cinema.** Scarecrow, 1985.

Larson discusses the scores of hundreds of SF, fantasy, and horror films from the earliest sound films to the 1980s, with special chapters on TV scoring, use of electronic and classical music, foreign films, and on four major composers. He provides many quotations from composers and critics and more than 200 pages of filmography and discography. Larson has gathered an enormous amount of information, but his criticism is suspect. He is enthusiastic about the large majority of the scores, in keeping with his conclusion that "music has always seemed to be at its best in fantastic films."

*10-29. LaValley, Al, ed. **Invasion of the Body Snatchers.** Rutgers, 1989.
Ignored by most mainstream critics when it was released in 1956, Don Siegel's *Invasion of the Body Snatchers* is now widely regarded as the best SF film of the 1950s. LaValley's collection includes the screenplay, heavily annotated with notes about changes made in successive versions; memos and correspondence from Siegel and the film's producer; two interviews with Siegel; a few contemporary reviews; and eight current essays and excerpts from other books. LaValley's 20-page introduction refutes some of the other contributors, demonstrating that investigation of a film's production process and of the backgrounds and intentions of the filmmakers is likely to yield better insights than a theoretical reading of the film. Several pieces consider the long-debated question of *Invasion*'s place in cold war politics; considerably fresher is Nancy Steffen-Fluhr's feminist treatment. LaValley has gathered essential information and a wide variety of critical views about a seminal film.

10-30. Lucanio, Patrick. **Them or Us: Archetypal Interpretations of Fifties Alien Invasion Films.** Indiana Univ. Press, 1987.
Examining not only films about aliens but also 1950s movies about terrestrial monsters such as giant insects, Lucanio seeks to show that SF is fundamentally distinct from horror, that the 1950s monster films are SF and not horror, and that SF films are best studied by Jungian analysis. Two films considered in detail are *Invaders From Mars* (1953) and Britain's *Fiend Without a Face* (1958). *Them or Us* is illustrated with frame enlargements, which are necessary to follow Lucanio's arguments but which are too tiny and sometimes printed too darkly. The text contains a good deal of theory but also perceptive observations on the films and such issues as the use of genre actors, special effects, stock footage, titles, and posters.

10-31. Mank, Gregory William. **It's Alive! The Classic Cinema of Frankenstein.** A. S. Barnes, 1981.
Mank's detailed accounts of the production of the eight Frankenstein films made by Universal from 1931 to 1948 may focus too much on studio politics, but the fascinating anecdotes, hundreds of quotations from veterans of the films, and dozens of illustrations make *It's Alive!* essential for the study of the Universal films, despite the lack of an index. The Universal Frankenstein movies were only the most famous of many film

versions of the Shelley story. More comprehensive and more analytical than Mank are four chapters on film and TV versions from 1910 to 1974 in *Mary Shelley's Monster* [9-102] by Martin Tropp. *The Endurance of Frankenstein* (1979), ed. by George Levine and U. C. Knoepflmacher, includes a useful survey of "The Stage and Film Children of Frankenstein" by Albert LaValley. Donald Glut's *Frankenstein Catalog* (1984) contains obsessively complete filmographic data on every film and TV version. Leslie Halliwell's *The Dead That Walk* (1988) compares the Universal and Hammer (1957–1974) cycles of Frankenstein films, always to Hammer's disadvantage. David Pirie's *A Heritage of Horror: The English Gothic Cinema, 1946–1972* (1973) defends the Hammer films. Stephen Jones's *The Illustrated Frankenstein Movie Guide* (1994) was not seen in time for annotation.

10-32. Mathews, Jack. **The Battle of Brazil.** Crown, 1987.

Terry Gilliam's dystopian *Brazil* (1985), like *Blade Runner*, failed at the box-office but has been championed by many in the SF community; Harlan Ellison called it "the best SF movie ever made and very likely one of the ten greatest films of any kind ever made." Mathews's *Battle* includes the annotated screenplay; a relatively brief recounting of the film's production; and a detailed, knowledgeable, persuasively fair account of the struggle between Gilliam and MCA/Universal executives over the final cut of the film. Mathews sees the conflict as a clash of lifestyles and principles as well as egos. Most unusually, the director won.

10-33. Peary, Danny, ed. **Omni's Screen Flights/Screen Fantasies: The Future According to Science Fiction Cinema.** Doubleday, 1984.

Short (42 pieces in 302 pages), original, mostly enlightening essays and interviews by directors, screenwriters, actors, film scholars, and authors (Ellison, Asimov, Pohl, Silverberg, Bloch), two of whom (Harry Harrison and Robert Sheckley) comment on screen adaptations of their work. Some essays are thematic; others cover 25 individual films (16 of them made after 1960), special effects, and futuristic art design. Many of the illustrations are unusual.

10-34. Penley, Constance, Elizabeth Lyon, and Lynn Spiegel, eds. **Close Encounters: Film, Feminism and Science Fiction.** Univ. of Minnesota Press, 1991.

Expanded version of a special issue of *Camera Obscura* (no. 15, fall 1986), with nine essays and a filmscript devoted to feminist analyses and critiques, heavily dependent on psychoanalytic methods. Two essays each on *Metropolis* and *The Terminator* reflect the importance of feminist issues in those films. Coverage of TV includes good essays on 1960s fantastic sit-coms and *Star Trek* fandom. The script for *Friendship's Death* (1987) is fasci-nating if out of place. Like Kuhn [10-26], focuses on a limited canon, and within a feminist context. Compare the broader treatment in Slusser [10-39]. (RL)

10-35.   Reemes, Dana M. **Directed by Jack Arnold.** McFarland, 1988.
Arnold was perhaps the most influential genre director of the 1950s. One of the few directors who actually read SF, he made eight SF films from 1953 to 1959, among them one much imitated film (*It Came From Outer Space*, 1953), one cult movie (*Creature From the Black Lagoon*, 1954), and one highly regarded film (*The Incredible Shrinking Man*, 1957). Reemes's book is informative, with detailed biographical information and many long excerpts from interviews with Arnold, but also excessively adulatory.

10-36.   Renzi, Thomas C. **H. G. Wells: Six Scientific Romances Adopted for Film.** Scarecrow, 1992.
*10-37.   Stover, Leon. **The Prophetic Soul: A Reading of H. G. Wells's Things to Come.** McFarland, 1987.

H. G. Wells believed in the power of film to effect fundamental social and political change. According to actor Raymond Massey, "No writer for the screen ever had or will have such authority as H. G. Wells possessed in the making of *Things to Come,*" produced from Wells's screenplay in 1936. The movie is the only major English-language futuristic film made before 1950 and probably is the most didactic, openly political SF film ever made in the West. Stover reprints the screenplay and Wells's film treatment "Whither Mankind?" and scours all Wells's previous writings, both famous and obscure, to paint an appalling picture of Wells's outlook. Influenced by Plato, Saint-Simon, and Lenin, Wells argued for a "world state," which would function as "a great machine," led by a master class of technocratic permanent revolutionaries who would share Wells's "qualified pity and unqualified contempt" for "the intellectually dull and morally base," the "quadrapeds" and "misbehaving children"; who would see "the spirit of opposition as purely evil, as a vice to be guarded against, as trouble in the machine"; and who would ensure that anyone indulging in "animal indi-vidualism" would be "socialized entirely against his disposition in the mat-ter." Stover's study of "a refreshingly candid antidemocratic mind at work" is a scholarly tour-de-force and a damning indictment of the politics of a major SF author. Renzi, who is interested primarily in the process of film adaptation, examines ten movies based on Wells's "scientific romances" but with screenplays by others. Renzi's criticism is sensible, but since the ten films vary greatly in tone, seriousness, and of course quality and have nothing in common except their loose adaptations of Wells's stories, he reaches no important conclusions. The significant films covered are *Island of Lost Souls* (1932), *The Invisible Man* (1933), *War of the Worlds* (1953), *The Time Machine* (1960), and *Time After Time* (1979).

10-38. Rubin, Steven Jay. **The Complete James Bond Movie Encyclopedia.** Contemporary, 1990.

The James Bond films have been more science fictional than the Ian Fleming novels from which they are loosely derived. Rubin's uncritical *Encyclopedia* documents the series from a 1954 TV film through *Licence to Kill* (1989). Every actor, character, and gadget receives an entry; many of the longest entries describe the work of behind-the-camera participants— writers, directors, designers, and editors. The alphabetical arrangement and several poorly chosen subject headings tend to scatter and bury information and Rubin's few insightful comments, but the *Encyclopedia* is irresistibly browsable and is the most detailed guide to the most long-lived of film series, which devoted unlimited financial and technical resources to the production of pure escapism.

*10-39. Slusser, George E., and Eric S. Rabkin, eds. **Shadows of the Magic Lamp: Fantasy and Science Fiction in Film.** Southern Illinois Univ. Press, 1985.

Fourteen essays from the 1982 Eaton Conference (see chapter 15), ranging from structural analyses of form to special effects to sexual politics and political ideology, with some of the best essays considering the cross-pollination of genres, especially SF and horror. The chronological and geographic scope is broad and the general level is high. The first and in many ways still the best collection to display the full range and sophistication of contemporary critical methods, from semiotic analyses to feminist critique, anticipating the later works of Kuhn [10-26] and Penley [10-34]. (RL)

*10-40. Sobchack, Vivian. **Screening Space: The American Science Fiction Film.** Ungar, 1987. 2nd, enl. ed.

Reprints the first three chapters of *The Limits of Infinity: The American Science Fiction Film 1950–1975* (Barnes, 1980) and adds a long fourth chapter, "Postfuturism," extending the coverage to the 1980s (the "Second Golden Age" in Sobchack's view). The original chapters systematically dissect visual and sound aesthetics, debate competing genre definitions, analyze iconography (especially the "alien"), and assess the significance of sound effects (compare the more detailed discussion in Larson [10-28]). Chapter 4 is heavily based on Fredric Jameson's Marxian views of "the cultural logic of late capitalism" and discusses the impact of electronic technology and a commodity culture's values on the aesthetics of mainstream (for example, *Star Wars*) and marginal (for example, *Repo Man, Buckaroo Banzai*) films. Her insights, though couched in a demanding critical vocabulary, are important and provide the most sophisticated treatment of contemporary SF film, strongly influencing Landon [10-27]. (RL)

10-41. Titelman, Carol, ed. **The Art of Star Wars.** Ballantine, 1979.
The Art of Star Wars is typical of many heavily illustrated promotional books released to accompany or in the aftermath of major films. Besides the screenplay, Titelman includes hundreds of production sketches, storyboards, matte paintings, photos of characters and artifacts, posters, comic art, and juvenile fan art. Some illustrations in this crowded book are too small. The script includes a few scenes not in the film. Some of the illustrations reveal interesting facts about the development of the movie; for instance, Chewbacca was less cuddly and more frightening in early sketches than in the film.

10-42. Warren, Bill. **Keep Watching the Skies! American Science Fiction Movies of the Fifties.** McFarland, 1982, 1986. 2 vols.
Warren's two volumes (1,300 pages) are the longest, most detailed books on 1950s SF films. Vol. 1 covers 134 films of 1950–1957; vol. 2, 153 films of 1958–1962. Warren concludes that the quality of the films declined sharply during the second period. For every SF film released in the United States, including several British and a few Japanese movies, Warren provides credits, a synopsis, and an "intensely personal" discussion. For major films, he discusses production history, careers of filmmakers, design, music, acting, camera work, and all other important aspects. These commentaries are chatty and colloquial but perceptive and hugely erudite. Warren is definitive (and sometimes too detailed) on the minor and middle quality films of the period and well worth reading on the major titles.

10-43. Weaver, Tom. **Interviews with B Science Fiction and Horror Movie Makers: Writers, Producers, Directors, Actors, Moguls and Makeup.** McFarland, 1988.
10-44. Weaver, Tom. **Science Fiction Stars and Horror Heroes: Interviews With Actors, Directors, Producers and Writers of the 1940s through 1960s.** McFarland, 1991.
Except for Richard Matheson, studio boss Samuel Z. Arkoff, and a few

actors who graduated to A films, most of the 57 film workers interviewed by Weaver in these two volumes are little known. Most of the films discussed are also individually obscure, but as a body they had a substantial impact on public perceptions of SF. Weaver's very well-informed questions elicit anecdotal but usually articulate and informative reminiscences about the colorful world of low-budget filmmaking.

Television and Radio

10-45. Cantril, Hadley. **The Invasion from Mars: A Study in the Psychology of Panic.** Princeton Univ. Press, 1940.
Radio drama was extremely popular in Depression-era America. Cantril estimates that about 6 million people heard Orson Welles's 1938 Mercury Theater of the Air broadcast of H. G. Wells's *War of the Worlds* and that at least 1 million were frightened. The panic caused many commentators to conclude that SF fans were of feeble mind, but Cantril found that listeners who had some familiarity with SF (mainly from magazines, comics, radio programs, and serial films) were likely to dismiss the broadcast as "that crazy Buck Rogers stuff" while most listeners who panicked were completely ignorant of SF. Cantril interviewed 135 people in depth. The small size of the sample may cast doubt on his conclusions, but *Invaders From Mars* is the most detailed study of the event. Many interviewees' accounts of absolute terror are far from funny. Cantril reprints the script of the broadcast by Howard Koch. Koch's book, *The Panic Broadcast* (1970), is superficial and padded. In his 1992 book of interviews with Peter Bogdanovich, *This Is Orson Welles*, Welles finally admitted that the broadcast was intended to frighten listeners. Joseph Bulgatz's *Ponzi Schemes, Invaders from Mars and More Extraordinary Popular Delusions and the Madness of Crowds* (1992) has a chapter on the panic, comparing it with later panics caused by *War of the Worlds* broadcasts in Ecuador (where people were killed), Peru, Europe, and local U.S. markets and with the 1835 New York Moon Hoax (p. 5 of this guide). *Handbook of Old-Time Radio* by Jon D. Swartz and Robert C. Reinehr (1993) is the most complete guide to U.S. radio series, including several SF programs. John Dunning's *Tune In Yesterday* (1976) has more detailed descriptions of the major series.

10-46. Fulton, Roger. **The Encyclopedia of TV Science Fiction.** Boxtree, 1990.
Fulton covers all SF seen on British television from 1951 to 1989—159 series and miniseries, 64 TV films, and 41 animated series, including most important U.S. series and all British programs. For each series, Fulton furnishes dates, producer, the regular cast, character names, and a brief descriptive/critical commentary; for each episode, he gives the title,

writer, director, guest actors and their character names, and a terse synopsis. The *Encyclopedia* is the largest source of genre TV episode synopses. Lentz [10-3], the other major reference source on SF on TV, has no synopses. Fulton and Lentz each list programs not in the other. *Variety Television Reviews* (1990) reprints terse contemporary reviews of representative episodes of most U.S. series, including reviews of 47 episodes of *Science Fiction Theater* (1955–1957), one of the better early anthology series. The index of George W. Woolery's *Children's Television: The First Thirty-Five Years, 1946–1981* (2 vols, 1983, 1985) lists 50 juvenile SF series; Woolery provides credits and descriptions for each series. Two nostalgic books about children's TV, Donald F. Glut's and Jim Harmon's *The Great Television Heroes* (1975) and Gary H. Grossman's *Saturday Morning TV* (1987) both include detailed reminiscences of the three most popular juvenile space series of the 1950s, *Space Patrol*, *Captain Video*, and *Tom Corbett, Space Cadet*. Grossman also covers several minor children's series. Glut and Harmon have a chapter on *The Adventures of Superman* and a charming chapter on the merchandise (helmets, ray guns, "secret decoder rings") used to promote the space shows. Baxter [10-10], Larson [10-28], and Penley [10-34] all consider aspects of SF on TV. *Starlog* magazine [10-59] provides coverage of both old and current series. Of several popular reference books on TV series in all genres, Harry Castleman's and Walter Podrazik's *Harry and Wally's Favorite TV Shows* (1989), despite its silly title, has the best combination of facts and informed opinion. Henry Jenkins's *Textual Poachers: Television Fans and Participatory Culture* (1992) is a well-informed and highly laudatory account of activist fans of many cult TV shows, most of them SF or fantasy; Jenkins, who is both a scholar and a fan, contends that committed fans are not passive consumers of their favorite shows but use the shows as raw materials for their own creative efforts.

10-47.   Gerani, Gary, and Paul H. Schulman. **Fantastic Television.** Harmony, 1977.

For each of sixteen series, some of which they admit are far from good, Gerani and Schulman provide one to seven pages of history and commentary (identifying outstanding episodes), several black-and-white illustrations, and credits and terse synopses for each episode. Each of several dozen other series and TV movies is described in one paragraph. Largely complete through 1977, except for selective coverage of British and children's shows, Gerani differs interestingly with Javna [10-50] on some series, such as Doctor Who, which Javna rates highly while Gerani relegates it to one dismissive paragraph.

10-48. Gerrold, David. **The World of Star Trek.** Bluejay, 1984. Rev. ed.
10-49. Trimble, Bjo. **The Star Trek Concordance.** Ballantine, 1976.

Three genre TV series, *The Adventures of Superman* (1953–1957), *The Twilight Zone* (1959–1964), and *Star Trek* (1966–1969), have added images, characters, and catch phrases to the permanent store of popular culture. After four successive TV series (one of them animated), seven films, and 27 years of fan activity, *Star Trek* has surpassed even *Doctor Who* in longevity. Gerrold, who wrote one *Trek* episode, is mildly critical of the show's dramatic and scientific shortcomings. He covers the program's production, the "Save *Trek*" campaign, the fans (including fan misbehavior), and the first three films. *The World of Star Trek* is about as serious as a fan-oriented book can be. Trimble's *Concordance* has detailed, uncritical episode synopses for the original series and the 1973 animated series and entries describing all characters, places, species, ships, and other named objects and concepts in *Trek*. Trimble's *On the Good Ship Enterprise* (1983) and Henry Jenkins's (*Textual Poachers,* 1992) are both informative about *Trek* fandom, the largest and most influential body of fans in either SF or TV. Susan R. Gibberman's *Star Trek: An Annotated Guide to Resources on the Development, the Phenomenon, the People, the Television Series, the Films, the Novels, and the Recordings* (1991) lists over 1,000 nonfiction books and articles by professionals, not fans, as well as *Trek* novels, sound recordings, and video recordings.

10-50. Javna, John. **The Best of Science Fiction TV.** Harmony, 1987.
Javna solicited comments and votes on SF TV series from a jury of 113 critics, fans, and SF authors. Four pages are devoted to each of the fifteen "best" shows and two pages to each of the ten "worst" series. Entries include each program's dates, number of episodes, actors, character names, descriptive and critical notes by Javna, brief comments by jurors, small black-and-white illustrations, "trivia," and some well-chosen quotes from the show (for example, from *Doctor Who,* "I'm a citizen of the Universe and a gentleman to boot"). The terse comments by Javna and jurors are often perceptive. Unlike Gerani [10-47] Javna has no episode synopses. Shorter entries describe 38 additional shows of special interest—British, Japanese, 1950s, anthology, and animated series. The section on Japanese animated series presents information not readily found elsewhere. Bibliography. Javna's book is more fannish than Gerani's, more up-to-date, and more in sympathy with its subject.

10-51. Lofficier, Jean-Marc. **The Doctor Who Programme Guide.** W. H. Allen, 1981, 1989. 2 vols.

10-52.   Tulloch, John, and Manuel Alvarado. **Doctor Who, The Unfolding Text.** St. Martin's, 1983.

Doctor Who (1963–1989), one of the longest-lived TV series in any genre, attempted with considerable success to appeal to both children and adults. For a while, its worldwide popularity seemed to rival that of *Star Trek.* As seven actors succeeded each other in the leading role, the tone and quality of episodes varied tremendously. Lofficier's *Programme Guide* furnishes the dates, writer, director, cast, and character names for each episode; his episode synopses are too terse. A two-volume set was published in 1981; only vol. 1, the episode guide, was updated in 1989. Vol. 2 is a reference guide to characters, places, species, and other names in *Doctor Who* from 1963 to 1981. Lofficier offers no criticism. By contrast, Tulloch's and Alvarado's *Doctor Who, The Unfolding Text* is one of the most serious, analytic books ever written about a popular TV series, so much so that casual fans will find it heavy going. The authors explore the show's roots in British pulp fiction, the differences among the first four Doctors and conflicts among writers, producers, and actors over the proper balance of the program's SF, comic, and adventure elements. The production of "Kinda," an unusually ambitious episode, is examined in detail. Large bibliography. Lofficier is unillustrated; Tulloch has a few illustrations. Many fannish, heavily illustrated *Doctor Who* books have appeared in Britain, several written by Peter Haining.

10-53.   Rogers, Dave. **The Complete Avengers.** St. Martin's, 1989.

The Avengers (1961–1969) began as an almost realistic crime series, then added increasingly audacious SF premises. The show is one of the most fondly remembered cult series, due to high quality production, writing, and cast and unrivaled élan and sense of style. Writing with justified enthusiasm, Rogers provides credits and synopses for all episodes of both *The Avengers* and *The New Avengers* (1976–1977). Unusually articulate commentary by Rogers and dozens of illustrations help to recapture the exhilaration of the series.

10-54.   Rogers, Dave. **The Prisoner & Danger Man.** Boxtree, 1989.

One of the shortest-lived series (17 episodes) to win an apparently permanent cult following, *The Prisoner* (1967) concerns an intelligence agent held captive in a futuristic detention "village" where no one can be trusted. Rogers's synopses and production history are extremely detailed. *Danger Man* was a spy series with no SF overtones, an earlier project of Patrick McGoohan, producer-star of *The Prisoner.*

10-55. Schow, David J., and Jeffrey Frentzen. **The Outer Limits: The Official Companion.** Ace, 1986.

The Outer Limits (1963–1965) was more science fictional and less oriented toward fantasy than the other major genre anthology series, *The Twilight Zone.* Although *Limits* does not have as large a cult following as *Zone,* Schow and Frentzen maintain that it was the best SF ever seen on TV. They provide credits, synopsis, and a genuinely critical appraisal of each episode, as well as a lengthy production history of the series. The many illustrations are small and poorly reproduced.

10-56. Zicree, Marc Scott. **The Twilight Zone Companion.** Bantam, 1989. 2nd ed.

The Twilight Zone (1959–1964) was the most popular TV anthology series and is second only to *Star Trek* in its impact on popular culture. The *Companion* has the usual features of a TV history—episode credits and synopses, illustrations, and production history. Zicree is genuinely critical. He examines the *Twilight Zone* film (1983) and the two *Zone* revival series (1985–1987, 1988–1990) briefly, finding them unworthy of the original.

Periodicals

*10-57. Cinefantastique. ISSN 0145-6032. 1970–. Bimonthly. Frederick S. Clarke, ed. (P.O. Box 270, Oak Park, IL 60303.) Circ.: 30,000. Indexed: *Film Literature Index.*

Cinefantastique is the highest quality English-language magazine on SF, fantasy, and horror films. Issues range from 60 to 90 pages, with in-depth articles and excellent illustrations. Short pieces profile forthcoming productions. Current films and TV programs are reviewed with independence and sophistication. *Cinefantastique*'s irreverence has led to feuds with some major filmmakers, which has hampered the magazine's ability to cover several productions. Recently *Cinefantastique* has taken a more popular approach, without sacrificing quality. After years of paying scant attention to television, *Cinefantastique* now provides selective coverage of both old and new TV shows. *Locus* [12-24], *Science Fiction Chronicle* [12-29], and *Magazine of Fantasy and Science Fiction* [12-6] all have frequent but not comprehensive coverage of films and TV. *Harlan Ellison's Watching* (1989) collected his rambling film columns from the last magazine. Two annuals, *International Index to Film Periodicals* and *Film Literature Index,* index reviews and articles in film magazines. *Film Review Index* (2 vols., 1986, 1987), ed. by Patricia King Hanson and Stephen L. Hanson, indexes both reviews in periodicals and discussions in hundreds of books of over 7,000 significant

films from the silents to 1985. Lee [10-2] and Willis [10-8] provide citations to periodical reviews.

10-58.   Cinefex. ISSN 0198-1056. 1980. Quarterly. Don Shay, ed. (P.O.
Box 20027, Riverside, CA 92516.) Circ.: 15,000. Indexed: *Film Literature
Index.*
Cinefex is the magazine of record for special effects. Each issue consists of
lengthy technical reports on all aspects of effects work in one to three current films. *Cinefex* is dependent on the cooperation of filmmakers and
does not criticize either effects or any other aspects of the films, but the
technical information is invaluable. *American Cinematographer* magazine
also often has articles on technical work in major genre films.

10-59.   Starlog. ISSN 0191-4626. 1976–. Monthly. David McDonnell, ed.
(475 Park Ave. S., New York, NY 10016.) Circ.: 250,000.
The most popular magazine in the field, *Starlog* covers SF and fantasy
films and TV—all fantastic media except horror, which is the subject of its
sister publication, *Fangoria*. Issues are about eighty pages, with informative
but uncritical, heavily illustrated articles and interviews. *Starlog* maintains
friendly relations with studios by not reviewing current films. Stronger
than *Cinefantastique* in coverage of TV series and low-budget films, *Starlog*
also includes interviews with fiction authors, reviews of novels, and
columns on video releases and computer games. Not as essential as
Cinefantastique, *Starlog* with its abundance of facts and paucity of analysis is
useful for large collections.

10-60.   Video Watchdog. ISSN 1070-9991. 1990–. Bimonthly. Tim Lucas,
ed. (P.O. Box 5283, Cincinnati, OH 45205-0283.)
Video Watchdog covers SF, fantasy, and horror films on videocassettes and
videodiscs, focusing on such problems as retitlings, fictitious credits, censorship, varying quality and running times, and treatment of films too
wide for TV screens. Each issue of about eighty pages has a wealth of
information on obscure, low-budget, and foreign films that have been
brought back to life by the insatiable video industry. A model of fan scholarship, combining industry, accuracy, enthusiasm, and extraordinary erudition. *The Video Watchdog Book* (1992) collects several columns by Lucas
originally published outside *Video Watchdog* and includes a detailed, much
needed index to the first twelve issues of the magazine.

CHAPTER 11

Science Fiction Illustration

Walter Albert and Neil Barron

Historians are not in agreement about the beginning of modern science fiction illustration. Robert Weinberg in his *Biographical Dictionary* [11-18] and Gary K. Wolfe in "The Iconography of Science-Fiction Art" in Volume 2 of Cowart and Wymer [7-24] place it at the end of the 19th century, in the futuristic drawings of Frenchman Albert Robida and in magazine and book illustrations for Verne (Wolfe) and Wells (Weinberg). They can't, however, agree on the important illustrators. Weinberg identifies Warwick Goble (illustrator of Wells's *War of the Worlds*), Fred Jane, and Henri Lanos as the "three finest artists" specializing in science fiction, while Wolfe refers to Hildibrand (illustrator of Verne) and several other artists (including Jane but not Lanos), but ignores Goble. Vincent Di Fate in his chapter, "Science Fiction Art: Some Contemporary Illustrators," in Marshall Tymn's *Science Fiction Reference Book* (1981) avoids the issue and begins his discussion with Frank R. Paul's work for *Amazing Stories* in 1926, with the brief comment that science fiction art is as old as the literature. Di Fate doesn't refer specifically to any literature before 1926, stating elliptically that its roots are "firmly embedded in reality and in the long ago beginnings of the human race."

What all three do agree on is the importance of the rise of the American science fiction pulp magazine in the development of the art form, and on Frank R. Paul (1884–1963) as the "father" of American science fiction illustration, a title bestowed on Paul at the first world science fiction convention in 1939.

If, however, the major pulp/magazine era began in 1926, it did not inaugurate a new style in fiction but continued and made available to a wider audience the scientific romance popularized by Wells in England and by Edgar Rice Burroughs in this country.

Burroughs's Mars and Venus series were illustrated by J. Allen St. John (1872–1957), whose romantic style featured dark-haired women in peril and muscular heroes in conflict with fantastic beasts and alien beings. Di Fate does not mention St. John, Weinberg calls him "influential" but without discussing the implications of that statement, and only Wolfe sees him as the "figure who most clearly epitomizes the transition from earlier book and magazine illustrations to the pulp era." Yet even Wolfe considers St. John's style "dated" by 1926. This style was, in the early years of the pulps, bypassed in favor of "gadget" or hardware art, in which space ships and towering cities of intricate architecture took precedence over character- and situation-based art.

Paul and his contemporaries have not always enjoyed critical appreciation of their work, with their covers characterized by Brian Aldiss in his *Trillion Year Spree* [8-5] as "gaudy but gorgeous." The stereotypical image of moldering pulp magazines hoarded by aging fans has translated into a dismissal of much of the art and fiction of the 1930s as chiefly of antiquarian interest. This is a point of view not only promoted by academic critics whose disdain of Burroughs and early pulp fiction style is well documented but also recently by the contemporary illustrator Boris Vallejo.

Vallejo, in his foreword to *The Fantasy Art Techniques of Tim Hildebrandt* [11-43], comments that only artists of "limited talent" worked in the field in the early years, a market that was "woefully underpaid." Then, in the 1960s and 1970s, artists often possessing "prodigious talent . . . opened the doors for an art form that now has millions of faithfully following fans all over the world." It is ironic that Boris—as he is known professionally—rose to popularity imitating the style of his gifted colleague Frank Frazetta who first came to notice in the field illustrating covers for Ace editions of novels by Edgar Rice Burroughs, a task he shared initially with Roy Krenkel, whose covers were very much in the tradition of J. Allen St. John. And the popular sword-and-sorcery genre with which both Frazetta and Boris came to be identified was squarely in the tradition of early pulp art.

The first era of the science fiction pulps (1926–1953) is dominated by two men, publisher Hugo Gernsback (*Amazing Stories, Air Wonder Stories,* and other pulps) and John W. Campbell, editor of *Astounding Science Fiction* from 1937 to 1971. Although their magazines and editorial policies were widely divergent, their art work, particularly that of the covers, was largely devoted to machine art, with human figures either primitively rendered (Gernsback) or featured as enigmatic or symbolic figures in a technocratic society (Campbell). Paul's colorful covers with their impressive alien and futuristic architectures have come to be synonymous with the early years of the pulps. His influence can be seen in the work of Hans Wessolowsky ("Wesso") in covers for the Clayton *Astounding* and even later in the work of Robert Fuqua for the Campbell-edited *Astounding.* Leo Morey was particularly skillful at capturing alien life forms in his work, while Howard V. Brown is often considered to have perfected the first space art style in his gleaming, austere projectiles.

Campbell favored a less imaginative, more "authentic" hardware style. However, when the Gernsback era waned in the mid-thirties, in spite of the importance of the *Astounding* "look," the most striking and popular magazine covers were those done for *Startling Stories, Thrilling Wonder Stories,* and *Fantastic Adventures.* These depicted heroic Flash Gordon space hunks and superbly endowed females threatened by and struggling with Bug-Eyed-Monsters (BEMs), a style brought to perfection by Earle K. Bergey, later a notable illustrator of paperback covers. This style, the aesthetic culmination of the space adventure pulp story, would later be updated and modernized in films (the *Star Wars* trilogy) and in the popular and enduring TV and film *Star Trek* series.

As the first generation of pulp magazines went the way of the dinosaur in the early fifties, it was succeeded by the digest pulps and by an explosion of paperback reprints and original fiction and small-press imprints. Here one found illustrators such as Kelly Freas, Ed Emsh, Edd Cartier, and Ed Valigursky, most of whom had begun their career in the pulps. The most prolific and innovative artist during this period may have been Richard Powers, whose surrealist-inspired paperback covers brought a new level of sophistication to pulp art, preparing the way for a generation of artists, many of them British, with affiliations with European art movements.

The more austere *Astounding* style culminated in the astronomical space art of Chesley Bonestell, prefiguring the artwork that would celebrate the achievements of American and Soviet space programs. Recent British illustrators have excelled in hardware illustration, often with little interest in the human figure, and have reflected relatively little influence of the early pulp art. Many American illustrators on the other hand have traveled from an infatuation with heroic fantasy, sword-and-sorcery art, fueled by the new popularity of Burroughs in the sixties and the discovery of Conan, the barbarian hero of Robert E. Howard, to a more fantasy-oriented art, influenced by such artists as Howard Pyle and Maxfield Parrish. This is especially true in the late seventies and eighties in the work of Michael Whelan and more recently in the highly decorative work of Don Maitz.

It is often extremely difficult to separate fantasy from science fiction. Both Whelan and Maitz move easily from one to the other, or combine the two in their work. The most influential postwar pulp magazine, *The Magazine of Fantasy and Science Fiction,* can be considered as the model for a genre in which crossover elements are the norm rather than the exception, although the New Wave writers of the sixties attempted to focus the genre on "hard" science wedded to stories of great technical skill that used fictional techniques usually associated with nongenre fiction, turning away from the fanciful, action-filled pulp universe.

If the fiction has managed to escape what it sees as its "humble" adventure epic beginnings and to produce writers who rival nongenre prose writers in their techniques and sophistication, the artists, also refusing to accept traditional categories, have increasingly explored the graphic novel, worked as storyboard illustrators for films, and returned to traditional book illustration. Their recognition has traditionally come from within the field, most commonly in the form of the Hugo to the best professional artist, awarded each year at the world science fiction convention. However, the artists now have exhibitions at art galleries, publish limited edition prints and portfolios, and are collected by knowledgeable fans for whom illustration is not a second-rate category. It can be hoped that this interest will be extended to the publication of more monographs on individual artists and that we may also have a comprehensive, well-illustrated study of this vigorous and increasingly accepted art form to complement Weinberg's fine *Biographical Dictionary* [11-18]. SF film poster art is the subject of two studies [10-16/17].

Table 11-1   Hugo Professional Artist Winners and Nominees, 1955–1994

Illustrator	*Entry*	*Winners*	*Nominations*	*= Rank[a]*
Frank Kelly Freas, 1922–	E, W	10	12	32
Michael Whelan, 1950–	E, W	11	6	28
Don Maitz, 1953–	E, W	2	11	15
Jack Gaughan, 1930–1985	E, W	2	8	12
John Schoenherr, 1935–	E, W	1	10	12
Vincent Di Fate, 1945–	E, W	1	10	12
Ed Emshwiller (Emsh), 1925–	E, W	3	5	11
Virgil Finlay, 1914–1971	E, W	1	6	8
Stephen E. Fabian, 1930–	E, W	0	7	7
Rick Sternbach, 1951–	E, W	2	3	7
Frank Frazetta, 1928–	E, W	2	3	7
Bob Eggleton, 1960–	W	1	4	6
Rowena Morrill, 1944–	E, W	0	5	5
David A. Cherry, 1949–	E, W	0	5	5
Barclay Shaw, 1949–	E, W	0	5	5
Leo and Diane Dillon, both 1933–	E, W	1	2	4
Thomas Canty, n.d.	E, W	0	4	4
James Burns, 1948–	E, W	1	2	4
Tom Kidd, 1955–	W	0	4	4
Mel Hunter, 1929–	W	0	3	3
Roy Krenkel, 1918–1983	E, W	1	1	3
Gray Morrow, 1934–	E, W	0	3	3
Jeff Jones, 1944–	W	0	3	3
Boris Vallejo (Boris), 1941–	W	0	3	3
Wally Wood, 1927–1981	E, W	0	2	2
Hannes Bok, 1914–1964	E, W	1	0	2
Vaughn Bodé, 1941–1975	E	0	2	2
Eddie Jones, 1935–	E, W	0	2	2
George Barr, 1937–	E, W	0	2	2
Paul Lehr, 1930–	E, W	0	2	2
Val Lakey [Lindahn], 1951–	W	0	2	2
J(effrey) K(night) Potter, 1956–	E	0	2	2
H. R. Van Dongen, n.d.	E, W	0	2	2
James Gurney, 1958–	E, W	0	2	2
Alex Schomburg, 1905–	E, W	0	1	1
Chesley Bonestell, 1888–1986	E, W	0	1	1
Mike Hinge, n.d.	W	0	1	1
Tim Kirk, 1947–	W	0	1	1
David Hardy, 1936–	E, W	0	1	1
Alicia Austin, 1942–	W	0	1	1
Carl Lundgren, 1947–	W	0	1	1
Darrell Sweet, 1934–	E, W	0	1	1

E=Encyclopedia of Science Fiction [7-22]; W=Weinberg [11-18]
[a] Rank equals winners times two plus nominations.

Bibliography

The author wishes to express his appreciation for the assistance of Neil
Barron and Robert E. Briney in the preparation of this bibliography. Contributions are identified with the initials (WA), (NB), and (REB).

General and Multiartist Studies

*11-1.   Aldiss, Brian W. **Science Fiction Art.** Crown, 1975.
An oversized (10½ x 14¾ inches) 128-page paperback, which showcases
the work of 30 American and British magazine illustrators from the 1920s
to the 1970s, while providing examples of cover and interior artwork by
another 50 or so artists. The subtitle of the book ("The Fantasies of SF")
expresses the difficulty historians of the field have in distinguishing science fiction and fantasy illustration. Aldiss's introduction concisely points
up the isolation of the illustrators of the 1930s and 1940s from artistic currents such as Surrealism and Expressionism that were themselves dealing
in imaginative ways with some of the themes of both science fiction and
fantasy illustration. The showcase for the 30 artists is followed by a longer
section organized by thematic materials, drawing on a wider range of
artists. One of the strong points of the book is that much of the cover
work is reproduced in color and the striking black-and-white interiors are
cleanly and usually sharply reproduced. A gallery of covers (in color and
in black-and-white) of 79 magazine titles shows changing styles of both
British and American titles. Index of artists and magazines. Compare
Frewin [11-6], whose historical scope is broader, and the more anecdotal
work of Sadoul [11-14]. (NB/WA)

11-2.   Ash, Brian. The Visual Encyclopedia of Science Fiction. Harmony, 1977.
It is frustrating to note that while there are a number of "illustrated" histories of science fiction, there is no history of science fiction illustration to
rival the breadth of the illustrated histories. Franz Rottensteiner's *The
Science Fiction Book* [8-121] does have two brief chapters on Albert Robida
and Hannes Bok but in spite of the profusion of illustrations in the two
Kyle histories, *A Pictorial History of Science Fiction* (1976) and *The Illustrated
Book of Science Fiction Ideas and Dreams* (1977), and in Gunn [8-62], there is
almost no discussion of science fiction illustration as a contributing factor
to the success of the pulp magazines. With relatively few exceptions, artists
are not identified in Rottensteiner's captions, and the use of illustrative

material is clearly designed as a merchandising ploy to make the text more attractive. This use of illustrations as supporting or complementary (separate and not equal) is less characteristic of Kyle (whose captions identify artists and often give biographical or other information), but there is no substantive engagement with illustration as a medium that often surpassed the stories it visualized. One of Ash's unidentified contributors provides a sweeping survey (pp. 286–92) of the first century of illustration, generally ignoring any distinction between fantasy and science fiction. Like most commentators, he identifies Paul as the most influential illustrator, but characterizes him as the "link" to the work of Warwick Goble (*War of the Worlds*) and J. Allen St. John, the great Burroughs illustrator. The comment appears to be inspired neither by chronology nor by affinity of style. (WA)

11-3. Dean, Martyn. **Dream Makers: Six Fantasy Artists at Work.** Paper Tiger, 1988.

These interviews with six American and British illustrators include Julek Heller, Michael Kaluta, and Chris Moore, who often incorporate science fiction iconography in their work. Their lives, ideas, and attitudes are clearly brought out by Dean's interviews, effectively rewritten by Chris Evans. Although Evans in his brief introduction claims that all the artists "work in an area which can be loosely called fantasy art," Evans describes the heroes of today's generation—and presumably the artists'—as "starship captains, warriors with magical weapons, bizarre but cuddly aliens" and refers to the artists' "soaring visions of human progress—gleaming spacecraft carrying a triumphant human race across the universe." This suggests once again the extent to which modern illustrators work in a universe of "dreams, nightmares and imagined futures," where fantasy and science fiction are not hostile or indifferent neighbors but co-inhabitants of a vast landscape of the imagination. Profusely illustrated in color and in black-and-white. (NB/WA)

11-4. Dean, Martyn. **The Guide to Fantasy Art Techniques.** Paper Tiger, 1984.

Like *Dream Makers* [11-3], this *Guide* consists of interviews with several contemporary illustrators, among them Jim Burns, Syd Mead, and Chris Foss, some of whose work is often science fiction rather than fantasy. Also among the artists interviewed are Philip Castle, who works principally in car and airplane advertising art, but who earlier did promotional art for Kubrick's *A Clockwork Orange* and incorporated Star Trek elements into billboard art, and Martin Bower, a maker of models for science fiction television shows and feature films. With numerous color and black-and-white illustrations and photographs. (NB/WA)

11-5.   del Rey, Lester. Fantastic Science-Fiction Art, 1926–1954. Ballantine, 1975.

A medium-sized (8³/₄ x 11³/₄ inches) trade paperback, which features a portfolio of forty, full-page color reproductions of magazine covers, introduced by del Rey, who attempts (in eight pages) to cover the history of science fiction illustration "from Frank R. Paul to Kelly Freas." Eighteen of the forty pulp covers reproduced in color are by Frank R. Paul, an imbalance that is not helped by a routine introduction. Prefer Sadoul [11-14]. (NB/WA)

***11-6.   Frewin, Anthony. One Hundred Years of Science-Fiction Illustration, 1840–1940.** Pyramid, 1975.

Because the early pulps are seldom seen today, this work provides a useful survey of SF illustration. The fascinating work of Grandville and Robida, two prolific 19th-century French artists, begins the book followed by selected illustrations from editions of Verne and Wells. The emphasis is on illustrations in the SF pulps from the 1920s and 1930s—Frank R. Paul, Eliot Dold, and others known only to aficionados. Over 40 covers are reproduced in color, some full-sized, some reduced. All illustrations have captions, and the remaining text, while succinct, is intelligent and helpful, putting SF illustration in a wider historical context. A very good introduction to the early years of SF illustration. Better coverage of the 19th-century than the Aldiss survey [11-1], and preferable to Sadoul [11-14]. (NB)

***11-7.   Hardy, David A. Visions of Space: Artists Journey Through the Cosmos.** Paper Tiger, 1989.

In his foreword, Arthur C. Clarke notes that the pulp-magazine artists first gave space art a "popular audience," even as he comments that they were concerned with entertainment rather than accuracy. He credits Chesley Bonestell with inspiring a new generation of space artists, characterized by a blend in which entertainment and accuracy were "combined." However, although Hardy's introduction on the "old masters" lists astronomical artists who do not figure in the usual histories of SF illustration, he also includes Alex Schomburg, Frank Tinsley, and Ed Valigursky, who do, and these illustrations, along with the obligatory Bonestell, suggest the links between the magazine illustrators and the so-called space artists who do not generally illustrate fiction. In addition, Hardy includes capsule career summaries of a number of the space artists, several of whom have illustrated fictional narratives. These biographies, along with the rich assortment of color reproductions (often indicating original size and medium), make

Visions of Space a highly recommendable reference source for both space and SF art. It should be the choice, then, among several similar books, such as Miller [11-12], Hartmann [11-8], and Ordway [11-13]. Robin Kerrod's *NASA: Visions of Space* (Courage, 1990) is a more conventional tribute to space art and the NASA program in which artists are often not identified and the concerns are more parochial. (WA)

*11-8.   Hartmann, William K., Andrei Sokolov, Ron Miller, and Vitaly Myagkov, eds. **In the Stream of Stars: The Soviet-American Space Art Book.** Chronicle, 1990.

At first glance, Ray Bradbury's very personal, visionary "historical" introduction may seem out of place in a volume ostensibly devoted to recording, with attention to scientific fact, man's obsession with the universe. But three of the editors are also artists, and *Stream* is a celebration of the artist's ability to transform scientific data into soaring works of the imagination. Ron Miller's chapter on space art is a record of a field, science "fact," that is often as imbued with a "sense of wonder" as the work of the illustrators of science fiction. Miller evokes a historical continuum in which the American Hudson River school and the British pre-Raphaelites are seen as major influences, and certainly Ron Miller's grandiose "Within Jupiter's Atmosphere" (p. 68) clearly demonstrates that lineage. Many of the illustrations would not be out of place gracing the covers of science fiction magazines, and these are landscapes that lift the soul to the horizon and beyond, and remind us of the pull of the heavens, probably as old as mankind itself. With numerous illustrations by artists including Robert McCall, Wayne Barlow, Vincent Di Fate, and Chesley Bonestell, and several 19th-century illustrators that open up an entire field of investigation and should challenge the standard histories with their focus on the pulp magazine illustrations. Many examples of Russian work are included, along with artist biographies. (WA)

11-9.   Holdstock, Robert, and Malcolm Edwards, eds. **Alien Landscapes.** Mayflower, 1979.

A variety of British artists have illustrated ten fictional worlds, from Clarke's *Rama* to Herbert's *Arrakis* to McCaffrey's *Pern*. A pseudo-encyclopedic text accompanies the pictures, which are large and colorful but far less credible than the detailed exactness of Barlowe's work [11-20]. Wingrove [11-19] is a companion volume. (NB)

11-10.   Lehmkuhl, Donald. **The Flights of Icarus.** Paper Tiger, 1977. Ed. by Martyn Dean and Roger Dean.

This oversize compilation features the work of 32 illustrators, mostly young Britons, much of which appeared on book covers and record jackets. The text is minimal and banal. The Holdstock and Edwards survey [11-9] includes a wider range of illustrators and emphasizes SF rather than fantasy, and has useful essays as well. Similar to but not nearly as good as the Summers compilation [11-17]. (NB)

11-11.   Miller, Ron. The Dream Machines: An Illustrated History of the Spaceship in Art, Science and Literature. Krieger, 1993.
Miller is well-qualified to write this fascinating history. With a BFA in illustration, he was active in the Smithsonian's Air and Space Museum as director for its Einstein Planetarium, has worked with NASA, won the Frank R. Paul award for outstanding achievement in SF art in 1988, and designed a ten-stamp set of commemorative space postage stamps for the U.S. Postal Service in 1991. When it was suspected there might be worlds other than ours, attempts to reach such worlds were made, first in imagination, then in expensive fact. The six parts chronologically trace such attempts, the text supplemented by a large variety of well-chosen illustrations, some of them in color, including schematic drawings of the many spaceships and rockets, fanciful and actual. Of interest to SF readers, aviation and astronautical historians, and model builders. About as accessible as one of the Jane's volumes devoted to aircraft, its high price will limit it to larger collections. Compare the works of Hardy [11-7], Hartmann [11-8], and Ordway [11-13]. (NB)

11-12.   Miller, Ron. Space Art. Starlog Magazine, 1978.
The former art director of the Smithsonian's National Air and Space Museum provides a comprehensive collection of astronomical art from the 19th century to the present, featuring the work of about 60 artists. The work is semiphotographic in most cases, but the best pieces share the same central concern as traditional religious art—mystery. As landscape and religious paintings are recognized genres, so space art in a secular age may take its place. The Hartmann/Miller *Stream* [11-8] makes an even stronger case for the genre. See also the collections of work by Bonestell [11-24] and by McCall [11-47–11-48]. (NB/WA)

11-13.   Ordway, Frederick I., III, and Randy Liebermann, eds. Blueprint for Space: Science Fiction to Science Fact. Smithsonian, 1992.
A tribute to the development of space exploration with the—by now—obligatory chapter by Ron Miller on space art. Sam Moskowitz traces the history of the American pulp magazines, an essay illustrated by some striking pulp covers and book jacket illustrations that depart from the usual selections, although artists are not always identified. There are several

illustrations by Camille Flammarion from *Les terres du ciel* (Paris, 1884) in Ben Bova's chapter on "The Vision of Spaceflight," while a potentially interesting chapter on "The *Collier*'s and Disney Series" is torpedoed by the absence of any reproductions of artwork from Disney's *Man in Space, Man and the Moon,* and *Mars and Beyond,* aired on the Disney program in 1955 and 1956. Less useful as a reference on space art than Miller [11-12] and Hartmann [11-8], but still a handsome volume on man's attempt to conquer space. (WA)

11-14.   Sadoul, Jacques. **2000 A.D.: Illustration from the Golden Age of Science Fiction Pulps.** Regnery, 1975. Trans. of *Hier, l'an 2000* (Denoël, 1973).

This affectionate study clearly reproduces several hundred black-and-white interior illustrations as well as many covers in full color, all with artist and issue indicated, from the 1926–1953 pulps. All the names familiar to fans and collectors are here. The illustrations are grouped in eight theme chapters, each introduced by a brief commentary. Frewin [11-6], although his coverage stops at 1940, has better-quality illustrations, more in color, and a livelier text. (NB)

11-15.   Sherwin, Mary, Ellen Asher, and Joe Miller, eds. **The New Visions: A Collection of Modern Science Fiction Art.** Doubleday, 1982.

Reproduces jacket paintings commissioned for SF Book Club editions: 46 images without the overprinted text, by 23 contemporary illustrators, who provide biographical notes often linked to the specific painting reproduced, which is always identified by the author and title of the book. (NB)

11-16.   Singer, Leslie. **Zap! Ray Gun Classics.** Chronicle, 1991.

Readers old enough to remember the phrase, "two boxtops and a dime," will love this book, although in most cases the ray guns were bought in stores, not by mail. Singer, an advertising creative director and copywriter, has collected toys and nostalgic Americana for years, and when you see his beautifully designed and photographed (by Dixie Knight) collection, you may think about becoming a collector yourself. The condition of the pieces varies enormously, from the first, a Buck Rogers Disintegrator from the 1930s that looks like it had been in the Martian deserts for a few centuries, to pristine multicolored specimens from the 1980s. The 97 pieces lovingly photographed are keyed to a price guide. In the land of yesteryear this would be called a Really Neato book; today the word might be Awesome. A complete delight for anyone. (NB)

*11-17. Summers, Ian, ed. **Tomorrow and Beyond: Masterpieces of Science Fiction Art.** Workman, 1978.

The former art director of Ballantine has assembled over 300 color reproductions from 67 primarily American illustrators. Much of the work depicted appeared on mass market paperback covers of the 1970s, as well as on LP jackets, in articles, and the like. No biographical information on the illustrators, nor are media and size of original shown. Yet the survey is a broad one and valuable for larger collections devoted to contemporary book illustration. (NB)

*11-18. Weinberg, Robert. **A Biographical Dictionary of Science Fiction and Fantasy Artists.** Greenwood, 1988.

The 279 biographical entries, with bibliographical information on magazine, paperback, and hardcover publication, are the heart of this impressive compilation. Although the entries emphasize the pulp era, 1926–1953, Weinberg's major interest, they include French and British artists, and a substantial number of entries from 1950 through the early 1980s. The lengthy introduction, which Weinberg calls "Science Fiction Art: A Historical Overview," surveys the changing market, tracing the field as it shifts from magazine to book and paperback publication. There is no attempt to distinguish between science fiction and fantasy art, a failure emphasized by the title. This is, however, understandable in a field in which artists cross over the imprecise boundary between fantasy and science fiction with bewildering ease. Weinberg's commentary is strongest in the biographical and historical elements, and less satisfactory in the thumbnail characterizations of style. Thus, the characterization of Bok's work as distinctive for its "style" and Finlay's for its "beauty" is tenuous at best. This is still the major reference tool for information about science fiction and fantasy artists, although Di Fate and Wolfe (see introductory essay) should be consulted for more authoritative discussions of stylistic and thematic traits. (WA)

11-19. Wingrove, David. **The Immortals of Science Fiction.** Pierrot, 1980.

Wingrove's mock-encyclopedic text discusses the central characters from the works of ten authors, such as Susan Calvin in Asimov's robot tales [3-13], Slippery Jim Digriz in Harrison's Stainless Steel Rat series (1961–), and others. The British illustrators are identified only as Young Artists. Colorful, little more. Intended as a companion to *Alien Landscapes* [11-9]. (NB)

Individual Artists

Wayne Barlowe

11-20. Barlowe, Wayne Douglas, and Ian Summers. **Barlowe's Guide to Extraterrestrials.** Workman, 1979.

11-21. Barlowe, Wayne Douglas. **Expedition.** Workman, 1990.

Barlowe's Guide is the Audubon for aliens. These color drawings are meticulous and lovingly rendered, and are carefully derived from a wide variety of stories, such as the Puppeteers from Niven's *Ringworld* [3-316] or the likable Mesklinites from Cement's *Mission of Gravity* [3-50]. The text describes the physical characteristics, habitat, culture, and reproductive systems of 50 aliens. Compare Holdstock and Edwards [11-9] for a similar account of fictional worlds. *Expedition* is the account of a voyage to Darwin IV, in a newly discovered "F-Class Binary System," some four centuries in the future. Barlowe's text describes the exploration of the planet, while his color and black-and-white drawings record the flora and fauna. The creatures verge on the whimsical, but without the wit Sidney H. Sime (1867–1941) brought to his fantastic creatures, although the illustrations are often attractively conceived and executed. (NB/WA)

George Barr

11-22. Barr, George. **Upon the Winds of Yesterday and Other Explorations.** Donald Grant, 1976.

Barr began as a commercial illustrator in Utah, had work published in fanzines, and won the 1968 Hugo for best fan artist. His professional SF work was first published in the early 1960s and he has had much work published since. More than 50 pieces are reproduced on glossy stock, a number of them first published here. Most are ballpoint pen, and watercolor, a technique explained by Stuart Schiff in his introduction. Barr's illustrations favor fantasy more than SF and tend toward whimsy. (NB)

John Berkey

11-23. Berkey, John. **John Berkey, Painted Space.** Friedlander, 1991.

John Berkey's work will be immediately familiar to movie fans for his promotional artwork for the *Star Wars* trilogy, the 1976 remake of *King Kong*, *The Towering Inferno*, and other films of the 1970s and 1980s, as well as the more recent *Star Trek VI*. Berkey began his career as a calendar artist in 1955 for Brown and Bigelow, although none of the early work is reprinted in this volume. *Painted Space*, however, is not intended as an overview of his work but rather as a representative collection of his science fiction illustrations for movie promotions and paperback covers. Although some of the illustrations feature human subjects, the majority of the illustrations (all of them in color) can be classified as "hardware" art, mostly of space ships, shuttles, and futuristic mammoth land vehicles. The artist's running commentary consists of remarks about the genesis and other circumstances of the paintings. Where other hardware artists attempt to capture the image with photographic accuracy, Berkey's images remind the viewer of imprecise reflections in a mirror. Thus, the effect shifts from detail to mass and color, with an impression of great energy in momentarily arrested movement. (WA)

Chesley Bonestell

*11-24. Durant, Frederick, III, and Ron Miller, eds. **Worlds Beyond: The Art of Chesley Bonestell.** Donning, 1983.

Bonestell (1888–1986) was the dean of astronomical artists; his paintings having a remarkable photographic realism. His first book, *The Conquest of Space* (1949), collected 48 paintings. Some are repeated here, along with landscapes, seascapes, and many other quasi-photographic paintings that originally appeared in *Life* and other magazines. He has painted murals for the Boston Museum of Science and the Flandrau planetarium of the University of Arizona. He has received various awards but none from traditional fine art museums. Selections from his work are collected in *Space Art* [11-12]. (NB)

Jim Burns

11-25. Burns, Jim. **Lightship.** Paper Tiger, 1986. Text by Chris Evans.

11-26. Burns, Jim. **The Jim Burns Portfolio.** Paper Tiger, 1990.

Welsh-born Burns (1948–), well-known for his designs for Ridley Scott's *Blade Runner*, uses an airbrush with great flair. *Lightship* collects 125 color and nine black-and-white illustrations, many used as covers for British and American books. His subjects are varied and include people, androids, and machines, all lovingly rendered in vivid color and careful detail. He extensively illustrated the odd novel by Harry Harrison, *Planet Story* (Pierrot, 1979). In the 1990 portfolio of 28 paintings, the textured surfaces glow with the tactile brilliance of ornate jewelry, while their photographic quality is haunted by a surrealist vision. The frequent human figures show little emotion. Even in groups, each figure will be turned away from other members of the group. But the avoidance of contact is occasionally breached and Burns's "Songbirds of Pain"—in which a white bird is drooped over a red rose that appears to be bleeding down the canvas—has an emotional power that is rare in work of the British artists published in similar format by Paper Tiger (Matthews, Pennington, and Foss). (NB/WA)

Edd Cartier

*11-27. Cartier, Edd. **Edd Cartier: The Known and the Unknown.** Gerry de la Ree, 1977.

One of the most popular illustrators for *Unknown* and *Astounding* in the 1940s and early 1950s was Cartier, whose work with brush and lithographic pencil is immediately recognizable. Much of his work has a whimsical quality, and he was especially skilled at depicting gnomes and aliens. This is one of de la Ree's out-of-print series of limited editions devoted mostly to artists specializing in fantasy subjects, such as Finlay and Fabian. (NB)

Roger Dean

11-28.   Dean, Roger. **Views.** Paper Tiger, 1975.

11-29.   Dean, Roger, and Martyn Dean. **Magnetic Storm.** Paper Tiger, 1984.

Dean's work in a variety of media is showcased here. *Views* shows his varied interests and methods, and the reproductions range from preliminary sketches to finished work. Book and record jackets, architectural and stage designs, are among the types of work shown, with the emphasis more on fantasy than SF. The text is by Dominy Hamilton and Carl Capalbo. *Magnetic Storm* shows the work of the brothers during the past decade in architecture, film, TV album covers, posters, and even video games. The interesting text is by Colin Greenland. (NB)

Vincent Di Fate

11-30.   Di Fate, Vincent, and Ian Summers. **Di Fate's Catalog of Science Fiction Hardware.** Workman, 1980.

Di Fate works in the tradition of Frank R. Paul (1884–1963), whose work was featured in the pulps from the 1920s on. Human figures are depicted infrequently and usually as accessories to the dominant machine. Approximately 50 works from the 1974–1980 period are reproduced here, along with engineering drawings, grouped by subject (transportation, environments, weapons, and so on). Compare the similar work by Robert

McCall [11-47–11-48]; contrast the colorful airbrushed work of British illustrators like Chris Foss [11-34–11-35]. (NB)

Peter Elson and Chris Moore

11-31.   Elson, Peter, and Chris Moore. **Parallel Lines: The Science Fiction Illustrations of Peter Elson & Chris Moore.** Paper Tiger, 1981.

Two British illustrators working in the tradition of Chris Foss [11-34–11-35], largely limited to space hardware. Pat Vincent's introduction suggests Elson is the more romantic of the two, but I found their work almost indistinguishable. Many similar books emphasizing space hardware have been published in the past few years, almost all designed as instant remainders and largely interchangeable. (NB)

Virgil Finlay

11-32.   Finlay, Virgil. **Virgil Finlay's Women of the Ages.** Underwood-Miller, 1992.

*11-33.   Finlay, Virgil. **Virgil Finlay's Strange Science.** Underwood-Miller, 1993.

These compilations of Finlay's illustrations for the pulps are the first volumes dedicated to his work since the extensive series of books edited and published by Gerry de la Ree in the 1970s. Like the de la Ree series, all the interior artwork consists of Finlay's black-and-white illustrations, although each of the dust jackets features an attractive color illustration. Finlay was perhaps the most popular and influential pulp artist of the 1930s and 1940s. He continued to work in the field until his death in 1971, but his time-consuming technique and meticulous craftsmanship undoubtedly reduced his commissions in the era of the digest pulps. The works are usually dated, but the arrangement appears to be haphazard and most of the material was originally published by de la Ree or Don Grant (1971). For a bibliography of the earlier collections, see the entry on Finlay in Barron [*Fantasy Literature*, 7-33].

Chris Foss

11-34.   Foss, Chris. **Science Fiction Art.** Hart-Davis, 1976. Text by Brian Aldiss.

*11-35.   Foss, Chris. **21st Century Foss.** Paper Tiger, 1978.

11-36.   Foss, Chris. **The Chris Foss Portfolio.** Paper Tiger, 1990.

21st Century Foss provides an extensive selection of work by one of the most popular British artists, who has done production sketches for films such as *Dune, Superman,* and *Alien.* His colorful space vehicles and other machines—humans rarely appear—have influenced the work of many contemporary British illustrators. Much of the work reproduced here originally appeared on the covers of British books, which are identified. The 1976 collection has ten 11 x 18 plates, while the 1990 collection has twenty-eight 11¼ x 16½ plates. In addition to the gleaming metallic ships of the earlier work, the more recent paintings often feature machines that are deadly juggernauts or are themselves threatened by gigantic creatures from some alien film set. (NB/WA)

Frank Kelly Freas

*11-37. Freas, Frank Kelly. **The Art of Science Fiction.** Donning, 1977.

*11-38. Freas, Frank Kelly. **The Astounding Fifties: A Portfolio of Illustrations.** Freas, 1971.

11-39. Freas, Frank Kelly. **A Separate Star.** Greenswamp, 1984.

Probably the best known of all SF illustrators (and winner of ten Hugos), Freas's work has been featured extensively in magazines and paperbacks since the early 1950s. *The Astounding Fifties,* a portfolio of 84 drawings from the more than 160 stories Freas illustrated in *Astounding,* represent "some of the best and . . . worst of my work." People are the center of his art, in contrast to the hardware emphasis of other illustrators. His anecdotal text in *The Art of Science Fiction* clearly explains the development of each illustration. The self-published *Separate Star* collects more recent work, from preliminary sketches to finished work. His commentary might be useful to aspiring illustrators. (NB/REB)

H. R. Giger

11-40. Giger, H. R. **H. R. Giger's Necronomicon.** Big O, 1978.

11-41. Giger, H. R. **H. R. Giger's Necronomicon 2.** Editions C, 1985.

Giger (1940–) is a Swiss artist and illustrator who achieved prominence with his set designs for the 1979 film *Alien,* for which he and others won an Oscar for visual effects. The autobiographical account in the 1978 volume reveals a preoccupation with death, the fantastic, and the morbid, evident in all his work. He strikingly juxtaposes or blends the human figure with mechanical structures to create biomechanoid images of great power, in which a decadent eroticism is prevalent. The 1985 collection is more of the same, unsettling and visceral in its impact. Giger is one of the more important artists working in nongenre fantastic art, and libraries with large art collections should consider one of his oversized collections. (NB)

Greg and Tim Hildebrandt

11-42. Hildebrandt, Greg, and Tim Hildebrandt. **The Art of the Brothers Hildebrandt.** Ballantine, 1978. Text by Ian Summers.

11-43. Norton, Jack E. **The Fantasy Art Techniques of Tim Hildebrandt.** Paper Tiger, 1991.

The Hildebrandts were first acclaimed for their Tolkien calendars and for their *Star Wars* film poster. The poster and selections from the calendars are reproduced in the Ballantine collection. The bulk of their collaborative work illustrates fantasy fiction, and the recent solo work of Tim Hildebrandt continues to reflect that emphasis, although there are a few accomplished pieces of science fiction art included. Greg Hildebrandt's *From Tolkien to Oz* (Unicorn, 1985) is almost entirely fantasy. (NB/WA)

Don Maitz

*11-44. Maitz, Don. **First Maitz: Selected Works by Don Maitz.** Ursus Imprints, 1988.

Maitz (1953–) has been in the eighties, with Michael Whelan [11-56–11-58], one of the most talented and influential of the new generation of illustrators. SF motifs are dominated by fantasy treatments of subjects such as battling heroes, exotic heroines, and fey children accompanied by supernatural creatures. The settings are notable for their wide-ranging color palette and decorative detail. His more recent work is included in *Dreamquests: The Art of Don Maitz* (Underwood-Miller, 1993). (WA)

Rodney Matthews

11-45. Matthews, Rodney. **In Search of Forever.** Paper Tiger, 1985.

11-46. Matthews, Rodney. **The Rodney Matthews Portfolio.** Paper Tiger, 1990.

Matthews (1945–) early developed an interest in nature and much of his often playful work has favored animals—often very fantastic animals—over people. He is particularly well known for his record album covers, and he has illustrated many of Michael Moorcock's works. The text by Matthews and Nigel Suckling in the 1985 collection provides interesting details about his work, which heavily favors the fantastic. A religious conversion in 1980 caused him to rethink his artistic goals, and he has increasingly incorporated Christian iconography into his paintings. There are, however, conventional SF icons (space ships and alien worlds) even though there are intrusions of prehistoric creatures and antiquated flying ships into the presumably futuristic landscapes. (NB/WA)

Robert McCall

11-47. Bova, Ben. **Vision of the Future: The Art of Robert McCall.** Abrams, 1982.

*11-48. McCall, Robert. **The Art of Robert McCall.** Bantam, 1992. Captions by Tappan King.

McCall (1919–) has had his work published in popular magazines for many years, with aviation and aerospace almost his sole subjects. His work is in the Johnson Space Center and the National Air and Space Museum. Included in the 1982 collection are sketches, rough drafts, watercolors, oils, and acrylics, to which Bova—a long-time space booster—contributes a laudatory text. Although his work is resolutely high tech, the Bantam collection also includes concept art for films, and the work celebrating America's space program casts an optimistic eye toward a future in which science has created a mechanistic context in support of mankind's work and play. While the paintings may lack any sense of mystery, they are often quite beautiful, in particular a series of serene, floating cities. McCall's art may in itself be a kind of futuristic fiction, ignoring the dark side of technology but capturing with great skill and confidence science's utopian conquest of the future. The Bantam edition has the advantage of a larger number of color illustrations, but both volumes are fine tributes to McCall's work. (NB/WA)

Syd Mead

11-49. Mead, Syd. **Sentinel.** Paper Tiger, 1979. Text by Strother MacMinn.

11-50. Mead, Syd. **Sentinel II.** Kodansha, 1987.

Syd Mead (1933–) is an industrial designer specializing in transportation. After graduating from the Art Center School in Los Angeles in 1958 he joined the staff of the Ford Advanced Vehicles Studio, then published a series of books and portfolios of his designs, and in 1970 formed Syd Mead Incorporated. The two *Sentinel* books are "visualizations of the American dream, taking the year A.D. 2000 as [their] time and place reference." At the time of the publication of the first edition (1979), Mead considered his work to be fantasy only in the sense that the designs had not yet been realized. Now, however, in the brief foreword to the second edition (for which he wrote all the text), he describes it as "a visual encyclopedia of possible fantasies." A number of illustrations have been dropped from the second edition, in particular a series of pencil sketches of alien beings in "ceremonial" dress. Most of the machines consist of advanced automobile designs, handsomely rendered. Science fiction is not a term that appears in either text, but the illustrations could function as designs for a science fiction film of the near future, and the comments on and sketches for alien beings and—in one painting—mutated horses clearly show some interest in alien cultures. The human figures are, not surprisingly, idealized advertising icons. Beautifully produced volumes (the second edition has one fold-out painting) and a tribute to a gifted illustrator in the lineage of the hardware and Bonestell space art tradition. (WA)

Bruce Pennington

11-51.   Pennington, Bruce. **Eschatus.** Paper Tiger, 1976–77.

11-52.   Pennington, Bruce. **The Bruce Pennington Portfolio.** Paper Tiger, 1990.

Some of the work of Pennington (1944–) shares with that of Rodney Matthews (11-45–11-46) a use of biblical and religious imagery. In *Eschatus*, Pennington's mystical nature found expression in illustrations for the prophecies of Nostradamus. In his *Portfolio*, cowled monk-like figures filing into a spiraling tower or alien figures of commanding power dominating ravaged landscapes seem to mediate between the setting and the viewer. Elsewhere, Frazetta-like warriors and horsemen brood over skeletal cities, while a relative of the ancient kraken guards the entrance to an island castle. Pennington's future is haunted by a barbaric past, and cities rise precariously from sandy deserts. In addition to commissioned works, the latest collection contains unpublished paintings based on his increasing interest in the paranormal. (WA)

Richard Powers

*11-53.   Powers, Richard. **Spacetimewarp.** Nelson Doubleday, 1983.

This portfolio of 16 loose plates, 13 of them book covers, was a premium of the SF Book Club. Powers has illustrated hundreds of books in many fields but, perhaps because of the variety of his work, has never received great acclaim for his paintings in the SF-fantasy fields, although he is considered by his peers to be the most influential SF artist of the 1950s. These plates, about 11 by 14 inches, showcase his talents well. His images tend toward the abstract/surrealistic, unlike the hard-edge photographic realism favored by many SF illustrators. (NB)

Alex Schomburg

11-54. Gustafson, Jon. **Chroma: The Art of Alex Schomburg.** Father Tree Press (5 Reno Road, Poughkeepsie, NY 12603), 1986.

Schomburg (1905–) is one of the oldest illustrators still active in SF and worked for, corresponded with, and dealt with Hugo Gernsback for almost 40 years, from the 1920s to the 1950s. His airbrushed work appeared on the covers of many pulps in the 1950s and 1960s as well as in comics, notably the Marvel line. Appreciations by Harlan Ellison, Stan Lee, Vincent Di Fate, Brian Aldiss, George Barr, and Frank Kelly Freas. Schomburg has received various awards but not a Hugo, for which he was nominated in 1962. (NB)

J. Allen St. John

*11-55. Richardson, Darrell C. **J. Allen St. John: An Illustrated Bibliography.** Mid-America Publishers (571 S. Highland Ave., Memphis, TN 38111), 1991.

Although Richardson does not include many examples of St. John's SF illustrations, this check list of his book and magazine illustrations is important as the first such compendium of St. John's work. As Wolfe rightly points out in his essay in Cowart and Wymer [7-24], St. John "epitomizes" the art of the transition period from earlier book and magazine work to the pulp era. Although St. John's work was largely absent from the covers of the early years of the American pulp era, in 1933–1934 he painted a series of striking covers for *Weird Tales*, Kline's *Buccaneers of Venus*, and Jack Williamson's *Golden Blood*, while in the early forties he did a number of cover and interior illustrations for *Amazing Stories* and *Fantastic Adventures*. The most substantial representation of his science fiction work can be found in volume one of the three-volume *Edgar Rice Burroughs Library of Illustration* (Russ Cochran; 1976, 1977, 1984). This set also includes examples of the work of Frank Schoonover in volume one and of Ed Emsch, Frank Frazetta, Reed Crandall, and Roy Krenkel in volume three. For corrections and additions to Richardson's ground-breaking work, see *Addenda and Errata* by Robert R. Barrett and Henry Hardy Heins, privately printed, 1991 (2040 Salina, Wichita, Kansas 67203).

Michael Whelan

11-56. Whelan, Michael. **The Art of Michael Whelan: Scenes/Visions.** Bantam, 1993.

*11-57. Whelan, Michael. **Michael Whelan's Works of Wonder.** Ballantine, 1987.

11-58. Whelan, Michael. **Wonderworks: Science Fiction and Fantasy Art.** Donning, 1979. Ed. by Polly Freas and Kelly Freas.

Whelan (1950–) is one of the best of today's illustrators, winner of 11 Hugos as best SF artist and an additional one for his 1987 book. He is possibly the most influential illustrator of the 1980s and dominated the Hugo voting during that decade. *Wonderworks* reproduces working sketches and the finished art, usually much larger than the American paperback covers it adorned. Comments by six writers he illustrated praise his skill in capturing key aspects of their works. *Works of Wonder* reproduces works done for Ballantine covers and features his comments, along with preliminary sketches. Fantasy illustrations predominate, but the stylistic unity of Whelan's work makes this of lesser importance than it might in another artist's work.

The Bantam hardcover (*Locus* award) rivals the books of Abrams and Abbeville in quality. More than a hundred color reproductions are included in this 11 x 12 inch volume, along with many sketches for the finished work, whose medium and size are shown. The larger part, Scenes, reproduces many of his cover illustrations for DAW and Ace. Visions is more personal, reproducing for the first time paintings he did for himself, not commissioned by others. Whelan's comments accompany each illustration, and he is the subject of three short interviews. The most expensive by far; libraries may prefer the Ballantine edition. (NB/WA)

Tim White

11-59. White, Tim. **Chiaroscuro.** Paper Tiger, 1988.

Chiaroscuro presents 105 full-color illustrations that showcase White's work since about 1980, thus documenting the period since the publication of *The Science Fiction and Fantasy World of Tim White* (New English Library, 1981; Paper Tiger, 1988). As the introduction points out, White's work has changed very little although he worked briefly in a medium known as "decalcomania." Fantasy dominates in more recent years, but the volume includes a number of SF landscapes, and spaceship and alien art. There is use of photography, and the perspectives and colors often remind the viewer of the work of Maxfield Parrish (1870–1966). The paintings are usually devoid of drama, and the human figures present untroubled profiles, as pure of emotion as the ships and fantastic creatures. (NB/WA)

Science Fiction Comics

Peter M. Coogan

Comic art has a long and varied history, going back to Pharaonic Egypt, Minoan Greece, Mayan Mexico, feudal Japan, and Europe. It has been intimately intertwined with the evolution and advances of printing.[1] The fathers of modern comics were Swiss educator and artist Rodolphe Topffer (1799–1846) and German poet, painter, and cartoonist Wilhelm Busch (1832–1908), who began to define the conventions we now recognize, such as panels and word balloons, in the European context. Early comic art publications were humor oriented and came from all over the European landscape, especially Britain, France, and Germany, in the early and mid-19th century, and a bit later in America. The rise of mass journalism and its attendant circulation wars brought comic strips to American newspapers in the 1890s.[2]

Science fiction in comics goes back to at least the early 19th century with "Le Roy de la Lune" (King of the Moon) in issue 932 of *Imagerie d'Epinal*[3] and Topffer's *Monsieur Pencil* (1840), in which a scientist traps and studies M. Jolibois in a cage, because he thinks his prisoner is a creature from another planet. The first American strip to significantly employ elements of SF was Winsor McCay's *Little Nemo in Slumberland* (1905–1914), chronicling the adventures of a little boy in his dreams, which even took him to other planets.

Pulp SF served as the source for early SF in comics, with Buck Rogers, Flash Gordon, and Superman all having roots in pulp novels. The first true SF came on January 7, 1929, with the debut of the daily *Buck Rogers in the Year 2429* (1929–1967 daily, 1930–1965 Sunday) adapted by Phil Nowlan from his *Amazing Stories* novelette "Armageddon 2419 AD" [2-93]. John Flint Dille, president of the National Newspaper Syndicate, convinced Nowlan to do the comic and hired former World War I pilot Dick Calkins, who took over the writing chores in 1940, to illustrate the adventures of pilot Buck Rogers, who awoke after 500 years of suspended animation to discover an America overrun by the Red Mongols. Other cartoonists handled both sides of the work until the strip's demise. Wildly popular and widely syndicated, *Buck Rogers* became the common reference point for Americans when thinking about SF, "that Buck Rogers stuff," and spawned radio and film serials, a television series, and several comic books, with both reprinted and original material. Buck Rogers began a long reprint run in one of the earliest modern comic books, *Famous Funnies*, beginning with no. 3 and running the life of the series (1933–1958).

The 1930s saw a slew of SF comics, both strips and books, following Buck Rogers' lead. The first specifically SF strip was Alex Raymond's *Flash Gordon*, debuting on January 7, 1934, as a Sunday (1934–), and May 27, 1940, as a daily (1940–1944, 1951–), drawn by Raymond's assistant Austin Briggs. Inspired by Philip Wylie and Edwin Balmer's novel *When Worlds Collide* [2-156], Flash Gordon was put forward by King Features Syndicate as a direct competitor to Buck Rogers.

Although American comic books reprinting collections of comic strips and cartoons had been around in one form or another since 1884, it was not until 1933 that comic books as we know them appeared. The most famous comic book creation of all came from two teenage SF fans from Cleveland, Jerry Siegel and Joe Shuster. Superman debuted in *Action Comics* no. 1 (June 1938–), starting the Golden Age of Superheroes. Like Flash Gordon and Buck Rogers before him, Superman's origins derive from SF, in this case Philip Wylie's novel *Gladiator* [2-155], which Siegel and Shuster reviewed in their fanzine and which began the integral connection between superheroes and SF. Several hundred imitators followed, many with SF origins: the Human Torch was an android, Captain America received a boost from a "super soldier formula," Starman tapped the power of the stars "scientifically."

Although SF comics had appeared since Centaur Publications' *Amazing Mystery Funnies* (1938–1940), with features like Bill Everett's "Skyrocket Steele" and "Dirk the Demon—24th Century Archaeologist," and Carl

Burgos's "Air-Sub DX," it wasn't until pulp publisher Fiction House spun off *Planet Stories* [12-14] into *Planet Comics* (1940–1953) that original SF found a successful home in comic books. Billed as "Weird Adventures on Other Worlds—The Universe of the Future," this series featured a mixture of big chested heroes and bigger chested heroines, space opera, and monsters. *Planet Comics* displayed the talents of many artists who would go on to greater fame later, like Murphy Anderson on "Star Pirate," George Evans on "Lost World," "Gashly" Graham Ingels and artists from the S. M. "Jerry" Iger shop, including Dick Briefer on "Auro, Lord of Jupiter," and Maurice Whitman on "Mysta of the Moon." Mysta was only one of *Planet's* pinups, which also included "Gale Allen and Her Girl Squadron," "Futura," and Lyssa of "Lost World."

EC produced the best SF in comics of the 1950s and arguably the best SF comics ever. The SF titles *Weird Fantasy* (1950–1953) and *Weird Science* (1950–1953) were consolidated into *Weird Science-Fantasy* (1954–1955), which changed to *Incredible Science Fiction* (1955–1956) following the Estes Kefauver hearings in the Senate, with testimony from *Seduction of the Innocent* (1953) author Fredric Wertham, and the creation by several publishers of the Comics Code Authority (CCA) to regulate the content of comics. With art by some of the best artists in comics—such as Wally Wood, Roy Krenkel, Bernie Krigstein, Joe Orlando, Al Williamson, George Evans, and Frank Frazetta—EC's science fiction frequently focused on the dark side of science and the dangers of exploring the boundaries of human knowledge. These artists were able to bring to vivid life the often gruesome consequences of scientific exploration. Writing highlights included the first published work of Harlan Ellison (the plot for "Upheaval!" in *Weird Science-Fantasy* 24), an adaptation of Otto (Eando) Binder's "Adam Link" stories, and a series of Ray Bradbury adaptations. Bradbury's "The Rocket Man" and "Kaleidoscope" were combined into "Home to Stay" in *Weird Fantasy* no. 13 without Bradbury's permission or knowledge. Instead of suing, he asked for payment, received it, and EC went on to authorized adaptations of two dozen Bradbury stories, including 14 SF tales. The Comics Code crippled EC's ability to distribute its comics, so in 1956 the publisher William Gaines canceled all his titles, with the exception of *Mad* (1955–), which, as a magazine, was exempt from the CCA's authority.

The 1957 launch of Sputnik caused the management at DC to see science fiction as the best way to attract readers. Superman prospered under this regime, and over the next three years editor Mort Weisinger and writer Otto Binder created the familiar Superman "mythos," including the bottled city of Kandor, villains like Brainiac, the scientific wonderland of

Krypton itself (reached through time travel), and the teen superheroes from the future, the Legion of Super-Heroes. The same regime turned Batman into a parody of himself, traveling to other planets and dimensions, and facing endless monsters and aliens.

The biggest boost from this new SF emphasis came on Julius Schwartz's two science fiction titles, *Mystery in Space* (1950–1966, 1980–1981) and *Strange Adventures* (1950–1973). Schwartz's approach to SF stressed the positive, beneficial aspects of technology and science and promised a bright future of jet packs and robot servants. Modeled after Buck Rogers, Adam Strange, an Earth archaeologist teleported to the distant planet Rann by the unpredictable Zeta-Beam, defeated menaces by applying scientific knowledge of chemistry and physics. *Strange Adventures* featured a mix of one shot stories and continuing series, like "Space Museum," "Star Hawkins," and "The Atomic Knights." These stories tended to promote a bright, clean, prosperous future, where mankind benefited from technology, except in "The Atomic Knights," set in a world nearly destroyed by atomic warfare, which the Knights explored, eventually settling in a postatomic pioneer village to start the climb back to civilization. A sense of wonder and fascination with gadgets, frequently enlarged to incredible proportions, pervaded the Schwartz SF universe.

In 1954 Julius Schwartz revived the Flash in *Showcase* no. 4, inaugurating the Silver Age of Superheroes. By the end of the 1950s several other Golden Age heroes were brought back with a new SF emphasis: Hawkman was now a visiting policeman from Thanagar, instead of a reincarnated Egyptian prince; Green Lantern came back as a member of an interplanetary corps of crime fighters, instead of gaining his powers from a mystic lantern; and the Atom returned as a scientist who could shrink to subatomic size, instead of a feisty, short scrapper. Marvel jumped on the superhero bandwagon with the Fantastic Four (1961), the Incredible Hulk (1962), and Spider-Man (1962), all of whom gained their powers from radiation, and all of which featured scientists as main characters. This revival returned superheroes to the dominant position in mainstream American comic books that they had during the late 1930s and early 1940s.

Three forces that would shape the future of comics, and science fiction in many ways, arose in the 1960s. The first was comics fandom. Early comics fandom began with EC fanzines, but it took the letter pages of the late 1950s and early 1960s at DC, Marvel, and Gold Key to give fans a forum to discuss their favorite comics for any sort of fan consciousness to arise among comics readers. Within SF fandom, comics fans began to focus on the Golden Age comics, and Jerry Bails and Roy Thomas, strictly comics fans, who got each other's address from *The Brave and The Bold* no. 35 (May 1961), the first comic book to print writers' addresses, began publishing *Alter-Ego*, the first comics fanzine. Inspired by SF conventions, Bails and other comics fans followed with comics conventions. The first fan to break into the majors, Roy Thomas inaugurated the tradition of comics fans moving into professional positions, the major source of new talent over the last three decades.

The second force was licensing. Many comics had featured adaptations of classic, and not so classic, SF, especially Gilberton's *Classics Illustrated*, which adapted the works of H. G. Wells, Jules Verne, Mary Shelley, and other 19th-century authors.[4] In the 1950s movies like *Destination Moon*, and television shows like *Captain Video* and *Tom Corbett, Space Cadet* showed up in comics as one shots or short run imitations of the TV shows. *Star Trek* changed all this when Gold Key issued *Star Trek* (1967–1979), which greatly outlasted the original show. Marvel (1980–1982) and DC (1984–1988, 1989–) have both presented new adventures of the original crew, and DC has the new series *Star Trek: The Next Generation* (1986–1988, 1989–). The big boost in licensing, and the real start of vertical integration of film and television adaptations, came with the *Star Wars* film series, which Marvel began adapting and expanding (*Star Wars* [1977–1986] and a newspaper strip [1981–1984]). Since then nearly every Hollywood SF film or TV series has found its counterpart comic book. The most recent example of this process has been Dark Horse's success with its *Alien* family of titles, which prompted the *Aliens 3* film. Dark Horse has made this sort of comic the core of its publishing line, with series adapting and based on *Robocop*, *The Terminator*, and *Predator*. They expanded the idea of adaptation even further with titles like *Aliens Vs. Predator* (1990), and *Robocop Vs. Terminator* (1992).[5]

The third important force from the 1960s is the underground comix revolution. Like the underground newspapers from which they took their name, underground comix provided a medium of free, uncontrolled expression, a perfect place for the exploratory side of SF. Additionally, and an important factor for future comics, underground cartoonists retained ownership over their creations and circumvented the Comics Code by being sold through headshops and the emerging comics specialty stores. Called "the key underground SF title" by horror artist Steve Bissette,[6] *Slow Death Funnies* (1970–1979) from Last Gasp Eco-Funnies was published on Earth Day, 1970, to benefit the Berkeley Ecology Center. Focusing on ecological themes, *Slow Death's* SF repoliticized the genre, discussing contemporary issues of pollution, racism, and the dangers of atomic power through the metaphor provided by science fiction. The underground artists used disturbing and frequently grotesque images to draw attention to these issues, as in Charles Dallas's "Book of Zee" (*Psychotic Adventure Illustrated* [1970–1974] no. 2) about insects living inside a postapocalyptic Earth breeding humans for food. Dallas's woodcut style made this story even more unsettling. George Metzger's *Moondog* (1970) was a hippie SF epic of sorts about the remnants of the counterculture living on steam technology after an atomic apocalypse.

The creative ferment of the undergrounds bore fruit in many diverse ways and inspired a range of creators in many media. Vaughn Bodé's "Cobalt 60" inspired Ralph Bhakshi's *Wizards*. Spain Rodriguez's "Trashman" influenced the creation of cyberpunk and was the germ of the film *Mad Max*.

In Europe the undergrounds sparked a renaissance of SF. Before the mid-1970s European SF comics had few high points. One was the first ten years of *Dan Dare, Pilot of the Future*, the two-page lead strip in *Eagle* (1950–1969). Written and drawn by Frank Hampson, who used custom built model spaceships, props, and life models in costumes, the early Dan Dare had a beautiful, highly modeled, realistic look. Another was Barbarella, Jean-Claude Forest's strip for *V-Magazine*, created in 1962. Barbarella was a barely, or rarely, dressed sex-loving blond astronaut, and was translated into the Jane Fonda film.

Influenced and inspired by the energy and freedom exhibited by the American undergrounds, a group of French cartoonists, Les Humanoïdes Associées, began publishing *Métal Hurlant* (1975–), which came to America as *Heavy Metal* (1977–). Moebius, the pen name of Jean Giraud, became the most influential European comics artist, with his beautifully colored, delicate line work. He went on to do the storyboards for films like *Tron* and *Alien*.

This highly stylized work found an American home in translated reprints in *Heavy Metal*. At the same time *Heavy Metal* brought the underground influence back to America, the groundlevel movement of the 1970s was picking up steam. Bud Plant published Jack Katz's SF epic *The First Kingdom* (1974) series of graphic novels. Mike Friedrich came out with *Star*Reach* (1974–1979), specifically with the idea of giving creators the ownership of characters, concepts, and artwork common to underground publishers, but with the idea of telling stories in the mainstream genres, although outside the control of the Comics Code. *Star*Reach* featured the work of both established and new artists, including Howard Chaykin, whose Cody Starbuck directly inspired the *Star Wars* character Han Solo.

Publisher Byron Preiss took up the concept of the graphic novel, a single-issue large comic book, usually on high quality paper and perfect bound rather than stapled, and through Baronet came out with Howard Chaykin's adaptations of Samuel Delany's *Empire* (1978) and Alfred Bester's *The Stars My Destination* (1979). The most important graphic novel publisher was *Heavy Metal,* who released the adaptation of the film *Alien* in 1979, by Archie Goodwin and Walter Simonson. This graphic novel made the *New York Times* bestseller list.

The success of *Heavy Metal* led to Marvel's imitation, *Epic Illustrated* (1980–1986), a more narrative driven anthology of SF and fantasy, under the direction of Archie Goodwin. At the same time a number of small comics publishers were springing up, offering creators ownership of their products and taking advantage of the direct-sales market that had sprung up to service comics specialty stores and their adult customers, fans who had grown up reading comics and had never abandoned them. The first comic book format comic to be sold direct was Jack Kirby's *Captain Victory and the Galactic Rangers* (1981–1982), a typical Kirby space opera, published by Pacific Comics. Many other well-known creators followed Kirby's lead and moved from the big two, DC and Marvel, to the independents in order to start series over which they had ownership. Bruce Jones, lately of Marvel, launched two anthology titles for Pacific, *Twisted Tales,* featuring horror, and the SF-oriented *Alien Worlds* (1982–1985), both of which looked back to EC for inspiration. Probably the most successful, both commercially and critically, was Howard Chaykin's *American Flagg!* (1983–1989) for First Comics. *American Flagg!* blended satire, sex, and action in telling of former video star Reuban Flagg, who tries to clean up a 21st-century hedonistic, consumer culture Chicago, with the political culture of 1980s Beirut. *American Flagg!* also received the second official recognition of comics by the SF community. In 1979 Jerry Siegel and Joe Shuster were given the Science Fiction Writers Association President's Award as the "Originators of Superman" and "For creating an American Myth."[7] *American Flagg!* nos. 4–12 was nominated by the SFWA for a Nebula in the category "Best Short Story of 1984."

The drain of creators engendered by the independents prompted Marvel to spin off *Epic Illustrated* into its Epic line of creator-owned comics, many of which were SF, including the beautifully painted coming-of-age story *Moonshadow* (1985–1986), a truly original and distinctive piece which pushed the boundaries of just what SF included and demonstrated the kind of craftsmanship and artistry the creator-owned comics revolution of the 1980s could produce. These recent titles show the value comic art can bring to SF, allowing creators to visualize futures and to blend words and images in ways unavailable to artists working in words alone.

DC was the home for the two most widely noted comic book series of the 1980s, both of which received Hugo awards. Following critical success at Marvel, Frank Miller produced his six-issue miniseries *Ronin* (1983–1984) about the battle between a masterless samurai in feudal Japan and the demon who resurrects him in a postapocalyptic New York City. His next effort, a four-issue miniseries centered on an aging Batman returning from retirement to save Gotham City, *Batman: The Dark Knight Returns* (1986), garnered the first ever Hugo award for a comic book, in the 1987 best nonfiction category, so placed because it was ruled an art book. Following on the heels of Miller, DC scored again with British writer Alan Moore and artist Dave Gibbons's 12-issue series *The Watchmen* (1986–1987), a postmodern graphic novel about the socially deforming consequences of superheroes. *The Watchmen* also picked up a Hugo, this time in the "Other Forms" category for 1988. The categorization troubles faced by these works points up the problems the SF community has integrating comics SF into its world. Moore then finished his series about a fascist, *Nineteen Eighty-Four*-style England, *V for Vendetta* (1988–1989), with its original artist David Lloyd, which he had begun for the British magazine *Warrior* (1982–1985). Moore's work exemplifies one of the strengths of the comics medium, in that his complex story lines rely on the pictures to provide visual clues and continuities, and frequent visual references to other comics materials are made, enriching the tale's visual dimension.

No discussion of comics and science fiction would be complete without at least mentioning the contributions made by the British and the Japanese. Following the death of *Eagle* in 1969, SF comics in England languished until February 23, 1977, with the debut of *2000 A.D.* (1977–), a weekly black and white from IPC Fleetway, followed by the short-lived *Warrior* (1982–1985). These comics featured the work of a rising generation of creators who would launch a British invasion of American comics, both through reprints and through original work in America. The most successful export of the last decade has been *2000 A.D.*'s "Judge Dredd," a stone faced policeman, judge, jury, and executioner, upholding the law in Mega City One. Dredd's adventures began the flood of *2000 A.D.* reprints in 1983, and his popularity helped bring the influx of talent from the United Kingdom.

Comic art in Japan goes back to the sixth century. Before World War II Japanese comics imitated American art, but during the postwar period stylistically distinct "manga" grew to account for 30 percent of all books and magazines published in Japan today. Early SF arose in the 1940s, and is now one of the dominant genres of the medium, including the *atimekomikkusu* (animation comics), which seek to retain the feel of animated cartoons. The most popular Japanese cartoonist is Osamu Tezuka, whose *Tetsuwan Atomu* (Mighty atom) came to America as *Astro Boy*. When *Akira*, the best selling Japanese comic book in America, was to be adapted for an animated film, its creator, Katsuhiro Otomo, was the only director considered for the job, an indication of how highly the Japanese regard comics artists.

Comics has always been a worldwide artistic medium, but only recently has this fact been recognized. SF has been and continues to be one of the most popular genres in comics, and each has added greatly to the other.

Notes

1. See Scott McCloud's *Understanding Comics* (Tundra, 1983) [11-69] for an analysis of comics theory and history. McCloud discusses Mayan and Egyptian art as comics, and using his analysis I have seen Minoan art that matches his definition. See also Frederik Schodt's *Manga! Manga!* (Kodansha, 1986) for more on Japanese comic art history, and both volumes of David Kunzle's *History of the Comic Strip* (Univ. of California Press, 1973, 1990) [11-67] for the evolution of comics and printing in Europe and America.

2. For more on the early history of comic strips in America see Richard Marschall's "History of the Comic Strip" in the *The Comics Journal* [11-75], nos. 57, 60, 62, 63, 68 (1980–1981), his *America's Great Comic Strip Artists* (1989), his essay in Maurice Horn's *The World Encyclopedia of Comics* [11-64], and Alan and Laurel Clark's *Comics: An Illustrated History* [11-61].

3. Denis Gifford reprints a page of this strip in *The International Book of Comics* (Crescent Books, 1984) p. 12, but gives no date. The publisher of *Imagerie d'Epinal* died in 1836.

4. For a complete list with artists, see Alex G. Malloy's *Comic Values Monthly: The Comic Book's Price Guide* (Attic Books, 1992) or Robert M. Overstreet's *The Overstreet Price Guide* [11-70] for a list without all the artists.

5. Many of the film adaptations appear in the guide and checklist of Mike Benton's *Science Fiction Comics: The Illustrated History* [11-60].

6. Phone conversation with author, Feb. 17, 1993.

7. *Comics Journal*, no. 47, July 1979, p. 15.

Bibliography

The emphasis in this bibliography is on relatively recent and accessible works from both general and specialty publishers, many of which were in print in 1993. Included are both general works on comics to provide the necessary historical perspective and works treating SF comics in more detail. Addresses are provided for sometimes elusive specialty publishers. Excluded are some of the earlier studies, many of which are largely of historical interest or which have been superseded. These include: Caulton Waugh's *The Comics* (Macmillan, 1947), Dick Lupoff and Don Thompson's *All in Color for a Dime* (Arlington House, 1970), and *The Comic Book Book* (Arlington House, 1973), Stephen Becker's *Comic Art in America* (Simon and Schuster, 1959), Pierre Couperie's *A History of the Comic Strip* (Crown, 1968), and James Sterenko's *The Sterenko History of Comics* (Supergraphics, 1970, 2 vols).

11-60.   Benton, Michael. **Science Fiction Comics: The Illustrated History.** Taylor Publishing, 1992.
Part of the Taylor History of Comics, begun with Benton's *The Comic Book in America* [11-61], Benton presents a copiously illustrated history of American mainstream science fiction comics, fleshing out publication histories with anecdotes from the creators and publishers involved in the SF titles. A popular, fan-oriented history, this work provides a good starting point and reference tool, although it suffers the major weakness of excluding underground comix and the influence of European SF comics on SF in all media. A guide and checklist of major, and many minor, mainstream SF comics published in the United States follows the text, although again most groundlevel and all underground works are excluded, weakening the value of the book as a true research tool. Benton's other titles in the Taylor history all suffer from the same limitations of coffee table book history, although the superhero titles show it less, and the horror history more: *Superhero Comics of the Golden Age: The Illustrated History* (1992), *Superhero Comics of the Silver Age: The Illustrated History* (1991), *Superhero Comics: The Illustrated History* (1991), *Horror Comics: The Illustrated History* (1991).

*11-61.   Clark, Alan, and Laurel Clark. **Comics: An Illustrated History.** Greenwood Press, 1991.
Well illustrated and indexed, this history gives a good overview of the medium, and follows with chapters on British, American, European, and international comics. Another good recent history is Mike Benton's *The Comic Book in America: An Illustrated History* (Taylor Publishing, 1989; rev. ed., 1993), which provides a brief history of the B.C. (Before Comic Books) period of 1896–1932, and then a short history of each year from 1933 to 1989, titled according to the year's highlight. Histories of 59 publishers and 17 genres, like SF, funny animals, superheroes, and underground comix, provide a good sense of the major elements of the

medium's development. An earlier work worth mentioning is Les Daniels' *A History of Comix in America* (Outerbridge & Dienstfry, 1971), which intersperses chapters focusing on historical periods with comics sections reprinting complete stories illustrating that period. Although not exactly a history, Hubert H. Crawford's *Crawford's Encyclopedia of Comic Books* (Jonathan David Publishers, 1978) provides plot summaries within the histories of 27 publishers, along with listings of each company's titles, and a chronology of American comics, including related developments in film and television. Published but not seen was *Masters of Imagination* (Taylor, 1994), which reproduces more than 250 illustrations of the 13 members of the Jack Kirby Hall of Fame or the Will Eisner Hall of Fame.

11-62. Crompton, Alastair, and Alan Vince. **The Man Who Drew Tomorrow.** Who Dares Publishing (3 Durrant Rd., Bournemouth, Dorset BH2 6NE, England), 1985.

A biography of Frank Hampson, who co-created *Eagle* and "Dan Dare, Pilot of the Future," the two-page strip leading the weekly *Eagle*. Crompton focuses primarily on Hampson's years of producing "Dan Dare," specifically detailing how he created complex photo-references, using models, actors, and scenery, to achieve the realistic look of the strip. Also included are Hampson's "lost years" from his departure from *Eagle* in 1961 to the 1975 International Comics Festival in Lucca, Italy, when he received a Yellow Kid Award. *Dan Dare Dossier: Celebrating the 40th Anniversary of Dan Dare, Pilot of the Future* by Norman Wright (Hawk Books, Suite 309, Canalot Studios, 222 Kensal Rd., London W10 5BN, England, 1990) gives more information on the series itself.

11-63. Dooley, Dennis, and Gary Engle, eds. **Superman at Fifty: The Persistence of a Legend.** Octavia Press, 1987.

Sixteen short essays on the origins, evolution, career, and place in American culture of Superman, with a closing chapter on "Unanswered Questions" about such topics as Superman's sign and his persistence as a virgin. This collection provides a nice popular overview of Superman's effect on and importance to American culture, throughout the media he has appeared in.

11-64. Horn, Maurice, ed. **The World Encyclopedia of Comics.** Chelsea House, 1976.

Horn's is a standard work, usefully supplemented and updated by Ron Goulart's *The Encyclopedia of American Comics* (Facts on File, 1990). Horn's effort provides a brief history and a chronology of comic books and strips and of newspaper syndication, a glossary of terms, a selected bibliography, and one of the few accessible printings of the Comics Code of America. For a long time one of the few good reference works on comics, its entries detail artists, titles, characters, and some writers. Unfortunately it does perpetuate a few of the myths of comics histories and contains some factual errors. Goulart's work is better on the factual matters, but suffers from the same conceptual weaknesses of the earlier encyclopedia. Both contain only name and title entries, are skimpy on writers, and, except for Goulart's entry on Romance Comics, completely ignore subject entries like genre. Horn focuses more on comic strips and includes foreign material, a strength, while Goulart concentrates more on comic books and limits himself to American subjects, but both nearly ignore underground and alternative writers, artists, and titles, and neither contain entries for companies. Despite these weaknesses, they represent the best general comics encyclopedias in English. Compare Horn and Goulart to Jerry Bail's *Who's Who of American Comics* (Pure Imagination, 88 Lexington Ave., 2E, New York, NY 10016, 1993–), a biographical listing of every known writer, artist, colorist, letterer, and publisher who has contributed to original American comics books. Volume A was to be published in 1993, and the completed work will become the preferred biographical source.

11-65. Jacobs, Will, and Gerard Jones. **The Comic Book Heroes: From the Silver Age to the Present.** Crown, 1985.
A history of superhero and hero-oriented comics at DC and Marvel from the 1956 revival of the Flash to the explosion of independent publishers in the 1980s. The authors go beyond the usual publication history typical of comics historians, and explain what was going on at the companies and with the creators, and how all that resulted in the comics. Compare the more scholarly and more recent study by Reynolds [11-71].

11-66. Kennedy, Jay. **The Official Underground and Newave Comix Price Guide.** Boatner Norton Press (99 Mt. Auburn St., Cambridge, MA 02138), 1982.
The only readily available source for information on many underground comics and an early source for groundlevel comics. The period of 1962 to 1982 is covered. Includes histories of titles and companies written by their founders, as well as a brief history by Kennedy. Entries list print runs, contributors, publishers, publication dates, contents, and so forth. An artist index is also included. The best known work on underground comics is Mark James Estren's heavily illustrated *A History of Underground Comix* (Straight Arrow Books, 1974, 1986 rev.), a disorganized history dealing with artists, their influences, the publishers, and comix predecessors during the glory years of the movement. A lesser known, but better, history is

Artsy, Fartsy, Funnies (Laren, Holland, Paranoia, 1974) by Patrick Rosenkranz and Hugo van Baren, which traces undergrounds back to college humor magazines and "Tijuana Bibles" (pornographic booklets), sources overlooked by many writers.

*11-67. Kunzle, David. **History of the Comic Strip**, Volume 1: **The Early Comic Strip: Narrative Strips and Picture Stories in the European Broadsheet From c. 1450 to 1825.** Univ. of California Press, 1973.
The single best scholarly treatment of the history of the comic strip. Kunzle traces the formal and cultural evolution of the early comic strip from the beginnings of printing in the 15th century down to the early 19th. In his second volume, *The History of the Comic Strip: The Nineteenth Century* (1990), he picks up the story in 1827 with Rodolphe Topffer's first comic strip/picture story, finishing in 1896 with the emergence of continuing comic strip characters in American newspapers. Well illustrated and annotated, these volumes are the definitive history of the medium. A third volume is in preparation.

11-68. McAlpine, Duncan. **The Official Comic Book Price Guide for Great Britain.** Price Guide Productions (Box 2541, London N16 OLT, England), 1992.
The fourth edition of this guide by McAlpine, who took it over from the former editors in 1989, is in many ways an improvement over Overstreet's guide [11-70]. Entries are grouped into four categories, Marvel, DC, Independents, and British, and an introduction and state of each is given. McAlpine expands the notion of a price guide by including features such as a first appearance index, a character index, a reprint index, and biographies of British writers and artists. British fandom is also covered. Each entry lists the title's dates, numbers, prices, and artist, character, and content information. The main advantage of this guide is its extensive listings of groundlevel and alternative comics, as well as British comics. Either this or Alex Malloy's *Comics Values Annual: The Comic Books Price Guide* (Attic Books, 15 Danbury Rd., Ridgefield, CT 06877, 1992) make a good companion for the Overstreet guide. The Malloy guide suffers from some shortcomings in organization and omissions, but does cover independents, undergrounds (written by Jay Kennedy), British, Australian, and international.

*11-69. McCloud, Scott. **Understanding Comics.** Tundra Publishing (320 Riverside Dr., Northampton, MA 01060), 1993. Reprinted Harper, 1994.
A groundbreaking work on comics theory in which McCloud sets out a definition, grammar, and vocabulary—the poetics, if you will, for the comics medium. In so doing, McCloud deeply and profoundly examines

the ways in which we perceive and interpret reality, and how those perceptions and interpretations can be visually and verbally expressed. His explanations of this definition of art, the artistic process, the effects of color and black-and-white printing on the artist and reader make clear how these elements affect artistic production and reception. Most importantly, he does all this using the comics medium itself instead of prose. In his *Comics & Sequential Art* (Poorhouse Press, 1985), Will Eisner does much the same thing, using text to explain, and his own classic and original artwork to illustrate, the unique aesthetics, of sequential art. Eisner's work was originally written as a series of essays in *The Spirit* magazine and grew out of teaching a course at the School of Visual Arts in New York City, so it is more instructive and less theoretical than McCloud's work. HN

*11-70. Overstreet, Robert M. **The Overstreet Comic Book Price Guide.** Avon, 1992. 22nd ed.

The standard comics price guide and basic research tool. Each alphabetically arranged title entry contains the series' beginning and end dates, publisher, alternate titles, and prices for good, fine, and mint. Most entries also include character cross-references, artist listings, issue contents, and other miscellaneous information. Included are articles on topics such as collector's information (grading, storage, market report), histories ("The First Wave of Comic Books," comics fandom, "A Chronology of the Development of the American Comic Book"), and foreign comics, and Canadian reprints, as well as an excellent explanation of the numbering system of *Classics Illustrated* and its related series. Each edition carries a new cover story and a new article or two. Overstreet does a superb job listing mainstream American comics, but underground, many groundlevel, and some alternative comics and comics publishers are not included, sometimes inexplicably. Unfortunately, to be comprehensive, a companion guide is needed, either McAlpine's *The Official Comic Book Price Guide for Great Britain* [11-68] or Malloy's *Comics Values Annual: The Comic Books Price Guide* [11-68].

11-71. Reynolds, Richard. **Superheroes: A Modern Mythology.** B. T. Batsford, 1992.

The only scholarly, major analysis of superheroes. Using a semiotic approach, Reynolds examines how superheroes constitute a modern mythology. From the story motifs of *Action Comics* no. 1, he constructs a working definition of the superhero, and then examines the meaning of continuity, and ever-more dominant feature of superhero comics, and the superhero costume. Four myths used by creators are deciphered, and the book ends with examinations of three "key texts," the *X-Men*, the *Dark*

Knight Returns, and the *Watchmen*. Reynolds concludes with the possibility that the superhero genre may have said all it has to say, and may be dead. Compare with Robert Jewett and John Shelton Lawrence's *The American Monomyth* (Anchor, 1977) for an analysis that ties the superhero into a much larger American mythology. For other excellent scholarly analyses of specific topics, try Martin Barker's *Comics: Ideology, Power, and the Critics* (Manchester Univ. Press, 1989) about British comics and the way theories of ideology construct communication, despite which it is very readable; his *A Haunt of Fears: The Strange History of the British Horror Comics Campaign* (Pluto Press, 1984), about the 1950s crusade against American comics in England; Joseph Witek's *Comic Books as History: The Narrative Art of Jack Jackson, Art Spiegelman, and Harvey Pekar* (Univ. Press of Mississippi, 1989), which discusses comics as a serious narrative art form; M. Thomas Inge's *Comics as Culture* (Univ. Press of Mississippi, 1990), 11 essays analyzing how comics have dealt with aesthetic and philosophical concerns of American culture; and the collection of essays that started comics scholarship, Caulton Waugh's recently reissued 1947 work, *The Comics* (Univ. Press of Mississippi, 1991), for which Inge wrote a new introduction. Compare the more popular, older account by Jacobs [11-65] and the heavily illustrated histories by Benton [11-60].

11-72. Robbins, Trina, and Catherine Yronwode. **Women and the Comics.** Eclipse Books (Box 1099, Forestville, CA 95436), 1985.
Written because of the paucity of coverage of women cartoonists in works like Jerry Robinson's *The Comics: An Illustrated History of Comic Strip Art* (Putnam, 1974), this work contains the names of more than 200 women cartoonists, writers, editors, and publishers. Arranged primarily chronologically and dealing with all areas of the medium, strips, undergrounds, magazines, foreign cartoonist, and so on, with photographs of several of the women comics workers, this book contains information available nowhere else and frequently overlooked by male authors. Robbins continued her research in *A Century of Women Cartoonists* (Kitchen Sink, 320 Riverside Dr., Northampton, MA 01060, 1993).

11-73. Schodt, Frederik L. **Manga! Manga! The World of Japanese Comics.** Kodansha International/USA Ltd., 1983. Recommended ed.: 1986 rev. ed.
A heavily illustrated overview and history of comics and comic art in Japan, with selections from four long-running Japanese series. Besides providing an excellent look at the history of Japanese comics, Schodt also goes a long way in explaining the cultural importance of manga (the Japanese word for comics) for the Japanese. A useful shorter survey is the

chapter on Japanese comics by John A. Lent in *Handbook of Japanese Popular Culture*, ed. by Richard Gid Powers and Hidetoshi Kato (Greenwood, 1989). For Canada, try *Canuck Comics: A Guide to Comic Books Published in Canada* (Matrix Books, Box 1141, Snowdon Station, Montreal H3X 3Y3, Canada, 1986), edited by John Bell, and *The Great Canadian Comic Book* (Peter Martin Associates, 1971), by Michael Hirsch and Patrick Laubert. Thirteen cartoonists are covered in *Cartoonists of Australia* (View Productions, GPO Box 1858, Sydney NSW 2001, Australia, 1983) by Richard Roe, and John Ryan provides *Panel by Panel: An Illustrated History of Australian Comics* (Cassell Australia, 1979), covering both newspaper strips and comic books.

*11-74. Scott, Randall W. **Comic Books and Strips: An Information Sourcebook.** Oryx Press, 1988.

A bibliography of the most important sources of information on comics: books, including reprint collections, periodicals, and library collections, from 1970 to 1988. This book is one of the few comics bibliographies widely available and is the best place to start any research. Scott's *The Comic Art Collection Catalog* (Greenwood Press, 1993) presents detailed information about the more than 70,000 cataloged items making up the Comic Art Collection at Michigan State University, the largest publicly owned comics research collection in the world. Because Scott, a special collections librarian at MSU, has made a concerted effort to obtain primary and secondary comics materials, this catalog presents the best bibliography of research materials yet available. M. Thomas Inge's chapter on comics in his *Handbook of American Popular Culture* (Greenwood Press, 1989, 2nd ed.) provides an excellent bibliographic essay and bibliography, and should be in the reference section of most college libraries.

Temple University's communications professor John Lent's long-awaited bibliographies should go a long way to filling research holes. Three volumes are: *Animation, Caricature, and Gag and Political Cartoons in the United States and Canada: An International Bibliography*, *Comic Books and Comic Strips in the United States: An International Bibliography*, and *Comic Art of Europe: An International, Comprehensive Bibliography* (Greenwood, 1994). The fourth volume, *Comic Art in Africa, Asia, Australia and Oceania, and Latin America and the Caribbean: A Comprehensive, International Bibliography*, is forthcoming.

11-75.   Stevens, Carol, ed. **Print.** November/December 1988.

A special issue of the graphic design magazine (104 Fifth Ave., New York, NY 10011) dealing with comics. With articles on several aspects of comics past and present, and a bibliography, the special issue provides an excellent overview of and introduction to the changes that have shaped the medium over the past decade. For ongoing comics publications look at *The Comics Journal* (Syndicate Pubs/Fantagraphics, 1974–) (7563 Lake City Way, NE, Seattle, WA 98115) and *The Comic Buyer's Guide* (Dynapub/Krause Publications, 1971–) (700 E. State St., Iola, WI 54990). The best places to investigate current publication, including collections and reprints, are the distributors' monthly catalogs, *Advance Comics* (Capital City, 1988–) (2537 Daniels St., P.O. Box 8156, Madison, WI 53708), and *Previews* (Diamond Distributors, 1988–) (1718 Belmont Ave. Baltimore, MD 21207). All these comics publications are available at local comics specialty stores.

CHAPTER 12

Science Fiction Magazines

Joe Sanders

The first science fiction magazines appeared early in the 20th century when a substantial part of the reading public was willing to at least glimpse fictional innovations that extended the rapid, real-life changes that were attracting and bothering them. For the better part of a century readers had been exposed to samples of SF in a context of mainstream, mass entertainment. It was magazines specializing in SF, however, that for decades both defined the genre and permitted its self-aware growth. Understanding SF's history and the nature of modern SF must include knowledge of the magazines.

Soon after mass-market magazines began to appear in the early-mid 1800s, SF began to appear among their contents. In America, Edgar Allan Poe and Fitz-James O'Brien wrote for pre-Civil War literary periodicals. Later, an assortment of West Coast writers published SF in more ephemeral newspapers, and still later it became one of the subcategories—"different stories"—of adventure fiction in pulp magazines. In Britain, publication of the anonymous future war tale "The Battle of Dorking" in the May 1871 issue of *Blackwood's Magazine* [1-21] led writers to do more truly extrapolative fiction so that SF became a popular vein of magazine fiction. In fact, by the turn of the century, H. G. Wells was only the foremost of many writers of the "scientific romance."

Reading these early stories, though, modern readers frequently notice a certain timidity. For one thing, though stories involve a disruption in the status quo, things usually are put back into place as each tale concludes; readers wanted to consider the prospect of change, but only from a safe, easily retreatable distance. Also, SF written for a general periodical had to take time to ease the readers into accepting the anomaly around which the story was built. It can be argued that these restrictions are no handicap for a writer as gifted as Wells, who plays ironically with the first and slides nimbly past the second. It also can be argued that fiction *should* strive to connect its truths to readers' mundane experience. In any event, these rules changed with the 1926 appearance of *Amazing Stories*, the first magazine whose entire contents were presented as science fiction.

Although he produced *Amazing* as part of a career in electronics/gadgeteering publishing, Hugo Gernsback knew that enough readers existed to support the magazine and that enough fiction had been written to fill it with reprints until he could attract new writers. However, the older fiction that Gernsback gleaned from various periodicals looked different when gathered together. Reading one SF story after another, both readers and writers saw new possibilities. For example, E. E. Smith had completed the manuscript of *The Skylark of Space* in 1919 but had been unable to find any market for it. Although editors such as Bob Davis of *Argosy* liked the novel, they were worried that readers couldn't accept a story that moved so fast and ventured so far from Earth. When Smith saw an issue of *Amazing* in 1927, he knew he had found his ideal audience, and when the delighted Gernsback serialized *Skylark* in 1928, he was confident that he had found a work that would satisfy his readers by stretching the range of SF imagination. Both men were right.

Writers could count on readers of an SF magazine to accept willingly notions that would have been more difficult for a general audience, such as the possibility of space flight and the existence of intelligent, nonhuman beings. In fact, such ideas become almost givens, as much a part of an SF story's background as railroads and sorority girls in a non-SF story. A few years later, John W. Campbell, Jr., the editor of *Astounding*, would describe the kind of fiction he was looking for as general fiction—from a magazine published in the next century. This attitude and body of shared conventions made possible works like Stanley G. Weinbaum's "A Martian Odyssey," which *begins* on Mars and describes a marooned human's encounters with native beings. It is impossible to imagine this impressive story, which leads off *The Science Fiction Hall of Fame* selected by the Science Fiction Writers of America, being published anywhere except an SF magazine, even assuming it could have been imagined and written otherwise.

Another, less aesthetic, measure of accomplishment is the popularity of the SF magazines. When *Amazing* was hijacked away from him by rival publisher Bernard Macfadden in early 1929, Gernsback was back two months later with *Science Wonder Stories*, first of several periodicals that were combined by mid-1930 into *Wonder Stories*. In the meantime, *Astounding Stories of Super Science* began, offering purer pulp fiction, fast-paced storytelling.

Whatever their specific intended readership, the SF magazines soon became aware that they shared a core audience of fans, people who gave more than casual attention to the wonderful brainstretching outlook of SF stories. Fandom has been important to SF out of proportion to its size, prodding magazines and writers to master new skills and try new steps. Fans soon began making direct contact and publishing magazines containing their own amateur fiction as well as news of professional activities. Without tracking down fanzines, though, we can get a sense of this ferment in the magazines' letter columns, where, for example, readers nagged E. E. Smith to write more Skylark stories and where Smith and younger writer John W. Campbell, Jr., debated the scientific accuracy of space adventures.

Self-aware SF fandom soon sprang up in Britain too, but publishers saw that the market was well supplied by imported back issues of American magazines and consequently failed to bring out a home-grown periodical. British SF writers could either send their work to the specialized American magazines or write stories that would reach a general audience. The effect of this was that British SF, for decades, was more "literary" and "serious" than the American variety. Rather than startling ideas it stressed smooth writing and complex characterization, and as part of the exploration of character it depicted personal frailty more frequently than did its brasher, more self-confident American relative. Escaping the "SF" label, it did some things genre SF evaded, while also accepting a niche closer to the mainstream.

During the mid-1930s, however, American SF continued to develop along its path. *Astounding Stories* had risen to dominance, partly because of its competitors' weakness but also because editor Orlin F. Tremaine was pushing his writers to try wilder ideas, in the "thought-variant" stories he began to feature each issue. Jack Williamson's "Born of the Sun" (March 1934), for example, takes up the question, What if the planets are actually eggs laid by our sun—and what happens when they hatch?

Whether it was successful missionary work by the existing SF magazines or external forces—the interest generated by Orson Welles's radio broadcast of *War of the Worlds*, the spreading uneasiness as the world political situation slid toward World War II—SF went through a brief boom in the late 1930s and early 1940s. There is little point in enumerating the magazines that fluttered about like mayflies during that time. They did give some valuable editing and writing experience to members of New York fandom such as Donald A. Wollheim, Frederik Pohl, C. M. Kornbluth, Robert A. W. Lowndes, and James Blish. However, they were imitative, underfinanced, poorly distributed, or all three, and if they had not expired naturally by 1942, they disappeared because of wartime paper and ink rationing.

After the dust from the publishing boomlet settled, through most of the 1940s, there remained a full range of magazines for SF readers. At the top, John W. Campbell, Jr.'s monthly *Astounding* published the most sophisticated fiction, including serialized novels. A step below were *Thrilling Wonder Stories* (descendent of *Wonder Stories*, after Gernsback left the field) and its younger sister, *Startling Stories*, which featured a complete short novel each issue. A few steps below was *Planet Stories*, whose wild, space opera fiction was uninhibited by any scientific plausibility but which published many of Ray Bradbury's early stories, including parts of what would later become *The Martian Chronicles*. A special case was *Famous Fantastic Mysteries*, which at the time reprinted "classic" novels that had appeared decades earlier in book form (many of them British). And the largest but most juvenile SF magazine was Ray Palmer's *Amazing Stories*.

Another way to look at this period is to see it as a contest between the kind of SF represented by the two leading editors. When Ray Palmer took over editorship of *Amazing* in mid-1938, he turned it into a lively and widely circulated magazine. In the process, he became the least understood figure in SF. Palmer was an extremely canny editor, and a decade or so later (in magazines that he both owned and edited) he showed that he could publish sophisticated, modern SF when he thought there was a market for it. He also was a fan with a genuine taste for slam-bang adventure and he was a person so much in tune with adolescent frustrations and desires that he could be drawn into that mind-set himself. In addition, he was a rogue who delighted in seeing how much mischief he could get away with. If outsiders sometimes had difficulty figuring out which role or combination of roles Palmer was filling at a given moment, it appears that Palmer didn't know either. After making *Amazing* popular with a diet of juvenile adventure and screwball humor, Palmer spun out of control with the Shaver Mystery, a series of paranoid fantasies that he presented as gospel truth beginning in 1945. At various times, Palmer justified the "mystery" as promotion, entertainment, or revelation. Eventually, publisher Ziff-Davis reined him in because fans were so vociferous in their hatred of what Shaverism was doing to SF's public image. Palmer didn't care about how SF might develop, and he certainly felt no responsibility to contribute to that development. He was too busy having fun.

John W. Campbell, Jr., had become editor of *Astounding* about half a year earlier, late in 1937. Besides the momentum established by Tremaine and the existence of a number of writers ready to try more mature, polished SF, the basis of Campbell's success was his skeptical, probing intelligence. After establishing himself as one of the best writers of planet-hurling interplanetary stories, Campbell had begun exploring a more restrained, reflective, even melancholy approach under the penname Don A. Stuart. When he became an editor, he gave up his own writing, but he became an expert at pushing others to explore their own talents and the limits of their ideas. He was uncomfortable with SF's juvenile appearance but since he couldn't change *Astounding*'s name right away he went about reshaping the genre from the inside. He insisted not only on scientific verisimilitude but also on attention paid to the social consequences of gadgets. Rather than lecturing about how a device worked, characters should show what a difference it made to people. Almost immediately, this focus both attracted thoughtful readers and drew together a recognizable school of writers. If sometimes, as with the prickly Robert A. Heinlein, Campbell benefited from simply being in the right place at the right time to publish a self-created writer's work, he also encouraged established writers such as Henry Kuttner and Clifford A. Simak to go on expanding their range. He worked especially hard with fledglings. Isaac Asimov in particular has spoken and written much [see 9-6/7] about how Campbell helped make him a writer by doing things like tossing him the idea for "Nightfall" and by suggesting that the idea that led to the *Foundation* series was too big for one short story. Over all, *Astounding* during those days was an exciting place to be; the mood was a pleasantly surprised "Hey, we can do almost *anything*!"

Though *Amazing* was the bestselling SF magazine at the height of Palmer's exploitation of Shaverism, Campbell and *Astounding* won the contest. SF would keep growing up, utilizing but extending the storytelling and thinking evolving within the magazines.

It would be a mistake to imagine that all writers were desperate to win Campbell's imprimatur, or that all the magazines were imitation *Astounding*s. Nevertheless, throughout the range of SF magazines the standard of writing and thinking improved. When, selecting more or less at random, I pick up the November 1948 *Startling Stories*, I see a typical pulp magazine cover, with a skimpily clad blonde grimacing while a young man struggles with a monster that looks like a cross between a hydra and a trash compactor. But the fiction that cover allegedly illustrates is Arthur C. Clarke's first novel, *Against the Fall of Night*, and five more stories (out of the seven shorter pieces in the issue) have been reprinted either in anthologies or single-author collections such as Bradbury's *The Illustrated Man*.

In the late 1940s, SF again experienced a publishing boom. As with the earlier boom, the causes may have been both external—as in public concern about the atom bomb or the V-2 rocket (which, German scientist Werner von Braun blithely commented, really had been designed as a spaceship but unfortunately had been aimed at the wrong planet)—and internal. The successful magazines had prepared readers for even more magazines. Whatever the cause, the boom that began in the late 1940s was larger than the 1938–1942 one. Like the earlier one, unfortunately, it contained many imitative and poorly financed titles that couldn't survive. One of the superior but ephemeral magazines, *Worlds Beyond*, is annotated below. Other notable but short-lived magazines included *Super Science Stories, Space Science Fiction, Rocket Stories*, and *Science Fiction Plus*, Hugo Gernsback's strange last hurrah. By the early-mid 1950s, this boom was also over, killed by difficulties with national newsstand distribution and by the spread of television which virtually wiped out the specialized fiction magazines, including the established pulps, *Thrilling Wonder, Startling, Planet*, and *Famous Fantastic Mysteries*.

Two digest-sized magazines that appeared early in the boom did establish readerships and survived the general collapse: *The Magazine of Fantasy and Science Fiction* and *Galaxy*. *F&SF* began life in late 1949 as *The Magazine of Fantasy*. It featured stories with more polish and depth than most pulp-derived SF; in its early years, it used many reprints from nongenre magazines and books. No other magazine was doing what *F&SF* set out to do, and it established a secure, if not especially dominant, place for itself. Most characteristically, as in stories such as Matheson's "Born of Man and Woman" and Keyes's "Flowers for Algernon," *F&SF* focused on human responses to strange experience rather than fully analyzing the strangeness. *Galaxy*'s first issue, dated October 1950, was a more direct challenge to *Astounding*. Editor H. L. Gold filled his first issues with stories by some of Campbell's favorite authors. Gold encouraged writers to deal more with soft sciences such as sociology, and he especially liked social criticism and satire. The most characteristic story from *Galaxy*'s early years is Pohl and Kornbluth's "Gravy Planet," published as *The Space Merchants* [3-147]. The high quality of *Galaxy*'s fiction, the fact that it was doing something different, and Campbell's temporary distraction by Dianetics (a pseudo-scientific cult created by SF writer L. Ron Hubbard), established *Galaxy* as a successful magazine.

Also beginning in the 1950s was another factor that affected the survival of SF magazines and that still is reshaping the genre: large-scale, commercial SF book publishing. Until the period after World War II, the SF that appeared in magazines stayed there, not just short works but all the novels of Smith, Williamson, Leiber, and others. Heinlein's *adult* fiction was contained in back issues of pulp magazines; he had begun writing juvenile novels at least partly because they would be published as books. When amateur, specialist fan publishers began to produce—and sell out—small editions of their favorite reading. However, major publishers began to see SF as a possibly profitable field. In addition to mining the back issues of magazines, they started publishing original books by recognized SF writers, novels or anthologies that never had been published anywhere else. And this shifted SF's aesthetic focus and (especially) economic base.

People who want to understand SF through the 1950s must examine the magazines. That is where the writers worked. Seeing the stories in context gives a fuller understanding than does reading collections or anthologies—even those drawn from individual magazines or representing some particular year or period. But the situation in recent decades is more complicated. The involvement of commercial book publishing changed what SF was written and the way it was written. For one thing, the magazines were not designed to publish full-length novels, so writers tended to concentrate on shorter works. Now they could think of writing longer stories, even *clusters* of novels. In addition, where formerly only a few people could support themselves as professional writers, it now became possible to sign enough contracts for novels to insure a comfortable living for years to come. But with all the factors encouraging longer fiction, there was less incentive to write the shorter works that magazines needed. Instead of dominating the field, magazines sometimes look like an afterthought. As one bizarre example, Frederik Pohl's *JEM* was serialized during the last, tottering issues of *Galaxy*, long after the novel had appeared in hardcover and even had been read, discussed, and voted awards by anyone interested.

The postwar period has also seen a strange, somewhat disillusioning rapprochement between SF and mainstream fiction. At one time, SF seemed such a subliterary genre that almost no one in a responsible position paid attention to it. Mass media, in particular, usually avoided it. After the war, general magazines began running more SF stories and movies discovered SF during the 1950s with (largely moronic) gusto. It seemed that the many real-life echoes of genre gadgets—and the very presence of genre SF even as an officially scorned subliterature for decades—had acclimated people in the mass audience to SF images. Even if *Star Trek* was not a TV network success, it became a lucrative cult franchise. SF fans expected that Trekkers would move on to contemporary written fiction, since the series itself seemed stuck in a late 1940s-mid-1950s groove. Still later, they waited for a flood of new readers to appear when Stephen Spielberg's anthology TV series, *Amazing Stories,* ran for two years. Certainly with the identically titled magazine right there on the newsstands, people would discover it and transfer to written SF! That did not happen. Apparently, the level of sophistication and indeed the attitudes toward reading are so different between SF readers and people in the mass audience that SF magazines can expect little benefit from SF's mass popularity. Readers must take what comfort they can from the general magazines that publish regularly: *Omni,* which publishes about as much deliberate fiction as it does UFOlogy, and *Pulphouse,* which includes SF as part of its eclectic, emotionally charged mix.

All this would seem to indicate that the SF magazines are at a dead end and may slowly fade away. That does not appear to be true. If some periodicals have failed, others have taken their places—or staked out new places. The SF magazines are surprisingly healthy and influential.

One major example of a magazine's influence showed up in Britain. During the first SF boom in America, the British fanzine *Novae Terrae* metamorphosed into *New Worlds,* its last three issues being edited by E. J. (Ted) Carnell in 1939. After the war, Carnell edited three issues of a professional magazine under that name before his publisher folded. Finally, in 1949, a group of fans incorporated to produce a regular magazine. Carnell was able to draw on a large number of British SF writers and without being a pastiche, *New Worlds* during the 1950s had something of the flavor of *Astounding* in the late 1930s and early 1940s: Everyone seemed delighted to be there and eager to do the best he or she could. By the early 1960s, however, sales had fallen, and Carnell became convinced that the future of short SF was in original anthologies, not magazines. At the last minute, *New Worlds* was saved, and Michael Moorcock took over as editor. What followed was an explosion of talent and acrimony, as Moorcock led the New Wave movement with the magazine as an extremely visible rallying point. The New Wave tried to liberate SF from restrictions that seemed natural to magazine editors, especially in America where SF's readership was sometimes pictured as adolescent males. Besides less inhibited language, the New Wave featured experimentation with structure and exploration of anomalies in consciousness—journeys into inner space rather than outer space. The results were mixed. On the one hand, as with any experimental movement, some silly things happened; Roger

Zelazny's "For a Breath I Tarry," for example, appeared in a seriously garbled form and nobody except the author noticed. On the other, writers such as Norman Spinrad, Thomas M. Disch, and Brian Aldiss produced powerful stories that could never have been written inside the restrictions of other magazines. For a time, all of SF seemed to be reacting either positively or negatively to *New Worlds*. That controversy included SF fandom. Not all fans are ready for all changes, especially when change involves questioning SF's basic attitude that the universe is or will be susceptible to human understanding and control. But Moorcock and his associates persisted. Throughout its energetic, erratic existence (even now a variety of paperback anthologies, etc., carry on the magazine's name), *New Worlds* certainly had a major influence on SF (see *The Entropy Exhibition* [8-61] for the details).

Another innovative magazine has taken a less confrontational approach that has made it a popular success. Beginning in early 1977, *Isaac Asimov's Science Fiction Magazine* cannily used Asimov's genial, rather conservative image as an umbrella sheltering a diverse body of fiction, including disturbing stories by such writers as Lucius Shepard, John Shirley, Bruce Sterling, and Michael Swanwick.

Strangely, the magazines' lesser importance in the overall flow of SF publishing may have given them some advantages over book publishers in budget and flexibility. As for price, SF magazines are very inexpensive— some would say absurdly so—at about half the price of a newsstand paperback. This can mean less profit but also less financial risk. As for contents, if innovation inside the magazines sometimes has been frustratingly slow, it has not thrived outside them either. It is hard to imagine an editor less open to innovation than the late Lester del Rey at Ballantine books. As SF has become a category of commercial publishing, it has become subject to the same rules that govern general book publishing: Don't disturb people; give them more of what they already enjoy; try to reach the biggest possible number with the highest priced product the traffic will bear. On the other hand, despite a magazine's general editorial personality, a given issue may include one or more pieces that will shake some readers. The magazine's familiar context calms, but at least some readers can move on with the writers to the next step. That is how SF advances, and the magazines appear better positioned to help do it than the frequently conservative, bottom-line-watching book publishers.

The SF magazines are still working out an economic and artistic role for themselves. In general, they perform two important services. First, they help new writers get started. It is easier to invest some time in a short story than to start out with a novel, and even writers who have moved on to multi-novel contracts usually have served an apprenticeship in the magazines. In addition, there are ideas that can't be done as novels, let alone trilogies. Established writers do write for the magazines when they feel they can afford the time. And thus new, live fiction keeps appearing.

The roles and accomplishments of current magazines are included in the survey below, along with descriptions of some especially significant magazines of the past. But overall the continued existence of SF magazines shows that they still deserve attention. They are still alive, still active and still influential in shaping SF's future.

Bibliography

This bibliography is arranged in five sections: current fiction magazines featuring SF; notable SF magazines from the past; major nonfiction magazines focused on SF; SF magazines in microform, and books about the history or contents of SF magazines. See, in particular, the authoritative handbook edited by Tymn and Ashley [12-46] for more thorough histories of most of the magazines discussed below. Addresses for currently published magazines are accurate as of summer 1993.

Holdings information was obtained from the libraries listed in chapter 14, to which the holdings statement is keyed. Not all libraries provided magazine holdings information. Following the holding library number is a letter denoting number of issues held: A (all), M (most), or S (some). All denotes a complete run, and a current subscription if the magazine is currently published. "Most" denotes ownership of at least half and, in many cases, almost all issues published. "Some" denotes that fewer than half the published issues were held, or that the library simply designated its holdings as "incomplete."

Current SF Magazines

12-1. **Aboriginal Science Fiction.** ISSN: 0895-3198. 1986. Quarterly. Charles Ryan, ed. (Box 2449, Woburn, MA 01888-0849.) Circ.: 20,000.

Format and size have varied in this struggling magazine. Contents, however, are usually the same: reviews and columns with a large number of short stories. Aimed at newer writers—and probably readers.

Holdings: 3(M), 8(A), 26(A), 28(S), 31(M), 50(M), 58(A), 65(M)

12-2. Amazing Stories. ISSN: 1058-0751. 1926. Quarterly. Kim Mohan, ed. (Box 5695, Lake Geneva, WI 53147.) Circ.: 6,500.

World's oldest SF magazine, discussed in the introductory essay. In addition to the tenures of Hugo Gernsback (1926–1929; important for showing the formation of conscious SF readership and writing nexus) and Ray Palmer (1938–1949; fascinating in the same way as a major traffic accident), two other editors have made distinctive contributions to the magazine: Cele Goldsmith (1957–1965; notable for encouragement of talented newcomers) and Ted White (1969–1979; singlehandedly and miraculously turning the magazine from a reprint zombie into a lively, cutting edge periodical). Since 1982, the magazine has been kept alive by TSR, the gaming publishers, who respect its heritage and have put a lot of money into it, but it suffers from terrible distribution. Has gone from an attractive, large-size magazine, with color illustrations and readable fiction, to an uncertain bare bones quarterly.

Derivative anthologies: Joseph Ross, ed., *The Best of Amazing* (1967); Ted White, ed., *The Best From Amazing* (1973); Isaac Asimov and Martin Harry Greenberg, eds., *Amazing Stories: 60 Years of the Best Science Fiction* (1985); *Amazing Stories: Visions of Other Worlds*; Martin Harry Greenberg, ed., *Amazing Science Fiction Stories: The Wonder Years: 1926–1935* (1987); *Amazing Science Fiction Stories: The War Years: 1936–1945* (1987); *Amazing Science Fiction Stories: The Wild Years: 1946–1955* (1987).

Holdings: 3 (A), 5(M), 6(M), 8(M), 10(M), 13(M), 14(A), 15(M), 21(M), 26(A), 28(A), 31(M), 32(M), 33(A), 34(M), 35(M), 41(M), 47(M), 57(A), 58(M), 59(M), 65(M)

*12-3. Analog: Science Fiction and Fact. ISSN: 1059-2113. 1930. 13 issues/year. Stanley Schmidt, ed. (Box 7061, Red Oak, IA 51591.) Circ.: 78,000.

Under its earlier name, *Astounding*, discussed extensively above. Besides John W. Campbell, Jr., notable editors have been F. Orlin Tremaine (1933–1939) and Ben Bova (1972–1978; revitalizing the magazine after Campbell's lethargic last years). Today, *Analog* is the last bastion of "hard" science fiction, which seems to mean stories whose problems can be stated and solved in quantifiable terms by characters who can control their emotions.

Derivative anthologies: John W. Campbell, Jr., ed., *The Astounding Science Fiction Anthology* (1952); *Prologue to Analog* (1962); *Analog 1* (1963); *Analog 2* (1964); *Analog 3*, paperback title *A World by the Tale* (1965); *Analog 4*, paperback title *The Permanent Implosion* (1966); *Analog 5*, paperback title *Countercommandment!* (1967); *Analog 6* (1968); *Analog 7* (1970); *Analog 8* (1971). Ben Bova, ed., *Analog 9* (1973); *The Best of Analog* (1978).

Retrospective anthologies: Harry Harrison and Brian W Aldiss, eds., *The Astounding-Analog Reader* 2 vols. (1972–1973). Tony Lewis, ed., *The Best of Astounding* (1978). Stanley Schmidt, ed., *The Analog Anthology #1: 50 Years of the Best* (1980), casebound as *Analog's Golden Anniversary Anthology* (1981). *The Analog Anthology #2: Readers' Choice* (1982). *The Analog Anthology #3: Children of the Future* (1982). *The Analog Anthology #4: Analog's Lighter Side* (1982, 1983). *The Analog Anthology #5: Writer's Choice* (1983). *The Analog Anthology #6: Analog's War and Peace* (1983). *The Analog Anthology #7: Aliens From Analog* (1983). *The Analog Anthology #8: Writer's Choice #2* (1984). *The Analog Anthology #9: From Mind to Mind* (1984). James Gunn, ed., *The Best of Astounding: Classic Short Novels From the Golden Age of Science Fiction* (1992). No ed., *Analog: The Best of Science Fiction* (1985).

Of additional interest: Martin Harry Greenberg, ed., *Astounding, July 1939* (1981), a facsimile of that issue with commentaries by three contributors; Harry Harrison, ed., *Astounding: John W. Campbell Memorial Anthology* (1973), 13 original stories by writers associated with the magazine, continuing series that Campbell helped direct. Readers should also note the bulk of many SF anthologies was drawn from *Astounding*. For example, Healy and McComas's *Adventures in Time and Space* [3-214] contains 33 stories and two articles—31 pieces drawn from *ASF*, 1934–1945.

Holdings: 2(M), 3(M), 5(A), 6(M), 8(M), 9(M), 13(M), 14(M), 15(A), 19(M), 21(M), 26(M), 28(M), 31(M), 32(M), 33(A), 34(M), 35(M), 41(M), 43(A), 46(M), 49(M), 53(M), 57(M), 58(M), 59(M), 63(M), 65(M)

*12-4. Asimov's Science Fiction. ISSN: 1065-2698. 1977. 13 issues/year. Gardner Dozois, ed. (Box 7058, Red Oak, IA 51591.) Circ.: 72,000.

Discussed above under original title, *Isaac Asimov's Science Fiction Magazine*. Currently the most consistently innovative and exciting SF magazine. Very few serialized novels but frequent longer stories.

Derivative anthologies: Early in the magazine's life, material was reprinted directly from the magazine's pages—illustrations, blurbs, and all—and published as paperback anthologies under the general title, *Asimov's Choice*, seven volumes between 1977 and 1982; volume 8, reissued as *A Space of Her Own* (1983), consisted of 22 stories by women writers, selected by then-editor Shawna McCarthy. A collection with no editor listed was published as *Asimov's Choice* in 1986. Other anthologies include Gardner Dozois, ed., *The Best of Isaac Asimov's Science Fiction Magazine*

(1988); *Transcendental Tales From Isaac Asimov's Science Fiction Magazine* (1989); *Isaac Asimov's Mars* (1991); Dozois and Sheila Williams, eds., *Isaac Asimov's Robots* (1991), *Isaac Asimov's Earth* (1992) and, by Dozois alone, *Isaac Asimov's SF Lite* (1993). Several brief anthologies were published as subscription premiums, all edited by Sheila Williams: *Isaac Asimov's Puzzles* (1984); *Science Fiction by Asimov* (1986); and *Robots From Asimov's* (1990).

Holdings: 3(M), 6(A), 8(M), 10(M), 13(M), 14(M), 21(M). 25(M), 26(M), 27(M), 28(M), 31(M), 33(A), 34(M), 35(M), 43(A), 46(M), 50(M), 58(A), 63(M), 65(M)

12-5. Galaxy Science Fiction. 1950–1980; 1994–.

Galaxy's outstanding debut is discussed above. H. L. Gold (editor 1950–1961), especially at the beginning, demanded lively, clear writing (even when it meant intrusive editorial rewriting; see the magazine and book [restored text 1990] versions of Heinlein's *The Puppet Masters*, for example) and strongly preferred wit and social awareness. Frederik Pohl (editor 1961–1969), whose own writing epitomized these qualities, worked hard to regain the magazine's preeminence, and James Baen (editor 1974–1977) also produced solid, seriously hopeful magazine. For most of its run, one of the top SF magazines. Gold's son revived the magazine in early 1994.

Derivative anthologies: H. L. Gold, ed., *Galaxy Reader of Science Fiction* (1952); *Second Galaxy Reader . . .* (1954); *Third Galaxy Reader . . .* (1958); *The Forth Galaxy Reader . . .* (1959); *The Fifth Galaxy Reader . . .* (1961); *The Sixth Galaxy Reader . . .* (1962); *Five Galaxy Short Novels* (1958); *The New World That Couldn't Be and Eight Other Novelets From Galaxy* (1959); *The Bodyguard and Four Other Short Novels From Galaxy* (1960); *The Mind Partner and Eight Other Novelets From Galaxy* (1961); Frederik Pohl, ed.: *The Seventh Galaxy Reader* (1964); *The Eighth Galaxy Reader* (1965); *The Ninth Galaxy Reader* (1966); *The Tenth Galaxy Reader* (1967); *The Eleventh Galaxy Reader* (1969); *Time Waits for Winthrop and Four Other Short Novels From Galaxy* (1962). Editors of *Galaxy*, *The Best From Galaxy*, Volume I (1972); Volume II (1974). Jim Baen, ed.: *The Best From Galaxy*, Volume III (1975); Volume IV (1976); *Galaxy: The Best of My Years* (1980). Frederik Pohl, Martin Henry Greenberg, and Joseph Olander, eds.: *Galaxy Magazine: Thirty Years of Innovative Science Fiction* (1980).

Holdings: 3(M), 6(A), 8(M), 10(M), 13(M), 14(M), 21(A), 26(A), 28(M), 31(M), 33(M), 35(M), 41(M), 43(A), 46(M), 49(M), 57(M), 58(A), 65(M)

*12-6. Interzone. ISSN: 0264-3596. 1982. Monthly. David Pringle, ed. (217 Preston Drive, Brighton BN1 6FL, England.) Circ.: 5,000–6,000.

The successor to *New Worlds,* discussed above, *Interzone* sometimes has stressed "radical" stories. In the context of 1990s SF, however, it looks like a rather middle-of-the-road magazine—though publishing stories like Blumlein's "Tissue Ablation and Variant Regeneration" shows that its furious heart is in the right place. A large-size, well-designed magazine with generally quite good stories. With issue 74, August 1993, *Interzone* absorbed Pringle's *Million: The Magazine About Popular Fiction* (14 issues, 1991–1993), whose 700 subscribers were too few by half to support this informal but informed bimonthly survey of both category fiction—fantastic, mystery, thrillers, romances, and so on—and some general fiction as well. Although Pringle says *Interzone* will print some material originally destined for *Million,* notably Brian Stableford's series on past bestsellers, its primary appeal will be to readers of fantastic literature. With the October 1994 issue *Interzone* absorbed a smaller, newer British magazine, *Nexus,* and was redesigned.

Derivative anthologies: John Clute et al., eds., *Interzone,* five anthologies, 1985–1991.

Holdings: 8(M), 26(M), 33(A), 50(M), 58(A), 63(A), 65(A)

*12-7. The Magazine of Fantasy and Science Fiction. ISSN: 0024-984X. 1949. Monthly. Kristine Kathryn Rusch, ed. (Box 56, Cornwall, CT 06753.) Circ.: 56,100.

Founding discussed above. Long known as the most "literary" SF magazine—that is, polished prose and emphasis on characterization. This standard was established by first editor Anthony Boucher (1949–1958) and has lasted through a series of editors; the Ferman family must deserve credit, as owners and editors, for the magazine's consistency. New editor Rusch was a risktaker as one of the founders of *Pulphouse,* and she may raise the magazine's energy level.

Derivative anthologies: *The Best From Fantasy and Science Fiction,* ed. by the following people—Anthony Boucher and J. Francis McComas, series one through three (1952–1954); Anthony Boucher, ed., series four through eight (1955–1959); Robert P. Mills, ed., series nine through eleven (1960–1962); Avram Davidson, ed., series twelve through fourteen (1963–1965); Edward L. Ferman, ed., series fifteen through twenty-four (1966–1982); *Best From Fantasy and Science Fiction: Twenty-fifth Anniversary Anthology* (1974) took the place of the 21st series. In addition, Annette Peltz McComas, ed., *The Eureka Years: Boucher and McComas's Magazine of Fantasy & Science Fiction 1949–1954* (1982); Robert P. Mills, ed., *A Decade of Fantasy and Science Fiction* (1960), contains 25 stories from 1949–1959 not selected for the annual series; Edward L. Ferman and Robert P. Mills, ed.,

Twenty Years of Fantasy and Science Fiction (1970); Edward L. Ferman, ed., *The Magazine of Fantasy and Science Fiction: A Thirty Year Retrospective* (1979); *The Best From Fantasy and Science Fiction: A 40th Anniversary Anthology* (1989); Edward L. Ferman and K. K. Rusch, eds., *The Best from Fantasy and Science Fiction: A 45th Anniversary Anthology*. Also note the facsimile of the April 1965 edition (1981), introduction by Ferman and brief memories by the writers represented.

Holdings: 3(A), 5(A), 6(A), 8(M), 13(M), 14(M), 15(M), 19(M), 21(M), 25(M), 26(A), 28(M), 31(M), 33(M), 34(M), 35(M), 41(M), 43(A), 47(M), 53(M), 57(M), 58(M), 63(M), 65(M)

12-8.   Science Fiction Age. ISSN: 1065-1829. 1992. Bimonthly. Scott Edelman, ed. (Box 749, Herndon, VA 22070.) Circ. unknown.

A canny mixture of mostly media-oriented features and varied fiction in a very attractively designed package. Hard to determine focus because thus far editor has concentrated on appealing to all possible interests/tastes.

Holdings: 8(M), 26(A)

12-9.   Tomorrow Speculative Fiction. ISSN: 1072-4990. 1993. Bimonthly. Algis Budrys, ed. (Unifont Company, Box 6038, Evanston, IL 60204.) Circ. unknown.

SF, fantasy, and horror short fiction, edited by an extremely knowledgeable writer/critic. Fiction thus far has stressed emotional intensity and gritty, noir atmosphere.

Holdings: 8(M)

SF Magazines No Longer Published

12-10.   Famous Fantastic Mysteries and **Fantastic Novels.** *FFM* 1939–1953; *FN* 1940–1941, 1948–1951.

FFM was intended to reprint fiction from the Frank A. Munsey Company's pulp magazines (*Argosy, All-Story*), and its mixture of short fiction and serialized novels was popular enough to spawn *FN* shortly thereafter. When *FN* ceased publication and *FFM* was sold to another publisher, the policy changed to reprinting novels that never had appeared in a magazine and to more frequent use of new short stories such as Clarke's "Guardian Angel" (April 1950), the seed of *Childhood's End* [3-44]. The magazines are important for making contemporary, American readers aware of other varieties of SF—older tales from the Munsey pulps and hardcover novels that were basically unavailable otherwise.

Derivative anthologies: Stefan R. Dziemianowicz et al., eds., *Famous Fantastic Mysteries* (1991).

Holdings: 5(M), 6(A), 8(M), 13(A), 14(M), 26(A), 28(S), 31(A), 32(M), 33(M), 35(M), 41(M), 43(A), 57(M), 58(M), 59(M), 65(M)

12-11. If / Worlds of If. 1952–1974.
Under publisher-editor James L. Quinn (1952–1958), *If* was always readable, sometimes more (it was, for example, the only magazine willing to publish "A Case of Conscience," the first section of Blish's novel [3-21]). When it was aquired by the publisher of *Galaxy*, however, it became more, especially under Frederik Pohl (editor 1961–1969). Pohl thought of *Galaxy* as his prestige magazine, and filled *If* with what he considered lighter-weight pieces; his playful attitude can be seen in an "All-Smith" issue, the contents of which ranged from adventure by E. E. Smith to surrealism by Cordwainer Smith. The public preferred the lighter fare, and *If* won three Hugo Awards as best SF magazine during those years, while *Galaxy* won none.

Derivative anthologies: James L. Quinn and Eve P. Wulff, eds.: *The First World of If* (1957); *The Second World of If* (1958). Frederik Pohl, ed: *The Best Science Fiction From If (1964); The If Reader of Science Fiction* (1966); *The Second If Reader* . . . (1968). "The Editors of If" [Ejler Jakobsson and Judy-Lynn Benjamin], eds.: *The Best From If*, Volume I (1973); Volume II (1974). Jim Baen, ed.: *The Best From If*, Volume III (1976).

Holdings: 6 (A), 8(M), 13(A), 14(M), 15(A), 21(M), 28(A), 31(M), 33(M), 35(M), 41(M), 43(A), 57(M), 58(A), 63(M), 65(M)

12-12. Infinity Science Fiction. 1955–1958.
Infinity was more impressive to read at the time than it is to look back at, but it still is an unusually interesting magazine for its sometimes outstanding fiction (such as Clarke's "The Star" in the first issue), its friendly, fannish tone, and its printing of Damon Knight's book reviews. If Knight had a larger sense of what SF could be, editor Larry Shaw did an intelligent job of putting together a nice variety of mid-1950s SF.

Holdings: Information not collected.

12-13. New Worlds. 1946–1979.
Discussed above. The magazine's run falls into two neat compartments: those edited by Ted Carnell (1946–1964) and those edited by Michael Moorcock and cohorts (1964–?). That oversimplifies somewhat, since many of the people identified with Moorcock's editorship (J. G. Ballard, for example) were first published by Carnell; still, it is the latter, in-your-

face complex of talents and viewpoints that most people have in mind when *New Worlds* is mentioned.

Derivative anthologies: John Carnell, ed.: *The Best from New Worlds Science Fiction* (1955); *Lambda I and Other Stories* (1964). Michael Moorcock, ed.: *The Best of New Worlds* (1965); *The Best SF Stories From New Worlds* 1–8 (1967–1974; in America only six volumes were published, 1969–1971). Judith Merril, ed.: *England Swings SF* (1968; abridged in the United Kingdom as *The Space-Time Journal*).

Holdings: 6(A), 8(M), 28(S), 31(M), 33(M), 43(M), 57(M), 58(M), 63(A), 65(M)

12-14.   Planet Stories. 1939–1955.

Discussed briefly above, *Planet* was the home of "space opera," the kind of adventure that pushed past plausibility to the verge of the absurd, but counted on readers being too swept along by emotion and colorful details to notice. At its best, as in the unplanned and unlikely collaboration of Leigh Brackett and Ray Bradbury on "Lorelei of the Red Mist" (Summer 1946), it actually achieved some of opera's larger-than-life power.

Derivative anthology: Leigh Brackett, ed.: *The Best of Planet Stories #1* (1975).

Holdings: 6(A), 8(M), 13(A), 14(M), 26(M), 28(S), 31(A), 33(M), 35(M), 41(M), 43(A), 47(M), 57(M), 58(M), 59(M), 65(M)

12-15.   Science Fiction/The Original Science Fiction Stories. 1939–1941, 1943, 1953–1958.

The publishing history of this title is almost impossible to summarize; see Tymn & Ashley [12-46] for details. It is typical, however, of the SF editorial production of Robert [A.] W. Lowndes: underfinanced but very intelligent. Lowndes's other magazines include *Future Fiction* and *Science Fiction Quarterly*. They all contain readable fiction and above-average nonfiction, especially Lowndes's editorials.

Holdings: 6(A), 8(M), 13(A), 14(M), 21(M), 28(S), 31(M), 33(M), 35(M), 41(M), 43(A), 57(M), 58(M)

12-16.   Startling Stories. 1939–1955.

For most of its run, a companion to *Thrilling Wonder Stories* but with the distinguishing feature of running a "complete novel" (45–60,000 words) each issue. Most are still readable action adventures, and several were reprinted (with source suitably disguised) as halves of Ace Double Novels by Donald A. Wollheim. Like its companion, *Startling* became a solid, mature magazine in the late 1940s and early 1950s, as shown by its being the only one willing to print Farmer's "The Lovers" (August 1952).

Derivative anthology: Samuel Mines, ed., *The Best From Startling Stories* (1953).

Holdings: 6(A), 8(M), 13(A), 14(A), 26(M), 28(S), 31(A), 32(M), 33(M), 35(M), 41(M), 43(A), 47(M), 53(M), 57(M), 58(M), 59(M)

12-17.   Wonder Stories/Thrilling Wonder Stories. 1929–1955.

Discussed briefly above. Actually begun as *Science Wonder Stories*, the magazine was first edited by Hugo Gernsback (1929–1936), a continuation of his pioneering efforts. Renamed after Gernsback's departure from SF, *TWS* concentrated on juvenile readers; beginning in 1945, however, editors Samuel Merwin, Jr. (1945–1951) and Samuel Mines (1951–1954) raised the level of the contents considerably.

Holdings: 6(A), 8(M), 13(A), 14(A), 28(S), 32(M), 33(M), 35(M), 41(M), 43 (M), 53 (M), 57 (M), 58 (M), 59 (M), 65 (M)

12-18.   Worlds Beyond. 1950–1951.

Damon Knight's first stint as SF editor shows the same features that have marked his later career: excellent taste in fiction, a desire to broaden the range of the field (here labeled "Science-Fantasy Fiction"), and vulnerability to marketing concerns that killed this magazine after three tantalizing issues.

Holdings: 5(M), 6(A), 8(M), 13(A), 14(A), 21(A), 26(A), 28(A), 31(A), 35(M), 41(M), 43(A), 57(M), 65(M)

Current Magazines About SF

12-19.   Burroughs Bulletin. ISSN: 0007-6333. 1990. Quarterly. George T. McWorter, ed. (The Burroughs Memorial Collection, University of Louisville, Louisville, KY 40292.)

For better or worse, Edgar Rice Burroughs probably is the most important American SF writer of this century—is there one better known worldwide or one who has been cited approvingly by a recent U.S. President? Each issue of the *Bulletin* concentrates on one of Burroughs's novels, in order of publication. Excellent reproduction of original and foreign illustrations.

Holdings: 8(M), 23(A), 28(S), 33(A), 65(M)

*12-20.   Extrapolation. ISSN: 0014-5483. 1959. Quarterly. Donald M. Hassler, ed. (Kent State Univ. Press, Journals Department, Kent, OH 44242.)
Oldest of the academic SF journals (founded by Thomas Clareson). Usually an assortment of mid-length critical essays, emphasizing SF but giving some attention to fantasy. Some reviews of scholarly books.

Holdings: 3(A), 6(A), 8(A), 9(A), 10(A), 13(M), 14(A), 15(A), 21(A), 26(A), 28(A), 31(A), 33(A), 41(A), 43(A), 46(A), 47(A), 53(A), 58(A), 59(A), 63(A), 65(M)

12-21.   Fantasy Commentator. No ISSN. 1943–1952, 1979–. Semi-annual. A. Langley Searles, ed. (48 Highland Circle, Bronxville, NY 10708.)
One of the relatively few surviving serious fanzines; rather than academics, most of the contributors to *FC* come out of SF fandom—and a seasoned and well-informed lot they are.

Holdings: 8(M), 31(M), 65(M)

*12-22.   Foundation. ISSN: 0306-4964. 1972. Three issues a year. Edward James, ed. (New Worlds, 71-72 Charing Cross Road, London WC2H 0AA, England.)
Britain's major SF journal, usually lively and frequently downright bloody-minded. Critical essays of varied lengths, many in-depth book reviews, and letters.

Holdings: 8(A), 9(M), 13(M), 15(M), 26(A), 28(M), 31(M), 33(M), 43(A), 46(M), 57(A), 58(A), 59(A), 63(A), 65(A)

12-23.   Futures Past: A Visual Guidebook to Science Fiction History. ISSN: 1068-1829. 1992. Irregular. Jim Emerson, ed. (Box 610, Convoy, OH 45832.)
This very irregular, one-man labor of love covers a year per issue, beginning in 1926. Includes listings (with brief summaries) of novels, films, and so on. Not much critical analysis, but fascinating glimpses of the past.

Holdings: No holdings reported

*12-24.   Locus: The Newspaper of the Science Fiction Field. ISSN: 0047-4949. 1968. Monthly. Charles Brown, ed. (Locus Publications, Box 13305, Oakland, CA 94661.)
Coverage of fantastic literature generally, including the most current and comprehensive reviews of general books and magazine fiction, interviews with SF pros, and lists of published and forthcoming U.S. and British books. Coverage of foreign-language SF has been a regular feature since the late 1980s. Has dominated the Hugo category for best semiprofession-

al magazine. Contrast the more fan-oriented *Science Fiction Chronicle* [12-29].

Holdings: 3(M), 5(M), 6(M), 8(A), 9(A), 13(M), 26(M), 28(M), 31(M), 33(A), 35(M), 43(M), 46(A), 58(A), 63(M)

*12-25. Monad. ISSN: 1061-1800. 1991. Irregular. Damon Knight, ed. (Pulphouse Publishing, Box 1227, Eugene, OR 97440.)
Substantial pieces, usually by active SF writers, on SF's nature and functions. Published only when Knight (winner of the Pilgrim Award in 1975) gets enough material to fill an issue; first three issues dated September 1990, March 1992, and September 1993.

Holdings: 8(M), 9(A), 58(A)

12-26. Nexus. ISSN: 1040-1157. 1991. Irregular. Paul Brazier, ed. (SF NEXUS, Box 1123, Brighton BN1 6JS, England.)
Nonfiction and SF-centered metafiction. Much space devoted to "The Users Guide to Science Fiction," a combination of publication list and brief reviews. Absorbed by *Interzone* [12-5] in 1994.

Holdings: Information not collected

*12-27. The New York Review of Science Fiction. ISSN: 1052-9438. 1988. Monthly. Donald G. Keller, and Robert K. J. Killheffer, eds. (Dragon Press, Box 78, Pleasantville, NY 10570.)
In-depth rather than comprehensive reviews, usually with feature essays each issue. Contributors include active writers and academic critics.

Holdings: 8(M), 26(M), 28(A), 31(A), 33(A), 43(A), 58(A)

12-28. The Science Fiction and Fantasy Writers of America Bulletin. ISSN: 0192-2424. 1965. Quarterly. Daniel Hatch, ed. (Pulphouse Publishing, Box 1227, Eugene, OR 97440.)
Began as a members-only journal but now available to the public. Usually short discussions of techniques, marketing, and whatever else concerns publishing SF&F writers. (Overlapping is *The Report: The Fiction Writer's Magazine*, edited by Christina F. York and J. Stephen York, same publisher, written largely by and for SF people.)

Holdings: 3(M), 8(M), 13(M), 28(S), 31(M), 33(A), 35(M), 43(M), 58(M), 63(M)

*12-29. Science Fiction Chronicle. ISSN: 0195-5365. 1979. Monthly. Andrew J. Porter, ed. (Box 2730, Brooklyn, NY 11202-0056.)
Locus's persistent rival as news magazine. Chief difference are *SFC*'s monthly columns on British and media news, much briefer book reviews,

quarterly market reports (listing fiction publishing opportunities in magazines and books), and greater attention to fan activities. Hugo award, 1993, 1994.

Holdings: 8(A), 10(M), 26(M), 28(A), 31(M), 33(A), 43(M), 58(A), 63(M), 65(M)

12-30. SF Commentary. ISSN: lacking. 1969. Irregular. Bruce Gillespie, ed. (GPO Box 5195AA, Melbourne, Vic. 3001, Australia.)

An outstanding example of one-man publishing. Reviews and essays by many people, attracted and held together by the intelligent, obsessive editor.

Holdings: 8(M), 58(M), 63(M)

*12-31. Science Fiction Eye. ISSN: lacking. 1987. Approximately three issues a year. Stephen P. Brown, ed. (Box 18539, Asheville, NC 28814.)

The SF scene from a countercultural perspective, frequently contemplating real-life application of SF themes. Longer essays, especially substantial interviews with SF writers. Absorbed *Thrust* (later *Quantum*), another critical journal, in 1993.

Holdings: 8(M), 33(A), 58(A), 63(A)

12-32. SFRA Review. ISSN: 1068-395X. 1970. Bimonthly. Amy Sisson, ed. (Robert J. Ewald, Treasurer, 552 W. Lincoln St., Findlay, OH 45840.)

Members of the Science Fiction Research Association (see chapter 15) receive this along with reduced price subscriptions to *Extrapolation* [12-20] and *Science-Fiction Studies* [12-33]. Includes SFRA news, lists of recent and forthcoming nonfiction, calls for papers, the acceptance speech of the annual Pilgrim winner (see awards in chapter 15), and reviews. Under Betsy Harfst's editorship in 1991 and 1992, when publication was ten issues yearly, coverage of nonfiction was comprehensive, with more than 200 reviews of books devoted to all types of fantastic literature, film, and illustration. Coverage of fiction was much weaker. The *SFRA Newsletter*, as it was called through the 1980s, was a negligible publication until Harfst's editorship. Major problems developed in 1993 under a new editor, who was replaced in 1994.

Holdings: 3(M), 8(A), 10(M), 13(M), 21(M), 28(A), 31(M), 43(M) 58(M), 63(M)

*12-33. Science-Fiction Studies. ISSN: 0091-7729. 1973. Three issues a year. R. D. Mullen, ed. (SF-TH, Inc., Arthur B. Evans, East College, DePauw University, Greencastle, IN 46135-0037.)

The most "academic" (theoretical, carefully documented, stiffly written) of the academic journals, though it recently has enlivened considerably without losing its solid content. Essays, review-essays, and reviews of scholarly works.

Holdings: 8(A), 9(A), 10(A), 13(A), 14(A), 15(M), 26(A), 28(A), 31(M), 33(A), 34(A), 41(A), 43(A), 53(M), 58(A), 59(A), 63(A), 65(M)

12-34. Utopian Studies. ISSN: 1045-991X. 1990. Semi-annual. Lyman Tower Sargent, ed. (Professor Hoda Zaki, Secretary-Treasurer, Society for Utopian Studies, Department of Political Science, Hampton University, Hampton, VA 23668.)
Critical essays and reviews on; utopian (and dystopian) themes and fiction, frequently overlapping SF.
Holdings: Information not collected

12-35. Vector. ISSN: 0505-0448. 1958. Bimonthly. Kev McVeigh and Catie Cary, eds. (British Science Fiction Association, Membership Secretary: Joanne Raine, 29 Thornville Road, Hartlepool, Clevelands TS26 8EW, U.K.); U.S. membership: (Cy Chauvin, 14248 Wilfred St., Detroit, MI 14248.)
The BSFA's critical journal, featuring essays and reviews. Accompanied by other BSFA newsletters, all-review magazines, and writers' 'zines.
Holdings: Information not collected

SF Magazines in Microform

U.M.I., 300 North Zeeb Road, Ann Arbor MI 48106-1346, lists the following as available on microfilm: *The Alien Critic* 1972–1974, *Analog* 1961–, *Asimov's Science Fiction* 1992–, *Astounding* 1938–1960, *Bulletin of the Science Fiction and Fantasy Writers of America* 1992–, *Bulletin of the Science Fiction Writers of America* 1970–1991, *Isaac Asimov's Science Fiction Magazine* 1977–1992, *Fantasy and Science Fiction* 1987–, *Magazine of Fantasy and Science Fiction* 1949–1987, *Science Fiction Chronicle* 1979–, *Science Fiction Review* 1975–1986, *Science-Fiction Studies* 1973–, *SFWA Bulletin* 1965–1969.

University Publications of America, 4520 East-West Highway, Bethesda, MD 20814-3389, offers sometimes incomplete files of the following magazines: *Amazing Stories, Amazing Stories Annual, Amazing Stories Quarterly, Comet, Cosmic Stories, Dynamic Science Stories, Extrapolation, Fantastic Adventures, Miracle Stories, Planet Stories, Science Stories, Science Fiction Quarterly, Science Wonder Stories/Wonder Stories, Science Wonder Quarterly/Wonder Quarterly, Stirring Science Stories, Startling Stories, Thrilling*

Wonder Stories, Extrapolation (series I); *Amazing Science Fiction, Astonishing Stories, Fantastic Stories; Extrapolation* (series II).

Books About SF Magazines

12-36. Ashley, Mike. **The History of the Science Fiction Magazine.** New English Library, 1974–1978. 4 vols.
Volume 1: 1926–1935; Volume: 2 1936–1945; Volume 3: 1946–1955; Volume 4: 1956–1965. Detailed introductions trace the magazines' history; especially valuable for information on British publications. Also includes selected stories (one per year) from the magazines discussed.

12-37. Berger, Albert I. **The Magic That Works: John W. Campbell and the American Response to Technology.** Borgo, 1993.
Careful study of what Campbell did and the context in which he worked. Extremely valuable. Also annotated as [9-29].

12-38. Carter, Paul. **The Creation of Tomorrow: Fifty Years of Magazine Science Fiction.** Columbia Univ. Press, 1977.
Information about the magazines themselves only in passing, but a thoughtful tracing of themes and motifs in SF stories in the magazines. Also annotated as [8-34]. For a more general perspective on SF magazines as one of many types, see the authoritative study by John Tebbel and Mary Ellen Zuckerman, *The Magazine in America, 1741–1990* (Oxford, 1991).

12-39. Gammell, Leon L. **The Annotated Guide to Startling Stories.** Starmont, 1986.
Basic information is available in Miller et al. [12-41], but this is valuable for listing which "novels" were later reprinted under different titles.

12-40. Greenland, Colin. **The Entropy Exhibition: Michael Moorcock and the British 'New Wave' in Science Fiction.** Routledge, 1983.
SF as exploring innerspace, turning away from hardware. What *New Worlds* accomplished, why it was resisted, whether it "failed." Also annotated as [8-61].

*12-41. Miller, Stephen T. and William G. Contento. **Science Fiction, Fantasy & Weird Magazine Index: 1890–1990.** Garland, 1995? 3 vols.
Because much of SF appeared only in magazines prior to about 1950, industrious fans prepared many indexes, beginning with Donald Day's pioneering *Index to the Science Fiction Magazines, 1926–1950* (1952: rev.

1982). Authoritative, detailed descriptions of all such indexes can be found in a chapter in Burgess [7-11]. Essentially superseding all these earlier indexes, this labor of love indexes more than 11,000 issues of 767 magazines, from the well-known to the rare or obscure one-shots known only to the most devoted collectors. Indexing was done directly from the issues themselves, and coverage is deliberately inclusive. Much new information is provided, such as previously unknown pseudonyms. Volumes will provide access by author, story title, and magazine contents, issue by issue, with full pagination. Vital for the handful of libraries whose magazine holdings are described in chapter 14, as well as selected university and public libraries and a handful of collectors. Important for anyone at all interested in the history of SF or the development of particular writers. A major achievement.

12-42. Rogers, Alva. **A Requiem for Astounding.** Advent, 1964.

Descriptive summary, issue by issue, story by story, 1930–1960, with some commentary about editorial policy, and so forth. See also Panshin [8-101].

12-43. Rosheim, David L. **Galaxy Magazine: The Dark and the Light Years.** Advent, 1986.

Descriptive summary, in efficient but plodding prose. Some efforts to add social context and comments from the people who produced the magazine.

12-44. Sampson, Robert. **Yesterday's Faces: A Study of Series Characters in the Early Pulp Magazines.** Bowling Green State Univ. Popular Press, 1983–1993.

First projected as a four-volume set, this work kept expanding, the sixth volume appearing after Sampson's death. More evocative than critical, savoring descriptions of pulp heroes and villains in action. Volume 2, *Strange Days* (1984) is of special interest; covers several "scientific detectives," Edgar Rice Burroughs's major characters, and E. E. Smith's Skylark of Space series.

12-45. Siegel, Mark. **Hugo Gernsback, Father of Modern Science Fiction: With Essays on Frank Herbert and Bram Stoker.** Borgo, 1988.

Note the subtitle and beware: The section on Gernsback is only 50 pages long. Nevertheless, it is at present the most substantial, readily available piece on Gernsback.

*12-46. Tymn, Marshall B. **Science Fiction, Fantasy, and Weird Fiction Magazines.** Greenwood, 1985.

The basic reference tool for all genre magazines as of 1984. Critical/historical essays for each magazine, including details of publication history, derivative anthologies, etc. Also includes a chapter on academic and major amateur magazines and one on non-English-language magazines.

12-47. Weinberg, Robert. **The Weird Tales Story.** FAX, 1977.

Of peripheral interest, as the title indicates; however, many SF writers also appeared in *Weird Tales*, and the magazine published a considerable amount of SF before and during the establishment of separate genre magazines. This book covers most important aspects of the magazine; of particular interest is the chapter on the letter column, including discussion of whether "interplanetary stories" should be included.

CHAPTER 13

Teaching Science Fiction

Dennis M. Kratz

As the 20th century draws to a close, teachers of science fiction find themselves confronting a situation rich in confusion, uncertainty, and opportunity. Science fiction now occupies a position in the academic world similar to its place in American culture. As James Gunn points out in the introduction to this volume, science fiction is currently in what we might call a "transitional" period, retaining its status as a minority literature while moving toward a new status as a significant part of everybody's experience.

Science fiction as an academic subject seems equally in transition. On one hand it has gained unprecedented acceptance as a field of study. SF courses are offered in many universities; conferences address works and issues of SF; and textbooks devoted to literature in general regularly include at least one work of SF. Indeed, never have more books or journal articles devoted to SF been published. In education, however, SF does not seem to be moving toward being a part of everyone's experience. On the contrary, it remains undeniably a minor and marginal part of the school and university curriculum. Many academics still regard SF as a lesser, even subliterary form of genre fiction. One troubling development in particular illustrates this marginal existence: the shrinking budgets of the past decade have led to a decline in the number of science fiction courses being offered in both secondary and higher education.

So what do we do now? No group is better suited by temperament and training, it seems to me, to confront uncertainty than readers and teachers of science fiction. The goal of this chapter is to help teachers of science fiction—both those new to the profession and those who have been practicing their craft for years—not only to improve their courses but also to find new arguments for the continuation, resurrection, and even the introduction of courses. The discussion primarily concerns courses devoted entirely to SF, but I hope that it will prove useful also to those teaching "units" of SF within other courses.

The first question facing anyone who is reading this chapter because he or she offers (or plans to offer) a course in science fiction is obvious: why? The answer will guide both the selection of material and the approach to it. It will guide the kinds of examinations, papers, and projects assigned. Like many of my colleagues, I construct my course from a belief in what Donald Lawler calls "the potential good effects upon the human imagination of science fiction and fantasy literature."[1] Most of us would add our conviction that SF can have an equally positive effect on our students' intellects (assuming that the two faculties of thought are inextricably intertwined).

Given the nature and the transitional status of science fiction, the instructor who dares to offer a course faces unusual challenges. Consider the students, for example. SF courses usually attract students ranging from those who have read a great deal of SF to those innocent (maybe even wary) of the genre. Some come attracted by popular films and television programs. In addition, college classes often mix students with a background in literature but little science and science students neither versed in nor accustomed to literary criticism.

This situation can be turned to instructional advantage. Many of the ideas presented in this chapter come from instructors who have developed ways to merge the different interests of students. The general principle is rather simple: positive discomfort. Science fiction almost inevitably involves some form of intellectual or cognitive displacement. Since many characters of SF will be encountering strange circumstances and ideas that force them to rethink their assumptions about the universe and themselves, it seems only fair to lure the students into experiencing, even enjoying similar encounters. I have found it particularly useful to form discussion groups where differing perspectives can lure the participants to a deeper and more complex understanding. In these groups I try to mix, after considering the particular work and idea under discussion, science and humanities students, long-time and neophyte readers, men and women. Much-taught shorter works such as "Flowers for Algernon" and "The Cold Equations" as well as complex novels like *Neuromancer* [4-184] and *Timescape* [4-46] are especially suited to this approach.

Most science fiction courses are designed to address three intertwined topics: the history of SF, what we might call the "esthetics" of SF, and SF as a means of philosophic examination. Some instructors stress SF as a form of literature; others teach it primarily as a means of exploring the implications of science and technology for human values; some base their courses on the role of the SF writer in creating alternative visions of society in order to comment on present values. Here is the outline of a current university course blending various aspects:

Science Fiction

I. Introduction: The Nature, History, and Themes of
   Science Fiction
   A. Some Stories and Ways to Read Them
   B. The History of SF
      1. *Frankenstein* to Gernsback
      2. The "Golden Age" of American SF
      3. The 1960s to the Present
II. The Dangerous Search for Knowledge
III. Rethinking Time
IV. The Alien
   A. Mutation and Manipulation
   B. Life on/From Other Planets
   C. A Blurred Boundary: The Living Machine
V. Conclusion: Science Fiction and the Implications of
   Change

Alternatives abound. The instructor might choose to arrange readings in a historical pattern, allowing the themes to emerge or provide a list of possible themes for the students to perceive. Or the instructor may design the course around the permutations of one specific theme.

One effective thematic approach to SF utilizes the "Frankenstein" effect, that is, the tendency of scientific or technological developments to have unforeseen results. The recent scientific interest in chaos theory could form an interesting complement to stories that explore this theme.

One intriguing pair of novels might be H. G. Wells's *The Island of Dr. Moreau* [1-100] and Michael Crichton's *Jurassic Park* [4-120]. Both explore scientific attempts to alter the natural course of evolution. Both take place on remote islands, and both directly address the moral question whether we should do what we can do.

Jack Williamson wisely states in his seminal book *Teaching Science Fiction* [13-16] that the subject can have no "standard" syllabus. SF is too rich and varied to be contained; but the instructor seeking a sample of how others teach SF will find valuable information in the works annotated as Instructional Guides at the conclusion of this essay. Williamson's anthology, for example, contains an illuminating discussion by Patricia Warrick on designing a course around the depiction of computers in SF. In the same book the reader will find advice on designing a course (or portion of a course) on "political" SF. Marshall Tymn's *Science Fiction: A Teacher's Guide and Resource Book* [13-15] contains one valuable essay by Tymn on structuring a course and another, by Lloyd Biggle, Jr., on using current events as the basis for an SF course.

As anyone who teaches SF knows, each of the approaches—historical, esthetic, philosophic—assumes the importance of the others. The history of SF is worth knowing because the genre provides esthetic and intellectual excitement; the pleasures of reading SF require an understanding of its history, particularly its origins and early development; and the primary pleasure of SF, especially in an academic setting, resides in its insistence on dealing with the implications of science and technology in our present and future. The meaning of this mutual dependence for anyone brash enough to teach science fiction is obvious: you will have to become interdisciplinary.

The advice given by Muriel Rogow Becker in the previous edition of *Anatomy of Wonder* still holds true for anyone interested in teaching science fiction. Build a personal reference collection. While the specific texts mentioned in this chapter provide a good beginning, the reader should consult chapters 7–11 for discussion of works of possible use in the classroom or for background reading. Subscribe to at least one academic journal devoted to science fiction. *Extrapolation* [12-20] in particular publishes numerous articles useful for teaching. Subscribe to *Locus* [12-24]; no better source of information about all aspects of SF exists.

If possible, attend at least one conference devoted to science fiction. The annual meetings of the Science Fiction Research Association and the International Association for the Fantastic in the Arts have sessions devoted to teaching. In addition, other academic organizations (for example the Popular Culture Association and the National Council of Teachers of

English) often include sessions on science fiction at their conventions. Perhaps the best advice for any teacher is to attend the Intensive English Institute on the Teaching of Science Fiction offered each July by the University of Kansas Center for the Study of Science Fiction (contact English Department, University of Kansas, Lawrence, KS 66045).

For the instructor interested in the history of science fiction, a range of valuable material is available. Concerning the social history of SF, the following titles are particularly useful: for literary history, Brian Aldiss's *Trillion Year Spree* [8-5]; for a more general illustrated history of the field and the major cultural influences that helped shape it, consult James Gunn's *Alternate Worlds: The Illustrated History of Science Fiction* [8-62]; and for the pulp heritage, still the most insightful source is Paul Carter's *Creation of Tomorrow: Fifty Years of Magazine Science Fiction* [8-34]. An invaluable source of information about every aspect of science fiction is *The Encyclopedia of Science Fiction* by Clute, Nicholls, and Stableford [7-22].

Perhaps the most common element of SF courses is the historical survey of the genre's development. Many instructors prefer to use one or more chronologically arranged anthologies for this aspect of their course. The two most popular and most used historically based anthologies are the first volume of *The Science Fiction Hall of Fame* [3-223] and the SFWA/SFRA anthology [13-23]. The fact that the *SF Hall of Fame* has remained in print so long seems to have given its stories almost a canonical status as essential to the history of American science fiction. Many instructors supplement these anthologies with others—usually either based on stories of a particular era or designed to explore a specific theme. Such anthologies, unfortunately, go out of print rather quickly. Instructors should monitor the various review media for new texts that might be useful.

SF is so vibrant a form of literature that I recommend including a recent "Best of the Year" anthology of the instructor's choice. Finally, I cannot recommend strongly enough including a current issue of one of the major SF magazines in any college SF course. Again, SF is a literature that celebrates the encounter with the new. I have found that students in such a course appreciate reading stories for which there exists no body of critical interpretation.

A problem that has always plagued (and can be counted on to continue to plague) courses in science fiction is that of out-of-print books. Here is one solution for instructors who teach SF on a regular basis. The instructor should develop an inclusive list of essential and desirable texts that he or she plans to use whenever the course is offered. Send or personally distribute this list to local booksellers, explaining that you have a continuing need for multiple reading copies of the books on the list. Without too much trouble you should be able to acquire a supply of used paperbacks that you could then rent to your students at a nominal fee. The rental fee will enable you to recover the expense that you incurred purchasing the books. Any additional money, of course, will go toward replacing books as they wear out.

If the local stores are unlikely to provide a sufficient number of the desired books, request free catalogs from national SF used book dealers. For example, Pandora's Books, Neche, ND 58265, provides free catalogs that list thousands of paperbacks, and some hardcovers at reasonable prices. Consider placing a standing order (at a negotiated maximum price) for copies of the books on your "essential" list. This solution should enable the instructor to teach a few essential texts regularly and at a negligible cost to students. I have personally implemented this suggestion and found the local dealers extremely receptive.

Most courses are either based on or at least include an approach to SF as a form of literature. What approach is most likely to evoke the most productive response from students? This issue has evoked a long debate among scholars in the field. Every instructor, of course, has an obligation to be aware of not only the most recent trends in criticism but also the critical tradition that has developed since the emergence of SF as an academic subject. Not surprisingly, some of the most insightful discussions of SF have come from writers themselves; some of the worst, from academic critics.

Above all, the instructors I contacted in preparing to write this chapter emphasized (rightly!) that SF in the classroom must be (a) enjoyable and (b) intellectually provocative. The instructor's "approach" should keep this fact constantly in mind. Remember, whatever text you are reading in class, people have bought and are reading on their own. Indeed, at my university I regularly encounter a problem unique to my courses in SF and fantasy. The books sell out before all those enrolled in the class can buy them. Other students see the SF titles (presumably after buying far more expensive textbooks) and purchase them before my students can get to them.

Inevitably the instructor will encounter the issue of definition. On the one hand, students will ask for a definition. On the other hand, SF is too protean and interesting a form of narrative to allow a single definition. That debate is not likely to end as long as there are academicians. One approach is to separate science fiction from fantasy and distinguish both from so-called realist literature. Another sees SF as the midpoint between fantasy and realism, embracing elements of both. I have based my courses on the idea of science fiction as "fantasy made plausible through the rhetoric of science." The diversity of available definitions (often contradictory) can be presented on a handout for students. Here too disagreement serves as a positive model. I have found that such handouts spark valuable interest and comments. Students can then read stories with the various definitions in mind to discover what scholarly perspectives offer more productive insights. Instead of discovering the "best" definition, they learn to think about the limitations of definition for any form of creative expression.

However we define SF, it is necessary for the instructor to recognize that the term embraces a spectrum of work ranging from serious literature to formulaic entertainment. In his introduction to *Nebula Awards 26*, James Morrow draws a distinction, perhaps seriously, between what he labels genuine SF, the "witty and subversive vision" of authors he respects, and sci-fi, "a branch of second-rate children's literature."[2] The diversity of SF—from space opera to philosophic fable—coupled with its double life as a branch of literature and a branch of popular fiction can be an advantage. For an interesting and provocative discussion of how to blend "high" and "popular" treatments of a theme, I recommend Harriett Hawkins's *Classics and Trash* [13-10]. Hawkins offers especially useful insights into the complementary use of film, television, and literary versions of the same theme.

No course in SF can ignore the mass media. During the past decade, in particular, film and television have played the major role in bringing science fiction to the attention of the public. Many major works of fiction have been made into films, and television versions of such important stories as "It's a *Good* Life," "The Cold Equations," and "Overdrawn at the Memory Bank" are available. Above all, I must emphasize that with the advent of videotape, theatrical films have ceased to be expensive or a frill. They are essential.

The most obvious use is to examine comparative versions of a novel and its film or television translation. Remakes of the same film place in sharp relief the way that science fiction portrays the present while seeming to portray the future. (The two versions of *Invasion of the Body Snatchers* work especially well.) Film also provides excellent examples of recurring science fiction themes. To illustrate the recurring contrast between the adventurous spirit and the fear of change, for example, an instructor can show scenes of opposition to space travel in *Things to Come* and *When Worlds Collide.*

Other instructors have confirmed my experience that students enjoy and learn from watching television programs and movies for examples of themes and techniques being examined in the class. The *Star Trek* series abounds in such examples, and the students gain a strong sense of involvement in the course when they bring them to the attention of the instructor and their classmates. (Consider assigning, in addition to or in place of a traditional paper, a journal of such SF reading/watching.) Again, videotape makes the use of these clips extremely easy.

For instructors wary of beginning with a definition, another entrance into science fiction involves simply reading one or more brief stories to the class as an introduction and eliciting from students their opinions as to whether (and how) the story is "science fiction." For example, in the very short story, by Dannie Plachta, "The Man From When" (reprinted in *World's Best Science Fiction:* 1967), a man relaxing in his home hears a loud noise outside. When he gets up to investigate he finds a a stranger at his door. The stranger turns out to be a time traveler with good and bad news: he has proved the possibility of time travel, but the expenditure of energy destroyed the Earth of his time. "Do you think the risk was worth it?" he asks his host. The host's answer, after learning that the visitor has traveled from eighteen minutes in the future is "no."

Brief as it is (a mere three pages), the story offers an introduction to several elements associated with science fiction: the encounter with an event that shatters a character's notion of what is possible, a scientific "explanation" of sorts for the event, and—at the core of the narrative—a question. The genre has produced a multitude of stories that would work as well.

The multilayered nature of science fiction invites a variety of instructional approaches. Several instructors with whom I have corresponded share my enthusiasm for what might best be called an "interactive" approach. This approach emerges from the desire to use SF as a means of enhancing students' imaginative and intellectual abilities. It reflects the eminently sensible advice of Inspector Dupin in Poe's "The Purloined Letter": to catch a thief one must learn to think like a thief. Ender Wiggin, hero of Orson Scott Card's novel *Ender's Game* [4-92], expresses a similar view while discussing the reasons for his ability to emerge victorious in the simulated war games of his military training: "Every time, I've won because I could understand the way my enemy thought. From what they *did* I could tell what they thought I was doing, how they wanted the battle to take shape. And I played off to that. I'm very good at that. Understanding how other people think."[3] I certainly do not want to adopt the metaphor of education as a battle. Our goal is to evoke appreciation and contemplation. Indeed, Ender goes on to argue that understanding nurtures affection: "And it came down to this: In the moment when I truly understand my enemy, understand him well enough to defeat him, then in that very moment I also love him. I think it's impossible to really understand somebody, what they want, what they believe, and not love them the way they love themselves."[4] One of the more positive developments in literary criticism urges a similar outlook—while taking the perspective of reading as an implied conversation between friends rather than a confrontation of foes.[5]

It follows from this perspective that to appreciate science fiction (or any form of creative expression) we must learn to think like an artist. To respond with intelligence to a science fiction narrative, we must think science-fictionally. What characterizes this mode of thought? And how can we as instructors nurture it in our students?

The most obvious source for information about the way science fiction writers think is the writer of science fiction. Many writers are willing to speak to classes. Dell Publishing offers, for example, to help bring authors to speak to classes. (Contact Dell Books, 1540 Broadway, New York, NY 10036.) Recent graduates of writing workshops such as Clarion provide intriguing insights into the ways stories are imagined and brought to completion. Other sources remain, including video and audio tape interviews of writers discussing their craft. The teacher may want to use, for example, *Arthur C. Clark: Starglider*, a filmed conversation with the famous author, or the interviews conducted by James Gunn for the series *Literature of Science Fiction*. See the audiovisual aids section for details.

To evoke the fusion of imagination and logical extrapolation that characterizes much science fiction, many instructors have devised exercises for their students. From published sources, material sent by other instructors, and my own experience, I list a few representative exercises:

1. Write a history of the future. Such an exercise, early in the semester, produces a number of useful results. It invites speculative thinking, gives students an idea of the boldness (or perhaps timidity) of their vision, and helps focus attention on what they think "important" enough to include.

2. Write a future history of a current technological feature. This exercise enhances students' abilities to understand how extrapolation works in SF. Some specific concepts that work well include genetic manipulation, computer technology (artificial intelligence) and, in the field of medicine, organ transplantation and the development of artificial organs.

3. A two-part *relativity* exercise: First, identify a repugnant behavior. Second, describe a planet whose environment and history make that behavior acceptable, even desirable. A connected exercise requires a group of students to imagine the environment and evolutionary history of another planet.

4. The following exercises are particularly effective for younger students. Imagine *new words* that will appear in the dictionary 50 (100, etc.) years from now; identify five items from contemporary life that a time traveler from the future would have trouble understanding.

For many instructors, the attempt to write science fiction plays an integral role in any class. For this reason I have annotated several writing guides. Even if writing does not play a role in your course, such guides (particularly since they are written by writers) provide additional insights into the creative thinking that created the stories the class is reading.

An intriguing recent development in SF is the franchise novel (also called "shared world" fiction). Such fiction is remarkably valuable in a classroom setting. The instructor, in conjunction with all or some students, can establish the outlines of a world. Another planet, an alternate universe, and a future Earth are three examples that work well. Students can then either imagine problems or write a series of connected stories that explore themes being discussed in class in the context of that specific world.

Given the idea-based nature of science fiction, instructors at every level (from elementary through graduate school) use stories as springboards for philosophic and moral explorations by the students. For example, a high school teacher assigns "The Veldt" (included in *The Stories of Ray Bradbury* [3-33]), which concerns the addictive powers of a room that can reproduce in sight, sound, and smell any place that a person can imagine. The students are then asked to imagine such a room waiting for them at home. How will they respond? Another instructor gives creative assignments called "interventions" or "variations," which involve extending or giving a new ending to stories.[6] Another approach involves allowing students to read only a portion of a story (or assigning only a portion), then asking them to enter a dialogue with what they have written and provide a range of possible continuations.

These exercises bring us naturally to the nature of science fiction as idea-based fiction. "While teaching a nine-week mini-course in science fiction and fantasy literature," writes a high school teacher, "I made an important discovery: this 'sub-genre' can be used to stimulate philosophical inquiry, that is, the ability to think critically and to make connections among disciplines."[7] In addition to the widely appreciated ability of science fiction to evoke thought about science and technology, it has become perhaps the most powerful medium to explore two issues currently at the center of curriculum reform in America: multiculturalism and gender issues. Courses or portions of courses using the medium of science fiction to explore these issues could mark a major contribution to American education in this decade. A course or unit based on gender issues might begin with *The Left Hand of Darkness* [4-254], which deals specifically with the impact of gender on thinking. The list of SF stories that deal directly with gender relations is long and varied. Works by Joanna Russ (for example, "When It Changed") and James Tiptree, Jr., (for example, "Houston, Houston, Do You Read?" and "The Screwfly Solution") come immediately to mind.

The encounter with the alien serves as an obvious and powerful metaphor for the engagement of differing cultures. Is the Other a threat to be conquered or another intelligence to be understood? I have found Octavia Butler's "Bloodchild" (1984; anthologized in *The New Hugo Winners* [1989], ed. by Isaac Asimov and others and in *Science Fiction: The SFRA Anthology* [13-23]) a provocative introduction to this theme. Obviously a novel like *Enemy Mine* [4-266] is appropriate, as are shorter stories ranging from John W. Campbell, Jr.'s "Who Goes There?" to Stanley Weinbaum's "A Martian Odyssey."

Finally, it is possible to build SF on the theme of "cognitive displacement," that is, the confrontation with a new idea or situation that demands a radical restructuring of our intellectual framework. This engagement of the new has long been recognized as a basic component of SF, however we define the genre. It deserves, therefore, to figure prominently in our teaching. Characters from works I have already mentioned can serve as positive models for students: Ender Wiggin, who learns that the aliens whom he destroyed were far from the intransigent enemies he has been led to believe, and Genly Ai in *The Left Hand of Darkness*.

In a landmark study, the psychologist William Perry demonstrated that students bring different attitudes and strategies to the classroom.[8] At one extreme, they see their role as discovering the "correct" answer that the professor knows but is hiding. Perry argues that a major function of the educator is to help students rise from this perspective to a more sophisticated conception of learning: to create for themselves a provisional interpretation among the many valid responses that are possible, always willing to revise that vision in light of new evidence, always willing to see the same event (text, problem) from a new perspective. SF, with the fusion of imaginative and analytical thinking required to create and respond to its narratives, seems uniquely suited to that task.

Teaching SF should be, as Gunn suggests, a daring act. It dares to explore the intersection of science and the humanities. It dares to deal directly with the inevitability (and desirability) of change. By exploring encounters with the alien and the Other, SF dares examine the essential issue of the humanities: What is it to be human? SF can move students to more sophisticated and complex readings of themselves and their world. The margin is no place for such a subject.

Notes

I wish to express my gratitude to a number of individuals for their help in preparing this chapter. Ruth Southard, associate director for Media Services of the University of Texas at Dallas Library, provided invaluable bibliographic information about audiovisual aids. The following colleagues shared with me, by letter and in person, their ideas about teaching SF: Muriel Rogow Becker, Barbara Bengels, Edra Bogle, James Gunn, Willis McNelly, Charles J. Pecor, David Samelson, Margaret Senatore, and Gary Westfahl.

1. Donald Lawler, "Certain Assistances: The Utilities of Speculative Fiction in Shaping the Future," *Mosaic* 13 (1980): 1.

2. James Morrow, "Introduction," *Nebula Awards 26* (Harcourt, 1992), p. xi.

3. Orson Scott Card, *Ender's Game* [4-92], pp. 260–61.

4. Ibid., p. 261.

5. For a discussion of the author as implied friend and the implications of this perspective for reading, see Wayne Booth, *The Company We Keep: An Ethics of Fiction* (Univ. of Chicago Press, 1988); on reading as a fusion of critical and creative thinking that attempts to recreate the process of writing, see Dennis M. Kratz and Peggy Brown, "Ways of Seeing Ways of Reading," *Translation Review* 24/25 (1987): 13–20.

6. James Prothero, "Fantasy, Science Fiction, and the Teaching of Values," *English Journal* (March 1990): 32–34.

7. Mitch Cox, "Engendering Critical Literacy Through Science Fiction and Fantasy," *English Journal* (March 1990): 35–37.

8. William G. Perry, Jr., *Forms of Intellectual and Ethical Development in the College Years* (Holt, Rinehart and Winston, 1970).

Bibliography

Instructional Guides

13-1. Allen, L. David. **The Ballantine Teachers' Guide to Science Fiction.** Ballantine, 1975.
This still-useful study offers analyses from a teacher's perspective of thirteen novels and two anthologies. Among the novels examined are *Dragonflight, Childhood's End, Fahrenheit 451, Rendezvous With Rama,* and *Ringworld.* Each analysis begins with a plot summary, then discusses important themes within the narrative. The postreading "topics and projects" sections are disappointing. The introduction is based on a four-part categorization (hard SF, soft SF, science fantasy, and fantasy) that might confuse students. Similar works by Allen, also out of print, are *Science Fiction: An Introduction* (Cliffs Notes, 1973) and *Science Fiction Reader's Guide* (Centennial Press, 1974).

13-2. Amelio, Ralph J. **HAL in the Classroom: Science Fiction Films.** Plaum, 1974.
A collection of nine essays, all originally published elsewhere, along with an annotated list of SF films and articles useful for teachers. The essays vary in quality. Frank McConnell's study of *The Creature From the Black Lagoon* and R. C. Dale's interpretation of *King Kong* should help instructors seeking topics for classroom discussion. The introduction is disappointingly vague. For the best general introduction to film in the classroom see Brooks Landon's chapter "Science Fiction in the Movies" in Tymn's teacher's guide [13-15].

13-3. Behrendt, Stephen C., ed. **Approaches to Teaching Shelley's Frankenstein.** Modern Language Association, 1990.
Highly recommended both as a guide to *Frankenstein* itself and as a stimulus for college instructors to develop similar collections for other SF novels. The essays examine *Frankenstein* from a wide range of perspectives, the majority with insight and intelligence but some with a heavy dose of jargon. Reading this book will not only enhance the instructor's understanding of the novel but also provide valuable topics for class discussion.

13-4. Brant-Kemezis, Ann. **Fahrenheit 451 Curriculum Unit.** Center for Learning (Box 910, Villa Marie, PA 16155), 1991.
Designed for high school teachers, this guide offers a wide range of suggested activities to enhance not only students' understanding of

Bradbury's challenging novel but also their ability to read in general. The activities address both the critical and the creative thinking necessary to respond to SF. Particularly valuable are the group projects. Bradbury's "coda" to the novel (a complaint against censorship) is included. Highly recommended, even for college instructors seeking ways to lure students into more enthusiastic involvement. The exercises can be adapted to other texts.

13-5.   Carratello, John, and Patty Carratello. **Literature and Critical Thinking: Fantasy and Science Fiction.** Teacher Created Materials (Box 1214, Huntington Beach, CA 92647), 1990.

Designed for grades 4–6, *Literature and Critical Thinking* offers teaching units for six excellent novels for the younger reader, of which two (*The Martian Chronicles* [3-32] and Pamela Service's *Stinker From Space*, 1988) are SF. The classroom activities are imaginative and enticing, aimed at enhancing students' ability to read and their pleasure in reading.

13-6.   Carratello, John, and Patty Carratello. **A Wrinkle in Time: Literature Unit.** Teacher Created Materials (Box 1214, Huntington Beach, CA 92647), 1991.

This book, devoted to *A Wrinkle in Time* [5-95], is a treasure trove of instructional ideas. It contains pre-reading activities, a plot summary, lesson plans, and suggested projects. It has the same virtues as the Carratellos' curriculum guide annotated above. Highly recommended.

*13-7.   Donelson, Kenneth, ed. **Science Fiction in the English Class.** NCTE, 1972.

This older, out-of-print collection will repay the effort of finding it. Reprinted from a special issue of the *Arizona English Bulletin*, it contains 19 articles on various aspects of teaching SF. Teachers of middle and high school students will find the essays particularly useful. Several outline curriculum units (for example, on the utopian/dystopian vision) while others offer practical advice on using films and old radio programs in the classroom. The general essays on SF have been supplanted by those in Tymn [13-15], but the instruction-based articles still offer a reservoir of ideas for the teacher to adopt and transform.

13-8.   Dubeck, Leroy W., Suzanne E. Moshier, and Judith E. Boss. **Science in Cinema: Teaching Science Fact Through Science Fiction Films.** Teachers College Press, 1988.

If used cautiously, a valuable source for instructors who teach any of the ten films discussed in detail by the authors, among them *Forbidden Planet,*

Them! and *The Day the Earth Stood Still.* Each discussion includes a plot summary, explanation of any scientific principles depicted, a scientific and literary "commentary," and some suggested classroom activities. The information about the scientific underpinning is welcome. Be warned, however. The book was written to serve as a companion to a course that uses science fiction films "as educational tools to build interest in and awareness of 'real' science." This restricted perspective leads the authors to label any deviation from current scientific practice or knowledge an error. It also results in unappreciative, often misleading interpretations of the films. Occasionally could be used as example of how not to read SF.

*13-9. Gunn, James. **Inside Science Fiction: Essays on Fantastic Literature.** Borgo, 1992.
This admirable collection of essays, all originally published elsewhere, is essential reading for every SF teacher. Gunn has made major contributions as a writer, critic, and teacher of SF. Four of the eighteen essays are clustered in the category "SF and the Teacher." Although the essays contain much practical advice, they offer something more valuable to the novice and experienced instructor alike: an insight into the overall philosophy that has guided Gunn's teaching over the years. Think of this book as a conversation with a Master Teacher. Also annotated as [8-63].

13-10. Hawkins, Harriett. **Classics and Trash: Traditions and Taboos in High Literature and Popular Modern Genres.** Univ. of Toronto Press, 1990.
The pulp origins of American SF often pose a problem for instructors. What if, Hawkins asks, all traditionally canonized works of literature were suddenly eliminated from every syllabus? Would not similar problems of priority, hierarchy, and comparable value arise with whatever works replaced them? She then offers a thoughtful discussion of these issues. Hawkins not only explores linkages that connect high and popular forms of art but also suggests ways of using those linkages to enliven contemporary education. Of particular value is her discussion comparing the depiction of heroism versus villainy. Recommended because it shows how a problem could become a strength of SF in the classroom.

13-11. Other Worlds: Fantasy and Science Fiction. *English Journal,* (March 1990), 25–46.
This admirable collection of four essays gives practical advice on a wide range of teaching issues. Anthony Wolk and James Prothero, in separate essays, both give valuable advice to instructors who wish to use "creative writing" assignments in SF courses. In an essay addressed to high school

teachers, Mitch Cox discusses the use of SF to stimulate discussion of philosophic questions. Finally Jane Donawerth describes her experience teaching SF by and about women. Her analysis of specific stories, combined with suggestions for teaching them, makes this an especially informative essay. Recommended for all teachers.

13-12.   Parrinder, Patrick. **Science Fiction: Its Criticism and Teaching.** Methuen, 1980.

Despite the title, Parrinder devotes only one brief chapter to teaching SF. The teacher should find his remarks on "consolidation and canon-formation" useful, if somewhat dated. More valuable are the implications for instruction to be found in the chapter on the style of SF titled "Imitation and Novelty: An Approach Through SF Language." Also annotated as [8-103].

13-13.   Smith, Johanna M., ed. **Frankenstein: Case Studies in Contemporary Criticism.** St. Martin's, 1992.

An excellent companion to Behrend's *Approaches to Teaching Frankenstein* [13-3], this book provides both a clear history of *Frankenstein* criticism and five essays representing different critical approaches: reader-response, psychoanalytic, feminist, Marxist, and cultural. Each essay defines its particular perspective, then applies that perspective to a reading of the text. Teachers will be able to use the complementary and occasionally conflicting assessments to good advantage. A glossary of terms (including those coined in the past decade for some of the new theoretical positions) is included.

*13-14. Spann, Sylvia, and Mary Beth Culp, eds. **Thematic Units in Teaching English and the Humanities.** NCTE, 1975, 1977, 1980.

An extremely valuable source for the high school teacher. The essay in the first volume, "The Future Arrives Before the Present Has Left," by Jane Everest, is especially recommended. It provides a clear and transferable approach to designing an SF unit for the high school class. An appendix suggests discussion questions for seven SF novels (most still being taught): *I, Robot* [3-13], *Childhood's End* [3-44], *The Gods Themselves* [4-20], *2001: A Space Odyssey* [4-110], *Planet of the Apes* [3-26], *Brave New World* [2-56], and *The Martian Chronicles* [3-32]. The projects and supplementary assignments retain their usefulness even after twenty years, and the guides are well worth searching for in libraries or from out-of-print dealers.

*13-15. Tymn, Marshall, ed. **Science Fiction: A Teacher's Guide and Resource Book.** Starmont, 1988.

A valuable work, especially for the beginning SF teacher. Tymn's brief introduction gives clear answers to some very basic concerns of the teacher designing a first course in SF. The text is divided into three sections. "Backgrounds" offers four essays on the history of SF as well as general discussions of children's SF, the fan movement, and films. A section of "Resources" offers annotated lists of essential reference texts. The final section, "Applications," includes general advice on structuring an SF course and a thoughtful essay by Lloyd Biggle, Jr., on how to connect SF to current events.

*13-16. Williamson, Jack, ed. **Teaching Science Fiction: Education for Tomorrow.** Owlswick, 1980.
Essential reading for every SF teacher at every level. The major section of the book consists of fourteen practical examples of teaching SF. For example, Robert Myers shows how to integrate philosophy and SF into a course, while Martin Greenberg and Joseph Olander take the reader through the design of a course on political SF. In addition, seven introductory essays discuss the origins of SF in the overall context of American culture. The value of the book resides in part in the breadth of its contributors' experience. Chapters by writers, scholars, teachers, an artist, and a publisher are included. Although it was published in 1980, and was still in print in 1993, only the bibliographies of this outstanding volume are dated. This is an essential work for any teacher or scholar interested in SF.

13-17. Wymer, Thomas L., ed. **Intersections: The Elements of Fiction in Science Fiction.** Bowling Green State Univ. Popular Press, 1978.
Although somewhat dated and out of print, this little book will prove useful to SF teachers who wish to use the traditional categories of literary criticism to analyze SF stories. After a brief introduction to SF, the authors devote a chapter to each of the following: plot, character, setting, point of view, language, tone, theme, and symbolism. Fortunately, many of the stories discussed are taken from the *Science Fiction Hall of Fame* [3-223], which is still widely used in SF courses.

Writing Guides

*13-18. Bretnor, Reginald, ed. **The Craft of Science Fiction.** Harper, 1976.
Included as much for its historical importance as for the insights it offers into current SF. The most valuable essays are those by Hal Clement (on the fictional use of technology and science), Jerry Pournelle (on constructing believable alternate societies), and Poul Anderson (on his specialty: adapting epics and sagas to new uses). A good supplementary text

for teachers who wish, as part of a survey of SF, to give students a feel for the state of the field in the 1970s.

*13-19. Card, Orson Scott. **How to Write Science Fiction and Fantasy.** Writer's Digest, 1990.

Card, who has won both the Nebula and Hugo awards for his fiction, provides a remarkably clear explanation of how to construct an SF story. He begins by situating both SF and fantasy in the larger context of speculative fiction (that is, all stories that take place in a setting contrary to known reality). He then takes the reader through the steps of creating a world, constructing a story, writing well, and even selling one's fiction. His concept of the MICE quotient (milieu, idea, character, event) is especially useful. Card provides invaluable insights into the intertwined arts of writing and reading SF. His book could serve as the main text in a course on writing and a supplementary text for any SF (or general fiction) course. Hugo winner, 1991

13-20. de Camp, L. Sprague, and Catherine Crook de Camp. **Science Fiction Handbook, Revised.** Owlswick Press, 1975.

The second edition of *Anatomy of Wonder* said of this handbook that it "continues to offer aspiring SF writers practical information about both the creative and the business aspects of writing SF." For business matters the reader is better served by more recent handbooks such as those by Card [13-19] and Dozois [13-21]. The essays still offer strong insights into the thinking that creates good fiction. The McGraw-Hill reprint is more likely to be found than the Owlswick edition.

*13-21. Dozois, Gardner, Tina Lee, and Stanley Schmidt, eds. **Writing Science Fiction and Fantasy: Twenty Dynamic Essays by Today's Top Professionals.** St. Martin's, 1991.

Although some of the twenty essays that comprise this excellent anthology were published previously, this is the best "new" comprehensive guide to writing and selling SF available. Contributors include writers and editors. The advice is divided into three areas: storytelling, ideas and foundations, and the business of writing. The last section is particularly well done. Especially recommended among the "creative" essays are Connie Willis on writing comedy and Stanley Schmidt's "Seeing Your Way to Better Stories." Teachers will find the various authors' comments on how they write very useful for getting students to think about productive ways of reading fiction.

*13-22. Longyear, Barry B. **Science Fiction Writer's Workshop: An Introduction to Fiction Mechanics.** Owlswick, 1980.

While most writing guides talk about the craft of writing, this essential book emphasizes practical exercises. Any SF teacher seeking to offer a writing workshop or to incorporate creative writing into a course should consult it. Longyear's "direct, illustrated approach" can be adapted for use in high school and college courses. Still in print in 1993.

*13-23. Warrick, Patricia, Charles G. Waugh, and Martin H. Greenberg, eds. **Science Fiction: The Science Fiction Research Association Anthology.** Harper and Row, 1988.

Along with the first volume of the *Science Fiction Hall of Fame* [13-223], the most popular anthology among college teachers. The stories are arranged chronologically from Nathaniel Hawthorne's "Birthmark" to Octavia Butler's "Bloodchild." Although it contains no teaching apparatus or suggestions, the alternate grouping of stories by theme (biological, technological, environmental, and psychosocial) is useful. The presence of H. G. Wells's "The Star" and E. M. Forster's "The Machine Stops" is especially welcome for the teacher trying to indicate the 19th-century roots of SF. The period from 1930–1960 is represented with such classic (and highly teachable) stories as Campbell's "Who Goes There?" and Stanley Weinbaum's "A Martian Odyssey." The selection of more recent SF, particularly by women authors, is a strong feature of the text. Such stories as Joanna Russ's "When It Changed," James Tiptree, Jr.'s "Houston, Houston, Do You Read?" and "Bloodchild" evoke strong, thoughtful response from students. A revised edition was in the planning stage in 1994.

13-24. Wilson, Robin Scott, ed. **Those Who Can: A Science Fiction Reader.** Mentor, 1973.

Long out of print, this text will reward the effort of finding it. The text is built around each of the traditional elements of fiction: plot, character, setting, theme, point of view, and style. For each element two widely known and respected authors (among them Delany, Ellison, Gunn, Le Guin, Pohl, and Russ) provide a story and a critical analysis of that element in the story. The discussions are valuable not only for courses on writing but also for any course on SF in which the instructor wishes the class to explore the way writers think. Compare the design of Wymer [13-17].

Textbooks and Anthologies

Most instructors use anthologies in their courses. The following include some of the most valuable for classroom use. Where an anthology is fully annotated elsewhere, comments are restricted to features relevant to its use for teaching. Only the most important out-of-print anthologies are included.

*13-25. Gunn, James, ed. **The Road to Science Fiction.** Mentor, 1977, 1979, 1982. 4 vols.

The best historical anthology of SF ever assembled. A teacher's guide, by Gunn and Stephen H. Goldman, was published for volumes 1–3. The guide poses questions concerning each story, discussions valuable for teachers, and suggestions on using the stories in thematic rather than chronological sequence. An essential acquisition for anyone interested in SF. Unfortunately, the series is no longer in print in English (a German translation is in print) but the teacher should obtain a copy for reference purposes.

13-26. Hipple, Theodore W., and Robert G. Wright, eds. **The Worlds of Science Fiction.** Allyn and Bacon, 1979.

Out-of-print. The editors include a thoughtful discussion on teaching short fiction to middle school and high school students. By explaining how they grouped stories thematically, they give insight into other kinds of groupings. Worth consulting by any high school teacher looking for well-conceived prereading and postreading activities that can be transferred to other SF stories.

13-27. Hollister, Bernard, ed. **You and Science Fiction.** National Textbook, 1976.

Like Hipple [13-26], this fine textbook retains its value as a model for presenting stories to high school students. Hollister links the stories in his anthology with provocative questions that belong in any literature course at any level: Who am I? What kind of society do I want? What kind of world do I seek? A discussion ("projection") precedes and questions ("probes") follow each tale. The stories are well chosen. The major authors (Bradbury, Simak, Pohl among them) are represented, but the stories are not the usual ones found in anthologies. The decision to include Daphne Du Maurier's "The Birds" is a masterstroke. Hope for this book's return to print. Meanwhile, it is well worth consulting by any teacher planning a high school SF course or unit.

*13-28. Silverberg, Robert, ed. **Science Fiction Hall of Fame**, Vol. 1. Doubleday, 1970.
Fully annotated as [3-223]. The first volume has remained in print and is one of the two anthologies most used in college courses today. An admirable selection of SF from the 1940s and 1950s. Instructors who take a historical approach will find *The Best of the Nebulas* (1979) edited by Ben Bova works well as a companion volume. A sharply contrasting new anthology is *The Norton Book of Science Fiction* [4-541], which is likely to be used in many classrooms.

13-29. Silverberg, Robert, ed. **The Mirror of Infinity: A Critics' Anthology of Science Fiction.** Harper, 1970.
Like Wilson's *Those Who Can* [13-24], this fine anthology links stories with criticism. In this case distinguished "critics" (among them Clareson and Franklin) provide the commentaries; but most of the critics are also writers of the first rank (for example, Budrys, Knight, and Aldiss). The stories range from Wells's "The Star" and Campbell's "Twilight" to Zoline's "Heat Death of the Universe."

Audiovisual Aids

The rapid development of videotape, along with the emergence of laser disk technology, is revolutionizing the role of audiovisual aids in the classroom. Videotape has essentially replaced the older film and film strip formats. It is more readily accessible, more economical, and in every way easier to use. The laser disk has joined videotape as a valuable instructional tool. Let us hope for the development of laser disk products for teaching SF similar to the *Perseus* project created for teaching classical literature and culture.

Three particularly useful explanatory guides are available in video format. For an insight into the mind of one of the best-known SF writers, instructors should consider *Arthur C. Clarke: Starglider* (Films for the Humanities, Box 2053, Princeton, NJ 08543). A new series from the Roland Collection (3120 Pawtucket Rd., Northbrook, IL 60062) features interviews with a wide range of well-known authors, including J. G. Ballard and Michael Moorcock. For grades 7–12 a useful product is *The Twilight Zone Project* (Sundance, Newtown Rd., Littleton, MA 01460). It combines a videocassette, videoscripts, supplementary activities, and learning guide.

Still the best general introduction to SF is *The Literature of Science Fiction: A Filmed Lecture Series*, available from the University of Kansas AV Center (746 Massachusetts Ave., Lawrence, KS 66044). Made in 1970–1975, this series does have a serious drawback. Contemporary students, accustomed to sophisticated television presentations, may be put off at first by its poor production values. But this problem is more than offset by the opportunity to see and hear John W. Campbell, Jr., Harlan Ellison, Poul Anderson, and others discuss their art.

Video provides an almost limitless supply of feature films and television programs that are important in the history of SF and deal with subjects worthy of extended discussion. Instructors should consult with the media specialist in their school or university about the availability of materials. The following regularly revised reference guides contain indispensable listings of entertainment and educational videos:

Bowker's Complete Video Directory. Bowker, 1994. Volume 1 is devoted to entertainment, with science fiction and fantasy films listed in a genre index. Volumes 2 and 3 list educational and special interest videos. In addition, 15 indexes provide access to the more than 95,000 listed videos.

The Video Source Book. Gale, 1994. Two volumes with an annual supplement, a competitor to the Bowker set.

Educational Film and Video Locator. 4th ed. Bowker, 1990. Two volumes list approximately 52,000 videos and films available for rental from 46 college and university media centers.

In addition, every SF teacher with access to cable television should subscribe, if it is offered, to *The Sci-Fi Channel,* a rich source of films and television programs. Although most are second-rate, the astute watcher can find valuable excerpts for classroom use as well as an occasional pearl. Write the following address for information on licensing off-air copies: Sci-Fi Channel, 1230 Ave. of the Americas, New York, NY 10020, telephone 212-408-9100.

The explosion of the audiocassette "books on tape" industry offers a new resource for SF teaching at every level. Works of fiction (read sometimes by the authors themselves) and interviews with writers are available. Caedmon, Spoken Arts, and the American Audio Prose Library are but three of many labels active in this area. Three forms of sound recording are especially useful: tapes of old radio programs, readings of SF novels/anthologies, and author interviews. The American Audio Prose Library, for example, has an insightful interview with Gene Wolfe as well as a tape of Wolfe reading "The Island of Dr. Death and Other Stories." *Radio's Golden Age of Science Fiction,* a four-tape collection of excerpts from more than 100 SF radio programs is available from Satellite Broadcasting (Box 5364, Rockville, MD 20851).

Instructors should consult *Words On Cassette* (Bowker, annual) to determine the availability of older recordings and the appearance of new recordings in this burgeoning field. This is the most comprehensive listing of audio cassettes and therefore the one indispensable source book. This reference work gives all the information necessary for building a strong audio cassette collection or finding specific titles. It contains more than 59,000 listings. SF and fantasy recordings are listed in a separate subsection.

CHAPTER 14

Research Library Collections of Science Fiction

Randall W. Scott

The first edition of *Anatomy of Wonder* in 1976 included a chapter similar to this one, except that the largest collections listed were the MIT Science Fiction Society Library with 30,000 items, and the Texas A&M University Library, with 13,000 items. The MIT listing now shows 35,000 items, the Texas A&M listing says 30,000, and while these continue to be outstanding collections they are no longer the largest. Science fiction and fantasy collecting has become institutionalized in the past quarter century to a degree we could only dream about in 1970, when most of the collections here were thought of as novelty collections and rather nervously held. Finally we can dispense with comparisons based on mere number of items held, and look at scope, specialties, and institutional support as the more important characteristics of a collection.

As the questionnaire responses for the new edition began arriving, a fairly clear geography of "more excellent" collections emerged. The Eaton Collection at the University of California, Riverside, is the premier collection in the United States, with Texas A&M and Bowling Green State University in Ohio the next two in importance. Canada has several collections, but the outstanding one is the Merril Collection at the Toronto

Public Library. The University of Sydney leads the Australian collections, and the University of Liverpool seems (newly) to be the place to visit in Great Britain. The city of Wetzlar in Germany owns the largest collection reported here, covering all German-language science fiction and fantasy, and the Maison d'Ailleurs in Switzerland has manuscripts of every French-speaking science fiction author. These are all enormous collections, remarkable hoards that rival the great private collections. These collections are good enough that we don't even need to list private collections in this edition. The current generation of researchers will find that most of their needs can be met by a library. They will take this for granted, of course, but it seems necessary to offer one last exclamation of delight that this has happened.

Not one of the very fine collections just mentioned exists in a national library. This is not to imply that the Library of Congress, the British Library, the Bibliothèque Nationale, and the National Library of Australia are not important and legitimate resources for science fiction research. These venerable institutions, however, were established long before science fiction became important to many people. Each collects massively in many areas, but none has developed the monomania for science fiction that is required to build a great collection. The researcher will find that much of value is held by these institutions, but unless the national libraries decide to organize and acquire retrospectively as science fiction specialty libraries, it is likely that the larger collections listed here will better serve our needs. In the United States the Library of Congress is increasingly willing to share primacy with other research libraries, due to budget restrictions and the overdue recognition that one institution cannot be all things to all people. This is probably the way things will continue to develop in years to come.

A fundamental difficulty with brief collection descriptions, such as those that follow, is that no matter how detailed they become they cannot tell a prospective user whether a given item is in a given collection. Yet even as recently as the third edition (1987), these little descriptions were about all we had. The next step was to write or call to get an idea whether a visit would be worth the effort. Times are changing, not suddenly but strikingly. In 1987 we were getting used to the idea that the OCLC network could give us a basic yes/no answer as to whether a book or magazine was held by a research library. We couldn't tell from OCLC whether the item was in a circulating collection, or was currently checked out, or was already stolen, but through the miracle of technology we had a kind of augury to go by. Now in 1993 most research library catalogs can be searched directly from a home or office computer anywhere in the world, and OCLC is no longer a logical option. As a special collections librarian in Michigan, I find that my users come not only from across campus, but from Pennsylvania and Indiana, with printouts that they made at home. They already know that the books are noncirculating, and they know which issues of a magazine are missing, and we don't think of it as a miracle anymore.

Although several of the research libraries described here sent dial-in or E-mail addresses for their catalogs, the situation is still in flux and these instructions and addresses have not been included here. Voice telephone numbers have been given for every collection, and if a library does not appear in the online directory that you use, a phone call will get you the appropriate information.

Two of the collections listed here do not have single locations that can easily be given discrete entries: The Science Fiction Writers of America Depository Program and the Science Fiction Oral History Association Regional Depositories. The SFWA depositories reporting are California State University, Fullerton (until 1986), University of California at Riverside, Northern Illinois University, University of Kansas, Michigan State University, Eastern New Mexico University, University of Dayton, Brigham Young University, University of New Brunswick, and University of Sydney. The SFOHA depositories are University of Kansas, Michigan State University, and Eastern New Mexico University. Most of these libraries have entries below.

The following five collections are active and of great potential value to researchers, but they are not part of supporting institutions and therefore need to be approached differently. Remember that the staff are volunteers.

The American Private Press Association (112 E. Burnett, Stayton, OR 97383. 503-769-6088) is a collection of 200,000 fanzines (primarily dated 1965–1980) and 3,000 letters, with extensive science fiction pulps and magazines. Photocopies available.

Corellian Archives (437 Via Roma, Santa Barbara, CA 93110. 805-967-4961) is an active circulating collection of fanzines, which began with George Lucas's collection of *Star Wars* fanzines, but currently holds material in most areas of fandom.

The Los Angeles Science Fantasy Society Library (11513 Burbank Blvd., North Hollywood, CA 91601. 818-760-9234) is a club collection primarily for members' use, with 12,000 volumes and over 120 magazine titles. Scholar use by appointment.

The MIT Science Fiction Society Library (W20-473 MIT Student Center, 84 Massachusetts Ave., Cambridge, MA 02139. 617-225-6453) is a club collection with a long history and reputation as one of the most complete science fiction magazine collections in North America. Around 35,000 total items. The hours are irregular, mostly evenings. Some material circulates to members, room use only for the public.

The San Francisco Academy of Comic Art (2850 Ulloa St., San Francisco, CA 94116. 415-681-1737) is a private collection of 4.5 million comic strips, with extensive books, magazines, fanzines, and reference material in science fiction, fantasy, and all other areas of popular culture studies. By appointment.

In general, the collections chosen for listing here are those that give science fiction some pride of place, either by making their material noncirculating or through other special handling or designation. Not every collection can be the largest of its kind, but even a small collection, proudly held, will attract the people and the further resources that produce good library service. It is always a good idea to call ahead before visiting a special collections department, to identify yourself and ask about hours and any special policies that may apply to the materials you need to see. The curators of the libraries listed here will go out of the way to be helpful in discussing your research or reading needs, and will provide photocopies of materials if they are not fragile. Sometimes legal restrictions will seem to interfere, either because of copyright law or because writers or their families have requested a certain privacy. Please be aware that librarians walk a thin line among public service, preservation, and fairness to donors of special collections materials.

The arrangement here is alphabetical by state for the United States, followed by other countries in alphabetical order.

Library Collections

Alabama

14-1.   University of Alabama in Huntsville Library. Special Collections, Box 2600, Huntsville, AL 35899. 205-895-6523.

The Willy Ley Memorial Collection in the Special Collections department maintains a small (350-volume) collection of science fiction books, and some magazines including most issues of *Analog* from 1947 to 1970. The books are all cataloged on OCLC. The local catalog is available via home computer and modem (call 205-895-6313 for information). Photocopies are available.

Arizona

14-2.   University of Arizona Library. Special Collections, Tucson, AZ 85721. 602-621-6423.

A science fiction collection of 18,000 volumes, with current acquisitions restricted to science fiction as opposed to fantasy and horror. The collection is based on the individual collections of Margaret Brown, Archibald Hanna, and Anthony Boucher. Holdings include complete runs of most American science fiction magazines and strong representation of early pulps. This is a noncirculating collection, and it is 90 percent cataloged. The University of Arizona is an OCLC library. Photocopies are sometimes available, but materials are not released for interlibrary loan.

California

14-3.   California State University, Fullerton—University Library. University Archives and Special Collections Unit, Box 4150, Fullerton, CA 92634. 714-773-3444.

The University Archives and Special Collections Unit holds a science fiction collection of about 4,000 paperback and 500 hardcover volumes, with 150 periodical titles and 71 fanzine titles at various levels of completeness. This is essentially a noncirculating collection, with some limited circulation of paperbacks through a Reserve Book Room. A larger circulating collection is distributed throughout the library. A science fiction manuscript collection is contained in 273 boxes (1,241 linear feet). The collection holds 146 film or TV scripts and a handful of recordings and pieces of art. The collection has particular strength in the manuscripts and papers of Avram Davidson, Philip K. Dick, Harry Harrison, Frank Herbert, and Robert Moore Williams. This collection was once part of what was called the Archive of Popular Culture (see *Fandom Directory*, 1984), and was a depository library of the Science Fiction Writers of America until about 1986. The Philip Dick holdings are described in "Philip K. Dick Manuscripts and Books: The Manuscripts and Papers at Fullerton," *Science-Fiction Studies* 2, no. 1 (March 1975), p. 4–5. The collection is relatively inactive at this time, adding about 15 items per year. Only a small portion of the collection is formally cataloged. Photocopies are available. Bibliography: McNelly, Willis E., "The Science Fiction Collection," p. 17–26 of *Very Special Collections: Essays on Library Holdings at California State University, Fullerton*, ed. by Albert R. Vogeler and Arthur A. Hansen, The Patrons of the Library, 1992.

14-4.   Huntington Library. 1151 Oxford Rd., San Marino, CA 91108. 818-405-2191.

The Huntington Library has a small collection of science fiction, supplemented by the following collections of correspondence: Brian Aldiss, 107 letters to his publishers, 1965–1973; Poul Anderson, 79 letters to his publishers, 1960–1977; Philip K. Dick, 61 pieces, including letters, outlines, and photographs; Frederik Pohl, 91 letters, 1959–1975; Robert Silverberg, 1,700 pieces, 1953–1992, including notes, drafts of short stories, and letters; Clifford D. Simak, 20 letters, 1961–1974. The manuscript holdings are described in: *Guide to Literary Manuscripts in the Huntington Library* (San Marino: the Library, 1979). The Huntington's material is noncirculating, but available to qualified scholars. Photocopying of some of the manuscripts is restricted.

14-5.   San Diego State University Library. Special Collections, San Diego, CA 92182. 619-594-6791.

The Special Collections section holds a 4,000-volume collection of science fiction, 34 magazine titles, and a few dozen manuscripts, letters, recordings, and artworks. Manuscripts or letters of Joan Vinge, Suzette Haden Elgin, Elizabeth Chater, and Jeff Sutton are held. The collection is fully cataloged, and the catalog can be accessed through Internet. Photocopies are available.

14-6.   San Francisco Public Library. McComas Collection of Fantasy and Science Fiction, Civic Center, San Francisco, CA 94102. 415-557-4545.

The McComas Collection holds 3,000 volumes of science fiction, plus a very strong collection of 92 periodical titles. About 10 percent of the collection was damaged beyond recovery in the 1989 earthquake, mostly periodicals at the beginning of the alphabet (*Amazing* and *Astounding*). The collection is noncirculating and fully cataloged. It is growing by about 30 volumes per year, plus several magazine subscriptions. Photocopying is available but not interlibrary loan.

14-7.   University of California, Los Angeles. Special Collections, University Library, 405 Hilgard Ave., Los Angeles, CA 90024. 213-825-4988.

This fantastic fiction collection has more than 10,000 monograph volumes, plus over 100 magazine titles with total holdings of about 5,000 issues. Holdings include Ray Bradbury manuscripts (1.5 linear feet), Jean Aroeste (Star Trek scripts), and single manuscripts of Henry Kuttner, Ward Moore, Margaret St. Clair, Fritz Leiber, and G. C. Edmondson. A collection of more than 400 early editions of H. Rider Haggard is maintained. The collection is fully cataloged, but with limited staff to answer written information requests. Some photocopying, no interlibrary loan.

14-8.   University of California at Riverside. Eaton Collection, Dept. of Special Collections, Tomas Rivera Library, University of California, Riverside, CA 92521. 909-787-3233.

The Eaton Collection holds approximately 63,000 volumes of science fiction, plus 100 shelf-feet of manuscripts, over 10,000 fanzines, 100 each of sound and video recordings, and extensive periodical holdings of over 175 science fiction or fantasy titles, microfilm of other pulp magazines, and 5,000 comic books. The collection includes the largest holdings of 17th–19th century utopian/dystopian fiction in North America, and holds almost 90 percent of all 20th-century American and British science fiction, fantasy, and horror. Also included are the largest collection of French science fiction in North America, strong representation of Japanese, Spanish, Russian, and German science fiction, and some Romanian, Chinese, South American, and Hebrew-language materials. The collection offers 10,000 reference, bibliographic, biographic, and index volumes pertaining to science fiction, and 75 pieces of science fiction art, including some original artwork.

The manuscript holdings include partial or full manuscript collections of: Gregory Benford, David Brin, Michael Cassutt, Philip K. Dick, G. C. Edmonson, Sheila Finch, Robert L. Forward, Diana G. Gallagher, Arthur Loy Holcomb, Gary Kern, Annette Y. Mallett, Daryl F. Mallett, Anne McCaffrey, George E. Slusser, Gary Westfahl, James White, Colin Wilson, and more. The collection catalog was published as: *Dictionary Catalog of the J. Lloyd Eaton Collection of Science Fiction and Fantasy Literature* (Boston: G. K. Hall, 1982), 3 vols. The collection is also cataloged on OCLC, except for the manuscripts. It is noncirculating, and is growing by more than 4,000 items per year. It is a Science Fiction Writers of America and a Science Fiction Research Association depository library. Photocopies are available depending on the item.

Colorado

14-9.   Colorado State University Libraries. Imaginary Wars Collection, Fort Collins, CO 80523. 303-493-1844.

The Imaginary Wars Collection consists of 1,800 volumes, including novels, short stories, and other fictional treatments of future wars, hypothetical wars, and people and societies who survive such wars. The collection has been described in *Extrapolation* (December 1974 and May 1975), *Alternative Futures* (Fall 1978), *Bulletin of Bibliography* (October/December

1978). *Future War Novels* [7-10] was based on this collection. The collection is 95 percent cataloged, 95 percent circulating, and growing by about 50 volumes per year. Photocopies and interlibrary loan are usually available.

Delaware

14-10. University of Delaware Library. Special Collections, Newark, DE 19717-5267. 302-831-2229.

The Special Collections section holds a 900-volume noncirculating collection of science fiction, with special emphasis on the published works of Ray Bradbury, Edgar Rice Burroughs, and Robert A. Heinlein. A strong representation of science fiction periodicals is also held. Photocopies are available, but not interlibrary loan.

District of Columbia

14-11. Library of Congress. Rare Book and Special Collections Division, Washington, DC 20540. 202-707-5434.

This collection is comprehensive for the works of Kingsley Amis, Ray Bradbury, Stephen King, Robert Nathan, and Colin Wilson. A collection of early English editions of Jules Verne is maintained. With the Serial and Government Publications Division, a pulp and periodical collection is held that is substantial, although gaps in the holdings are common because of the uneven way copyright deposits are received. Bibliography: Mistichelli, Judith, "Science Fiction at the Library of Congress," in *Science Fiction Collections* (Haworth Press, 1983), p. 9–24.

Florida

14-12. Rollins College, Olin Library. 1000 Holt Ave. Campus Box 2744, Winter Park, FL 32789. 407-646-2421.

A bibliographic collection of the works of M. P. Shiel. All 450 volumes of the collection relate to or refer to Shiel. A noncirculating collection, which includes a small number of periodicals as well as hardcover books. The collection is listed in OCLC. Photocopies are available, but interlibrary lending is not.

Georgia

14-13. University of Georgia Libraries. Humanities Dept., Athens, GA 30602. 706-542-0677.

A circulating collection of 6,041 volumes of science fiction, including reference materials and 50 videotapes. Manuscripts: Michael Bishop (9 boxes), Brad Strickland (2 boxes), Sharon Webb (21 boxes). A major strength is an extensive collection of pulps. Manuscripts and back issues of fragile magazines are in Special Collections, and noncirculating. The collection is cataloged on OCLC, and the local catalog is available through dial-in or Internet. Interlibrary loan and photocopying are available.

Illinois

14-14.   Northern Illinois University Libraries. Special Collections, DeKalb, IL 60115. 815-753-9838.

The Special Collections section holds a collection of more than 1,000 volumes of science fiction. One hundred five magazine titles are held, and a few H. P. Lovecraft letters. The collection has been a Science Fiction Writers of America Depository library since 1983. Complete holdings are listed on OCLC. Photocopies are available, but the collection does not circulate and will not be loaned through interlibrary loan. The collection is active and adds about 100 items annually.

14-15.   Northwestern University Library. Special Collections Department, 1937 Sheridan Rd., Evanston, IL 60208-2300. 708-491-3635.

A noncirculating collection of "several thousand" science fiction paperbacks and magazines, along with 14,500 comic books. The collection is not cataloged and not currently growing. Some photocopying is available, but not interlibrary loan.

14-16.   University of Illinois at Urbana-Champaign. Library Rare Book Room, Urbana, IL 61801. 217-333-3777.

The H. G. Wells Collection of over 1,000 volumes includes Wells's library and correspondence, with his inscribed and corrected first editions. The Wells manuscripts are in 145 boxes, of which 24 boxes are science fiction related. The Wells collection was purchased in 1954, except for a small number of papers held back by the family and finally acquired by the library in 1993. All of Wells's works are being cataloged (on OCLC) and microfilmed as a grant project. Another collection, the Jaffee Collection, specializes in first edition science fiction in dust jacket. The Jaffee Collection is actively growing, and includes over 500 volumes. Photocopies are available.

14-17.   Wheaton College. Special Collections, Buswell Memorial Library, Wheaton, IL 60187-5593. 708-752-5705.

The library holds more than 160 published volumes by or about Madeleine L'Engle, and more than 200 linear feet of her papers and writings. Also included are numerous audio and video tapes and other media materials. The Madeleine L'Engle Collection is added to regularly through purchases and gifts and accessible by written permission only. The World Science Fiction Conference (Chicon) Collection contains the files (more than three linear feet) of Chicon IV, held in Chicago in 1982. The Coleman Luck Collection contains scripts and other materials related to the *Otherworld* television series, which aired on CBS in the late 1980s.

Indiana

14-18. Indiana University, Lilly Library. Bloomington, IN 47405. 812-337-2452.

The Lilly Library has no separate SF/fantasy collections, but has extensive holdings in these areas. Authors' papers in the library include those of Anthony Boucher, Fritz Leiber, August Derleth, and Robert Bloch. Correspondence from many SF/fantasy writers is scattered throughout the collections, especially in publishers' files such as those of Bobbs-Merrill and Capra Press. First edition collections of many authors are held, including Wells, Verne, Haggard, Chesterton, Derleth, and Lovecraft. A separate catalog of the collection is available. An exhibition catalog highlights some of the holdings (*Science Fiction and Fantasy,* David R. Randell, S. C. Fredericks, and T. Mitchell, comps. Lilly Library, 1975). The collection is fully cataloged on OCLC, and new materials are acquired regularly.

Iowa

14-19. Iowa State University Library, Parks Library. Department of Special Collections, Ames, IA 50010-2140. 515-294-6672.

The Parks Library has a small (479-volume) collection of science fiction as a special collection, a one-time gift from a single donor. Some science fiction magazines are also held. In 1980 the library prepared an exhibit on science fiction art using examples from its collection, and published a brochure (*In the Mind's Eye: Science Fiction Art and Illustration,* Ames, Iowa, ISU Library Special Collections, 1980, 13 pages). The collection is fully cataloged on OCLC, and the catalog can be reached through Internet.

Kansas

14-20. Pittsburg State University, Leonard H. Axe Library. Pittsburg, KS 66762. 316-235-4883.

The Irene P. Ertman Science Fiction Collection is a noncirculating, fully cataloged special collection of 1,850 science fiction paperbacks. A few magazines are also held. The cataloging is on OCLC, and the collection is active and growing through gifts at a rate of 300 volumes per year.

14-21.   University of Kansas, Kenneth Spencer Research Library. Dept. of Special Collections, Lawrence, KS 66045-2800. 913-864-4334.

The Spencer Library holds over 7,000 volumes of science fiction, and more than 80 reference or critical volumes. One hundred twenty-eight magazine titles are held, as well as a large collection of fanzines. The collection holds at least 500 recordings, both audio and visual, miscellaneous convention literature, buttons, posters, prospectuses, and so forth, and one Hugo award statuette. Over 140 linear feet of manuscripts and papers include the following: Brian Aldiss (13 feet), Lloyd Biggle (17), Algis Budrys (1), Thomas Easton (2), J. Hunter Holly (4), Lee Killough (12), P. Schuyler Miller (5), T. L. Sherred (4), Cordwainer Smith (3), A. E. van Vogt (1), Robert Mills Agency/Richard Curtis Agency (29), Science Fiction Research Association (5). The collection has particular strength in the works of James Gunn, Lloyd Biggle, and Theodore Sturgeon.

Begun in 1969, the collection is built primarily through gifts. The Biggle and part of the Gunn manuscript materials are deposits only. The collection is the official repository for the archives of the Science Fiction Research Association and the Science Fiction Oral History Association (audio tapes only received so far). It includes SFWA official papers from the presidencies of Gunn, Williamson, and Pohl. The collection is the North American Repository for World SF, which deposits non-English-language books and has participated in the SFWA depository scheme since 1970. The collection is described in "The Library of the Future: Science Fiction and the Department of Special Collections," by Ann Hyde, *Books and Libraries at the University of Kansas* 13, no. 3 (Spring 1976): 1–5, and "Records of the Time Patrol: SF at KU," by Ann Hyde, *Books and Libraries at the University of Kansas* 20 (Spring 1988): 1–8.

The collection is active, adding 400 items annually by gift. The collection is noncirculating, and about 30 percent cataloged. Materials on-site are accessible by donor lists and shelf arrangement. Photocopies are available.

Kentucky

14-22.   University of Kentucky Library. Special Collections, Lexington, KY 40506. 606-257-8611.

A collection of 5,550 volumes of science fiction, with 54 English-language magazine titles but without substantial runs of magazines. This collection is active, growing through large gifts every three or four years. The cataloging is minimal, with some presence on OCLC. Photocopies are available.

14-23. University of Louisville Library. Rare Books and Special Collections, Louisville, KY 40292. 502-588-6762.

An Edgar Rice Burroughs collection of 60,000 items, with special collections of Ambrose Bierce, L. Frank Baum, and Ursula Le Guin, and a pulp magazine collection of some 10,000 issues. The Burroughs collection is the largest of its kind in any institutional library, and includes first editions, personal memorabilia, scrapbooks, Burroughs's school textbooks, comics, posters, photos, manuscripts, fanzines, toys, movies, and related material about Burroughs. The library publishes a journal (*Burroughs Bulletin* [12-19]) and a monthly newsletter (*The Gridley Wave*). Collecting is active, with regular additions through purchase and gift. Materials are for room use only. Photocopies can be provided, but no interlibrary loan.

Bibliography: McWhorter, G. T., *Edgar Rice Burroughs Memorial Collection: A Catalog*. Ltd. first ed. (House of Greystoke, 1991), 190 p. McWhorter, G. T., "Edgar Rice Burroughs," *Library Review* 30 (May 1980).

Louisiana

14-24. Louisiana State University. Middleton Library, Clarence J. Laughlin Library of the Arts, Baton Rouge, LA 70803. 504-388-6572.

The Laughlin Library is an extensive collection of the literary output of major American and British trade publishers from the late 19th century to the mid-20th century. From that point, the focus narrowed to science fiction, fantasy, and mystery fiction. The collection is based heavily on Bleiler's *The Checklist of Fantastic Literature* [7-1]. The large fiction holdings, the runs of many pulps, and the output of specialty presses such as Gnome Press and Arkham House make this a major potential resource. Collecting is not very active, and much of the collection is still boxed and uncataloged.

14-25. Tulane University. Howard-Tilton Memorial Library, Special Collections, New Orleans, LA 70118-5682. 504-865-5685.

This is an active special collection of 4,600 books, plus 2,500 magazine issues, and 400 fanzine issues. Specialties include the works of Rosel George Brown, who began the collection, and Robert Heinlein first editions. The collection is growing at a rate of about 200 volumes per year. The materials are all noncirculating, with some interlibrary loan (not serials, only monographs) and photocopying available. Recent cataloging (less than 20 percent) can be seen through Internet, older materials have in-house cataloging only.

Maryland

14-26.   University of Maryland. Baltimore County, Albin O. Kuhn Library and Gallery, 5401 Wilkens Ave., Catonsville, MD 21228. 410-455-2353.

The Azriel Rosenfeld Science Fiction Research Collection includes 10,000 volumes of science fiction and 600 volumes of reference and critical work. More than 100 magazine titles are held, along with 15,000 fanzine issues, 790 manuscripts, 4,000 letters, 42 sound recordings, 17 visual recordings, 31 filmscripts, and 100 pieces of SF art. The collection is particularly strong for authors Roger Zelazny, Thomas F. Monteleone, and David Bischoff. The David Bischoff collection of manuscripts, correspondence, personal papers, books, and journals was acquired recently. Other manuscripts by Roger Zelazny, Thomas F. Monteleone, Charles L. Harness, Brian M. Stableford, E. C. Tubb, and 18 other authors are held. The Walter Coslet fanzine collection is a major strength, mostly dating from before 1960 and including many from the 1930–1950 period. A catalog of the fanzine collection is available in the library. The collection is active, adding 400 items annually. Cataloging of the books is 75 percent complete, on OCLC, and the on-line catalog can be reached through Internet. Photocopies are available, but no interlibrary loan.

Massachusetts

14-27.   Boston University. Mugar Memorial Library, Dept. of Special Collections, 771 Commonwealth Ave., Boston, MA 02215. 617-353-3696. FAX 617-353-2838.

A science fiction collection of 1,800 volumes and two magazine titles. Manuscripts in linear feet: Isaac Asimov (220), Marion Zimmer Bradley (50), Arthur C. Clarke (2), L. Sprague de Camp (22), Samuel R. Delany (60), Alan Nourse (60), Edgar Pangborn (18), Curt Siodmak (10), Jack Vance (10). The collection is active, adding about 100 books annually. The collection is partially cataloged in-house. Photocopies are available.

Michigan

14-28.   Michigan State University Libraries. Special Collections Division, East Lansing, MI 48824-1048. 517-355-3770.

Part of the Russel B. Nye Popular Culture Collection is a 10,000-volume science fiction collection that is mostly monographs, but includes samples of most science fiction pulps and magazines. All manuscripts of the Clarion Workshop from 1973 to the present are held. The Clarion manuscripts are arranged by year and by author. A fanzine collection of about 2,000 issues is arranged by title. A comic book collection of more than 75,000 items includes at least 1,000 science fiction comics, depending on definition. The Vincent Voice Library is a regional depository for the Science Fiction Oral History Association collection, which numbers more than 350 tapes. The books, pulps, magazines, comics, and sound recordings are cataloged on OCLC, and the local online catalog can also be reached through direct dial or Internet. Cataloging has been enhanced to include publishers' series designations and names of illustrators, cover and jacket artists whenever possible. The collection grows by gifts at a rate of about 300 items per year, and has been an SFWA depository since 1972. The materials are noncirculating. Some photocopies are available, but no interlibrary loan.

14-29. University of Michigan. Harlan Hatcher Graduate Library, Special Collections Library, Ann Arbor, MI 41109-1205. 313-764-9377.

The Hubbard Collection of Imaginary Voyages consists of 3,000 volumes of fiction and 130 volumes of reference and critical material, largely of various editions, translations, adaptations, abridgments, and imitations of *Robinson Crusoe* and *Gulliver's Travels*. A few books by such authors as Verne, Bellamy, and Cyrano de Bergerac are included. Almost entirely limited to imaginary voyages on Earth with few interplanetary trips. The collection is active, adding three to five items annually. It is noncirculating, fully cataloged, and photocopies are available.

Minnesota

14-30. University of Minnesota Libraries. Manuscripts Division, 826 Berry St., St. Paul, MN 55114. 612-627-4199.

The Manuscripts Division holds a *Star Trek* collection of about 9 linear feet of scripts and related materials, including 50 published volumes of *Star Trek* fiction, 100 reference and critical volumes, and nine sound recordings. The scripts are a pilot script and complete set of shooting scripts for the original television series, and shooting scripts for the first two movies. Manuscripts and papers of Gordon R. Dickson (60 boxes), Clifford D. Simak (17 boxes), Carl Jacobi (5 boxes), E. Hoffman Price (1 box), and H. P. Lovecraft (17 items) are maintained. The focus of the collection is authors having Minnesota connections. (Exceptions are Price and Lovecraft.) An attempt is being made to collect materials from the old pulp writers, such as Price and Jacobi, but the pulp magazines themselves are not retained in the division. The collections contain notes, correspondence, manuscript drafts, and some galley proofs. The collection is actively maintained and cataloged for use within the Division. Acquisitions are by gift only.

New Mexico

14-31.   Eastern New Mexico University. Golden Library, Special Collections, Station 32, Portales, NM 88130. 505-562-2635.

The Williamson Science Fiction Library originated with gifts from Jack Williamson and now consists of more than 20,000 items. Fully cataloged and circulating are 12,800 volumes of fiction. The magazine collection (including fanzines) includes 11,695 issues of 900 titles. The manuscript collection is measured in linear feet: Jack Williamson (47), Leigh Brackett (8), Edmond Hamilton (4), Forrest J. Ackerman (13.5), Piers Anthony (1), *Analog* files 1954–1975 (various authors) (21), James Blish, SFWA Presidential (1), Marcia Howl (1), Woody Wolfe (1). The Williamson collection is a regional depository for the Science Fiction Oral History Association, and 44 sound recordings from the SFOHA are held. The collection is active, adding at least 400 titles per year, and has been an SFWA depository since 1969. The books are cataloged on OCLC, and internal lists and indexes are used to keep track of the rest of the material. Circulating materials will be lent on interlibrary loan, and photocopies are available.

14-32.   University of New Mexico. Center for Southwest Research, Zimmerman Library, Albuquerque, NM 87131. 505-277-6451.

The Donald Day Science Fiction Collection consists of a virtually complete collection of 52 American and three British magazines published between 1926 and 1950. The magazines are those indexed in Donald B. Day's *Index to the Science Fiction Magazines, 1926–1950.* The collection includes Day's original card index. The collection is noncirculating, inactive, and not cataloged in the library sense, although the index serves the purpose. An inventory is available from the center. Some photocopying available, depending on the condition of the original.

New York

14-33.   New York Public Library. General Research Division, 5th Ave. and 42nd St., New York, NY 10018. 212-930-0830.

The General Research Division has over 5,000 volumes of science fiction in closed stacks. Current science fiction paperbacks are being filmed routinely in the Microforms Division, and over 2,000 are on film. The Microforms Division (separate from the General Research Division but at the same address) holds most commercial science fiction microforms available (pulps and magazines), and 212 sample fanzine titles filmed in-house. The collection is growing by 500 volumes per year. The cataloging is visible on OCLC, RLIN, and through Internet. Photocopies and interlibrary loan are available.

14-34. State University of New York. University Libraries, Dept. of Special Collections and Archives, 1400 Washington Ave., Albany, NY 12222. 518-442-3544.

A special collection of 3,266 volumes of science fiction, 229 reference and critical volumes, and 18 magazine titles. The monographic collection is under controlled usage: only hardcover books may circulate. The majority of items date from 1950 to present. The collection is active, adding 80 to 100 purchased items and some gifts annually. Cataloging is on OCLC and visible through Internet. Interlibrary loan and photocopies are available.

14-35. Syracuse University Library. Special Collections Dept., Room 600, Bird Library, Syracuse, NY 13244-2010. 315-443-2697.

A noncirculating collection of 4,100 monograph volumes of science fiction, 5,800 magazine issues, 25 manuscript collections, and 50 fanzines. The manuscripts (in linear feet) are of authors Forrest J. Ackerman (79), Piers Anthony (10), Hal Clement (2.5), Galaxy Publishing Corporation (31.8), Hugo Gernsback (33), Gnome Press (0.5), William F. Jenkins (35), David Keller (5), Damon Knight (10), David A. Kyle (0.5), Keith Laumer (8.5), Anne McCaffrey (1.8), Mercury Press (20), Andre Norton (16.25), Frederik Pohl (6.5), Robert Silverberg (2.5), Universal Publishing Corporation (0.8), Kate Wilhelm (6), Richard Wilson (17.25), Donald A. Wollheim (0.25), and Roger Zelazny (3.5). A description of the collection, "Syracuse University," by Fred Lerner, appears in H. W. Hall, ed. *Science Fiction Collections: Fantasy Supernatural and Weird Tales* (Haworth Press, 1983). The book collection is partially (30 percent) cataloged on OCLC, and the manuscripts are on RLIN. The catalog can be accessed through direct dial-in. Acquisitions are occasional. Some photocopying is done, but no interlibrary loan.

North Carolina

14-36. Duke University. Special Collections Library, Durham, NC 27708-0185. 919-660-5820.

The Negley Collection consists of 1,600 volumes of utopian fiction. The basic description of the collection is found in Glen Negley's *Utopian Literature: A Bibliography, With a Supplementary Listing of Works Influential in Utopian Thought* (1978). (Note: The frequently cited Folcroft edition is reprinted from a partial checklist and should be avoided, according to the library.) This major utopian collection is active, adding 15–20 items annually. It is cataloged, and a separate shelf list is maintained.

Ohio

14-37.   Bowling Green State University. Popular Culture Library, Bowling Green, OH 43403. 419-372-2450.

The Popular Culture Library is the flagship collection of the popular culture studies world, with amazing accumulations in every imaginable category. Science fiction and fantasy holdings include 15,000 volumes of fiction and several hundred related reference and critical volumes; 500 magazine titles; 1,000 fanzine issues; 5,200 pulp magazine issues, and many manuscripts. Manuscripts (extent in linear feet) are by: Daniel Cohen (18), Alexi Panshin (19.5), Joanna Russ (7.5), Carl Jacobi, and Sheldon R. Jaffery, with a major Ray Bradbury collection. A special strength of the collection is American magazines, 1926–1960. Especially notable are the Michael L. Cook Collection of fanzines and the H. James Horvitz Science Fiction Collection of pulp magazines. The Ray Bradbury collection consists of over 700 books and 15 linear feet of nonbook materials. There are rare Bradbury pamphlets, comic book adaptations, original art by Bradbury, sound recordings, maps, broadsides, photographs, galley proofs, scripts, programs, screenplays, diary notes, posters, promotional material, interviews, speeches, and more than 400 periodicals. The centerpiece of the manuscript collection is the heavily revised 221-page typed draft of *Fahrenheit 451.* Also included are 120 manuscripts in 160 drafts of Bradbury short stories and verse. An unusual item is a 135,000-word manuscript transcribed from tapes forming a complete Bradbury autobiography. The Jaffery collection includes nearly complete sets of Arkham House and DAW books. The collection is very active, adding 200 to 1,000 items annually. Cataloging is on OCLC and available through Internet. Photocopies are available, but not interlibrary loan.

14-38.   Kent State University Library. Special Collections and Archives, Kent, OH 44242. 216-672-2270.

A collection of 1,000 volumes of paperback science fiction, mostly dating from 1950 to 1980, and a Stephen R. Donaldson collection that includes 11 boxes of Donaldson's manuscripts. An exhibit in 1981, "Ohio's Contribution to Science Fiction & Fantasy," featured authors born in Ohio. In 1986 the library published *Epic Fantasy in the Modern World: A Few Observations*, a booklet by Donaldson. The collection is noncirculating, and relatively inactive. The books are partially cataloged on OCLC.

14-39. Ohio State University. Special Collections, 1858 Neil Ave. Mall, Columbus, OH 43210-1286. 614-292-6151.

The Special Collections include 105 science fiction magazine titles from 1926 to the present, including a nearly complete set of *Weird Tales*. Under the designation "The William Charvat Collection of American Fiction," Ohio State has been working for years to assemble a complete American fiction collection up to the year 1926, and has been collecting new fiction comprehensively since 1986, and the intervening years are substantially represented as well. The goal is to fill them in where possible. The collection also includes a sizable number of *Star Trek* (original series) TV scripts. Cataloging is on OCLC, and photocopies are available.

14-40. University of Dayton. Archives and Special Collections, Roesch Library, Room 317, Dayton, OH 45469-1360. 513-229-4267.

A collection of 1,500 SFWA depository books, fully cataloged and noncirculating. The cataloging is on OCLC, and available through Internet and direct dial. This library has been a SFWA depository since 1973, and is growing regularly.

Oklahoma

14-41. University of Tulsa. McFarlin Library, Special Collections Dept., 600 S. College Ave., Tulsa, OK 74104-3189. 918-631-2496.

A large collection of R. A. Lafferty manuscripts and a small science fiction collection of books and magazines. Cataloging is on OCLC, and available through direct dial and Internet. Interlibrary loan and photocopies are available.

Pennsylvania

14-42. Pennsylvania State University. Pattee Library, Special Collections, University Park, PA 16802. 814-865-1793.

A science fiction collection of 4,200 volumes, with 150 reference and critical volumes and 155 magazine titles. The strength of the collection is in the 3,000-issue magazine collection, which includes complete runs of many titles. The monograph collection includes a near-complete file of

Arkham House books. A separate utopian collection of 2,000 items supplements this collection. The collection is active, adding 100 items annually. It is 45 percent cataloged on OCLC, with no interlibrary loan and limited photocopying. A bibliography of the utopia collection is available for $10.

14-43.   Temple University Libraries. Special Collections Dept., Philadelphia, PA 19122. 215-204-8230. FAX 215-204-2501.

A collection of 15,000 books, 5,000 magazine issues, 2,000 fanzines, and 130 feet of manuscripts. Manuscripts (linear feet) include: Ben Bova (32), Gardner Dozois (7), Lloyd A. Eshbach/Fantasy Press (5.8), Jack Dann (12), Tom Purdom (4), Pamela Sargent (13), George Zebrowski (14), Felix Gotschalk (1), John Varley (2), Oswald Train/Prime Press (2), Miriam DeFord (0.5), Richard Peck (0.5), Stanley Weinbaum. Of particular note are strong collections of the published works of H. P. Lovecraft, Robert Howard, Ben Bova, George Zebrowski, Pamela Sargent, Jack Dann, and Stanley Weinbaum. This was formerly called the David C. Paskow Collection, and is now referred to as the Science Fiction & Fantasy Collection (Paskow/Knuth). It has been through some important changes. The focus has shifted from strictly science fiction to include fantasy materials. Although most of the collection (90 percent) was cataloged by 1984, the influx of gifts has since reduced to the proportion of cataloged material to about half. The collection is active, currently adding about 250 items per year. Cataloging for published items is being added to OCLC and for manuscript material to RLIN.

14-44.   University of Pittsburgh. Special Collections, 363 Hillman Library, Pittsburgh, PA 15260. 412-642-8191.

The Archive of Popular Culture includes 2,200 science fiction paperback novels and 320 fanzine issues. The collection is noncirculating, and not cataloged, although there are local inventories. The collection is active, growing through donations. Photocopies are available.

Rhode Island

14-45.   Brown University. John Hay Library, Providence, RI 02912. 401-863-2146.

The definitive H. P. Lovecraft collection, with more than 700 printed and more than 5,000 manuscript items, half by Lovecraft himself and half by Lovecraft correspondents such as August Derleth, Frank Belknap Long, C. L. Moore, E. Hoffmann Price, and Clark Ashton Smith. A separate Clark Ashton Smith collection includes more than 5,000 manuscripts and 5,000 letters. A complete run of *Weird Tales* is held. Publisher collections include the complete works of Arkham House including most ephemera, and complete Donald W. Grant and Necronomicon Press collections. The collection is active, and cataloged.

Texas

14-46.   Dallas Public Library. 1515 Young St., Dallas, TX 75201. 214-670-1667.

Since 1974, this library has been building a research collection of science fiction that now includes over 16,000 volumes, and 187 fantasy and science fiction periodical titles. Some 2,350 of the volumes are in the Brian Aldiss Collection, which also includes personal correspondence, photographs, speeches, illustrations, introductions, posters and cover art, book and film reviews, radio plays, and notes and typescripts for short stories, novels, and poetry. The collection is growing at a rate of about 300 volumes per year by gift and purchase. The collection is cataloged, and most of it circulates. Photocopies and interlibrary loan are available.

14-47.   Texas A&M University Library. College Station, TX 77843. 409-845-1951.

The Science Fiction Research Collection was begun in 1970, and now exceeds 30,000 items. An important strength of the collection is a pulp magazine collection, containing more than 200 titles of American and British science fiction magazines from 1923 to the present, plus a growing sample of foreign-language titles including near complete runs of *Fiction* (France), *Galactika* (Hungary), and *Robot* (Italy). The monograph collection of 25,000 volumes is strongest from 1950 to the present, but includes much pre-1950 material. The manuscript collection (20 linear feet) includes works by Moorcock, Sladek, Silverberg, Davidson, and Burgess. George R. R. Martin donated a collection of his papers, books, and correspondence in late 1993. A special effort is made to collect all historical, critical, and reference materials in all languages, including master's theses and doctoral dissertations. A particularly valuable segment of the collection is the "Science Fiction: Collected Papers" file, consisting of more than 10,000 pages of articles about science fiction collected by a local professor in his research. A representative collection of more than 6,000 fanzine issues is maintained. The collection is described in Hall, H. W., ed. *Science Fiction Collections: Fantasy Supernatural and Weird Tales* (Haworth Press, 1983). The collection is active, adding 1,000 or more items annually. The books are about 70 percent cataloged. Photocopies are available, but not interlibrary loan.

14-48.   University of Texas at Austin. Harry Ransom Humanities Research Center, Box 7219, Austin, TX 78713. 512-471-9119.

The Harry Ransom Humanities Research Center has nearly 8,000 volumes of fiction and hundreds of magazines, manuscripts, and letters. The core of the collection is the L. W. Currey Science Fiction and Fantasy Collection, which was the basis for his book on science fiction first editions [7-7]. Supplementing the Currey collection is the Selznik Archive, which includes extensive material on *King Kong* and other fantastic films, and a large collection of motion picture promotional material and lobby cards. The center has hundreds of letters to or from science fiction writers throughout its collections, by Ambrose Bierce, Stapledon, Čapek, Lewis, Orwell, and many others. Manuscript collections include L. Sprague de Camp, Arthur Conan Doyle (23 boxes), Lord Dunsany (6 boxes), Arthur Machen (23 boxes), Ernest Bramah Smith (25 boxes), and T. H. White (36 boxes). The collection is developing along the lines of established strength through purchase and regular gifts. Most of its books are cataloged. Photocopies are available, but not interlibrary loan.

Utah

14-49.   Brigham Young University. Harold B. Lee Library, Provo, UT 84607. 801-378-6218.

A collection of more than 12,000 volumes of science fiction, of which all but 1,000 volumes are circulating. This is the official Orson Scott Card depository and includes more than 40 cubic feet of his manuscripts and papers. Collecting began in 1964 with a large purchase, and the materials are used in support of university science fiction classes. Special interests include Arkham House publications, Edgar Rice Burroughs and Orson Scott Card first editions, and Science Fiction Book Club editions. The collection is an SFWA depository, and is growing by purchase as well, adding more than 600 items annually. Cataloging is complete, on RLIN. Interlibrary loan and photocopies are available.

Virginia

14-50.   Virginia Commonwealth University. James Branch Cabell Library, 901 Parke Ave., Box 2033, Richmond, VA 23284-2033. 804-367-1108.

A collection of 1,750 volumes of science fiction, mostly paperbacks, kept in a restricted circulation area, with a few of the materials available for faculty circulation. Some magazines are held, and 1.5 linear feet of manuscripts called the Robert Adams Papers. The collection is cataloged on OCLC, and accessible through direct dial or Internet. New volumes are being added through gift and purchase.

Wisconsin

14-51. State Historical Society of Wisconsin. Archives Division, 816 State St., Madison, WI 53706. 608-264-6460.

The August Derleth collection is composed of fantasy and science fiction pulp magazines, together with many detective and genre pulps to which Derleth contributed. The collection also includes some Arkham House books and the bulk of Derleth's manuscripts and personal papers, and some papers of Arkham House. The collection can be examined in the Archives Reading Room. No appointment is necessary, but it is recommended that researchers call ahead or write.

14-52. University of Wisconsin, La Crosse. Murphy Library, La Crosse, WI 54601. 608-785-8511.

The Paul W. Skeeters Collection of fantasy, science fiction, and horror literature contains more than 1,100 items ranging from 1764 to the mid-1960s, primarily first editions. Greatest strength is in the 1900–1926 period, and in Arkham House books, about 100 titles. The books are for room use only. The collection is active, adding five items annually, and is fully cataloged on OCLC. Photocopies are available, but not interlibrary loan.

14-53. University of Wisconsin, Milwaukee. Golda Meir Library, Special Collections, Box 604, Milwaukee, WI 53201. 414-229-4345.

A collection of science fiction magazines published from 1926 to the present, 11 titles. The collection is still growing, and fully cataloged in the online catalog. Photocopies are available.

Wyoming

14-54. University of Wyoming. Coe Library, Box 3924, Laramie, WY 82071. 307-766-6385.

Primarily a collection of science fiction and fantasy manuscripts, about 300 cubic feet in extent. Author manuscripts collected, and number of boxes each: Robert Bloch (234+), Sam Peeples (222), Forrest J. Ackerman (140+), Martin Caidin (54+), Fritz Lang (30), H. L. Prosser (19), Donald A. Wollheim (14), Michael Kurland (8), Hugo Gernsback (6), Philip José Farmer (6), A. E. van Vogt (3), Stanley B. Hough (2). The collections contain books, correspondence, magazines, and fan material collected by Wollheim, Bloch, Shea, and Ackerman. Of particular note in the

Wollheim material are much data on early fandom in the United States, and voluminous correspondence relating to Wollheim's editorial experience, extremely valuable in the study of the development of the anthology. The correspondence also reflects important aspects of the market conditions for science fiction over a long period. Much correspondence with well-known writers is included. Some material is restricted. The collection is active, growing through gifts. Catalogs and finding aids are available on site. The collection may be used in-house only, and interlibrary loan is not offered. Photocopying is available.

Australia

14-55.   Murdoch University Library. Box 14, Willetton, Western Australia 6155.

The Alternative and Contemporary Documents collection holds about 5,000 volumes of science fiction, and good periodical runs since 1950. Over 300 titles of Australian fanzines are represented. The collection began to support course work and a Ph.D candidate, and the fanzines were donated by a library staff member active in fan publishing. The collection is currently inactive. Photocopies and interlibrary loan are available.

14-56.   University of Queensland Library. Special Collections, St. Lucia, Queensland 4067. Phone: Brisbane 377-3249.

This library holds the Donald Tuck collection of science fiction and fantasy, used to compile his *Encyclopedia of Science Fiction and Fantasy Through 1968* [7-9]. The collection includes both monographs and serials as listed in Tuck's work. It is growing through purchase of materials, and is fully cataloged. Hardcover books circulate and are available for interlibrary loan. Photocopies are available.

14-57.   University of Sydney Library. Rare Books and Special Collections, Sydney, NSW 2006. 02-692-2992.

The Science Fiction and Fantasy Collection holds 38,200 volumes (hardcover 14,200, paperback 24,000) and 800 reference and critical volumes. One hundred seventy titles of English-language magazines, and 40 in foreign languages, with a total of more than 17,000 issues. Two thousand fanzine titles, and 1,426 comic book titles (over 14,000 issues). Some audiovisual material. Manuscripts and typescripts (10 boxes) of Aldiss, Brunner, Chandler, Coney, Cowper, Ellison, Lovecraft, Leiber, Priest, Tubb, Wilhelm, Wollheim, and others. Original illustrations by Virgil Finlay (6), Kelly Freas, Jack Gaughan, Rick Sternbach, Donald Wollheim.

The collection was established in 1974 as a research collection for scholars. In 1979, holdings were greatly increased with the bequest of the Ron Graham SF Collection, one of the largest private collections in the world. Holdings for most major science fiction magazines (U.S., U.K., and Australian) are complete up to 1978; a representative collection of English fanzines is also held with strengths in early Australian (mainly N.S.W.) fanzines. Also held are the fanzines of Donald Wollheim and the Futurians. Primary strength in the monograph collection lies after 1945, but the earlier period is well covered. Holdings include a comics collection relating to the weird or fantastic.

The collection is active, adding 150 items annually. The library has been a Science Fiction Writers of America Depository since 1981. Cataloging is about 25 percent complete, and the Graham collection has a title card catalog devised by Graham. Material is not for loan, but photocopies can often be provided.

Canada

14-58. Toronto Public Library. 40 St. George St., Toronto, ON M5S 2E4.

The Merril Collection of Science Fiction, Speculation and Fantasy holds 22,400 volumes of fiction, 3,797 volumes of reference and critical material, and 17,659 issues of English-language magazines (85 subscriptions). The collection includes 500 foreign-language periodicals, and more than 1,200 fanzine titles; 350 audio recordings, 360 videocassettes, 60 fantasy games plus modules, and original fantasy art. Manuscripts include Andre Norton, Eric Frank Russell, Donald H. Tuck, and Poul Anderson.

Established in 1970 with the donation of Judith Merril's 5,000-item collection as the "Spaced Out Library," it was renamed the Merril Collection of Science Fiction, Speculation and Fantasy on January 1, 1991. Holdings are now in excess of 54,000 items. In addition to collecting SF specialty press materials, a Verne Collection is maintained. The fanzine collection and the periodical collection are both indexed by subject. All anthologies are indexed by author and title of each individual short story. The collection is described in H. W. Hall, ed. *Science Fiction Collections: Fantasy Supernatural and Weird Tales* (Haworth Press, 1983). Collecting is active, adding approximately 1,000 books and 1,200 periodical issues annually. A small circulating paperback collection is kept (8,700 volumes). Photocopies are available.

14-59. University of British Columbia Library. Special Collections, 1956 Main Mall, Vancouver, BC V6T 1Z1. 604-822-2521. FAX 604-822-9587.

A collection of 30 titles of science fiction pulps and magazines, dating mainly from the 1940s and 1950s. Described in John McKinley, "The Science Fiction Collection at the University of British Columbia" (*British Columbia Library Quarterly* 34, no. 4 (April 1971). Interlibrary loan is not available, and photocopies are not usually available because of the fragility of the pulps.

14-60.   University of New Brunswick. Ward Chipman Library, Box 5050, Saint John, NB E2L 4L5. 506-648-5703.

The Science Fiction and Fantasy Collection includes more than 16,000 books including very substantial reference and critical materials, and 11,000 issues of periodicals including microfilm serial holdings, with some audiovisuals and other related material, including science fiction comic books. Manuscripts include three short stories by John Wyndham and *Rite of Passage* by Alexei Panshin. The collection began in 1966 and has been growing actively since through gifts and purchases. It is an SFWA depository, fully cataloged with an index to its vertical files. Items that are not rare circulate locally and through interlibrary loan. Photocopies are available.

14-61.   University of Winnipeg Library. 515 Portage Ave., Winnipeg, Manitoba, R3B 2E9. 204-786-9804.

Collection of 2,870 volumes (plus 150 volumes of reference and critical works) includes detective, horror, weird, ghost, and fantasy fiction. A separate children's book collection also includes sample science fiction and fantasy titles. A few fantasy and horror periodicals are held (eight titles, and three microform titles of science fiction magazines, for example, *Fantastic Adventures*, 1939–1945 on microfilm). The collection is active, adding 60 volumes annually through purchases and gifts. The books are fully cataloged. This is a circulating collection, but with closed stacks. Interlibrary loan and photocopies are available.

England

14-62.   Oxford University. Bodleian Library, Dept. of Western Manuscripts, Oxford OX1 3BG. (0865) 277000. FAX (0865) 277182.

The Department of Western Manuscripts holds papers and books of James Blish, Michael Moorcock, and Brian Aldiss, plus a large general collection of printed science fiction received through copyright deposit.

14-63.University of Liverpool. Librarian/Administrator Andy Sawyer, Science Fiction Foundation Collection, Sydney Jones Library, Special Collections, Box 123, Liverpool L69 3DA. 051-794-2696.

The Science Fiction Foundation Research Library, formerly located at the University of East London (formerly called Polytechnic of East London, earlier North East London Polytechnic) moved from Essex to Liverpool in the summer of 1993. The Research Library is housed in the same special collections area as the Olaf Stapledon Archive. The Stapledon collection includes about 350 books (including first editions of Stapledon's works, presentation copies from other authors, and books from Stapledon's personal library), 800 manuscripts, and 2,400 letters and miscellaneous other primary material. Additional details are in the *SFRA Newsletter* no. 117 (December 1983), p. 8–10 and *Locus,* December 1993, p. 7. The Science Fiction Foundation brings at least 25,000 total items to the University of Liverpool, of which the majority are books and magazines. The magazine collection includes over 100 titles. Manuscripts include works of John Wyndham, Ian Watson, Bob Shaw, Christopher Priest, Brian Stableford, Arthur Sellings, Barrington J. Bayley, and Ramsey Campbell. Publication of the journal *Foundation, the Review of Science Fiction* [12-22] continues. The policy at Liverpool in the past has been to offer photocopies, but no interlibrary loan.

Germany

14-64. Phantastische Bibliothek Wetzlar. Domplatz 7, Box 2120, D-W-6330 Wetzlar 1. 06441-405-490.

The Fantastic Library of Wetzlar holds more than 85,000 books, paperbacks, booklets, and magazines of all fantastic genres (science fiction, fantasy, weird, fairy tales, utopias, and so on) of the 19th and 20th centuries in the German language. Manuscripts, nonfiction, games, catalogs, dictionaries, and fanzines are included, also a complete set of German-language pulps and magazines. All German fantastic authors are collected in depth. The materials are noncirculating, but the collection is open to the public and for research. The collection is actively growing, adding more than 5,000 items per year.

Switzerland

14-65. Maison d'Ailleurs. Case postale 3181, CH-1401 Yverdon-les-Bains. 24-21-6438.

The Maison d'Ailleurs holds some 35,000 volumes of science fiction in 34 languages, of which about one-fifth make up a lending library. The magazine collection is substantial, with more than 150 titles in English as well as more than 50 in other languages. Fanzines (more than 300 titles), audiovisual items (more than 1,700), and manuscripts of nearly every French author and some English. More properly a museum than a library, the Maison d'Ailleurs contains more than 60,000 items. The remainder includes posters, paintings, music, postage stamps, toys, games, comics, art, autographs, calendars, photographs, and much more, all relating to science fiction. The collection was amassed by Pierre Versins and Martine Thome, and is the essential collection for the study of French or European science fiction. The collection is described in Roger Gaillard's "The Maison d'Ailleurs, a Museum for Science-Fiction," in *Foundation*, no. 53 (1991), p. 7–23, and more recently in *Locus*, January 1994, p. 40. The collection is active, growing at a rate of about 1,000 items per year. Photocopies are available, but not interlibrary loan.

CHAPTER 15

Listings

Neil Barron

Best Books

Of the several thousand works of fiction and nonfiction annotated in this guide, some are clearly of greater distinction or historical importance than others. Since libraries, like individuals, have limited budgets, any library wanting to develop a core collection of the best books should begin by checking their holdings against this listing (a procedure complicated by the fact that some books in the following list may be uncataloged paperbacks).

Contributors were asked to asterisk the best books they annotated, and these asterisks precede entry numbers of annotations throughout the book. Asterisked entries were considered for inclusion in this best books listing, and to insure balance, three outside readers reviewed the lists submitted by contributors. If they concurred with the contributor's judgment, their initials follow the title. If they did not, their choices are listed without a star, followed by their initials and, in a few cases, by the year of publication if the book was not annotated. New to this edition is a benefit for smaller libraries with more limited budgets: two stars identify the most essential books. The outside readers for this edition selected those chapter lists they felt most qualified to judge, and those chapter numbers follow their sketches:

Brian W. Aldiss, one of Britain's most distinguished authors, not only of SF, but of criticism, autobiography, and a variety of other works (2–4)

Peter Nicholls, co-editor of *The Encyclopedia of Science Fiction* [7-22] and of one of the best histories of fantastic cinema [10-13] (1–5, 7, 8, 10–12)

David Wingrove, co-author of *Trillion Year Spree* [8-5] and author of the multivolume Chung Kuo saga [4-507] (3, 4, 7, 8, and 12)

Books are listed in the same sequence as annotated, with only the first author/editor shown. See the annotations for more details. And see the awards listing later in this chapter for additional recommendations. See also table 10-1 for best films.

1: The Emergence of Science Fiction: The Beginnings Through 1915

(Note: Brian Stableford selected the ** books)
**Bellamy, Edward. *Looking Backward* (BA, PN)
**Beresford, J. D. *The Hampdenshire Wonder* (BA, PN)
Bergerac, Cyrano de. *Other Worlds* (PN)
*Burroughs, Edgar Rice. *At the Earth's Core* (BA, PN)
*———. *A Princess of Mars* (BA, PN)
*Butler, Samuel. *Erewhon* (BA, PN)
*Chesney, Sir George. *The Battle of Dorking* (BA, PN)
*Childers, Erskine. *The Riddle of the Sands* (PN)
**Clemens, Samuel Langhorne. *A Connecticut Yankee in King Arthur's Court* (BA, PN)
*De Mille, James. *A Strange Manuscript Found in a Copper Cylinder* (BA, PN)
*Donnelly, Ignatius. *Caesar's Column* (PN)
**Doyle, Arthur Conan. *The Lost World* (BA, PN)
*———. *The Poison Belt* (PN)
*Forster, E. M. "The Machine Stops" (BA, PN)
*Franklin, H. Bruce. *Future Perfect* (BA, PN)
*Gilman, Charlotte Perkins. *Herland* (BA, PN)
*Greg, Percy. *Across the Zodiac* (BA, PN)
*Haggard, H. Rider. *She* (BA, PN)
*Holberg, Ludwig. *A Journey to the World Under-Ground* (BA, PN)
Jefferies, Richard. *After London* (PN)
*Kepler, Johannes. *Somnium* (BA, PN)
*London, Jack. *Before Adam* (BA, PN)
*———. *The Science Fiction of Jack London* (BA, PN)

*Lytton, Edward Bulwer. *The Coming Race* (BA, PN)

Mercier, Louis Sebastian. *Memoirs of the Year Two Thousand Five Hundred* (PN)

*More, Thomas. *Utopia* (BA, PN)

*O'Brien, Fitz-James. *Supernatural Tales of Fitz-James O'Brien*

*Poe, Edgar Allan. *The Narrative of Arthur Gordon Pym of Nantucket* (BA, PN)

**———. *The Science Fiction of Edgar Allan Poe* (BA, PN)

*Rhodes, W. H. *Caxton's Book*

*Seaborn, Adam. *Symzonia* (BA, PN)

*Serviss, Garrett P. *Edison's Conquest of Mars* (BA, PN)

*———. *The Second Deluge* (BA, PN)

**Shelley, Mary. *Frankenstein* (BA, PN)

———. *The Last Man* (BA, PN)

Shiel, M. P. *The Purple Cloud* (1901) (BA, PN)

**Stevenson, Robert Louis. *The Strange Case of Dr. Jekyll and Mr. Hyde* (BA, PN)

**Swift, Jonathan. *Gulliver's Travels* (BA, PN)

**Verne, Jules. *A Journey to the Center of the Earth* (BA, PN)

**———. *Twenty Thousand Leagues Under the Sea* (BA, PN)

Wells, H. G. *The First Men in the Moon* (PN)

———. *The Island of Doctor Moreau* (BA, PN)

*———. *A Modern Utopia* (BA, PN)

**———. *The Short Stories of H. G. Wells* (BA, PN)

**———. *The Time Machine* (BA, PN)

**———. *The War of the Worlds* (BA, PN)

*White, Stewart Edward. *The Mystery*

———. *The Sign at Six* (PN)

2: Science Fiction Between the Wars: 1916–1939

**Asimov, Isaac. *Before the Golden Age* (BA, PN)

*Bell, Neil. *The Seventh Bowl* (BA, PN)

*Burroughs, Edgar Rice. *The Land That Time Forgot* (BA, PN)

*Campbell, John W., Jr. *Who Goes There?* (BA, PN)

**Čapek, Karel. *The Absolute at Large* (BA, PN)

*———. *Krakatit* (PN)

*———. *R.U.R.* (BA, PN)

*———. *War With the Newts* (BA, PN)

*Cummings, Ray. *The Girl in the Golden Atom* (PN)

*Dent, Guy. *Emperor of the If* (PN)

*Farrère, Claude. *Useless Hands*

*Gloag, John. *To-Morrow's Yesterday* (BA, PN)
*———. *Winter's Youth*
**Huxley, Aldous. *Brave New World* (BA, PN)
*Karinthy, Frigyes. *Voyage to Faremido and Capillaria* (BA, PN)
*Large, E. C. *Sugar in the Air* (PN)
*Lindsay, David. *A Voyage to Arcturus* (BA, PN)
Llewellyn, Alun. *The Strange Invaders* (1934) (PN)
Marvell, Andrew. *Minimum Man* (PN)
*Maurois, André. *The Weigher of Souls* (BA, PN)
Merritt, A. *The Metal Monster* (PN)
Nowlan, Philip F. *Armageddon 2419 A.D.* (PN)
**Odle, E. V. *The Clockwork Man* (BA, PN)
O'Neill, Joseph. *Land Under England* (PN)
*Shaw, George Bernard. *Back to Methuselah* (BA, PN)
**Shiel, M. P. *The Young Men Are Coming!*
*Smith, E. E. *The Skylark of Space* (BA, PN)
**Stapledon, Olaf. *Last and First Men* (BA, PN)
*———. *Odd John* (BA, PN)
**———. *Star Maker* (BA, PN)
*Taine, John. *The Time Stream* (PN)
*Weinbaum, Stanley G. *A Martian Odyssey and Other Science Fiction Tales* (BA, PN)
*———. *The New Adam* (PN)
*Wells, H. G. *The Shape of Things to Come* (BA, PN)
*Williamson, Jack. *The Legion of Time* (BA, PN)
*Wright, S. Fowler. *Deluge* (BA, PN)
*———. *The New Gods Lead* (PN)
**———. *The World Below* (BA, PN)
*Wylie, Philip. *Gladiator* (BA, PN)
**Zamiatin, Evgenii. *We* (BA, PN)

3: From the Golden Age to the Atomic Age: 1940–1963

Aldiss, Brian. *The Airs of Earth* (1963) (DW)
**———. *Hothouse* (BA, DW)
———. *Non-Stop* (PN, DW)
Anderson, Poul. *Brain Wave* (PN)
**———. *The Enemy Stars* (BA, DW)
*Asimov, Isaac. *The Caves of Steel* (BA, DW)
———. *The End of Eternity* (1955) (DW)
**———. *The Foundation Trilogy* (BA, PN, DW)
*———. *I, Robot* (PN, DW)

————. *The Naked Sun* (PN, DW)
*Ballard, J. G. *The Drowned World* (BA, PN, DW)
————. *The Wind From Nowhere* (DW)
**Bester, Alfred. *The Demolished Man* (BA, PN, DW)
*————. *The Great Short Fiction of Alfred Bester* (PN, DW)
————. *Tiger! Tiger!* (PN, DW)
*Blish, James. *A Case of Conscience* (BA, PN, DW)
**————. *Cities in Flight* (BA, PN, DW)
Borges, Jorge. *Labyrinths* (1962; rev. 1964) (DW)
*Brackett, Leigh. *The Long Tomorrow* (BA, PN)
Bradbury, Ray. *Fahrenheit 451* (DW)
————. *The Illustrated Man* (1951) (DW)
*————. *The Martian Chronicles* (BA, PN, DW)
**————. *The Stories of Ray Bradbury* (BA, PN, DW)
Brown, Fredric. *The Lights in the Skies Are Stars* (1953) (DW)
*Budrys, A. J. *Rogue Moon* (BA, PN)
*Burgess, Anthony. *A Clockwork Orange* (BA, PN, DW)
Christopher, John. *The Death of Grass* (PN)
**Clarke, Arthur C. *Against the Fall of Night* (PN)
*————. *Childhood's End* (BA, PN, DW)
————. *The City and the Stars* (PN, DW)
**Clement, Hal. *Mission of Gravity* (BA, PN, DW)
**de Camp, L. Sprague. *Lest Darkness Fall* (BA)
*del Rey, Lester. *Early del Rey*
**Dick, Philip K. *The Collected Stories of Philip K. Dick* (BA, PN, DW)
*————. *The Man in the High Castle* (BA, PN, DW)
————. *Time Out of Joint* (1959) (DW)
*Farmer, Philip José. *The Lovers* (PN, DW)
————. *Strange Relations* (DW)
*Fast, Howard. *The Edge of Tomorrow* (BA)
*Finney, Jack. *The Third Level* (PN)
Frank, Pat. *Alas, Babylon* (PN)
*Galouye, Daniel. *Dark Universe* (BA, PN, DW)
Golding, William. *The Inheritors* (1955) (DW)
Harness, Charles. *Flight Into Yesterday* (1953) (PN, DW)
————. *The Rose* (1966) (DW)
Harrison, Harry. *Deathworld* (PN)
Heinlein, Robert A. *Beyond This Horizon* (DW)
————. *Double Star* (DW)
————. *Orphans in the Sky* (PN)
**————. *The Past Through Tomorrow* (BA, PN, DW)

————. *Starship Troopers* (DW)

*————. *Stranger in a Strange Land* (BA, PN, DW)

*Herbert, Frank. *The Dragon in the Sea* (BA, PN, DW)

Hesse, Hermann. *The Glass Bead Game* (1943; trans. 1969) (DW)

Hoyle, Fred. *The Black Cloud* (PN)

*Hubbard, L. Ron. *Final Blackout* (PN)

Huxley, Aldous. *Ape and Essence* (BA)

*Keyes, Daniel. *Flowers for Algernon* (BA, PN, DW)

*Knight, Damon F. *The Best of Damon Knight* (BA, PN, DW)

*Kornbluth, C. M. *The Best of C. M. Kornbluth* (BA, PN, DW)

*Kuttner, Henry. *The Best of Henry Kuttner* (BA, PN, DW)

————. *Fury* (1950) (BA, PN)

*Leiber, Fritz. *The Best of Fritz Leiber* (BA, PN, DW)

*————. *The Change War* (PN, DW)

**Lem, Stanislaw. *Solaris* (BA, PN, DW)

**Lewis, C. S. *The Space Trilogy* (BA, PN, DW)

*Matheson, Richard. *Born of Man and Woman* (BA)

McKenna, Richard. *Casey Agonistes* (PN, DW)

*Merril, Judith. *The Best of Judith Merril* (BA)

**Miller, Walter M., Jr. *A Canticle for Leibowitz* (BA, PN, DW)

*Moore, C. L. *The Best of C. L. Moore* (BA, PN, DW)

*Moore, Ward. *Bring the Jubilee* (BA, PN, DW)

*Neville, Kris. *The Science Fiction of Kris Neville* (PN)

*Oliver, Chad. *Shadows in the Sun* (BA, PN)

**Orwell, George. *Nineteen Eighty-Four* (BA, PN, DW)

*Pangborn, Edgar. *A Mirror for Observers* (BA, PN, DW)

*Pohl, Frederik. *The Best of Frederik Pohl* (BA, PN, DW)

**————. *The Space Merchants* (BA, PN, DW)

*Reynolds, Mack. *The Best of Mack Reynolds* (BA)

*St. Clair, Margaret. *Change the Sky*

*Sarban. *The Sound of His Horn* (BA)

Sheckley, Robert. *Immortality Inc.* (DW)

————. *Pilgrimage to Earth* (DW)

*————. *Untouched by Human Hands* (BA, PN, DW)

**Shute, Nevil. *On the Beach* (BA, PN, DW)

**Simak, Clifford. *City* (BA, PN, DW)

*————. *Way Station* (BA, PN, DW)

*Smith, E. E. The Lensman series (BA, PN)

**Stapledon, Olaf. *Sirius* (BA, PN, DW)

**Stewart, George R. *Earth Abides* (BA, PN, DW)

*Sturgeon, Theodore. *E Pluribus Unicorn* (BA, PN, DW)

**————. *More Than Human* (BA, PN, DW)
*————. *Without Sorcery* (PN)
*Tenn, William. *Of All Possible Worlds* (BA, PN, DW)
van Vogt, A. E. *Slan* (PN)
————. *Voyage of the Space Beagle* (PN)
————. *The Weapon Shops of Isher* (PN)
*————. *World of Null A* (BA)
Vance, Jack. *Big Planet* (1957) (PN)
————. *The Dying Earth* (DW)
————. *The Languages of Pao* (PN)
*————. *To Live Forever* (BA)
Vonnegut, Kurt. *Cat's Cradle* (DW)
**————. *Player Piano* (BA, PN, DW)
————. *The Sirens of Titan* (BA, PN, DW)
Williamson, Jack. *Darker Than You Think* (DW)
*————. *The Humanoids* (BA, PN, DW)
*Wolfe, Bernard. *Limbo* (BA, PN)
Wyndham, John. *The Day of the Triffids* (PN)
————. *The Midwich Cuckoos* (1957) (DW)
————. *Re-Birth* (PN)

Anthologies
Aldiss, Brian. *The Penguin Science Fiction Omnibus* (1973) (BA, PN)
**Asimov, Isaac. *The Hugo Winners* (PN, DW)
*————. *Isaac Asimov Presents the Great Science Fiction Stories* (PN, DW)
*Conklin, Groff. *A Treasury of Science Fiction* (PN)
*Healy, Raymond J. *Adventures in Time and Space* (PN)
*Merril, Judith. *SF: The Year's Greatest* (PN, DW)
*Pohl, Frederik. *Star Science Fiction Stories* (PN, DW)
**Silverberg, Robert. *The Science Fiction Hall of Fame* (PN, DW)

4: The New Wave, Cyberpunk, and Beyond: 1964–1994
Aldiss, Brian W. *Barefoot in the Head*
*————. *Greybeard* (BA, PN, DW)
**————. Helliconia series (BA, PN, DW)
————. *The Malacia Tapestry* (1976) (DW)
————. *The Moment of Eclipse* (1970) (DW)
Amis, Kingsley. *The Alteration* (DW)
*Anderson, Poul. *Tau Zero* (PN, DW)
*Asimov, Isaac. *The Complete Stories*
*————. *The Gods Themselves* (BA, PN, DW)

*Atwood, Margaret. *The Handmaid's Tale* (BA, PN)

**Ballard, J. G. *Chronopolis and Other Stories* (BA, PN, DW)

**———. *The Crystal World* (BA, DW)`

*———. *The Drought*

———. *The Terminal Beach* (1964) (BA)

Bayley, Barrington. *The Knights of the Limits* (DW)

**Bear, Greg. *Blood Music* (BA, PN, DW)

———. *Eon* (DW)

*———. *Queen of Angels* (BA, PN, DW)

*Benford, Gregory. *Great Sky River* and *Tides of Light* (BA, PN, DW)

———. *In Alien Flesh* (1986) (DW)

———. *In the Ocean of Night* (DW)

*———. *Timescape* (BA, PN, DW)

Bishop, Michael. *Close Encounters With the Deity* (1986) (DW)

———. *A Funeral for the Eyes of Fire* (1975) (DW)

**———. *No Enemy but Time* (BA, PN)

———. *Transfigurations* (DW)

Blish, James. *Black Easter* (DW)

*Brin, David. *Earth* (BA)

*———. *Startide Rising* (DW, PN)

*———. *The Uplift War* (DW, PN)

*Brunner, John. *The Sheep Look Up* (BA, PN, DW)

**———. *Stand on Zanzibar* (BA, PN, DW)

*Bujold, Lois McMaster. *Barrayar* (DW)

*———. *Falling Free* (PN)

*Bunch, David. *Moderan* (DW)

*Butler, Octavia. *Dawn* (PN)

———. *Wild Seed* (DW)

*Cadigan, Pat. *Patterns* (PN)

Card, Orson Scott. *Ender's Game* (DW)

———. *Seventh Son* (1987) (DW)

*Carter, Angela. *The Infernal Desire Machines of Doctor Hoffman*

*Cherryh, C. J. *Cyteen* (PN)

*———. *Downbelow Station* (BA, PN, DW)

*Clarke, Arthur C. *The Fountains of Paradise* (BA)

*———. *Rendezvous With Rama* (BA, PN, DW)

*Compton, D. G. *The Continuous Katherine Mortenhoe* (PN, DW)

Coney, Michael. *Hello Summer, Goodbye* (1975) (DW)

Cowper, Richard. *The Custodians* (1976) (DW)

———. *The Road to Corlay* (DW)

———. *The Twilight of Briareus* (1974) (DW)

Crowley, John. *Beasts* (DW)

*———. *The Deep* (1975) (DW)

*———. *Engine Summer* (BA, PN, DW)

*Delany, Samuel R. *Babel-17* (BA, DW)

*———. *Dhalgren* (DA, DW)

———. *Driftglass* (DW)

*———. *The Einstein Intersection* (BA, PN, DW)

**———. *Nova* (PN, DW)

*Denton, Bradley. *Buddy Holly Is Alive and Well on Ganymede* (PN)

**Dick, Philip K. *Do Androids Dream of Electric Sheep?* (BA, PN, DW)

———. *Dr. Bloodmoney* (DW)

———. *Flow My Tears, the Policeman Said* (DW)

**———. *Ubik* (BA, PN, DW)

Dickson, Gordon. *Dorsai!* (DW)

**Disch, Thomas M. *Camp Concentration* (BA, PN, DW)

———. *The Man Who Had No Idea* (DW)

*———. *On Wings of Song* (DW)

**———. *334* (PN)

Donaldson, Stephen. *Lord Foul's Bane, The Illeath War,* and *The Power That Preserves* (all 1977; trilogy) (BA)

*Effinger, George Alec. *When Gravity Fails* (PN, DW)

Elgin, Suzette Elgin. *Native Tongue* (DW)

**Ellison, Harlan. *Deathbird Stories* (BA, PN, DW)

**———. *The Essential Ellison* (PN, DW)

*Farmer, Philip José. *To Your Scattered Bodies Go* (BA, PN, DW)

*Fowler, Karen Joy. *Sarah Canary* (BA, PN, DW)

**Gibson, William. *Burning Chrome* (BA, PN, DW)

*———. *The Difference Engine* (PN)

*———. *Mona Lisa Overdrive* (PN)

*———. *Neuromancer* (BA, PN, DW)

Gunn, James. *The Listeners* (DW)

**Haldeman, Joe. *The Forever War* (BA, PN, DW)

Harrison, Harry. *Bill, the Galactic Hero* (1965) (BA)

**Heinlein, Robert A. *The Moon Is a Harsh Mistress* (PN, DW)

*Herbert, Frank. **Dune* (BA, PN, DW) and *Dune Messiah* (BA, PN, DW) and *Children of Dune* (BA, PN)

Holdstock, Robert. *Mythago Wood* (1984) (DW)

Kavan, Anna. *Ice* (DW)

*Kessel, John. *Good News From Outer Space*

*Lafferty, R. A. *Fourth Mansions* (BA, PN)

*———. *Nine Hundred Grandmothers* (PN, DW)

*Le Guin, Ursula K. *Always Coming Home* (PN)
**———. *The Dispossessed* (BA, PN, DW)
**———. *The Left Hand of Darkness* (BA, PN, DW)
———. *Orsinian Tales* (DW)
**———. *The Wind's Twelve Quarters* (BA, PN, DW)
*Leiber, Fritz. *The Leiber Chronicles* (BA, PN, DW)
———. *The Wanderer* (DW)
Lessing, Doris. *The Marriage Between Zones Three, Four and Five* (DW)
———. *Shikasta* (DW)
*Malzberg, Barry. *Beyond Apollo* (BA, PN, DW)
Mann, Philip. *The Eye of the Queen* (DW)
———. *The Fall of the Families* (1987) (DW)
———. *Master of Paxwax* (1986) (DW)
Martin, George R. R. *Dying of the Light* (DW)
———. *A Song for Lya* (DW)
Masson, David. *The Caltraps of Time* (BA, DW)
McDevitt, Jack. *The Hercules Text* (1986) (DW)
*Moorcock, Michael. *Behold the Man* (BA, PN, DW)
**Niven, Larry. *Ringworld* (BA, PN, DW)
*Pangborn, Edgar. *Davy* (BA, PN, DW)
*Panshin, Alexei. *Rite of Passage* (PN)
**Piercy, Marge. *Woman on the Edge of Time* (BA, PN)
**Pohl, Frederik. *Gateway* (BA, PN, DW)
———. *JEM* (DW)
*———. *Man Plus* (BA, PN, DW)
*Powers, Tim. *The Anubis Gates* (PN, DW)
Preuss, Paul. *Broken Symmetries* (DW)
Priest, Christopher. *An Infinite Summer* (DW)
———. *Inverted World* (DW)
Roberts, Keith. *The Chalk Giants* (DW)
*———. *Pavane* (BA, PN, DW)
**Robinson, Kim Stanley. *Red Mars* (BA, PN)
*———. *The Wild Shore* and *The Gold Coast* and *Pacific Edge* (PN)
**Russ, Joanna. *The Female Man* (BA, PN, DW)
*Ryman, Geoff. *The Child Garden* (PN)
Schenck, Hilbert. *At the Eye of the Ocean* (DW)
———. *A Rose for Armageddon* (DW)
Shaw, Bob. *Other Days, Other Eyes* (DW)
Sheckley, Robert. *Dimension of Miracles* (DW)
———. *Mindswap* (1966) (DW)
**Shephard, Lucius. *The Jaguar Hunter* (BA, PN, DW)

Wilhelm, Kate. *And the Angels Sing* (BA)

*———. *Children of the Wind*

**———. *The Clewiston Test* (PN)

*———. *The Infinity Box* (PN, DW)

**Willis, Connie. *Doomsday Book* (BA, PN, DW)

Wingrove, David. Chung Kuo series (BA)

**Wolfe, Gene. The Book of the New Sun series (BA, PN, DW)

*———. *The Fifth Head of Cerberus* (BA, PN, DW)

———. *The Island of Doctor Death and Other Stories and Other Stories* (DW)

*Zelazny, Roger. *The Doors of His Face, The Lamps of His Mouth and Other Stories* (BA, PN, DW)

*———. *The Dream Master* (PN, DW)

**———. *Lord of Light* (PN, DW)

**———. *This Immortal* (PN, DW)

Anthologies

*Aronica, Lou. *Full Spectrum* (PN, DW)

**Asimov, Isaac. *The New Hugo Winners* (BA, PN, DW)

**Carr, Terry. Best Science Fiction of the Year series (BA, PN, DW)

*———. Universe series (BA, PN, DW)

Dann, Jack. *In the Field of Fire* (BA, PN)

**Dozois, Gardner. The Year's Best Science Fiction series (BA, PN, DW)

**Ellison, Harlan. *Dangerous Visions* and *Again, Dangerous Visions* (PN, DW)

Harrison, Harry. *Nova* series (1970–1974) (DW)

*Hartwell, David. *The World Treasury of Science Fiction* (PN, DW)

*Knight, Damon F. *Orbit* series (BA, PN, DW)

*Le Guin, Ursula K. *The Norton Book of Science Fiction*

**Morrow, James. Nebula Awards series (BA, PN, DW)

Science Fiction Poetry

*Ackerman, Diane. *The Planets* (PN)

*Ballentine, Lee. *POLY* (PN)

*Green, Scott E. *Contemporary Science Fiction, Fantasy and Horror Poets* (PN)

*Lucie-Smith, Edward. *Holding Your Eight Hands* (BA, PN)

*Martinson, Harry. *Aniara* (BA, PN)

*Murphy, Patrick D. *The Poetic Fantastic* (PN)

**Star*Line* (PN)

**Tem, Steve Rasnic. *The Umbral Anthology of Science Fiction Poetry* (PN)

5: Young Adult Science Fiction

*Anthony, Piers. *Race Against Time*

*Benford, Gregory. *Jupiter Project* (PN)

**Bethancourt, T. Ernesto. *The Mortal Instruments*

*Bond, Nancy. *The Voyage Begun*
*Bova, Ben. *Exiled From Earth* (PN)
*Christopher, John. *The Guardians* (PN)
**———. *The White Mountains* (PN)
*Corlett, William. *Return to the Gate* (PN)
*Cross, John Keir. *The Angry Planet* (PN)
**Dickinson, Peter. *Eva* (PN)
*———. *The Weathermonger* (PN)
*du Bois, William Pene. *The Twenty-One Balloons* (PN)
*Engdahl, Sylvia Louise. *Enchantress From the Stars* (PN)
*Fisk, Nicholas. *Trillions* (PN)
*Hamilton, Virginia. *Dustland* (PN)
*———. *The Gathering* (PN)
*———. *Justice and Her Brothers* (PN)
*Harding, Lee. *Misplaced Persons* (PN)
Heinlein, Robert A. *Citizen of the Galaxy* (PN)
*———. *Rocket Ship Galileo*
*———. *Starman Jones* (PN)
———. *Time for the Stars* (1956) (PN)
*———. *Tunnel in the Sky* (PN)
*Hoover, H. M. *Another Heaven, Another Earth* (PN)
*———. *The Rains of Eridan* (PN)
**Huddy, Delia. *Time Piper* (PN)
*Jacobs, Paul Samuel. *Born Into Light*
Jones, Diana Wynne. *Archer's Goon* (1984) (PN)
———. *The Homeward Bounders* (1981) (PN)
———. *A Tale of Time City* (1987) (PN)
*Karl, Jean E. *The Turning Place* (PN)
*Lawrence, Louise. *Andra*
**L'Engle, Madeleine. *A Wrinkle in Time* (PN)
*Maguire, Gregory. *I Feel Like the Morning Star*
**Mayne, William. *Earthfasts* (PN)
*McCaffrey, Anne. *Dragonsong* (PN)
*McKillip, Patricia. *Moon-Flash* (PN)
*North, Eric. *The Ant Men*
Norton, Andre. *Catseye* (PN)
*———. *Operation Time Search* (PN)
**———. *Star Man's Son* (PN)
*Nourse, Alan E. *Star Surgeon* (PN)
**O'Brien, Robert C. *Mrs. Frisby and the Rats of NIMH* (PN)
**———. *Z for Zachariah* (PN)
Pešek, Luděk. *The Earth Is Near* (PN)

*Randall, Florence Engel. *A Watcher in the Woods* (PN)
**Rubinstein, Gillian. *Beyond the Labyrinth* (PN)
**————. *Skyway* (PN)
**————. *Space Demons* (PN)
*Sargent, Pamela. *Earthseed* (PN)
*Schlee, Ann. *The Vandal* (PN)
*Sleator, William. *House of Stairs*
*Snyder, Zilpha Keatley. *And All Between* (PN)
*————. *Below the Root* (PN)
*————. *Until the Celebration* (PN)
*Stone, Josephine Rector. *The Mudhead* (PN)
**Stoutenburg, Adrien. *Out There*
**Suddaby, Donald. *Village Fanfare* (PN)
*Swindells, Robert. *Brother in the Land*
Townsend, John Rowe. *Noah's Castle* (PN)
*Ure, Jean. *Plague*
Vance, Jack. *Vandals of the Void* (PN)
*Vinge, Joan. *Psion* (PN)
**Westall, Robert. *Futuretrack 5* (PN)
*————. *Urn Burial* (PN)
Wilder, Cherry. *The Luck of Brin's Five* (PN)
**Yep, Laurence. *Sweetwater* (PN)
*Zebrowski, George. *Sunspacer*

7: General Reference Works

*Brown, Charles N., and William G. Contento. *Science Fiction, Fantasy, &
  Horror* annual (DW)
Clareson, Thomas D. *Science Fiction in America, 1870s–1930s* (PN)
*Reginald, R. *Science Fiction and Fantasy Literature* (DW)
*Burgess, Michael. *Reference Guide to Science Fiction, Fantasy, and Horror*
*Contento, William G. *Index to Science Fiction Anthologies and Collections* (2
  vols.)
*Hall, H. W. *Science Fiction and Fantasy Reference Index* (2 vols.)
*Bleiler, Everett F. *Science Fiction Writers* (DW)
*————. *Science-Fiction: The Early Years* (DW)
**Clute, John, Peter Nicholls, and Brian Stableford. *The Encyclopedia of
  Science Fiction* (DW)
*Magill, Frank. *Survey of Science Fiction Literature* (DW)
Sargent, Lyman Tower. *British and American Utopian Literature 1516–1975*
  (PN)

8: History and Criticism

**Aldiss, Brian W., and David Wingrove. *Trillion Year Spree* (PN, DW)
Atheling, William [James Blish]. *The Issue at Hand* (PN)
————. *More Issues at Hand* (PN)
**Bailey, J. O. *Pilgrims Through Space and Time*
*Bleiler, Everett F. *Science-Fiction: The Early Years* (DW)
**Brians, Paul. *Nuclear Holocausts*
**Carter, Paul A. *The Creation of Tomorrow* (PN)
**Clareson, Thomas D. *Some Kind of Paradise* (PN)
**Clarke, I. F. *Voices Prophesying War* (PN)
*Delany, Samuel R. *The Jewel-Hinged Jaw* (PN, DW)
*Fredericks, Casey. *The Future of Eternity*
*Greenland, Colin. *The Entropy Exhibition* (PN)
**Gunn, James. *Alternate Worlds* (PN)
**Hillegas, Mark R. *The Future as Nightmare* (PN)
*Ketterer, David. *New Worlds for Old* (PN)
Knight, Damon. *In Search of Wonder* (PN)
**Le Guin, Ursula K. *The Language of the Night* (PN, DW)
*Lefanu, Sarah. *In the Chinks of the World Machine* (PN, DW)
*Lem, Stanislaw. *Microworlds* (PN)
*Malmgren, Carl. *Worlds Apart*
*Malzberg, Barry. *The Engines of the Night* (PN)
*Manlove, Colin. *Science Fiction: Ten Explorations* (PN, DW)
*Meyers, Walter E. *Aliens and Linguists* (PN)
Moskowitz, Sam. *Strange Horizons* (PN)
*Nicholls, Peter. *Science Fiction at Large* (PN, DW)
*Panshin, Alexei and Cory. *The World Beyond the Hill* (PN)
**Pringle, David. *Science Fiction: The 100 Best Novels* (DW)
**Rose, Mark. *Alien Encounters* (PN)
*Ruddick, Nicholas. *Ultimate Island* (PN)
————. *Structural Fabulation* (PN)
**Scholes, Robert. *Science Fiction: History/Science/Vision* (PN)
**Spinrad, Norman. *Science Fiction in the Real World* (PN, DW)
*Stableford, Brian M. *Scientific Romance in Britain, 1890–1950* (PN, DW)
**Suvin, Darko. *Metamorphoses of Science Fiction* (PN)
*————. *Victorian Science Fiction in the UK* (PN)
*Wagar, W. Warren. *Terminal Visions* (PN)
**Wolfe, Gary K. *The Known and the Unknown* (PN)

9: Author Studies

Brian W. Aldiss
*Aldiss, Margaret. *The Work of Brian W. Aldiss*

J. G. Ballard
*Pringle, David. *Earth Is the Alien Planet*
*———. *J. G. Ballard*

James Blish
*Ketterer, David. *Imprisoned in a Tesseract*
*Stableford, Brian M. *A Clash of Symbols*

Ray Bradbury
*Mogen, David. *Ray Bradbury*

John W. Campbell, Jr.
*Berger, Albert I. *The Magic That Works*

Orson Scott Card
*Collings, Michael R. *In the Image of God*

Arthur C. Clarke
*Slusser, George Edgar. *The Space Odysseys of Arthur C. Clarke*

Samuel R. Delany
*Barbour, Douglas. *Worlds out of Words*

Philip K. Dick
*Mackey, Douglas A. *Philip K. Dick*
*Mullen, R. D. *On Philip K. Dick*
*Sutin, Lawrence. *Divine Invasions*

Harlan Ellison
*Slusser, George Edgar. *Harlan Ellison*

William Gibson
**Olsen, Lance. *William Gibson*

Robert A. Heinlein
**Franklin, H. Bruce. *Robert A. Heinlein*

Ursula K. Le Guin
*Cummins, Elizabeth. *Understanding Ursula K. Le Guin*

Fritz Leiber
*Byfield, Bruce. *Witches of the Mind*

C. S. Lewis
**Downing, David C. *Planets in Peril*
*Manlove, C.N. *C. S. Lewis*
*Murphy, Brian C. *C. S. Lewis*

Jack London
*Beauchamp, Gorman. *Jack London*

*Labor, Earle. *Jack London*

A. Merritt
*Foust, Ronald. *A. Merritt*

George Orwell
*Howe, Irving. *Orwell's Nineteen Eighty-Four*
*Orwell, George. *Nineteen Eighty-Four*, ed. by Bernard Crick
**Sheldon, Michael. *Orwell*
**Reilly, Patrick. *Nineteen Eighty-Four: Past, Present, and Future*

Christopher Priest
*Ruddick, Nicholas. *Christopher Priest*

Mary Shelley
*Baldick, Chris. *In Frankenstein's Shadow*
**Mellor, Ann K. *Mary Shelley*
**Sunstein, Emily W. *Mary Shelley*
**Tropp, Martin. *Mary Shelley's Monster*

Olaf Stapledon
*Kinnard, John. *Olaf Stapledon*
*McCarthy, Patrick A. *Olaf Stapledon*
*McCarthy, Patrick A., et al. *The Legacy of Olaf Stapledon*

Mark Twain
*Cummings, Sherwood. *Mark Twain and Science*

Jules Verne
*Evans, Arthur B. *Jules Verne Rediscovered*

Kurt Vonnegut
*Klinkowitz, Jerome. *Kurt Vonnegut*
*Merrill, Robert. *Critical Essays on Kurt Vonnegut*

H. G. Wells
*Crossley, Robert. *H. G. Wells*
*Huntington, John. *The Logic of Fantasy*
*Smith, David. *H. G. Wells*
*Suvin, Darko. *H. G. Wells and Modern Science Fiction*

Jack Williamson
*Williamson, Jack. *Wonder's Child*

Collective Biography
*Jakubowski, Maxim. *The Profession of Science Fiction*

Interviews
**McCaffery, Larry. *Across the Wounded Galaxies*
Moskowitz, Sam. *Explorers of the Infinite* (1963) (PN)
**Platt, Charles. *Dream Makers*

10: Science Fiction in Film, Television, and Radio

Reference Works
*Hardy, Phil. *Science Fiction* [film encyclopedia] (PN)

General Studies
**Brosnan, John. *The Primal Screen* (PN)
**Nicholls, Peter. *The World of Fantastic Films* (PN)

Specialized Studies
*LaValley, Al. *Invasion of the Body Snatchers*
*Slusser, George. *Shadows of the Magic Lamp* (PN)
*Sobchack, Vivian. *Screening Space* (PN)
Warren, Bill. *Keep Watching the Skies!* (PN)

Periodicals
* *Cinefantastique* (PN)

11: Science Fiction Illustration

General and Multiartist Studies
**Aldiss, Brian W. *Science Fiction Art* (PN)
**Frewin, Anthony. *One Hundred Years of Science Fiction Illustration, 1840–1940* (PN)
*Hardy, David A. *Visions of Space*
*Hartmann, William K. *In the Stream of Stars*
*Summers, Ian. *Tomorrow and Beyond*
*Weinberg, Robert. *A Biographical Dictionary of Science Fiction and Fantasy Artists* (PN)

Individual Artists
*Bonestell, Chesley. *Worlds Beyond* (PN)
Burns, Jim. *Lightship* (PN)
*Cartier, Edd. *The Known and the Unknown* (PN)
*Finlay, Virgil. *Virgil Finlay's Strange Science* (PN)
*Foss, Chris. *21st Century Foss* (PN)
 *Freas, Frank Kelly. *The Art of Science Fiction* (PN)
*———. *The Astounding Fifties*
*Maitz, Don. *First Maitz* (PN)

*McCall, Robert. *The Art of Robert McCall*
*Powers, Richard. *Spacetimewarp* (PN)
*Richardson, Darrell C. *J. Allen St. John* (PN)
*Whelan, Michael. *Michael Whelan's Works of Wonder* (PN)
White, Tim. *The Science Fiction and Fantasy Worlds of Tim White* (1981) (PN)

Comics
*Clark, Alan. *Comics: An Illustrated History*
Gravett, Paul. *The New Penguin Book of Comics* (1993) (PN)
*Kunzle, David. *History of the Comic Strip*, Volume 1 (PN)
**McCloud, Scott. *Understanding Comics* (PN)
*Overstreet, Robert M. *The Overstreet Comic Price Guide* (PN)
*Scott, Randall W. *Comics Books and Strips*

12: Magazines

Current SF Magazines
Amazing Stories (PN)
**Analog* (PN)
***Asimov's Science Fiction* (PN)
**Interzone* (PN)
**The Magazine of Fantasy and Science Fiction* (PN)

Current Magazines About SF
***Extrapolation* (PN)
**Foundation* (PN)
***Locus* (PN)
**Monad* (PN)
**The New York Review of Science Fiction* (PN)
**Science Fiction Chronicle*
**Science Fiction Eye* (PN)
**Science-Fiction Studies*

Books About SF Magazines
*Miller, Stephen T., et al. *Science Fiction, Fantasy & Weird Magazine Index*
*Tymn, Marshall B., and Mike Ashley. *Science Fiction, Fantasy, and Weird Fiction Magazines* (PN)

13: Teaching Science Fiction

Instructional Guides
*Donelson, Kenneth. *Science Fiction in the English Class*
*Gunn, James. *Inside Science Fiction*

*Spann, Sylvia, and Mary Beth Culp. *Thematic Units in Teaching English and the Humanities*
**Tymn, Marshall. *Science Fiction: A Teacher's Guide and Resource Book*
**Williamson, Jack. *Teaching Science Fiction*

Writing Guides
*Bretnor, Reginald. *The Craft of Science Fiction*
*Card, Orson Scott. *How to Write Science Fiction and Fantasy*
*Dozois, Gardner. *Writing Science Fiction and Fantasy*
*Longyear, Barry B. *Science Fiction Writer's Workshop I*
*Warrick, Patricia. *Science Fiction: The SFRA Anthology*

Textbooks and Anthologies
*Gunn, James. *The Road to Science Fiction*
*Silverberg, Robert. *Science Fiction Hall of Fame*

Awards

Most of the awards described below are likely to be unknown to the general reader. They were created to recognize distinguished work in science fiction because the more prestigious literary awards usually ignore popular fiction to concentrate on what is believed to be "serious" work. Those voting for these awards range from a committee to a few hundred readers, sometimes members of the organizations discussed later.

Only a handful of the better known or more "significant" awards are discussed below. An authoritative listing of winners (only) for all categories of all awards is found in Mallett and Burgess [7-17]. Listing runners-up would greatly lengthen this already detailed listing. However, winners and runners-up for the Hugo and Nebula awards are found in Donald Franson and Howard De Vore's *A History of the Hugo, Nebula, and International Fantasy Awards*, last revised in 1985. (An updated edition has been promised.)

Winners for novels and shorter fiction (the latter in quotes) are shown by year of publication, with the abbreviation of the award following the winner, so that the reader can easily compare awards, and to consolidate what would otherwise be long, repetitious lists. This listing is a supplement to the best books listing created by contributors and outside readers, who naturally considered these award winners as candidates for their best books, although they did not select all of them for annotation. Consult the indexes for entry numbers of annotated books. The shorter fiction has been collected not only in author collections but in anthologies, especially the best-of-the-year anthologies. Collections and anthologies containing the earlier short fiction are indexed by Contento [7-13], the later fiction indexed in the *Locus* annuals [7-2]. For award-winning films and TV programs, see table 10-1.

British Science Fiction Association Awards [BSFA]. Members nominate the candidates, and a panel makes the final selections, with winners receiving engraved plaques.

John W. Campbell, Jr., Memorial Award [JWC]. Given in memory of the long-time editor of *Astounding*, now *Analog*, it is presented each year at the University of Kansas for the best SF novel. This award is distinct from the John W. Campbell Award for the best new author.

Arthur C. Clarke Award [ACC]. A panel of judges selects the best SF novel published in the United Kingdom, and the writer receives a £1,000 cash prize.

Philip K. Dick Memorial Award [PKD]. Created soon after Dick's death in 1982, selected by a five-person jury, first and second winners receive $1,000 and $500 respectively for the best original American SF paperback. Only first winners are listed.

Hugo Award [H]. Named after Hugo Gernsback, founding editor of *Amazing Stories*, this is the best known award in its field. It was officially called the Science Fiction Achievement Award until its name was formally changed to the Hugo Award at the 1992 world SF convention. Attending and supporting members of the convention vote by mail.

Locus Award [L]. Voted by readers of *Locus* [12-24], these awards generate more votes than any other single award.

Nebula Award [N]. About a third of the active membership of the Science-Fiction and Fantasy Writers of America votes this award in various categories, including several for shorter fiction. The awards are announced a few months before the Hugos and probably have some influence on them.

Academic Awards. Just as academics founded organizations devoted to the study of SF, so they began to bestow awards for scholarly distinction. The SF Research Association was the first to offer such awards, beginning in 1970 with the **Pilgrim Award** for sustained contribution to the study of SF and continuing more recently with the **Pioneer Award** for best article. The **J. Lloyd Eaton Memorial Award** is given to the best scholarly book about SF published two years previously; listed by year of publication. The **International Association for the Fantastic in the Arts Distinguished Scholarship Award** is given to an individual by judges appointed by the IAFA. These awards are listed following the awards for fiction.

Fiction Awards

Note: From 1952 through 1964 all stories were Hugo winners. With 1965 the Nebula awards began, with other awards following.

1952   *The Demolished Man* by Alfred Bester
1954   *They'd Rather Be Right* by Frank Riley and Mark Clifton
      "The Darfsteller" by Walter M. Miller, Jr.
      "Allamagoosa" by Eric Frank Russell
1955   *Double Star* by Robert A. Heinlein
      "Exploration Team" by Murray Leinster
      "The Star" by Arthur C. Clarke
1957   *The Big Time* by Fritz Leiber
      "Or All the Seas With Oysters" by Avram Davidson
1958   *A Case of Conscience* by James Blish
      "The Big Front Yard" by Clifford D. Simak
      "The Hell-Bound Train" by Fritz Leiber
1959   *Starship Troopers* by Robert A. Heinlein
      "Flowers for Algernon" by Daniel Keyes
1960   *A Canticle for Leibowitz* by Walter M. Miller, Jr.
      "The Longest Voyage" by Poul Anderson
1961   *Stranger in a Strange Land* by Robert A. Heinlein
      "Hothouse" series by Brian W. Aldiss
1962   *The Man in the High Castle* by Philip K. Dick
      "The Dragon Masters" by Jack Vance
1963   *Way Station* by Clifford D. Simak
      "No Truce With Kings" by Poul Anderson
1964   *The Wanderer* by Fritz Leiber
      "Soldier, Ask Not" by Gordon R. Dickson
1965   *This Immortal* (a.k.a. *And Call Me Conrad*) by Roger Zelazny (H)
      Dune by Frank Herbert (H, N)
      "'Repent, Harlequin!' Said the Ticktockman" by Harlan Ellison (H, N)
      "He Who Shapes" by Roger Zelazny (N)
      "The Saliva Tree" by Brian Aldiss (N)
      "The Doors of His Face, the Lamps of His Mouth" by Roger Zelazny (N)
1966   *The Moon Is a Harsh Mistress* by Robert A. Heinlein (H)
      Babel-17 by Samuel R. Delany (N)
      Flowers for Algernon by Daniel Keyes (N)
      "The Last Castle" by Jack Vance (H, N)
      "Neutron Star" by Larry Niven (H)

"Call Him Lord" by Gordon R. Dickson (N)

"The Secret Place" by Richard McKenna (N)

1967   *Lord of Light* by Roger Zelazny (H)

The Einstein Intersection by Samuel R. Delany (N)

"Weyr Search" by Anne McCaffrey (H)

"Riders of the Purple Wage" by Philip José Farmer (H)

"Gonna Roll Them Bones" by Fritz Leiber (H, N)

"I Have No Mouth, and I Must Scream" by Harlan Ellison (H)

"Behold the Man" by Michael Moorcock (N)

"Aye, and Gomorrah" by Samuel R. Delany (N)

1968   *Stand on Zanzibar* by John Brunner (H, BSFA)

Rite of Passage by Alexei Panshin (N)

"Nightwings" by Robert Silverberg (H)

"The Sharing of Flesh" by Poul Anderson (H)

"Dragon Rider" by Anne McCaffrey (N)

"Mother to the World" by Richard Wilson (N)

"The Planners" by Kate Wilhelm (N)

1969   *The Left Hand of Darkness* by Ursula K. Le Guin (H, N)

"Ship of Shadows" by Fritz Leiber (H)

"Time Considered as a Helix of Semi-Precious Stones" by Samuel
    R. Delany (H, N)

"A Boy and His Dog" by Harlan Ellison (N)

"Passengers" by Robert Silverberg (N)

1970   *Ringworld* by Larry Niven (H, L, N)

The Jagged Orbit by John Brunner (BSFA)

"Ill Met in Lankhmar" by Fritz Leiber (H, N)

"Slow Sculpture" by Theodore Sturgeon (H, N)

"The Region Between" by Harlan Ellison (L)

1971   *To Your Scattered Bodies Go* by Philip José Farmer (H)

A Time of Change by Robert Silverberg (H)

The Moment of Eclipse by Brian Aldiss (BSFA)

The Lathe of Heaven by Ursula K. Le Guin (L)

"The Queen of Air and Darkness" by Poul Anderson (H, L, N)

"Inconstant Moon" by Larry Niven (H)

"The Missing Man" by Katherine MacLean (N)

"Good News From the Vatican" by Robert Silverberg (N)

1972   *The Gods Themselves* by Isaac Asimov (H, L, N)

Beyond Apollo by Barry N. Malzberg (JWC)

"The Word for World Is Forest" by Ursula K. Le Guin (H)

"Goat Song" by Poul Anderson (H, N)

"Eurema's Dam" by R. A. Lafferty (H)

"The Meeting" by Frederik Pohl and C. M. Kornbluth (H)

"A Meeting With Medusa" by Arthur C. Clarke (N)
"When It Changed" by Joanna Russ (N)
"The Gold at Starbow's End" by Frederik Pohl (L)
"Basilisk" by Harlan Ellison (L)

1973   *Rendezvous With Rama* by Arthur C. Clark (BSFA, JWC, H, L, N)
Malevil by Robert Merle (JWC)
"The Girl Who Was Plugged In" by James Tiptree, Jr. (H)
"The Ones Who Walk Away From Omelas" by Ursula K. Le Guin (H)
"The Death of Dr. Island" by Gene Wolfe (L, N)
"Of Mist, and Grass, and Sand" by Vonda N. McIntyre (N)
"Love Is the Plan, the Plan Is Death" by James Tiptree, Jr. (N)
"The Death Bird" by Harlan Ellison (L)

1974   *The Dispossessed* by Ursula K. Le Guin (H, L, N)
Orbitsville by Bob Shaw (BSFA)
Flow My Tears, the Policeman Said by Philip K. Dick (JWC)
"A Song for Lya" by George R. R. Martin (H)
"Adrift, Just off the Islets of Langerhans . . ." by Harlan Ellison (H, L)
"The Hole Man" by Larry Niven (H)
"Born With the Dead" by Robert Silverberg (L, N)
"The Stars Are Gods" by Gregory Benford (N)
"The Day Before the Revolution" by Ursula K. Le Guin (L, N)

1975   *The Forever War* by Joe Haldeman (H, L, N)
"Home Is the Hangman" by Roger Zelazny (H, N)
"Borderland of Sol" by Larry Niven (H)
"Catch That Zeppelin" by Fritz Leiber (H, N)
"San Diego Lightfoot Sue" by Tom Reamy (N)
"The Storms of Windhaven" by George R. R. Martin (L)
"The New Atlantis" by Ursula K. Le Guin (L)
"Croatoan" by Harlan Ellison (L)

1976   *Where Late the Sweet Birds Sang* by Kate Wilhelm (H, L)
Brontomek! by Michael G. Coney (BSFA)
Man Plus by Frederik Pohl (N)
The Alteration by Kingsley Amis (JWC)
"Houston, Houston, Do You Read?" by James Tiptree, Jr. (H, N)
"By Any Other Name" by Spider Robinson (H)
"The Bicentennial Man" by Isaac Asimov (H, L, N)
"Tricentennial" by Joe Haldeman (H, L)
"A Crowd of Shadows" by Charles L. Grant (N)
"The Samurai and the Willows" by Michael Bishop (L)

1977   *Gateway* by Frederik Pohl (H, JWC, L, N)
       The Jonah Kit by Ian Watson (BSFA)
       "Stardance" by Spider and Jeanne Robinson (H, L, N)
       "Eyes of Amber" by Joan D. Vinge (H)
       "Jeffty Is Five" by Harlan Ellison (H, L, N)
       "The Screwfly Solution" by James Tiptree, Jr. (N)

1978   *Dreamsnake* by Vonda N. McIntyre (H, L, N)
       Gloriana by Michael Moorcock (JWC)
       "The Persistence of Vision" by John Varley (H, L, N)
       "Hunter's Moon" by Poul Anderson (H)
       "Cassandra" by C. J. Cherryh (H)
       "A Glow of Candles, a Unicorn's Eye" by Charles L. Grant (N)
       "Stone" by Edward Bryant (N)
       "The Barbie Murders" by John Varley (L)
       "Count the Clock That Tells Time" by Harlan Ellison (L)

1979   *The Fountains of Paradise* by Arthur C. Clarke (H, N)
       The Unlimited Dream Company by J. G. Ballard (BSFA)
       On Wings of Song by Thomas M. Disch (JWC)
       Titan by John Varley (L)
       "Enemy Mine" by Barry B. Longyear (H, N)
       "Sandkings" by George R. R. Martin (H, L, N)
       "The Way of Cross and Dragon" by George R. R. Martin (H, L)
       "giANTS" by Edward Bryant (N)
       "Palely Loitering" by Christopher Priest (BSFA)

1980   *The Snow Queen* by Joan D. Vinge (H, L)
       Timescape by Gregory Benford (BSFA, JWC, N)
       "Lost Dorsai" by Gordon R. Dickson (H)
       "The Cloak and the Staff" by Gordon R. Dickson (H)
       "Grotto of the Dancing Deer" by Clifford R. Simak (H, L, N)
       "Unicorn Tapestry" by Suzy McKee Charnas (N)
       "The Ugly Chickens" by Howard Waldrop (N)
       "The Brave Little Toaster" by Thomas M. Disch (BSFA, L)
       "Nightflyers" by George R. R. Martin (L)

1981   *Downbelow Station* by C. J. Cherryh (H)
       The Claw of the Conciliator by Gene Wolfe (N)
       The Shadow of the Torturer by Gene Wolfe (BSFA)
       Riddley Walker by Russell Hoban (JWC)
       The Many Colored Land by Julian May (L)
       "The Saturn Game" by Poul Anderson (H, N)
       "Unicorn Variation" by Roger Zelazny (H)
       "The Pusher" by John Varley (H, L)

"The Quickening" by Michael Bishop (N)
"The Bone Flute" by Lisa Tuttle (N)
"Mythago Wood" by Robert Holdstock (BSFA)
"Guardians" by George R. R. Martin (L)
"Blue Champagne" by John Varley (L)

1982 *Foundation's Edge* by Isaac Asimov (H, L)
No Enemy But Time by Michael Bishop (N)
Helliconia: Spring by Brian W. Aldiss (BSFA, JWC)
Software by Rudy Rucker (PKD)
"Souls" by Joanna Russ (H, L)
"Fire Watch" by Connie Willis (H, N)
"Melancholy Elephants" by Spider Robinson (H)
"Another Orphan" by John Kessel (N)
"A Letter From the Clearys" by Connie Willis (N)
"Kitemaster" by Keith Roberts (BSFA)
"Djinn, No Chaser" by Harlan Ellison (L)
"Sur" by Ursula K. Le Guin (L)

1983 *Startide Rising* by David Brin (H, L, N)
Tik-Tok by John Sladek (BSFA)
The Citadel of the Autarch by Gene Wolfe (JWC)
The Anubis Gates by Tim Powers (PKD)
"Cascade Point" by Timothy Zahn (H)
"Blood Music" by Greg Bear (H, N)
"Speech Sounds" by Octavia E. Butler (H)
"Hardfought" by Greg Bear (N)
"The Peacemaker" by Gardner Dozois (N)
"After Images" by Malcolm Edwards (BSFA)
"Her Habiline Husband" by Michael Bishop (L)
"The Monkey Treatment" by George R. R. Martin (L)
"Beyond the Dead Reef" by James Tiptree, Jr. (L)

1984 *Neuromancer* by William Gibson (PKD, H, N)
Mythago Wood by Robert Holdstock (BSFA)
The Years of the City by Frederik Pohl (JWC)
The Integral Trees by Larry Niven (L)
"Press ENTER" by John Varley (H, L, N)
"Bloodchild" by Octavia E. Butler (H, L, N)
"The Crystal Spheres" by David Brin (H)
"Morning Child" by Gardner Dozois (N)
"Unconquered Country" by Geoff Ryman (BSFA)
"Salvador" by Lucius Shepard (L)

1985 *Ender's Game* by Orson Scott Card (H, N)

Helliconia Winter by Brian W. Aldiss (BSFA)

The Postman by David Brin (JWC, L)

Dinner at Deviant's Palace by Tim Powers (PKD)

"Twenty-Four Views of Mt. Fuji, by Hokusai" by Roger Zelazny (H)

"Paladin of the Lost Ark" by Harlan Ellison (H, L)

"Fermi and Frost" by Frederik Pohl (H)

"Sailing to Byzantium" by Robert Silverberg (N)

"Portraits of His Children" by George R. R. Martin (N)

"Out of All Them Bright Stars" by Nancy Kress (N)

"Cube Root" by Dave Langford (BSFA)

"The Only Neat Thing to Do" by James Tiptree, Jr. (L)

"With Virgil Oddum at the East Pole" by Harlan Ellison (L)

1986   *Speaker for the Dead* by Orson Scott Card (H, L, N)

The Ragged Astronauts by Bob Shaw (BSFA)

A Door Into Ocean by Joan Slonczewski (JWC)

The Handmaid's Tale by Margaret Atwood (ACC)

Homunculus by James P. Blaylock (PKD)

"Gilgamesh in the Outback" by Robert Silverberg (H)

"Permafrost" by Roger Zelazny (H)

"Tangents" by Greg Bear (H, N)

"R and R" by Lucius Shepard (L, N)

"The Girl Who Fell Into the Sky" by Kate Wilhelm (N)

"Kaeti and the Hangman" by Keith Roberts (BSFA)

"Thor Meets Captain America" by David Brin (L)

"Robot Dreams" by Isaac Asimov (L)

1987   *The Uplift War* by David Brin (H, L)

The Falling Woman by Pat Murphy (N)

Grainne by Keith Roberts (BSFA)

Lincoln's Dreams by Connie Willis (JWC)

The Sea and the Serpent by George Turner (ACC)

Strange Toys by Patricia Geary

"Eye for Eye" by Orson Scott Card (H)

"Buffalo Gals, Won't You Come Out Tonight" by Ursula K. Le Guin (H)

"Why I Left Harry's 11-Night Hamburgers" by Lawrence Watt-Evans (H)

"The Blind Geometer" by Kim Stanley Robinson (N)

"Rachel in Love" by Pat Murphy (L, N)

"Forever Yours, Anna" by Kate Wilhelm (N)

"Love Sickness" by Geoff Ryman (BSFA)

"The Secret Sharer" by Robert Silverberg (L)

"Angel" by Pat Cadigan (L)

1988   *Cyteen* by C. J. Cherryh (H, L)
Falling Free by Lois McMaster Bujold (N)
Islands in the Net by Bruce Sterling (JWC)
Unquenchable Fire by Rachel Pollack (ACC)
Wetware by Rudy Rucker (PKD)
"The Last of the Winnebagos" by Connie Willis (H, N)
"Schrödinger's Kitten" by George Alec Effinger (H, N)
"Kirinyaga" by Mike Resnick (H)
"Bible Stories for Adults, #17: The Deluge" by James Morrow (N)
"The Scalehunter's Beautiful Daughter" by Lucius Shepard (L)
"The Function of Dream Sleep" by Harlan Ellison (L)
"Eidolons" by Harlan Ellison (L)

1989   *Hyperion* by Dan Simmons (H, L)
The Healer's War by Elizabeth Ann Scarborough (N)
Pyramids by Terry Pratchett (BSFA)
The Child Garden by Geoff Ryman (ACC, JWC)
Subterranean Gallery by Richard Paul Russo (PKD)
"The Mountains of Mourning" by Lois McMaster Bujold (H, N)
"Enter a Soldier. Later: Enter Another" by Robert Silverberg (H)
"Boobs" by Suzy McKee Charnas (H)
"At the Rialto" by Connie Willis (N)
"Ripples in the Dirac Sea" by Geoffrey A. Landis (N)
"In Translation" by Lisa Tuttle (BSFA)
"The Father of Stones" by Lucius Shepard (L)
"Dogwalker" by Orson Scott Card (L)
"Lost Boys" by Orson Scott Card (L)

1990   *The Vor Game* by Lois McMaster Bujold (H)
Tehanu: The Last Book of Earthsea by Ursula K. Le Guin (N)
Take Back Plenty by Colin Greenland (BSFA, ACC)
Pacific Edge by Kim Stanley Robinson (JWC)
Points of Departure by Pat Murphy (PKD)
The Fall of Hyperion by Dan Simmons (L)
"The Hemingway Hoax" by Joe Haldeman (H, N)
"The Manamouki" by Mike Resnick (H)
"Bears Discover Fire" by Terry Bisson (H, L, N)
"The Original Dr. Shade" by Kim Newman (BSFA)
"A Short, Sharp Shock" by Kim Stanley Robinson (L)
"Entropy's Bed at Midnight" by Dan Simmons (L)

1991   *Barrayar* by Lois McMaster Bujold (H, L)
Stations of the Tide by Michael Swanwick (N)

The Fall of Hyperion by Dan Simmons (BSFA)
Buddy Holly Is Alive and Well on Ganymede by Bradley Denton (JWC)
Synners by Pat Cadigan (ACC)
King of Morning, Queen of Day by Ian McDonald (PKD)
"Beggars in Spain" by Nancy Kress (H, N)
"Gold" by Isaac Asimov (H)
"A Walk in the Sun" by Geoffrey A. Landis (H)
"Guide Dog" by Mike Conner (N)
"Ma Qui" by Alan Brennert (N)
"Bad Timing" by Molly Brown (BSFA)
"The Gallery of His Dreams" by Kristine Kathryn Rusch (L)
"All Dracula's Children" by Dan Simmons (L)
"Buffalo" by John Kessel (L)

1992   *Doomsday Book* by Connie Willis (N, L)
Body of Glass by Marge Piercy (ACC)
Through the Heart by Richard Grant (PKD)
Red Mars by Kim Stanley Robinson (BSFA)
Brother to Dragons by Charles Sheffield (JWC)
"Danny Goes to Mars" by Pamela Sargent (N, L)
"Even the Queen" by Connie Willis (N, L)
"Barnacle Bill the Spacer" by Lucius Shepard (L)
"The Innocents" by Ian McDonald (BSFA)

1993   *Red Mars* by Kim Stanley Robinson (H, N)
Green Mars by Kim Stanley Robinson (L)
Aztec Century by Christopher Evans (BSFA)
Growing Up Weightless by John M. Ford & *Elvissey* by Jack Womack
    (PKD, tie)
Vurt by Jeff Noon (ACC)
"Georgia on My Mind" by Charles Sheffield (H, N)
"The Night We Buried Road Dog" by Jack Cady (N)
"Graves" by Joe Haldeman (N)
"Down in the Bottom Lands" by Harry Turtledove (H)
"The Ragthorn" by Robert Holdstock & Garry Kilworth (BSFA)
"Death in Bangkok" by Dan Simmons (L)
"Close Encounters" by Connie Willis (L)
"Mefisto in Onyx" by Harlan Ellison (L)

Academic Awards

Note: Pilgrim awards 1970–date, Eaton awards 1977–date, IAFA scholarship awards, 1986–date. Listed in that sequence.

1970   J. O. Bailey
1971   Marjorie Hope Nicolson
1972   Julius Kagarlitski
1973   Jack Williamson
1974   I. F. Clarke
1975   Damon Knight
1976   James E. Gunn
1977   Thomas D. Clareson
       The Creation of Tomorrow by Paul A. Carter
1978   Brian W. Aldiss
       Future Tense: The Cinema of Science Fiction by John Brosnan
1979   Darko Suvin
       The Known and the Unknown: The Iconography of Science Fiction by
          Gary K. Wolfe
1980   Peter Nicholls
       Robert A. Heinlein: America as Science Fiction by H. Bruce Franklin
1981   Sam Moskowitz
       Alien Encounters by Mark Rose
1982   Neil Barron
       The Logic of Fantasy by John Huntington
1983   H. Bruce Franklin
       The Entropy Exhibition by Colin Greenland
1984   Everett F. Bleiler
       Fantasy and Mimesis by Kathryn Hume
1985   Samuel R. Delany
       Some Kind of Paradise by Thomas R. Clareson
       Scientific Romance in Britain by Brian Stableford
1986   George E. Slusser
       Trillion Year Spree by Brian W. Aldiss and David Wingrove
       Brian W. Aldiss
1987   Gary K. Wolfe
       Origins of Futuristic Fiction by Paul Alkon
       Brian Stableford
1988   Joanne Russ
       Jules Verne Rediscovered by Arthur B. Evans
       Kathryn Hume
1989   Ursula K. Le Guin
       Science Fiction, Fantasy, & Horror: 1988 by Charles N. Brown and
          William G. Contento
       Colin Manlove

1990 Marshall B. Tymn
The Last Frontier: Imagining Other Worlds by Karl Guthke
H. Bruce Franklin
1991 Pierre Versins
Isaac Asimov by Donald M. Hassler
The Second Marxian Invasion by Stephen W. Potts
Brian Attebery
1992 Mark R. Hillegas (SFRA)
L'Obscur objet d'un savoir by Roger Bozzetto
Jack Zipes (IAFA)
1993 Robert Reginald (SFRA)
Devendra P. Varma (IAFA)
1994 John Clute (SFRA)
James Flannery (IAFA)

Series

Listed here are series of three or more books, at least one of which is annotated in this guide. Some books require or at least benefit from a reader's knowledge of earlier books in the series. Books are therefore listed in their internal reading sequence or by year of publication if the sequence is unimportant. Included here are prequels, works describing earlier events involving characters or settings from a previous work. Reginald's bibliography [7-8] provides fuller details, including listings of omnibus volumes and books with variant titles not listed here.

Following the author listing is an index by keywords in the series titles, cross-referenced to the author. Series titles are sometimes not fixed. I have therefore used the "standard" title, if any, or followed the series listing in Reginald's bibliography. Three series in chapter 1 by Burroughs (Tarzan), Haggard (Quatermain), and Verne (the *voyages extraordinaires*) are not listed because most books within the series are not SF; see Reginald for complete listings. Consult the index for entry numbers.

Adams, Douglas. Hitchhiker
The Hitch Hiker's Guide to the Galaxy, 1979
The Restaurant at the End of the Universe, 1980
Life, the Universe and Everything, 1982
So Long, and Thanks for All the Fish, 1984
Mostly Harmless, 1992

Aldiss, Brian W. Helliconia
Helliconia Spring, 1982
Helliconia Summer, 1983
Helliconia Winter, 1985

Anderson, Chester. Greenwich Village
The Butterfly Kid, 1967
The Unicorn Girl (by Michael Kurland), 1969

The Probability Pad (by T. A. Waters), 1970

Anderson, Poul. Technic Civilization
War of the Wing-Men, 1958
Trader to the Stars, 1964
The Trouble Twisters, 1966
Satan's World, 1969
Mirkheim, 1977
The Earth Book of Stormgate, 1978
The People of the Wind, 1973
Ensign Flandry, 1966
A Circus of Hells, 1969
The Rebel Worlds, 1969
The Day of Their Return, 1973
Agent of the Terran Empire, 1965
Flandry of Terra, 1965
A Knight of Ghosts and Shadows, 1975
The Game of Empire, 1985
Let the Spacemen Beware! 1963
The Long Night, 1983

Anthony, Piers. Tarot
God of Tarot, 1979
Vision of Tarot, 1980
Faith of Tarot, 1980

Appleton, Victor. Tom Swift
Tom Swift and His Motor Cycle, 1910
Tom Swift and His Motor Boat, 1910
Tom Swift and His Airship, 1910
Tom Swift and His Submarine Boat, 1910
Tom Swift and His Electric Runabout, 1910
Tom Swift and His Wireless Message, 1911
Tom Swift among the Diamond Makers, 1911
Tom Swift and the Caves of Ice, 1911
Tom Swift and His Sky Racer, 1911

Tom Swift and His Electric Rifle, 1911
Tom Swift in the City of Gold, 1912
For remaining titles through 1935, see Reginald [7-8] or Bleiler [7-21] for plot summaries and evaluation.

Asimov, Isaac. Foundation
Prelude to Foundation, 1988
Forward the Foundation, 1993
Foundation, 1951
Foundation and Empire, 1952
Second Foundation, 1953
Foundation's Edge, 1982
Foundation and Earth, 1986

Asimov, Isaac. Robot
I, Robot, 1950
The Rest of the Robots, 1964
The Caves of Steel, 1954
The Naked Sun, 1957
The Robots of Dawn, 1983
Robots and Empire, 1985
Isaac Asimov's Caliban by Roger McBride Allen, 1993
Isaac Asimov's Inferno by Roger McBride Allen, 1994

Attanasio, A. A. Radix
Radix, 1981
In Other Worlds, 1984
Arc of the Dream, 1986
The Last Legends of Earth, 1989

Bell, Clare. Ratha
Ratha's Creature, 1983
Clan Ground, 1984
Ratha and the Thistle-Chaser, 1990
Ratha's Challenge, 1994

Benford, Gregory, Great Sky River
Great Sky River, 1987
Tides of Light, 1989
Furious Gulf, 1994

Biemiller, Carl L. The Hydronauts
The Hydronauts, 1970
Follow the Whales, 1973
Escape From the Crater, 1974

Blish, James. Cities in Flight
They Shall Have Stars, 1956
A Life for the Stars, 1962
Earthman, Come Home, 1955
The Triumph of Time, 1958

Bova, Ben. Exiles
Exiled From Earth, 1971
Flight of Exiles, 1972
End of Exile, 1975

Bradley, Marion Zimmer. Darkover
Darkover Landfall, 1972
The Spell Sword, 1974
Star of Danger, 1965
The Winds of Darkover, 1970
The Bloody Sun, 1964, 1979
The Heritage of Hastur, 1975
The Sword of Aldones, 1962
The Planet Savers, 1971
The Shattered Chain, 1976
The Forbidden Tower, 1977
Stormqueen! 1978
Two to Conquer, 1980
Sharra's Exile, 1981
Hawkmistress! 1982
Thendara House, 1983
City of Sorcery, 1984
Oath of the Renunciates, 1984
The Heirs of Hammerfell, 1989
Rediscovery, 1993 (with Mercedes
Lackey)
Anthologies based on Darkover
omitted; see Reginald [7-8].

Bujold, Lois McMaster. Vorkosigan
Shards of Honor, 1986
Barrayar, 1991
The Warrior's Apprentice, 1986
Borders of Infinity, 1989
The Vor Game, 1990

Brothers in Arms, 1989
Mirror Dance, 1994

Burroughs, Edgar Rice. Mars
A Princess of Mars, 1917
The Gods of Mars, 1918
The Warlord of Mars, 1919
Thuvia, Maid of Mars, 1920
The Chessmen of Mars, 1922
The Master Mind of Mars, 1928
A Fighting Man of Mars, 1931
Swords of Mars, 1936
Synthetic Men of Mars, 1940
Llana of Gathol, 1948
John Carter of Mars, 1964

Burroughs, Edgar Rice. Pellucidar
At the Earth's Core, 1922
Pellucidar, 1923
Tanar of Pellucidar, 1930
Tarzan at the Earth's Core, 1930
Back to the Stone Age, 1937
Land of Terror, 1944
Savage Pellucidar, 1963

Burroughs, Edgar Rice. Venus
Pirates of Venus, 1934
Lost on Venus, 1935
Carson of Venus, 1939
Escape on Venus, 1946
The Wizard of Venus, 1970

Busby, F. M. Bran Tregare
Star Rebel, 1984
The Alien Debt, 1984
Rebel's Quest, 1985
Rebel's Seed, 1986

Butler, Octavia. Patternist
Patternmaster, 1976
Mind of My Mind, 1977
Survivor, 1978
Wild Seed, 1980
Clay's Ark, 1984

Butler, Octavia. Xenogenesis
Dawn, 1987

Adulthood Rites, 1988
Imago, 1989

Campbell, John W., Jr. Arcot, Wade and Morley
The Black Star Passes, 1953
Islands of Space, 1956
Invaders From the Infinite, 1961

Card, Orson Scott. Ender Wiggins
Ender's Game, 1985
Speaker for the Dead, 1986
Xenocide, 1991

Charnas, Suzy McKee. Holdfast
Walk to the End of the World, 1974
Motherlines, 1978
The Furies, 1994

Cherryh, C. J. Chanur
The Pride of Chanur, 1982
Chanur's Venture, 1984
The Kif Strike Back, 1985
Chanur's Homecoming, 1986
Chanur's Legacy, 1992
Tripoint, 1994

Cherryh, C. J. Downbelow Station
Downbelow Station, 1981
Merchanter's Luck, 1982
Forty Thousand in Gehenna, 1983

Christopher, John. Fireball
Fireball, 1981
New Found Land, 1983
Dragon Dance, 1986

Christopher, John. Luke
The Prince in Waiting, 1970
Beyond the Burning Lands, 1973
The Sword of the Spirits, 1972

Christopher, John. Tripod
When the Tripods Came, 1988
The White Mountains, 1967
In the City of Gold and Lead, 1967
The Pool of Fire, 1968

Clarke, Arthur C. Rama
Rendezvous With Rama, 1973
Rama II, 1989
The Garden of Rama, 1991
Rama Revealed, 1993

Clark, Arthur C. 2001
2001, 1968
2010: Odyssey Two, 1982
2061: Odyssey Three, 1988

Claudy, Carl H. Adventures in the Unknown
The Mystery Men of Mars, 1933
A Thousand Years a Minute, 1933
The Land of No Shadows, 1933
The Blue Grotto Terror, 1934

Coney, Michael. Greataway: Song of Earth
The Celestial Stream Locomotive, 1983
Gods of the Greataway, 1984
Fang, the Gnome, 1988
King of the Scepter'd Isle, 1989

Constantine, Storm. Wraeththu
The Enchantments of Flesh and Spirit, 1987
The Bewitchments of Love and Hate, 1988
The Fulfillments of Fate and Desire, 1989

Corlett, William. Gate
The Gate of Eden, 1975
The Land Beyond, 1976
Return to the Gate, 1977

Cowper, Richard. Bird of Kinship
The Road to Corlay, 1978
A Dream of Kinship, 1981
A Tapestry of Time, 1982

Dick, Philip K. VALIS
VALIS, 1981
The Divine Invasion, 1981

The Transmigration of Timothy Archer, 1982

Dickinson, Peter. Changes
The Devil's Children, 1970
Heartsease, 1969
The Weathermonger, 1968

Dickson, Gordon R. Childe Cycle
Necromancer, 1962
No Room for Man, 1963
Tactics of Mistake, 1971
Soldier, Ask Not, 1967
The Genetic General, 1960
Dorsai! 1976
The Spirit of Dorsai, 1979
Young Bleys, 1991
The Final Encyclopedia, 1984
The Chantry Guild, 1988
Other, 1994

Effinger, George Alec. Marid Audran
When Gravity Fails, 1987
A Fire in the Sun, 1989
The Exile Kiss, 1991

Elgin, Suzette Haden. Coyote Jones
Communipath Worlds, 1970
Furthest, 1971
At the Seventh Level, 1972
Star Anchored, Star Angered, 1979
Yonder Comes the Other End of Time, 1986

Elgin, Suzette Haden. Native Tongue
Native Tongue, 1984
The Judas Rose, 1987
Earthsong, 1994

Farmer, Philip José. Riverworld
To Your Scattered Bodies Go, 1971
The Fabulous Riverboat, 1971
The Dark Design, 1977
The Magic Labyrinth, 1980
Gods of Riverworld, 1983
River of Eternity, 1983

Farmer, Philip José. World of Tiers
The Maker of Universes, 1965
The Gates of Creation, 1966
A Private Cosmos, 1968
Behind the Walls of Terra, 1970
The Lavalite World, 1977

Foster, Alan Dean. Flinx
For Love of Mother-Not, 1983
The Tar-Aiym Krang, 1972
Orphan Star, 1977
The End of the Matter, 1977
Bloodhype, 1973
Flinx in Flux, 1988

Foster, Alan Dean. Morphodite
The Morphodite, 1981
Transformer, 1983
Preserver, 1985

French, Paul. Lucky Starr
David Starr: Space Ranger, 1952
Lucky Starr and the Pirates of the Asteroids, 1953
Lucky Starr and the Oceans of Venus, 1954
Lucky Starr and the Big Sun of Mercury, 1956
Lucky Starr and the Moons of Jupiter, 1957
Lucky Starr and the Rings of Saturn, 1958

Gibson, William. Neuromancer
Neuromancer, 1984
Count Zero, 1986
Mona Lisa Overdrive, 1988

Giesy, J. U. Palos trilogy
Palos of the Dog-Star Pack, 1918
The Mouthpiece of Zitu, 1919
Jason, Son of Jason, 1921

Haldeman, Joe. Worlds
Worlds, 1981
Worlds Apart, 1983
Worlds Enough and Time, 1992

Pournelle, Jerry. Falkenberg's
Legion
The Mercenary, 1977
West of Honor, 1976
Prince of Mercenaries, 1989
Go Tell the Spartans, 1991

Rankin, Robert. Armageddon
Armageddon: The Musical, 1990
*They Came and Ate Us:
Armageddon II: The B-Movie*,
1991
*The Suburban Book of the Dead:
Armageddon III: The Remake*,
1992

Reynolds, Mack. Lagrange
Lagrange Five, 1979
The Lagrangists, 1983
Chaos in Lagrangia, 1984
Trojan Orbit, 1985

Robinson, Kim Stanley. Mars
Red Mars, 1992
Green Mars, 1993
Blue Mars, 199?

Robinson, Kim Stanley. Orange
County
The Wild Shore, 1984
The Gold Coast, 1988
Pacific Edge, 1990

Rockwood, Roy. Great Marvel
Through the Air to the North Pole,
1906
Under the Ocean to the South Pole,
1907
Five Thousand Miles Underground,
1908
Through Space to Mars, 1910
Lost on the Moon, 1911
On a Torn-Away World, 1913
The City Beyond the Clouds, 1925
By Air Express to Venus, 1929
By Space Ship to Saturn, 1935

Saberhagen, Fred. Berserker
Berserker, 1967
Brother Assassin, 1969
Berserker's Planet, 1975
Berserker Man, 1979
The Ultimate Enemy, 1979
Berserker Base, 1985
The Berserker Throne, 1985
Berserker: Blue Death, 1985
The Berserker Attack, 1987
Berserker Lies, 1991
Berserker Kill, 1993

Shaw, Bob. Land and Overland
The Ragged Astronauts, 1986
The Wooden Spaceships, 1988
The Fugitive Worlds, 1989

Shaw, Bob. Orbitsville
Orbitsville, 1975
Orbitsville Departure, 1983
Orbitsville Judgement, 1990

Shirley, John. Song Called Youth
Eclipse, 1985
Eclipse Penumbra, 1988
Eclipse Corona, 1990

Simmons, Dan. Hyperion
Hyperion, 1989
The Fall of Hyperion, 1990
Endymion, 199?

Slonczewski, Joan. Shora
A Door into Ocean, 1986
Daughter of Elysium, 1993
The Children Star, 199?

Smith, E. E. Lensman
Triplanetary, 1948
First Lensman, 1950
Galactic Patrol, 1950
Grey Lensman, 1951
Second-Stage Lensman, 1953
Children of the Lens, 1954
The Vortex Blaster, 1960

Snyder, Zilpha Keatley. Green Sky
  Beyond the Root, 1975
  And All Between, 1976
  Until the Celebration, 1977

Sucharitkul, Somtow. Chronicles of
  the High Inquest
  Light on the Sound, 1982
  The Throne of Madness, 1983
  Utopia Hunters, 1984
  The Darkling Wind, 1985

Turner, George. Ethical Culture
  Beloved Son, 1978
  Vaneglory, 1981
  Yesterday's Men, 1983

van Vogt, A. E. Null-A
  The World of Null-A, 1948
  The Pawns of Null-A, 1956
  Null-A Three, 1985

Vance, Jack. Cadwal Chronicles
  Araminta Station, 1987
  Ecce and Old Earth, 1991
  Throy, 1992

Varley, John. Gaea
  Titan, 1979
  Wizard, 1980
  Demon, 1984

Vinge, Joan. Snow Queen
  The Snow Queen, 1980
  World's End, 1984
  The Summer Queen, 1991

Wallace, Ian. Croyd
  Croyd, 1967
  Dr. Orpheus, 1968
  Deathstar Voyage, 1969
  A Voyage to Dari, 1974
  Z-Sting, 1978
  Heller's Leap, 1979
  The Lucifer Comet, 1980
  Megalomania, 1989

Walters, Hugh. Chris Godfrey
  Blast Off at Woomera, 1957
  The Domes of Pico, 1958
  Operation Columbus, 1960
  Moon Base One, 1961
  Expedition Venus, 1962
  Destination Mars, 1963
  Terror by Satellite, 1964
  Journey to Jupiter, 1965
  Spaceship to Saturn, 1967
  The Mohole Mystery, 1968
  Nearly Neptune, 1969
  First Contact? 1971
  Passage to Pluto, 1973
  Tony Hale, Space Detective, 1973
  Murder on Mars, 1975
  Boy Astronaut, 1977
  Caves of Drach, 1977
  The Last Disaster, 1978
  The Blue Aura, 1979
  First Family on the Moon, 1979
  The Dark Triangle, 1981
  School on the Moon, 1981
  P-K, 1986

Watson, Ian. Black Current
  The Book of the River, 1984
  The Book of the Stars, 1984
  The Book of Being, 1985

Webb, Sharon. Earthchild
  Earthchild, 1982
  Earth Song, 1983
  Ram Song, 1984

Wilder, Cherry. Torin
  The Luck of Brin's Five, 1977
  The Nearest Five, 1980
  The Tapestry Warriors, 1983

Williams, Walter Jon. Hardwired
  Hardwired, 1986
  Voice of the Whirlwind, 1987
  Solip: System, 1989

Williamson, Jack. Legion of Space
The Legion of Space, 1947
The Cometeers, 1967
One Against the Legion, 1967
The Queen of the Legion, 1983

Wilson, Robert Anton. Schrödinger's Cat
The Universe Next Door, 1979
The Trick Top Hat, 1981
The Homing Pigeons, 1981

Wingrove, David. Chung Kuo
The Middle Kingdom, 1989
The Broken Wheel, 1990
The White Mountains, 1991
The Stone Within, 1992
Beneath the Tree of Heaven, 1994
White Moon, Red Dragon, 1994

Wolfe, Gene. Book of the Long Sun
Nightside the Long Sun, 1993
Lake of the Long Sun, 1994
Caldé of the Long Sun, 1994

Wolfe, Gene. Book of the New Sun
The Shadow of the Torturer, 1980
The Claw of the Conciliator, 1981
The Sword of the Lictor, 1981
The Citadel of the Autarch, 1983
The Urth of the New Sun, 1987

Womack, Jack. Terraplane
Ambient, 1967
Terraplane, 1988
Heathern, 1990
Elvissey, 1993

Wright, Austin Tappen. Islandia
Islandia, 1970
The Islar (by Mark Sexton), 1969
The Two Kingdoms (by Mark Sexton), 1979
Havoc in Islandia (by Mark Sexton), 1982

Wright, S. Fowler. Dream
Dream, 1931
Vengeance of Gwa, 1935
Spider's War, 1954

Series Index

Note: Series named after a person are listed by the first name of the person.

Adventures in the Unknown (Claudy)

Arcot, Wade and Morley (Campbell)

Armageddon (Rankin)

Berserker (Saberhagen)

Bird of Kinship (Cowper)

Black Current (Watson)

Book of the Long Sun (Wolfe)

Book of the New Sun (Wolfe)

Bran Tregare (Busby)

Cadwell Chronicles (Vance)

Canopus in Archives (Lessing)

Changes (Dickinson)

Chanur (Cherryh)

Childe Cycle (Dickson)

Chris Godfrey (Walters)

Chronicles of the High Inquest (Sucharitkul)

Chung Kuo (Wingrove)

Croyd (Watson)

Cities in Flight (Blish)

Conquest of the United States (Hancock)

Coyote Jones (Elgin)

CV (Knight)

Dancers at the Edge of Time (Moorcock)

Darkover (Bradley)

Davy (Pangborn)

Dr. Adder (Jeter)

Downbelow Station (Cherryh)

Dune (Herbert)

Dustland (Hamilton)

Earthchild (Webb)

Eden (Harrison)

Ethical Culture (Turner)

Ender Wiggins (Card)

Exiles (Bova)

Falkenberg's Legion (Pournelle)

Fireball (Christopher)

Flinx (Foster)

Forerunner (Norton)

Foundation (Asimov)

Four Hundred Billion Stars (McAuley)

Future History (Heinlein)

Gaea (Varley)

Galactic Warlord (Hill)

Gate (Corlett)

Great Marvel (Rockwood)

Great Sky River (Benford)

Greataway: Song of Earth (Coney)

Green Sky (Snyder)

Greenwich Village (Anderson)

Hardwired (Williams)

Harper Hall (McCaffrey)

Heechee (Pohl)

Helliconia (Aldiss)

High Inquest, Chronicles of (Sucharitkul)

Hitchhiker (Adams)

Holdfast (Charnas)

Huntsman (Hill)

The Hydronauts (Biemiller)

Hyperion (Simmons)

Imperium (Laumer)

Isis (Hughes)

Islandia (Wright)

Janus (Norton)

Jeremy Grant (MacVicar)

Jerry Cornelius (Moorcock)

Known Space (Niven)

Lagrange (Reynolds)

Land and Overland (Shaw)

Legion of Space (Williamson)

Lensman (Smith)

Logan (Nolan)

Long Sun, Book of the (Wolfe)

Lucky Starr (French)

Luke (Christopher)

Man-Kzin Wars (Niven)

Marid Audran (Effinger)

Mars (Burroughs)

Mars (Robinson)

Minervan Experiment (Hogan)

Morphodite (Foster)

Native Tongue (Elgin)

Neuromancer (Gibson)

New Sun, Book of the (Wolfe)

Null-A (van Vogt)

Orange County (Robinson)

Orbitsville (Shaw)

Palos (Giesy)

Pandora (Herbert)

Patternist (Butler)

Pellucidar (Burroughs)

Pern (McCaffrey)

Pliocene Exiles, Saga of (May)

Radix (Attanasio)

Rama (Clarke)

Ratha (Bell)

Retief (Laumer)

Riverworld (Farmer)

Robot (Asimov)

Rock (Lightner)

Saga of Pliocene Exile (May)

Schrödinger's Cat (Wilson)

Ship Who Sang (McCaffrey)

Snow Queen (Vinge)

Song Called Youth (Shirley)

Space Trilogy (Lewis)

Starbridge Chronicles (Park)

Tarot (Anthony)

Technic Civilization (Anderson)

Terraplane (Womack)

Time (L'Engle)

Tom "Red Clay" (Ore)

Tom Swift (Appleton)

Tripod (Christopher)

2001 (Clarke)

VALIS (Dick)

Venus (Burroughs)

Viriconium (Harrison)

Vorkosigan (Bujold)

Winterlong (Hand)

World of Tiers (Farmer)

Worlds (Haldeman)

Wraeththu (Constantine)

Xenogenesis (Butler)

Translations

English-language science fiction has often been translated into other languages and has frequently served as a model for writers in non-English languages. The reverse has rarely occurred, and few non-English-language SF writers are well-known in North America or Britain. Verne and Lem are the principal exceptions. Readers desiring to read SF in non-English languages should consult the third edition of *Anatomy of Wonder* for the sections discussing SF in 13 languages; the *Encyclopedia of Science Fiction* [7-22] for its entries on more than 300 authors and national literatures; the *Survey of Science Fiction Literature* [7-27] for essays on novels and short fiction of 93 authors; and the surveys that appear several times yearly in *Locus* [12-24].

The reasons for excluding untranslated SF from this edition are explained in the preface. To give some sense, however inadequate, of the range of foreign-language SF, translations of annotated fiction are listed below, preceded by comments by Dennis Kratz, who teaches fantastic literature and is actively involved in the American Literary Translators Association (ALTA). He has starred those translations he judges of superior quality. William Weaver won the National Book Award for his translation of Calvino's *Cosmicomics*. Several of the annotated anthologies include translated SF, notably those by Aldiss and Lundwall [4-520], Merril and others [4-543], and Nolane [4-545].

A Note on Translation by Dennis Kratz

Literary translation, always a complex and problematic endeavor, presents additional challenges when the literature involved is science fiction. Stated most simply and ambitiously, the goal of translation is to recreate in a new language the totality of what was expressed in the original language. Where the original is dull, the translation should be dull; where the original crackles with intellectual and esthetic power, so should the translation.

Translation deals, then, not with words themselves but with the artistic vision the words were meant to express and the esthetic response the words were intended to evoke. A translation recreates not what is "there" but what the translator interprets as being there.

The translator, in other words, is attempting the impossible: to create an equivalent text. Ideally this equivalence will manifest itself both in the new text and in the response of the new readers. What characterizes the "equivalent" nature of a translation? A comparison of the two texts will reveal that the translator has found a way to recreate the mode of thinking as well as the use of language found in the original.

For the translator, the text is a complex system of dynamically interconnected parts. Meaning cannot be separated from presentation. Most discussions of translation, interestingly enough, use metaphors of friendship and marriage. We speak of the translator's "fidelity" to the text. But translation also leads to a recognition that this fidelity will be at best partial; for the work of fiction is a complex system that is not only telling a story but also (in all likelihood) impressing the reader with the author's virtuosity. This complexity of the text combined with the differences separating any two languages precludes the ideal goal of total fidelity. Every translator, as a result, is faced with this constant choice: to what part of the text should the translation be faithful? Faithful in what ways?

This issue of fidelity leads to the second goal of the translator: creating a work of art that evokes an equivalent level and quality of response from its new readers. Imagine the challenge of translating a joke from one language to another. Can we really claim to have translated a statement that evokes laughter in one language if it does not also cause laughter in its new version? Consider the choices to which this goal leads the translator, especially if fidelity to the literal meaning of the words would destroy the humor.

The translator of science fiction faces a challenge analogous to that posed by comedy. The best science fiction evokes a sense of wonder that emerges from the author's attempt to describe a setting contrary to known reality in language clear enough to make this new reality plausible and appealing enough to lure to the reader into re-envisioning what was in the author's mind. A successful translation would recreate, however imperfectly, both these aspects of the work.

Translation is essential to the growth of science fiction as an international literature. It makes English-language science fiction available throughout the world and brings to the American reader works that might expand the possibilities of the genre. Writers like Stanislaw Lem, the Strugatskii brothers, and Jules Verne are known to most American readers only in translation. In recent years both the number and quality of translations in science fiction have increased, and I have starred the best in the following list. World SF (see next section) gives the Karel Award to translators but not for individual translations. (See Mallett [7-17] for a list of the Karel Award winners.)

Czech

Čapek, Karel. *The Absolute at Large*
————. *Krakatit*
————. *R.U.R.*
————. *War With the Newts*
Nesvadba, Josef. *The Lost Face*

Danish

Jensen, Johannes V. *The Long Journey*

French

Bergerac, Cyrano de. *The Comical History of the States and Empires of the Worlds of the Moon and Sun*
Boulle, Pierre. *Planet of the Apes*
Farrère, Claude. *Useless Hands*
Gary, Romain. *The Gasp*
Klein, Gérard. *The Day Before Tomorrow*
Knight, Damon, ed. *Thirteen French Science Fiction Stories*
Maurois, André. *The Thought-Reading Machine*
————. *The Weigher of Souls*
Mercier, Louis Sebastian. *Memoirs of the Year Two Thousand Five Hundred*
Merle, Robert. *Malevil*
Roger, Noëlle. *The New Adam*
Rosny aîné, J. H. *The Giant Cat*
Tarde, Gabriel de. *Underground Man*
Vercors. *You Shall Know Them*

Verne, Jules. *The Adventures of Captain Hatteras*
————. *From the Earth to the Moon*
————. *A Journey to the Center of the Earth*
————. *Twenty Thousand Leagues Under the Sea* (*Mickel translation [1-95])
Vonarburg, Élisabeth. *The Silent City*

German

Gail, Otto Willi. *The Shot Into Infinity*
Jeschke, Wolfgang. *The Last Day of Creation*
Kaul, Fedor. *Contagion to the World*
Moszkowski, Alexandr. *The Isles of Wisdom*
Pešek, Luděk. *The Earth Is Near*
————. *Trap for Perseus*
von Hanstein, Otfrid. *Electropolis*
von Harbou, Thea. *Metropolis*
Winterfeld, Henry. *Star Girl*

Hungarian

Karinthy, Frigyes. *Voyage to Faremido and Capillaria*

Italian

*Calvino, Italo. *Cosmicomics*
————. *Invisible Cities*
*————. *t zero*

Japanese

Murakami, Harumi. *Hard-Boiled Wonderland and the End of the World*

Latin

Campanella, Tommaso. *Civitas Solis*
Holberg, Ludwig. *A Journey to the World Under-Ground*
Kepler, Johannes. *Somnium*

Polish

*Lem, Stanislaw. *The Cyberiad*
————. *The Futurological Congress*
————. *The Investigation*
————. *Mortal Engines*

————. *Solaris*
*————. *The Star Diaries*

Russian

Beliaev, Aleksandr. *The Amphibian*
Bulgakov, Mikhail. "The Fatal Eggs"
Magidoff, Robert, ed. *Russian Science Fiction*
Merril, Judith, ed. *Path Into the Unknown*
Strugatskii, Arkadi and Boris. *Definitely Maybe*
*————. *Roadside Picnic & Tale of the Troika*
————. *The Snail on the Slope*
————. *The Ugly Swans*
Sturgeon, Theodore, ed. *New Soviet SF*
Tolstoi, Aleksei. *Aelita*
Tsiolkovsky, Konstantin. *Beyond the Planet Earth*
Zamiatin, Evgenii. *We*

Organizations

All hobbies and areas of specialized interest generate organizations of like-minded individuals. Perhaps the earliest such group in SF was the Science Fiction League, founded by Hugo Gernsback to enlarge the subscriber base for *Amazing Stories* [12-2] in the 1920s. With this magazine fans had a focus for their interest and used the letters column to correspond with one another, and to found amateur magazines (fanzines) in which appeared some of the work of writers later well-known.

Described below are some of the many organizations having SF as a core interest or one of several major interests. The date of foundation follows the name of the organization. More information can be obtained from the person whose address is shown. The addresses are current as of mid-1994, and listed individuals, almost all volunteers, will probably forward queries to their successors if they don't respond directly.

Association of Science Fiction & Fantasy Artists. 1976
Todd Cameron Hamilton, 2208 W. Rosemont Ave., Chicago, IL 60659

An organization of about 250 members, about half of them fan (amateur) artists, collectors, and a small number of professional illustrators/artists and art directors. The former *ASFA Quarterly* has been superseded by an irregular newsletter emphasizing convention and gallery art show reports, interviews, and market news, with convention news predominating.

Awards called Chesleys (after Chesley Bonestell, 1888–1986) are given each year in a variety of categories.

British Science Fiction Association. 1958
Cy Chauvin, 14248 Wilfred, Detroit, MI 48213
Keith Freeman, 269 Wykeham Rd., Reading RG6 1PL, England

An outgrowth of several shorter-lived organizations dating back to the 1930s, the BSFA had about 2,000 members in 1993. Among the several publications is *Vector* [12-35]. The BSFA presents several awards at the annual National Science Fiction Convention, informally known as the Eastercon (see awards above).

First Fandom. 1959
Mark Schulzinger, 601 E. Delmar, Springfield, MO 65807

As noted above, organizations celebrating SF were founded in the 1920s. Individuals active in the field by January 1939 are eligible to be members of one of the first fan organizations, which currently has approximately 200 full members. Associate members qualify with at least 30 years' activity in SF. A First Fandom award is presented at the annual worldcons (see conventions below).

International Association for the Fantastic in the Arts. 1982
Mary Pharr, English Department, Florida Southern College, Lakeland, FL 22801

The IAFA's scope is broader than that of the SFRA (see below), as the name suggests. Each organization has about the same number of members, 300+, mostly academics. Members receive the *IAFA Newsletter*, the *Journal of the Fantastic in the Arts*, and an annual member directory. An annual conference is held each winter in Florida at which more than 200 papers, panels, and discussions are presented, along with the IAFA Distinguished Scholarship Award (see awards section). A selection of the papers have been published for several years by Greenwood Press (see chapter 8).

Popular Culture Association. 1970
Popular Culture Center, Bowling Green State Univ., Bowling Green, OH 43403, 419-372-7861

The systematic study of popular culture has attracted a wide variety of specialists from many fields, reflected in the diverse membership of the PCA, which currently numbers about 3,000 members. The annual conferences, held each spring, typically attract 2,000 registrants, at which many hundreds of papers, panels, and discussions are presented. Awards are given for the outstanding published article and for work for the PCA. Although no proceedings volumes result, the association is closely linked to the *Journal of Popular Culture* and *Journal of American Culture*, both published at BG State University.

Science-Fiction and Fantasy Writers of America, Inc. 1965
Peter Pautz, 5 Winding Brook Drive, #1B, Guilderland, NY 12084

Although many of the approximately 1,300 members write only SF, many also write fantasy, a fact recognized by a change in name from the SFWA to the current name in 1991. (There is also a Horror Writers Association founded in 1987, outside this guide's scope.) Affiliate, active, and associate memberships are available. Members receive the quarterly *SFWA Bulletin* (market reports, how-to articles, and so on), the bimonthly *SFWA Forum* (for associate and active members only), and an annual directory, which lists the agents of the authors. One of the most important of the awards, the Nebulas, are presented at the annual spring conventions, usually held on either the East or West Coast. See awards.

Science Fiction Foundation. 1971
Rob Meades, 75 Hecham Close, Walthamstow, London E17 5QT, England

Originally founded to support teaching and research at what was then called North East London Polytechnic (now the University of East London), this semi-autonomous body publishes the most important British journal about SF, *Foundation* [12-22], and has assembled the largest publicly accessible library of SF in the UK [14-63]. The SFF moved from London to Liverpool University in 1993, and the library was integrated with the University of Liverpool library system. A charitable trust established to support the SFF is Friends of Foundation, whose members receive *Foundation* and the *Friends of Foundation Newsletter*, both three times yearly.

Science Fiction Oral History Association. 1977
Nancy Tucker, 695 Judd Road, Saline, MI 48176

Organized by SF writer Lloyd Biggle, Jr., and local fans, the association is concerned with assembling audio and video recordings of important events in SF and making them available through library depositories (see chapter 14). It invites donations of tapes, will make copies of tapes, and will instruct anyone interested in the techniques of interviewing. The approximately 75 members receive a house organ, *S.F.O.R.A. Newsletter,* three times yearly and may borrow or purchase copies of tapes, a catalog of which is available to members.

Science Fiction Poetry Association. 1978
SFPA, C/o Marge B. Simon, 1412 NE 35th St., Ocala, FL 34479

Enough SF poetry has appeared in recent years to justify the inclusion of a section devoted to it (see end of chapter 4). The SFPA embraces SF, fantasy, horror, and "speculative" poetry and gives the Rhysling awards for the best short and long poem. (Rhysling was a blind singer/engineer in Heinlein's "The Green Hills of Earth," 1947.) The award winners are reprinted in the SFWA's annual Nebula anthologies [4-544], and winners and nominees in the SFPA's Rhysling anthologies. The 182 members of the SFPA receive *Star*line* (bimonthly) [4-569] and *The Rhysling Anthology* [annual], including special publications such as the "All-Horror" and "All-Prose-Poetry" special issues, and several broadsides and chapbooks on craft are occasionally made available to members.

Science Fiction Research Association. 1970
Robert J. Ewald, 552 W. Lincoln St., Findlay, OH 45840

Founded in 1970 by Thomas Clareson and other academics, this is the oldest organization devoted to the study and teaching of SF. Scholarship is recognized by the annual Pilgrim and Pioneer awards (see above), presented at the SFRA's June conferences. The 300+ members, mostly academics (academic affiliation isn't a requirement), receive the *SFRA Review* [12-32], *Extrapolation* [12-20], *Science-Fiction Studies* [12-33], and an annual membership directory.

Society of Utopian Studies. 1975
Hoda Zaki, Political Science Dept., Hampton Univ., Hampton, VA 23668

An international, interdisciplinary group devoted to the study of literary and experimental utopias. Papers are presented at the annual fall meetings, some of them collected in the *Utopian Studies* volumes published by Univ. Press of America. Awards include the Arthur O. Lewis Award for the best paper delivered by a junior scholar at the meeting and the Eugenio Battista Award for the best article in each volume of the journal *Utopian Studies*. Members receive *Utopus Discovered,* a newsletter, a directory of utopian scholars, and the semi-annual *Utopian Studies* (also available to non-members; write *Utopian Studies,* Univ. of Missouri, St. Louis, MO 63121).

H. G. Wells Society. 1960

Mary C. Mayer, Membership Secretary, H. G. Wells Society, 75 Well-meadow Road, London SE13 6TA, England

Founded to promote appreciation of the life and works of H. G. Wells, the 300 members receive a quarterly newsletter, an annual scholarly journal, *The Wellsian*, and meet regularly, with an annual conference held in London, site of the H. G. Wells Centre at the Kentish Town precinct of the Polytechnic of North London, where the society maintains a large collection of books and other materials by and about Wells.

World SF. 1976

Elizabeth Ann Hull, 855 S. Harvard Drive, Palatine, IL 60067

Organized at the first World SF writer's conference in Dublin, its goal is to promote communication among SF writers and editors worldwide. An irregular newsletter is sent to the approximately 700 members (150 of whom are American), who try to meet annually, political conditions permitting. Awards presented at the conferences include the Karel award for translation (after Karel Čapek), the President's Award for independence of thought in SF, and the Harry Harrison award for individuals who have most improved the international image of SF.

Conventions

The American pulp magazines of the 1920s and 1930s provided a focus for readers with an interest in SF, and the letters columns enabled them to correspond with one another. Conventions were inevitable, from casual gatherings in one another's homes to more formal gatherings at which speakers, panels, and other activities were scheduled. This fan subculture has been crucially important to the development of SF, originally mostly in English-speaking countries, now worldwide.

Almost every issue of *Locus* [12-24] and *Science Fiction Chronicle* [12-29] has a detailed list of forthcoming conventions, from small, local gatherings to those that attract thousands, such as the world SF convention (Worldcon) or the American Booksellers Association convention, at which publishers that feature SF actively promote their wares. If you had the interest, time, and money, you could attend a convention every week throughout the year.

The Worldcons, which began in 1939, are scheduled over the Labor Day weekend each year. They now attract 5,000 to 7,000 registrants when held in the United States. Those attending comprise fans, including an increasing number whose primary interest is not printed SF but media adaptions (films, TV) or comic books, plus editors, writers, publishers, hucksters (as dealers are affectionately known), illustrators/artists, and assorted SF groupies. Masquerades have become a prominent part of Worldcons, and *Locus* includes many photos of the elaborate costumes, which range from the gorgeous to the grotesque to the whimsical. The programming is varied and nonstop for almost a week, with many fans arriving early and leaving late. There are various types of guests of honor (GoH)—writer, artist, fan—who appear on panels, are interviewed, autograph books, and so forth. Various awards are presented, of which the Hugos are the best known. (At the 50th Worldcon, the 1992 MagiCon in Orlando, Florida, it was formally decided to drop the former official name for the Hugo, the "Science Fiction Achievement Award.") Intersection, the 1995 Worldcon, will be held in Glasgow, Scotland. The 1996 Worldcon is scheduled for the Anaheim convention center, near Disneyland in California.

Regional conventions vary in size, from several hundred to several thousand. Their names suggest their location: Boskone (Boston), Midsouthcon (Nashville), Westercon (West Coast cities), and so on. England's National Science Fiction Convention, the Eastercon, is the largest in the United Kingdom. The SF conventions became the model for the World Fantasy Convention and the World Horror Convention.

As academic interest in SF developed in the 1960s, conventions (or conferences, to dignify the gatherings a bit) inevitably followed. The first to hold a convention was the Science Fiction Research Association, which met in New York in 1970. These conferences are held each June and attract 75–100 people, among them guest writers and scholars. Papers and panels are presented, and the Pilgrim and Pioneer awards are presented. The J. Lloyd Eaton conferences are held at the University of California, Riverside, each spring. Begun in 1979, the conference is organized around a theme. The Eaton award is presented, and many of the papers have been published in collections (see chapter 8). The International Association for the Fantastic in the Arts meets each winter in Florida and offers nonstop, mostly academic programming from Wednesday through Sunday. It attracts the largest number of the academic gatherings, 300+. A selection of the papers has been published for several years (see chapter 8), and a scholarship award is also presented.

A two-week Intensive English Institute on the Teaching of Science Fiction is offered by the University of Kansas as part of a varied July SF program. Although valuable for teachers, it also has enrolled aspiring writers and interested readers. It concludes with the Campbell Conference, which discusses a single topic relating to the teaching, writing, and publishing of SF, and with the awarding of the John W. Campbell Memorial Award for the best SF novel of the year and the Theodore Sturgeon Award for the best short SF. The conference also marks the beginning of a Writers Workshop in Science Fiction, which offers a two-week intensive program.

.

Author/Subject Index

This index provides access to all books and other material having named authors or editors annotated or substantively mentioned. Substantively means at least some critical or descriptive information is included; simple mentions, such as in the compare/contrast statements, are excluded. Cross-references are selectively provided from better-known pseudonyms to real names or vice versa. References to authors as subjects immediately follow the author's name. Annotations are cited by entry numbers, easily identified by the hyphen, such as 2-86, meaning entry 86 in chapter 2. All other references, such as to the introductory essays, are cited by page numbers.

Certain categories were not indexed: variant titles are listed in the annotations but not under the author's name in this index or in the title index; books discussed within annotations, most commonly sequels, are indexed only in the title index (the "parent" entry is shown here as well as in the title index); stories in collections or anthologies (see Contento [7-13] for such indexing); references to authors of essays in the introductions, notes or chapter 8 (the comprehensive indexes by Hall [7-16] provide ready access to this secondary literature); translators; and editors of authored books (as distinct from edited books like anthologies).

Subject indexing includes authors as subjects (see above) and selected other topics. See also the separate theme index, new to this edition.

Alphabetization is word by word, e.g., van Vogt before Vance. Mackey comes before McCarthy (i.e., Mac and Mc are not interfiled).

Title Index

Short fiction is not normally indexed here for reasons explained in the introductory note to the Author/Subject index. Variant titles are not normally indexed but are shown in the annotation. Subtitles are included only when it is necessary to distinguish between works having the same title; books with the same title are followed by the author's surname to distinguish between them. SF is alphabetized as if spelled out as science fiction and numerals are alphabetized as if spelled out. Alphabetization is word by word. Translated books are indexed only by the translated title. Film and TV titles are not normally indexed (see chapter 10). See also the series index in chapter 15.

Theme Index

This index lists recurrent themes in science fiction and the main entry titles in which each theme appears. Notes amplify the theme headings. Titles are listed with entry numbers, which are easily identified by the hyphen, e.g. 3-231 in chapter 3. (Numbers that follow headings are to references in text, not to main entry titles.) Related headings are linked by *see also* references. This list supplements the "compare" and "contrast" statements in the individual annotations, which refer the reader to other books with similar themes, structures, narrative devices, and so forth.

ALTERNATE WORLDS/HISTORIES

Properly, alternative worlds, but the usage is fixed. Might-have-been worlds or history. *See also* HISTORY IN SF, PARALLEL WORLDS

ANDROIDS

Artificial creations that look and act like humans. *See also* CYBORGS, ROBOTS

ANTHROPOLOGY

Stories exploring humankind's essential nature. *See also* ALIENS, EVOLUTION

Anti-Utopia. *See* DYSTOPIA

Apocalyptic stories. *See* END OF THE WORLD

Artificial intelligence. *See* INTELLI-GENCE, COMPUTERS

Atlantis. *See* LOST RACES/WORLDS

Bildungsroman. *See* COMING OF AGE

BIOLOGY

Stories in which biological developments are prominent. *See also* CLONES/CLON-ING, EVOLUTION, GENETIC ENGI-NEERING, MEDICINE, MUTANTS

Cosmic Disaster. *See* DISASTER

CRIME AND PUNISHMENT

Including SF detective stories.

CYBERPUNK, 232

Label usually applied to stories by a group of writers who became prominent in the mid-1980s. The "cyber" presumably comes from cybernetics, the study of control and communication in machines (including "cyberspace" linking computers), and is combined with a downbeat, punk sensibility echoing that of the hardboiled school of detective fiction writers. *See also* HARD SF

CYBORGS

Man-machine hybrids (from cybernetic organism). The machine may be a pros-

FEMINIST SF, 230

Usually stories in which female roles are atypical and/or women are dominant and/or men are viewed with suspicion or are absent. *See also* WOMEN IN SF

First Contact. *See* ALIENS and INVASION

Flying saucers. *See* INVASION

FUTURE HISTORY, 9

The historical milieu in which a writer's stories are set, such as the works of Asimov or Heinlein. *See also* HISTORY, GALACTIC EMPIRES

Rimrunners, 4-107
The Robots of Dawn, 4-21
War of the Wing-Men, 3-9

Future War. *See* WAR

GALACTIC EMPIRES

Human empires writ large. *See also* COL-
ONIZATION OF OTHER WORLDS,
FUTURE HISTORY, HISTORY

Agent of the Unknown, 3-154
Aristoi, 4-498
Barrayar, 4-78
Battle for the Stars, 3-81
Becoming Alien, 4-322
Citizen of the Galaxy, 3-85
Federation, 3-144
Flandry of Terra, 3-7
The Foundation Trilogy, 3-12
Foundation's Edge, 4-19
Hyperion, 4-419
Judgment Night, 3-130
The Lensman Series, 3-167
Light on the Sound, 4-447
Pebble in the Sky, 3-15
Shadows in the Sun, 3-138
Stars in My Pocket Like Grains of
  Sand, 4-131
The Tar-Aiym Krang, 4-169

GENERATION STARSHIPS

If pseudoscientific explanations involving
faster-than-light travel are rejected, then
the time required for interstellar travel
will encompass many human generations. *See also* SPACE TRAVEL

Captive Universe, 4-198
The Dark Beyond the Stars, 4-363
The Dream Millennium, 4-490
Non-Stop, 3-4
Orphans of the Sky, 3-88
Rendezvous with Rama, 4-109

GENETIC ENGINEERING, 234

The idea of biological engineering
appeared early in SF and is prominent
today. Includes artificial creation of life,
as in *Frankenstein*. *See also* CLONES/
CLONING, CYBORGS, EVOLUTION

The Amphibian, 2-3
Andra, 5-91

Beasts, 4-121
Beggars in Spain, 4-238
Beyond This Horizon, 3-84
Black Milk, 4-353
Blind Voices, 4-351
Blood Music, 4-38
Bone Dance, 4-81
The Child Garden, 4-377
The Death Guard, 2-18
The Divide, 4-505
The Dragon Masters, 3-184
Earthchild, 5-167
Earthseed, 5-136
Exiled from Earth, 5-18
Falling Free, 4-79
The Food of the Gods, 1-99
The Forever Formula, 5-17
Frankenstein, 1-84
Geek Love, 4-151
The Island of Dr. Moreau, 1-100
Jurassic Park, 4-120
The Keeper of the Isis Light, 5-76
The Mercy Men, 5-120
Mirabile, 4-223
The Rediscovery of Man, 4-427
The Seedling Stars, 3-23
The Silent City, 4-477
Solarion: A Romance, 1-34
The Sound of His Horn, 3-156
Startide Rising, 4-67
The Uplift War, 4-68

Gods and demons. *See* MYTHOLOGY

HARD SF

Stories in which the author adheres with
varying degrees of rigor to scientific principles believed to be true at the time of
writing, principles derived from the hard
(physical, biological) rather than soft
(social) sciences. Sometimes hardcore SF.

Beyond Apollo, 5-154
Bound for Mars, 5-8
Broken Symmetries, 4-342
Close to Critical, 3-47
Cycle of Fire, 3-48
Dragon's Egg, 4-168
The Enemy Stars, 3-6
Eon, 4-39
Falling Free, 4-79

HISTORY IN SF

HOLOCAUST AND AFTER
More serious than DISASTER, less serious than END OF THE WORLD. Usually
results from human folly, such as nuclear
war, rather than natural events.

HUMOROUS SF

Including parodies. *See also* SATIRICAL SF

Imaginary voyage. *See* FANTASTIC VOYAGE

IMMORTALITY

See also RELIGION

Inner space. *See* PSYCHOLOGY

INTELLIGENCE

For machine intelligence, *see* COMPUTERS. For superhuman intelligence, *see* SUPERMEN/WOMEN

Interplanetary romance. *See* PLANETS, LIFE ON OTHER WORLDS

INVASION

Most commonly of the Earth by extraterrestrials, often transported in UFOs. *See also* ALIENS

ROBOTS
Traditionally mechanical or electro-
mechanical in nature. *Compare*
ANDROIDS, CYBORGS

SATIRICAL SF
See also HUMOROUS SF

SCIENCE FANTASY
Stories combining "rational" elements
from SF and magical or fanciful elements
from fantasy. Excludes heroic fantasy and
sword and sorcery, which generally fall
outside SF.

SCIENTISTS AND ENGINEERS, 25–26
In which the character of a
scientist/engineer is a key element.
Includes "mad" scientists.

SEX IN SF
Including gender, sexual stereotypes and
roles. *See also* FEMINIST SF, WOMEN IN
SF

SOCIOLOGY

The study of social relationships on Earth or elsewhere. *See also* ANTHROPOLOGY, POLITICS, UTOPIAS

SPACE FLIGHT

A classic theme in earlier SF overtaken by history. Distinct from SPACE OPERA, GENERATION STARSHIPS, and FANTASTIC VOYAGES.